Children Act Private Law Proceedings:
A Handbook

Children Act Private Law Proceedings: A Handbook

Third Edition

John Mitchell

Published by Family Law
a publishing imprint of
Jordan Publishing Limited
21 St Thomas Street
Bristol BS1 6JS

Whilst the publishers and the author have taken every care in preparing the material included in this work, any statements made as to the legal or other implications of particular transactions are made in good faith purely for general guidance and cannot be regarded as a substitute for professional advice. Consequently, no liability can be accepted for loss or expense incurred as a result of relying in particular circumstances on statements made in this work.

British Library Cataloguing-in-Publication Data

A catalogue record for this book is available from the British Library.

ISBN 978 1 84661 238 1

Typeset by Letterpart Ltd, Reigate, Surrey

Printed in Great Britain by CPI Antony Rowe, Chippenham and Eastbourne

FOREWORD

The Handbook is intended to serve two purposes. The first is to introduce the law and practice of the Private Law relating to children to practitioners who have little experience of the subject.

The second purpose is to provide experienced practitioners with easy access not only to summaries of the law in specific areas but also to policy reports, research and articles not always found in standard practice books.

Since the second edition of this valuable Handbook, the role of the court in relation to private disagreements relating to children has continued to be closely scrutinised. The recommendations of the Family Justice Review, which reported in November 2011, are designed to create a process which enables people, wherever possible and safe to do so to resolve these cases without court involvement. John Mitchell looks closely at the recommendations and considers them in the context of recent developments, including the revised Private Law Programme and the guidance issued by myself in relation to split hearings. In his discussion of the key issues, including that of violence within the family, he calls upon his own deep knowledge and experience as a highly respected family judge and upon the wide range of literature and research which has been commissioned in this vitally important area of the law.

The Handbook is primarily intended for legal and social work practitioners, although I am aware that previous editions have also been welcomed by and useful to litigants in person. By placing his discussion of the Children Act 1989 in the context both of policy and socio-legal research, in order to produce an holistic model of law and practice, John Mitchell ensures that this highly practical publication will also be of interest to students and to the wider 'family' community, to whom I am very glad to commend it.

Nicholas Wall
President of the Family Division
March 2012

PREFACE

In the Preface to the second edition of the Handbook, I wrote in 2006 that 'these are exciting and challenging times for private family law'. 'New' family arrangements were being made and the Private Law Programme and the new contact provisions inserted into the Children Act 1989 offered a hope of making better provision for disputed contact cases. And, so it proved. Courts have been challenged to apply the principles of the Act to novel problems in same-sex families. What part, for example, should donor fathers play in the life of the child and how can family life between his father and his father's same-sex partner be secured? Courts have tackled the issues and will continue to do so. Intractable contact disputes are a perennial challenge but Parenting Information Programmes and First Hearing Dispute Resolution appointments have helped to divert some families from litigation. The Family Procedure Rules have created a unified Family Court in all but name, completing part of the project suggested by Sir Morris Finer and the Committee on One-Parent Families in 1974. Interestingly, the Committee saw that it was of fundamental importance that the advantages to be derived from the family court should be seen primarily in terms of 'its capacity to help [families] make the best decisions and reach the best solutions over the whole range of problems which the fact of family breakdown produces in the circumstances of each ... case.'

The next years, however, appear more daunting than exciting. The proposals of the *Family Justice Review* may assist the resolution of some family problems but research cited in the Handbook consistently points to the many difficulties including the risk of domestic violence encountered in a significant proportion of cases which come to court and the long entrenched positions of parents in 'high conflict' cases. These are unlikely to be resolved by the use of parenting agreements or child arrangement orders. They require experienced judges supported by child guardians and access to expert advice. Even with specialist lawyers they make great demands on all resources. And yet, in the future, courts will be expected to deal with such cases when both parents are normally litigants in person, guardians will be in short supply and possibly unrepresented, with no means of paying for hair-strand testing, psychiatric advice or specialist contact centres. The problems resulting from self-representing litigants are, of course, not confined to family courts. The recent Civil Justice Council report, *Access to Justice for Litigants in Person* warns that in many cases, 'members of the public with good claims will be left with no option but to abandon their rights and leave problems unresolved and potentially worsening, unless they are prepared to attempt to represent themselves'. The same may come to be true of family justice.

On a happier note, I am very grateful to Sir Nicholas Wall P for writing such a generous Foreword. The editorial team at Jordans – Greg Woodgate, Kate Hather and Gillian Wright and my wife have, as always, been encouraging and supportive even when their patience has been tested and I am pleased to be able to thank them once again.

The law is stated as at 7 March 2012.

John Mitchell

CONTENTS

Chapter 10
Residence Orders

Contents

TABLE OF CASES

References are to paragraph numbers.

TABLE OF STATUTES

References are to paragraph numbers.

TABLE OF STATUTORY INSTRUMENTS

References are to paragraph numbers.

TABLE OF EUROPEAN MATERIALS

References are to paragraph numbers.

TABLE OF OTHER MATERIALS

References are to paragraph numbers.

TABLE OF ABBREVIATIONS

CA 1989   Children Act 1989
CAFCASS   Children and Family Advisory and Support Service
CPR 1998   Civil Procedure Rules 1998
DSM–III   Diagnostic and Statistical Manual of Mental Disorders
FAO   Family Assistance Order
FHDRA   First Hearing Dispute Resolution Appointment
FPR 2010   Family Procedure Rules 2010
ICD   International Classification of Diseases
LSC   Legal Services Commission
PAS   Parental Alienation Syndrome
PD   Practice Direction (of the Civil Procedure Rules 1998 and the
                   Family Procedure Rules 2010)
SDQ   Strengths and Difficulties Questionnaire

Chapter 1

PRIVATE LAW PROCEEDINGS IN THE TWENTY-FIRST CENTURY

INTRODUCTION

1.1 The creators of the Children Act 1989 – the members of the Law Commission[1] who wrote *Family Law: Review of Children Law: Guardianship and Custody*[2] – and Lord McKay of Clashfern,[3] the Lord Chancellor, and the judges[4] who first applied the Act were born at a time when most children were born within marriage and relatively few parents, with the exception of the period immediately following the Second World War, divorced. When they practised law, they would have encountered few if any cases in which parents disputed the arrangements concerning their children following divorce. Stephen Cretney suggests that after the War the issue of 'custody' was secondary to whether a decree of divorce would be granted or not and because 'winning' the divorce had an influence on any orders made, this would lead to behind-the-scenes bargaining,[5] what, in these days when litigants have little need to fear the Queen's Proctor and there was no law forbidding collusion, is now called 'private ordering'. Wardship was there for the unusual case but until the development of the modern child protection system following the case of Maria Colwell in 1973, it was little used by most of the population

1.2 The creators of the Act were able to sweep away the 'complicated, confusing and unclear'[6] details of the law relating to children and replaced it with a framework, which nearly a quarter of a century after it was passed, can be applied to families very different from those envisaged at the time. The Law Commission commented that most orders relating to children are made in the course of divorce or other matrimonial proceedings and 'that will clearly continue'.[7] Now, nearly half of children are born outside marriage, a significant number of whose parents will not be living together. They may be

---

1   Most notably, Professor Brenda Hoggett, now Baroness Hale of Richmond, born 1945, to the Bar 1969. 'When I started out as a family lawyer, marriage was the central institution on which everything else depended … Separation and divorce were viewed as pathology.' Hale 'Practising family law: outside the box' [2011] Fam Law 1341.

2   (1988) HC 594.

3   Born 1927, admitted to The Faculty of Advocates 1955.

4   For example, the President of the Family Division Lord Justice Stephen Browne, born 1924, called to the Bar 1949, and Mrs Justice Bracewell, born 1934, called to the Bar 1955, who had special responsibility for supervising the introduction of the Act.

5   Cretney *Family Law in the Twentieth Century* (Oxford University Press, 2004), at pp 576–577.

6   *Family Law: Review of Children Law: Guardianship and Custody* op cit, at para 1.1.

7   Ibid, at para 1.8.

born into or become members of same-sex families. Some will have two mothers and one, possibly two, father figures. Yet the substantive law, for the most part, remains satisfactory. Complaints about private family law proceedings are mainly about the process, perceived – largely erroneously – as encouraging litigation in cases which can readily be resolved by attendance at parenting information programmes or mediation. Important extensions to the Act have been made – for example, the introduction of special guardianship in 2002 and contact activity and conditions in 2006 – but these have been to enhance rather than to repair the Act. Although the statutory definition of 'harm' was amended in 2002[8] to include impairment suffered from seeing or hearing the ill-treatment of others,[9] the Court of Appeal in *Re L, V, M, H (Contact: Domestic Violence)*[10] in 2000 was able, without the need for legislation, to embed in the s 1 welfare checklist the importance of a court taking into account the effect of past or the risk of future domestic violence.

FAMILIES IN THE TWENTY-FIRST CENTURY

1.3　The traditional family structure of a married couple and their co-resident children is declining, largely due to an increase in the number of households containing cohabiting or lone parents.[11]

Marriage and cohabitation

1.4　In the last 40 years there has been a continuing fall in the number of marriages in England and Wales, from 480,285 in 1972 to 231,490 in 2009, the lowest since 1895.[12] During the same period, unmarried cohabitation has increased to unprecedented levels. In the early 1960s fewer than one in a hundred adults under 50 were estimated to have been cohabiting at any one time compared with one in six currently. In 2004–07 three in five men and two in three women aged between 24 and 44 had cohabited at some point.[13] Cohabitation is no longer seen as socially deviant[14] and many consider themselves as having the same status and rights as if they were married[15] despite Government campaigns to make people more aware of the difference. However, cohabitation remains a relatively short-term relationship. At the tenth

---

8　　By the Adoption and Children Act 2002 but not brought into force until 2005.

9　　See **5.30**.

10　　[2000] 2 FLR 334. See **5.20**.

11　　Panico, Bartley and others 'Changes in family structure in early childhood in the Millenium Cohort Study' (*Population Trends* No 142 Winter 2010).

12　　Office for National Statistics (ONS). See also 'Marriages Down in 2009' [2011] Fam Law 449.

13　　Beaujouan and Bhrolcháin 'Cohabitation and marriage in Britain since the 1970s' (*Population Trends* No 145 Autumn 2011).

14　　See Probert 'Looking back on the overlooked: cohabitants and the law' in Douglas and Lowe (eds) *The Continuing Evolution of Family Law* (Jordans, 2009), ch 3. Probert cites the British Social Attitudes Survey which found that the percentage of respondents who thought that people who wanted to have children ought to marry fell from 70% in 1989 to 54% in 2000.

15　　Smart and Stevens *Cohabitation Breakdown* (Family Policy Studies Centre, 2000) summarised in *Cohabiting Parents' Experience of Relationships and Separation* Findings 460 (Joseph Rowntree Foundation).

anniversary of moving in together, half of cohabiting couples have married each other, just under four in ten have separated, and slightly over one in ten are still living together as a couple.[16]

Births

1.5 In parallel with these two trends there has been a steady rise in the proportion of births outside marriage although marriage or civil partnership remains the most common family setting for births in England and Wales. In 2010 just over half of births occurred within marriage or civil partnership (53%) compared with 61% in 2000 and 88% in 1980. The percentage of births occurring outside marriage or civil partnership varies considerably by age. Almost all women (96%) aged under 20 giving birth in 2010 were not married or in civil partnership. In contrast, at ages 30–39 the majority of women giving birth were either married or in a civil partnership, with only 30% of births outside marriage/civil partnership, the lowest percentage across all the age groups.[17] Of the total birth registrations, only the mother and not the father is named in around 7% of birth registrations, sole registration was much more common among younger mothers and particularly common for those who gave birth under the age of 21.[18]

Separation

1.6 In part because the chance of a couple divorcing is linked to the age at which they marry and this age having increased, the divorce rate has fallen to 10.5 people per thousand.[19] A significant proportion of children, born within marriage, will experience parental divorce in their childhood. A lack of clarity about what 'cohabiting' means and how it can be identified as having ended makes it difficult to obtain statistics about the proportion of cohabitations which end other than in marriage or death. However, it appears that a significantly higher proportion of cohabitations than marriages are terminated in any given period.[20] Until they are 3, children born into cohabiting households are most likely to see a change in parents or parental figures, with 17% having experienced such a change by age 3. By age 5, just under a quarter (24%) of children born to lone parents are slightly more likely than those born into cohabiting households (21%) to experience a change in parents or parental figures. By contrast, married couple households have much lower rates of just under 7% by the age of 5.[21]

---

[16] Beaujouan and Bhrolcháin op cit.
[17] *Live births in England and Wales by characteristics of mother* (ONS, 2011).
[18] *Births, further parental statistics* (ONS, 2009). See also **7.12**.
[19] (ONS, 2011). See also 'Divorce at 32 year low' [2011] Fam Law 433.
[20] Allan and Crow *Families, Households and Society* (Palgrave, 2001) at p 72.
[21] Panico, Bartley and others op cit.

Family structure

1.7   These trends have changed the structure of family households. In 2009, just over three-quarters (77%) of families with dependent children in Great Britain were headed by a married or cohabiting couple compared with 92% in 1971. The percentage of families headed by a lone mother had increased from 7% in 1971 to one in five in 2009, little changed since 1998. The proportion headed by a lone father has increased marginally since the early 1970s, but since the mid-1990s has remained at about 2 to 3%. In total, the proportion of families headed by a lone parent was 8% in 1971, but was nearly three times higher in 2009.[22]

1.8   Currently around one in ten families with dependent children are now step-families. Because children tend to stay with their mothers following separation, in 2006 over four in five (84%) of stepfamilies in Great Britain consisted of a stepfather and a natural mother compared with 10% with a stepmother and a natural father.[23]

Same-sex families

1.9   Hidden behind these statistics is an emergence of same-sex families. These are formed in a variety of ways. A couple, if in a civil partnership or living as partners in an enduring family relationship,[24] may adopt. A child may be born to another person, possibly as a result of impregnation by the intended male parent and then be placed in the care of the intended parents by way of surrogacy, a parental order under s 54 of the Human Fertilisation and Embryology Act 2008 (HFEA 2008) possibly being made to confer legal parenthood.[25] One of the intended female parents may become pregnant as a result of formal treatment, whether under the HFEA 2008 or abroad (in which case the male donor will probably be anonymous) or informally by an arrangement with a male donor.[26] In some cases it will be agreed prior to conception that the male donor – and his same-sex partner if he has one – will play some role in the child's life.[27] Finally, a step-same-sex family may be established by the two partners bringing their children born into other relationships into the family.[28]

1.10   Research indicates that children brought up by lesbian or gay parents do equally well as those brought up by heterosexual parents in terms of emotional well-being, sexual responsibility, academic achievement and avoidance of crime.[29] Informal arrangements for conception are a relatively recent

---

22   General Lifestyle Survey, (ONS, 2009).
23   *Social Trends 37* 2007. See also **10.98**.
24   Adoption and Children Act 2002, ss 50 and 144(4).
25   See **6.49**.
26   See **7.36**.
27   Ibid.
28   See **10.94**. See also *Ghaidan v Godin-Mendoza* [2004] UKHL 30, [2004] 2 FLR 600, per Baroness Hale of Richmond at [141].
29   Equal Treatment Bench Book Judicial College, at para 7.1.6. See also **10.97**.

development and there appears to be little research into how they work in the long term. Courts see only those cases where there are problems and not the successes, but a number of cases in the last 7 or so years show that problems may occur over issues such as parental responsibility,[30] shared residence[31] and contact. Other cases, most notably *Re G (Residence: Same-Sex Partner)*,[32] show that even where male donors are not involved in the life of the family, same-sex parents are not immune from post-separation disputes about contact or the greater importance that one may have as the birth mother.

1.11 In summary, demographic and social changes[33] have meant the traditional concept of a family which includes children, namely a heterosexual couple married to each other and bringing up children born to them both, is no longer the only model. These changes and the impact of international conventions and the European Union have resulted in much academic and political discussion about what, in law, does or should constitute a family.[34] Save for issues concerning a person's right under Art 8 of the European Convention for the Protection of Human Rights and Fundamental Freedoms 1950 to respect for private and family life,[35] the structure and definition matters little.

THE CHILDREN ACT 1989 AND THE FAMILY

1.12 In an evidence paper in 2008 the Department for Schools and Families[36] stated that 'All children need a "stable and harmonious home" in which to grow up'.[37]

> 'Families are the bedrock of our society, providing a wide range of functions. They nurture children, help to build strength, resilience and moral values in young people, and provide the love and encouragement that helps them lead fulfilling lives. Families are vital in ensuring all children have good life chances and the opportunities to get on in life.'

1.13 The Ministerial Foreword also added that:

> 'Extended family members provide one another with support throughout life, especially in difficult times and during critical moments, such as when a child is

---

30   See **7.37** and **10.41**.
31   See **10.41**.
32   [2005] EWCA Civ 462, [2005] 2 FLR 957. See **10.45**.
33   For a further discussion of which, see Douglas and Lowe *The Continuing Evolution of Family Law* op cit, ch 1, pp 3–10.
34   See, for example, Diduck *Law's Family* (LexisNexis, 2003), ch 2; McGlynn *Families and the European Union: Law, Politics and Pluralism* (Cambridge University Press, 2006), ch 4.
35   See, for example, **3.14**.
36   *Families in Britain: An Evidence Paper* (Department for Schools and Families, 2008), at p 4. The Paper makes it clear that it is 'an analytical discussion paper and not a statement of government policy'.
37   *Re P (Adoption; Unmarried Couple)* [2008] UKHL 38, [2008] 2 FLR 1084, per Baroness Hale of Richmond at [108].

born, when a couple is separating or when relatives need caring for. It is within families that a sense of identity develops, and cultural and social values are passed on from one generation to the next ... The family has also shown itself able to endure, shape and adapt to changes in social and economic circumstances, and it continues to do so today. So we see an increasing range of family structures, to the extent that there is arguably no longer a one size fits all family in Britain today. But this is diversity and not decline. Warm, loving and stable relationships matter more for our happiness and wellbeing than the legal form of a relationship. And while marriage will remain of central importance, the reality in many people's everyday lives is that more and more families experience a range of family forms throughout their life time. There is no single family form that guarantees happiness or success. All types of family can, in the right circumstances, look after their family members, help them get on in life and, for their children, have high hopes and the wherewithal to put them on the path to success.'

1.14 It is surprising therefore to realise that in Parts I and II of the Act which deal with private law proceedings, the word 'family' occurs in only two sections, namely s 10(5)(a) and (aa) in relation to the spouse or civil partner of a parent where the child is 'a child of the family' and s 16 which confers the power to make a 'family assistance order'.[38] Rather, the Act is concerned with relationships between the child and other individuals – those in direct biological relation with the child (parents) or in a legal relationship with a parent (spouses or civil partners); others who hold parental responsibility or who have residence or contact orders in their favour. Members of the extended family are mentioned only insofar as they are 'relatives'[39] and then only in relation to being able to apply for a residence or special guardianship order without requiring the permission of the court provided the child has lived with him or her for a period of at least one year immediately preceding the application.[40] But because the Act allows others to apply for residence, contact, specific issue and prohibited steps orders (the 's 8 orders') with permission of the court, courts have been able to make orders governing the relationship between children and all those who are important to them regardless of whether or not they share a genetic relationship. An important example is the 'psychological parent', someone unknown in statute but recognised by the courts. This person will share a 'relationship which develops through the child demanding and the parent providing for the child's needs, initially at the most basic level of feeding, nurturing, comforting and loving, and later at the more sophisticated level of guiding, socialising, educating and protecting'.[41] Needing

---

[38] The public law provisions do concern themselves to some extent with the family, for example CA 1989, s 23(6) which states that when a local authority is providing a home for the child it shall, so far as is consistent with his welfare, enable him to live with a list of specified people including a relative. See also, for example, *G and B (Children)* [2007] EWCA Civ 358, [2007] 2 FLR 140 and *Re A (A Child) (Care Order)* [2006] All ER (D) 247 (Oct) CA, which emphasise the importance of investigating whether family members are able to look after children who are the subject of care proceedings.

[39] Ie a grandparent, brother, sister, uncle or aunt (whether of the full blood or half blood or by marriage or civil partnership) or step-parent – CA 1989, s 105.

[40] Ibid, ss 10(5B) and 14A(5).

[41] *Re G (Children)* [2006] UKHL 43, [2006] 2 FLR 629, per Baroness Hale of Richmond at [33]–[37]. See also **6.62**.

permission to apply is, however, a continuing source of frustration for some family members, especially grandparents[42].

1.15 Extra-legally, the possible importance to the child of members of the wider family playing a part in resolving disputes and, arguably, to the family in being able to play such a part, can be seen in the support given to dispute resolution by way of family conferences.[43]

1.16 Whether the state should be concerned with family status has been the subject of political and academic debate, prompted by an increasing pluralism in society which contains ethnic groups for whom kinship is a primary reference point for social relations[44] and the normalisation of same-sex families.

> 'One prevalent view is that status is of decreasing importance and the new emphasis is rather on contract and on the appropriate ordering of family affairs. At its most basic, this is an approach which would treat those connected by personal, intimate relationships as if they were not so connected … [However, for others there is] a pervasive concern about the social acceptability of personal and family relationships and the need to secure for them the imprimatur of the law.'[45]

1.17 Whatever future policy decisions are taken, currently the law is concerned not with rights of the family or kinship group but with relationships between individuals, so much so that John Eekelaar has suggested that as in truth the law is dealing with people's 'personal' or 'private' lives, it would seem appropriate 'and could perhaps be liberating' to abandon the label 'family' law and replace it with the expression 'personal law'.[46]

THE CHILDREN ACT 1989 AS LAW

1.18 If the Parts I and II of the Act contain little about the family, they also contain little substantive law. The keystone of private law relating to children is parental responsibility.[47] Section 3 deals with what it is and ss 2, 4, 4ZA, 4A and 12B with how it is acquired. Sections 5 and 6 deal with the status of a guardian when the child has no parent or special guardian with parental

---

[42] See **15.34** and the Family Justice Review Final Report (Ministry of Justice 2011), at paras 4.41–4.48.

[43] See **16.18**.

[44] See, for example Iqbal and Simpson 'Kinship, infertility and new reproductive technologies: a British Pakistan Muslim experience' in Ebtehaj, Lindley, Richards (eds) *Kinship Matters* (Hart Publishing, 2006).

[45] Bainham 'Status anxiety? The rush for family recognition' in *Kinship Matters* op cit, at p 47. Both this paper and the others in the collection are valuable and interesting contributions to the questions which Bainham suggests might be considered by the Law Commission including what legal importance should be attached to kinship and whether the current legal effects arising from kinship remain appropriate or are in need of adjustment (at p 62). See also *The Law's Families* op cit and *Families and the European Union: Law, Politics and Pluralism* op cit.

[46] *Family Law and Personal Law* (Oxford University Press, 2007), at p 31.

[47] See **Chapter 7**.

responsibility[48] and ss 14A–14F with special guardianship.[49] Other than that, the sections are concerned with procedural remedies – the orders which can be made to govern the exercise of parental responsibility (the 's 8 orders'[50]), how decisions are made (the s 1 paramouncy principle that when a court determines any question with respect to the upbringing of a child, the child's welfare shall be the court's paramount consideration and the s 1(2) 'welfare checklist' of the circumstances to which the court in particular has to have regard when considering whether to make, vary or discharge a s 8 or special guardianship order[51]), and supplemental provisions for procedure,[52] investigation,[53] support[54] and the enforcement of contact.[55] When the Act was passed, it was easy to define who a parent was (although sometimes less easy to decide whether an individual male was or was not the father[56]) but scientific developments in the field of assisted reproduction has necessitated detailed provision defining who is or is not to be treated as a parent[57] and it was more appropriate for the legislature to set this out in the Human Fertilisation and Embryology Act 1990[58] than to amend the 1989 Act.

1.19 The lack of substantive law – usually conceived in terms of rights and remedies – in the Private law parts of the Act was deliberate.

> 'Family law is now largely a law of remedies, not rights. The circumstances of families vary so much that it is not possible to lay down in advance what the outcome of any dispute will be. Instead a wide variety of applications may be made for various forms of relief …'[59]

1.20 This had not always been the case. However by 1969 this watershed had been passed as shown by the decision in 1969 of the House of Lords in *J v C*:[60]

> 'While there is now no rule of law that the rights and wishes of unimpeachable parents must prevail over other considerations, such rights and wishes, recognised as they are by nature and society, can be capable of ministering to the total welfare of the child in a special way, and must therefore preponderate in many cases. The

---

48   See **Chapter 12**.
49   Ibid.
50   See **1.14**.
51   See **Chapter 2**.
52   Controlling who can apply for orders (s 10, see **Chapter 15**) and restricting future applications (s 91(14), see **Chapter 21**).
53   The power to direct s 7 and s 37 welfare reports (see **Chapter 19**).
54   The power to direct monitoring of contact orders (s 11H, see **Chapter 11**), to impose contact activity directions (ss 11A–11G) and to make Family Assistance orders in order to 'advise, assist and (where appropriate) befriend' any person named in a s 8 or special guardianship order (s 16, see **Chapter 13**).
55   Including making an unpaid work order or ordering compensation for financial loss (ss 11J–11P, see **Chapter 23**).
56   See **6.82**. However, the Law Commission commented (at para 2.20) that 'our present law has no coherent concept of parenthood as such'.
57   See **Chapter 6**.
58   Now the Human Fertilisation and Embryology Act 2008.
59   *Family Law: Review of Children Law: Guardianship and Custody* op cit, at para 1.8.
60   [1970] AC 668, per Lord MacDermott at 715.

parental rights, however, remain qualified and not absolute for the purposes of the investigation, the broad nature of which is still as described in the fourth of the principles enunciated by FitzGibbon LJ in *In re O'Hara* [1900] 2 IR 232 [namely that in ignoring the parental right the Court must act cautiously, not as if it were a private person acting with regard to his own child and acting in opposition to the parent only when judicially satisfied that the welfare of the child requires that the parental right should be suspended or superseded].'

1.21 By the time the Law Commission reported in 1988, talk of parental 'rights' had diminished further.

'Scattered through the statute book at present are such terms as "parental rights and duties" or the "powers and duties" or "the rights and authority" of a parent. However ... to talk of parental "rights" is not only inaccurate as a matter of juristic analysis but also a misleading use of ordinary language. The House of Lords in *Gillick v West Norfolk and Wisbech Area Health Authority*[61] has held that the powers which parents have to control or take decisions for their children are simply the necessary concomitant of their parental duties. To refer to the concept of "right" in the relationship between parent and child is therefore likely to produce confusion ...'[62]

Furthermore such parental powers are surrendered to the court when a legal dispute concerning their exercise arises. As noted above, the 'paramouncy principle' governs all decisions concerning any question with the respect to the upbringing of a child.

'Litigants might still be tempted to introduce evidence and arguments which [have] no relevance to the child's welfare in the hope of persuading the court to balance one against the other ... We recommend therefore that in reaching any decision about the child's upbringing [or] care ... the welfare of any child likely to be affected by the decision should be the court's only concern ... [The] new formulation [of the welfare checklist] still allows and indeed requires the court to take into account *all* the relevant circumstances and factors bearing upon the children's welfare ... [The] strength of a parent's natural "wishes and feelings" which can stem from parenthood itself[63] may be "capable of ministering to the welfare of a child in a very special way".[64]They may also blind the parent to the overall needs of the child which must always prevail.'[65]

1.22 The special place that a biological parent may occupy in the checklist is still recognised. For example, in *Re G (Children)*,[66] Lord Nicholls said that:

'In reaching its decision the court should always have in mind that in the ordinary way the rearing of a child by his or her biological parent can be expected to be in the child's best interests, both in the short term and also, and importantly, in the longer term.'

---

61 [1986] AC 112. See also **7.5**.
62 Op cit, at para 2.4.
63 *Re C (MA) (An Infant)* [1966] 1 WLR 646.
64 *J v C* [1970] AC 668, per Lord MacDermott at 715.
65 Op cit, at para 3.16.
66 [2006] UKHL 43, [2006] 2 FLR 629, at [3].

1.23   In the subsequent case of *Re B (A Child)*[67] Lord Kerr pointed out that it is only 'as a contributor to the child's welfare that parenthood assumes any significance. In common with all other factors bearing on what is in the best interests of the child, it must be examined for its potential to fulfil that aim.' As regards *Re G (Children)*:

> '[Lord Nicholls] was careful to qualify his statement, however, by the words "*in the ordinary way* the rearing of a child by his or her biological parent *can be expected* to be in the child's best interests"[68]. In the ordinary way one *can* expect that children will do best with their biological parents. But many disputes about residence and contact do not follow the ordinary way. Therefore, although one should keep in mind the common experience to which Lord Nicholls was referring, one must not be slow to recognise those cases where that common experience does not provide a reliable guide.'[69]

1.24   Family justice professionals share a settled view that the courts should be unfettered when considering the welfare of the child. Parents and others have their rights for respect for the family life protected by Art 8 of the Convention but this right has to be balanced against the rights of the child and may be subject to interference by the courts if required in the interests of the child.[70] It is not a settled view necessarily held by others. For example, the Family Justice Review ('the Norgrove Committee') in 2011 received a large response to its consultation about whether there should be a shared parenting presumption post-separation. Charities, legal and judicial organisations and academics supported the Committee's provisional stance that it should not. Against this, many individuals – typically grandparents and fathers – said that a presumption of shared parenting is necessary in order to ensure that both parents remain involved with their children post separation. The Committee remained firm in its view that 'any legislation that might risk creating an impression of a parental "right" to any particular amount of time with a child would undermine the central principle of the Children Act 1989 that the welfare of the child is paramount'.[71]

THE ROLE OF THE COURT

1.25   All contested applications which come before the courts in private law proceedings share a common feature. They are about the role the applicant should play in the life of a child. Should he or she have parental responsibility and be able to share in decision making about such matters as a choice of school or upbringing? Should the child live with the applicant and, if not what if any contact between the applicant and child should there be? For example, a mother with whom the child lives is able to emigrate with the child without the

---

67   [2009] UKSC 5, [2010] 1 FLR 551, at [37].
68   Emphasis added to the original in the citation.
69   *G (Children), Re* [2006] UKHL 43, at [34]. See also **10.68**.
70   See **Chapter 3**.
71   *Family Justice Review: Final Report* (Ministry of Justice, 2011), at paras 4.24–4.27. See also **10.27**.

consent of anyone unless there is a residence order in her favour, in which case the written consent of everyone with parental responsibility is required.[72] It is only if there is not consent, that the court becomes involved. Disputes of this kind commonly involve questions about how relocation will diminish the non-carer's relationship with the child by reducing contact or terminating shared care and whether this can be justified as being in the child's best interests.[73]

1.26 Courts attempt to assist the parties to solve the issue by negotiation. Leaving aside the benefits of alternative dispute resolution,[74] this is a legally principled approach because the court's powers can normally be invoked and the welfare checklist comes into play[75] only where there is a dispute. Where such resolution is impossible, the court has to determine what order, if any, is in the child's best interests. It is an essentially pragmatic process.

> 'Family court orders are meant to provide practical solutions to the practical problems faced by separating families. They are not meant to be aspirational statements of what would be for the best in some ideal world which has little prospect of realisation. Ideally there may be many cases where it would be best for the children to have a home with each of their parents. But this is not always or even usually practicable. Family courts have no power to conjure up resources where none exist.'[76]

1.27 Often the hearing cannot be described as a trial. In 1999[77] researchers[78] studying family proceedings in four county courts found that all had highly developed systems for managing cases. While these provided for formal case management, they were also occasions when often the parties could meet a Cafcass officer and, with an input, sometimes in the form of a quite powerful intervention from the judge, were negotiating opportunities. A high proportion of applications settled.

> 'We had gone looking for an old-fashioned, red in tooth and claw, welfare officer reporting and district judge adjudicating court and we could not find one.'

1.28 A recognisable trial will, however, take place in two circumstances. First, it is recognised that if allegations are made of domestic violence[79] (including

---

72   CA 1989, s 13(1).
73   See **Chapter 9**.
74   See **16.4**.
75   CA 1989, s 1(4)(a). See also *Family Law: Review of Children Law: Guardianship and Custody* op cit, para 3.19.
76   *Holmes-Moorhouse v Richmond-Upon-Thames London Borough Council* [2009] UKHL 7, [2009] 1 FLR 904, per Baroness Hale of Richmond at [38]. See **10.58**.
77   Ie before the institution of the Private Law Programme in 2004 – see **17.30**.
78   Davis and Pearce 'A view from the trenches – practice and procedure in section 8 applications' [1999] Fam Law 457; Bailey-Harris and others 'Settlement culture and the use of the "no order" principle under the Children Act 1989' [1999] CFLQ 53.
79   Ie threatening behaviour, violence or abuse (psychological, physical, sexual, financial or emotional) between adults who are or have been intimate partners or family members, regardless of gender or sexuality: *Domestic Violence: A National Report* (Home Office, 2005).

sexual abuse) which might affect the outcome of the case, these should be investigated at a fact-finding hearing to be held as quickly as possible.[80]

1.29 Second, if the dispute cannot be resolved during the case-management period a trial will be held in which the arguments of the parties, for example concerning relocation, will be examined and the factual and, if necessary, expert evidence[81] and welfare reports will be tested before the court decides the issues, applying the welfare checklist to the facts as found.

1.30 The checklist was designed by the Law Commission to assist greater consistency, clarity and a more systematic approach to decisions:

> 'Perhaps most important of all, we are told that such a list could assist both parents and children in endeavouring to understand how judicial decisions are made. At present, there is a tendency for advisers and clients (and possibly even courts) to rely on "rules of thumb" as to what the court is likely to think best in any given circumstances. A checklist would make it clear to all what, as a minimum would be considered by the court.'[82]

> 'While the checklist may provide a clear statement of what society considers the most important factors in the welfare of children, it must not be applied too rigidly or be so formulated as to prevent the court from taking into account everything which is relevant in the particular case.'[83]

However, it can only be practicable if it is 'confined to major points leaving others to be formulated elsewhere'.[84]

1.31 'Formulated elsewhere' has tended to mean guidance given by the Court of Appeal, for example in relation to changes in a child's name,[85] international relocation[86] or restrictions being placed on the making of further applications pursuant to s 91(14).[87] The guidance is based on judicial experience in other cases and proves useful. However, there are dangers that guidance may not hold its value much beyond the times in which it was expressed and, despite warning, that it may be treated as creating a presumption, inhibiting or distorting the rigorous search for the welfare solution.[88] That the danger is not just theoretical is demonstrated by the protracted debate on relocation and the

---

80 See **5.53** and **11.69**.
81 See **Chapter 18**.
82 Op cit, at para 3.18.
83 Ibid, at para 3.19.
84 Ibid.
85 In *W (A Child) (Illegitimate Child: Change of Surname), Re* [1999] 2 FLR 930; see **9.14**.
86 In *Payne v Payne* [2001] EWCA Civ 166, [2001] 1 FLR 1052, see **9.29**.
87 In *Re P (Section 91(14) Guidelines) (Residence and Religious Heritage)* [1999] 2 FLR 573, see **21.4**. For a discussion of guidance, see also **2.42**.
88 *Re L (Contact: Domestic Violence); Re V (Contact: Domestic Violence); Re M (Contact: Domestic Violence); Re H (Contact: Domestic Violence)* [2000] 2 FLR 334, per Thorpe LJ at 364.

guidance given in *Payne v Payne*.[89] In 2011 the Court of Appeal revisited the issue in *MK v CK*.[90] Moore-Bick LJ made the point that:

> 'The only principle of law enunciated in *Payne v Payne* is that the welfare of the child is paramount; all the rest is guidance. Such difficulty as has arisen is the result of treating that guidance as if it contained principles of law from which no departure is permitted. Guidance of the kind provided in *Payne v Payne* is, of course, very valuable both in ensuring that judges identify what are likely to be the most important factors to be taken into account and the weight that should generally be attached to them. It also plays a valuable role in promoting consistency in decision-making. However, the circumstances in which these difficult decisions have to be made vary infinitely and the judge in each case must be free to weigh up the individual factors and make whatever decision he or she considers to be in the best interests of the child.'

1.32 There are similar problems in regard to the application of guidance for making orders under s 91(14), restraining further applications. The guidance given in *Re P (Section 91(14) Guidelines) (Residence and Religious Heritage)*[91] states that such orders are generally to be seen as an exceptional weapon of last resort to be used when there is a history of repeated and unreasonable applications. However , in practice it tends to be applied by allowing the section to be used only where there is a such a history whereas, as the guidance states, the matter is governed by the welfare principle.[92]

1.33 The court's functions extend beyond the voluntary resolution, case management and determination stages. The court has the power to direct monitoring of contact orders by the Children and Family Advisory and Support Service (Cafcass).[93] Where contact disputes are seen as 'long-term', 'high conflict', 'intractable' or 'conflicted',[94] the court itself is expected to monitor contact by way of review hearings. 'Swift, efficient, enforcement of existing court orders' is required at the first sign of non-compliance.

> 'A flabby judicial response sends a very damaging message to the defaulting parent, who is encouraged to believe that court orders can be ignored with impunity, and potentially also to the child.'[95]

THE COURT PROCESS

1.34 In general, informed complaints about private law proceedings have not been about the application of the welfare checklist – although there were complaints pre-*Re L (Contact: Domestic Violence); Re V (Contact: Domestic*

---

[89]   See **9.22**.
[90]   [2011] EWCA Civ 793.
[91]   Op cit
[92]   See also **Chapter 21**.
[93]   See **11.65**.
[94]   See **11.172**.
[95]   *Re D (Intractable Contact Dispute: Publicity)* [2004] EWHC 727 (Fam), [2004] 1 FLR 1226, per Munby J at [56].

Violence); Re M (Contact: Domestic Violence); Re H (Contact: Domestic Violence)[96] about a perceived reluctance to address the issue of domestic violence and about the application of the *Payne* Guidelines. Rather they have been about the court process.

1.35 The *Family Justice Review: Interim Report*[97] discussed a range of issues that drove a need for reform. These included:

- the view (which might or might not be right) that lawyers generally took an adversarial approach that inflamed rather than reduced conflict;

- a perception that the system favours mothers over fathers;

- a fear that wider family members may lose contact;

- the difficulty of navigating the system;

- children not understanding processes or feeling listened to;

- questioning whether courts are the best place to resolve private law disputes;

- arrangements that may break down in the long term, at a high emotional cost to both children and adults;

- the time cases took; and

- changes to legal aid.

The Review made detailed recommendations with the aim of creating:

'… a supportive, clear process for private law cases that promotes joint parental responsibility at all stages, provides information, manages expectations and that helps people to understand the costs they face. The emphasis throughout should be on enabling people to resolve their disputes safely outside court wherever possible.'[98]

1.36 The Private Law Programme, now embedded in the Family Procedure Rules 2010,[99] shares this aim. Judicial continuity is expected to be the norm[100] and attendance at Parenting Information Programmes (PIPs)[101] and mediation,[102] strongly encouraged.

---

[96] Op cit.
[97] As cited in the *Family Justice Review: Interim Report* (Ministry of Justice, 2011), at para 4.2.
[98] Ibid, at para 4.69.
[99] Practice Direction 12B. see **Chapter 17**.
[100] See **16.109**.
[101] See **11.66**.
[102] See **16.8**.

1.37 Trinder, Bryson and Coleman, who have researched the effectiveness of PIPs,[103] caution that:

'The "one size fits all" approach was ill-suited to dealing with cases raising serious risk issues and could be coercive. The rapid processing of cases and focus on settlement also meant that children were excluded from the process or risked becoming responsible for decisions.'[104]

1.38 There remains, however, a significant proportion of cases where it is unsafe to promote private ordering or alternative dispute resolution, for example because of domestic violence, or where, despite every effort the parties or one of them refuse to engage in a genuine attempt to resolve their difficulties. As regards the first category, a survey[105] found a high level of reported violence with just under two-fifths of women citing domestic abuse/violence as a reason for separation and three-tenths, mental or verbal abuse. At the time of the application for contact, three-fifths of women and a quarter of men reported that a fear of violence from an ex-partner or ex-partner's new partner made it more difficult to sort out problems with the ex-partner. And, as regards the second, many parents involved in legal disputes are experiencing multiple problems and difficulties in caring for the children.[106]

1.39 Some parents will have long lasting personal or inter-personal problems.

'I have already expressed how limited is the capacity of the family justice system to produce good outcomes in disputed areas of personal relationship. Yet a great deal of the resources of the system are taken up with contested contact cases. The disputes are particularly prevalent and intractable. They consume a disproportionate quantity of private law judicial time. The disputes are often driven by personality disorders, unresolved adult conflicts or egocentricity. These originating or contributing factors would generally be better treated therapeutically, where at least there would be some prospect of beneficial change, rather than given vent in the family justice system.'[107]

The court cannot refuse to deal with such cases and although they might, in theory, be better dealt with through services such as the NHS as Lord Justice Thorpe suggested, those resources are limited and an adult cannot be compelled to take part in therapy. If the non-resident parent and the child are

---

[103] Trinder, Bryson, Coleman and others *Building bridges? An evaluation of the costs and effectiveness of the Separated Parents Information Programme (PIP)* (Department for Education Research Report DFE-RR140, 2011), summarised in Trinder, Smith, Bryson and others 'The Separated Parent Information Programme: Current effectiveness and future potential' [2011] Fam Law 998. See **11.66**.

[104] *Making contact happen or making contact work?* at p 100.

[105] Trinder, Connolly and others *Making contact happen or making contact work?* (Department for Constitutional Affairs DCA Research Series 3/06, 2006) at pp 85–88, summarised in [2006] Fam Law 416. See also Trinder 'Conciliation, the Private Law Programme and children's well-being: Two steps forward, one step back?' [2008] Fam Law 338.

[106] See **10.66**.

[107] *Re L (Contact: Domestic Violence); Re V (Contact: Domestic Violence); Re M (Contact: Domestic Violence); Re H (Contact: Domestic Violence)* [2000] 2 FLR 334, per Thorpe LJ at 366.

to have the contact which the child's welfare requires, in some cases this can be secured only by the exercise of the court's authority.[108]

THE FUTURE

1.40 The Family Justice Review recommends that all new parents are provided with information at the time their child is born about the meaning and practical implications of parental responsibility. If disputes later arrive, parents need to be helped to find routes to resolve their disputes short of court proceedings by an online 'information hub', the use of mediation and PIPs, and the use of parenting agreements setting out the practical arrangements for the care of the child.

The Family Justice Review also recommends the introduction of a child arrangements order in place of orders for residence and contact. This would set out the arrangements for the upbringing of the child and would:

'... focus all discussions on resolving issues related to their care, rather than on labels such as residence and contact. It would of course, be necessary either in a Parenting Agreement or a court order to provide clarity on where a child would normally live and with whom a child would spend time.'[109]

Whether this will amount to more than 're-badging' and how it will work in practice remains to be seen. There is the risk that instead of dealing with broad issues of residence and whether there should be direct contact and if so, of what kind, courts will be expected to deal with the minutiae of a child's life more often than at present.

1.41 The Review, possibly influenced by civil procedure, proposes a twin-track system for resolving disputes which remain contested.[110]

1.42 The simple track would be used to determine narrow and (most likely) single issues, without allegations of domestic abuse, and those where no findings of fact are required. The court would undertake a tightly-managed hearing (limited, say, to 2 hours), held at short notice and during which each party could be heard. It should allow the court flexibility to proceed in whichever manner it considers practical and fair in order to support the parties to reach agreement. Instructions would be given to enable the parties to understand the process and to minimise the scope for delay. They would be required to submit all documents relating to the case within deadlines before each hearing. Tailored case-management rules and principles would apply. These could include:

● informal hearings;

---

[108] And see the comments of Coleridge J at **11.172**.
[109] Op cit, at para 4.60.
[110] Ibid, at paras 4.124–4.129.

- limited cross-examination;

- removal of strict rules for evidence; and

- limitations on numbers of hearings and indeed the expectation of only one in the majority of cases.

Presumably these would be cases where no s 7 report or expert evidence was required.

1.43 Other cases would be allocated to the complex track.

1.44 The Review contains no suggestion as to how many and what proportion of cases would be suitable for the simple track. However, it is a valuable suggestion. District judges are well used to dealing with civil claims on a similar Small Claims track.[111] There will, however, be considerable difficulties with the complex track because, as a result of changes to Legal Aid, there will be a sharp increase in the already growing proportion of litigants in person. The Civil Justice Council's report, *Access to Justice for Litigants in Person*[112] described the future for civil justice.

> 'In many other cases, members of the public with good claims will be left with no option but to abandon their rights and leave problems unresolved and potentially worsening, unless they are prepared to attempt to represent themselves.'

1.45 It identified the difficulties encountered by litigants in person, not only in presenting but also formulating their cases and on the demands that they legitimately make on those representing the other party, the judiciary and the court staff. It made a number of valuable recommendations[113] but bluntly stated that:

> 'Even if all the recommendations we make are acted upon, they will not prevent the reality that in many situations, as a result of the reductions and changes in legal aid, there will be a denial of justice. There must be no misunderstanding about this. Put colloquially, the recommendations are about making "the best of a bad job".'[114]

1.46 Within the Family Justice System litigants in person will face all the difficulties encountered within the civil system but with the additional highly aggravating factor that their emotions are deeply engaged.

Problems will include:

- negotiating with the other party;

---

[111] See the Civil Procedure Rules 1998, Pt 27.
[112] (2011), at para 2.
[113] See, for example, **17.157**.
[114] Op cit, at para 19.

- preparing the case (whether or not they have educational or language difficulties);

- identifying, instructing and paying for experts;

- conducting any trial sensitively and in a way which does not exacerbate feelings;

- instituting and pursuing enforcement proceedings appropriately.

1.47 The family judges' role which is already quasi-inquisitorial will become more so. A number of questions readily identify themselves. Will the judge have any part to play in identifying an expert and if not, will Cafcass have such a role? Will the judge be expected to draft the letter of instruction? It might be argued that experts in private law proceedings are not usually required but they are in intractable contact cases. Where fact-finding hearings are to be held, how will important third party information, for example from the police or health authorities be obtained? Will the Court Service be expected to do this?

1.48 Access to Justice for Litigants in Person warned that 'if there is not an increase in litigants in person, the reason will be that the individual was resigned to accepting that the civil justice system was not open to them even if they had a problem it could solve or it could give access to the rights they were entitled to'.[115] The same will be true for the family justice system.

Research: a warning note

1.49 Fifty years ago, family law was firmly rooted in a legalistic framework and 'was seen apart from the values it embodied and helped to structure and restructure'.[116] Now, as Professors Douglas and Lowe have pointed out:[117]

'Empirical data and the insights of non-legal disciplines are used as a means of understanding how and why the law developed in the ways it has ... The socio-legal approach ... has come to be relied on to a major extent not only by legal scholars and policy makers but also by practitioners and the judiciary ... Research into how laws operate and how the family justice system operates plays an increasingly important role in influencing opinions and decision making.'

It is for this reason that the Handbook contains references not only to policy documents (such as *The Family Justice Review*) but also to socio-legal research (for example, *Making Contact Happen or Making Contact Work?*)[118] and literature reviews of social research (such as *Caring for children after parental*

---

[115] Ibid, para 15.
[116] Freeman 'Fifty years of family law: an opinionated review' in Douglas and Lowe (eds) *The Continuing Evolution of Family Law* (2009), at p 153.
[117] Ibid, at p 2.
[118] Op cit.

separation: would legislation for shared parenting time help children?)[119] as well as individual pieces of research. It is hoped that they will be found useful by both legal or social worker practitioners and provide them with possibilities for further investigation. However, there must be warnings. This is a legal handbook for practitioners and not a literature review. Not every important domestic – let alone foreign – study is included. Nor is it a substitute for expert evidence focused on the specific circumstances of the individual case. It will not provide a foundation for successfully asserting that 'judicial knowledge' will be taken of any 'fact' contained in it.

---

[119] Fehlberg, Smyth, Maclean and Roberts (Oxford University: Department of Social Policy and Intervention, Family Policy Briefing 7, 2011).

Chapter 2

THE WELFARE TEST

INTRODUCTION

2.1 Private law decisions about the future of children are strikingly different from civil disputes where most legal rules are 'act orientated', requiring a determination of a past event. Instead there is a 'person orientated' approach in which the court evaluates the attitudes, capacities, strengths and shortcomings of each adult and the needs of the child. Proof of what happened in the past is relevant only insofar as it enables the court to decide what is likely to happen in the future.[1]

2.2 This approach is made clear by s 1 of CA 1989 which governs the approach of the court to all applications which concern the upbringing of a child. The child's welfare has to be the court's paramount consideration ('the paramountcy principle'). In deciding what is in the best interests of the child, the court has to have regard to all the circumstances including those in what is known as 'the s 1 checklist'. The decision has to be based on the circumstances of the individual child and there are no presumptions, for example that a young child should live with his mother as opposed to his father. In addition, the court has to have regard to two matters of general application: the 'no delay' and the 'no order' principles. First, there is the principle that any delay in determining the question is likely to prejudice the welfare of a child. Secondly, the court must not make an order unless it considers that doing so would be better for the child than making no order at all.

THE WELFARE TEST

2.3

'When a court determines any question with respect to –

(a)   the upbringing of a child or
(b)   the administration of a child's property or the application of any income arising from it

the child's welfare shall be the court's paramount consideration.'[2]

---

[1]   Mnookin 'Child-custody adjudication: judicial functions in the face of indeterminacy' (1975) 39 *Law and Contemporary Problems* 226.

[2]   Children Act 1989, s 1(1).

'Welfare' has to be construed in the widest sense. It has to be measured not only by material standards but also in terms of the child's moral and emotional well-being.[3] The classic exposition of the paramountcy principle was given by Lord MacDermott in *J v C*:[4]

> 'Reading these words in their ordinary significance and relating them to the various classes of proceedings [in which they are to be applied], it seems to me that they must mean more than that the child's welfare is to be treated as the top item in a list of items relevant to the matters in question. I think they connote a process whereby, when all the relevant facts, relationships, claims and wishes of parents, risks, choices and other circumstances are taken into account and weighed, the course to be followed will be that which is most in the interests of the child's welfare as that term now has to be considered. That is the first consideration because it is of first importance and the paramount consideration because it rules upon or determines the course to be followed.'

2.4   Although the court takes account of 'child welfare science' derived from medical and social scientific discourses about child health and development, either directly by way of expert medical evidence or from 'judicial knowledge' of prevailing beliefs about how a family should be structured and what role its members should play, the process cannot directly import all the sometimes contradictory factors which science would recognise as being capable of affecting children's welfare.[5] Nor is it a scientific process. It is not one of precision, with values being attributed to the different factors, but rather calls for a quality of judgment and this is not susceptible to detailed analysis. As Megarry J commented in *Re F (An Infant)*:[6]

> 'There is a limit to the extent to which the court can fairly be expected to expound the process which leads to a conclusion, not least in the weighing of imponderables.[7] In matters of discretion it may at times be impossible to do much more than ensure that the judicial mind is brought to bear, with a proper emphasis on all that is relevant to the exclusion of all that is irrelevant.'

The wishes of the parent, whether what used to be called the 'unimpeachable parent'[8] or otherwise, cannot dictate the course to be followed:

> 'The role of the court is to exercise an independent and objective judgment. If that judgment accords with that of the devoted and responsible parent, well and good. If not, then it is the duty of the court, after giving due weight to the view of the

---

3   *Re McGrath (Infant)* [1893] 1 Ch 143.
4   [1970] AC 668, at 710.
5   Barnett 'The welfare of the child re-visited: in whose best interests?' [2009] Fam Law 50, 135
6   [1969] 2 All ER 766, at 768.
7   Judges should 'approach each case in a position of uncertainty, respecting the complexity and ambiguity of a client's life'. Piper 'Assumptions about children's best interests' (2002) 24 *Journal of Social Welfare and Family Law* 261 at 265. See also Rhoades 'Revising Australia's parenting laws' [2010] CFLQ 172.
8   And see the comments of Ormrod LJ in *S (BD) v S (DJ) (Infants: Care and Consent)* [1977] 1 All ER 656 at 661: 'I have never known and still do not know what [the phrase] means', discussed in **Chapter 10**.

devoted and responsible parent, to give effect to its own judgment ... Once the jurisdiction of the court is invoked, its clear duty is to reach and express the best judgment it can.'[9]

When does the test apply?

2.5 The test is to be applied when a court decides any question with respect to a child's upbringing or the administration of a child's property or the application of any income arising from it.[10] It will not apply when a statute stipulates another test or when the question to be decided does not involve the child's upbringing. Sometimes sophisticated analysis is required to decide whether the issue concerns the upbringing of the child. For example, in *Re Z (A Minor) (Freedom of Publication)*[11] the Court of Appeal refused to allow a mother to co-operate with the making of a television programme whose subject was the way in which her child was being raised. Whether or not the child should take part was a matter concerning her upbringing and therefore the welfare of the child was the paramount consideration. If, however, the programme had been made without the mother's co-operation and the child's participation, and an injunction was then sought to prevent it being broadcast, the issue would concern the publicity to be given to the upbringing of the child and not the upbringing itself. The welfare of the child, while still a consideration, would not be paramount and would have to be balanced against the importance of the freedom of publication.

2.6 Procedural issues rather than substantive ones do not involve questions of a child's upbringing.[12] The test does not apply when the court is considering an application for leave to apply for a s 8 order,[13] to be joined as a party,[14] or for the ordering of a blood test.[15] Absent cases involving Brussels bis II or the Hague Convention and the European Convention on the Recognition and Enforcement of Decisions Concerning Custody of Children and on the Restoration of Custody of Children 1980, the test applies when a court is deciding whether to remit cases to another jurisdiction on grounds of forum conveniens or because the child has been abducted from a non-Convention country.[16]

Even when the test does not apply, the court will still regard the welfare of the child as one of the factors to be taken into account.

Where two siblings are involved in the same proceedings, the welfare test must be applied separately to each. See **10.118**.

---

9   *Re Z (A Minor) (Freedom of Publication)* [1996] 1 FLR 191, per Sir Thomas Bingham at 217.
10   CA 1989, s 1(1).
11   [1996] 1 FLR 191.
12   *Re A and W (Minors) (Residence Order: Leave to Apply)* [1992] 2 FLR 154.
13   Ibid.
14   *G v Kirklees Metropolitan Borough Council* [1993] 1 FLR 805.
15   *S (An Infant, by her Guardian ad Litem the Official Solicitor to the Supreme Court) v S; W v Official Solicitor (acting as Guardian ad Litem for a Male Infant named PHW)* [1972] AC 24.
16   *Re J (Child Returned Abroad: Convention Rights)* [2005] UKHL 40, [2005] 2 FLR 802.

THE WELFARE TEST AND ARTICLE 8

2.7 There is potential for conflict between s 1 and Art 8 of the European Convention for the Protection of Human Rights and Fundamental Freedoms 1950. This is discussed in **Chapter 3**.

DELAY

2.8

> 'In any proceedings in which any question with respect to the upbringing of a child arises, the court shall have regard to the general principle that any delay in determining the question is likely to prejudice the welfare of the child.'[17]

The Overriding Objective in the Family Procedure Rules 2010[18] emphasises this by stating that dealing with a case justly includes, so far as is practicable, ensuring that it is dealt with expeditiously and fairly by active case management.[19]

2.9 In addition, Art 6(1) of the European Convention for the Protection of Human Rights and Fundamental Freedoms 1950 requires that proceedings should be determined 'within a reasonable time'. The European Court of Human Rights has recognised that the reasonableness of the length of proceedings must be assessed in the light of the circumstances of the particular case, in particular to its complexity, the conduct of the applicant and to the importance to the applicant of what is at stake but it is essential for custody cases to be dealt with speedily.[20]

The importance of avoiding delay

2.10 In its Working Paper,[21] the Law Commission proposed that any dispute about a child's upbringing should be heard within a maximum of 3 months. The final report reluctantly drew back from stipulating a time-limit because it recognised the resource implications but nevertheless emphasised the importance of the principle:

> 'The case for a scheme along these lines is very strong indeed. Prolonged litigation about their future is deeply disturbing [to children] not only because of the uncertainty it brings for them but because of the harm it does to the relationship between the parents and their capacity to cooperate with one another in the future. Moreover, a frequent consequence is that the case of the parent who is not living with the child is severely prejudiced by the time of the hearing. Regrettably it is

---

17 CA 1989, s 1(2).
18 SI 2010/2955 (L.17) Pt 1.1(2), r 1.4.
19 See **17.6**.
20 *Nuutinen v Finland* (2002) 34 EHRR 15; *Adam v Germany* [2009] 1 FLR 560.
21 *Care, Supervision and Interim Orders in Custody Proceedings* (1987) Working Paper No 100.

almost always to the advantage of one of the parties to delay the proceedings as long as possible and, what may be worse, to make difficulties over contact in the meantime.'[22]

2.11 A sense of time is relative. What may be a short period for an adult may seem an eternity for a young child and delay in the resolution of disputes therefore has to be viewed not just in terms of objective measurements of weeks and months but according to what has been called 'the child's sense of time':[23]

> 'Too often adults forget how things look to children. They think about systems, what is logical and what are acceptable timescales from an adult's point of view. Adults forget how time appears to pass more slowly to children. Adults tend no longer to remember the confusion of entirely new issues and the worry of questioning those who are grownup and logical.'[24]

2.12 Take, for example, delay in deciding whether or not there should be contact between a father and his child following separation. Goldstein, Freud and Solnit[25] commented that:

> 'For most children under the age of five years, an absence of parents for more than two months is ... beyond comprehension. For the younger school-age child, an absence of six months or more may be similarly experienced. More than one year of being without parents and without evidence that there are parental concerns and expectations is not likely to be understood by the older school-age child and will carry with it the detrimental implications of the breaches in continuity ,,, After adolescence is fully launched an individual's sense of time closely approaches that of most adults.'

2.13 The point in the child's development at which the unresolved dispute occurs is also significant. Growth in different areas – physical, intellectual, emotional and social and educational – does not take place at an even pace. Although, in most areas of development, the period of most rapid growth occurs in the first 6 years with a 'spurt' at puberty, for some characteristics there is as much quantitive growth in a single year as there are in 8 or 10 years at other stages. Studies suggest that there are periods when children respond more readily to various environmental opportunities and setbacks during these periods may have a lasting, although not necessarily irreversible, effect on the child's development.[26]

2.14 Disputes often adversely affect the child and his parents, not only during the course of the litigation but for some time afterwards. One study, *Families in*

---

[22] *Family Law Review of Child Law: Guardianship and Custody* (1988) Law Com No 172, para 4.55.

[23] Goldstein, Freud, Solnit *Beyond the Best Interests of the Child* (Macmillan, 1973).

[24] *Adoption: A New Approach* (Department of Health, 2000).

[25] Goldstein, Freud, Solnit *Beyond the Best Interests of the Child* (Macmillan, 1973) at p 41.

[26] Pringle *The Needs of Children* (3rd edn, 1986), pp 19–24.

Conflict,[27] measured the well-being of parents and children both at the end of disputed residence or contact proceedings and one year later. They found that, after the proceedings, four in five (84%) of parents were experiencing disruption in the way in which they normally functioned. Just under half (46%) of the children had borderline or abnormal scores on a Strengths and Difficulties questionnaire (SDQ), indicating a significant level of emotional and behavioural difficulties.[28] One year later, the well-being of parents had improved but over two in five (43%) of fathers and a third of mothers were still experiencing emotional problems. The well-being of the children, on the other hand, had deteriorated during the year, more than half (56%) having borderline or abnormal SDQ scores. Thirty-eight per cent of girls still had significant difficulties (nearly twice that expected in the general population) but the percentage of boys in these ranges had increased to over three in five (62%), three times that expected. Overall, younger children were more likely to be affected than older ones.

Causes of delay

2.15 Two studies commissioned by the Lord Chancellor's Department, that by Dame Margaret Booth in 1996[29] and a scoping study in 2002,[30] examined the causes of delay. They identified a number of causes, aggravated by the unpredictable number of applications being made each year. These included:

- a lack of adequate resources, including what the scoping study called 'not having the right judges in the right place at the right time';

- poor administration;

- lax procedures on transfer from the family proceedings courts;

- lack of proper control by the courts through case management;

- too many parties being joined;

- overuse of experts and insufficient experienced experts of the level required.

2.16 In private law proceedings, there has to be added to the list, insufficient Cafcass officers. Following the Booth report, the Children Act Advisory

---

[27] Buchanan and Others *Families in Conflict* (The Policy Press, 2001) summarised in Buchanan and others 'Families in conflict – perspectives of children and parents on the Family Court Welfare Service' [2001] Fam Law 900.

[28] In the general population of children, it would be expected that 80% would score in the normal range, 10% in the borderline and 10% in the abnormal range.

[29] *Avoiding Delay in Children Act Cases* (Lord Chancellor's Department, 1996).

[30] *Scoping Study on Delay in Children Act Cases* (Lord Chancellor's Department, 2002), summarised in [2002] Fam Law 492. See also Finlay 'Delay and the challenges of the Children Act' in Thorpe and Cowton (eds) *Delight and Dole – The Children Act 10 Years On* (Family Law, 2002).

Committee produced a *Handbook of Best Practice in Children Act Cases*,[31] whose recommendations were designed to reduce delay in many of these areas. The specific recommendations are discussed in **Chapters 18, 19** and **20**.

Acceptable delay

2.17 Not all delay prejudices the child. It can be acceptable, provided it furthers the child's interests:

> 'Delay is ordinarily inimical to the welfare of the child, but ... planned and purposeful delay may well be beneficial. A delay of a final decision for the purpose of ascertaining the result of an assessment is proper delay and is to be encouraged.'[32]

For example, ordering a s 7 Cafcass report may delay the final hearing, but the child will benefit by the court having a fuller picture of the circumstances of the case and an independent and professional recommendation as to the risks and benefits of various options. Delay caused by ordering contact between a young child and her father with the final hearing being adjourned for, say, 4 months to see how contact progressed can also be beneficial.[33]

THE WELFARE CHECKLIST

2.18 A court, when considering whether to make, vary or discharge a s 8 order in contested proceedings, must have regard in particular to a number of matters listed in s 1(3). This quickly became known as 'the welfare checklist'.

2.19 The Law Commission proposed a checklist as a means of providing greater consistency, clarity and a more systematic approach to decisions:

> 'Perhaps most important of all, we are told that such a list could assist both parents and children in endeavouring to understand how judicial decisions are made. At present, there is a tendency for advisers and clients (and possibly even courts) to rely on "rules of thumb" as to what the court is likely to think best in any given circumstances. A checklist would make it clear to all what, as a minimum would be considered by the court.'[34]

2.20 The Law Commission recognised the limits of a checklist. There was a need to ensure that it should not increase the burden on courts in uncontested cases 'and thus encourage them to intervene unnecessarily'. Hence the provision that it applies only in contested cases. Further:

> 'While the checklist may provide a clear statement of what society considers the most important factors in the welfare of children, it must not be applied too

---

31 The Lord Chancellor's Department, July 1997. See Appendix C.
32 *C v Solihull Metropolitan Borough Council* [1993] 1 FLR 290, per Ward J at 304.
33 *Re B (Minor) (Contact: Interim Order)* [1994] 2 FLR 269.
34 *Family Law Review of Child Law: Guardianship and Custody* (1988) Law Com No 172.

rigidly or be so formulated as to prevent the court from taking into account everything which is relevant in the particular case.'

The checklist could only be practicable if it was 'confined to major points leaving others to be formulated elsewhere'. Finally, because knowledge and understanding of children and their needs were progressing all the time, courts had to be able to keep pace with change and free of fetters imposed by too detailed or rigid a list.

2.21 Like the checklist of matters to be considered when a court makes an order for financial relief which are set out in s 25 of the Matrimonial Causes Act 1973, the checklist contains no hierarchy:

'It is one of the functions of the Court of Appeal, in appropriate cases, to lay down general guidelines on the relative weights to be given to various factors in different circumstances ... These guidelines, not expressly stated by Parliament, are derived by the courts from values about family life which it considers would be widely accepted in the community. But there are many cases which involve value judgements on which there are no such generally held views ... Since judges are also people, this means that some degree of diversity in their application of values is inevitable and, within limits, an acceptable price to pay for the flexibility of the discretion conferred by the ... Act. The appellate court must be willing to permit a degree of pluralism in these matters.'[35]

2.22 Nor are the factors given a generally applicable weight. 'Each case turns on its own facts and the weight to be given to various factors will change from case to case.'[36]

2.23 The section 1 test is founded on the welfare of a specific child, the child who is the subject of the adjudication. 'The focus [of the trial judge] has to be on the individual child in the particular circumstances of the case'[37] and general propositions of policy, for example that comity requires that a child abducted from a non-Convention country should be returned to that country, must give way to the interests of the individual child.

---

[35] *Piglowska v Piglowski* [1999] 2 FLR 763, per Lord Hoffmann at 785–786, discussing the financial relief checklist.

[36] *Re W (Children) (Relocation: Removal Outside the Jurisdiction)* [2011] EWCA Civ 345 per Wall P at [117]. See also *Payne v Payne* [2001] 1 FLR 1052 per Butler-Sloss P at 1078; *Re M* [2009] EWHC 2525 (Fam), [2010] 3 All ER 682 per Munby J at [35]; *MK v CK (Relocation: Shared Care Arrangement)* [2011] EWCA Civ 793 per Black LJ at [144].

[37] *Re J (Child Returned Abroad: Convention Rights)* [2005] UKHL 40, [2005] 2 FLR 802 per Baroness Hale at para 29.

The wishes and feelings of the child

The ascertainable wishes and feelings of the child concerned (considered in the light of his age and understanding)

2.24 The topic of a child's wishes and feelings, how they are ascertained, the weight to be given to them and the linked topic of the circumstances in which a child can or should be made a party is the subject of **Chapter 4**.

> 'The weight to be attached to [the child's] wishes and feelings will always be case-specific and fact-specific. In some cases, in some situations, they may carry much, even on occasions, preponderant, weight. In other cases, in other situations, and even where the circumstances may have a superficial similarity, they may carry very little weight.'[38]

'Wishes and feelings' will normally be investigated by way of a Cafcass report, although in appropriate but exceptional cases, the child may be joined as a party and represented by a guardian or next friend. In rare cases, when the child is able (having regard to his understanding) to give instructions in relation to the proceedings, he may be allowed to act without a guardian/next friend.

Wishes and feelings do not determine the issue to be decided, being only one of the factors in the welfare checklist.

Needs

His physical, educational and emotional needs

2.25 Physical and educational needs require little elaboration. A child needs adequate nutrition, hygiene and safety from injury, whether caused deliberately or by neglect.

2.26 The Department of Health in its *Framework for the Assessment of Children in Need and their Families*[39] defines 'health' including growth and development as well as physical and mental wellbeing.

> 'The impact of genetic factors and of any impairment should be considered. It involves receiving appropriate health care when ill, an adequate and nutritious diet, exercise, immunisations where appropriate and developmental checks, dental and optical care and, for older children, appropriate advice and information on issues that have an impact on health, including sex education and substance misuse.'

2.27 Parents are under a duty to cause their child of compulsory school age to receive efficient full-time education suitable to his age, ability and aptitude and

---

[38] *Re M* [2009] EWHC 2525 (Fam), [2010] 3 All ER 682 per Munby J at [35], a case involving an adult lacking capacity.
[39] (HMSO, 2000) chapter 2.

to any special educational needs he may have whether by ensuring he attends school 'or otherwise'.[40] The *Framework* adds that education:

> '... covers all areas of a child's cognitive development which begins from birth'. The child's needs include 'opportunities: for play and interaction with other children; to have access to books; to acquire a range of skills and interests; to experience success and achievement ... an adult interested in educational activities, progress and achievements, who takes account of the child's starting point and any special educational needs.'

2.28   Emotional needs are less obvious. Dr Mia Kellmer Pringle, the former Director of the National Children's Bureau, suggested that there are four basic emotional needs which have to be met from the very beginning of life to enable a child to grow 'from helpless infancy to mature adulthood'.[41] These are:

• The need for love and security – this is probably the most important because it provides the basis for all later relationships:

> 'The security of a familiar place and a known routine make for continuity and predictability in a world in which the child has to come to terms with so much that is new and changing. Also, a stable family life provides him with a sense of personal continuity, of having a past as well as a future, and of a coherent and enduring identity.'

• The need for new experiences:

> 'Just as the body requires food for physical development and just as an appropriate balanced diet is essential for normal growth, so new experiences are needed for the mind.'

The most important experiences are play and language. Play helps the child learn and the child's language environment – not just how much he is talked and listened to but also how relevant and rich the conversation is – is probably the most crucial factor which promotes intellectual growth.

• The need for praise and recognition:

> 'Because growing up is beset by difficulties, conflicts and setbacks, a strong incentive is needed. This is provided by the pleasure shown at success and the praise given to achievement by the adults who love the child and whom he in turn loves and wants to please.'

The level of expectation cannot, of course, be the same for all children.

---

[40]   Education Act 1944, s 36, as amended.
[41]   Pringle *The Needs of Children* (3rd edn, 1986). This book was commissioned by the Department of Health in the early 1970s and is still in print. All quotations are from Chapter 7.

- *The need for responsibility* – this is met by allowing the child to gain personal independence, by learning to look after himself, for example, feeding, washing and dressing himself, and later expending his responsibility so that ultimately he has freedom over his own actions:

  > 'Granting increasing independence … does [not] mean opting out from participating in and guiding the lives of children nor, indeed, cordoning everything they do. On the contrary, children need a framework of guidance and of interests. They are helped by knowing what is expected or permitted, what the rules are, together with the reasons for them, and whether these are in their interests or in the interests of others.'

2.29   The *Framework* provides a different but equally useful analysis.

- *Emotional and Behavioural Development* – 'the appropriateness of response demonstrated in feelings and actions by a child, initially to parents and caregivers and, as the child grows older, to others beyond the family'; it includes 'nature and quality of early attachments, characteristics of temperament, adaptation to change, response to stress and degree of appropriate self control'.

- *Identity* – involves the child's growing sense of self as a separate and valued person and includes 'the child's view of self and abilities, self image and self esteem, and having a positive sense of individuality' with contributions from race, religion, age, gender, sexuality and disability. Also included are feelings of belonging and acceptance by family, peer group and wider society, including other cultural groups.

- *Family and Social Relationships* – development of empathy and the capacity to place self in someone else's shoes. They include 'a stable and affectionate relationship with parents or caregivers, good relationships with siblings, increasing importance of age appropriate friendships with peers and other significant persons in the child's life and response of family to these relationships'.

- *Social Presentation* – a child's 'growing understanding of the way in which appearance, behaviour, and any impairment are perceived by the outside world and the impression being created'. Included are 'appropriateness of dress for age, gender, culture and religion; cleanliness and personal hygiene; and availability of advice from parents or caregivers about presentation in different settings'.

- *Self Care Skills* – the acquisition by a child of practical, emotional and communication competencies required for increasing independence. His needs include 'early practical skills of dressing and feeding, opportunities to gain confidence and practical skills to undertake activities away from the family and independent living skills as older children'. Encouragement is needed to enable the child to acquire social problem solving approaches.

'Special attention should be given to the impact of a child's impairment and other vulnerabilities, and on social circumstances affecting these in the development of self care skills.'

2.30 The court has to consider both the child's temporary and long-term needs and these may differ. For example, in *Re H (A Minor) (Custody: Interim Care and Control)*,[42] a 9-year-old child was living with her terminally ill mother who, a week before she died, arranged for her to go to live with her maternal grandmother. The girl's father applied for an order that she should live with him. The Court of Appeal held that she should remain with her grandmother pending a final hearing in 3 months' time when the trial judge would have the benefit of a welfare report:

> '... there is some danger in this case of confusing the long-term and the short-term needs of this child ... at this moment of time, with the devastation to her of the tragic loss of her mother, her grandmother ... is a very good person with whom to live. She will find, no doubt, the period of bereavement a great deal easier with grandmother.'[43]

Change of circumstances

The likely effect on him of any change in his circumstances

2.31 The extent and possible effect of any change should not be underestimated. For example, a residence order causing a child to move from one parent to another will not only involve a change in carer but possibly a change of home, school, neighbourhood and friends:[44]

> 'Some of the authorities convey the impression that the upset caused to a child by a change of custody is transient and a matter of small importance. For all I know that may have been true in the cases containing dicta to that effect. But I think a growing experience has shown that it is not always so and that serious harm even to young children may, on occasion, be caused by such a change ... a child's future happiness and sense of security are always important factors and the effect of a change of custody will often be worthy of ... close and anxious attention ...'[45]

Courts favour the status quo and one of the most experienced family judges of the twentieth century, Ormrod LJ, called it 'one of the most important single factors in deciding what is in the best interests of young children'.[46] Clear evidence is required to show that a change of carer is in the child's interests.[47]

---

[42] [1991] 2 FLR 109.
[43] Ibid, per Butler-Sloss LJ at 111–112.
[44] For a more detailed discussion in relation to residence orders, see **10.67**.
[45] *J and Another v C and Others* [1970] AC 668, per Lord MacDermott at 715.
[46] *S (BD) v S (DJ) (Infants: Care and Consent)* [1977] 1 All ER 656 at 663.
[47] See, for example, *Re A (A Minor) (Custody)* [1991] 2 FLR 394.

Characteristics of the child

His age, sex, background and any characteristics of his which the court considers significant

2.32 There are no universal guidelines and each child has to be considered as an individual. Nor is there, any longer, any presumption or assumption that a child (as opposed to a young baby)[48] should be with its mother.[49] Nor is there a general assumption that girls should be raised by their mothers.[50] The child's cultural, racial and religious background[51] may need to be considered. In *Re M (Section 94 Appeals)*,[52] the Court of Appeal held that the court below should have taken account of the fact that a child, living with her white mother, and who was of mixed race, was confused about her racial identity when deciding an application for contact by her black father. In *Re J (Specific Issue Orders: Muslim Upbringing and Circumcision)*[53] and *Re S (Change of Names: Cultural Factors)*,[54] the court had to consider whether boys born to one Muslim parent should be circumcised and brought up as Muslims.[55] Another example is provided by *Re A (Leave to Remove: Cultural and Religious Considerations)*[56] when the mother of a 9-year-old Iraqi child was given permission to relocate with her new husband, despite his father arguing that this would have a detrimental effect on the child succeeding as the head of the family group. In considering these issues, courts act pragmatically rather than having regard to niceties, for example, of religious law.[57]

Risk of harm

Any harm which he has suffered or is likely to suffer

2.33 'Harm' means ill-treatment or the impairment of health or development. 'Ill-treatment' includes sexual abuse and forms of ill-treatment which are not physical. 'Health' means physical or mental health, including harm a child 'has suffered or is at risk of suffering as a result of seeing or hearing the ill-treatment of another person'.[58] 'Development' means physical, intellectual, emotional, social or behavioural development. When the court considers

---

48 *K and T v Finland* [2001] 2 FLR 707, ECHR at 737 and *Re W (A Minor) (Residence Order)* [1992] 2 FLR 332.
49 *Re S (A Minor) (Custody)* [1991] 2 FLR 388 but see *Brixey v Lynas* [1996] 2 FLR 499. The matter is discussed more fully at **10.84**.
50 *Re A (A Minor: Custody)* [1991] 2 FLR 394.
51 See **9.94**.
52 [1995] 1 FLR 546.
53 [1999] 2 FLR 678.
54 [2001] 2 FLR 1005.
55 See **9.110**.
56 [2006] EWHC (Fam) 421, [2006] 2 FLR 572.
57 *Re C (Adoption: Religious Observance)* [2002] 1 FLR 1119, where Wilson J had to deal with the adoption of a child whose background had Jewish, Irish Roman Catholic and Turkish-Cypriot Muslim elements, the mother describing herself as Church of England. See also *Ismailova v Russia* [2008] 1 FLR 533 (ECHR).
58 CA 1989, s 105(1) and s 31(9) inserted by Adoption and Children Act 2002, s 120.

whether harm suffered by a child is significant to the child's health or development, his health or development has to be compared with what could reasonably be expected of a similar child.[59]

2.34 When a court is considering whether a child is 'likely' to suffer harm, it does not have to be satisfied that it is more likely than not to suffer harm. Rather, it has to be satisfied on evidence (as opposed to suspicion) that there is a real possibility of harm, 'a possibility that cannot sensibly be ignored having regard to the nature and gravity of the feared harm in the particular case'.[60] Difficulties can arise when a judge cannot be satisfied that harm has occurred in the past but he thinks that there is a substantial possibility that it has. This lingering doubt cannot by itself justify a conclusion that harm is likely to occur in the future. In *Re P (Sexual Abuse: Standard of Proof)*,[61] for example, the trial judge could not find on the evidence that a father had probably sexually abused his young daughters but considered that there was a substantial risk that he had and so directed supervised contact. The Court of Appeal held that he was wrong to do so:

> 'The judge has plainly confused an analysis of past harm ... which has to be established on the balance of probabilities, with the need to make an assessment of risk of future harm.'[62]

However, evidence which is insufficient to prove past harm may be sufficient to establish a real possibility of harm in the future. For example, the judge may not be satisfied that a father has sexually abused his child but the evidence may disclose paedophile tendencies which could justify a need for closely supervised contact.

Capability of parents and others

How capable each of his parents, and any other person in relation to whom the court considers the question to be relevant, is of meeting his needs

2.35 There is no room for stereotypical judgments. A father may be more able to meet a child's needs than the mother.[63] The court has to consider *this* parent in relation to the needs of *this* child. The strain which parents may be under at the time of the hearing or following a separation from a former partner may temporarily affect or disguise his or her parenting ability. This may cause difficulties in assessing the parent's ability to meet both the child's long-term and short-term needs.

---

[59]   CA 1989, 105(1), 31(9) and (10).
[60]   *Re H and R (Child Sexual Abuse: Standard of Proof)* [1996] 1 FLR 80, per Lord Nicholls of Birkenhead at 95.
[61]   [1996] 2 FLR 333.
[62]   Ibid, per Wall J at 343.
[63]   *Re S (A Minor) (Custody)* [1991] 2 FLR 388.

2.36 The Department of Health's *Framework* lists various dimensions of parenting capacity.[64]

- *Basic care* – providing for the child's physical needs, and appropriate medical and dental care including provision of food, drink, warmth, shelter, clean and appropriate clothing and adequate personal hygiene.

- *Ensuring safety* – ensuring the child is adequately protected from harm or danger, including providing protection from significant harm or danger, and from contact with unsafe adults/other children and from self-harm. Recognition of hazards and danger both in the home and elsewhere.

- *Emotional warmth* – ensuring the child's emotional needs are met, giving the child a sense of being specially valued and a positive sense of own racial and cultural identity. This includes:

   '... ensuring the child's requirements for secure, stable and affectionate relationships with significant adults, with appropriate sensitivity and responsiveness to the child's needs. Appropriate physical contact, comfort and cuddling sufficient to demonstrate warm regard, praise and encouragement.'

- *Stimulation* – promoting the child's learning and intellectual development through encouragement and cognitive stimulation and promoting social opportunities. Facilitating the child's cognitive development and potential through interaction, communication, talking and responding to the child's language and questions, encouraging and joining the child's play, and promoting educational opportunities. Enabling the child to experience success and ensuring school attendance or equivalent opportunity. Facilitating the child to meet the challenges of life.

- *Guidance and boundaries* – enabling the child to regulate their own emotions and behaviour.

   'The key parental tasks are *demonstrating and modelling* appropriate behaviour and control of emotions and interactions with others, and *guidance* which involves setting boundaries, so that the child is able to develop an internal model of moral values and conscience, and social behaviour appropriate for the society within which they will grow up. The aim is to enable the child to grow into an autonomous adult, holding their own values, and able to demonstrate appropriate behaviour with others rather than having to be dependent on rules outside themselves. This includes not overprotecting children from exploratory and learning experiences.'

- *Skills* – 'social problem solving, anger management, consideration for others, and effective discipline and shaping of behaviour'.

---

[64] *Framework for the Assessment of Children in Need and their Families* (2000) chapter 2. See also Balbernie 'Law and child development' [2003] Fam Law 508.

- *Stability* – providing a sufficiently stable family environment to enable a child to develop and maintain a secure attachment to the primary caregiver(s) in order to ensure optimal development and ensuring children keep in contact with important family members and 'significant others'. This requires ensuring secure attachments are not disrupted, 'providing consistency of emotional warmth over time and responding in a similar manner to the same behaviour'.

The Department notes that parental responses change and develop according to a child's developmental progress.

2.37 The relative importance of parents to other adults is discussed at **10.68**. Put shortly, judicial comments about the rearing of a child by a biological parent or psychological parent are set firmly in the context of the child's welfare.

> '[This] must be the dominant and overriding factor that ultimately determines disputes about residence and contact and there can be no dilution of its importance by reference to extraneous matters. When Lord Nicholls said [in *Re G*[65]] that courts should keep in mind that the interests of a child will normally be best served by being reared by his or her biological parent, he was doing no more than reflecting common experience that, in general, children tend to thrive when brought up by parents to whom they have been born. He was careful to qualify his statement, however, by the words *'in the ordinary way* the rearing of a child by his or her biological parent *can be expected* to be in the child's best interests' (emphasis added). In the ordinary way one *can* expect that children will do best with their biological parents. But many disputes about residence and contact do not follow the ordinary way. Therefore, although one should keep in mind the common experience to which Lord Nicholls was referring, one must not be slow to recognise those cases where that common experience does not provide a reliable guide.'[66]

2.38 The importance (or otherwise) of the sexual orientation of potential carers is examined at **10.94**.

Range of powers available

The range of powers available to the court under this Act in the proceedings in question

2.39 When a court is considering an application in any family proceedings (and this includes applications for ouster/occupation or non-molestation orders under Pt IV of the Family Law Act 1996) it can make any s 8 order – a residence order, contact order, specific issue order or prohibited steps order – without an application needing to be made.[67] Likewise, ouster/occupation and non-molestation orders can be made in any family proceedings, including

---

65   [2006] UKHL 43, [2006] 2 FLR 629 at [2].
66   *Re B (A Child)* [2009] UKSC 5, [2010] 1 FLR 551, per Lord Kerr at [35].
67   CA 1989, s 10(1).

proceedings under the CA 1989, without the need for an application.[68] In addition, in s 8 proceedings under the CA 1989, the court can make a family assistance order in order to provide help to the family from Cafcass or a local authority.[69]

THE NO ORDER PRINCIPLE

2.40

> 'Where a court is considering whether or not to make one or more orders under the Act with respect to a child, it shall not make the order or any of the orders unless it considers that doing so would be better for the child than making no order at all.'[70]

Prior to the Children Act 1989 coming into force, there had been a tendency for orders to be made regarding children whenever divorce or separation cases came to court, whether those orders were necessary or not. This was thought to be detrimental to the relationship between the child and his parents:

> 'Where a child has a good relationship with both parents, the law should seek to disturb this as little as possible. There is always a risk that orders allocating custody and access (or even deciding upon residence and contact) will have the effect of polarising the parent's roles and perhaps alienating the child from one or other of them.'[71]

Furthermore, disputes between parents over the welfare of their child should be resolved by the courts only as a matter of last resort:

> 'A fundamental principle which guided both the Review of Child Care Law and the Government's response to it was that the primary responsibility for the upbringing of children rests with their parents. The State should be ready to help them discharge that responsibility and should intervene compulsorily only where the child is placed at unacceptable risk. Although these views were expressed in the context of local authority care and social services, we consider that they are equally valid in the context of the private law.'[72]

2.41 In *Re G (Children) (Residence: Making of order)*[73] Lord Justice Ward noted that although there seemed to be considerable academic learning on the sub-section, the provision was 'perfectly clear'. It did not create a presumption one way or the other. 'It merely demanded of the court that it ask itself the question whether to make an order would be better for a child than making no

---

68 Family Law Act 1996, ss 39(2) and 42(2).
69 CA 1989, s 16. See **Chapter 13**.
70 Ibid, s 1(5).
71 *Family Law Review of Child Law: Guardianship and Custody* (1988) Law Com No 172, para 3.2.
72 Ibid, para 2.1.
73 [2005] EWCA Civ 1283, [2006] 1 FLR 771. See also Doughty, 'The "no order principle": a myth revived?' [2008] Fam Law 561.

order at all.' In the instant case although there was no factual dispute because the parents had agreed that the children reside with their mother, a residence order would be advantageous and had been an important part of their negotiations. In contested cases 'no order' is often not an option, especially where there are cross-applications. For example, a mother with care may apply for leave to remove the child from the jurisdiction and the father may counter with an application for a residence order. The court then has to make one order or another.[74] In uncontested cases, orders may still be necessary – for example, residence orders being granted to a parent and step-parent in order to give the step-parent parental responsibility.[75]

PRESUMPTIONS, ASSUMPTIONS OR GUIDANCE?

2.42 In the past, judges have occasionally expressed themselves in language which suggested that in a given set of circumstances, 'other things being equal', it was in the best interests of the child for a particular course to be taken. For example, that a mother was the 'obvious' person to look after a girl of 4 unless there was a good reason to the contrary.[76] Sometimes, the word 'presumption' was used.[77] It was inevitable that this should happen because little guidance was given by the predecessors of s 1 as to what 'the best interests' of the child meant or how it was to be determined. Judges would draw on what, in their opinion, was 'the law of nature and of society'[78] to make good the deficit. Yet this sat uneasily with the requirement that the court should decide what was best for the individual child who was the subject of the application.

2.43 It has now been clearly stated, both by the House of Lords and the Court of Appeal, that there is no room for presumptions in children cases. In *Dawson v Wearmouth*,[79] Lord Hobhouse said that while a factor may need to be considered in each case of a particular type:

> '... it should not be treated as an "all-important" factor which requires to be "displaced by strong countervailing considerations". Each case depends on its own facts. In any given case all the facts and circumstances relevant to the welfare of the child need to be taken [into] account and weighed up against each other. Whether or not any one factor tips the balance one way or the other will vary from one case to another.'

2.44 In the Court of Appeal, Thorpe LJ has stressed on a number of occasions that presumptions have no place in disputes involving children. In *Re*

---

[74] *Re H (Children) (Residence Order: Condition)* [2001] EWCA Civ 1338, [2001] 2 FLR 1277 per Thorpe LJ at 1283. See also *Re P (A Child) (Parental Dispute: Judicial Determination)* [2002] EWCA Civ 1627, [2003] 1 FLR 286.

[75] *G v F (Shared Residence: Parental Responosibility)* [1998] 2 FLR 799 but otherwise in *Re WB (Residence Orders)* [1995] 2 FLR 1023. See **10.39**.

[76] For example, *M v M* (1980) 1 FLR 77.

[77] As in *MH v GP (Child: Emigration)* [1995] 2 FLR 106.

[78] *Re O'Hara* [1900] 2 IR 232.

[79] [1999] 1 FLR 1167, at 1181.

L (Contact: Domestic Violence); *Re V (Contact: Domestic Violence)*; *Re M (Contact: Domestic Violence)*; *Re H (Contact: Domestic Violence)*[80] he said that:

'... [I am] wary of presumptions. Again the word has a special value in the context of adversarial litigation. There is a danger that the identification of a presumption will inhibit or distort the rigorous search for the welfare solution. There is also the danger that a presumption may be used as an aid to determination when the individual advocate or judge feels either undecided or overwhelmed.'

In *Payne v Payne*,[81] he explained:

'Generally in the language of litigation a presumption either casts a burden of proof upon the party challenging it or can be said to be decisive of outcome unless displaced. I do not think that such concepts of presumption and burden of proof have any place in the Children Act 1989 where the judge exercises a function that is partly inquisitorial.'

2.45 The Court of Appeal has now said that there is, for example, no presumption that, unless there are good reasons to the contrary, a parent guilty of domestic violence should not have contact,[82] that the carer who makes reasonable proposals should be able to take a child abroad to live[83] or that young children should live with their mother.[84]

2.46 At the same time as retreating from 'presumptions' or 'assumptions', the Court of Appeal has offered 'guidance', supplementing the checklist by providing a list of matters which should be considered in particular classes of cases. These are:

'... factors, among others which [are not] enumerated, which have to be given appropriate weight in each individual case and weighed in the balance.

... They are not and could not be exclusive of the other important matters which arise in the individual case to be decided.'[85]

Guidance has been given on contact when domestic violence is an issue,[86] on applications to remove children from the jurisdiction[87] and on the change of surnames.[88]

---

[80]   [2000] 2 FLR 334, at 364.
[81]   [2001] EWCA Civ 166, [2001] 1 FLR 1052, at 1060.
[82]   *Re L (Contact: Domestic Violence); Re V (Contact: Domestic Violence)*; *Re M (Contact: Domestic Violence)*; *Re H (Contact: Domestic Violence)* [2000] 2 FLR 334.
[83]   *Payne v Payne* [2001] EWCA Civ 166, [2001] 1 FLR 1052.
[84]   *Re S (A Minor) (Custody)* [1991] 2 FLR 388.
[85]   *Payne v Payne* [2001] EWCA Civ 166, [2001] 1 FLR 1052, per Dame Elizabeth Butler-Sloss P at 1079.
[86]   *Re L (Contact: Domestic Violence); Re V (Contact: Domestic Violence)*; *Re M (Contact: Domestic Violence)*; *Re H (Contact: Domestic Violence)* [2000] 2 FLR 334. See **Chapter 5**.
[87]   *Payne v Payne* [2001] EWCA Civ 166; [2001] 1 FLR 1052. See **9.42**.
[88]   *W (A Child) (Illegitimate Child: Change of Surname), Re* [1999] 2 FLR 930. See **9.14**.

2.47 It is important to distinguish between legal principle and guidance. As Lord Justices Moore-Bick and Black pointed out in *MK v CK (Relocation: Shared Care Arrangement)*[89] the guidance given for example in *Payne v Payne*[90] is very valuable both in ensuring that judges identify what are likely to be the most important factors to be taken into account and the weight that should generally be attached to them. It also plays a valuable role in promoting consistency in decision-making. However, the circumstances in which these difficult decisions have to be made vary infinitely and the judge in each case must be free to weigh up the individual factors and make whatever decision he or she considers to be in the best interests of the child. In *Payne* the only principle of law was that the welfare of the child was paramount: all else is guidance.

2.48 Nevertheless, while guidance from the Court of Appeal does not have statutory force, judges at all levels must pay heed to it and depart from it only after careful deliberation and when it is clear that the particular circumstances of the case require them to do so in order to give effect to fundamental principles.[91] It must be heeded as guidance, not as rigid principle or so as to dictate a particular outcome in a sphere of law where the facts of individual cases are so infinitely variable.[92]

2.49 But whatever the guidance, the court must not start from any a priori assumptions about what is best for any individual child.

> 'It looks at the child and weighs a number of factors in the balance, now set out in the well-known "check-list" in s 1(3) of the Children Act 1989; these include his own wishes and feelings, his physical, emotional and educational needs and the relative capacities of the adults around him to met those needs, the effect of change, his own characteristics and background, including his ethnicity, culture and religion, and any harm he has suffered or risks suffering in the future. There is nothing in those principles which prevents a court from giving great weight to the culture in which a child has been brought up when deciding how and where he will fare best in the future. Our own society is a multi-cultural one. But looking at it from the child's point of view, as we all try to do, it may sometimes be necessary to resolve or diffuse a clash between the differing cultures within his own family.'[93]

2.50 Moreover guidance is however a reflection of the values sought to be expressed at the time it is given and may and will change as the values or their weight change.

> 'In a world which values difference, one culture is not inevitably to be preferred to another. Indeed, we do not have any fixed concept of what will be in the best interests of the individual child. Once upon a time it was assumed that all very

---

89   [2011] EWCA Civ 793, per Moore-Bick at [86] and Black LJ at [141]–[142].
90   [2001] EWCA Civ 166, [2001] 1 FLR 1052 and see **1.31** and **9.45**.
91   *MK v CK* [2011] EWCA Civ 793, per Moore-Bick LJ.
92   Ibid, per Black LJ.
93   *Re J (Child Returned Abroad: Convention Rights)* [2005] 2 FLR 802, per Baroness Hale of Richmond at [38].

young children should be cared for by their mothers, but that older boys might well be better off with their fathers. Nowadays we know that some fathers are very well able to provide everyday care for even their very young children and are quite prepared to prioritise their children's needs over the demands of their own careers. Once upon a time it was assumed that mothers who had committed the matrimonial offence of adultery were only fit to care for their children if the father agreed to this. Nowadays we recognise that a mother's misconduct is no more relevant than a father's: the question is always the impact it will have on the child's upbringing and well-being. Once upon a time it may have been assumed that there was only one way of bringing up children. Nowadays we know that there are many routes to a healthy and well-adjusted adulthood. We are not so arrogant as to think that we know best.'[94]

2.51 There remain two situations where a stipulated course will be followed unless there are good reasons to the contrary. Neither offends the 'no presumption' rule because both are derived from statute. The first is that children should remain in contact with a parent or reside with a parent unless it is in their best interests not to do so. Although this originated in the courts' belief in 'the ties of nature',[95] it finds strength from the Art 8(2) requirement that any interference with the right to family life has to be justified. The second is that there should be no change in the status quo unless the change is in the best interests of the child. This is derived from the 'no order' principle of s 1(5) discussed above. Both topics are discussed further in **Chapter 10**.

---

[94] Ibid, at para 37.
[95] *Re K (A Minor)* [1990] 2 FLR 64.

Chapter 3

CHILD LAW AND HUMAN RIGHTS

3.1 The provisions of the Human Rights Act 1998 mean that courts are now required to interpret and apply primary and secondary legislation in a way which is compatible with rights under the European Convention for the Protection of Human Rights and Fundamental Freedoms 1950.[1] Some lawyers, both practitioners and academics, have seen potential for conflict between s 1 of the Children Act 1989 and Art 8 of the Convention. Is the welfare principle compatible with Art 8 or does the implementation of the Human Rights Act 1998 require a change in the way s 1 is applied?[2] Courts in England and Wales hold that it is. Nevertheless the Act has meant that Arts 8 and 6 (which guarantees the right to a fair trial) receive closer attention than hitherto.

3.2 In addition, international conventions on the rights of children, although not directly binding on domestic courts, are used to inform decisions on the way in which the courts' discretion should be exercised.

ARTICLE 8

3.3 Article 8 provides that:

'1 Everyone has the right to respect for his private and family life, his home and his correspondence.

2 There shall be no interference by a public authority with the exercise of this right except such as is in accordance with the law and is necessary in a democratic society in the interests of national security, public safety or the economic well-being of the country, for the prevention of disorder or crime, for the protection of health or morals, or for the protection of the rights and freedoms of others.'

---

[1] Human Rights Act 1998, s 3. For a useful description of Art 8, see Prest 'The right to respect for family life: obligations of the state in private law children cases' [2005] Fam Law 124.

[2] The issues are discussed in Swindells 'Crossing the rubicon – family law post the Human Rights Act 1998' in Cretney (ed) *Family Law: Essays for the New Millennium* (Family Law, 2000) and Herring 'The Human Rights Act and the welfare principle in family law: conflicting or complementary?' in Butler (ed) *Human Rights for the New Millennium* (Kluwer Law International, 2000).

WHEN DOES FAMILY LIFE EXIST?

3.4 Both the European Court of Human Rights in Strasbourg and domestic courts have recognised that family life can exist in a wide variety of circumstances. In *X, Y and Z v United Kingdom*[3] the ECHR held that there was family life between a woman (Y) living with a female-to-male transsexual (X) and also between X and a child (Z) born to Y by donor insemination.

> '[The] notion of family life in Article 8 is not confined solely to families based on marriage and may encompass other de facto relationships. When deciding whether a relationship can be said to amount to "family life", a number of factors may be relevant, including whether the couple was living together, the length of their relationship and whether they have demonstrated their commitment to each other by having children together or by any other means.'[4]

Likewise in *Ghaidan v Godin-Mendoza*[5] where the House of Lords held that the defendant who had a longstanding, monogamous homosexual relationship with a tenant, protected under the Rent Act 1977, could succeed to the tenancy on his partner's death on the ground that they had been living together as 'husband or wife', Baroness Hale of Richmond said at 141:

> '[The] presence of children is a relevant factor in deciding whether a relationship is marriage-like but if the couple are bringing up children together, it is unlikely to matter whether or not they are the biological children of both parties. Both married and unmarried couples, both homosexual and heterosexual, may bring up children together. One or both may have children from another relationship: this is not at all uncommon in lesbian relationships and the court may grant them a shared residence order so that they may share parental responsibility. A lesbian couple may have children by donor insemination who are brought up as the children of them both: it is not uncommon for each of them to bear a child in this way. A gay or lesbian couple may foster other people's children. When the relevant sections of the Adoption and Children Act 2002 are brought into force, they will be able to adopt: this means that they will indeed have a child together in the eyes of the law.'[6]

3.5 Whether or not there is family life is essentially a question of fact 'depending upon the real existence in practice of close personal ties'.[7] However, both the European Court of Human Rights and domestic courts have recognised a number of situations in which it can usually be said that family life exists.

---

[3]   (1997) 24 EHRR 143, [1997] 2 FLR 892.
[4]   At [36].
[5]   [2004] UKHL 30, [2004] 2 FLR 600.
[6]   See also *Pawandeep Singh v Entry Clearance Officer, New Delhi* [2004] EWCA Civ 1075, [2005] QB 608, per Munby J at paras [57]–[88] and Munby 'Families old and new – the family and Article 8' [2005] CFLQ 487.
[7]   *Lebbink v The Netherlands* (Application No 45582/99) [2004] 2 FLR 463, at para 36, *Pawandeep Singh v Entry Clearance Officer, New Delhi* 2004] EWCA Civ 1075, [2005] QB 608, per Dyson LJ at [20].

3.6 Mothers, and fathers who are married to mothers, are in a special position, being treated automatically as having Art 8 rights with the child. It is likely that a mother's civil partner who is treated as being the child's parent under s 45 of the Human Fertilisation and Embryology Act 2008 (HFEA 2008) as a parent will likewise have such rights. Other biological or legal parents will find it easy to acquire rights by a period of having a relationship with the child, whether as a result of living with the child or not. Article 8 is not confined however to a relationship between children and their parents. Relatives can enjoy family life as can non-relatives. In considering whether such a relationship exists in the circumstances of a particular case, the quality of the relationship and its duration may be important as may any legal or biological ties between the child and the other person.

3.7 It is important to remember that Art 8 accords respect to *family* life. A close relationship which does not exist within family life, perhaps between the child and a friend, a teacher or social worker will not be protected unless it attracts the protection accorded to privacy.

Mother and child

3.8 A mother shares a family life with her child even if they are separated at the moment of birth: 'The carrying and giving birth to a child brings with it a relationship between them both which is entitled to respect.'[8]

Father with parental responsibility

3.9 There can be no doubt but that the father, if married to the mother, shares family life with the child.[9] Likewise, although there is no direct authority on the point, a father with parental responsibility, whether because of his registration as the father on the child's birth certificate or by registered agreement with the mother or by court order (see **7.18**), is likely to be treated as sharing family life. In law he has the same responsibility as the father who is or was married to the mother and because the parents not being married carries little weight, there is no valid reason for differentiating between the two groups of fathers.

Father without parental responsibility

3.10 The mere fact that parents are not married carries little weight[10] but the difference between the automatic recognition of family life to fathers married to the mother and those who are not has been held by the European Court of Human Rights to be justified. 'The relationship between unmarried fathers and their children varies from ignorance and indifference to a close stable

---

8   *Re B (Adoption by One Natural Parent to Exclusion of Other)* [2001] 1 FLR 589, per Hale LJ at 599.
9   But quaere if the marriage was a sham, for example, for immigration purposes and there was no cohabitation. See *Human Rights Law and Practice* (3rd edn, 2009), para 4.8.44.
10   *Berrehab v Netherlands* [1988] 11 EHRR 322.

relationship indistinguishable from the conventional family-based unit'
(*McMichael v UK*[11]). For this reason the Court has held that there exists an
objective and reasonable justification for the difference in treatment between
married and unmarried fathers with regard to the automatic acquisition of
parental rights.'[12] Something more than mere paternity has to be shown. This
can be:

Cohabitation

3.11   There is a bond amounting to family life between a child and its parents
who are cohabiting[13] or have previously cohabited even if at the time of the
birth their relationship has ended.[14]

Other children

3.12   A child born to a couple who have not cohabited but who have other
children in common is part of the family unit from the moment of birth 'and
by the very fact of it'.[15]

Social relationship

3.13   The mutual enjoyment of contact without cohabitation, for example, can
create family life.

Other circumstances

3.14   The question of whether a father, not married to the mother, enjoys a
right to family life with his child from birth, because of their biological
relationship, and independent of any actual enjoyment of family life is more
difficult.

3.15   In *Soderback v Sweden*[16] F, the father of the child had never lived with or
had a stable relationship with the mother. The child and her mother had lived
with the mother's new partner, P, since the child was 6 months old and he
became the child's psychological father. However F saw her 'from time to time'.
P applied to adopt the child and F objected. The ECHR held that the adoption
constituted an interference with F's Art 8 rights but was justified under
Art 8(2). It was not disputed before the Court that F had Art 8 rights and the
Commission had held that family life covered a potential relationship which
might develop.

---

11   Series A no 307-B, p 58(98).
12   *B v United Kingdom* [2000] 1 FLR 1, at 5.
13   *Johnston v Ireland* (1986) 9 EHRR 203.
14   *Keegan v Ireland* (1994) 18 EHRR 342.
15   *Kroon v Netherlands* (1995) EHRR 263.
16   [1999] 1 FLR 250, [1999] Fam Law 87. See also *Anayo v Germany* (Application No 20578/07)
     [2011] 1 FLR 1883.

3.16 In *Re H; Re G (Adoption: Consultation of Unmarried Fathers)*,[17] the President, relying on *McMichael v United Kingdom*, held that in the absence of marriage, cohabitation or siblings there is no family life between the father and the child at birth. Likewise in *Re J (Adoption: Contacting Father)*[18] Bennett J held that there was no family life between a father of a child, unmarried to the mother, and his child, where the parents did not have a strong commitment to each other, had never cohabited and who had not seen each other since the child was born. Hale LJ in *Re B (Adoption by One Natural Parent to Exclusion of Other)*[19] seemed to disagree: 'The child is in any event, and independently of parental responsibility, a full member of his family'. In *Z County Council v R*,[20] Holman J appeared to agree with Hale LJ because he was prepared to assume that a mother's brothers and sisters with whom she was not living were part of her child's family.

Adoptive parents

3.17 The relations between an adoptive parent and an adoptive child are 'as a rule' of the same nature as family relations protected by Art 8. Such a relationship, arising from a lawful and genuine adoption, may be deemed sufficient to attract respect.[21]

3.18 Conversely, the Court of Appeal has expressed the view, but without deciding the matter, that 'it is far from obvious' that natural parents have any Art 8 rights post-adoption.[22]

Relatives

3.19 Family life can exist between children and their siblings and near relatives[23] although the relationship between the child and near relatives, such as grandparents, is different in nature and degree from that between a child and its parents.[24] See also **15.16**.

3.20 What is required, however, is more than just a blood tie. In most cases, an actual social relationship which can be broadly described as a 'shared family life' will be required. In *Boyle v United Kingdom*[25] an uncle had acted as a father figure to his nephew but when the boy was taken into care, the local authority refused the uncle contact. The European Commission of Human Rights held that his Art 8 rights had been infringed.

---

17   [2001] 1 FLR 646.
18   [2003] EWHC 199 (Fam).
19   [2003] EWHC 199 (Fam), [2003] 1 FLR 933.
20   [2001] 1 FLR 365, at 593.
21   *X v France* 31 DR 241 (1992) E Com HR; *Kurochkin v Ukraine* [2010] 2 FLR 943, ECHR.
22   *Oxfordshire CC v X, Y and J* [2010] EWCA Civ 581, at [43].
23   *Marckx v Belgium* (1979–80) 2 EHRR 330.
24   *Price v United Kingdom* (1988) 55 DR 199, E Com HR.
25   [1994] 2 FCR 822.

Step parents

3.21 Although there appears to be no Strasbourg authority directly on the point, there is no reason why a family relationship cannot exist between a step-parent – whether married to or in a civil partnership with the child's natural parent and a child. However, it is unlikely that the mere fact of the marriage/civil partnership will be sufficient to establish the relationship. It is uncertain whether the marriage/partnership together with the grant of parental responsibility under s 4A of the Children Act 1989 (see **7.29**) would be.

3.22 In most cases cohabitation for a more than short period of time is likely to be required. The grant of parental responsibility to the spouse/partner is under s 4. In _Sonderback_[26] the ECHR noted that 'de facto' family ties had existed between a mother and the adoptive father for five years until they married and 'the adoption consolidated and formalised' those ties.

Cohabitees

3.23 Family life is not confined to marriage. Nor is the role of parenthood restricted to those who are biological or legal parents.

> 'Social and psychological parenthood [is] the relationship which develops through the child demanding and the parent providing for the child's needs, initially at the most basic level of feeding, nurturing, comforting and loving, and later at the more sophisticated level of guiding, socialising, educating and protecting. ... [There] are ... parents who are neither genetic nor gestational, but who have become the psychological parents of the child and thus have an important contribution to make to their welfare. Adoptive parents are the most obvious example, but there are many others. This is the position of CW [born to M who was in a same sex relationship, but not a civil partnership with W at the time C was born as a result of non-licensed treatment, W living with C from her birth until C was 3] in this case.'[27]

3.24 Factors such as cohabitation and the length of the relationship are important.[28] Therefore a parent's cohabitee might be able to establish family life with a child in the same household but given the transient nature of some relationships a longer period of cohabitation is likely to be required than where there is marriage/civil partnership. There is no proper reason why a cohabitee of the opposite sex of the child's parent should start from a stronger position than a same sex cohabitee.

Same sex partner

3.25 It is no longer unusual for a child to be born to a mother who is in a same sex relationship at the time the child was conceived as a result of sperm or

---

[26] [1999] 1 FLR 250, [1999) Fam Law 87.
[27] _Re G (Children)_ [2006] UKHL 43, [2006] 2 FLR 629, per Baroness of Richmond at [35] and [37].
[28] _X, Y and Z v United Kingdom_ [1997] 2 FLR 892.

gamete donation.[29] Strasbourg was slow to recognise that Art 8 might protect the relationship between the child (C) and the mother's partner (W), if only because of the margin of appreciation allowed to signatory countries. In 1992, for example, the Commission in *Kerkhoven v Netherlands*[30] refused to recognise family life in these circumstances. However, five years later in *X, Y and Z v United Kingdom*[31] the Court recognised that Art 8 applied to the relationship between X, a female-to-male transsexual who had undergone gender reassignment surgery and Z, a child born to X's female partner as a result of artificial insemination. The Court held that the notion of family life was not confined to marriage. Factors such as cohabitation and length of the relationship were important. There was no common European standard with regard to granting parental rights to transsexuals and the community as a whole had an interest in maintaining a coherent system of family law. Nonetheless X had lived with Y to all intents and purposes as her male partner for 13 years. The couple applied together for treatment by AID. X was involved in the process and had acted as Z's 'father'. In those circumstances de facto ties linked X, Y and Z and Art 8 was engaged.

3.26 Conversely, in *G v Netherlands*[32] the Commission refused to recognise that there was family life between the biological father who had donated his sperm to the lesbian mother notwithstanding that he had helped to care for the child for seven months.

3.27 While there is no domestic authority directly on the point, it is likely that in some circumstances family life between W and C will be recognised by family courts. Where W was in a civil partnership with M at the time M received treatment by a person licensed under HFEA 2008 by being artificially inseminated or an embryo was placed in her, W may, subject to the provisions of s 45 of the HFEA 2008, be treated as the child's parent.[33] As she was a civil partner of M, she will be treated in same way as a father who was married to M and Art 8 would apply automatically.

3.28 Where W was not in a civil partnership with M at the time of the treatment, she may still be treated as a parent if M had agreed at the time of the fertilisation treatment that she should be treated as a parent.[34] However, unless W was in a civil marriage with M at the time of the birth, the child will not be regarded as being legitimate[35] and W will not automatically have parental responsibility. Logically W should be treated for the purposes of establishing family life in the same way as a father who is not married to the mother (see **3.11**, living with the child and the grant of parental responsibility being important factors).

---

[29] See **6.19**.
[30] Unreported.
[31] [1997] 2 FLR 892.
[32] (1993) 16 EHRR CD 38.
[33] Human Fertilisation and Embryology Act 2008 (HFEA), s 42.
[34] HFEA 2008, s 43.
[35] HFEA 2008, s 48(6).

3.29   Where ss 42 and 43 of the HFEA 2008 do not apply, perhaps because the mother was not in a civil partnership, or because there was no shared parenthood agreement or because the treatment was not carried out in the United Kingdom by a person licensed under the Act, W logically should be treated in the same way as a male cohabitee (see **3.32**). Article 8 was not considered by the House of Lords in *Re G (Children)*[36] but there would be little doubt but that W who had lived with C1 and C2 from the time of their birth until they were 3 and 1 and with whom the children had developed a good and close relationship[37] would have been held to have a family life with them.

Foster parents

3.30   The authors of *Human Rights: Law and Practice*[38] argue that in some circumstances family life may exist in a foster family relationship. In *X v Switzerland*[39] the Commission left the matter unresolved. However, because the carer will in most cases be acting as an agent for a local authority, cohabitation for a considerable period is likely to be required. As a rough guide, the length of period in domestic law is likely to be at least one year, that being the period of time required under s 10(5) to relieve foster carers of the need to seek permission before applying for a residence order (see **15.7**).

PRIVATE LIFE

3.31   Most of the consideration of Art 8 in family proceedings in England and Wales has focused on the right to respect for family life. However, the right to respect for a private life is of similar, considerable relevance and is much wider than what might loosely be termed a right to privacy.

In *Bensaid v United Kingdom*[40] the European Court of Human Rights commented:

> 'Private life is a broad term not susceptible to exhaustive definition. The court has already held that elements such as gender identification, name and sexual orientation and sexual life are important elements in the personal sphere protected by Article 8. Mental health must also be regarded as a crucial part of private life associated with the aspect of moral integrity. Article 8 protects a right to identity and personal development and the right to establish and develop relationships with other human beings and the outside world. The preservation of mental stability is in that context an indispensable precondition to effective enjoyment of the respect for private life.'[41]

---

[36]   [2006] UKHL 43, [2006] 2 FLR 629.
[37]   Ibid, at [16].
[38]   Op cit, at para 4.8.47.
[39]   13 DR 248 (1978) E Com HR.
[40]   (2001) 33 EHRR 10, at [47].
[41]   See also Munby 'Families old and new' (2005) 17 CFLQ 487, at 504–508.

This raises two important aspects of application. First, it is a right to positive respect, to the promotion of what is entailed in a private life, not merely a protection from interference with one's privacy. The state – and this of course includes the court – may be under a duty to do something rather than merely refrain from action. Secondly, it can apply in family situations even where there is at present no family life. A child may have no family life with a father who is not married to his mother and has had no contact with him. However, the right to personal development may include the right to come to know one's father or one's child.[42] It is clearly engaged when the court is considering the establishment of paternity, whether there should be contact and whether the child's name should be changed.

3.32 In *Mikulic v Croatia*[43] the ECHR held that a child's Art 8 rights were engaged when she sought to establish the identity of her father even though her parents were not married and she had no existing relationship with him.

'[No] family tie has been established between the applicant and her alleged father. The court reiterates, however, that Art 8, for its part, protects not only 'family' but also 'private' life. Private life, in the court's view, includes a person's physical and psychological integrity and can sometimes embrace aspects of an individual's physical and social identity. Respect for "private life" must also comprise to a certain degree the right to establish relationships with other human beings (see, mutatis mutandis, *Niemietz v Germany* (1992) 16 EHRR 97 at 111 (para 29)).There appears, furthermore, to be no reason of principle why the notion of "private life" should be taken to exclude the determination of the legal relationship between a child born out of wedlock and her natural father ...'

3.33 Likewise in *Rose v Secretary of State for Health*[44] Scott Baker J held that Art 8 was engaged when a child, born by artificial insemination by an anonymous donor, sought identifying information from the Secretary of State or the establishing of a contact register.

'[Counsel for the Secretary of State] analysed the meaning of family life and private life within Art 8. He did so separately with regard to each expression and sought to show that the claimants fall within neither. In my judgment it is more helpful to look at the one expression "respect for his private and family life" to see whether the claimants fall within that. This case is really about respect for the claimants' personal identity within that context ... Respect for family life has been interpreted by the European court to incorporate the concept of personal identity (see *Gaskin*[45]). Everyone should be able to establish details of his identity as a human being (*Johnston v Ireland* (1987) 9 EHRR 203 para 55). That, to my mind, plainly includes information about a biological parent who will inevitably have contributed to the identity of his child.'[46]

---

42   See also **6.66**.
43   [2002] 1 FCR 720.
44   [2002] EWHC 1593 (Admin), [2002] 2 FLR 962.
45   (1990) 12 EHRR 36 ECHR.
46   [2002] EWHC 1593 (Admin), [2002] 2 FLR 962, at paras [41] and [48].

ARTICLE 8 AND THE EUROPEAN COURT OF HUMAN RIGHTS

3.34 The European Court of Human Rights has declined to interpret Art 8 as incorporating the principle that the interests of a child are paramount. Indeed, given the wording of Art 8, it is difficult to see how it could have done, Art 8 clearly providing that where the interests or rights of individuals conflict, a proper balance has to be struck. This was emphasised in *Johansen v Norway*[47] (a case which concerned a child being taken into care) in which the Court said that: 'a fair balance has to be struck between the interests of the child in remaining in public care and those of the parent in being reunited with the child'.

> 'In carrying out this balancing exercise, the Court will attach particular importance to the best interests of the child, which, depending on their nature and seriousness, may override those of the parent. In particular, as suggested by the Government, the parent cannot be entitled under Article 8 of the Convention (Art 8) to have such measures taken as would harm the child's health and development.'[48]

The Court has also indicated that the best interests of the child have 'particularly' to be taken into account[49] and 'consideration of what is in the best interests of the child is in every case of crucial importance'.[50]

3.35 Strasbourg's approach can be illustrated by *Hendriks v Netherlands*,[51] a case in which the Commission had to examine a claim by a father that domestic courts had denied him contact with his child in breach of his Art 8 rights:

> 'The natural link between a parent and a child is of fundamental importance and that, where the actual "family life" in the sense of "living together" has come to an end, continued contact between them is desirable and should in principle remain possible. Respect for family life within the meaning of Article 8 thus implies that this contact should not be denied unless there are strong reasons ... which justify such an interference.
>
> ... Feelings of distress and frustration because of the absence of one's child may cause considerable suffering to the non-custodial parent. However, where ... there is a serious conflict between the interests of the child and one of its parents which can only be resolved to the disadvantage of one of them, the interests of the child must, under Article 8(2), prevail.'

3.36 Nonetheless a fair balance has to be struck between the interests of the child and those of the parents and the margin of appreciation enjoyed by states

---

[47] (1997) 23 EHRR 33.
[48] Ibid, at para 78.
[49] *Hokkanen v Finland* (1995) 19 EHRR 139 and see also *Olsson v Sweden (No 2)* (1994) 17 EHRR 134.
[50] *L v Finland* [2000] 2 FLR 118, at 138.
[51] (1983) 5 EHRR 223, ECHR.

is narrower in relation to striking this balance in contact disputes than issues about residence. In *Süss v Germany*[52] the ECHR held that:

'... a stricter scrutiny is called for as regards any further limitations, such as restrictions placed by ... authorities on parental rights of access ... Such further limitations entail the danger that family relations between a young child and one or both parents would be effectively curtailed.'

3.37   A fair balance has to be struck between the competing Art 8 rights of all individuals, not just the biological parents and the child. For example when considering a promotion of family life in the future between a child and his biological father who currently enjoys no such life, consideration must also be given to the existing family life between the child, his mother and step-father.[53]

3.38   Conversely the question has been raised whether the paramountcy principle of s 1 of the Children Act 1989 is compatible with the Convention. Jonathan Herring, for example has pointed out that there are fundamental differences between the approach of the Act and the Convention. Under the Convention, a case concerned with denying a parent contact with a child starts with the parent's right to contact and clear and convincing evidence is required to justify the interference with this right. Under the Act, the approach may start with a factual presumption that the child's welfare is generally promoted but this can be rebutted in a particular case on less evidence than is necessary to rebut the Art 8 right.[54] Others have expressed a concern lest a rights based approach will 'constitute a damaging step back from a world in which the welfare of the child is the focus of decision making to a world in which parental rights are privileged and prioritised'.[55] Sir James Munby has written that:

'We need, before it is too late, to examine whether the principle that the child's rights are paramount is really compatible with the Convention. This is something too readily assumed, on occasions asserted, but rarely subjected to very convincing analysis.'[56]

ARTICLE 8 AND ENGLISH COURTS

3.39   The domestic courts adopted what has been called a conservative or minimalist approach to the Convention.[57] Before the advent of the Human Rights Act 1998, the House of Lords twice expressed the view that s 1 and

---

52   [2006] 1 FLR 522.
53   *Anayo v Germany* (Application No 20578/07) [2011] 1 FLR 1883.
54   Herring 'The Human Rights Act and the welfare principle in family law: conflicting or complementary?' in Butler (ed) *Human Rights for the New Millennium* (Kluwer Law International, 2000).
55   Harris-Short 'Family law and the Human Rights Act 1998: judicial restraint or revolution?' [2005] CFLQ 329, at 350.
56   Munby 'Families old and new – the family and Article 8' [2005] CFLQ 487.
57   Harris-Short 'Family Law and the Human Rights Act 1998: Judicial Restraint or Resolution?' [2005] CFLQ 329, at 336.

Art 8 were not in conflict. In *Dawson v Wearmouth*,[58] a case concerning the change of a child's surname, Lord Hobhouse said:

> 'It is submitted that the father's rights under Art 8 are being infringed. There is no basis for this submission. The present case is concerned with the welfare of the child not with the rights of the father. There is nothing in the Convention which requires the courts of this country to act otherwise than in accordance with the interests of the child.'

Earlier, in *Re KD (A Minor) (Access: Principles)*,[59] Lord Oliver of Aylmerton had said that if there was any conflict (which he doubted):

> '... [it] is, I think, semantic only and lies only in differing ways of giving expression to the single common concept that the natural bond and relationship between parent and child gives rise to universally recognised norms which ought not to be gratuitously interfered with and which, if interfered with at all, ought to be so only if the welfare of the child dictates it.'

3.40   However, the implementation of the Act was welcomed by the judiciary. Sir James Munby, writing extra-judicially,[60] suggested that it provided 'new tools with which to meet the emerging needs of our changing society'. Post-implementation, judges, both at first instance and in the Court of Appeal, and more recently the House of Lords and now the Supreme Court, were willing to consider Art 8 rights alongside the welfare test, although holding to the position that when the rights of adults conflict with the best interests of the child, those of the child must prevail, not just because of s 1, but also under Art 8.[61] This has produced a conscious and conscientious examination, more detailed than hitherto, of the interests of the adults involved as well as those of the child and in a re-examination of the way the courts should approach classes of case. Take, for example, *Payne v Payne*,[62] when the Court of Appeal dealt with a mother's application for permission to take her daughter to live in New Zealand:

> 'All those immediately affected by the proceedings, that is to say the mother, the father and the child have rights under Art 8(1). Those rights inevitably in a case such as the present appeal are in conflict and, under Art 8(2) have to be balanced against the rights of the others. In addition and of the greatest significance is the welfare of the child which, according to European jurisprudence, is of crucial importance, and where in conflict with a parent is overriding (see *Johansen v Norway* (1996) 23 EHRR 33 at 67 and 72). Article 8(2) recognises that a public authority, in this case the court, may interfere with the right to family life where it

---

[58]   [1999] 1 FLR 1167, at 1181 and see also Lord Mackay of Clashfern at 1174.
[59]   [1988] 2 FLR 139, at 153.
[60]   Munby 'Families old and new – the family and Article 8' [2005] CFLQ 487, at 509.
[61]   See *Re L (Contact: Domestic Violence)*; *Re V (Contact: Domestic Violence)*; *Re M (Contact: Domestic Violence)*; *Re H (Contact: Domestic Violence)* [2000] 2 FLR 334, per Dame Elizabeth Butler-Sloss P at 345.
[62]   [2001] EWCA Civ 166, [2001] 1 FLR 1052, per Dame Elizabeth Butler-Sloss P at [82]. For a consideration of the effect of the Convention and Act on child law, see also Fortin 'A decade of the HRA and its impact on children's rights' [2011] Fam Law 173.

does so in accordance with the law, and where it is necessary in a democratic society for, inter alia, the protection of the rights and freedoms of others and the decision is proportionate to the need demonstrated. That position appears to me to be similar to that which arises in all child-based family disputes and the European case-law on children is in line with the principles set out in the Children Act 1989. *I do not, for my part, consider that the Convention has affected the principles the courts should apply in dealing with these difficult cases. Its implementation into English law does however give us the opportunity to take another look at the way the principles [governing leave-to-remove cases] have been expressed in the past and whether there should now be a reformulation of those principles.*' (emphasis added)

3.41 In *Re T (Paternity: Ordering Blood Tests)*,[63] Bodey J was concerned with a putative father trying to establish his paternity of a child born to a married woman and seeking contact with him. He examined the individual rights of the child, the applicant and those of the mother and her spouse before concluding that it was in the child's best interests that his paternity be established:

'I find that any such interference as would occur in the right to respect for the family/private life of the mother and her husband, to be proportionate to the legitimate aim of providing T with the possibility of certainty as to his real paternity ...'

3.42 Courts have taken account of Arts 8 and 6 when considering whether fathers without parental responsibility should be joined as parties to proceedings freeing children for adoption.[64]

There has also been an increased awareness of the desirability of taking the child's independent rights and interests into account.[65] The possible impact of Art 8 on procedural matters has also been considered.[66]

It is important, however, to recognise the distinction in jurisdiction between considering applications under the Children Act 1989 and those under the Human Rights Act 1998 which are in reality, an application for judicial review of decisions taken by public authorities.

'The Human Rights Act 1998 has not collapsed the fundamental distinction between public law proceedings and private law proceedings ... Save for any High Court judge's residual jurisdiction to hear cases of great urgency which may fall outside his assigned position, any judicial review proceedings ... must, in my view,

---

63   [2001] 2 FLR 1190, at 1198.
64   See, for example, *Z County Council v R* [2001] 1 FLR 365 and *Re H; Re G (Adoption: Consultation of Unmarried Fathers)* [2001] 1 FLR 646. They are not always joined: see *Re J (Adoption: Contacting Father)* [2003] EWHC 199 Fam, [2003] 1 FLR 933 and *C (A Child) v XYZ County Council* [2007] EWCA Civ 1206, [2008] 1 FLR 1294. For other examples, see Moylan 'What have human rights done for family justice?' [2010] Fam Law 810, and Munby 'The Human Rights Act and family law – 10 years on' (2010) available at: www.legalscholars.ac.uk/southampton.
65   See **4.10**.
66   See **15.19**.

be determined within the Administrative Court or by a judge of the Family Division who is a nominated judge of the Administrative Court.'[67]

CONSIDERING ARTICLE 8

3.43   When an Art 8 point is being put forward, the following questions need to be asked:

- Is there 'family life' shared by the relevant adult and the child?

- Does the proposed order interfere with a right to that life?

- Is the interference in accordance with the law?

  - Does it have a basis in law?
  - Does it enable the parties to foresee with a reasonable degree of certainty the circumstances in which and the conditions on which the court will act?[68]

- Is the interference necessary for the protection of the rights and freedoms of others?

   'Whilst the adjective "necessary" ... is not synonymous with "indispensable" neither has it the flexibility of such expressions as "admissible", "ordinary", "useful", "reasonable" or "desirable".'[69]

- Is the interference proportionate? Is there a reasonable relationship between the goal pursued and the means used?[70]

   'The more drastic the interference, the greater must be the need to do it.'[71]

In *De Freitas v Permanent Secretary of Ministry of Agriculture, Fisheries, Lands and Housing*[72] the Privy Council adopted a three-stage test, that in determining whether a limitation (by an act, rule or decision) is arbitrary or excessive the court should ask itself whether:

(i)   the legislative objective is sufficiently important to justify limiting a fundamental right;

---

[67]   *Re T (Wardship: Review of Police Protection Decision) (No 2)* [2008] EWHC 196 (Fam), [2010] 1 FLR 1026, per McFarlane J at [64]–[65].

[68]   *Malone v United Kingdom* (1985) 7 EHRR 14.

[69]   *Handyside v United Kingdom* (1979–80) 1 EHRR 737.

[70]   *Ashingdane v United Kingdom* (1985) 7 EHRR 528.

[71]   *Re B (Adoption by One Natural Parent to Exclusion of Other)* [2001] 1 FLR 589, per Hale LJ at 599. See also *R (Mahmood) v Secretary of State for the Home Department* [2001] 1 FLR 756, per Lord Phillips of Worth Matravers MR at 772.

[72]   [1999] 1 AC 69, per Lord Clyde at 80.

(ii)   the measures designed to meet the legislative objective are rationally connected to it and

(iii) the means used to impair the right or freedom are no more than is necessary to accomplish the objective.[73]

3.44   By way of example, in *Hoppe v Germany*[74] the ECHR found that the domestic court was justified in interfering with a father's Art 8 rights when it refused to grant him joint parental authority on the ground that the parents were in conflict. It had the benefit of expert reports and took into account not just the opposition of the mother but also the father's insistence on the recognition of his rights and his disregard for the child's psychological health. 'The court is satisfied that the contested decisions were based on reasons which were not only relevant but also sufficient.'

PRACTICE

3.45   When the Human Rights Act 1998 is relied on, the court must be provided with a list of authorities it is intended to cite and copies of the reports, either as part of the bundle in cases to which the *Practice Direction (Family Proceedings: Court Bundles) (10 March 2000)*[75] applies or no less than 2 clear days before the hearing. Any authority which is to be cited must be an authoritative and complete report. Reports obtained from the European Court of Human Rights database (HUDOC) may be used.[76]

3.46   The application of Art 8 to particular issues in private law applications is discussed further in relation to contact in Chapter 11, applications for s 8 orders by non-parents (Chapter 15), the child's wishes and feelings (Chapter 4) and enforcement (Chapter 23).

OTHER CONVENTION RIGHTS

3.47   Other conventions, ratified by the United Kingdom, confer rights in a family setting. Domestic courts have occasionally referred to them but less frequently than the European Convention on Human Rights and Fundamental Freedoms.

---

[73]   Approved by Lord Steyn in *R (Daly) v Secretary of State for the Home Department* [2001] UKHL 26, [2001] AC 532, at [27].

[74]   [2003] 1 FLR 384.

[75]   [2000] 1 FLR 536 (now Family Procedure Rules 2010 (FPR 2010), SI 2010/2955, Practice Direction 29A) and see **20.01**.

[76]   *Practice Direction Human Rights Act* (24 July 2000) [2000] 2 FLR 429 (now FPR 2010, PD 29B).

3.48 When reliance is placed on these rights, it is important to distinguish whether they are incorporated into domestic law and can therefore be enforced by individuals or whether they are merely persuasive, being binding only on the state.

European Community Law

3.49 McGlynn argues that the European Union has yet to create a fully fledged children's policy. It is, at present, 'a policy of "bits and pieces" with no cohering theme or approach'.[77] Fortin, however, takes the view that despite lacking a specific remit to protect children's rights, the Council of Europe has played a direct part in encouraging important reforms in the area of family law, many of which have promoted children's rights.[78]

3.50 Under European law some children have the right to freedom of movement within the Community and are entitled to the same 'tax and social advantages'[79] and access to the educational system of the host state under the same conditions as nationals.[80] It should be noted that these rights are conferred not just on the nuclear family of migrant workers, that is their birth children and adopted children who are unmarried and under the age of majority,[81] but also dependent step-children in the custody of the worker. However, the receiving state need not admit step-children who are in the joint custody of their migrant worker parent and their other non-migrant parent even if the non-migrant parent consents.[82]

3.51 Directives are replicated in national legislation and are therefore indirectly enforceable in domestic law.

The United Nations Convention on the Rights of the Child 1989

3.52 The 1989 United Nations Convention is the successor to the Declaration of the Rights of the Child 1959, ('the Declaration of Geneva') which has been described as 'the first serious attempt to describe in a reasonably detailed manner what constitutes children's overriding claims and entitlements'.[83] As Fortin illustrates, it emphasises that states must not only protect children and safeguard their fundamental freedoms they must also provide resources to ensure that they realise their potential for maturing into healthy and happy adulthood.[84]

---

[77]   *Families and the European Union: Law, Politics and Pluralism* (2006), at p 43.
[78]   Fortin (ed) *Children's Rights and the Developing Law* (3rd edn, 2009), at p 72.
[79]   Art 7(2) of Regulation 1612/68.
[80]   Art 12 of Regulation 1612/68. See generally *Families and the European Union: Law, Politics and Pluralism* op cit, ch 3.
[81]   *Family Reunification Directive* Council Directive 2003/86/EC, art 4(1)(a) and (b).
[82]   Ibid, at 4(1)(c) and (d).
[83]   Op cit p 38.
[84]   Ibid.

3.53   The articles of the Convention most relevant to the private law relating to children are set out in Appendix 1. The Committee on the Rights of the Child[85] has raised four articles on the status of general principles.

• **Art 2 The obligation to respect and ensure the rights set forth in the Convention to each child within the jurisdiction without discrimination of any kind.**

> 'This non-discrimination obligation requires States actively to identify individual children and groups of children for whom recognition and realisation of their rights may demand special measures. For example, the Committee highlights in particular the need for data collection to be disaggregated to enable discrimination or potential discrimination to be identified. Addressing discrimination may require changes in legislation, administration and resource allocation as well as educational measures to change attitudes. It should be emphasised that the application of the non-discrimination principle of equal access to rights does not mean identical treatment. A General Comment by the Human Rights Committee has underlined the importance of taking special measures in order to diminish or eliminate conditions that cause discrimination.'[86]

• **Art 3(1) The best interests of the child to be a primary consideration in all actions concerning children.**

> 'The article refers to actions undertaken by "public or private social welfare institutions, courts of law, administrative authorities or legislative bodies". The principle requires active measures throughout government, parliament and the judiciary. Every legislative, administrative and judicial body or institution is required to apply the best interests principle by systematically considering how children's rights and interests are or will be affected by their decisions and actions – by, for example, a proposed or existing law or policy or administrative action or court decision, including those which are not directly concerned with children, but indirectly affect children.'[87]

• **Art 6 The child's inherent right to life and States' obligation to ensure to the maximum extent possible the survival and development of the child.**

> 'The Committee expects States to interpret "development" in the broadest sense as an holistic concept, embracing the child's physical, mental, spiritual, moral, psychological and social development. Implementation measures should be aimed at achieving the optimal development for all children.'[88]

• **Art 12 The child's right to express his or her views freely on 'all matters affecting the child' and to have those views given due weight.**

---

85   (2003) *General Measures of Implementation of the Convention on the Rights of the Child* General Comment No 5 CRC/C/GC 9 Centre for Human Rights Geneva.
86   Ibid, para 12.
87   Ibid.
88   Ibid.

'This principle, which highlights the role of the child as an active participant in the promotion, protection and monitoring of his or her rights, applies equally to all measures adopted by States to implement the Convention. Opening government decision-making processes to children is a positive challenge which the Committee finds States are increasingly responding to ... If consultation is to be meaningful, documents as well as processes need to be made accessible. But appearing to "listen" to children is relatively unchallenging; giving due weight to their views requires real change. Listening to children should not be seen as an end in itself, but rather as the means by which States make their interactions with children and their actions on behalf of children ever more sensitive to the implementation of children's rights ... The emphasis on "matters that affect them" in article 12(1) implies the ascertainment of the views of particular groups of children on particular issues – for example children who have experience of the juvenile justice system on proposals for law reform in that area, or adopted children and children in adoptive families on adoption law and policy.'[89]

3.54 The Convention was ratified by the United Kingdom on 16 December 1991.

3.55 These rights are not directly enforceable in domestic courts but can be persuasive when the courts are considering how to exercise any discretion. Indeed, the so called 'Bangalore Principles',[90] derived from the deliberation of Commonwealth judges. state that although in common law countries the national court is obliged to give effect to national law where it is clear but inconsistent with the international obligation of the state concerned:

'It is within the proper nature of the judicial process and well-established judicial functions for national courts to have regard to international obligations which a country undertakes – whether or not they have been incorporated into domestic law – for the purpose of removing ambiguity or uncertainty from national constitutions, legislation or common law.'

Subsequent colloquia have suggested that it is a duty of judges to interpret domestic legislation and to develop the common law in the light of values expressed in Conventions.[91] This approach is unlikely to find favour in the courts of the United Kingdom. In *Re H (A Child)*[92] Wilson LJ commented that arguments that such approaches are binding lack 'elementary legal discipline'.

---

[89] Ibid.

[90] *Developing Human Rights Jurisprudence Volume 7 Seventh Colloquium on the Domestic Application of International Human Rights Norms* (1998) Commonwealth Secretariat and Interrights available at: www.chr.up.ac.za/test/images/files/documents/ahrdd/theme24/judiciary_bangalore_principles_1988.pdf.

[91] *Human Rights Law and Practice* op cit, para 9.03. See also Macdonald 'Bringing rights home for children: arguing the UNCRC' [2009] Fam Law 851.

[92] [2010] EWCA Civ 915.

3.56 Nevertheless, the United Nations Convention has been treated as persuasive and cited by the senior judiciary both to test domestic rules against international obligations and to buttress the domestic approach on a particular issue. For example, in *Re R (A Minor) (Contact)*[93] Butler-Sloss LJ said that:

'It is the right of a child to have a relationship with both parents wherever possible. This principle has been stated again and again in the appellate courts. It is underlined in the United Nations Convention on the Rights of the Child and endorsed in the Children Act 1989 ...'

In *Mabon v Mabon*[94] Thorpe LJ considered Art 12 in relation to the representation of children in private law proceedings.

'In my judgment the [domestic] Rule is sufficiently widely framed to meet our obligations to comply with both Article 12 of the United Nations Convention and Article 8 of the ECHR, providing that judges correctly focus on the sufficiency of the child's understanding and, in measuring that sufficiency, reflect the extent to which, in the 21st Century, there is a keener appreciation of the autonomy of the child and the child's consequential right to participate in decision making processes that fundamentally affect his family life.'

3.57 The argument reached flying-buttress proportions in *Re ZH (Tanzania) v Secretary of State*[95] in the Supreme Court where Baroness Hale of Richmond said:

'For our purposes the most relevant national and international obligation of the United Kingdom is contained in article 3(1) of the UNCRC: "In all actions concerning children, whether undertaken by public or private social welfare institutions, courts of law, administrative authorities or legislative bodies, the best interests of the child shall be a primary consideration." This is a binding obligation in international law, and the spirit, if not the precise language, has also been translated into our national law. Section 11 of the Children Act 2004 places a duty upon a wide range of public bodies to carry out their functions having regard to the need to safeguard and promote the welfare of children ...'

'Further, it is clear from the recent jurisprudence that the Strasbourg Court will expect national authorities to apply article 3(1) of UNCRC and treat the best interests of a child as "a primary consideration". Of course, despite the looseness with which these terms are sometimes used, "a primary consideration" is not the same as "the primary consideration", still less as "the paramount consideration". The UNHCR, in its Guidelines on Determining the Best Interests of the Child (May 2008), explains the matter neatly, at para 1.1:

"The term 'best interests' broadly describes the well-being of a child ... The CRC neither offers a precise definition, nor explicitly outlines common factors of the best interests of the child, but stipulates that: the best interests must be the determining factor for specific actions, notably adoption

---

93 [1993] 2 FLR 762.
94 [2005] EWCA Civ 634, [2005] 2 FLR 1011, at [26].
95 [2011] UKSC 4, [2011] 1 FLR 2170.

(Article 21) and separation of a child from parents against their will (Article 9); the best interests must be a primary (but not the sole) consideration for all other actions affecting children, whether undertaken by public or private social welfare institutions, courts of law, administrative authorities or legislative bodies (Article 3)."

This seems to me accurately to distinguish between decisions which directly affect the child's upbringing, such as the parent or other person with whom she is to live, and decisions which may affect her more indirectly, such as decisions about where one or both of her parents are to live. Article 9 of UNCRC, for example, draws a distinction between the compulsory separation of a child from her parents, which must be necessary in her best interests, and the separation of a parent from his child, for example, by detention, imprisonment, exile, deportation or even death.'

'Nevertheless, even in those decisions, the best interests of the child must be a primary consideration.'

'We now have a much greater understanding of the importance of these issues in assessing the overall well-being of the child. In making the proportionality assessment under Article 8, the best interests of the child must be a primary consideration. This means that they must be considered first. They can, of course, be outweighed by the cumulative effect of other considerations.'[96]

3.58   The Convention, as well as the European Convention, may also influence other bodies, for example, Cafcass, when providing their services.[97]

---

[96]   Ibid, at [23], [24], [25] and [33].
[97]   See, for example, *Children's Rights Policy* (Cafcass, 2008).

Chapter 4

CHILDREN'S WISHES AND FEELINGS

INTRODUCTION

4.1   When a court decides any question with respect to a child's upbringing, it is under a duty to have regard to 'the ascertainable wishes and feelings of the child concerned (considered in the light of his age or understanding)'.[1] Those wishes and feelings will normally be investigated by way of a Cafcass report although, in appropriate but exceptional cases, the child may be joined as a party under Part 16.2 of the Family Procedure Rules 2010 (FPR 2010)[2] and represented by a guardian or next friend under Part 16.4 (formerly rule 9.5 of the Family Proceedings Rules 1991). In rare cases, when the child is able, having regard to his understanding, to give instructions in relation to the proceedings, he may be allowed to act without a guardian/next friend. Wishes and feelings do not determine the issue to be decided, being only one of the factors in the welfare checklist.

4.2   Despite a recognition in recent years that children may need to be consulted more than hitherto[3] and a consultation by the Department of Constitutional Affairs in 2006 into the question of whether children who are the subject of private law proceedings should be granted party status,[4] the approach of the Law Commission in 1988[5] remains a good summary of the current position of courts:

> 'The opinion of our respondents was almost unanimously in favour of the proposal to give statutory recognition to the child's views. Obviously there are dangers in giving them too much recognition. Children's views have to be discovered in such a way as to avoid embroiling them in their parents' disputes, forcing them to "choose" between their parents or making them feel responsible for the eventual decision. This is usually best done through the medium of a court welfare officer's report although most agreed that courts should retain their present powers to see children in private. Similarly, for a variety of reasons the child's views may not be reliable, so that the court should only have to take due account of them in the light of his age and understanding. Nevertheless, experience has shown that it is pointless to ignore the clearly expressed views of older children. Finally, however, if the parents have agreed on where the child will live and made their arrangements accordingly, it is no more practicable to try to

---

[1]   CA 1989, s 1(3).
[2]   SI 2010/2955.
[3]   As in *Re A (Contact: Separate Representation)* [2001] 1 FLR 715.
[4]   DCA *Separate Representation of Children* (2006) CP 20/6.
[5]   *Family Law: Review of Child Law: Guardianship and Custody* Law Com No 172.

alter these to accord with the child's views than it is to impose the views of the court. After all, united parents will no doubt take account of the views of their children in deciding upon moves of house or employment but the children cannot expect their wishes to prevail.'[6]

Often, decisions, for example about contact, will be reached by agreement between the adults at the First Hearing Dispute Resolution Appointment (FHDRA) (see **Chapter 17**) without the views of the child necessarily being known. Practice Direction 12B[7] states that at the FHDRA the court must consider:

- whether the child is aware of the proceedings and how the wishes and feelings of the child are to be ascertained (if at all);

- how the child is to be involved in the proceedings, if at all, and whether at or after the FHDRA;

- if consideration is given to joining of the child as a party to the application, the current Guidance from the President of the Family Division, who will inform the child of the outcome of the case where appropriate.

WHY SHOULD WISHES AND FEELINGS BE ASCERTAINED?

4.3   There are three reasons for a child's wishes being ascertained and then considered. The first is protective, the second, utilitarian and the third, rights-based.

Any order which causes a child harm by reason of emotional disturbance needs to be avoided. Secondly, the wishes and feelings of the child may be relevant to the effectiveness of the order proposed. A 2-year-old child removed from the care of his mother and placed with someone who is a psychological stranger for a day's contact may become distraught, protest and, irrespective of the distress suffered by the child, contact will not be successful. The feelings of a child of this age about separation from his carer in circumstances which cannot effectively be explained to him are obviously relevant to the issue. Likewise, forcing a course of action on an unwilling teenager may be doomed to failure. In *Re P (A Minor) (Education)*,[8] for example, the Court of Appeal overturned a decision that a 14-year-old boy should attend a boarding school rather than a local day school which was his clear preference. He was mature, sensible and intelligent and at his age his views should have been given great weight. On a practical level, forcing him to board carried real dangers:

---

6   *Family Law: Review of Child Law: Guardianship and Custody* Law Com No 172, para 3.23.
7   The Revised Private Law Programme para 5.5
8   [1992] 1 FLR 316.

'He may be very resentful, not only resentful of the court, but resentful of his mother, resentful of authority; he may not settle well and he may be very unhappy.'[9]

4.4 In some cases the utilitarian argument meets the separate issue of the child being able legally to veto or refusing to consent to a course of action. In *Re D (Paternity)*[10] an 11-year-old boy, T, opposed an application that a sample be taken for DNA testing to establish whether or not his father was the applicant, or another person whom he believed to be his father. Mr Justice Hedley gave permission under s 20 of the Family Law Reform Act 1969 (see **6.89**) for testing but stayed it in relation to T without limit of time with permission to restore the application.

'I am satisfied that although T could not be described as being competent in the *Gillick*[11] sense of that term, he does understand what testing means and what its conclusions might be; that his strong opposition to it is essentially a view of his own and that this whole issue of paternity is a big issue for him at a highly emotive stage of his life.'

The last reason is the growing belief that it is important that children as individuals ought to be able to contribute to decisions about their futures, whether or not this can be termed a 'right'.[12] A sub-committee of the Family Justice Council summarises it as: 'Essentially ... the child needs to feel included in the process in an age appropriate manner'.[13] Baroness Hale of Richmond added that it is a big mistake to think that children's views can be effectively communicated through the adult parties to any dispute.[14]

4.5 In domestic law, any right children have to make a contribution is to be found in Art 6 of the European Convention on Human Rights. The European Court of Human Rights has recognised that courts ought to take into account the wishes and feelings of children when making decisions about their welfare. In *Hokkanen v Finland*,[15] for example, it held that the wish of a mature 10-year-old of an above-average intelligence to remain with her grandparents,

---

9   Ibid, per Butler-Sloss LJ at 322; and see also *Re T (Contact: Alienation: Permission to Appeal)* [2002] EWCA Civ 1736, [2003] 1 FLR 531.
10   [2006] EWHC 3545 (Fam), [2007] 2 FLR 26, at [26].
11   *Gillick v West Norfolk and Wisbech Area Health Authority and Department of Health and Social Security* [1986] 1 FLR 224.
12   For summaries of the argument, see Fortin *Children's Rights and the Developing Law* (3rd edn, 2009) ch 7, Lowe and Murch 'Children's participation in the Family Justice System – translating principles into practice' [2001] CFLQ 137 and Piper 'Barriers to seeing and hearing children in private law proceedings' [1999] Fam Law 394; Sir Nicholas Wilson 'The ears of the child in family proceedings' [2007] Fam Law 808; Fortin 'Representation through the looking glass' [2007] Fam Law 500; Hale 'Can you hear me Your Honour?' [2012] Fam Law 30.
13   'Enhancing the participation of children and young people in family proceedings: starting the debate?' [2008] Fam Law 431.
14   'Can you hear me Your Honour?' op cit, at 31.
15   (1994) 19 EHRR 139, [1996] 1 FLR 289.

with whom she had lived since she was 2, and her feeling that their home was her home were not only relevant but were sufficient to justify dismissing her father's application for custody.

However, the current emphasis placed by the European Court of Human Rights is not so much on the right of the child to be heard in the sense of his wishes being taken into account but on the need to investigate all relevant circumstances before deciding whether any interference with family life was justified. Nor has the Court prescribed steps which must be taken in every case. In *Sahin v Germany; Sommerfield v Germany*[16] the Fourth Section of the Court held that in a contact case a domestic court's failure to hear directly from the child in the first case (although there had been a psychological report) and to direct a report by a psychologist in the second infringed the *father's* right to be sufficiently involved in the proceedings. However the Grand Chamber[17] took a different view, recognising that domestic courts had a margin of appreciation when deciding what was required by the circumstances of the particular case.

> '[As] a general rule it is for the national courts to assess the evidence before them, including the means to ascertain the relevant facts (see *Vidal v Belgium* (22 April 1992), Series A, No 235-B 17 at para 33). It would be going too far to say that domestic courts are always required to hear a child in court on the issue of access to a parent not having custody, but this issue depends on the specific circumstances of each case, having due regard to the age and maturity of the child concerned.'[18]

Furthermore any requirement that a child's views should be considered, does not equate with the child having a right to be a party. What is guaranteed by Art 6 is an overall fair hearing within a reasonable time by an independent and impartial tribunal. Any right to be a party to the proceedings is not absolute and may be subject to limitations. Under the so-called '*Ashingdane* principles',[19] States enjoy a certain margin of appreciation in regulating the right of access, 'regulation which may vary in time and place according to the needs and resources of the community and of individuals'. Accordingly, the European Commission of Human Rights in the case of *M v United Kingdom*[20] recognised that:

> 'In the majority of the contracting states, the right of access to court is regulated in respect of minors, vexatious litigants, persons of unsound mind and persons declared bankrupt. Such regulations are not in principle contrary to Article 6 of the Convention where the aim pursued is legitimate and the means employed to achieve the aim is proportionate.'

Given these principles and because the European Court of Human Rights in practice seemingly accords children a lower status than adults, it is unlikely that

---

[16] [2002] 1 FLR 119.
[17] [2003] 2 FLR 671.
[18] Para [73].
[19] *Ashingdane v United Kingdom* (1985) EHRR 528.
[20] [1985] 52 DR 269.

the Court would hold that children had to be made parties to private law cases provided the domestic courts have the discretion (as they do in England and Wales) to order representation, if appropriate, having regard to the circumstances of the individual case.

4.6 There are other international Conventions which acknowledge that the views of children should be considered and given due weight and that when a child is capable of forming its own views, the child should have the opportunity of being heard by the court either directly or indirectly.

4.7 Article 12 of the UN Convention on the Rights of the Child 1989 provides that:

> 'States parties shall assure to the child who is capable of forming his or her own views the right to express those views freely in all matters affecting the child, the views of the child being given due weight in accordance with the age and maturity of the child ... the child shall in particular be provided the opportunity of being heard in any judicial and administrative proceedings affecting the child either directly or through a representative or appropriate body, in a manner consistent with procedural rules of national law.'

4.8 Article 3 of the European Convention on the Exercise of Children's Rights 1996 (which has not yet been ratified by the United Kingdom) provides that a child:

> '... considered by internal law as having sufficient understanding shall in judicial proceedings affecting him be granted and be entitled to request the following rights:
>
> (a) to receive all relevant information;
> (b) to be consulted and express his or her own views;
> (c) to be informed of the possible consequences of compliance with these views and the possible consequences of any decision.'

Article 4 provides the further right:

> '... to apply, in person or through other persons or bodies, for a special representative in proceedings before a judicial authority affecting the child where internal law precludes the holders of parental responsibilities from representing the child as a result of conflict of interests with the latter.'

4.9 Both domestic and Convention law agree therefore that courts should consider the wishes and feelings of children, that these should be given weight according to the age and maturity of the child and that, in order to protect rights, it may be necessary for them to be allowed to be parties. The existence of Convention rights, however, has encouraged courts in England and Wales to revisit their traditional approach that children should not be made parties in private law cases. In *Re A (Contact: Separate Representation)*,[21] Dame Elizabeth Butler-Sloss said:

> 'There are cases when they do need to be separately represented and I suspect as a result of the European Convention for the Protection of Human Rights and Fundamental Freedoms 1950 becoming part of domestic law and the increased view of the English courts, in any event, that the children should be seen and heard in child cases and not always sufficiently seen and heard by the use of a court welfare officer's report, there will be an increased use of guardians in private law cases. Indeed, in the right case I would welcome it.'

However, she added that, 'in the majority of cases, in private law proceedings, children do not need to be separately represented'.

4.10   The impact of the various Rights conventions was further acknowledged by the Court of Appeal in 2005. In *Mabon v Mabon*[22] Thorpe LJ spoke of 'the need to reflect the extent to which, in the twenty-first century, there is a keener appreciation of the autonomy of the child and the child's consequential right to participate in the decision-making processes that fundamentally affect his family life'.

4.11   Speaking extra-judicially in 2007,[23] Sir Nicholas Wilson (as he then was) expressed the view that in some but certainly not all cases, a report to the court under s 7 of the 1989 Act probably sufficed to comply with the duty under the UN Convention to provide the right for children to participate in proceedings.

> 'However, when we learn that the UK has not signed, still less ratified, the European Convention, our suspicions arise that, no doubt for economic reasons, we are not committing ourselves to acceptable procedures for enabling children to exercise their rights. Such scepticism is born of dispiriting experience of the failure of our governments to give reasonable priority to family justice; but in this respect it may be misplaced. Other EU States, including France, have also failed to ratify the European Convention and, in the words of one commentator, it has 'gathered nothing but dust'.[24]

Despite this, he expressed the view that the absence of an express duty to grant the child's application for separate representation must mean that no such duty is intended.[25]

---

21   [2001] 1 FLR 715, at para [22].
22   [2005] EWCA Civ 634, [2005] 2 FLR 1011, at para 26.
23   'The ears of the child in family proceedings' op cit, at 810.
24   Geary 'A child's right to expression in the courtroom under international conventions on the rights of children and French national law' (2006) www.crin.org/docs/Right_to_Expression_Geary.doc. See also Sawyer 'International developments: one step forward, two steps back' [1999] CFLQ 151.
25   See also Parkes 'The right of the child to be heard in family law proceedings: Art 12 UNCRC' [2009] IFL 238.

4.12 Whatever the origins of the beliefs which have been variously expressed about the importance of involving children in proceedings which concern them, judicial opinion is that they should be involved to an appropriate extent. In *Re D (Abduction: Rights of custody)*[26] Baroness Hale of Richmond said:

> 'As any parent who has ever asked a child what he wants for tea knows, there is a large difference between taking account of a child's views and doing what he wants. Especially in Hague Convention[27] cases, the relevance of the child's views to the issues in the case may be limited. But there is now a growing understanding of the importance of listening to the children involved in children's cases. It is the child, more than anyone else, who will have to live with what the court decides. Those who do listen to children understand that they often have a point of view which is quite distinct from that of the person looking after them. They are quite capable of being moral actors in their own right. Just as the adults may have to do what the court decides whether they like it or not, so may the child. But that is no more a reason for failing to hear what the child has to say than it is for refusing to hear the parents' views.'

WHAT DO CHILDREN WANT?

4.13 In 2000, Ann O'Quigley carried out a literature review on the representation of children's views for the Lord Chancellor's Advisory Board on Family Law.[28] The literature contains a mixture of factual reporting mixed with untested assertions by the researchers as to what would be desirable. It appears, however, that children are bewildered by what is happening when parents separate, confused about what has been decided and unable to talk to their parents or ask them questions for fear of upsetting them.

4.14 In *Your Shout Too!*[29] researchers investigated the views of children aged 11 and over who had been the subject of private law proceedings where either a section 7 report had been ordered or the child had been made a party. Forty per cent agreed they had been able to 'have a say' and 16% that they had not. In general there was an association between feeling involved and feeling they had been able to influence the outcome. Only 2% had attended court and half of these children spoke to the judge. Nearly a fifth (90%) had not gone to court but would have liked to speak to the judge. Over half (55%) did not want to go to court.

4.15 The authors concluded that the findings clearly confirmed that different children require a range of different services. Younger children in particular

---

[26]   [2006] UKHL 51, [2007] 1 FLR 961, at [57].

[27]   The Hague Convention on the Civil Aspects of International Child Abduction 1980.

[28]   *Listening to Children's Views: The Findings and Recommendations of Recent Research* (Joseph Rowntree Foundation). The review is summarised in 'Where Are the Children's Voices?' [2000] Fam Law 439.

[29]   Timms, Bailey and Thorburn NSPCC Policy Practice Research Series (2007). The cohort may not be representative of children involved in private law proceedings. Questionnaires were sent to the parents of 1,690 children but only 141 replied. In addition, as the authors point out, the children were aged 11 and over and in only a small proportion of cases are reports ordered.

were more satisfied with the service they received than were older children, who wanted more information and more proactive help in achieving satisfactory residence and contact arrangements. The children and young people valued particular aspects of the Cafcass service. They appreciated a Cafcass officer who:

- listened;

- showed understanding;

- was friendly;

- was supportive;

- enabled the young person to express their views;

- facilitated contact with a parent with whom the young person wished to keep in contact;

- assisted the young person with their decision as to with whom to live;

- respected their confidentiality and privacy.

The Report recommended that for a service to be seen as satisfactory by children and young people, it should be composed of a number of elements, of which listening to children is a valued prerequisite, but was not sufficient on its own. Other elements of the task were:

- to give the child accurate information about their situation;

- to inform and facilitate family communication;

- to negotiate on the child's behalf;

- to represent their views and interests effectively and accurately, both in court and within their families;

- to achieve the best possible outcomes for them.

4.16 One strand which emerges from the studies is the need for adults to talk to children about what is happening and a need for general information to be made available to children from outside agencies.

4.17 The second strand which emerges from the literature[30] is that, while many children are used to participating in family life about decisions which

---

[30] See also Smart, Neale and Wade *The Changing Experience of Childhood: Families and Divorce* (Polity, 2001), at pp 167–168.

affect them, they are aware of the difficulties of actually taking the responsibility of making decisions for themselves. In fact, some children see it as not merely difficult but unfair for parents to ask them to make decisions about matters such as residence or contact. Nor do they welcome being asked about their wishes by outsiders. Most children feel loyalty and attachment to both parents and want these feelings respected. They are overwhelmingly concerned that things should be fair for their parents.

4.18 The third strand of conclusions concerns difficulties in ascertaining children's views and communicating them to the court. Researchers have found that children are generally reluctant to talk to 'outsiders' about family issues, seeing this as both disloyal and liable to lead to an escalation of problems. Professionals are seen as interventionist, judgmental and intrusive, and their discussions with children feel like interrogations. Children want their discussions to be confidential, but because this cannot be offered, the lack of confidentiality needs to be made clear to them at the outset. They should have the right not to participate if that is what they want.

4.19 A further study conducted in three county courts in 2000[31] found that s 7 reports were ordered in just under half (47%) of residence or contact cases and children were consulted in half of these. This meant that they had been consulted in only a quarter of all cases examined. Cases where they were not consulted were mainly those where they were too young to express a view, where the issues were 'cut and dried' or where there had been early agreement. 'In other words, children were only given the opportunity to be influential when there was serious conflict.' The researchers gained the impression that the views of children over the age of 7 were taken seriously, especially where they were old enough to 'vote with their feet'. The wishes and feelings of younger children could also have an impact but only where they confirmed other evidence. Many children were aware of the conflict between their parents and despite adult concern about involving children:

> 'It seems that the agenda was indeed about asking them to express a preference. We do not suggest that court welfare officers asked the children in such a direct fashion, but it does seem that many children took the opportunity to state their preferences clearly.'

4.20 Children will need adequate information if they are to express their views and opportunities need to be provided for exploring options. Professionals also need to be aware of developmental and cultural factors which may affect children, although they should not make assumptions about the individual child based on this knowledge. It may be appropriate to use drawing, sentence completion and other activities rather than direct question and answers.

---

[31] Smart, May and others *Residence and Contact Disputes in Court* Vol 1 (2003) Department of Constitutional Affairs, summarised in May and Smart 'Silence in court? Hearing children in residence and contact disputes' [2004] CFLQ 305.

Interviews with an adult who is a relative stranger may be too pressurising for younger children, who may find it much easier to speak if they have a friend with them.

COMMUNICATING CHILDREN'S WISHES AND FEELINGS

4.21   The tensions between the desirability and even the right of children to have their wishes taken into account when a decision about welfare has to be made have been discussed already. The problems in ascertaining those wishes and the reluctance of children to become involved in taking sides against a parent are mirrored in the approach adopted by courts. Although there may be an increasing willingness to allow an expression of children's wishes, courts remain, in theory at least, unwilling to allow them to 'enter the arena':

> 'The reason for this approach is principally the belief that it is inappropriate for children to be involved directly in, or to have the conduct of, litigation. The courts are deeply reluctant to allow children to give evidence in Family Proceedings and to be cross-examined. In addition, if children are the applicants in proceedings, they will have access to all the court documentation, which may include statements by the parties and medical reports and records which it may not be appropriate for them to see. Plainly, the older the child, the more readily permission [for them to make s 8 applications] may be granted, although the view remains that that litigation is a matter for adult parties, not the children who are usually the subject of the proceedings.'[32]

The view of the majority who responded to the Advisory Board on Family Law Children Act Sub-Committee's Working Paper[33] was that, in most cases, the wishes and feelings of children in relation to contact could be ascertained by a Children and Family Reporter. As the Sub-Committee said in its final report:[34]

> 'Being heard does not necessarily mean being represented: what it means is giving children the confidence that their wishes and feelings have been fully made known to the court and that the court has taken them fully into account.'

4.22   Given the different reasons put forward to justify considering the wishes and feelings of children and the difficulties experienced in ascertaining them in practice, not least because of financial restraints, it is not surprising that there has been some academic criticism of a perceived failure to do more and of the present practice of the courts. Professor Fortin, for example, points to 'five rungs' to the ladder of children's involvement.

> 'On the ladder's bottom rung there is no court hearing because the parents' dispute is resolved in its early stages under the in-court conciliation procedures

---

[32]   *Making Contact Work: A Consultation Paper* (The Children Act Sub-Committee of the Lord Chancellor's Advisory Board on Family Law, 2001).
[33]   Ibid.
[34]   Ibid, para 12.12.

established under the Private Law Programme. On the next rung up, the case has proceeded to litigation but the court relies on the parents' own assessments of what is in the child's best interests. On the third rung of the ladder is the child regarding whom a welfare report is prepared by the children and family reporter. This will include an account of the child's own wishes and feelings. On the fourth rung of the ladder are children provided with party status and separate representation. On the top rung children litigate on their own behalf possibly even having initiated the proceedings themselves. Disappointingly, despite the reorganization of the system for representing children in family proceedings, the rules regarding these situations remains arcane.'[35]

Children as witnesses

4.23 Prior to 2010, courts started from the position not only that it is undesirable for children to give evidence but also that it would be rare for them to do so.[36]

4.24 In the vast majority of cases, courts will not allow children to give evidence and any attempt to adduce evidence from them, for example, by having them make statements is likely to be seriously deprecated.[37] The Family Law Protocol[38] states that solicitors should advise clients that it will not assist them to produce statements written by their children nor to bring their children to speak with solicitors acting for one or other parent. Solicitors should not see the children who are the subject of any case in which they are advising unless they are acting for the child.

Competency

4.25 Section 96(1) of the Children Act 1989 provides that a child is competent to give evidence and either understands the nature of an oath or if, in the opinion of the court she understands that it is her duty to speak the truth and has sufficient understanding to justify her evidence being heard.

4.26 Guidance was also given in criminal proceedings (where the test set out in s 53 of the Youth Justice and Criminal Evidence Act 1999 is different) by the Court of Appeal in *R v Barker*.[39]

---

[35] Op cit, at 248.

[36] *LM (By her guardian) v Medway Council RM and YM* [2007] EWCA Civ 9, [2007] 1 FLR 1698. See also *R v B Council ex parte P* [1991] 1 FLR 470; *Re P (A Minor) (Witness Summons)* [1997] 2 FLR 447; *SW v Portsmouth City council: Re W (Care Order: Sexual Abuse)* [2009] EWCA Civ 644, [2009] 2 FLR 1106 and *Re W (Children) (Family Proceedings: Evidence)* [2010] EWCA Civ 57, [2010] 2 FLR 256.

[37] *Re M (Family Proceedings: Affidavits)* [1995] 2 FLR 100.

[38] (3rd edn, The Law Society, 2010), para 5.9.12.

[39] [2010] EWCA Crim 4.

Re W (Children) (Abuse: Oral Evidence)[40]

4.27 In 2010 the Supreme Court in *Re W (Children) (Family Proceedings: Evidence)* held that a presumption that a child should not give evidence in care proceedings could not be reconciled with the approach of the European Court of Human Rights, which always aims to strike a fair balance between competing Convention rights. Article 6 requires that the proceedings overall be fair and this normally entails an opportunity to challenge the evidence presented by the other side. However, account also had to be taken of the Art 8 rights of the perceived victim:

> 'Striking that balance in care proceedings may well mean that the child should not be called to give evidence in the great majority of cases, but that is a result and not a presumption or even a starting point.'[41]

Subsequently, in *Re H (A Child) (Abuse: Oral Evidence)*[42] Lord Justice Thorpe said that:

> 'The guidance given by the Supreme Court ... does not turn the world on its head: it still requires a measured balance between the demands of justice and the needs of child welfare'.

The experience of judges is that post-*Re W* there has been an increase in applications for children to give evidence but no increase in the numbers who do.

4.28 The issue of a child giving evidence most commonly arises in care proceedings and it must not be forgotten that the judgments in *Re W* were given in such a context. However, the issue can also be raised in private law proceedings. The principle is the same but in private law proceedings the child may not have the same protection from the risk of harm inherent in giving evidence. She may not have a guardian or be legally represented and the alleged perpetrator may be more likely to be unrepresented. Moreover the Supreme Court was dealing specifically with cases where factual allegations made by a child need to be investigated. The decision may be of little help in persuading family courts in private law to allow children to give evidence, for example, in relation to their wishes. In both jurisdictions anecdotal evidence suggests that although post-*Re W* there may have been an increase in the number of applications for children to give evidence, this is not matched by an increase in the number of cases where a child in fact gives evidence.[43] In *Re M (Sexual Abuse: Evidence)*[44] Hughes LJ when refusing permission to appeal a finding of fact based on hearsay evidence from children aged between 10 and 3 said that:

---

40   [2010] UKSC 12, [2010] 1 FLR 1485.
41   See also *Re M (Minors) (Sexual Abuse Evidence)* [1993] 1 FLR 822. For a discussion of *Re W*, see Hall 'The misfortune of being brought forward? The impact of *Re W* on children giving evidence in care proceedings' [2010] CFLQ 499.
42   [2011] EWCA Civ 741, at [8].
43   Mitchell 'Children giving evidence: the practical implications of *Re W*' [2011] Fam Law 817.
44   [2010] EWCA Civ 1030, at [5].

'Whatever [*Re W*] may say about a necessary change in practice in relation to the starting point in relation to children of that age, I have no doubt at all that there would never have been and should not be even now any question of any of these children being expected to give oral evidence, at least in a family court. Indeed elsewhere the criminal courts have had to consider on numerous occasions the real difficulties which arise where in criminal cases young children have to give evidence, and it is quite apparent, for example from *R v Barker* [2010] EWCA Crim 4, that the criminal courts as well as the family courts need to adjust to recognise the profound limitations that court proceedings and conventional cross examination have in relation to very young children.'

For a discussion of when the issue should be considered and the effect of any concurrent criminal proceedings, see **17.77**.

Considerations

4.29 In *Re W* Baroness Hale of Richmond said that:

'The object of the proceedings is to achieve a fair trial in the determination of the rights of all the people involved. Children are harmed if they are taken away from their families for no good reason. Children are harmed if they are left in abusive families. This means that the court must admit all the evidence which bears upon the relevant questions: whether the threshold criteria justifying state intervention have been proved; if they have, what action if any will be in the best interests of the child? The court cannot ignore relevant evidence just because other evidence might have been better. It will have to do the best it can on what it has.

When the court is considering whether a particular child should be called as a witness, the court will have to weigh two considerations: the advantages that that will bring to the determination of the truth and the damage it may do to the welfare of this or any other child. A fair trial is a trial which is fair in the light of the issues which have to be decided ... The welfare of the child is also a relevant consideration, albeit not the paramount consideration in this respect ... [The] object of the proceedings is to promote the welfare of this and other children. The hearing cannot be fair to them unless their interests are given great weight.'[45]

The need for the evidence

4.30 Relevant factors in weighing the advantages that calling the child to give evidence may bring to the fair and accurate determination of the case include:

- the issues to be decided in order properly to determine the case;

- the quality of the evidence the court already has;

- the quality of any pre-recorder ('Achieving Best Evidence') interview;

---

[45] [2010] UKSC 12, [2010] 1 FLR 1485, at [23]–[24]. The Family Justice Council has also issued guidance: *Guidelines in relation to children giving evidence in family proceedings* [2012] Fam Law 79.

- the age, maturity and intellectual ability of the child;

- the length of time since the events in question, for these will have a bearing on whether an account now can be as reliable as a near-contemporaneous account, especially if given in a well-conducted ABE interview.

4.31 In *Re X (A Child) (Evidence)*[46] Theis J refused to allow a 17-year-old child to give evidence. The grounds for doing so included the fact that, against the background that he had been diagnosed as having severe Asperger's Syndrome and was immature, vulnerable and had difficulties with understanding, the challenge to his evidence was likely to involve matters which had not been covered in his ABE interview and were likely to cover a considerable period of time. 'In all likelihood [his evidence] would be of limited if any evidential value.'

The welfare of the child and the support which can be provided

4.32 The impact on children of having to give evidence cannot be underestimated. In a study of children who had given evidence in criminal trials as witnesses[47] Plotnikoff and Woolfson found that of those in full-time education nearly two-fifths said their studies or attendance were affected in the pre-trial period, 8% dropped out altogether and 3% changed schools due to intimidation. Nearly one in eight reported that their concentration was affected and 4% said they got into trouble at school for poor behaviour which they attributed to the offence and the court case. Half were anxious about giving evidence; a quarter were scared. By the time the study was conducted, just over half felt better but only a third felt they had put the experience behind them. According to the authors, giving evidence was 'a lengthy process that was, for many, distressing and disenchanting'.

4.33 It is therefore essential that the court considers the support which can be provided, not only after the decision is taken but as part of the decision as to whether the child should give evidence. 'The family court will have to be realistic in evaluating how effective it can be in maximising the advantage while minimising the harm.'[48]

4.34 Relevant factors in weighing any risk to the child include:

- the age and maturity of the child;

- the support which the child has from family or other sources, or the lack of it;

---

[46] [2011] EWHC 3401 (Fam).
[47] Plotnikoff and Wilson *Measuring Up?* (Nuffield Foundation, 2009).
[48] [2010] UKSC 12, [2010] 1 FLR 1485, per Baroness Hale at [28].

- the child's own wishes and feelings about giving evidence. An unwilling child should rarely, if ever, be obliged to give evidence;

- the views of the child's guardian and, where appropriate, those with parental responsibility;

- any risks specific to the particular child, eg the need to give evidence in criminal proceedings;

- general evidence of the harm which giving evidence may do to children.

Difficulties may arise where an older child wants to give evidence. In *Re J (Child Giving Evidence)*[49] a boy aged either 17 or 13 was allowed to give evidence against his mother in care and private law proceedings. He had potentially relevant evidence on factual issues, wanted to give evidence and would feel a profound sense of injustice if he was not permitted to. In *Re X (A Child) (Evidence)*[50] permission was refused even though the child wanted to give evidence.

The trial process

4.35 Relevant factors may include:

- the risk of further delay to the proceedings;

- whether the child's evidence can be given in advance of the trial.

'There are things that the [Family] court can do but they are not things that it is used to doing at present. It is not limited by the usual courtroom procedures or to applying the special measures by analogy ... One possibility is an early video'd cross examination as proposed by Pigot. Another is cross-examination via video link. But another is putting the required questions to her through an intermediary. This could be the court itself, as would be common in continental Europe and used to be much more common than it is now in the courts of this country.'[51]

There is no obvious reason why this could not be appropriate in family proceedings, perhaps being conducted by a child and adolescent psychiatrist or psychologist. There would be no court style cross-examination but as Baroness Hale pointed out, 'the important thing is that the questions which challenge the child's account are fairly put to the child so that she can answer them, not that counsel should be able to question her directly'.[52]

4.36 Before deciding the issue the judge is likely to need to read the transcript of any ABE interview to view the recording.

---

[49]   [2010] EWHC 962 (Fam), [2010] 2 FLR 1080. The boy's age was in dispute.
[50]   [2011] EWHC 3401 (Fam).
[51]   *Re W (Children) (Abuse: Oral Evidence)* [2010] UKSC 12, [2010] 1 FLR 1485, at [27]–[28]. See also Mitchell op cit, at p 821.
[52]   *Re W (Children) (Abuse: Oral Evidence)* [2010] UKSC 12, [2010] 1 FLR 1485, at [28].

4.37 For examples where the trial judge systematically decided the issue of children giving evidence, see *Re J (Child Giving Evidence)*[53] and *Re X (A Child) (Evidence)*.[54]

Special Measures

4.38 The so called 'special measures' which are used in criminal proceedings to reduce the strain on a child and other vulnerable witnesses of giving evidence can also be used in Family Courts. These are:

- screening the child from the alleged perpetrator;[55]

- evidence being given by live link either from within the same building or elsewhere;[56]

- evidence being given in private.[57] This will normally be the case in all family proceedings but the court will have to consider whether the press should be excluded. The court can also limit the number of persons present;

- the child being examined through an intermediary;[58]

- the use of communication aids such as sign or symbol boards.[59]

Intermediaries

4.39 Intermediaries are specialists in assessing communication needs and facilitating communication with a witness who has difficulty understanding questions or giving evidence.[60] Under s 29 of the Youth Justice and Criminal Evidence Act 1999 the function of an intermediary is to communicate to the witness the questions put, to communicate to the person asking the questions, the answers given in reply and to explain such questions or answers so far as necessary to enable them to be understood by the witness or person in question. However, it is not an intermediary's role to assess or comment upon a witness's competence to give evidence, nor does the intermediary act as an advocate.

In practice, all intermediaries will be intermediaries registered with the Ministry of Justice. Many guardians and social workers will not be registered and may not have the necessary language skills. Therefore family courts will

---

53   [2010] EWHC 962 (Fam), [2010] 2 FLR 1080.
54   [2011] EWHC 3401 (Fam).
55   Youth Justice and Criminal Evidence Act 1999, s 23.
56   Ibid, s 24.
57   Ibid, s 25.
58   Ibid, s 29.
59   Ibid, s 30.
60   For their background, see Cooper 'Child witnesses in family proceedings: should intermediaries be showing us the way?' [2011] Fam Law 397.

need to ensure that registered intermediaries are booked in advance. For an account of the difficulties which may be encountered in securing and paying for an intermediary, see *Re X (A Child) (Evidence)*.[61]

Witness supporters

4.40 In contrast to the intermediary who plays an active part during the trial, the role of the court witness supporters is 'by their presence, to provide emotional support to the witness and to reduce their anxiety and stress when giving evidence, thereby ensuring that the witness has the opportunity to give their best evidence'.[62] Their task is to provide emotional support 'in a neutral but sympathetic manner' but they cannot influence the proceedings in any direct way. *The National Standards for the Court Witness Supporter*[63] lists the obligatory key characteristics as being:

- someone not involved in the case, who has no knowledge of the evidence and who has not discussed the evidence with the witness;

- someone who has received suitable training in their role and conduct; and

- someone with whom the witness has a relationship of trust. 'Ideally, this should be the person preparing the witness for court, but others may be appropriate.'

The ways in which supporters can assist children in family proceedings include:

- providing emotional support and information;

- understanding the child's views, wishes, concerns, and any particular vulnerabilities that might affect them during the trial process (including the child's views on special measures), and conveying these to the relevant agency;

- helping the child to become familiar with the court and its procedures;

- supporting the child through court hearings;

- undertaking court preparation and passing on information about the forthcoming trial;

- accompanying the witness on a pre-trial visit to court;

- being with the child when she views the ABE interview before giving evidence;

---

[61]   [2011] EWHC 3401 (Fam).
[62]   *Achieving Best Evidence* (Ministry of Justice and Crown Prosecution Service, 2011).
[63]   Ibid, Appendix L.

- being with the child when she gives evidence in court or the live link room.

4.41 Because the child's parent, guardian or social worker will be involved in the case and have knowledge of the evidence, they cannot, in the criminal courts at least, be appropriate supporters. Experienced child supporters may be found through local Witness Care Units and organisations such as the NSPCC and Barnado's. Resources may however be scarce and arrangements should be made as soon as possible after it is decided that the child will be giving evidence. To avoid uncertainty about whether support will in fact be available, it would be useful if the directions order named the supporter.

Cross-examining the child

4.42 The experience of being cross-examined is likely to be stressful for the child and both the stress and the nature of the questioning may make answers unreliable.[64] Of the child witnesses interviewed for *Measuring Up*[65] nearly a half said they did not understand some questions. Sixty-five per cent reported one or more problems of comprehension, complexity, pace of questions that were too fast or having their answers talked over. Of these, two in five, had been told they could tell the court if they did not understand but only less than half actually did so. A quarter said defence lawyers talked over some of their answers. Nearly three in five said the cross-examiner had accused them of lying and of these, 70% said it happened more than once.

4.43 Some of these difficulties are caused by advocates failing to understand and take into account the level of the child's verbal and intellectual development. Common pitfalls include using vocabulary which is too complex, complicated or multiple questions, unnecessary narrative, negatives, tag questions, for example, 'You stayed at home that day, didn't you?' and prefacing questions with 'Do you remember …?'

4.44 To some extent these difficulties can be lessened by advocates being trained and by the tribunal intervening to prevent inappropriate questioning. In *R v Barker*[66] the Lord Chief Justice said that while the right of the defendant to a fair trial must be undiminished the trial process must cater for the needs of child witnesses.

> 'When the issue is whether the child is lying or mistaken … it should not be over-problematic for the advocate to formulate short, simple questions which put the essential elements of the defendant's case to the witness, and fully to ventilate … the areas of evidence which bear on the child's credibility. Aspects of evidence which undermine or are believed to undermine the child's credibility must, of course, be revealed to the [tribunal], but it is not necessarily appropriate for them to form the subject matter of detailed cross-examination of the child and the

---

[64] See Mitchell 'Do you ever tell fibs? Cross-examining children' [2011] Fam Law 962.
[65] Plotnikoff and Wilson op cit.
[66] [2010] EWCA Crim 4, at [42].

advocate may have to forego much of the kind of contemporary cross-examination which consists of no more than comment on matters which will be before the [court] in any event from different sources.'

Baroness Hale likewise commented in *Re W*[67] that the court is unlikely to be helped by 'generalised accusations of lying, or by a fishing expedition in which the child is taken slowly through the story yet again in the hope that something will turn up, or by a cross-examination which is designed to intimidate the child and pave the way for accusations of inconsistency in a future criminal trial'. However, focused questions which put forward a different explanation for certain events may help the court to do justice between the parties but the court should not assume that:

'... an "Old Bailey style" cross examination is the best way of testing that evidence. It may be the best way of casting doubt upon it in the eyes of a jury but that is another matter. A family court would have to be astute both to protect the child from the harmful and destructive effects of questioning and also to evaluate the answers in the light of the child's stage of development.'

4.45 Valuable assistance in phrasing questions is given in *Raising the Bar: The Handling of Vulnerable Witnesses, Victims and Defendants in Court*.[68]

Cross-examination and the litigant in person

4.46 See **17.163**. The Family Justice Council Guidelines[69] state that a child should never be questioned directly by a litigant in person who is an alleged perpetrator.

Letters from children

4.47 The court may deprecate any attempt to encourage a child to express his views in a letter, whether to the court, a Cafcass reporter or the other parent. The residential parent runs the risk of being suspected of having dictated the letter or having encouraged it.[70] This is not to say the court will not take account of a letter written by the child of his own volition.

Judges or magistrates meeting children

4.48 It has long been recognised that judges may interview the child, but caution needs to be exercised. Not every judge has the ability to communicate readily with a child during a solitary interview.[71] Moreover, there is an inherent contradiction in seeing a child in order to ascertain his wishes while at the same time being required to report to his parents anything material which is said.

---

67 [2010] UKSC 12, [2010] 1 FLR 1485, at [25] and [27].
68 (Advocacy Training Council, 2011). Its list of Do's and Don'ts is set out in 'Do you ever tell fibs? Cross-examining children' op cit, at p 968.
69 Op cit, at para 17.
70 See, for example *Re S (Minors) (Access: Religious Upbringing)* [1992] 2 FLR 313 at 320.
71 See *Making Contact Work*, paras 12.10 and 12.11.

Any expression by the child of a preference for one parent inevitably involves disloyalty to the other. Until recently, the tendency of judges was against meeting the child. In *B v B (Minors) (Interviews and Listing Arrangements)*[72] in 1994 Wall J, sitting in the Court of Appeal, pointed out:

'... In these circumstances ... a child could only express true feelings if promised absolute confidentiality. Yet that is the one promise which the judge cannot give.'

He explained that seeing a child represents a complete departure from the normal forensic process and what the child says cannot be tested in cross-examination. Ascertaining a child's wishes and feelings is normally the role of the Cafcass reporter who can be cross-examined. This process should not be automatic or routine.

4.49 However, by 2007 there was a growing debate about whether this reluctance by judges to speak to children was justified. Professor Hunter, for example, while neither arguing for or against judicial interviews, suggested that there was a need for 'clear and critical thinking' about why the debate about the respective roles of Cafcass officers and the judiciary in understanding children's wishes and feelings had arisen.[73] Evidence from Scotland[74] and New Zealand[75] seemed to suggest that many judges thought that speaking directly to children could make a difference.[76] Judges who were reluctant to do so identified the main barriers as a lack of training, a perceived susceptibility to children being coached and the complications of handling sensitive information where children sought confidentiality. In 2009 a summary of international research[77] made similar findings:

- judges and parents agreed that the welfare officer had a primary role and any interview with the judge should be an adjunct with the welfare officer present;

- most judges and parents were concerned about the capacity of judges to make an accurate assessment of children's views during a short interview;

- non-resident parents were concerned about the children's vulnerability to manipulation by the resident parent;

---

72 [1994] 2 FLR 489, per Wall J at 495; and see also the comments of Wall J in *Mabon v Mabon* [2005] EWCA Civ 634, [2005] 2 FLR 1011, at para [38].

73 'Close encounters of a judicial kind: "hearing" children's voices in family law proceedings' (2007) CFLQ 283 at 303. See also the report of the Voice of the Child sub-committee of the Family Justice Council *Enhancing the Participation of Children and Young People in Family Proceedings* (2008) and 'The voice of the child and the judge as an interviewer of children' [2010] IFL 141.

74 Raitt 'Hearing children in family law proceedings: can judges make a difference?' (2007) CFLQ 204.

75 Caldwell 'Common law judges and judicial interviewing' (2011) CFLQ 41.

76 See also Bellamy, Platt and Crichton 'Talking to children: the judicial perspective' (2010) Fam Law 647.

77 Parkinson and Cashmore 'The child's voice: Australian research' [2009] IFL 11. See also 'The children's voice: research' [2008] Fam Law 1170.

- judges were concerned about the risk to due process;

- all judges agreed the process could not be confidential.

Raitt[78] comments that none of these difficulties are insurmountable 'but it does take a serious degree of purpose, will and creativity to tackle them'.

4.50 Senior judges in England and Wales were divided. In *Re W (Leave to Remove)*[79] Lord Justice Thorpe thought it unfortunate that the trial judge had not spoken to three children aged 15, 13 and 11 before refusing their mother's application to relocate to Sweden, noting that the children had wanted the Cafcass officer to advance the formulation of their wishes which they had agreed (which she had done) but 'she did not return to them to explain her intention to finesse away their stated position by her own analysis'.

> 'The participation of children in private law Children Act proceedings is a matter of particular topical concern. The Family Justice Council has created a sub-committee, 'The Voice of the Child', to advise government and to stimulate professional debate as to the way forward. As a generalisation it can be said that the committee is strongly in favour of judges seeing children much more frequently than has been our convention. This case well illustrates the argument. J in particular, at nearly 15 years of age, would in another context be judged *Gillick* competent. She is an autonomous person with clear rights. If major issues are to be decided, determining the whole course of her remaining minority, she is at a minimum entitled to be heard. That can be achieved in three ways, separate representation, discussion with the judge or through a *CAFCASS* intermediary. Each of these methods has different advantages and disadvantages. The one selected in the present case has the obvious disadvantage that at the conclusion of the process J can only feel that her wishes and feelings were insufficiently considered by the judge because they were diminished by the very professional whom she trusted to advance them. This conclusion might have been avoided had the judge had a meeting with the children, and particularly with J. He suggested that course and, in my judgment, it is regrettable that he was dissuaded from it.'[80]

4.51 Lord Justice Wilson[81] took a different view.

> 'It may be that, presumably under the guidance of a set of fully debated and carefully drawn principles and perhaps following a degree of judicial training, the practice of the family courts in England and Wales will come to encompass such meetings (at any rate for some purposes) more frequently. Presently, however, the discretion of our judges to meet children privately is largely untrammelled by authority; and all that is clear is that such is currently the exception rather than the norm.'

---

[78] Op cit, at 223.
[79] [2008] EWCA Civ 538, [2008] 2 FLR 1170.
[80] Ibid, at [33].
[81] Now a member of the Supreme Court.

Not wishing to pre-empt the debate by expressing an opinion which was unnecessary to the decision before the court he indicated that had he been conducting the hearing of the mother's application and had reached the decision which the trial judge reached:

> '(a) I would have met the children, albeit not for the purpose, nor at the stage, commended by Thorpe LJ. (b) I would have met the children very shortly after giving judgment in order to explain to them the reasons for my decision; I would have done so in the light of their ages and intelligence and in particular because my decision was contrary to their wishes. (c) In the light of the ages and intelligence of A and of C, it would not have crossed my mind to meet J without them. (d) I would not have met the children prior to judgment, for the purpose of collecting their wishes and feelings, because at present I am unpersuaded that the potentially important evidence collected in such strained circumstances would be either a balanced and comprehensive reflection of their views or easily susceptible of later forensic examination.'[82]

4.52 Previously Lord Justice Wilson, speaking extra-judicially in a lecture,[83] had expressed 'a multitude' of objections to current practice being changed. Judges unlike guardians and Cafcass officers were untrained; in order to protect the judge from later allegations that he had misrepresented the child's views, another adult would need to be present and a short interview would be likely to present children with 'a wholly inadequate' opportunity to express their wishes.

4.53 After *Re W (Leave to Remove)*, Lord Justice Thorpe, also speaking extra-judicially[84] maintained his position.

> 'Comparative glances sideways must not always be given exaggerated importance. Every justice system reflects its own tradition and the traditions of the societies of which it serves. [I am confident] that we could and should progress to achieving greater participation for children ... For me there are a number of principles that underline future progress. These in particular I emphasise:
>
> a) The participation of the child is multi-faceted and careful thought should be given in any individual case to its almost unique requirements.
>
> b) In our system the CAFCASS officer must bear the primary responsibility for eliciting the wishes and feelings of the child and for exploring whether some enhanced participation and, if "yes", in what form? That is not to exclude the possibility of a judge seeing the child without a report from the CAFCASS officer. Given that CAFCASS reports now take over 12 weeks in preparation, there may well be cases in which time and tide do not allow the luxury of waiting for that contribution.
>
> c) Whatever the child's participation, the child must be protected from any sense that he or she is responsible for the outcome.

---

[82] Ibid, at [57].
[83] 'The ears of the child in family proceedings' op cit, at 815.
[84] 'The voice of the child in family proceedings' [2010] IFL 136.

d) No enhanced participation can ever establish confidentiality between child and judge. Natural justice prohibits that ... That consideration also points to the advisability of a transcript or at least a careful note of what passes in the Judge's meeting with the child.

e) The introduction of change should be at a measured pace to enable those judges who do not feel comfortable at the prospect of meeting the child to abstain from the process. At the same time judicial training should be made available to those who are willing but feel the need for expert preparation.'

4.54 In 2010 the Family Justice Council produced *Guidelines for Judges Meeting Children* who are subject to Family Proceedings[85] approved by the President of the Family Division, whose purpose was 'to encourage Judges to enable children to feel more involved and connected with proceedings in which important decisions are made in their lives and to give them an opportunity to satisfy themselves that the Judge has understood their wishes and feelings and to understand the nature of the Judge's task'. The Guidelines expressly state that nothing in the guidance was intended to replace or undermine the current position that in most cases a child's needs, wishes and feelings are brought to the court in written form by a Cafcass officer. However, based on the FJC's understanding that it was Cafcass practice to discuss with a child in a manner appropriate to their developmental understanding whether their participation in the process included a wish to meet the judge:

'If the child does not wish to meet the Judge discussions can centre on other ways of enabling the child to feel a part of the process. If the child wishes to meet the Judge, that wish should be conveyed to the Judge where appropriate. The primary purpose of the meeting is to benefit the child. However, it may also benefit the Judge and other family members.'

4.55 The Guidelines are as follows.

• The judge is entitled to expect the lawyer for the child and/or the Cafcass officer:

  (i) to advise whether the child wishes to meet the judge;
  (ii) if so, to explain from the child's perspective, the purpose of the meeting;
  (iii) to advise whether it accords with the welfare interests of the child for such a meeting to take place; and
  (iv) to identify the purpose of the proposed meeting as perceived by the child's professional representative/s.

• The other parties shall be entitled to make representations as to any proposed meeting with the judge before the judge decides whether or not it shall take place.

---

[85] [2010] 2 FLR 1872.

- In deciding whether or not a meeting shall take place and, if so, in what circumstances, the child's chronological age is relevant but not determinative. Some children of 7 or even younger have a clear understanding of their circumstances and very clear views which they may wish to express.

- If the child wishes to meet the judge but the judge decides that a meeting would be inappropriate, the judge should consider providing a brief explanation in writing for the child.

- If a judge decides to meet a child, it is a matter for the discretion of the judge, having considered representations from the parties [to decide]:

    (i)   the purpose and proposed content of the meeting;
    (ii)   at what stage during the proceedings, or after they have concluded, the meeting should take place;
    (iii)   where the meeting will take place;
    (iv)   who will bring the child to the meeting;
    (v)   who will prepare the child for the meeting (this should usually be the Cafcass officer);
    (vi)   who shall attend during the meeting – although a judge should never see a child alone;
    (vii)   by whom a minute of the meeting shall be taken, how that minute is to be approved by the judge, and how it is to be communicated to the other parties.

    'It cannot be stressed too often that the child's meeting with the judge is not for the purpose of gathering evidence. That is the responsibility of the CAFCASS officer. The purpose is to enable the child to gain some understanding of what is going on, and to be reassured that the judge has understood him/her.'

- If the meeting takes place prior to the conclusion of the proceedings:

    (i)   The judge should explain to the child at an early stage that a judge cannot hold secrets. What is said by the child will, other than in exceptional circumstances, be communicated to his/her parents and other parties.
    (ii)   The judge should also explain that decisions in the case are the responsibility of the judge, who will have to weigh a number of factors, and that the outcome is never the responsibility of the child.
    (iii)   The judge should discuss with the child how his or her decisions will be communicated to the child.
    (iv)   The parties or their representatives shall have the opportunity to respond to the content of the meeting, whether by way of oral evidence or submissions.

Although the Guidelines are not binding, they are persuasive. They differ little from the guidance given by the President, Sir Nicholas Wall P, in *B v B (Minors) (Interviews and Listing Arrangements)*.[86]

4.56 Although justices have a discretion to see the child in private, it was previously considered rare if ever that they should do so. The extent to which this position has changed as a result of the Guidelines is uncertain.[87]

Children's views communicated by others

By a party

4.57 There is no rule of evidence that a party or any other lay witness cannot give evidence about what a child wants but any such evidence is open to attack as being partial and the witness open to criticism that the child has been questioned and possibly leading questions put. In *Re C (Children: Disclosure)*[88] the Court of Appeal doubted the wisdom of children being taken to speak to the father's Member of Parliament in order that he could gauge their wishes and feelings.

By a Children and Family Reporter

4.58 This is the normal manner in which evidence of a child's wishes and feelings is adduced. See **Chapter 19**.

The Cafcass *Reporting to Court Handbook* states that 'practitioners should be clear with the child/ren about the purpose to which … a report will be put, enabling the child/ren more fully to participate in the court process and to be aware of the potential for sharing.'

By a child psychiatrist or psychologist

4.59 Normally, a child psychiatrist or psychologist will not be used to report a child's wishes to the court unless one is instructed for other reasons (see **Chapter 18**). However, instructing an expert may be useful when the child has emotional, mental or physical difficulties in communicating with a Children and Family Reporter.

Children's wishes and feelings communicated by their guardian or legal representative

4.60 See below.

---

[86] Op cit.
[87] *Re M (A Minor) (Justices' Discretion)* [1993] 2 FLR 706.
[88] [2010] EWCA Civ 209, [2010] 2 FLR 22.

THE CHILD AS A PARTY

4.61   In some cases a child[89] will be a party to the proceedings because he or she is the applicant or a necessary respondent. In these circumstances, a guardian must be appointed for the child.[90] In other cases he may be a necessary respondent but not be the child who is subject to the proceedings. For example, he may be a parent of the subject child. In these circumstances the party must have a litigation friend.[91]

Other than this, the court's permission will be required before the subject child is made a party. In order to assist the court when a report is ordered under s 7 of the Act, the Reporter, whether or not a Cafcass officer or a local authority officer has an express duty to consider whether it is in the best interests of the child for the child to be made a party to the proceedings. If it is considered that the child should be made a party, the Children and Family Reporter has to notify the court and give his reasons.[92]

Should a child be joined as a party?

4.62   The general view of the courts is that children should not be joined as parties in private law proceedings unless their welfare specifically requires it. However in recent years there has been a greater willingness to consider joining children and in 2004 the President of the Family Division issued a Practice Direction[93] giving guidance on when children might be joined under the then rule 9.5 of the Family Proceedings Rules 1991. This Practice Direction has since been replaced by Practice Direction 16A Part 4 which is in identical terms.

4.63   In 2006 academics from Cardiff University carried out research on behalf of the Department for Constitutional Affairs into children being joined as parties, *Research into the operation of Rule 9.5 of the Family Proceedings Rules 1991.*[94] The authors concluded that a number of children need a concerned impartial person accessible to them to support them and help them manage the critical family transitions following the breakdown of their parents' relationship. There were a number of roles which this person could play and it was important to distinguish between them, not least to avoid children and their parents becoming confused. First, there was the role of ascertaining the voice of the child to assist in the court's decision-making. Second, there was the way in which the child representation process could be used by the court and the children's representatives as part of their efforts to moderate the intractability of parental disputes (what some solicitors referred to as 'unlocking the case'). Third, there was the role of providing children with a

---

89   That is, someone under the age of 18: Family Procedure Rules 2010, r 2.3.
90   Ibid, r 16.4.
91   Ibid, r 16.5.
92   Practice Direction 16A, para 11.3.
93   *President's Direction (Representation of Children in Family Proceedings Pursuant to Family Proceedings Rules 1991 Rule 9.5)* [2004] 1 FLR 1188.
94   Douglas, Murch, Miles and Scanlan, DCA, summarised in Douglas, Murch, Miles and Scanlan 'Special Representation Report' [2006] Fam Law 385.

source of reliable information and support during the course of the proceedings to help them cope with the associated anxieties and uncertainties ('a passage agent'). Although there might be many more children in need of these specific supports than was currently the case, not all of the roles required the child to be separately represented.

> 'In intractable and complex cases, we recognise that the combined skills of a guardian and solicitor working in tandem may well be the most effective means of ensuring that the child's viewpoint and interests are put centre stage – sometimes where necessary with a view to moderating the parents' mutual antipathy[95] as part of a strategy of proactive judicial case management assisted by judicial continuity. Yet there may also be less difficult cases where the court may conclude that the tandem model is unnecessary; that what the child needs first and foremost is a source of reliable neutral information and support while the litigation proceeds.'[96]

4.64   Practice Direction 16A gives the following guidance.

•   The proper conduct and disposal of proceedings concerning a child may require the child to be made a party.

•   Making the child a party to the proceedings is a step that will be taken only in cases involving an issue of significant difficulty and consequently will occur in only a minority of cases. Before taking the decision to make the child a party, consideration should be given to whether an alternative route might be preferable, such as asking an officer of Cafcass to carry out further work or by making a referral to social services or possibly, by obtaining expert evidence.

•   The decision to make the child a party will always be exclusively that of the judge, made in the light of the facts and circumstances of the particular case. The following are offered, solely by way of guidance, as circumstances which may justify the making of an order.

•   Where a Cafcass officer has notified the court that in his opinion the child should be made a party.

•   Where the child has a standpoint or interests which are inconsistent with or incapable of being represented by any of the adult parties.

•   Where there is an intractable dispute over residence or contact, including where all contact has ceased, or where there is irrational but implacable hostility to contact or where the child may be suffering harm associated with the contact dispute.

---

[95] For a discussion of a strategy which might be used, see Robinson 'Resolving entrenched child litigation Part One: the child's solicitor's role in resolving conflict in Rule 9.5 cases' (2006) Fam Law 48.

[96] Douglas, Murch et al op cit, paras 7.46–7.47.

- Where the views and wishes of the child cannot be adequately met by a report to the court.

- Where an older child is opposing a proposed course of action.

- Where there are complex medical or mental health issues to be determined or there are other unusually complex issues that necessitate separate representation of the child.

- Where there are international complications outside child abduction, in particular where it may be necessary for there to be discussions with overseas authorities or a foreign court.

- Where there are serious allegations of physical, sexual or other abuse in relation to the child or there are allegations of domestic violence not capable of being resolved with the help of a Cafcass officer.

- Where the proceedings concern more than one child and the welfare of the children is in conflict or one child is in a particularly disadvantaged position.

- Where there is a contested issue about blood testing.

The Practice Direction pointed out that separate representation of the child may result in a delay in the resolution of the proceedings. 'When deciding whether to direct that a child be made a party, the court will take into account the risk of delay or other facts adverse to the welfare of the child. The court's primary consideration will be the best interests of the child.'

4.65 The Practice Direction merely indicates the kind of cases where a child might appropriately be made a party. It does not say that in the circumstances an order must be made. For example, the fact that the case involves serious issues whose resolution will permanently affect the child does not seem by itself to be sufficient justification for separate representation. In *Re J (Specific Issue Orders: Muslim Upbringing and Circumcision)*,[97] for example, the child was not separately represented, even though the issues involved whether he should be brought up as a Muslim and circumcised.

In *Re W (Contact: Joining Child as Party)*[98] the Court of Appeal criticised a decision to join a 7-year-old child in contact proceedings because the child had expressed concerns about contact as 'an unusual course'. 'The normal course would be for there to be a … court reporter's report. If a report is not adequate the question is should the child be represented.'[99]

---

[97] [1999] 2 FLR 678.
[98] [2001] EWCA Civ 1830, [2003] 1 FLR 681.
[99] Per Butler-Sloss P at para [5].

In order to avoid unnecessary delay, a decision about joining a child should be made as soon as possible. In the set of six cases concerning contact between children and their fathers who suffered unusual psychological problems such as Asperger's Syndrome or who had undergone gender reassignment (see **11.144**) no child was represented although in two cases it was said that the children would have benefited from this had time permitted.

> 'It does seem to me, as a matter of principle, that where the court is faced with contact issues as difficult as those which arise in this case, consideration should be given to the children being separately represented and, where appropriate, expert advice being sought on their behalf. In such cases children quite frequently have particular interests and standpoints which do not coincide with and are not necessarily capable of being adequately represented by their parents. Absence of separate representation in the present case means, in my judgment, that the court cannot give the children all the assistance they need.'[100]

A small survey of cases carried out in 2004 by the National Youth Advocacy Service (NYAS)[101] found that a quarter of children who were granted separate representation were 5 and under and nearly three-fifths were between 6 and 11. Just over a third had a guardian appointed because of adversarial and hostile parents and just under three-tenths because the case was an entrenched and protracted one. Almost all cases involved an intractable dispute over contact and just under three-fifths of children were very reluctant to express an opinion because it was not consistent with their parents' views. However, in just under nine-tenths of cases reports of the children's views coincided with the order made. In 80% of cases NYAS recommended that there be contact.

Examples of cases where a child has been joined as a party

Re S (Minors) (Access: Religious Upbringing)[102]

4.66 The unrepresented, non-resident father who was applying for a contact order was obsessed by his wish that his teenage children should practice the Roman Catholic faith. The children were made parties so that the Official Solicitor could investigate.

Re A (Contact: Separate Representation)[103]

4.67 The mother was refusing contact between a father and his 4½-year-old daughter. There were allegations of sexual abuse. The father had a criminal record, including convictions for possessing and supplying drugs. The mother had a history of emotional ill-health:

---

[100] *Re H (Contact Order) (No 2)* [2002] 1 FLR 22, per Wall J at 36.
[101] Fowler and Stewart 'Rule 9.5 separate representation and NYAS' [2005] Fam Law 49.
[102] [1992] 2 FLR 313.
[103] [2001] 1 FLR 715.

'There may be a conflict of interest between each parent and the child and the child's interests in this case are quite separate to the parents to a degree, more marked, perhaps, than in some cases.'

L v L (Minors) (Separate Representation)[104]

4.68   Three children aged between 9 and 14 and living in England with their father were made parties to an application for contact by their mother who lived in Australia because the Children and Family Reporter formed the view that she could not adequately represent their views, because the father appeared to have a dominant personality such that the children were unable to express to him their views about contact and because of the international element.

Re M (Intractable Contact Dispute: Interim Care Order)[105]

4.69   There was an intractable contact dispute involving two children aged 13 and 10. After contact was ordered, the children's mother alleged that the father had physically and sexually abused them. All contact ceased. The allegations were found to be untrue. The mother again refused to comply with the order and again made an allegation of sexual abuse which was dismissed. An application was made for the mother to be committed to prison. The children were joined as parties and were eventually placed in the care of their father by means of an interim care order.

'It is in my view, that one of the prime categories for the tandem model of separate representation in private law proceedings is where all contact has ceased and the issue of contact has become intractable. Children in this situation frequently have an interest in the proceedings which is independent from the view point being advanced by each of their parents.'[106]

Mabon v Mabon[107]

4.70   Following parental separation the three elder children (aged 17, 15 and 13) remained with their father and the younger three with their mother. The mother applied for residence orders in respect of the three older children. The six children were joined as parties, a course which the Court of Appeal approved.

'There are a number of factors which point strongly towards the grant of separate representation in the present case. The [boys] were aged ... 17, 15 and 13 ... How were they to know what their parents were contending for: were there cross-applications for residence, what were the contact applications? It was simply unthinkable to exclude young men from the knowledge of and participation in legal proceedings that affected them so fundamentally.'[108]

---

[104]   [1994] 1 FLR 156.
[105]   [2003] EWHC 1024 (Fam), [2003] 2 FLR 636.
[106]   Per Wall J at para [15].
[107]   [2005] EWCA Civ 634, [2005] 2 FLR 1011.
[108]   Per Thorpe LJ at para [23].

The child as a party with a guardian

4.71 A child who is made a party to the proceedings will normally be represented by a guardian who will instruct a solicitor to act for the child.

In deciding whether to join a child in cases in the county court, the court may consider whether the nature of the case, its complexity or importance of the issues require the case to be transferred to another court.[109]

Previously, the family proceedings court had no power to make the child a party and therefore any case which required this had to be transferred to the county court.[110] But the introduction of the Family Procedure Rules 2010, which do not distinguish between the tiers of courts when using the phrase 'the court', means that such appointments can be made. However the *Guidance Note to Family proceedings Courts*[111] observes that the content of Practice Direction 16A 'points to the conclusion that it will be unusual if not rare for magistrates sitting in the family proceedings courts to retain jurisdiction where there is a proposal to make a child a party'.

Practice Direction 16A[112] states that where a child is made a party and a guardian is to be appointed, consideration should first be given to appointing a Cafcass officer. Before the appointment, preliminary enquiries must be made of a Cafcass manager regarding the appointment and the timescale involved. The court must take into account the demands on the resources of Cafcass that such appointment would make.[113] Following the Cafcass Practice Note[114] (see below), if it is not appropriate to appoint Cafcass, then the Official Solicitor or another person may be appointed provided they consent.[115] However, the court may not appoint a person as a guardian unless it is satisfied that he can fairly and competently conduct proceedings on behalf of the child and has no interest adverse to that of the child. In addition, save where the Official Solicitor is appointed, the person must undertake to pay any costs ordered to be paid by the child subject to a right to be repaid from the child's assets.[116]

4.72 If Cafcass cannot help, it may be appropriate to take advantage of the professional services of a charitable organisation such as the National Youth

---

[109] Practice Direction 16A, para 7.5.
[110] See the Allocation and Transfer of Proceedings Order 2008, SI 2008/2836, art 15(1) and **16.75**.
[111] Justices Clerks Society (July 2011) [2011] Fam Law 1024.
[112] Para 7.4.
[113] Practice Direction 12B, para 5.5.
[114] *Cafcass and the National Assembly for Wales Practice Note (Appointment of Guardians in Private Law Proceedings) June 2006* [2006] 2 FLR 143.
[115] FPR 2010, r 16.24.
[116] Ibid.

Advocacy Service (NYAS).[117] It would not normally be appropriate to use a solicitor as guardian with an independent social worker for a child as young as 7.[118]

4.73 A Protocol has been agreed between Cafcass and NYAS for deciding whether NYAS will accept an appointment as a guardian. Cafcass should be approached first and will usually provide a guardian. However, NYAS may, for example, be asked by the court to provide a guardian in any matter (likely to be long standing) where, despite the best efforts of Cafcass staff, one or more members of the family can no longer work with the organisation. Both agencies are committed to effective communication in the best interests of the child in accordance with the law. The normal points of contact should be the Cafcass service manager and the nominated NYAS lawyer. If any case moves between the two agencies it is particularly important to pass on information which may assist the work with the child and family, eg aspects of risk management, conflict of interest issues and any particular needs of the child. If NYAS is invited to provide r 9.5 representation where Cafcass has not been approached, NYAS will discuss the matter with Cafcass and will be responsible for notifying the court in the first instance. Cafcass and NYAS will work together to advise the court whenever there appears to be good reason for a guardian not to be appointed, eg when there is an alternative preferable route such as a s 37 report from the local authority.[119] In *Re H (National Youth Advocacy Service)*[120] the Court of Appeal stressed the importance of the court consulting NYAS where the criteria is made out before deciding an application for NYAS to be appointed.

4.74 The procedure for inviting Cafcass to act is set out in the Cafcass *Practice Note* of 2006.[121]

- The order should simply state that '[name of child] is made party to the proceedings and pursuant to [FPR 2010, r 16.24] an officer of Cafcass be appointed as his/her guardian'.

- The decision about which particular officer of Cafcass to allocate as guardian is a matter for Cafcass.[122] It is also helpful for Cafcass to know whether the court considers there is any reason why any Cafcass officer who has dealt with the matter so far should not continue to deal with it in the role of guardian.

---

[117] *Re A (Contact: Separate Representation)* [2001] 1 FLR 715, per Dame Elizabeth Butler-Sloss P at 718. For the work of NYAS, see Mullin and Singleton 'NYAS: Representing children and Rule 9.5' [2006] Fam Law 975.

[118] *Re W (Contact: Joining Child as Party)* [2001] EWCA Civ 1830, [2003] 1 FLR 681.

[119] (2006) Fam Law 243.

[120] [2006] EWCA Civ 896, [2007] 1 FLR 1028.

[121] Op cit.

[122] Cafcass is not under a duty to make an officer available immediately on receiving a request from the court: *R v Children and Family Court Advisory and Support Service* [2003] EWHC 235 Admin, [2003] 1 FLR 953.

- In cases proceeding in the county court, the order should be sent to the Cafcass/Cafcass CYMRU office responsible for private law cases in the area in which the child is currently living. For county court cases proceeding in the Principal Registry, the order and the court file should be sent to the Cafcass office at the Principal Registry for referral to the relevant local office. The Cafcass High Court Team does not undertake work proceeding in the county court.

- In the High Court, the case will be referred either to the Cafcass High Court Team (where child is resident in England); the Assembly lawyers (where child is resident in Wales) or to the relevant local Cafcass office.

- The following categories of case involving an appointment should be referred to the Cafcass High Court Team/Assembly lawyers:

  - reporting restriction orders arising in a children's case;
  - exceptionally complex adoption cases including exceptionally complex cases involving inter-country adoption;
  - all medical treatment cases where the child is old enough to have views which need to be taken into account, or where there are particularly difficult ethical issues such as the withdrawal of treatment, unless the issue arises in existing proceedings already being handled locally when the preferred arrangement will usually be for the matter to continue to be dealt with locally but with additional advice provided by Cafcass Legal/Assembly lawyers if necessary;
  - any free-standing human rights applications pursuant to s 7(1)(a) of the Human Rights Act 1998 in which it is thought that it may be possible and appropriate for any part to be played by Cafcass/Cafcass CYMRU or its officers;
  - exceptionally complex international cases particularly where there is a dispute as to which country's courts should have jurisdiction over the child's affairs;
  - applications in wardship and applications made under the High Court's inherent jurisdiction.

- In cases referred to the Cafcass High Court Team where the appointment is urgent, the judge is encouraged to phone the Team to discuss the matter before an order is made.

- In cases falling outside the above categories, the order making the appointment should be sent to the Cafcass office/Cafcass CYMRU office for the area where the child is currently living or, where the case is proceeding in the Principal Registry, to the Cafcass office at the Principal Registry for referral to the relevant local office.

- The office that is to be responsible for the matter will notify the court of the name and contact details of the nominated guardian. If for whatever reason there is likely to be any significant delay in an officer being made available Cafcass will notify the court accordingly to enable the court to consider whether some other proper person should be appointed instead.

• Where the guardian is a member of the Cafcass High Court Team there may be no need for a solicitor for the child also to be appointed as the litigation may be conducted in house.

Duties of the guardian

4.75 The duties of the guardian are set out in Practice Direction 16A, Part 3.

> 'It is the duty of a child's guardian fairly and competently to conduct proceedings on behalf of the child. The child's guardian must have no interest in the proceedings adverse to that of the child and all steps and decisions the child's guardian takes in the proceedings must be taken for the benefit of the child.'[123]

The guardian acts as an individual, independently both of Cafcass (if employed by Cafcass)[124] and of the child.[125]

4.76 The guardian's specific duties cover investigations, the appointment of a solicitor, giving such advice to the child as is appropriate having regard to the child's understanding, attendance at court and providing advice to the court and, unless the court directs otherwise, a written report. The guardian is also under a duty to ensure that a child is told in an appropriate manner about any decision made by the court if the guardian considers it appropriate to the age and understanding of the child to do so.

For the court's power to replace a guardian, see *Re B (Contact: Appointment of Guardian)*.[126]

Duties of the child's solicitor

4.77 A solicitor appointed by the guardian must represent the child in accordance with the guardian's instructions. However, where he considers, having had regard to the views of the guardian and any direction given by the court, that the child wishes to give instructions which conflict with those of the guardian and the child is able, having regard to his understanding, to give such instructions, he must conduct the proceedings in accordance with the child's instructions. Where there is no guardian he must act in accordance with the child's instructions. In either instance, where no instructions are given, he must represent the child in furtherance of the child's best interests.[127]

---

[123] Practice Direction 16A, para 7.6.
[124] *A County Council v K, C and T* [2011] EWHC 1672. See also Timms 'Yielding to no-one: the independence of the Children's Guardian' [2011] Fam Law 783.
[125] *Re A (Contact Order)* [2010] EWCA Civ 208, [2010] 2 FLR 577.
[126] [2009] EWCA Civ 435, [2009] 2 FLR 999.
[127] FPR 2010, r 16.29. The Law Society has issued a Practice Note to assist solicitors where the

Child as a party without a guardian

4.78 There is a fundamental difference between a child having a guardian and acting without one. As explained by Thorpe LJ in *Mabon v Mabon*:[128]

'In our system, we have traditionally adopted the tandem model for the representation of children who are parties to family proceedings, whether public or private. First, the court appoints a guardian ad litem, who will almost invariably have a social work qualification and very wide experience of family proceedings. He then instructs a specialist family solicitor who, in turn, usually instructs a specialist family barrister. This is a "Rolls Royce" model and is the envy of many other jurisdictions. However, its overall approach is essentially paternalistic. The guardian's first priority is to advocate the welfare of the child he represents. His second priority is to put before the court the child's wishes and feelings. Those priorities can in some cases conflict. In extreme cases the conflict is unmanageable. That reality is recognised by the terms of [Pt 16.6]. The direction set by [Pt 16.6(3)] is a mandatory grant of the application provided that the court considers "that the minor concerned has sufficient understanding to participate as a party in the proceedings concerned". Thus the focus is upon the sufficiency of the child's understanding in the context of the remaining proceedings.'

4.79 The procedure whereby a child can be a party without a guardian/next friend is set out in FPR 2010, r 16.6:

- the child does not have to have a guardian/next friend if he has a solicitor who is acting for him in the proceedings and that solicitor considers that the child is able, having regard to his understanding, to give instructions in relation to the proceedings;

- the court may permit the child to proceed without a guardian/next friend being appointed. The court must grant permission for the child to proceed without a guardian/next friend if it considers that the child has sufficient understanding to participate in the proceedings as a party without one.[129] Once the court is so satisfied, it cannot impose a guardian/next friend against the child's will, even by the device of making the child a ward;[130]

- where a guardian/next friend has already been appointed, the court may discharge the appointment and allow the child to continue without a guardian/next friend. However:

  –   if a solicitor acting for a child without a guardian/next friend does not consider, or no longer considers, that the child is able to give

---

child is to have a guardian but none has yet been appointed or the guardian is not immediately available: *Law Society Practice Note: Acting in the Absence of a Children's Guardian 25 August 2009* [2010] 1 FLR 1632.
[128] [2005] EWCA Civ 634, [2005] 2 FLR 1011, at para [25].
[129] FPR 2010, r 16.6(6).
[130] *Re T (A Minor) (Wardship: Representation)* [1993] 2 FLR 278.

instructions in relation to the proceedings, he must inform the court forthwith, whereupon the court will consider appointing a guardian/next friend;

– where the court, having granted permission to proceed without a guardian/next friend, considers that a child does not have sufficient understanding to participate as a party without a guardian/next friend, it may revoke any permission to proceed without a guardian/next friend and appoint one to act for the child.

4.80 The correct approach to ascertaining the child's understanding was set out by the Court of Appeal in *Re S (A Minor) (Independent Representation)*.[131] Although there is a difference in the test to be satisfied if the child has a solicitor who is prepared to act ('able, having regard to his understanding, to give instructions') and that when the court's permission is being sought ('sufficient understanding to participate in the proceedings as a party without one'), the difference is more apparent than real because, save in a relatively straightforward case or in the case of an older child, the court is unlikely (in the absence of consent by any existing guardian/next friend) to grant permission unless the child proposes to be legally represented and in that event, the real issue would again be whether the child had sufficient understanding to give coherent instructions. The test is the child's understanding and not his age. The judge has to do his best, on the evidence before him, to assess the understanding of the individual child in the context of the proceedings in which he seeks to participate:

'Where any sound judgment on these issues calls for insight and imagination which only maturity and experience can bring, both the court and the solicitor will be slow to conclude that the child's understanding is sufficient.'[132]

4.81 The Court of Appeal approved the dicta of Thorpe J in *Re H (A Minor) (Care Proceedings: Child's Wishes)*,[133] in which he rejected the submission that almost any child of nearly 16 years must be taken to have sufficient understanding and his comment that when there was any real question as to whether a child's emotional disturbance was so intense as to destroy the capacity to give coherent and consistent instructions, specific expert opinion should be sought. However as Thorpe LJ recognised in 2005 in *Mabon v Mabon*,[134] *Re S (A Minor) (Independent Representation)* the child was now 12 years old.

'Although the tandem model has many strengths and virtues ... unless we in this jurisdiction are to fall out of step with similar societies as they safeguard Art 12 rights, we must in the case of articulate teenagers accept that the right to freedom of expression and participation outweighs the paternalistic judgment of welfare.'

---

[131] [1993] 2 FLR 437.
[132] Ibid, per Sir Thomas Bingham MR at 444G.
[133] [1993] 1 FLR 440.
[134] [2005] EWCA Civ 634, [2005] 2 FLR 1011. See also Fortin 'Children's representation through the looking glass' [2007] Fam Law 500.

Welfare however may have a place in the decision.

'If direct participation would pose an obvious risk of harm to the child, arising out of the nature of the continuing proceedings and, if the child is incapable of comprehending that risk, then the judge is entitled to find that sufficient understanding has not been demonstrated. But judges have to be equally alive to the risk of emotional harm that might arise from denying the child knowledge of and participation in the continuing proceedings.'

4.82 The degree of understanding required to be shown by the child is uncertain. In *Re N (Contact: Minor Seeking Leave to Defend and Removal of Guardian)*[135] Coleridge J held that the 11-year-old who was the subject of the proceedings did not have sufficient understanding 'to participate in the proceedings and give instructions which are *fully* considered in the sense of *fully* [emphasis added] as to their implications'. But as Professor Fortin has commented,[136] 'if adults were obliged to overcome a similarly worded hurdle before commencing litigation, the legal aid bill would be very small indeed'. Building on this comment, it might be argued that an appropriate test of 'sufficient understanding' could be: 'Would the child if over the age of eighteen, have capacity so as not to require a litigation friend?'

Although a court will be very slow to go behind or question the professional judgment of a solicitor that a child has the requisite understanding, a judge's overriding duty is to protect the interests of the child and he is not precluded from exercising his power to appoint a guardian/next friend by the solicitor's refusal to accept that the condition in FPR 2010, r 16.6(3)(b)(i) is or is no longer satisfied.[137]

4.83 When a child is permitted to proceed without a guardian/next friend, the court can invite CAFCASS Legal Services to continue as amicus but its services in that capacity should be resorted to sparingly and in the knowledge that it would be unlikely to be able to assist the court to the same extent as if one of its officers had been appointed as a guardian/next friend.[138]

Examples

Re S (A Minor) (Independent Representation)[139]

4.84 The Court of Appeal upheld a refusal by a trial judge to allow a child of 11 to proceed without a guardian in private law proceedings as to contact and residence. There was expert evidence that it was possible that the child's wishes might be the product of influence exerted by his father and any other conclusion 'would have bordered on the perverse'.

---

[135] [2003] 1 FLR 652. The Court of Appeal in *Mabon* was careful not to treat the decision as being based on its own facts, see Thorpe LJ at [27] and Wall LJ at [45].

[136] Op cit at 508.

[137] *Re T (A Minor) (Wardship: Representation)* [1993] 2 FLR 278.

[138] Ibid and *Re H (A Minor) (Care Proceedings: Child's Wishes)* [1993] 1 FLR 440.

[139] [1993] 2 FLR 437.

Re H (A Minor) (Role of Official Solicitor)[140]

4.85 Permission was granted. Booth J discharged the Official Solicitor from acting for a 15-year-old in wardship proceedings brought by his parents against a drama teacher, R, who it was alleged was a malign influence on him. One psychiatrist thought that H had sufficient understanding but another that he had been brainwashed by R. In the exceptional circumstances of the case, including the extent to which the boy had already been involved and the divergence between his own settled views as to what was in his best interests and those of the Official Solicitor, the judge held that H should have permission to proceed without a guardian. It would be very difficult for the Official Solicitor to present H's case and it was unlikely that H would accept any decision which was contrary to his wishes.[141]

Mabon v Mabon[142]

4.86 Following parental separation the three elder children (aged 17, 15 and 13) remained with their father and the younger three with their mother. The mother applied for residence orders in respect of the three older children. The Court of Appeal allowed an appeal against a refusal to allow the three older children to proceed without a guardian although they had sufficient understanding.

> 'The judge seems to me, with all respect to him, to have perceived the case from the perspective of the adults. From the boys' perspective, it was simply impossible for the guardian to advance their views or represent them in the proceedings. He would, no doubt, faithfully report to the judge what the boys were saying, but in the case he would be (or was likely to be) directly opposed to what the boys were actually saying. In these circumstances, I do not agree with the judge that the only advantage from independent representation was "perhaps the more articulate and elegant expression of what I already know". That analysis overlooks, in my judgment, the need for the boys, on the facts of this particular case, to emerge from the proceedings (whatever the result) with the knowledge that their position had been independently represented and their perspective fully advanced to the judge.'[143]

Re A (Contact Order)[144]

4.87 In care proceedings the local authority sought to terminate contact between R, a 12-year-old boy, and his mother. His parents sought to remove

---

[140] [1993] 2 FLR 552.

[141] The outcome was an unhappy one. The trial judge found that H had 'developed an enthusiasm for ... Mr R which became eventually obsessive and in my judgment morally unhealthy'. In subsequent proceedings Thorpe J considered that an affidavit filed by H showed that his perceptions were 'far removed' from reality. See *Re H (Publication of Judgment)* [1995] 2 FLR 542.

[142] [2005] EWCA Civ 634, [2005] 2 FLR 1011. See also *Children, Guardians and Rule 9.5* Whybrow [2004] Fam Law 504.

[143] Per Wall LJ at paras [43] and [44].

[144] [2010] EWCA Civ 208, [2010] 2 FLR 577.

the guardian and replace his solicitor on the basis that the guardian, while supporting R's wish to continue to have contact was presenting the case as she saw it and not as R saw it. The trial judge refused the application on the basis that although the child was bright and articulate, he lacked the maturity to comprehend and weigh all the complex considerations involved and to reach a proportionate, balanced consideration. The appeal was dismissed. Lord Justice Thorpe was clear the trial judge's decision was the correct one.

> 'There are cases involving children in post-pubertal adolescent rebellion for whom it is very difficult for a guardian to act. Their position, their wishes, their feelings, their opinions so conflict with an objective view of welfare that there has to be a parting of the ways, and our system generously provides for two distinct and equally constituted litigation teams thereafter. That is an extremely expensive solution, and in present days when the family justice system is obliged to seek economy wherever and whenever it can, orders granting separate representation under this rule should, in my opinion, be issued very sparingly. This was a perfectly standard situation in which the child's wishes were only an ingredient within the review of the guardian and only one element upon which the guardian had to report to the court.'[145]

While agreeing with the decision, Lady Justice Arden expressly did not adopt what Thorpe LJ said about the resource implications.[146]

4.88 A child who is allowed to conduct proceedings without a guardian/next friend is bound by the rules which govern other parties, including rules as to confidentiality[147] and the court can direct that he is not allowed to keep copies of the case papers.[148]

Applications by a child

4.89 A child requires permission and permission may be granted only if the court is satisfied that the child has sufficient understanding to make the proposed application.[149] Permission to make an application for permission to bring a s 8 order is discussed further in **Chapter 15**.

THE CHILD IN COURT

4.90 Under FPR 2010, r 12.12(2)(d) the court may give directions for the attendance of the child at a hearing. This does not give the child a right to be present however. Where proceedings are held in public, the child has the same right as any member of the public to attend subject to the court's power to exclude anyone who disrupts the proceedings. Likewise, arguing from first principles, as the point has never been decided, the child may have a right to

---

[145] Ibid, at [5].
[146] Ibid, at [9].
[147] *Re H (Publication of Judgment)* [1995] 2 FLR 542 at 555.
[148] Ibid, at 543.
[149] CA 1989, s 10(8).

attend proceedings held in private if he is a party. In practice, courts adopt a commonsense approach. Baroness Hale, writing extra-judicially, has said that that the Strasbourg court might well see difficulty in the routine exclusion of children.

> 'I myself always took the view that if a child was deemed mature enough to instruct her own solicitor (or to make her own application in private law proceedings) she was mature enough to attend court and ought to be expected to do so unless there was a very good reason to the contrary. It is all part of accepting that rights bring responsibilities too.'

4.91 In *A City Council v T, J and K (by her Children's Guardian)*[150] Mr Justice Peter Jackson allowed a 13-year-old girl to attend a hearing at which a secure accommodation order was being sought.

> 'In the generation that has passed since the decision in *Re W (Secure Accommodation Order: Attendance at Court)*,[151] thinking about these issues has undoubtedly evolved ... [In] considering child welfare and children's rights we would, I think, give more weight to the potential benefits of greater involvement by children who want to be present when important decisions about their future are made. It can no longer be presumed that attendance in court is likely to be harmful: if this is so, thought must surely first be given to adapting court procedures to meet children's needs before deciding to exclude them. Nor should children have to prove that their attendance at proceedings about them is in their interests. The starting point should be an open evaluation of the consequences of attendance or non-attendance in terms of the welfare of the child and the court's ability to manage its proceedings fairly.'

4.92 Each case will depend on its own circumstances, but the following factors will generally be relevant:

- The age and level of understanding of the child.

- The nature and strength of the child's wishes.

- The child's emotional and psychological state.

- The effect of influence from others.

- The matters to be discussed.

- The evidence to be given.

- The child's behaviour.

- Practical and logistical considerations.

---

[150]   [2011] EWHC 1082 (Fam), [2011] 2 FLR 803.
[151]   [1994] 2 FLR 1092.

- The integrity of the proceedings.

The court always retains the power to manage proceedings in a way that achieves overall fairness. Other considerations, such as the interests of other parties, may influence decisions about a child's attendance.

'The above evaluation may well lead to the conclusion that a child of sufficient understanding who wants to attend an important hearing about his or her future should be allowed to do so for at least part of the time, unless there are clear reasons justifying refusal. This situation will most often be found in, but is not limited to, public law proceedings. In cases where attendance at the hearing itself is not thought appropriate, a meeting with the judge is a possible alternative.'

THE WEIGHT TO BE GIVEN TO A CHILD'S WISHES AND FEELINGS

4.93 When a court is deciding any question with respect to a child's upbringing, it is under a duty to have regard to the ascertainable wishes and feelings of the child[152] which should be considered separately.[153] The weight to be given to the wishes and feelings has to be ascertained according to the child's age or understanding. Although, in the past, courts have commented on the weight to be given to the wishes of a child of a particular age, the current approach is to consider the maturity and understanding of the particular child rather than to adopt the assumed understanding of a hypothetical child of the particular child's age. Allowance has to be made for the possibility that the wishes and feelings may have been influenced, whether indirectly or intentionally, by an adult but remembering that such wishes and feelings are nevertheless real. What may be of greater importance is whether those wishes are based on a substratum of supporting fact, how carefully the child has considered the situation, how much the child can appreciate the benefits and demerits of alternative possibilities, long as well as short term, and how far those wishes and feelings may change. For example, a child of 3 may be reluctant to leave his mother for a few hours for contact. However, that reluctance may quickly disappear once a relationship is established with the person with whom he spends that period, whether a non-resident parent or a nursery assistant. On the other hand, a child of 14 may be firmly rooted in the demonstrably mistaken belief that a parent is not deserving of contact with it or poses a threat and it may be very difficult for those views to change.

4.94 The weight to be given to a child's wishes was discussed by the Court of Appeal in the case of *Re T (Abduction: Child's Objection to Return)*,[154] which was brought under the Hague Convention on the Civil Aspects of International Child Abduction 1980. In that case, unlike in cases brought under s 8, one of

---

[152] CA 1989, s 1.
[153] *Re H (Care Order: Contact)* [2008] EWCA Civ 1245, [2009] 2 FLR 55, per Ward LJ at [11].
[154] [2000] 2 FLR 192, per Ward LJ at 203. See also *Re J (Abduction: Child's Objections to Return)* [2004] EWCA Civ 428, [2004] 2 FLR 64.

the matters the court had to consider was whether it was appropriate to take the child's views and objection to a return to the country of her habitual residence into account at all. However, the court's approach as to the weight to be given to the child's views is equally applicable to s 8 cases:

'It seems to me [said Thorpe LJ] that the matters to establish are:

(1)   Whether the child objects [to a particular course of conduct].

(2)   The age and degree of maturity of the child. Is the child more mature or less mature than or as mature as her chronological age? ...

(3)   ... the strength and validity of those views [need to be ascertained] which will call for an examination of the following matters among others:

(a)   What is the child's own perspective of what is in her interests, short, medium and long term? Self-perception is important because it is *her* views which have to be judged appropriate.

(b)   To what extent, if at all, are the reasons for objection rooted in reality or might reasonably appear to the child to be so grounded?

(c)   To what extent have those views been shaped or even coloured by undue influence and pressure, directly or indirectly exerted by the abducting party?

(d)   To what extent will the objections be mollified on return and, where it is the case, on removal from any pernicious influence from the abducting parent?'

4.95   While the views of each individual child have to be considered separately they cannot be assessed in isolation from the family dynamics. 'The child's place within the family and the consequences of the exercise of the [judicial] discretion must be considered.'[155]

4.96   One matter is clear as a matter of principle. The child's wishes and feelings are never the sole consideration. All the other s 1 factors have to be considered as well and the course to be taken must be in the child's best interests.

4.97   In *C v Finland*,[156] for example, the European Court of Human Rights held that the wishes of children, even those aged 12 or more, were not determinative: all other factors including the rights of adults have to be considered and balanced before deciding what is in the children's best interests. The decision by the Finnish Supreme Court to allow an appeal against a decision awarding custody of two children aged 12 and 9 to their father, the children wishing to remain with their mother, breached the father's Art 8 rights. However, in some cases the strength of the wishes may be such as to effectively determine the matter.

---

[155]   *Z v Z (Abduction: Children's Views)* [2005] EWCA Civ 1012, [2006] 1 FLR 410, per Wall LJ at [34].

[156]   [2006] 2 FLR 597.

Chapter 5

DOMESTIC VIOLENCE

INTRODUCTION

5.1 Domestic violence can be defined as threatening behaviour, violence or abuse (psychological, physical, sexual, financial or emotional) between adults who are or have been intimate partners or family members, regardless of gender or sexuality.[1] It is widespread, common and likely to cause both physical and emotional injury not only to the victim but to children caught up in violence perpetrated on their parent. It is highly relevant when a court is considering making residence or contact orders and, as the Practice Direction on Residence and Contact Orders: Domestic Violence and Harm[2] emphasises the court must, at all stages of the proceedings, consider whether domestic violence is raised as an issue, either by the pies or otherwise, and if so must:

- identify at the earliest opportunity the factual and welfare issues involved;

- consider the nature of any allegation or admission of domestic violence and the extent to which any domestic violence which is admitted, or which may be proved, would be relevant in deciding whether to make an order about residence or contact and, if so, in what terms;

- give directions to enable the relevant factual and welfare issues to be determined expeditiously and fairly.

In summary:

- Allegations of domestic violence must be investigated if they may be relevant to the issue of contact.

- It is for the court and not the parties to decide whether the allegations may be relevant.

- The investigation should take place as quickly as possible with consideration being given to having the allegations tried as a preliminary issue.

- If the allegations are found proved there is no presumption against contact.

---

[1]   A definition used by the Home Office: see **5.3**.
[2]   FPR 2010, PD 12J, para 3.

- The decision as to contact must be made by applying the welfare test and the checklist to the circumstances of the particular case.

- The following factors may be particularly relevant:

  - the ability of the offending parent to recognise his past conduct;
  - the ability of the offending parent to be aware of the need to change;
  - the ability of the offending parent to make genuine efforts to change;
  - the offending parent's reasons for seeking contact.

- Particular consideration must be given, especially when considering interim contact, to the likely risk of harm to the child, whether physical or emotional. The court must ensure, so far as it can, that any risk to the child and the carer, before, during and after contact is minimised. The court should consider granting a non-molestation order. If there is a risk of violence, a supported contact centre should not be used.

BACKGROUND

The nature of domestic violence

5.2 In recent decades as domestic violence has become part of public consciousness,[3] a more comprehensive understanding of what it involves has developed and, in parallel, both international and domestic definitions have changed.[4] According to Chester and Streather in 1972, for example, the concept of 'cruelty' in divorce law involved danger to 'life, limb and health' and the concept of 'mental cruelty' was not recognised.[5] Following the Report of the House of Commons Select Committee on Violence in Marriage,[6] the Domestic Violence and Matrimonial Proceedings Act 1976 was enacted to provide some protection. A year later, Lord Denning commented in *Davies v Johnson*[7] that:

> '"Battered wives" is a telling phrase. It was invented to call the attention of the public to an evil. Few were aware of it. It arose when a woman suffered serious or repeated physical injury from the man with whom she lived ... "Battered wives" are now a matter of public concern.'

When the case was heard by the House of Lords, Lord Salmon adopted a broad approach to the mischief at which the Act was aimed.

---

3 Chiswick Women's Aid, now Refuge, was founded in 1971; Pizzey *Scream Quietly or the neighbours will hear* was published in 1974 (Penguin).
4 Edwards 'Domestic violence: not a term of art but a state of consciousness' [2011] Fam Law 1244, at p 1246.
5 'Cruelty in English Divorce: some empirical Findings' (1972) 34(4) *Journal of Marriage and Family* 706, cited by Williams ibid.
6 Select Committee on Violence in Marriage, 1975.
7 [1979] AC 264, at 272.

'Physical violence, or the threat of it, is clearly within the mischief. But there is more to it than that. Homelessness can be as great a threat as physical violence to the security of a woman (or man) and her children. Eviction – actual, attempted or threatened – is, therefore, within the mischief: likewise, conduct which makes it impossible or intolerable, as in the present case, for the other partner, or the children, to remain at home.'

5.3 In 1992 the United Nations Committee which monitors the Convention on the Elimination of all Forms of Discrimination against Women (CEDAW), adopted General Recommendation 19, which included in its definition of discrimination in relation to gender-based violence 'acts that inflict physical, mental or sexual harm or suffering, threats of such acts, coercion and other deprivations of liberty'. The following year, the General Assembly adopted the Declaration on the Elimination of Violence against Women, defined as 'any act of gender-based violence that results in, or is likely to result in, physical, sexual or psychological harm or suffering to women ...'.

In 1992 the Law Commission in its Report on Domestic Violence and Occupation of the Family Home[8] had explained domestic violence thus.

'The term "violence" itself is often used in two senses. In its narrower meaning it describes the use or threat of physical force against a victim in the form of an assault or battery. But in the context of the family, there is also a wider meaning which extends to abuse beyond the more typical instances of physical assaults to include any form of physical, sexual or psychological molestation or harassment which has a serious detrimental effect upon the health and well-being of the victim.'

The following year, the House of Commons Home Affairs Committee[9] adopted as a definition of domestic violence:

'... any form of physical, sexual or emotional abuse which takes place within the context of a close relationship.'

In 1998 the House of Lords held in *R v Burstow; R v Ireland*[10] that a defendant who refused to accept a decision by the victim to end their social relationship and proceeded to harass her over an 8-month period by making silent telephone calls, distributing offensive cards in the street where she lived, surreptitiously taking photographs of her and her family and sending her a menacing note as a result of which she suffered severe depression, was guilty of assault occasioning actual bodily harm under s 47 of the Offences Against the Person Act 1861.

The 2005 Home Office report, *Domestic Violence: A National Report* referred to a common definition of domestic violence used by the police as being:

---

8   (1992, Law Com No 207, at para 2.3.
9   Report on Domestic Violence Session 1992-93, Third Report, HC 245-I, para 5.
10   [1998] AC 147, [1998] 1 FLR 105.

'Any incident of threatening behaviour, violence or abuse (psychological, physical, sexual, financial or emotional) between adults who are or have been intimate partners or family members, regardless of gender or sexuality.'[11]

As Baroness Hale of Richmond noted in *Yemshaw v Hounslow BC*,[12] this or a similar definition was adopted by many official and governmental bodies.

The Practice Direction on Residence and Contact Orders: Domestic Violence and Harm[13] uses, for the purpose of family proceedings a definition of 'domestic violence' which includes:

'physical violence, threatening or intimidating behaviour and any other form of abuse which, directly or indirectly, may have caused harm to the other party or to the child or which may give rise to the risk of harm.'

5.4 Each definition has been drafted for and takes its meaning from a specific context, whether homelessness applications, immigration legislation or the criminal or family law but all[14] now recognise that domestic violence can be physical, emotional, sexual, intimidating and is not limited to either male or female. In *Yemshaw* Baroness Hale, talking in the context of Part VII of the Housing Act 1996 made the point that 'domestic violence' is not a term of art. 'It is capable of bearing several meanings and applying to many different types of behaviour.'[15] She continued:

'There may also be a concern that an expanded definition is setting the threshold too low. The advantage of the definition adopted by the President of the Family Division is that it deals separately with actual physical violence, putting a person in fear of such violence, and other types of harmful behaviour. It has been recognised for a long time now that it is dangerous to ignore what may appear to some to be relatively trivial forms of physical violence. In the domestic context it is common for assaults to escalate from what seems trivial at first. Once over the hurdle of striking the first blow, apologising and making up, some people find it much easier to strike the second, and the third, and go on and on. But of course, that is not every case. Isolated or minor acts of physical violence in the past will not necessarily give rise to a probability of their happening again in the future. This is the limiting factor.'[16]

Research on domestic violence in the community

5.5 The 2001 British Crime Survey (BCS) included a detailed self-completion questionnaire designed to ascertain: the most accurate estimates of the extent and nature of domestic violence, sexual assault and stalking for

---

11   These reports were cited by Baroness Hale of Richmond in *Yemshaw v Hounslow BC* [2011] UKSC 3, [2011] 1 FLR 1614, at [20]–[24].
12   Ibid, at [24].
13   [2008] 2 FLR 103, reissued as FPR 2010, PD 12J.
14   With the exception of the Green Paper on Legal Aid (2010) Cm 7967, at para 4.67 which restricts it for the purpose of qualifying for Legal Aid to physical harm.
15   [2011] UKSC 3, [2011] 1 FLR 1614, at [27].
16   Ibid, at [34].

England and Wales.[17] There were an estimated 12.9 million incidents of domestic violence acts against women and 2.5 million against men in England and Wales in the year prior to interview.

The authors found that inter-personal violence is widespread with over one-third (36%) of people experiencing domestic violence (abuse, threats or force), sexual victimisation or stalking. A minority, largely women, suffer multiple attacks, severe injuries and experience more than one form of inter-personal violence and serious disruption to their lives. Nearly a half (45%) of women and just over a quarter of men (26%) aged between 16 and 59 could recall being subject to domestic violence,[18] sexual victimisation or stalking at least once in their lifetimes.

The BCS estimated that 4% of women and 2% of men had been subject to domestic violence (non-sexual domestic threats or force) in the 12 months prior to interview. If the definition was extended to include financial and emotional abuse, the figures increased to 6% and 5% respectively. Among women subject to domestic violence the average number of incidents was 20, while 28% experienced one incident only. Of men, the mean average number of incidents was seven, while one incident was experienced by 47%.

While some experience of inter-personal violence was widespread, a minority, overwhelmingly women, were subject to extreme levels of violence, consistent with exceptional degrees of coercive control. Among people subject to four or more incidents of domestic violence from the perpetrator of the worst incident nearly nine in ten (89%) were women. Just under a third (32%) of women had experienced domestic violence from this person four or more times compared with only 11% of men.

Injuries were often sustained, especially among women. During the worst incident of domestic violence experienced in the previous year, just under half (46%) of women sustained a minor physical injury, a fifth , a moderate physical injury, and 6%, severe injuries. Just under a third (31%) suffered emotional problems. Among men, just under half (41%) sustained a minor physical injury, 14% a moderate physical injury, 1% severe injuries and 9% mental or emotional problems. Only 30% of women and 14% of men who reported injuries sustained in domestic violence, said that they consulted a doctor or some other health professional.

Domestic violence had a detrimental impact on employment. Among employed women who suffered domestic violence, a fifth (21%) took time off work and 2% lost their jobs. Among men in this situation, 6% took time off work and 2% lost their jobs.

---

[17] Walby and Allen *Domestic Violence, Sexual Assault and Stalking: Findings from the British Crime Survey* (Home Office Research Study 276, 2004).

[18] Defined as abuse, threats or force.

The perception of the seriousness of what had happened was low. Nearly two-thirds of women (64%) of women and most men (94%) subjected to domestic violence did not think that what had happened to them was a crime. However two-thirds of women who had been victimised many times were more likely to think that what had happened to them was 'domestic violence'. There was a greater likelihood of applying the concepts of domestic violence and crime to the incident if injuries were sustained and the acts were severe and repeated.

The authors found the following risk factors.

* Women are more at risk than men of inter-personal violence and especially of sexual assault.

* Younger people are more at risk of all forms of inter-personal violence than older people.

* Women in households with an income of less than £10,000 are three and a half times more likely to suffer domestic violence than those living in households with an income of over £20,000, while men were one and a half times more likely. However the nature of the links between poverty and risk of inter-personal violence is unclear. It may be that poverty is associated with the onset of domestic violence, or it may be that in fleeing domestic violence women are reduced to poverty.

* The presence of children in the household is associated with nearly double the risk of domestic violence for women.

5.6 The BCS found little ethnic variation in inter-personal violence. However, violence among minority communities appears to have special features, as is illustrated by a recent post-separation study of South Asian and African-Carribean women and children who had suffered domestic violence. The authors[19] concluded that the respondents had lived with high levels of severe abuse over long periods. In most cases, the abuse began as psychological or emotional before becoming physical and increasing in frequency and severity. The majority of women suffered daily abuse before separation. Two-thirds could be categorised as being at 'high risk'. For several South Asian women the abuse was also perpetrated by other family members. Control and isolation was a feature for all the women but women who lacked family and social support, or knowledge of how things worked in the UK, were more vulnerable. Fear of abduction and/or separation from their children was a significant issue for all, but especially South Asian, women. The threat of and actual abduction of children as a tactic of abuse, whilst hard to quantify and prove, was extremely commonly reported by a significant number of women. The undermining of the women's parenting by their partners and in-laws was

---

19   Thiara and Gill *Domestic Violence, Child Contact and Post-Separation Violence: Issues for South Asian and African-Caribean women and Children* (University of Warwick/NSPCC, 2011).

an issue reported by several South Asian women. Where undermining of African-Caribbean women took place , it was at the hands of their partners.

5.7 Domestic violence is not confined to heterosexual relationships. Donovan and Hester[20] comment that domestic violence was identified as a problem in North America and Europe over 20 years ago and it is only recently that there has been any serious commitment to addressing the problem.

5.8 In the 1996 BCS half of the respondents who had suffered violence from a partner or ex-partner were living with children. Three-tenths said that their children had been aware of what was going on and, not surprisingly, the more assaults, the more children were likely to have seen or heard what happened. Just under half (45%) of women who suffered repeated violence said their child had been aware of the last incident.

Thiara and Gill found that when living with domestic violence, children became involved in men's abusive behaviour in a range of ways. It was evident from women's accounts that many men paid little heed to children's presence when being abusive or deliberately abused children in the process. Even very young children were often aware of men's behaviour.[21]

5.9 A literature review, *Understanding what children say: Children's experiences of domestic violence, parental substance misuse and parental health problems*[22] found that children were often more aware of violence and arguments than their parents thought, or hoped. They often worried more than their parents recognised and although they were aware of problems, they did not always understand what was happening and why. They reported seeing or witnessing or themselves experiencing violence which was sometimes extreme. They said that fear of violence was made worse by the unpredictability of parents' moods and behaviour, feeling they were 'walking on eggshells'. Some children, particularly boys, would not talk to anyone about it and many children spoke of coping by emotionally or physically avoiding problems, or by distracting themselves. Any sadness and isolation they experienced could be perpetuated by the stigma and secrecy surrounding domestic violence. However they frequently described close relationships with parents and love and loyalty towards them, expressing a desire to help them overcome their problems.

Research into domestic violence post separation

5.10 Government guidance, *Working Together to Safeguard Children*[23] warns that danger does not automatically end on separation and the point of leaving is the time of highest risk. Contact arrangements can be used by violent men

---

20 'Seeking help from the enemy: help-seeking strategies of those in same sex relationships who have experienced domestic abuse' [2011] CFLQ 26.
21 Thiara and Gill op cit, at pp 39–40.
22 Gorin National Children's Bureau, summarised in *Findings* 514 (Joseph Rowntree Foundation, 2004).
23 (2010) Department for Children Schools and Families, at para 9.20.

not only to continue their controlling, manipulative and violent behaviour but also as a way of establishing the whereabouts of the victim.

5.11 In Thiara and Gill's study[24] women experienced a great deal of pressure from both professionals and family members to give the perpetrator a chance and agree to contact. In the case of professionals, most of the women in these situations stated that decisions were made without full consideration of their cases, especially if they only wanted supervised contact. The authors concluded that in many cases pressures to agree informal contact – to keep things out of the courts as contact would be awarded anyway, not bring shame on the family, to do it for the children's sakes, not to dishonour black men – resulted in compromising women's safety.

5.12 A study[25] in which 29 children from 13 families who were killed as a result of contact arrangements assessed the cases against a list of 15 significant risk factors identified by Cardiff's Women's Safety Unit, the NSPCC and South Wales Police.[26] On very limited information, there were 10–12 indicators present in three cases, 5–8 in seven, in two, 4 and in one, 3. The indicators were:

- There had been or was going to be a separation: (present in 13 cases)

- There was conflict over child contact: (12)

- The assailant had problems with alcohol (2), drugs (2) or mental illness (9)

- The assailant was expressing or behaving in a jealous (7) or controlling (8) way

- The abuse was becoming worse/happening more often (7)

- The assailant had threatened or attempted suicide (6)

- The victim considered there was a risk? (4)

- Weapons had been used (3)

- Injuries had been inflicted (3)

- Threats to kill had been made (3)

- The assailant had a criminal record (3)

- The victim was pregnant (2)

- There had been sexual abuse (2)

---

24 Op cit at p 78.
25 Saunders *Twenty-nine child homicides* (Women's Aid, 2004).
26 Available at: www.crarg.org.uk.

- There were financial problems (2)

- There had been an attempt to strangle/choke (1)

5.13 In 2005 Lord Justice Wall examined all available court files for the five cases in which there had been court involvement. In his subsequent report[27] to the then President of the Family Division, he examined in detail each of the five cases where the courts were involved and provided his opinion as to how each matter was conducted by the courts. He concluded that:

> 'These cases, therefore, tragic as they are, represent a tiny proportion of the many thousands of contact orders which are made each year ... I am in no doubt that all the contact orders in the cases concerned were made in good faith and that the judges did their best conscientiously to apply section 1 of the Children Act 1989 ... However I am the first to accept that contact cases involving domestic violence need the most rigorous examination by judges and magistrates who are properly trained in and alert to the risk factors posed by domestic violence.'[28]

He also identified lessons to be learned.

- The responsibility for making an order remains that of the judge, and judges can only make orders in relation to children if they consider that the order is in the best interests of the child. A judge cannot therefore abnegate responsibility for an order because it is made by consent. Judges have the responsibility to scrutinise any proposed consent order and satisfy themselves that the particular order is in the interests of the child.[29]

- It is essential that the court satisfies itself that each party had entered into any consent order freely and without pressure being placed upon them. 'It is a frequent complaint that because of what is perceived as the court's bias towards contact, lawyers pressurise reluctant mothers into consent orders for contact which they do not believe to be safe for their children.'[30]

- Being concerned to read at a number of places in the files that reliance was being placed on the proposition that it may be safe to order contact where domestic violence had been perpetrated on the mother, but not on the child, he stated that an application of the principles set out by Drs. Sturge and Glaser (see **5.18**) was necessary to ensure that the risks of

---

[27] A Report to the President of the Family Division on the Publication by the Women's Aid Federation of England Entitled *Twenty-nine Child Homicides: Lessons Still to be Learnt on Domestic Violence and Child Protection* (2006) availablel at: www.judiciary.gov.uk/NR/rdonlyres/888661BA-06A4-4CAE-8D00-A2E412834763/0/report_family.pdf.

[28] Ibid, at paras 8.6–8.7.

[29] Ibid, at para 8.20.

[30] Ibid, at para 8.21. See also Masson 'Consent orders in contact cases: a survey of Resolution members' [2006] Fam Law 1041 which found that 'some solicitors could take more account of domestic violence when advising on children matters' and that 'courts do not currently appear to support the identification of cases where violence is an issue or to enquire into the safety and suitability of arrangements for children when making consent orders'.

contact to their violent father by children who have not themselves been physically assaulted are better appreciated and taken into account.[31]

- Where criminal proceedings involving violence by the father against the mother are outstanding at the date of the contact application, especial care is required before an order is made. While it was impossible to say that there should never be contact in such circumstances because there may be cases in which the seriousness of the criminal change is outweighed by the children's need for contact with their non-residential parents, any order in these circumstances (whether by consent or otherwise) requires a rigorous examination, which can involve the use of the Children Act Sub-Committee Guidelines,[32] of the risks posed by the father and should not be made unless the court is satisfied that the child can be fully protected against such risks.[33]

Research into domestic abuse in the context of litigation

5.14 Between 1999 and 2001 Buchanan and Hunt also investigated the incidence of domestic violence in their survey of parents involved in proceedings in which court welfare reports had been ordered.[34] Over half (56%) of parents reported physical violence at some stage in the past. Just under half (49%) said they had suffered physical injury. Two-thirds of women reported violence as a frequent occurrence and for a half, violence was continuing at the commencement of the proceedings. In more than two-thirds of cases, children were said to have witnessed arguments and just under a third, violence. Children were interviewed and more than a third said that their parents had 'pushed' or 'shoved' the other. Parents may therefore underestimate what children in fact see or view what occurs as less serious.

5.15 A high level of reported violence was also found by Trinder and Connolly in their study of contact disputes in Essex in 2003.[35] Just under two-fifths of women cited domestic abuse/violence as a reason for separation and three-tenths, mental or verbal abuse. At the time of the application for contact, three-fifths of women and a quarter of men reported that a fear of violence from an ex-partner or ex-partner's new partner made it more difficult to sort out problems with the ex-partner.[36]

---

[31]   Ibid, at paras 8.22–8.23.
[32]   See **5.19**.
[33]   *Twenty-nine Child Homicides: Lessons Still to be Learnt on Domestic Violence and Child Protection* op cit, at paras 8.25–8.26.
[34]   *Families in Conflict* (The Policy Press, 2001).
[35]   Trinder, Connolly and others *A Profile of Applicants and Respondents in Contact Cases in Essex* (DCA Research series 1/05, 2005), at pp 85–88.
[36]   Trinder found similar results in her survey of in-court conciliation: Trinder, Connolly and others *Making Contact Happen or Making Contact work?* (DCA Research Series 3/06, 2006), p 34. See also Hunt and McLeod *Outcomes of Applications to Court for Contact Orders After Parental Separation or Divorce* (Oxford Centre for Family Law & Policy/Ministry of Justice, 2008).

5.16 The experience of domestic violence can make it difficult to assess the ability of the victim to meet the needs of the children and the court process can perversely make it more difficult for them. A study of a small sample of women who have experienced domestic violence[37] found that after arrival at a refuge women were in a state of shock and confusion for the first days, weeks and sometimes months, with feelings of numbness and unreality. Gradually this changed to a recognition of what had happened and an acceptance of a need to take responsibility for themselves and their children, but this was not marked by a fluid and dynamic progress but rather by oscillating emotions. They experienced material loss of a regular income and most of their possessions which may have had emotional significance for them, an emotional loss of not just the relationship with the abuser but also of older children, pets, family and support network and a personal loss of self.

Women identified six factors which were important in helping them progress. Most important was physical safety, mental security and a need to build a sense of trust in those around them. The remaining factors rated equally in terms of importance were being treated with respect, being believed, not being judged, having time to talk and be heard and mutual support from women in the same situation. Being involved in contested contact proceedings may operate to nullify the positive existence of at least some of these factors.

The effect of domestic violence on children

5.17 As shown above even young children are likely to witness domestic violence in a home where it exists and more than their parents believe.

Some children involved in Thiara and Gill's study were extremely clear about not liking their father's behaviour towards their mothers, especially when they had witnessed the violence. However, after separation they had mixed feelings about their fathers with girls aged between 6 and 8 appearing to be more mixed in their feelings and whilst not liking their father's behaviour they still considered them to be 'my dad'. All of the older girls said they wished their mothers had left earlier.[38]

5.18 In a report for the Court of Appeal in *Re L, V, M, H*,[39] two child and adolescent psychiatrists, Sturge and Glaser, commented that research is needed into how domestic violence affects children, but advised that all children are affected by 'significant and repeated' violence, even if they are not directly involved:

> "'Even when children do not continue in that violent situation, emotional trauma continues to be experienced; the memories of the violence continue as persecutory images." Children may also have a continuing fear of the perpetrating parent and

---

[37] Abrahams 'Worth it in the end: a new look at refuge support' (2005) 2 *Counselling and Psychotherapy Research* 160.
[38] Thiara and Gill op cit, at p 64.
[39] [2000] 2 FLR 334.

may continue to be aware of the fear that the other parent has. Domestic violence may impact on contact in other ways. The resident parent may continue to suffer the effects of past violence and children's own behaviour and their long term attitude towards violence can be affected.'[40]

Sturge and Glaser argued that there should be no automatic assumption that contact with a previously or currently violent parent is in a child's interests:

> 'If anything the assumption should be in the opposite direction ... We would go so far as to suggest ... a position in which a father (or mother in certain circumstances) who has been found to have been ... violent to the child's carer should need to show positive grounds as to why, despite this, contact is in the child's interests in order for an application to be even considered.'

They saw the balance tipping against contact unless the following features were present:

- some (preferably full) acknowledgement of the violence;

- some acceptance (preferably full if the non-resident parent was the sole instigator) of responsibility for the violence;

- a full acceptance of the inappropriateness of the violence and of the likely effects on the child;

- a genuine interest in the child's welfare, not imposing the conditions under which contact takes place;

- a wish to help the child recognise the inappropriateness of violence;

- an expression of regret and showing some understanding of the past and present impact of their behaviour on the other parent;

- indications that the non-resident parent can reliably sustain contact.

5.19 *Working Together to Safeguard Children*[41] also emphasises that prolonged and/or regular exposure to domestic violence can have a serious impact on children's safety and welfare. An analysis of Serious Case Reviews[42] found evidence of past or present domestic violence present in over half (53%) of cases. Domestic violence rarely exists in isolation. Many parents misuse drugs or alcohol, experience poor physical and mental ill health and have a history of poor childhood experiences themselves. 'The co-morbidity of issues compounds the difficulties parents experience in meeting the needs of their

---

[40] See also Mills 'Effects of domestic violence on children' [2008] Fam Law 165.

[41] Op cit, paras 9.18–9.26.

[42] Brandon, M., Bailey, S., Belderson, P., Gardner, R., Sidebottom, P., Dodsworth, J., Warren, C. and Black, J. *Understanding Serious Case Reviews and their Impact: A Biennial Analysis of Serious Case Reviews 2005–07* (Department for Children Schools and Families, 2009).

children, and increases the likelihood that the child will experience abuse and/or neglect.' Domestic violence impacted on children in a number of ways.

- They are at increased risk of physical injury during an incident, either by accident or because they attempt to intervene.

- They are greatly distressed by witnessing the physical and emotional suffering of a parent. This can lead to serious anxiety and distress which may express itself in anti-social or criminal behaviour.

- It impacts on parenting capacity. A parent may have difficulty in looking after the children when domestic violence results in injuries, or in extreme cases, death. Exposure to psychological and emotional abuse has profound negative effects on women's mental health resulting in a loss of confidence, depression, feelings of degradation, problems with sleep, isolation, and increased use of medication and alcohol. These are all factors that can restrict her capacity to meet the developmental needs of her child. 'Moreover, belittling and insulting a mother in front of her children undermines not only her respect for herself, but also the authority she needs to parent confidently.'

- A mother's relationship with her children may also be affected because, in attempts to avoid further outbursts of violence, she prioritises her partner's needs over those of her children.

No age group is particularly protected from or damaged by the impact of domestic violence but may suffer in different ways. Children's ability to cope with parental adversity is related to their age, gender and individual personality. However, regardless of age, support from siblings, wider family, friends, school and community can act as protective factors.

'Key to the safety of women and children subjected to violence and the threat of violence is an alternative, safe and supportive residence.'[43]

LEGAL POLICY

The Advisory Board on Family Law: Children Act Sub-Committee: Report on Contact and Domestic Violence

5.20 Following some years of increasing academic and extra-legal pressure for courts to take greater account of the impact of domestic violence when deciding issues of contact,[44] the Children Act Sub-Committee of the Lord Chancellor's Advisory Board on Family Law reported in 2000.[45] It

---

[43]   Ibid, at 9.22.
[44]   See Kaganas and Sclater 'Contact and Domestic Violence – the Winds of Change?' [2000] Fam Law 630.
[45]   *A Report to the Lord Chancellor on the Question of Parental Contact in Cases where there is*

reached the clear view that steps needed to be taken to ensure that the issue was both properly addressed and seen to be properly addressed. However, it thought that it could be addressed within the framework of the Children Act 1989 and did not require immediate legislation. Courts should recognise that domestic violence takes many forms. A broad definition which is gender-neutral should be adopted which enables them to identify violence in a given case and assess its impact on the residential parent and the children. The Sub-Committee produced draft Guidelines for Good Practice which are set out in Appendix 5. These were not written to tell the court what to do in any particular case (it did not, for example, recommend that there should be a presumption against contact in cases of violence) but to ensure that the question of violence was properly addressed, assessed and taken into account when considering what was best for the child in a particular case. In summary, the Guidelines state in every case where domestic violence is put forward as a reason for refusing or limiting contact, the court should at the earliest opportunity consider the allegations made (and any answer to them) and decide whether the nature and effect of the violence as alleged was such as to make it likely that the order for contact would be affected if the allegations were proved. Appropriate directions should be given in order for the facts to be ascertained as quickly as possible. Consideration should be given to having the allegations tried as a preliminary issue. A Cafcass report should be directed unless the court was satisfied that it was not necessary and subject to the seriousness of the allegations and the difficulty of the case, consideration should be given to the child being separately represented. Where cases were proceeding in a family proceedings court, a transfer to the county court should be considered and, where in a county court, a transfer to the High Court. When considering interim contact, the court must give particular consideration to the likely risk of physical or emotional harm to the child, consider whether to make a non-molestation order and consider whether the person seeking contact should seek advice and/or treatment as a precondition of contact taking place. At the final hearing, the court should make findings of fact as to the nature and degree of the violence and its effect on the child and the resident parent. The s 1 checklist should be applied and in particular the harm the child has and is likely to suffer should be taken into account. The court should make an order for contact only if it is satisfied that the safety of the residential parent and the child can be secured.[46]

Domestic Violence (Lord Chancellor's Department, 2000). The chairman, Wall J, had played an important part in considering the issues in a number of reported cases. He later discussed his views on the subject in 'Domestic Violence at the Millennium – Contact between Children and Violent Parents' in Cretney (ed) *Essays for the New Millennium* (Jordans, 2000).

[46] For the views of the Sub-committee chairman, Sir Nicholas Wall, on the refusal of the then President to translate the Guidelines into a Practice Direction, see Lord Justice Wall 'Making contact work in 2009' [2009] Fam Law 590, at p 591.

Re L, V, M, H (Contact: Domestic Violence)[47]

5.21 A few months after the publication of the Report on Contact and Domestic Violence, the Court of Appeal took the opportunity of four appeals to give guidance on how contact applications should be approached when allegations of violence were made. Extracts from the judgments are reproduced in Appendix 5.

5.22 The President adopted the approach of the Sub-Committee. She emphasised that courts needed to have a heightened awareness of the consequences on children of exposure to domestic violence. Violence to a partner involved 'a significant failure in parenting – failure to protect the child's carer and failure to protect the child emotionally'. Courts have to decide whether any allegations of domestic violence which are made are true and are not grossly exaggerated. Where they are found to be true, however, there is no presumption that there should not be contact. Rather, the seriousness of the violence, the risks to the child and the carer and its impact on the child have to be weighed against the positive benefits (if any) of contact. When this balancing exercise is carried out, the ability of the offending parent to recognise his past conduct, to be aware of the need to change and to make genuine efforts are likely to be an important consideration. The non-resident parent's reason for seeking contact is also important. Is it a desire to promote the best interests of the child or a means to continue violence and/or intimidation and/or harassment of the carer? When considering an application for interim contact, the court should give particular consideration to the likely risk of harm to the child, whether physical or emotional, and should ensure, so far as it can, that any risk to the child and the carer, before, during and after contact is minimised.

5.23 Thorpe LJ rejected the Sturge/Glaser approach that there should be no automatic assumption that contact to a previously or currently violent parent is in a child's interests, and 'If anything the assumption should be in the opposite direction'. He commented that there is a spectrum within the broad categorisation 'from the slap which may have been provoked to premeditated murder'. There was also a distinction between past, acknowledged and addressed violence and the continuing risk of future violence:

> 'In my opinion, the only direction that can be given to the trial judge is to apply the welfare principle and the welfare checklist ... to the facts of the particular case.'

---

[47] [2000] 2 FLR 334. The decision is extensively discussed in Kaganas '*Re L (Contact: Domestic Violence); Re V (Contact: Domestic Violence); Re M (Contact: Domestic Violence); Re H (Contact: Domestic Violence)*' [2000] CFLQ 311. Piper and Kaganas discuss the judgment further in Hunter, McGlynn and Rackley (eds) *Feminist Judgments: From Theory to Practice* (Hart Publishing, 2010), ch 7. In an interesting re-writing of the judgment from a feminist perspective, Kaganas suggests that rather than there being no presumption for or against contact, where domestic violence is shown to have occurred, the courts should assume that there will be no contact.

5.24 The President later expanded on this guidance extra-judicially. In guidance to the judiciary in December 2001, she stressed the importance of the issue of domestic violence being tackled as early as possible in the proceedings. The court has to decide whether, if proved, the alleged violence would be relevant to the issue of contact. Where the allegations may have an effect on the outcome, the court must adjudicate on them:

'Tightly constructed directions and careful timetabling must be achieved at the earliest possible stage to identify and deal expeditiously with the issues raised. An early exchange of statements may enable the court to determine whether or not the alleged violence may be relevant to the issue of contact ...'

She pointed out that domestic violence covers a wide range of unacceptable behaviour:

'Indirect violence, threats and verbal abuse may, in certain circumstances, be as detrimental as actual violence. Violence is a form of emotional or psychological abuse as well as physical assault.'

She added that the carer may not understand the effect which domestic violence can have on children and:

'It is not, therefore, open to that parent to decide that contact should take place notwithstanding the violence.'

If a court is asked to make an order, it must be satisfied that to do so is in the child's interests.

This approach has been the basis for all subsequent guidance from the Court of Appeal resulting in the Practice Direction: Residence and Contact Orders: Domestic Violence and Harm[48] the aim of which is 'to make contact safe'.[49]

SAFEGUARDING IN THE COMMUNITY

Child protection services

5.25 Concerns about a child being at risk of harm as a result of exposure to domestic violence may result in professionals referring families to social services with a view to the child's needs being assessed and action taken to meet those needs including support for the abused parent, a child protection plan being agreed or, in extreme cases where the carer is unable to protect the child, care proceedings being issued. For further information see chapter 5 of *Working Together to Safeguard Children*.[50]

---

[48]   9 May 2008 [2008] 2 FLR 103, revised 14 January 2009 [2009] 2 FLR 1400, and reissued as FPR 2010, PD 12J.

[49]   Lord Justice Wall *Making Contact Work in 2009* op cit, at p 595. Sir Nicholas added at p 592: 'Please read, digest and, so far as it is within your gift, put it into practice.'

[50]   Op cit.

Independent domestic violence advisors

5.26 Independent domestic violence advisors (IDVAs) are specialist case workers who focus on working predominantly with high-risk victims, those most at risk of homicide or serious harm. They have a well-defined role underpinned by an accredited training programme and offer intensive short- to medium-term support. They also mobilise multiple resources on behalf of victims by coordinating the response of a wide range of statutory and voluntary agencies who might be involved with a case, including those working with perpetrators and children. Although working in partnership with these agencies, they are independent of any single agency.[51] In each case a safety plan is drawn up which involves measures to improve a family's safety such as changing a phone number, planning what to do if a perpetrator gains entry and changing the route taken to a child's school. IDVAs also help families to access advice on matters such as housing, benefits, counselling and family and criminal court matters.

Multi Agency Risk Assessment Conferences

5.27 During the last 4 years local Multi Agency Risk Assessment Conferences (MARACs) have been established to provide regular and frequent opportunities for different agencies, from both the statutory and voluntary sectors to identify and share information about the highest risk victims in the area and to create and implement a plan to protect them.[52] Links are made with local safeguarding boards[53] in relation to children and vulnerable adults and to Multi Agency Public Protection Arrangements (MAPPAs)[54] in relation to offenders.[55]

MARACs' essential purposes are:

- to share information about risk;

- to devise a co-ordinated safety plan for the adult victim;

- to liaise with the appropriate agencies to address the safety of children;

- to address the behaviour of the alleged perpetrator; and

---

[51] Howarth, Stimpson, Barran and Robinson *Safety in Numbers: A Multi-site Evaluation of Independent Domestic Violence Advisor Services* (2009) www.henrysmithcharity.org.uk/documents/SafetyinNumbersFullReportNov09.pdf.

[52] For a detailed description of the work of MARACs, see Barran 'Developments in Protecting Victims of Domestic Abuse' [2009] Fam Law 416. See also *MARACs and Disclosure into Court Proceedings* (Family Justice Council, 2011).

[53] See *Working Together to Safeguard Children* op cit, ch 3.

[54] Formed under s 37 of the Criminal Justice and Courts Services Act 2000 as amended.

[55] See also *Supporting high risk victims of domestic violence: a review of Multi-Agency Risk Assessment Conferences (MARACs)* (Home Office Research Report 55, 2001).

- to address the safety of staff working with the family.[56]

MARACs use common risk identification tools, the CAADA Risk Assessment Checklist,[57] comprising 24 questions based on aspects of physical abuse, sexual abuse, coercion, threats and intimidation, emotional abuse and isolation, economic abuse and children and pregnancy.

Guidance to courts on requesting disclosure of information from MARACs has been given by the Family Justice Council.[58] It emphasises that generally the details of the MARAC safety plan need to be kept confidential if it is to be effective for to do otherwise would be to increase risk. Furthermore a MARAC is not a legal entity and therefore the owner of information shared at a MARAC is the original supplying agency. MARACs should be required to disclose information only by an order of the court. Any request for information should set out the nature of the information sought – there should be no 'fishing expeditions' – and should be considered well in advance of final hearings . Notice should be given to the chair of the MARAC who is under a duty to raise formal objection if any disclosure will interfere significantly with a safety plan or may cause harm to any relevant child.

THE LAW

European Convention for the Protection of Human Rights and Fundamental Freedoms

5.28 The European Court of Human Rights has noted that domestic violence is a general problem which concerns all Member States and which does not always surface since it often takes place within personal relationships or closed circuits and it is not only women who are affected.[59]

The Committee of Ministers of the Council of Europe has recommended that Member States should introduce, develop and/or improve where necessary national policies against violence based on maximum safety and protection of victims, support and assistance, adjustment of the criminal and civil law, raising of public awareness, training for professionals confronted with violence against women and prevention.[60]

In particular, that Member States should penalise serious violence against women such as sexual violence and rape and abuse of the vulnerability of pregnant, defenceless, ill, disabled or dependent victims, as well as penalising any abuse of position by the perpetrator. They should ensure that all victims of

---

[56] 'MARACs and Disclosure into Court Proceedings' op cit, at para 3.
[57] See the Co-ordinated Action Against Domestic Abuse (CAADA) website , www.caada.org.uk/dvservices/resources-for-domestic-abuse-practitioners.html.
[58] 'MARACs and Disclosure into Court Proceedings' op cit.
[59] *Opuz v Turkey* (Application 33401/02) [2009] ECHR 870, at [132].
[60] Recommendation Rec (2002) 5 of 30 April 2002 on the protection of women against violence. See also *A v Croatia (*Application No 55164/08) [2011] 1 FLR 407, at [45]–[47].

violence are able to institute proceedings, encourage prosecutors to regard violence against women as an aggravating or decisive factor in deciding whether or not to prosecute in the public interest, ensure where necessary that measures are taken to protect victims effectively against threats and possible acts of revenge and take specific measures to ensure that children's rights are protected during proceedings. All forms of violence within the family should be classified as criminal offences and envisage the possibility of taking measures in order, inter alia, to enable the judiciary to adopt interim measures aimed at protecting victims, to ban the perpetrator from contacting, communicating with or approaching the victim, or residing in or entering defined areas, to penalise all breaches of the measures imposed on the perpetrator and to establish a compulsory protocol for operation by the police, medical and social services.[61]

5.29 These Recommendations do not have the force of law and it is for individual states, within the margin of appreciation allowed them under the Convention, to decide the most appropriate methods of protecting individuals from attack.[62] However, as stated by the European Court of Human Rights in *Hajduová v Slovakia*,[63] the concept of private life includes a person's physical and psychological integrity. Under Art 8 states have a duty to protect the physical and moral integrity of an individual[64] from other persons. Children and other vulnerable individuals, in particular, are entitled to effective protection.[65] To that end states are under a duty to maintain and apply in practice an adequate legal framework affording protection against acts of violence by private individuals.[66]A failure to afford protection may breach Art 2 (Right to Life), Art 3 (Prohibition of torture and inhuman or degrading treatment) Art 8 (respect for private and family life) and Art 14 (freedom from discrimination) – but not, in relation to the prosecution of the alleged perpetrator, Art 6 (right to fair trial).[67]

Recent examples of where the ECHR has found breaches include *Opuz v Turkey*,[68] *A v Croatia*[69] and *Hajduová v Slovakia*.[70]

---

[61]   For other European reports, see *Opuz v Turkey* (Application 33401/02) [2009] ECHR 870, at [72]–[90].

[62]   *A v Croatia* (Application No 55164/08) [2011] 1 FLR 407, at [75]; *Hajduová v Slovakia* (Application No 2660/03) [2011] 1 FLR 1247.

[63]   *Hajduová v Slovakia* (Application No 2660/03) [2011] 1 FLR 1247, at [45]–[46].

[64]   The Court has acknowledged that it is not only women who are affected and men may also be victims: *Opuz v Turkey* (Application 33401/02) [2009] ECHR 870, at [132].

[65]   *X and Y v The Netherlands* (1986) 8 EHRR 235, 26 March 1985, at paras 23–24 and 27, and *August v United Kingdom* (Application No 36505/02) (unreported) 21 January 2003).

[66]   *X and Y v the Netherlands* (1986) 8 EHRR 235, at [22]–[23]; *Costello-Roberts v United Kingdom* (Application No 13134/87) (1995) 19 EHRR 112, [1994] ELR 1, at para 36; *DP and JC v United Kingdom* (Application No 38719/97) (unreported) 10 October 2002, at [118]; *MC v Bulgaria* (Application No 39272/98) 4 December 2003, at [150] and [152] and *A v Croatia* (Application No 55164/08) [2011] 1 FLR 407, at [60].

[67]   *A v Croatia* (Application No 55164/08) [2011] 1 FLR 407, at [81]–[83].

[68]   (Application 33401/02) [2009] ECHR 870.

[69]   *A v Croatia* (Application No 55164/08) [2011] 1 FLR 407.

[70]   (Application No 2660/03) [2011] 1 FLR 1247. See also Burton 'The human rights of victims of domestic violence: *Opuz v Turkey*' [2010] CFLQ 131.

Children Act 1989, Section 1

5.30 The welfare checklist requires a court to have regard to any harm which the child has suffered or is at risk of suffering and 'harm' is now defined as including 'impairment suffered from seeing or hearing the ill-treatment of another'.[71]

Family Law Act 1986

Non-molestation orders

5.31 Section 42 of the Family Law Act 1996 provides a useful aid in cases where a court needs to protect the child or its carer by doing more than imposing a condition on contact. In any family proceedings, the court can make a non-molestation order against a party in order to protect another party or a 'relevant child', whether or not an application for such an order has been made.[72] There is no need for the person in whose favour the order is made to be 'associated' within the meaning of s 62(3). A 'relevant child' means any child who is living with or might reasonably be expected to live with any of the parties to the proceedings.[73]

5.32 In deciding whether or not to make an order, the court has to have regard to all the circumstances, including the need to safeguard the health, safety and well-being of the person for whose benefit the order will be made and any relevant child.

A person who without reasonable excuse does anything that he is prohibited from doing by a non-molestation order at a time when he was aware of the existence of the order is guilty of an offence.[74]

The offence is punishable on conviction on indictment, to imprisonment for a term not exceeding 5 years, or a fine, or both and on summary conviction, to imprisonment for a term not exceeding 12 months, or a fine not exceeding the statutory maximum, or both.[75]

Where a person is convicted of an offence under s 42A in respect of any conduct, that conduct is not punishable as a contempt of court[76] and a person cannot be convicted of an offence under s 42A in respect of any conduct which has been punished as a contempt of court.[77]

5.33 The decision to make breaches of non-molestation orders a criminal offence, thereby effectively removing the family court's powers to deal with

---

[71] CA 1989, s 31(9) inserted by Adoption and Children Act 2002, s 120.
[72] Family Law Act 1996, s 42.
[73] Ibid, s 62(2).
[74] Ibid, s 42A(1), (2).
[75] Ibid, s 42A(5), (6).
[76] Ibid, s 42A(3).
[77] Ibid, s 42A(4).

breach and preventing powers of arrest being added to orders was controversial.[78] Post-implementation of the Domestic Violence Crime and Victims Act 2004 there was a strong suspicion that the removal of the power of arrest acts deterred victims from using the civil route for protection.[79]

The court will not save in exceptional proceedings grant a child permission to make an application for a non-molestation order where such an application could be made by one of his parents.[80]

Occupation orders

5.34 In addition to the power to make non-molestation orders, the court may also make occupation orders under ss 33–40 of the Act but an application is required.[81]

If the court makes an occupation order at a hearing of which the respondent has been given notice and it appears to the court that the respondent has used or threatened violence against the applicant or a relevant child, the court must attach a power of arrest to one or more provisions of the order unless satisfied that in all the circumstances of the case the applicant or child will be adequately protected without such a power of arrest.[82]

Where the order is made without notice the court may attach a power of arrest to one or more provisions of the order if it appears to it:

(a) that the respondent has used or threatened violence against the applicant or a relevant child; and

(b) that there is a risk of significant harm to the applicant or child, attributable to conduct of the respondent, if the power of arrest is not attached to those provisions immediately.[83]

In such a case the court may provide that the power of arrest is to have effect for a shorter period than the other provisions of the order[84] and any period may be extended by the court (on one or more occasions) on an application to vary or discharge the occupation order.[85]

---

[78] For an account of the changes see Gore 'The Domestic Violence, Crime and Victims Act 2004 and the Family Law Act 1996 injunctions' [2007] Fam Law 738.

[79] Platt 'The Domestic Violence Crime and Victims Act 2004: Is it working?' [2008] Fam Law 642. See also Hester, Westmarland, Pearce and Williamson *Early Evaluation of the Domestic Violence, Crimes and Victims Act 2004* (Ministry of Justice Research series 14/08, 2008) noted sub nom 'Domestic Violence Report' [2008] Fam Law 962.

[80] *Re Alwyn (Non-Molestation Proceedings by a Child)* [2009] NI Fam 22, [2010] 1 FLR 1363, a decision of the High Court of Northern Ireland.

[81] For which see Family Procedure Rules 2010 Pt 10 and Practice Direction 10A.

[82] Domestic Violence Crime and Victims Act 2004, s 47(2).

[83] Ibid, s 47(3).

[84] Ibid, s 47(4).

[85] Ibid, s 47(5).

If, a power of arrest is attached to certain provisions of an order, a constable may arrest without warrant a person whom he has reasonable cause for suspecting to be in breach of any such provision.[86] The person arrested must be brought before a judge within the period of 24 hours[87] beginning at the time of his arrest and if the matter is not then disposed of forthwith, the judge before whom he is brought may remand him.[88]

Breach of an occupation order is not an offence but a contempt of court and may be punishable by a fine or committal to prison for a period of up to 2 years.[89]

Undertakings

5.35 In any case where the court has power to make an occupation order or non-molestation order, the court may accept an undertaking from any party to the proceedings.[90]

However the court may not accept an undertaking instead of making a non-molestation order in any case where it appears to the court that:

(a) the respondent has used or threatened violence against the applicant or a relevant child; and

(b) for the protection of the applicant or child it is necessary to make a non-molestation order so that any breach may be punishable under s 42A.[91]

The court may not accept an undertaking instead of making an occupation order in any case where apart from this section a power of arrest would be attached to the order (see **5.34**).[92]

No power of arrest may be attached to any undertaking.[93]

An undertaking is enforceable as if the court had made an occupation order or a non-molestation order in terms corresponding to those of the undertaking.[94] A breach is not an offence but is a contempt of court and punishable as such.

---

[86] Domestic Violence Crime and Victims Act 2004, s 47(6).
[87] In reckoning for the purposes of this subsection any period of 24 hours, no account is to be taken of Christmas Day, Good Friday or any Sunday: ibid, s 47(7).
[88] Ibid, s 47(7).
[89] For a consideration of sentencing criteria, see *Hale v Tanner* [2001] 1 WLR 2377, [2000] 2 FLR 879 (see **23.63**); *H v O (Contempt of Court: Sentencing)* [2004] EWCA Civ 1691, [2005] 2 FLR 329; *Murray v Robinson* [2005] EWCA Civ 935, [2006] 1 FLR 365.
[90] Domestic Violence Crime and Victims Act 2004, s 46(1).
[91] Ibid, s 46(3A).
[92] Ibid, s 46(3).
[93] Ibid, s 46(2).
[94] Ibid, s 46(4).

SAFEGUARDING PRE-COMMENCEMENT

Solicitors

5.36 Chapter 4 of the *Family Law Protocol*[95] provides valuable guidance for solicitors. It notes that their role in identifying abuse can be invaluable.[96] In order to respond effectively they should:

- recognise that domestic abuse is a serious problem and always prioritise the safety of victims. 'It is important not to collude with perpetrators';

- recognise that domestic abuse occurs irrespective of class, race or ethnicity, sex or sexuality, age, mental or physical ability and be sensitive to different needs and experiences of clients from different backgrounds and culture;

- ask questions about domestic abuse directly and routinely as part of the normal interview procedures. 'Solicitors should be aware that disclosure may be piecemeal and so questions should be asked sensitively and appropriately at each interview';

- not be judgemental;

- have information about the sources of help and support available within the local area and keep such information up to date.[97]

5.37 Resolution has produced a Domestic Abuse Screening Toolkit.[98]

- Have you been arguing a lot recently?

- Do you generally have a lot of arguments?

- When you argue, what usually happens?

- Have you or your partner ever been convicted of any criminal offence, in particular those including violence and/or drugs or alcohol?

- What happens when your partner loses their temper and/or you lose your temper?

- When you and/or your partner drink alcohol does this ever result in arguments?

---

95 (3rd edn, The Law Society, 2010).
96 Masson 'Consent orders in contact cases: A survey of Resolution members' [2006] Fam Law 1041 which found that 'some solicitors could take more account of domestic violence when advising on children matters'.
97 *Family Law Protocol* op cit, at para 4.1.9.
98 Available at: www.resolution.org.uk.

- Do you and/or your partner ever become violent after consuming alcohol or any other substance?

- How safe or afraid do you and/or your partner feel in your current relationship?

- Has your partner ever threatened you with a weapon and have you ever threatened them with a weapon?

- Has your partner threatened to harm himself or herself and/or the children and have you ever threatened to harm yourself and/or the children?

- Has your partner ever stalked you and have you ever stalked your partner?

5.38   If domestic abuse emerges as an issue, the Protocol advises that:

- there should be a needs assessment;[99]

- a record of evidence should be compiled;[100]

- clients should be advised how to protect themselves and their children;[101]

- the limits of confidentiality should be explained;[102]

- where clients are in hiding or face particular risk, solicitors should discuss possible dangers from disclosure of their whereabouts and consider ways in which this can be kept confidential.[103]

Mediation

5.39   Mediation may be inappropriate in private law cases where domestic abuse has occurred or is still occurring.[104] If clients still wish to mediate, the Protocol advises that the risks should be considered and discussed as should steps which can be taken to make them feel safe.

Mediation Information and Assessment Meeting

5.40   An applicant in Private Law Proceedings is not expected to attend a Mediation Information and Assessment Meeting (MIAM) – see **16.25** – where any party has, to the applicant's knowledge, made an allegation of domestic

---

99   See *Family Law Protocol* op cit, para 4.1.15.
100   Ibid, para 4.1.16
101   Ibid, para 4.1.20.
102   Ibid, para 4.1.21.
103   Ibid, para 4.1.22–4.1.24.
104   Ibid, para 2.2.11.

violence against another party and this has resulted in a police investigation or the issuing of civil proceedings for the protection of any party within the last 12 months.[105]

COMMENCEMENT OF PROCEEDINGS

5.42 One difficulty about the application of *Re L, V, M, H (Contact: Domestic Violence)* is that victims may be reluctant to report it or think that contact should take place despite the violence.[106] There is a further difficulty in that the family justice system has lacked a strategy for making sure that the court process and not just contact is safe. In October 2005 HM Inspectorate of Court Administration[107] concluded that the nature of domestic abuse was insufficiently understood by most Cafcass practitioners and routine ways of working did not assess risk. Moreover the practice of courts' administration was largely reactive based and while front line staff used their experience, skills and initiative, policies needed to be developed.

The Green Paper, *Parental Separation: Children's Needs and Parents' Responsibilities*[108] stated that:

'It is vital – particularly if we are to provide for better enforcement of contact orders – that issues of domestic violence are fully and properly dealt with by the courts. Contact arrangements which put the safety of the child or the resident parent at risk should not be put in place. All contact must be safe for all involved.'

5.41 Applications are generally commenced by filing Form C1. Question 7 asks whether the applicant believes that a child named in the application has suffered or are at risk of suffering any harm from:

- any form of domestic abuse;

- violence within the household;

- child abduction;

- other conduct or behaviour

by any person who is or has been involved in caring for the child or lives with, or has contact with, the child. If the answer is 'yes, the applicant must also complete Form C1A which includes a request for details of the nature and frequency of the abuse experienced by the applicant or the child and whether

---

[105] FPR 2010 PD 3A, Annex C, para 4.

[106] Hester and Radford *Domestic Violence and Child Contact in England and Denmark* (The Policy Press, 1996) summarised in *Findings: Social Policy Research* 100 (Joseph Rowntree Foundation).

[107] *Domestic Violence, Safety and Family Proceedings* (HM Inspectorate of Court Administration, 2005).

[108] Cm 6273 (2004), para 45.

this has led to any involvement with the police, social services, children's services, your doctor (GP) or any other outside agency. Form C1A must also be completed by any Respondent who answers a similar question in Form C7 in the affirmative.

Research into the use of Form C1A[109] found that although issues of violence were identified, there were many omissions and anomalies despite most having been completed by solicitors. In three in ten cases where applicants answered 'no' to question 7 on C1 which would trigger having to complete C1A, the court case file contained evidence of a high level of violence. 'This urges caution about reliance on the form alone to screen for violence and supports awareness that other sources of evidence may also need to be considered.' The authors also found that judges who were interviewed were not wholly convinced about the rationale or need for C1A and thought the form had a number of drawbacks, including being too long and complex, applicants without English as their first language and its inquisitorial nature possibly being counterproductive and inadvertently exacerbating already difficult situations.

Unless the court directs otherwise, a party is not required to reveal

- the party's home address or other contact details;

- the address or other contact details of any child; or

- the name of a person with whom the child is living, if that person is not the applicant.

A party who does not wish to reveal any of these particulars must give notice of those particulars to the court.[110]

SAFEGUARDING POST-COMMENCEMENT AND PRE-FHDRA

5.43   Practice Direction 12B contains detailed provisions relating to domestic violence.

No later than 24 hours after the proceedings are issued or, where the applications are first considered on paper, no later than 48 hours after issue, Form C1 and, where one has been filed, C1A and other documents are sent by the court to Cafcass.[111]

---

[109]   Aris and Harrison *Domestic violence and the supplemental Information Form C1A* (Ministry of Defence, Research Series 17/07, 2007).
[110]   Form C8.
[111]   FPR 2010, PD 12B, para 3.2.

Before the First Hearing Dispute Resolution Appointment (FHDRA; see **17.25**) Cafcass must identify any safety issues by the following steps which shall be confined to matters of safety.

(a)   In order to inform the court of possible risks of harm to the child in accordance with its safeguarding framework Cafcass will carry out safeguarding enquiries, including checks of local authorities and police, and telephone risk identification interviews with parties.

(b)   If risks of harm are identified, Cafcass may invite parties to meet separately with the Cafcass Officer before the FHDRA to clarify any safety issue. However, neither Cafcass nor a Cafcass Officer may discuss any matter other than relates to safety with either party before the FHDRA. The parties will not be invited to talk about other issues, for example relating to the substance of applications or replies or about issues concerning matters of welfare or the prospects of resolution. If such issues are raised by either party they will be advised that such matters will be deferred to the FHDRA when there is equality between the parties and full discussion can take place which will also be a time when any safety issues that have been identified also can be taken into account.

(c)   Cafcass must record and outline any safety issues for the court.

(d)   The Cafcass officer will not initiate contact with the child prior to the FHDRA. If contacted by a child, discussions relating to the issues in the case will be postponed to the day of the hearing or after when the Cafcass officer will have more knowledge of the issues.

(e)   At least 3 days before the hearing the Cafcass officer must report the outcome of risk identification work to the court by completing the Form at Schedule 2.[112]

In addition to these checks, s 16A of the Children Act 1989 provides that if, in carrying out any function in relation to family proceedings in which the court has power to make an order in relation to any child or in connection with an order made in such proceedings,[113] a Cafcass officer is given cause to suspect that the child concerned is at risk of harm, he must:

(a)   make a risk assessment (ie an assessment of the risk of that harm being suffered by the child) in relation to the child; and

(b)   provide the risk assessment to the court.

5.44   The duty to provide the risk assessment to the court arises irrespective of the outcome of the assessment. Where an officer is given cause to suspect that

---

[112]   Ibid, para 3.9.
[113]   This applies at any time and not just to pre-FHDRA checks.

the child concerned is at risk of harm and makes a risk assessment in accordance with s 16A, he must provide the assessment to the court, even if he reaches the conclusion that there is no risk of harm to the child. The fact that a risk assessment has been carried out is a material fact that should be placed before the court, whatever the outcome of the assessment. In reporting the outcome to the court, the officer should make clear the factor or factors that triggered the decision to carry out the assessment.[114]

5.45 A disclosure protocol[115] has been agreed between Cafcass and the Association of Chief Police officers by which the police will disclose information to Cafcass and under which it is acknowledged that Cafcass is under a duty to comply with the Data Protection Act 1998 whenever it processed sensitive personal information. It has to observe two principles: that personal data has to be processed fairly and lawfully and that personal data has to be obtained only for one or more specified and lawful purposes and is not to be further processed in any manner incompatible with those purposes.[116] Cafcass is not permitted to refer in reports to police information which was not relevant to the child or to give a copy of police information in its original form to any of the parties or their legal representatives. Cafcass has thus to extract and make use only of the information considered to be relevant to the child. A draft report which does not observe these principles cannot be filed with the court or served on the parties.[117]

5.46 Cafcass's current and very detailed procedure for its safeguarding role is set out in *Cafcass Safeguarding Framework 2010 Working Together Update*.[118] In relation to risk assessments, it states that the identification of risks should prompt a more detailed assessment. In some private law situations, there will be a need for an expert assessment. 'The identification of risks should also prompt a consideration of the need for an immediate referral of a child protection nature.'[119]

For Cafcass's duties to inform other professional agencies if it is concerned about children on whom it is making enquiries, see **19.31**.

At the FHDRA, the court must inform the parties of the content of any screening report or other information which has been provided by Cafcass or Cafcass Cymru, unless it considers that to do so would create a risk of harm to a party or the child.[120]

---

[114]   PD 12L, paras 3 and 4.
[115]   *Disclosure Protocol with CAFCASS and CAFCASS Cymru in Private Law Cases 2008*.
[116]   For the Guidance Note to Cafcass, summarising Cafcass's duties, see the Appendix to *Re G and B (Disclosure: Protocol)* [2010] EWHC 2630 (Fam), [2011] 1 FLR 1089.
[117]   Ibid.
[118]   www.cafcass.gov.uk.
[119]   Ibid, paras 3.11–3.14.
[120]   PD 12J, para 10.

SAFEGUARDING — THE COURT'S DUTIES

The General Principles

5.47 The 'General Principles' the court must adopt when considering applications for residence and contact orders are set out in Practice Direction 12J: Residence and Contact Orders: Domestic Violence and Harm.

The court must, at all stages of the proceedings, consider whether domestic violence is raised as an issue, either by the parties or otherwise, and if so must:

(a) identify at the earliest opportunity the factual and welfare issues involved;

(b) consider the nature of any allegation or admission of domestic violence and the extent to which any domestic violence which is admitted, or which may be proved, would be relevant in deciding whether to make an order about residence or contact and, if so, in what terms;

(c) give directions to enable the relevant factual and welfare issues to be determined expeditiously and fairly.[121]

In all cases it is for the court to decide whether an order for residence or contact accords with s 1(1) of the 1989 Act . Any proposed order, whether to be made by agreement between the parties or otherwise must be scrutinised by the court. The court shall not make a consent order for residence or contact or give permission for an application for a residence or contact order to be withdrawn, unless the parties are present in court, except where it is satisfied that there is no risk of harm to the child in so doing.[122]

In considering whether there is any risk of harm to the child, the court must consider all the evidence and information available. The court may direct a report under s 7 of the CA 1989 either orally or in writing before it makes its determination; in such a case, the court may ask for information about any advice given by the officer preparing the report to the parties and whether they or the child have been referred to any other agency, including local authority children's services. If the report is not in writing, the court shall make a note of its substance on the court file.[123]

These Principles find their origin in *Re L, V, M, H (Contact: Domestic Violence)*[124] and the Children Act Sub-Committee Guidelines. Subsequent cases have shown the need for the Guidelines to be constantly reinforced both by the Judicial College and by the Court of Appeal.[125]

---

[121] Ibid, para 3.
[122] Ibid, para 4.
[123] Ibid, para 5.
[124] [2000] 2 FLR 334.
[125] See, for example, *Re H (Contact: Domestic Violence)* [2005] EWCA Civ 1404, [2006] 1 FLR 943.

'The Guidelines were designed to be applied selectively and intelligently to the facts of the individual case. They represent good practice and they are to be used. It is bad practice to ignore them. I append them to this judgment in the hope that this court will not again be presented with a case such as the present, which not only ill-serves the parties and the child, but does the system discredit, and helps to devalue the valuable and conscientious work which courts up and down the country are undertaking in an attempt to tackle the scourge of domestic violence and to minimise the effect which it has on parties and children.'[126]

First Hearing Dispute Resolution Appointment

5.48 At the FHDRA, the court must ascertain at the earliest opportunity whether domestic violence is raised as an issue and must consider the likely impact of that issue on the conduct and outcome of the proceedings. In particular, it should consider whether the nature and effect of the domestic violence alleged is such that, if proved, the decision of the court is likely to be affected.[127]

Admissions

5.49 Where at any hearing an admission of domestic violence to another person or the child is made by a party, the admission should be recorded in writing and retained on the court file.[128]

Considering the need for a fact-finding hearing

5.50 When considering at the FHDRA the possible risk to a child, the court is essentially carrying out a limited risk screening: if the allegations are true, *might* the child be placed at risk if a contact residence order were made? There is no authorised screening tool and family judges are not trained in the techniques of carrying out such screenings. There are tools available – for example, those used by the authors of *Twenty-nine child homicides*,[129] the CAADA Risk Assessment Checklist[130] and the Resolution Domestic Abuse Screening Toolkit[131] which Cafcass's *Safeguarding Framework* states should always be used by its practitioners.[132]

It should be born in mind that a screening exercise is not a risk assessment. A risk assessment essentially asks five questions:

- What harmful outcome is potentially present in this situation?

- What is the *probability* of this outcome coming about?

---

126 Ibid, per Wall LJ at [140].
127 PD 12J, para 11.
128 Ibid, para 12.
129 Op cit, see **5.12**.
130 Op cit, see **5.27**.
131 Op cit, see **5.37**.
132 Op cit, para 4.3.18.

- What risks are *probable* in this situation in the short, medium and long term?

- What are the factors that could increase or decrease the risk that is probable?

- What measures are available whose deployment could mitigate the risks that are probable?[133]

A screening assessment on the other hand asks:

- What are the *possible* risks to the child if the allegations are true?

- Are there any protective measures which *can* be put in place which *will* reduce the risk to an acceptable level?

- Is there currently enough information to decide the probability of the risk and the likely effect of the protective measures?

The screening tools are an aid to answering these questions but as the author of *Twenty-nine child homicides* warns:

> 'Any risk assessment tool based on checklist categories will provide only a limited picture of the nature, severity and danger of a particular domestic violence situation. Previous assault is one of the most robust and straightforward indicators for domestic violence.'

Common sense dictates that the list cannot indicate that there is no risk or that any risk is acceptable, especially when applied by non-professionals (including lawyers and judges). If there is any concern, contact should be refused or strictly supervised until a full investigation and professional risk assessment have taken place.

Where a screening assessment indicates a need for a risk assessment, two questions arise:

- Is there a sufficient factual foundation on which a risk assessment can be based either because of admissions or because of judicially determined facts? Such facts may already have been determined in earlier proceedings but if not, and the risk assessment is to be carried out by someone other than a court, for example, Cafcass or a psychiatrist or psychologist the allegations will need to be investigated at a fact finding hearing in advance of the assessment. If however, the judge is unlikely to need expert evidence, it may be appropriate for the facts to be determined at the final hearing when the court will consider whether to make the substantive orders.

---

[133] Mahendra 'Psychiatric risk assessment in family and child law' [2008] Fam Law 569. See also *Risk: Analysis, Perception, Management* (The Royal Society, 1992).

- Who should carry out the assessment? This question is discussed further at **5.79**.

Practice Direction 12J states that the court should determine as soon as possible whether it is necessary to conduct a fact-finding hearing in relation to any disputed allegation of domestic violence before it can proceed to consider any final order for residence or contact. If it determines that a finding of fact hearing is not necessary, the order must record the reasons for that decision.[134]

Section 7 Report

5.51 In any case where domestic violence is raised as an issue, the court should consider directing that a s 7 report on the question of contact, or any other matters relating to the welfare of the child, be prepared by Cafcass or a Welsh family proceedings officer or, if appropriate, a local authority, unless the court is satisfied that it is not necessary to do so in order to safeguard the child's interests. If the court so directs, it should consider the extent of any enquiries which can properly be made at this stage and whether it is appropriate to seek information on the wishes and feelings of the child before findings of fact have been made.[135]

FACT-FINDING HEARINGS

5.52 If allegations of physical or sexual abuse are made and are deemed by the court to be relevant, it is important that findings are made as quickly as possible for four reasons. First, unresolved issues act as a clog on any progress or resolution which is attempted. Second, the welfare checklist cannot properly be applied if there are unresolved, relevant issues. Third, the more time passes, the more difficult it will be to make reliable findings. Last, it makes it more difficult for a parent who is opposed to contact to attempt to frustrate the operation of an order by renewing allegations or making fresh ones. Reported cases of intractable contact disputes (see **11.166**) contain many examples of cases which have continued for years without a proper investigation of the facts taking place. In *Re O (Contact: Withdrawal of Application)*,[136] for example, a judge had the difficult task of assessing an 8-year-old boy's reluctance to see his father because of alleged memories of violence towards his mother, no later than December 1997 (when the boy was 6), the allegations being made no later than March 1999 but still untried in March 2001. In *Re M (Intractable Contact Dispute: Interim Care Order)*[137] Wall J said:

---

[134] PD 12J, para 13.
[135] Ibid, para 15V.
[136] [2003] EWHC 3031 (Fam), [2004] 1 FLR 1258.
[137] [2003] EWHC 1024 (Fam), [2003] 2 FLR 636.

'In an intractable contact dispute where the residential parent is putting forward an allegedly factual basis for contact not taking place, there is no substitute in my judgment for findings by the court as to whether or not there is any substance to the allegations.'

Subsequently Munby J in *Re D (Intractable Contact Dispute: Publicity)*[138] added:

'The court should grasp the nettle. Such allegations should be speedily investigated and resolved, not left to fester unresolved and a continuing source of friction and dispute. Court time must be found – and found without delay – for fact finding hearings. Judges must resist the temptation to delay the evil day in the hope that perhaps the problem will go away. Judges must also resist the temptation to put contact "on hold", or to direct that it is to be supervised, pending investigation of the allegations. And allegations which could have been made at an earlier stage should be viewed with appropriate scepticism. Once findings have been made, everybody must thereafter approach the case on the basis of the facts as judicially found. As Wall J said in *Re M* at para [128], "these are not questions which can be reopened". He went on to point out that if a parent persists in assertions contrary to such judicial findings, that is plain evidence of a refusal to recognise reality and what is in the interests of the children.'

5.53 Where the court considers that a fact-finding hearing is necessary, it must give directions to ensure that the matters in issue are determined expeditiously and fairly and in particular it should consider:

- directing the parties to file written statements giving particulars of the allegations made and of any response in such a way as to identify clearly the issues for determination;

- whether material is required from third parties such as the police or health services and may give directions accordingly (see **17.62**); and

- whether any other evidence is required to enable the court to make findings of fact in relation to the allegations and may give directions accordingly.[139]

Where the court fixes a fact-finding hearing, it must at the same time fix a further hearing for determination of the application ('the final hearing'). The hearings should be arranged in such a way that they are conducted by the same judge or, in the magistrates' court, by at least the same chairperson of the justices.[140]

---

[138] [2004] EWHC 727 (Fam), [2004] 1 FLR 1226, at [54].
[139] Practice Direction 12J, para 14.
[140] Ibid, para 15.

These requirements are based on practice developed in Public and Private Law proceedings on a case-by-case basis by the Court of Appeal and the High Court. A failure to follow them can amount as a serious deficiency in the trial process.[141]

Identifying suitable cases

5.54 The problems facing a court when deciding whether a fact finding hearing is necessary was considered by the Court of Appeal In *Re W (Care Order: Sexual Abuse)*.[142]

> 'Domestic violence and other forms of child abuse must be properly addressed by the courts. They are, in essence, issues of fact which must be brought to the attention of the court, and resolved by the court. Nobody else can do it, and no decision relating to a child's welfare can properly be made when such issues remain outstanding. At the same time, the intellectual rigour which needs to be brought to all proceedings relating to children needs to be applied with particular diligence when it comes to the *Practice Direction*. We all know that findings of fact hearings are time-consuming and can cause delay. The judge who directs one, and the advocates who seek it, both owe a duty to the children in the case and to the system itself to ensure that such a hearing is strictly necessary, and that in the terms of the overriding objective such a hearing, where required, addresses appropriate issues and is given an appropriate share of the court's resources. It follows that all those engaged in care proceedings (albeit in this instance that I have particularly in mind the advocates and the case managing judge) must apply their minds rigorously to the question of the need for a separate fact-finding hearing in any proceedings relating to children.'[143]

5.55 The following year in *AA v NA (Appeal: Fact-Finding)*[144] Mostyn J emphasised that a fact-finding hearing should only be ordered if the court can discern 'a real purpose' for such a hearing.

> 'The finite resources of the court do not exist simply to provide a free-standing medium for one party to obtain, for no reason other than vindication, findings of matrimonial misconduct against the other.'[145]

McFarlane J in *A County Council v DP*[146] suggested that in care proceedings the following factors are likely to be relevant:

(a)   the interests of the child (which are relevant but not paramount);

---

[141]   *Re K and S (Children) (Contact: Domestic Violence)* [2005] EWCA Civ 1660, [2006] 1 FCR 316.

[142]   [2009] EWCA Civ 644, [2009] 2 FLR 1106.

[143]   Ibid, per Wall LJ at [31]–[33]. For a district judge's view of fact-finding hearings, see Grand 'Allegations of violence: prove it' [2009] Fam Law 522.

[144]   [2010] EWHC 1282 (Fam), [2010] 2 FLR 1173, at [18].

[145]   This is an example of a fact-finding hearing which took on a life of its own. There were 89 allegations covering a 6-year period, 15 witnesses and lasted a total of 17 days over a period of 9 months.

[146]   [2005] EWHC 1593, [2005] 2 FLR 1031.

(b)   the time that the investigation will take;

(c)   the likely cost to public funds;

(d)   the evidential result;

(e)   the necessity or otherwise of the investigation;

(f)   the relevance of the potential result of the investigation to the future plans for the child;

(g)   the impact of any fact finding process upon the other parties;

(h)   the prospects of a fair trial on the issue;

(i)   the justice of the case.[147]

5.56 The President of the Family Division has given guidance in relation to split hearings in which he emphasised that a decision to direct a split hearing or to conduct a fact-finding hearing is a judicial decision, not one for Cafcass or the parties. The court should not direct a fact-finding hearing simply because the parties agree that one is necessary or because Cafcass says that it cannot report without one. 'Such considerations are, of course, to be taken into account, but they are not conclusive.' Judges and magistrates should always remember that a fact-finding hearing is a working tool designed to assist them to decide the case and a fact-finding hearing should only be ordered if the court takes the view that the case cannot properly be decided without such a hearing. Even when the court comes to the conclusion that a fact-finding hearing is necessary, it by no means follows that such a hearing needs to be separate from the substantive hearing.[148]

5.57 Courts and practitioners need to be alert to identify those cases which are suited to a split hearing. In general, they are likely to be cases in which there is a clear and stark issue, such as sexual abuse or physical abuse.[149]

Preparations for the final hearing

5.58 The court should consider what directions are required for the final hearing, not just its listing but also directions for s 7 reports, the instructions of experts, for example as to risk (see **5.79**), the availability of treatment programmes such as anger management courses see **5.81**), in case they are required. The purpose of any such direction is simply to ensure that time is not wasted and that the parties do not have to wait until findings are made by the

---

[147]   These were approved in the context of Private Law proceedings by Mostyn J in *AA v NA (Appeal: Fact-Finding)* [2010] EWHC 1282 (Fam), [2010] 2 FLR 1173, at [26].

[148]   *The President's Guidance In Relation To Split Hearings May 2010* [2010] 2 FLR 1897. See also *Re C (Children)* [2009] EWCA Civ 994.

[149]   *Re S (Care Proceedings: Split Hearing)* [1996] 2 FLR 773.

court before putting in place the structure which will enable the second stage of the hearing to take place as quickly as possible: it is not to facilitate inappropriate psychiatric or psychological evidence being given at the first stage.[150]

Judicial continuity

5.59 Where the court has made findings of fact on disputed allegations, any subsequent hearing in the proceedings should be conducted by the same judge or, in the magistrates' court, by at least the same chairperson of the justices. Exceptions may be made only where observing this requirement would result in delay to the planned timetable and the judge or chairperson is satisfied, for reasons recorded in writing, that the detriment to the welfare of the child would outweigh the detriment to the fair trial of the proceedings.[151]

5.60 In *Re B (Care Proceedings: Standard of Proof)*[152] Baroness Hale of Richmond said:

> '[The] finding of ... facts is merely part of the whole process of trying the case. It is not a separate exercise. And once it is done the case is part heard. The trial should not resume before a different judge, any more than any other part heard case should do so. In the particular context of care proceedings, where the character and personalities of the parties are important components in any decision, it makes no sense at all for one judge to spend days listening to them give evidence on one issue and for another judge to send more days listening to them give evidence on another. This is not only a wasteful duplication of effort. Much useful information is likely to fall between the gaps. How can a judge who has not heard the parents give their evidence about how the child's injuries occurred begin to assess the risk of letting them care for the child again? The experts may make their assessments, but in the end it is for the judge to make the decision on all the evidence before him. How can he properly do that when he has heard only half of it?'

Representation of the child

5.61 Subject to the seriousness of the allegations made and the difficulty of the case, the court must consider whether it is appropriate for the child who is the subject of the application to be made a party and be separately represented. If the case is proceeding in the magistrates' court and the court considers that it may be appropriate for the child to be made a party to the proceedings, it may transfer the case to the relevant county court for determination of that issue and following such transfer the county court shall give such directions for the further conduct of the case as it considers appropriate.[153]

---

150 *Re N (Sexual Abuse Allegations: Professionals not Abiding by Findings of Fact)* [2005] 2 FLR 340.
151 PD 12J, para 23. See also *Re G (Care Proceedings: Split Trials)* [2001] 1 FLR 872; *M v A (Contact: Domestic Violence)* [2002] 2 FLR 921.
152 [2008] UKHL 35, [2008] 2 FLR 141, at [76].
153 PD 12J, para 17. The draftsman of the Practice Direction (which adopts the pre-2010 FPR

Preparations for the fact-finding hearing

5.62

- A schedule of allegations should be prepared at the earliest opportunity.

- The parties and the court should at all times maintain their focus on the factual issue or issues and not allow themselves to be diverted from them without very good reason.[154]

- The parties and the court must concentrate their energies upon assembling the evidence that will enable that issue to be tried. The court will require the best first-hand evidence available whether from a witness or in a document and attention should always be given to corroborative evidence.[155] Tight directions must be given and the case timetabled to ensure that the factual issue is heard speedily. These directions and timetable must be adhered to.[156]

- Full statements by the parties are needed to identify which facts are in issue between them, and, therefore, need proof, and which are accepted.

- Evidence which is relevant to the assessment of the parents or others at the later stage should not be permitted unless for some reason it is of direct relevance to the factual issue being tried. It is the essence of a split hearing that assessments of the parties need to be carried out on the basis of the facts found by the court.[157]

- Evidence of propensity or a psychiatric or psychological assessment of one of the parties is unlikely to be of any assistance in resolving a purely factual issue.[158]

5.63   In *Re A (Contact: Risk of Violence)*[159] Black J gave valuable guidance concerning the preparation of the case.

'When a finding of fact is sought, the court expects and requires the best possible evidence on which to make its decision. Where this is not made available, or is made available only far too late, the decision making process may be impaired. It may even be necessary for the judge to refuse to hear the matter until there has been proper preparation. It is impossible to provide a blueprint for preparation that will serve in all domestic violence cases. It is the obligation of the lawyers to do whatever is necessary in the particular case. This will involve them in reviewing,

---

Practice Direction) may have overlooked that the family proceedings courts now have the power to make the child a party – see PD 16A which refers to 'the court'.

[154] *Re B (Care Proceedings; Guidelines)* [1998] 2 FLR 211, at 217.
[155] *Re A (Contact: risk of Violence)* [2005] EWHC 851 (Fam), [2006] 1 FLR 283.
[156] Ibid.
[157] Ibid.
[158] Ibid.
[159] [2005] EWHC 851 (Fam), [2006] 1 FLR 283, at [8]–[15].

at an early stage, what it is that they seek to establish (or to cast doubt upon) and by what means, what evidence, they can best do so. Case management by judges does not transfer the responsibility for the preparation of the case to the judge; it remains with the parties' legal representatives, whose obligation it is to gather together and present the evidence, seeking specific directions when problems are encountered. When it is necessary to seek such directions, the judge should be presented by the party applying with a precise draft of the order sought by way of a solution for the particular problem, not simply with the problem and an invitation to solve it.'

- Where first-hand evidence is available, either from a witness or in documentary form, it should be presented.

- In some cases, the court will draw an adverse inference from the absence of supporting witnesses. 'It is, however, much more difficult to know what to make of such a lacuna where it is clear that there have been gaps in the preparation of the case.'

- Attention must always be given to the issue of evidence that may be corroborative or give rise to doubt about important allegations.

- It is normally sensible to give some thought to whether the police have records of reports of domestic incidents and whether there may be material police witnesses, just as consideration should be given to whether there may be medical evidence to corroborate an assertion that a particular assault took place and caused injuries.

    However, 'Bruising does not normally need medical treatment and it is not at all uncommon for women to keep quiet about violence in the home, not even telling their general practitioner. Even rape need not necessarily require medical treatment.'

- If there are tapes of relevant interviews, the advocates should listen to them before the hearing.

Dispensing with a final hearing which has been ordered

5.64 It is not unknown for a fact-finding hearing to be listed only for the allegations or the application to be withdrawn. If permission to withdraw the application is given, the consequence is straightforward. There is no need for an investigation provided that the terms of the compromise, for example that there should be only indirect contact, do not expose the child to risk of harm. Parties should be warned that allegations which are later renewed may be viewed with appropriate scepticism[160] and that the court may not allow them to be investigated. However, even if the resident parent seeks to withdraw the allegations, the judge may well have to proceed with the investigation despite the absence of the principal defence evidence if the allegations remain relevant

---

[160] See *Re D (Intractable Contact Dispute: Publicity)* [2004] EWHC 727 (Fam), [2004] 1 FLR 1226.

to the child's welfare.[161] In addition the court may engage child protection procedures either by directing Cafcass to refer the matter to social services or directing that a s 37 report (see **Chapter 19**) be prepared.

5.65 The court also needs to be alert to the possibility that the application or allegations are being withdrawn out of a sense of frustration or because of undue pressure from the other party or family.

The authors of *Domestic Violence, Child Contact and Post-Separation Violence Issues for South Asian and African-Caribbean Women and Children*[162] discuss in detail the pressure from family, community and professionals placed on African-Caribbean and South Asian women to concede contact despite allegations of abuse.

5.66 A decision to dispense with a fact-finding hearing already listed should only be made with great caution, especially where the judge listed to try the allegations is not the judge who directed the hearing.

'There is no doubt that in family proceedings the court has a discretion [even at a late stage] whether to hear evidence in relation to disputed matters of fact with a view to determining them ... Nevertheless in my view ... considerations [additional to those applying to the initial decision as to whether to order a hearing] fall to be weighed by a judge who is considering, at the outset of a prearranged fact-finding hearing, whether in effect to abort it. That judge should weigh, with appropriate respect, the previous decision that the exercise should be undertaken and should ask whether any fresh circumstances, or at least any circumstances freshly discovered, should lead her or him to depart from the chosen forensic course. Equally she or he should weigh the costs already incurred in the assembly of the case on all sides and the degree to which a refusal at that stage to conduct the hearing would waste them. Furthermore she or he should weigh any special features such as, in the present case, the facts that a girl then aged 16 had been shown the court room, that she had participated in discussions with the guardian as to the way in which she would prefer to give evidence and that she was thus expecting that she would imminently be giving oral evidence in some way or another, although the judge should not on the other hand ignore the girl's likely apprehension at that prospect. What needs, however, to be avoided at all costs is a sudden decision to abort the hearing in circumstances in which, later, the findings not then made might after all be considered to be necessary.'[163]

The hearing

5.67 The NSPCC publish a series of information leaflets on aspects of physical child abuse based on a collaborative project by the NSPCC and the Welsh Child Protection Systematic Review Group at the Department of Child Health, Cardiff University. They cover Bruises on children; Fractures in

---

[161] *Re F (Children) (Contact Orders: Domestic Violence)* [2005] EWCA Civ 499, [2005] 2 FLR 950.

[162] Op cit (see **5.11**).

[163] *Re F-H (Dispensing with Fact-finding Hearing)* [2008] EWCA Civ 1249, [2009] 1 FLR 349, per Wilson LJ at [26].

children; Head and spinal injuries; Oral injuries and bites on children and Thermal injuries on children.[164] Although useful guides for advocates they are not –and are not intended to be – a substitute for expert evidence based on the facts of a particular case.

5.68 For a discussion of the need for any photographic evidence of bruising to be taken as soon as possible after the injuries have been identified and for them to be of good quality, see *Re C and D (Photographs of Injuries)*.[165] Bruises are very difficult to age and photographs taken other than by medical photographers are unlikely to be of much assistance. The court is likely to deprecate a parent taking photographs of bruising as evidence against the other in all but the most exceptional circumstances.

The standard of proof is discussed at **20.49**.

The court must hear all the evidence. The judge cannot say he has heard one side, does not think much of it, and therefore is not going to permit cross-examination of the other side of the issues involved, particularly where the safety and welfare of children are concerned. There is no equivalent for a submission of 'no case to answer' in proceedings relating to children.[166]

Findings

5.69 At the fact-finding hearing the court should, wherever practicable, make findings of fact as to the nature and degree of any domestic violence which is established and its effect on the child, the child's parents and any other relevant person. The court must record its findings in writing, and shall serve a copy on the parties. A copy of any record of findings of fact or of admissions must be sent to any officer preparing a report under s 7.[167]

Cost orders in fact-finding hearings

5.70 Notwithstanding the practice that it is unusual to make a costs order in Private Law proceedings (see **Chapter 24**) the Court of Appeal in *Re J (Costs of Fact-Finding Hearing)*[168] allowed a mother's appeal against a refusal to make a costs order against a father because the hearing fell into a separate and unusual category being devoted exclusively to the court's consideration of serious and relevant allegations against the father. Over two-thirds of the mother's allegations were true and less than one-third of them were not established but were not found to be untrue. Of the true allegations, nine had been falsely denied by the father; and all but one of the remainder had been admitted by

---

[164] www.nspcc.org.uk/Inform/trainingandconsultancy/learningresources.
[165] [2011] 1 FLR 990, at [264]–[273].
[166] *Re Z (Unsupervised Contact: Allegations of Domestic Violence)* [2009] 2 FLR 877; *Re K (Children) (Sexual Abuse: Evidence)* [2008] EWCA Civ 1307, [2009] 1 FLR 921; *Re R (Family Proceedings: No Case to Answer)* [2009] EWCA Civ 1619, [2009] 2 FLR 83.
[167] PD 12J, para 22.
[168] [2009] EWCA Civ 1350, [2010] 1 FLR 1893.

him only in part. Because of the unproven allegations and the limited admissions made by the father prior to the hearing, the order was limited to two-thirds of the mother's costs of the fact-finding hearing.

Appeals

5.71 In appropriate cases the Court of Appeal will hear appeals in relation to issues determined at a split hearing before the second part of the proceedings is heard.[169] See also **25.65**.

If the appellate court is to review facts found at a preliminary hearing, it must be asked to do so before the trial judge embarks on the final, welfare hearing.

If the final hearing has taken place and the appellant has been successful, it may be 'questionable' whether his right of appeal survives.[170]

Should further evidence become available before the final hearing the court at first instance may, and must, if the interests of the child require it, revisit the earlier findings made.

> '[The judge] must remain alive to the possibility of mistake and be prepared to think again if evidence emerges which casts new light on the evidence which led to the earlier findings. It is now well settled that a judge in care proceedings is entitled to revisit an earlier identification of the perpetrator if fresh evidence warrants this …'[171]

If an appeal against the findings is successful the Court of Appeal can direct a rehearing before a different judge.[172] However, it will be reluctant to change judges unless necessary because such a course would not only be contrary to the principles laid down in *Re B (Children) (Sexual Abuse: Standard of Proof)*,[173] it would also be a waste of 'valuable and all too limited' resources.[174] A change may be necessary where a litigant has legitimately lost confidence in the judge, or where there is an appearance of bias.[175]

---

[169] *Re B (Split Hearings: Jurisdiction)* [2000] 1 FLR 334.
[170] *Re H (Abuse: Oral Evidence)* [2011] EWCA Civ 741, [2012] 1 FLR 186, per Thorpe LJ at [4]. However, this was said in the context of care proceedings which had been dismissed. There might be an argument that there is a difference in private law proceedings whether or not residence or contact orders are made.
[171] *Re SB (Children)* [2009] UKSC 17, [2010] 1 FLR 1161, per Baroness Hale of Richmond at [46]. See also *North Yorkshire County Council v SA* [2003] EWCA Civ 839, [2003] 2 FLR 849, per Butler-Sloss P at [37]. For an example, see *Re I (A Child)* [2009] UKSC 10.
[172] As was done in *Re G (Children) (Fact-Finding Hearing)* [2009] EWCA Civ 10, [2009] 1 FLR 1145.
[173] [2008] UKHL 35, [2008] 2 FLR 141.
[174] *Re D (Care Proceedings: Preliminary Hearing)* [2009] EWCA Civ 472, [2009] 2 FLR 668.
[175] *Re G and B (Fact-Finding Hearing)* [2009] EWCA Civ 10, [2009] 1 FLR 1145, per Wall LJ at [25].

INTERIM ORDERS

5.72 Where the court gives directions for a fact-finding hearing, it should consider whether an interim order for residence or contact is in the interests of the child; and in particular whether the safety of the child and the residential parent can be secured before, during and after any contact.[176]

In deciding any question of interim residence or contact pending a full hearing the court should

- take into account the matters set out in the welfare checklist as appropriate;

- give particular consideration to the likely effect on the child of any contact and any risk of harm, whether physical, emotional or psychological, which the child is likely to suffer as a consequence of making or declining to make an order.[177]

5.73 Where the court is considering whether to make an order for interim contact, it should in addition consider:

- the arrangements required to ensure, as far as possible, that any risk of harm to the child is minimised and that the safety of the child and the parties is secured; and in particular

  - whether the contact should be supervised or supported, and if so, where and by whom; and
  - the availability of appropriate facilities for that purpose;

- if direct contact is not appropriate, whether it is in the best interests of the child to make an order for indirect contact.[178]

See also **11.111**.

5.74 In *Re M (Interim Contact: Domestic Violence)*[179] the Court of Appeal allowed an appeal against an order for interim visiting contact at a contact centre when the mother of the 15-month-old child alleged that the father had treated her violently throughout the relationship:

'[Too] much reliance is placed on the fact that T is still a baby. The fact is that an order of this sort impacts heavily upon the primary carer, the mother. She is entitled not to have such an order put upon her without a full investigation of her contrary submissions. Anything else seems a prejudgment of the case. This is a

---

[176] PD 12J, para 18.
[177] Ibid, para 19.
[178] Ibid, para 20. For an example of the balancing exercise in circumstances where the fact-finding hearing meant a significant delay, see *S v S (Interim Contact)* [2009] EWHC 1575 (Fam), [2009] 2 FLR 1586.
[179] [2000] 2 FLR 377.

father who had an undeniable record of domestic violence. In addition there was the largely disputed territory of further domestic violence. This was a father whose irresponsibility in relation to the court proceedings [he had failed to keep appointments with the court welfare officer] was manifest to the judge, and only unimpressively explained. The possibility of the judge at the final hearing determining that a regime of continuing and progressive contact was not in the interests of the child is patently obvious.'

5.75 Depending on the nature of the allegations it may not be appropriate to use contact centres, specially supported contact centres, as a venue for contact prior to a fact-finding hearing.[180]

ORDERS AT THE CONCLUSION OF THE FACT FINDING

5.76 At the conclusion of the fact-finding hearing, the court must consider, notwithstanding any earlier direction for a s 7 report, whether it is in the best interests of the child for the court to give further directions about the preparation or scope of any report under s 7. Where necessary, it may adjourn the proceedings for a brief period to enable the officer to make representations about the preparation or scope of any further enquiries. The court should also consider whether it would be assisted by any social work, psychiatric, psychological or other assessment of any party or the child and if so (subject to any necessary consent) make directions for such assessment to be undertaken and for the filing of any consequent report.[181]

5.77 The court should take steps to obtain or direct the parties or Cafcass to obtain information about the facilities available locally to assist any party or the child in cases where domestic violence has occurred.[182]

5.78 Following any determination of the nature and extent of domestic violence, whether or not following a fact-finding hearing, the court should consider whether any party should seek advice or treatment as a precondition to an order for residence or contact being made or as a means of assisting the court in ascertaining the likely risk of harm to the child from that person, and may (with the consent of that party) give directions for such attendance and the filing of any consequent report.[183]

RISK ASSESSMENTS

5.79 Based on the findings of fact the court should consider directing Cafcass and the parties to instruct an expert witness, such as a psychiatrist or psychologist to assess the risk to the child of making the order sought.

---

[180] See **5.83** and **11.90**.
[181] PD 12J, para 22.
[182] PD 12J, para 24.
[183] Ibid, para 25.

5.80 Before disposing of the application for contact or residence[184] the court may also give a contact activity direction under s 11A of the Children Act 1989 (see **11.59**) requiring any party who is a perpetrator to take part in an activity that promotes contact with the child concerned. The activities that may be required include, in particular programmes, classes and counselling or guidance sessions of a kind that may, by addressing a person's violent behaviour, enable or facilitate contact with a child.[185] However, no one may be required to undergo medical or psychiatric examination, assessment or treatment.[186]

There are a variety of such activities such as Domestic Violence Perpetrator Programmes or Integrated Domestic Abuse Programmes which may be available privately or through Cafcass or the Probation Service. Many programmes will provide a court report.

In order to avoid delay, information should be sought about such programmes, their availability, length, cost and requirements, at the same time as directions are given for fact-finding hearings (see **5.58**). It should not be assumed that all or even part of the cost will be borne by Cafcass or the Legal Services Commission.

5.81 Perpetrators can offer to attend anger management courses but care should be taken before the court approves such attendance. It may not be specifically directed at domestic violence. However, the comments of Lord Justice Thorpe in *Re C*[187] should be noted. In that case, the last act of violence had occurred 3 years earlier; there had never been allegations that the father had been violent to the child and contact was taking place at a contact centre. Lord Justice Thorpe, when upholding a decision of the trial judge that the father, having attended an anger management course, should not be directed to attend a Domestic Violence Intervention Programme (DVIP), said that the detail of what a reference to a domestic violence intervention project involves was highly relevant to the exercise of the judge's discretion.

> 'A programme of this duration and intensity is another significant cost to the public purse. This father has successfully completed an anger management course, and I simply cannot follow and certainly not accept the assertion of the CAFCASS officer to the effect that the issues tackled in an anger management programme have no relevance to the issues that would be tackled in the DVIP programme. The modules in the DVIP programme include stopping physical violence, emotional abuse, effects of domestic violence on partners and children, responsible parenting, harassment and stalking, sexual abuse, jealousy and tactics of isolation. They may indeed be said to be separate ingredients but obviously the control of passion is part and parcel of each programme.'

---

[184] Children Act 1989, s 11A(7).
[185] Ibid, s 11A(5).
[186] Ibid, s 11A(6).
[187] [2009] EWCA Civ 994, at [19].

5.82 Felicity Kaganas has examined success rates for anger management and alcohol abuse programmes[188] and argues that the drop-out rate is particularly high in relation to voluntary programmes and it is the most dangerous men who fail to maintain attendance. Unstructured programmes targeting general health problems and those narrowly focusing on emotions such as anger are less likely to bring about change than those which aim to change the perpetrator's attitude, for example, towards those of the opposite gender. Married, employed, older men are more likely to succeed in reducing violence than younger, unmarried, unemployed men.[189]

DOMESTIC VIOLENCE AND CONTACT CENTRES

5.83 In 2001 Dame Elizabeth Butler-Sloss P emphasised the importance of the safety of the child.

'If there is any danger of misbehaviour by the offending parent, it is NOT appropriate to make an order for contact to take place at a supported contact centre.[190] The supervised contact centres may be appropriate ... They are however thin on the ground and the facilities may not be available.'[191]

This is underlined by subsequent research into contact centres.[192] The authors of the report were concerned about the way low vigilance, supported centres were being used to manage highly contentious child contact problems that arise in the context of domestic violence. Although all centres are screened for domestic violence, information provided by the parties (and in particular, the non-resident parent's solicitors) frequently failed to mention issues of domestic violence even when they were the main source of contention. Violent incidents occurred regularly at many centres and created anxiety for other users but centre coordinators did not necessarily take assertive action against the perpetrators. Despite a long-standing history of domestic violence many women found themselves having to be present in the building particularly when very young children or babies were involved. In spite of a history of abuse and a lack of comprehensive risk and safety assessment there were strong pressures at centres from both non-resident parents and co-ordinators for contact to move to a less supervised setting. Moreover, even if the centres knew of the

---

[188] '*Re L (Contact: Domestic Violence)*; *Re Y (Contact: Domestic Violence)*; *Re M (Contact: Domestic Violence)*; *Re H (Contact: Domestic Violence)*' [2000] CFLQ 311.

[189] See also Dobash and others *Re-education Programmes for Violent Men –An Evaluation* (Home Office Research findings No 46, 1996).

[190] For which see **11.84**.

[191] 'Contact and Domestic Violence' [2001] Fam Law 355.

[192] Aris, Harrison and Humphreys *Safety and Child Contact: An Analysis of the Role of Child Contact Centres in the Context of Domestic Violence and Child Welfare Concerns* (Department for Constitutional Affairs, 2002) summarised in Humphreys and Harrison 'Focusing on Safety – Domestic Violence and the Role of Child Contact Centres' [2003] 15 CFLQ 237, [2003] Fam Law 7 and Humphreys and Harrison 'Squaring the Circle' [2003] Fam Law 419.

history, it became easy for the issue to be lost, partly if there was a high turnover of staff and also because it became easier to focus on the present. Finally:

> 'Children in highly conflicted contact situations are some of the most distressed children in the population. Their needs for physical and psychological safety are very high given their past experience. In supported contact centres consultation with children about their needs in relation to contact rarely happened. While many children enjoy contact, some children are unhappy ... and our research showed that two thirds of the 21 children who filled in the child-friendly interview sheet wanted their mothers close by.'

MAKING SUBSTANTIVE ORDERS

5.84 When deciding the issue of residence or contact the court should, in the light of any findings of fact, apply the individual matters in the welfare checklist with reference to those findings; in particular, where relevant findings of domestic violence have been made, the court should in every case consider any harm which the child has suffered as a consequence of that violence and any harm which the child is at risk of suffering if an order for residence or contact is made and should only make an order for contact if it can be satisfied that the physical and emotional safety of the child and the parent with whom the child is living can, as far as possible, be secured before during and after contact.[193]

In every case where a finding of domestic violence is made, the court should consider the conduct of both parents towards each other and towards the child. In particular, the court should consider:

(a)   the effect of the domestic violence which has been established on the child and on the parent with whom the child is living;

(b)   the extent to which the parent seeking residence or contact is motivated by a desire to promote the best interests of the child or may be doing so as a means of continuing a process of violence, intimidation or harassment against the other parent;

(c)   the likely behaviour during contact of the parent seeking contact and its effect on the child;

(d)   the capacity of the parent seeking residence or contact to appreciate the effect of past violence and the potential for future violence on the other parent and the child;

---

[193]   PD 12J, para 26.

(e)   the attitude of the parent seeking residence or contact to past violent conduct by that parent; and in particular whether that parent has the capacity to change and to behave appropriately.[194]

5.85   As Baroness Butler-Sloss, the then President, made clear in the Court of Appeal in *Re L (Contact: Domestic Violence)*; *Re V (Contact: Domestic Violence)*; *Re M (Contact: Domestic Violence)*; *Re H (Contact: Domestic Violence)*,[195] although the family courts need to have a heightened awareness of the existence of and consequences on children of exposure to domestic violence between their parents or other partners:

'There is not, however, nor should there be, any presumption that, on proof of domestic violence, the offending parent has to surmount a prima facie barrier of no contact. As a matter of principle, domestic violence of itself cannot constitute a bar to contact. It is one factor in the difficult and delicate balancing exercise of discretion. The court deals with the facts of a specific case in which the degree of violence and the seriousness of the impact on the child and on the resident parent have to be taken into account. In cases of proved domestic violence, as in cases of other proved harm or risk of harm to the child, the court has the task of weighing in the balance the seriousness of the domestic violence, the risks involved and the impact on the child against the positive factors (if any), of contact between the parent found to have been violent and the child. In this context, the ability of the offending parent to recognise his past conduct, be aware of the need to change and make genuine efforts to do so, will be likely to be an important consideration. Wall J in *Re M (Contact: Violent Parent)*[196] suggested that often in cases where domestic violence had been found, too little weight had been given to the need for the father to change. He suggested that the father should demonstrate that he was a fit person to exercise contact and should show a track record of proper behaviour. Assertions, without evidence to back it up, may well not be sufficient.'

Examples

Re L (Contact: Domestic Violence)[197]

5.86   Allegations which amounted to 'a catalogue of sadistic violence' were found proved against the father of a mixed-race toddler. The mother had genuine fears based on reasonable grounds and direct contact would affect the mother in such a way that the child would be put at serious risk of major emotional harm. The Court of Appeal upheld a refusal of direct contact, the granting of indirect contact with a family assistance order and a refusal at the present time to grant a parental responsibility order.

---

[194]   Ibid, para 27. These factors are derived from the judgments of the Court of Appeal in *Re L (Contact: Domestic Violence); Re V (Contact: Domestic Violence); Re M (Contact: Domestic Violence); Re H (Contact: Domestic Violence)* [2000] 2 FLR 334.

[195]   [2000] 2 FLR 334, at 342.

[196]   [1999] 2 FLR 321, at 333.

[197]   [2000] 2 FLR 334.

Re V (Contact: Domestic Violence)[198]

5.87 Following a conviction for causing grievous bodily harm to the mother, and serving a sentence of imprisonment, the father underwent counselling in anger management and 'was a changed person'. The court refused an order for direct contact in the present because the child, aged 9 at the time of the appeal, who had witnessed the attack on his mother 5 years earlier, rejected the idea of direct contact and was still showing considerable distress. The Court of Appeal upheld the order which involved 'a difficult and delicate balance'.

Re M (Contact: Violent Parent)[199]

5.88 The father behaved violently towards the children's mother and drank to excess. Following the separation of the parents, the father harassed the mother and assaulted her both during an occasion of contact and, again, when she was pregnant with their second child. The elder child, who had witnessed some of the incidents, remembered them and remained disturbed. Wall J rejected the father's appeal against a refusal of direct contact by justices. He emphasised the need to show change and not just a willingness to change:[200]

> 'It is important for the father to understand that if he is to make a further application for direct contact ... he must address the findings which the justices have made. He needs to be able to satisfy the mother than he is no longer a threat to her security and stability or [that] of the children. He needs to satisfy her and the court that he no longer has a problem with alcohol and violence ... He will have to show a track record of proper behaviour. That will, in my judgment, include taking up the offer of indirect contact.'

Re A (Children: Contact)[201]

5.89 In 1997 the father stabbed the mother 16 times with a pair of scissors. He went to ground but in 2003 he re-appeared and sought contact with the children (aged 11 and 9 at the time of the hearing), denying responsibility for the attack. On the morning of the hearing he admitted responsibility. His appeal against the rejection of his application for direct contact, an order for contact by way of cards on the children's birthday and at Eid and a s 91(14) direction that he should make no application without permission for 3 years was dismissed. The order represented a significant development and was the best the father could hope for.

---

[198] Ibid.
[199] [1999] 2 FLR 321, FD; [2000] 2 FLR 334, CA.
[200] See also Dobash and others *Re-education Programmes for Violent Men – An Evaluation* (Home Office Research Findings No 46, 1996).
[201] [2005] All ER (D) 289 (Nov) (22 November 2005, CA).

Re H (A Child) (Contact: Domestic Violence)[202]

5.90 In 2001 the father of the child born in 1999 subjected the mother to a serious assault which required hospital treatment. In 2002 he applied for contact and in 2005 the court ordered six supervised contact sessions. The mother's appeal was allowed. It was wholly unacceptable for the judge to make an incomplete and selective reference to *Re L (A Child) (Contact: Domestic Violence)*[203] and he had not appeared to address the critical areas of the capacity of the father to appreciate the effect of past and future violence on the other parent and the child and his capacity to change. Retrial ordered.

Re F (Indirect Contact)[204]

5.91 Violence had been inflicted on the child's mother and witnessed by the child on a number of occasions by a father who had been at all times loving and affectionate towards the child. Direct contact as ordered. The father was later committed to prison for 68 breaches of non-molestation orders and the mother and child had had to move ten times to escape his attentions. The Court revoked an order for direct contact and a parental responsibility order and made an order under s 91(14) restraining further applications. However, it ordered indirect contact by cards and gifts, to be vetted by Cafcass, the judge being satisfied that such contact would not allow the father to trace the mother and child. The Court of Appeal dismissed the mother's appeal. Lord Justice Thorpe recognised that the critical question was not whether the means of transmission were proof against the discovery of the mother by the father, but whether subjectively she could feel confident that she would be secure. Without that sense of security her capacity to make the child feel secure would be reduced. Such a fundamental consideration should not go by default simply because it was not raised before the judge but the arrangements were working and if the feared consequences began to develop an application could be made for variation.

SEXUAL ABUSE

5.92 Sexual abuse is a form of domestic violence and allegations of sexual abuse need to be investigated in the same way as other forms of violence.

The continuing effect on the child of past sexual abuse by the applicant and the risk of abuse in the future are relevant considerations. However, as in the case of domestic violence, past sexual abuse does not give rise to a presumption that there should be no contact.[205]

---

202 [2005] EWCA Civ 1404.
203 [2000] 2 FLR 334.
204 [2006] EWCA Civ 1426, [2007] 1 FLR 1015.
205 *H v H (Child Abuse: Access)* [1989] 1 FLR 212.

5.93 If the allegations are disputed, the issue should normally be tried as a preliminary issue in the same way as disputed allegations of domestic violence.

5.94 The standard of proof for allegations of sexual abuse is the same as for other issues, namely the balance of probability:

'The balance of probability standard means that the court is satisfied an event occurred if the court considers that, on the evidence, the occurrence of the event was more likely than not. When assessing the probabilities the court will have in mind as a factor, to whatever extent is appropriate in the particular case, that the more serious the allegation the less likely it is that the event occurred and, hence, the stronger should be the evidence before the court concludes that the allegation is established on the balance of probability. Fraud is usually less likely than negligence. Deliberate physical injury is usually less likely than accidental physical injury. A stepfather is usually less likely to have raped and had non-consensual oral sex with his under-age stepdaughter than on some occasion to have lost his temper and slapped her. Built into the preponderance of probability standard is a serious degree of flexibility in respect of the seriousness of the allegation.

Although the result is much the same, this does not mean that where a serious allegation is in issue the standard of proof required is higher.'[206]

5.95 In cases brought under s 8, the court is assessing the risk to the child of there being contact. It does not have to be proved on the balance of probabilities that abuse will occur, only a risk that it will, and this is akin to the requirement for the making of a care order that harm is 'likely'. In the leading care case of *Re H and R (Child Sexual Abuse)*,[207] Lord Nicholls of Birkenhead defined 'likely' as 'a real possibility, a possibility which cannot sensibly be ignored having regard to the nature and gravity of the foreseen harm'. If the court cannot find the allegations of past abuse proved on the evidence, any unresolved judicial doubts and suspicions cannot be used to find that there is a risk of future abuse.[208] However, there may be other evidence relating to the applicant, for example a conviction for possessing child pornography, or a lack of appreciation of sexual boundaries, which would justify a finding of risk.

Where there is a risk, this has to be weighed together with all the other circumstances in deciding whether there should be no contact at all,[209] supervised contact,[210] or indirect contact. Even where the court finds that there is no risk, some degree of supervision albeit for a limited time may be necessary to allay any fears the child has or any reasonable anxiety of the resident parent which may adversely affect the child.[211]

---

[206] *Re H (Minors) (Sexual Abuse: Standard of Proof)* [1996] 1 FLR 80, per Lord Nicholls of Birkenhead at 96.

[207] Ibid, at 95.

[208] Ibid, at 99.

[209] As in the case of *Re R (A Minor) (Child Abuse: Access)* [1988] 1 FLR 206.

[210] As in the case of *H v H (Child Abuse: Access)* [1989] 1 FLR 212 and *Re P (Parental Responsibility)* [1998] 2 FLR 96.

[211] *Re P (Minors) (Sexual Abuse: Standard of Proof)* [1996] 2 FLR 333.

5.96 It is rare but not impossible for children to give evidence in support of allegations (see **4.23**). This makes fact-finding especially difficult especially when the only evidence is allegations by the child, given as hearsay evidence by a parent opposing contact. As the trial judge commented in a particularly difficult case, *D v B and Others (Flawed Sexual Abuse Enquiry)*[212] where the allegations against the father were based entirely upon what the children have said to their mother and repeated to others:

> 'Cases that turn on such evidence are invariably complex, especially where, as here, there is no physical or direct evidence to support the allegations. What the children say is hearsay (admissible but needs to be scrutinised with great care – see e.g. *Re N (child abuse: Evidence)*[213] and Butler-Sloss LJ in *Re P (child: compellability as witness)*[214] where she said: "A court presented with hearsay evidence has to look at it anxiously and consider carefully the extent to which it can properly be relied upon"). It is necessary to examine with particular care:
>
> a) What the children have said;
> b) The circumstances in which they said it;
> c) The circumstances in which any alleged abuse might have occurred (e.g. what happened during contact when abuse is said to have occurred? Who was present? etc).'

5.97 Even where the evidence about what the child is alleged to have said is extremely unsatisfactory, the fact-finding hearing should not be abandoned (see **5.68**). Thorpe LJ commented in *Re K (Sexual Abuse: Evidence)*[215] that on the facts of the particular case, it was crucial for the judge to hear the evidence of the person to whom the child spoke and the evidence of each parent. The judge had the responsibility for the management of a very difficult family breakdown and needed to evaluate each of the parents, both in relation to the primary issue and possibly in relation to the wider issues raised. The concerns inevitably flowing from the child's words should be weighed against the considerable detail to be found within the father's police statement.

5.98 In *Re B (Care Proceedings: Practice)*[216] Wall J commented that evidence of propensity or a psychiatric or psychological assessment of one of the parties is unlikely to be of any assistance in resolving a purely factual issue. Such an expert instructed to undertake an assessment of a parent for the first stage of a split hearing is unlikely to have a complete knowledge of the facts. Furthermore, such a witness may express opinions as to propensity or as to responsibility for a child's injuries which are both prejudicial and wrong. The assessment of adult credibility as to the responsibility for a child's injuries (often the critical factual issue) remains the function of the judge. In his judgment, he states:

---

[212] [2006] EWHC 2987 (Fam), [2007] 1 FLR 1295, at [15].
[213] [1996] 2 FLR 214.
[214] [1991] FCR 337, at 344; *sub nom R v B CC, ex p P* [1991] 2 All ER 65, at 72.
[215] [2008] EWCA Civ 1307, [2009] 1 FLR 921, at [18].
[216] [1998] 2 FLR 211, at 217–218.

'... a psychiatric or psychological assessment of the parties should not be permitted at the first stage of a split trial unless the particular facts of the case demonstrate that such evidence is or is likely to be directly relevant to the factual issue to be tried.'

Chapter 6

PATERNITY AND PARENTHOOD

INTRODUCTION

6.1   The last 30 years has seen a dramatic change in biological parenthood. Hitherto those unable to conceive had few ways of becoming parents, adoption – both formal after the passing of the Adoption of Children Act 1926 and informal – being the most common. Now assisted reproduction – either under regulated schemes or, again informal – and surrogacy have not only helped those unable to conceive but also those who have no opposite-sex partner. Legislation both to regulate these practices and to determine issues of parentage and parental responsibility has been required because, as Baroness Hale of Richmond wrote extra-judicially in 1996, 'some would think it a disadvantage for a child to be legally deprived of one half of the usual network of family and kin [and] the State might also suffer if there is only one parent legally liable to support the child'.[1] No longer can it always be assumed that the biological parent is the legal parent or vice versa.

6.2   Legal provision has had to be made to decide which of the participating adults should be treated or not treated as the mother, father or parent of the child. This is regulated by the Human Fertilisation and Embryology Act 2008 (HFEA 2008) which enables someone to be deemed to be the mother, father or parent of a child even there is no genetic parentage.[2] The Act also makes provision for deciding the legal status of adults who arrange for a child to be conceived in the course of surrogacy arrangements. Parental orders under s 54 can be granted in specified circumstances which have the effect of making the commissioning adults the child's parents.

6.3   The question of who is the child's mother, father or parent is not identical with whether that parent has parental responsibility. That issue is dealt with in **Chapter 7**.

6.4   An example of the legal, ethical and social problems which can arise from 'the widening of the frontiers of human existence'[3] by the use of assisted reproduction techniques is provided by *Leeds Teaching Hospitals NHS Trust v*

---

[1]   Hale *From the Test Tube to the Coffin* (The Hamlyn Lectures) (1996), at p 37. See also Herring 'Parents and children' in Herring (ed) *Family Law: Issues, Debate, Policy* (Willan, 2001).

[2]   For a critique of the Act and in particular its enabling same-sex families to be legitimated, see Smith 'Clashing symbols? Reconciling support for fathers and fatherless families after the Human Fertilisation and Embryology Act 2008' [2010] CFLQ 46.

[3]   *Re R (IVF: Paternity of Child)* [2005] UKHL 33, [2005] 2 FLR 843, per Lord Hope of Craighead at [5].

A.[4] Mr and Mrs A, a white couple underwent sperm injection treatment which was supposed to involve using the wife's egg and the husband's sperm. Mr and Mrs B, a black couple, were also undergoing treatment. By mistake, Mr B's sperm was used to fertilise Mrs A's eggs. After children were born to the couples the mistake was discovered. It was agreed that the children born to Mrs A should remain with the As but Mr B applied for a declaration of parentage, seemingly for the sole purpose of allowing the legal issues to be clarified. It was held that Mr A could not be treated as the father of the children under s 28(2) of the Human Fertilisation and Embryology Act 1990[5] because he had not consented to the actual treatment carried out, namely his wife's eggs being fertilised by another man's sperm, and consent could not be given retrospectively. Nor could he be treated as the father under s 28(3) because he was married to the woman receiving treatment. Mr B was the biological father and could not be excluded from legal paternity under s 28(6) because he had not consented to the treatment which in fact had been carried out. However, as only the use of his sperm connected him to the children, he did not have family life with the children so as to afford him Art 8 rights.

6.5   The State, society, kinship groups and the children themselves all have interests in knowing who the parents of children are both biologically and legally. Developments in science during the last 40 years have allowed this question to be determined with ever increasing reliability, moving from unreliable testimony and reliance on subjective evaluation of photographs, through blood testing which could exclude or not exclude the putative father from a group of men who could be the child's father, to the certainty of DNA testing (assuming the tests were properly carried out).[6] Issues also arise as to children's rights to know their parents, both in terms of knowing who their parents are and receiving information about them and to have a relationship with them (in the terms of Art 8 of the European Convention for the Protection of Human Rights and Fundamental Freedom, the right to family life).[7]

6.6   The determination of parentage does not remove all problems. Conception under regulated schemes will usually result in someone being deemed to be a parent and all others being deemed not to be, but where informal methods of reproduction have been used, disagreements between adults can arise as to the role the genetic donor or the biological parent's partner should play.[8] 'Courts also have to take into account not just biological and legal parentage but also psychological parenthood, '... one based on a

---

4   [2003] EWHC 259 (QB), [2003] 1 FLR 1091. See also Terry and Campbell 'Delicate bonds and blunt instruments' [2003] Fam Law 599 and Ford and Morgan '*Leeds Teaching Hospitals NHS Trust v A* – Addressing a misconception' [2003] CFLQ 199.

5   Now HFEA 2008, s 35.

6   See Freeman and Richards 'DNA testing and kinship: paternity, genealogy and the search for the "truth" of our genetic origins' in Ebtehaj, Lindley and Richards (eds) *Kinship Matters* (Hart Publishing, 2006).

7   See, for example, Booth and Bond 'Who is my parent and what does it mean anyway?' [2006] Fam Law 578.

8   See for example Didduck 'If only we can find the appropriate terms to use the issue will be

day-to-day interaction, companionship, shared experiences. The role can be fulfilled either by a biological parent or an adoptive parent or by any other caring adult-but never by an absent, inactive adult, whatever his biological or legal relationship to the child may be.'[9]

THE RIGHT TO BE A PARENT

6.7 Article 12 of the European Convention on Human Rights protects the right of 'men and women of marriageable age ... to marry and to found a family according to the national laws governing the exercise of this right'. However the European Court of Human Rights (ECtHR) has intervened little in how states choose to regulate this, holding for example in a Dutch case[10] that the rights of a couple to found a family were not infringed because they had failed to fulfil conditions in domestic law as regards the difference in age between them and the child.[11] Moreover a distinction is drawn between married couples and those who are not married. Unmarried couples are not recognised as having a right to found a family.[12]

6.8 In *Dickson v United Kingdom*[13] the ECtHR explained that a certain margin of appreciation is, in principle, accorded by the Court to states but the breadth of the margin varied depending on a number of factors, including the nature of the activities restricted and the aims pursued by the restrictions. Where a particularly important facet of an individual's existence or identity was at stake (such as the choice to become a genetic parent), the margin of appreciation would in general be restricted. Where, however, there was no consensus within the member states either as to the relative importance of the interest at stake or as to how best to protect it, the margin will be wider. This was particularly so where the case raises complex issues and choices of social strategy: 'the authorities' direct knowledge of their society and its needs means that they are in principle better placed than the international judge to appreciate what is in the public interest.' In such a case, the Court would generally respect the legislature's policy choice unless it is 'manifestly without reasonable foundation'. A wide margin would usually be accorded if the state was required to strike a balance between competing private and public interests or Convention rights. On the facts of the instant case the Court found that the

---

solved: Law, identity and parenthood' [2007] CFLQ 458 and Scherpe 'Tensions between legal, biological and social conceptions of parenthood' [2009] CFLQ 127 and also **7.36** and **10.46**).

[9] Goldstein, Freud and Solnit *Beyond the Best Interests of the Child* (The Free Press, 1973), at p 19.

[10] 8896/80 (Dec) March 10 1981 24 DR 177.

[11] Reid, *The Practitioner's Guide to the European Convention of Human Rights* (Sweet & Maxwell, 1998), at p 290 and Lester, Pannick and Herberg (ed) *Human Rights: Law and Practice* (LexisNexis Butterworths, 3rd edn, 2009), at paras 4.12.8 and 4.12.9.

[12] *Emonet v Switzerland* (Application 39051/03) 13 December 2007.

[13] (Application No 44362/04) [2008] 1 FLR 1315. The question of prisoners' rights to create a family is discussed in Williams 'Prisoners and artificial insemination: have the courts got it right?' [2002] CFLQ 217 and Jackson 'Prisoners, their partners and the right to family life' [2007] CFLQ 239.

UK had violated a married couple's right to found a family when it refused to allow artificial insemination facilities to be made available because the husband was serving a sentence of life imprisonment for murder with a tariff of 15 years. There was no place under the Convention system, 'where tolerance and broadmindedness are the acknowledged hallmarks of democratic society' for automatic forfeiture of rights by prisoners based purely on what might offend public opinion. While the maintaining of public confidence in the penal system had a role to play in the development of policy and punishment remains one of the aims of imprisonment, the Court underlined the evolution in European penal policy towards the increasing relative importance of the rehabilitative aim of imprisonment, particularly towards the end of a long prison sentence. The state, when developing and applying the policy, should concern themselves, as a matter of principle, with the welfare of any child but that could not go so far as to prevent parents who so wish from attempting to conceive a child in circumstances like those of the present case, especially as the second applicant was at liberty and could have taken care of any child conceived until such time as her husband was released.

6.9   In *Evans v United Kingdom*[14] a couple who were not married signed forms under the Human Fertilisation and Embryology Act 1990 consenting to treatment for the creation of embryos which would be stored and then used for in vitro fertilisation (IVF) treatment in which they would be implanted into the woman's uterus. After the relationship broke down the man withdrew his consent to the future use of the embryos, stating they should be destroyed. Both the judge at first instance and the Court of Appeal held that the consent could be validly withdrawn. The ECtHR found that there had been no violation of the woman's right to family life. The use of IVF treatment gave rise to sensitive moral and ethical issues on which there was no clear common ground between member states. The Act was the culmination of an exceptionally detailed examination of the issues and the fruit of much reflection and debate. The general interests it pursued were legitimate and consistent with Art 8. There was an irreconcilable conflict between the Art 8 rights of the woman and her former partner and her right to respect for the decision to become a parent should not be accorded greater weight than the man's right to respect for his decision not to have a genetically related child.[15]

6.10   Domestically, in *R v Human Fertilisation and Embryology Authority ex parte Blood*[16] and *L v Human Fertilisation and Embryology Authority*[17] courts have upheld decisions of the Human Fertislisation and Embryology Authority (HFEA) based on the Act not to permit the use of the deceased husband's sperm to be used for IVF treatment of his widow, the sperm in *Blood* being removed before death and in *L*, after death. Here, there might be thought to be

---

[14]   (Application No 6339/05) [2007] 1 FLR 1990; see also [2004] 1 FLR 67 (at first instance) and [2004] 2 FLR 766 in the Court of Appeal in domestic courts.

[15]   Although Art 12 had been argued in the domestic courts it was apparently not relied on before the ECtHR, presumably because the couple were not married.

[16]   [1997] 2 FLR 742 (first instance) and see at 758 for the Court of Appeal decision.

[17]   [2008] EWHC 2149 (Fam).

no competing Art 8 rights and the matter also fell within Art 12. *Blood* predated the Human Rights Act 1998 and the Convention was not mentioned in the judgments at first instance or in the Court of Appeal. In *L* Charles J rejected the submission made on behalf of the widow that because the man had died before any retrieval took place there is no balancing act to be carried out, or that his autonomy is not engaged.

'[In] my view, the nature of gametes and the purpose of their storage and use (ie to produce a child) means that in respect of issues relating to their retrieval, storage and use both: (a) the autonomy of the donor; and (b) the potential knock-on effects of their use without express and informed consent, are engaged after the death of the provider.'

The essential ingredients of the reasoning of the Grand Chamber in *Evans* relating to the HFEA rules by reference to a withdrawal of consent – the sensitive nature of the issues, the width of the margin of appreciation, the close consideration given to the legislation and the existence of competing rights – applied with at least equal force to the instant situation. The judge found that the differences between the impact and potential impact of the need for a continuing express consent in *Evans* and the instant case fell 'well short' of founding an argument that, on the facts of the case, the need for effective consent to storage in the UK, for subsequent use in the UK, was incompatible with the claimant's Convention rights.[18]

6.11 These problems have been resolved by the enactment of ss 39 and 40 of HFEA 2008 (see **6.35**).

6.12 In *Re R (IVF: Paternity of Child)*[19] the House of Lords had to deal with the problem caused by a change in circumstances during treatment. A woman (M) and her unmarried male partner (A) sought IVF treatment under the provisions of the Human Fertilisation and Embryology Act 1990 using donor sperm. A signed a consent stating that he intended to become the legal father of any resulting child. During the treatment but before M became pregnant, the relationship ended. M attended further treatment with her new partner P. She signed a new consent form but left the 'partner's name' blank. She conceived and gave birth to C. A applied for a declaration that he was C's father. The House of Lords upheld the decision of the Court of Appeal to refuse the declaration. In conferring the relationship of parent and child on people who were related neither by blood or marriage the rules must be applied very strictly. Important though legal certainty was it as even more important that the very significant relationship of parenthood should not be based on a fiction, in this

---

18   In *Blood* the widow was eventually able to rely on Arts 59 and 60 of the European Community Treaty to secure the removal of the sperm from the UK so that she could receive treatment in another member state of the European Community.

19   [2005] UKHL 33, [2005] 2 FLR 843. The decision of the Court of Appeal which was upheld by the House of Lords is reported at [2003] EWCA Civ 182, [2003] 1 FLR 1183. See also Lind '*Re R (Paternity of IVF Baby)* – unmarried paternity under the Human Fertilisation and Embryology Act 1990' [2003] CFLQ 327 and Fovargue '*Re R (IVF: Paternity of Child)*: assisting conception for the single infertile' [2006] CFLQ 423.

case that the child was born as a result of treatment provided for M and A together.[20] Nor did Art 8 assist. The assertion that A had a right to family life with the child when he was neither her social nor biological father assumed that there was already family life whereas this had to be established for the purpose of Art 8.[21]

6.13 Domestic courts have also had to consider the right to found a family in cases where their consent was sought for the sterilisation of children or adults who lacked capacity to consent. In *Re B (Minor) (Wardship)*,[22] for example, the House of Lords upheld decisions of the High Court and the Court of Appeal that a severally mentally handicapped 17-year-old girl who lacked the capacity to consent could be sterilised. 'It is clear beyond argument that for F her pregnancy would be a disaster. The only question is how she may best be protected against it.'[23] Lord Oliver of Aylmerton stressed that:

> 'No one of us is likely to forget that we live in a century which, as a matter of relatively recent history, has witnessed experiments carried out in the name of eugenics or for the purpose of population control, so that the very word 'sterilisation' has come to carry emotive overtones. It is important at the very outset, therefore, to emphasise as strongly as it is possible to do so, that this appeal has nothing whatever to do with eugenics. It is concerned with one primary consideration and one alone, namely the welfare and best interest of this young woman, an interest which is conditioned by the imperative necessity of ensuring, for her own safety and welfare, that she does not become pregnant.'[24]

In *Re F (Mental Patient: Sterilisation)*[25] the House of Lords affirmed the trial judge's decision to declare that a sterilisation of a woman of 36 who suffered from serious mental disability and who had the mental capacity of a child of 4 or 5 was in her best interests and was lawful.[26]

WHO ARE THE PARENTS?

6.14 There is a difference between birth parentage and legal parentage. In addition a distinction has to be drawn between being a mother or father and being a parent. The HFEA 2008 makes provision for some who are assisted to reproduce being treated as or not being treated as the child's mother or father and for some who are associated with those persons being treated as the child's parent or who have been provided with a child by way of surrogacy. The adoption of a child under the Adoption and Children Act 2002 may (and usually does) change its legal parentage. It has to be noted though that the

---

20 [2005] UKHL 33, [2005] 2 FLR 843, per Lord Walker of Gestingthorpe at [42].
21 Ibid, at [44].
22 [1988] AC 199, [1987] 2 FLR 314. See also *Re E (A Minor) (Medical Treatment)* [1991] 2 FLR 585 and *Re GF (Medical Treatment)* [1992] 1 FLR 293.
23 [1987] 2 FLR 314, per Lord Bridge of Harwich at 324.
24 Ibid, at 325.
25 [1990] 2 AC 1.
26 Cases involving adults would not be considered under the Mental Capacity Act 2005 by the Court of Protection.

provisions of HFEA 2008, ss 33 to 53 apply only to births brought about by a course of treatment services provided in the UK under licence. They do not apply where the births are as a result of 'self help' procedures where the donor of the sperm will be rated as both the biological and legal father. There will be cases where psychological parents lack the legal parentage they might have been afforded had the HFEA 2008 or its predecessor been in force at the time of conception. In *J v C (Void Marriage: Status of Children)*[27] for example, the mother (M) and the applicant (A) went through a ceremony of marriage. A had lived for many years as a man but was in fact a woman. Two children (C1 and C2) were born as a result of donor insemination. Between M's conception of C2 HFEA 1990 came into force. Three years after the birth of C2 M and A separated, M discovered that A was a woman and obtained a decree of nullity.[28] A changed gender and obtained a gender recognition certificate showing his gender to be male. In section 8 proceedings, the High Court held that A was neither the father nor a parent of C2. For the Act to have effect the time of conception had to be post-commencement. Furthermore to be a parent the applicant had to be married to the mother. A, being a woman, could not be married to her. A's appeal was dismissed by the Court of Appeal

6.15 Gamble and Ghevaert have commented that although the Act contains some positive advances, it continues to be based on the norm of two-parent families. Gay and lesbian parents involved in co-parenting may become caught in odd ways and single parents too remain poorly catered for.[29]

6.16 If persons are deemed under the Act to be the child's mother, father or parent despite lacking a genetic tie with the child, they will be able to register – and may be required to register – the child's birth with the Registrar of Births Deaths and Marriage showing themselves as the child's parents. Unlike adoption where there is a separate register, there will be nothing to show a lack of genetic relationship. Andrew Bainham has criticised this, arguing that the fundamental aim of birth registration is to uphold the right of the child to an accurate account of the event of the birth and to the identification of the two birth parents.[30]

Mothers and female parents

Birth parent

6.17 At common law the birth and legal mother of a child is not necessarily the genetic parent but the woman who carried the child to parturition.[31]

---

27 [2006] EWCA Civ 551 [2006] 2 FLR 1098.
28 *J v S-T (Formerly J) (Transsexual: Ancillary Relief)* [1997] 1 FLR 402.
29 Gamble and Ghaevert 'The Human Fertilisation and Embryology Act 2008: Revolution or evolution' [2009] Fam Law 730.
30 Bainham 'What is the point of birth registration?' [2008] CFLQ 449. See also 'Arguments about parentage' (2008) Cambridge Law Journal 322. For a rebuttal of some of the arguments in these papers, see Fortin 'Children's right to know their origins – too far, too fast? [2009] CFLQ 336.
31 *The Ampthill Peerage* [1977] AC 547, per Lord Simon of Glaisdale at 577.

6.18 Occasionally there are factual disputes about who is the mother of the child. Recently in *Haringey LBC v E*[32] parents claimed that although doctors had told them they could not have children of their own, the wife gave birth in Kenya to three 'miracle' children as a result of prayers said in their church. An attempt to have one child's birth videoed by a representative of the Red Cross failed as the 'birth' took place after the representative left the clinic. In care proceedings relating to one of the children Ryder J held that the child was not born to the mother but had had his true identity 'stolen from him by a cruel deception perpetrated by adults who are involved in international child trafficking'.[33]

Deemed maternity under the Human Fertilisation and Embryology Act 2008

6.19 Under HFEA 2008, s 33 the woman who is carrying or has carried a child as a result of the placing in her of an embryo or of sperm and eggs, and no other woman, is to be treated as the mother of the child. This applies whether the woman was in the United Kingdom or elsewhere at the time of the placing in her of the embryo or the sperm and eggs.

Deemed parenthood under the Human Fertilisation and Embryology Act 2008

6.20 Under s 42 of the Act if at the time of the placing in her of the embryo or the sperm and eggs or of her artificial insemination, W was a party to a civil partnership, the other party to the civil partnership is to be treated as a parent of the child unless it is shown that she did not consent to the placing in W of the embryo or the sperm and eggs or to her artificial insemination (as the case may be). This section applies whether W was in the UK or elsewhere at the time of the placing in her of the embryo or the sperm and eggs or of her artificial insemination. However, this does not affect any common law presumption in England and Wales and Northern Ireland that a child is the legitimate child of the parties to a marriage and in Scotland, does not apply in relation to any child who, by virtue of any enactment or other rule of law, is treated as the child of the parties to a marriage.[34]

6.21 Under s 43 of the Act if no man is treated by virtue of s 35 as the father of the child (see **6.32**) and no woman is treated by virtue of s 42 as a parent of the child (see **6.20**) but:

---

[32]   [2004] EWHC 2580, [2005] 2 FLR 47. See also *Lewisham CBC v D (Local Authority Disclosure of DNA Samples to Police)* [2010] EWHC 1238 (Fam), [2011] 1 FLR 895 and [2010] EWHC 1239 (Fam), [2011] 1 FLR 908. See also *Re P (Identity of Mother)* [2011] EWCA Civ 795, [2012] 1 FLR 351.

[33]   In order to prevent deception when a possible heir to the throne is born, it was the practice for many centuries for the birth to take place in the presence of officials including the Lord Chancellor.

[34]   HFEA 2008, ss 42(1) and 45(2) and (3).

- the embryo or the sperm and eggs were placed in W, or W was artificially inseminated, in the course of treatment services provided in the UK by a person to whom a licence applies;

- at the time when the embryo or the sperm and eggs were placed in W, or W was artificially inseminated, the agreed female parenthood conditions were met in relation to another woman (P), in relation to treatment provided to W under that licence; and

- P remained alive at that time,

then P is to be treated as a parent of the child. However, this does not affect any common law presumption in England and Wales and Northern Ireland that a child is the legitimate child of the parties to a marriage and in Scotland, does not apply in relation to any child who, by virtue of any enactment or other rule of law, is treated as the child of the parties to a marriage.[35]

6.22 'The agreed female parenthood conditions' are met in relation to P in relation to treatment provided to W under a licence if but only if:

- P has given the person responsible a notice stating that P consents to P being treated as a parent of any child resulting from treatment provided to W under the licence;

- W has given the person responsible a notice stating that W agrees to P being so treated;

- neither W nor P has, since giving notice given the person responsible notice of the withdrawal of P's or W's consent to P being so treated;

- W has not, since the giving of the notice, given the person responsible:

  - a further notice stating that W consents to a woman other than P being treated as a parent of any resulting child; or
  - a notice under s 37(1)(b) stating that W consents to a man being treated as the father of any resulting child; and

- W and P are not within prohibited degrees of relationship in relation to each other.[36]

Notices must be in writing and must be signed by the person giving it.[37]

---

[35] HFEA 2008, ss 43 and 45(2) and (3).
[36] Ibid, s 44(1).
[37] Ibid, s 44(2). Section 44(3) makes special provision a person who is unable to sign because of illness, injury or physical disability.

6.23 The section does not automatically confer parental responsibility on the woman deemed to be a parent. However she can acquire it under s 4ZA of the Children Act 1989 by:

- becoming registered as a parent of the child;

- making an agreement with the child's mother providing for her to have parental responsibility for the child; or

- by the court, on her application, ordering that she shall have parental responsibility for the child.

See **Chapter 7**.

6.24 Section 46 makes provision for what should happen under ss 42 and 43 if the embryo is transferred after the death of the civil partner or intended female parent.

6.25 If:

- the child has been carried by W as the result of the placing in her of an embryo;

- the embryo was created at a time when W was a party to a civil partnership;

- the other party to the civil partnership died before the placing of the embryo in W;

- the other party to the civil partnership consented in writing (and did not withdraw the consent):

  - to the placing of the embryo in W after the death of the other party; and
  - to being treated for the purpose of enabling the deceased woman's particulars to be entered as the particulars of the child's other parent in a relevant register of births as a parent of the child as the parent of any resulting child;

- W has elected in writing not later than the end of the period of 42 days (21 days in Scotland) from the day on which the child was born for the other party to the civil partnership to be treated for the purpose mentioned above as the parent of the child; and

- no one else is to be treated:

  - as the father of the child by virtue of s 35 or 36 or by virtue of s 45(2) or (3); or

‒ as a parent of the child by virtue of s 42 or 43 or by virtue of adoption,

then the other party to the civil partnership is to be treated for the purpose of enabling the deceased woman's particulars to be entered as the particulars of the child's other parent in a relevant register of births as a parent of the child.[38]

6.26 If:

• the child has been carried by W as the result of the placing in her of an embryo;

• the embryo was not created at a time when W was a party to a marriage or a civil partnership, but was created in the course of treatment services provided to W in the UK by a person to whom a licence applies;

• another woman consented in writing (and did not withdraw the consent):

‒ to the placing of the embryo in W after the death of the other woman; and
‒ to being treated for the purpose of enabling the deceased woman's particulars to be entered as the particulars of the child's other parent in a relevant register of births as a parent of the child as the parent of any resulting child;

• the other woman died before the placing of the embryo in W;

• immediately before the other woman's death, the agreed female parenthood conditions set out in s 44 were met in relation to the other woman in relation to treatment proposed to be provided to W in the UK by a person to whom a licence applies;

• W has elected in writing not later than the end of the period of 42 days (21 days in Scotland) from the day on which the child was born for the other woman to be treated for the purpose mentioned above as the parent of the child; and

• no one else is to be treated:

‒ as the father of the child by virtue of s 35 or 36 or by virtue of s 45(2) or (3); or
‒ as a parent of the child by virtue of s 42 or 43 or by virtue of adoption,

---

[38] HFEA 2008, s 46(1), (4) and (5).

then the other woman is to be treated for the purpose of enabling the deceased woman's particulars to be entered as the particulars of the child's other parent in a relevant register of births.[39]

Deemed parenthood by reason of adoption

6.27   Section 67(3) of the Adoption and Children Act 2002 provides that an adopted person is to be treated in law:

- as if born as the child of the adopters or adopter;

- the legitimate child of the adopters or adopter; and

- if adopted by a couple or the partner over the age of 21 of one of the child's parent as the child of the relationship of the couple in question.

Deemed parenthood by reason of a parental order

6.28   See **6.50**.

Fathers and male parents

Birth parent

6.29   At common law the birth father is the genetic father.

6.30   Figures from the Child Support Agency regarding DNA tests performed between 1 April 1998 and 31 March 2005 apparently revealed that DNA tests on men named by mothers as the father of the child showed positive results in just over four in five cases (83.9%). Many of the namings of those not shown to be the father may have been innocent mistakes on the part of mothers but there are cases in the law reports of fathers being deceived for years into believing they were the father of the child. In *P v B (Paternity: Damages for Deceit)*[40] it was determined by consent that the claimant was not the father of the child in question despite believing for 2 years that he was. The mother denied making any representations as to paternity and said that any representations which were made were honestly made. The man brought a claim for damages based on deceit, the claimant alleging he had spent over £90,000 supporting the child and the mother. As a preliminary issue the Court decided that the fact could give rise to an action based on deceit. In a similar case of *A v B (Damages: Paternity)*[41] where the claimant had believed for 7 years he was the father, the claim was tried and the claimant was awarded general damages of £7,500 on account of the substantial distress caused the claimant by the mother's

---

[39]   HFEA 2008, s 46(2), (4) and (5).
[40]   [2001] 1 FLR 1041.
[41]   [2007] 2 FLR 1051.

fraudulent representations and special damages of £14,900. In family proceedings Hogg J had refused the man's application for contact because of the mother's opposition.[42]

6.31 In *Re WB (Residence Orders)*[43] two children were born to an unmarried couple. The man discovered that he was not their father only after the couple separated and in the course of contact proceedings, the children then being aged 11 and 8. On appeal Thorpe J upheld the refusal by the family proceedings court to grant shared residence orders which would have had the effect of granting him parental responsibility. See also **10.39**.

Deemed parenthood under the Human Fertilisation and Embryology Act 2008

6.32 Under s 35 of the Act if at the time of the placing in her of the embryo or of the sperm and eggs or of her artificial insemination, W was a party to a marriage and the creation of the embryo carried by her was not brought about with the sperm of the other party to the marriage, then the other party to the marriage is to be treated as the father of the child unless it is shown that he did not consent to the placing in her of the embryo or the sperm and eggs or to her artificial insemination (as the case may be). This section applies whether W was in the UK or elsewhere at the time of the placing in her of the embryo or the sperm and eggs or of her artificial insemination. However, this does not affect any common law presumption in England and Wales and Northern Ireland that a child is the legitimate child of the parties to a marriage and in Scotland, does not apply in relation to any child who, by virtue of any enactment or other rule of law, is treated as the child of the parties to a marriage.[44]

6.33 Under s 36 of the Act, if:

- the embryo or the sperm and eggs were placed in W, or W was artificially inseminated, in the course of treatment services provided in the UK by a person to whom a licence applies;

---

[42] See also the Australian case of *McGill v McGill orse Magill v Magill* [2006] 231 ALR 277 and cases from the United States: *W v W* (1999) CS-98-2422 (Minnesota Court of Appeals), *Koelle v Zwiren* (1996) 672 NE2d 868 (Illinois Appellant Court), *Doe v Doe* (1998) 712 A2d 132 (Maryland Court of Appeals) and *Miller v Miller* (1998) 956 P2d 887 (Oklahoma Supreme Court) where recovery was permitted and *Nagy v Nagy* (1988) 258 Cal Rptr 787 (Californian Court of Appeal) and *Pickering v Pickering* (1988) 434 NW 2d 758 (S Dakota Supreme Court) where recovery was denied. References up to date as at the date of *A v B (Damages: Paternity)* 3 April 2007. See also Sterling 'DNA, paternity deceit and reliability of the birth certificate as historical document' [2009] Fam Law 701 and Wikely and Young 'Secrets and lies: no deceit down under for paternity fraud' [2008] CFLQ 81 (which discusses *Magill*) for useful discussions of the issue.
[43] [1995] 2 FLR 1023.
[44] HFEA 2008, s 35.

- at the time when the embryo or the sperm and eggs were placed in W, or W was artificially inseminated, the agreed fatherhood conditions (as set below) were satisfied in relation to a man, in relation to treatment provided to W under the licence;

- the man remained alive at that time; and

- the creation of the embryo carried by W was not brought about with the man's sperm,

then the man is to be treated as the father of the child. However this does not affect any common law presumption in England and Wales and Northern Ireland that a child is the legitimate child of the parties to a marriage and in Scotland, does not apply in relation to any child who, by virtue of any enactment or other rule of law, is treated as the child of the parties to a marriage.[45]

6.34 The 'agreed fatherhood conditions' are met in relation to a man (M) in relation to treatment provided to W under a licence if, but only if:

- M has given the person responsible a notice stating that he consents to being treated as the father of any child resulting from treatment provided to W under the licence;[46]

- W has given the person responsible a notice stating that she consents to M being so treated;

- neither M nor W has, since giving notice under either of the above provisions given the person responsible notice of the withdrawal of M's or W's consent to M being so treated;

- W has not, since the giving of the notice stating she consents to M being treated given the person responsible:

  - a further notice under that paragraph stating that she consents to another man being treated as the father of any resulting child; or
  - a notice stating that she consents to a woman being treated as a parent of any resulting child; and

- W and M are not within prohibited degrees of relationship in relation to each other.[47]

---

45 HFEA 2008, ss 36, 38(2) and (3).
46 Consent cannot be given retrospectively – *Leeds Teaching Hospitals NHS Trust v A* [2003] EWHC 259 (QB), [2003] 1 FLR 1091 and see **6.4**.
47 HFEA 2008, s 37(1).

Notice must be in writing and must be signed by the person giving it.[48]

6.35 Sections 39 and 40 make provision for what should happen under ss 35, 36 and 43 if the embryo is transferred after the death of the man providing the sperm or of the husband or another man who did not provide the sperm.

6.36 If:

- the child has been carried by W as a result of the placing in her of an embryo or of sperm and eggs or her artificial insemination;

- the creation of the embryo carried by W was brought about by using the sperm of a man after his death, or the creation of the embryo was brought about using the sperm of a man before his death but the embryo was placed in W after his death;

- the man consented in writing (and did not withdraw the consent):

  − to the use of his sperm after his death which brought about the creation of the embryo carried by W or (as the case may be) to the placing in W after his death of the embryo which was brought about using his sperm before his death; and
  − to being treated for the purpose of enabling the man's particulars to be entered as the particulars of the child's father in a relevant register of births as the father of any resulting child;

- W has elected in writing not later than the end of the period of 42 days (21 days in Scotland) from the day on which the child was born for the man to be treated for the purpose of enabling the man's particulars to be entered as the particulars of the child's father in a relevant register of births; and

- no-one else is to be treated:

  − as the father of the child by virtue of s 35 or 36 or by virtue of s 38(2) or (3); or
  − as a parent of the child by virtue of s 42 or 43 or by virtue of adoption,

then the man is to be treated for the purpose mentioned above as the father of the child. This applies whether W was in the UK or elsewhere at the time of the placing in her of the embryo or of the sperm and eggs or of her artificial insemination.[49]

---

[48] HFEA 2008, s 37(2). Section 37(3) makes special provision where a person who is unable to sign because of illness, injury or physical disability.
[49] Ibid, s 39.

6.37 If:

- the child has been carried by W as a result of the placing in her of an embryo;

- the embryo was created at a time when W was a party to a marriage;

- the creation of the embryo was not brought about with the sperm of the other party to the marriage;

- the other party to the marriage died before the placing of the embryo in W;

- the other party to the marriage consented in writing (and did not withdraw the consent):

    – to the placing of the embryo in W after his death; and
    – to being treated for the purpose of enabling the man's particulars to be entered as the particulars of the child's father in a relevant register of births as the father of any resulting child;

- W has elected in writing not later than the end of the period of 42 days (21 days in Scotland) from the day on which the child was born for the man to be treated for the purpose mentioned above as the father of the child; and

- no-one else is to be treated:

    – as the father of the child by virtue of s 35 or 36 or by virtue of s 38(2) or (3); or
    – as a parent of the child by virtue of s 42 or 43 or by virtue of adoption,

then the man is to be treated for the purpose of enabling the man's particulars to be entered as the particulars of the child's father in a relevant register of births as the father of the child.

This applies whether W was in the UK or elsewhere at the time of the placing in her of the embryo.[50]

6.38 If:

- the child has been carried by W as a result of the placing in her of an embryo;

---

50   HFEA 2008, s 40(1), (4) and (5).

- the embryo was not created at a time when W was a party to a marriage or a civil partnership but was created in the course of treatment services provided to W in the UK by a person to whom a licence applies;

- a man consented in writing (and did not withdraw the consent):

  – to the placing of the embryo in W after his death; and
  – to being treated for the purpose of enabling the man's particulars to be entered as the particulars of the child's father in a relevant register of births as the father of any resulting child;

- the creation of the embryo was not brought about with the sperm of that man;

- the man died before the placing of the embryo in W;

- immediately before the man's death, the agreed fatherhood conditions set out in s 37 were met in relation to the man in relation to treatment proposed to be provided to W in the UK by a person to whom a licence applies;

- W has elected in writing not later than the end of the period of 42 days (21 days in Scotland) from the day on which the child was born for the man to be treated for the purpose mentioned above) as the father of the child; and

- no-one else is to be treated:

  – as the father of the child by virtue of s 35 or 36 or by virtue of s 38(2) or (3); or
  – as a parent of the child by virtue of s 42 or 43 or by virtue of adoption,

then the man is to be treated for the purpose of enabling the man's particulars to be entered as the particulars of the child's father in a relevant register of births as the father of the child.

This applies whether W was in the UK or elsewhere at the time of the placing in her of the embryo.[51]

Deemed parenthood by reason of adoption

6.39 See **6.27**.

---

51 HFEA 2008, s 40(2), (3), (4) and (5).

Deemed parenthood by reason of a parental order

6.40   See **6.50**.

Persons deemed not to be the child's mother, father or parent

Adoption

6.41   Under section 67(3) of the Adoption and Children Act 2002 an adopted person if adopted by one of a couple under section 51(2) (the adopter's partner being the child's parent), is to be treated in law as not being the child of any person other than the adopter and the other one of the couple, and in any other case, is to be treated in law, subject to subsection (4), as not being the child of any person other than the adopters or adopter.

Effect of Human Fertilisation and Embryology Act 2008, ss 33–53

6.42   These sections do not apply where a child is subsequently adopted.

Where by virtue of the Act a person is to be treated as the mother, father or parent of a child, that person is to be treated in law as the mother, father or parent (as the case may be) of the child for all purposes.[52]

6.43   In relation to England and Wales and Northern Ireland, a child who:

- has a parent by virtue of s 42 (see **6.20**); or

- has a parent by virtue of s 43 (see **6.21**), who is at any time during the period beginning with the time mentioned in s 43(b) and ending with the time of the child's birth a party to a civil partnership with the child's mother,

is the legitimate child of the child's parents.[53] That person will therefore have parental responsibility for the child.[54] Where, however, a child has a parent by virtue of s 43 but the parent was not at the relevant time the civil partner of the mother, the child is not legitimate.[55]

6.44   Where by virtue of the Act a person is not to be treated as a parent of the child, that person is to be treated in law as not being a parent of the child for any purpose.

- Where a person is to be treated as the father of the child by virtue of s 35 or 36, no other person is to be treated as the father of the child.[56]

---

[52]   HFEA 2008, s 48(1).
[53]   Ibid, s 48(6).
[54]   Children Act 1989, s 2(1A).
[55]   Ibid, s 2(2A).
[56]   HFEA 2008, s 38(1).

- Where the sperm of a man who had given such consent as is required by para 5 of Sch 3 to the 1990 Act (consent to use of gametes for purposes of treatment services or non-medical fertility services) was used for a purpose for which such consent was required, he is not to be treated as the father of the child.[57]

- Where the sperm of a man, or an embryo the creation of which was brought about with his sperm, was used after his death, he is not, subject to s 39, to be treated as the father of the child whether W was in the UK or elsewhere at the time of the placing in her of the embryo or of the sperm and eggs or of her artificial insemination.[58]

- Where a woman is treated by virtue of s 42 or 43 as a parent of the child, no man is to be treated as the father of the child.[59]

- A woman is not to be treated as the parent of a child whom she is not carrying and has not carried, except where she is so treated:

  – by virtue of s 42 or 43; or
  – by virtue of s 46 (for the purpose mentioned in subs (4) of that section)).[60]

Surrogacy and parental orders

6.45 Surrogacy can be defined as an arrangement whereby a woman agrees with a couple that she will conceive using the sperm of a male member of the couple and will hand the child to the couple at birth with the intention that they will become the child's parents.[61] In *Re P (Surrogacy: Residence)*[62] Coleridge J commented that:

> 'Surrogacy arrangements are now a feature of contemporary life and are regulated by statute: the Human Fertilisation and Embryology Act [2008]. When all goes according to plan, they are a way of remedying the agony of childlessness. However, when the arrangements do not go according to plan the result, in human and legal terms is, putting it simply, a mess.'

6.46 Surrogacy arrangements will fall into two categories: those where it is possible for the commissioning parents to obtain a parental order under HFEA 2008, s 54 and those where it is not. In the latter cases the often complex situation will be governed by the normal provisions of common law and the Children Act 1989, assisted in some cases by adoption under the Adoption and Children Act 2002 (ACA 2002).

---

[57] HFEA 2008, s 41(1).
[58] Ibid, s 41(2).
[59] Ibid, s 45(1).
[60] Ibid, s 47.
[61] See Horsey 'Challenging presumptions: legal parenthood and surrogacy arrangements' [2010] CFLQ 449.
[62] [2008] 1 FLR 177, at [3].

Surrogacies where parental orders cannot be made

6.47 In *Re G (Surrogacy: Foreign Domicile)*[63] for example where a couple could not be granted a parental order because they were domiciled in Turkey, the child's mother, separated from her husband living in England, McFarlane J suggested that possibilities included:

- making an order under s 84 of ACA 2002, namely an order made by the High Court granting them parental responsibility, the court being satisfied that they intended to adopt the child under the law of a country or territory outside the British Islands;

- a residence order to the applicants with permission to take the child out of the jurisdiction;

- a special guardianship order;

- a Convention Adoption Order;

- orders under the inherent jurisdiction.

6.48 In *Re P (Surrogacy: Residence)*[64] a woman (M) entered into two separate surrogacy arrangements with two separate sperm donor fathers. In each case she falsely informed the donors and their wives that she had miscarried, raising both children as her own. The fathers discovered the true situation when child A was 6 years old and child B, 18 months. Child A's father reached an agreement with M that A would be told the true situation at an appropriate time in the near future and that he would then have contact. Child B's father applied for and was granted a residence order, supported by expert psychiatric evidence. M's appeal was dismissed.

6.49 In *Re TT (Surrogacy)*[65] the surrogate mother, M, decided to keep the child, T, after her birth and breast fed her. The donor father, Mr W, applied for residence when the child was 7 days old. There was no expert evidence other than evidence from the child's guardian. Baker J was concerned about a number of matters relating to M, Mr W and Mr W's wife. After a classic analysis using the welfare checklist he made a residence order in favour of M and a defined contact order in favour of Mr W with a review after a month.

> 'On balance, I have reached the clear conclusion that T's welfare requires her to remain with her mother. In my judgment, there is a clear attachment between mother and daughter. To remove her from her mother's care would cause a measure of harm. It is the mother who, I find, is better able to meet T's needs, in particular her emotional needs. I am satisfied that the mother would foster contact

---

63   [2007] EWHC 2814 (Fam), [2008] 1 FLR 1047.
64   [2008] 1 FLR 177 (first instance); [2007] EWCA Civ 1053, [2008] 1 FLR 198 (sub nom *Re P (Surrogacy: Appeal)* on appeal).
65   [2011] EWHC 33 (Fam), [2011] 2 FLR 392.

and a close relationship between T and her father. I am less confident that Mr and Mrs W would respect the relationship between T and her mother were they to be granted residence.'

Surrogacy and parental orders

6.50 Section 54 of HFEA 2008 provides that on an application made by two people the court[66] may make an order providing for a child to be treated in law as the child of the applicants if:

- The child has been carried by a woman who is not one of the applicants, as a result of the placing in her of an embryo or sperm and eggs or her artificial insemination whether the woman was in the UK or elsewhere at the time of the placing in her of the embryo or the sperm and eggs or her artificial insemination.

- The gametes of at least one of the applicants were used to bring about the creation of the embryo.

- The applicants are:
  - husband and wife;
  - civil partners of each other; or
  - two persons who are living as partners in an enduring family relationship and are not within prohibited degrees of relationship in relation to each other.

- The application for the order is made during the period of 6 months beginning with the day on which the child is born unless transitional provisions[67] apply.

- At the time of the application and the making of the order the child's home must be with the applicants; and either or both of the applicants must be domiciled in the UK or in the Channel Islands or the Isle of Man.[68]

- At the time of the making of the order both the applicants have attained the age of 18.

- The court must be satisfied that both:

---

[66] In England and Wales, this is any family court, in Northern Ireland the High Court or county court and in Scotland the Court of Session or Sheriff Court: s 54(9). In practice in England and Wales, applications will be heard by the High Court.

[67] HFEA 2008, s 54(11).

[68] No order may be made where this is not satisfied- see *Re G (Surrogacy: Foreign Domicile)* [2007] EWHC 2814 (Fam) [2008] 1 FLR 1047. See also *Z v B and C* [2011] EWHC 3181 (Fam) where a same sex couple were found to have domicile.

– the woman who carried the child; and

– any other person who is a parent of the child but is not one of the applicants (including any man who is the father by virtue of s 35 or 36 or any woman who is a parent by virtue of s 42 or 43;

have freely, and with full understanding of what is involved, agreed unconditionally to the making of the order. However the agreement of a person who cannot be found or is incapable of giving agreement is not required. The agreement of the woman who carried the child is ineffective if given by her less than 6 weeks after the child's birth.

- The court is satisfied that no money or other benefit (other than for expenses reasonably incurred) has been given or received by either of the applicants for or in consideration of:

  – the making of the order;
  – any agreement required above;
  – the handing over of the child to the applicants; or
  – the making of arrangements with a view to the making of the order,

  unless authorised by the court.[69]

6.51 A parental order transfers parental responsibility for a child in respect of whom it is made to the persons who obtained the order.[70]

6.52 The procedure for applying under s 54 is set out in Part 13 and Practice Direction 13 of the Family Procedure Rules 2010 (FPR 2010).[71]

In England and Wales the proceedings have to commence in the family proceedings court but if the application involves an international element it should be transferred at the first hearing to a nominated intercountry adoption court or the High Court as the issues raised could be of a similar standard of complexity and importance to those in cases of intercountry adoption.[72] Where the grant of the order may confer British citizenship on the child, notice of the proceedings should be given to the Home Office.[73]

6.53 The discretion to make a parental order is governed by s 1 of the Adoption and Children Act 2002 which provides that 'the paramount consideration of the court ... must be the child's welfare throughout his life'. When considering whether to make an order the court must have regard to all relevant matters including those set out in s 4 of the 2002 Act.[74]

---

[69]   HFEA 2008, s 54.

[70]   Adoption and Children Act 2002, s 46(1) as amended by Sch. 1 of the Human Fertilisation and Embryology (Parental Orders) Regulations 2010, SI 2010/985.

[71]   SI 2010/2955.

[72]   *Re G (Surrogacy: Foreign Domicile)* [2007] EWHC 2814 (Fam), [2008] 1 FLR 1047.

[73]   *Re IJ (Foreign Surrogacy Arrangement: Parental Order)* [2011] EWHC 921 (Fam), [2011] 2 FLR 646.

[74]   Human Fertilisation and Embryology (Parental Orders) (Consequential, Transitional and Saving Provision) Order 2010 (SI 2010/986); *Re L (Commercial Surrogacy)* [2010] EWHC 3146 (Fam), at [9].

6.54 In *Re G (Surrogacy: Foreign Domicile)*[75] McFarlane J suggested that the following principal matters needed to be borne in mind.

- Non-commercial surrogacy arrangements where neither of the commissioning couple is domiciled in the UK, whilst not illegal, are to be discouraged on the ground that it will not be open to the commissioning parents to apply for a parental order.

- Agencies involved in facilitating surrogacy arrangements, whether they are statutory or run by well-motivated volunteers, must ensure that they are fully familiar with the basic requirements of the area of the law within which these arrangements are made.

- Courts charged with determining an application under the Act have a duty to ensure that each of the qualifying conditions required of applicants is met in a case that has, or may have, an international element.

- Where a prospective surrogate mother is a married woman who has separated from her husband, all reasonable attempts should be made before the surrogacy process begins to establish that the husband does not consent to the proposed surrogacy arrangement.

- In the event that any agencies or solicitors involved in facilitating or advising on surrogacy arrangements are approached by a couple who are not domiciled in the UK must advise that the 'court may at any time make such orders as to costs as it thinks just'. Such orders for costs can be made against the commissioning non-domiciled couple and can include payment of the legal costs of the proceedings and payment for the costs incurred by Cafcass. Whether such costs should be ordered will depend upon the circumstances of each case given that the court takes the view that the provision for surrogacy arrangements for non UK domiciled couples are to be discouraged, it follows that the legal aspects to such arrangements should not become the financial responsibility of the British taxpayer. Any court faced with an application such as that which has been considered in this case should give active consideration to the making of a costs order.

6.55 In *Re IJ (Foreign Surrogacy Agreement: Parental Order)*[76] Hedley J added that those who travel abroad to make these arrangements should take advice from those knowledgeable in the domestic law of England and Wales so to be sure as to the problems that will confront them (not the least of which is immigration) and how they can be addressed. 'Reliance on advice from overseas agencies is dangerous as the provisions of our domestic and immigration law are often not fully understood.'

---

[75]   [2007] EWHC 2814 (Fam), [2008] 1 FLR 1047.
[76]   [2011] EWHC 921 (Fam), [2011] 2 FLR 646.

6.56 The Court has power to grant a parental order in favour of both applicants even if one of the applicants has died after the application is made but before the order is granted.[77]

6.57 The requirement that the court must be satisfied that no money or other benefit other than expenses reasonably incurred has been given causes perennial difficulties. Altruistic donation can mean that donors can incur financial loss (for example, loss of wages) or expenses (for example in relation to travel). However, the shortage of donors and the number of people seeking children means that there is a risk that there is a risk of commercial arrangements. The legislature decided as a matter of policy to outlaw such payments.[78]

6.58 In October 2011 the HFEA revised its guidance to clinics after extensive consultation in order to reflect the value of donation and set a level of compensation which would not deter those interested in donation but would retain donors already in the system, without attracting those who are merely financially motivated.[79] The guidance applies only to licensed clinics but may be taken into account when a court considers whether to authorise payments.[80]

6.59 The court has to deal not with arrangements made by licensed clinics whether in the UK but also informal arrangements made here or abroad. Retrospective authorisation is possible.[81] No matter how much commercial arrangements may be deplored the court is faced with a situation where a child is already living with the applicants and his welfare is paramount (see **6.53**). In all but the most exceptional cases therefore retrospective approval of the payments will be given.[82]

6.60 Previously as Hedley J commented in *Re X (Foreign Surrogacy)*[83] the statute offers no guidance as to the basis for approval.

> 'It is clearly a policy decision that commercial surrogacy agreements should not be regarded as lawful. Equally there is clearly a recognition that sometimes there may be reasons to do so. It is difficult to see what reason Parliament might have in mind other than the welfare of the child under consideration.'

---

[77] *A v P (Surrogacy: Parental Order: Death of Applicant)* [2011] EWHC 1738 (Fam), [2011] Fam Law 1080.

[78] For a philosophical and utilitarian argument against payments regarding donation of human tissue, see , for example, Titmuss *The Gift Relationship* (Pantheon, 1970).

[79] Available at: www.hfea.gov.uk/6700.html. Also see the HFEA Guidance Section 13A.

[80] Ibid.

[81] *Re C (Surrogacy: Payments)* [2002] EWHC 157 (Fam), [2002] 1 FLR 909; *Re X (Children) (Parental Order: Foreign Surrogacy)* [2008] EWHC 3030 (Fam), [2009] 1 FLR 733.

[82] See also Gamble 'International Surrogacy Law Conference in Las Vegas October 2011' [2012] Fam Law 198.

[83] Ibid. See also Gamble and Ghevaert *'Re X and Y (Foreign Surrogacy)*: "A trek through a thorn forrest" Thesis', [2009] Fam Law 239 for a discussion of the problems illustrated by the case.

Given that there was a wholly valid public policy justification lying behind s 30(7), welfare considerations cannot be paramount but 'of course, are important'. Such an approach accorded with that adopted in previous cases and with the approach adopted towards the authorising of breaches of the adoption legislation.[84]

Hedley J suggested that that the court should ask:

- Was the sum paid disproportionate to reasonable expenses?

- Were the applicants acting in good faith and without 'moral taint' in their dealings with the surrogate mother?

- Were the applicants party to any attempt to defraud the authorities?

In *Re S (Parental Order)*[85] Hedley J added that the following matters should also be considered where the arrangements were made abroad. The court must be astute to ensure that:

- commercial surrogacy agreements are not used to circumvent childcare laws in this country, so as to result in the approval of arrangements in favour of people who would not have been approved as parents under any set of existing arrangements in this country;[86]

- it does not become involved in anything that looks like a simple payment for effectively buying children overseas. That has been ruled out in this country and the court should not be party to any arrangements which effectively allow that.

- sums of money which might look modest in themselves are not in fact of such a substance that they overbear the will of a surrogate.

See also *Re X (Children) (Parental Order: Retrospective Authorisation of Payments)*.[87]

6.61 In case where approval is sought, the child should ordinarily be separately by a guardian.[88]

---

84   For example *Re AW (Adoption Application)* [1993] 1 FLR 62.
85   [2009] EWHC 2977 (Fam), [2010] 1 FLR 1156.
86   See also *Re K (Foreign Surrogacy)* [2010] EWHC 1180 (Fam), [2011] 1 FLR 533; *Re L (Parental Order: Foreign Surrogacy)* [2010] EWHC 3146 (Fam); *Re IJ (Foreign Surrogacy Agreement: Parental Order)* [2011] EWHC 921 (Fam), [2011] 2 FLR 646; *A v P (Surrogacy: Parental Order: Death of Applicant)* [2011] EWHC 1738 (Fam), [201]] Fam Law 1080.
87   [2011] EWHC 3147 (Fam), [2012] Fam Law 286.
88   Ibid.

PSYCHOLOGICAL PARENTS

6.62 The phrase 'psychological parent' was, if not coined, at least given circulation by Goldstein, Freud and Solnit in *Beyond the Best Interests of the Child*[89] who defined it as:

> '... one based on a day-to-day interaction, companionship, shared experiences. The role can be fulfilled either by a biological parent or an adoptive parent or by any other caring adult-but never by an absent, inactive adult, whatever his biological or legal relationship to the child may be.'[90]

The direct cause of this emotional relationship is not the biological relationship:

> 'This attachment results from day-to-day attention to his needs for physical care, nourishment, comfort, affection and stimulation. Only a parent who provides for these needs will build a psychological relationship to the child ... and will become his "psychological parent" in whose care the child can feel valued and "wanted".'[91]

6.63 In *Re G (Children)*[92] Baroness Hale of Richmond, referring to *Beyond the Best Interests of the Child*, described the various meanings of 'parent' as follows.

> 'There are at least three ways in which a person may be or become a natural parent of a child, each of which may be a very significant factor in the child's welfare, depending upon the circumstances of the particular case. The first is genetic parenthood: the provision of the gametes which produce the child. This can be of deep significance on many levels. For the parent, perhaps particularly for a father, the knowledge that this is 'his' child can bring a very special sense of love for and commitment to that child which will be of great benefit to the child (see, for example, the psychiatric evidence in *Re C (MA) (An Infant)*.[93] For the child, he reaps the benefit not only of that love and commitment, but also of knowing his own origins and lineage, which is an important component in finding an individual sense of self as one grows up. The knowledge of that genetic link may also be an important (although certainly not an essential) component in the love and commitment felt by the wider family, perhaps especially grandparents, from which the child has so much to gain.

> 'The second is gestational parenthood: the conceiving and bearing of the child. The mother who bears the child is legally the child's mother, whereas the mother who provided the egg is not: 1990 Act, s 27. While this may be partly for reasons of certainty and convenience, it also recognises a deeper truth: that the process of carrying a child and giving him birth (which may well be followed by breast-feeding for some months) brings with it, in the vast majority of cases, a very special relationship between mother and child, a relationship which is different from any other.

---

89   (The Free Press, 1973).
90   Ibid, at p 19.
91   Ibid, at p 17.
92   [2006] UKHL 43, [2006] 2 FLR 629, at [33]–[37].
93   [1966] 1 WLR 646.

The third is social and psychological parenthood: the relationship which develops through the child demanding and the parent providing for the child's needs, initially at the most basic level of feeding, nurturing, comforting and loving, and later at the more sophisticated level of guiding, socialising, educating and protecting.

Of course, in the great majority of cases, the natural mother combines all three. She is the genetic, gestational and psychological parent. Her contribution to the welfare of the child is unique. The natural father combines genetic and psychological parenthood. His contribution is also unique. In these days when more parents share the tasks of child rearing and breadwinning, his contribution is often much closer to that of the mother than it used to be; but there are still families which divide their tasks on more traditional lines, in which case his contribution will be different and its importance will often increase with the age of the child.

But there are also parents who are neither genetic nor gestational, but who have become the psychological parents of the child and thus have an important contribution to make to their welfare. Adoptive parents are the most obvious example, but there are many others.'

6.64   In a dispute about the status to be given to a particular person, the result will depend to some extent on his psychological relationship with the child but also on the child's psychological relationship with his parents. Unlike biological parentage, children can have more than two psychological parents.

Unless the psychological parent is married or in a civil partnership with a parent of the child in circumstances in which the child is treated as a 'child of the family',[94] the psychological parent will have no present or future liability to maintain the child, for example, by way of an order being made under Sch 1 to the Children Act 1989.[95]

6.65   The issue of whether or not weight and, if so, how much weight, should be given in proceedings under the Act to a party who is the child's legal or biological parent is discussed in detail at **10.68**. In *Re G (Children)*[96] Baroness Hale commented that 'the fact that CG is the natural mother of these children in every sense of that term, while raising no presumption in her favour, is an important and significant factor in determining what will be the best for them now and in the future'.[97]

---

[94]   See Matrimonial Causes Act 1973, s 41(3) and Civil Partnership Act 2004, s 75(3).
[95]   *T v B* [2010] EWHC 1444 (Fam), [2010] 2 FLR 1966. See also Gamble and Ghevaert 'Lesbian Mothers in Dispute: *T v B*' [2010] Fam Law 1203.
[96]   Ibid, at [44].
[97]   See also Everett and Yeatman 'Are some parents more natural than others?' [2010] CFLQ 290.

A CHILD'S RIGHT TO KNOWLEDGE ABOUT HIS PATERNITY

The child's right to know

6.66 Professionals have long held the view that it is important for a child to have knowledge of his or her origins. In 1972, the Houghton Committee on Adoption[98] observed that:

'The importance of telling a child that it has been adopted has long been recognised and there is a growing recognition that the child should be told early and helped to understand it more fully as he grows older. It is also increasingly recognised that at some stage the child will need to know about his origins – the positive factors about his parents, such as any special qualities, gifts or interests; their appearance; their reasons for giving him up and any medical background which may be relevant. This kind of information helps the proper development of a sense of identity and gives the child ... a fuller understanding of him as an individual with his own unique combination of characteristics, both inherited and acquired from his upbringing and environment.'

Consequently, the Adoption Acts (now ss 60 and 74 of the Adoption and Children Act 2002) give an adult who has been adopted some right of access to his original birth certificate. In 1979, the Law Commission observed that the right to know the facts about one's origins was increasingly recognised.[99] By 1992, the *Interdepartmental Review of Adoption Law*[100] expressed the view that 'For many years now there has been increasing recognition that a child's knowledge of his or her background is crucial to the formation of positive self-identity'. It continued by saying that:

'It is essential that an adopted child of sufficient age and understanding is told that he or she is adopted and what this means ... Some adopted people experienced considerable trauma to discover by chance – and sometimes at quite a late age – that they were adopted.'

6.67 However Professor Jane Fortin has argued that although adopted children may certainly benefit from information about their biological parents, this is not necessarily so for other groups such as children conceived by donor. She suggests that arguments that there is ' a right to know' are prompted by what are essentially adult concerns over the extent to which putative fathers should be allowed to develop relationships with children they claim to have produced. 'If indeed all children really did have a "right" to have their parents' identity established, the next logical step would be to introduce compulsory DNA testing for all adults and babies prior to the birth registration process.'[101]

---

[98] Report of the Departmental Committee on the Adoption of Children Cmnd 5107.
[99] *Family Law: Illegitimacy* (Working Paper No 74).
[100] (Department of Health), at paras 4.1 and 27.4.
[101] Fortin 'Children's right to know their origins – too far, too fast?' [2009] CFLQ 336. Professor Fortin examines the issue in depth in *Children's Rights and the Developing Law* (Cambridge University Press, 3rd edn, 2009), ch 13.

6.68 Since the decision of the House of Lords in *S (an Infant, by her Guardian ad Litem the Official Solicitor to the Supreme Court) v S; W v Official Solicitor (acting as Guardian ad Litem for a Male Infant named PHW)* (henceforward *S v S*),[102] (see **6.92**) most courts which have considered the issue of directing blood tests have regarded a child knowing who his genetic father is as normally being in his best interests.

6.69 In *Mikulic v Croatia*,[103] this 'right to know' has been recognised by the European Court of Human Rights as being an Art 8 right.

> '[Respect] for private life requires that everyone should be able to establish details of their identity as individual human beings and that an individual's entitlement to such information is of importance because of its formative implications for his or her personality (see the *Gaskin v United Kingdom* judgment [1990] 1 FLR 167).'

It was also recognised by the domestic court in *R (Rose) v Secretary of State for Health*[104] when Scott-Baker J ruled that Art 8 was engaged when two claimants who had been born as a result of artificial insemination sought information about the anonymous donors.

> 'Respect for family life ... plainly includes the right to obtain information about a biological parent who will inevitably have contributed to the identity of his child.'

In *B v A (Parental Responsibility)*[105] a man whose sperm was used to father a child born to a lesbian couple was granted parental responsibility.

Conversely a child has the right not to have the identity of the person assumed to be her father changed unilaterally. In *Re L (Family Proceedings Court) (Appeal: Jurisdiction)*[106] the court set aside a declaration of non-paternity which had been made in the Family Proceedings Court, without the knowledge or participation of the child or her mother, on an appeal by the mother's husband against a decision by the Child Support Agency (CSA) that he was the child's father.

> 'The order made [by the FPC] has brought into question the issue of her parentage ... [The decision] is an affront to justice. L has been the victim ... of a miscarriage of justice in a matter going ... to the very heart of her identity as a human being. Her human rights have been infringed.'[107]

The topic is discussed further at **6.94**.

---

102 [1972] AC 24.
103 *Mikulic v Croatia* [2002] 1 FCR 720.
104 [2002] EWHC 1593 (Admin), [2002] 2 FLR 962.
105 [2006] EWHC 0002 (Fam).
106 [2003] EWHC 1682 (Fam), [2005] 1 FLR 210.
107 Per Munby J at [23]–[24].

The father's right to know

6.70   In *Re T (Paternity: Ordering Blood Tests)*,[108] Bodey J held that a child had a right of respect for his private life under Art 8 of the European Convention for the Protection of Human Rights and Fundamental Freedoms 1950 in the sense of having knowledge of his identity which encompassed his true paternity. In the light of the comments of Butler-Sloss LJ in *Re R (A Minor) (Contact)*[109] (see below), it is likely that this statement will be generally accepted by the courts. The father has a right to family life but it is uncertain whether the right to be acknowledged as the father forms part of this right other than as an adjunct to being afforded the opportunity of a relationship with the child by way of contact and being kept informed of his progress. It can be argued that the article recognises the right to the status as father, for example, being given the opportunity of taking part in adoption proceedings.[110] In *Dawson v Wearmouth*,[111] a case involving the change of surname of a child born to unmarried parents, Lord Jauncey of Tullichettle said:

> 'The father's wish that his son should bear his surname rather than that of this man [with whom he has no connection either biological or directly familial] is understandable. The child has after all not a drop of Wearmouth blood in his veins.'

He also suggested that the matter was important to society generally:

> 'The surname is ... a biological label which tells the world at large that the blood of the name flows in its veins.'

6.71   There are, however, competing rights including the right of the child, the mother and her partner that their life and privacy should not be intruded upon or interfered with.[112] A balance therefore has to be struck and in striking the balance the court has to consider the welfare of the child.[113]

The family's right to know

6.72   Currently there is little support from reported cases to support a proposition that members of a family have the right to know that a child has been born to another member. Any discussion that there has been has

---

108   [2001] 2 FLR 1190.
109   [1993] 2 FLR 762. And see *R (Rose) v Secretary of State for Health and Human Fertilisation and Embryology Authority* [2002] EWHC 1593 (Admin), [2002] 2 FLR 962.
110   See *Re H; Re G (Adoption: Consultation of Unmarried Fathers)* [2001] 1 FLR 646 and *Re J (Adoption: Contacting Father)* [2003] EWHC 199 (Fam), [2003] 1 FLR 933.
111   [1999] 1 FLR 1167, at 1175.
112   *Re T (Paternity: Ordering Blood Tests)* [2001] 2 FLR 1190 and *Yousef v The Netherlands* (Application No 33711/96) [2003] 1 FLR 210 and *Anayo v Germany* (Application No 20578/07) [2011] 1 FLR 1883.
113   *Re L (Contact: Domestic Violence); Re V (Contact: Domestic Violence); Re M (Contact: Domestic Violence); Re H (Contact: Domestic Violence)* [2000] 2 FLR 334 and *Hendriks v The Netherlands* (1983) 5 EHRR 223.

approached the issue by considering the risks and benefits to the child of family members being informed. In *Birmingham City Council v S, R and A*[114] for example, an application by a father that a local authority should be restrained from informing his devout Muslim parents of his child's birth out of wedlock and the fact that she was subject to care proceedings was dismissed. If her mother was unable to care for her the only prospect she might have of growing up within her own family, and retain links with both her father and mother was if her father's family could care for her. The court would wish to preserve the father's position within his own family and to avoid upset to him and them if that were in A's best interests and her rights permitted it. However in the circumstances of the case, they did not. Whilst rejection by her family would be damaging for A when she learned of it in the future it was less likely to occur and it would be less damaging for her than losing the opportunity to remain in the care of her family. By way of comparison in *Re X (Care: Notice of Proceedings)*[115] M, an unmarried Bangladeshi 17-year-old girl, gave birth to C. The father, her brother in law, was unaware of the birth. The court heard evidence that if the liaison between M and F became known in the wider community, she would face ostracism and F's family would be placed under great strain. 'The overall effect could be catastrophic'. The court held that on balance it was in the best interests of C and the wider family that F should not be given notice of adoption proceedings.[116]

ESTABLISHING PATERNITY

6.73 The right to challenge or prove paternity by recourse to court proceedings is protected by Arts 6(1), 8 and 14 of the European Convention on Human Rights. A fair balance has to be struck between a general interest in protecting legal certainty in family relationships and an individual's right, for example, to have at least one occasion to reject or prove one's paternity of a child[117] or the child's legitimate interest in knowing the identity of her father.[118] There is no absolute rule as to whether or not respect for family life requires that biological and social reality prevails over a legal presumption of paternity. In *Kroon v Netherlands*,[119] the European Court of Human Rights held that it

---

114 [2006] EWHC 3065 (Fam), [2007] 1 FLR 1223, per Sumner J.

115 [1996] 1 FLR 186.

116 See also Mitchell *Adoption and Special Guardianship: a Permanency Handbook* (2009), at paras 17.64–17.86 for a discussion of when courts have permitted a local authority to withhold information of the birth of a child and subsequent adoption proceedings from fathers who do not have parental responsibility and members of the wider family. The position is different for fathers with parental responsibility – see *A Local Authority v M and F; The Children (By Their Guardian)* [2009] EWHC 3172 (Fam), [2010] 1 FLR 1355 and *Re A (A Father: Knowledge of Child's Birth)* [2011] EWCA Civ 273, [2011] 2 FLR 123.

117 *Mizzi v Malta* (Application No 26111/02) [2006] 1 FLR 1048; *Shofman v Russia* (Application No 74826/01) [2006] 1 FLR 680 (both cases where a husband sought to rebut the presumption of paternity based on his marriage to the child's mother; *Rózanski v Poland* (Application No 55339/10) [2006] 2 FLR 1163 (putative father who was not married to but cohabited with the child's mother seeking to prove paternity).

118 *Tavli v Turkey* (Application No 11449/02) [2007] 1 FLR 1136.

119 (Application No 18535/91) [1994] ECHR 35.

did but in *Rózanski v Poland*[120] the Court drew a distinction between cases where parents were in agreement (as in *Kroon*) and those where they were not.

6.74   Under s 55A of the Family Law Act 1986 any person may apply to the High Court, a county court or a magistrates' court for a declaration as to whether or not a person named in the application is or was the parent of another person so named.[121] The court shall have jurisdiction to entertain the application if, and only if, either of the persons named in it:

*   is domiciled in England and Wales on the date of the application; or

*   has been habitually resident in England and Wales throughout the period of one year ending with that date; or

*   died before that date; and either:

    –   was at death domiciled in England and Wales; or
    –   had been habitually resident in England and Wales throughout the period of one year ending with the date of death.[122]

The court must refuse to hear the application unless:

*   it considers that the applicant has a sufficient personal interest in the determination of the application (but this is subject to Child Support Act 1991, s 27);

*   the applicant is the parent of a named person;

*   a named person is the parent of the applicant; or

*   a named person is the other parent of a named child of the applicant.[123]

Where one of the persons named in it is a child, the court may refuse to hear the application if it considers that the determination of the application would not be in the best interests of the child.[124]

Where a court refuses to hear an application it may order that the applicant may not apply again for the same declaration without leave of the court.[125]

---

[120]   [2006] 2 FLR 1163.
[121]   See, for example, *M v W (Declaration of Parentage)* [2006] EWHC 2341 (Fam), [2007] 2 FLR 270.
[122]   Family Law Act 1986, s 55A(2).
[123]   Ibid, s 55A(3) and (4).
[124]   Ibid, s 55A(5).
[125]   Ibid, s 55A(6).

Where a declaration is made by a court on an application the court must notify the Registrar General that it has been made.[126]

6.75 The only relief available under the section is the granting of a declaration. Absent other statutory powers, the court cannot stay other proceedings, for example, staying enforcement of child support liabilities, pending the investigation of the paternity issue.[127]

6.76 In addition any person may apply to the High Court or a county court for a declaration under s 56 of the Act that:

- he is the legitimate child of his parents;[128]

- he has become a legitimated person;

- he has not become a legitimated person.[129]

6.77 A court shall have jurisdiction to entertain an application under this section if, and only if, the applicant:

- is domiciled in England and Wales on the date of the application; or

- has been habitually resident in England and Wales throughout the period of one year ending with that date.[130]

Where a declaration is made the court must notify the Registrar General.[131]

6.78 On an application for a declaration under s 55A or 56 the court may at any stage of the proceedings, of its own motion or on the application of any party to the proceedings direct that all necessary papers in the matter be sent to the Attorney-General. The Attorney-General, whether or not he is sent papers in relation to the application may intervene in the proceedings on that application in such manner as he thinks necessary or expedient and argue before the court any question in relation to the application which the court considers it necessary to have fully argued.

Where any costs are incurred by the Attorney-General in connection with any such application the court may make such order as it considers just as to the payment of those costs by the parties.[132]

---

[126]   Ibid, s 55A(7).
[127]   *Law v Inostroza Ahumuda* [2010] EWCA Civ 1149, [2011] 1 FLR 708.
[128]   Ibid, s 56(1).
[129]   Ibid, s 56(2).
[130]   Ibid, s 56(3).
[131]   Ibid, s 56(4).
[132]   Ibid, s 59.

6.79 When considering applications made under s 55A or 56 and the truth of the proposition to be declared is proved to the satisfaction of the court, the court must make that declaration unless to do so would manifestly be contrary to public policy.[133]

If the court dismisses the application it does not have power to make any declaration for which an application has not been made.[134]

Any declaration made under s 55A or 56 is binding on everybody and not just the parties to the application.[135]

6.80 Under s 27 of the Child Support Act 1991 where a child support officer is considering whether to make a maintenance assessment with respect to a person who is alleged to be a parent of the child in question and the alleged parent denies that he is one of the child's parents and the child support officer is not satisfied that the case falls within one of those grounds set out in s 26(2) (adopted child, paternity by gamete donation or previous finding by a court) the Secretary of State or the person with care may apply to the court for a declaration as to whether or not the alleged parent is one of the child's parents. If, on hearing the application the court is satisfied that the alleged parent is, or is not, a parent of the child in question it shall make a declaration to that effect. However a declaration under this section has effect only for the purposes of the Child Support Act.

6.81 Courts may also make findings about paternity in other proceedings where the matter is in issue but the findings will bind only the parties to the proceedings.

PROVING PATERNITY

6.82 In *The Ampthill Peerage*,[136] Lord Simon said that while motherhood is based on fact, 'fatherhood, by contrast, is a presumption'. This reflected the state of scientific knowledge in 1976 but the introduction of DNA testing of blood has now made it possible to establish paternity with near certainty, bringing about what Professor Cretney has called 'a profound revolution in forensic practice'.[137] However, the inability of the courts to compel an adult to provide a sample means that paternity in some cases is still a matter of presumption or inference from evidence.

---

[133]   Ibid, s 58(1).
[134]   Ibid, s 58(3).
[135]   Ibid, s 58(2).
[136]   [1977] AC 547.
[137]   Cretney *Family Law in the Twentieth Century* (Oxford University Press, 2003), at p 540.

Standard of proof

6.83 The standard of proof is the civil standard of probability but the strength of evidence required to prove a fact may change according to the seriousness of the issue.[138] The degree of proof involved in the burden of establishing paternity was summarised by Waite LJ in *Re A (A Minor) (Paternity: Refusal of Blood Test)*:[139]

(1) The question raised by an issue of paternity is a serious one – more serious in the scale of gravity than, for example, proof of debt or minor negligence.

(2) The balance of probability has to be established to a degree of sureness in the mind of the court which matches the seriousness of the issue.

(3) The weighing process involved in (2) must not however be over-elaborate. The court should not attempt, in a precise – almost mathematical – way to determine precisely what degree of probability is appropriate to the gravity of the issue. There is still ample scope for the influence of common sense and the insight gained by first impression.

Presumption of legitimacy

6.84 At common law, it is presumed that a child born to a married woman is the child of her husband. In the *Banbury Peerage Case*,[140] the House of Lords held that before the presumption could be rebutted it had to be shown that no sexual intercourse took place between the couple during the (wide) possible period within which the child was conceived. This could be done by proof that either sexual intercourse between them was impossible either because of impotency or physical absence or that the circumstances were such as to render it highly improbable that intercourse took place. The presumption can now be rebutted by evidence which shows that it is more probable than not that the person is legitimate or illegitimate and it is not necessary to prove that fact beyond reasonable doubt.[141] In the light of this statutory amendment, which does not limit the nature of the evidence required, it is doubtful whether the *Banbury Peerage Case* has any modern applications. In *Re H and A (Paternity: Blood Tests)*,[142] Thorpe LJ said:

'As science has hastened on and as more and more children are born out of marriage it seems to me that the paternity of any child is to be established by science and not by legal presumption or inference.'

---

[138] *Re H and R (Child Sexual Abuse: Standard of Proof)* [1996] 1 FLR 80, per Lord Nicholls of Birkenhead at 96; and see Chapter 19.

[139] [1994] 2 FLR 463, at 470.

[140] (1811) 1 Sim & St 153.

[141] Family Law Reform Act 1987, s 26.

[142] [2002] EWCA Civ 383, [2002] 1 FLR 1145, at 1154.

Evidence

6.85 The nature of the evidence required to establish or disprove paternity is unrestricted. It may be evidence showing that it was unlikely that intercourse took place between the couple at the time when conception took place. It is generally accepted that pregnancy lasts about 280 days from the first day of the last menstrual period. In exceptional cases, there may be considerable variation but it is generally agreed that the shortest duration of a normal pregnancy is 240 days and the longest, 313 days. It may be evidence showing that the father is incapable of producing children. Evidence may show that contraceptives were used but this will not necessarily be conclusive. Photographic evidence showing a likeness between the child and the alleged father is admissible,[143] but nowadays is unlikely to be given any, weight. A finding that a person has been found to be the father of a child in proceedings under specified Social Security Acts or the Children Act 1989 or its predecessors or in affiliation proceedings in any court in the UK is admissible to prove paternity, whether or not he offered any defence to the earlier allegations and whether or not he is a party to the present proceedings.[144] Moreover, such a finding raises a presumption that he is the father unless the contrary is proved. In most cases, however, evidence derived from bodily samples will be the best evidence available.

The absence of DNA evidence does not prevent the court making a finding. It is manifestly unacceptable to leave an issue of a child's parentage unresolved and it will usually be in the child's interest for it to be resolved.[145]

SEROLOGICAL/DNA TESTS

6.86 Family Law Reform Act 1969, s 20 provides that in any civil proceedings in which the paternity of a person falls to be determined, a court has power to direct the use of bodily tests to ascertain whether such tests show that a party to the proceedings is or is not excluded from being the father.[146] Part III of the Act provides a code for the formal aspects of the carrying out of the tests. The report of the tester is received by the court as evidence in the proceedings. Within 14 days of receiving the report, a party may serve notice on the other parties that he wishes to call the tester to give evidence. Originally, the testing envisaged by the legislature was serological testing but the wording of the section is wide enough to encompass DNA testing of samples,[147] which provides a higher degree of reliability.

6.87 The Act originally did not give the court the express power to direct the taking of a sample from a child for the purpose of establishing paternity unless

---

[143] *C v C and C (Legitimacy: Photographic Evidence)* [1972] 3 All ER 577.
[144] Civil Evidence Act 1968, s 12.
[145] See *Re P (Identity of Mother)* [2011] EWCA Civ 795, [2012] 1 FLR 351, per Sir Nicholas Wall P at [15]–[16]. See also **6.89**.
[146] Samples other than blood may now be taken (Blood Tests (Evidence of Paternity) (Amendment) Regulations 2001, SI 2001/773).
[147] See *Re H (Paternity: Blood Test)* [1996] 2 FLR 65.

the person with the care and control of the child consented. This caused difficulties[148] and the section was amended. The section now provides that where the person having control of the child does not consent, the court may authorise a taking of the sample if it considers that it is in the best interests of the child.[149]

6.88 The importance of following the correct procedure was emphasised in *Re F (Children) (DNA Evidence)*[150] where problems arose when the testing company was unable to link the donor to his or her sample.

- Any order for DNA testing made by the family courts should be made pursuant to the Family Law Act 1969 and the order should specify this.

- Either the company who is to undertake the testing should be named or the Order should direct that the company identified to undertake the testing is selected in accordance with the Act, from the Ministry of Justice Accredited List. Only accredited companies may be instructed.

- The taking of samples from children should only be undertaken pursuant to the express order of the court. If a need arises for further samples to be taken, that should be arranged only with the approval of the court. If all the parties agree on the need for further samples to be taken, the application may be made in writing to the judge who has conduct of the matter. These requirements should be communicated to the identified DNA company in the letter of instruction.

- Save in cases where the issue is solely confined to paternity testing, where the identified company may have its own standardised application form, all requests for DNA testing should be by letter of instruction.

- The letter of instruction should emphasise that the responsibilities on DNA experts are identical to those of any expert reporting in a family case and that their overriding obligation is to the court. Further, if any test carried out in pursuance of their instruction casts any doubt on, or appears relevant to the hypothesis set by their instructions, they should regard themselves as being under a duty to draw that to the attention of the court and the parties.

- Any letter of instruction to a DNA company should set out in clear terms precisely what relationships are to be analysed and, where the information is available, the belief of the parties as to the extent of their relatedness.

'In recent decades British society has become much more culturally diverse. Some cultures have different attitudes to consanguine relationships, others

---

[148] See, for example, *Re R (Blood Test: Constraint)* [1998] 1 FLR 745 and *Re O and J (Paternity: Blood Tests)* [2000] 1 FLR 418.

[149] Family Law Reform Act 1969, s 21(3).

[150] [2007] EWHC 3235 (Fam), [2008] 1 FLR 348.

include children within the family for a variety of reasons (usually highly laudable) who may have remote or indeed no genetic connection to the adults. In these cases, separate statements from the parties setting out the family history and dynamics is likely to be helpful.'

- The letter of instruction should always make clear that if there appears to the DNA expert to be any lack of clarity or ambiguity in their written instructions, or if they require further guidance, they should revert to the solicitor instructing them. The solicitor should keep a note or memorandum of any such request.

- DNA experts preparing reports for the court should bear in mind that they are addressing lay people. The report should strive to interpret their analysis in clear language. Whilst it will usually be necessary to recite the tests undertaken and the likely ratios derived from them, care should be given to explain those results within the context of their identified conclusions.

- Particular care should be taken in the use of relative phrases such as 'this result provides good evidence'. Such expressions should always be set within the parameters of current DNA knowledge and should identify in plain terms the limitations as to the reliability of any test carried out. A 'likelihood ratio' by definition is a concept which has uncertainty inherent within it. The extent of uncertainty will vary from test to test and the author of the report must identify and explain those parameters (eg it is not always possible to demonstrate half sibling relationship by DNA testing, even where it is given that a biological relationship exists).

- Where any particular test and subsequent ratio of likelihood is regarded as in any way controversial within the mainstream of DNA expertise, the use of the test and the reasons for its use should be signalled to the court within the report.[151]

6.89 In *Re D (Paternity)*[152] the court refused to direct the taking of a sample from D, a disturbed boy of 11, who refused to give a sample which might show whether A was his father, the boy stating that he wanted nothing to do with A. Although there were reasonable grounds for believing that A was D's father and it was in D's best interests to know the truth about his disputed parentage, it was not in his best interests to press the issue now given the other disturbance in his life and his deep resistance to testing. However the court directed that samples from A be taken and stored. The taking of a sample from D was also ordered but that part of the order was stayed with permission to restore.

---

[151] Ibid, at [32].

[152] [2006] EWHC 3545 (Fam), [2007] 2 FLR 26. Following *Re F (Children) (DNA Evidence)* the Department of Health issued a consultation paper on the revision of its Code of Practice on Genetic Paternity Testing Services (2001) which it withdrew (see [2008] Fam Law 371). It appears that the Department did not publish a new guide but relies on *A Common Framework of Principles for direct-to-consumer genetic testing services* (2010) issued by the Human Genetics Commission www.hgc.gov.uk.

In *Re P (Identity of Mother)*[153] the maternity of S, aged 15, was in dispute. S refused to provide a DNA sample. Although s 21(3) of the Family Law Reform Act 1969 gave the court power to direct that a sample from a child under the age of 16 if it considered it to be in the child's best interest, it was not envisaged that one would be taken from S without her consent. The trial judge decided that in the circumstances a finding of maternity would not be able to be made. The Court of Appeal disagreed. It was open to the court under s 23(1) to draw an inference from S's refusal and it was in her best interests for the issue to be resolved and for her to know the truth.

6.90 'The child' is the child whose paternity is to be ascertained. Section 21(3)(b) would not assist the court to order a sample should be taken from another child whose DNA might contribute to the determination of the paternity of a sibling unless she agreed.[154]

6.91 Bodily samples taken by police during a criminal investigation under s 64 of the Police and Criminal Evidence Act 1984 cannot be used in family proceedings to establish paternity because by virtue of s 64(1A) they 'shall not be used by any person except for purposes related to the prevention or detection of crime, the investigation of an offence or the conduct of a prosecution'.[155] Conversely however, family courts may disclose samples taken under s 20 of the Family Law Reform Act 1969 to police to enable them to carry out investigations, for example into child trafficking.[156] Such a disclosure would be an interference with the child's Art 8 rights but might be justified as being necessary for the prevention of crime or for the protection of the rights and freedoms of others.

Should a test be ordered?

6.92 The court has a discretion to refuse to direct blood testing and indeed may refuse to allow an issue of paternity to be tried at all. It will rarely do this nowadays if paternity is a real issue, because of the weight given to the child's right to know the true facts about his paternity.

When the court is considering how to exercise its discretion, the s 1 welfare test does not apply, because the issue is not one concerning the upbringing of the child.[157] However, the welfare of the child is a matter to be considered. As Lord Reid said in the leading case of *S v S*:[158]

---

[153] [2011] EWCA Civ 795, [2012] 1 FLR 351. See also **6.85**.
[154] See *Re L (Paternity Testing)* [2009] EWCA Civ 1239, [2010] 2 FLR 188.
[155] *Lambeth LBCv S, C, V and J (By His Guardian)* [2006] EWHC 326 (Fam), [2007] 1 FLR 152; *Lewisham LBC v D (Local Authority Disclosure of DNA Samples to Police)* [2010] EWHC 1238 (Fam), [2011] 1 FLR 895.
[156] *Lewisham LBC v D (Local Authority Disclosure of DNA Samples to Police)* [2010] EWHC 1238 (Fam), [2011] 1 FLR 895.
[157] *S v S* [1972] AC 24.
[158] Ibid, at 45.

'I would, therefore, hold that the court ought to permit a blood test of a young child to be taken unless satisfied that that would be against the child's interests.'

Lord McDermott agreed that the court could refuse to direct a test if the child's interests required it:

'... [but this] would not ordinarily afford ground for refusing a blood test merely because it might, in revealing the truth, prove the infant's illegitimacy ...'[159]

A number of factors have influenced courts in the past.

The interests of justice

6.93 Courts have been unanimous in holding that the interests of justice almost always require that the truth be established by the most reliable means possible:

'The interests of justice in the abstract are best served by the ascertainment of the truth and there must be few cases where the interests of children can be shown to be best served by the suppression of truth. Scientific evidence of blood groups has been available since the early part of this century and the progress of serology has been so rapid that in many cases certainty or near certainty can be reached in the ascertainment of paternity. Why should the risk be taken of a judicial decision being made that is factually wrong and may later be demonstrated to be wrong?

Failure to submit the child to a blood test may eventually lead the child to unnecessary doubt as to his paternity and the chance of removing that doubt may be lost in the passing of time. There may be genetic consequences in some cases which could have been avoided if the blood test had been taken.'[160]

This argument has grown even stronger with the availability of DNA testing. As Waite LJ said in *Re A (A Minor) (Paternity: Refusal of Blood Test)*:[161]

'Genetic testing, already advanced to a high degree of probability through the negative techniques of exclusion, has now moved on to the point where it has become possible to achieve positive certainty.'

The interests of the child in knowing the true identity of its father

6.94 As discussed above, most courts which have considered the issue of directing blood tests have regarded it as normally being in the best interests of a child to know who its father is. In *S v S*,[162] Lord Morris of Borth-y-Gest considered that in most cases the interests of the child are best served if the truth is known and courts considering the issue since then have usually

---

[159]   Ibid, at 48.
[160]   [1972] AC 24, per Lord Hodson at 57–58.
[161]   [1994] 2 FLR 463, at 472.
[162]   [1972] AC 24.

expressed the same view. For example, in *Re G (Parentage: Blood Sample)*,[163] Ward LJ said that it was 'the entitlement' of the child to know who her father was.

The interests of the child in not having a settled life disturbed

6.95 The possibility of the loss of a status of being legitimate was not considered sufficient justification by their lordships in *S v S*, nor is the possibility that the person whom the child believes to be his father will be shown not to be. If no purpose is to be achieved by the tests, this is a reason for not allowing the issue of paternity to be tried at all. *Re JS (A Minor) (Declaration of Paternity)*[164] is a rare example of the Court of Appeal stating that tests should not be taken. At the time of conception, the mother was having a sexual relationship with her partner but also had a very brief relationship with J, a work colleague. She became pregnant and gave birth to a child who was brought up by her and her partner, R, as though he was the child of both of them. J became obsessed with the thought of the child, insisted on seeing him and applied for a declaration that he was the father and for contact. Informal blood tests did not preclude him from being the father, R refusing to undergo tests. The trial judge dismissed J's applications. The Court of Appeal dismissed J's appeal, holding that even if there was jurisdiction to grant a declaration (and at that time the Family Law Act 1996 was not in force), it was wrong to entertain the application on two grounds. The first was that it would bind only the parties and not R, the second that a declaration would 'transmute a mathematical probability into a forensic certainty' when there was no need to:

> '... there were strong reasons for not embarking on the enquiry in the first place ... With hindsight it is now clear that it was unnecessary to consider the biological parentage of this child in order to reach a conclusion about access, which was the only live issue. The child is securely based in a two-parent family with the mother and Mr R, who fully accepts his role as de facto father, with the knowledge of the doubt of his being the biological father; [J] is, to all intents and purposes, a stranger to the child. To allow the paternity issue to disturb this settled relationship was, in our view, an undoubted mistake ...'[165]

Given the emphasis now placed on the importance of a child knowing the truth about its origins, it is doubtful whether *Re JS* would be decided in the same way today.

6.96 The test may prejudicially affect the health of the child. Lord MacDermott, who suggested this in *S v S*,[166] was considering the physical health of the child but it might be that the test could affect the child's psychological well-being, either because of a fear of needles or if it knew of the reason for the test. However, samples for DNA testing are normally obtained by taking a

---

[163]   [1997] 1 FLR 360.
[164]   (1981) 2 FLR 146 and also *K v M (Paternity: Contact)* [1996] 1 FLR 312.
[165]   (1981) 2 FLR 146, per Ormrod LJ at 152.
[166]   [1972] AC 24.

mouth swab. Lord MacDermott also suggested that a refusal might be justified if the application was of a fishing nature, designed for some ulterior motive to call into question the legitimacy, otherwise unimpeached, of a child.

Balancing the factors

6.97   The court will need to balance all these factors, but given the decision of the House of Lords in *S v S*, a test will normally be ordered unless it can be clearly demonstrated that there is a likelihood of harm being caused to the child. In *Re T (Paternity: Ordering Blood Tests)*,[167] blood tests were ordered in an application for contact and parental responsibility, even though it was far from certain that such orders would be made:

> 'The applicant's application ... cannot, simply, be "wished away". Those applications are going to have to be heard, whether or not blood tests are ordered. In that event, how much more satisfactory must it be in principle for the evidence to be the best that science can provide (probably certainty) as compared to the unsatisfactory situation of the court being left with presumptions and inferences.'

Inferences to be drawn from a refusal to undergo a blood test

6.98   The Family Law Reform Act 1969, s 21(3) states that samples may not be taken from anyone other than the child, except with his or her consent. However, when a direction has been given for tests, the court may draw such inferences, if any, as appear proper from any failure to take the test or to consent to the test being taken by a person named in the direction.[168] Where there is a presumption of legitimacy in favour of the person who fails to take any step required of him in the direction, the court may adjourn the proceedings and may, if at the end of the period of adjournment the person has still refused without reasonable cause to comply, dismiss his claim for relief notwithstanding the absence of evidence to rebut the presumption.[169] The Court of Appeal has held that an indication by a party that he or she will refuse, made in advance of a direction, also permits an adverse inference to be drawn:[170]

> 'It should be remembered that [at the time the Law Commission reported in 1968 (*Blood Tests and the Proof of Paternity* Law Co No 16)] blood testing served only to exclude paternity: it did not establish it. It seems to me that a refusal to comply after the solemnity of the court's decision is more eloquent testimony of an attempt at hiding a truth than intransigent objection made as a forensic tactic. Science has now advanced. The whole truth can now be known. As Waite LJ said in *Re A (A Minor) (Paternity: Refusal of a Blood Test)*:[171]

---

167   [2001] 2 FLR 1190, per Bodey J at 1196.
168   Family Law Reform Act 1969, s 23(3). This includes drawing an inference from the child's refusal: *Re P (Identity of Mother)* [2011] EWCA Civ 795, [2012] 1 FLR 351 – see **6.89**.
169   Ibid, s 23(2).
170   *Re H (A Minor) (Paternity: Blood Test)* [1996] 2 FLR 65, per Ward LJ at 76.
171   [1994] 2 FLR 463, at 473. See also *Secretary of State for Work and Pensions v Jones* [2003]

"Against that background of law and scientific advance, it seems to me to follow, both in justice and in common sense, that if a mother makes a claim against one of the possible fathers, and he chooses to exercise his right not to submit to be tested, the inference that he is the father of the child should be virtually inescapable. He would certainly have to advance very clear and cogent reasons for this refusal to be tested – reasons which it would be just and fair and reasonable for him to be allowed to maintain."'

6.99 In *Re G (Parentage: Blood Sample)*,[172] the petitioner had cohabited with the mother but they separated when she started a relationship with another man, the child being conceived around the time of the separation. They later resumed their cohabitation, the child was born and they married. They separated and the child, who was then 2½, remained in the care of the petitioner. The child later went to live with the mother, but following divorce proceedings, in the course of which the petitioner sought an order for contact, an order for testing was given. The petitioner refused to comply, arguing first that the child would be upset if she were told he was not the father and secondly, that if he were shown not to be the father, the mother would use the finding to thwart contact. At first instance, the judge refused to draw any inference from the petitioner's failure to comply, holding on the rest of the evidence that the mother had not displaced the presumption of legitimacy. The Court of Appeal held that he was wrong:

'The mother asserted paternity for 2½ years. Since then she has asserted her belief that another man is the father. The petitioner, whatever doubts he may have harboured about his paternity given the fractured relationship during the time of the separation, has since [the resumption of the cohabitation] persistently held the belief that he is the father. She is willing for her belief to be put to the test; he is not. In those circumstances, it seems to me that the only inference the court can properly draw is an inference that the petitioner is not in fact the father ...'[173]

Thorpe LJ added:

'The court must be astute to discern what are the real motivations behind the refusal. It should look critically at any proffered explanation or justification. It should only uphold an explanation that is objectively valid, demonstrating rationality, logicality and consistency. Anything less will usually lead to an adverse inference.'

And yet, it is suggested the court should also be cautious about drawing adverse inferences let alone allowing the refusal to stand in place of factual evidence.[174] A putative father may refuse a test not only because he knows that he is or is not the father but also because he fears he is or is not. Great weight

---

EWHC 2163 (Fam), [2004] 1 FLR 282 where the court said that the refusal of a possible father to be tested led to the 'virtually inescapable' inference that he was the father.

[172] [1997] 1 FLR 360.

[173] [1997] 1 FLR 360, per Ward LJ at 367. See also *Re P (Identity of Mother)* [2011] EWCA Civ 795, [2012] 1 FLR 351.

[174] But see *Re P (Identity of Mother)* [2011] EWCA Civ 795, [2012] 1 FLR 351, per Sir Nicholas Wall P at [15]–[16] and **6.85**.

is given in the cases to the need to ascertain the truth, and a major purpose of testing nowadays is to ensure that the truth about his or her paternity is available to the child (see Ward LJ at 365: 'It is her entitlement to know who her father is'). Drawing adverse inferences may be a just way of preventing a tactical advantage being gained when pecuniary interests are at stake, but that is a separate issue from using a refusal to make a finding which binds everyone including the child. The Law Commission[175] recognised that a power to draw adverse inferences had its imperfections but thought that in practice the provision would effectively deter parties from refusing to be tested for purely tactical reasons.

GIVING EFFECT TO PATERNITY: PRACTICAL CONSIDERATIONS

6.100 Paternity sometimes has to be ascertained in circumstances where the child has no knowledge that the putative father may be his father or even knows of his existence. Sometimes he believes that another person, perhaps his mother's partner, is his father. Such cases raise delicate issues of when a DNA test should be ordered (see **6.95**) and, following establishing that the putative father is the child's biological parent, whether and how the existence of that adult, or the fact that he is the father can be introduced to the child. The third area of difficulty is the role which that person should play in the child's life. This is considered at **11.115**.

6.101 No matter how difficult are the problems which are raised in the individual case, it is the court's responsibility to make the decision. If a parent is unwilling to comply with a decision that the child should be told by taking advice and ensuring that she or someone tells the child, the court can enforce its decision by means of a specific issue order under s 8 of the Children Act 1989 requiring the parent to cooperate with the child being told by a guardian, Cafcass officer, psychiatrist or other professional.[176] If the parent is unwilling to tell the child herself 'it would be quite pointless to order the reluctant parent to do the job. Such a parent is the worst possible person to carry out the delicate task and in reality the court would meet the challenge by simply putting in place alternative mechanisms for the imparting of the sensitive information.'[177]

6.102 Each case has to be decided on its own circumstances, the individual child's welfare being paramount. However from reported cases it appears that

---

[175] Blood Tests and the Proof of Paternity in Civil Proceedings (1968) Law Com No 16, para 47.

[176] *Re F (Paternity: Jurisdiction)* [2007] EWCA Civ 873, [2008] 1 FLR 225 where NYAS were invited to assist. The suggestion in *J v C (Void Marriage: Status of Child)* [2006] EWCA Civ 551, [2006] 2 FLR 1098 that it was doubtful whether the manner in which children should be told is justiciable was not followed. In *J v C* the issue as to how children who believed that A was their father should be told that he had been born a woman and was not their father. See **11.147**. See also *Re C (Contact: Moratorium: Change of Gender)* [2006] EWCA Civ 1765, [2007] 1 FLR 1642.

[177] *Re F (Paternity: Jurisdiction)* [2007] EWCA Civ 873, [2008] 1 FLR 225, per Thorpe LJ at [18].

the court will start from the position that it is normally in the child's best interests to be told the true position notwithstanding difficulties in arranging the telling.[178] Considerations of the child's welfare may not however justify making an order. In *Re J (Paternity: Welfare of Child)*,[179] for example, a father whose identity had been established by DNA tests applied for contact. The child, aged 10, believed that his mother's long-term partner was his father. The father then disappeared and played no subsequent part in the proceedings. Sumner J held that no order should be made. He noted expert evidence that the mother was vulnerable and would experience difficulties telling the child but added that she obtain advice. The longer the boy remained in ignorance the greater the chance he would learn the truth from another source and the greater the upset. In reaching the decision all the relevant evidence should be considered including evidence from any psychiatrist or other relevant professional involved with the family.[180] In other cases it may be in the child's interests to be told but that the telling should be postponed, for example, perhaps until the child had taken important exams.[181]

Examples

Re R (A Minor) (Contact: Biological Father)[182]

6.103 Married parents separated when their daughter was 1. Contact between father and child ceased soon afterwards, when the mother formed a relationship with a new partner, the child being brought up to believe that the partner was her father. When the child was 5, the father applied for contact which the mother opposed because of the danger of destabilising the family unit. Contact was ordered but when the mother was unable or unwilling to co-operate in preparing the child for the first period of contact, the order was revoked. The Court of Appeal held that the trial judge had been wrong to do so. Butler-Sloss LJ said:

'It is the right of a child to have a relationship with both parents wherever possible. This principle has been stated again and again in the appellate courts. It is underlined in the United Nations Convention on the Rights of the Child and endorsed in the Children Act 1989 ...

... I agree with the judge that the child and her father cannot meet at this moment. But I differ from the judge in leaving the long-term decision in limbo. I believe the child has not only the right to see her father; if this can eventually be realised without causing her damage, she also has a right ... to know the truth.'[183]

---

[178] See, for example, *Re K (Specific Issue Order)* [1999] 2 FLR 280 (see **6.105**) and *Re P (Surrogacy: Residence)* [2008] 1 FLR 177, at [2].
[179] [2006] EWHC 2837 (Fam), [2007] 1 FLR 1064.
[180] See, for example, *Re L (Identity of Birth Father)* [2008] EWCA Civ 1388, [2009] 1 FLR 1152.
[181] See for example, *Re L (Identity of Birth Father)* [2008] EWCA Civ 1388, [2009] 1 FLR 1152, at [4].
[182] [1993] 2 FLR 762.
[183] [1993] 2 FLR 762, at 767.

The Court of Appeal invited the Official Solicitor to represent the child and to instruct a child psychiatrist to assist the mother to inform the child of her true parentage or, if that proved impossible, to do so himself if considered appropriate.

A v L (Contact)[184]

6.104 The parents were unmarried. As in *Re R (A Minor) (Contact: Biological Father)*, there had been no contact for some time and the mother had a partner whom the 3-year-old boy thought was his father. The father, who was serving a long prison sentence, applied for indirect contact, accepting that the boy should not be told his true parentage until older. The justices dismissed the application. On appeal, Holman J held they were wrong to do so:

> 'It is precisely because J is still young and has no understanding of the facts of life that it is more appropriate and better to introduce him, very gently, and in age-appropriate ways, at this stage, to the fact that he in fact has two fathers. That is not to say that he should be given any encouragement not to regard and address D as "Daddy" or that he needs to think LA is "Daddy". But he needs to know now, whilst he is still sufficiently young that it is in no way threatening to him, that there is another father so that, in due course, as he begins to learn the biological facts of life he can gently assimilate this truth about his parentage. To do and say nothing now is in truth storing up a potential bombshell for the future, which might be very damaging for J to learn and might indeed seriously undermine his sense of trust in his mother and D who are otherwise parenting him so well.'[185]

An order was made for indirect contact by letters, cards and modest presents and the judge directed that the mother must ensure that the child opened them and had the messages read to him. The applicant was not however to refer to himself as the child's father.

Re K (Specific Issue Order)[186]

6.105 The parents, who were unmarried, separated soon after the child was born. There was no contact and the mother brought the child up to believe that his father was dead. When the boy was 12, the father applied for contact and a specific issue order that his son be told that his father was alive and who he was. The mother adamantly opposed this and the Official Solicitor recommended that if the mother co-operated, it was in the child's best interests to be told, but not otherwise. The deputy High Court judge refused to make the order on the grounds that, because of the mother's obsessional hatred of the father, informing the child about his father would cause an emotional upset in the child's life which would be seriously detrimental. The Court of Appeal invited the Official Solicitor to represent the child and to instruct a child psychiatrist to assist the mother to inform the child of her true parentage or, if that proved

---

184   [1998] 1 FLR 361.
185   Ibid, at 366.
186   [1999] 2 FLR 280.

impossible, to do so himself if considered appropriate. (Now, the appropriate order would be for a Cafcass guardian to be appointed.)

Chapter 7

PARENTAL RESPONSIBILITY

INTRODUCTION

7.1 'Parental responsibility' means all the rights, duties, powers, responsibilities and authority which by law a parent has in relation to the child and his property.[1] It was described by Lord Mackay of Clashfern who, as Lord Chancellor, was responsible for the passage of the Children Bill through Parliament as running 'through the Bill like a golden thread, knotting together parental status and the effect of orders about a child's upbringing whether in private family proceedings or in care proceedings ...'[2] The mother has parental responsibility automatically, as does the father if he is married to her either at the time of the birth or later. Otherwise, it can be acquired in a variety of ways including by agreement with the child's mother or by court order. Not all those who have parental responsibility are the child's parents and not all parents have parental responsibility. A significant number of fathers, unmarried to the child's mother but playing a full role in their child's life, do not have parental responsibility, but are unaware of this.[3]

WHAT IS PARENTAL RESPONSIBILITY?

7.2 The Children Act 1989, s 3 defines the concept of 'parental responsibility' as meaning all the rights, duties, powers, responsibilities and authority which by law a parent has in relation to the child and his property. As the report of the Law Commission on *Family Law: Review of Child Law: Guardianship and Custody*[4] recognised, although it would be superficially attractive to provide a list of these duties and powers, it is practically impossible to do so. They include common law duties to maintain, protect and educate the child and such powers as enable the parent to perform these duties[5] as well as rights conferred by statute, such as the right to consent, or withhold consent, to the child marrying or being adopted. The list in respect of children in general changes from time to time as it is extended or restricted by statute and, in

---

[1]   Children Act 1989, s 3.

[2]   'Perceptions of the Children Bill and beyond. The Joseph Jackson Memorial Lecture' NLJ Ap 14 (1989) 505.

[3]   See, for example, Lewis, Papacosta and Warin, *Cohabitation, Separation and Fatherhood* (2002) summarised in *Findings* 552 (Joseph Rowntree Foundation).

[4]   Law Comm No 172 (1988).

[5]   Blackstone *Commentaries on the Laws of England* (1st edn, 1765), Bk 1, Ch 16.

respect of a particular child, as the child's needs and circumstances change and as the child matures. In the words of Lord Denning in *Hewer v Bryant*:[6]

> '... the legal right of a parent to the custody of a child ends at the 18th birthday: and even up till then, it is a dwindling right which the courts will hesitate to enforce against the wishes of the child, and the more so the older he is. It starts with the right of control and ends with little more than advice.'[7]

7.3 The Family Justice Review[8] listed the elements of parental responsibility as including:

- naming the child;

- providing a home for the child;

- having contact with the child;

- protecting and maintaining the child;

- administering the child's property;

- consenting to the taking of blood for testing;

- allowing the child to be interviewed;

- taking the child outside of the jurisdiction of the UK and consenting to emigration;

- agreeing to and vetoing the issue of the child's passport;

- agreeing to the child's adoption;

- agreeing to the child's change of surname;

- consenting to the child's medical treatment and

- arranging the child's education.

It added:

---

6   [1970] QB 357, at 369.

7   For a discussion of the nature of parental rights and responsibility, see *Gillick v West Norfolk and Wisbech Area Health Authority and Another* [1986] AC 112, [1986] 1 FLR 224. See also Probert, Gilmore and Herring (eds) *Responsible Parents and Parental Responsibility* (Hart Publishing, 2009), Part I. For parental responsibility in relation to an adolescent, see Fortin *Children's Rights and the Developing Law* (3rd edn, Cambridge University Press, 2009) ch 3 and Gilmore 'The limits of parental responsibility' in *Responsible Parents and Parental Responsibility*.

8   Ministry of Justice Final Report (2011), at para 4.6.

'This arid list does no justice to the warmth and caring needed if parents are to nurture their children successfully. But understanding it is particularly important in the legal context of a separation and that needs to start before separation. We recognise the limits of what the law can do in this area, and the effectiveness of government action more widely also has limits. Yet it is right to do what can be done. All our recommendations on the process of separation are governed by the aim to strengthen shared parental responsibility and to emphasise its importance as parents make arrangements for their child's upbringing post separation. The aim is to focus both parents on the needs of their child and, where they both have parental responsibility, that they each share equal status as parents of their child.[9]

7.4 One change which was brought about by the Act is an emphasis on responsibilities instead of 'rights'. In the leading case of *Re S (Parental Responsibility)*,[10] Ward LJ said:

'It is unfortunate that the notion of "parental responsibility" has still to be defined by s 3 of the Children Act 1989 to mean "... all the rights, duties, powers, responsibilities and authority which by law a parent has in relation to the child and his property" which gives outmoded pre-eminence to the "rights" which are conferred ... The significant change that the Act has brought about [is to move the emphasis] from rights and to concentrate on responsibilities.'

7.5 In *Gillick v West Norfolk and Wisbech AHA and Department of Health and Social Security*[11] Lord Fraser said:

'Parental rights to control a child do not exist for the benefit of a parent. They exist for the benefit of the child and they are justified only in so far as they enable the parent to perform his duties towards the child and towards other children in the family.'

7.6 Yet the concept of parental responsibility is more than a bundle of rights and responsibilities. It confers a status on the parent which is important both for the child and the parent. For the child, the recognition of a parent as having parental responsibility is just as, if not more, important. In *Re S (Parental Responsibility)*, Ward LJ added:

'I have heard, up and down the land, psychiatrists tell me how important it is that children grow up with good self-esteem and how much they need to have a favourable positive image of the absent parent. It seems to me important, therefore, wherever possible, to ensure that the law confers upon a committed father that stamp of approval, lest the child grow up with some belief that he is in some way disqualified from fulfilling his role and that the reason for the disqualification is something inherent which will be inherited by the child, making her struggle to find her own identity all the more fraught.'[12]

---

9   Ibid, at para 4.7.
10 [1995] 2 FLR 648. Ward LJ's judgment contains a valuable review of cases reported up to 1995.
11 [1986] 1 AC 112, at 170.
12 [1995] 2 FLR 648, at 657.

ACQUIRING PARENTAL RESPONSIBILITY

7.7   Parental responsibility can be acquired in a number of circumstances, by non-judicial or judicial acts. It is acquired by:

- the mother, on the birth of the child;[13]

- the father or a man treated as the father under s 35 of the Human Fertilisation and Embryology Act 2008 (HFEA 2008) (see **6.32**), who is married to the mother on the birth of the child;[14]

- the father or a man treated as the father under HFEA 2008, s 36 (see **6.33**), on the marriage of the parents;[15]

- the father or a man treated as the father under HFEA 2008, s 36 (see **6.33**), by the parents both agreeing in a prescribed form which is recorded in the prescribed manner that he should have parental responsibility[16] (see below);

- the father or a man treated as the father under HFEA 2008, s 36 (see **6.33**), on an order of the court on an application by him[17] (see below);

- the child's father or a man treated as the father under HFEA 2008, s 36 (see **6.33**), if he is registered as the child's father under the Births and Deaths Registration Act 1953 on or after 1 December 2003 (see **7.16**);[18]

- a woman who is a parent by virtue of s 43 of the HFEA 2008 (see **6.21**) and is the civil partner of the mother at the time the embryo or sperm and eggs were placed inside the mother or she was artificially inseminated, or was her civil partner at the time the child was born, who is registered as the child's parent under the Births and Deaths Registration Act 1955, or she and the mother both agree in a prescribed form recorded in the prescribed manner (see above) that she should have parental responsibility or is granted responsibility by order of the court;[19]

- a step-parent,[20] or a parent with parental responsibility agreeing (or, if both parents have parental responsibility, both agreeing) in a prescribed form which is recorded in the prescribed manner that his or her spouse (or, if both have parental responsibility, the spouse of one of them) shall have parental responsibility;[21]

---

13   CA 1989, s 2(1).
14   Ibid.
15   Family Law Reform Act 1987, s 1(3), read with Legitimacy Act 1976, s 2.
16   CA 1989, s 4(1)(b).
17   Ibid, s 4(1)(a).
18   Ibid, s 4(1)(a).
19   Ibid, s 4ZA; Family Law Reform Act 1987, s 1(3).
20   Ie the mother's husband or civil partner: CA 1989, s 4A.
21   Ibid, s 4A(1)(a).

- a step-parent,[22] on an order of the court on an application by the step-parent;[23]

- a special guardian, on a court making a special guardianship order;[24]

- adopters, on adoption;[25]

- anyone named in a parental order made under s 54 of the HFEA 2008 (see **6.51**);[26]

- the person in favour of whom a residence order is made;[27]

- a guardian, on the appointment of the guardian coming into force or on the appointment by a court of a guardian;[28]

- a local authority on the making of a care order;[29]

- an adoption agency on the making of a placement order;[30]

- prospective adopters when the child is placed with them by a local authority or other adoption agency.[31]

LOSING PARENTAL RESPONSIBILITY

7.8   Parental responsibility is lost:

- when the order which resulted in it being acquired (e g a residence order or care order) is discharged;

- when the court, on an application brought by a person who has parental responsibility or the child, makes an order under CA 1989, s 4(3) , s 4A(3) or s 4ZA(5) discharging an agreement for parental responsibility or an order for parental responsibility or revoking parental responsibility which was acquired by the registration of the father or step-parent;

---

22   Ie the mother's husband or civil partner: CA 1989, s 4A.
23   Ibid, s 4A(1)(b). 'Step-parent' means the spouse or the civil partner of a parent.
24   See Chapter 11.
25   Adoption Act 1976, s 12(1).
26   Adoption and Children Act 2002, s 46(1) as amended by Sch 1 of the Human Fertilisation and Embryology (Parental Orders) Regulations 2010, SI 2010/985.
27   CA 1989, s 12(2). This is one way in which, for example, partners of lesbian mothers can acquire parental responsibility – see **Chapter 10**.
28   CA 1989, s 5(6).
29   Ibid, s 33.
30   Adoption and Children Act 2002, s 25.
31   Ibid, s 25(3).

- on the making of an adoption order;[32]

- by the revocation or disclaimer of the appointment of a guardian;

- when a court discharges the appointment of a guardian or special guardian.

A mother or the father, if married to the mother, or persons in whose favour a parental order has been made, can lose parental responsibility only on the making of an adoption order although their ability to exercise parental responsibility is limited if a placement order is made.[33]

MARRIED PARENTS

7.9   Where the grant of parental responsibility to the father depends on his being married to the mother, the parents must be or have been legally married. Thus a father who has undergone a religious marriage with the mother which did not create a legal marriage under domestic law does not automatically have parental responsibility.[34]

ACQUISITION BY REGISTRATION OF NAME OF FATHER

7.10   Principle 3.8 of *The Principles of European Family Law Regarding Parental Responsibilities*[35] states that 'Persons whose legal parentage has been established should have parental responsibilities for the child'. In practice though, there needs to be some form of recognition of the holding of parental responsibility so that a claim to have parental responsibility can easily be verified without the need for a DNA test. The marriage certificate of the mother and the person deemed to be the father, the birth certificate naming the father as an informant, a registered agreement entered into under ss 4, 4ZA or 4A or a court order all provide evidence of the status.

7.11   In 2008 the previous Government issued a White Paper, *Joint Birth Registration: Recording Responsibility*,[36] which proposed new legislation to make unmarried mothers and fathers jointly responsible for registering the births of their children, thereby resulting in the father being granted parental responsibility under CA 1989, s 4(1)(a).

---

[32]   Adoption and Children Act 2002, s 46.

[33]   Ibid, s 27.

[34]   *AAA v ASH, Registrar General for England and Wales and the Secretary of State for Justice* [2009] EWHC 636 (Fam), [2010] 1 FLR 1.

[35]   Commission on European Family Law (2007). The CEFL is an international group of scholars. The Principles have no binding international or domestic force. See Scherpe 'Establishing and ending parental responsibility: A comparative view' in Probert, Gilmore and Herring (eds) *Responsible Parents and Parental Responsibility* (Hart Publishing, 2009).

[36]   Cmd 7293.

'The point at which a birth is registered is ... a key moment for parents, when a mother and father publicly acknowledge that they have responsibility for their child – not only as its legal representative, but also in the expectation that they will safeguard and promote their child's health, development and welfare. Birth registration can also be the time at which fathers, in particular, realise that they have a real influence in their child's life, and that they are playing an extremely privileged and important role ...

'At the heart of our reforms is a desire to promote child welfare and the right of every child to know who his or her parents are. In most cases, a child's right to be acknowledged and cared for by his or her father should not be dependent on the relationship between the parents. To support this right we will ensure that fathers who want to take responsibility for their children do not have to overcome unnecessary obstacles. We intend that joint birth registration should play a key part in developing the Government's determination to develop a culture in which the welfare of children is paramount and people are clear that fatherhood as well as motherhood always comes with rights as well as responsibilities.'

The previous Green Paper[37] had noted that in the UK, the large majority of birth certificates have both parents' names on them and there has been a significant increase in the number of joint birth registrations outside marriage over the last 30 years. Registration where only the mother's name appeared on the birth certificate) accounted for around 7% of the total birth registrations in England and Wales.[38] Research showed that sole registration was much more common among younger mothers, and particularly common for those who gave birth under the age of 21. The choices exercised, and the decisions made, seemed to be informed by three broad sets of factors related to the rights of the child, involvement in parenting and the relationship between the parents. There were a number of reasons, including fear of domestic violence, why some mothers made a deliberate decision not to register the birth jointly with the father. However, the research indicated that there is a group of mothers who do not make a conscious choice about sole or joint registration. In some of these cases the father has regular contact with the child even though the birth was not registered jointly. The Government believed these couples would be more likely to register jointly if there was a legal requirement, or they were encouraged to do so.

7.12 The proposals met with some opposition. For example, Julie Wallbank[39] argued that the potential impact of the proposal as to identify and single out those who fail to conform to the norm and to marginalise further those who cannot or did not want to identify the father. In contrast to the hopes of the Government that joint registration would strengthen commitment:

---

[37] Cmd 7160 (2007).

[38] 93.8%. See Births, further parental statistics (Office of National Statistics, 2009).

[39] Wallbank 'Bodies in the shadows: joint birth registration, parental responsibility and social class' [2009] CFLQ 267, at 281. See also Barton 'Joint birth registration: "recording responsibility" responsibly?' [2008] Fam Law 789.

'There is little if anything to be gained from children being able to name the man who was biologically responsible for the birth. Indeed there may be more damage to the developing child who starkly realises that the named man has never had and perhaps never will have any relationship whatsoever with the child.'

7.13 The proposals were enacted in Sch 6 to the Welfare Reform Act 2009 with the effect of amending the Births and Deaths Registration Act 1953 by introducing s 2A (information concerning birth of child whose parents are not married). However it does not require the mother to provide information relating to the father if she makes, in the presence of the registrar, a declaration in the prescribed form stating:

- that by virtue of HFEA 2008, s 41 the child has no father;

- that the father has died;

- that she does not know the father's identity;

- that she does not know the father's whereabouts;

- that the father lacks capacity (within the meaning of the Mental Capacity Act 2005) in relation to decisions under this Part of the Act;

- that she has reason to fear for her safety or that of the child if the father is contacted in relation to the registration of the birth; and

- any other conditions prescribed by the Minister.

The amendment is not yet in force.

7.14 Currently where the child's father and mother were not married to each other at the time of his birth, the registrar must not enter in the register the name of any person as father of the child except:

- at the joint request of the mother (M) and the person (F) stating himself to be the father of the child, in which case that person must sign the register together with the mother; or

- at the request of M on production of:

    - a declaration in the prescribed form made by M stating that that F is the father of the child; and
    - a statutory declaration made by F stating himself to be the father of the child; or

- at the request of F on production of:

– a declaration in the prescribed form by F stating himself to be the father of the child; and
– a statutory declaration made by M stating that that F is the father of the child; or

• at the request of M or F on production of:

– a copy of a parental responsibility agreement between them in relation to the child; and
– a declaration in the prescribed form by the person making the request stating that the agreement was made in compliance with the Children Act 1989, s 4 and has not been brought to an end by an order of a court; or

• at the request of M or F on production of:

– a certified copy of an order under s 4 giving F parental responsibility for the child; and
a declaration in the prescribed form by the person making the request stating that the order has not been brought to an end by an order of a court; or

• at the request of M or F on production of:

– a certified copy of an order under s 15(1) of and Sch 1, para 1 to the Children Act 1989 which requires F to make any financial provision for the child and which is not an order falling within Sch 1, para 4(3); and
– a declaration in the prescribed form by the person making the request stating that the order has not been discharged by an order of a court; or

• at the request of M or F on production of:

– a certified copy of an order made in relation to the child under Family Law Reform Act 1987, s 4, Guardianship of Minors Act 1971, s 9 or 11B, or Affiliation Proceedings Act 1957 s 4 – all of which have been repealed; and
– a declaration in the prescribed form by the person making the request stating that the order has not been brought to an end or discharged by an order of a court.[40]

7.15 Where the birth of a child whose father and mother were not married to each other at the time of the birth has been registered but no person has been

---

[40] Births and Deaths Registration Act 1953, s 10(1) (substituted by the Family Law Reform Act 1987, s 24 as amended by CA 1989, s 108(4), Sch 12, para 6(1), (2).

registered as the father of the child, the registrar shall re–register the birth so as to show a person as the father if one of the circumstances set out above are satisfied.[41]

7.16 Where the father is named and the registration or re-registration took place on or after 1 December 2003, he will have parental responsibility under s 4(1)(a) of the 1989 Act.

ACQUISITION BY AGREEMENT

7.17 In 1996, the year in which 649,485 children were born outside marriage, only about 3,000 parental responsibility agreements were registered.[42]

7.18 Parental responsibility can be acquired by the father if the parents agree, using a form prescribed by the Parental Responsibility Agreement Regulations 1991,[43] and which is filed in the Principal Registry.[44] Parental responsibility can also be acquired by the spouse or civil partner of one parent with responsibility if the spouse or civil partner and all parents with parental responsibility agree in a prescribed form which is recorded in the prescribed manner.[45]

Parents can agree to the acquisition of parental responsibility even when the child is subject to a care order and even when the local authority, which also has parental responsibility by virtue of s 33, disagrees.[46]

ACQUISITION BY ORDER

7.19 In 2010, 6,740 applications for parental responsibility orders were dealt with by courts. Ninety per cent were granted, 5.4% were withdrawn, 1.6% were refused or no orders were made. Parental responsibility was granted in 98% of the cases which were not withdrawn.[47]

Acquisition by a father

7.20 When the court grants a residence order, the grantee automatically acquires parental responsibility which will last as long as the order.[48] However, when a father who does not have parental responsibility is granted a residence order, the court must also make an order under s 4 which will last until it is

---

[41]   Births and Deaths Registration Act 1953, s 10A.
[42]   *Procedures for the Determination of Paternity and on the Law on Parental Responsibility for Unmarried Fathers* (Lord Chancellor's Department, 1998).
[43]   SI 1991/1478.
[44]   CA 1989, s 4(1)(b).
[45]   Ibid, s 4A as amended.
[46]   *Re X (Parental Responsibility Agreement: Children in Care)* [2000] 1 FLR 517.
[47]   *Judicial Statistics 2011* (Ministry of Justice).
[48]   CA 1989, s 12(2).

terminated under the same section.[49] Other than this, the grant of a s 4 order is discretionary and the exercise of the discretion is governed by the welfare test.[50] In 1991, Balcombe LJ in *Re H (Illegitimate Children: Father: Parental Rights)*[51] rephrased the test in a way which has been consistently followed by the Court of Appeal:

'In considering whether to make an order ... the court will have to take into account a number of factors, of which the following will undoubtedly be material (although there may well be others, as the list is not meant to be exhaustive):

(1) the degree of commitment which the father has shown towards the child;
(2) the degree of attachment which exists between the father and the child;
(3) the reasons of the father for applying for the order.'

7.21 As was made clear by Butler-Sloss LJ in *Re H (Parental Responsibility)*,[52] this tripartite test is only the starting point and cannot replace s 1. In some cases, it might be right to make an order even though the test is not satisfied and in other cases the welfare of the child may require that the order is not made, even though it was. In *Re C and V (Contact: Parental Responsibility)*[53] Ward LJ pointed out that the test included some, though not all, of the factors which might be material in answering 'a much more general' question as to whether or not the particular father showed 'genuine concern for the child and a genuine wish to assume the mantle of responsibility in law which nature had already thrust on him.' The phrasing of the wording of the test, however, enables the court to approach the issue of whether or not to grant the order by taking into account the situation of many applicants.[54] For a father, the legal status of having parental responsibility may be important only when his relationship with the child's mother (whether or not this is cohabitation or a non-cohabiting but co-operative parenting partnership) breaks down. Indeed, in many cases, he may be unaware that he does not have the same rights as a father who is married to the mother. In many cases, the lack of legal responsibility does not imply a failure or an unwillingness to take responsibility for the child's welfare. Research in 1999 found no differences between married and cohabiting fathers as regards their involvement with their children and almost all were very positive about being a father.[55] A study of a group of single fathers aged 16–24 who did not live with their children which was conducted in 1997 reported that the majority were proud that they were

---

[49]   Ibid, s 12(1).
[50]   *Re H (Parental Responsibility)* [1998] 1 FLR 855.
[51]   [1991] 1 FLR 214, at 218.
[52]   [1998] 1 FLR 855.
[53]   [1998] 1 FLR 392, at 397.
[54]   For a critical account of how *Re H* has been applied, see Gilmore 'Parental responsibility and the unmarried father – a new dimension to the debate' [2003] CFLQ 21.
[55]   Pickford *Fathers, Marriage and the Law* (Family Policy Studies, 1999), summarised in 'Fathers, Marriage and the Law' *Findings* 989 (Joseph Rowntree Foundation).

fathers and wanted to be good fathers.[56] As the Lord Chancellor's Consultation Paper on the Law of Parental Responsibility[57] commented:

> 'Discrimination between married and unmarried fathers in respect of parental responsibility is increasingly seen as unacceptable, in view of the large number of children who are now born to unmarried parents, many of whom are likely to be in stable relationships. It is clearly impossible to assume that most unmarried fathers are irresponsible or uninterested in their children and do not deserve a legal role as parents.'[58]

7.22 Although involved fathers need to prove that it is in the child's interest that an order is made, they can easily do this. At the other end of the spectrum are fathers of children born as a result of rape, transient or coercive relationships or fathers who are indifferent to their child's welfare or even existence. The tripartite test allows applications by such fathers to be rejected. The European Court of Human Rights in the case of *B v United Kingdom*[59] held that this spectrum of situations provides an objective and reasonable justification for the difference in treatment between married fathers who automatically had parental responsibility and unmarried fathers who did not.

Examples of cases where parental responsibility was granted

7.23 Commitment has to be viewed in the round and an order will not be refused solely, for example, because the father fails to provide maintenance[60] or has been convicted of possessing obscene literature[61] or is a transsexual.[62] In *Re P (Parental Responsibility)*,[63] Hirst LJ commented that the order will not be refused where a father has shown commitment and has sound and genuine reasons for wanting it simply because, through hostility towards the mother or an excess of zeal, the father might seek to exercise his responsibility inappropriately. In such a case, any inappropriate exercise of parental responsibility can be controlled by prohibited steps orders or orders for supervised contact. A parental responsibility order will not be refused merely because the father will be unable to exercise responsibility in the immediate future, for example, because the child is subject to a care order and in foster

---

56   Speak, Cameron and Gilroy *Young, Single Fathers: Participation in Fatherhood – Bridges and Barriers* (Family Policy Studies Centre), summarised in 'Young, single, non-residential fathers: their involvement in fatherhood', *Findings* 137 (Joseph Rowntree Foundation).

57   *Procedures for the Determination of Paternity and on the Law of Parental Responsibility for Unmarried Fathers* (Lord Chancellor's Department, 1998).

58   It has been argued, however, that having parental responsibility does not alter the position of the unmarried father very much. See Eekelaar 'Rethinking parental responsibility' [2001] Fam Law 426.

59   [2000] 1 FLR 1.

60   *Re H (Parental Responsibility: Maintenance)* [1996] 1 FLR 867.

61   *Re S (Parental Responsibility)* [1995] 2 FLR 648.

62   *Re L (Contact: Transsexual Applicant)* [1995] 2 FLR 438.

63   [1997] 2 FLR 722.

care.[64] Even if there is little prospect of parental responsibility being exercised, it may still be appropriate to grant it to enable a father to oppose the making of an order freeing the child for adoption. He would still have the right to receive progress reports and to apply to revoke the freeing order.[65] As Waite LJ neatly put it in *Re C (Minors) (Parental Rights)*,[66] he has 'rights in waiting'.

7.24 The granting of a parental responsibility order is a different matter from granting contact and it may be appropriate to grant parental responsibility even though a contact application is dismissed. Because it grants status and responsibilities which may not immediately be exercisable or the exercise of which may be controlled by a prohibited steps order, the hostility of the parent with care and hostility without good grounds, is less of an obstacle than when contact is being considered. In *Re J-S (Contact: Parental Responsibility)*[67] the Court of Appeal criticised a judge who had refused to grant a father parental responsibility on the ground that he had harassed the four-year-old child's mother by referrals to social services but had failed to take into account important aspects of the case including the father's genuinely held concerns for the child and the fact that the mother had not been affected by the referrals.

> 'Here we have a father who has played an important part in the life of this young child, certainly during his first 2 years ... The parents then had a shared care regime. The father is clearly devoted to him and the boy responds in turn ... In my judgement the case is overwhelming that he should be granted parental responsibility.'[68]

In *B v A (Parental Responsibility)*[69] the father of a child born to a lesbian couple was granted parental responsibility upon giving undertakings not to exercise it in certain areas without the consent of the couple.

7.25 Normally, therefore, an application for parental responsibility should not be deferred. Exceptionally, this was done in *Re D (Parental Responsibility: IVF Baby)*[70] to allow a man who had undergone treatment with the mother under the Human Fertilisation and Embryology Act 1990 and who was accordingly to be treated as the child's father under s 28(3) to demonstrate commitment through maintaining indirect contact.

---

64   *D v Hereford and Worcester County Council* [1991] 1 FLR 205, *Re CB (A Minor) (Parental Responsibility Order)* [1993] 1 FLR 920 and *Re G (A Minor) (Parental Responsibility Order)* [1994] 1 FLR 504.

65   *Re H (Illegitimate Children: Father: Parental Rights) (No 2)* [1991] 1 FLR 214. A decision to the opposite effect was made by *W v Ealing London Borough Council* [1993] 2 FLR 788.

66   [1992] 1 FLR 1.

67   [2002] EWCA Civ 1028, [2003] 1 FLR 399.

68   Per Ward LJ at [53].

69   [2006] EWHC 2 (Fam), [2006] 1 FCR 556. See **8.26**.

70   [2001] EWCA Civ 230, [2001] 1 FLR 972.

7.26 A parental responsibility order cannot be suspended.[71] In *Re G (Parental Responsibility Order)*[72] a child (G) was conceived following a 'one night' stand between his mother, (M) and his father, (F). F and G never formed a relationship and G grew up with his stepfather (P) as his psychological parent. M and P were hostile towards F and resisted his attempts to form a relationship with G. When G was 7, F applied for parental responsibility and contact. The trial judge made an order for limited contact and granted F parental responsibility but suspending the order on terms that M provided him with information about G's health, education and whereabouts. F appealed. His appeal was dismissed but the parental responsibility order was discharged on two grounds, first that there was no jurisdiction to suspend it although the same result might be achieved by a raft of specific issue orders and secondly, that although F had satisfied the tripartite test, it was ultimately a matter of welfare which could not be resolved in F's favour. Instead the application was adjourned with liberty to restore, M being invited to give undertakings to provide the information the judge had indicated. If they were not given or complied with, he could restore the application.

Examples of refusal to grant parental responsibility

7.27 Courts have refused to grant parental responsibility, for example, on the grounds of lack of commitment when the father has treated the mother with hatred and violence, failed to maintain and has abducted the child,[73] when he has inflicted injuries and deliberate cruelty on the child[74] and when he was serving 15 years' imprisonment for robbery whilst on home leave from a sentence imposed for robbery prior to the birth of his child.[75] Parental responsibility has been refused on the ground that the order would be used inappropriately, when the judge found that the father intended to use the order to interfere with and possibly undermine the mother's care, because he had no understanding of sexual boundaries and because he posed a risk to his daughter.[76]

7.28 In *M v M (Parental Responsibility)*,[77] the court refused to grant parental responsibility to a father who had serious deficiencies in his intellectual functioning as a result of an accident. Sections 3 and 4 presupposed that a father with parental responsibility would be capable of exercising his powers and fulfilling his duties whereas the father in the case could not.

---

[71] [2006] EWCA Civ 745, [2006] 2 FLR 1092.

[72] Ibid.

[73] *Re T (A Minor) (Parental Responsibility: Contact)* [1993] 2 FLR 450: 'He needs urgently to understand that he has to do something pretty dramatic to revise his approach to the mother and to revise his approach to what are real parental duties', per Butler-Sloss LJ at 460.

[74] *Re H (Parental Responsibility)* [1998] 1 FLR 855.

[75] *Re P (Parental Responsibility)* [1997] 2 FLR 722.

[76] *Re P (Parental Responsibility)* [1998] 2 FLR 96.

[77] [1999] 2 FLR 737.

Acquisition by a step-parent

7.29 Despite some years of government and judicial discouragement of step-parent adoptions, in 2004 23% of all adoptions were made to step-parents.[78] The authors of the *Review of Adoption Law: Report to Ministers of an Interdepartmental Working Group*[79] were concerned that some applications for adoption were made without a full consideration of the needs of the child:

> 'Where the prime motivation behind an adoption application is the wish to cement the family unit and put away the past, this may be confusing and lead to identity problems for the child especially (as is statistically not unlikely) the new marriage breaks down. As divorce becomes more common, it is less necessary for families to pursue step-parent adoption in order to avoid embarrassment and difficult explanations ... It is likely that in many circumstances a residence order would be a better way of confirming a step-parent's responsibility for a child because it does not alter a child's legal relationship with his or her parents and family.'

7.30 The White Paper *Adoption: A New Approach*[80] did not comment on step-parent adoptions but it is likely that this thinking lay behind the introduction of CA 1989, s 4A in the same form as a clause in an Adoption Bill introduced in 1996. The consultative document which accompanied it, *Adoption – A Service for Children*,[81] stated that it was intended to provide new alternatives to adoption.

7.31 The extent to which s 4A is used is uncertain. Are step-parents concerned enough, even if they know about the amendment, to seek parental responsibility when all is going well with their spouse? If there are problems with the absent parent, how will the grant of parental responsibility add anything of benefit? Parental responsibility can be granted under s 4A only if the applicant is married to or in a civil partnership with, rather than just living with, one of the child's parents. However, by virtue of ss 49(1) and 144(4) of the Adoption and Children Act 2002, an adoption order can be granted to 'a couple' in an 'enduring relationship' who need not be married. The number of step-parent adoptions may not fall. Hitherto, courts have been able to justify refusing to grant an adoption order by granting a residence order which conferred parental responsibility. Is it likely that the ability to make a free-standing order will change matters? How will courts approach the issue that second marriages, on average, last a shorter period than first marriages? If applications are made after the step-parent and the parent separate, an order can be made only if the applicant has remained married to the child's natural parent. Courts may be reluctant to grant orders when the marriage upon which

---

78 Judicial Statistics 2004.
79 Department of Health and Welsh Office, 1992.
80 HMSO, December 2000.
81 Department of Health and Welsh Office, 1996.

the application is based is in the process of being dissolved.[82] An alternative route is to grant the step-parent a shared residence order.[83]

7.32 It is unlikely that courts will impose an easier test for step-parents than the tripartite test. Requiring the step-parent to demonstrate commitment and attachment will be likely to mean that usually the applicant will have had to live with the child, whether before or after marriage to the child's parent for some time. When the absent parent plays little or no part in the child's life, an order is likely to be readily granted to a committed applicant in order to ensure that there are at least two people who are able and willing to exercise parental responsibility. Where the absent parent plays a full part in the child's life, emphasis may be placed on the requirement imposed by CA 1989, s 1(5) that the court must be satisfied that granting the order is better for the child than not granting it, thereby requiring the applicant to show that an order is needed.

7.33 In *Re R (Parental Responsibility)*,[84] seemingly the only reported case concerning s 4A, a child, G, was born to a man (S) and M who was married to R, a much older man. M persuaded both S and R that R was G's father. When G's birth was registered, R was named as the father. When G was 2, M left R taking G with her and went to live with S. R applied for parental responsibility. The order was refused but M was ordered to provide R with regular information about G and contact was ordered.

> 'It can ... be seen that in normal circumstances the beneficiary of such an order will be a person who might be described as an incoming step-parent who wishes to bring up a child together with the parent with parental responsibility and will be centrally participating in the upbringing of the child in future. [However] on behalf of the mother, [it is accepted] that the court's power to grant parental responsibility is not limited to such paradigm circumstances. However, [counsel] argues that the other situations in which an order might be made are likely to be limited. I agree. One can foresee a situation in which an order might be made following separation in favour of the parent of a much older child, who turns out at a late stage not to be the biological parent, but who will continue with the child's approval to carry on a full parental role. What is important is what is in the child's best interests for the future.'[85]

R had G's psychological parent for nearly 3 years and had continued to fulfil that role, though in a much diminished way with 'limitless' commitment to G and a strong desire to play as great a part as possible in his life, not excluding removing him from the care of his mother.

> 'However, he is not G's biological father and I do not consider that it is in G's true interests to invest (or reinvest) R with parental responsibility. It would place him at the heart of all future important decisions about G in a way that is, in my view,

---

82   See also Masson 'The impact of the Adoption and Children Act 2002' [2003] Fam Law 580 and Booth 'Parental responsibility – what changes' [2004] Fam Law 353.
83   See **8.28–8.32**.
84   [2011] EWHC 1535 (Fam), [2011] 2 FLR 1132.
85   Ibid, per Peter Jackson J at [36] to [37].

likely to lead to conflict with the mother. I do not foresee R playing such an
important role in G's future development that it would be beneficial to G for him
to have equal status with the mother. I do not see this as a case in which the power
under s 4A should be exercised for a purpose that was probably not intended. It is
only by chance that the power exists at all. It would not do so if R and M were
already divorced, as well they might have been.'

It remains to be seen whether this decision, which leaves open the question how
long the psychological parent has to live with a child before he or she will be
granted parental responsibility on separation, is an indication of an approach
which will generally be adopted.

7.34 Where the parent is not married to or in a civil partnership with a
partner, the only ways in which the partner can obtain parental responsibility is
by an adoption order, a special guardianship order or a residence order. In *Re
A (Joint Residence: Parental Responsibility)*[86] H was born to M who was living
with but not married to A. For 2 years A believed that he was H's father and
when he and M separated he applied for parental responsibility. H's biological
father played no part in the proceedings. The trial judge made a shared
residence order to A and M in order to give A parental responsibility and said
that A should be regarded for all purposes as H's father. However M was to be
H's prime carer. An order was made prohibiting M from introducing H to his
biological father for 2 years without the agreement of A or permission from the
court. M appealed against the joint residence order but her appeal was
dismissed. However the Court of Appeal considered the judge's remarks about
A being regarded for all purposes to be H's father, 'unfortunate'.

> 'The fact is, Mr A is not H's father or parent either in common parlance or under
> any definition contained in the Children Act 1989 or other legislation (cf *J v J (A
> Minor: Property Transfer)*.[87] He is not a father by biological paternity or adoption,
> nor a stepfather by marriage. He is a person entitled, by reason of the role he has
> played and should continue to play in H's life, to an order conferring parental
> responsibility upon him. He is thus a person who, jointly with the mother, enjoys
> the rights, duties, powers, responsibilities and authority which by law a parent of a
> child has in relation to that child (see s 3(1) of the Children Act 1989) but he does
> not thereby become the father of that child.'

7.35 For the use of shared residence orders in order to grant parental
responsibility, see **10.39**.

Donor fathers

7.36 Difficult problems can occur when a mother either singly or as half of a
lesbian couple seeks a donor so that she can have children. What should be
done if despite assurances to the contrary, the donor seeks to play a role in the
life of the child?

---

[86] [2008] EWCA Civ 867, [2008] 2 FLR 1593.
[87] [1993] 2 FLR 56.

7.37 In *Re D (contact and parental responsibility: lesbian mothers and known father)*[88] the donor sought parental responsibility but undertook not to exercise his parental responsibility to involve himself without the consent of A (the mother) and C (her partner) in particular areas of the child's life where they might anticipate that problems might be caused, namely her medical treatment and her schooling. A and C objected to the grant of parental responsibility, fearing B's influence on the stability of their family and relationship. By the time of the order the man was having contact with the child. Having heard detailed expert evidence from Dr Sturge, a consultant child psychiatrist, who thought the decision 'pretty finely balanced', Mrs Justice Black (as she then was) granted the man parental responsibility. She recorded her anxiety about whether making a parental responsibility order would potentially threaten the stability of the child's immediate family from 'interference' from the applicant as well as the impact on society's perception of the family if he were, in fact, to use it to become more visible in the child's life. On the other hand, she was very mindful of the authorities which stressed the status aspect of parental responsibility and those which indicated that it is not appropriate to refuse to grant it because of a feared misuse which should more properly be controlled by s 8 orders. In addition, the man's actions towards D's family fell far short of the sort of activity that had previously been seen by the courts as sufficient to found a refusal of parental responsibility.

> 'Perhaps most importantly of all, I am considerably influenced by the reality that Mr B is D's father. Whatever new designs human beings have for the structure of their families, that aspect of nature cannot be overcome. It is to be hoped that as society accepts alternative arrangements more readily, as it seems likely will happen over the next few years, the impulse to hide or to marginalise a child's father so as not to call attention to an anomalous family will decline, although accommodating the emotional consequences of untraditional fatherhood and motherhood and of the sort of de facto, non-biological parenthood that is experienced by a step-parent or same sex partner will inevitably remain discomfiting.'

The dilemma facing the judge had been 'greatly eased' by Mr B's offer to be bound by conditions which would prevent him from being intrusive in the obvious situations which might be anticipated as problem areas and allowed her to take 'a creative approach to parental responsibility in an attempt to make it serve the novel demands of a case such as this ...'. The applicant was granted parental responsibility on the basis that he would not visit or contact the child's school or any health professional involved in the child's care without, in each case, the prior written consent of Ms A or Ms C. If the conditions were not observed, the court might be invited to reconsider the whole question of parental responsibility.

7.38 In *Re B (Role of Biological Father)*[89] two civil partners agreed with a donor that the child would grow up in a nuclear family which would not

---

[88]   [2006] EWHC 2 (Fam), [2006] 1 FCR 556.
[89]   [2007] EWHC 1952 (Fam), [2008] 1 FLR 1015.

include him. However, after the birth he applied for contact and parental responsibility. Mr Justice Hedley, having heard evidence from Dr Sturge made no order on the application for parental responsibility but ordered direct contact four times a year. There was no purpose in imposing conditions of the kind Mrs Justice Black imposed in *Re D (Contact and Parental Responsibility: Lesbian Mothers and Known Father)*[90] as the applicant would undoubtedly seek to exercise parental responsibility and forcefully advance his views. His role would be that as uncle.

> '[He] has a dual role: as uncle and biological father. The fulfilment of an avuncular role needs no contribution from the court; that must be worked out in the ordinary course of extended family life. It is his unique biological position that commands attention for all the reasons set out as I tried to view this through [the child's] growing eyes ... The court needs to be clear about the purpose of contact. It is not to give [the applicant] parental status in the eyes of [the child] or indeed anyone else. It is not to allow the development of a relationship which would amount to parental. That would threaten [the mother and her partner] and would not be consistent with their autonomy as a nuclear family. It follows that contact must not have a feel of regularity to it. On the other hand, it is essential that the door is kept open for [the child] so that without artificiality he can picture [the applicant] as someone significant but not ordinarily important in his life yet someone with whom (in time and if he so wishes) he can explore the implications of the kind man who enabled him to be and he can ask questions to satisfy his own natural curiosity.'

7.39 In a third case, *R v E and F (Female Parents: Known Father)*[91] the mother was in a civil partnership and the North American donor father in a same-sex marriage. The father and his partner were involved in the child's life from birth but after a falling out when the child was 5 the relationship between the four adults deteriorated. The donor father applied for parental responsibility. After receiving advice from Dr Sturge, Mr Justice Bennett refused to grant the application but ordered contact. Both men were asserting that there was 'one family' which was not the reality. The reality had been that since the child's birth he had been parented by both women. The father, whilst being committed and loving to the child was not undertaking the role of a parent. The child's nuclear family comprised the child and the two women, who had his daily care and had taken all the decisions relating to his upbringing and welfare. The women had good reason to perceive the application for parental responsibility as being a direct threat to the autonomy of their family.

7.40 In all three cases the child already had two parent figures who had parental responsibility either through a shared residence order or by a s 4ZA(1)(b) agreement. No additional person with parental responsibility was required nor did the child require someone with the status of father. This might be thought to be the a key welfare factor. However, the distinguishing rationale behind the decisions was that in *Re B (Role of Biological Father)* and *R v E and F (Female Parents: Known Father)* the court was satisfied that granting

---

[90]   [2006] EWHC 2 (Fam).
[91]   [2010] EWHC 417 (Fam), [2010] 2 FLR 383.

parental responsibility would upset the family whereas in *Re D (Contact and Parental Responsibility: Lesbian Mothers and Known Father)* the court was persuaded it would not. This indicates that in cases of this kind – and possibly any s 4A(1)(b) cases – more weight will be placed on the risk of disturbance than in the more conventional s 4(1)(c) cases. A decision in a case where the mother is not in a civil partnership or the applicant is exemplary in his approach to the mother and child will be even more difficult to reach.

7.41   When s 2A of the Births and Deaths Registration Act 1953 comes into force (see **7.13**) a donor in this type of case would have to be registered as a father and would thereby gain parental responsibility. If he is not, he would be able to apply for the child's birth to be re-registered under s 14A after a declaration of parentage has been made. There appears to be no reason why even before the section comes into force the putative father cannot seek a declaration of paternity and then apply for re-registration. Both stages require the exercise of discretion – the first by the court and the second by the Registrar General. This was not explored in any of the three cases because s 4A of the 1989 Act was not in force at the time of the child's birth.

7.42   For a discussion of other aspects of similar donor arrangements, see **10.46**.

Acquisition of parental responsibility by second female parent

7.43   Where a child has a parent by virtue of s 43 of the Human Fertilisation and Embryology Act 2008 (see **6.21**) and is not a person to whom s 1(3) of the Family Law Reform Act 1987 applies,[92] that parent shall acquire parental responsibility for the child if:

(a)   she becomes registered as a parent of the child;[93]

(b)   she and the child's mother make an agreement providing for her to have parental responsibility for the child; or

(c)   the court, on her application, orders that she shall have parental responsibility for the child.

REVOKING THE ORDER

7.44   Principle 3.32 of *The Principles of European Family Law Regarding Parental Responsibilities*[94] states that 'The competent authority should discharge the holder of parental responsibilities wholly or in part where his or her behaviour or neglect causes serious risk to person or property of the child'.

---

[92]   Ie not treated as having been adopted or legitimated.
[93]   Under paragraphs (a), (b) and (c) of s 10(1B) and of s 10A(1B) of the Births and Deaths Registration Act 1953 and similar provisions for Scotland and Northern Ireland.
[94]   See **7.10**.

7.45 A parental responsibility order can be revoked by the court on an application made by any person who has parental responsibility or, with leave of the court, by the child himself. The court may grant leave for the child to make an application only if it is satisfied that the child has sufficient understanding to make the application.

7.46 The test to be applied is the s 1 test. Where the court was required by s 4 to grant parental responsibility to a father because it made a residence order in his favour, it may not revoke the order for responsibility while the residence order remains in force.[95]

7.47 The Court Service does not provide statistics for the number of orders which are discharged or agreements terminated each year, but they are likely to be very low indeed because, since 1991, only one case has been reported. In *Re P (Terminating Parental Responsibility)*,[96] Singer J terminated a parental responsibility agreement in circumstances in which a father was convicted of causing serious injury to his 9-week-old daughter. The agreement had been entered into after the injuries had been caused, at a time when, according to the mother, she believed the father to be innocent. Singer J held that parental responsibility, once obtained, should not be terminated on less than solid grounds, with a presumption for continuance rather than termination. Nor should the ability of the mother to apply for an order be allowed to become a weapon in her hands:

> '[Termination] should be used by the court as an appropriate step in the regulation of the child's life where the circumstances really do warrant it and not otherwise.'

In the instant case, the father's lack of commitment, the difficulties which continuation would have caused the child's foster parents and the local authority in whose care she had been placed and the absence of any prospect that the father would be able to exercise responsibility in a way which would be beneficial to the child justified terminating the agreement.

---

[95] CA 1989, s 12(4).
[96] [1995] 1 FLR 1048.

Chapter 8

CONTROLLING THE EXERCISE OF PARENTAL RESPONSIBILITY

INTRODUCTION

8.1   Parental responsibility comprises an ill-defined bundle of rights and responsibilities which extend from clearly defined and well established rights, albeit not absolute – for example, the right to withhold consent to the child being adopted but subject to the power of the court to dispense with consent on the ground that the child's welfare requires adoption[1] – to vague responsibilities such as to control a child's day-to-day life. In recent decades, perhaps marked by a move from thinking in terms of 'rights' to 'responsibilities',[2] parental autonomy has increasingly been restricted by a recognition that rights or responsibilities have to be exercised for the benefit of the child, justifying state interference. Such interference can be in relation to particular acts, for example prohibiting female genital mutilation[3] or banning corporal punishment in schools.[4] In *Williamson v Secretary of State for Education and Employment and Others*,[5] for example, Lord Bingham of Cornhill held that the legislature was entitled to take the view that all corporal punishment of children at school was undesirable and unnecessary and that other means of discipline were available and preferable.

> 'On this Parliament was entitled, if it saw fit, to lead and guide public opinion. Parliament was further entitled to take the view that a universal ban was the appropriate way to achieve the desired end. Parliament was entitled to decide that, contrary to the claimants' submissions, a universal ban is preferable to a selective ban which exempts schools where the parents or teachers have an ideological belief in the efficacy and desirability of a mild degree of carefully-controlled corporal punishment.'

Or, the interference can be by way of care proceedings based on the treatment of individual children, provided they have suffered or are likely to suffer significant harm attributable to the care they have received or are likely to

---

[1]   Adoption and Children Act 2002, s 52(1).

[2]   A discourse complicated by the growing importance attached to Conventional human rights.

[3]   Prohibition of Female Circumcision Act 2003, s 1 and see *K v Secretary of State for the Home Department, Fornah v Secretary of State for the Home Department* [2006] UKHL 46, [2007] 1 AC 412.

[4]   Education Act 1996, ss 548–549. See also Choudhry 'Parental responsibility and corporal punishment' in Probert, Gilmore and Herring (eds) *Repsonsible Parents and Parental Responsibility* (Hart Publishing, 2009).

[5]   [2005] UKHL 15, [2005] 2 AC 246, at [50].

receive not being what it would reasonable to expect a parent to give.[6] However, absent this, a sole holder of parental responsibilities is unlikely to face challenges to any parental decisions.[7]

8.2   Challenge may however arise if another person, parent or otherwise, or, possibly the child herself objects to the way in which the other parent is exercising or proposes to exercise the responsibility. Then, an application can be made under s 10 of the Children Act 1989 for a specific issue or prohibited steps order as defined by s 8(1).

8.3   Lord Mackay of Clashfern who, as Lord Chancellor, was responsible for sponsoring the Children Bill, hoped that:

> '... the professionals and the courts seize the opportunity to bring home to the parties at the outset of a dispute that [s 8] orders do not affect their status as parents, that they remain responsible for their child's upbringing and that, except in so far as the court orders may settle certain issues, they are expected to continue to play a full part in that upbringing in cooperation with the other parent.'[8]

Some exercise of parental responsibility relating to children requires the consent of all persons with parental responsibility. Others can be exercised by one person independently but (according to one view of the law) only after consulting the others. However, other than special guardians no person with parental responsibility can out-vote another (see **8.7** and **12.43**).

8.4   Courts are able to control the exercise of parental responsibility by two kinds of orders under s 8 of the Act. They can grant a prohibited steps order, that is, an order that no step can be taken by a parent in meeting his parental responsibility which is of a kind specified in the order without the consent of the court.[9] Or they can make a specific issue order, that is, an order giving directions for the purpose of determining a specific question which has arisen or which may arise in connection with any aspect of parental responsibility.[10] Orders of both types are commonly used together. For example, a court may decide that a child should be known by a particular name (a specific issue order) and prohibit a parent from changing the name or causing the child to be known by a different name (a prohibited steps order). In addition, the High Court can control the exercise of parental responsibility by the use of wardship, which vests in the court an overriding control of major decisions

---

6   Children Act 1989, s 31.
7   Herring 'Introduction: parental responsibility – law, issues and themes' in Probert, Gilmore and Herring (eds) *Responsible Parents and Parental Responsibility* (Hart Publishing, 2009), at p 17.
8   'Perceptions of the Children Bill and beyond. the Joseph Jackson Memorial Lecture' (1989) 14 NLJ Ap 505.
9   CA 1989, s 8(1).
10   Ibid.

relating to the child. For example, if a child is a ward, his mother, even if she has sole parental responsibility, cannot change his name without the permission of the court.[11]

8.5 The ability to apply to the court for a prohibited steps or specific issue order is not unregulated. A parent or special guardian or most people with parental responsibility may apply without first seeking the permission of the court. Others, including the child, will need to apply for permission under s 10(1)(a)(ii) (see **Chapter 15**).

8.6 The authors of the influential *Beyond the Best Interests of the Child*[12] argued that 'once it is determined who will be the custodial parent, it is that parent, not the court, who must decide under what conditions he or she wishes to raise the child'.[13] However, courts have never adopted this approach. While recognising that parental responsibility does not give the right to challenge decisions made by the carer in relation to 'all matters which arise in the course of the day-to-day management of the child's life'[14] the court retains the power to decide whether and to what extent it should intervene.

> 'In the event of disagreement between them on a specific issue relating to the child, the court will have to resolve it. If the father were to seek to misuse the rights given him under s 4 such misuse could, as a second to last resort, be controlled by the court under a prohibited steps order against him and/or a specific issue order. The very last resort of all would presumably be the discharge of the parental responsibility order.'[15][16]

Where permission is required, it can be refused if, for example, the matter is not one of importance. In *Re C (A Minor) (Leave to Seek section 8 Orders)*,[17] for example, the court refused permission for a girl aged nearly 15 to apply for an order directing her parents to allow her to go to Bulgaria for a holiday.

CONSENT OR CONSULTATION?

8.7 The law relating to whether one of a number of people can unilaterally exercise a power relating to parental responsibility is confused. Certain decisions, by statute, require the consent of all persons with parental responsibility, even though that consent is given by each of them individually. The most important of these is an adoption order, or an order placing a child for adoption, which requires the agreement of both parents or guardians with parental responsibility while making provision for the court to dispense with

---

[11] For an example of the use of wardship in a situation of sustained parental conflict, see *T v S (Wardship)* [2011] EWHC 1608 (Fam), [2012] 1 FLR 230.

[12] Goldstein, Freud and Solnit (Free Press, 1973).

[13] Ibid, at p 38.

[14] *Re P (A Minor) (Parental Responsibility Order)* [1994] 1 FLR 578.

[15] If possible: see **7.43**.

[16] *Re P (A Minor) (Parental Responsibility Order)* [1994] 1 FLR 578, per Wilson J at 585.

[17] [1994] 1 FLR 26.

the consent of each parent individually.[18] The exercise of certain powers requires the consent of all persons with parental responsibility. Section 13(1) of CA 1989, for example, provides that when a residence order is in force, no person may cause the child to be known by a new surname or remove him from the United Kingdom (except, in the case of the person in whose favour the residence order was made, for a period of less than 1 month) without the written consent of every person who has parental responsibility or the leave of the court.

8.8   In the absence of such provisions, the position is unclear. For example, can one parent with parental responsibility change the child's name (when no residence order is in force) or school, consent to major medical treatment which is not required immediately (for example, sterilisation or circumcision) to take him abroad to live, without the consent of the other parent or even without consultation?

The Law Commission

8.9   It is important for the child and the parents that the extent of their powers is clear. The Law Commission in its report *Review of Child Law: Guardianship and Custody*[19] examined the matter in detail and recommended that parental responsibility should be able to be exercised without the consent of or consulting others:

> 'In most cases there are two people, usually the child's parents, with parental responsibility, but the present law is not clear about whether they may act independently. The Guardianship of Minors Act 1973 provides that married parents may do so but the Children Act 1975 provides that "joint" holders of any parental right may act alone only if another holder has not signified disapproval. As we explained in our Working Paper on Custody, we believe it important to preserve the equal status of parents and their power to act independently of one another unless and until a court orders otherwise. This should be seen as a part of the general aim of encouraging both parents to feel concerned and responsible for the welfare of their children. A few respondents suggested that they should have a legal duty to consult one another on major matters in their children's lives, arguing that this would increase parental co-operation and involvement after separation or divorce. This is an objective which we all share. However, whether or not the parents are living together, a legal duty of consultation seems both unworkable and undesirable. The person looking after the child has to be able to take decisions in the child's best interests as and when they arise. Some may have to be taken very quickly. In reality, as we pointed out in our Working Paper on Custody, it is that person who will have to put these decisions into effect and that person who has the degree of practical control over the child to be able to do so. The child may well suffer if that parent is prevented by the other's disapproval and thus has to go to court to resolve the matter, still more if the parent is inhibited by the fear that the other will disapprove or by difficulties of contacting him or of deciding whether

---

18   Adoption and Children Act 2002, ss 19 and 21.
19   (1988) Law Com No 172, at para 2.10. One of the commissioners was Professor Brenda Hoggett, later to become Baroness Hale of Richmond.

what is proposed is or is not a major matter requiring consultation. In practice, when the parents disagree about a matter of upbringing the burden should be on the one seeking to prevent a step which the other is proposing or to impose a course of action which only the other can put into effect, to take the matter to court. Otherwise the court might be inundated with cases, disputes might escalate well beyond their true importance, and in the meantime, the children might suffer. We recommend, therefore, that the equal and independent status of parents be preserved and, indeed, applied to others (principally guardians) who may share parental responsibility in future. This will not, of course, affect any statutory provision which requires the consent of both parents, for example, to the adoption of the child.'

8.10 The recommendation was carried into effect by the legislation. Section 2(7) provides that:

'Where more than one person has parental responsibility for a child, each of them may act alone and without the other (or others) in meeting that responsibility but nothing in this Part shall be taken to affect the operation of any enactment which requires the consent of more than one person in a matter affecting the child.'

The cases

8.11 The effect of the section seems clear, but in *Re PC (Change of Surname)*[20] Holman J held that the consent of more than one person might still be required by some other source of law other than an enactment. Thus, a mother with whom the children of the marriage were living but in respect of whom no residence order had been made was held not to have the right to change their surname without the consent of their father. In *Re G (Parental Responsibility: Education)*,[21] Glidewell LJ held, obiter, that a mother should have been consulted before her son was removed from the school which he was attending and sent to a boarding school. This approach has been criticised[22] and resurrects the difficulty alluded to by the Law Commission. Which responsibilities can be exercised independently and which carry a duty to consult? How are they to be recognised? This confusion raises difficulties not just for parents but also third parties. Is the consent of both parents with parental responsibility required before a child is circumcised? The Court of Appeal in *Re J (A Minor) (Prohibited Steps Order: Circumcision)*[23] held, again obiter, that it was. The operation was of considerable consequence and irreversible and 'it must, therefore, join the exceptional categories where disagreement between holders of parental responsibility must be submitted to the court for determination'.[24] But suppose the father had arranged for the child to be circumcised during contact without the mother's consent. Would the

---

[20] [1997] 2 FLR 730.
[21] [1994] 2 FLR 964.
[22] See Eekelaar 'Do parents have a duty to consult?' (1998) 114 LQR 337; Eekelaar 'Re-thinking parental responsibility' [2001] Fam Law 426; and Maidment 'Parental responsibility – duty to consult?' [2001] Fam Law 518.
[23] [2000] 1 FLR 571.
[24] Ibid, per Thorpe LJ at 576.

doctor be liable in tort for assault or even guilty of assault? On the authority of *Re D (A Minor) (Wardship: Sterilisation)*,[25] probably yes. If he is, can the child's mother as a litigation friend sue him on the child's behalf without the consent of the father?

8.12 A source of the confusion may lie in the desire which was shared by the Law Commission that parents and those with parental responsibility should co-operate and consult. In *Re J (A Minor) (Prohibited Steps Order: Circumcision)*,[26] the President said that:

> 'The decision to circumcise a child ... should only be carried out where the parents together approve of it or, in the absence of parental agreement, where a court decides that the operation is in the best interests of the child.'

8.13 This suggestion that there should be a legal duty to act in concert or, at least, consult has been criticised by John Eekelaar who argues that it is a mistake to 'cast into legal form an aspiration of good conduct'.[27] Where the relationship between parents is good, it is not needed and where it is poor, how could it be enforced? He also raises questions such as what amounts to consultation? Is provision of information enough or must there be agreement about outcome? What if the non-resident parent has demonstrated no interest in the child?

8.14 Helen Reece adds that 'although one view is that this case law has augmented the authority aspect of paternal responsibility, the better view is that these precedents have further diluted parental responsibility since they are likely to lead to more decisions being taken by courts as opposed to parents.'[28] This overstates the case. Undoubtedly the decisions provide parents with a greater opportunity to litigate but in practice, these opportunities are seldom taken, save as regards change of names and relocation (see **Chapter 9**). Despite the nice legal problems posed by the decisions, the approach of the courts that such decisions are better taken after at least consultation if not agreement may influence the approach of parents and will influence family lawyers and serve to discourage litigation.

8.15 The dicta of Dame Elizabeth Butler-Sloss P and Thorpe LJ were obiter because the court was being asked to decide the matter on its merits on an application for a specific issue order. 'Ought' might therefore have been intended to mean 'it is desirable that ...' and not 'it is requisite that ...'. If this is correct, then the only decision which is legally binding is that of Holman J which is limited to a change of name. If this interpretation is wrong, the list of powers which can only be exercised with the consent of all persons with parental responsibility include:

---

25 [1976] 1 All ER 326.
26 [2000] 1 FLR 571.
27 Eekelaar 'Rethinking parental responsibility' [2001] Fam Law 426.
28 'The degradation of parental responsibility' in *Responsible Parents and Parental Responsibility* op cit, at p 93.

- change of name (even if there is no residence order);

- removing the child from the jurisdiction for a period of more than 1 month;

- a serious and irreversible operation such as circumcision, abortion or sterilisation, save in circumstances where the operation has to be carried out in an emergency or medical necessity;

- change of school;

- immunisation.[29]

If, as the cases seem to suggest, these powers are those which would require the consent of the High Court if the child was a ward, they will also include:

- commencing proceedings on behalf of the child or making an application to the Criminal Injuries Compensation Board;[30]

- allowing the child to be interviewed by the police.[31]

8.16 In comparison, in Germany, for example, and under the *Principles of European Family Law Regarding Parental Responsibility*[32] all holders of parental responsibility are free to take day-to-day decisions but have to agree on decisions of 'significance' or of 'importance'.[33]

8.17 Parents, it seems, may be in favour of at least a moral if not a legal duty to consult. A survey of the public[34] found respondents strongly in favour. However, when it came to who should take the final decision, they were less inclined to support the court taking it save (by a slim majority) in cases of relocation, favouring instead the parent with care having control. It should be noted though that the sample was unrepresentative of separated parents.

Practical considerations

8.18 In most circumstances, it does not matter in practice whether powers can be exercised independently or not. In so far as acts are reversible, for example, changes of name, the court can reverse them whether or not the original act was a valid exercise of parental responsibility. The fact that this may mean a

---

29   *Re C (Welfare of Child: Immunisation)* [2003] EWCA Civ 1148, [2003] 2 FLR 1095.
30   *Re G (A Ward) (Criminal Injuries: Compensation)* [1991] 1 FLR 89.
31   *Re S (Minors) (Wardship: Disclosure of Material)* [1988] 1 FLR 1.
32   (2007) Commission on European Family Law available at: www.ceflonline.net/Reports/ Principles%20PR%20English.pdf.
33   See Scherpe 'Establishing and ending parental responsibility' in *Responsible Parents and Parental Responsibility* op cit, at p 58.
34   Potter and Williams 'Parental responsibility and the duty to consult' [2005] CFLQ 207.

change for the child will of course be a valid consideration,[35] but so too will be whether the other parent had agreed or been consulted. A failure to consult will inevitably make the court more willing to exercise its discretion.

8.19 When a parent is considering making any important decision involving a child, it is important therefore that the other parent is consulted, both to demonstrate reasonableness and, more importantly, because the child's interests are best served if both parents are able to contribute to a major decision about his life. If agreement cannot be reached, the parent wanting to make a change should consider whether or not to apply to the court for a specific issue order and should be prepared to justify not making an application. Whether or not an application is made will depend on the nature of the issue. How serious is it? Is it reversible and, if so, will reversing it be likely to adversely affect the child? How urgent is the matter? From a tactical point of view, the parent should also ask whether the other parent will be likely to challenge the decision. If, for example, a mother with sole parental responsibility wants to emigrate, a father who has regular contact with the child is likely to apply for a prohibited steps order. A failure by the mother to consult him about her plans and, if necessary, to apply to the court before putting her plans into action, selling her home, etc can well lead to court action which will cause her great inconvenience and delay her move as well as raising doubts about her willingness to foster contact between father and child and to consult him about future decisions if she moves.

8.20 Where parents disagree about an important issue, the court has to decide the matter on the welfare principle and making 'no order' is not an option.[36] In *Re P (Parental Dispute: Judicial Determination)*,[37] for example, divorced parents were in dispute as to the choice of senior school for their daughters. The trial judge found that both parents were fully alive to the academic needs of the children and ordered that future questions in respect of their education, including the choice of schools, should be decided by the mother (with whom the girls were living) in consultation with the father. The Court of Appeal allowed the father's appeal and directed a rehearing. A choice of school was fundamental and it was the duty of the court to reach a clear decision in the absence of parental agreement.

SPECIAL GUARDIANSHIP

8.21 Section 14C(1)(b) of the Children Act 1989 provides that 'a special guardian is entitled to exercise parental responsibility to the exclusion of any other person with parental responsibility for the child (apart from another

---

[35]　See, for example, *Re C (Change of Surname)* [1998] 2 FLR 656.

[36]　*Re H (Children) (Residence Order: Condition)* [2001] EWCA Civ 1338, [2001] 2 FLR 1277, disapproving *Re X and Y (Leave to Remove from Jurisdiction: No Order Principle)* [2001] 2 FLR 118.

[37]　[2002] EWCA Civ 1627, [2003] 1 FLR 286.

special guardian)'. The meaning of this sub-section is unclear unless it emphasises that where there is a special guardian, s 2(7) is to be strictly applied. See further **12.43**.

WARDSHIP

8.22 If a child is a ward, no major decision may be made about the child without the consent of the High Court, whether or not the person making the decision has sole parental responsibility. Making the child a ward therefore automatically prevents parental responsibility being validly exercised. Since the Children Act came into force however, the High Court has been reluctant to allow wardship to be used if the s 8 powers are sufficient. As Waite LJ put it in *Re CT (A Minor) (Wardship: Representation)*:[38]

> 'The courts' undoubted discretion to allow wardship proceedings to go forward in a suitable case is subject to their clear duty, in loyalty to the scheme and purpose of the Children Act legislation, to permit recourse to wardship only when it becomes apparent to the judge in any particular case that the question the court is determining in regard to the minor's upbringing or property cannot be resolved under the statutory procedures in Part II of the Act in a way which secures the best interests of the child; or where the minor's person is in a state of jeopardy from which he can only be protected by giving him the status of a ward of court; or where the court's functions need to be secured from the effects, potentially injurious to the child, of external influences (intrusive publicity for example) and it is decided that conferring on the child the status of a ward will prove the more effective deterrent than the ordinary sanctions of contempt of court which already protect all family proceedings.'[39]

Examples

C v Salford City Council and Others[40]

8.23 Roman Catholic foster parents who had, for 2 years, looked after a 3-year-old orthodox Jewish girl with Down's Syndrome applied for a residence order. Hale J discharged the wardship on the ground that the foster parents' application for a residence order gave the court all the powers it needed in the circumstances of the particular case.

Re W (Wardship: Discharge: Publicity)[41]

8.24 Children who had been warded prior to the Act coming into force were living with their father who some years later applied for the wardship to be discharged. The parties agreed that the wardship should not be continued

---

[38] [1993] 2 FLR 278, at 282.
[39] See also *Re M and J (Wardship: Supervision and Residence Orders)* [2003] EWHC 1585 (Fam), [2003] 2 FCR 541 and *T v S (Wardship)* [2011] EWHC 1608 (Fam), [2012] 1 FLR 230.
[40] [1994] 2 FLR 926.
[41] [1995] 2 FLR 466.

unless it offered advantages to the boys which could not be secured under the Children Act. In the circumstances of the case, the court found that wardship did offer such advantages. The father had 'fanned the flames' of the children's concern about their mother, had unilaterally changed their school, had used his home as 'a refuge for men' and had sought publicity. Even though prohibited steps orders had been made at first instance, the Court of Appeal held that it was not possible to frame a prohibited steps order or one under the general inherent jurisdiction which could anticipate every way in which the father might seek publicity or act in a way which could be harmful to the boys. Wardship would afford the boys some degree of protection from his actions.[42]

Re W and X (Wardship: Relatives Rejected as Foster Carers)[43]

8.25 In care proceedings the local authority wished to allow the children to live with their maternal grandparents under a residence order coupled with a supervision order. It was held that the circumstances of the case including the need for external control of the placement and the inability to achieve this because the grandparents could not be approved as foster parents justified the use of wardship.

UNDERTAKINGS

8.26 In *B v A (Parental Responsibility)*[44] the father of a child born to a lesbian couple undertook not to exercise parental responsibility in particular areas of the child's life where the couple might anticipate that problems might be caused, namely her medical treatment and schooling.

---

[42] For a discussion of the interplay between wardship and the Children Act, see Mitchell 'Whatever happened to wardship?' [2001] Fam Law 130, at 212.
[43] [2003] EWHC 2206 (Fam), [2004] 1 FLR 415.
[44] [2006] EWHC 0002 (Fam).

Chapter 9

CONTROLLING PARENTAL RESPONSIBILITY: COMMON PROBLEMS

INTRODUCTION

9.1 Specific issue and prohibited steps orders can be used by the court in order to resolve disputes relating to the exercise of parental responsibility. As 'parental responsibility' is an imprecise term (see **7.2**) the court in practice has a wide, but not unlimited, discretion to decide most if not all disputes relating to the care of a child.

9.2 Some categories of dispute come before the courts more frequently than others. Of these, two – change of names and international relocation – have been so frequent in the past that the Court of Appeal has given guidance on how the exercise of the judicial discretion should be approached. No statistics are available as to the frequency with which such disputes arise but anecdotally, change of name cases come before the courts less frequently than previously, possibly because of the increase in the numbers of children whose parents are not married to each other and who may be registered with their mother's surname at birth. However, there is a perception that disputed cases of international relocation are increasing as individuals become more likely to move between countries and therefore children are more likely to have one or both parents with close connections with other countries.

9.3 Cases involving the granting or withholding of consent to a child between the ages of 16 and 18 marrying or entering a civil partnership are extremely rare if they occur at all but the issues involved are discussed briefly in case they arise in applications relating to forced marriages.

9.4 Whatever the nature of the dispute or whether the Court of Appeal has given guidance, the welfare of the child concerned remains of paramount importance and, as emphasised by the Court of Appeal in *MK v CK (Relocation: Shared Care Arrangements)*[1] the weight to be given to each factor in the s 1(3) checklist will vary according to the circumstances of the individual child. This lodestar is of as great importance when deciding issues relating to the exercise of parental responsibility as it is when deciding issues of residence and contact. While many cases concern cases of genuine disagreement between parents as to what is best – most of which will require mediation at the outset in an attempt to avoid unnecessary litigation – there are all too many where the

---

[1] [2011] EWCA Civ 793, per Moore-Bick LJ at [86] and Black LJ at [144]. See also **9.45**.

dispute is merely an indication of more extensive disagreement and rivalry between parents.[2] In *Surtees v Kingston-upon Thames RBC*[3] Browne-Wilkinson VC said that:

> 'The studied calm of the Royal Courts of Justice, concentrating on one point at a time, is light years away from the circumstances prevailing in the average home.'

In his introduction to a collection of academic papers which examine the scope of parental responsibility,[4] Jonathan Herring comments that this judicial acknowledgement of the reality of family life reveals that 'although there are dicta indicating that high standards are expected, the judiciary here acknowledge that parents cannot always promote their children's welfare nor protect them from harm.'[5] Herring is writing here about the fact that parents, unlike courts, are not required to put the interests of their child first when making decisions but the passage also serves to underline their inability to do so on occasions.

CHANGE OF NAME

The importance of names

9.5   Names are powerful things. They identify us as individuals but at the same time can place us within contexts of our family, race and religion.[6] It is recognised that their loss can affect our whole sense of our personality. According to the sociologist, Erving Goffman:

> 'Persons invest self feelings in their possessions. Perhaps the most significant of these possessions is not physical at all [but] one's full name. Whatever one is called thereafter, loss of one's name can be a great curtailment of the self.'[7]

9.6   A change of name engages the child's right to a private life. In the Strasbourg case of *Bensaid v United Kingdom*,[8] the European Court of Human Rights commented:

> 'The court has already held that elements such as gender identification, *name* and sexual orientation and sexual life are important elements in the personal sphere protected by Article 8 ... [which] protects a right to identity and personal development ...'

---

2   See, for example, *T v S (Wardship)* [2011] EWHC 1608 (Fam), [2012] 1 FLR 230.
3   [1992] PIQR 101, at 124.
4   Probert, Gilmore and Herring (eds) *Responsible Parents and Parental Responsibility* (Hart Publishing, 2009).
5   Ibid, at p 19.
6   See, for example Herring 'The shaming of naming' in *Responsible Parents & Parental Responsibility* op cit, at p 113, citing the French psychologist and psychiatrist, Jacques Lacan.
7   Goffman *Âsylums* (Penguin, 1961), at p 27.
8   (2001) 33 EHRR 10, at [47].

Domestic courts too regard a change of name as 'a profound and not merely a formal matter'.[9] In *Re D, L and LA (Care: Change of Forename)*[10] Dame Elizabeth Butler-Sloss P said in relation to foster parents that the principle is the same in private law situations:

> 'To change a child's name is to take a significant step in a child's life. Forename or surname, it seems to me that the principles are the same, in general. A child has roots. A child has names given to him or her by parents. The child has a right to those names and retains that right, as indeed, the parents have rights to retention of the name of the child which they chose. Those rights should not be set to one side, other than for good reasons. It may be that foster parents do not appreciate the underlying importance for the child of a name, and it is significant. You would not, for instance, be likely to change the forename of a child of 7, 8 or 9, I suggest even, 5, 6 or 7, because by that time the child has made that name part of his or her identity and very young children know what their names are. You ask a very young child "what's your name?", and they will certainly be able to give you the name he or she is called by. To change that is to affect the child's identity. The right of the child and both parents to respect for that part of family life still exists, even though the child has gone into a foster placement. It may be that foster carers have not yet been sufficiently made aware that this is not a technical point. There is an underlying importance to the principle that the name should not be changed.'

Surnames

9.7   Adults can change their name freely (usually evidenced by deed poll, statutory declaration or merely by usage) because they do not like their old name, for professional reasons, as a tribute to another person or sometimes to embarrass or annoy someone. Parents name their children or change their names for similar reasons, although subject to some restriction as to when this can be done. The Births and Deaths Registration Act 1953 requires the child to be registered within 42 days of his birth. Currently, if the parents of the child are married, both are under a duty and either can register and thereby choose the child's name. If they are unmarried, only the mother may do so unless either she consents to the father doing so or he already has parental responsibility granted by agreement or court order.[11] As Ward LJ said in *Re C (Change of Surname)*:[12]

> 'The father ... has no right. His input into that necessary process is limited to that which he can procure by agreement with the mother. With her consent but not otherwise, he can be named as the father of the child and may sign the birth certificate accordingly.'

9.8   Subject to the restrictions noted below a child's name may be changed in the same way as adults may change their names by usage or deed poll. Additionally a child's name may be changed upon adoption. However, by

---

9   *Re C (Change of Surname)* [1998] 2 FLR 656.
10   [2003] 1 FLR 339, at 346.
11   Children Act 1989, Sch 12, para 6.
12   [1998] 2 FLR 656.

virtue of the Births and Deaths Registration Act 1953 the registered name remains the same with one exception. The child's name (and by reason of the current implementing regulations, this means only his first name) may be altered within 12 months of the initial registration if it has been changed by baptism or, if the child has not been baptised) by the mother, father, guardian 'or other person procuring the name of the child to be altered'.[13] The courts' powers therefore are limited to determining the name by which the child is to be known. They do not include the power to change the child's registered name,[14] although where a parent may apply under the Births and Deaths Registration Act 1953 to change a name, the court would presumably have the power to direct a parent to make such an application.

9.9 By virtue of ss 13(1) and 14C(3) of CA 1989, nobody may cause the child to be known by a new surname when a residence or special guardianship order is in force without either the written consent of every person who has parental responsibility for the child or leave of the court. In *Re PC (Change of Surname)*,[15] Holman J held that this statutory prohibition was a mere precaution because, where two or more persons have parental responsibility, none can change the child's name without the consent of the others. Departmental guidance to head teachers states that a child's name on the school role should not be changed unless the school is provided with evidence – independent of the parent making the request – that the other parent consents.[16]

9.10 At one time there may have been some uncertainty about whether an application for permission to change a child's name should be brought under s 13(1) or by seeking a specific issue order under s 10.[17] However, in practice this does not cause any difficulties and applications are treated (correctly it is submitted) under s 10.[18]

Importance of names

9.11 The test to be applied when a court considers permitting or prohibiting a change of name is the welfare test and there must be some evidence that changing the name will lead to an improvement in the child's life.[19] However, the application of the welfare test brings its own problems because there appears to be little professional knowledge of the effect on a child of a change

---

13 Births and Deaths Registration Act 1953, s 13.
14 See further Gosden 'Children's surnames – how satisfactory is the current law?' [2003] Fam Law 186.
15 [1997] 2 FLR 730.
16 DfEE Guidance 92/2000, para 15.
17 See George 'Changing names, changing places: reconsidering s 13 of the Children Act 1989' [2008] Fam Law 1121.
18 One reason why it is submitted that this is the correct approach is that s 10(4) and (5) contain a code regulating who requires or does not require the court's permission to apply for a s 8 order. It would be strange if applications concerning change of names and removal from the jurisdiction were not subject to the code.
19 *Dawson v Wearmouth* [1999] 1 FLR 1167.

of name. Assertions as to the effect it has on the child are commonly made but can be contradictory. Anecdotal evidence can be misleading. In *Re B (Change of Surname)*,[20] the mother sought permission to change the names of her children from that of their father, B (from whom she had separated 9 years earlier and who had no contact with the children) to that of her second husband who had lived with the children for 7 years. In evidence, the mother said that R, aged 14, had once failed to answer to a new teacher who had addressed him by the name of B and that, when corrected, he had explained 'that's not my name'. Some teachers, however, report children behaving quite differently, refusing to use their new name. 'Judicial knowledge' which lacks an empirical base can be outdated or just wrong. In *Re C (Change of Surname)*,[21] the trial judge said that 'it would very foreseeably cause eyebrows to be raised among small children if she is registered and known at school as GC when her mother is named H'. On appeal, Ward LJ disagreed:

> 'The unhappy fact in the light of which these applications, in this day and age, have to be judged is sadly quite different. The breakdown in relationships is now of such magnitude that there is nothing at all unusual in children having names different from their mother.'

It seems to be agreed, however, that names can be important in a child's sense of his identity. Some children can be disturbed by a change in name and, bearing in mind the likelihood of the parent with care changing partners during the child's childhood, the possibility of multiple changes should be avoided.

> 'All too easily because an issue is seen as important to an adult, it is seen as important to a child. Although whether a child has one name or another matters a great deal to some parents, it is not obvious that it matters enormously to children's welfare.'[22]

9.12 A further complication is the paucity of research into name changing.[23] There is some limited research into naming .One study of a small number of lesbian couple found that many favoured double-barrelled names to reflect the equality of both parents.[24] However admirable such agreements may be, the practice does not necessarily serve as a guide for what should happen later in the child's life if disagreements arise.

9.13 A decision can be made, therefore, only after a detailed analysis of the family circumstances of the individual child. *Re S (Change of Names: Cultural*

---

20 [1996] 1 FLR 791.
21 [1998] 2 FLR 656.
22 Herring 'The Shaming of Naming' op cit, at p 122.
23 Morris 'Change of names and the adoptive process' (1995) Adoption and Fostering 41 is concerned with practicalities.
24 Almack 'What's in a name? The significance of the choice of surnames given to children born within lesbian-parent families' (2005) 8 *Sexualities* 239. See also 'Naming names: kinship, individuality and personal names' (2008) 42 *Sociology* 709; 'Children's surnames, moral dilemmas: accounting for the predominance of father's surnames for children' (2010) 24 *Gender and Society* 499.

Factors)[25] provides an example of the issues which a change of name may involve. The mother was Muslim and the father, a Sikh. Their marriage had caused a rift between her and her family. When the mother returned to live with her family and divorced the father, she sought the court's permission to change the Sikh names of the boy (then aged 3½) to Muslim names. For some time, she had informally called him by a Muslim first name but because her Sikh nickname for the father was similar to this she wanted to abandon it. Expert evidence was unanimous that a child with a Sikh name living in a Muslim community in East London would find it difficult to be accepted by that community. Wilson J found that the birth of the boy conceived outside marriage and the mother's past relationship with a Sikh were continuing sources of distress and social denigration. He held that in order for the child and his mother to integrate into the Muslim community, he had to be known both formally and informally in the community by Muslim names. Accordingly, he granted the mother permission to allow him to be known by Muslim names, to be brought up in the Muslim faith and to be circumcised. However, it was not in his best interests for his existing Muslim name to be changed:

> 'It seems to me that the mother's proposal to eliminate that name and to give him an entirely different Muslim first name shows a limited insight into his emotional need to have an enduring sense of who he is.'[26]

Nor was it appropriate for his name to be changed by deed poll to enable him to obtain a passport in a Muslim name. This would contribute to a:

> '... comprehensive elimination of his half Sikh identity. As [father's counsel] submits, the mother is attempting to do the impossible. She is attempting to re-write his genetic identity.'[27]

The approach to be adopted

9.14 The approach of the courts to issues of change of surnames was summarised by the Court of Appeal in *Re W (A Child) (Illegitimate Child: Change of Surname)*.[28]

- If parents are married, they both have the power and the duty to register their child's name.

- If they are not married, the mother has the sole duty and power to do so.

---

25 [2001] 2 FLR 1005.
26 Ibid, at 1013.
27 Ibid, at 1015.
28 [1999] 2 FLR 930.

- After registration of the child's names, the grant of a residence order obliges any person wishing to change the surname to obtain the leave of the court or the written consent of all those who have parental responsibility.

- In the absence of a residence order, the person wishing to change the surname from the registered name ought to obtain the relevant written consent or the leave of the court by making an application for a specific issue order.

- On any application, the welfare of the child is paramount and the judge must have regard to the s 1(3) criteria.

- Among the factors to which the court should have regard is the registered surname of the child and the reasons for the registration, for instance, recognition of the biological link with the child's father. Registration is always a relevant and important consideration but is not in itself decisive. The weight to be given to it by the court will depend on the other relevant factors or valid countervailing reasons which may tip the balance the other way.

- The relevant considerations should include factors which may arise in the future as well as the present situation.

- Reasons given for changing or seeking to change a child's name based on the fact that the child's name is or is not the same as the parent making the application do not generally carry much weight.

- The reasons for an earlier unilateral decision to change a child's name may be relevant.

- Any change of circumstances of the child since the original registration may be relevant.

- In the case of a child whose parents were married to each other, the fact of the marriage is important and there would have to be strong reasons to change the name from the father's surname if the child were so registered.

- Where the child's parents were not married to each other, the mother has the control over registration. Consequently, on an application to change the surname of the child, the degree of commitment of the father to the child, the quality of the contact, if it occurs, between father and child, and the existence or absence of parental responsibility are all relevant factors to take into account.

Dame Elizabeth Butler-Sloss P added:

'I cannot stress too strongly that these are only guidelines which do not purport to be exhaustive. Each case has to be decided on its own facts with the welfare of the child the paramount consideration and all the relevant factors weighed in the balance by the court at the time of the hearing.'[29]

9.15   Other cases make the following points:

- an order for a change of name ought not to be made unless there is some evidence that this will lead to an improvement from the point of view of the welfare of the child;[30]

- bearing the father's name preserves a link between the child and the non-resident parent. This link is as important when there is good contact as when there is none;[31]

- the time which has passed between the original change of name and the application is likely to be an important consideration because a further change may confuse the child;[32]

- the wishes of the child are not decisive.[33]

Where the application is made by a *Gillick*-competent child the court should give very careful consideration to the wishes, feelings, needs and objectives of the applicant. If the judge has the advantage of advice from a guardian who has had the opportunity to make a thorough investigation of the family dynamics he should pay particular heed. Next he must give 'searching scrutiny' to the motives and stated objectives of the respondent.[34] The court should be particularly loathe to refuse applications which are consistent with the wishes of mature children, even though those wishes are neither paramount nor determinative.[35]

There has been a recent trend in courts seeking a middle way of allowing a child to use a new name informally while retaining the registered name[36] or combining the names of both parents.[37] Herring comments that:

'... surnaming has been used to normalise and symbolise male power over women and children. This can be avoided by the courts advocating the use of double surnames.'[38]

---

[29]   [1999] 2 FLR 930, at [10].
[30]   *Dawson v Wearmouth* [1999] AC 308, per Lord Mackay of Clashfern.
[31]   *Re C (Change of Surname)* [1998] 2 FLR 656.
[32]   Ibid and *Re PC (Change of Surname)* [1997] 2 FLR 730.
[33]   *Re B (Change of Surname)* [1996] 1 FLR 791.
[34]   *Re S (Change of Surname)* [1999] 1 FLR 672, per Thorpe LJ at 674.
[35]   *Re M, T, P, K and B* [2000] 2 FLR 645, at 651.
[36]   *Re PC (Change of Surname)* [1997] 2 FLR 730, *Re S (Change of Names: Cultural Factors)* [2001] 2 FLR 1005.
[37]   *Re R (A Child) (Surname: Using Both Parents)* [2001] EWCA Civ 1344, [2001] 2 FLR 1358.
[38]   Herring 'The shaming of naming' op cit, at p 122.

Examples

9.16 In one of the appeals in *Re W, Re A, Re B (Change of Name)*,[39] a parent was permitted to change a child's name because the father's imprisonment for a number of serious offences and manslaughter and his notoriety made it desirable for the name to be changed and, in another, a change was permitted where the father had been imprisoned for a number of offences of indecency and as a result was likely to play only a peripheral part in the life of his daughters.

9.17 In *Re S (Change of Surname)*[40] a 15-year-old girl was granted permission on her own application to change her surname when her farther had been acquitted of charges of sexually abusing her sister.

> 'The acquittal probably retards rather than advances the prospects of any contact between K and her father. K is now 15. The letter of 1 September 1998 is sad but determined in her rejection of her father. Her right to determine her surname without the leave of the court is likely to arrive before there has been a change sufficient to weigh in the scale which we balance.'

9.18 Likewise in *Re M, T, P, K and B*[41] a local authority was granted permission to change the surnames of five children aged between 15 and nearly 10 who were in their care, following 'a reign of terror and tyranny' by their father who had sexually and physically abused them, the children not having any contact with their parents and expressing fear that they would be found by members of their large extended family.

9.19 An unusual example is *Re A (Change of Name)*.[42] A was born to unmarried Somali parents, the mother recently having been divorced. The mother registered A with two names, a given name and the name of her ex-husband. A's father applied for an order changing his registered name. The mother argued that if A bore the name of his father she would lose dignity and prestige in her community, whereas the father argued that the Somali patrilineal naming principle required that after his given name A's second name be that of his father, and the third that of his paternal grandfather. The judge had no expert evidence other than a s 7 report to the effect that the Imam at the local mosque had advised that any child conceived, like A, within 4 months after a divorce should bear the name of the mother's former husband. The trial judge ordered that the name be changed but on appeal the Court of Appeal directed that expert reports be obtained as to the conventions in the Somali community. The reports were not entirely satisfactory but one expert advised that when a child was conceived within 4 months of his mother's divorce he would be regarded as 'belonging' to the former husband and would be named accordingly. The Court of Appeal accordingly allowed the mother's appeal,

---

39 [1999] 2 FLR 930.
40 [1999] 1 FLR 672, per Thorpe LJ at 675.
41 [2000] 2 FLR 645.
42 [2003] EWCA Civ 56, [2003] 1 FCR 493.

giving due regard to the consideration that a registered name was not lightly to be altered. Interestingly despite the importance normally attached to a child knowing his true identity (see **6.66**), Chadwick LJ said for his part he would not think it right, without very good reason, to deny A the benefit of the fiction that he was the child of the former husband 'which is conferred by custom and practice within a community for whom, as Professor Lewis[43] points out in his report, illegitimacy is regarded as a much more serious stigma than divorce'.[44]

Special guardianship

9.20 In *S v B and Newport City Council: Re K*[45] Hedley J granted grandparents special guardianship in relation to their 6-year-old grandson who had lived with them since he was 6 months old and, in the absence of opposition from his parents, allowed them to change his surname to theirs. No reasons for this were given. However, the following year in *Re L (Special Guardianship: Surname)*[46] in similar but not identical circumstances[47] but with the guardian expressing 'major' concerns about the child's identity needs in the context where the grandparents were seemingly not going to raise the issue of her parentage with the child until she asked, the trial judge granted a special guardianship order but refused permission for the child's surname to be changed.

> 'In a case where there is as much anxiety as there is here about the way in which [E's] identity is dealt with, it would be completely contrary to her interests, in my view, for her now to be known by a different surname. Her welfare is most likely to be secured, it seems to me, by keeping her circumstances as faithful to reality and the truth of the situation as possible. Whilst I accept that some explanation of names will be required, for instance, doctors and schools, I do not consider that would be an insuperable problem in the context of a special guardianship order.'

The Court of Appeal dismissed the grandparents' appeal. The child's welfare was the litmus test and overwhelmingly justified the refusal to allow a change of name.

> 'Sympathetic as I am to [the predicament of the grandparents] and their hurt, their concerns overlook the value of the lesson ... honesty is the best policy ... It avoids the much more difficult questions that will be asked when [E] wishes to know, "why am I S if my parents are L?"'[48]

---

[43]   An academic at the London School of Economics. The report does not identify his discipline.
[44]   [2003] EWCA Civ 56, at [20].
[45]   [2007] 1 FLR 1116.
[46]   [2007] EWCA Civ 196, [2007] 2 FLR 50.
[47]   The child was of mixed race.
[48]   [2007] EWCA Civ 196, [2007] 2 FLR 50, per Ward LJ at [39].

First names

9.21 In *Re H (Child's Name: First Name)*,[49] the Court of Appeal held that none of the authorities which guided a court in determining surnames was of any application to a dispute as to the child's first name. The surname by which a child was registered and known was of particular significance but given names were of a much less concrete nature. The court could not prevent a parent from using a particular name at home or in the community. While this is a pragmatic decision it does not sit easily with the judgment of Dame Elizabeth Butler-Sloss P a year later in *Re D, L and LA (Care: Change of Forename)*[50] when she said that 'Forename or surname, it seems to me that the principles are the same, in general'.

In *Re D, L and LA (Care: Change of Forename)* the President noted that *Re H (Child's Name: First Name)* was a very rare example of the courts having to decide the issue of first name and that in a private law rather than a public setting. This, it is submitted is a distinction of only limited relevance. It may be that in some cases, for example when the carers are foster parents with the local authority exercising some control, it will be easier to prevent the use of a new first name but in other cases, where, as in *Re D, L and LA (Care: Change of Forename)*, the carers are proposed adopters, it may be less easy. However, the reason why it is generally not in the child's best interests to change either a first name or surname is the same whatever the setting.

RELOCATION

Background

9.22 Parental separation commonly results in both parents moving from the former matrimonial home. The study *How parents cope financially on marriage breakdown*[51] found that 2 years after divorce two-fifths of the respondents who had children living with them had left the former matrimonial home. There may be subsequent moves when a parent forms a new relationship. A survey conducted in 2000–01[52] reported that a tenth of households in England had moved in the previous year and a tenth of these had moved because of divorce. Nearly 20% of owner-occupiers moved more than 20 miles, 10% more than 50 miles and 2% emigrated. It is self-evident that such moves by either parent will interfere with a child's contact with his non-resident parent. Another study, *Non-Resident Parental Contact*,[53] for example, found, unsurprisingly, that the distance between a non-resident parent's home and that of their child is an important factor governing the frequency of direct contact. Over one-eighth of children who lived within 10 miles of their non-resident parent saw them daily.

---

49 [2002] EWCA Civ 190, [2002] 1 FLR 973.
50 [2003] 1 FLR 339, at 346.
51 Perry, Douglas and others (Family Policy Studies Centre, 2000) summarised in *Findings 480* (Joseph Rowntree Foundation).
52 *Social Trends 2002*.
53 Blackwell and Dawe (Office for National Statistics, 2003).

If children lived 50 miles or more away they were most likely never to see their non-resident parent and if contact took place this was more likely to be monthly rather than a greater frequency. Whether or not this distance resulted in less indirect contact is uncertain. There appears to be no difference when reports by non-resident parents are considered but according to reports from resident parents, 40% of children whose non-resident parents lived 50 or more miles away never had indirect contact, twice the proportion of children who lived nearer.

9.23 The frequency and intensity of parental disputes over relocation are a relatively modern phenomenon being a by-product of communication and travel technology lowering national frontiers and creating a global world and the continuing expansion of the European Union which enlarges the choice of countries to which every EU citizen has the right of entry and residence.[54] As Lord Justice Thorpe, the Head of International Family Justice has said extra-judicially:

> 'In many of our jurisdictions relationships are easily formed and children follow. But the relationships are as easily unformed and the family fractured. In such a painful process one of the parents may well at some level need to distance himself or herself physically as well as emotionally from the other. Dissention results and the contested relocation case is born. Judges in several jurisdictions have said that these are some of the most difficult cases that a trial judge has to decide.'[55]

He added that the relocation case is but one aspect of the international movement of children, another being the unlawful removal or abduction of a child from a jurisdiction where he is habitually resident to another without the consent of those having parental responsibility or judicial permission.

9.24 Relocation cases concern both married and unmarried parents and occur for a variety of reasons. As Dr Marilyn Freeman has pointed out,[56] very often, as with cases of abduction, those wishing to relocate are returning to their family home to receive practical support at a time of emotional stress. Sometimes, the relocating parent wants to move to be with a new partner who comes from another country; in other cases the relocating parent simply wishes to start afresh in a new country, with which she has no connections, sometimes with the offer of employment, schooling for the children, and accommodation to tempt her. It is also possible that the relocating parent wishes to go quite literally to the other side of the world in order to escape the obligations of co-parenting. In some cases this wish is justified, reflecting the same inability for some women and children to be fully protected by the legal systems in their States of habitual residence which has been seen in cases of child abduction.

---

[54] Thorpe 'Relocation: The Search for Common Principles' [2010] IFL 241.
[55] Ibid.
[56] Freeman *Relocation* (Reunite, 2009), at p 5.vii available at: www.reunite.org/pages/leave_to_remove.asp.

Others, however, will merely seek to lead independent lives, away from any practical connection with the other parent in both their own, and their child's lives.

9.25 Judge Brasse[57] has categorised relocation cases into re-marriage cases[58], carer/lifestyle choice[59] and a return to family roots.[60] However, while these categories usefully illustrate a variety of situations in which applications are made, the legal principles which are to be applied are the same.[61] If permission is sought to remove a child from the jurisdiction, the test is the s 1 welfare test. If a child is brought to the country from another without the consent of the other parent or judicial permission from the courts of that other country, the court has to consider whether or not the child should be returned to the country of his former residence either under the provisions of the Child Abduction and Custody Act 1985 if the other country is a signatory to the Convention on the Civil Aspects of International Child Abduction 1980 ('the Hague Convention') or the European Convention on the Recognition and Enforcement of Decisions concerning Custody of Children and on the Restoration of Custody of Children 1980 ('the Luxembourg Convention') or under the court's inherent power to decline jurisdiction of the welfare of the child which requires that any issue relating to the child should be determined in the courts of his former residence.

9.26 The problems created for contact and the relationship between the child and his non-resident parent by any relocation are compounded if the relocation is international, not just because of the distance and expense involved but also because the jurisdiction to resolve any future problems is transferred to the courts of the new place of abode (see **9.56**). Dr Freeman carried out research for Reunite, an organisation founded to assist families involved with child abduction.[62] Nearly all cases involve sacrifice and readjustment for the left-behind parent and family. Many parents will bear those emotions with resigned realism but in some cases, the grief and despair are too much to bear, resulting in a complete loss of the parent-child relationship.

> 'The consequences that may result from the relocation of … children may impact as seriously and as negatively on the children as a mother's unhappiness in being where she does not want to be. These are two sides of the same story.'

---

[57] Brasse 'The Payne threshold: leaving the jurisdiction' [2005] Fam Law 780. See also Freeman *Relocation* op cit, at p 5.vii.

[58] For example, *Poel v Poel* [1970] 1 WLR 1469; *Re H (Application to Remove from the Jurisdiction)* [1998] 1 FLR 848; *Re B (Removal from Jurisdiction)* [2003] EWCA Civ 1149, [2003] 2 FLR 1043.

[59] For example, *Re B (Leave to Remove: Impact of Refusal)* [2004] EWCA Civ 956, [2005] 2 FLR 239.

[60] *A v A (Child: Removal from the Jurisdiction)* (1980) 1 FLR 380; *Payne v Payne* [2001] EWCA Civ 166, [2001] 1 FLR 1052; *Re C (Permission to Remove from Jurisdiction)* [2003] EWHC 596 (Fam), [2003] 1 FLR 1066; *Re G (Removal from Jurisdiction)* [2005] EWCA Civ 170, [2005] 2 FLR 166.

[61] *Re B (Leave to Remove: Impact of Refusal)* [2004] EWCA Civ 956, [2005] 2 FLR 239.

[62] Freeman *Relocation* op cit. See also Freeman 'Relocation: the Reunite research project' [2010] IFL 161.

The problems, perhaps most clearly seen in cases of joint/shared residence, relate to all cases where there are two involved parents, both wanting to follow different paths in their lives following the failure of their own relationship, both wanting their children, and both likely to suffer significantly if their plans are not accepted. 'Both outcomes have the potential to negatively, and severely, impact on the child's life.'

9.27 The common problems identified by Freeman relate to contact and are both practical as well as related to a lack of desire on the part of some relocated parents to promote contact. Many parents in the sample interviewed reported that there were constant problems in exercising the contact that had been ordered by the court granting permission to relocate. There was no monitoring system in place after the relocation despite assurances that Cafcass would be involved to ensure that contact arrangements work. In reality, Cafcass is unable to assist once the child leaves the jurisdiction.[63] Several parents reported that indirect contact, which is often part of a contact order and is designed to supplement the infrequent physical visits between a parent and child, rarely happened and could not be relied upon as a method of maintaining contact. Phone conversations were difficult to organise at convenient times .When they do take place, they are strained and truncated. The internet is not a suitable method of communication for most young children who would require parental assistance which may not be forthcoming, and the same is true of webcams which regularly are included within contact orders. Similarly, pre-paid mobile phones which have been programmed with the telephone numbers of the left-behind father and family are only useful where the residential parent will allow their use. Older children are very comfortable with using the internet as a means of communication, but will only do so if they know that it is supported by the residential parent and will not cause a problem with that parent. Difficulties were experienced in enforcing contact in the courts of the new residence.

> 'Mirror orders are not routinely granted, especially if, as is very often the case because of the costs involved in the type of multiple litigation which such cases produce, the parent opposing relocation is self representing. This has required the left-behind parent to engage the assistance of the court in the new jurisdiction, with all the personal, time and financial considerations that this involves, often to find at the end of the process that contact is not reinstated by the new court which takes a different view of the best interests of the child concerned.'

Regularly trips by the non-resident parent may cause severe financial problems or prove impossible. Freeman recommends that the costs of international contact must be realistically considered by a court ordering contact, and should not be brushed aside as one of the burdens that a left-behind father must bear. 'It may not be possible for him to do so, and the child may suffer as a result.'

---

[63] See *Enquiries Abroad/Overseas Travel Policy* (July 2006) www.cafcass.gov.uk, especially para 25.

9.28 While the research focused in the relationship between the child and the non-resident parent, relocation has the potential for affecting relationships with other family and friends. The relocating parent may have close family in England and Wales and the child may return to the jurisdiction for holidays providing some opportunity for contact with the non-resident parent and his family. However, where the parent relocates to a country where her parents live, loss of contact with the non-resident parent is likely to mean loss of the relationship with his family.

The domestic debate

9.29 Undoubtedly courts can control moves by the resident parent either by the use of conditions imposed on residence orders, prohibited steps or specific issue orders or by refusing permission to emigrate if the resident parent has a residence order and therefore requires permission under s 13(1). The debate centres on whether or not permission is too readily granted.[64] One school of thought argues that if the welfare test is properly applied, permission should be granted only if it can be shown to positively benefit the child and, if the child enjoys a good relationship with the non-resident parent, supported by frequent and good quality contact, a strong case needs to be shown before permission should be granted. Mere assertions that the resident parent will be so unhappy if compelled to remain in England or their present home that their care of the children is likely to suffer, are not enough. The other school of thought contends that this is no 'mere assertion' and a refusal will result in 'almost inevitable bitterness'.[65] Although Art 2 of Protocol No 4 of the European Convention for the Protection of Human Rights (freedom of movement) has not been ratified by the United Kingdom, a refusal to allow free movement to the parent is in breach of his or her common law rights and a strong case has to be made to justify this.[66] Whatever the merits and strengths of the opposing arguments,[67] 'the strength and longevity of the approach of the English courts [which inclines towards the later argument] is a product of the very powerful arguments in favour of upholding the status quo [of *Payne v Payne*[68]]' (see **9.42**).[69] Indeed in *Payne v Payne*[70] Thorpe LJ said that 'Few guidelines for the determination of individual cases, the facts of which are never replicated, have stood so long in our family law'.

The debate about relocation cases is not confined to the United Kingdom. There is a diversity of approaches in other jurisdictions.[71] Australia, for

---

[64]   See 'The leave to remove debate' [2005] Fam Law 911.

[65]   *Chamberlain v De la Mare* (1983) 4 FLR 434, per Ormrod LJ.

[66]   *Poel v Poel* [1970] 1 WLR 1469; *Payne v Payne* [2001] EWCA Civ 166, [2001] 1 FLR 1052, per Thorpe LJ at [37].

[67]   And see Perry '*Payne v Payne*: Leave to remove children from the jurisdiction' [2001] 13 CFLQ 455.

[68]   [2001] EWCA Civ 166, [2001] 1 FLR 1052].

[69]   Brasse 'The Payne threshold: leaving the jurisdiction' [2005] Fam Law 780.

[70]   [2001] EWCA Civ 166, [2001] 1 FLR 1052, at [27].

[71]   Worwood 'International relocation – the debate' [2005] Fam Law 621 which usefully summarises the approaches in a variety of jurisdictions.

example has adopted the *Payne* approach[72] while New Zealand has rejected it because it is inconsistent with the wider all-factor child-centred approach required under New Zealand law.[73]

9.30 An international common law conference in Washington DC in 2000 concluded that:

'Courts take significantly different approaches to relocation cases which are occurring with a frequency not contemplated in 1980 when the Hague Child abduction Convention was drafted. Courts should be aware that highly restrictive approaches to relocation can adversely affect the operation of the Hague Child abduction Convention.'[74]

9.31 A review of the approaches in both Common Law and Civil Law countries by Thomas Foley in 2006[75] suggested that the varying approaches can be categorised under three general headings:

- *pro-relocation*, which generally accepted a proposal to relocate unless it was unreasonable or detrimental to the child's best interests, an approach adopted by England, France, Spain, South Africa, probably Scotland and certain States of the United States;

- *anti-relocation*, which reflected 'a strong and almost unwavering commitment to not frustrating in any way' the relationship of both parents, the approach of New Zealand, Sweden and some States of the United States;

- *neutral*, being neither a presumption in favour of nor against relocation and which applies a fresh inquiry into each case, for example the approach of Canada, Germany, Belgium, other US States and probably Australia.[76]

9.32 In 2008 the Hague Conference on Private International Law resulted in a report, *Transfrontier Contact concerning Children: General Principles and a Guide to Good Practice*.[77] Its core principles were that:

'all possible steps should be taken to secure the rights of children to maintain personal relationships and have regular contact with both of their parents and of parents to maintain personal relationships and have regular contact with their children, unless it is determined that such contact is contrary to the interests of the

---

[72] *U v U* [2002] HCA 36.
[73] *D v S* [2002] NZFLR 116.
[74] Cited in Foley *International Child Relocation* (2006).
[75] Ibid.
[76] For other reviews see Bryant 'Freedom of movement in an era of shared parenting: the differences in judicial approaches: a critique' [2010] IFL 10; Hanson 'Relocation applications: recent developments in the Channel Islands' [2006] Fam Law 370; Chamberland 'The Canadian law of parental relocation' [2010] IFL 17; Messitte 'Relocation of children: law and practice in the United States' [2010] IFL 73; Young 'Resolving relocation disputes: the "interventionist" approach in Australia' [2011] CFLQ 203.
[77] (Jordans) available at: www.hcch.net/upload/guidecontact_e.pdf.

children. This is equally applicable when the parents live in different countries. Restrictions on contact should be proportional. Legal restrictions on contact between parents and children should be no more than are necessary to protect the interests of the child.'

It also contained detailed proposals on promoting contact and agreement, enforcing contact orders and relocation. In relation to the latter, it emphasised the importance of ensuring that the terms and conditions of a contact order made in the country of origin are given maximum respect in the country of relocation and that considering the possibility of obtaining a mirror order should be made a condition of relocation.[78]

9.33 In 2010 an International Judicial Conference on Cross-Border Family Relocation was convened in Washington in March 2010 by the Hague Conference, the US State Department and the International Centre for Missing and Exploited Children, to explore a wide range of issues surrounding the relocation of a parent and child following the breakdown of co-habitation and to explore the development of common principles to guide the exercise of any judge's discretion in granting or refusing a relocation application. Twelve jurisdictions were represented.[79] Their deliberations resulted in the 'Washington Declaration'[80] whose recommendations based on research findings concerning children's needs and development in the context of relocation included the following:

Reasonable Notice of International Relocation

2. The person who intends to apply for international relocation with the child should, in the best interests of the child, provide reasonable notice of his or her intention before commencing proceedings or where proceedings are unnecessary, before relocation occurs.

Factors Relevant to Decisions on International Relocation

3. In all applications concerning international relocation the best interests of the child should be the paramount (primary) consideration. Therefore, determinations should be made without any presumptions for or against relocation.
4. In order to identify more clearly cases in which relocation should be granted or refused, and to promote a more uniform approach internationally, the exercise of judicial discretion should be guided in particular, but not exclusively, by the following factors listed in no order of priority. The weight to be given to any one factor will vary from case to case:
     i)   the right of the child separated from one parent to maintain personal relations and direct contact with both parents on a regular basis in a manner consistent with the child's development, except if the contact is contrary to the child's best interest;

---

[78]   Ibid, ch 8.
[79]   Thorpe 'Relocation development' [2010] Fam Law 565.
[80]   Available at: www.hcch.net/upload/decl_washington2010e.pdf

ii) the views of the child having regard to the child's age and maturity;

iii) the parties' proposals for the practical arrangements for relocation, including accommodation, schooling and employment;

iv) where relevant to the determination of the outcome, the reasons for seeking or opposing the relocation;

v) any history of family violence or abuse, whether physical or psychological;

vi) the history of the family and particularly the continuity and quality of past and current care and contact arrangements;

vii) pre-existing custody and access determinations;

viii) the impact of grant or refusal on the child, in the context of his or her extended family, education and social life, and on the parties;

ix) the nature of the inter-parental relationship and the commitment of the applicant to support and facilitate the relationship between the child and the respondent after the relocation;

x) whether the parties' proposals for contact after relocation are realistic, having particular regard to the cost to the family and the burden to the child;

xi) the enforceability of contact provisions ordered as a condition relocation in the State of destination;

xii) issues of mobility for family members; and

xiii) any other circumstances deemed to be relevant by the judge.'

9.34 In *Re H (A Child)*[81] Wilson LJ drew attention to the fact that the Declaration did not include as a factor to be considered the effect on the child of the negative impact upon the applicant of refusal of the application.

'Some may share my initial perplexity even at the terminology of (viii) in that it appears to train the consideration of the court upon impact not only "on the child" but also, and by way of contradistinction, "on the parties" apparently irrespective of impact on the child. It is axiomatic that our notion of paramountcy excludes from consideration all factors which have no bearing on the child.'

9.35 It is important to note that while the Washington Declaration may prove to be a valuable means of harmonising the approaches of different jurisdictions and become the foundation of some reform of English domestic law, it is no more than a declaration and not law.[82]

Article 8

9.36 When a court is considering whether to permit or prohibit the relocation of a child, the Art 8 rights of the child and his parents are undoubtedly engaged. In another sphere, that of immigration, the Court of Appeal[83] has found that a decision to deport a mother and her two young children to

---

[81] [2010] EWCA Civ 915, [2010] 2 FLR 1875, at [27].

[82] Ibid, per Wilson LJ at [26]. See also *RF v M* [2010] EWHC 1346 (Fam), per Mostyn J at [12].

[83] *Edore v Secretary of State for the Home Department* [2003] EWCA Civ 716, [2003] 3 All ER 1265.

Nigeria, thus depriving them of their relationship with their father, who could not accompany them, was disproportionate to the aim of controlling immigration.

> '[The adjudicator] seems to me to have explained perfectly plainly how the children would be adversely affected: they are "emotionally dependent" upon their father who provides "a stable influence" in their lives; if sent to Nigeria they would be permanently deprived of his love and support. What clearer or more convincing reason could one have for not imposing this separation upon them?'[84]

9.37 In *ZH (Tanzania) v Secretary of State for The Home Department*[85] the Supreme Court held that in any immigration case the state had to take into account the need to safeguard and promote the welfare of any child involved as required by Art 3(1) of the United Nations Convention on the Rights of the Child 1989 and in order to avoid a breach of Art 8(2) of the ECHRFF. The child's best interests were a primary but not a sole or paramount consideration.

> 'Specifically, as Lord Bingham indicated in *EB (Kosovo)*[86], it will involve asking whether it is reasonable to expect the child to live in another country. Relevant to this will be the level of the child's integration in this country and the length of absence from the other country; where and with whom the child is to live and the arrangements for looking after the child in the other country; and the strength of the child's relationships with parents or other family members which will be severed if the child has to move away.'[87]

9.38 The Court of Appeal when considering relocation cases has recognised this engagement but has said that it adds little to the traditional approach.

> '[The] advent of the Convention within our domestic law does not necessitate a revision of the fundamental approach to relocation applications formulated by this court and consistently applied over so many years. The ... court's approach is and always has been to apply child welfare as the paramount consideration. The court's focus upon supporting the reasonable proposal of the primary carer is seen as no more than an important factor in the assessment of welfare. In a united family the right to family life is a shared right. But once a family unit disintegrates the separating members' separate rights can only be to a fragmented family life. Certainly the absent parent has the right to participation to the extent and in what manner the complex circumstances of the individual case dictate.

> [36] But despite the fact that this appeal has raised only the asserted Art 8 rights of the secondary caring parent, we should not lose sight of the Art 8 rights of the primary carer, although not specifically asserted in argument. However an appeal may well arise in which a disappointed applicant will contend that s 13(1)(b) of the

---

84   Ibid, per Simon Brown LJ at [25].
85   [2011] UKSC 4, [2011] 2 LR 2170.
86   *EB (Kosovo) v Secretary of State for the Home Department* [2008] UKHL 41, [2008] 3 WLR 178.
87   [2011] UKSC 4, [2011] 2 LR 2170, per Baroness Hale of Richmond at [29].

Children Act 1989 imposes a disproportionate restriction on a parent's right to determine her place of habitual residence.'[88]

Permanent removal

Restrictions on removal

9.39 When a residence or special guardianship order is in force, no person may remove the child from the United Kingdom (except, in the case of the person in whose favour the residence order was made, for a period of less than one month) without the written consent of every person who has parental responsibility or the leave of the court.[89] This applies whether or not the removal is intended to be permanent or for the purpose of a holiday. For the purpose of the section, 'the United Kingdom' includes Northern Ireland.[90] The statutory prohibition has been extended by the courts to include a prohibition on a parent changing the habitual residence of a child without the consent of all persons holding parental responsibility, even when no residence order is in force. In the words of Lord Donaldson of Lymington MR in *C v S (A Minor) (Abduction)*:[91]

> '... in the ordinary case of a married couple ... it would not be possible for one parent unilaterally to terminate the habitual residence of the child by removing the child from the jurisdiction wrongfully and in breach of the other parent's rights.'

In addition, it is an offence for a parent, anyone who has custody of the child and any other person 'connected' with a child under the age of 16 to remove him from the United Kingdom without the consent of each parent with parental responsibility, any person who has his custody or the leave of the court.[92]

The test

9.40 There can be no doubt but that the test to be applied is the s 1 welfare test in which all the relevant circumstances have to be considered and the weight to be applied to the different factors will be determined by the circumstances of the individual case.

> 'The principle – the *only* authentic principle – that runs through the entire line of relocation authorities is that the welfare of the child is the court's paramount

---

88   *Payne v Payne* [2001] EWCA Civ 166, [2001] 1 FLR 1052, per Thorpe LJ at [35] and [36]. See also Herring and Taylor 'Relocation relocation' [2006] CFLQ 517.

89   CA 1989, ss 13(1) and 14C(3) – 3 months rather than 1 when a special guardianship order is in force.

90   *Re H (Children) (Residence Order: Condition)* [2001] EWCA Civ 1338, [2001] 2 FLR 1277.

91   [1990] 2 FLR 442, at 449.

92   Child Abduction Act 1984, s 1. See for example, *R v CS* [2012] EWCA Crim 389 where the Court of Appeal held that a defence of necessity was not available to a mother who wrongly removed a child from the jurisdiction because, she said, the child was being sexually abused by her father.

consideration. Everything that is considered by the court in reaching its determination is put into the balance with a view to measuring its impact on the child.'[93]

However, difficulties arose because the Court of Appeal offered 'guidance' (see **2.42**) in two cases, the first that of *Poel v Poel*[94] and the second that of *Payne v Payne*[95] which resulted in both the Court and lower courts placing what some thought as a misplaced emphasis on the likely or possible effect on the resident parent being refused permission to relocate. The guidance rested on dicta of the Court of Appeal in *Poel v Poel*:[96]

'When a marriage breaks up, a situation normally arises when a child of that marriage, instead of being in the joint custody of both parents, must of necessity become one who is in the custody of a single parent. Once that position has arisen and the custody is working well, this court should not lightly interfere with such reasonable way of life as is selected by that parent to whom custody has been rightly given. Any interference may, as my Lord has pointed out, produce considerable strains which would not only be unfair to the parent whose way of life is interfered with but also to any new marriage of that parent. In that way it might well in due course reflect on the welfare of the child. The way in which the parent who properly has custody of a child may choose in a reasonable manner to order his or her way of life is one of those things which the parent who has not been given custody may well have to bear, even though one has every sympathy with the latter on some of the results.'

9.41 Although an application of this dicta meant that leave to remove the child was granted in almost all the reported cases in the 30 years after 1970, the Court of Appeal in *Payne v Payne*[97] was careful to point out that there was no presumption in favour of the parent who wanted to emigrate.

9.42 In *Payne* Thorpe LJ said that there was a danger that if the reasonable proposals of the primary carer were elevated into a legal presumption then there would be an obvious risk of the breach not only of the respondent's rights under Art 8 but also his rights under Art 6 to a fair trial. To guard against this he suggested the following approach.

- Pose the question: is the mother's application genuine in the sense that it is not motivated by some selfish desire to exclude the father from the child's life? Then ask: is the mother's application realistic, by which I mean founded on practical proposals both well researched and investigated? If the application fails either of these tests refusal will inevitably follow.
- If however the application passes these tests then there must be a careful appraisal of the father's opposition: is it motivated by genuine concern for

---

93 *MK v CK (Relocation: Shared Care Arrangement)* [2011] EWCA Civ 793, per Black LJ at [141]. See **9.46**.
94 [1970] 1 WLR 1469.
95 [2001] EWCA Civ 166, [2001] 1 FLR 1052.
96 [1970] 1 WLR 1469, per Sachs LJ at 1473.
97 [2001] EWCA Civ 166, [2001] 1 FLR 1052. For a critical assessment of *Payne*, contemporary with the judgment, see the case note by Perry in [2001] 4 CFLQ 455.

the future of the child's welfare or is it driven by some ulterior motive? What would be the extent of the detriment to him and his future relationship with the child were the application granted? To what extent would that be offset by extension of the child's relationships with the maternal family and homeland?

- What would be the impact on the mother, either as the single parent or as a new wife, of a refusal of her realistic proposal?[98]

- The outcome of the second and third appraisals must then be brought into an overriding review of the child's welfare as the paramount consideration, directed by the statutory checklist insofar as appropriate.'[99]

Dame Elizabeth Butler-Sloss P summarised the position as follows. Where there is a real dispute as to which parent should be granted a residence order, and the decision as to which parent is the more suitable is finely balanced, the future plans of each parent are relevant.[100] If one parent intended to emigrate and to remove the child from school, surroundings, the other parent and family, it may in some cases be an important factor to weigh in the balance. But where the balance clearly lay in favour of the emigrating parent or residence was not a live issue, the following considerations would be relevant:

- the welfare of the child is always paramount;

- there is no presumption granted by CA 1989, s 13(1)(b);

- the reasonable proposals of the parent with a residence order wishing to live abroad carry great weight;

- consequently the proposals have to be scrutinised with care and the court needs to be satisfied there is a genuine motivation for the move and not the intention to bring contact between the child and the other parent to an end;

- the effect upon the applicant parent and the new family of the child of a refusal of leave is very important;

- the effect upon the child of the denial of contact with the other parent and in some cases his family is very important;

- the opportunity for continuing contact between the child and the parent left behind may be very significant.

The President added:

---

[98]   In *Re B (Leave to Remove: Impact of Refusal)* [2004] EWCA Civ 956, [2005] 2 FLR 239 the Court of Appeal ordered a retrial because this had not adequately been investigated by the trial judge.

[99]   [2001] EWCA Civ 166, [2001] 1 FLR 1052, at [40].

[100] See for example, *Re J (Leave to Remove: Urgent Case)* [2006] EWCA Civ 1897, [2007] 1 FLR 2033.

'[These] are not and could not be exclusive of the other important matters which
arise in the individual case.'[101]

Indeed, the wishes and feelings of the child, for example, need to be
considered,[102] as will the question of whether the child's residence should be
transferred to the parent who is not emigrating.

9.43   In the years since *Payne* criticism of the guidance grew,[103] Wall LJ noted
this in *Re D (Leave to Remove: Appeal)*:[104]

> 'There has been considerable criticism of *Payne v Payne* in certain quarters, and
> there is a perfectly respectable argument for the proposition that it places too great
> an emphasis on the wishes and feelings of the relocating parent, and ignores or
> relegates the harm done of children by a permanent breach of the relationship
> which children have with the left behind parent ... [This] is a perfectly respectable
> argument, and would, I have no doubt, in the right case constitute a 'compelling
> reason' for an appeal to be heard.'

However, he expressed the view that principles and guidelines in a decision of
the Court of Appeal can be altered only by legislation or by it being overruled
by a decision of the Supreme Court. The House of Lords and the Supreme
Court have never heard a relocation case and what their approach would be is a
matter of conjecture although in *Re J (Child Returned Abroad: Convention
Rights)*[105] Baroness Hale of Richard had commented in relation to another
area of child law:

> 'As this is the first time that the issue has come before this House, it seems right to
> remind ourselves of first principles ... our law does not start from any *a priori*
> assumptions about what is best for any individual child. It looks at the child and
> weighs a number of factors in the balance, now set out in the well-known
> 'check-list' in section 1(3) of the Children Act 1989 ...'[106]

9.44   As criticism of *Payne* grew[107] the Court of Appeal was perceived to
become more cautious in overturning a refusal of permission to relocate made

---

101   [2001] EWCA Civ 166, [2001] 1 FLR 1052 at [85]. See, for example, *M v M (Removal from
       Jurisdiction)* [1993] 1 FCR 5.
102   See Perry 'Payne v Payne: leave to remove children from the jurisdiction' [2001] 13 CFLQ 455.
103   For recent criticism, see, for example, Freeman 'Relocation and the child's best interests' [2010]
       IFL 247.
104   [2010] EWCA Civ 50, [2010] 2 FLR 1605, at [33]. See also *Re W (Relocation: Removal Outside
       Jurisdiction)* [2011] EWCA Civ 345, [2011] 2 FLR 409.
105   [2005] UKHL 40, [2005] 2 FLR 802.
106   Ibid, at [18] and [33].
107   See, for example, Hayes 'Relocation cases: Is the Court of Appeal applying the correct
       principles?' [2006] CFLQ 351. For an argument which supports the relocating parent from a
       rights-based perspective, see Herring and Taylor 'Relocating relocation' [2006] CFLQ 517.

by the trial judge.[108] However, the Court remained reluctant to re-visit *Payne*.
For example, in *Re H (Leave to Remain)*[109] Wilson LJ acknowledged the
criticisms of *Payne* but added:

> 'Nevertheless one must beware of endorsing a parody of the decision. Both
> Thorpe LJ, at [26(a)], and the President, Dame Elizabeth Butler-Sloss, at [85(a)],
> stressed that, in the determination of applications for permission to relocate, the
> welfare of the child was the paramount consideration. It is only against the
> subsidiary guidance to be collected from *Payne* that criticisms can perhaps more
> easily be leveled.'

9.45   However, in 2011 the Court eventually revisited the issue in *MK v CK*.[110]
Moore-Bick LJ[111] made the point that while *Payne* bound all courts apart from
the Supreme Court, it was binding in the true sense only for its *ratio decidendi*.
Nonetheless, where the Court gave guidance on the proper approach to take in
resolving any particular kind of dispute, judges at all levels must heed it and
depart from it only after careful deliberation and when it is clear that the
particular circumstances of the case require them to do so in order to give
effect to fundamental principles. However:

> 'The only principle of law enunciated in *Payne v Payne* is that the welfare of the
> child is paramount; all the rest is guidance. Such difficulty as has arisen is the
> result of treating that guidance as if it contained principles of law from which no
> departure is permitted. Guidance of the kind provided in *Payne v Payne* is, of
> course, very valuable both in ensuring that judges identify what are likely to be the
> most important factors to be taken into account and the weight that should
> generally be attached to them. It also plays a valuable role in promoting
> consistency in decision-making. However, the circumstances in which these
> difficult decisions have to be made vary infinitely and the judge in each case must
> be free to weigh up the individual factors and make whatever decision he or she
> considers to be in the best interests of the child. As Hedley J said in *Re Y*[112], the
> welfare of the child overbears all other considerations, however powerful and
> reasonable they may be. I do not think that the court in *Payne v Payne* intended to
> suggest otherwise.'[113]

9.46   Black LJ considered *Poel* and *Payne* in their historical context.

> 'In these early cases I detect a struggle to reconcile a disinclination to interfere
> with the reasonable choice of the parent with custody as to how, and in particular
> where, they should live with the undoubted principle that the welfare of the child
> is the primary consideration in deciding whether to give that parent permission to

---

108   For example, *Re H (A Child)* [2007] EWCA Civ 222, [2007] 2 FLR 317 and *Re B (Leave to
      Remove)* [2008] EWCA Civ 1034, [2008] 2 FLR 2059.
109   [2010] EWCA Civ 915, at [21]. See also, for example, *Re G (Leave to Remove)* [2007] EWCA
      Civ 1497, [2008] 1 FLR 1587.
110   [2011] EWCA Civ 793. See also Gilmore 'The Payne saga: precedent and family law cases'
      [2011] Fam Law 970.
111   Moore-Bick LJ described himself as 'one who has little familiarity with family law and
      practice' [2011] EWCA Civ 793, at [86].
112   *Re Y (Leave to Remove from the Jurisdiction)* [2004] 2 FLR 330.
113   [2011] EWCA Civ 793, at [86].

move to live outside the jurisdiction. The answer to the conundrum was found in the conviction that the child's welfare was inextricably bound up with the happiness of the custodial parent and the stability of the home that he or she could provide and that that happiness and stability would be likely to be threatened if the parent was compelled to adopt a manner of life that he or she reasonably did not want.'[114]

9.47 She then emphasised as Moore-Bick LJ had done the limited status of the decision in *Payne*.

'The first point that is quite clear is that, as I have said already, the principle – the *only* authentic principle – that runs through the entire line of relocation authorities is that the welfare of the child is the court's paramount consideration. Everything that is considered by the court in reaching its determination is put into the balance with a view to measuring its impact on the child. Whilst this is the only truly inescapable principle in the jurisprudence, that does not mean that everything else – the valuable guidance – can be ignored. It must be heeded for all the reasons that Moore-Bick LJ gives but as guidance not as rigid principle or so as to dictate a particular outcome in a sphere of law where the facts of individual cases are so infinitely variable. Furthermore, the effect of the guidance must not be overstated. Even where the case concerns a true primary carer, there is no presumption that the reasonable relocation plans of that carer will be facilitated unless there is some compelling reason to the contrary, nor any similar presumption however it may be expressed. Thorpe LJ said so in terms in *Payne* and it is not appropriate, therefore, to isolate other sentences from his judgment, such as the final sentence of paragraph 26 ("Therefore her application to relocate will be granted unless the court concludes that it is incompatible with the welfare of the children") for re-elevation to a status akin to that of a determinative presumption. It is doubly inappropriate when one bears in mind that the judgments in *Payne* must be read as a whole, with proper weight given to what the then President said. She said that she wished to reformulate the principles since they may have been expressed from time to time in too rigid terms with the word "presumption" over-emphasising one element of the approach (paragraph 82) whereas the criteria in s 1 Children Act govern the application (paragraph 83) and there is no presumption in favour of the applicant (paragraph 84) ...

'*Payne* therefore identifies a number of factors which will or may be relevant in a relocation case, explains their importance to the welfare of the child, and suggests helpful disciplines to ensure that the proper matters are considered in reaching a decision but it does not dictate the outcome of a case. ... The weight attached to the relevant factors alters depending upon the facts of the case.'[115]

Shared residence

9.48 The difficulties in any relocation case are intensified where the parents are sharing the care of the child whether informally or under an order granting each of them shared care (see **Chapter 10**). In *Re Y (Leave to Remove From*

---

[114] Ibid, at [97].
[115] Ibid, at [141]–[145].

Jurisdiction)[116] Y, a 5-year-old child, spent four nights a week with his North American mother and three with his English (but Welsh-speaking) father. Although the parents found their mutual relationship difficult, Hedley J found that they had 'achieved remarkable harmony' so far as the care and upbringing of Y was concerned which undoubtedly benefited him. Y's mother applied for permission to relocate to the United States. Hedley J held that the circumstances of the case fell outside the main run of cases founded on *Payne* and directed himself that he had to take into account a number of matters touching Y's welfare which 'is the lodestar by which the court at the end of the day is guided'. He refused permission. He adopted a similar approach in *Re D (Leave to Remove: Shared Residence)*[117] and not only allowed the mother to relocate to the United States but granted both parents shared residence.

9.49 A similar approach was adopted by Theis J in *C v D*[118] where the mother sought to relocate to the United States to join her new partner.

> 'I recognise that this will be devastating for the mother but I have come to this conclusion primarily based on the evidence that the children ([aged 13 and 8] are thriving under the regime the parents have devised in this jurisdiction [20 days with their mother followed by 10 days with their father] and the adverse impact on their time and relationship with their father if they did move to south USA. For the reasons set out above I do not believe it can be effectively replicated if the children move to south USA and that any different regime will not meet the children's needs. With the welfare of these children as the lodestar by which I am guided I am satisfied that the move to south USA would not meet the welfare needs of these children, however disappointing that decision will be for the mother.'[119]

9.50 In *MK v CK*[120] Thorpe LJ while holding to the *Payne* approach agreed that it should not be used in a *Re Y* type case.

> 'What is significant is not the label "shared residence" because we see cases in which for a particular reason the label is attached to what is no more than a conventional contact order. What is significant is the practical arrangements for sharing the burden of care between two equally committed carers. Where each is providing a more or less equal proportion and one seeks to relocate externally then I am clear that the approach which I suggested in paragraph 40 in *Payne v. Payne* should not be utilised. The judge should rather exercise his discretion to grant or refuse by applying the statutory checklist in section 1(3) of the Children Act 1989. What is significant is not the label "shared residence" because we see cases in which for a particular reason the label is attached to what is no more than a conventional contact order. What is significant is the practical arrangements for sharing the burden of care between two equally committed carers. Where each is providing a more or less equal proportion and one seeks to relocate externally then I am clear that the approach which I suggested in paragraph 40 in *Payne v. Payne*

---

[116] [2004] 2 FLR 330.
[117] [2006] EWHC 1794 (Fam), [2006] Fam Law 1006.
[118] [2011] EWHC 335 (Fam), sub nom *C v C* [2011] 2 FLR 701.
[119] Ibid, at [65]. See also Geekie 'Relocation and shared residence: one route or two?' [2007] Fam Law 446.
[120] [2011] EWCA Civ 793, at [57].

should not be utilised. The judge should rather exercise his discretion to grant or refuse by applying the statutory checklist in section 1(3) of the Children Act 1989.'

9.51   Black LJ, however, saw the *Re Y* approach not as being an exception to *Payne* but rather the approach which should be adopted in all relocation cases.

'I see [*Re Y*] as a decision within the framework of which *Payne* is part. It exemplifies how the weight attached to the relevant factors alters depending upon the facts of the case. Accordingly, I would not expect to find cases bogged down with arguments as to whether the time spent with each of the parents or other aspects of the care arrangements are such as to make the case "a *Payne* case" or "a *Re Y* case", nor would I expect preliminary skirmishes over the label to be applied to the child's arrangements with a view to a parent having a shared residence order in his or her armoury for deployment in the event of a relocation application. The ways in which parents provide for the care of their children are, and should be, infinitely varied. In the best of cases they are flexible and responsive to the needs of the children over time. When a relocation application falls to be determined, all of the facts need to be considered.'[121]

9.52   In some cases there will be a cross-application by the non-relocating parent, seeking a sole residence order in which case, as Dame Elizabeth Butler-Sloss indicated in *Payne*[122] the issue will have to be determined in the usual way.

Section 7 Reports

9.53   Although Cafcass reports are often ordered in relocation cases this is not invariably so. The Cafcass officer is usually in no position to assess the merits of the applicant's proposals for life abroad and it is sometimes said that as a result such reports have less of a role in relocation cases. However when the age of the child is such that his wishes need to be ascertained the Cafcass report is the conventional conduit for them. Equally the officer may be able to assess the relationship between the child and the non-relocating parent.[123]

Applications for financial relief

9.54   Where an application to relocate is closely linked to an application for financial relief, both applications should be heard together by an experienced specialist judge but where this is not possible, the financial application should be heard first to enable the rival contentions on finance in the context of relocation to be evaluated in the light of the mother's actual rather than potential entitlement.[124]

---

[121]   [2011] EWCA Civ 793, at [144]–[145].
[122]   [2001] EWCA Civ 166, [2001] 1 FLR 1052, at [86].
[123]   *Re R (A Child) (Leave to Remove: Contact)* [2010] EWCA Civ 1137, [2011] 1 FLR 1336.
[124]   *Re W (Children) (Leave to Remove)* [2008] EWCA Civ 538, [2008] 2 FLR 1170.

Summary

9.55

- The only test is the s 1 welfare test.

- There is no presumption either in favour of or against relocation.

- All circumstances which may affect the welfare of the child have to be considered. As a general rule no actor in the welfare checklist outweighs another. The weight to be attached to a particular factor will depend on the circumstances of the individual case.

- There is no different approach for shared residence cases.

- The first two questions posed in *Payne* by Thorpe LJ remain valuable guidance as to a preliminary approach: Is the mother's application genuine and realistic? Is the father's opposition genuine? If these are not passed a fuller inquiry may not be necessary.

Loss of jurisdiction

9.56   A court in England and Wales has jurisdiction to make a s 8 order only if:

- the child is habitually resident in another European Community Country and the courts in England and Wales has jurisdiction under Council Regulation (EC) No 2201/2003 (Brussels IIA otherwise known as Brussels II bis);[125] or

- the Council Regulation does not apply but the question of making the order arises in connection which matrimonial or civil partnership proceedings and those proceedings are continuing;[126] or

- the Council Regulation does not apply but the child is habitually resident in the jurisdiction or is present in the jurisdiction and not habitually resident in any other part of the United Kingdom or a specified dependent territory.[127]

In summary, because habitual residence can be quickly lost (see **16.61**) once a child leaves England and Wales pursuant to permission to relocate, the courts in England and Wales lose their jurisdiction to make s 8 orders or even to enforce the orders. Some limited relief is granted by Art 9 of the Council Regulation which provides that:

---

[125]   Family Law Act 1986, s 2(1)(a); Art 8 Brussels IIA.
[126]   Family Law Act 1986, s 2(1)(b)(i).
[127]   Ibid, ss 2(1)(b)(ii), 3.

'1. Where a child moves lawfully from one Member State to another and acquires a new habitual residence there, the courts of the Member State of the child's former habitual residence shall, by way of exception to Article 8, retain jurisdiction during a three-month period following the move for the purpose of modifying a judgment on access rights issued in that Member State before the child moved, where the holder of access rights pursuant to the judgment on access rights continues to have his or her habitual residence in the Member State of the child's former habitual residence.

2. Paragraph 1 shall not apply if the holder of access rights referred to in paragraph 1 has accepted the jurisdiction of the courts of the Member State of the child's new habitual residence by participating in proceedings before those courts without contesting their jurisdiction.'

A parent who agrees under Brussels IIA, Art 12(3) that the courts of England and Wales should retain jurisdiction to deal with contact disputes cannot unilaterally withdraw her agreement; nor is the jurisdiction terminated by the decision of the court of her habitual residence.[128]

9.57   For the difficulties caused by loss of jurisdiction, see **9.26**.

Conditions on removal

9.58   If permission is granted to remove the child, the court will normally make orders relating to contact, can require 'mirror' orders to be obtained in the country the child is being removed to and may require undertakings to be given by the removing parent that she will assist in funding of contact.

9.59   While contact orders may be enforced in the jurisdiction of the country where the child acquires habitual residence under Brussels IIA this will involve delay, practical difficulties and expense for the non-resident parent and the original domestic order is vulnerable to being changed by the enforcing courts.[129] They will however remain in force and circumstances might arise – for example the child returning to this jurisdiction – which permit enforcement here. 'Mirror orders' provide either an alternative or an additional safeguard but these too can be difficult to obtain, some countries, for example, India, not recognising 'mirror' orders but requiring original orders to be obtained in its own courts.[130] Sometimes these orders cannot be obtained until the child has relocated and obtained residence within their jurisdiction. Some provision for the expense in enforcing orders can be obtained by the court requiring the relocating parent, as a condition to relocation, to lodge a bond securing a

---

[128]   *AP v TD (Relocation: Retention of Jurisdiction)* [2010] EWHC 2040 (Fam), [2011] 1 FLR 1851.

[129]   But see Damrell 'It's just an expensive bit of paper' (ICACU) [2010] Fam Law 842. For a case where a child relocated to England from Australia with the permission of the Australian Court and the English Court of Appeal suspended the Australian contact order, see *Re G (A Child)* [2006] EWCA Civ 1507, [2007] 1 FLR 1663.

[130]   In *Re W (Jurisdiction: Mirror Orders)* [2011] EWCA Civ 703, the Court of Appeal held that a request to courts in England and Wales for minor orders, the child being abroad, did not amount to an acceptance of jurisdiction under Art 12(3) of Brussels IIA.

specified sum of money which can be used for legal, travel and subsistence costs incurred in an attempt to enforce the orders. However, as Freeman's research makes clear (see **9.26**), unless the relocating parent can be trusted voluntarily to promote the child's relationship with the other parent, the price of relocation may well be the loss of the relationship.

Mediation

9.60   Parties are expected to attempt to resolve problems by way of mediation (see **16.8**). Mediation is becoming seen as appropriate for translocation cases as well as other family disputes although Freeman's respondents reported being advised that there was little mediation could do because the positions were polarised or they were encountering difficulties in obtaining funding.[131] However as a Reunite study into mediation in child abduction cases found:[132]

'... there is a clear role for mediation in resolving these highly contentious and emotional disputes, and that parents are willing to embrace the use of mediation ... Whilst it would be true to say that mediation would not be appropriate, or suitable, in every case, and that mediation cannot resolve all cases where it is attempted, it is a facility that should be offered in all cases of international parental child abduction.'

The study found that three-quarters of parents were able to agree a Memorandum of Understanding focused on the best interests of their child, ensuring that the child continued to have a positive relationship with both parents and their extended family and avoiding a court-enforced decision and future litigation. Even where it was not possible to agree a Memorandum of Understanding, parents reported that mediation assisted in reducing the conflict and was helpful in improving communication, and in some cases the parents continued to work together and eventually arrived at their own agreement.

9.61   There would seem to be no reason why similar results could not be obtained in non-abduction relocation cases. A number of alternative dispute resolution processes are available including early neutral evaluation as well as mediation.[133]. Resolution has its own mediation service.[134]

---

[131]   Op cit, at p 23.

[132]   *Mediation In International Parental Child Abduction* (2006) www.reunite.org.

[133]   Thomas 'Relocation dispute resolution hearings' [2010] Fam Law 872. See also Vigers 'Mediating cross-border disputes concerning children' [2010] IFL 118.

[134]   See www.reunite.org/pages/mediation.asp.

Examples of permission not being granted

Re K (A Minor) (Removal from the Jurisdiction)[135]

9.62 There was an adverse effect on the child's relationship with her father and ill thought-out proposals by the mother.

MH v GP (Child: Emigration)[136]

9.63 The mother's proposals were incompatible with the maintenance and development of the child's relationship with his father and wider family.

Re C (Leave to Remove from Jurisdiction)[137]

9.64 The Court of Appeal was unwilling to intervene with the trial judge's conclusion that it would be detrimental to the child for contact to be reduced from staying contact every third weekend, half terms and holidays to once a year, despite the effect refusal would have on the mother and her new partner.

R v R (Leave to Remove)[138]

9.65 The mother did not have the necessary emotional stability to establish a new life in another country. Her plans had not been adequately considered. The children's contact with their father and with both sets of their grandparents probably would be adversely affected.

Temporary removal

9.66 When the purpose for the removal is a holiday, the parent taking the child abroad will normally be required to undertake to return him to the jurisdiction at the end of the holiday. Where a failure by a parent to return a child could mean the irretrievable separation of a child from its roots, the court has to achieve what security it can by building in all practical safeguards.[139] Extra conditions, including the requirement of obtaining 'mirror' orders (those are orders from a court in the country where the holiday will take place, directing the child to be returned at the end of the holiday, and if the child is residing with the other parent, recognising the rights of that parent) may be imposed if there is genuine concern that the children may not be returned. Bonds or security for their child's return or notarised agreements can also be required.[140]

---

[135] [1992] 2 FLR 98. See *also H v F (Refusal of Leave to Remove a Child from the Jurisdiction)* [2005] EWHC 2705 (Fam), [2006] 1 FLR 776.
[136] [1995] 2 FLR 106.
[137] [2000] 2 FLR 457.
[138] [2004] EWHC 2572 (Fam), [2005] 1 FLR 687 (Baron J).
[139] *Re K (Removal from Jurisdiction: Practice)* [1999] 2 FLR 1084.
[140] *DS v RS* [2009] EWHC 1594 (Fam), [2010] 1 FLR 576; *Re K (Removal from Jurisdiction: Practice)* [1999] 2 FLR 1084.

In *Re A (Foreign Contact Order: Jurisdiction)*[141] the mother wanted to go to South Africa for 2 years in order to carry out research to complete her PhD. She wanted to take her 4-year-old daughter, who spent two nights a week with her father, with her. The Court of Appeal allowed her appeal against a refusal of permission, holding that:

> '... the considerations relevant to an application for permission to relocate permanently are simply not automatically, or perhaps at all, applicable to applications for temporary removal.'[142]

Had the difference between the instant case and a request for permanent removal been appreciated by the trial judge there could have been a greater focus on the long-term benefits of the move and the detriment to the mother's career of not moving and more attention could have been paid to ways in which contact by phone, email, text messaging, DVD and digital photographs could have overcome the child's loss of her father's presence.

9.67 It is for the trial judge to assess not only the magnitude of risk of breach of the contact order but also the magnitude of the consequence of breach of the contact order and consider 'whatever butresses can be devised' to secure the child's return including all the options listed above, especially where the holiday is to take place in a country which is not a signatory to the Hague Convention.[143] In *Re M (A Child) (Removal From Jurisdiction: Adjournment)*[144] Black LJ, while not saying that no application could proceed without expert evidence to deal with the practicalities of the foreign legal system and how a return from a non-Hague Convention country could proceed if the child were not returned, commented that:

> '... it is in my view incumbent on a judge to approach the matter in accordance with *Re K* with an inclination that such expert evidence will be necessary and, if he or she concludes it is not necessary, to explain very clearly why what might be classed as the normal practice is not required in a particular case.'[145]

9.68 Applications which involve the consideration of the legal system in foreign states and which may require 'mirror' orders should ordinarily be heard by a judge of the Family Division.[146]

---

[141] [2004] EWCA Civ 1587, [2005] 1 FLR 639.

[142] Ibid, per Thorpe LJ at [10].

[143] *K (Removal from Jurisdiction: Practice)* [1999] 2 FLR 1084, per Thorpe LJ.

[144] [2010] EWCA Civ 888, [2011] 1 FLR 1943.

[145] Ibid, at [24].

[146] *Re K (Removal from Jurisdiction: Practice)* [1999] 2 FLR 1084. Where the intended removal is to Pakistan, see *Family Division: Guidance to Judges on the Implementation of the UK-Pakistan Judicial Protocol on Child Contact and Abduction* (2004).

Examples

Re T (Staying Contact in Non-Convention Country)[147]

9.69 A father was allowed to have contact in Egypt subject to a number of conditions including a mirror order being obtained there giving custody to the mother and providing for the child's return to England at the end of contact, the father entering into a bond of £50,000 to guarantee her return to England and the father undertaking, inter alia, not to obtain a travel document in his daughter's name and not to make any application in respect of her in any court other than the English High Court.

Re L (Removal from Jurisdiction: Holiday)[148]

9.70 A mother proposed taking her son on holiday in the United Arab Emirates. She was required to deposit £50,000 with the court as a bond, to enter, with her brother, into a solemn declaration on the Koran to return the boy and to provide the father with details of her journey and copies of the tickets.

Re S (Leave to Remove from Jurisdiction: Securing Return from Holiday)[149]

9.71 A mother who sought leave to take the children on holiday to India was required to return the children to the jurisdiction by a particular date and not to return them to India thereafter save with the father's consent, to seek only a short-term visa for entry to India, to serve the order on the Indian High Commission and on the British High Commission in Delhi and not to seek Indian passports or citizenship for the boys while they were in India. In addition, the boys were made wards of court and declarations were made that their habitual residence was in England and Wales and that they were British citizens.

Emergency applications

9.72 Where it is feared that the child is about to be removed from the jurisdiction an application for a prohibited steps order can be made without notice to the other party. This, however, places important duties on the applicant, which are discussed at **10.122**. Care should be taken not to leap to unjustified assumptions. In *Re S (Ex Parte Orders)*[150] a non-resident father was told by his daughter's childminder and by someone at her school that she was not going to be in school the following day and that her mother (who had a partner who came from St Lucia) was going away. This was factually correct but his assumption that his daughter was being taken to St Lucia was not. In

---

[147] [1999] 1 FLR 262.
[148] [2001] 1 FLR 241.
[149] [2001] 2 FLR 507.
[150] [2001] 1 FLR 308.

fact, the mother who was employed in a senior financial position in the City of London and therefore unlikely suddenly to emigrate was taking the child to Norfolk for the weekend.

Surrender of passports

9.73   By virtue of s 37 of the Family Law Act 1986 when an order has been made prohibiting the removal of a child from part of the United Kingdom, the court may require the surrender of any United Kingdom passport which has been issued to or contains particulars of the child.

The Passport Agency can be asked not to issue a passport in respect of a child without the permission of the court or the consent of the other parent.[151] The application to the agency can be made if the following orders are in force:

* a prohibited steps order forbidding removal;

* an order confirming that the removal is contrary to the wishes of the court;

* a residence order in favour of the objector or an order confirming that the consent of the objector is required;

* an order prohibiting the removal of the child;

* an order under s 37 of the Family Law Act 1986.

In addition an objection can be made in the absence of an order:

* by the mother if she and the father have not been married to each other;

* by the police if they notify the Agency that they intend to exercise their power of arrest under the Child Abduction Act 1984.

The registration of the child's details will be effective for only 12 months. In *Hamilton Jones v David & Snape*[152] general damages of £20,000 and £25,500 were awarded against a mother's solicitors who had failed to re-register the children's names or advise that they should be re-registered, the children's father having obtained UK passports and removed them to Tunisia.

---

[151]   *Passports for Children: Guidance* (The United Kingdom Passport Agency).
[152]   [2003] EWHC 3147 (Ch), [2004] 1 FLR 774.

Guidance on communicating with the Passport Agency[153] and on applying for passports in the absence of the signature of a person with parental responsibility[154] has been given by the President's Office.

Port alert

9.74 The police may be requested to institute a port alert if there is a real risk that a child is about (ie within 24–48 hours) to be removed unlawfully from the United Kingdom.[155] The removal must be unlawful, that is in contravention of the Child Abduction Act 1984, which states that a person connected with the child (ie a parent, a man who is not married to the mother but in respect of whom there are reasonable grounds for believing him to be the father, a guardian, a person in whose favour a residence order is in force or who has custody of the child)[156] commits an offence if he takes or sends a child out of the United Kingdom without 'appropriate consent'.[157] 'Appropriate consent' is the consent of each of the following: of the mother, the child's father if he has parental responsibility, a guardian, a person in whose favour a residence order is in force or any person with custody or the leave of the court.[158] However, the removal is not unlawful if it is permitted under CA 1989, s 13(b). The child's name will remain on the stop list for 4 weeks and will be removed automatically unless a further application to the police is made.

The application should be made to the applicant's local police station or if it is urgent or a court order has just been made, to any police station.

The police will need:

- full details of the child including his passport number if known;

- full details of the abductor and whether the child is likely to assist him;

- details of the applicant including contact details;

- likely destination;

- likely time of travel and port of embarkation;

- grounds for alert including details of any court order.

---

[153] *Protocol from the President's Office (Communicating with the Passport Service)* [2004] 1 FLR 640. Similar guidance has been given for communication with the Home Office: *Protocol from the President's Office (Communicating with the Home Office)* (March 2012). See **17.67**.

[154] *Guidance from the President's Office (UK Passport Applications on behalf of Children in the Absence of the Signature of a Person with Parental Responsibility)* [2004] 1 FLR 746.

[155] *Registrar's Direction: Children – Removal from the Jurisdiction* [1986] 2 FLR 89.

[156] Child Abduction Act 1984, s 1(2).

[157] Ibid, s 1(1).

[158] Ibid, s 1(2).

Electronic tagging

9.74A In some cases, electronic tagging of the parent with care might be considered.[159]

INTERNAL RELOCATION IN ENGLAND AND WALES

9.75 In some cases the resident parent moving within the United Kingdom will have as great if not greater impact on the relationship between the child and the other parent than emigrating would have. In some cases, as in *Re F (Shared Residence Order)*[160] when a mother moved to Edinburgh, shared residence can ensure that the other party's role in the child's life is recognised and maintained. A similar order was made in *Re H (Agreed Joint Residence: Mediation)*[161] where, following separation, the child's father was his main carer. When the father decided to move from Kent to Devon to enhance his work prospects, the mother decided to move to Kent in order that her son, now aged 5, could live with her and continue to attend his school. The parents agreed that there should be a joint residence order and the court decided that it was in the child's best interests to move to Devon. In other cases, it may be in the child's best interests for residence to pass to the other parent, especially if close links with a locality and, for example, grandparents, need to be maintained. None of these may be possible though and the court has to decide whether some restraint on the move should be imposed. A shared residence order is not however a 'trump card' if one parent subsequently wishes to relocate.[162]

9.76 Although courts can prevent a parent moving the child's home within the jurisdiction, either by a prohibited steps order or by imposing conditions on a residence order under s 11(7) of the Act requiring the parent in whose favour the order is made to live in a particular place, they are very reluctant to do so. As the Court of Appeal said in *Re E (Residence: Imposition of Conditions)*,[163] to do so in most cases would be 'an unwanted imposition' upon the right of a parent to choose where he/she will live and with whom. The correct approach is to look at the issue of where the child will live as one of the relevant factors in the context of cross-applications for residence. If the case is finely balanced, but one parent's plan for where the child will live is less suitable than the other's, that will be an important factor and may persuade the court to make a residence order in favour of the other. If it is not in the best interests of the child to reside with his other parent a current paucity of authority makes it impossible to offer more than general guidance on the approach to be taken. The mere fact that contact with his non-resident parent will be adversely affected is not enough. The detriment must be exceptional so as to make it necessary rather than just desirable that the proposed move does not take place.

---

[159] See *Re C (Abduction: Interim Directions: Accommodation by Local Authority)* [2003] EWHC 3065 (Fam); *Re A (Family Proceedings: Electronic Tagging)* [2009] 2 FLR 891.
[160] [2003] EWCA Civ 592, [2003] 2 FLR 397.
[161] [2004] EWHC 2064 (Fam), [2005] 1 FLR 8.
[162] *Re L (Shared Residence Order)* [2009] EWCA Civ 20, [2009] 1 FLR 1157.
[163] [1997] 2 FLR 638, per Butler-Sloss LJ at 642.

Second, the likely effect of the prohibition on the resident parent will need to be carefully examined and its impact on her future care of the child assessed. Third, the harm that is likely to be suffered by the child if the move takes place must be balanced against the harm which is likely to occur if the move is prevented. Finally, any decision which is not based on detailed findings of fact and which is unsupported by cogent evidence, including expert evidence where appropriate, will be vulnerable on appeal.

The Court added that the guidance in Payne did not apply to internal relocation.

9.77 In *Re B (Prohibited Steps Order)*[164] the Court of Appeal cited with approval a passage in *International Movement of Children*:[165]

> 'The correct approach, therefore, is to look at the issue of where the children will live as one of the relevant factors in the context of the cross-applications for residence, and not as a separate issue divorced from the question of residence. If the case is finely balanced between the respective advantages and disadvantages of the parents, the proposals put forward by each parent will assume considerable importance. If one parent's plan is to remove the children against their wishes to a part of the country less suitable for them, it is an important factor to be taken into account by the court and might persuade the court in some cases to make a residence order in favour of the other parent.'

9.78 Although the principles in *Re E (Residence: Imposition of Conditions)* have been followed by the Court of Appeal in a number of subsequent cases, Wilson LJ revisited them in *Re F (Internal Relocation)*.[166] First, in relation to *Payne* he queried whether it was so obvious that there should be a complete dichotomy between the principles apt to each of the two types of determination. In *Re S (A Child) (Residence Order: Condition)*,[167] Thorpe and Clarke LJJ both observed that it was desirable to have some consistency between the two sets of principles. In *Re H (Children) (Residence Order: Condition)*,[168] Thorpe LJ had said:

> 'What is the rationalisation for a different test to be applied to an application to relocate to Belfast, as opposed to, say, an application to relocate from Gloucester to Dublin? All that the court can do is to remember that in each and every case the decision must rest on the paramount principle of child welfare.'

While not meaning to suggest, particularly in the light of the then current controversy surrounding the aptness of the principles in *Payne* that they should or could be applied to cases of internal relocation:

---

164 [2007] EWCA Civ 1055, [2008] 1 FLR 613.
165 Everall, Lowe, Nicholls (2004), at 6.4.
166 [2010] EWCA Civ 1428, [2011] 1 FLR 1382.
167 [2001] EWCA Civ 847, [2001] 3 FCR 154.
168 [2001] EWCA Civ 1338, [2001] 2 FLR 1277.

'Nevertheless, even if, for example, the effect upon the aspiring parent, and thus indirectly upon the child, of a refusal of permission to remove was one day to be considered to have been afforded too great an emphasis in our principles governing external relocation, I would expect our principles governing internal relocation to allow at any rate for some weight to be attributed to that factor.'

9.79 Wilson LJ's second observation related to the 'early insinuation' into the principles governing internal relocation of a test of exceptionality. No one could quarrel with a proposition that it would rarely be in the interests of a child for the residential parent to be prevented from moving home with the child within the UK. However there was a danger that a decision-maker's attempt to explain his decision in terms which include reference to exceptionality gives rise to the subsequent elevation of a concept of exceptionality as the governing criterion.[169]

'It is too late for it to be permissible for this court to rule that, in internal relocation cases, the analysis of the child's welfare, informed by consideration of the matters specified in section 1(3) of the Act, should not be conducted through the prism of whether the circumstances are exceptional ... But ... had I not felt bound by authority, I might have wished to suggest that a test of exceptionality was an impermissible gloss on the enquiry mandated by section 1(1) and (3) of the Act.'

9.80 In *Re F (Internal Relocation)*[170] Wilson LJ expressed the provisional view that internal relocation should be prevented where appropriate by making a prohibited steps order rather than by placing a condition upon a residence order.[171]

9.81 For an example of an order preventing internal relocation being breached, see *Re G (Residence: Same-Sex Partner)*.[172]

Examples

Re H (Children) (Residence Order: Condition)[173]

9.82 The Court of Appeal, in what it described as 'a highly exceptional case' upheld an order preventing a father with a residence order from returning to Northern Ireland (from where the parent originated) from Gloucester where the mother (M) lived. M had a residence application which was pending while she received treatment for alcohol abuse and the trial judge had held that, other things being equal, she would be the preferred carer.

---

[169] See *Currey v Currey (No 2)* [2006] EWCA Civ 1338, [2007] 1 FLR 946, at [19], and *Haringey Independent Appeal Panel v R (M)* [2010] EWCA Civ 1103.

[170] [2010] EWCA Civ 1428, [2011] 1 FLR 1382.

[171] See also *Re B (Prohibited Steps Order)* [2007] EWCA Civ 1055, [2008] 1 FLR 613, per Thorpe LJ at [4].

[172] [2006] EWCA Civ 372, [2006] 2 FLR 614.

[173] [2001] 2 FLR 1277.

Re S (A Child) (Residence Order: Condition)[174]

9.83 V was born with a congenital heart and lung defect. She suffered from Down's Syndrome and had a much shortened life expectancy. When she was 3 her parents separated, V remaining with her mother (M). When M and her new partner decided to move from Croydon to Cornwall, her father (F) objected and sought to prevent the move. The trial judge imposed a condition on M's residence order requiring her to live in Croydon, having heard evidence from an educational psychologist that reducing contact with F would have a detrimental effect on V and the long gaps between the visits would make her anxious. She would also find it difficult if she were to lose contact with her extended family and to move school. The Court of Appeal directed a rehearing, holding that insufficient attention had been given to the effect on the family of forbidding the move. At the rehearing evidence was called to show that M suffered from depression and would be very distressed if she could not move. Nevertheless the trial judge found that there was a very real risk that V would suffer emotional harm if she moved to Cornwall and re-imposed the same condition. M again appealed but this time unsuccessfully. A differently constituted Court of Appeal held that the judge had been entitled to treat the case as exceptional. He had considered the principles in *Re E (Residence: Imposition of Conditions)*[175] and carried out 'the unusually difficult balancing exercise' and come to a conclusion which could not be faulted.

B v B (Residence: Condition Limiting Geographic Area)[176]

9.84 The 6-year-old child lived with her mother (M) who had made two applications, both withdrawn, for permission to emigrate to Australia. There had been protracted litigation about contact between the parents and the district judge hearing the litigation had expressed firm views about the mother's intransigence. When M decided to move from Middlesex to Newcastle, the child's father who lived in West Sussex objected and applied for a specific issue order to determine his daughter's schooling. The judge found that M's proposals were unclear and lacked purpose other than to create as much physical and emotional distance between the child and her father as possible. Moreover, the move would have a detrimental effect on the child's education. Finding that this was a highly exceptional case, the trial judge imposed a condition on the residence order to the effect that the child had to live until further order in an area bounded by the A4 to the north, the M25 to the west and the A3 to the south and east.

MEDICAL INTERVENTION

9.85 The Court of Appeal is clear that non-urgent serious operations (especially those of a non-therapeutic kind) require the consent of all parties

---

[174] [2001] EWCA Civ 847, [2001] 3 FCR 154; [2002] EWCA Civ 1795, [2003] 1 FCR 134.
[175] [1997] 2 FLR 638.
[176] [2004] 2 FLR 979.

with parental responsibility or, failing that, the approval of the court.[177] The majority of the recently reported decisions involve disputes between parents and medical professionals,[178] but disputes can arise between those with parental responsibility and then the court has to decide on the basis of medical evidence as to where the best interests of the child lie. The resident parent cannot veto the operation or treatment but the effect on her care of the child of the treatment taking place against her wishes will need to be assessed and any possible detriment to the child balanced against the benefits.

9.86 When the operation is non-therapeutic, non-reversible and carries some physical or psychological risk, albeit small, for example male circumcision, there have to be clear benefits to the child which show that the operation will be in his best interests.[179]

9.87 It is clear from *Re C (Welfare of Child: Immunisation)* that there is no general principle that a court will not order non-essential invasive medical treatment in the face of strong opposition from the child's primary carer[180] but in some cases, for example *Re J (Specific Issue Orders: Muslim Upbringing and Circumcision)*[181] the effect on the child of a carer's opposition will persuade a court that the operation is not in the child's best interests. However, the greater the medical indication for the operation, the less weight will be placed on the opposition. The cases where the dispute lay not between the parents, but between the medical professionals and the parents, contain only one example of an operation being held not to be in the child's best interests because of the opposition.[182]

---

[177] See, for example, *Re J (Specific Issue Orders: Child's Religious Upbringing and Circumcision)* [2000] 1 FLR 571 and **Chapter 8**.

[178] See, for example, *Royal Wolverhampton Hospitals NHS Trust v B* [2000] 1 FLR 953 (declaration that a chronically sick premature baby could be treated in accordance with the advice of her paediatrician); *Re A (Conjoined Twins: Medical Treatment)* [2001] 1 FLR 1 (decision that conjoined twins should be separated notwithstanding the refusal of their parents to consent); and *Portsmouth NHS Trust v Wyatt and Wyatt, Southampton NHS Trust Intervening* [2004] EWHC 2247 (Fam), [2005] 1 FLR 21, [2005] EWHC 693 (Fam), [2005] 2 FLR 480, [2005] EWHC 2293 (Fam), [2006] 1 FLR 652 and [2006] EWHC 319 (Fam), [2006] 2 FLR 111. See also Pedain 'Doctors, parents and the courts: legitimising restrictions on the continuing provision of lifespan maximising treatments for severely handicapped, non-dying babies' [2005] 17 CFLQ 535.

[179] *Re J (Specific Issue Orders: Muslim Upbringing and Circumcision)* [1999] 2 FLR 678, per Wall J at 699.

[180] [2003] EWCA Civ 1148, [2003] 2 FLR 1095, at [22].

[181] [2000] 1 FLR 571.

[182] *Re T (Wardship: Medical Treatment)* [1997] 1 FLR 502, a case with very unusual features, not least that the child was no longer within the jurisdiction. 'This has been seen as an aberrant decision or, conversely, as more progressive than most: aberrant if viewed as a reversion to the idea of parents; natural rights; progressive because it took into account the important aspect of the caring relationship.' Hagger 'Parental Responsibility and Children's Health Care Treatment' in *Responsible Parents & Parental Responsibility* op cit, at p 189.

Male circumcision

9.88 Most reported cases of inter-parental disputes over operations concern male circumcision and are considered in the section on religion below. Female circumcision (female genital mutilation) is illegal (see **9.112**).

Immunisation

9.89 In *Re C (Welfare of Child: Immunisation)*[183] the court was concerned with two families in which the fathers sought specific issue orders that their daughters each receive childhood immunisations including the triple vaccine MMR (measles, mumps and rubella). Both mothers opposed the immunisations arguing that they involved unacceptable risks and that imposing them against their wishes would cause them undue distress. Because the trial judge rejected the expert evidence called on behalf of the mothers on the ground that the expert had allowed her deeply held feelings on immunisation to overrule the duty owed as an expert witness to the court (see **18.34**), the acceptable medical evidence was all one way. Following the advice of the doctors whose evidence he accepted, Sumner J held that it was in the interests of the two girls to receive most of the immunisations (some being contra-indicated). He considered the argument that imposing immunisation against the mothers' wishes would impact on their care of the children but found that it would not have a significant effect.

9.90 The judge set out his approach in a way which provides guidance for other cases where parents disagree about treatment.

'Art 8 of the European Convention giving respect to private and family life is considered. There is an exception permitting the interference by the court for the protection of health … The opposition of the mothers is of considerable concern. Both mothers and fathers have equal rights before the court. The parent with whom a child is living, whether mother or father, does not have greater rights than an absent parent who is entitled to be consulted on major decisions in the child's life. But the court does attach importance to the bond between a child and the parent with whom they are living and will take care to safeguard and preserve it in the best interests of the child … Where a proposed course is beneficial for a child but may cause damage to that relationship, the court will balance the issue with care. It may prevent a course otherwise beneficial to the child being ordered. This is especially where the proposal is for invasive medical intervention to which that parent is opposed. Compelling evidence is required … Where medical intervention is concerned the more scope there is for genuine debate the less likely is the court to take a decision. Difficult decisions should be taken by parents.'[184]

The mothers appealed unsuccessfully, the Court of Appeal holding that the trial judge's approach was 'above criticism'.

---

[183] [2003] EWHC 1376 (Fam), [2003] 2 FLR 1054 and, on appeal [2003] EWCA Civ 1148, [2003] 2 FLR 1095. See O'Donnell '*Re C (Welfare of Child: Immunisation)* – Room to refuse?' [2004] 16 CFLQ 213.

[184] [2003] EWHC 1376 (Fam) [2003] 2 FLR 1054, at [365] to [371].

Blood transfusion

9.91   Conditions can be placed on a residence order to the effect that the child should have treatment, for example, a blood transfusion if advised by a doctor. See **10.11**.

HIV testing

9.92   In *Re C (HIV Test)*[185] a local authority applied for a specific issue order that a baby born to an HIV positive mother should be tested for HIV. The order was granted, the application being opposed by the parents. Although the issue revolved only around testing its apparent simplicity proved deceptive. It was necessary for the court to investigate the likely medical reaction to a positive or a negative result, as well as the likely consequences of the continued absence of any testing.

> 'The advantages of the proposed test [are] very substantial. The principal disadvantage is the effect of its imposition on the parents: the affront to them; the stress of medical and legal intrusion into their lives ... and the prospect of further conflict with orthodox medicine, and even perhaps with the law, in the wake of the result ... But this case is not at its heart about the rights of the parents. This baby has rights of her own. They can be considered nationally or internationally. Under our national law I must determine the case by reference to her welfare (s 1(1)); and, in particular, I must have regard to her physical needs (s 1(3)(b)); to her background, namely her mother's infection (s 1(3)(d)); and to the harm which she is at risk of suffering (s 1(3)(e)).'[186]

Permission was granted and the Court of Appeal refused the parents leave to appeal.

9.93   The President has given guidance on the HIV testing of children.[187] The need to make an application is likely to arise only rarely in the absence of parental disagreement. If there are proceedings concerning the child pending in the Family Proceedings Court these should be transferred to the county court. Where a child of sufficient understanding opposes the testing and there are no pending proceedings, the application should be made under the inherent jurisdiction in the High Court.

RELIGION

Introduction

9.94   There are differing concepts of religion. For Christianity, at least in Western Europe, 'religion' means primarily a system of beliefs to which the

---

185   [1999] 2 FLR 1004.
186   Ibid, per Wilson J at 1006.
187   *President's Direction HIV Testing of Children* [2003] 1 FLR 1299 replacing guidance given in *Note: Re (HIV) Test* [1994] 2 FLR 116.

believer is required to assent. One becomes a Christian by choice or conversion. In comparison, to be a Jew means first and foremost to belong to a group, the Jewish people, and religious beliefs are secondary.[188] Like Judaism, Islam means much more than what is usually meant by the Western concept of religion but unlike Judaism, it is not necessarily primarily a matter of birth. Whether one is a Muslim appears to depend on a combination of belief and practice and how one sees oneself and is seen by others.[189]

9.95 In practice though the distinction between Western and non-Western religions is not clear cut and there are similarities. A child may become a Christian through infant baptism but for his believing parents, his Christianity may be as much a part of his identity as if a Christian by birth. One study,[190] which examined a group of parents who were predominantly from Christian and Muslim backgrounds, found that most thought that religion was a way of life, transmitted between generations and believed that it was part of their parenting responsibility to pass on their faith. In both groups of believers, the prospect of the child being adopted outside the faith may cause considerable distress. In practice therefore it has been assumed that a child shares his parents' religion or cultural identity from birth, regardless of whether the child has undergone any rite of acceptance.

9.96 Irrespective of whether the child is born into a religion, background of parental influence is obviously important in producing religious attitudes, belief and behaviour. Young children, up to about the age of 12, readily take to religion and accept what they are told without difficulty[191] Their beliefs are therefore likely to mirror those of their parents. It is with the onset of adolescence that the young person starts to take an independent stance.[192] The phase starts with a high level of religious activity, followed typically by period of questioning and doubt in which overt religious activity may decline. Many may 'drop out' from the church in which they were brought up and many are converted to a new faith. 'This is an age of both conversion and deconversion.'[193]

9.97 Courts are reluctant to engage in assessing the relative merits of religions or even the merits of following one particular religion as opposed to following none, provided that the doctrines are legally and socially acceptable.[194] However, there are occasions when a child's religious upbringing is the subject of dispute between parents, either as a factor in deciding with whom the child should live or as an issue as to whether the non-resident parent may encourage

---

[188]   de Lange *Judaism* (Penguin, 1986), at pp 3–4.
[189]   Pearl and Menski *Muslim Family Law* (3rd edn, Sweet & Maxwell, 1998), ch 5.
[190]   Howarth, Lees and others *Religion, Beliefs and Parenting Practices* Summarised Findings 2265 (Joseph Rowntree Foundation, 2008).
[191]   Argyle *Psychology and Religion* (Routledge, 2000), at pp 25–29.
[192]   See, for example, *Re S (Minors) (Access: Religious Upbringing)* [1992] 2 FLR 313, at 320.
[193]   Argyle op cit, at p 26. See also *Re A and D (Local Authority: Religious Upbringing)* [2010] EWHC 2503 (Fam), [2011] 1 FLR 615, per Baker J at [73].
[194]   *Re R (A Minor) (Residence: Religion)* [1993] 2 FLR 163, per Purchas LJ at 171.

the child to take part in religious activity during contact or as to how the child is to be brought up by the resident parent.

The test to be applied is the welfare test and all the factors in the checklist have to be considered.

Freedom of choice

9.98 As Rachel Taylor has pointed out, the question of whether a child should be brought up to adhere to a particular religion or no religion is one upon which reasonable people deeply disagree and the state has no tools[195] – nor standing – to resolve the disagreement. However while a parent has no obligation to raise a child to have religious knowledge,[196] the right to determine a child's religious upbringing is undoubtedly an aspect of parental responsibility.[197]

9.99 Specific guidance emerges from the reported cases and statutes. A parent or a child has the right to follow a religion of their choosing:

> 'The court ... should recognise that each [parent] is entitled to his or her own beliefs and way of life and that the two opposing ways of life [may be] both socially acceptable and certainly consistent with a decent and respectable life.'[198]

9.100 The child and each parent has the right under Art 9(1) of the European Convention on Human Rights to freedom of thought, conscience and religion, including the freedom, either alone or with others and in public or private, to manifest his religion or belief in worship, teaching, practice and observance. The Article covers religions, including Druidism, sects, including Scientology[199] and beliefs, such as pacifism,[200] as well as atheism and agnosticism.[201] However, the freedom to manifest religion or belief, unlike the freedom to hold a belief is subject to such limitations as are prescribed by law and necessary in a democratic society in the interests of public safety, for the protection of public order, health or morals or for the protection of the rights or freedoms of others.[202] In *Re J (Specific Issue Orders: Muslim Upbringing and Circumcision)*,[203] Wall J, not unsurprisingly, held that it is not inconsistent with Arts 8 and 9 for a court to prevent one parent manifesting his religion in such a

---

[195] It was not always so. Prior to 1957 a judge when granting an adoption order in favour of two active communists made it a condition of the order that the child should be sent regularly to church. James 'The illegitimate and deprived child' in Graveson and Crane (eds) *A Century of Family Law* (1957), at p 52, n 3.

[196] *Re J (Specific Issue Orders: Muslim Upbringing and Circumcision)* [1999] 2 FLR 678, per Wall J at 685.

[197] Taylor 'Parental responsibility and religion' in *Responsible Parents and Parental Responsibility* op cit, at p 123.

[198] *Re T (Custody: Religious Upbringing)* (1981) 2 FLR 239, per Scarman LJ at 245.

[199] *Church of Scientology v Sweden* [1979] ECC 511.

[200] *Arrowsmith v UK* [1978] 19 DR 5.

[201] *Kokkinakis v Greece* (1994) 17 EHRR 397.

[202] Art 9(2).

[203] [1999] 2 FLR 678.

way that it is not in the best interests of his child.[204] Because the child's rights are engaged, particular attention will have to be paid to the views of a mature and informed child.

Welfare test

9.101 Section 1(3)(d) of the Children Act 1989 requires the court to have regard, 'in particular', among other matters to the child's background and any characteristics which the court considers relevant. These include the child's 'religious and cultural heritage'. It is a relevant consideration, the weight of which will vary according to the facts of each case.[205] In *Re P (Section 91(14) Guidelines)*[206] the Court of Appeal had to consider whether an 8-year-old girl born with Down's syndrome to Jewish Orthodox parents should be moved from non-practising Catholic foster parents with whom she had been living from the age of 17 months to her parents. Her parents' application was dismissed on the grounds that her stability required that she should remain with her foster parents.[207] However, Butler-Sloss LJ commented that:

> '[In this case her religion] is an important factor. No one would wish to deprive a Jewish child of her right to her Jewish heritage. If she had remained with a Jewish family it would be almost unthinkable, other than in an emergency, to remove her from it ... But in the unusual circumstances of this case her parents were not able to accommodate her within her community ... and it was then, not now, that she was deprived of her opportunity to grow up within the Jewish community.'

Ward LJ added that a court can take the religious factor into consideration whether or not the child has an understanding of the value of the religious life but conversely the court may also have regard to the child's level of understanding[208]

9.102 The court is concerned not with the beliefs of the particular religion or sect but with the impact of those beliefs on the welfare of the child, viewed not only in the immediate but also in the medium- and long-term future. There is no difficulty in judges reaching the view that adhering to a particular religion will not harm the child in any case which concerns mainstream religion but they are more ready to examine the doctrines and rules of other sects, such as the Plymouth Brethren[209] or Scientology.[210] However, they have to be aware that there is a great risk, merely because they are dealing with an unpopular

---

[204] See also the New Zealand case of *Re J (An Infant)*; *B and B v Director-General of Social Welfare* [1996] 2 NZLR 134 – parents' rights to practise their religion cannot extend to imperilling the life or health of their child.

[205] *Re P (Section 91(14) Guidelines)* [1999] 2 FLR 573, per Butler-Sloss LJ at 585, and Ward LJ at 595.

[206] Ibid.

[207] See **10.78**.

[208] [1999] 2 FLR 573, at 601.

[209] *Re R (A Minor) (Residence: Religion)* [1993] 2 FLR 163.

[210] *Re B and G (Minors) (Custody)* [1985] FLR 134, FD and [1985] FLR 493, CA. 'Scientology is both immoral and socially obnoxious ... It is corrupt, sinister and dangerous', per Latey J at 157.

minority sect, of overplaying the dangers to the welfare of the child inherent in the possibility that it might follow one parent's beliefs.[211] Care has to be taken that findings, for example, about the effect a parent's belief will have on the child's care, are based on direct concrete evidence and not mere assertions of generalities, and that there is a reasonably proportionate relationship between the order and the legitimate aim sought.[212]

9.103 In *M v H (Educational Welfare)*,[213] for example, Charles J said that:

> 'It cannot be said that the beliefs and practices of a parent who is a Jehovah's Witness creates a situation that is so inimical to good family life that ordinary considerations have to give way to it in determining what will best promote the welfare of the relevant child. The position is that the two opposing ways of life that are relevant in this case are both socially acceptable and certainly consistent with a decent and respectable life and one in which the welfare of children can be promoted (see in *Re T*).[214] Rather the relevance of the religious difference relates to the impact in all the circumstances of the case on S's welfare of the respective beliefs of the parents and thus of their respective lifestyles and attitudes based thereon. This is an exercise that can only be carried out in all the circumstances of a given case and it naturally has many comparative elements.'

Having carried out this exercise the Court granted residence of S, a 5-year-old child to her father in part because the mother's beliefs and practices regarding parties and Christmas were likely to limit the width of S's friends of her own age and her contact with adults, who could help and influence her. However, absent the child's emotional insecurity following parental conflict:

> 'those effects would have far less weight ... They are not the most important or magnetic considerations in this case. Rather they constitute a factor that supports the conclusion based on those most important and magnetic considerations.'

9.104 Likewise in *Re A and D (Local Authority): Religious Upbringing)*[215] the Court dismissed an application by the Muslim father of a 5-year-old boy who had lived with his maternal grandmother since he was 6 months old. The grandmother was Roman Catholic but her daughter, the boy's mother, had converted to Islam. The grandmother was raising the boy with information about Catholicism and Islam but he was receiving no formal instruction about Islam.[216] Notwithstanding an insufficient focus by the local authority on the child's religious heritage which had to be addressed it was not in the child's best interests to be placed in the care of his father.

---

[211] *Re T (Custody: Religious Upbringing)* (1981) 2 FLR 239.
[212] *Palau-Martinez v France* (Application No 64927/01) [2004] 2 FLR 810. Granting residence in favour of a father because of generalised concerns about the mother being a Jehovah's Witness was in breach of her Art 8 and Art 14 rights.
[213] [2008] EWHC 324 Fam.
[214] (1979) 10 December Court of Appeal (unreported), per Scarman LJ at pp 8 and 10.
[215] [2010] EWHC 2503 (Fam), [2011] 1 FLR 615.
[216] It should be noted that, the child being in care, the local authority was prohibited from causing the child 'to be brought up in any religious persuasion other than that in which he would have been brought up if the order had not been made' (CA 1989, s 33(6)(a)).

Steps the court can take

9.105 If the court decides that either the parent or the child adhering to the religion poses a risk to the child, it will need to consider whether the risk can be avoided by the parent giving undertakings or by the imposition of conditions on a residence order. For example, the risk to a child's life because a parent who is a Jehovah's Witness will be unwilling to consent to blood transfusion may be avoided by an undertaking either to consent or to give medical staff the written consent of the other parent or a specific issue order that the child may receive a transfusion if the doctor having charge of its treatment considers it desirable. This involves not only the parent being willing to give the undertakings but an assessment of whether or not the undertakings will be honoured.[217] Restrictions as to the observance of, for example, Christmas, can be avoided by contact taking place at that time. An order can be made that the child attend a secular school. Conversely, a contact or specific issue order can be granted to allow the child to take part in religious activities. In *Re Z (A Child) (Specific Issue Order: Religious Education)*,[218] for example, the Court of Appeal granted a specific issue order which allowed a boy born to a Muslim father and a non-Muslim mother to attend the mosque on two weekdays as well as at weekends when he was staying with his father.

9.106 When parents have decided to bring their children up in two religions it may be difficult to persuade a court later that this decision should be changed. In *Re S (Specific Issue Order: Religion: Circumcision)*[219] the Muslim mother and the Hindu, Jainite, father agreed that their two children should be brought up as Hindus with Islamic influences and this agreement was put into effect. When they separated their daughter was 8 and their son 6. They lived with their mother who wanted them to be brought up as practising members of the Islamic faith and her son to be circumcised. Their father objected. The trial judge refused to grant the mother a specific issue order. A further 2 years had passed and it was too late to seek to replace one of the children's religions of origin in favour of the other. The problem stemmed not directly from their needs but from the need of the mother and her family to portray her marriage as being to a Muslim man. This deception should not be sanctioned by the court particularly when the children knew of their cultural heritage. Furthermore, children of a mixed heritage should be allowed to choose for themselves which, if any, religion they wished to follow. Circumcision could not be reversed and could prevent the boy practising Jainism when he was older. When he became *Gillick* competent he could make his own, informed, decision.[220]

---

[217] In *Re B and G (Minors) (Custody)* [1985] FLR 134, the court was unable to accept a father's undertakings that he would not involve the children in Scientology until they were old enough to decide for themselves.

[218] [2002] All ER (D) 145 (Mar).

[219] [2004] EWHC 1282 (Fam), [2005] 1 FLR 236.

[220] [2005] EWHC 2769 (Fam).

9.107   A non-resident parent can be prevented from using contact for religious ends. *Re S (Minors) (Access: Religious Upbringing)*[221] concerned a fervent Roman Catholic father and two children aged 13 and 11 who lived with their atheist mother. During the marriage, the girls were brought up as Roman Catholics but their father became increasingly obsessed with religious observances. Following a divorce, the father sought orders that the children should not attend religious or sex education classes at their schools, that they should be returned to private Catholic education and that the mother should encourage them in the practice of their faith. The children made it very clear to the court and family reporter that they did not want contact with their father or to attend church. The Court of Appeal upheld the refusal of the trial judge to order contact and Butler-Sloss LJ indicated that it would be 'an absolute requirement' of any future application for contact that he did not make his religion the basis of his case. Although the court did not grant the directions the father sought, the President thought it too soon for children to decide that they wanted nothing to do with their religion and in the exceptional circumstances of the case invited the Official Solicitor to represent the children so that he could explore the possibility of continuing with the observances of their baptised faith.

9.108   In some cases, the court will prohibit the person with care bringing the child up in a particular faith. The fact that the child has habitually been following the religion may be of relevance but it cannot be decisive.[222]

9.109   The court can not only prohibit a parent with care bringing a child up in a particular religion but can direct that the child is brought up in another. In *J v C*,[223] Protestant foster parents of a child born to Roman Catholic parents were ordered to raise the child as a Roman Catholic. In *Re K (Adoption and Wardship)*,[224] directions were given in wardship that a Bosnian Muslim child, brought to the United Kingdom as a baby by a non-Muslim English couple, was to receive instruction in the Muslim religion. The fact that such directions are required does not necessarily mean that the child should be a ward. The powers of the court under the Children Act are sufficient in many cases.[225]

Male circumcision

9.110   In some cases, the religious observances of one parent may lead him or her to seek to have a male child circumcised.[226] Two cases involving Muslim parents who had conceived a child with a non-Muslim partner provide

---

[221]   [1992] 2 FLR 313.

[222]   *Re B and G (Minors) (Custody)* [1985] FLR 134.

[223]   [1970] AC 668.

[224]   [1997] 2 FLR 221.

[225]   *C v Salford City Council* [1994] 2 FLR 926 (application by Roman Catholic foster parents for a residence order in respect of a young girl born to orthodox Jewish parents).

[226]   Taylor (op cit, p 130) comments that this is 'an unusual right: the right to submit their child to a surgical procedure involving permanent change to the child's body despite the lack of a medical need for such a procedure'. See also *The Law and Ethics of Male Circumcision: Guidance for Doctors* (British Medical Association, 2008).

examples. In *Re J (Specific Issue Orders: Muslim Upbringing and Circumcision)*,[227] a child, J, was born to a father who was a non-practising Muslim and a notionally but non-practising Christian mother. Before they married, the mother promised that she would convert to Islam (she did not) and when she was pregnant she agreed that any male child would be circumcised. They separated when J was 2½, the boy remaining with his mother. J was not raised in any faith. When he was 5, his father sought specific issue orders that J be brought up as a Muslim and circumcised. Wall J had to balance the importance of a child being familiar with his cultural and religious heritage and the impact that following the Muslim religion would have on his daily life with a non-believer. Only in unusual circumstances would the court require that a child be brought up in a faith which was not that of the parent with whom he was living. J would have the opportunity of learning about the Muslim faith and culture through contact with his father but was unlikely to have much contact with the Muslim world even when having contact with his father. It would not be appropriate to require his mother to follow religious practices but would be wise to respect the father's wish that J should not eat pork. Although circumcision would firmly identify J with his father and confirm him as a Muslim in the eyes of Islam, the operation carried some risk and was painful. The mother strongly opposed it and would have difficulty in presenting the operation to J in a positive light. It would make him an exception in the eyes of his peers. Therefore, Wall J refused to grant either order and an appeal by the father was dismissed. Permission for circumcision was also refused in *Re S (Specific Issue Order: Religion: Circumcision)*[228] where an 8-year-old boy had been brought up, prior to his parents' separation, as a Hindu with Islamic influences.[229]

9.111 In *Re S (Change of Names: Cultural Factors)*,[230] a boy was born to a Muslim mother and Sikh father. They separated when he was 15 months old, S remaining with his mother, living in the Bangladeshi community of East London. The mother applied to the court for permission to change S's names from Sikh to Muslim ones and for permission to have him circumcised before he was 10 years old. Wilson J held that in the circumstances of the case, which included great personal and social difficulties of the mother, both she and S had to be enabled to integrate into their community. He gave permission for S to be informally known by Muslim names, although he refused permission for his names to be changed by deed poll. He gave permission for S to be brought up in the Muslim faith, not only at home (which his father did not oppose) but also in the wider community. He granted permission for the child to be circumcised in order that he would not experience embarrassment in the community. Although a child could not be brought up in two faiths

---

227 [1999] 2 FLR 678, FD and *Re J (Specific Issue Orders: Child's Religious Upbringing and Circumcision)* [2000] 1 FLR 571, CA.
228 [2004] EWHC 1282 (Fam), [2005] 1 FLR 236.
229 See also *T v S (Wardship)* [2011] EWHC 1608 (Fam), [2012] 1 FLR 230 where both parents agreed.
230 [2001] 2 FLR 1005. See also *Re S (Specific Issue Order: Religion: Circumcision)* [2004] EWHC 1282 (Fam), [2005] 1 FLR 236.

simultaneously, the decisions about his religion did not preclude S from becoming aware of his Sikh identity through contact with his father.

Female circumcision

9.112 Female circumcision is illegal under the Female Genital Mutilation Act 2003.[231]

EDUCATION

9.113 The parent with whom the child does not live is entitled to be consulted about his or her child's education. Section 36 of the Education Act 1944 imposes a duty on parents to cause their child to receive efficient full-time education suitable to his age, ability and aptitude and to any special needs he may have, either by regular attendance at school or otherwise. No distinction is drawn between parents who reside with their child and those who do not or those with parental responsibility and those without it.[232] Likewise, no distinction is drawn as regards parents' rights and duties under the sections of the Education Act 1996 and the Education (Special Educational Needs) Regulations 1994, SI 1994/1047 which deal with the assessment of and meeting any special educational needs. These rights include the right to be consulted.

Courts are able to impose conditions on the grant of residence orders that the resident parent provide copies of school reports, notices of parents' evenings and school events but, on a practical level, head teachers are normally willing to send these directly to the non-resident parent and this should be the first line of enquiry.[233] Departmental guidance advises headteachers that non-resident parents and others with parental responsibility should be sent annual reports and invitations in the same way as resident parents.[234]

> 'Everyone who is a parent whether they are a resident or non-resident parent has the same right to participate in decisions about a child's education and receive information about the child. However for day to day purposes the school's main contact is likely to be with the parent who lives with whom the child lives on school days ... Schools and [local education authority] staff must treat all parents equally unless there is a court order limiting an individual's exercise of parental responsibility.'

9.114 Parents can be prevented from visiting the child's school.[235]

---

[231] See also *Working together to Safeguard Children* (Department for Children, Schools and Education, 2010), at p 195 and *K v Secretary of State for the Home Department* [2006] UKHL 46, [2007] 1 AC 412.

[232] Under s 114 of the Act, 'parent' includes any person who is not a parent of the child but who has parental responsibility or the care of him. This can include a foster parent (see *Fairpo v Humberside County Council* [1997] 1 FLR 339).

[233] See Piper 'Parental responsibility and the Education Acts' [1994] Fam Law 146.

[234] DfEE Guidance 92/2000, para 12.

[235] For example *Harris v Harris*; *Attorney-General v Harris* [2001] 2 FLR 895 (father prevented

Which school?

9.115 A non-resident parent with parental responsibility is entitled to be consulted about a change of school[236] and whether or not a parent without responsibility is legally entitled to be consulted, a failure to involve such a parent who is showing commitment to a child runs the risk that plans for the move will be halted or even put into reverse if the non-resident parent takes the matter to court.

9.116 There are few reported cases where courts have had to decide how and where a child is to be educated. For most parents, there is little choice concerning schools, either at primary or secondary level. The choice between private or state education or the decision as to which private school a child is to attend features as an issue usually, if at all, in applications for ancillary relief when the cost of the various choices will be a very important if not determinative factor.

Examples

Re A (Specific Issue Order: Parental Dispute)[237]

9.117 This concerned a dispute between a French father and English mother about whether their daughters should move from their private schools to a *lycée* in London where teaching was in French and on the French system. The Court of Appeal held that there could be no general principle about the education of children of separated parents of different nationalities other than that imposed by s 1(3) of the Act. The trial judge had considered all relevant matters when he decided that the children should attend the *lycée* and refused to interfere with the order.

Re P (A Minor) (Education)[238]

9.118 The Court of Appeal overturned a decision that a 14-year-old boy should attend a boarding school rather than a local day school which was his clear preference. He was mature, sensible and intelligent and at his age his views should have been given great weight. On a practical level, forcing him to board carried the very real danger that he would not settle well and be very unhappy.

Re P (Parental Dispute: Judicial Determination)[239]

9.119 Divorced parents were in dispute as to the choice of senior schools for their daughters. The trial judge found that both parents were fully alive to the

---

from loitering outside any school where his children were pupils or entering the school premises or attending an event organised by the school unless none of the children was present and he had arranged in writing and in advance with staff).

[236] *Re G (Parental Responsibility: Education)* [1994] 2 FLR 964.
[237] [2001] 1 FLR 121.
[238] [1992] 1 FLR 316.
[239] [2002] EWCA Civ 1627, [2003] 1 FLR 286.

academic needs of the children and were capable of deciding their future. He therefore ordered that future questions in respect of their education, including the choice of schools, should be decided by the mother (with whom the girls were living) in consultation with the father. The Court of Appeal allowed the father's appeal and directed a rehearing. A choice of school was fundamental and it was the duty of the court to reach a clear decision in the absence of parental agreement.

M v M (Specific Issue: Choice of School)[240]

9.120   In a protracted contact case there was a dispute between the parents as to whether their 7-year-old son should attend a cathedral choir school. The court directed that the boy should attend a voice test which might result in his being awarded a scholarship. The potential upset of taking the test would be small and without it the proceedings would be more protracted and difficult to resolve.

MARRIAGE AND CIVIL PARTNERSHIP

9.121   Canon law required parental consent before minors could marry and this requirement was introduced into civil law by the Clandestine Marriages Act 1753. The current relevant legislation is the Marriage Act 1949 (as amended).[241]

9.122   A child between the ages of 16 and 18 who is not a widow or widower requires the consent of the following people to marry[242] or who is not a surviving civil partner, to enter a civil partnership:[243]

(a)   each parent (if any) of the child who has parental responsibility for him and each guardian[244] (if any) of the child;

(b)   where a residence order is in force with respect to the child, the consent of the person or persons with whom he lives, or is to live, as a result of the order (in substitution for the consents mentioned in paragraph (a));

Where a care order is in force with respect to the child, the consent of the local authority designated in the order is required in addition to the consents mentioned in para (a). Other provisions relate to a child subject to a placement order whether or not placed for adoption.

---

[240]   [2005] EWHC 2769 (Fam).

[241]   See Probert 'Parental responsibility and children's partnership choices' in *Responsible Parents & Parental Responsibility* op cit for an interesting account of the requirement.

[242]   Marriage Act1949, s 3.

[243]   Civil Partnership Act 2004, s 4.

[244]   Includes special guardian.

Where neither para (a) nor (b) applies but a residence order was in force with respect to the child immediately before he reached the age of 16, the consent of the person or persons with whom he lived, or was to live, as a result of the order is required in substitution for the consents mentioned in para (a).

9.123 If the superintendent registrar is satisfied that the consent of any person whose consent is so required cannot be obtained by reason of absence or inaccessibility or by reason of his being under any disability, the necessity for the consent of that person is dispensed with if there is any other person whose consent is also required. If there is no such person the Registrar General may dispense with the necessity of obtaining any consent, or the court may, on application being made, consent to the marriage, and the consent of the court so given has the same effect as if it had been given by the person whose consent cannot be obtained.

9.124 If any person whose consent is required refuses his consent, the court may, on application, consent to the marriage, and the consent of the court so given has the same effect as if it had been given by the person whose consent is refused.[245]

9.125 The procedure for applying to the court for consent is set out in Chapter 9 of Pt 8 of the Family Procedure Rules 2010.

9.126 No test is prescribed by either the Marriage Act 1949 or the Civil Partnership Act 2004 for giving consent and 'giving consent' does not fall easily into the phrase 'the upbringing of a child' in s 1(1)(a) of the Children Act 1989. However, if the issue arose there is no doubt but that a welfare paramountcy test would be applied. In *Re K: A Local Authority v N*[246] Munby J said:

> 'No doubt the determinative principle is the best interests of the child, and as the current editors of Rayden & Jackson on *Divorce and Family Matters*[247] said 'No doubt the court would continue to afford such reasonable protection as it can'. But how is a judge in today's society really supposed to decide, and by reference to what criteria, whether or not it is in a 16 or 17-year-old ward's best interests to marry some particular suitor. And supposing the judge says no. Is that really likely to serve the child's best interests? The only effect of what may be perceived by a defiant teenager as paternalism of the most patronising kind is likely to be either a continuation of the relationship, openly or clandestinely,without the benefit of matrimony or a hardening of attitude with the child merely counting off the days until she or he can escape from the court's fetters.'

9.127 In theory, there could be cases where those with parental responsibility disagreed about whether the child should marry. Although such a dispute could be the subject of a specific steps or prohibited steps order, any application for consent (as opposed to an order forbidding consent) would have to be brought under s 3 of the 1945 Act or s 4 of the 2004 Act.

---

[245] Marriage Act 1949, s 3(1)(b).
[246] [2005] EWHC 2956 (Fam); [2007] 1 FLR 399.
[247] (Lexis Nexis UK, 18th edn) vol 1(2), para 42.50.

9.128 In recent years there appear to have been no cases brought under either Act, in part because fewer and fewer people under the age of 18 marry. In 2004, for example, only 78 males married under the age of 18 and 434 females.[248] The Court Service last published statistics for applications under s 3 in 1973. In *Re K: A Local Authority v N*[249] Munby J referred to the jurisdiction as 'being little more than a dead letter'. However, arranged marriages, particularly in the South Asian communities, mean that issues relating to marriages of those under 18 are coming before the court. Hitherto the cases have involved issues of child protection rather than disputes between those with parental responsibility.

9.129 The consent to the marriage of those with parental responsibility does not dispense with the need for the child to consent. In *Re E (An Alleged Patient); Sheffield City Council v E*[250] Munby defined the capacity to marry required by an adult as being:

> '... mentally capable of understanding the duties and responsibilities that normally attach to marriage. What then are the duties and responsibilities that in 2004 should be treated as normally attaching to marriage? In my judgment the matter can be summarised as follows: Marriage, whether civil or religious, is a contract, formally entered into. It confers on the parties the status of husband and wife, the essence of the contract being an agreement between a man and a woman to live together, and to love one another as husband and wife, to the exclusion of all others. It creates a relationship of mutual and reciprocal obligations, typically involving the sharing of a common home and a common domestic life and the right to enjoy each other's society, comfort and assistance.'

There is no reason why the same test should not be applied to someone under 18. However, there the issues are wider. When viewing an adult's capacity the court is concerned with the person's capacity as a general question. It is distinct from the question of whether the decision is a wise one whether to marry at all or whether to marry X rather than Y.[251] When a child is involved the court is not only deciding the factual question of whether the child has capacity but also whether it should exercise its discretion to allow or prevent the marriage and here, the issue of whether the marriage is or is not in the child's best interests is relevant.

9.130 *Re K: A Local Authority v N*[252] Munby J said that in its protective rather than its custodial jurisdiction orders restraining marriage are to be made if they are needed to protect the child, in particular, if they are needed to protect the child from parental default or worse. However, the court should not normally:

---

[248] Marriage, Divorce and Adoption Statistics (Office for National Statistics, 2008).

[249] [2005] EWHC 2956 (Fam); [2007] 1 FLR 399.

[250] [2004] EWHC 2808 (Fam), [2005] 1 FLR 965, at [132]. See also Gaffney-Rhys *'Sheffield City Council v E* – Capacity to marry and the rights and responsibilities of married couple' [2006] CFLQ 139. See also *City of Westminster v IC* [2008] EWCA Civ 198, [2008] 2 FLR 267 and Probert 'Hanging on the telephone' [2008] CFLQ 395.

[251] *Re K: A Local Authority v N* [2005] EWHC 2956 (Fam); [2007] 1 FLR 399, at [85].

[252] Ibid.

'... invade the sphere of parental obligation and parental responsibility unless there is real reason to fear that the child will not be adequately protected by the parents or indeed, as in cases of forced marriages, that the child requires to be protected from the parents. In short, in cases such as this the protective jurisdiction will normally be appropriately invoked only where there is a failure or abuse of parental power.'

9.131   Since *Re K: A Local Authority v N* in 2005 the Forced Marriage (Civil Protection) Act 2007 has amended the Family Law Act 1996 by giving the court powers for the purpose of protecting any person, whatever their age, from being forced into a marriage or from any attempt to be forced into a marriage or a person who has been forced into a marriage. In deciding whether and how to exercise its powers the court must have regard to all the circumstances including the need to secure the health, safety and well-being of the person to be protected.[253]

---

[253]   Family Law Act 1996, s 63A(2).

Chapter 10

RESIDENCE ORDERS

INTRODUCTION

10.1 A residence order is an order settling the arrangement to be made as to the person with whom the child is to live.[1] Joint residence orders may be made in favour of people living in the same household and shared residence in favour of those living in different households. Accordingly, CA 1989, s 11(4) provides that an order may specify the periods during which the child is to live in the different households.

10.2 A residence order confers parental responsibility on the person in whose favour it is made for the period the order remains in force.[2] The responsibility granted under s 12(2) is limited in that it does not confer the right to withhold consent to the making of an order freeing the child for adoption or an order for adoption or the right to appoint a guardian. When a residence order is made in favour of the father of a child who does not already have parental responsibility, the court must make a s 4 order granting him responsibility and this order will continue notwithstanding that the residence order comes to an end.[3] An order for parental responsibility granted under s 12(1) may not be brought to an end under s 4 so long as the residence order remains in force.

10.3 A residence order may be subject to conditions, both those imposed by the court and those imposed by statute.[4]

10.4 Decisions about residence are governed by the welfare test and the checklist factors must be applied to the circumstances of the individual child. Nonetheless, courts have adopted general assumptions. For example, a child needs to be brought up, if possible, by a parent as opposed to a non-parent and brothers and sisters should, wherever possible, be brought up together. The strength of these assumptions is such that the Court of Appeal will expect a trial judge to justify any departure from them and will examine with care the strength of the evidence justifying such departure.

10.5 The current debate about co-parenting, and advice that it is normally in the best interests of children whose parents do not live together if their parents do co-operate in making decisions about them and are committed to being

---

1   CA 1989, s 8(1).
2   Ibid, s 12(2).
3   Ibid, s 12(1).
4   Ibid, s 11(7).

involved in their children's lives, appear to have lead to an increase in separated parents agreeing that their children should divide their time and living arrangements between each of them. Anecdotally, more parents, usually fathers, than previously seem to apply for shared residence orders in the absence of agreement by the other parent. Many of the reported decisions in the last 8 years which involve disputes of residence concern questions of when courts can make shared residence orders, when they should and attempts to resolve the problems which shared residence can create. A second strand of cases involves questions of a child's residence being changed because of a failure by the resident parent to comply with orders or contact between the child and the non-resident parent.

BACKGROUND

10.6   In 2004, 36,970 applications for residence were made in all tiers of court in private law proceedings. Orders were made in 96% of all applications and in nearly 98.6% of all cases which were not withdrawn.[5] Three per cent of applications were withdrawn, orders were refused in 0.032% of the cases and no orders were made in 1% of the cases.

10.7   A number of socio-legal studies have examined the pattern which lies behind these figures.

A small scale study, *Separating from cohabitation: making arrangements for finances and parenting*[6] examined the parenting arrangements which are made when cohabiting but non-married parents separated. There was sometimes initially some dispute about who the children would mainly live with but this seemed to be a reflection of bitterness and anger at the separation rather than a genuine dispute about residence. In all but two of the 29 cases examined the children mostly lived with their mother. There seemed to be a high degree of flexibility in how contact worked. Parents were sometimes motivated by their memories of their own parents' separations. They also recognised the value to their children of a sustained relationship with both parents and seemed genuinely keen to facilitate this.[7]

Just as with contact there is a difference between families who resolve any difficulties without recourse to litigation and those who do not. Between 1999 and 2001, a study examined a selection of the more difficult cases in which court welfare reports had been ordered.[8] Applications were made for a variety of reasons. In only 45% of cases were the applications seeking a change in the status quo. In 25% of cases, the applicant wanted to confirm or reverse a recent change. The main reason for bringing the case in 10% of cases was a fear that

---

5   *Judicial and Court Statistics* 2004 (Ministry of Justice, 2011).
6   Tennant, Taylor and Lewis (2006) Department for Constitutional Affairs Research Series 7/06.
7   Ibid, at pp 75–76.
8   Buchanan and Others *Families in Conflict* (The Policy Press, 2001).

the other parent would remove the child. Shared residence was the issue in 10% of cases and in a further 10% it was to establish arrangements, the child still living with both parents.

Residence orders were made in favour of mothers in seven out of ten (71%) of cases and to fathers in a fifth (19%). However, this was largely a reflection of the status quo rather than a prejudice in favour of mothers. In just under two-thirds (62.5%) of cases, residence remained with the mother and a fifth (19%) with the father. There was a change in residence in just over a third (37.5%) of cases, equally divided between mother and father.

Although the main purpose of applications in nearly half the cases was to change a child's residence, there was no change in just under two-thirds of cases. Residence orders were nearly four times more likely to be made to mothers but when there was a change in residence, no distinction could be made between the parents. A follow-up a year later showed stability. There had been a change of residence in only one out of 80 cases (1.25%).

10.8 In 2003 a further study, *Residence and Contact Disputes in Court*,[9] sponsored by the Department for Constitutional Affairs, which examined a number of residence cases in 3 county courts, found that half the applications were made by mothers, a third by fathers and the rest predominantly by grandparents. Applications were more likely to be made by a parent who was or had been married to the other parent. There were two main reasons why parents applied for orders. The first was a fear that the child would be removed by the other parent. This reason was present in nearly a half of all cases and tended to occur in cases where there was high conflict between the parents. In over a quarter of cases the non-resident parent had a home or family abroad. The second reason was whether the care provided by the resident parent was adequate. This was most common when the application was made by the father. The application was justified in less than a tenth of cases by the allegation that the child wanted to move.

The researchers found that the application succeeded in 44% of cases. It made little difference to the prospect of success whether the applicant was the mother or father. In general, the status quo was preserved. An order changed residence in only 13% of cases. Where the child moved from mother to father, it was usually because the mother had a serious mental health, alcohol or drug problem.

Just under half of the cases resolved in less than 3 months and three-quarters in less than 6 months.

---

9   Smart, May and Wade [2003] Research Series 6/03 (Department for Constitutional Affairs), summarised in Smart and May 'Residence and contact disputes in court' [2004] Fam Law 36.

Summary

10.9

*   Most residence applications are made by mothers who are seeking to preserve the status quo, often because they fear that the child will be removed by the other parent.

*   When fathers apply, it is usually because they consider the mother's care to be inadequate.

*   The status quo will be preserved in about two-thirds of all cases and it makes little difference whether the applicant was the father or mother.

*   In half the cases, presumably those where the purpose of the application is to make sure the child remains with the residential parent, the application will be resolved at the first appointment or shortly afterwards with only a quarter lasting 6 months or more.

CONDITIONS

10.10   When a residence order is in force, no person may:

*   cause a child to be known by a new surname;

*   remove him from the United Kingdom (save, in the case of the person in whose favour the order is made for a period of less than 1 month) without the written consent of every person with parental responsibility or the leave of the court.[10]

10.11   Section 11(7) of the Children Act 1989 allows a residence order to contain directions about how it is to be carried out and to impose conditions which must be complied with by any person:

(1)   in whose favour the order is made;

(2)   who is a parent of the child concerned;

(3)   who has parental responsibility for the child; or

(4)   with whom the child is living.

The conditions or their provisions can be made to have effect for a specified period.

---

10   CA 1989, s 13.

Conditions which can be imposed include conditions as to the child being brought up in a particular faith[11] and conditions about receiving medical treatment, most commonly as regards receiving blood transfusions when living with a parent who is a Jehovah's Witness.

The topics of restricting the exercise of parental responsibility are more fully discussed in **Chapters 8** and **9**.

Section 11(7) has been drawn very widely and its scope has been left deliberately vague. However it is apparent from a number of authorities that there are limits to its use and matters which go beyond the kind of matters that it ought to address.[12]

Courts are careful not to impose restrictions which overrule parents' right to live their lives as they choose and to distinguish issues of conditions from those which are fundamentally ones relating to residence. For example, when a judge was concerned about violence perpetrated on the mother by a partner, he should not have granted a residence order in her favour with a condition that she should not allow the partner to live with her children. Rather, he should have considered the matter as a contested residence application between the children's parents and given the mother an opportunity of electing whether to live with the partner or her children.[13]

10.12 In *Re E (Residence: Imposition of Conditions)*,[14] the Court of Appeal held that the trial judge was wrong in imposing a condition on a mother that she should live at a named address. This was an unwarranted imposition on her right to choose where she should live in the United Kingdom. If one parent planned to move the children to somewhere less suitable, that was a factor to be considered when deciding the issue of which parent the child should live with. The same applies when a parent proposes to move abroad with the child. However, it may be appropriate to impose conditions where the court has concerns about the ability of the resident parent to be a suitable carer but there is no better solution but to place the child with that parent.

For a discussion of relocation within England and Wales see **9.75**.

10.13 In *Re H (Residence Order: Placement Out of Jurisdiction)*[15] Hedley J held that where a child will be living outside England and Wales it would be wrong in principle to insert conditions into a residence order because they would be unenforceable. Thus where children were placed with their maternal

---

11   For example, in *J v C* [1970] AC 668, foster parents were directed to raise the child as a Roman Catholic and in *Re K (Adoption and Wardship)* [1997] 2 FLR 221, a child was to receive instruction in the Muslim religion.
12   *Re H (Residence Order: Placement Out of Jurisdiction* [2004] EWHC 3243 (Fam), [2006] 1 FLR 1140.
13   *Re D (Residence: Imposition of Conditions)* [1996] 2 FLR 281.
14   [1997] 2 FLR 638.
15   2004] EWHC 3243 (Fam), [2006] 1 FLR 1140, at [23].

uncle and aunt who lived in the United Arab Emirates under a residence order after one of them had suffered serious injuries whilst in their parents' care, he refused to impose conditions that they should not be in the care of their parents until they reached the age of at least six and that contact with their parents should be limited to twice weekly until they reached the age of at least four. In addition:

> 'It seems to me that the making of such conditions is in fact contrary to the principle that these children are now living in a different family, in a different culture, in a different country to which family, culture and country they forthwith must be seen to belong. For those reasons, I do not think it would be a proper use of s 11(7) and would be contrary to the principle of the care plan in this case to make conditions of that sort.'

However, the judge made it clear that the uncle and aunt should understand that they had the sole primary responsibility for ensuring the safety and general welfare of these children and they should exercise their rights. Further, it was crucial that the children were given the time and space necessary to become attached to their primary carers and it was incumbent on all adults involved to ensure that the children did not have their loyalties divided between their parents and their primary carers.

The High Court of Northern Ireland[16] has held that conditions should not be used to exclude a parent from their home or to prohibit molestation. Rather domestic violence legislation should be used to make appropriate orders.[17]

THE NEED FOR A RESIDENCE ORDER

10.14 Section 1(5) provides that a court shall not make a s 8 order unless it considers that doing so would be better for the child than making no order at all. This is not to say, however, that a court would be justified in refusing a residence order when there is no dispute about where a child is to live because an order may confer other advantages to the child.[18] The grant of parental responsibility is one example (see **10.39**). There are others, notably the restrictions it places upon the exercise of certain powers held by anyone with parental responsibility:

- where a residence order is in force, no person may cause the child to be known by a new surname or removed from the United Kingdom (save for a period of less than 1 month by the person in whose favour the order was granted) without the written consent of every person with parental responsibility or the leave of the court;[19]

---

16   *Re Alwyn (Non-Molestation Proceedings by a Child)* [2009] NIFam 22, [2010] 1 FLR 1363.
17   Family Law Act 1996, Pt IV. See **Chapter 5**.
18   See Grand 'Residence Order or Package Order?' [1995] Fam Law 201.
19   CA 1989, s 13.

- when a local authority is providing a child with accommodation under s 20, no person with parental responsibility may remove the child from the care of the authority without the consent of the person in whose favour a residence order is in force;[20]

- the Child Support Agency can assess only a parent who is 'not living in the same household as the child'. While this seems to be a matter of fact, the existence of a residence order might be of some assistance in showing that the child had his home with the person with a residence order.[21]

SHARED RESIDENCE ORDERS

Background

10.15 In many western countries shared time arrangements have been steadily increasing this century without legal orders particularly among parents who co-operate with each other.

> 'However the pace of change within families is less rapid than we might like to think; it is still very much a minority of parents who share care equally even in 'intact' families where parents live together.'[22]

The change in part reflects social and cultural changes with more women in paid employment and an increased involvement of fathers in their children's daily lives. In 1985 (the year before *Riley v Riley*[23]) only 30% of women with children under five were in part-time and 8% in full-time employment outside the home.[24] By 1995 a third were engaged in part-time employment and the percentage in full-time, more than doubled. However there are also philosophical and political factors. Parents not only became aware of the possibility of shared care, some believed it was best for children. Over recent years there has been a continual discourse centred on a model of 'the good divorce'. For example, the Green Paper, *Parental Separation: Children's Needs and Parents' Responsibilities: Next steps, Report on the responses to consultation and agenda for action*[25] advised parents that:

> 'A child's welfare is usually best promoted by a continuing and constructive relationship with both parents, as long as it is in the child's best interests and safe for all concerned. Both parents have a responsibility to ensure their child has constructive contact with the other parent where contact is in the child's best interests.'

---

[20] Ibid, s 20(8).

[21] See *Re R (Residence Order: Finance)* [1995] 2 FLR 612.

[22] Fehlberg, Smyth, Maclean and Roberts *Caring for children after parental separation: would legislation for shared parenting time help children?* (Oxford University: Department of Social Policy and Intervention Family Policy Briefing 7, 2011), at p 4.

[23] [1986] 2 FLR 429; see **10.30**.

[24] Beechy and Perkins *A Matter of Hours* (Polity Press, 1987).

[25] Cm 6452 (Department for Constitutional Affairs, Department for Education and Skills and the Department for Trade and Industry, 2005), at p 7.

10.16   Julie Wallbank of the University of Leeds has commented that whilst behaving in this way is part of the 'doing' role associated with parental responsibility, the passage also speaks to the 'thinking' part of the responsible parent with the message that 'Contact is quite simply not enough: it must be "constructive" and both parents are responsible for ensuring that it is so.'[26] For some parents it may only be a short step to deciding that it would be best for children to divide their time more or less equally between them both. There is also a political discourse where much of the debate is adult-centred. 'Men's groups argue from a perspective of fathers' rights and feminist lobbies are often based on arguments about the abilities and rights of women to raise their children.'[27] Fathers may argue for the 'right' of equal time, albeit dressed in the clothing of an argument based on the welfare of children[28] and mothers argue for no contact in similar fashion.

Where parents are in agreement about shared care, there may be an informal agreement and the matter never comes before the courts unless either the arrangement breaks down or there is a dispute with an outside agency, for example about the payment of welfare benefits or the provision of social housing.

10.17   Despite the increase in shared parenting, its prevalence still remains low, a recent study for England and Wales[29] suggesting that only 3.1% of children in separated families spend half their time with each parent. This is lower than other Western countries and some states in the US with Sweden at 28% (and see footnote to **10.37**) Washington DC 16% and Canada 9–15%.[30] However, rather than the early adopters of the idea of shared care who were typically economically-advantaged, co-operative and flexible there now seem to be at least three groups: the classic co-operators; those who obtained a rigid pattern

---

[26]   'Parental responsibility and the responsible parent: managing the "problem" of contact' in Probert, Gilmore and Herring (eds) *Responsible Parents and Parental Responsibility* (Hart Publishing, 2009), at p 307.

[27]   Pryor and Rodgers *Children in Changing Families (Understanding Children's Worlds)* (Wiley-Blackwell, 2001), at p 272.

[28]   See Collier 'Fathers 4 Justice, law and the new politics of fatherhood' [2006] CFLQ 511. In 2009 Families Need Fathers published a series of four sets of guidance on *Shared Parenting: For CAFCASS Case Officers, for Teachers and Schools, for Sure Start and for Litigants in Person.* Hunt, Masson and Trinder criticised the guidance as containing deficiencies in what was said about current law and 'of particular concern ... was the inclusion in each, of an effective presumption of equal parenting time': 'Shared parenting: the law, the evidence and guidance from Families Need Fathers' [2009] Fam Law 831. The guidance no longer appears on FNF's website (as at 4 March 2012). It was withdrawn from the Cafcass website: Gilmore 'Shared residence: a summary of the courts' guidance' [2010] Fam Law 285, at 285.

[29]   Ermisch, Iacovou & Skew 'Family Relationships' in McFall (ed) *Understanding Society* (Economic and Social Research Council, 2011), available at: http://research. understandingsociety.org.uk.

[30]   *Caring for children after parental separation: would legislation for shared parenting time help children?* op cit, at p 4.

of shared care through litigation with high levels of pre- and post-litigation conflict and a higher conflict group who tried shared care but reverted to other patterns.[31]

10.18 As a result there has been a semi-legal debate for some years about whether or not shared residence orders should be made or whether arrangements should be by way of the more conventional order granting residence to one parent and contact to the other. It is important to distinguish between 'shared parenting', namely that both parents have responsibility for the child, and 'shared residence', when a child has its home at separate times with each parent.[32]

In support of shared residence,[33] it is argued that:

> 'the system denigrates, disrespects and demeans that parent who no longer has "possession" of the children. This is damaging for the child concerned.'

The introduction and expectation of shared care would set the tone for future arrangements and send a clear message to children that their relationship with both parents is respected and protected. There should be a presumption of shared parenting irrespective of the parents' ability or willingness to work with the other and irrespective of the fact that the time spent with each parent may not be equal. Contrary arguments suggest that children need a single settled home and that the principal carer needs autonomy. In its most extreme form, it is argued that the parent without care should have no legally enforceable right to visit the child:

> 'Once it is determined who will be the custodial parent it is that parent and not the court who must decide under what conditions he or she wishes to raise the child.'[34]

Welfare considerations

10.19 A number of studies have been conducted into 'shared custody'. These are summarised in two recent literature reviews, *Caring for children after parental separation: would legislation for shared parenting time help children?*[35] and *Shared residence: a review of recent research literature.*[36]

---

[31] Trinder 'Shared residence: a review of recent research literature' [2010] CFLQ 475 at 494. See also a summary of the article in [2010] Fam Law 1192.

[32] *Re F (Shared Residence Order)* [2003] EWCA Civ 592, [2003] 2 FLR 397.

[33] See, for example, the responses to the Sub-Committee of the Advisory Board on Family Law in *Making Contact Work* (Lord Chancellor's Department, 2002), Appendix 3; Johnson 'Shared residence orders: for and against' [2009] Fam Law 131; Evans 'Shared residence: fact or fantasy?' [2009] Fam Law 200; Bond 'Shared panacea – a mistake' [2011] Fam Law 1016.

[34] Goldstein, Freud, Solnit *Beyond the Best Interests of the Child* (1973), p 38. See also Kaganas and Piper 'Shared parenting – a 70% solution' [2002] CFLQ 365.

[35] Fehlberg et al op cit.

[36] [2010] CFLQ 475. See also a summary of the Review in [2010] Fam Law 1192.

Warnings about the research

10.20   Both Reviews warn that caution must be exercised when considering the research. First, definitions of shared parenting vary widely. In the United Kingdom, 'shared parenting' generally refers to an equal division of time whereas in the United States 'joint physical custody', dual residence' and 'shared physical placement' are all used to describe shared care arrangements but rarely mean an equal division of time as opposed to possibly 30% or more time with one parent.[37] Next, there are still gaps in the knowledge base, including the financial implications of shared parenting, and researchers have tended not to differentiate between consensual arrangements and those imposed by order. There is a significant difference between these types of families.[38] 'They enter on a different track and stay on that track by different means with different outcomes.'[39] There is also an over-reliance on the reports of parents as to their children's well-being which typically affect their own well-being.[40]

The Australian experience

10.21   The literature reflects the particular importance of the issue of shared parenting in Australia which followed the enactment of the Family Law Amendment (Shared Parental Responsibility) Act 2006. The objects of the Act were ensuring that the best interests of children were met by:

- ensuring that children have the benefit of both of their parents having a meaningful involvement in their lives, to the maximum extent consistent with the best interests of the child;

- protecting children from physical or psychological harm from being subjected or exposed to abuse, neglect or family violence;

- ensuring that children receive adequate and proper parenting to help them achieve their full potential; and

- ensuring that parents fulfil their duties, and meet their responsibilities, concerning the care, welfare and development of their children.[41]

The principles underlying these objects were that (except when it was or would be contrary to a child's best interests):

---

37   Fehlberg et al op cit, at p 2, Trinder op cit, at p 477.
38   Fehlberg et al op cit, at p 9; Trinder op cit, at p 477.
39   McIntosh et al *Post-separation parenting arrangements and developmental outcomes for infants and children. Collected Reports* (2010) Australian Attorney-General's Department www.ag.gov.au.
40   Trinder op cit, at p 477.
41   Section 60B(1).

- children had the right to know and be cared for by both their parents, regardless of whether their parents are married, separated, have never married or have never lived together;

- children had a right to spend time on a regular basis with, and communicate on a regular basis with, both their parents and other people significant to their care, welfare and development (such as grandparents and other relatives);

- parents jointly shared duties and responsibilities concerning the care, welfare and development of their children;

- parents should agree about the future parenting of their children; and

- children had a right to enjoy their culture (including the right to enjoy that culture with other people who share that culture).[42]

The Act stated that when making a parenting order in relation to a child, the court must apply a presumption that it is in the best interests of the child for the child's parents to have equal shared parental responsibility.[43] The presumption did not apply if there were reasonable grounds to believe that a parent of the child (or a person who lives with a parent of the child) had engaged in:

- abuse of the child or another child who, at the time, was a member of the parent's family (or that other person's family); or

- family violence.[44]

If a parenting order provided that the parents were to have equal shared parental responsibility the court had to consider whether the child spending equal time with each of the parents would be in the best interests of the child and reasonably practicable and if so, consider making an order for equal time.[45]

The Act has been criticised for reducing judicial discretion, discouraging the use of legal processes as a first resort, placing less reliance than previously on empirical evidence and research findings, making family law increasingly complex 'well beyond even the specialist legal practitioner' and politicising family law.[46] According to Helen Rhoades[47] 'warnings of potential harm to

---

[42] Section 60B(2).
[43] Section 61DA(1).
[44] Section 61D(2).
[45] Section 65DAA(1).
[46] Dewar 'Can the centre hold? Reflections on two decades of family law reform in Australia' [2010] CFLQ 377, at p 380.
[47] Associate Professor in the Melbourne School of Law, University of Melbourne.

children's wellbeing caused by the Act were evident from the outset'[48] and by 2010 there were calls for the legislation to be amended.[49] Evaluations[50] suggested that while shared care had not become the norm, there had been a marked increase in the arrangements being ordered by the courts with harmful results for many children whose parents were unable to manage the daily negotiations and interactions required to make it work.[51] A number of the key principles were hard for lay people to understand and there was continuing confusion in reported cases[52] about the meaning of the 'meaningful relationship' provision.[53]

Messages from research

10.22 The literature reviews by Trinder and Ehlberg make similar points.

• On the whole shared care parents are not typical of the broader separating population. They are older and are more economically secure.[54] Those who have agreed shared care are also atypical. They tend to have undergone further education; enjoy some flexibility in working hours; live near each other; if fathers, were involved in the child's daily care prior to separation. Also, the children are of primary school age.[55]

• Shared care arrangements do not last as long as other arrangements, most reverting to the mother being the primary carer.[56]

• There is no clear relationship between shared care and the child's well-being.[57]. Research consistently has found that the quality of the relationship between each parent and between them and the children as well as the level of resources are more important than an equal division of time.[58]

• Shared care parents tend to communicate and share decisions better but are no more and are sometimes less friendly than those with primary care arrangements.[59]

---

48 'Revising Australia's parenting laws: a plea for a rational approach to children's best interests' [2010] CFLQ 172, at p 173.
49 Ibid, at p 183.
50 Including Chisholm *Family Courts Violence Review* (Family Law Council, 2009) – 'the Chisholm Report'. See also Fehlberg et al op cit, at p 10.
51 Rhoades op cit, at p 172.
52 See *McCall v Clark* [2009] Fam CAFC 92.
53 Rhoades *Family Justice Review* (2011) Annex G, at p 218.
54 Trinder op cit, at p 494.
55 Fehlberg et al op cit, at p 6.
56 Trinder op cit, at p 494.
57 Fehlberg et al opcit, at p 6; Trinder op cit, at p 494.
58 Fehlberg et al op cit, at p 12; Trinder op cit, at p 488.
59 Trinder, op cit, at p 494.

- In high conflict families there is some evidence that shared care is associated with hyperactivity, especially for boys and where arrangements are rigid.[60]

- A significant number of mothers report a lot of conflict and have serious concerns about safety and violence. Such concerns are strongly associated with poorer outcomes for the child.[61]

- A recent study has found a cluster of developmental problems for infants with weekly overnight contact and those aged 2–3 who experience shared care.[62]

- Fathers have a higher level of satisfaction with shared care and mothers, less. Mothers have high levels of dissatisfaction with litigated and rigid arrangements.[63]

- Children are less satisfied with shared care than their parents especially where arrangements are rigid and inflexible and focus on the needs of adults rather than their own and where they have little say in the arrangements.[64]

Some studies[65] have asked children what they would want if their parents were to separate. Consistently, more than half said they would prefer to spend half their time with each parent but within this broad statement lie variations. More girls than boys favour sole custody. More children over 14 favoured sole custody than those who were 12 years old. This suggests that what may be appropriate for a young child *may* be less appropriate when the child becomes a teenager. Experience of separation also affects preferences. One study of young adults found that three-fifths of those whose parents had not divorced would have wanted joint custody compared to one-fifth whose parents had separated.

In Trinder's opinion:

> 'It seems that early or pre-existing parent or family characteristics predict subsequent pathways and outcomes. Co-operative parents tend to develop flexible shared care arrangements with positive outcomes. High conflict parents tend to develop rigid arrangements, often through litigation, that are associated with poorer child adjustment and lower levels of child satisfaction. In mediated arrangements shared care seemed to maintain or exacerbate rather than reduce conflict over time.'[66]

---

[60] Fehlberg et al op cit, at p 8; Trinder op cit, at p 494.
[61] Fehlberg et al op cit, at p 8; Trinder op cit, at p 494 .
[62] McKintosh, op cit Study Two. See Fehlberg et al op cit, p 8; Trinder op cit, at p 494.
[63] Fehlberg et al op cit, at p 12; Trinder op cit, at p 494.
[64] Trinder et al op cit, at p 494; Fehlberg et al op cit, at p 6.
[65] For a summary of the studies, see Pryor and People 'Adolescent attitudes towards living arrangements after divorce' [2001] CFLQ 197; Neale, Flowerdew and Smart 'Drifting towards shared residence' [2003] Fam Law 904.
[66] Trinder, at p 495.

Fehlberg concluded that assisting parents to think carefully about the arrangements which will best serve the interests of their children's changing needs and to put those needs above their own is more important than legislating to prioritise shared time.'[67]

> 'Research consistently finds that the best interests of children are closely connected to parental capacities and skills and to practical resources, such as adequate housing and income. The quality of relationships between parents and between parents and their children, as well as the level of resources, are more important determinants of children's well-being than equal or near equal parenting time.'[68]

Policy

The Law Commission

10.23   The Law Commission report which preceded the Children Act 1989[69] pointed out that the main difference between the proposed residence order and the existing custody order was that 'the new order should be flexible enough to accommodate a much wider range of circumstances'. In some cases, a child might live with both parents who did not share the same household:

> 'It was never our intention [in the Working Paper] to suggest that children should share their time more or less equally between their parents. Such arrangements will rarely be practicable, let alone for the children's benefit. However, the evidence from the United States is that where they are practicable they can work well and we see no reason why they should be actively discouraged. None of our respondents shared the view expressed in a recent case [*Riley v Riley* [1986] 2 FLR 429] that such an arrangement, which had been working well for some years, should never have been made. More commonly, however, the child will live with both parents but spend more time with one than the other. Examples might be where he spends term time with one and the holidays with the other or two of three holidays from boarding school with one and the third with the other. It is a far more realistic description of the responsibilities involved in that sort of arrangement to make a residence order covering both parents than a residence order for one and a contact order for the other. Hence, we recommend that where a child is to live with two (or more) people who do not live together, the order may specify the periods during which the child is to live in each household. The specification may be general rather than detailed and in some cases may not be necessary at all.'

---

[67]   Fehlberg et al op cit, at p 13.
[68]   Fehlberg et al op cit, at p 12.
[69]   *Family Law Review of Child Law Guardianship and Custody*, Law Com No 172 (1988) at para 4.12.

Children Act 1989 Guidance and Regulations[70]

10.24 In 1991, the Department of Health published guidance on CA 1989 which has been cited with approval by the Court of Appeal:[71]

'A residence order may be made in favour of more than one person at the same time even though they do not live together, in which case the order may specify the periods during which the child is to live in the different households concerned (s 11(4)). A shared residence order could therefore be made where the child is to spend, for example, weekdays with one parent and weekends with the other, or where the child is to spend large amounts of time with each parent. This latter arrangement was disapproved of by the Court of Appeal in *Riley v Riley* ... which must now be taken to have been over-ruled by s 11(4), but it is not expected that it will become a common form of order, partly because most children will still need the stability of a single home, and partly because in the cases where shared care is appropriate there is less likely to be a need for the court to make any order at all. However a shared care order [sic] has the advantage of being more realistic in those cases where the child is to spend considerable amounts of time with both parents, brings with it certain other benefits (including the right to remove the child from accommodation provided by the local authority under s 20) and removes any impression that one parent is good and responsible whereas the other parent is not.'

The revised version published in 2008 is more limited.

'A residence order may be made in favour of more than one person at the same time even though they do not live together, in which case the order may specify the periods during which the child is to live in the different households concerned (section 11(4)). A shared residence order may be appropriate in those cases where the child is to spend considerable amounts of time with both parents.[72]

Making contact work

10.25 The Sub-Committee of the Advisory Board on Family Law in *Making Contact Work*[73] considered the issue of shared residence briefly in 2002. In essence, it echoed the arguments of the Law Commission 14 years earlier. It supported an ethos which encouraged the sharing of parental responsibility and the maintenance of maximum contact with the non-resident parent but it could see a number of practical objections. In some cases, parents lived substantial distances apart which made it difficult to have meaningful shared parenting. Parents do not always behave rationally and in some cases one parent or even the child may need protection from the other:

---

[70] Vol 1, Court Orders (HMSO, 1991), para 2.2(8).

[71] *A v A (Minors) (Shared Residence Order)* [1994] 1 FLR 669 'helpful' – Butler-Sloss LJ at 677
– and *Re D (Children) (Shared Residence Order)* [2001] 1 FLR 495 – 'a very helpful passage' –
Butler-Sloss LJ at 501.

[72] Para 2.34.

[73] See, for example, the responses to the Sub-Committee of the Advisory Board on Family Law in
Making Contact Work (Lord Chancellor's Department, 2002), Appendix 3.

'While we understand the argument that an expectation of shared parenting as the norm should restrict the scope for acrimonious disagreement, we doubt its efficacy in practice.'

However, the Sub-Committee welcomed the comments made by the Court of Appeal in *Re D (Children) (Shared Residence Order)*,[74] discussed below.

Next Steps

10.26 *Parental Separation: Children's Needs and Parents' Responsibilities: Next Steps*[75] considered the arguments for shared residence or, as it was more usually phrased, a presumption of equal contact, against its declared aim that 'It should be unacceptable that non-resident parents absent themselves from their child's development and upbringing following separation'.[76] However the Government was not persuaded that any legislative change to introduce a presumption of equal contact would benefit children nor would it have any significance in practice. The House of Commons Constitutional Affairs Committee[77] pointed out that there might be accommodation and financial difficulties and children might not want it.

'The concept of a pre-determined statutory template for the division of time a child is to spend with each parent is not one we favour ... An arbitrary "template" imposed on all families, whatever the needs of the child, would regulate the welfare of individual children to a secondary position.'[78]

Family Justice Review

10.27 *The Family Justice Review*[79] – 'the Norgrove Report' – in its interim report had opposed legislation to encourage 'shared parenting'.

'The evidence showed that people place different interpretations on this term, and that it is interpreted in practice by counting hours spent with each parent, disregarding the quality of the time. The thorough and detailed evidence from Australia showed the damaging consequences for many children.'[80]

This position attracted a large response in consultation. Charities, legal and judicial organisations and academics (including Professors Rhoades, and Trinder) supported it. Many other individuals – typically grandparents, fathers – opposed it on the basis that a presumption of shared parenting was necessary in order to ensure that both parents remained involved with their children. It was argued that decisive steps and a clear message were required. Many contributors took strong positions, citing gender imbalance, bias and

---

74   [2001] 1 FLR 495.
75   Cm 6452 (Department for Constitutional Affairs, 2005).
76   Ibid, Ministerial Foreword.
77   Family Justice: the operation of the family courts [2005] HC 116–1.
78   Ibid, at para 60.
79   (Ministry of Justice and the Department for Health and Social Services, 2011).
80   Ibid, para 4.23

institutional wrongdoing within family justice. Others maintained that there is insufficient evidence against shared parenting to suggest that it should not be the primary consideration of the court.

The Panel concluded that:

> 'Having thoroughly reconsidered the evidence, we remain firm in our view that any legislation that might risk creating an impression of a parental 'right' to any particular amount of time with a child would undermine the central principle of the Children Act 1989 that the welfare of the child is paramount. We also believe that legislation is a poor instrument for social change in this area. We were told in Sweden[81] for example that shared parenting arrangements after separation have been increasing, but only because they are now more common before separation. So we maintain our view that the focus should instead be on supporting and fostering a greater awareness of shared parental responsibility and on the duties and roles of both parents from birth onwards. Legislation is not the means through which to achieve this'[82]

Cafcass

10.28 For whatever reason, Cafcass does not include advice about shared residence on its website[83] other than to note that a shared residence order may be granted and the topic is not discussed in its publications for parents, such as *Parenting Plans: Putting your children first: a guide for separating parents.*

The approach of the courts

Background

10.29 In the last 16 years, there has been a gradual shift in the willingness of courts to make orders for shared residence, from a refusal save in the most exceptional circumstances, through a willingness[84] to find exceptions to the present position as set out in *Re D (Children) (Shared Residence Order)*. However, there has been a consistent awareness that shared orders are unlikely to work unless there is a reasonable prospect of co-operation and in the absence of major unresolved disputes.

10.30 In 1986, in *Riley v Riley*,[85] the parents of the child separated and arranged that their daughter, then aged 4, should spend alternate weeks with each of them. They lived about a mile apart and the child attended a school midway between the two homes. Following the divorce, the court made a joint

---

81 For the position in Sweden, see Newnham 'Shared Residence: lessons from Sweden' [2011] CFLQ 251 and Harris-Short 'Building a house upon sand: post-separation parenting, shared residence and equality – lessons from Sweden' [2011] CFLQ 344.

82 Op cit, paras 2 4.27–28.

83 Viewed on 28 January 2012.

84 Or, as Ward LJ put it in *Re H (Shared Residence: Parental Responsibility)* [1995] 2 FLR 883, 'grudging approval'.

85 [1986] 2 FLR 429.

custody order by consent. Five years after the separation, the mother applied for the order to be varied to give her sole custody. Her application was dismissed but the Court of Appeal allowed her appeal:

> 'It was an unusual order to make in the first place. Fortunately, so far as one can see, it has worked well up to date and naturally there is a reluctance in children cases where things are going well to disturb that situation. But, with respect to the recorder, I think that the conclusion to which he came was clearly wrong. In my judgment to keep a child of nearly 9, not far off puberty, going backwards each week between mother and father, with no single settled home, is prima facie wrong ... The [original] order ought not to have been made in those terms to start with.'[86]

As the Law Commission noted in 1988,[87] none of its respondents supported this view but it still received the support of the Court of Appeal, 6 years later, in *Re H (A Minor) (Shared Residence)*:[88]

> 'A child, as was emphasised in the case of *Riley v Riley* ... should have one home, and the other place of spending time, including overnight, is not the home but a place where visits may regularly and frequently be made. The establishment, as it were, of two competing homes only leads to confusion and stress and would be contrary to the paramount concept of the welfare of the child himself.'

10.31 In the same year, however, a differently constituted Court of Appeal in *A v A (Minors) (Shared Residence Order)*[89] held that *Riley v Riley* could no longer be considered good law because of the changes brought about by ss 8 and 11(4). Notwithstanding this, there remained a 'general principle' that shared orders are not appropriate in 'normal conventional circumstances where parents are separated. They should only be made where there is something unusual about the case which justifies making such an order in the best interests of the child or children concerned'.[90] Shared orders were exceptional, but whether or not to make one was always at the discretion of the trial judge on the special facts of the individual case:

> 'However, a shared residence order would, in my view, be unlikely to be made if there were concrete issues still arising between the parties which had not been resolved, such as the amount of contact, whether it should be staying or visiting contact or another issue such as education, which were muddying the waters and which were creating difficulties between the parties which reflected the way in which the children were moving from one parent to the other in the contact period.
>
> If a child, on the other hand, has a settled home with one parent and substantial staying contact with the other parent, which has been settled, long-standing and working well, or if there are future plans for sharing the time of children between two parents where all the parties agree and where there is no possibility of

---

86   [1986] 2 FLR 429, per May LJ at 431.
87   *Family Law Review of Child Law Guardianship and Custody*, Law Com No 172 (1988).
88   [1994] 1 FLR 717, per Purchas LJ at 728.
89   [1994] 1 FLR 669.
90   Ibid, per Connell J at 672.

confusion in the mind of the child as to where the child will be and the circumstances of the child at any time, this may be, bearing in mind all the other circumstances, a possible basis for a shared residence order, if it can be demonstrated there is a positive benefit to the child.'[91]

In *A v A (Minors) (Shared Residence Order)*, the children had stayed with their mother in the former family home when the parents separated but, after 3 months, interim care and control was granted to the father for a short period because the mother required surgery. After they returned to her care, an order was made whereby their time was shared equally with both parents. Their father then applied for joint residence. The mother opposed the application and, when it was granted, appealed. The Court of Appeal dismissed the appeal. The trial judge had found that the children were not confused by the situation, the father had an exceptional relationship with them, communication between the parents, although poor, was improving and the court welfare officer supported the order. There was no justification, when applying the principles in *G v G (Minors: Custody Appeal)*,[92] for the Court of Appeal to hold that he was plainly wrong.

10.32 In 2001, in *Re D (Children) (Shared Residence Order)*,[93] the Court of Appeal moved closer to accepting shared orders, justifying the move by reference to CA 1989. They do not require exceptional circumstances and the sole criterion is what is best for the child concerned. If it is either planned or it has happened that the child is spending substantial amounts of time with both parents, then a shared order may be entirely appropriate. If there are major matters still unresolved, then 'it stands to reason' that there could not be a shared order.[94] In this case, the children had spent substantial periods of time with both parents (the father calculated 38% of their time with him) but the arrangements were subject to a high degree of animosity between the parents and there were frequent applications to the court. The father (who had parental responsibility) applied for a shared order, arguing that he was being treated as a second-class parent by authorities, the children's schools and doctors. The children appeared to be coping exceptionally well with the situation, although there was no guarantee this would continue. The trial judge granted his application and the Court of Appeal rejected the mother's appeal:

'In those circumstances it seems to me that there is indeed a positive benefit to these children in those facts being recognised in the order that the court makes. There is no detriment or disrespect to either parent in that order. It simply reflects the reality of these children's lives. It was entirely appropriate for the judge to make it in this case ...'[95]

---

91   [1994] 1 FLR 669, per Butler-Sloss LJ at 677.
92   [1985] FLR 894, see Chapter 21.
93   [2001] 1 FLR 495. See also *Re R (Residence Order: Finance)* [1995] 2 FLR 612.
94   [2001] 1 FLR 495, per Hale LJ at 501.
95   [2001] 1 FLR 495, per Hale LJ at 501.

The current position

10.33 Since *Re D Children (Shared Residence Order)* in 2001 there has been what Thorpe LJ has called a 'significant shift in case law'.[96] While of course a need remains for the demonstration of circumstances which positively indicate that the child's welfare would be served, by a shared residence order, there is no need for the circumstances to be 'unusual' or 'exceptional'.[97] However, in *T v T (Shared Residence)*[98] Black LJ observed it is going 'too far' to say as Mostyn J said in *Re AR (A Child: Relocation)*,[99] that a joint or shared residence order is nowadays the rule rather than the exception even where the quantum of care undertaken by each parent is unequal.

> 'Whether or not a joint or shared residence order is granted depends upon a determination of what is in the best interests of the child in the light of all the factors in the individual case.'[100]

Decisions of the Court of Appeal have shown that objections to shared residence, distance between the homes, unresolved issues or lack of agreement or even co-operation between parents are not absolute bars to the making of an order. 'Indeed, the presence of [an] ... harmonious relationship is a contraindication of a shared residence order since such parents would fall within the no order principle emphasised by s 1(5) of the Act'.[101] However, it is clear that while an inability to work in harmony is not a reason for declining to make an order for shared residence if the welfare of the child required it rather than no order being made, a possible consequence of their inability to do so, namely the deliberate and sustained marginalisation of one parent by the other, may sometimes do so.[102] Nor does an order for shared residence mean that time will be shared equally.[103] In *Re R (Residence Order)*,[104] for example, the Court of Appeal upheld a shared residence order where a 7-year-old was to spend the school week with her father and weekends with her mother. In *Re M (Residence Order)*[105] the Court of Appeal seemed to suggest that equality is 'if not indicated, certainly a starting point'. The phrase was however used in the context of the particular case and might not have been intended to have general application.

---

[96]   *Re R (Children) (Shared Residence Order)* [2005] EWCA Civ 542, at para [11].
[97]   *Re D (Children) (Shared Residence Order)* [2001] 1 FLR 495, per Hale LJ at [31]–[32]; *Re W (Shared Residence Order)* [2009] EWCA Civ 370, [2009] 2 FLR 436.
[98]   [2010] EWCA Civ 1366.
[99]   [2010] EWHC 1346 (Fam).
[100] *T v T (Shared Residence)*[2010] EWCA Civ 1366, at [26].
[101] Ibid. See also *Re H (Residence: Shared Care: Children's Views)* [2005] EWCA Civ 542, [2006] 1 FLR 491.
[102] *Re W (Shared Residence Order)* [2009] EWCA Civ 370, [2009] 2 FLR 436, per Wilson LJ at [15].
[103] *Re F (Shared Residence Order)* [2003] EWCA Civ 592.
[104] [2010] EWCA Civ 303, [2010] 2 FLR 1138.
[105] [2008] EWCA Civ 66, [2008] 1 FLR 1087, per Thorpe LJ at [12].

10.34 There are two aspects of an application involving the decision of shared care: whether or not a shared residence order should be made and second, whether there should be an equal division of time.

> 'The two aspects of the application, namely for a ruling in favour of an equal division of time and for a shared residence order, do not stand or fall together. On the contrary, they have to be considered separately; and the convenient course is for the court to consider both issues together but to rule first upon the optimum division of the child's time in his interests and then, in the light of that ruling, to proceed to consider whether the favoured division should be expressed as terms of a shared residence order or of a contact order.'[106]

In making such orders, courts have sometimes stressed the psychological benefits of the orders in recognising cases where 'parents have a joint and equal responsibility' and the residence is shared between them[107] and confirming 'a parent's equal authority and competence'[108] and the practice of reflecting the realities of the situation 'unless there [are] some counterbalancing welfare considerations that prevented that sensible outcome'.[109]

10.35 Where there is a need for an order because parents are not in agreement, a shared residence order may be made on the ground that it reflects the reality of what is already happening. Thus in *Re P (Shared Residence Order)*[110] where parents had agreed on separation that the care of their child, then aged 3, should be shared more or less equally but with the father agreeing a residence order in favour of the mother, the Court of Appeal granted the father a shared residence order 2 years later despite Cafcass recommending that the sole residence order remain because of a deterioration in the parents' relationship, described by Thorpe LJ as 'the skirmishing ground [which] ... seems ... to be confined to the practical arrangements for transition during the operation of the rota'.[111]

> '[The] making of such an order plainly involves the exercise of a judicial discretion and does not automatically follow because children divide their time between their parents in proportions approaching equality. However, where that does happen, as here, and where a child in Megan's position lives for nearly 50 per cent of the time with her father, it seems to me ... firstly that a shared residence order is most apt to describe what is actually happening on the ground; and secondly that good reasons are required if a share residence order is not to be made. Such an order emphasises the fact that both parents are equal in the eyes of the law, and that they have equal duties and responsibilities as parents. The order can have the

---

[106] *Re K (Shared Residence Order)* [2008] EWCA Civ 526.
[107] *A v A (Shared Residence)* [2004] EWHC 142 (Fam), [2004] 1 FLR 1195, per Wall J at [126].
[108] *Re A (Children)(Shared Residence)* [2002] EWCA Civ 1343, [2003] 3 FCR 636.
[109] Ibid, per Thorpe LJ at [16].
[110] [2005] EWCA Civ 1639, [2006] 2 FLR 347.
[111] Ibid, at [351].

additional advantage of conveying the court's message that neither parent is in control and that the court expects parents to co-operate with each other for the benefit of their children.'[112]

Examples

Re F (Shared Residence Order)[113]

10.36 The parents of two children aged 5 and 4 made cross-applications for residence. The mother intended to move eventually from the West Country to Edinburgh. The Court of Appeal refused the mother's appeal from an order for shared residence, the children spending one weekend in four and one day each week in term time with the father and half the school holidays with a detailed alteration if the mother moved to Scotland. The distance between the homes and the fact that time was not divided equally did not invalidate the decision which reflected the underlying reality of the children's lives.

A v A (Shared Residence)[114]

10.37 An intractable contact dispute involving 2 children aged 9 and 11 in which the mother had made allegations of sexual abuse against the father which had been rejected. The children moved to live with the father on an interim basis and by the time of the final hearing were spending half their time with each parent. A shared residence order was justified despite the parents being able to work in harmony because it was important to reflect the reality of their lives and the fact that the parents were equal in the eyes of the law. There was a risk that a sole residence order could be interpreted as giving only one parent control.

Re R (Children) (Shared Residence Order)[115]

10.38 Children now aged 10 and 8. In 2003 when the parents separated there was an agreement for shared care, the children spending periods of 5 days with alternate parents who lived about a 30-minute car journey apart. While the children were happy with the arrangements, these were difficult to sustain for practical reasons. The trial judge followed the recommendation of the s 7 report and made a sole residence order in favour of the mother, the father having contact for less than alternate weekends and the school holidays. Although the Court of Appeal criticised the trial judge for having a 'closed mind to [the] very serious option [of shared residence], given that it was on foot, ... had operated to the benefit of the children for the preceding six months and ... the fact that it was the children's strong wish to see it continue',

---

[112] Wall LJ at [22]. For another account of the approach of the Court of Appeal to shared residence, see Gilmore 'Shared residence: a summary of the courts' guidance' [2010] Fam Law 285.

[113] [2003] EWCA Civ 592 [2003] 2 FLR 397.

[114] [2004] EWHC 142 (Fam), [2004] 1 FLR 1195.

[115] [2005] EWCA Civ 542.

with some hesitation it dismissed the father's appeal because the new arrangements had been in place for 11 months and it was not in the children's interests for there to be further litigation.

Shared residence orders and parental responsibility

10.39 One situation where shared residence orders may be appropriate is where the applicant does not have and cannot be granted parental responsibility without a residence order because he or she is not a parent. However much, and perhaps all, depends on the needs of the particular child. In *Re H (Shared Residence: Parental Responsibility)*,[116] the mother's husband was not the father of her elder son (now 14) but treated the boy as his own throughout the child's life. Indeed, the boy learned the truth about his paternity only after the mother and stepfather separated. After the separation, a residence order was made by consent with the intention that the children should spend alternate weeks with the mother and stepfather/father. This arrangement was never implemented and the mother applied for a sole residence order. Her application was dismissed, as was her appeal:

'The essential element of the judge's decision was to alleviate the confusion that would arise in the children's minds if they did not have the comfort and security of knowing not only that the father wished to treat the boy as if he was his father, but that the law would give some stamp of approval to that de facto situation.

This is a case where a shared residence order is not artificial but of important practical therapeutic importance. This is a case where its making does reflect the reality of the father's involvement and reflect the need for him to be given some status with the school to continue to play his part as both parties wish to do.'[117]

10.40 In contrast, in *Re WB (Residence Orders)*,[118] an application for a shared order failed. The children (aged 11 and 8) had been born during the marriage and the husband treated them as his own, the fact that he was not the father being established only during proceedings. Thorpe J refused his appeal against the justices' refusal to make a shared residence order. In the circumstances of that case, the children were confused and their welfare required that their primary home with their mother should be established and confirmed. It would have been quite wrong for the justices to grant a shared residence order 'for no other reason than to arrive at a finding of parental responsibility in the appellant'.

10.41 Sections 4A and 4ZA of the Act (see **7.29** and **7.43**) remove the need for a shared residence order to be granted solely to give the step-parent or the parent's civil partner, including a female civil partner where treatment is given to the mother under the Human Fertilisation and Embryology Act 2008 (HFEA 2008), if they are to have parental responsibility (although of course it

---

[116] [1995] 2 FLR 883.
[117] [1995] 2 FLR 883, per Ward LJ at 888.
[118] [1995] 2 FLR 1023.

may be justified on other grounds). It will not deal with the situation of a step-parent who is not married to or in a civil partnership with the parent. These will still need a shared residence order. In *G v F (Contact and Shared Residence: Applications for Leave)*,[119] a child was born to a lesbian couple, the mother being artificially inseminated. After the couple separated, the mother's former partner applied for leave to apply for a shared residence order. Bracewell J granted the partner leave, despite the mother indicating that she would object to the final order being made. There appeared to be very genuine reasons for the application which was not a device in order to obtain parental responsibility. It was conceded by the mother that the applicant had undertaken the role of parent even after the separation, had supported the child financially and had a good and close relationship with the child. There was nothing which suggested that the making of the order would disrupt, confuse or harm the child. The conception in this case was not carried out under the HFEA 2008 but now, if the partner is in a civil partnership with the mother, the partner has parental responsibility under s 4A of the 1989 Act. However, the case remains a good illustration of how shared residence can promote parental responsibility.[120]

10.42   *X, Y and Z v UK*[121] was an unusual case in which X, a female-to-male transsexual had undergone gender reassignment surgery and lived with Y who had conceived a child by means of artificial insemination. X applied to the European Court of Human Rights, complaining that his inability to be registered as the child's father violated his Art 8 rights. In dismissing the application, the court held that X was not prevented from acting as the child's father in a social sense and that he and Y could apply for a shared residence order, noting that Douglas Brown J had made a joint residence order in favour of two cohabiting lesbians in an unreported case in Manchester on 24 June 1994.

In these circumstances it may be possible to utilise the provisions of s 12(2) of the Act which provides that the person in whose favour a residence order – shared or otherwise – has parental responsibility while the order remains in force.

10.43   No matter how great the psychological importance of a shared order, it must be intended to reflect the real position on the ground and not just status. In *Re A (Children) (Shared Residence)*[122] two girls lived with their mother and the boy, who refused to see his mother, with his father. The trial judge made a shared residence order to both parents with 'care and control' of the boy to his father. The Court of Appeal held that this was inappropriate. Shared residence orders were not necessarily exceptional but they were orders which settled the arrangements to be made as to the person with whom a child was to live. It was difficult to make such an order about a child who was not only not living with

---

[119]   [1998] 2 FLR 799.
[120]   See also *Re G (Residence: Same Sex Partner)* [2005] EWCA Civ 462, [2005] 2 FLR 957.
[121]   [1997] 2 FLR 892.
[122]   [2001] EWCA Civ 1795, [2002] 1 FCR 177.

one of the parents but was, for the foreseeable future, unlikely even to visit that parent. The court's order had to be designed to reflect the real position on the ground. Accordingly, the shared residence order in relation to M was inappropriate.

Shared responsibility and same-sex families

10.44 When a single person or a same-sex couple seek to start a family, there are various means by which this can be achieved with important but differing legal consequences. Same-sex couples, unable to conceive a child together, may seek to found a family either by adoption or one giving birth as a result of treatment abroad or under the Human Fertilisation and Embryology Act 2008 (see **Chapter 6**) or by an informal arrangement, one becoming pregnant by a known or unknown sperm donor or by a surrogacy arrangement. The legal implications for parental responsibility in these circumstances are considered in **Chapters 6** and **7**.

In some cases where conception results from an informal arrangement the mother, although in a relationship with a partner, may not be in a civil partnership and therefore the partner cannot be granted parental responsibility under s 4A. In addition, the donor will in law be the child's father and be able to apply for parental responsibility under s 4.[123] As with unmarried heterosexual parents, little thought may be given to the partner or the donor's parental responsibility until disagreement arises. In addition there may be an agreement or no agreement about the prospective role, or lack of it, which the donor – and in some cases, his partner – may play in the child's life. In some cases there may be no agreement as to the donor's role either before or at the time of the conception or birth but he may later seek a role.

The situations of the mother's partner and of the donor need to be considered separately.

The mother's partner

10.45 Where the mother's partner is not in a civil partnership with the mother and is not deemed to be the child's parent under s 43 of the HFEA 2008, the only way that she can obtain parental responsibility, short of adopting the child, is by way of a joint residence order when they are still cohabiting or a shared residence order post-separation. In *Re G (Residence: Same-Sex Partner)*[124] the mother (M) and her same-sex partner W cohabited for 8 years during which time M conceived two children by way of anonymous donor insemination. The children were cared for jointly by M and W. They separated

---

[123] In order to avoid further complication in this analysis by introducing subconscious overtones, I use the word 'donor' rather than 'father' although the word 'father' may be used in the authorities.

[124] [2005] EWCA Civ 462, [2005] 2 FLR 957. See also Smith 'Principle or pragmatism? Lesbian parenting, shared residence and parental responsibility after *Re G (Residence: Same-Sex Partner)*' [2006] CFLQ 125.

when the children were 3 and about one but W continued to have extensive contact until M began to restrict it following forming a new relationship. W applied for shared residence both because she wanted parental responsibility and also because she wanted alternate weekend contact and shared school holidays. The trial judge refused to grant a shared residence order but made a series of specific issue orders designed to ensure W retained a significant role in the children's lives. W appealed. Allowing the appeal Thorpe LJ cited dicta of Baroness Hale of Richmond in *Ghaidan v Godin-Mendoza*:[125]

> '... The presence of children is a relevant factor in deciding whether a relationship is marriage-like but if the couple are bringing up children together, it is unlikely to matter whether or not they are the biological children of both parties. Both married and unmarried couples, both homosexual and heterosexual, may bring up children together. One or both may have children from another relationship: this is not at all uncommon in lesbian relationships and the court may grant them a shared residence order so that they may share parental responsibility. The lesbian couple may have children by donor insemination who are brought up as the children of them both: it is not uncommon for each of them to bear a child in this way ... It follows that a homosexual couple whose relationship is marriage-like in the same ways that an unmarried heterosexual couple's relationship is marriage-like are indeed in an analogous situation. Any difference in treatment is based upon their sexual orientation.'

Thorpe LJ continued by accepting the submission made on behalf of Ms W that that had the case concerned the two children of a heterosexual couple who had cohabited between 1995 and 2003 and the father, being the absent parent, had sought the parental responsibility order on the strength of the same degree of past and proposed future commitment as had been demonstrated by Ms W, 'the outcome would have been evident'.[126]

The donor

10.46 Some early research suggested that a tendency among lesbian women to enter into informal arrangements with known donors could be attributed to experiencing difficulty in accessing fertility treatments[127] but in a survey carried out in 2005 the majority of the women interviewed said that their decision to use a known donor was because they believed it was important for the child to be able to trace his or her genetic roots.[128] Despite the complications which the presence of a biological parent might bring, it appeared that lesbian parents may be more likely than heterosexual mothers to encourage links between the child and the donor.[129] Sometimes, it is agreed prior to conception that the donor will play a part in the child's life. Leanne Smith has commented that:

---

125 [2004] UKHL 30, [2004] 2 FLR 600, at [141] and [143].
126 Sadly, the difficulties continued. See *Re G (Children)* [2006] UKHL 43, [2006] 2 FLR 629.
127 See, for example, Douglas 'Assisted reproduction and the welfare of the child' (1993) 43 Current Legal Problems 53.
128 Smith 'Is three a crowd? Lesbian mother's perspectives on parental status in law' [2006] CFLQ 231, at 239.
129 Ibid, at 240. However in *Re G (Children)* [2006] UKHL 43, [2006] 2 FLR 629, Baroness of

'The popular choice to use and maintain contact with a known donor dictates that there are almost always three adults with a potential claim to parental status in lesbian parenting arrangements. Thus, for many lesbian families the problem of establishing securely the role of the co-parent is further complicated by the need to negotiate another role for and with a genetic father.'[130]

In fact, the issue is even more complicated than Smith suggests. The hopes and motives of the lesbian couple may be mirrored by the donor who, if homosexual, may see the arrangement, not just as a service to the mother but as a legitimate means for creating a family of his own. He also may have a partner and because the donor in an informal arrangement is in law the child's father, his civil partner may, like the mother's civil partner, apply for a parental responsibility order under s 4A or, in the absence of a civil partnership, apply for leave to apply for a shared residence order.

10.47 Such arrangements may give rise to incomprehension amongst heterosexuals but it is important to remember that the difficulties encountered in the reported cases may be representative only of the families where difficulties arise. One can no more judge the wisdom of such arrangements from these cases as one can judge heterosexual families by looking at reports concerning intractable contact. Nevertheless, as in heterosexual families the arrangements carry a potential for serious emotional harm to the child if difficulties emerge. In *MR and AL v RW and SW*[131] the 9-year-old girl, P, who was at the centre of the dispute said that she wished she could move far away from all the 'horrible' conflict which had lasted 3 years. She did not feel as if D (the donor) was a father to her. She liked D and his partner and liked seeing them too, but she did not think of them as her family because she has family. Namely, her two mothers and her younger sister. She could not pretend that D was her father in order to make him happy. Hedley J was satisfied that P had suffered significant emotional harm as a result of the conflict but detected no basis on which she might look for any resolution of those conflicts in the future. 'It must follow from that that the four adults in this case regard the price paid by these two children as an acceptable price for the pursuit of their own adult disputes.'

10.48 As illustrated by the three reported cases discussed in **Chapter 7**, (*Re D (Contact and Parental Responsibility: Lesbian Mothers and Known Father)*,[132] *Re B (Role of Biological Father)*[133] and *R v E and F (Female Parents: Known Father)*[134]) there is currently no certainty about the view the courts will take as

---

Hale of Richmond commented, at [8], that many might regard receiving treatment at a clinic, using an anonymous donor, as 'the more responsible choice not only for safety reasons but also to avoid the sort of confusion and conflict' which arose in *Re D (Contact and Parental Responsibility: Lesbian Mothers and Known Father)* [2006] EWHC 2 (Fam), [2006] 1 FCR 556.

130 Ibid.
131 [2011] EWHC 2455 (Fam).
132 [2006] EWHC 2 (Fam), [2006] 1 FCR 556.
133 [2007] EWHC 1952 (Fam) [2008] 1 FLR 1015.
134 [2010] EWHC 417 (Fam) [2010] 2 FLR 383.

regards applications by donors for parental responsibility. In the first, parental responsibility was granted but not in the other two.

Applications for parental responsibility in such cases are sometimes accompanied by applications for shared residence either in an attempt to secure recognition of the role of the donor or to secure genuine shared residence.

In *T v T*[135] Black LJ observed that there was no universal solution for cases of this type, which depend on their individual features and, as Hedley J commented in *Re B (Role of Biological Father)*,[136] are 'shaped by the personalities, strengths and weaknesses of the individual human beings involved'. Her Ladyship noted that it is now possible to grant parental responsibility under ss 4 and 4A in situations where in the past where they could be granted only by means of shared residence orders. It was 'profoundly disappointing' to see how, in practice, instead of bringing greater benefits for children, shared/joint residence could simply serve as:

> '... a further battlefield for the adults in the children's lives so that even when the practicalities of how the child's time should be split are agreed or determined by the court, they continue to fight on over what label is to be put on the arrangement. This can never have been intended when shared/joint residence orders were commended by the courts as a useful tool.'[137]

Examples

Re B (Leave to Remove)[138]

10.49 A lesbian mother (M) with a partner (but not a civil partner) conceived by sperm donation from her partner's brother (D). There was disagreement as to D's future role: M alleged he was to act as an uncle to the child (P) whereas D claimed that it had been agreed he would play an equal role in Ps life. D obtained an order for contact but contact was acrimonious; there was constant litigation (over 20 court appearances in 4 years) and M made allegations that D had sexually abused P. When P was 4, D applied for a sole or shared residence order and M applied for permission to take P to live permanently in the United States. Sumner J granted M's application but dismissed D's on the ground that there was no justification for changing P's carer and relocation was in P's best interests. As regards shared residence, the judge accepted the evidence of a child and adolescent psychiatrist, Dr Berelowitz, that it was known that discord harms children. 'Research showed that children do much better if their parents get on and that the quality of the relationship between the parents is paralleled by the relationship the child has with the absent parent.' He did not see how handover could work with children of this age when the parents do not speak.

---

135 [2010] EWCA Civ 1366.
136 [2007] EWHC 1952 (Fam) [2008] 1 FLR 1015.
137 [2010] EWCA Civ 1366, at [27].
138 [2006] EWHC 1783 (Fam), [2007] 1 FLR 333.

Equally he did not see how a child could survive psychologically when 'he lives on one side of an iron curtain with each parent profoundly hostile to the other'.

R v E and F (Female Parents: Known Father)[139]

10.50 The mother was in a civil partnership and the North American donor (D), in a same-sex marriage. D and his partner were involved in the child's life from birth but after a falling out when the child was 5 the relationship between the four adults deteriorated. D applied for parental responsibility and shared residence. For reasons discussed at **7.39**, Bennett J refused the application for parental responsibility. He also dismissed the application for shared residence which D admitted was not his main application, being uncertain whether there was any difference between parental responsibility with an order for defined contact and shared residence. In addition, the judge adopted the evidence of another child and adolescent psychiatrist, Dr Sturge,[140] that shared residence 'said nothing' as to where the child's central home would be and would lead to complications.[141]

T v T (Shared Residence)[142]

10.51 The mother, M, was in a civil partnership with L and the donor, D, in a stable same-sex partnership. D advertised that he would like to become a father and M and L, who wanted to have children, responded. Two children were born, 3 years apart. The children lived primarily with M and L but D had parental responsibility and had been a presence in their lives through contact on alternate weekends and an additional night once a fortnight as well as increased contact during school holidays. Relationships between M, D and L deteriorated. When the children were 7 and 10, L was granted parental responsibility and shared residence orders were made whereby D had contact on approximately 152 days and 110 overnight stays. The Court of Appeal dismissed M's appeal against the shared residence orders on the ground that no error in the judgment had been demonstrated. Black LJ commented that one might be forgiven for thinking that someone who has been granted parental responsibility has truly been recognised as a parent of the child. In this case, three people had parental responsibility, M, D and L, and they had thereby been recognised as parents. 'It seems to me that that probably accords with how things look at the moment from the children's point of view'.[143]

---

[139] [2010] EWHC 417 (Fam) [2010] 2 FLR 383.
[140] For a detailed summary of Dr Sturge's general approach to such arrangements, see also Sturge 'Gay and Lesbian Parenting in the UK: Biological, Societal and Psychological Issues Relevant to the Children' [2008] IFL March.
[141] Ibid at [61]–[63].
[142] [2010] EWCA Civ 1366.
[143] [2010] EWCA Civ 1366, at [22]–[23].

MR and AL v RW and SW[144]

10.52 The mother, M conceived two children, on separate occasions, by IVF using the sperm of D. After the children were born, D and M's civil partner, S, were granted parental responsibility by agreement. Both D and A, D's civil partner were acknowledged as having a secondary parenting role to fulfil for at least three purposes. The first was to give a clear sense of identity to the children; the second was to provide the male component of parenting and third, there was a more general role of benign involvement which would have, but would not be confined to, an avuncular aspect. When the children were aged 6 and 3, the relationship between the adults deteriorated and there followed 3 years of litigation in which M and S sought to reassert their primary role and D and A to extend their secondary role. By the time the case reached an interim hearing, Hedley J said the primary role of M and S should be restored. Although D shared parental responsibility with them, the day-to-day decisions must be taken by M and S. D should contribute to decisions concerning health, elective treatment, education, moves of home-'the major events of life'. Once that is recognised, the role of D and A needed to be formalised in practical arrangements for contact.

His Lordship added that 'The relationships are uniquely crafted in this case and they are not, in my view, assisted by borrowing concepts from traditional but separated families.'[145]

Criticism of the approach of the Court of Appeal

10.53 The use of shared residence as a carriage for parental responsibility has been criticised. Helen Reece has noted that the categories of people who hold parental responsibility automatically or who may acquire it has expanded and this expansion has been increased by the use of shared residence which has encouraged litigation.

> 'Part of the hope behind the Children Act 1989 was that after separation or divorce the endurance of parental responsibility would lead orders about children to be made less frequently than had been the case. As parental responsibility has been diluted, shared residence orders have arguably come to represent the new way of giving separated parents equal authority.'[146]

She argues that this is a trend away from parental responsibility as parental authority towards parental responsibility in at least some cases was 'nothing more than official approval'.[147]

---

[144] [2011] EWHC 2455 (Fam).

[145] Ibid, at [41].

[146] 'The degredation of parental responsibility' in Probert, Gilmore and Herring (eds) *Responsible Parents and Parental Responsibility* op cit, at p 94.

[147] Ibid, at p 102.

Peter Harris and Robert George[148] likewise argue that the trend has created a number of risks.

> 'First it has become increasingly uncertain what the purpose and effect of parental responsibility is. Secondly, some judges are again becoming willing to make orders even where none is needed to resolve a dispute between those with parental responsibility. Third, that willingness to make unnecessary orders encourages parents to seek orders even where they are not needed and this promotes litigation and conflict; it also results in widely varying practices, depending on the views of the individual judge.'[149]

10.54 As is shown at **10.33** the Court of Appeal since *Re D (Shared Residence Order)* has engaged in identifying circumstances which do not exclude shared residence. However, it has failed – at least until now – to examine critically in the light of domestic and international research the circumstances where shared residence may be inappropriate. An obvious example is shared residence in the context of parental disharmony. Another is parents living at a distance. It may be that following the *Family Justice Review's* rejection of a presumption in favour of equal time, decisions post-*Re D* will be revisited. Lord Justice May's comment in *Riley*[150] that 'to keep a child of nearly 9 … going backwards between mother and father with no single settled home', albeit informed not by research but by common sense – may again be influential.

Shared residence, accommodation, state benefits and child support

10.55 Research has linked the well-being of a child in a shared care arrangement with there being a harmonious relationship between each carer and a sufficient level of resources. Cases brought in courts other than family courts indicate the difficulties which shared carers may encounter in securing housing and state benefits. Unless possible difficulties are addressed at the time shared care arrangements are being agreed or ordered, the arrangements may prove impractical or prove a fertile ground for disagreement.

Accommodation

10.56 Both carers will need suitable accommodation. Where they can supply it from their own resources either by purchase or renting privately they will need to apply to a housing authority or social landlord such as a housing association. It is unlikely that accommodation will be provided without a considerable wait. An application can be made for accommodation to be made available by the local authority under Part 7 of the Housing Act 1996 on the grounds that the applicant:

---

[148] 'Parental responsibility and shared residence orders' [2010] CFLQ 151.
[149] Ibid, at p 170.
[150] See **10.30**.

- is homeless, ie has no accommodation which is available for occupation by him together with any other person who normally resides with him as a member of his family or who might reasonably be expected to reside with him;[151] and

- has a priority need for accommodation, defined as including being a person with whom dependent children reside or might reasonably be expected to reside.[152]

A question common to both heads is whether the applicant has children residing with him or who might reasonably be expected to reside with him.

10.57   When exercising their functions under Part 7, housing authorities are required to have regard to the statutory *Homelessness Code of Guidance for Local Authorities*.[153] Social services in England are also required to have regard to the Code when exercising their functions relating to homelessness and the prevention of homelessness.[154]

Paragraph 10.6 of the Code states that:

> 'There must also be actual residence (or a reasonable expectation of residence) with some degree of permanence or regularity, rather than a temporary arrangement whereby the children are merely staying with the applicant for a limited period (see paragraphs 10.9 and 10.10). Similarly, the child need not be wholly and exclusively resident (or expected to reside wholly and exclusively) with the applicant.'

Paragraph 10.9 advises that where a court makes a residence order indicating with which parent the child normally resides 'the child may be considered to reside with the parent named in the order, and would not normally be expected to reside with the other parent.'

The Code also considers the situation where no order is made but the parents agree how the child is to be cared for.

> 'Residence does not have to be full-time and a child can be considered to reside with either parent even where he or she divides his or her time between both parents. However, as mentioned above, there must be some regularity to the arrangement. If the child is not currently residing with the applicant, the housing authority will need to decide whether, in the circumstances, it would be reasonable for the child to do so.'[155]

10.58   As regards shared residence:

---

151   Housing Act 1996, ss 175, 176.
152   Ibid, s 189(1).
153   (Department for Local Government; Secretary of State for Health; Secretary of State for Education and Skills, 2006.)
154   Housing Act 1996, s 182(2).
155   Para 10.10.

'An agreement between a child's parents, or a joint (sic) residence order by a court, may not automatically lead to a conclusion that it would be reasonable for the child to reside with the parent making the application, and housing authorities will need to consider each case individually. However, housing authorities should remember that where parents separate, it will often be in the best interests of the child to maintain a relationship with both parents.'[156]

The House of Lords considered Part 7 in relation to shared residence in *Holmes-Moorhouse v Richmond-Upon-Thames London Borough Council*.[157] A shared residence order was made, apparently in contested proceedings under Part IV of the Family Law Act 1996,[158] whereby three children divided their time equally between their parents, spending alternate weeks with each during the school term. The father's application for housing under Part 7 was rejected by his local housing authority. He succeeded before the Court of Appeal[159] but the House allowed the authority's appeal.[160] The House pointed out that while the family court and the housing authority were applying criteria which superficially appeared similar, they were not deciding the same questions and the two procedures should not become entangled. In particular, the family court regarded the child's welfare as paramount whereas the authority's duty required them to have regard to any scarcity of resources and the demands of others who are homeless.[161] A shared residence agreement or order will not automatically lead to a conclusion that it would be reasonable for the child to reside with the applicant.[162]

The version of the Code in use at the time of the housing authority's decision had stated that it would only be in very exceptional cases that a child might be considered to reside with both parents. While expressing some criticism of the phrase Lord Hoffman said it would be only in exceptional circumstances that it would be reasonable to expect a child who has a home with one parent to be provided with Part 7 accommodation so that he can reside with the other parent as well. 'I do not say that there may not be such a case ... [but] such cases ... will be unusual.'[163]

Baroness Hale of Richmond agreed.

'Family court orders are meant to provide practical solutions to the practical problems faced by separating families. They are not meant to be aspirational statements of what would be for the best in some ideal world which has little prospect of realisation. Ideally there may be many cases where it would be best for the children to have a home with each of their parents. But this is not always or even usually practicable. Family courts have no power to conjure up resources

---

[156] Para 10.10.
[157] [2009] UKHL 7, [2009] 1 FLR 904.
[158] But probably without a Cafcass report – see Baroness Hale of Richmond, ibid at [35].
[159] [2007] EWCA Civ 970, [2008] 1 FLR 1061.
[160] See also *R (Bibi) v Camden London Borough Council* [2004] EWHC 2527 (Admin), [2005] 1 FLR 413.
[161] [2009] UKHL 7, [2009] 1 FLR 904, per Lord Hoffmann at [8] and [13].
[162] Ibid, at [19].
[163] Ibid, at [21].

where none exist. Nor can they order local authorities or other public agencies to provide particular services unless there is a specific power to do so ...'[164]

Lord Hoffman and Baroness Hale gave as examples of cases where a child might reasonably be expected to live with a parent in accommodation provided under Part 7 despite also having a suitable home with the other parent, a disabled child, whose parents might be better able to look after him properly if they shared his care between them and a child where a shared residence order had been working extremely well for some time one of whose parents had unexpectedly and unintentionally become homeless, perhaps because of domestic violence from a new partner.[165] However, they emphasised the word 'might'.

The House also agreed the family court should not use a residence order as a means of putting pressure upon a local housing authority to allocate their resources in a particular way.[166] Furthermore, 'it should not make a shared residence order unless it appears reasonably likely that both parties will have accommodation in which the children can reside'.[167] Without seeking to influence the housing authority, it might be appropriate for the court to give the applicant permission to disclose any s 7 or 37 report to the housing authority and a transcript of any judgment for the purpose of the Part 7 application.[168]

State benefits

10.59   The fact that there is a shared residence order does not mean that the Benefits Agency or the Treasury will divide child benefit or child tax credit between the parents when paying it.[169]

Only one amount of child benefit is payable in respect of a child but it is possible for more than one person to be entitled to it. In these circumstances, it is paid according to the priority established by Sch 10 to the Social Security Contributions and Benefits Act 1992.[170] As between persons not falling within the scheme of priority (and separated parents with joint residence orders will not fall within the scheme), they can jointly elect who is to receive the benefit and in default of agreement, the Secretary of State may decide.[171] In *R (Chester) v Secretary of State for Social Security*,[172] a contact order was in force under which the mother was to have her two children each weekend and for half the school holidays. She applied for child benefit and this was refused on the basis that it was already being paid to the children's father. The

---

164   [2009] UKHL 7, [2009] 1 FLR 904, at [38].
165   Ibid, per Lord Hoffman at [21] and Baroness Hale at [41].
166   Ibid, per Lord Hoffman at [17] and Baroness Hale of Richmond at [39].
167   Ibid, per Lord Hoffman at [17].
168   And see Baroness Hale at [40].
169   Mitchell 'Shared care – shared benefits' [2003] Fam Law 321.
170   See *Welfare Benefits and Tax Credit Handbook 2011/12* (Child Poverty Action Group), at pp 68–69.
171   Sch 10, para 5.
172   [2001] EWHC Admin 1119.

Administrative Court allowed her application for judicial review, holding that in principle there was nothing to prevent the Secretary of State taking the view that, for example, during the school holidays the mother should receive the benefit for one child and the father for the other. The Secretary of State had failed to have regard to the relevant consideration that he could have approached the case in a way which reflected more exactly the division of care which had taken place.[173]

10.60 This power allows the benefit to be paid to different people for different periods but does not permit it to be split for the same period. However, under reg 34 of the Social Security (Claims and Payments) Regulations 1987,[174] the Secretary of State can direct that benefit is paid wholly or in part to another person if 'such a direction as to payment appears to the Secretary of State ... to be necessary for protecting the interests of the beneficiary or any child ... in respect of whom benefit is payable'. Although Collins J in *R (Chester) v Secretary of State for Social Security* thought that the benefit in that case might be divided, Sir Richard Tucker in *R (Barber) v Secretary of State for Work and Pensions*[175] took a more restrictive approach. In that case, following a divorce, care of the children was shared equally between the parents. The father applied for a share of the child benefits. This was refused and his application for judicial review was unsuccessful. Sir Richard Tucker held that reg 34 was an exceptional measure designed to cover situations where the parent was unwilling or unable to apply the benefit in the interests of the child or squandered it. To allow benefit to be split in the circumstances of the case would be to encourage a proliferation of claims and their administration would become complex and expensive.

There were similar difficulties with regard to the payment of a child supplement to income-based jobseekers allowance. However, when the Secretary of State refused to pay Mr Hockenjos (who shared the care of his two children with their mother who received child benefit) the supplement to his jobseekers allowance which he would have received if he had been in receipt of child benefit, the Court of Appeal[176] held that the regulations were unlawfully discriminatory and both parents were entitled to the supplement.[177]

10.61 There are similar difficulties in relation to Child Tax Credit (CTC). Under the Tax Credits Act 2002 and the Child Tax Credit Regulations 2002 a claimant may be granted child tax credits if the child normally lives with him or her (the 'normally living with' test) or he or she has the main responsibility for the child (the 'main responsibility' test). Section 9 of the 2002 Act allows the Secretary of State to make provision for CTC to be divided between two

---

[173] See also *R (Ford) v Board of Inland Revenue* [2005] EWHC 1109 (Admin).
[174] SI 1987/1968.
[175] [2002] 2 FLR 1181.
[176] *Hockenjos v Secretary of State for Social Security (No 2)* [2004] EWCA Civ 1749, [2005] 1 FLR 1009.
[177] The House of Lords refused the Secretary of State permission to appeal: [2005] 2 FLR 402.

claimants but currently no such provision is in force.[178] The 'single payment' rule means that only one parent will receive the credit even if there is a shared residence order in which case the credit will go to the parent who is the majority carer.[179]

The position is more uncertain where care is shared equally. If parents cannot decide who should receive the credit, the Revenue will decide.[180] In *Commissioner's Case No CTC 4390 2004* the Social Security Commissioner emphasised that it is in the interest both of the public and the child that agreement is reached where possible. 'Agreement may also be to the mutual advantage of the claimants as well as their mutual advantage because that may maximise total potential entitlement to the credits.'[181] In remitting the case to the Commissioners for decision the Social Security Commissioner indicated that in the particular circumstances of the case, the best outcome in terms of the maximum payment was for the mother to receive the tax credit.

> 'It is for the Commissioners and the Tribunal to decide ... [but]as a matter of law I see no reason why the Commissioners should not take this approach ... I would certainly regard the converse approach – that [they] award credits to the person who would cost the public purse least- both outside the spirit and the intent of the 2002 Act and against any decision that rational conflicting claimants would agree and therefore irrelevant in law.'[182]

However in *CM v HMRC*[183] in 2010, a decision of equal standing, an Upper Tribunal Judge disagreed.

> 'It would be both illogical and wrong to prefer one parent over the other for the purposes of the credit on the basis of their respective incomes and the effect that these would have in the calculation of any award. It is not a factor which is pertinent to a decision as to which parent has main responsibility, neither is consideration as to an award to which parent would save the public purse.'

The fact that benefits are made by way of single payments does not mean that they cannot be divided once received. The message is clear. As in all areas of shared residence, parents need to cooperate.

---

[178] For a discussion of the section and the review carried out by the Revenue post-*Hockenjos*, see *Humphries v Revenue and Customs Commissioners* [2010] EWCA Civ 56, at [6]–[8], [32]–[34] and [64]–[66] for a recognition by the Court of Appeal of the difficulties in changing the single-payment rule.

[179] *Humphries v Revenue and Customs Commissioners* [2010] EWCA Civ 56.

[180] See *Welfare Benefits and Tax Credits Handbook 2011/12* (Child Poverty Action Group), at p 1247 for a discussion of the factors taken into account.

[181] At [18].

[182] Ibid, at [35].

[183] [2010] UKUT 400 (AAC).

Child support

10.62 Maintenance payable under the Child Support Act 1991 (as amended) where the amount of maintenance depends in part on the number of days a year the child lives with the paying parent.

Shared residence and relocation

10.63 The issues raised when one parent seeks to move with the child to live in another part of the country or abroad, are considered in detail in **Chapter 9**. In brief, and as stated by Black LJ in *MK v CK (Relocation: Shared Care Arrangements)*:[184]

> '... the *only* authentic principle ... is that the welfare of the child is the court's paramount consideration. Everything that is considered by the court in reaching its determination is put into the balance with a view to measuring its impact on the child. ... Even where the case concerns a true primary carer, there is no presumption that the reasonable relocation plans of that carer will be facilitated unless there is some compelling reason to the contrary, nor any similar presumption however it may be expressed.'[185]

A decision by a primary carer to relocate may prompt the other parent to seek a shared residence order[186]. The court will then decide the matter carrying out the classic welfare checklist exercise. It should be noted that if the relocating parent makes plans in secret without consulting the other, the court may conclude that this demonstrates the primary carer's view that the other parent is in a second class role.[187]

10.64 There is a risk of similar applications where there is already a shared residence arrangement or order.[188] The court may have to decide a number of issues. Where the only dispute is as to relocation, these may be:

- Is it in the best interests of the child to relocate?

- In light of the answer to the first issue, should the shared care remain albeit with the arrangements being varied or should there be sole residence to the relocating or, as it may be, to the non-relocating parent?

---

[184] [2011] EWCA Civ 793.

[185] Ibid, at [141]–[145].

[186] See, for example, *Re L (Shared Residence Order)* [2009] EWCA Civ 20, [2009] 1 FLR 1157 and *Re C (Residence)* [2007] EWHC 2312 (Fam), [2008] 1 FLR 826 where the relocating mother proposed shared residence as an alternative to the father obtaining sole residence.

[187] As in *Re L (Shared Residence Order)* 2009] EWCA Civ 20, [2009] 1 FLR 1157, at [37]–[40] and *Re C (Residence)* [2007] EWHC 2312 (Fam), [2008] 1 FLR 826, at [27].

[188] See, for example, *Re R (Residence: Shared Care: Children's Views)* [2005] EWCA Civ 542, [2006] 1 FLR 491.

In the first reported case involving relocation and shared care, *Re Y (Leave to Remove from Jurisdiction)*[189] Hedley J reminded himself that 'the welfare of this child is the lodestar by which the court at the end of the day is guided'. He refused the mother permission to relocate from Wales to the USA, her country of origin, in part because the child was bi-lingual in English and Welsh (his preferred language) and making excellent progress in his Welsh medium school. The long-running debate about *Payne v* Payne[190] resulted in a line of jurisprudence developing which held that different considerations from the *Payne* guidance applied when there was currently shared care.[191] Insofar as post-*K v K* if there remains any difference in the approach of Hedley J and the general approach to be adopted to relocation where there is not shared care,[192] *Re Y* remains the appropriate approach to shared care cases.

> 'What is significant is not the label "shared residence" because we see cases in which for a particular reason the label is attached to what is no more than a conventional contact order. What is significant is the practical arrangements for sharing the burden of care between two equally committed carers. Where each is providing a more or less equal proportion and one seeks to relocate externally then I am clear that the approach which I suggested in paragraph 40 in *Payne v. Payne* should not be utilised. The judge should rather exercise his discretion to grant or refuse by applying the statutory checklist in section 1(3) of the Children Act 1989.'[193]

The proper approach to internal relocations is identical for shared and non-shared care cases.[194] Relocation proposals may result in further litigation under the Matrimonial Causes Act 1973 if the parents were married or under Sch 1 to the Children Act 1989 for financial assistance in rehousing or the variation of existing financial orders where this is possible.[195]

CONTESTED APPLICATIONS

10.65 Decisions are decided by the s 1 welfare test and the consideration of all the checklist factors as they apply to the individual child. Decisions reached in similar circumstances will be no more than guides as to the courts' general approach. However, some topics have received detailed consideration on a number of occasions. These include the weight to be given to the status quo, the preference to be given to a child living with a parent and whether or not there is a presumption favouring mothers.

---

189 [2004] 2 FLR 330.
190 [2001] 1 FLR 1052.
191 See *MK v CK* [2011] EWCA Civ 793, per Black LJ at [28].
192 See Black LJ, ibid, at [144].
193 Ibid, per Thorpe LJ at [57].
194 *Re L (Shared Residence Order)* [2009] EWCA Civ 20, [2009] 1 FLR 1157.
195 See, for example, *E v E (Shared Residence: Financial Relief: Yardstick of Equality)* [2006] EWCA Civ 843, [2006] 2 FLR 1228.

THE STATUS QUO

Background

10.66 Residence disputes arise in a variety of situations. They can occur at a time when parents separate, either in anticipation of the actual separation when the child is still living with both parents or shortly after the separation when one parent has left. Or they can occur after a period when the child has lived for some time with one parent and the non-resident parent proposes a change. In all these situations, any change will involve discontinuity in relationships, at least with the carer and possibly with siblings, other important relatives such as grandparents or non-relatives such as step-parents or the partners of the carer. There will be a discontinuity of the daily regime and possibly a discontinuity of environment such as home, school, neighbourhood and even country. If the change involves a change in home or school, there may be a loss of relationships with friends and teachers. In a study of the financial arrangements made by separating couples,[196] Perry and others found that less than 3 years after decree nisi, only three in five (58%) of parents who had children living with them were still living in the former matrimonial home. Parents separating brings about other changes. Mothers either began to work full-time or increased their hours of work. It would be reasonable to suppose that this would of necessity change their pattern of child care. The dispute will inevitably be a time of strain and conflict both for the child and the adults who are involved. If the dispute arises at a time when the parents are separating, this strain will come on top of the distress and turmoil of feelings caused by the separation. If some time after the initial separation, the dispute can reawaken the distress of the separation.

In their study, *Families in Conflict*,[197] Buchanan and her colleagues measured the well-being of parents and children both at the end of disputed residence and contact proceedings and 1 year later. They found that most parents and nearly half of the children showed emotional disturbance immediately following the hearing. Although parents improved during the following year, a significant number remained affected. Over the same period, the percentage of children who were disturbed actually increased. Immediately after the proceedings, 84% of parents were experiencing disruption to the way in which they normally functioned with little difference between mothers and fathers and between applicants and respondents. The researchers assessed the children involved using a standardised Strengths and Deficiencies Questionnaire (SDQ). If the SDQ was administered to the general population of children, it would be expected that 80% would score in the normal range, 10% in the borderline and 10% in the abnormal range. In these children, however, 46% had borderline or abnormal scores, indicating a significant level of emotional and behavioural

---

[196] Perry, Douglas and Others *How Parents Cope Financially on Marriage Breakdown* (Family Policy Foundation, 2000), summarised in 'How Parents Cope Financially on Marriage Breakdown', *Findings* 480 (Joseph Rowntree Foundation). See also Douglas and Perry, 'How parents cope financially on separation and divorce – implications for the future of ancillary relief' [2001] CFLQ 67.

[197] Buchanan and Others *Families in Conflict* (The Policy Press, 2001).

difficulties. In the year following the proceedings, the well-being of parents improved but nearly two in five (38%) were still experiencing emotional problems, more fathers than mothers (43%:33%) and more applicants than respondents (43%:34%). High scores were associated with complex situations such as a history of domestic violence, low income and a relationship with the other parent which had not involved marriage. The well-being of the children, on the other hand, deteriorated during the year, over half (53%) having borderline or abnormal SDQ scores. Thirty-eight per cent of girls still had significant difficulties (nearly twice that expected in the general population) but the percentage of boys in these ranges had increased to 62%, three times that expected. Overall, younger children were more likely to be affected than older ones. High scores for parents were associated with the level of children's distress, especially if domestic violence was present. When domestic violence was an issue in the proceedings, the children involved had an SDQ score more than three times higher than the level expected.

Any parent proposing to change the arrangements for the care of children will have to present the court with details of his or her proposed arrangements, home, school, health care, etc.[198] Proposals and even the most settled way of life are vulnerable to change. There may be a change of employment, health, a move of home or a new partner, unforeseen at the time of the proceedings and likely to aggravate existing emotional difficulties.

Most parents are able to offer their children at least adequate, loving care and resolving the dispute involves a subjective choice between parents with different strengths and weaknesses.

Section 1(5) of the Children Act 1989 provides that the court may not make an order 'unless it considers that doing so would be better for the child than making no order at all'. This does not create a presumption in favour of the status quo (see **2.41**) but provides a starting point. The important question though is how much weight should be attached to status quo in the circumstances of the particular case. 'Compelling' reasons are not required to disturb the status quo.[199]

The approach of the courts

10.67 Against a background of discontinuity, proposed change and uncertainties, disturbance and subjective strengths and weaknesses, it is unsurprising that courts favour the status quo, a very experienced family judge, Ormrod LJ, calling it 'one of the most important single factors in deciding what is in the best interests of young children'.[200] As a result, clear evidence is required to show that a change of carer is in the child's interests:

---

[198] For an example of a detailed examination of such proposals, see *Re K (Application to Remove from Jurisdiction)* [1998] 2 FLR 1006.

[199] See *Re B (A Child)* [2009] UKSC 5, [2010] 1 FLR 551 where Lord Kerr at [16] implicitly accepted that none were required.

[200] *S (BD) v S (DJ) (Infants: Care and Consent)* [1977] 1 All ER 656, at 663. Sir Roger Ormrod

'This little girl [aged 6] has lived all her life in her present home with her brothers … She has remained with her father and, he with the help of [his housekeeper] whom [she] has known since birth, has looked after her … She has been and has been accustomed to being, the youngest of a large family. She has grown accustomed to the present position and the loss of her mother and sister on a day-to-day basis, and clearly is settled where she is. She has been affected, inevitably, by the breakdown of her parents' marriage, and is not doing as well at school as might otherwise be expected, and she needs urgently to settle down … The proposal is to move her to a new home with her mother with whom she has not lived now for 18 months, with an older sister with whom she has not had a great deal of contact other than, of course, on access … Her mother is working out a relationship with a potential stepfather who brings his children, about whom we know very little, into the mother's family, and in respect of whom there may be problems in the future. There is an air of change and some degree of uncertainty about the mother's household which renders it less than entirely stable. How will [the child] settle into this new family? …

The status quo argument cannot be carried too far, but in this case it has, for me at least, great force …'[201]

Where there is continuity of care, there is also likely to be family life within Art 8 of the European Convention for the Protection of Human Rights and Fundamental Freedoms 1950 (ECHR). Disruption of that continuity will interfere with that life and will require justification under Art 8(2).[202]

Examples of the importance placed on continuity can also be found in more recent cases. In *Re H*[203] the Court of Appeal overturned an interim residence made in favour of the children's father in part because the trial judge failed to give any weight to the fact that the children had been settled with their mother throughout their lives; she was a satisfactory if not a good mother; they were settled in local schools and their whole routine was established, part of which was staying with their father on a fortnightly basis.

It is incumbent on the judge to adequately explain his reasons for changing the child's settled residence. However it would be better to address the checklist factors than rely on any presumption of fact which may arise from status quo.

'The status quo argument means no more than that, if the children are settled in one place, then the court is to have regard to section 1(3)(b) of the Act and consider the likely effect on them of any change in his circumstances.'[204]

---

is a qualified doctor as well as a lawyer. See Cretney *Family Law in the Twentieth Century: A History* (Oxford University Press, 2003), p 802.

[201] *Re A (A Minor) (Custody)* [1991] 2 FLR 394, per Butler-Sloss LJ at 402. See also *Re M (Residence)* [2004] EWCA Civ 1574, [2005] 1 FLR 656.

[202] See, for example, *Jucius and Juciuviene v Lithuania* (Application No 14414/03) [2009] 1 FLR 403.

[203] [2007] EWCA Civ 529.

[204] *Re F (Shared Residence Order)* [2009] EWCA Civ 313, [2010] 1 FLR 354, per Wall LJ at [9].

PREFERENCE FOR PARENTS?

Background

10.68 Although the welfare checklist is neutral as regards applications made by parents compared to those made by non-parents, courts use the 'needs' factor to give effect to the principle that a child should be brought up, if possible, by a parent as opposed to a non-parent. They will give such weight to this factor as to allow it to trump all the other factors save in cases where the welfare of the child demands otherwise.

The Law Commission in its Review of Child Law[205] wrote:

> 'We conclude, therefore, that the welfare of each child in the family should continue to be the paramount consideration whenever their custody or upbringing is in question between private individuals. The welfare test itself is well able to encompass any special contribution which natural parents can make to the emotional needs of their child, in particular to his sense of identity and self-esteem, as well as the added commitment which knowledge of their parenthood may bring. We have already said that the indications are that the priority given to the welfare of the child needs to be strengthened rather than undermined. We could not contemplate making any recommendation which might have the effect of weakening the protection given to children under the present law.'[206]

10.69 In *Re KD (A Minor) (Access: Principles)*,[207] Lord Oliver of Aylmerton emphasised:

> '... the single common concept that the natural bond and relationship between parent and child gives rise to universally recognized norms which ought not to be gratuitously interfered with and which, if interfered with at all, ought to be so only if the welfare of the child dictates it.'

In his speech, Lord Templeman said:

> 'It matters not whether the parent is wise or foolish, rich or poor, educated or illiterate, provided the child's moral and physical health are not endangered. Public authorities cannot improve on nature.'[208]

Re KD (A Minor) (Access: Principles) concerned a mother seeking contact with her child who was in care, but these statements were later applied by the Court of Appeal in a private law residence case (*Re K (A Minor) (Custody)*).[209] It granted a father's appeal against a refusal to make a residence

---

205 Working Paper No 96. Family Law: Review of Child Law: Custody (1986), at para 6.22.
206 Cited with approval in In *Re G (Children)* [2006] UKHL 43, [2006] 2 FLR 629 and *Re B (A Child)* [2009] UKSC 5, [2010] 1 FLR 551 (see **10.71**).
207 [1988] 2 FLR 139, at 153.
208 [1988] 2 FLR 139, at 141.
209 [1990] 2 FLR 64.

order in his favour in respect of his 4¹/₂-year-old son who had been living with his maternal aunt for a year, his mother having died:

'The speeches in the House of Lords [in *Re KD (A Minor) (Access: Principles)*] make it plain that the term "parental right" is not there used in any proprietary sense, but rather as describing the right of every child, as part of its general welfare, to have the ties of nature maintained wherever possible with the parents who gave it life.

... [The trial] judge proceeded ... as though the question before him had been: which claimant will provide the better home? The question he ought of course to have been asking was: are there any compelling factors which require me to override the prima facie right of this child to an upbringing by its surviving natural parent?

[His] approach led him to embark upon a careful and detailed assessment of the merits of the two competing households with a view to deciding in which of them R would have a better prospect of achieving a sense of security and stability, qualities, certainly, which he will badly need after his sufferings. That comparative exercise was conscientiously undertaken and involved the most careful weighing of minutiae such as the age differences between the parties, of imponderables such as the father's future marriage prospects, and even of wholly unknown quantities such as the emotional effect of a change of primary carer, which the judge undertook, in the absence of any medical or psychiatric evidence one way or the other. It was, despite its thoroughness, an exercise misconceived in law.'[210]

This approach reflects that required by Art 8 of the European Convention for the Protection of Human Rights and Fundamental Freedoms 1950:

'The natural link between a parent and a child is of fundamental importance and ... Respect for family life within the meaning of Article 8 thus implies that this contact should not be denied unless there are strong reasons ... which justify such an interference.'[211]

10.70 Notwithstanding this, the welfare test governs any decision about the future residence of the child regardless of whether both the contesting parties are the parents of the child or not. In *Re G (Children)*[212] Baroness Hale of Richmond emphasised that the statutory position is plain: the welfare of the child is the paramount consideration.

'As the Law Commission explained, "the welfare test itself is well able to encompass any special contribution which natural parents can make to the emotional needs of their child" or, as Lord MacDermott put it, in [*J v C*[213]] the claims and wishes of parents "can be capable of ministering to the total welfare of the child in a special way".'

---

[210] [1990] 2 FLR 64, per Waite J at 70.
[211] *Hendriks v Netherlands* (1983) 5 EHRR 223.
[212] [2006] UKHL 43, [2006] 2 FLR 629, at [30].
[213] [1970] AC 668.

Lord Scott of Foscote agreed:

'Thorpe LJ [in the Court of Appeal] failed to give the gestational, biological and psychological relationship between [their mother] and the girls the weight that that relationship deserved. Mothers are special and ... [the mother] was, on the evidence, a good and loving mother.'[214]

Lord Nicholls of Birkenhead observed:

'In this case the dispute is not between two biological parents. The present unhappy dispute is between the children's mother and her former partner ... In this case, as in all cases concerning the upbringing of children, the court seeks to identify the course which is in the best interests of the children. Their welfare is the court's paramount consideration. In reaching its decision the court should always have in mind that in the ordinary way the rearing of a child by his or her biological parent can be expected to be in the child's best interests, both in the short term and also, and importantly, in the longer term. I decry any tendency to diminish the significance of this factor. A child should not be removed from the primary care of his or her biological parents without compelling reason. Where such a reason exists the judge should spell this out explicitly.'[215]

10.71   The House of Lords, or rather, the Supreme Court returned to the issue in *Re B (A Child)*.[216] Lord Kerr, giving the judgment of the court, commented that Lord Nicholl's dicta in *Re G* did no more than reflect common experience that, in general, children tend to thrive when brought up by parents to whom they have been born.

'He was careful to qualify his statement, however, by the words "*in the ordinary way* the rearing of a child by his or her biological parent *can be expected* to be in the child's best interests" (emphasis added). In the ordinary way one *can* expect that children will do best with their biological parents. But many disputes about residence and contact do not follow the ordinary way. Therefore, although one should keep in mind the common experience to which Lord Nicholls was referring, one must not be slow to recognise those cases where that common experience does not provide a reliable guide.'[217]

His Lordship continued:

'[The] central point of the *In re G* case ... is a message which should not require reaffirmation but, if and in so far as it does, we would wish to provide it in this judgment. All consideration of the importance of parenthood in private law disputes about residence must be firmly rooted in an examination of what is in the child's best interests. This is the paramount consideration. It is only as a contributor to the child's welfare that parenthood assumes any significance. In

---

214   [2006] UKHL 43, [2006] 2 FLR 629, at [3].
215   Ibid, at [2].
216   [2009] UKSC 5, [2010] 1 FLR 551.
217   Ibid, at [34].

common with all other factors bearing on what is in the best interests of the child, it must be examined for its potential to fulfil that aim.'[218]

In practice there remain a number of difficulties. The first is one of semantics. There appears to be no difference for practical purposes between a presumption in favour of adequate parents and there being no presumption, but the ability of that parent being given extra weight. This can be overcome by the judge starting not from a rebuttable presumption in favour of a biological parent but from a neutral position but, when considering the ability of the contenders to meet the child's needs, considering whether the parent in question has something to add as a result of being a parent. The second poses a greater problem. Baroness Hale's dicta were in the context of her discussion of the various types of parenthood, biological (genetic and/or gestational), legal, social and psychological (see **6.62**). Most parents are all these but there are some, for example, adoptive parents who are legal, social and psychological but not gestational or genetic and others, for example step-parents who may be solely psychological. In same sex families the mother's partner may be solely the child's psychological parent as was the case in *Re G*. In that case, the court placed special weight on the biological parent, Baroness Hale commenting that 'to be the legal parent of a child gives a person legal standing to bring and defend proceedings about the child and makes the child a member of that person's family, but it does not necessarily tell us much about the importance of that person to the child's welfare.'[219] Presumably it would have made no difference if the children had been conceived as a result of treatment under the Human Fertilisation and Embryology Act 2008 and the mother's partner was to be treated as a parent by reason of s 43.[220] But what makes this proposition so obvious? And as Everett and Yeatman have commented:[221] 'The difficulty is that if the genetic relationship between parent and child "must count for something" as Baroness Hale stated, how much weight should be attached to it.' They argued that the law 'should seek to recognize all natural (sic) parents equally regardless of their route to parenthood. The crucial factor should be the love and commitment shown by the adults in the child's life, not the source of the love be it genetic or social'.

A tentative summary of the position

10.72

• The child's welfare is the paramount consideration.

---

[218] [2009] UKSC 5, [2010] 1 FLR 551, at [37].

[219] Ibid, at [32].

[220] See **6.21**.

[221] 'Are some parents more natural than others?' [2010] CFLQ 290, at p 308. *Re G* and its application to same-sex parenting is the subject of an interesting discussion by Monk and Diduck in Hunter, McGlynn and Rackley (eds) *Feminist Judgments: From Theory to Practice* (Hart Publishing, 2010) ch 6. In it *Re G* is re-written as a feminist judgment in which Diduck suggests that formal equality of treatment between heterosexual and same-sex couples obscures what is different about same-sex couples.

- By virtue of the application of s 1(5) the court starts from the position of having to consider whether it is the child's best interests to disturb the status quo (see **10.67**). In practice this may favour a parent if the child is already living with that person.

- When considering the ability of any person to meet the child's needs, the court should consider what a biological parent has to offer by reason of being the biological parent. Consideration must also be given to what each party has to offer by, for example, being the child's psychological parent whether or not that person is also the biological parent.

- The weight to be given to the attributes of each contender will depend on the circumstances of each case which will focus on the child's wishes, feelings and needs and the risks involved in each choice. It may be, however, that the biological contribution should be given some extra weight. The quantum of the weight, if any, will depend on the circumstances of each individual case and not be the product merely of the parent's status.'

- When the court decides what it should do after consideration of the welfare checklist, there is no presumption in favour of a parent whether legal, biological or psychological.

10.73 However, both under domestic and Convention law, it is recognised that the welfare of a particular child may require an order to be made in favour of a non-parent. The leading case is *J v C*:[222]

'While there is now no rule of law that the rights and wishes of unimpeachable parents must prevail over other considerations, such rights and wishes, recognised as they are by nature and society, can be capable of ministering to the total welfare of the child in a special way, and must therefore preponderate in many cases. The parental rights, however, remain qualified and not absolute for the purposes of the investigation, the broad nature of which is still as described in the fourth of the principles enunciated by FitzGibbon LJ in *In re O'Hara* [1900] 2 IR 232 [namely that in ignoring the parental right the Court must act cautiously, not as if it were a private person acting with regard to his own child and acting in opposition to the parent only when judicially satisfied that the welfare of the child requires that the parental right should be suspended or superseded].'

10.74 In *In re O'Hara*,[223] FitzGibbon LJ gave examples of 'exceptional cases' justifying ignoring parental claims, involving:

'... the risk of moral or material injury to the child, such as the disturbance of religious convictions or of settled affections, or the endurance of hardship or destitution with a parent as compared with solid advantages offered elsewhere. The court, acting as a wise parent, is not bound to sacrifice the child's welfare to the fetish of parental authority, by forcing it from a happy and comfortable home

---

[222] [1970] AC 668.
[223] [1900] 2 IR 232.

to share the fortunes of a parent, however innocent, who cannot keep a roof over its head or provide it with the necessities of life.'

Examples

10.75 Most reported instances of courts granting residence to non-parents are cases where the child has developed a deep bond with the successful applicants, such that they could properly be called his psychological parents.

J and Another v C and Others[224]

10.76 The House of Lords dismissed an appeal by Spanish Roman Catholic parents against a refusal to grant them care and control of their son. He was 10 years old and had been cared for by foster parents since he was a baby with the exception of a period of 17 months. They wanted to bring him up as a member of the Church of England. He had a close relationship with the foster parents' own child, had become very English in his ways and his parents would be unable to cope with the problems of his adjusting to life in Spain.

Re M (Child's Upbringing)[225]

10.77 The Court of Appeal allowed an appeal by Zulu parents, living in South Africa, against a refusal to grant them a residence order in respect of their son. He was 10 years old and had lived with a white, South African foster mother since he was a baby. Until he was 6, he also lived with his mother, but then his foster mother moved with him from South Africa to England, since when he had had no contact with his parents. The court held that it was in his best interests to be brought up as a Zulu in South Africa and that he would cope with the change. The harm of emotional upset was offset by the benefits offered by his cultural heritage. This decision was widely criticised. The foster mother planned to petition the European Commission of Human Rights.[226] The boy did not settle in South Africa and was later voluntarily returned to the care of his foster mother.

Re P (Section 91(14) Guidelines) (Residence and Religious Heritage)[227]

10.78 The Court of Appeal dismissed an appeal by Orthodox Jewish parents against a refusal to grant them a residence order in respect of their daughter. She was 8 years old and suffered from Down's Syndrome and serious respiratory problems which required constant attention. She had been cared for by non-practising Roman Catholic foster parents since she was 17 months old. She was more strongly attached to the foster parents than a normal child to his

---

[224] [1970] AC 668.
[225] [1996] 2 FLR 441.
[226] *Re M (Petition to European Commission of Human Rights)* [1997] 1 FLR 755.
[227] [1999] 2 FLR 573. See also *C v Salford CC* [1994] 2 FLR 926, an earlier decision in the case.

parents and a move from them carried not only a certainty of short-term emotional harm but also a grave risk both of long-term harm and a deterioration in her physical health.

Re N (Residence: Appointment of Solicitor: Placement With Extended Family)[228]

10.79 The Court of Appeal allowed an appeal by a father against a refusal to grant him a residence order in respect of his son, to the extent of ordering a rehearing. The boy was 2½ years old. When he was just 1, he had been injured in a car crash in which his mother was killed. He went to live with his maternal uncle and aunt, his two older brothers living with his father. After the father remarried, he applied for a residence order. There had been contact between the father and his son, who had a comfortable relationship with him. The trial judge granted the uncle and aunt residence because moving the boy was 'a high risk strategy'. The Court of Appeal directed a rehearing because the medium- and long-term factors which indicated that the child should be brought up with his father had not been addressed.

Re G (Children)[229]

10.80 The mother (M) and her same-sex partner (CW) decided to start a family. M was inseminated by using sperm from an anonymous donor and gave birth to two children. CW played a full part in looking after the children and developed a good and close relationship with them. When the children were 3 and about one year old, M and CW separated, the children remaining with M. CW was granted a shared residence order whereby most of the children's time would be spent with M.[230] M then moved with the children to Cornwall in breach of an order that they should remain in Leicester. About 4 years after the separation Bracewell J, having no confidence that M would promote the children's relationship with CW, reversed the arrangements under the shared residence order. M's appeal was rejected by the Court of Appeal.[231] However, the House of Lords allowed her further appeal. The children were settled in Cornwall and doing well in the care of M notwithstanding her faults; contact was continuing as ordered and ('an important and significant factor') M was their natural mother.

Re B (A Child)[232]

10.81 A 3-year-old child, H, had lived with his maternal grandmother all his life and had regular contact with his father (F) and mother (M). F remarried. Both M and F applied separately for residence orders. The family proceedings

---

[228] [2001] 1 FLR 1028.

[229] [2006] UKHL 43, [2006] 2 FLR 629.

[230] *Re G (Children) (Shared Residence Order: Parental Responsibility)* [2005] EWCA Civ 462, [2005] 2 FLR 957; see **10.70**.

[231] [2006] EWCA Civ 372, [2006] 2 FLR 614.

[232] [2009] UKSC 5, [2010] 1 FLR 551.

court found that M could not provide a safe and stable environment for H but both the grandmother and F could. They concluded that H should remain with his grandmother largely on the basis that there was no compelling reason to disturb the continuity of care. F successfully appealed to the High Court. The grandmother then appealed to the Court of Appeal but her appeal was dismissed. Her subsequent appeal to the Supreme Court was however successful. The justices' decision could not be characterised as 'plainly wrong'. They had carefully evaluated the evidence and weighted the various competing factors. Importantly, they recognised that H's welfare was the paramount consideration.[233]

PREFERENCE FOR MOTHERS?

Background

10.82 If children live with only one parent, the vast majority live with their mother. In 1991, one-quarter of all children in Great Britain lived in lone parent families. Of these, 92% lived with their mothers. Fifty-eight per cent of children living with their mothers did so because their parents had divorced or separated.[234] In the small-scale study by Buchanan and others,[235] two-thirds of children were living with their mother at the start of disputed cases and the same proportion at the end. An equal proportion (15%) of children moved from their mother to their father or vice versa. Do the courts then favour mothers? One answer is that they do not, the statistics merely demonstrating the weight given to the status quo. If a child initially remains with his mother when the parents separate, it is to be expected that the months spent with her pending the final hearing will reinforce the mother's case. On the other hand, courts have historically favoured mothers, recognising the social situation in which the majority of mothers did not work outside the home and fathers did not participate in child rearing.[236]

The pattern of working and child care has changed in the last 30 years. Two-thirds of mothers with dependent children now work, compared with fewer than half in the early-1970s, although fathers, on average, earn two-thirds of the family income. While surveys suggest that mothers in two-parent families still typically carry the major share of routine household responsibilities, including looking after children, the 'gender gap' has narrowed. Three-fifths of

---

[233] See also *B v B (Residence: Forced Marriage: Child's Best Interests)* [2008] EWHC 938 (Fam), [2008] 2 FLR 1588 where a child of 12, despite her wish to live with her mother, was left in the care of her paternal uncle because a return to her mother's care was potentially dangerous.

[234] Haskey 'Estimated numbers of one-parent families and their prevalence in Great Britain in 1991' (1994) *Population Trends* 5.

[235] Buchanan and Others *Families in Conflict* (The Policy Press, 2001), op cit.

[236] For a discussion of the historical approach, see Maidment *Child Custody and Divorce* (1984), chapter 6.

mothers who worked full time and half of those working part time told one researcher that responsibilities were shared equally with fathers.[237]

It can be argued that courts have recognised this change and that whatever the historical approach, there is no simple presumption, at least in higher courts, that women are better able to look after children, at least in those cases where the child is not 'very young' (a very flexible term).

Articles 8 and 14

10.83   The ECHR accords mothers and fathers similarity of treatment. Very weighty reasons need to be put forward before a difference in treatment on the ground of sex or birth within or without wedlock can be justified under the Convention. The same is true for a difference in treatment of the father of a child born out of wedlock as compared with a father born within wedlock.[238] However, it is justifiable for a state to attribute parental authority over a child born out of wedlock initially to the mother in order to ensure that there is a person at birth who will act for the child in a legally binding way.[239]

The approach of the courts

10.84   The leading decision of the House of Lords (Scotland) in *Brixey v Lynas*[240] is a mixture of both the traditional approach and some recognition of changes in society:

'To determine what is in the best interests of a very young child [in the instant case the child was 4] regard must necessarily be had to its relationship with the mother with whom it is living. To suggest that any recognition of the normal mother's natural ability to look after a very young child amounts to sexual discrimination is absurd. Nature has endowed men and women with very different attributes and it so happens that mothers are generally better fitted than fathers to provide for the needs of very young children. This is no more discriminatory than the fact that only women can give birth.'

'... My Lords, to summarise, the advantage to a very young child of being with its mother is a consideration which must be taken into account in deciding where lie its best interests in custody proceedings in which the mother is involved. It is neither a presumption nor a principle but rather a recognition of a widely held belief based on practical experience and the workings of nature. Its importance will vary according to the age of the child and to the other circumstances of each individual case such as whether the child has been living with or apart from the mother and whether she is or is not capable of providing proper care. Circumstances may be such that it has no importance at all. Furthermore it will

---

[237]   Lewis 'A man's place in the home: fathers and families in the UK', *Foundations* (Joseph Rowntree Foundation, 2000).

[238]   *Sporer v Austria* (Application No 35637/03) [2011] 1 FLR 2134, at [75].

[239]   *Zaunegger v Germany (Application No 22028/04)* (2010) 50 EHRR 38; *Sporer v Austria* [2011] 1 FLR 2134, at [85].

[240]   [1996] 2 FLR 499.

always yield to other competing advantages which more appropriately promote the welfare of the child. However, where a very young child has been with its mother since birth and there is no criticism of her ability to care for the child only the strongest competing advantages are likely to prevail.'[241]

10.85 The Court of Appeal adopted a similar approach in *Re S (A Minor) (Custody)*[242] and *Re A (A Minor) (Custody)*:[243]

'[It is argued that] it was natural for a mother to have the care of a 6-year-old girl. This was, in my judgment, a misunderstanding of the decision of this court in *Re S (A Minor) (Custody)* ... where I said that: "it is natural for young children to be with mothers but, where it is in dispute, it is a consideration but not a presumption".

In cases where a child has remained throughout with its mother and is young, particularly when a baby or a toddler, the unbroken relationship of the mother and child is one which it would be very difficult to displace, unless the mother was unsuitable to care for the child. But where the mother and child have been separated, and the mother seeks the return of the child, other considerations apply, and there is no starting-point that the mother should be preferred to the father and only displaced by a preponderance of evidence to the contrary.

... at the age of 6 [this child] is not within the category of very young children.'[244]

In *Re S (A Minor) (Custody)*,[245] Lord Donaldson of Lymington MR recognised the change in social arrangements for looking after children:

'What is clear is that there is a change in the social order, in the organisation of society, whereby it is much more common for fathers to look after young children than it used to be in bygone days. It must follow that more fathers are equipped to undertake these sorts of duties than was formerly the case. From that it must follow that courts could more readily conclude in an individual case that it was in the interests of a young child that it be with its father than they would have done previously.'

10.86 However, the importance of babies being with their mother, save in exceptional circumstances, is still recognised. Principle 6 of the United Nations Declaration of the Rights of the Child 1959 provides that 'a child of tender years shall not, save in exceptional circumstances, be separated from its mother'. The relevance and value of this Principle in residence disputes is doubtful. It is over 40 years old and it is not reflected in the 1989 Convention

---

[241] [1996] 2 FLR 499, per Lord Jauncey of Tullichettle at 504.
[242] [1991] 2 FLR 388.
[243] [1991] 2 FLR 394.
[244] [1991] 2 FLR 394, per Butler-Sloss LJ at 399.
[245] [1991] 2 FLR 388, at 392.

on the Rights of the Child, which is gender neutral.[246] However, very compelling reasons will be needed before a young baby is removed from its mother.[247]

10.87 In the past, it has been argued that girls reaching puberty ought, other things being equal, to be in the care of their mothers. The matter has not been directly in dispute in recent reported cases but it no longer seems to be accepted as a general proposition. As Butler-Sloss LJ said in *Re A (Minor) (Custody)*:[248]

> 'The conflict of guidance over matters peculiar to her sex is, in the context of a case like this, and probably generally, unimportant and ought not to be placed in the balance, unless there were recognisable difficulties which had already occurred or were likely to occur.'

Examples

Re A (A Minor) (Custody)[249]

10.88 The Court of Appeal allowed an appeal by a father against a refusal to grant him a residence order in respect of his 6-year-old daughter. The parents separated when the girl was 5, the mother leaving her with her father and older siblings, one older sibling going with the mother. The trial judge was wrong to start with the proposition that little girls go to their mothers. The factors in favour of her not being uprooted were very strong indeed, as was the sibling relationship with one of the children living with the father.

Re W (A Minor) (Residence Order)[250]

10.89 The Court of Appeal allowed an appeal by a mother against a refusal to grant her an interim residence order in respect of her 4-week-old son. The parents never lived together and prior to the birth agreed that the father would look after the child. Two days after the birth, the mother discharged herself from hospital in order to look after her 3-year-old child. The father collected his son from hospital. The Court of Appeal held that 'it hardly requires saying that a baby of under 4 weeks would normally be with his or her natural mother'.

---

[246] *Re A (Children: 1959 UN Declaration)* [1998] 1 FLR 354.

[247] *K and T v Finland* (Application No 25702/94) (No 2) [2001] 2 FLR 707, at 737; *Re W (A Minor) (Residence Order)* [1992] 2 FLR 332; *P, C and S v United Kingdom* (Application No 56547/00) [2002] 2 FLR 631; *R (D) v Secretary of State for the Home Department* [2003] EWHC 155 (Admin), [2003] 1 FLR 979; *Haase v Germany* (Application No 11057/02) [2004] 2 FLR 39; *CF v Secretary of State for the Home Department* [2004] EWHC 111 (Fam), [2004] 2 FLR 517; *Kirklees MBC v S (Contact to Newborn Babies)* [2006] 1 FLR 333.

[248] [1991] 2 FLR 394, at 400.

[249] [1991] 2 FLR 394.

[250] [1992] 2 FLR 332.

Re K (Residence Order: Securing Contact)[251]

10.90 The Court of Appeal dismissed an appeal by a mother against a refusal to grant her a residence order in respect of her 2-year-old son. The mother took the child to India when he was one, decided to divorce the father and returned to England leaving the child in India with her maternal grandmother. When ordered to return the child to England, she did so. She was refused permission to remove the child permanently from the jurisdiction and a residence order was made in favour of the father. The order was justified because there was a real risk that if the child resided with his mother, he would be removed to India. In addition, the boy's speech was delayed, which the father, but not the mother, accepted. The father could offer a better emotional and a broader-based family background.

Re T (A Child) (Residence Order)[252]

10.91 Child, four, had a German father living in England and an Italian mother who had returned to live in Italy when they separated. The Court of Appeal refused to set aside a residence order made in favour of the father. Both parents were admirable parents but there were likely to be fewer difficulties about contact if the child lived with her father.

ATTRIBUTES OF THE CARERS

10.92 Courts, with the help of Cafcass reports, need to assess the attributes of the rival carers and their abilities to look after the child in a variety of situations. Day-to-day caring will, of course, be important: feeding, housekeeping, ability to care for a temporarily sick child or one with permanent health problems. But the parent's ability to handle the child's distress at a move, to manage change, choosing a future partner sensibly as well as a willingness and ability to promote a good relationship between the child and the other parent will also be important. These matters are difficult to assess and the difficulty may be compounded by the fact that the parent is under stress and perhaps behaving in an atypical manner (see **10.66**).

The 'unimpeachable parent'

10.93 In the past, courts have given great weight to the so-called 'unimpeachable parent', traditionally a father who had not committed adultery or whose behaviour was not seen as being responsible for the marriage break-up. Whatever the views of parents who consider that they were not to blame for the separation, courts no longer take this into account, first because it is difficult, if not impossible, in some cases to allot blame and, secondly, because the concept does not fit easily with an application of the welfare test:

---

[251] [1999] 1 FLR 583.
[252] [2005] All ER (D) 58 (Oct), CA.

'It is clear from *J v C* that if the interests of the children require a decision in favour of one parent, the perfectly proper interests and wishes of the other parent, unimpeachable or impeachable, must yield to the interests of the children. The phrase "unimpeachable parent" seems to exercise a certain fascination over judges and advocates from time to time. I think it is a most misleading phrase. It is hurtful to the other parent in whom it invariably creates an immediate resentment and a bitter sense of injustice, and, in my experience, it is a most potent stimulus for appeals to this court. I have never known and still do not know what it means. It cannot mean a parent who is above criticism because there is no such thing. It might mean a parent against whom no matrimonial offence has been proved. If so, it adds nothing to the record which is before the court and in any event it is now outmoded. I think in truth it is really an advocate's phrase. It is to be found in some cases but only, I think, in those where a parent was trying to recover custody of the child from a non-parent or stranger and there the concept of unimpeachability may have some place [but not] where the dispute is between one parent and the other ...'[253]

Thus, in *Re K (Minors) (Wardship: Care and Control)*,[254] the Court of Appeal dismissed an appeal by a clergyman father against a decision granting control of his two young children to their mother who had committed adultery and was living with her lover.

Gay/lesbian parents[255]

Background

10.94 Although it is 29 years since the House of Lords dispensed with the consent of a father to the adoption of his son by his former wife and her new husband because he was a practising homosexual[256] and despite changes in the law, homosexuality is still not viewed with equanimity in some sections of society. Nor can some parents be expected to be neutral if they see the separation from their former partner as having been caused by the other's sexual orientation. It is not surprising, therefore, if parents and their advocates use the homosexuality of the other parent as being a ground for denying them a residence order. However, a number of studies have revealed no reason to suppose that making residence orders in favour of lesbian mothers will disadvantage children, by adversely affecting their mental state or by influencing their sex-role behaviour.[257] Research by Golombok[258] compared children with an average age of 10–11, who had been conceived and raised in

---

[253] *S(BD) v S(DJ) (Infants: Care and Consent)* [1977] 1 All ER 656, per Ormrod LJ at 659.

[254] [1977] 1 All ER 647.

[255] For a full discussion of family law issues involving lesbian and gay families, see Bailey-Harris 'Third Stonewall Lecture – Lesbian and gay family values and the law' [1999] Fam Law 560 and Bailey-Harris 'New families for a new millennium' in Cretney (ed) *Essays for a New Millennium* (2000).

[256] *In re D (An Infant) (Adoption: Parent's Consent)* [1977] AC 602.

[257] A summary of research until 1991 is found in Tasker and Golombok 'Children raised by lesbian mothers' [1991] Fam Law 184.

[258] Summarised in Golombok 'Lesbian mother families' in Bainham, Slater and Richards (ed) *What is a Parent?* (1999).

their early years in a heterosexual relationship but were currently being raised by a lesbian mother with children raised by a single heterosexual mother. Golombok found that children in lesbian families were no more likely to suffer psychological disorder than children of single heterosexual mothers. All the boys and girls had a secure gender identity as male or female respectively. Children of lesbian mothers were no more likely to be teased or bullied by their peers, although when asked about this on follow-up 14 years later, the children in the lesbian mother households were more likely to recall having been teased about being gay or lesbian themselves. By the time of the follow-up, all but one heterosexual mother had had at least one male partner and all but one of the lesbian mothers, a female partner. The two groups of young adults did not differ in terms of the quality of their relationships with their fathers and mothers. In terms of sexual attraction, there was no significant difference between the two groups.[259]

The courts' approach

10.95 There are no reported residence cases between a heterosexual mother and a gay father, but in the past courts have experienced cases where the father is heterosexual and the mother is lesbian. In *C v C (A Minor) (Custody: Appeal)*,[260] the Court of Appeal allowed a father's appeal against an order giving custody of a girl aged 7 to her mother who was living with a woman who had served a 12-month prison sentence for unlawful wounding and theft:

'Despite the vast change over the past 30 years or so in the attitudes of our society generally to the institution of marriage, to sexual morality, and to homosexual relationships, I regard it as axiomatic that the ideal environment for the upbringing of a child is the home of loving, caring and sensible parents, her mother and her father. When the marriage between father and mother is at an end, that ideal cannot be attained. When the court is called upon to decide which of two possible alternatives is then preferable for the child's welfare, its task is to choose the alternative which comes closest to that ideal.

Even taking account of the changes of attitude to which I have referred, a lesbian relationship between two adult women is an unusual background in which to bring up a child ...

[The judge] seems to have disregarded the effect on C of her school friends learning of the relationship. If or when they do, she is bound to be asked questions which may well cause her distress or embarrassment.

... I make it clear that I am not saying that the fact that the mother is living in a lesbian relationship is conclusive, or that it disqualifies her from ever having the care and control of her child. A court may well decide that a sensitive, loving, lesbian relationship is a more satisfactory environment for a child than a less

---

[259] See also the evidence cited in *B v B (Minors) (Custody, Care and Control)* [1991] 1 FLR 402 and Murray 'Same-sex families: outcomes for children and parents' [2004] Fam Law 136.
[260] [1991] 1 FLR 223, per Glidewell LJ at 228.

sensitive or loving alternative. But that the nature of the relationship is an important factor to be put into the balance seems to me to be clear.'

10.96   In the same year, in *B v B (Minors) (Custody, Care and Control)*,[261] another judge granted care and control of a 2-year-old boy to his mother who was living in a lesbian relationship rather than to his father who was engaged to be married and who was living with the boy's siblings. He accepted that there was no evidence to the effect that there was an increased incidence of homosexuality among children of homosexual parents and that it was rare for peers to show an interest in other children's parents. The difference between the two cases may be explained in part by the fact that in *C v C (A Minor) (Custody: Appeal)* the trial judge had to rely on what Balcombe LJ called 'the moral standards which are generally accepted in society' and on his own experience whereas, in *B v B (Minors) (Custody, Care and Control)*, the judge had evidence from a professor of psychiatry to the effect that 'the dangers to the child of living in a lesbian household tend to be overestimated and there are, of course, widespread prejudices about lesbianism'.

10.97   Since 1991, there have been further changes in terms of legislation and government policy towards gays and lesbians. Same-sex couples can now adopt.[262] In *Ghaidan v Godin Mendoza*[263] the House of Lords recognised that a same-sex couple could have a 'marriage-like' relationship. Courts have been willing to dispense with a parent's consent to adoption and freeing for adoption where the child was going to be placed with a gay or lesbian adopter.[264] In *G v F (Contact and Shared Residence: Applications For Leave)*,[265] Bracewell J granted the lesbian former partner of the mother leave to apply for a shared residence order despite the mother indicating that she would object to the final order being made. A shared residence order was granted to the lesbian former partner of the mother in *Re G (Residence: Same-Sex Partner)*.[266]

It may be that a relative absence of recent reports concerning homosexuality and disputed residence cases indicates a willingness to be guided by research and the interests of the particular child. Guidance to the judiciary from the Judicial College[267] states that:

> 'Extensive psychological research has demonstrated that children brought up by lesbian or gay parents do equally well as those brought up by heterosexual parents in terms of emotional well-being, sexual responsibility, academic achievement and avoidance of crime. There is no body of respectable research which points convincingly to any other conclusion ...

---

[261]   [1991] 1 FLR 402.

[262]   Adoption and Children Act 2002, s 50.

[263]   [2004] UKHL 30, [2004] 2 FLR 600.

[264]   See, for example, *Re W (Adoption: Homosexual Adopter)* [1997] 2 FLR 406 and *Re AMT (Known as AC) (Petitioners for Authority to Adopt SR)* [1997] Fam Law 225, a decision of the Court of Session (Inner House).

[265]   [1998] 2 FLR 799.

[266]   [2005] EWCA Civ 462, [2005] 2 FLR 957.

[267]   *Equality Before the Courts* (Judicial Studies Board, 2002), p 15.

Upon divorce, issues of residence and contact may need to be resolved in relation to children of the family. It would be wrong for a judge to make any value judgements based on the sexuality of the parties. The heterosexual party may feel superior or suppose that a heterosexual home will generally be regarded by the judiciary as better than a home with a lesbian, gay or bisexual parent. Judges should reject stereotypical notions and clearly focus on the evidence and the interests of the child.'[268]

The Equal Treatment Bench Book notes that In *McClintock v Department of Constitutional Affairs*,[269] a Justice of the Peace, resigned from membership of the Family Panel because the Department of Constitutional Affairs refused to relieve him of the duty to sit in cases in which he might have to place children with civil partners or same-sex partners. The Employment Appeal Tribunal upheld a tribunal's decision that he had not suffered direct or indirect discrimination or harassment on grounds of his religion or belief. The basis on which he had asked to be excused was that children were being treated as part of an unacceptable social experiment. In any event, the requirement for him to uphold the judicial oath to apply the law 'without fear or favour' was justified.

Step-parents/cohabitees

Background

10.98 Currently around a quarter of children are growing up in lone parent households,[270] whereas one in ten families with dependent children are now step-families.[271] Because children tend to stay with their mothers following separation, most (84%[272]) of step-families in Great Britain consist of a stepfather and a natural mother compared with 10% of families with a stepmother and a natural father. The proportion of children living with their natural mother and a stepfather remained fairly stable (between 83 and 88%) over the last 10 years. However, there has been an increase (albeit with fluctuations) in the proportion of children living with their natural father and a stepmother from 6% in 1991 to 10% in 2006.[273]

10.99 There are variations in the way step-families are formed. A man may join a mother and her children. He may come alone or with his own children. The same is true for the woman. In 6% of cases, the family will contain children from both partner's previous marriage/cohabitation[274] and in this case, both the man and the woman will be in a step-parent role. In addition further children may be born to the couple.

---

[268] Equal Treatment Bench Book, para 7.1.6.
[269] UKEAT/0223/07.
[270] *Social Trends 37* 2007. The exact figure is 24%.
[271] Ibid.
[272] Figures for 2006.
[273] *Social Trends 38* 2008.
[274] *Social Trends 38* 2008 op cit.

10.100 The step-parent may have the same gender as the biological parent. A quarter of women and one in ten men forming a civil partnership in the UK in 2006 had previously been in a legal partnership, the large majority having previously been married.[275] At least some of these will have children from their former relationship.

10.101 If the non-resident parent has also formed a new relationship, the child may belong to two step-families – mother/stepfather and father/stepmother. Step-parents may also introduce the children into their extended families, perhaps including other nuclear step-families at the same or different generational levels (for example step-grandparents).

10.102 The high rates of divorce and separation mean that the chances that a step-family will dissolve are higher than for first marriages or cohabitation.[276]

10.103 There are also variations in the role played by the non-resident birth parent. Two models of the role have been suggested: the 'substitute model' in which the birth parent is replaced by the step-parent and the 'accumulation model' in which children add a parent to their lives by gaining a step-parent.[277]

Relationships within the step-family

10.104 A number of studies have examined relationships in step-families both between the adults and the children. For example, in the 1990s, Ferri and Smith;[278] at the end of the decade, Dunn and Deater-Deckard[279] and a study by Smith in 2003.[280] In addition Rodgers and Pryor conducted a literature review, *Divorce and Separation: The Outcomes for Children*,[281] in 1998.

Are step-families different?

10.105 In some areas, step-families are very much like birth families. The majority of adults indicated they were happy in their partnership but the proportion reporting unhappiness was higher than for partners in first families. Likewise a higher proportion of those who said they disagreed about the way children should be brought up was reported.[282]

---

[275] *Social Trends 38* 2008.
[276] Rodgers and Pryor *Divorce and Separation: The Outcomes for Children* (Joseph Rowntree Foundation, 1998) summarised in *Foundations* 6108 (Joseph Rowntree Foundation)., at p 43.
[277] White and Gilbreth 'When Children have Two Fathers' (2001) 63 *Journal of Marriage and the Family* 155; Pryor 'Children and their Changing Families' in Ebtehaj, Lindley and Richards (ed) *Kinship Matters* (Hart Publishing, 2006), at p 102.
[278] Ferri and Smith *Step-parenting in the 1990s* (1998) summarised in *Findings* 658 Joseph Rowntree Foundation.
[279] *Children's Views of their Changing Families* (2001) summarised in *Findings* 931 Joseph Rowntree Foundation.
[280] *New stepfamilies- a descriptive study of a largely unseen group* op cit.
[281] Rodgers and Pryor *Divorce and Separation: The Outcomes for Children* op cit.
[282] Ferri and Smith op cit.

How do children view step-families?

10.106 Most parents, step-parents and children did not identify themselves as being in a 'step-family'. An identification as a step-family did not appear to be associated with the length of time the family had been in existence nor with marital status.[283] Just over half of the children studied by Smith denied that their family was a step-family even when the definition was explained to them.

The non-resident birth parent

10.107 Children tended to have inclusive views about their family. Nearly two-thirds of the children in Smith's sample included their non-residential parent as part of the family and where there had been contact within the last year, this proportion was as high as 85%.[284] Many children greatly missed their other birth parent and wanted to see him/her more.[285] Smith found no association between contact and child well-being but there was some evidence that the nature of the children's relationship with the non-resident parent was important. Those children who viewed it as 'the same as before' showed significantly better scores when their 'well-being' was assessed.[286]

The step-parent

10.108 According to Dunn and Deater-Deckard, feelings of warmth, closeness, companionship and confiding were less common between children and their step-parents than with their birth parents. However they varied in the way they saw the role of step-parents. Some stressed that the step-parent should be a friend; others said, a parent. Many found it difficult to accept discipline from a step-parent.[287] In Smith's sample, three-quarters called their step-parent by his/her first name.

The presence of other children

10.109 The studies found that the existence of other children in the family, whether born to the birth parent and the step-parent or previously born to the step-parent made a real difference. Children in Smith's sample where the step-parent had no biological children were more likely and those with shared biological children were less likely to describe their family as a 'step-family'. Higher levels of conflict were more common in step-families in which children had been born to the couple.[288] Half the children studied by Dunn and Deckard felt they took second place to children born jointly to their parent and step-parent and three in ten felt displaced by the step-parents own children. 'This suggests that far from "cementing" the new family unit there are stresses associated with the more complex relationships created by its expansion.'[289]

---

[283] Smith op cit.
[284] Ibid.
[285] Dunn and Deater-Deckard op cit.
[286] Smith op cit.
[287] Dunn and Deater-Deckard op cit.
[288] Ferri and Smith op cit.
[289] Ibid.

Legal relationships

10.110 Smith examined the legal relationship between children and step-parents. Only one child of the 233 in the study had been adopted by his step-parent. Five per cent of adults did not know that adoption as a possibility while just over half said they had not considered it. A quarter of families had considered it but had rejected it while 13% were still considering it. Decisions on changing the child's name were only slightly more common. Most adults had not thought about it. The children's names had been legally changed in 4% of families and informally in a further 9%.

The children's wellbeing

10.111 Smith found few variables concerning the children's well-being related to the structure of the step-family but there was a strong association with the quality of relationships within the household, particularly between the child and his biological parent and between the adults and to some extent, but less so, between the child and step-parent.

Rogers and Pryor's literature review found that studies suggest that, in a number of ways, children in step-families fare less well than those in intact families and in some instances those in single-parent families. They are, for example, likely to have lower self-esteem and high levels of distress at 16. They are more likely than children from single-parent families to leave school without qualifications. They are more likely to leave home by the age of 18 and to form early partnerships. Young children, however, seem to fare better, possibly because it is easier to adapt to a new family structure at an early age.

What are the issues?

10.112 As a result of her study Smith posed a number of questions which lie at the root of a proper legal approach to stepfamilies.

* What sort of a relationship is it appropriate for a step-father to develop with his stepchild?

* Should this relationship be the same as a parental relationship or how should it differ?

* What sort of contact arrangements and financial arrangements should be agreed with non-resident parents?

The law

10.113 Step-parents are able, if married to or in a civil partnership with the child's parents obtain parental responsibility either by agreement or by order under s 4A of the 1989 Act (see **Chapter 7**). This is so whether or not they are living with the child. Otherwise, parental responsibility can be obtained by way of a shared residence order (see **7.29** and **10.39**).

10.114 Step-parents with parental responsibility are able to apply for a s 8 order without first obtaining the permission of the court.[290] Even without parental responsibility they can apply for a contact or residence order without the need for permission if they are married to or in a civil partnership with a parent and the child is a child of the family or they have lived with the child for a period of at least 3 years or the other conditions in s 10(5) are met. Otherwise he will require leave.

The welfare checklist

10.115 The capabilities of the partners of the parents in respect of meeting the needs of the child will be a relevant matter under the welfare checklist. The children and family reporter will be expected to interview them and in most cases the court will expect them to be called to give evidence. It may be that the customs of the new partner, adopted by the parent with whom he or she may be living, differ from those of the two parents when living together. In such situations, courts have to be careful not to pass judgment on matters of private taste and judgment which lie within the broad boundaries of acceptable behaviour[291] but to concentrate on how a change in mores will effect the children. At the same time, partners and parents have to be careful not to fuel misunderstandings by the non-resident parent which can lead to allegations of abuse. In *Re W (Residence Order)*,[292] where children aged 9 and 6 saw their mother and new partner naked and had shared a bath with the new partner:

> 'A balance has to be struck between the behaviour within families which is seen by them as natural and with which the family is comfortable and the sincerely held views of others who are shocked by it. Nudity is an obvious example … Communal family bathing is another …
>
> In a happy and well-run family how the members behave in the privacy of their home is their business and no one else's. But when the family life is the subject of proceedings … there is a danger that the grownups who act in an uninhibited way, however innocently and naturally they may do so, may be misunderstood. It would seem to me wise, in all cases where partners change and children move between the new adult families, for those accustomed to a less inhibited approach to be careful not to raise concerns among the other family who may not share that free attitude.'

SEPARATION OF SIBLINGS

10.116 Courts consider that it is normally in the interests of all siblings to remain together after their parents separate:

---

[290] CA 1989, s 10(4).
[291] It may be difficult to judge what is deemed acceptable by a significant proportion of society. See, for example, a survey of parental behaviour and attitudes on sexual matters in Smith and Grocke *Normal Family Sexuality and Sexual Knowledge in Children* (Royal College of Psychiatrists, 1995) summarised in *Child Protection: messages from Research* (HMSO, 1995).
[292] [1999] 1 FLR 869, per Butler-Sloss LJ at 873.

'It is really beyond argument that unless there are strong features indicating a contrary arrangement that brothers and sisters should, wherever possible, be brought up together, so that they are an emotional support to each other in the stormy weathers of the destruction of their family.'[293]

'... In the normal course of events it is clearly in the interests of children that they should live together. Where parents are in dispute, children give each other enormous moral support and emotional support. It is only in the unusual case that one has to separate children, and any judge who separates children does so with a heavy heart.'[294]

In *B v B (Residence Order: Restricting Applications)*, Butler-Sloss LJ added that it is an error to confuse frequent contact with living together so as to lessen the weight to be given to the importance of living together.

10.117 Neither Purchas LJ nor Butler-Sloss LJ was saying that siblings should never be separated. In some cases, each parent may have accommodation for only one child. In another, the children may already be living apart and the benefit of living together may be outweighed by the disruption of a move. In others, the age difference may mean that the relationships are less strong than in cases where they are close in age.[295]

10.118 Where two or more children are involved in the same proceedings, for example an application by child A for contact with child B, it is only the interests of the one who is the subject of the proceedings (ie child B) which are paramount, although the interests of the other child fall to be considered as part of all the circumstances of the case.[296] Where they are each subject to concurrent proceedings, the interests of each are paramount in the proceedings in which they are the subject. Thus, where A and B were subject to care orders and there was no opposition to A being freed for adoption but the father applied for a residence order in respect of B, the order was granted notwithstanding that it was in A's best interests to be adopted with B.[297] The Law Commission had recommended that the welfare test be amended to provide that the interests of the child whose future was being decided by the court should not in principle prevail over those of other children likely to be affected by the decision but this was not accepted by the legislature.[298]

---

[293] *C v C (Minors: Custody)* [1988] 2 FLR 291, per Purchas LJ at 302.

[294] *B v B (Residence Order: Restricting Applications)* [1997] 1 FLR 139, per Butler-Sloss LJ at 144. See also Edwards, Hadfield and Mauthner *Children's Understanding of Their Sibling Relationships* (National Children's Bureau) summarised in *Findings* 0245 (Joseph Rowntree Foundation).

[295] See also *Re M (Residence Order)* [2008] EWCA Civ 66, [2008] 1 FLR 1087.

[296] *Birmingham City Council v H (No 3)* [1994] 1 FLR 224.

[297] *Re T and E (Proceedings: Conflicting Interests)* [1995] 1 FLR 581.

[298] *Family Law Review of Child Law: Guardianship and Custody* (1988) Law Com No 172, para 3.13.

10.119 Where, however, two or more children are the subject of the same proceedings, the interests of each are paramount and the court has to carry out a balancing exercise:[299]

> 'While the welfare of [the two children], taken together, is to be considered as paramount to the interests of any adults concerned in their lives, as between themselves the court must approach the question of their welfare without giving one priority over the other. You start with an evenly balanced pair of scales. Of course, when you start to put into the scales the matters relevant to each child – and in particular those listed in s 1(3) – the result may come down in favour of the one rather than the other, but that is a balancing exercise which the court is well used to conducting in cases concerning children.'[300]

> 'But the welfare of the two individuals cannot both be "paramount" in the ordinary and natural meaning of that word. If that is the requirement of s 1(1) in the circumstances, then the Act presents the court with an impossible task. For this reason, I agree with Balcombe LJ that the requirement must be regarded as qualified, in the cases where the welfare of more than one child is involved, by the need to have regard to the potential detriment for one in the light of potential benefit for the other. Only in this way, it seems to me, can the subsection be applied and the manifest objects of the Act achieved.'[301]

This does not mean that the interests of both do not initially have to be weighed separately. It may be in the interests of A to live with her father and B with her mother, the needs of each child to be with the other being outweighed by the needs of each to be with a particular parent. The problem arises where A has a need to be with her father, that need being the same as that for B to be with her mother but the need of each to be with the other outweighs their needs to be with their respective parents. Where an even balance between their needs remains, the court should choose the least detrimental alternative.[302]

INTERIM RESIDENCE ORDERS

10.120 When the court is precluded from making a final order either because there has been insufficient time for a full investigation or because other matters remain unresolved or uncertain, for example a decision about which parent is to occupy the former matrimonial home,[303] it can make a residence order which is intended to be interim.

10.121 Interim orders should be made only if the welfare of the child requires it and should never be applied for in order to gain a tactical advantage:

---

[299] *Birmingham City Council v H (No 2)* [1993] 1 FLR 883.
[300] Ibid, per Balcombe LJ at 891. See also *Re S (Relocation: Interests of Siblings)* [2011] EWCA Civ 454, [2011] 2 FLR 678.
[301] *Birmingham City Council v H (No 2)* [1993] 1 FLR 883, per Evans LJ at 899.
[302] *Re A (Conjoined Twins: Medical Treatment)* [2001] 1 FLR 1, per Ward LJ at 49. This was a case where the interests of twins were fundamentally and tragically opposed.
[303] As in *Re B (A Minor: Custody)* [1991] 2 FLR 405.

'What is more important than anything else is that [children] should not be treated as packages and removed from one place to another and back again because the grown-ups are involved in a dispute and have overlooked that children have rights and that children's rights are to remain somewhere until after calm and sensible consideration and a decision by a court that the particular place in which they are living is changed by the decision of the court to them living somewhere else.'[304]

The status quo will usually be maintained by an interim order.[305] However a trial judge was criticised by the Court of Appeal in *Re H (Children)*[306] for making an interim residence order in favour of a child's father who kept her after contact because the child was suffering from a tooth abcess which the father thought indicated maternal neglect.

'[The judge] should not have countenanced a change of residence of the children on an interim basis unless there was a really compelling reason to do so on welfare grounds. She should have had in the forefront of her mind that this was a court order entered into by consent some years earlier which recognised the status quo, after a full investigation by the circuit judge, and it was going to call for very careful thought before any disruption was countenanced and only following a proper investigation. The allegations made by the husband simply did not begin to justify the kind of peremptory switch of interim residence that is sometimes and in emergency acceded to by the court.'[307]

Thorpe LJ added:

'Where, under order of the court, children are in the primary care of one parent and the other parent, who has staying contact, wrongfully retains the children at the end of a contact visit, the principled order is for peremptory return. There will be exceptional cases in which events happening or circumstances emerging during the contact visit suggest that the children would be at risk of significant harm if returned; then the retention may not be wrongful.'[308]

Examples of the Court of Appeal upholding an interim change of carer include *Re W (A Minor) (Residence Order)*,[309] where the court made an interim order in favour of the mother in respect of her 4-week-old son who had been in the care of his father. In *Re G (Minors) (Ex Parte Interim Residence Order)*,[310] an order was justified because the mother admitted that she and her boyfriend took drugs and that her children, aged between 5 and 10, knew this. There were serious and worrying matters which needed investigation.[311]

---

[304] *Re B (A Minor) (Residence Order: Ex Parte)* [1992] 2 FLR 1, per Butler-Sloss LJ at 5.
[305] *Re G (Minors) (Ex Parte Interim Residence Order)* [1993] 1 FLR 910.
[306] [2007] EWCA Civ 529.
[307] Ibid, per Coleridge J at [26].
[308] Ibid, at [29]. See also *Re K (Procedure: Family Proceedings Rules)* [2004] EWCA Civ 1827, [2005] 1 FLR 764.
[309] [1992] 2 FLR 332.
[310] [1993] 1 FLR 910.
[311] See also Brown 'Retention of children after contact' [2011] Fam Law 497, 623, 708.

Re R (Family Proceedings)[312] provides an example of the difficulties which can occur if interim orders are made too readily. A 7-year-old boy, T, was living on the Isle of Wight with his father (F) and his older brother. His mother (M) removed him from school and took him to Dorset when F applied for residence. A request in the Isle of Wight family proceedings court for an urgent hearing was not heeded and the case was transferred to Bournemouth. After a one-day hearing the FPC in Bournemouth refused an order returning T to F but did not expedite a final hearing. F's appeal to a circuit judge was dismissed. Later a three-day, fact-finding hearing into M's allegations of domestic abuse was listed, the earliest date being in 6 months' time. F appealed to the Court of Appeal who directed an urgent hearing if one could be arranged.

> 'The first and perhaps principal error is that the team reaction to the removal of T on the 29th was not an immediate application for an order of peremptory return; it was a reliance upon the pre-issued C100 and an application that existing court time should be either expedited or extended to deal with the crisis … The lesson to be learnt from this case is 1) that seemingly unlawful removal of a child from the home of a primary carer ordinarily speaking calls for a peremptory order for return; 2) any application for a peremptory return order must be issued at once to a court which has the facility to offer a 24-hour service, or at least a service on every court sitting day, for the issue of an immediate order on a without notice basis and for accommodating the necessary inter partes hearing within days thereafter; 3) if there is no such application issued and the court is not engaged for peremptory return order, but weeks are allowed to pass between the date of removal and the date of any judicial investigation or determination, then the ordinary rule is unlikely to be equally applicable.'[313]

Orders made without notice

10.122 Applications for s 8 orders without notice to all parties is governed by FPR 2010, r 12.16.

An application may, in the High Court or a county court, be made without notice in which case the applicant must file the application:

(a) where the application is made by telephone, the next business day after the making of the application; or

(b) in any other case, at the time when the application is made.

An application may, in a magistrates' court, be made with the permission of the court, without notice, in which case the applicant must file the application at the time when the application is made or as directed by the court.

Where a s 8 order, an emergency protection order, an order for the disclosure of information as to the whereabouts of a child under s 33 of the Family Law Act 1986 Act or an order authorising the taking charge of and delivery of a

---

[312] [2011] EWCA Civ 558.
[313] Ibid, per Thorpe LJ at [16] and [22].

child under s 34 of the 1986 Act, is made without notice, the applicant must serve a copy of the application on each respondent within 48 hours after the order is made.

Within 48 hours after the making of an order without notice, the applicant must serve a copy of the order on:

(a)   the parties, unless the court directs otherwise;

(b)   any person who has actual care of the child or who had such care immediately prior to the making of the order; and

(c)   in the case of an emergency protection order and a recovery order, the local authority in whose area the child lives or is found.

Where the court refuses to make an order on an application without notice it may direct that the application is made on notice in which case the application will proceed in accordance with rr 12.13 to 12.15.

Where the hearing takes place outside the hours during which the court office is normally open, the court or court officer will take a note of the proceedings.

Practice Direction 12E applies to applications in the High Court.

Urgent or out-of-hours applications, particularly those which have become urgent because they have not been pursued sufficiently promptly, should be avoided. A judge who has concerns that the urgent or out-of-hours facilities may have been abused may require a representative of the applicant to attend at a subsequent directions hearing to provide an explanation. Urgent applications should whenever possible be made within court hours. The earliest possible liaison is required with the Clerk of the Rules who will attempt to accommodate genuinely urgent applications (at least for initial directions) in the Family Division applications court, from which the matter may be referred to another judge.

When it is not possible to apply within court hours, contact should be made with the security office at the Royal Courts of Justice[314] who will refer the matter to the urgent business officer. The urgent business officer can contact the duty judge. The judge may agree to hold a hearing, either convened at court or elsewhere, or by telephone. When the hearing is to take place by telephone it should, unless not practicable, be by tape-recorded conference call arranged (and paid for in the first instance) by the applicant's solicitors. Solicitors acting for potential applicants should consider having standing arrangements with their telephone service providers under which such conference calls can be arranged. All parties (especially the judge) should be informed that the call is being recorded by the service provider. The applicant's solicitors should order a

---

[314]   Tel: 020 7947 6000 or 020 7947 6260.

transcript of the hearing from the service provider. Otherwise the applicant's legal representative should prepare a note for approval by the judge.

10.123 Interim orders ought not to be made without giving both parents an opportunity to be heard save in the most exceptional cases and on very strong evidence, even when one parent alleges that the other has injured the child.[315] Ex parte orders may be justified if a child has been removed from a settled home by the non-resident parent, but it is preferable that the hearing takes place on notice, if necessary with the notice being abridged.[316] The court should take account of any involvement by social services and give weight to the fact that they had not taken emergency action, presumably because they thought that none was required.[317]

> 'There is almost always the potential for serious injustice when courts are invited to make orders without hearing both sides of the case. The courts have, perforce, to rely heavily on those who apply for or obtain such orders to behave with scrupulous care in relation both to the application itself and to the implementation of any order which is made.'[318]

10.124 Guidance on the practice to be followed was given by Hale J in *Note: Re J (Children: Ex Parte Orders)*[319] and Munby J in *Re S (Ex Parte Orders)*.[320] This, together with other guidance from both civil and family cases, is summarised as follows.

Duty on applicant when applying

10.125

* Informal notice to the other party, for example, by phone, is better than no notice at all.[321]

* The applicant must make the fullest and most candid disclosure to the court of all relevant factors known.[322]

* The applicant must make all proper enquiries for any additional facts which might be relevant.[323]

---

[315] *Re H (A Minor) (Interim Custody)* [1991] 2 FLR 411 – the judge was wrong to make an ex parte residence order in favour of a father who had discovered a bruise on his child's buttocks during contact.
[316] *Re B (A Minor) (Residence Order: Ex Parte)* [1992] 2 FLR 1.
[317] *Re P (A Minor) (Ex Parte Interim Residence Order)* [1993] 1 FLR 915.
[318] *Re J (Children: Ex Parte Orders)* [1997] 1 FLR 606, per Hale J at 611B.
[319] [1997] 1 FLR 606.
[320] [2001] 1 FLR 308.
[321] *G v G (Ouster: Ex Parte Application)* [1990] 1 FLR 395.
[322] *Re S (Ex Parte Orders)* [2001] 1 FLR 308.
[323] *Bloomfield v Serenyi* [1945] 2 All ER 646.

- If a sworn statement cannot be provided in time, an undertaking must be given to file it as soon as possible.[324]

The Order

10.126

- The order should recite or list in the schedule all statements and other evidential material read by the court.[325]

- An order made without notice must be strictly limited in time and for the shortest possible time 'which means within a matter of days not a matter of weeks.'[326] A hearing date 7 weeks after the first hearing is completely unacceptable.[327]

- The court should consider imposing conditions, for example, as to contact[328] .

- The order should state that the respondent is at liberty to apply to vary or discharge the order on notice. Where the applicant is represented by a local solicitor there is no justification for inserting a provision that 48 hours' notice need be given.[329]

- The applicant's advocate would be prudent to keep a proper note of the proceedings lest they are embarrassed by a request for information they are unable to provide.[330]

After the hearing

10.127

- The applicant's lawyers must satisfy themselves that the order is correct and sets out all the necessary information including a schedule of the statements read by the court. If it is not accurate, they must take urgent steps to have it amended.[331]

- The applicant's lawyers must ensure they understand the order.[332]

---

[324] *Re S (Ex Parte Orders)* [2001] 1 FLR 308.
[325] Ibid.
[326] *Re B (A Minor) (Residence Order: Ex Parte)* [1992] 2 FLR 1, per Butler-Sloss LJ at 5.
[327] *G v G (Ouster: Ex Parte Application)* [1990] 1 FLR 395.
[328] *Re P (A Minor)(Ex Parte Interim Residence Order)* [1993] 1 FLR 915.
[329] *G v G (Ouster: Ex Parte Application)* [1990] 1 FLR 395.
[330] *Re S (Ex Parte Orders)* [2001] 1 FLR 308.
[331] Ibid.
[332] *Re J (Children: Ex Parte Orders)* [1997] 1 FLR 606.

- The applicant and his lawyers must be scrupulously accurate in the way they interpret the order to others. They should generally not give advice about it without having read a copy.[333]

- The applicant and his lawyers must comply meticulously with undertakings.[334] Pressure of other work is no excuse and 'apologies, however sincere and humble will not of themselves always suffice to call forth the exercise of judicial mercy'.[335]

- The order must be served as soon as possible. In addition, the application must be served within 48 hours of the making of the order.[336]

- Applicants are under a duty to bring the evidential and other persuasive materials to the notice of the respondent at the earliest possible opportunity, to provide information about what happened at the hearing and to respond forthwith to a reasonable request for copies of the material which was before the judge.[337]

- The applicant must inform the court immediately if he becomes aware that the court has been misinformed at the time of making the application or has been given incomplete information or there has been any material change of circumstances while the proceedings remain on a 'without notice' basis.[338]

Challenging orders

10.128 Save in wholly exceptional cases, an application to vary or set aside the order should be made on notice rather than 'without notice' or by way of appeal.[339]

10.129 A failure by an applicant's lawyers to comply with any of the above duties is a very serious matter which can result in a referral being made to the relevant professional body with a view to disciplinary proceedings, a wasted costs order or even contempt proceedings. However, the welfare of the child remains paramount and a breach will not necessarily result in the order not being renewed or continued.[340]

---

[333] Ibid.
[334] *Re S (Ex Parte Orders)* [2001] 1 FLR 308, per Munby J at 319.
[335] Ibid, at 323.
[336] FPR 2010, r 12.16(5).
[337] *Re S (Ex Parte Orders)* [2001] 1 FLR 308.
[338] *Commercial Bank of the Near East plc v A, B, C and D* [1989] Lloyds Rep 319.
[339] *G v G (Ouster: Ex Parte Application)* above, *Re P (A Minor) (Ex Parte Interim Residence Order)* [1993] 1 FLR 915.
[340] *Re S (Ex Parte Orders)* [2001] 1 FLR 308.

CHANGE OF RESIDENCE

10.130 For a discussion of the issue of whether a child's residence should change because the primary carer fails to promote contact with the non-resident parent, see **Chapter 11**.

TERMINATION OF RESIDENCE ORDERS

10.131 A residence order can normally be varied or discharged by way of application, made with leave if required by s 10[341] or if a s 91(14) direction has been given.[342] However, where a residence order is made in favour of someone who is not the child's parent or guardian, the court may direct, at the request of that person, that the order is to last until the child is 18 rather than the usual 16.[343] Where such a direction has been given, an application to vary or discharge the order can be made only with leave, regardless of who is applying.[344]

10.132 Residence orders will end:

- when discharged;

- when the child reaches the age specified in the order or, if none, 16.[345] It can be directed to last until the child is 18 if the order is not made in favour of the child's parent or guardian;[346]

- when a care order is made in relation to the child;[347]

- on the making of a placement order;[348]

- on the making of an adoption order;

- when the parents, each of whom have parental responsibility, live together for a continuous period of more than 6 months.[349]

---

[341] See Chapter 15.
[342] See Chapter 21.
[343] CA 1989, s 12(5).
[344] Ibid, s 12(6).
[345] Ibid, s 9(6).
[346] Ibid, s 12 as amended by the Adoption and Children Act 2002, s 114(1).
[347] CA 1989, s 91(2).
[348] Adoption and Children Act 2002, s 29(2).
[349] CA 1989, s 11(5).

Chapter 11

CONTACT

INTRODUCTION

11.1   No area of private family law has received more attention in recent years than contact. Under s 8 of the Children Act 1989, contact can be ordered in a variety of forms, either with or without conditions. Great weight is attached to children having contact with parents with whom they do not live but every decision about contact must be taken after considering all the circumstances of the individual child and after applying the welfare checklist. If direct contact is not appropriate, the court should always consider ordering indirect contact. Although a residential parent cannot veto contact, the reasons for his or her objections and the effect the opposition may have on the child will need to be examined. Cases where there has been violence on the part of non-resident parents require special attention.

In recent years attention has focused on the proceedings not as traditional, 'find the facts, decide the order' litigation but more as a dynamic process in which parties can be assisted to resolve their difficulties, preferably without but, if not, within, court proceedings, often without any adjudication taking place. In this way, parties can discover ways in which they can resolve future contact difficulties without further proceedings. This may be effective in many cases – although families who bring contact disputes to court appear to face more problems than those who do not – but where the dispute is intractable or there are allegations of domestic violence or abuse, the traditional approach is required to make findings of relevant facts as quickly as possible.

THE IMPORTANCE OF CONTACT

11.2   The importance of contact between parents and children is recognised widely, internationally through Conventions, in domestic case-law and by parents and children themselves. There is a common theme that contact should be the norm but that the interests of a child in the circumstances of a particular case may dictate that there should not be contact.

International Conventions

11.3   Article 9(3) of the UN Convention on the Rights of the Child declares that:

> 'States Parties shall respect the right of the child who is separated from one or both parents to maintain personal relations and direct contact with both parents on a regular basis, except if it is contrary to the child's best interests.'

The issue of contact engages the right to respect for family life and a private life under Art 8 of the European Convention for the Protection of Human Rights and Fundamental Freedoms 1950.

> 'The natural link between a parent and a child is of fundamental importance and ... where the actual "family life" in the sense of "living together" has come to an end, continued contact between them is desirable and should in principle remain possible. Respect for family life within the meaning of Article 8 thus implies that this contact should not be denied unless there are strong reasons ... which justify such an interference
>
> ... feelings of distress and frustration because of the absence of one's child may cause considerable suffering to the non-custodial parent. However, where there is a serious conflict between the interests of the child and one of its parents which can only be resolved to the disadvantage of one of them, the interests of the child must, under Article 8(2) prevail.'[1]

Denying contact[2] not only needs to be justified as necessary for one of a variety of reasons, including the protection of the rights and freedoms of others, but also has to be proportionate to the aim which it is sought to achieve. A fair balance has to be struck between the interests of the child and those of the parents and particular importance should be attached to the best interests of the child which, depending on their nature and seriousness may override those of the parents. In particular, a parent is not entitled to contact under Art 8 which would harm the child's health or development.[3]

The motives of legal parents for refusing the biological father contact do not necessarily have to be based on considerations relating to the child's best interests.[4]

11.4 It is generally accepted that courts must take into account the wishes of children in such proceedings. On a practical basis, there may also come a stage where it becomes pointless, if not counter-productive and harmful, to attempt to force a child to conform to a situation which, for whatever reasons, he or she resists. However courts have to be careful not to place exclusive weight on the

---

1 *Hendriks v Netherlands* (Application No 8427/78) (1983) 5 EHRR 233, ECHR.
2 This includes failing to enforce contact: *SI v Slovenia* (Application No 45082/05) [2012] 1 FLR 356.
3 *Sahin v Germany, Sommerfield v Germany* (Applications Nos 30943/96 and 31871/96) [2003] 2 FLR 671, at [66].
4 *Anayo v Germany* (Application No 20578/07) [2011] 1 FLR 1883, at [69]. It may be unclear whether the ECHR was commenting on the legal parents' rights to respect for their family life or whether it was pointing out that their reasons were not to be assumed as necessarily being in the child's s interests.

views expressed by the child without considering any other factors, in particular the applicant's rights as a father, effectively giving the child an unconditional veto power.[5]

11.5 The obligation of the national authorities to take measures to facilitate contact by a non-custodial parent with children after divorce is not, however, absolute since the reunion of a parent with a child who has lived for some time with other persons may not be able to take place immediately and may require preparatory measures being taken to this effect. The nature and extent of such preparation will depend on the circumstances of each case, but the understanding and co-operation of all concerned will always be an important ingredient. Whilst national authorities must do their utmost to facilitate such co-operation, any obligation to apply coercion in this area must be limited since the interests as well as the rights and freedoms of all concerned must be taken into account, and more particularly the best interests of the child and his or her rights under Art 8 of the Convention. Where contacts with the parent might appear to threaten those interests or interfere with those rights, it is for the national authorities to strike a fair balance between.[6]

11.6 Contact applications also engage the parties' rights under Art 6(1) to a hearing within a reasonable time. The reasonableness of the length of proceedings must be assessed in the light of the circumstances of the case and with reference to the following criteria: the complexity of the case, the conduct of the applicant and the relevant authorities and what was at stake for the applicant in the dispute.[7] In cases relating to civil status, special diligence is required in view of the possible consequences which the excessive length of proceedings may have, notably on enjoyment of the right to respect for family life.[8]

The approach of the domestic courts

11.7 Domestic case-law contains many similar statements. In *Re K (A Minor) (Access Order: Breach)*,[9] Latey J said:

> 'Save in comparatively rare and exceptional cases, where a marriage has broken down it really is of the first importance in the interests of the children that they should have, and know that they have, the love and support of both parents; and that they can only know that, especially if they are very young, if they have real and regular contact with the non-custodial parent.'

---

[5]   *C v Finland* (Application No 18249/02) [2006] 2 FLR 597.The child in the case was 12.
[6]   *Olsson v Sweden (No 2)* judgment, (1994) 17 EHRR 134; *Hokkanen v Finland* (Case No 50/1993/445/524) (1995) 19 EHRR 139, [1996] 1 FLR 289; *Kaleta v Poland* (Application No 11375/02) [2009] 1 FLR 927.
[7]   See for example, *Frydlender v France* (Application No 30979/96) (2001) 31 EHRR 52.
[8]   *Laino v Italy* (Application No 3158/96) [1999] ECHR 10; *Adam v Germany* (Application No 44036/02) [2009] 1 FLR 560, at para 61.
[9]   [1977] 2 All ER 737.

11.8   Until perhaps the 1980s most contact applications were made by parents who had previously lived with the child but now contact applications are often made in the context of the parent never having lived with the child. In some cases, the child lives in a family with a person whom he erroneously believes to be his natural father (see **6.95**). Nevertheless contact with the biological parent is seen as being in the child's best interests unless his welfare requires otherwise. The development of same-sex families where the child was conceived as a result of sperm donation by a known donor (see **10.46**) has provided further examples of courts holding that whatever the circumstances of the conception or the family, contact has an important function in enhancing the child's welfare. In *Re B (Role of Biological Father)*[10] Hedley J said that the experience of adoption should not be neglected in other less conventional forms of parenting. Children often develop a real interest in their natural parents which is hardly surprising. The other 'powerful lesson' from adoption is the need for truth and the avoidance of deceit from the earliest days. Young children rarely had trouble with the truth although the adults around them may do so. However, the discovery in adolescence that they have been duped or misled (as they may choose to see it) may have serious ramifications for family relationships.

11.9   The importance of contact does not imply the need for a particular type of relationship between the child and the adult. Courts need to be clear about the purpose of contact. It may not necessarily be to give the applicant parental status in the eyes of the child or to allow the development of a parental relationship. Its sole purpose may be to enable the child to picture the applicant as someone significant but not ordinarily important in his life, yet as someone with whom in the future (and if he wishes) he can develop a relationship.[11]

11.10   Whether or not these judicial views about the importance of contact can be justified by evidence is discussed at **11.13**.

The views of the children

11.11   Children in a number of studies indicate that they want continuing contact, especially if conflict between their parents is absent or contained: 'Children are distressed and saddened by their parents divorce and want to remain in contact with their non-residential parent.'[12] In 2000, a team from Kings College London interviewed 467 children aged between 5 and 16 from a variety of family situations.[13] Many children who were not living with both

---

10   [2007] EWHC 1952 (Fam), [2008] 1 FLR 1015, at [24].

11   See, for example, *Re B (Role of Biological Father)* [2007] EWHC 1952 (Fam), [2008] 1 FLR 1015, at [29].

12   Rodgers and Pryor *Divorce and Separation: The Outcomes for Children* (Joseph Rowntree Foundation, 1998). See also Chapter 1.

13   Dunn and Deater-Deckard *Children's Views of their Changing Families* (Joseph Rowntree Foundation, 2001) summarised in *Findings* 931.

parents said that they missed their non-resident parent very much and wanted to see more of him, making practical suggestions as to how this might be achieved.

THE BENEFITS AND RISKS OF CONTACT

11.12 In 2000, a psychiatric review of the issues involved in contact in circumstances where there has been or is a risk of domestic violence was commissioned by the Official Solicitor when he was instructed in the appeals of *Re L (Contact: Domestic Violence)*; *Re V (Contact: Domestic Violence)*; *Re M (Contact: Domestic Violence)*; *Re H (Contact: Domestic Violence)*[14] (hereafter referred to as *Re L, V, M, H*). In the review, *Contact and Domestic Violence: the Experts' Court Report*,[15] Dr Claire Sturge and Dr Danya Glaser prepared a list of the purposes of contact from the point of view of the child.

Benefits of contact

11.13 Benefits to the child include:

- sharing information and knowledge about the child's roots;

- maintaining meaningful and beneficial relationships or forming and building relationships which have the potential for benefiting the child;

- providing experiences which can be the foundations for healthy emotional growth and development;

- providing role models;

- repairing broken or problematic relationships;

- providing opportunities for testing fantasy and idealisation against reality;

- facilitating the assessment of the quality of the relationship or contact when a return to the care of that parent is being considered;

- helping to sever relationships when contact is to cease in the long term.

A list of the benefits of contact from the adult's view (not discussed in the review) would include:

- providing the benefits for the child set out above or (to put it colloquially) 'being there' for the child;

- sharing information and knowledge about the child;

---

[14] [2000] 2 FLR 334.
[15] [2000] Fam Law 615.

- maintaining meaningful and beneficial relationships or forming and building relationships which have the potential for benefiting the adult;

- providing the means for the adult to maintain a sense of his or her role as a parent;

- providing some continuity after a separation.

Risks of contact

11.14 Sturge and Glaser list the risks of contact as follows:

- escalating the climate of conflict around the child thereby undermining a sense of stability and well-being, causing tugs of loyalty and a sense of responsibility for the conflict and affecting the relationships between the child and both parents;

- direct experiences of physical, sexual or emotional abuse, neglect and being placed in a situation of danger, emotional abuse by way of the child or his or her carer being denigrated;

- continuing unhealthy relationships including situations where the child is aware of the carer's fear of contact;

- undermining the child's sense of security by deliberately or inadvertently setting different moral standards or standards of behaviour;

- experiences lacking in endorsement of the child as a valued individual, for example, where little or no interest is shown in the child;

- unstimulating experiences;

- continuing unresolved situations, for example if the child has a memory or belief about a negative aspect of the non-resident parent where this is denied or the parent refuses to acknowledge the memory or to apologise or help the child;

- unreliable contact in which the child is frequently let down or feels rejected;

- contact which the child does not want to attend;

- significantly difficult contact situations where there is little potential for or prospect of change;

- contact which causes stress to the child and/or his carer:

'Proceedings often mean a standstill in the child's overall life and development while his or her carer's emotional energies are taken up with the case and the child is only too aware that he or she is the centre of attention and somehow responsible for this and the resulting distress.'

11.15 A literature review carried out by Kelly in 2000[16] concluded that after parental separation, contact with the non-resident parent has a 'buffering' effect. Large-scale studies have found no relationship between frequency of contact and child adjustment. What is important is the quality of the relationship between the child and the non-resident parent. The extent of any benefit appears to be linked to the degree of conflict, the type of paternal involvement, maternal acceptance and the regular payment of child support. Visiting schedules that permit both school-week and leisure-time involvement with the non-resident parent may enable 'real parenting'. Kelly also draws attention to an analysis of 57 recent studies,[17] which showed stronger evidence of the benefits of father–child contact than was thought previously.[18]

11.16 The benefits of contact cannot be assessed in isolation from the circumstances of the child's life which are unlikely to remain static. The separation of parents is not a single event but a process beginning, for many, years before the physical separation and its repercussions reverberate into adulthood.[19] Parents need to renegotiate their own relationship and despite early good intentions[20] may find this easier to acknowledge as an ideal than to achieve in practice. Just as the stress of conflict and hardship and aspects of the parents' personalities affect adult behaviour, the personality and attributes of the child also impact.[21] The child grows older and becomes more reliant on a widening circle of friends and activities outside the home. The circumstances of the parents change. They may move or relocate, domestically or abroad. They may take new partners; step-siblings may be born; these new partnerships may themselves end. Decisions about whether contact will benefit a particular child and if so, what type of contact this will be, must take all this into account, looking not just to the past but assessing the present and predicting the future while acknowledging the imprecision of all three exercises. As a general rule, all research and commentators agree that it is the quality of contact which is important: not the quantity.

'With few exceptions children want their fathers around and the loss of them from their lives can be an ongoing source of pain. In situations of total absence,

---

[16] Kelly 'Children's Adjustment in Conflicted Marriage and Divorce: a Decade Review of Research' (2000) *Journal of the American Academy of Child and Adolescent Psychiatry* vol 39, no 39, pp 963–973, summarised in Buchanan and Others *Families in Conflict* (The Policy Press, 2001).

[17] Amato and Gilbreth 'Non-resident Fathers and Children's Well Being: a Meta-analysis' (1999) *Journal of Marriage and the Family* vol 61, no 3, at pp 557–573.

[18] See also Chapter 1.

[19] *Divorce and Separation: The Outcome for Children* op cit, at p 51

[20] See Tennant, Taylor and Lewis *Separating from cohabitation: making arrangements for finances and parenting* (DCA Research Series 7/06, 2006), at para 5.2; see **11.23**.

[21] Pryor and Rodgers *Children in Changing Families: Life after Parental Separation* (Blackwell, 2001), at p 151.

children are likely to idealize their fathers or reject them as totally bad.[22] The mere presence of fathers, though, is not enough. Children benefit from having them in their lives when the relationship is positive, supportive and involved and this is true whether parents are together or apart. Conversely negative, intrusive and abusive father-child relations are not good for children, regardless of family structure.'[23]

BACKGROUND

11.17 The approach of the courts and policy makers to contact cannot be understood without taking into account the extensive research which has been carried out into contact both without and as a result of court intervention and into the court process.

How much contact is there?

11.18 The proportion of children who are not in care and who have contact with their non-resident parents is uncertain. In 1991, one study reported that only above three in five (57%) of children had contact with an absent parent and, of those who did, a quarter had contact less than once a month.[24] Another in 1997 stated that just under half (48%) of children saw their non-resident fathers at least once a week.[25] A summary of research into the role of fathers carried out in 2000 by Professor Lewis on behalf of the Joseph Rowntree Foundation[26] found that 70% of non-resident fathers had contact with their children. Figures may be inaccurate because there is a reporting bias according to whether they are obtained from resident or non-resident parents. A study of fathers in 1997,[27] for example, found that while seven out of ten non-resident fathers reported having contact with their children and almost half reported seeing them every week, mothers reported lower levels of contact between non-resident fathers and children.

11.19 Since the publication of the consultation paper *Making Contact Work*[28] in 2001, a number of specially commissioned research studies on contact have been published. Details are given in **Appendix 5**.

In 2002 the Office of National Statistics interviewed about 1,000 resident and non-resident parents.[29] At least half of the children had direct (ie face to face)

---

[22]   See also, for example Smart, Neale and Wade, *The Changing Experience of Childhood: Families and Divorce* (Polity, 2001), at p 69: 'At the core of children's ... negotiation of their relationships with parents after divorce or separation is the experience of absence'.

[23]   *Children in Changing Families: Life after Parental Separation* op cit, at p 220.

[24]   Bradshaw and Millar *Lone Parent Families in the UK* (DSS Research Report No 6).

[25]   *Social Focus on Families* (ONS, 1997).

[26]   Lewis 'A Man's Place in the Home: Fathers and Families in the UK' (2000) *Foundations* 440.

[27]   Burgess and Others *Fathers and Fatherhood in Britain* (Family Policy Studies Centre), summarised in 'Fathers and Fatherhood in Britain' *Findings* 120 (Joseph Rowntree Foundation).

[28]   Children Act Sub-Committee of the Lord Chancellor's Advisory Board on Family Law (2001).

[29]   Blackwell and Dawe *Non-Resident Parental Contact* (Office of National Statistics (ONS), 2002).

or indirect (by phone, email, texting or letters) contact at least once a week. Between just over two in five and three in five (depending on whether reports came from resident or non-resident parents) had direct contact and a further one in ten/just under one in five, indirect contact at least once a week. Children who saw their non-resident parent at least weekly were also more likely to have indirect contact each week. Over half of all children stayed overnight with the non-resident parent, just under a third doing so weekly. A quarter/a tenth of children had no contact.

Another study[30] took as its sample over 2,400 parents who were involved with the Child Support Agency. When interpreting its results it has to be borne in mind that both parents were in contact with each other, if only through the agency, and nearly two-thirds lived within 10km of each other, a factor which has a bearing on the frequency of contact (see below). Just over two in five (reports from resident parents) and just under three in five (non-resident parents) had weekly direct contact and three in five/three-quarters, at least fortnightly. Where contact took place, about three in five parents reported that there was some staying contact. There was no contact in about 5% of cases.

11.20 It seems therefore that at any one time two-thirds of non-resident parents have some contact with their children[31] and between 40 and 50% have direct contact at least weekly. It is difficult to know whether these rates are increasing or, less likely, decreasing. More contact does seem to take place but, as a Family Policy Briefing by Oxford University's Department of Social Policy and Social Work[32] commented:

> 'Some non-resident parents are still disappearing from children's lives and others have insufficient contact to develop the type of parenting likely to yield demonstrable benefits.'

What is generally agreed is that contact is likely to diminish over time. The ONS survey, for example, found that non-resident parents who had separated for at least 3 years were also more likely never to have contact than parents who had separated more recently. The consultation paper, *Making Contact Work* noted that certain transitions involve particular vulnerability for contact:

- the initial breakdown and separation;

- the introduction of new partners by either parent;

- changes of residence by either parent;[33]

---

[30] Wikeley, Barnett and others *National Survey of Child Support Agency Clients* (Research Report No 152 Department of Work and Pensions, 2001 (CSA)).

[31] See Hunt and Macleod *Outcomes of Applcations to Court for Contact Orders after Parental Separation or Divorce* (Oxford Centre for Family Law and Policy/Ministry of Justice, 2008), at pp 2–3.

[32] Hunt and Roberts *Child Contact with Non-Resident Parents* (Family Policy Briefing 3, University of Oxford Dept of Social Policy and Social Work, 2004).

[33] And see **Chapter 9**.

- adolescent testing out of parental authority;

- changes of job of either parent;

- negotiations over financial issues.

Unless these difficulties are overcome contact may decrease or cease altogether. Trinder, Beek and Connolly[34] comment:

> 'Above all what is apparent is the degree of circularity about making contact with family members acting and reacting to the behaviour of others within a context of relationships, the ongoing reaction between different processes ... challenges and mediating factors and the pattern of contact over time in the form of vicious and virtuous circles.'

11.21 Both the ONS and the CSA surveys as well as other surveys have examined factors which might be thought to be associated with contact.

- Distance between the non-resident parent's home and that of the child is an important factor for direct contact.[35]

- Non-resident parents who blamed themselves for the relationship breakdown were more likely to maintain contact.[36] However, there is no evidence for a clear linkage between the reason for the separation and contact.[37]

- Non-resident parents who were homeowners were more likely to maintain contact.[38]

- Higher income and education appear to be associated with more contact.[39]

- The fact that the parents had been married to each other rather than cohabiting or 'never lived together' is positively associated with contact.[40]

- Whether or not either parent had a new partner seems to be a factor but there were differences between the two groups of parents. If the responding parent was a resident parent, contact was likely to be adversely influenced by whether or not that parent had children in their current

---

[34]   Trinder, Beek and Connolly *Making Contact: How Parents and Children Negotiate and Experience Contact after Divorce* (Joseph Rowntree Foundation 2002) at p 45.

[35]   ONS.

[36]   CSA.

[37]   Trinder, Beek and Connolly *Making Contact: How Parents and Children Negotiate and Experience Contact after Divorce* (Joseph Rowntree Foundation, 2002).

[38]   CSA.

[39]   Stephens "Will Johnny see daddy this week?" (1996) *Journal of Family Issues* Vol 17, p 466; Cooksey and Craig *Parenting from a distance* (1998) Demography Vol 35, p 187.

[40]   Maclean and Eekelaar *The Parental Obligation* (Hart Publishing, 1997).

relationship. However, when the responding parent was a non- resident parent, the influencing factor was whether or not that parent had a partner.[41]

- Children who had direct contact at least weekly were more likely to receive maintenance payments. Children who had no contact were least likely to receive maintenance payments.[42] However, dealings with the CSA did not affect contact.[43]

- The age of the child or that of the non-resident parent had little influence.[44]

Trinder, Beek and Connolly[45] suggest that the factors discussed above can be analysed as:

- Direct determinants

  - commitment to contact
  - role clarity
  - relationship quality between parents and between parents and children

- Challenges

  - nature of separation
  - new adult partners
  - financial settlements/child support
  - logistics e g distance, money
    parenting style/quality
  - risk/safety issues

- Mediating factors – how challenges are met

  - beliefs about the value of contact
  - relationship skills, empathy and insight
  - involvement of families and outside agencies

- Time

  - child age and stage
  - time post-separation.

---

41 ONS.
42 ONS.
43 CSA.
44 ONS.
45 Trinder, Beek and Connolly *Making Contact: How Parents and Children Negotiate and Experience Contact after Divorce* (Joseph Rowntree Foundation, 2002).

Court applications

11.22 In 1994, 46,728 applications for contact were made in all tiers of court. By 2004, the figure had risen to 76,426.[46] Judicial statistics are however notoriously inaccurate.[47] *Judicial and Court Statistics* for 2010[48] show that 46,350 children were the subject of contact applications, a fall of 13% from 2009.[49] However, Table 2.4 gives the figure of 95,460 children involved in disposals. It is unlikely that the difference results from disposals accumulating from previous years. Just over 2% of applications were withdrawn; far less than 1% were refused; no order was made in just under 1% and orders for some contact were made in nearly 97% of cases.

Parental attitudes to contact

11.23 A study of separating couples who had cohabited but not married[50] found that there were arrangements for contact, including overnight stays, in all the cases involving children from the relationship, and there generally seemed to be a high degree of flexibility in how contact worked. People were sometimes motivated here by memories of their own parents' separations. They also recognised the value to their children of a sustained relationship with both parents, and seemed genuinely keen to facilitate this. There was also a desire to avoid disputes to keep the courts and legal processes out of their arrangements. The situation was more varied when it came to children from one partner's previous relationship. In some cases contact had dwindled or ceased, either reflecting the children's decision or that of the other partner, and if the latter it was viewed with some regret. Other people had stayed in touch.

11.24 It is widely accepted that parental attitudes both to each other and in the way contact is viewed are important, but not the sole factors in determining that amount and quality of contact. In *Re O (Contact: Withdrawal of Application)*[51] the then Wall J said:

> 'Contact in my experience works best when parents respect each other and are able to co-operate, when the children's loyalties are not torn and they can move between their parents without tension.'

The ONS survey examined the relationship between the parents. Nearly half had no relationship with their previous partner, although nearly three in ten non-resident parents and one in five resident parents said they spoke at least once a week, about a further one in eight speaking at least once a month. Perhaps surprisingly over 60% of all parents reported that they were 'very

---

[46]   Judicial Statistics 2004 (Department for Constitutional Affairs, 2004).
[47]   See Haskey 'Research in Family Law: The Need for Better Statistical Information' [2001] Fam Law 159.
[48]   Judicial and Court Statistics (Ministry of Justice, 2010).
[49]   Ibid, Table 2.3.
[50]   Tennant, Taylor and Lewis *Separating from cohabitation: making arrangements for finances and parenting* (DCA Research Series, 7/06, 2006), at para 5.2.
[51]   [2003] EWHC 3031 (Fam), [2004] 1 FLR 1258.

friendly' or 'fairly friendly' with the other and nearly a half reported that their relationship had improved since separation. However, 30% described their relationship as 'tense'. Just over a third of non-resident parents and over a quarter of resident parents told the researchers that they found negotiating contact issues with the other 'very easy' or 'fairly easy', but 30% of resident parents where there was contact said they did not negotiate directly. About two in five non-resident parents and a quarter of resident parents reported that there had been disputes about contact. Three in five parents said that they could not trust the other to keep arrangements.

11.25 Trinder, Beek and Connolly[52] identified three broad groupings of contacting arrangements.

- *Consensually committed* where parents and children are committed to regular contact

  – Inter-parental conflict is low.
  – Parents agreed that children should be put first and about the importance of contact and amicability.
  – Parents had a balanced view of the other parent, recognising their strengths and weaknesses. They either had a good relationship with each other or were prepared to work hard to manage conflict and endorse the other's role with the children.

- *Faltering contact* where contact is irregular or has ceased without court involvement

  – Both parents are ambivalent about the importance of contact and no contact schedule had ever been established or adhered to.
  – No maintenance or child support was being paid.
  – The parent with care had been the parent most involved with the children prior to separation.
  Significantly, none of the children wanted all contact to finish.

- *Conflicted contact* with significant disputes about the amount or form of contact or where past or present violence or abuse impacted on contact. A number of sub-groups and different factors/symptoms appeared to be involved

  – Parents either battle over their respective roles, whether in private or at court, or cease all communication.
  – One parent may be more committed to contact than the other.
  – Parents analyse the dispute in terms of their own 'rights'.
  Children were inevitably involved in the conflict and contact was a significant source of stress for both children and the adults involved.

---

[52] Trinder, Beek and Connolly *Making Contact: How Parents and Children Negotiate and Experience Contact after Divorce* (Joseph Rowntree Foundation, 2002).

The study argues that one of the most striking aspects was the presence of 'two common trajectories of either a virtuous or vicious circle over time established early in the contact process'. Where parents had a workable relationship in the beginning, the parental relationship continued to improve, but where contact was problematic to begin with, it continued to decline.

> 'Once contact had become problematic it was extremely difficult to get it back on track whilst conversely, once contact was established in a relatively conflict-free manner, then the reasonably good relationships between participants reinforced each other and enabled parents to ride out challenges such as the arrival of new partners.'

BACKGROUND TO CONTACT DISPUTES

Causes of contact disputes

11.26 The increase in contact applications has been attributed to a number of causes.[53] Most divorces being undefended, adults are less able to obtain a formal validation of their lack of responsibility for the break-up of the marriage elsewhere in the judicial system. While this may explain why some people contest contact applications, it cannot explain an increase in applications, there having been virtually no divorce hearings for a number of years. More men think differently about their role as fathers and are less willing to forgo this role. Also, an increased awareness of the relevance of domestic violence may make women less willing to agree to contact.

11.27 A further reason may be found in the increase in the divorce rate since the divorce law reforms of 1969. Those who are parents now were children in a society with a high divorce and separation rate and, given the proportion of fathers who fail to maintain contact, a significant number of parents who separate will have suffered loss of contact with one of their parents in their own childhood. A number of studies have reported an association between parental separation and offspring experiencing separation from their own partners.[54] Practitioners may find it illuminating to ask their clients whether they and their former partners had regular and consistent contact with their own parents in childhood.

11.28 As the Children Act Sub-Committee of the Lord Chancellor's Advisory Board on Family Law commented,[55] parental resistance to contact cannot be understood as a single phenomenon but the intense emotional nature of divorce and separation must be recognised as a factor:

---

[53] See, for example, Freeman 'Disputing Children' in Katz, Eekelaar and Maclean (eds) *Cross Currents: Family Law and Policy in the US and England* (2000).

[54] Rodgers and Pryor *Divorce and Separation: The Outcomes for Children* (Joseph Rowntree Foundation, 1998).

[55] *Making Contact Work: A Consultation Paper* (Lord Chancellor's Department, 2001).

'It is surprisingly easy in the rationally based environment of the law, to become bewildered and irritated by what appears to be plainly irrational behaviour on the part of one parent against the other, when other aspects of the same parent's conduct appear perfectly rational. Furthermore, irrational behaviour is easily communicated in ways that can elicit similarly irrational responses from the other parent.'

Although co-operation of parents is likely to be best for the children:

'It is simply not realistic to expect the majority of separated parents to be able to establish and sustain a cooperative parental relationship, particularly during the emotional process of divorce ... Post-divorce parenting is demanding.'

And not just emotionally demanding. Parents may suffer lethargy. The parent who leaves is likely to be in temporary accommodation, less inviting than his or her former home. One study found that 68% of men moved at least twice following separation.[56] The parent who remains may have to look after children who are possibly distressed, without support. Both are likely to experience financial difficulties, cutting back on expenditure as well as incurring debt.[57]

Fathers may be unreliable and irresponsible over contact or mothers may be obstructive. In addition, the parents may just dislike each other. Smart and Neale have commented that during a relationship, a couple may be prepared to tolerate the aspects of the other that they dislike but after separation any incentive to do this may fade.[58]

11.29 Where there are problems about contact, they are often linked to other arguments, for example about the payment/non-payment of child support. This is discussed at **11.103**.

11.30 A number of studies report a high incidence of allegations of domestic violence. The topic is discussed at **5.14**.

Going to court

11.31 A team of researchers from Leeds University has investigated contact disputes in court on behalf of the Department for Constitutional Affairs.[59] They found that parents often initiated proceedings out of a sense of insecurity, no longer being able to handle the problem themselves. As the cases unfolded it became clear that complex issues involving matters which the courts did not

---

[56] Douglas and Perry 'How Parents Cope Financially on Separation and Divorce' [2001] CFLQ 67.

[57] Ibid, summarised in *Findings* (Joseph Rowntree Foundation, April 2000).

[58] *Family Fragments* (Polity, 1999). See also Rhoades 'The "No Contact Mother": Reconstructions of Motherhood in the Era of the "New Father"' (2002) *Int Jo of Law, Policy and the Family* 71.

[59] Smart, May, Wade and Furniss *Residence and Contact Disputes in Court* Vol 1 (DCA Research Series No 6/03, 2003), Vol 2 (DCA Research Series 4/05, 2005) (Department for Constitutional Affairs).

consider relevant to the welfare checklist, for example disputes about financial support, often underlay the dispute about contact and parents found it difficult to understand why the law did not take account of matters they viewed as highly relevant.

It is sometimes suggested that courts only serve to make matters worse. Carol Smart could not say whether this was so from her data but concluded that 'It is impossible to isolate "going to court" as a sole causal factor in what is a complex process of human relationships'.[60]

11.32 A study by Trinder, Connolly and others, *Making Contact Happen or Making Contact Work?*[61] found that resident and non-resident parents had concerns that were different in kind or in degree. In the run up to the court application nearly all resident parents were satisfied with residence arrangements and with their involvement with the children and about half were satisfied with the level of contact. In contrast, only half of non-resident parents were satisfied with residence and fewer than a fifth were satisfied with the quantity or quality of contact.

11.33 Both resident and non-resident parents were fairly dissatisfied with the quality of contact. Three quarters questioned the other parent's commitment to contact; more than four in ten parents reported their ex-partner had threatened to stop allowing or having contact and a quarter had made that threat themselves. Non-resident parents were significantly more likely to report problems. Problems with keeping to the contact timetable were also very common and nearly three-quarters of both resident and non-resident parents said they experienced problems with the other parent's punctuality. The sample as a whole also expressed high levels of concern about children's reaction to contact and about the parenting quality of the other parent. More than three in ten parents thought that their children were not being given enough attention or appropriate discipline whilst with the other parent, and over two in ten of parents thought that the other parent might have been too harsh or might harm the child. Finally, around half of the sample reported problems on four 'conflict' items:

- the presence of third parties;

- the ex-partner controlling or interfering;

- conflicts over money; and

- fear of violence impacting on contact. More than half of resident parents reported that fear of violence made it more difficult to sort out contact problems.

---

[60]   Ibid, Vol 1, p iii.
[61]   (2006) Trinder, Connolly, Kellet, Notley and Swift (Department for Constitutional Affairs DCA Research Series 3/06, 2006), at pp 31–36.

Non-resident parents were significantly more likely to report that the ex-partner attempted to control or interfere with their relationship with the children while in contrast resident parents were significantly more likely to report a fear of violence.

11.34 A previous study of applicants and respondents in contact cases in three county courts in Essex by Trinder and others[62] found that typically parents had run into contact problems soon after separation and once informal negotiations had been exhausted they turned rapidly to lawyers and the courts rather than mediation. 'The relative brevity of most disputes might indicate that effective early intervention could prevent cases becoming entrenched.' However, on all the measures where a comparison could be made with community as opposed to court-based studies of post-separation families, the court sample were facing difficulties 'of an entirely different magnitude'. The level of parental and child distress was high even before they entered the court system. Equally worrying was the presence of multiple risk factors, such as economic adversity, parental conflict, reports of domestic violence, all of which are associated with poorer outcomes for children.

> 'Although involvement with the courts may exacerbate the conflict and increase levels of stress,[63] it is clear that parents are highly conflicted and polarised before they enter the court system ... This does mean that the courts are only dealing with cases which do require external intervention. Reasonably effective filters appear to be in place preventing families being drawn into the court process which do not need to be there.'[64]

11.35 Trinder's subsequent study[65] found a similar picture. The level of distress reported by parents was very high. Three-quarters (77.5%) of parents scored above the threshold on the General Health Questionnaire, a figure that almost matches a recent study of parents involved in the court welfare report process by Buchanan (see **10.66**). The Strengths and Difficulties Questionnaire showed levels of difficulties for children substantially higher than general population norms.

11.36 Looking at the sample as a whole it is clear that the parents, and children, were facing significant difficulties, with fraught or tenuous contact, conflicted and distrustful parental relationships, very limited shared decision making, high levels of dissatisfaction with arrangements and numerous contact problems. It is therefore no surprise that this translates into high levels of adult and child distress. The cases therefore present a significant challenge to the courts and to the potential effectiveness of in-court conciliation.

---

[62] Trinder, Connolly and others *A Profile of Applicants and Respondents in Contact Cases in Essex* (DCA Research series 1/05, 2005).
[63] For a discussion of the stress involved, see **10.66**.
[64] Trinder, Connolly and others *A Profile of Applicants and Respondents in Contact Cases in Essex* op cit, at p v.
[65] *Making Contact Happen or Making Contact Work?* op cit, at pp 37–39.

The court process

11.37   Carol Smart[66] examined the time taken from the issue of the application for contact to the making of the last order. In her sample, just under a fifth of cases had concluded in less than 3 months, just under a half in less than 6 months and three-fifths in less than 9 months while a fifth took between 9 and 12 months, 17% between 1 and 2 years and 13% more than 2 years.[67] The researchers warn that it is important not to rush to the conclusion that cases dealt with swiftly are necessarily managed with greater efficiency. In some instances the application may be made as an emergency measure, in others one party may withdraw either the application or their opposition. Moreover the 'cost' of shorter cases is that children are rarely consulted. Rather, 'protracted' disputes, that is those which took more than 12 months, differ from those which settled earlier and it is not clear whether speedy legal solutions are possible.[68] They were marked by the following features.

- The cases tended to involve allegations of:

    - violence;
    - harassment;
    - drug use;
    - concerns over the care of children;
    - child sexual abuse;

    which changed over time, tending to become more serious with social services becoming involved. The allegations were often corroborated and the researchers do not suggest that they were exaggerations or 'strategic falsehoods' but rather that they reflect the problems facing the family.

- What seemed to be at stake was less the presenting issue and more the relationship between the parents.

- The relationship between parents remained poor.

- The non-resident parent felt that the other was obstructing contact.

- The resident parent felt that the other was irresponsible or unreliable.

11.38   In *Making Contact Happen or Making Contact Work?*[69] Trinder was primarily looking at the process of in-court conciliation. There was a high level of agreement and any variation reflected the different conciliation models rather than case characteristics. The agreements typically resulted in a

---

[66]   *Residence and Contact Disputes in Court* op cit; see **11.31**.

[67]   Smart, May, Wade and Furniss *Residence and Contact Disputes in Court* Vol 1 (DCA Research Series No 6/03, 2003), p 35. An earlier study of county courts in the west of England – Bailey-Harris and others 'Settlement Culture and the Use of the "No Order" Principle Under the Children Act 1989' (1999) CFLQ 53 – found a swifter rate of settlement, half the cases settling within three months.

[68]   Smart, May, Wade and Furniss *Residence and Contact Disputes in Court* Vol 1 op cit, chapter 4.

[69]   Op cit.

restoration and/or extension of the quantity of contact. Unsurprisingly non-resident parents were significantly more satisfied with the agreements than resident parents. There were examples of agreements resulting from pressure. It seemed that whilst parents reaching an agreement expressed fairly modest levels of satisfaction, not reaching an agreement attracts even more dissatisfaction.

11.39 Another study by Hunt and Macleod, *Outcomes of applications to court for contact orders after parental separation or divorce*[70] examined 308 cases. They found the following.[71]

- Outcomes were typically agreed. It was rare for the court to have to make a final ruling.

- Most cases ended with face-to-face contact. Where they did not this was usually because the applicant withdrew from proceedings.

- Contact typically involved at least fortnightly overnight stays with some children having additional visiting contact. Visiting contact was usually weekly or more and almost always unsupervised.

- Non-resident parents were largely successful in getting direct contact where there had been none and in getting the type of contact sought.

- Those who achieved staying contact usually got the amount they sought; those with visiting contact mainly did not. Applications to enforce previous orders were unusual and rarely wholly successful.

- Non-resident parents were almost twice as likely to succeed in getting the type of contact they wanted as resident parents who initially opposed staying, unsupervised contact or any contact.

- Four in five resident parents who opposed unsupervised contact raised serious welfare concerns.

- The initial position of the resident parent and whether they raised serious welfare issues were significantly related to outcome, as were the age of the child, whether there was any contact at the point the application was made and the interval since the child was last seen.

- There was no evidence that non-resident parents as a group were systematically unreasonably treated by the courts. On the contrary, courts start from the position that contact is generally in the interests of the child; they made great efforts to achieve this and in most instances they

---

[70] (Oxford Centre for Family Law and Policy/Ministry of Justice, 2008). Summarised in 'Courts on contact' [2008] Fam Law 1072.

[71] Summarised by the authors in *Outcomes of applications to court for contact orders after parental separation or divorce: Briefing Note.*

were successful. In a small minority of cases, however, it might be argued that the outcome was unfair to the non-resident parent.

Outcomes

Outcomes at six months

11.40   Trinder and her fellow researchers interviewed parents 6 months after the conciliation hearings. This presented a mixed picture. In some respects there had been quite a marked impact. Only a fifth of agreements did not work at all; most agreements were intact or had been extended; most cases were closed with low relitigation rates. Many more children were having more contact, more parents were satisfied with the quantity and quality of contact and parents and children were doing better than at baseline, although the overall level remained low.

> 'What is significant, instead, is having an agreement or the case being closed. It seems that having an agreement generates its own momentum, at least in the short term, and parents whose cases were closed scored better on almost all measures than parents where the court battle was ongoing or had been resurrected.'[72]

Conciliation appeared to work best with what were the less entrenched cases.

11.41   Trinder notes that although this is an impressive list of achievements, 'the analysis also highlighted real and enduring problems'. The relitigation rate was low, but the majority of cases required more professional input than a single conciliation session, raising concerns about the ongoing ability of parents to adapt arrangements to suit changing needs and circumstances.

Outcomes at two years

11.42   Trinder carried out a follow-up study 2 years after the conciliation hearing.[73] Conciliation, or at least going to court, appeared to have a marked impact on contact. Significantly more (four-fifths) children were having contact, broadly similar to the numbers of children having contact in the general population. It seemed that attending court significantly increased both the chance of overnight contact and the amount of contact.

> '[Our] analysis does suggest that there is quite a strong court effect and that the more expansive arrangements are not simply about the restoration of contact or the ageing of children.'[74]

Nevertheless approximately 10% of 'hard cases' proved resistant. Contact was more likely to be taking place if the case had been easier at the outset. The

---

[72]   Op cit, p 85.
[73]   Trinder and Kellett *The Longer-Term Outcomes of In-Court Conciliation* (Ministry of Justice Research Series 15/07, 2007).
[74]   Ibid, at p 20.

strongest determinant of the amount of contact was how much contact had been occurring before the proceedings started.[75]

11.43   Parental relationships seemed to have improved a little for about 15% of parents but the majority still reported a negative relationship which had not improved or had worsened. Shared decision-making levels remained low but the number of parents sharing major decisions had increased, this increase most likely reflecting the quality of the relationship prior to conciliation. Further litigation did not appear to have influenced relationship quality or shared decision making but being involved in a current dispute had a marked and adverse impact.[76]

11.44   Nearly half (43%) of parents reported that contact problems had improved. Problems relating to threats to stop contact, commitment and reliability dropped, disputes over money declined significantly, but half still had concerns about their ex-partner's reliability and commitment. Although contact appeared more stable, there was no real change in concerns about the ex-partner's parenting or children's reactions to 'contact transitions'. Encouragingly, there was a significant fall in the fear of violence. As in other areas, the presence of problems at the time of the conciliation tended to predict continuing problems 2 years later.[77]

11.45   There was a 'stark contrast' between levels of parent well-being which had improved remarkably (and was now at the same level as those in the general community) and child well-being. A disproportionately high number of children had borderline or abnormal scores. 'Having contact, further litigation and current adult well-being did not predict child well-being at the two-year follow-up.'[78]

11.46   Trinder was able to identify predictors for successful outcomes.

> 'Put simply, the easier cases at baseline, those with some shared decision-making and without domestic violence concerns, were more likely to reach agreement and consequently more likely to stay settled and to report improved relationships two years later. The difficult cases tended to stay difficult, regardless of whether contact was resolved or not.'[79]

Nearly half of the sample was classified as 'settled and conflicted' ie dissatisfied with contact arrangements but with some cases 'bubbling away prior to re-litigation.' More appeared to have given up on litigation as a means of resolving matters because of its perceived ineffectiveness and the financial and emotional cost. In contrast, some parents had found a way of moving on, identifying the key factors in this as the passage of time, new partnerships and

---

[75]   Ibid.
[76]   Ibid, at p 24.
[77]   Ibid, at p 28.
[78]   Ibid, at p 32.
[79]   Ibid, at p 41.

maturing children able to make their own decisions. Parents who identified the court process as helpful did so on the basis that it provided a framework for contact rather than assistance with working together.[80]

The authors concluded that:

'We now have evidence that even after two years most co-parental relationships are not improved simply by the exercise of contact. About a quarter of parents in this study reported that things were getting better but these tended to be the cases where relationships had been easier to start with. For the majority, however, co-parental relationships were competitive or non-existent, trust was low and conflict was high. Agreements and court orders alone are likely to increase significantly the chances of contact occurring but are far less likely to shift parental attitudes and behaviour.'[81]

Summary

11.47

- Many families involved in litigation have multiple problems in the relationship between parents.

- Contact following an application to court is usually agreed, not resolved by judicial decision.

- Litigation secures contact where none is taking place.

- The type of contact agreed or ordered is usually maintained or has improved by the time of follow-up.

- Post-litigation, any improvement in the relationship between parents tends to occur where there was some existing co-parenting.

- At the time of the litigation the welfare of the parents and the child is poor. Post-litigation, parents recover but children do not.

THE POLICY OF THE GOVERNMENT AND JUDICIARY

Reports

11.48 The public interest in contact disputes in recent years has been reflected not only in research projects, with major ones being sponsored by the Department for Constitutional Affairs in order to try to discover 'what works' but also by a series of influential reports, new legislation and procedural initiatives.

---

[80] Ibid, at p 49.
[81] Ibid, at p 50.

In 1999 the Children Act Sub-Committee of the Lord Chancellor's Advisory Board on Family Law, chaired by Mr Justice Wall (as he then was) issued a consultation paper on *Contact between Children and Violent Parents*.[82] The Sub-Committee reported in 2000 – *A Report to the Lord Chancellor on the Question of Parental Contact in Cases Where There is Domestic Violence*.[83] The Sub-Committee then decided to examine the wider issue of contact and a further consultation paper, *Making Contact Work: The Facilitation of Arrangements for Contact Between Children and Their Non-Residential Parents; and the Enforcement of Court Orders for Contact*[84] was published in 2001. The report, *Making Contact Work: A report to the Lord Chancellor*[85] followed in 2002.

The Government programme

11.49 In July 2004 the Government published its Green Paper *Parental Separation: Children's Needs and Parents' Responsibilities*[86] which was followed by *Parental Separation: Children's Needs and Parents' Responsibilities: Next Steps*.[87] In February 2005 the Government published the draft Children (Contact) and Adoption Bill which contains powers for making contact more effective including provisions for enforcing orders. Taken together these documents constituted a programme of reform, sharing the common aims of minimising the harmful effects on children of parental separation and promoting their welfare throughout their childhood.[88] A commentary on the programme is provided by *Family Justice: the operation of the family courts*,[89] the report of the House of Commons Constitutional Affairs Committee published in March 2005.

The foundation of *Next Steps* was clear.

> 'The Government firmly believes that both parents should continue to have a meaningful relationship with their children after separation as long as it is safe and in the child's best interests. Most parents are able to make arrangements between themselves for the care of their children.'[90]

The stated aim of the programme was to help parents make their own arrangements but 'for those who do ask the courts to decide on arrangements for their children, we intend to improve the legal services and service delivery.'

---

82   Lord Chancellor's Department.
83   Lord Chancellor's Department.
84   Lord Chancellor's Department.
85   Lord Chancellor's Department.
86   Department For Constitutional Affairs Cm 6273.
87   Cm 6273, (Department of Constitutional Affairs) summarised in [2005] Fam Law 96.
88   Ibid, Ministerial Foreword.
89   HC 116–1.
90   *Parental Separation: Children's Needs and Parents' Responsibilities: Next Steps* Cm 6273 (Department of Constitutional Affairs), Ministerial Foreword.

There were four corners to the plan: helping parents to make their own arrangements, if at all possible without litigation, through mediation if necessary; efficient and effective court processes; ensuring the safety of the child and making sure that agreed or ordered contact takes place. There were inevitably tensions between the four, for example the time required for mediation and the subsequent delay in establishing contact. Moreover, the plan attempted two separate things: to change post-separation parenting generally and to assist individual families. The Government recognises that the first must be a long-term aim.

> 'In time it needs to become socially unacceptable for one parent to impede a child's relationship with its other parent wherever it is safe and in the child's best interests. Equally it should be unacceptable that non-resident parents absent themselves from their child's development and upbringing following separation.'[91]

To this end *Next Steps* stated that the Government 'will determine the best way in which parties can be strongly encouraged to attend mediation and other alternative dispute resolution sessions'. Mediation would however not be made compulsory. 'An essential part of the process is that people come to it voluntarily and are therefore willing to participate.'[92] In parallel, advice would be provided in a number of ways and in particular through the Family Advice and Information Networks (FAInS) in order to enable parents to access a range of services, for example, mediation, through a single point of reference.[93]

11.50 In November 2004 Dame Elizabeth Butler-Sloss P issued *The Private Law Programme*, guidance to the judiciary, HM Court Service and CAFCASS managers on best practice in managing contact applications.

11.51 The *Family Justice Review Final Report*,[94] noted that only 10% of separating couples litigate contact but these disputes account for a significant number of private law applications made to court each year. It agreed that judicial determination is unavoidable in the most difficult cases 'but it tends to be a blunt instrument'. Despite the best efforts of judges, lawyers and Cafcass it concluded that 'the process of achieving a determination may itself further inflame things and court ordered arrangements are necessarily likely to be less flexible than agreements made by the parties'.[95]

The Report concentrated its recommendation about Private Law on the need to avoid litigation by education, for example, parents being given literature on the responsibilities of parenting.[96] Parents who separate should be encouraged to agree arrangements between themselves and the use of Parenting Agreements

---

91   Ibid.
92   Ibid, para 50.
93   See Walker 'FAInS – a new approach for family lawyers?' [2004] Fam Law 436.
94   (Ministry of Justice, 2011).
95   Ibid, at para 4.3. The evidence for this assertion is not cited and it does not appear to describe whether or not an occurrence of such 'inflammation' is more likely than not.
96   Ibid, at paras 4.18, 4.28e.

should be encouraged.[97] Prior to any issue of proceedings they should attend a mediation information and assessment meeting (MIAM – see **16.25**), followed, if agreement is not reached by alternative dispute resolution (ADR) such as mediation (see **16.8**) which should be centred on the best interests of the child and embody the principles of shared parental responsibility. If ADR failed to result in agreement they would then be able to apply to court.

11.52 Although the authors of the Report were in favour of shared parental responsibility[98] they opposed legislation to encourage 'shared parenting'.

> 'The evidence showed that people place different interpretations on this term, and that it is interpreted in practice by counting hours spent with each parent, disregarding the quality of the time. The thorough and detailed evidence from Australia showed the damaging consequences for many children. So we recommended that: no legislation should be introduced that creates or risks creating the perception that there is a parental right to substantially shared or equal time for both parents.'[99]

Such legislation would undermine the central principle of the Children Act 1989 that the welfare of the child is paramount.[100]

11.53 The Interim Report[101] had recommended that a statement should be inserted into legislation to reinforce the importance of the child continuing to have a meaningful relationship with both parents, alongside the need to protect the child from harm. There was disagreement about this among those responding to the Interim Report. Norgrove points to the anger that such a statement could mistakenly be seen as importing a presumption of shared time. Having considered evidence about the experience of a similar provision in Australia, the Final Report stated that:

> 'We have concluded that the core principle of the paramountcy of the welfare of the child is sufficient and that to insert any additional statements brings with it unnecessary risk for little gain. As a result, we withdraw the recommendation that a statement of 'meaningful relationship' be inserted in legislation.'

11.54 The Final Report reached a conclusion that although it is difficult to point to clear evidence either way, the terms 'residence' and 'contact' should cease to apply.

> '[A] broader, new order should be developed that would encompass all arrangements for children's care in private law. This could be termed a "child arrangements order", which would set out the arrangements for the upbringing of the child. It would focus all discussions on resolving issues related to their care,

---

97 Ibid at paras 4.12, 4.49–4.54.
98 By which they seem to mean both sharing legal responsibility and taking decisions – para 4.6 – and practical sharing of parental tasks – para 4.19.
99 Ibid, at para 4.23. See also **10.27**.
100 Ibid, at para 4.27.
101 *Family Justice Review: Interim Report* (Ministry of Justice, 2011).

rather than on labels such as residence and contact. It would of course, be necessary either in a Parenting Agreement or a court order to provide clarity on where a child would normally live and with whom a child would spend time.'[102]

Although the implications of Norgrove are still being worked out, it is difficult to see what practical difference these recommendations will make to family courts having to determine visiting arrangements between children and their non-resident parents if, despite encouragement, agreement cannot be reached.

11.55 In its *Response to the Review*,[103] the Government rejected the Norgrove position that a statement about the importance of 'an ongoing relationship' should not be enshrined in legislation.

> 'Both Governments believe that children benefit from both parents being as fully involved as possible in their child's upbringing, unless there are safety or welfare concerns ... the Government believes that there should be a legislative statement of the importance of children having an ongoing relationship with both their parents after family separation, where that is safe, and in the child's best interests.'[104]

It would however be mindful of the lessons which must be learnt from the Australian experience.

> 'We will therefore consider very carefully how legislation can be framed to avoid the pitfalls of the Australian experience, in particular that a meaningful relationship is not about equal division of time, but the quality of parenting received by the child.'[105]

THE LAW

Contact orders

11.56 Under s 10(1) of the Children Act 1989 in any family proceedings in which a question arises with respect to the welfare of any child, the court may make a contact order if an application for such an order is made or if it considers that the order should be made even though no such application has been made. A 'contact order' means an order requiring the person with whom a child lives, or is to live, to allow the child to visit or stay with the person named in the order, or for that person and the child otherwise to have contact with each other.[106]

11.57 A contact order can be made only if it is attached to a residence order by which the child is to live with the person who is ordered to allow the child

---

[102] Ibid, at para 4.60.
[103] *The Government Response to the Family Justice Review* Cm 8273 (Ministry of Justice/Department for Education, 2012).
[104] Ibid, at paras 59 and 61.
[105] Ibid, para 62.
[106] CA 1989, s 8(1).

contact with another[107] or if it is agreed where the child should live.[108] Nothing in the Act gives a court power to order the child to live with a person or to spend time with a person other than by way of a residence order or contact order respectively.[109]

The test

11.58 The test is the s 1 welfare test and the checklist must be applied.

Contact activity directions

11.59 Sections 11A–11B of the 1989 Act provide that where the court is considering whether to make provision about contact with a child by making, varying or discharging a contact order which is not an exempted order[110] and there is a dispute as regards the provision which should be made,[111] it may make a contact activity direction in connection with that provision about contact.[112]

11.60 A contact activity direction is a direction requiring an individual who is a party to the proceedings to take part in an activity that promotes contact with the child concerned.[113] The individual cannot be a child unless the individual is a parent of the child in relation to whom the court is considering provision about contact.[114]

The direction must specify the activity and the person providing the activity.[115]

Contact activity directions are the prelude to making a contact order and not an adjunct to such an order. A court may not on the same occasion make a contact activity direction and dispose finally of the proceedings as they relate to contact with the child concerned.[116] For contact activity conditions imposed post-contact orders, see **11.78**.

The activities

11.61 The activities that may be required include, in particular:

(a) programmes, classes and counselling or guidance sessions of a kind that:

---

[107] *Re B (A Child: Contact)* [2001] EWCA Civ 1968; *Re S (Contact Order)* [2010] EWCA Civ 705, [2011] 1 FLR 183.
[108] *Re H (Contact: Adverse Findings of Fact)* [2011] EWCA Civ 585, [2011] 2 FLR 1201.
[109] *Re S (Contact Order)* [2010] EWCA Civ 705, [2011] 1 FLR 183.
[110] Ie many orders involving adoption; CA 1989, ss 11B(3), (5).
[111] Ibid, s 11B(1).
[112] Ibid, s 11A(1)
[113] Ibid, s 11A(3).
[114] Ibid, s 11B(2).
[115] Ibid, s 11A(4).
[116] Ibid, s 11A(7).

(i)   may assist a person as regards establishing, maintaining or improving contact with a child;

(ii)   may, by addressing a person's violent behaviour, enable or facilitate contact with a child;

(b)   sessions in which information or advice is given as regards making or operating arrangements for contact with a child, including making arrangements by means of mediation.[117]

However, no one may be required to undergo medical or psychiatric examination, assessment or treatment or to take part in mediation.[118]

Care needs to be taken before any information is communicated to providers. The court's permission is required before court documents including reports are sent.[119] However, where the activity is to allow the party making the disclosure to receive counselling, consent is not required.[120]

The test

11.62 When considering whether to make a contact activity direction, the welfare of the child concerned is to be the court's paramount consideration.[121]

Before making a contact activity direction the court must satisfy itself that:

•   the activity proposed is appropriate in the circumstances of the case;

•   the person proposed as the provider of the activity is suitable to provide the activity;

•   the activity proposed is provided in a place to which the individual who would be subject to the direction can reasonably be expected to travel.[122]

11.63 The court must also obtain and consider information about the individual who would be subject to the direction (or the condition) and the likely effect of the direction (or the condition) on him.[123] It may, in particular, include information as to:

(a)   any conflict with the individual's religious beliefs;

(b)   any interference with the times (if any) at which he normally works or attends an educational establishment.

---

117   Ibid, s 11A(5).
118   Ibid, s 11A(6).
119   *A v Payne and Williams; A v G and N* [2009] EWHC 736 (Fam), [2009] 2 FLR 463.
120   FPR 2010, PD 12G, para 2.1.
121   CA 1989, s 11A(9).
122   Ibid, s 11E(1)–(4).
123   Ibid, s 11E(5).

The court may ask an officer of Cafcass to provide the court with information as to the above matters and the officer must comply with the request.[124]

Finance

11.64 The Secretary of State may by regulations make provision authorising him to make payments to assist individuals subject to a contact activity direction in paying relevant charges or fees.[125] All fees have been scrapped for PIPS (see **11.66**).

Monitoring

11.65 The court may on making the direction ask an officer of Cafcass:

(a) to monitor, or arrange for the monitoring of, the individual's compliance with the direction;

(b) to report to the court on any failure by the individual to comply with the direction;

and the officer must comply with the request.[126]

Parenting Information Programmes

11.66 The *Separated Parents Information Programme*, otherwise known as Parenting Information Programmes (PIPs) are one example of contact activity programmes. The programmes are designed to improve parents' awareness of the potential impact their dispute has on their children, and to improve their relationship with each other to reach amicable agreements about their children's future care, without the continued involvement of the courts. In 2010–11 there were 102 providers delivering the programmes, with coverage across England good in most areas.[127]

11.67 In 2010–11 more than 13,000 parents attended PIPs, compared to fewer than 1,000 in 2009–10. In this year Cafcass provided £2,457 million worth of PIPs, as well as commissioning £2,400 million worth of services and grants to external providers to help families to improve their relationships following separation or divorce.[128]

11.68 PIPs are not suitable for cases involving domestic violence, where there are serious mental health issues or substance abuse.[129]

---

[124] CA 1989, s 11E(7).
[125] Ibid, s 11F(1).
[126] Ibid, s 11G.
[127] Cafcass Annual Report 2010/11 p 17.
[128] Ibid.
[129] Dancey and Jones *Contact Activities: Parenting Information Programmes* [2010] Fam Law 1101, at p 1102.

11.69   PIPs normally comprise two group sessions totalling four hours. They are available both during the evening and day time. To provide different perspectives, groups are mixed to include both male and female participants, applicants and respondents. The parties do not attend the same sessions.

The content of the programme is determined nationally by Cafcass/ Department for Education and involves a mix of exercises and discussions interlinked by a workbook. According to DJ Dancey and Roni Jones of Relate, perhaps the part of the programme with the greatest emotional impact is a video of a family going through separation, with child actors commenting on the experience.

> 'Parents find this powerful and for many it is the first time they have been enabled to see their family situation through the eyes of the child. It is a mantra of the programme that making small changes encourages change in the other parent – you cannot make another change but you can be responsible for your own input.'[130]

11.70   Research into PIPs[131] was carried out in 2010. The results of the evaluation are mixed. Whilst participants' experience of attending a PIP tends to be very positive, this does not necessarily translate into mutually satisfactory contact arrangements regarding the child. The main findings[132] were:

- Just over a third (38%) of participants thought participation improved their ability to discuss issues with their ex-partner. Just under half (46%) thought they had a better understanding of their ex-partner's perspective.

- Less than one-tenth (8%) thought the PIP played a 'big' role in reaching an agreement. Twice as many said it had played 'some' role.

- Less than one tenth (8%) of respondents who were previously having no contact with their child started to have some contact attendance at a PIP. One in 20 (6%) parents said they were happy with the agreement in place.

- The evidence indicates that PIPs are most effective when they are undertaken early but PIPs can have a good impact on older cases as well.

- PIPs are more effective in improving contact where there was no arrangement in place before the parent participated in a PIP.

The authors concluded that:

---

130   Ibid, at p 1103.
131   Trinder, Bryson, Coleman and others *Building bridges? An evaluation of the costs and effectiveness of the Separated Parents Information Programme (PIP)* (Department for Education Research eport DFE-RR140, 2011) summarised in Trinder, Smith, Bryson and others 'The Separated Parent Information Programme: Current effectiveness and future potential' [2011] Fam Law 998.
132   As summarised in the Brief version of the Report.

'It is clear that the programme resonates with many parents and that, despite initial reservations, most parents report finding the experience of attending a parenting programme entirely acceptable and generally supportive. Parents were positive about the purpose and focus of the programme, the group interaction and the way the programme was facilitated.'

11.71 However, the findings of the impact study offered a more sober estimate of the effectiveness of the programme when compared to the standard non-PIP case pathways. Participation had a positive impact on contact rates of about 8%, seemingly by converting 'no contact' into some, but not frequent, contact. It did not seem to have any impact on the quality of the parental relationship.

11.72 Their recommendations included the following.

- PIPs should be made available at an earlier stage. It should be voluntary self-referral and linked with mediation as a mandatory step before proceedings in appropriate cases.

- More effective and systematic screening and assessment is required.

- More attention needs to be paid to ensuring that all parents have full, clear and accurate explanations about PIPs before attending the course.[133]

- The process for transferring information to providers requires attention. Some courts have devised forms that could be developed into a standard form.

- A single national collection and allocation point should be considered.

- The aims and content of the PIP should be reviewed to ensure a more focused programme which could address different needs. The course materials should be available in a range of languages.

- More effective mechanisms are needed for follow up and to provide a bridge between the PIP and the dispute resolution process.

The Family Justice Review[134] supported these recommendations. It added that suitability assessment for PIPs, currently carried out as part of the court process, should form part of the mediation assessment as happens in Australia. It was not necessary or even appropriate for Cafcass to carry out safeguarding checks before attendance at PIPs. However, mediators would need training to identify risks when carrying out MIAMs.[135]

---

[133] See for example, *Separated Parents Information Programme* (Cafcass) www.cafcass.gov.uk/publications.
[134] Op cit, at para 4.89.
[135] See **5.39**.

Domestic violence

11.73 A party is not expected to attend a MIAM where there are allegations of domestic violence (see **5.40**) and similar caution is necessary when considering whether to give Contact Activity Directions.

Conditions

11.74 Section 11(7) of the Children Act 1989 allows a contact order to contain directions about how it is to be carried out and to impose conditions which must be complied with by any person:

(1)　in whose favour the order is made;

(2)　who is a parent of the child concerned;

(3)　who has parental responsibility for the child; or

(4)　with whom the child is living.

The conditions or their provisions can be made to have effect for a specified period.

11.75 Commonly imposed conditions deal with the manner in which the child is to be collected from and returned to the residential parent. It may be appropriate to include a condition that the visiting parent arrives promptly at the beginning of contact and returns the child promptly at the end of contact in order to avoid concern to the resident parent and anxiety to the child about whether contact will take place. If the resident parent is going to incur cost in taking the child to the place where contact is to start, a condition can be imposed as to who will pay the travel costs.[136] Where there is dispute about the aspects of the contact which the court has still to resolve or which have been resolved by agreement, other conditions may also be imposed, for example, about who may or may not come into contact with the child during contact and the manner in which the child is to be transported ('only when strapped into an approved toddler seat') or the food he may not be given. This may be a dietary necessity, for example the child having a nut allergy, a religious necessity (the child eating only kosher food) or, for example, to prevent the child being poisoned, as in cases of Fictitious (and Induced) Illness by Proxy (FII) (formerly known as Münchausen's Syndrome by Proxy).[137]

11.76 In order to alleviate a subjective fear on the part of a parent with care that the child may be abducted during contact, it may be appropriate to impose

---

[136]　*Re O (A Minor) (Contact: Imposition of Conditions)* [1995] 2 FLR 124, per Swinton Thomas LJ at 135.

[137]　See *DH (A Minor) (Child Abuse)* [1994] 1 FLR 679. For an account of a case involving FII and guidance on the forensic strategy to be adopted, see *A County Council v A Mother, A Father and X, Y and Z (By Their Guardian)* [2005] EWHC 31 (Fam), [2005] 2 FLR 129.

a condition that the non-resident parent deposits his passport with a responsible person, such as a party's solicitor, during contact.[138] Courts should not agree to retain passports because it lacks the means for keeping them secure. If there is an objective risk of abduction, the court will have to consider whether there is a means of sufficiently reducing the risk and this may include conditions for the retention of the non-resident parent's passport and directions that he or she not apply for passports to be issued on behalf of the child. See also **9.73**.

11.77 A condition such as 'the children have to decide for each contact whether to take it up or not' is a highly unusual provision and burdens them with a responsibility that 'they should not be asked to bear at the ages of 12 and 13'.[139]

Contact activity conditions

11.78 Section 11C permits a court, when making or varying a contact order which is not an exempted order,[140] to impose a condition requiring the person with whom the child concerned lives or is to live, the person whose contact with the child is provided for in the order, or a person upon whom that order imposes a condition under s 11(7)(b) (see above), to take part in an activity that promotes contact with the child concerned).

However a contact activity condition may not be imposed on an individual who is a child unless the individual is a parent of the child concerned.[141] Nor may such a condition be imposed unless the individual is habitually resident in England and Wales. A condition ceases to have effect if the individual ceases to be so habitually resident.[142]

The requirements and provisions made by sections 11E, F and the monitoring provisions made by s 11G in respect of contact activity directions (see **11.65**) also apply to contact activity conditions. Also see **11.61** for the disclosure of information to providers.

11.79 Conditions should be imposed only if there is a dispute between the parties on the issue and the court needs to resolve the issue in order to try to avoid the dispute continuing. In deciding the content of the condition, the court has to tread a delicate path between not interfering with the visiting parent's autonomy in deciding how to look after his own child and the resident

---

[138] See, for example, *R v P (Contact: Abduction: Supervision)* [2008] EWHC 937 (Fam), [2008] 2 FLR 936t.

[139] *Re S (Contact: Intractable Dispute)* [2010] EWCA Civ 447, [2010] 2 FLR 1517, per Thorpe LJ at [2].

[140] CA 1989, s 11D(2); see **11.59**.

[141] Ibid, s 11D(1).

[142] Ibid, s 11D(3).

parent's reasonable concerns that her standard of care is maintained. As Sir Thomas Bingham MR said in *Re O (A Minor) (Contact: Imposition of Conditions)*:[143]

> 'It is not, however, as I think, for the court to act as governess in these matters, but where possible to enable the parties to work out their own salvation.'

Conditions imposed in relation to indirect contact are discussed at **11.135**.

Monitoring contact

11.80 Section 11H makes provision for contact orders to be monitored. When the court makes or varies a contact order which is not an exempted order[144] or at any time during the subsequent course of the proceedings as they relate to contact with the child concerned,[145] it may ask a Cafcass officer:

(a)   to monitor whether the person who is required by the order to allow contact or is named as the person having contact with the child complies with the order or on whom a contact condition has been imposed;

(b)   to report to the court on such matters relating to the individual's compliance as the court may specify.[146]

If the contact order includes a contact activity condition, the request is to be treated as relating to the provisions of the order other than the contact activity condition.[147] The court may also order any individual specified above to take such steps as may be specified with a view to enabling the officer to comply with the court's request.[148] However, it may not make such an order with respect to an individual who is a child unless he is a parent of the child with respect to whom the order was made.[149]

The officer must comply with any request.[150]

Supervised contact

11.81 When direct contact carries a risk of harm to the children which can be moderated or removed by the contact being supervised by a third party, a court can impose a condition that the contact be supervised. Sometimes the risk is such that limited supervision such as that provided at 'supported' Contact Centres (see below) will be sufficient. Sometimes much closer supervision is

---

143   [1995] 2 FLR 124, at 131.
144   See **11.59**.
145   CA 1989, s 11H(5).
146   Ibid, s 11H(2), (3).
147   Ibid, s 11H(4).
148   Ibid, s 11H(8).
149   Ibid, s 11H(9).
150   Ibid, s 11H(7).

required (for example if there is a risk of the child being abused) when either contact at a supervised Contact Centre or supervision by a nominated third person will be necessary. While a Cafcass officer may be an appropriate supervisor for a few introductory visits (see above), the court ought not to impose an open-ended obligation to supervise in the absence of special circumstances and the agreement of Cafcass. Nor should a family assistance order be used solely to provide a supervisor.[151] The supervisor must be told about the reason supervision is being imposed and must be made aware of any restrictions imposed on the contact.

Supervision from Cafcass or a specialist organisation may be of considerable importance in offering help and guidance to reduce, if not eliminate, anger in one of both parents of children where the relationship has broken down.[152]

Family Assistance Orders

11.82 In some cases an order for more formal supervision by way of a family assistance order may be required. See **Chapter 13**.

CONTACT CENTRES

11.83 There are about 350 Centres which subscribe to the National Association of Child Contact Centres (NACCC) Code of Practice. This defines Centres as neutral meeting places where children of a separated family can enjoy contact with one or both parents and sometimes other family members in a comfortable and safe environment where there is no viable alternative. In the main, they are staffed by volunteers, although a few are run by Social Services or Cafcass.[153]

What are Contact Centres?

11.84 The distinction between 'supported contact centres' and 'supervised contact centres' is very important. Most Centres provide only 'supported' contact which involves low vigilance with several families in the same room at a time. Doors to all rooms remain open for observation but conversations are not monitored. However, a few Centres provide 'supervised' contact with high vigilance and only one family in a room at once. Conversations are monitored and behaviour is closely observed. Issues arising from the visit are addressed at a later stage. Two-way mirrors may be used.

All Centres affiliated to the NACCC are based on the premises that:

- contact is child-centred;

---

[151] *S v P (Contact Application: Family Assistance Order)* [1997] 2 FLR 277.
[152] *Re W (Contact)* [2007] EWCA Civ 753, [2007] 2 FLR 1122, at [15].
[153] For further guidance on the use of Centres, see *Family Law Protocol* (3rd edn, The Law Society, 2010).

- impartiality is fundamental;

- Centres operate a confidentiality policy;

- Centres will have a complaints procedure.

The basic elements of supported contact are:

- Impartiality.

- Staff and volunteers are available for practical assistance (for example calming a tearful child) and keeping a watchful eye. They do not monitor or evaluate individual contact/conversations.

- Several families are usually together in one or a number of rooms.

- Families are encouraged to develop mutual trust and consider more satisfactory family venues.

- Apart from confirmation of attendance dates and times, no report will be made to a referrer, Cafcass, a party's solicitor or court.

- Supported child contact centre staff and volunteers are not available to be called as witnesses unless it is a criminal matter.

- It is acknowledged that the supported child contact centre is a temporary arrangement, to be reviewed after an agreed period of time.[154]

How are Centres used?

11.85 In 2011 over 15,000 children from 9,000 families used a Centre. The majority of children attend to see a parent after the parents have separated, but many meet grandparents, siblings or parents following care proceedings. Research carried out in 1998 into a cross-section of Centres by Clare Furniss[155] found that a stereotypical view of users – white, lower class, probably unemployed, poor, children living with their mother and using the Centre to see their father – was not borne out. There were a significant number of people from different ethnic backgrounds. Ten per cent of non-resident parents were mothers with the children living with their fathers. The background of users ranged from the unemployed to professional classes. About half the children were under 5, 85% were 8 or under and about 6% were 11 or older.

---

[154] *Revised Protocoal for Referrals of Families to Supported Child Contact Centres by Judges and Magistrates* [2010] Fam Law 858.
[155] Furniss 'The process of referral to a Family Contact Centre: Policy and practice' [2000] CFLQ 255.

11.86 While it is generally accepted that Centres are a short-term provision enabling families to move to contact away from the Centres, Furniss found that there were long-term users with the following characteristics:

- special circumstances, such as mental illness, drug or alcohol dependency, on the part of the visiting parent;

- cases which had been allowed to drift;

- cases which were taking a greater than average time to reach a final court hearing.

Most resident parents told Furniss they did not trust the non-resident parents and had agreed to contact at a Centre because of a perceived element of control. Most thought the Centre was safe. Both resident and non-resident parents described being in conflict with the other parent and only a small proportion could talk to the other parent about their children. A period of time at a Centre seemed to have little effect on improving communication between parents and some spoke of their fears at contact taking place away from the centre. However, the limited research which Furniss was able to conduct about contact after the use of the Centre stopped suggests that over two-thirds of parents may still have direct contact at least 6 months later.

11.87 Centres rely on the goodwill of volunteers and their resources are limited. Although doors remain open, visiting rooms are monitored and the volunteers will intervene if a child shows distress, contact is not usually supervised. Centres operate a policy of confidentiality. Of necessity, therefore, the use of Centres is limited to the primary aim of providing facilities for contact.

How should Centres be used?

11.88 Centres are not always suitable where there has been domestic violence or there are child protection issues and should not be used for such cases.[156] Centre co-ordinators expect referrers to screen out those cases which are too difficult or volatile for Centres to handle. They also need information on family backgrounds, including warnings of potential violence and convictions relating to abuse. For a discussion on Contact Centres and domestic violence see **5.83**.

11.89 Centres will rarely provide reports for the court, although most are willing to confirm details from their register as to who attended and when.

> 'Contact Centres are neutral venues for use in situations where it has been agreed or ordered that it is in the child's best interests to have contact. The volunteers are not qualified to give opinions about family relationships. Their role is to provide the facilities to enable contact to happen when there are practical or other obstacles to contact taking place. If there are serious doubts about whether a child

---

[156] Dame Elizabeth Butler-Sloss P 'Contact and Domestic Violence' [2001] Fam Law 355.

would benefit from contact, given the history, then a referral to a supported contact centre is inappropriate. It may be appropriate to refer the family to a supervised centre but to make other arrangements for therapy, assessments and reports if they are also required.'[157]

The President of the Family Division, Sir Nicholas Wall has said that:

'Supported child contact centres are integral to the better working of the wider family justice system. It is crucial that they are used appropriately. This means that the safety of the children being referred, the other families using the centre as well as the staff and volunteers must be considered before an order is made. They offer a voluntary service and must be able to decide whether to accept or refuse a referral. Furthermore, courts recognise that supported contact centres are charities and nearly all the staff are volunteers. They can only undertake their work if free of any risk of being drawn into individual cases or disputes. Accordingly courts and parties will not require or seek their involvement in resolving disputes, writing reports, noting events or attending, in any capacity, any family court hearing.'[158]

Protocol

11.90   There is a *Protocol for Referrals of Families to Supported Child Contact Centres by Family Courts*.[159] Before making an order for contact at a supported contact centre courts should ensure the following steps have been taken.

- The question of whether referral to a supported as opposed to a supervised contact centre is appropriate must be addressed where any one or a combination of the following are present:

  (a)   domestic violence;
  (b)   drug or substance misuse;
  (c)   alcohol misuse;
  (d)   mental illness.

- The child contact centre co-ordinator has been contacted and should have confirmed that:

  (a)   The centre is an accredited member of NACCC.
  (b)   The referral appears to be suitable for that particular centre, subject to a satisfactory pre-visit or equivalent. (In line with its safeguarding policy a supported child contact centre can refuse to accept families if the circumstances appear to them to be inappropriate for the centre.)
  (c)   The intended day and times are available at the particular centre concerned.

---

[157]   Halliday 'Reports to courts by Contact Centres – why they rarely happen' [1999] Fam Law 112. Eunice Halliday was the Director of the NACCC.
[158]   *Revised Protocol for Referrals of Families to Supported Child Contact Centres by Judges and Magistrates* op cit, at p 858.
[159]   Ibid.

(d)   A vacancy is available or a place on a waiting list has been allocated.

- The Court should direct that a copy of the order is provided to the centre by one or other of the parties within a specified time together with any other injunctive or relevant orders on the court file.

- It has been agreed who will have responsibility for completing and returning the centre's referral form. Solicitors for both parties should agree the contents and it should be forwarded to the child contact centre within 24 hours of the court hearing.

- It has been confirmed that the parties understand that the child contact centre offers supported contact only; and that parties and their solicitors are aware that apart from attendance dates and times, no report will be made to a referrer, Cafcass, a party's solicitor or court; and that the parties understand that the centre staff and volunteers are not available to be called as witnesses unless it is a criminal matter.

- If contact is to be observed at the child contact centre by a Cafcass officer or other third party it has been confirmed in advance that this is a facility offered by that centre and that the centre has agreed to this course of action. Many do not permit such attendance.

- Where there may be a communication problem related to language, it has been confirmed that arrangements have been made for the provision of an independent interpreter. This is not the responsibility of the supported child contact centre.

- The order clearly defines whether or not any other family members are to be a part of the contact visit.

- It has been agreed who is going to tell the children where and when they will see their non-resident parent.

- It has been agreed who will be responsible for informing the centre when the place is no longer required.

- A date has been set for a review of contact, including the use of the supported child contact centre and of any other steps parties have been ordered or undertaken to take which are relevant to contact and for further directions if necessary. Only in exceptional circumstances should an order be made allowing for the open-ended use of a supported child contact centre.

The order should be worded 'Subject to the parties attendance at a pre-contact meeting or equivalent, the availability of a place and the parties abiding by the rules of the centre ...'

The form of the order

11.91 It is important for purposes of enforcement that the order states precisely what it is that the resident parent is required to do[160] and it needs to be drafted for the specific circumstances of each case. A sample order might read:

> '[Name] shall ensure that [name of child] has contact with [name of non resident parent] every Saturday from [time] until [time], the first contact to take place on [date]. [Name] shall deliver [name of child] to [name of non resident parent] at [place] promptly at the start of contact and shall collect [him] from the same place at the end of contact.'

For a detailed discussion of the importance of this, see **23.19**.

11.92 Where the court makes (or varies) a contact order, it has to attach to the contact order (or the order varying the contact order) a notice warning of the consequences of failing to comply.[161] See for the terms of the notice **23.18**.

THE COURTS' APPROACH TO CONTACT

11.93 In the leading case of *Re O (A Minor) (Contact: Imposition of Conditions)*,[162] Sir Thomas Bingham MR set out the 'very familiar but nonetheless fundamental' principles which apply to contact cases. These are reproduced in Appendix 4.

- The welfare of the child is the paramount consideration. The court is concerned with the interests of the mother and the father only in so far as they bear on the welfare of the child:

> 'Where the parents have separated and one has the care of the child, access by the other often results in some upset to the child. Those upsets are usually minor and superficial. They are heavily outweighed by the long term advantages to the child of keeping in touch with the parent concerned so that they do not become strangers, so that the child in later life does not resent the deprivation and turn against the parent who the child thinks, rightly or wrongly, has deprived him and so that the deprived parent loses interest in the child and therefore does not make the material and emotional contribution to the child's development which that parent by its companionship and otherwise would make.'[163]

> 'But before concluding this judgment I would like to make three general points. The first is that judges should be very reluctant to allow the

---

[160] *Re S-C (Contempt)* [2010] EWCA Civ 21, [2010] 1 FLR 1478, per Wall LJ at [17] and *Re L-W (Enforcement and Committal: Contact); CPL v CH-W* [2010] EWCA Civ 1253, [2011] 1 FLR 1095, per Munby LJ at [34].

[161] CA 1989, s 11I.

[162] [1995] 2 FLR 124.

[163] *M v M (Child: Access)* [1973] 2 All ER 81, per Latey J at 87.

implacable hostility of one parent (usually the parent who has a residence order in his or her favour), to deter them from making a contact order where they believe the child's welfare requires it. The danger of allowing the implacable hostility of the residential parent (usually the mother) to frustrate the court's decision is too obvious to require repetition on my part.'[164]

- The court should not hesitate to exercise its powers to enforce orders for contact where it judges that it will promote the welfare of the child overall to do so.

- A court may be compelled to conclude that in existing circumstances, an order for immediate contact should not be ordered, because to so order would injure the welfare of the child. However, it should not at all readily accept that the child's welfare will be injured by direct contact. A medium-term view should be taken and excessive weight should not be accorded to what appears likely to be short-term or transient problems. Neither parent should be encouraged or permitted to think that the more intransigent, the more unreasonable:

  'Courts should remember that in these cases they are dealing with parents who are adults, who must be treated as rational adults, who must be assumed to have the welfare of the child at heart, and who have once been close enough to each other to have produced the child. It would be as well if parents were also to bear these points in mind.'[165]

- If direct contact cannot for the time being be ordered, it is usually very desirable that there should be indirect contact. This calls for a measure of restraint, common sense and unselfishness on the part of both parents. The object of indirect contact is to build up a relationship with the absent parent and the child, not to enable the absent parent to pursue a feud with the caring parent in a manner not conducive to the welfare of the child. It is entirely reasonable that a parent with the care of the child should be obliged to report on the progress of the child to the absent parent but judges must not impose duties which parents cannot reasonably be expected to perform:

  'Some means of communication, directly or indirectly, is essential if indirect contact is to be meaningful, and if the welfare of the child is not to suffer.'[166]

Since the introduction of the Human Rights Act 1998, Sir Thomas Bingham's comment that 'It cannot be emphasised too strongly that the court is concerned with the interests of the mother and the father only in so far as they bear on the welfare of the child' needs some modification. Under the welfare principle, the welfare of the child is paramount but the

---

[164] *Re J (A Minor) (Contact)* [1994] 1 FLR 729, per Balcombe LJ at 736B–C.
[165] *Re O (A Minor) (Contact: Imposition of Conditions)* [1995] 2 FLR 124, per Sir Thomas Bingham MR at 130.
[166] Ibid.

rights of both parents to respect for their private and family life under Art 8 have to be respected. However, as *Hendriks v Netherlands*[167] makes clear, where these rights conflict with the welfare of the child, the welfare of the child prevails in all cases where this is proportionate to any risk involved.

IS THERE A PRESUMPTION OF CONTACT?[168]

11.94 Sturge and Glaser argue that 'the purpose of any proposed contact must be overt and abundantly clear. Contact can only be an issue where it has the potential for benefiting the child in some way'. As a bald statement, this does not represent the present legal position either as set out in Convention law or domestic authorities. Article 8 of the European Convention on Human Rights affords parents the right to contact with their child unless the welfare of the child requires otherwise and the limitation of contact is proportional to the harm to be avoided:

'Respect for family life within the meaning of Article 8 thus implies that this contact should not be denied unless there are strong reasons ... which justify such an interference.'[169]

11.95 In domestic law, courts have repeatedly stated that a refusal of contact to a parent must be justified. For example, *M v M (Child: Access)*:[170]

'No court should deprive a child of access to either parent unless it was wholly satisfied that it was in the interests of the child that access should cease, and that was a conclusion at which the court should be extremely slow to arrive.'

Alternatively, see Waite LJ in *Re D (A Minor) (Contact: Mother's Hostility)*:[171]

'[Are there] any cogent reasons why this child should, exceptionally, be denied the opportunity of access to his father[?]'

11.96 Is there, then, a presumption of contact? In Scotland, s 3(2) of the Law Reform (Parent and Child) (Scotland) Act 1986 expressly states that 'the court shall regard the welfare of the child involved as paramount and shall not make any order relating parental rights unless it is satisfied that to do so will be in the interests of the child'. So, no presumption there; but in *S v M (Access*

---

167   (1983) 5 EHRR 233.
168   For an academic discussion of the issue, see Bailey-Harris and others 'From Utility to Rights? The Presumption of Contact in Practice' (1999) *International Journal of Law, Policy and the Family* vol 13, p 111, Kaganas and Sclater 'Contact and Domestic Violence – The Winds of Change? [2000] Fam Law 630, Bailey-Harris 'Contact – Challenging Conventional Wisdom' [2001] CFLQ 361. See also **Chapter 1**.
169   *Hendriks v Netherlands* (1983) 5 EHRR 233.
170   [1973] 2 All ER 81.
171   [1993] 2 FLR 1.

Order)[172] Lord Hope of Craighead left open the question about what the common law was. In England and Wales, there was a presumption in waiting. Section 11(4) of the Family Law Act 1996 required the court to have particular regard to 'the general principle that, in the absence of evidence to the contrary, the welfare of the child will best be served by his having regular contact with those who have parental responsibility for him'. But that section was never brought into force and the statutory presumption died when the Act was repealed.

11.97 There are decisions in English and Welsh courts which specifically use the word 'presumption'. In *M v M (Child: Access)*,[173] for example, in 1973, Wrangham J spoke of a 'very strong presumption in favour of maintaining contact between the child and both parents'. There has been a gradual change in terminology. In *Re M (Contact: Welfare Test)*,[174] Wilson J in the Court of Appeal spoke of 'the fundamental need of *every* child to have an enduring relationship with both parents' (my emphasis). In *Re L, V, M, H*, the President referred to 'the general principle that contact with the non-resident parent is in the interests of the child'.[175] In the same case, however, Thorpe LJ adopted a different approach and summarised the authorities in this way:

'So whilst some comparative study demonstrates a spectrum from rights through presumption to simple application of the welfare principle the significance of the distinction is reduced by what appears to be universal judicial recognition of the importance of contact to the child's development'.[176]

He pointed out that any benefit of contact will vary according to the circumstances of each case:

'I would not assume the benefit with unquestioning confidence where a child has developed over its early years without knowledge of the father, particularly if over these crucially formative years a psychological attachment to an alternative father has been achieved.'

He added that:

'There is a danger that the identification of a presumption will inhibit or distort the rigorous search for the welfare solution. There is also a danger that a presumption may be used as an aid to determination when the individual advocate or judge feels either undecided or overwhelmed.'

11.98 The current answer to the question: 'Is there a presumption that contact is of benefit for every child?' therefore appears to be 'No'.[177] The court has to decide what is in the best interests of *this* child, bearing in mind all the

---

[172] [1997] 1 FLR 980.
[173] [1973] 2 All ER 81.
[174] [1995] 1 FLR 274, at 278.
[175] [2000] 2 FLR 334, at 341.
[176] Ibid, at 364.
[177] See also Gillmore 'Disputing contact: Challenging some assumptions' [2008] CFLQ 285.

circumstances of the case, those factors set out in the welfare checklist and the Art 8 rights of all those concerned. Where there is evidence of the needs of the child who is the subject of the application, derived from a CAFCASS report, expert evidence or that deduced from factual evidence, the emotional needs of the child will be determined in the light of that evidence. Where there is insufficient evidence, the court will take judicial knowledge of the general proposition that contact with a non-residential parent is often beneficial to a child. However, as illustrated by the Sturge/Glaser report, contact may carry different types of benefits as well as different kinds of disadvantage.

11.99 The *Family Justice Review*[178] emphasised its view that children 'benefit from a relationship with both parents post separation' where this is safe.

> 'The question is how best to achieve this without inadvertently encouraging arrangements which involve frequent changes of carer or home for a very young child, or exposing children to ongoing parental conflict. In particular the issue for us was to recommend what role the law and the courts should play.'

As noted at **11.52** it did not accept that there should be a presumption of contact.

> 'We remain firm in our view that any legislation that might risk creating an impression of a parental "right" to any particular amount of time with a child would undermine the central principle of the Children Act 1989 that the welfare of the child is paramount.'[179]

IS THERE A PRESUMPTION OF EQUAL CONTACT?

11.100 The Government Green Paper, *Parental Separation: Children's Needs and Parents' Responsibilities*[180] sought views on whether or not a presumption of contact should be introduced to give parents equal rights to equal time with their child after separation. However, it also expressed the view that it did not believe that an 'automatic 50:50' division of the child's time between the two parents would be in the best interests of most parents.

> 'In many separated families, such arrangements would not work in practical terms, owing to living arrangements or work commitments. Enforcing this type of arrangement through legislation would not be what many children want and could have a damaging impact on some of them. Children are not a commodity to be apportioned equally after separation. The best arrangements for them will depend on a variety of issues particular to their circumstances: a one-size-fits-all formula will not work.'[181]

Gillmore argues that unless courts emphasise that there is a respect for contact between the child and the non-resident parent as an element for respect for family life, they should avoid any assumption that contact is beneficial.

[178] Op cit, at para 4.22.
[179] Ibid, at para 4.27.
[180] Cm 6273 (2004).
[181] Ibid, para 42.

In its response the Government stated that it was not persuaded that any fundamental change to the principles of the CA 1989 would benefit children.[182] The House of Commons Constitutional Affairs Committee took the same view.[183]

There is currently no presumption of equal time and in 2008 the senior judiciary were opposed to one being introduced, pointing out that such a presumption would be in opposition to the welfare presumption of CA 1989, s 1.[184]

The support which some give the presumption is reflected in an increase of interest in the concept of 'shared residence' (see **10.15**).

The *Family Justice Review*[185] did not support any presumption of equal time being introduced into legislation.[186]

For the Government's position, see **11.55**.

CAN A PARENT BE COMPELLED TO HAVE CONTACT?

11.101 A parent with whom the child is living, far from wanting to stop contact, may want the court to direct that an unwilling parent sees the child. The court, however, has no power to make such an order no matter, in the words of Thorpe LJ, 'how much the child may yearn for his company and the mother desire respite'.[187] A contact order is an order which 'requires the person with whom a child lives'[188] to allow contact between the child and a named person. It is not an order requiring a named person to have contact. As Wall J said in *Re M (A Minor) (Contact: Conditions)*,[189] 'orders for ... contact are permissive and not mandatory'.

11.102 Julie Wallbank has noted the disparity in approach this brings to the discourse about parental responsibility.

> 'Faced with a mother who is hostile to contact, the courts have constructed her as "implacably hostile" ... However in respect of the father who fails to have contact with his child, no equivalent label ... such as "implacably irresponsible' [has] been employed.'[190]

---

182 *Parental Separation: Children's Needs and Parents' Responsibilities Report of the Responses to Consultation and Agenda for Action* (Cm 6452, 2005), paras 10–12.
183 *Family Justice: The Operation of the Family Courts* (HC 116–1, 2005), paras 60–61.
184 Ibid, paras 42–44.
185 Op cit, at para 4.22.
186 Ibid, at para 4.27.
187 [2000] 2 FLR 334, at 364.
188 CA 1989, s 8(1).
189 [1994] 1 FLR 272.
190 Probert, Gilmore and Herring (eds) *Parental Responsibility and the Responsible Parent* in *Responsible Parents & Parental Responsibility* (Hart Publishing, 2009), at p 304.

CONTACT AND CHILD SUPPORT

11.103 The Lord Chancellor's Advisory Board on Family Law in its report, *Making Contact Work*,[191] noted the injustice felt by some men when they are paying maintenance and being unreasonably denied contact.

Furthermore, there appears to be a connection between the regularity of contact and paying maintenance and between the level of satisfaction over contact felt by both parents. However, this is not a straightforward link predicated on a simple 'contact-pay' basis.[192] A recent study of parents in contact with the Child Support Agency[193] found that two-fifths of non-resident parents having contact once a week or more felt the Child Support Agency assessment was fair, compared with three-fifths of parents having less contact. When contact took place once a week or more, half of resident parents thought the assessment fair, compared with one-third when contact was less frequent. Conversely, problems with child support can cause problems with contact. In a third of the county court cases closely examined by Smart,[194] contact was said to be restricted because child support was not being paid. Although residential mothers knew that according to the law they should not link the issue of contact with child support, they felt very strongly that it should be known when fathers did not support their children financially and pointed out that fathers applied for contact only after they had been approached by the Child Support Agency. Fathers, on the other hand, argued that mothers stopped contact in order to force them to pay more. Smart recognised that there were arguments both for keeping the two issues separate and for linking them. Similar findings were made by Trinder[195] although in her sample, half of the respondents reported that financial conflicts made contact more difficult.

11.104 The Children Act Sub-Committee recognised that there was a genuine sense of injustice but felt unable to make any recommendations on the issue but invited the Government to consider the desirability and practicability of legislating for an inter-relationship between maintenance and contact.[196]

The response of the Government was clear and firm:[197]

> 'We reject this recommendation. Contact is not a commodity to be bartered for money. The meeting of a non-resident parent's financial obligation towards their

---

[191] (Lord Chancellor's Department, 2002.)

[192] Douglas 'Contact is not a commodity to be bartered for money' [2011] Fam Law 491, at p 493.

[193] Wikely *National Survey of Child Support Agency Clients* Research Report No 152 (DWP, 2001), discussed in Davis and Wikely 'National Survey of Child Support Clients – The Relationship Dimension' [2002] Fam Law 522.

[194] Smart, May, Wade and Furniss *Residence and Contact Disputes in Court* Vol 1 (DCA Research Series No 6/03, Department for Constitutional Affairs, 2003), at pp 81–85.

[195] Trinder, Connolly and others *A Profile of Applicants and Respondents in Contact Cases in Essex* (DCA Research series 1/05, Department for Constitutional Affairs, 2005), p 77.

[196] *Making Contact Work* (Lord Chancellor's Department, 2002), para 14.43.

[197] *Government's Response to the Report of the Children Act Sub-Committee of the Lord Chancellor's Advisory Board on Family Law 'Making Contact Work'* (Lord Chancellor's Department, 2002).

children ensures the children's welfare is maintained as far as possible. This obligation remains regardless of whether contact is taking place. Contact cannot be made conditional on the payment of maintenance as it could deprive children of beneficial contact e g a parent may be unable to support the child financially because they have a long term illness and so be unable to work. There are also occasions when contact is not in the best interests of the children e g where there has been violence or other abuse. These children should not suffer additional deprivation as a result.'

11.105 The *Family Justice Review*[198] had been asked by the Government to consider whether there might be circumstances when it would be right to link maintenance and contact. In its Interim Report it had recommended:

'... there should be no automatic link between contact and maintenance but when contact was continually frustrated and it was in the child's best interests, the courts should have an additional enforcement mechanism available to enable them to alter or suspend the payment of maintenance. Responses to the Proposal were mixed.'

Having reconsidered its recommendation Norgrove concluded that to introduce any connection between contact and maintenance would risk reinforcing this problem, even if it is at the discretion of a judge.

'For the sake of a power that may be rarely if ever used it would in our view be wrong to risk strengthening the view that it is acceptable not to pay maintenance when there are contact difficulties or for that matter, that contact can be withheld when maintenance is not being paid. The existence of the power could also undermine private arrangements and encourage litigation. For these reasons we recommend there should be no link of any kind between contact and maintenance.'[199]

11.106 The Government's Response[200] was that simply restricting contact if maintenance was not paid or reducing the maintenance payable if a parent withheld contact would undermine the fundamental principle that decisions about arrangements for the care of the child must be based on the child's best interests. However, it recognised the importance of effective enforcement and will consider how existing provisions and practice might be strengthened.

11.107 Subsequently the Department of Work and Pensions issued a consultation paper, *Strengthening families, promoting parental responsibility: the future of child maintenance*[201] which, while recognising the welfare principle, was 'keen to explore approaches that allow maintenance agreements to be considered in the round when determining appropriate enforcement measures.' In a paper criticising this approach,[202] Professor Gillian Douglas welcomed the Norgrove recommendation.

---

[198] Op cit.
[199] Ibid, at para 4.161.
[200] *The Government Response to the Family Justice Review* op cit, at p 80.
[201] Cm 7990 (2011).
[202] 'Contact is not a commodity to be bartered for money' op cit, at p 496.

'Our firm conclusion is that sometimes the "prevailing wisdom" does make good sense and the long-standing policy to keep contact and maintenance quite separate (and this child-rather than adult-focused) in more in line with the government's objective of encouraging consensual family-based decision-making whilst liking the two is extremely likely to produce the opposite effect.'

Nevertheless, the issues remain interlinked for many parents and if they are to make mutually satisfactory and effective arrangements for contact, any problems relating to child support also need to be addressed. If disputes reach the court, there is nothing to preclude enquiries being made about whether maintenance is being paid, to encourage agreements to be reached and possibly recorded on the order and the non-resident's payment record being taken into account if his/her commitment to the child needs to be assessed.[203]

11.108 As long ago as 1981, the Divisional Court of the Queens Bench held that a magistrate's court was wrong to remit arrears of maintenance as a penalty for withholding contact.[204]

'[There] is absolutely no connection between the remission of payments of maintenance and the wife's failure or non-failure to allow access. The two are wholly different. If payment is not a reward to the wife for allowing access, the order of remission is not a penalty on the wife for not allowing access. The two are wholly distinct and separate.'[205]

11.109 Similarly, but in a converse situation, in *Re H (Parental Responsibility: Maintenance)*[206] the Court of Appeal held that a parental responsibility order should not be withheld as a punishment for not paying maintenance.

'The court ought not, in my judgment, to use the weapon of withholding a parental responsibility order for the purpose of exacting from the father what may be regarded as his financial dues. That approach fails to give him proper credit for his sustained attempts to have contact with both children whenever he could. Though he is failing the children by not putting his money where he says his heart is, it must, in my judgment, be in the children's best interest that their natural father should at least be accorded that voice in their future which is implicit in a parental responsibility order.'[207]

In *Re B (Contact: Child Support)*[208] a father complained that the child's mother wanted to restrict contact so as to maximise child support payments. She responded by alleging that his prime motive for seeking an increase in contact was to reduce payments. The Court of Appeal held that the effect which the quantum of contact had on the amount of child support payable was irrelevant. While there were anomalies in the child support legislation then in force which could properly be said to give rise to substantial injustice, these

---

[203] See also Brasse 'Contact and money' [2002] Fam Law 691.
[204] *R v Halifax Justices ex parte Woolverton* (1981) 2 FLR 369.
[205] Ibid, per Lord Widgery CJ at 371.
[206] [1996] 1 FLR 867.
[207] Per Leggatt LJ at 872.
[208] [2006] EWCA Civ 1574, [2007] 1 FLR 1949.

were irrelevant to determination of the optimum level of a parent's contact with a child. It would be inappropriate to exercise the jurisdiction to make an order for contact with a view to reversing or mitigating the consequences of the statutory provisions. 'Indeed it would be positively unlawful to do so because it would be to introduce a consideration unrelated to the child's welfare.'[209]

11.110 Commenting on the issue, Professor Wikeley recognised that the legal principle that contact and child support are entirely separate is long-standing but nevertheless the child support system, by linking the amount of child support to the number of nights spent with each parent, contributed to the persistence of the widespread view that they were mutually interdependent.[210]

INTERIM CONTACT

11.111 The court can make interim orders pending a final and full hearing but, as Wall J pointed out in *Re D (Contact: Interim Order)*,[211] this presents particular difficulties:

'By their very nature, they are unlikely to be made with a full understanding of all the facts, and equally there will not normally have been full evidence given, with cross-examination as to all the relevant issues. It follows, in my judgment, that interim orders for contact ... need to be approached with a degree of caution.'

Whether or not the principle of contact is in issue or not, the test to be applied is the welfare test.

11.112 In *Re D (Contact: Interim Order)* Wall J laid out a series of principles. Where the principle of the type of contact sought is not in issue, interim orders can be and are often properly made without detailed investigation or oral evidence, either by seeking the lowest common denominator which is acceptable to the parties or by imposing an interim regime which does not prejudice the child.[212]

11.113 Where the principle of contact is in issue, there is the risk that an interim order will prejudge the final decision. Before making an interim order, therefore, courts need to take the greatest care that, on the facts as they currently present themselves, contact is truly in the interests of the child, is as neutral as possible[213] and that the order does not prejudice the issue, for example, by ordering interim staying contact where staying contact is imposed. Contact might be justified where it is to be part of the overall adjudication

---

[209] Ibid, per Wilson LJ at [18].

[210] 'Contact and child support – Putting the horse before the cart' [2007] Fam Law 343. See also Wikeley 'Financial support for children after parental separation: Parental responsibility and responsible parenting' in Probert, Gilmore and Herring (eds) *Responsible Parents and Parental Responsibility* (Hart Publishing, 2009) ch 15.

[211] [1995] 1 FLR 495, at 504.

[212] Ibid, at p 504 and *Re B (A Minor) (Contact: Interim Order)* [1994] 2 FLR 269.

[213] *Re H (Contact Order)* [2010] EWCA Civ 448.

process, for example, allowing contact to be observed by a Cafcass officer or a child psychiatrist,[214] but, where such a report is required before taking the disputed step, an interim order for such contact should not be made. In *Re W (Staying Contact)*,[215] for example, a 4-year-old child was having staying and visiting contact with her father but the mother stopped all contact, first, because she was concerned that the father had sexually abused the child and, secondly, because the child was showing behavioural difficulties. After an investigation by social services, the judge directed the joint instruction of a child psychologist to investigate the behavioural difficulties and ordered interim staying contact. The Court of Appeal held that he was wrong to do so pending the assessment.

11.114 A second broad category where contact might be ordered is where the court has sufficient information to be satisfied that an interim order is in the child's best interests even though a possibility exists that at the final hearing the court may come to a different conclusion. An example of this is where contact had been taking place satisfactorily but the resident parent terminates it for no apparent good reason.[216]

For interim contact where there are allegations of domestic violence, see **5.72**.

INTRODUCING CONTACT

11.115 When there is no existing relationship between the child and the non-resident parent, an introductory programme of contact will be needed. In some cases, the child will not know the parent to be his parent and may even believe someone else, for example, a step-parent, to be his parent.[217] In others, the child may have a relationship with the parent but one based on erroneous beliefs, for example, that the parent has abused the child in the past and is not to be trusted.

11.116 The fact that the child believes someone else to be his father is not an insurmountable objection to contact even if the residential parent is unwilling for contact to take place.[218]

11.117 The first stage in introducing contact will normally be for the child to be told as quickly as possible that he has another parent and to be helped to come to terms with this. This can best be done by a child psychiatrist with supervision being provided either by a family assistance order (in which case all adults named in the order will have to consent) or by the child being joined as a party to the proceedings and a guardian being appointed (as happened in *Re R (A Minor) (Contact)*). Once the child knows he has another father, indirect

---

[214]   *Re D (Contact: Interim Order)* [1995] 1 FLR 495.
[215]   [1998] 2 FLR 450.
[216]   *Re D (Contact: Interim Order)* [1995] 1 FLR 495.
[217]   See **Chapter 6**.
[218]   See for example, *Re R (A Minor) (Contact)* [1993] 2 FLR 762, **6.104**.

contact may then be appropriate as in *A v L (Contact)*,[219] if necessary with the resident parent being directed to ensure that the child received the presents and had the messages read. The next stage would be some direct contact. However, the sensitivity of the situation may require each stage to be monitored by the court.

11.118 When the child already knows that the applicant is his father or is too young to be affected by the knowledge, direct contact may be appropriate at the first stage, the child meeting the applicant for, initially, short periods, in the company ideally of the resident parent but, if that is impracticable, another person with whom he is at ease. Gradually, the child can be left in the sole company of the applicant, usually in a familiar place or a place the child has come to know, such as a contact centre.

11.119 When the children have had a relationship with the absent parent and know who he is, then the court is likely to order a few periods of contact supervised by someone like a CAFCASS officer.[220]

11.120 Whatever the problem, courts do not favour a 'wait for a few years until the child is older' approach, regarding it as being both dangerous and driven by a desire to put off a difficult decision.[221]

DIRECT CONTACT

11.121 There is no formula for the amount or frequency of contact and the order which is made will depend on the circumstances of each individual case.[222] However, because orders will be made only when there is a dispute between the person with residence and the applicant, the court will try to establish a framework of contact to avoid frequent returns to court while at the same time leaving scope for adjustment by agreement. Regularity of contact is desirable, not just because it makes it easier to establish a framework but, more importantly, because it meets the child's need for security through predictability. In addition, it assists the adults and, as they develop a life away from the family home, children to organise their lives. Frequency of contact is also important because it enables a relaxed relationship between the adult and child to continue without breaks. This is particularly relevant in the case of young children. It also helps the child and the non-resident parent to keep track of what is happening in each other's lives. The length of the contact needs to be considered. The immediate purpose of contact will be to allow the non-resident parent and the child to spend an enjoyable time together and shortness of contact, especially when the non-resident parent collects the child from the

---

[219] [1998] 1 FLR 361. See **6.104**.
[220] See, for example, *Re H (Minors) (Access)* [1992] 1 FLR 148.
[221] Ibid, at 152; *Re R (A Minor) (Contact)* [1993] 2 FLR 762 at 768 and *A v L (Contact)* [1998] 1 FLR 361, at 366.
[222] General advice on contact arrangements is given by Cafcass in *Putting Your Children First* available at www.cafcass.gov.uk/publications.

child's home and returns the child afterwards, may adversely affect this. For this reason and because longer periods will enable the parent and child to share everyday social activities such as meal times and 'just being together' without 'special' activities such as outings and to enable the child to see the non-resident parent in his or her own home, staying contact is seen not only as beneficial but one of the important targets, the most important being the parents being able to organise contact without resort to the courts.

11.122 In the circumstances of the individual case, these aims may be impossible to achieve, at least in the short term, especially where there is a lack of trust and co-operation between parents. In such circumstances, an order is a compromise. Where there is an absence of a relationship between the parent and child, for example, an introductory programme of contact may need to be established before establishing a more permanent pattern. The non-resident parent may live such a distance from the child, even in another country, that frequent contact cannot take place. A child under nursery age may not be used to being away from his carer for any length of time and the non-resident parent may be unfamiliar. Short but frequent periods of contact may be needed before the length of contact is increased and the frequency possibly diminished. The non-resident parent may be living in a series of temporary accommodations. He may have no suitable accommodation for over-night stays. In *M v B (Ancillary Proceedings: Lump Sum)*,[223] Thorpe LJ said in relation to ancillary relief proceedings that, while the prime carer needs whatever is available to make the main home for the children:

> '... it is of importance, albeit it is of lesser importance, that the other parent should have a home of his own where the children can enjoy their contact time with him. Of course there are cases where there is not enough to provide a home for either ... But in any case where there is, by stretch and a degree of risk-taking, the possibility of a division to enable both to rehouse themselves, that is an exceptionally important consideration ...'

11.123 The optimal arrangements for contact must be considered against the wider background of the child's life. The majority of the child's life will be spent with the resident parent and both the child and that parent need time together. During the week with the child at school and the parent perhaps working, such time will be limited. Contact, for example, at weekends, will reduce that period further. The child also needs time exclusively for himself and, as he grows older, to spend with his peers. A balance will therefore need to be struck. When making a contact order the court should have regard to the realities of the parents' and the child's lives, for example, their work schedule.[224]

As circumstances change, the order may need to be varied. For example, the Court of Appeal suspended a contact order when it became apparent that contact ordered by an Australian court would not work.[225]

---

[223] [1998] 1 FLR 53, at 60.
[224] See *Gluhaković v Croatia* (Application No 21188/09) [2011] 2 FLR 294.
[225] *Re G (Contact)* [2006] EWCA Civ 1507, [2007] 1 FLR 1663.

Staying contact

11.124 When the principle of contact is accepted, disputes about whether there should be staying contact are often caused by the resident parent needing to be assured that the arrangements are suitable. Relevant factors include the availability of accommodation, whether the accommodation is suitable, whether the non-resident parent is reasonably able to look after the child during the period of contact and whether the child is able to spend time away from the other parent without undue distress. If there is a serious dispute about whether the accommodation is suitable, a s 7 report can be ordered. If the resident parent merely needs to be reassured that the accommodation is suitable, the issue could be dealt with more speedily by that parent visiting the accommodation and, if necessary, filing a short statement stating why the accommodation is not suitable. Unless the child has special care needs or the non-resident parent is deficient in caring skills or there is a risk to the child's safety by reason of the parent drinking to excess or abusing drugs, the court is likely to take a robust view of whether the parent can cope, especially if the contact is for only one or two nights. If the child is young or inexperienced at spending a night away from home, both the child and the resident parent can be reassured by an agreement or a condition being imposed that he will phone the resident parent during the contact.

11.125 A structure for deciding holiday dates well in advance needs to be established, both so that the non-resident parent can make the necessary arrangements and that the resident parent can make arrangements for his or her holiday with the child. Resident parents need to be reassured that the arrangements are appropriate. Details should be provided in advance.

11.126 Under the current regime for child support, the assessment is affected only if the child stays overnight with the non-resident parent for more than two nights a week. Under the new regime proposed but delayed, the assessment is reduced by one-seventh for every night stayed with the non-resident parent.

Contact abroad

11.127 For contact abroad, see **9.66**.[226]

Visiting contact

11.128 When the principle of contact is accepted, disputes about non-staying contact are usually about the length of contact or the practicalities of the 'handover'. The most relevant factors will be the child's age and familiarity with the parent having contact. For a child under 4, two or three hours may be more appropriate than a whole day if the child may be unused to being away from the other parent, bearing in mind the possibility that the child may tire more quickly than an older one. Practitioners need to exercise considerable

---

[226] See also *Transfrontier Contact Concerning Children: General Principles and a Guide to Good Practice* (Hague Conference on Private International Law, 2008).

ingenuity over the handover arrangements but the ideal to aim for – and some might say, expect – is the non-resident parent collecting the child from and returning him to his home.

Contact in prison

11.129 Difficulties about visiting contact may arise when the person in whose favour the order is made is serving a prison sentence. Many prisons have facilities for children to visit but not all are satisfactory. In addition, the Prison Governor has a discretion whether or not to allow visits. The Publication Protection Manuel (PPM) which sets out the prison service's written policy, Chapter 2, deals with Child Contact Procedures. On one hand, contact with family members is to be encouraged. Rules 3 and 4 of the Prison Rules 1999 (as amended)[227] state:

> '3. The purpose of the training and treatment of convicted prisoners shall be to encourage and assist them to lead a good and useful life.
>
> 4. (1) Special attention shall be paid to the maintenance of such relationships between a prisoner and his family as are desirable in the best interests of both.
>
> (2) A prisoner shall be encouraged and assisted to establish and maintain such relations with persons and agencies outside prison as may, in the opinion of the governor, best promote the interests of his family and his own social rehabilitation.'

The welfare of the child, too, must be considered and is paramount. The governor must request an assessment in the form of a report in writing from children's services and that assessment must be in accordance with the *Framework for the Assessment of Children in Need and their Families.*[228] A referral from a prison governor will trigger an initial assessment which should address the dimensions of the assessment framework and that initial assessment will determine whether a further, more detailed core assessment should be undertaken. Having regard to the factors which the PPM requires a governor to consider in coming to a contact decision which specifically include a child's needs, wishes and feelings and the capacity of the parent/carer to protect the child from likely harm, it is to be expected that an initial assessment will suffice unless that assessment itself reveals a need for more in-depth consideration. There is an initial assessment record which children's services are to use and which can be communicated to the governor in response to the referral.[229]

---

[227] SI 1999/728.

[228] (2000) Department of Health. See also *Westwater v Secretary of State for Justice* [2010] EWHC 2403 (Admin), [2011] 1 FLR 1989, at [36]; *Bryan v Secretary of State for Justice* [2010] EWHC 2507 (Admin), [2011] 1 FLR 1902, at [44].

[229] *Westwater v Secretary of State for Justice* [2010] EWHC 2403 (Admin), [2011] 1 FLR 1989, at [38].

11.130 In deciding whether to permit contact, the Governor has to balance these two factors. The PPM provides a procedure[230] which establishments must follow, the main stages of which are:

- Prisoners are made aware of procedures. This includes asking those prisoners who present a possible risk of harm whether they intend to request child contact and making a record which is to be kept with the prisoner's records.

- A request made for contact. There is an application form for the prisoner to complete and specific provision for requests made by a parent or child which must be put to the prisoner so that s/he can decide whether to make an application for contact. Requests made by a parent or child must be put to the prisoner so that s/he can decide whether to make an application for contact.

- A record is maintained.

- The availability of parental Support for Contact is ascertained. The parent or carer of a child is to be asked whether they support contact or not and at what level.

- A multi-agency assessment is carried out. This includes the wishes and feelings of the child being ascertained by children's services during a home visit so that they can be taken into account.

- The Governor makes a decision based on the best interests of the child.

- The level of contact is decided.[231]

Before deciding that direct contact is not in the child's best interests, the court should examine all options including parental activity directions, the parents undergoing counselling and referring the family to an organisation which is dedicated to assisting children cope with the impact of family breakdown.[232]

Where direct contact is not in the child's best interests, the court should consider making an order for indirect contact.

---

[230] At para 3.2.

[231] For a judicial review of a decision not to allow contact, see *Westwater v Secretary of State for Justice* [2010] EWHC 2403 (Admin), [2011] 1 FLR 1989 and *Bryan v Secretary of State for Justice* [2010] EWHC 2507 (Admin), [2011] 1 FLR 1902.

[232] See, for example, *Re M (Contact: Longterm Best Interests)* [2005] EWCA Civ 1090, [2006] 1 FLR 627; *Re W (Contact)* [2007] EWCA Civ 753, [2007] 2 FLR 1122; *Re P (Children)* [2008] EWCA Civ 1431, [2009] 1 FLR 1056.

INDIRECT CONTACT

11.131   Indirect contact in its various forms may be appropriate either in place of direct contact where such contact is not in the child's best interests or as an adjunct to direct contact.

11.132   When, for whatever reason, direct contact cannot for the time being be ordered, it is ordinarily highly desirable that there should be indirect contact[233] which, at least, will maintain some relationship between parent and child and can lead to direct contact being established. In *Re M (A Minor) (Contact: Conditions)*,[234] Wall J allowed a father who had allegedly been violent towards the child's mother and who was serving a sentence of 3 years' imprisonment for crimes of dishonesty to send his 3-year-old son Christmas and Easter cards and presents (the father was going to be released before the boy's next birthday).[235] However, even indirect contact may be inappropriate. In *Re C (Contact: No Order for Contact)*,[236] Connell J upheld a refusal by magistrates to continue indirect contact by cards and letters with a boy who was nearly 9 and was upset by the communications and destroyed them.

11.133   The Sub-Committee's report, *Making Contact Work*, recommended imaginative and creative use of orders:

> 'Indirect contact can take a very wide variety of forms. Apart from letters, cards and presents, contact by e-mail and videos, to take only two examples, should be considered.'[237]

Texting and messaging are also possibilities.

Although orders for indirect contact typically refer to 'cards and letters', parents may have difficulty writing or knowing what to write to a child and the child may have little or no reading ability. Drawings or photographs might in some cases be a substitute or addition.

11.134   In *Re A (Contact: Witness Protection Scheme)*[238] a father was allowed indirect contact by way of a video link against the background of violence towards the mother by a member of the father's family and the mother being on a witness protection scheme. The father had behaved with restraint and the risk to the child of any contact could be kept under review. Such contact would be in the child's best interests and it would not prejudice his and the mother's security. There should be a time lag in the link to allow intervention should the

---

[233]   See *Re O (A Minor) (Contact: Imposition of Conditions)* [1995] 2 FLR 124.
[234]   [1994] 1 FLR 272 and likewise *A v L (Contact)* [1998] 1 FLR 361 and *Re P (Contact: Indirect Contact)* [1999] 2 FLR 893.
[235]   See also *Re F (Indirect Contact)* [2006] EWCA Civ 1426, [2007] 1 FLR 1015.
[236]   [2000] 2 FLR 723.
[237]   *Making Contact Work* (Lord Chancellor's Department, 2002), para 13.9.
[238]   [2005] EWHC 2189 (Fam), [2006] 2 FLR 551.

child inadvertently say anything which might reveal his whereabouts[239] and the father would not be permitted to take any photos of the screen or retain any images if they were stored in any way on the computer he was using to see the child.

11.135 In most cases, a limit on the frequency of the correspondence should not be imposed.[240] Sometimes there is concern that letters will contain inappropriate messages or presents will be attempts to buy the child's affection. As Sir Thomas Bingham MR said in *Re O (A Minor) (Contact: Imposition of Conditions)*:[241]

> 'The object of indirect contact is to build up a relationship between the absent parent and the child, not to enable the absent parent to pursue a feud with the caring parent …'

Where there are grounds for such concern, the court can set a limit on the price of the present and Cafcass may be prepared to act as a post office and censor.

11.136 In *Re M (A Minor) (Contact: Conditions)*,[242] Wall J doubted that the court had jurisdiction, not only to direct that the resident parent gives the child letters but also reads them to him, but a different view was later taken by the Court of Appeal in *Re O (A Minor) (Contact: Imposition of Conditions)*:[243]

> '[That passage in *Re M*] is tantamount to saying that a mother's withholding of consent and expression of unwillingness to do something is enough to defeat the court's power to order that something should be done.'

In addition, Sir Thomas Bingham MR pointed out that the court has power to order a resident parent to send the other photographs, school reports and medical reports (if there are any) and to keep that parent generally informed of the child's progress 'in order to promote meaningful contact between the father and the child which would almost certainly wither and die if the father received no information about the child's progress'. Likewise, the court has the power to direct a parent to encourage the child to communicate with the absent parent and to facilitate such contact. However, in order to be effective, especially when the child is young, indirect contact depends on the co-operation of the residential parent and can be difficult to monitor. Other ways of conveying information may have to be tried. Guidance from the Department of Education advises head teachers that non-resident parents and others with parental responsibility should be sent annual reports and invitations to school events in the same way as resident parents.[244]

---

[239] For an example of other indirect contact taking place following an assessment of whether it might enable the child's whereabouts to be discovered , see *Re F (Indirect Contact)* [2006] EWCA Civ 1426, [2007] 1 FLR 1015.

[240] *Re O (A Minor) (Contact: Imposition of Conditions)* [1995] 2 FLR 124, at 131.

[241] Ibid, at 130.

[242] [1994] 1 FLR 272.

[243] [1995] 2 FLR 124, at 131.

[244] DfEE Guidance 92/2000, para 12.

11.137 Even minimal indirect contact should be considered before refusing all contact.[245]

Example

Re K (Contact: Mother's Anxiety)[246]

11.138 The father had been imprisoned for kidnapping the child (now nearly 6) before its second birthday. On his release, he applied for direct contact. Two periods of interim supervised contact went well. The mother found this contact very stressful and her distress was very apparent to the child, who felt guilty for enjoying contact. The court ordered indirect contact only.

REFUSING CONTACT

11.139 Courts should be very slow before concluding that no contact with a non-resident parent is in the child's best interests. In *Re S (Contact: Promoting Contact with Absent Parent)*[247] Dame Elizabeth Butler-Sloss P said:

> 'No parent is perfect but 'good enough parents' should have a relationship with their children for their own benefit and even more in the best interests of the children. It is, therefore, most important that the attempt to promote contact between a child and the non-resident parent should not be abandoned until it is clear that the child will not benefit from continuing the attempt.'

11.140 Deciding whether attempts at securing contact should cease, albeit to allow a period of respite, is an exercise in proportionality. If the problem is the recalcitrant attitude of the carer, the court can commit to prison for contempt or fine. However:

> 'Most mothers do not have enough money to pay a significant fine and this sanction is seldom used, particularly since she is the primary carer of the child. Equally the sanction of prison for mothers who refuse to allow contact is a heavy one and may well be a self-defeating one. It will hardly endear the father to the child who is already reluctant to see him to be told that the father is responsible for the mother going to prison. Prison is a sanction of last resort and there is little else the court can do. At this stage also the court may have the evidence that the continuing efforts to persuade the mother to agree to contact are having a disproportionately adverse effect upon the child whose welfare is paramount and the court may find it necessary, however reluctantly, to stop trying to promote contact.'[248]

---

[245] See, for example, *Re G (Restricting Contact)* [2010] EWCA Civ 470, [2010] 2 FLR 692.
[246] [1999] 2 FLR 703.
[247] [2004] EWCA Civ 18, [2004] 1 FLR 1279, at [33].
[248] Ibid, at [29].

If the difficulty lies in the behaviour of the person seeking contact, and there is no prospect of that behaviour moderating, for example, with counselling, then contact may have to cease.[249]

11.141 In other situations proportionality is to be weighed in deciding the lengths to which a court should go to force contact on an unwilling child and on the apprehensive primary carer.

> 'At this point the factor of proportionality becomes all-important since there is a limit beyond which the court should not strive to promote contact and the court has the overriding obligation to put the welfare of the child at the forefront and above the rights of either parent.'[250]

Before taking such a decision the court should consider what steps if any can be taken to ameliorate the positive including making contact activity directions such as requiring attendance at PIPs, encouraging counselling, appointing a guardian for the child (see **4.61**) seeking advice from a child psychiatrist, psychologist or specialist organisation and indirect contact.

Examples

Re H (A Minor) (Parental responsibility)[251]

11.142 A father was refused contact with his 2-year-old son because the mother's new husband's objection to contact was such that the marriage and the child's welfare would be placed at risk. The Court of Appeal dismissed the father's appeal.

Re K (Children: Refusal of Direct Contact)[252]

11.142A A father (F) of three children aged 7, 5 and 1 had convictions for sexual offences against children as young as 8 and for accessing child pornography. He was made the subject of a Sexual Offenders Prevention Order and subsequently imprisoned for breaching the order. Their mother (M) failed to understand the seriousness of his behaviour. In care proceedings, the court ordered that the children should continue to live with M and, on the recommendation of their Guardian, refused direct contact. The Court of Appeal dismissed F's appeal. The order preventing F having any direct contact with his children was at the extreme end of the interventions that a court can

---

[249] See, for example, *Re F (Contact)* [2007] EWHC 2543 (Fam), [2008] 1 FLR 1163. 'I have sought in vain for an alternative ... Taking the children's welfare as my paramount consideration and having regard to the welfare checklist, I am forced with reluctance to conclude that continuing contact even supervised is not at this time in the children's best interests. It surely cannot take much for the father to understand how readily he could change the position. If his personality makes that too difficult then it is a real tragedy.' Per Sumner J at [215]–[216].

[250] *Re S (Contact: Promoting Contact with Absent Parent)* [2004] EWCA Civ 18, [2004] 1 FLR 1279, at [29].

[251] [1993] 1 FLR 484 and see also *Re B (Contact: Stepfather's Opposition)* [1997] 2 FLR 579.

[252] [2011] EWCA Civ 1064, [2012] 1 FLR 195.

make in ordinary private family life. The impact upon him and upon the children in not having any face-to-face contact was significant. However, F's behaviour could not be divorced from the issue of contact because of the effect that it would have upon the children when they got to know about it, and the judge had found that was likely to produce devastating results.

CONTACT AND THE UNUSUAL APPLICANT

11.143 In some cases, the applicant may have unusual characteristics which may affect contact.[253] In *Re B (Minors: Access)*,[254] the father was a very anxious and socially awkward figure and at times his behaviour was eccentric to the point of being bizarre. The applicant might suffer from a condition, such as Asperger's syndrome, an autistic-like condition which impairs reciprocal social interaction,[255] or Huntingdon's disease, a disorder leading to adverse effects on mood and personality.[256] The applicant may have suffered brain damage with loss of memory and self-control, as in the case of *M v M (Parental Responsibility)*.[257] The applicant may experience delusional beliefs, whether or not as a result of schizophrenia.[258] The father may have undergone a gender reassignment after his child has come to know him as a male.[259]

11.144 Such conditions do not give rise to a presumption that there should be no contact. As in more ordinary cases, there is an assumption that it is in the best interests of children to have contact with a non-resident parent and there is the additional belief that it will often be best for them gradually to understand their parent's condition, 'perhaps even coming eventually to accept and appreciate them as something of which neither he nor they should feel ashamed'.[260] Rather, the situation requires very careful analysis and investigation and the decision reached by applying the welfare checklist. In addition to a CAFCASS report, a psychiatric report on the applicant will normally be required and the impact of the parent's condition on the child may require a report from a child psychiatrist.[261] In some cases, but not all, it may be appropriate for the child to be joined as a party and represented by a guardian.[262] The complexity of the issues and the involvement of adult and

---

253 See Mitchell 'Contact and the unusual parent' [2003] Fam Law 169.
254 [1992] 1 FLR 140.
255 See Young 'Encounters with Asperger's Syndrome in the solicitor's office' [2001] Fam Law 695 and Henderson and Hackett 'Asperger's Syndrome in child contact cases' [2002] Fam Law 119. See also Fish 'Representing parents with mental health problems' [2005] Fam Law 375.
256 For example, *Re H (Contact Order) (No 2)* [2002] 1 FLR 22.
257 [1999] 2 FLR 737.
258 See, for example, *Re W (Contact: Parent's Delusional Beliefs)* [1999] 1 FLR 1263.
259 *Re F (Minors) (Denial of Contact)* [1993] 2 FLR 677; *Re L (Contact: Transsexual Applicant)* [1995] 2 FLR 438 and *Re C (Contact: Moratorium: Change of Gender)* [2006] EWCA Civ 1765, [2007] 1 FLR 1642.
260 *Re B (Minors: Access)* [1992] 1 FLR 140, per Waite J at 146.
261 As for example in *Re C (Contact: Moratorium: Change of Gender)* [2006] EWCA Civ 1765, [2007] 1 FLR 1642.
262 As in *Re W (Contact: Parent's Delusional Beliefs)* [1999] 1 FLR 1263 and *M v M (Parental Responsibility)* [1999] 2 FLR 737.

child psychiatrists may make the matter appropriate for the High Court but before transferring a case the court should consider any delay which may be caused.[263]

11.145 Where the facts justify the need for supervision, the court will have to consider both whether long-term supervision is available and whether supervision is likely to prevent the child suffering harm. In *Re H (Contact Order) (No 2)*,[264] for example, the father's condition manifested itself in violence against the mother and threats to kill the children. In the light of evidence that there remained a risk of physical injury to the children even during supervised contact and that it could not be guaranteed that professional supervisors would spot a change in mood, Wall J refused direct contact. Similar considerations arise when the risk posed by the father is not violence to the child but behaviour which is likely to cause the child distress or there is a risk that the father may not respond appropriately.[265]

11.146 The views of the child must be considered but, as in all cases, the weight given to them will depend on the age of the child and the other circumstances. In *Re H (Contact Order) (No 2)*, for example, the children wanted to continue seeing their father, although not suffering harm because they were not seeing him, but direct contact was refused on the basis that it carried too great a risk. In *Re F (Minors) (Denial of Contact)*[266] 'very considerable weight' was given to the reluctance of two children, aged 12 and 9, to see their father, who had changed his social gender. Likewise, the weight given to the attitude of the child's carer will depend on an assessment of the overall circumstances. In *Re H (Contact Order) (No 2)*, the court found there was a likelihood of the mother suffering a nervous breakdown if an order for face-to-face contact was imposed on her.

11.147 In some cases, it may be justified to impose a moratorium on contact to allow the child and his or her carer a respite and an opportunity for counselling or other professional assistance but before doing this all the circumstances in the welfare checklist should be considered. In *Re C (Contact: Moratorium: Change of Gender)*[267] the Court of Appeal allowed an appeal by a father who had undergone gender reassignment against the imposition of a 20-month moratorium. The judge should have distinguished between the question of the children being told the truth about their father and the question of whether contact should be reinstated. To delay telling them the truth would put them at risk of finding out the truth by accident. As regards the second question, they would need professional help dealing with the fact that their father was now a woman and they should be provided with assistance from NYASS (see **4.73)** which should begin as soon as possible with NYAS then providing an interim report.

---

[263] *Re W (Contact: Parent's Delusional Beliefs)* [1999] 1 FLR 1263.
[264] [2002] 1 FLR 22.
[265] *M v M (Parental Responsibility)* [1999] 2 FLR 737, at 742.
[266] [1993] 2 FLR 677.
[267] [2006] EWCA Civ 1765, [2007] 1 FLR 1642.

11.148 In *Re L (Contact: Transsexual Applicant)*[268] a family assistance order was made together with an order for indirect contact. Finally, when direct contact is not possible or desirable, indirect contact should always be considered.

INTRACTABLE CONTACT

11.149 Despite a full and concluded forensic examination and a finding that contact is in the best interests of the child, some residential parents remain steadfastly opposed to contact. In *Re K (Contact: Psychiatric Report)*,[269] Ward LJ said:

'It is my unhappy experience, borne out by other anecdotal evidence and confirmed by the Official Solicitor's department that there seems to be an increasing number of cases coming before the family courts where contact between a young child and the absent parent has become bedevilled by stubborn opposition to contact being shown by the child which may, or may not, be evidence of some implacable hostility on the part of the other parent for good reason or for no reason at all.'

11.150 In such cases, the courts face a very real difficulty. On the one hand, there will be or has been a full investigation into the child's need for contact. In *Re O (A Minor) (Contact: Imposition of Conditions)*,[270] Sir Thomas Bingham MR quoted with approval the dicta of Balcombe LJ in *Re J (A Minor) (Contact)*:[271]

'But before concluding this judgment I would like to make three general points. The first is that judges should be very reluctant to allow the implacable hostility of one parent (usually the parent who has a residence order in his or her favour) to deter them from making a contact order where they believe the child's welfare requires it. The danger of allowing the implacable hostility of the residential parent (usually the mother) to frustrate the court's decision is too obvious to require repetition on my part.'

Sir Thomas Bingham MR added that:

'... neither parent should be encouraged or permitted to think that the more intransigent, the more unreasonable, the more obdurate and the more unco-operative they are the more likely they are to get their own way.'

11.151 On the other hand, the fact of the opposition remains and there may be a risk that to enforce contact in the face of such opposition may be more detrimental to the child than deciding that there should be no or only restricted contact.

---

[268] [1995] 2 FLR 438.
[269] [1995] 2 FLR 432.
[270] [1995] 2 FLR 124.
[271] [1994] 1 FLR 729, at 736B–C.

11.152 Such disputes can be called 'long-term'[272],' high conflict',[273] 'intractable',[274] 'conflicted',[275] or 'chronically litigated'.[276] Parents either battle over their respective roles or cease all communication. Despite perhaps verbal acknowledgement of the paramountcy principle, they analyse the dispute in terms of their 'rights'. One may apparently be more committed to contact than the other. Allegations about behaviour reaching into the far past are made and fresh allegations are made whether of domestic violence or sexual abuse or the risk of either. Litigation extends beyond the 2-year period during which about nine-tenths of cases are resolved (see **11.37**). Difficulties are compounded if there is a lack of judicial continuity.[277]

11.153 Intractable contact disputes may be caused by mothers, fathers or the child or a combination of all three. And, as Trinder describes,[278] a 'vicious circle' is created.

11.154 Fathers' complaints that mothers interfere with contact may have a basis in fact. The literature review by Kelly[279] notes one study which found that mothers sabotaged visits between 25% (mothers' reports) and 35% (fathers' reports) of the time.

On the other hand, fathers can be unreliable and irresponsible,[280] for example, failing to attend contact, to keep to orders preventing him contacting the child or the mother outside the contact schedule, making inappropriate remarks during contact.[281]

> '[The] father may believe that an order by the court for unrestricted contact would have the result of a happy resumption of a loving relationship between him and the child. Such a father is able to see the beam in the eye of the mother but is wholly unable to see that there is a beam in his eye also and that his conduct has not been perfect. He may well have been responsible for unfortunate scenes with

---

[272] Adams 'Parents' rights v children's needs in private cases' [2007] Fam Law 257.
[273] Weir 'High conflict contact disputes: evidence of the extreme unreliability of children's expressed wishes and feelings' (2011) *Family Court Review* 788.
[274] *Re D (Intractable Contact Dispute: Publicity)* [2004] EWHC 727, [2004] 1 FLR 1226.
[275] See Trinder, Beek and Connolly *Making Contact: How Parents and Children Negotiate and Experience Contact After Divorce* (Joseph Rowntree Foundation, 2002).
[276] Hunt and Trinder *Chronically Litigated Contact Cases: How Many Are There and What Works?* (Family Justice Council, 2011)
[277] See, for example, *Re D (Intractable Contact Dispute: Publicity)* [2004] EWHC 727, [2004] 1 FLR 1226 and *Re Bradford; Re O'Connell* [2006] EWCA Civ 1199, [2007] 1 FLR 530.
[278] *Making Contact: How Parents and Children Negotiate and Experience Contact After Divorce* op cit.
[279] 'Children's adjustment in conflicted marriage and divorce: A decade review of research' (2000) *Journal of the American Academy of Child and Adolescent Psychiatry*, vol 39, no 39, pp 963–973.
[280] Rhoades 'The "no contact mother": Reconstructions of motherhood in the era of the "new father" (2002) Int Jo of Law, Policy and the Family 71.
[281] For an example of the kind of extreme behaviour which can occur, see *Re F (Contact)* [2007] EWHC 2543 (Fam), [2008] 1 FLR 1163, at [210]; *Hammerton v Hammerton* [2007] EWCA Civ 248, [2007] 2 FLR 1133 and *Re W (Family Proceedings: Applications)* [2011] EWHC 76 (Fam), [2011] 1 FLR 2163.

the mother in the presence of the child, from inappropriate behaviour under increasing frustration, and that behaviour has added more fuel to the flames of opposition by the mother and often by the child to contact. If the father becomes unreasonable there is a risk for him that his behaviour may become so unacceptable that he may, himself, make it impossible for contact to be resumed.'[282]

11.155   In the leading case of *Re D (Contact: Reasons for Refusal)*,[283] Hale J in the Court of Appeal said that:

'It is important to bear in mind that the label "implacable hostility" is sometimes imposed by the law reporters and can be misleading. It is, as Miss MacGregor points out, an umbrella term that sometimes is applied to cases not only where there is hostility, but no good reason can be discerned either for the hostility or for the opposition to contact, but also to cases where there are such good reasons. In the former sort of case the court will be very slow indeed to reach the conclusion that contact will be harmful to the child. It may eventually have to reach that conclusion but it will want to be satisfied that there is indeed a serious risk of major emotional harm before doing so. It is rather different in the cases where the judge or the court finds that the mother's fears, not only for herself but also for the child, are genuine and rationally held.'[284]

11.156   Some, possibly most, cases are not simply divided into reasonable or unreasonable opposition. There may be some grounds for concern because of the non-resident's behaviour, for example, drinking too much, while the resident parent's opposition to contact, even with safeguards, is in itself unreasonable.[285] In *Re S (Contact: Promoting Relationship with Absent Parent)*[286] Dame Elizabeth Butler-Sloss P summed the matter up in this way.

'Some situations remain extremely difficult to manage from the point of view of the court and the CAFCASS reporter who may be advising the court. One example is the unreasonable mother who is implacably opposed to contact and without any good reason wants to cut the father out of her and the child's future life. An even more difficult situation is the child who, either influenced by the mother or by his own viewpoint or a combination of both, refuses to see the father. The third situation, which may be combined with the first two situations, or may arise entirely separately, is the father who believes that he is "perfect", that the mother is to blame for everything and the child is prevented from a natural, loving relationship with him solely by the intransigence of the mother.

11.157   In recent years, there has been a move towards an analytical approach which attempts to tease out the issues, whether there are objective grounds for

---

[282] *Re S (Contact: Promoting Relationship With Absent Parent)* [2004] EWCA Civ 18, [2004] 1 FLR 1279, per Butler-Sloss P, at [28].

[283] [1997] 2 FLR 48, at 53.

[284] And see also *Re P (Contact: Discretion)* [1998] 2 FLR 696, per Wilson J at 703.

[285] For example, *Re T (A Child) (Contact: Alienation: Permission to Appeal)* [2002] EWCA Civ 1736, [2003] 1 FLR 531 where against a background of the father's drug and alcohol problems, the Court of Appeal directed an investigation of the possibility that the mother was responsible in part at least for the child's alienation from the father.

[286] [2004] EWCA Civ 18, [2004] 1 FLR 1279, at [27].

opposition to contact, whether the resident parent's subjective grounds have any objective basis and whether the risk to the child of ordering contact outweighs any harm in not having contact. One parent may object to contact on the grounds that the non-resident parent has treated her with violence in the past and poses a risk to the child and maintains that stance regardless of a finding that there has never been violence in the past and there are no grounds for supposing it will happen in the future. This is different from the mother who makes the same allegations and maintains them in the face of findings that the non-resident parent has behaved violently in the past but there is little risk of it happening in the future.

11.158 The Sub-Committee of the Lord Chancellor's Advisory Board on Family Law in *Making Contact Work: A Consultation Paper*[287] commented that the 'hostile parent' is not always acting as an individual but can be part of a wider family involvement in a dispute. 'Families can sometimes take an extreme position from which the individual parent fears to diverge' and they may feel that a compromise will harm their relationships within their wider family:

> 'Cultural factors can be important here, so that irreconcilable differences concerning child contact hide wider breaches of cultural breaches and understandings.'[288]

11.159 The European Commission on Human Rights also recognised the importance of taking into account the effect of a contact order on the resident parent. A refusal to order contact which 'would place the child in a situation which could be detrimental to his mental development owing to the existence of a loyalty conflict *vis-à-vis* one or both of the parents and the inevitable parental pressure put on him causing feelings of insecurity and distress', which amounts to an interference with the non-resident parent's Art 8(1) right can amount to a legitimate aim under Art 8(2).[289] The question in each case will therefore be, is the refusal a proportionate response to the risk to the child?

Parental Alienation Syndrome

11.160 There has been interest in recent years in so-called 'Parental Alienation Syndrome' (PAS) in which the resident parent, whilst ostensibly supporting contact, covertly creates anxiety in the child so that it appears that it is the child who is opposed to contact.[290] PAS was first described by the late Richard Gardner, a child psychiatrist in the United States in 1985. He defined it as:

> 'A childhood disorder which that arises almost exclusively in the context of child-custody disputes. Its primary manifestation is the child's campaign of denigration against a parent, a campaign that has no justification. It results from

---

[287] At para 2.20.
[288] See, for example Hasan 'Contact and illegitimacy in the Muslim community' [2000] Fam Law 928, which explores the problems faced by a Muslim mother of an illegitimate child living within her community.
[289] *Hendriks v Netherlands* (1983) 5 EHRR 233.
[290] See Willbourne and Cull 'The emerging problem of parental alienation' [1997] Fam Law 807.

the combination of a programming (brainwashing) parent's indoctrinations and the child's own contributions to the vilification of the target parent. When true parental abuse and/or neglect is present, the child's animosity may be justified and so the parental alienation syndrome explanation for the child's hostility is not applicable.'[291]

According to Gardner, PAS is characterised by a cluster of symptoms which usually appear together in the child, including a campaign of denigration, weak, absurd or frivolous rationalisations for the denigration, lack of ambivalence towards the parent, 'the independent-thinker' phenomenon, reflexive support of the alienating parent, absence of guilt, the presence of borrowed scenarios and the spread of animosity towards the friends or extended family of the alienated parent.

11.161 Critics of Gardner assert that there is no such thing as PAS. Carol Bruch, a law professor in California, suggests that the deficiencies in the theory are manifest, identifying five main ones.[292] First, Gardner confuses a child's reaction to high-conflict parental separation with psychosis. Next, he overstates the frequency of cases in which parents or children manufacture false allegations. In addition, PAS shifts attention away from the behaviour of the non-resident parent, which may present a risk to the child and the other parent. Fourthly, Gardner overstates his case when he asserts that in serious cases the relationship between the child and the father will be irreparably damaged. Last, his proposed remedy in extreme cases of removing the child from the care of the alienating parent endangers children.

11.162 Dr Kirk Weir, a British child and adolescent psychiatrist with considerable experience in conflicted cases, notes that a child may show complete resistance to any form of contact and freely, stridently and without guilt or ambivalence express unreasonable negative feelings such as anger and hatred which are significantly disproportional to his or her actual experience.[293] His assessment of such families routinely includes attempted observation of the child at a visit with the non-resident parent. Despite their previously stated views most children have a positive experience in those visits that took place despite the fact that most had not seen that parent for a long time. Overall there was a statistical association between increased resistance to contact and the greater age of the child and the longer the time during which no contact had occurred. However, the responses of children and young people were unpredictable and it was impossible to conclude that apparent maturity or intelligence was a guide to the reliability of their expressed resistance. He advises that courts should exercise caution when evaluating the views of children in this situation.

---

[291] *Definition of the Parental Alienation Syndrome* (2001) www.rgardner.com/refs.
[292] Bruch 'Parental Alienation Syndrome and Alienated Children – Getting it Wrong in Child Custody Cases' [2002] CFLQ 381.
[293] 'High conflict contact disputes: evidence of the extreme unreliability of children's expressed wishes and feelings' (2011) *Family Court Review* 788.

11.163 The syndrome is not recognised as a manifestation of personality disorder suffered by the resident parent with a categorisation in the International Classification of Diseases (ICD) or the Diagnostic and Statistical Manual of Mental Disorders (DSM-III) in the way that Münchausen's Syndrome and Münchausen's Syndrome by Proxy are. Despite enthusiastic pressure by its proponents,[294] courts in the United Kingdom have been reluctant to investigate whether a refusal to allow contact in a particular case is or is not a manifestation of the syndrome. In one of the cases, reported as *Re L, V, M, H (Contact: Domestic Violence)*,[295] the President said:

> 'There is, of course, no doubt that some parents, particularly mothers, are responsible for alienating their children from their fathers without good reason and thereby creating this sometimes insoluble problem. That unhappy state of affairs, well known in the family courts, is a long way from a recognised syndrome requiring mental health professionals to play an expert role.'

In some subsequent cases the Court of Appeal and High Court judges have alluded to 'parental alienation' while omitting the word 'syndrome'.[296] However, emphasis has remained centred on the circumstances of the particular case rather than on accepting or rejecting the existence of a 'syndrome' let alone affirming Gardner. In *Re O (Contact: Withdrawal of Application)*[297] Wall J said:

> 'Parental alienation is a well-recognised phenomenon. In the recent case of *Re M (Intractable Contact Dispute: Interim Care Orders)*[298] a mother had persuaded her children, quite falsely, that their father had physically and sexually abused them, and that their paternal grandparents were also a danger to them. She refused to allow their father to have any contact with them, and disobeyed court orders for contact. I found that her conduct was causing the children significant harm, and invited the local authority to take care proceedings, the outcome of which was the removal of the children from their mother, and residence orders in favour of their father. That, in my judgment, was a clear case of parental alienation. [However] I agree with Dr Claire Sturge and Dr Danya Glaser in their report for the Court of Appeal in the seminal case of *In Re L (A Child) (Contact: Domestic Violence); In Re V (A Child); In Re M (A Child); In Re H (Children)* ... that the term "parental alienation syndrome" is a misnomer.'

11.164 The Sub-committee of the Lord Chancellor's Advisory Board on Family Law in *Making Contact Work: A Report*[299] stated that 'for the purposes of this report and, we suspect, for those faced with these cases, what matters is not the label which is attached to the phenomenon, but the principled approach which is required to address it'. Thus, discussions of the syndrome may be

---

[294] See, for example, Hobbs 'Parental alienation syndrome and UK family courts' [2002] Fam Law 182 and 381.

[295] [2000] 2 FLR 334, at 351.

[296] For example, *Re T (Contact: Alienation: Permission to Appeal)* [2002] Civ 1736, [2003] 1 FLR 531.

[297] [2003] EWHC 3031 (Fam), [2004] 1 FLR 1258, at [91]–[92].

[298] [2003] EWHC 1024 (Fam), [2003] 2 FLR 636.

[299] At 2.7.

useful in drawing the attention of professionals to the possibility that the overtly supportive parent may be undermining contact but in actual court cases, investigation needs to be directed at whether this is happening in fact in any particular case.[300]

11.165 Professor Harry Zeitlin, another consultant child and adolescent psychiatrist, has tentatively suggested a model which recognises the phenomenon of parental alienation but avoids labelling a parent, recommending instead that the family dynamics need to be analysed and addressed.[301] Often the resident parent, usually the mother, feels abused in the relationship with the other parent and wishes to be free from all traces of the relationship. Because the child's presence is a legacy of the relationship, she continues to feel the father's intrusion and projects her feelings onto the child/father relationship alleging that he will abuse or remove the child. Not all of her statements may be unreasonable. The child, who is often close to the resident parent, cannot resolve the impossible choice between two parents other than by rejecting one in a way which is disproportionate to any threat which the non-resident parent may pose, the difficulty being compounded for younger children because they lack a mature ability to test the reality behind the resident parent's beliefs. Zeitlin suggests that an intervention strategy can be based on obtaining an understanding of the resident parent's feelings and 'hidden reasons' and explaining them to both parents, helping them to state their own fears while addressing the fears of the other. The non-resident parent, for example, should affirm that he does not intend to remove the child, be pro-active by offering rather than resisting supervision of contact and be prepared to demonstrate his willingness to be inconvenienced. Above all however, the resident parent must be prepared to work on the problem.

Case management

11.166 In the past intractable contact disputes have continued for years without resolution and in many cases, without anything approaching a trial of the issues or allegations, in the hope that matters will improve. Allegations of violence or sexual abuse are made after some time rather than at the start of the proceedings, sometimes when committal proceedings are pending against a resident parent who has not complied with a contact order. The longer the proceedings, the more likely it is that there will not be judicial continuity. *Re D (Intractable Contact Dispute: Publicity)*[302] is but one example. The parents separated in November 1998 and the child, then aged 2, lived with her mother. Contact was problematical from the start and the father had not seen his daughter since December 2001. The mother continually sabotaged contact arrangements by means of groundless assertions, over a period of 5 years, of violence, the child being force fed and threats that the child would not be

---

[300] See, for example, *Re C (Prohibition on Further Applications)* [2002] 1 FLR 1136. See also, Mitchell 'Parental Alienation Syndrome: The Debate' (2002) NLJ.
[301] Zeitlin 'Acrimonious contact disputes and so-called Parental Alienation Syndrome: A model of understanding to assist with resolution' (2007) 75 Med Leg J 143.
[302] [2004] EWHC 727 (Fam), [2004] 1 FLR 1226.

returned. Orders for contact were made, penal notices were attached, suspended prison sentences imposed and finally a period of imprisonment for 14 days was implemented in 2001. There were 43 hearings conducted by 16 different judges including four High Court judges after numerous adjournments including 'final hearings' being adjourned four times. The parents' and experts' evidence totalled 950 pages including 338 pages of expert reports. Although an independent social worker became involved, this was not until 2001 and a guardian for the child was not appointed until 2002. When the case came before Munby J in November 2003 the father abandoned his application (aptly described by the judge as 'a battle') for contact. In a judgment which received wide publicity[303] Munby J commented:

> 'From the father's perspective the last 2 years of the litigation have been an exercise in absolute futility. His counsel told me that the father felt very let down by the system ... He has every right to express that view. In a sense it is shaming to have to say it, but I personally agree with his view. Those who are critical of our family justice system may well see this case as exemplifying everything that is wrong with the system. I can understand such a view. The melancholy truth is that this case illustrates all too uncomfortably the failings of the system. There is much wrong with our system and the time has come for us to recognise that fact and to face up to it.'[304]

11.167 Not all cases are like this. In *Re T (Order for Costs)*[305] the Court of Appeal commended a circuit judge on her handling of a dispute during the course of which the mother three times made allegations of abuse including harassment, domestic violence and the sexual abuse of the child.

> 'From the moment it first came before [the judge] ... she rightly reserved it to herself and took a firm procedural grip of it. She made swift and impeccable findings of fact, and when those did not have the desired effect, responded immaculately by an equally swift and effective investigation of the sexual abuse allegations, in relation to which she appropriately engaged expert assistance. Handled differently, this case could well have spiralled into a wholly intractable dispute through a combination of ill feeling, frustration, delay and an absence of proper case management. Instead, effective case management and firm judicial control have produced a clear resolution, and one which is plainly in the interests of J. We can say that with some confidence, because we were told at the hearing of this appeal that, by agreement, the parents have arrived at [an agreed regime of contact with which] both are broadly content. The father in particular was appreciative of the fact that there was judicial continuity. The mother had found [the psychologist's] intervention particularly welcome. The case ... is in our view a paradigm example of how a difficult contact dispute should be handled.'[306]

11.168 One difficulty is that the potential in the case for it to become intractable may not be obvious at the outset. Shaw and Bazley suggest that signs may include:

---

303 For example, 'Judge: law fails love split dads' (The Sun).
304 [2004] EWHC 727 (Fam) [2004] 1 FLR 1226, at [2] and [4].
305 [2005] EWCA Civ 1029, [2005] 2 FLR 681.
306 Ibid, per Wall LJ at [29]–[30].

- allegations of physical, emotional or sexual abuse;

- mental illness in a family member;

- one or other parent losing sight of the child's emotional needs.[307]

Other clues may be:

- one parent demonstrating signs of a personality disorder;

- both or either parent not having had or losing a relationship with one of their parents during their own childhood (see **11.27**).

There is the possibility that the process of the litigation may result in the case becoming intractable.

Effective and firm judicial control is required. It can be divided into three stages:

- assessing and deciding what contact, if any, is in the child's best interests;

- making the order;

- enforcing the subsequent order for contact.

In both stages three rules should be observed:

- Judicial continuity is essential. Every case of any complexity should be allocated to a single or, at most, two judges.[308]

- Whenever the court makes a decision whether of a case management or of a substantive nature, it should be expressly stated that it is being taken as being in the child's best interests.

- All directions whether of a case management or of a substantive nature should be enforced and any failure should be notified to the court and dealt with promptly. 'Swift, efficient, enforcement of existing court orders' is required at the first sign of non-compliance.

> 'A flabby judicial response sends a very damaging message to the defaulting parent, who is encouraged to believe that court orders can be ignored with impunity, and potentially also to the child.'[309]

---

[307] 'Effective strategies in high conflict contact disputes' [2011] Fam Law 1129.

[308] *Re D (Intractable Contact Dispute: Publicity)* [2004] EWHC 727 (Fam), [2004] 1 FLR 1226. See **16.109**.

[309] *Re D (Intractable Contact Dispute: Publicity)* [2004] EWHC 727 (Fam), [2004] 1 FLR 1226, per Munby J at [56].

Assessment stage[310]

11.169

- The allocated judge must set a timetable at the earliest practicable stage so that the cases conclude in months rather than years.[311]

- Disputed allegations, eg of domestic violence or sexual abuse must be tried speedily and resolved.

  > 'In an intractable contact dispute, where the residential parent is putting forward an allegedly factual basis for contact not taking place, there is no substitute, in my judgment, for findings by the court as to whether or not there is any substance to the allegations.'[312]

  For a summary of directions which are required, see **5.53**.

- Once findings have been made, the case must be approached on the basis of the facts as judicially found.

  > 'These are not questions which can be reopened.'[313]

- Allegations which could have been made at an earlier stage should be viewed with appropriate scepticism.[314]

- If a parent persists in assertions contrary to such judicial findings, that is plain evidence of a refusal to recognise reality and what is in the interests of the children.[315]

- Judges must resist the temptation 'to delay the evil day in the hope that perhaps the problem will go away. Judges must also resist the temptation to put contact "on hold", or to direct that it is to be supervised, pending investigation of the allegations'.[316]

- A report under s 7 will always be required. A report can be ordered from a local authority under s 37 of the Act (see **19.3**) if the facts of the case meet its criteria. It must appear to the court that 'it may be appropriate for a care or supervision order to be made' with respect to the children in question. The court must be satisfied that there are reasonable grounds for

---

[310] See also 'Effective strategies in high conflict contact disputes' op cit.
[311] Ibid.
[312] *Re M (Intractable Contact Dispute: Interim Care Orders)* [2003] EWHC 1024 (Fam), [2003] 2 FLR 636, per Wall J at [12].
[313] Ibid.
[314] *Re D (Intractable Contact Dispute: Publicity)* [2004] EWHC 727 (Fam), [2004] 1 FLR 1226.
[315] *Re M (Intractable Contact Dispute: Interim Care Orders)* [2003] EWHC 1024 (Fam), [2003] 2 FLR 636.
[316] *Re D (Intractable Contact Dispute: Publicity)* [2004] EWHC 727 (Fam), [2004] 1 FLR 1226, per Munby J at [55].

believing that the circumstances with respect to the children meet the
threshold criteria under s 31(2) that the child is suffering or is likely to
suffer significant harm.

> 'Section 37 is, accordingly, a well-focused tool, to be used only when the case
> fits its criteria.'[317]

• Intractable contact disputes may justify the child being made a party and
the appointment of a guardian.[318] This should not be delayed. See
Practice Direction 16A and **4.64**.

• The instruction of experts provides an opportunity to assist the family
and not just to provide an opinion.[319]

• Mediation should not be overlooked.[320]

> 'There is no case, however conflicted, which is not potentially open to
> successful mediation. [It is vital] for there to be judicial supervision of the
> process of mediation. It is not enough, in a difficult case such as this, for [the
> judge] directing mediation simply to make the order and thereafter that there
> will be a smooth passage to the initial meeting. The selection of the
> appropriate mediator in a difficult case is crucial and the availability of the
> supervising judge to deal with crisis is equally important.'[321]

• Contact activity directions should be made unless inappropriate and
parents should be directed to attend PIPS (see **11.66**). The parents can
agree to receive counselling, family therapy or other professional help.[322]

> 'Manifestly there are between these adults unresolved areas of conflict
> which, unless resolved, will continue down the years to resound to the
> prejudice and harm of these two children. A process of family therapy is
> infinitely more likely to lead to resolution than continuing litigation between
> them ... Whilst the court has no power to order the respondent to re-engage
> in a process of family therapy, it is relevant to observe that her present
> condition, signed off work, at least gives her plenty of opportunity, plenty of
> availability, and if it emerges before the judge of the Division that reasonable
> proposals, reasonable both as to time and location, have been advanced for

---

[317] *Re M (Intractable Contact Dispute: Interim Care Orders)* [2003] EWHC 1024 (Fam), [2003]
2 FLR 636, per Wall J at [8]. See also *C v C (Children) (Investigation of Circumstances)* [2005]
EWHC 2935 (Fam).

[318] *President's Direction (Representation of Children in Family Proceedings Pursuant to Family
Proceedings Rules 1991 Rule 9.5)* [2004] 1 FLR 1188; *Re M (Intractable Contact Dispute:
Interim Care Orders)* [2003] EWHC 1024 (Fam), [2003] 2 FLR 636; *Re D (Intractable Contact
Dispute: Publicity)* [2004] EWHC 727 (Fam) [2004] 1 FLR 1226.

[319] *Re D (Intractable Contact Dispute: Publicity)* [2004] EWHC 727 (Fam), [2004] 1 FLR 1226.

[320] *Re S (Contact: Promoting Relationship With Absent Parent)* [2004] EWCA Civ 18, [2004]
1 FLR 1279.

[321] *Al-Khatib v Masry* [2004] EWCA Civ 1353 [2005] 1 FLR 381, per Thorpe LJ at [17].

[322] *Re S (Contact: Promoting Relationship With Absent Parent)* [2004] EWCA Civ 18, [2004]
1 FLR 1279, per Thorpe LJ at [47].

the revival of the family therapy and she has continued to refuse, then she must understand that the court may draw adverse inferences against her.[323]

Making the order

11.170 Despite the difficulties posed by intractable contact disputes, it is very important that the attempt to promote contact between a child and the non-resident parent should not be abandoned until it is clear that the child will not benefit from continuing the attempt.[324] At the same time, it has to be remembered that although 'there is a tendency in family law to see an outcome such as this as a panacea – a one-size-fits-all solution ... this is not the case'.[325]

It is important that families are given the assistance they require to give orders the best possible chance of being effective.

- The court should consider whether the following are required:

  - contact activity conditions (see **11.78**);
  - a direction under s 11H for contact to be monitored (see **11.80**);
  - a family assistance order.

- Should a contact centre be used for a limited period to secure regular albeit restricted contact as a platform for more extensive contact?

- Reviews should be pre-listed before the allocated judge at stages where the contact arrangements change, for example contact moves outside a contact centre in order to ensure that there is no delay dealing with problems.

Example

Re P (Contact: Supervision)[326]

11.171 Both parents of the children (aged 8 and 6) had histories of psychiatric illness combined with alcohol and drug abuse. Direct contact went well but the mother objected. The trial judge terminated direct contact on the ground that there was a possible detriment to the children through a threat to the mother's health caused by stress and anxiety over contact. The Court of Appeal allowed the father's appeal on the grounds that there was no evidence that contact to date had had any adverse effect on the children or on the mother's capacity to

---

[323] *Re S (Uncooperative Mother)* [2004] EWCA Civ 597, [2004] 2 FLR 710, per Thorpe LJ at [20] and [22].

[324] *Re S (Contact: Promoting Relationship With Absent Parent)* [2004] EWCA Civ 18, [2004] 1 FLR 1279, per Butler-Sloss P at [32].

[325] *Re M (Intractable Contact Dispute: Interim Care Orders)* [2003] EWHC 1024 (Fam), [2003] 2 FLR 636, per Wall J at [6].

[326] [1996] 2 FLR 314.

care for them and there was insufficient psychiatric or other evidence to justify the finding that there was such a risk in the future as to outweigh the benefits of contact.

Enforcing the order

11.172   In a speech in 2010, Mr Justice Coleridge said of intractable contact disputes:

> '[The] question remains ... how have we reached the situation where these cases are the scourge of the courts both in terms of their quantity and the time they occupy; what is the real underlying cause of the problem? The answer is, I suggest, in large part, a lack of clear and sufficient judicial authority exercised swiftly.'[327]

Seven years earlier in *Re D (Intractable Contact Dispute: Publicity)*[328] Munby J said:

> 'Other things being equal, swift, efficient, enforcement of existing court orders is surely called for at the first sign of trouble. A flabby judicial response sends a very damaging message to the defaulting parent, who is encouraged to believe that court orders can be ignored with impunity, and potentially also to the child. Thus, it may in some cases be appropriate for a judge who has concerns as to whether the contact ordered for Saturday will take place to include in the order a direction requiring the father's solicitor to inform the judge on Monday morning by fax or email if there have been any problems, on the basis (also spelt out in the order so that the mother can be under no illusions as to what will happen if she defaults) that the mother will thereupon be ordered to attend court personally on Tuesday morning and immediately arrested if she fails to attend.'

11.173   There are two messages in the authorities. The first is that given by Sir Nicholas Wall.

> 'The message is that if, in the forensic process we get to the enforcement stage, we have failed. The order we have made is not working. The first proposition therefore is that we should try never to get to the stage of enforcement.'[329]

The second is that the court must deal firmly and swiftly with any breach of an order. To make no order if an option exists and if an unsatisfactory state of affairs exists when the case is returned to court is an abdication of responsibility.[330]

11.174   A number of options are available in the event of breach. Save for committal or a fine – and even there the primary aim is to ensure compliance rather than punishment[331] – the court will be concerned with securing

---

[327]   'Let's hear it for the child' [2011] Fam Law 96.
[328]   [2004] EWHC 727 (Fam), [2004] 1 FLR 1226, at [56].
[329]   'Enforcement of contact orders' [2005] Fam Law 26, at p 30.
[330]   *Re C (Residence Order)* [2007] EWCA Civ 866, [2008] 1 FLR 211, per Ward LJ at [26].
[331]   See *Hale v Tanner* [2000] 2 FLR 879.

compliance with an order which it made because it considered tit o be in the child's best interest and not to punish recalcitrance.[332] Although changing circumstances have to be considered and orders should not be enforced if they are no longer in the child's interests, parents should not be allowed to think that orders can be re-negotiated in some way.

11.175 The options available to the court include:

- Further attempts at therapy etc.[333]

- An order for compensation for financial loss under s 11O. See **23.22**.

- An enforcement order under s 11J. See **23.28**.

- A fine or committal. This is a matter of last resort.[334] See **23.47**.

- Changing a child's residence.

- Placing the child in the interim care of a local authority as a prelude to a move to the care of the other parent.

Change of residence

11.176 Although in some cases a persistent refusal by a parent to co-operate with contact may justify changing a child's residence if overall that is in the child's best interests, such an order should not be made merely to enforce a contact order. The Lord Chancellor's Sub-Committee disapproved of the use or threat of a residence application as a means of achieving contact:

> 'It is a legitimate complaint by women's groups that abused women are sometimes induced to agree to unsuitable and unsafe contact with violent fathers by their belief in unfounded threats that their children will either be transferred to the father or taken into care. At the same time there will be cases in which a refusal of contact will be sufficiently damaging to the child as to outweigh the trauma caused by removing the child from the care of the residential parent. [Cases may include a mother who has placed herself in a socially isolated position with the child and is thoroughly over-protective of him], where children are being brought up in the false belief that they have been sexually abused by the absent parent or where children of mixed race are being brought up in the belief that the race to which the absent parent belongs consists of people who are dangerous and/or bad.'[335]

---

[332] *Re W (Residence: Leave to Appeal)* [2010] EWCA Civ 1280, [2011] 1 FLR 1143, per Wall P at [52].

[333] For, example, *Re C (Residence Order)* [2007] EWCA Civ 866, [2008] 1 FLR 211.

[334] *Re M (Intractable Contact Dispute: Interim Care Orders)* [2003] EWHC 1024 (Fam), [2003] 2 FLR 636.

[335] *Making Contact Work*, op cit, at para 14.27.

For this reason, a change of residence is a 'judicial weapon of last resort'.[336] A graduated approach to a change may be appropriate and in the child's best interests if the resident carer's care is, apart from an unwillingness to allow contact, satisfactory. For example the court can postpone a decision to change residence until a review to give the carer time to consider her situation.[337] A residence order can be made but suspended on terms.[338]

11.177 Before such an order is made, the welfare test and checklist must, of course, be carefully applied. The order should not be made to punish the mother.[339] Even if the order is justified and the child can move to the other parent's care, the difficult issue of contact with the former resident parent has to be considered. In *Re M (Intractable Contact Dispute: Interim Care Orders)*[340] the children, having been moved to their father, stated that they did not want to see their mother. Wall J stressed that they needed to receive skilled help.

> 'I would be bitterly disappointed at the end of this case if, having rescued the children from the significant harm in which we found them in the earlier part of this year, the court were then to be left with a situation in which they had found their father and restored their relationship with him, only to lose it with their mother.'

For an example of continued attempts to secure contact including an attempt to change residence which failed, see *Re S (Transfer of Residence)*.[341]

Interim care order

11.178 Changing residence if a prolonged resistance to contact by the resident parent has damaged the parent/child relationship is obviously very difficult.[342] In extreme cases, as illustrated by *Re M (Intractable Contact, Interim Care Order)*[343] a child can be placed in the interim care of a local authority as a prelude to being moved to the other parent. In that case Wall J gave detailed guidance on how this should be approached. The s 38 criteria must be met and the court must spell out the reasons for making the s 37 order very carefully and a transcript (or very full note) of the judgment should be made available to the local authority at the earliest opportunity. It is preferable that the s 37 report is supported by professional or expert advice.

---

[336] *Re A (Residence Order)* [2009] EWCA Civ 1141, [2010] 1 FLR 1083, per Wall LJ at [18] and per Coleridge J at [21].

[337] *Re C (Residence)* [2007] EWHC 2312 (Fam), [2008] 1 FLR 826.

[338] *Re A (Suspended Residence Order)* [2009] EWHC 1576 (Fam), [2010] 1 FLR 1679.

[339] *Re K (Contact: Committal Order)* [2002] EWCA Civ 1559, [2003] 1 FLR 277, per Hale LJ at [28].

[340] [2003] EWHC 1024 (Fam), [2003] 2 FLR 636, at [170].

[341] [2010] EWHC 192 (Fam), [2010] 1 FLR 1785; [2010] EWCA Civ 219; [2010] EWCA Civ 325, [2011] 1 FLR 1789.

[342] See, for example, *Re K (Contact: Committal Order)* [2002] EWCA Civ 1558, [2003] 1 FLR 277, per Hale J at para 28.

[343] [2003] EWHC 1024 (Fam), [2003] 2 FLR 636.

11.179 See *Re H (Care Order: Contact)*[344] for an example of a final care order being revoked on appeal in part because the 10-year-old child wished to return to the care of her mother and in part because it could not be said that her living with a foster carer would secure direct contact with her father and maternal grandmother.

Examples

Re O (A Minor) (Contact: Imposition of Conditions)[345]

11.180 The mother was not prepared to participate in contact between the 2-year-old child and his father. The trial judge directed her to send the father photographs of the child every 3 months, copies of progress reports and to accept delivery of cards and presents pending a review after 6 months. The Court of Appeal dismissed the mother's appeal.

Re M (Intractable Contact Dispute: Interim Care Orders)[346]

11.181 Children aged 13 and 10. Four years of disputes. Mother twice made false allegations against father and paternal grandparents that they had physically and sexually abused the children. Suspended committal order was made which was breached. Child applied for prohibited steps order against contact. Children's residence transferred to father by way of an interim care order.

A v A (Shared Residence)[347]

11.182 An intractable contact dispute involving two children aged 9 and 11 in which the mother had made allegations of sexual abuse against the father, which had been rejected. The children moved to live with the father on an interim basis and by the time of the final hearing were spending half their time with each parent. A shared residence order was justified despite the parents being able to work in harmony because it was important to reflect the reality of their lives and the fact that the parents were equal in the eyes of the law. There was a risk that a sole residence order could be interpreted as giving only one parent control.

V v V (Contact: Implacable Hostility)[348]

11.183 Children aged 8 and 6. Four years of disputes. Mother made a number of false allegations of sexual, physical and emotional abuse against the father and his relatives. Residence transferred to father.

---

[344] [2008] EWCA Civ 1245, [2009] 2 FLR 55.
[345] [1995] 2 FLR 124.
[346] [2003] EWHC 1024 (Fam), [2003] 2 FLR 636.
[347] [2004] EWHC 142 (Fam), [2004] 1 FLR 1195.
[348] [2004] EWHC 1215 (Fam), [2004] 2 FLR 851.

'This is a case in which, but for the mother's malign influence, the children would have benefited by having ... regular and substantial contact ... The false allegations by M ... are likely to continue as long as the children live with her. She will continue to refer the children to social services, the police and hospital. She will continue to involve them in lies, to coach them, to subject them to intrusive investigations in respect of those whom they want to love and respect. She provides a very bad example to the children by her manipulation and deceit. She seems oblivious to the harm which she is causing. I find that, if left with M, there will be increasing emotional harm to the children and ... M's conduct is likely to continue. The use of enforcement procedures, such as penal notice, may have the effect of causing M to deliver contact but it will not prevent her from continuing to poison the children's minds against their father and family and building up a case against him ... The capability of the parents means that F and his wider family are able to provide a more balanced and emotionally secure basis for the children in the future.'[349]

Re W (Residence: Leave to Appeal)[350]

11.184 A mother refused to comply with a contact order and failed to attend hearings. She made a number of very serious allegations against the father which were found to be unsubstantiated. At one stage she was committed for 7 days. After 3 years in which she had failed to allow contact on 28 out of 34 occasions, the judge made a residence order in favour of the paternal grandmother. The Court of Appeal refused the mother leave to appeal.

'[The] course which the judge took was one which was properly open to her on the evidence. In my view, the contrary is unarguable. The judge plainly did not move P as an act of frustration or irritation at the mother's contumelious conduct. She moved P because she took the view that P's welfare in the longer term required such a move ... The mother is not left without a remedy. No residence or contact order is even final. The judge has [listed a review]. However, if the mother is to seek to disturb the order made by the judge, she will need both to satisfy the judge that she really has changed, (in other words that she really and genuinely recognises the value of P's relationship with her father) and also that it is in P's best interests to live with her rather than with her paternal grandmother.'[351]

TERMINATION OF CONTACT ORDERS

11.185 Contact orders will end:

- when discharged;

- when the child reaches the age specified in the order or, if none, 16;[352]

---

[349] Ibid, per Bracewell J at [49]–[50].
[350] [2010] EWCA Civ 1280, [2011] 1 FLR 1143.
[351] Per Wall P at [57] and [60].
[352] CA 1989, s 9(6).

- when a care order is made in relation to the child;[353]

- if the order requires a parent with whom the child lives to allow the child to have contact with the other parent, when the parents live together for a continuous period of more than 6 months.[354]

---

[353] Ibid, s 91(2).
[354] Ibid, s 11(6).

Chapter 12

GUARDIANSHIP AND SPECIAL GUARDIANSHIP ORDERS

INTRODUCTION

12.1 Parental responsibility is the keystone to the private law relating to children. Usually, it can be gained permanently only by parents and step-parents. However, in the case of the death of both parents or if the child's need for permanence cannot be met by adoption, guardianship and a recent creation, special guardianship, enable it to be granted to someone who is not the child's parents.

GUARDIANSHIP ORDERS

Background

12.2 The orphaned child, once familiar both in the real world[1] and in fiction,[2] is now much less common and is far less visible. Falling death rates meant that by 1971 the proportion of children living in one-parent families had fallen to about 10% and a quarter of these had lost one parent. In 1974 the Finer Committee on One-Parent Families could comment that '[Divorce] has replaced death as the major factor in disposing of marriages of couples in the younger age groups'.[3] However, bereavement – in the sense of losing someone with whom they have a significant relationship – is still a common experience for young people. One study has found that as many as 92% of young people will experience what they see as a 'significant' bereavement before the age of 16[4] and between 4 and 7% will lose a parent.[5] Yet there is little research on the extent and impact of bereavement, either socially or legally. Although many practitioners will have been involved in at least one case arising from the death

---

[1]   In Clayworth, a village in Nottinghamshire, in 1688, 35.5% of all children had lost one or both parents through death; Laslett *The World We have Lost – Further Explored* (2005) chap 5.

[2]   David Copperfield's father died 6 months before David was born and his mother when he was about 10.

[3]   *Report of the Committee on One-Parent Families* (Cmnd 5629) para 3.32.

[4]   Harrison and Hartington 'Adolescents' bereavement experiences: prevalence, association with depressive symptoms and use of services' *Journal of Adolescence* 24(2) 159.

[5]   *Young People, Bereavement and Loss: Disruptive Transitions?* (McCarthy National Children's Bureau, 2005) summarised in *The Impact of Bereavement and Loss on Young People* (Findings Ref 0315, Joseph Rowntree Foundation).

of a child's parent, save in relation to foreign guardians being able to consent to adoption there is only one reported authority concerning guardianship post the Children Act 1989.[6]

12.3 Prior to the enactment of the Children Act 1989 the legal framework dealing with the custody of a child after the death of one or both parents was a 'patchwork of common law and statute'.[7] By virtue of the Guardianship Act 1973, for example, the mother's rights and authority were the same as the father's but no statute equated her position to the natural guardianship of the father. Each parent could appoint a guardian to replace him on his death but if the survivor then objected, the guardian had to apply to the court. The guardian could also apply if he thought the surviving parent unfit. If the appointment took effect, the guardian would have the same rights as the survivor, creating the possibility of disagreement. The Law Commission suggested abolishing 'these archaic and confusing rules'[8] and replacing them by 'a coherent modern structure'[9] within the general framework proposed for parental responsibility. Its suggestions were based on three principles.

- Guardians should have full and complete legal responsibility for the child if the parents die and this should be accomplished by granting them parental responsibility.[10]

- Appointments should generally only take effect after the death of the surviving parent unless there was a residence order in favour of the deceased parent, in which case both parent and guardian would have parental responsibility.[11]

- There should be a simpler method of appointment, by any document, not just a deed or will. The power of the court to appoint a guardian should mirror that of a parent and the court should also have the power to remove a guardian.[12]

The status of guardianship

12.4 A guardian has parental responsibility for the child,[13] that is 'all the rights, duties, powers, responsibilities and authority which by law a parent of a child has in relation to the child and his property'.[14] Parental responsibility is discussed more fully in **Chapter 7**.

---

6   *Re SH (Care Order: Orphan)* [1995] 1 FLR 746.
7   Family Law Review of Child Law, Guardianship and Custody (1988) Law Com No 594 para 2.22.
8   Ibid, para 2.3.
9   Ibid, para 2.22.
10   Ibid, para 2.23.
11   Ibid, para 2.27.
12   Ibid, paras 2.29–2.30.
13   CA 1989, s 5(6).
14   Ibid, s 3(1).

The appointment normally takes effect on the death of the person making the appointment if the child no longer has a parent who has parental responsibility for him.[15] However, it takes effect at once if immediately before the death there was either a residence order in force in favour of the person making the appointment which was not shared with any surviving parent, or he was the child's only or surviving special guardian.[16]

The appointment of a guardian

Appointment by a parent, guardian or special guardian

12.5 A guardian can be appointed by a parent with parental responsibility,[17] a guardian,[18] either before or after his own appointment takes effect,[19] or a special guardian.[20]

The appointment must be made in writing, dated and:

(1) be signed by the person making the appointment; or

(2) in the case of an appointment made by a will which is not signed by the testator, be signed at the direction of the testator in accordance with the requirements of s 9 of the Wills Act 1837, namely that it must appear that the testator intended by the signature to give effect to the will, the signature was acknowledged by the testator in the presence of two or more witnesses present at the same time, and each witness either attested or signed the will or acknowledged his signature in the presence of the testator; or

(3) in any other case be signed at the direction of the person making the appointment, in his presence and in the presence of two witnesses who each attest the signature.[21]

An appointment may be revoked in a number of ways.

• by a subsequent appointment, unless it is clear, whether expressly or by necessary implication, that the purpose of the subsequent appointment was to appoint an additional guardian;[22]

---

15 CA 1989, s 5(7)(a).
16 Ibid, s 5(7)(b) as amended by Adoption and Children Act 2002, s 115.
17 Ibid, s 5(3).
18 Ibid, s 5(4).
19 Ibid, s 5(7) and (8).
20 Ibid, s 5(4) as amended by Adoption and Children Act 2002, s 115.
21 Ibid, s 5(5).
22 Ibid, s 6(1).

- by a written and dated instrument, either signed by the person making the appointment or signed by another at his direction, in his presence and in the presence of two witnesses each of whom attest the signature;[23]

- if made other than in a will or codicil, if the person making the appointment, with the intention of revoking it, either destroys the instrument or has some other person destroy it in his presence;[24]

- if the person appointed is the spouse of the person who made the appointment and the marriage is dissolved or annulled in England and Wales (or elsewhere if the divorce or annulment is recognised in England and Wales) unless a contrary intention appears by the appointment.[25]

A person who is appointed guardian may disclaim the appointment by an instrument in writing signed by him and made within a reasonable time of his first knowing that the appointment has taken effect.[26]

Appointment by the court

12.6 A court may appoint one or more[27] individuals as guardian(s)[28] if:

- the child has no parent with parental responsibility for him; or

- a residence order has been made with respect to the child in favour of a parent or guardian or special guardian of his who has died while the order is in force; or

- there is no residence order in favour of a parent, guardian or special guardian and the child's only or last surviving special guardian dies.[29]

The order can be made either on the application by any individual who wishes to be appointed guardian, or by the court of its own motion in any family proceedings,[30] if the court considers the order should be made.[31]

The test is the section 1 welfare test. One of the only two modern authorities on the topic[32] states that even if, which was doubted, the court has power to make a guardianship order if the child is a ward, it should not be made if the

---

23   CA 1989, s 6(2).
24   Ibid, s 6(3).
25   Ibid, s 6(3A) inserted by Law Reform (Succession) Act 1995, s 4(1).
26   Ibid, s 6(5).
27   Ibid, s 5(10).
28   But not a local authority or other body: *Re SH (Care Order: Orphan)* [1995] 1 FLR 746. However, a named individual, for example an individual who is the director of social services, can be, and to the knowledge of the author, has been, appointed.
29   CA 1989, s 5(1).
30   As defined by ibid, s 8(3).
31   Ibid, s 5(1) and (2).
32   *Re C (Minors) (Wardship: Adoption)* [1989] 1 FLR 222.

wardship is to continue. Furthermore, even though it may not be an absolute bar, it would be unusual, to say the least, to appoint a guardian who had never seen the child.

Revocation of guardianship

12.7 Once guardianship has taken effect, an appointment, whether made by the court or otherwise, may be brought to an end by the court at any time:

- on the application of any person who has parental responsibility for the child; or

- on the application of the child concerned, with the leave of the court; or

- in any family proceedings if the court considers that those proceedings should be brought to an end even though no application has been made.[33]

SPECIAL GUARDIANSHIP

12.8 The provisions relating to special guardianship orders are contained in ss 14A–14G of the Children Act 1989, inserted by the Adoption and Children Act 2002, s 115(1) which came into effect on 30 December 2005. The creation of special guardianship arose from a major review of adoption law and special guardianship orders commonly are made in public law care proceedings. However its status, vesting parental responsibility in private individuals rather than a public authority while at the same time preserving the status of the child's parents as joint holders of parental responsibility, is planted in private law proceedings.

Background

Custodianship

12.9 The problem of how to provide a permanent family placement for older children in local authority care or living with relatives for whom adoption is not an option has been recognised for over 30 years. In 1972 the Departmental Committee on the Adoption of Children ('the Houghton Committee') reported that:

> 'There are many children not being brought up by their natural parents but are in the long-term care of foster parents or relatives. These people normally have no legal status in relation to the child, and the law provides no means by which they can acquire it without cutting his links with his natural family by adoption. They are faced with the choice of doing without legal security, which may be damaging

---

[33]   CA 1989, s 6(7).

to the child or applying for an adoption order. This is one reason why … adoption is frequently applied for in inappropriate circumstances, particularly by relatives.'[34]

The Committee recommended that the right to apply for 'guardianship' should be granted to relatives and (although it had some reservations) to foster parents. It might be appropriate for foster parents where the parents were out of the picture, the foster parents and the child wanted to secure their relationship and be independent of the local authority but the child was old enough to have a sense of identity and wished to keep this (sic) and retain his own name. It might also be appropriate in a few cases where the natural parents were in touch with the child and their bond with the child was secure, but they recognised they would never be able to provide him with a home. In other cases, foster parents might be precluded from applying for adoption because of financial constraints.[35]

The order would differ from adoption in a number of ways.[36]

- It would not be irrevocable.

- It would not permanently extinguish parental rights although these would be suspended.

- It would not alter the child's relationship with the members of his natural family.

- The child's natural parents could have contact with him but under the control of the court.

- The child would retain his own name unless he wanted to change it.

- There would be no right to inherit under intestacy.

These are all features of special guardianship.

12.10 The proposals of the Houghton Committee were enacted in Part II of the Children Act 1975 with the status being referred to as 'custodianship' rather than 'guardianship'. Professor Cretney has commented that had the provisions actually been brought into force with minimal delay 'it would have been seen as a landmark in the history of child law'.[37] Unfortunately, there was delay in its coming into force because of lack of resources, both staffing and financial, including the cost of providing for Legal Aid.[38] In the event, it did not come

---

[34] *Report of the Departmental Committee on the Adoption of Children* (Cmnd 5107, 1972) at para 116.
[35] Ibid, para 121.
[36] Ibid, para 123.
[37] Cretney *Family Law in the Twentieth Century* (2004), at p 707.
[38] *The Cost of operating the Unimplemented Provisions of the Children Act 1975* (DHSS, 1980); Cretney (above), at p 707.

into force until 1 December 1985 and even then, the provisions of the Act which required local authorities to establish a comprehensive adoption service were delayed for another 3 years. One contemporary commentator, Professor Bevan, wrote in 1988, 'waiting for something for over a decade may diminish one's enthusiasm for it'.[39] In fact, by 1985, 'it was all but dead on arrival'.[40] It was given its quietus by being repealed by Sch 15 of the Children Act 1989. An official verdict was that the legislation was 'complicated and technical and its impact appears to have been small. This was probably due to its complexity and late implementation.'[41]

Judicial attitudes to custodianship

12.11 Judicial attitudes towards custodianship were on the whole supportive.[42] It was welcomed in advance of enactment as filling a gap in the existing law[43] and Balcombe LJ in *Re C*[44] stated that 'when the custodianship provisions of Part II of the Children Act are brought into force ... in some cases at any rate, contested applications for adoption may become things of the past'. In cases where parents opposed adoption on the ground that custodianship would be available, courts took this into account. In *Re H*[45] the foster parents of children aged 11 and 9 who had continuing contact with their father and paternal grandmother commenced adoption proceedings to prevent their feared removal by the local authority. The Court of Appeal held that this was a misuse of the procedure and Sir John Arnold P commented that 'if ever there was a case which cried out for the consideration of custodianship [yet to be brought into force] this is that case'. The possibility of custodianship meant that the father could not be said to be unreasonably withholding his consent to adoption. On the other hand there were cases where the absolute security of adoption was seen as being important for the child concerned and the possibility of custodianship was rejected in favour of adoption.[46] One difficulty in drawing much guidance from this experience is that courts in the main were dealing with adoption applications being made in advance of the custodianship provisions coming into force and the practicalities of the status did not have to be examined critically against the factual background of the cases.

---

[39] Bevan *Child Law* (1989), at para 6.94.
[40] Cullen 'Adoption- a (fairly) new approach' (2005) CFLQ 476, at 478.
[41] *Inter-Departmental Review of Adoption Law – Discussion Paper Number 1: The Nature and Effect of Adoption* (Department of Health, 1990) para 42. See also Bullard, Malos and Parker *Custodianship Research Project: a report to the Department of Health* (Socio-Legal Centre for Family Studies, University of Bristol, 1990).
[42] See Montgomery 'Custodianship: Twelve months on' [1987] Fam Law 214; Hershman and McFarlane 'Child in care: adoption, custodianship, access' [1988] Fam Law 31.
[43] See, for example, *Re M (Minors) (Adoption: Parents' Agreement)* [1985] FLR 921.
[44] [1986] 1 FLR 315, at 318.
[45] [1985] FLR 519.
[46] *Re J (A Minor)* [1987] 1 FLR 455; *Re S (A Minor) (Adoption or Custodianship)* [1987] 2 FLR 331.

Adoption – a new approach

12.12   The problem of what to do with children in need of a permanent home
did not go away. In 1993, another White Paper, *Adoption: The Future*[47]
proposed introducing a 'new guardianship order' to be known as 'Inter-Vivos
Guardianship'.[48] It would extend to the age of 18 and allow a guardian to
appoint another in the event of his death. Foster parents who obtained an
order might regard it as giving them 'Foster-plus' status. However, the idea
never reached the statute book. It was revived again in 2000 by the Prime
Minister's Performance and Innovation Unit (PIU)[49] which made comments
similar to those of the Houghton Committee 28 years earlier.

'One specific message to be voiced during the study was that the range of legal
options to provide the spectrum of permanence is at present not complete. In
particular, there was a need identified for an intermediate legal status for children
that offered greater security than long term fostering without the absolute legal
severance from the birth family associated with adoption.

While planned long term fostering could offer some degree of security, and might
suit some children, it still lacks real security and a proper sense of permanence in
a family. Children are still subject to monthly visits by social workers and annual
medical inspections, and permission from a social worker is needed, for example,
before a child can 'sleep over' at a friend's house. Residence Orders were
acknowledged to provide some of what was required, but are still open to legal
challenge at any time, and usually ended when the child was 16. Those consulted
were of the view that a new option would in particular fulfil the needs of a distinct
group of older children who did not wish to be adopted. The precise nature of a
new option will need careful consideration.'[50]

A further White Paper in the same year, *Adoption – a new approach*,[51] adopted
and widened this.

'Ethnic communities have religious and cultural difficulties with adoption as it is
set out in law. Unaccompanied asylum-seeking children may also need secure,
permanent homes, but have strong attachments to their families abroad. All these
children deserve the same chance as any other to enjoy the benefits of a legally
secure, stable permanent placement that promotes a supportive, lifelong
relationship with their carers, where the court decides that is in their best interests.
In order to meet the needs of these children where adoption is not appropriate,
and to modernise the Government believes there is a case to develop a new
legislative option to provide permanence short of the legal separation involved in
adoption. ... The Government will legislate to create this new option, which could
be called "special guardianship". It will be used only to provide permanence for
those children for whom adoption is not appropriate, and where the court decides
it is in the best interests of the child or young person.'[52]

---

[47]   Cm 2288.
[48]   Above, paras 5.23–5.27.
[49]   *Prime Minister's Review of Adoption* (The Cabinet Office, 2000).
[50]   Ibid, paras 8.5–8.7.
[51]   Cm 5017.
[52]   Ibid, paras 5.8–5.10.

The main points about the new status would be that it would:

- give the carer clear responsibility for all aspects of caring for the child or young person, and for taking the decisions to do with their upbringing. The child or young person will no longer be looked after by the council;

- provide a firm foundation on which to build a lifelong permanent relationship between the carer and the child or young person;

- be legally secure;

- preserve the basic legal link between the child or young person and their birth family;

- be accompanied by proper access to a full range of support services including, where appropriate, financial support.

These proposals were enacted by the Adoption and Children Act 2002.

Special guardianship – the future

12.13 In 1988 Professor Bevan had prophesied that 'four closely integrated factors' would determine the future of custodianship: its attractiveness as an alternative to adoption, the crucial role of the local authority, judicial attitudes and the availability of advice and resources.[53] The PIU reported that those consulted were of the view that special guardianship would fulfil a need[54] and the White Paper, that it was 'strongly supported'.[55] Whether it will prove to be popular in practice, falling short of adoption which has a psychological resonance both with children and carers, will be seen in time. The provision of resources will play an important role and unlike custodianship, regulations will set out the services which local authorities must provide, not only for the duration of the order but also after the child reaches the age of 18. Deborah Cullen[56] has commented that 'if properly publicised and supported by local authorities, it could be a really important option for some children'. However 'there is detectable some ambivalence in the government, perhaps a fear that special guardianship will be too readily seen by the courts as a less controversial option than adoption'. As for custodianship, special guardianship has been welcomed by the judiciary as an additional option, especially as there is greater awareness of the disadvantages of growing up in care[57] and the importance of the child's autonomy.[58]

---

[53]   *Child Law* (1989) para 6.94.

[54]   *Prime Minister's Review of Adoption* (The Cabinet Office, 2000) para 8.6.

[55]   Cm 5017 para 5.9.

[56]   The Secretary to the Legal Group of the British Association for Adoption and Fostering (BAAF) but writing in her own right in *Adoption – a (fairly) new approach* (above at para **10.10**). See also Johnstone 'Special Guardianship orders: a guide' (2006) Fam Law 116.

[57]   See, for example, *People Like Us* (Utting Stationery Office, 1997).

[58]   For example, *Mabon v Mabon* [2005] EWCA Civ 634, [2005] 2 FLR 1011.

12.14 Research by Ananda Hall into the first year in which special guardianship was available found that 372 orders were made in England and Wales in 2006 excluding orders made in Family Proceedings Courts.[59] Nearly three-quarters (74%) were made in care proceedings and 26% in private law proceedings.

An analysis of a sample of 70 cases found that kinship carers were by far the most common special guardians (87%) compared to local authority foster parents (12%). Of the kinship carers just over two-thirds (68%) were of the 'grandparent' generation, 17% were aunts and uncles and the remaining 15%, cousins, step-parents or siblings. A quarter of the special guardians had not previously cared for the child. The children in the sample ranged from 6 months to 17 years and Hall found no evidence that special guardianship was being used for older children. Contact orders were made in 30% of cases and orders permitting a change of name in 10%.

12.15 In 2010, 410 applications for special guardianship orders were made in public law proceedings and 1,320 in private law proceedings.[60] In the same year 1,970 special guardianship orders were made in public law proceedings and 900 in private law proceedings. No such orders were refused or withdrawn in public law proceedings, an indication that family members are unlikely to apply for orders without the local authority indicating their support at a stage where it is unlikely that the child will return to a parent. In private law proceedings 30 applications (3% of those made) were withdrawn or refused, perhaps because most applications in private law proceedings are unlikely to be opposed.[61]

The status of special guardianship

12.16 The order lasts until the child's 18th birthday.

The effect of the order is that while the order is in force:

- the special guardian has parental responsibility for the child;[62]

- subject to any other order, the special guardian is entitled to exercise parental responsibility to the exclusion of any other person with parental responsibility apart from another special guardian,[63] unless any enactment or rule of law requires the consent of more than one person with parental responsibility.[64] In the absence of judicial guidance it is

---

[59]   'Special Guardianship: A missed opportunity – findings from research' [2008] Fam Law 148 and 'Special Guardianship and permanency planning: unforeseen circumstances and missed opportunities' [2008] CFLQ 359.

[60]   *Judicial and Court Statistics 2010* (Ministry of Justice), Table 2.3.

[61]   Ibid, Table 2.4.

[62]   CA 1989, s 14C(1)(a).

[63]   Ibid, s 14C(1)(b).

[64]   Ibid, s 14C(2)(a).

uncertain whether a special guardian needs the agreement of all with parental responsibility before authorising a non-therapeutic operation such as circumcision;

- making the order discharges any care order which is in force;[65]

- no person may cause the child to be known by a new surname or to remove him from the UK (save in the case of a special guardian, for less than 3 months[66]) without either the written consent of every person who has parental responsibility or the leave of the court.[67] This may create a difficulty where there are two special guardians and a residence order has been made in respect of one. Can the special guardian with residence remove the child for more than 1 but less than 3 months without the consent of the other? As s 14C(4) only states that s 14C(3) does not prevent the removal and not s 14C(3) and s 13, presumably not;

- if the child dies, the special guardian must take reasonable steps to give notice of the fact to each parent with parental responsibility and each guardian;[68]

- no application may be made for a residence order made without leave whether or not the applicant would otherwise require leave.[69]

The order does not affect any rights which a parent has in relation to the child's adoption or placement for adoption.[70] Nor does it affect rights held by a parent as parent and not just as someone with parental responsibility, for example the right to apply for a residence order without first seeking leave.[71]

12.17 The status of special guardians lies somewhere between carers with a residence order who have limited legal autonomy, and natural parents and adopters who have absolute autonomy. Where there is a residence order the general rule on the exercise of parental responsibility is governed by s 2(7) of the 1989 Act which provides that:

'Where more than one person has parental responsibility for a child, each of them may act alone and without the other (or others) in meeting that responsibility but nothing in this Part shall be taken to affect the operation of any enactment which requires the consent of more than one person in a matter affecting the child.'

Where there is a special guardian, the general rule is extended to a limited extent and the special guardian is entitled to exercise parental responsibility to

---

[65] CA 1989, s 91(5A).
[66] Compare ibid, s 13 where a person with a residence order may remove the child for less than one month.
[67] Ibid, s 14C(3).
[68] Ibid, s 14C(5).
[69] Ibid, s 10(7A).
[70] Ibid, s 14C(2)(b).
[71] Ibid, s 10(4)(a).

the exclusion of any other person with parental responsibility apart from another special guardian,[72] unless any enactment or rule of law requires the consent of more than one person with parental responsibility.[73] If there is a dispute in relation to any exercise of parental responsibility, the parent or special guardian or anyone with a residence order[74] (and others who have obtained leave under s 10(8)) may apply under s 10 for a specific issue or prohibited steps order. Special guardians are protected from unmeritorious claims for residence orders by the requirement that applicants, including parents, need to the leave of the court (see **15.1**). Curiously, natural parents do not require leave to apply for contact orders, or specific issue or prohibited steps orders. In *Re S (Adoption Order or Special Guardianship Order)*[75] Wall LJ commented:

> 'The absence of a requirement that parents obtain leave may seem surprising because special guardianship orders are designed to promote finality but if so, one might expect similar considerations to apply to other forms of orders under s 8. An essential component of the advantages produced by an adoption order for both adopters and children is that they are in most cases then free from the threat of future litigation. If the same protection is not available in respect of special guardianship orders, this may be a substantial derogation from the security provided.'

In comparison, adoption orders are irrevocable and all applications by the natural family for section 8 orders require the leave of the court.

12.18   The – at least semi-permanent – nature of the status was underlined by in *Birmingham City Council v R*,[76] by Wall LJ.

> '[Special guardianship] is plainly not something to be embarked upon lightly or capriciously, not least because the status it gives the special guardian effectively prevents the exercise of parental power on the part of the child's natural parents ... In this respect it is substantially different from a residence order which ... does not confer on any person who holds the order the exclusivity in the exercise of parental responsibility which accompanies a special guardianship order.'

Notwithstanding the comment that the status 'effectively prevents' the exercise of parental responsibility by the child's parents, there has been little by way of reported cases to support or disprove the proposition. Is it really the case that special guardians will easily obtain permission to emigrate where there is a close relationship between a child and his parents supported by frequent contact? Much may depend on the circumstances of the individual case. Writing extra judicially Baroness Hale of Richmond has stated that:

---

72   CA 1989, s 14C(1)(b).
73   Ibid, s 14C(2)(a).
74   Ibid, s 10(2).
75   [2007] EWCA Civ 54, [2007] 1 FLR 819, at [65].
76   [2006] EWCA Civ 1748, [2007] 1 FLR 564, per Wall LJ at [78].

'The message for us all … must be that the legal status should follow from the answers to the key questions about the child's future rather than the other way around. The legal status is a means and not an end. The end is the successful upbringing of the child.'[77]

Who can be a special guardian?

12.19   A special guardian (s) can be:

- one or more individuals, who

- must be aged 18 or over, but

- who is not a parent of the child in question.[78]

Who can apply?

Applicants who need no leave to apply

12.20   These are:[79]

- any guardian of the child;

- any individual in whose favour a residence order is in force;

- any person with whom the child has lived for a period of at least 3 years. This need not be continuous but must not have begun more than 5 years before or ended more than 3 months before the making of the application;[80]

- any person who in a case where a residence order is in force has the consent of each person in whose favour the order was made;

- any person who in a case where the child is in the care of the local authority,[81] has the consent of that authority;

- any person who has the consent of each person who has parental responsibility for the child;

- a local authority foster parent with whom the child has lived for a period of at least 1 year immediately preceding the application;

---

[77]   Jordan and Lindley (eds) *Special Guardianship: What Does It Offer Children Who Cannot Live With Their Parents?* (Family Rights Group, 2006), Foreword at p iv.

[78]   CA 1989, s 14A(1) and (2).

[79]   Ibid, s 14A(5).

[80]   Ibid, s 14A(12) and s 10(10).

[81]   Ie is subject to a care order: ibid, s 31(1).

- a relative with whom the child has lived for a period of at least 1 year immediately preceding the application.

Applicants who need leave

12.21 Anyone else, including the child, requires leave and s 9(3) applies in relation to an application for permission.[82] Taking into account s 10A(5) this means that a person who is or was at any time in the last 6 months a local authority foster parent of the child who does not qualify under s 10A(5) may not apply for leave unless:

- if the child is being looked after, he has the consent of the local authority to apply (if the child is subject to a care order and the local authority consents to the order being granted, he does not need to apply for permission[83]); or

- he is a relative of the child.

Where the applicant is the child concerned, the court may grant leave only if it is satisfied that he has sufficient understanding to make the proposed application.[84]

Where the applicant is not the child concerned the court must have particular regard to:

(a)   the nature of the proposed application;

(b)   the applicant's connection with the child;

(c)   any risk there might be of the application disrupting the child's life to such an extent that he would be harmed by it; and

(d)   where the child is being looked after by the local authority:

   (i)   the authority's plans for the child; and
   (ii)   the wishes and feelings of the child's parents.[85]

Orders without an application

12.22 The court may make a special guardianship order in any family proceedings[86] in which a question arises as to the welfare of the child, if it considers that it should be made even though no application has been made.[87]

---

[82]   CA 1989, s 14A(4).
[83]   Ibid, s 14A(5)(c)(ii).
[84]   Ibid, s 14A(12) and s 10(8). See also Chapter 15.
[85]   Ibid, s 14A(12) and s 10(9). See also Chapter 15.
[86]   As defined by ibid, s 8(3).
[87]   Ibid, s 14A(6)(b).

12.23 If no application for a special guardianship has been made by any party, one reason may be that no one wants it. As Wall LJ stated in *Re S (Adoption Order or Special Guardianship Order)*[88] the statute therefore envisages an order being made against the wishes of the parties.

> 'Whether or not it will do so will depend upon the acts of the individual case including the nature of the refuser's case and its interrelationship with the welfare of the particular child. What seems to us clear is that if the court comes to the view on all the facts and applying the welfare checklist under the 1989 Act (including the possible consequences to the child of the refuser implementing the threat to refuse to be appointed a special guardian) that a special guardianship order will best serve the welfare interests of the child in question, that is the order the court should make.'[89]

In that case, the court rejected the appeal in of a foster mother who had not agreed to being granted a special guardianship order, preferring an adoption order.

The test

12.24 The test is the welfare test,[90] but in addition to the usual checklist the court must also consider whether, if the special guardianship order is made, a contact order should also be made with respect to the child and whether any s 8 order in force should be varied or discharged.[91]

In addition to making the order the court may give leave for the child to be known by a new surname and also order as to whether the guardian should be given leave to remove the child from the UK without the consent of others for a period of 3 months or more (either generally or for specified purpose).[92]

12.25 As the order suspends parental responsibility, making the order as opposed to merely granting a residence order will have to be justified under Art 8 of the European Convention for the Protection of Human Rights and Fundamental Freedoms (ECHR). In particular, it must be necessary and proportionate.[93] The essential benefit of the order (as compared with a residence order) is the limited protection from parental interference provided by the need for anyone other than the special guardian to have leave to apply for a residence order or to vary or discharge the order, and the ability to apply for special guardian support services (see below).

12.26 In the case of *Re S (Adoption Order or Special Guardianship Order)*[94] the Court of Appeal examined the question of whether or not the various

---

[88] [2007] EWCA Civ 54, [2007] 1 FLR 819, at [73].
[89] Ibid, at [77].
[90] CA 1989, s 1(1).
[91] Ibid, s 14B(1).
[92] Ibid, s 14B(2).
[93] See Chapter 3.
[94] [2007] EWCA Civ 54, [2007] 1 FLR 819.

orders could or should be ranked in order so that, having regard to Art 8 of the ECHR, the court could select the least intrusive order which was appropriate. Giving the judgment of the court,[95] Wall LJ said:

> 'There is nothing in the statutory provisions themselves which limits the making of a special guardianship order or an adoption order to any given set of circumstances. The statute itself is silent on the circumstances in which a special guardianship order is likely to be appropriate, and there is no presumption contained within the statute that a special guardianship order is preferable to an adoption order in any particular category of case. Each case must be decided on its particular facts; and each case will involve the careful application of a judicial discretion to those facts. The key question which the court will be obliged to ask itself in every case in which the question of adoption as opposed to special guardianship arises will be: which order will better serve the welfare of this particular child?'[96]

He added that although the 'no order' principle[97] as such is unlikely to be relevant, it is a material feature of the special guardianship regime that it is 'less intrusive' than adoption.

> 'In other words, it involves a less fundamental interference with existing legal relationships. The court will need to bear Article 8 of ECHR in mind, and to be satisfied that its order is a proportionate response to the problem, having regard to the interference with family life which is involved. In choosing between adoption and special guardianship, in most cases Article 8 is unlikely to add anything to the considerations contained in the respective welfare checklists. Under both statutes the welfare of the child is the court's paramount consideration, and the balancing exercise required by the statutes will be no different to that required by Article 8. However, in some cases, the fact that the welfare objective can be achieved with less disruption of existing family relationships can properly be regarded as helping to tip the balance.'[98]

---

[95]   The case was heard in the same period as *Re AJ (Adoption Order or Special Guardianship Order)* [2007] EWCA Civ 55, [2007] 1 FLR 507 and *Re M-J (Adoption Order or Special Guardianship Order)* [2007] EWCA Civ 56, [2007] 1 FLR 691. Each of the three appeals was heard by a different constitution and on a different date. Only one member of the court (Wall LJ) sat in each constitution. Because it was the first time that the question of the relationship between adoption and special guardianship was considered by the Court of Appeal, all five members of the court involved in the three appeals took the opportunity to consider the underlying principles to be applied in making one or other of the two orders and to give guidance to courts of first instance. Each judgment was a judgment of the court. In addition, each member of each constitution read, contributed to and expresses agreement with the commentary on the statutory provisions and general considerations, which were set out in the judgment in *Re S* at [40]–[77] and which should be read as part of each of the other judgments. Given the importance and likely prevalence of the question in adoption, care and private law proceedings, the three judgments were shown to the President, who authorised the court to say that he agreed with that commentary. Per Wall LJ at [3]–[4].

[96]   Ibid, at [47].

[97]   ACA 2002, s 1(6).

[98]   See also *Down Lisburn Health and Social Services Trust v H* [2006] UKHL 36, [2007] 1 FLR 121, per Baroness Hale of Richmond at [34].

12.27 However, in *Re M-J (Adoption Order or Special Guardianship Order)*,[99] the Court of Appeal said that it goes too far to say that it is 'incumbent' on the court to adopt 'the least interventionist option'.

> 'It is true that section 1(5) of the 1989 Act (the terms of which we have set out in paragraph 26 of the judgment in *Re S*) requires the court to make an order under the Act only if it considers that doing so would be better for the child than making no order at all. However, in the instant case, an order is manifestly necessary. Indeed, MJ is already subject to a care order. The recorder was right to consider whether the order was a 'proportionate' response to the child's needs. In that context, it may be material for the court to be required to consider which order is less 'interventionist'. However, in so far as any such consideration is allowed to derogate from the welfare principle, it is plainly unacceptable. The danger of the recorder's formulation is that because a special guardianship order is less 'interventionist' than an adoption order, that is the order which the court will feel constrained to make. That would be wrong as a matter of law, because it would be a clear derogation from the paramountcy of the welfare principle. It is also not the decision which the recorder ultimately reached.'

12.28 One importance of special guardianship for kinship placements is that it avoids a stark choice between the impermanency of a residence order and the disadvantages, perceived by some, of some kinship adoptions, at least where the adoptors are grandparents. Such situations are complex and there is no universally accepted approach other than that all options should be considered and the decision will depend on the best interests of the child in his or her particular circumstances.

12.29 There is no prohibition on a child being adopted by relatives but caution has long been advised especially where the relatives are the child's grandparents, not least because of their age. It has been argued that relatives may have their own particular motives such as a desire for secrecy or arising from feelings of guilt, the wish to make reparation or 'sheer possessiveness'. On the other hand there may be a genuine sense of responsibility and a wish to work out the problem within the family.[100] Such adoptions may pose acute problems of identity and 'skewed' relationships,[101] if, for example, his mother becomes his sister and his grandparents, his parents[102] especially if, as was apparently going to be the case in *S v B and Newport City Council*[103] the child might not be told the true situation.

12.30 The Review *of Adoption Law: Report to Ministers of an Interdepartmental Working Group*[104] shared some of these concerns.

---

[99]   [2007] EWCA Civ 56, [2007] 1 FLR 691, at [19].
[100] *A Guide to Adoption Practice* (Advisory Council on Child Care 1970), para VIII.12.
[101] As submitted in *Re M-J (Adoption Order Or Special Guardianship Order)* [2007] EWCA Civ 56, [2007] 1 FLR 691, at [29].
[102] *A Guide to Adoption Practice* op cit, para VIII 13.
[103] [2007] 1 FLR 1116.
[104] (Department of Health and the Welsh Office, 1992), at para 6.3.

'We are particularly concerned that a number of adoption applications particularly by relatives and step-parents, are made without giving proper consideration to the needs of the child and the effect of being cut-off from his or her birth family. Adoption is too often regarded as the only way of securing permanence, in part, no doubt because it is more familiar than other orders and because its long term implications are not always understood. We therefore recommend that the court should have a duty[105] ... to consider the alternative orders available ... Of course, it is important that these alternatives are explored before the application is made and discussed fully with the child, his family, the applicants and other relevant persons. The knowledge that the court will expect to know why adoption is considered more appropriate for the child than other orders should encourage agencies and guardians ... to ask this type of question from a much earlier stage in the process.'

12.31 In *Re S (Adoption Order or Special Guardianship Order)*[106] Wall LJ commented that:

'A particular concern is that an adoption order has, as a matter of law, the effect of making the adopted child the child of the adopters for all purposes. Accordingly, where a child is adopted by a member of his wider family, the familial relationships are inevitably changed. This is frequently referred to as the 'skewing' or 'distorting' effect of adoption, and is a factor which the court must take into account when considering whether or not to make an adoption order in such a case. This is not least because the checklist under section 1 of the 2002 Act requires it to do so – see section 1(4)(f) ('the relationship which the child has with relatives.'). However, the weight to be given to this factor will inevitably depend on the facts of the particular case, and it will be only one factor in the overall welfare equation.[107] As will be seen, the three appeals before this court illustrate the different weight to be placed on this factor in different circumstances, and that in some it may be of only marginal importance. In particular, as the case of *Re AJ*[108] demonstrates, both children and adults are capable of penetrating legal forms and retaining hold of the reality.'

12.32 In the linked case of *Re AJ (Adoption Order Or Special Guardianship Order)*[109] Wall LJ commented further that 'the question of the likely distortion of family relationships by an adoption order is very fact specific and should not be overplayed'. In that case, the boy, AJ, who was nearly 6, knew 'precisely who he is'.

'He knows that his birth parents are Mr and Mrs J and that they are unable to look after him. He knows he is living with his aunt and uncle. He is not confused, nor is he likely to be in the future. What matters for him is that he should be fully accepted and cared for by his aunt and uncle as a member of their household, and as a brother to W. The difference between brother and cousin on the facts of this case is readily understandable: what matters is the relationship between the two

---

[105] Supplied by CA 1989, s 1(3)(g) and now, as regards adoption by ACA 2002, s 1(6).
[106] [2007] EWCA Civ 54, [2007] 1 FLR 819, at [51].
[107] And see also *Re AJ (Adoption Order or Special Guardianship Order)* [2007] EWCA Civ 55, [2007] 1 FLR 507, at [44].
[108] [2007] EWCA Civ 55, [2007] 1 FLR 507.
[109] Ibid, at [51].

children. In our view it is not a major or negative distortion of family relationships in this case for cousins to grow up together as brothers.'[110]

12.33 The issue of familial adoption was also considered by Hedley J in *S v B and Newport City Council*[111] when he granted a special guardianship order in respect of a 6-year-old boy to his grandparents who he had lived with since he was 6 months old. After considering the risk of 'skewing',[112] he drew attention to the fact that adoption was formulated principally as the means by which a child could be given security in a home 'where otherwise he would be a stranger'.

> 'One purpose of adoption is ... to give lifelong status to carers where otherwise it would not exist. In a familial placement that is not necessary because family status exists for life in any event. That is not to say that a familial status may never be secured by adoption. One can imagine a case where the need for security against aggressive parents including forensic aggression, may be overwhelming or where the child has such disabilities that the need for carer to have parental status may last long into majority where adoption may still be right and necessary. No doubt there will be other cases too.'

12.34 In the reported cases since ACA 2002 came into force, there are no examples of grandparents being granted adoption orders although examples do exist pre-2002 where there were special circumstances – see, for example, *Re B (Adoption Order: Nationality)*.[113] Whether the apparent objection to grandparents is because they belong to a generation older than the child's parents or because the child is in a direct line of descent from them is uncertain. These two features do not exist when aunts and uncles are considered and adoption orders in favour of uncles and aunts have been made under the 2002 Act.[114]

Contact

12.35 Before making a special guardianship order, the court has to consider:

- whether a s 8 contact order, which may contain conditions[115] should also be made;

- whether any s 8 order, including a contact order, should be discharged;

---

[110] Per Wall LJ at [51].
[111] [2007] 1 FLR 1116.
[112] The case was decided before *Re AJ* and the other two cases were heard by the Court of Appeal.
[113] [1999] 1 FLR 907.
[114] *Re MJ (Adoption Order or Special Guardianship)* [2007] EWCA Civ 56, [2007] 1 FLR 691 and *Re AJ (Adoption Order or Special Guardianship Order)* [2007] EWCA Civ 55, [2007] 1 FLR 507.
[115] CA 1989, s 11(c).

- where a contact order is not discharged, whether any enforcement order[116] should be revoked;

- whether any contact activity direction[117] should be discharged.[118]

The report to the court made by the applicant's local authority under subs 14A(8) or (9) must contain a recommendation as to what arrangements there should be for contact between the child and his relatives or any person the authority considers relevant.[119]

12.36 When a court is considering making, varying or discharging a contact order it may make a contact activity direction requiring a party to take part in an activity that promotes contact with the child.[120] The activity may include programmes, classes, counselling or guidance sessions which may assist a person to establish, maintain or improve contact with a child or may, by addressing a person's violent behaviour, enable or facilitate contact.[121]

The purpose of making such a direction is both to facilitate contact and to provide a court with information as to whether a contact order should be made and the form it should take. Therefore s 11A(7) provides that a court cannot, on the same occasion, make a contact activity direction and dispose finally of the proceedings .[122]

12.37 Local authority provision of services to support contact is discussed at **12.96**.

12.38 Special guardianship is such a recent innovation that there is no research on how contact generally works. However, there are studies of contact where the child is living with a relative. Children placed with kin-carers have higher levels of contact with other relatives including parents than those living with non-kin foster carers. This may only typically be with the side of the family with whom they are living. Evidence about whether contact causes difficulties for the child and the extent of the difficulties is unclear. It frequently appears to cause difficulties for the carer. Richards[123] found that grandparents caring for children following family crisis repeatedly stressed the impact on children of poor quality contact with their birth parents and said they had not known who to contact for help. In another study[124] Hunt found most children

---

[116] See CA 1989, s 11J.
[117] See ibid, s 11A.
[118] Ibid, s 14B(1).
[119] Special Guardianship Regulations 2005 (SI 2005/1109), Sch, para 10.
[120] CA 1989, s 11A(2).
[121] Ibid, s 11A(5).
[122] Ibid, s 11A(7).
[123] *Second Time around- A Survey of Grandparents Raising Their Grandchildren* (Family Rights Group, 2001) [2003] Fam Law 749.
[124] Hunt, Waterhouse and Lutman *Keeping Them in the Family: Outcomes for Abused and Neglected Children Placed with Family or Friends Carers Through Care Proceedings* (BAAF, 2008).

were in touch with at last one parent, usually the mother, but contact, particularly paternal contact, diminished over time. Problems with contact were common and in a substantial minority of cases contact appeared to be entirely negative for the child. This is likely to be more common where local authorities have been the instigators of the placement. Families seemed to have assistance in less than half of cases. The authors cautioned that:

'It should not be assumed that the family can make contact arrangements [work] smoothly themselves. There needs to be more focus on contact planning at the assessment stage and perhaps more use of formal written agreements'.[125]

12.39 In 2007 Ananda Hall studied a sample of 70 of 372 of the special guardianship orders which had been made in the first year of the implementation of s 14A.[126]

Of the 60% or more of parents having contact in her survey only 5% of visits were unsupervised. This reflected the high proportion of parents with personal problems. Over half of the parents had substance misuse problems, a third involved a history of domestic violence, a third of the parents had mental health problems and a fifth involved a history of sexual or physical abuse of the child.

12.40 There is, at present, only limited guidance on how issues of contact should be approached when a special guardianship order is in place or is intended. When contact orders are made when parents separate, the parent with whom the child lives cannot veto contact although the effect contact may have on the parent's care of the child may be a factor to be considered. In comparison, courts have historically been reluctant to impose contact on unwilling adopters.[127]

12.41 There are arguments that contact applications where a special guardianship order is in force should be treated more like other applications for contact under s 8 rather than those involving an adopted child. One of the purposes behind the introduction of special guardianship orders was to enable the relationship between the child and his parents and siblings to continue.[128] Moreover, only adopters have parental responsibility whereas the making of a special guardianship order does not remove a parent's parental responsibility, although special guardians may exercise their parental responsibility to the exclusion of any other person.[129] It will be difficult for parental responsibility

---

[125] Ibid, at p 439.
[126] Hall 'Special Guardianship: A missed opportunity – findings from research' [2008] Fam Law 148; Hall 'Special Guardianship – themes emerging from case law' [2008] Fam Law 244 and 'Special Guardianship and permanency planning: unforeseen circumstances and missed opportunities' [2008] CFLQ 359.
[127] See, for example, *Re C (A Minor) (Adoption Order: Conditions)* [1989] AC 1, [1988] 2 FLR 159, per Lord Ackner at 167 and *SB and County Council: P (A Child)* [2008] EWCA Civ 535 sub nom *P (A Child)* [2008] 2 FLR 625.
[128] *Adoption – A New Approach* (Cm 5017), para 5.8.
[129] CA 1989, s 14C(1). See also **12.16**.

to be exercised if there is no contact. However, at the same time, special guardianship is intended to provide the child with a permanent home. The child is likely to have a greater need for stability than the ordinary child[130] and caution will have to be exercised to avoid a risk of the home being destabilised.

12.42 In *Re L (Special Guardianship: Surname)*,[131] an appeal brought by grandparents who had been granted a special guardianship order but objected, amongst other matters, to the grant of contact orders to the children's parents which required the continued involvement of social workers who would arrange and supervise contact which would take place away from their home and in their absence. The Court of Appeal pointed out that when a special guardianship order is made, links with the birth parents are not severed as in adoption but undoubtedly the purpose was to give the special guardians freedom to exercise parental responsibility in the best interests of the child. 'That however does not mean that the special guardians are free from the exercise of judicial oversight.' The trial judge clearly had the jurisdiction to make the contact orders she did and in the circumstances of the case, the exercise of her discretion was unobjectionable. However, the orders would be varied so that the supervision of contact would last for only one year.

Parental responsibility

12.43 As explained in **12.16**, s 14C(1) extends the general rule concerning the exercise of parental responsibility. However, even a special guardian may not change the child's surname or remove him from England and Wales for more than 3 months without the written consent of every person who has parental responsibility or the leave of the court.[132]

12.44 There have been no reported decisions concerning the translocation of a child subject to a special guardianship order and it remains to be seen whether the increased status given to special guardians over others with guardianship requires guidance further to that given in *Payne v Payne*[133] and *Re W (Relocation: Removal Outside Jurisdiction)*[134] (see **9.40**).

12.45 Early indications seem to show that when making a special guardianship order courts will exercise the power to permit a change of name very cautiously. In *S v B and Newport City Council: Re K*[135] Headley J made a special guardianship order in favour of maternal grandparents who had been looking after their 6-year-old grandson since he was 6 months old. He rejected the grandparents' preference for an adoption order on the ground that it would skew familial relationships but he nevertheless gave permission for the child to be known by their surname. In contrast, in *Re L (Special Guardianship:*

---

[130] See **13.74**.
[131] [2007] EWCA Civ 196, [2007] 2 FLR 50, at [66].
[132] CA 1989, s 14C(3).
[133] [2001] EWCA Civ 166, [2001] 1 FLR 1052.
[134] [2011] EWCA Civ 345, [2011] 2 FLR 409.
[135] [2007] 1 FLR 1116.

Surname)[136] the Court of Appeal upheld a refusal by the trial judge to allow maternal grandparents in very similar circumstances to change the 3-year-old's surname. The two cases might be distinguished by the fact that the grandparents in *S v B* may (it is not clear) have been bringing the child up as their grandchild whereas in *Re L* the grandparents, at least in the past, had been perceived as being reluctant to clarify to the child who her biological parents were. On the other hand, the difference might have been that the two cases were heard by different judges who had formed their own assessment of the different parties.

12.46 In *Re L (Special Guardianship: Surname)* the trial judge found that:

'In a case where there is as much anxiety as there is here about the way in which [E's] identity is dealt with, it would be completely contrary to her interests, in my view, for her now to be known by a different surname. Her welfare is most likely to be secured, it seems to me, by keeping her circumstances as faithful to reality and the truth of the situation as possible. Whilst I accept that some explanation of names will be required, for instance, doctors and schools, I do not consider that would an insuperable problem in the context of a special guardianship order.'[137]

In the Court of Appeal Ward LJ added:

'Sympathetic as I am to [the predicament of the grandparents] and their hurt, their concerns overlook the value of the lesson ... honesty is the best policy ... It avoids the much more difficult questions that will be asked when [E] wishes to know, "why am I S if my parents are L?"'[138]

Examples

12.47 Reported cases concerning whether a special guardianship order should or should not be made are limited in number and may not provide an accurate sample of decisions being made in uncontested cases or where parents, whilst contesting care proceedings, argue that if their child is not to return home, he should be placed with members of the extended family rather than be adopted outside the family.

Re M-J (Adoption Order or Special Guardianship)[139]

12.48 M was placed with foster carers at the age of about 6 months because of his mother's drug and alcohol dependency, as a result of which he had suffered foetal growth retardation. Following the making of a care order he was placed with his maternal aunt at the age of 2 with a view to adoption and contact apparently ceased. His mother completed a three-stage detoxification programme and when her son was just over 3, applied for the care order to be discharged and for contact. At the hearing she withdrew her applications but

---

[136] [2007] EWCA Civ 196, [2007] 2 FLR 50.
[137] Ibid, per Black J at [36].
[138] Ibid, at [39].
[139] [2007] EWCA Civ 56, [2007] 1 FLR 691.

unsuccessfully opposed the making of an adoption order, arguing that special guardianship was more appropriate. The Court of Appeal dismissed her appeal. The trial judge, supported by expert evidence, had been entitled to conclude that although many of M's needs could be met by special guardianship, the fact that he was a vulnerable child because of his small stature, his emotional history of inadequate parenting and many changes of carer meant that adoption with its clarity and certainty was required.

Re AJ (Adoption Order or Special Guardianship Order)[140]

12.49 AJ's parents engaged in criminal activities and their relationship was violent and unstable. When he was 6 months old AJ was removed from their care and placed with his paternal uncle and aunt, Mr and Mrs T. A care order was made on the basis that AJ would remain with them as a long-term foster child having contact with his parents. However, when AJ was 5, after a threat from AJ's father and the parents ceasing to attend contact for a period, Mr and Mrs T applied to adopt him .His parents did not oppose AJ remaining with the Ts but argued, unsuccessfully, that a special guardianship order was more appropriate given their family connection. Dismissing the appeal, the Court of Appeal held that the existence of a family tie did not preclude the making of an adoption order. AJ had been with the Ts since the age of 6 months and needed the assurance that the security of the placement could not be disturbed. This could be provided only by adoption.

Re S (Adoption Order or Special Guardianship Order)[141]

12.50 S was placed under a care order at the age of 3 because she suffered a non-accidental injury (the perpetrator not being identified) when living with her parents and because of violence and drug taking within the home. At the age of 4 she moved from her foster carer to live with members of her extended family but this placement broke down after 6 months and she returned to her former foster carer who applied to adopt her. It was agreed that S's mother who had a good relationship with the carer should continue to have frequent and regular contact with S and that her father should continue to have some contact. The trial judge dismissed the adoption application, instead making a special guardianship order of her own volition. The Court of Appeal dismissed the carer's appeal holding that the trial judge was entitled to find on the facts of the finely balanced case that special guardianship met both S's needs for stability and provide 'a legal expression for S's loyalty both to the appellant and her mother'. The carer would have the day-to-day management of the decisions relating to S's life and the parents would not be given leave to challenge them unless something major occurred such as indicated that the whole basis of the arrangement had been changed or undermined. Both parents had agreed to an

---

[140] [2007] EWCA Civ 55, [2007] 1 FLR 507.
[141] [2007] EWCA Civ 54, [2007] 1 FLR 819.

order being made under s 91(14) of the 1989 Act and this would provide 'a further level of protection from the [carer] having her autonomy over S undermined'.

S v B and Newport City Council[142]

12.51 K had lived with his maternal grandparents under a care order since he was 6 months old because his father was a long-term drug abuser who suffered from a borderline personality disorder and was violent and unpredictable. Contact between K and his parents ended and when K was 6, his grandparents applied for an adoption order and, in the alternative a special guardianship order. The parents did not actively oppose the proceedings. Hedley J granted a special guardianship order, a prohibited steps order preventing the parents having contact with K without a court order, a s 91(14) order without limitation of time and an order giving leave for K to be known by his grandparents' surname. He held that the case was one of those for which special guardianship was specially designed. The order permitted familial carers to have all the practical authority and the standing of parents while leaving intact real and readily comprehensible relationships within the family and avoiding the child having to learn that the apparent relationship was not a 'real' one.

Re L (Special Guardianship: Surname)[143]

12.52 When E was 3 months old she was placed with her maternal grandparents under a residence order because of the highly volatile relationship between her parents, both of whom were drug takers. The grandmother and the mother had a particularly complex relationship and both grandparents suffered hostility from E's father. When E was nearly 3 her grandparents applied to adopt her. This was opposed by the local authority who were concerned about the grandparents' reluctance to clarify for E who her birth parents were. The grandparents, 'under considerable pressure', did not pursue the application. Black J made a special guardianship order, refused permission for E's surname to be changed and ordered some direct contact for the mother and some indirect contact for the father. The Court of Appeal dismissed the grandparents' appeal against the last two orders. E's welfare was the litmus test and overwhelmingly justified the refusal to allow a change of name. Honesty was the best policy.

Notice to the local authority

12.53 No individual may apply for an order without giving the local authority who is looking after the child or, if the child is not being looked after, the local

---

[142] [2007] 1 FLR 1116.
[143] [2007] EWCA Civ 196, [2007] 2 FLR 50.

authority in whose area the applicant is ordinarily resident,[144] written notice of his intention to apply and without 3 months having expired from the date the notice was given.[145]

Local authority report

12.54   On receipt of the notice the local authority must investigate and provide the court with a report dealing with:

(a)   the suitability of the applicant to be a special guardian;

(b)   such other matters as may be prescribed by the Secretary of State; and

(c)   such other matter as the local authority considers relevant.[146]

The court may also require the local authority to provide a report[147] and, because no order can be made without a report,[148] where a court is considering making an order without an application under s 14A(6), it will have to order such a report.

12.55   If no application has been made but the court is considering making the order under its powers under s 14A(6), it will have to order a report under s 14A(9).[149]

> 'There is no provision either in the statute or the regulations for any restriction, reduction or alteration in the information which the local authority is required to cover. We do, however, think it important to pause to reflect why this is so. In our judgment it is because special guardianship is an issue of very great importance to everyone concerned with it, not least, of course, the child who is its subject. It is plainly not something to be embarked upon lightly or capriciously, not least because the status it gives the special guardian effectively prevents the exercise of parental responsibility on the part of the child's natural parents, and terminates the parental authority given to a local authority under a care order (whether interim or final). In this respect, it is substantially different from a residence order which, whilst it also brings a previously subsisting care order in relation to the same child to an end, does not confer on any person who holds the order the exclusivity in the exercise of parental responsibility which accompanies a special guardianship order.'[150]

---

[144]   In *O v Orkney Island Council* [2009] EWHC 3173 (Fam), [2010] 1 FLR 1449 a child form Orkney was fostered in England by the Orkney Island Council. When the couple applied for a special guardianship order in England, the order not being available in Scotland, the court directed the English local authority to prepare a s 14A(4) report.

[145]   CA 1989, s 14A(7).

[146]   Ibid, s 14A(8).

[147]   Ibid, s 14A(9).

[148]   Ibid, s 14A(11).

[149]   *Birmingham City Council v R* [2006] EWCA Civ 1748, [2007] 1 FLR 564 at [97] and *Re S (Adoption Order or Special Guardianship)* [2007] EWCA Civ 54, [2007] 1 FLR 819, at [11].

[150]   *Birmingham City Council v R* [2006] EWCA Civ 1748, [2007] 1 FLR 564, per Wall LJ at [77]–[78].

However a judge should not use s 14A(9) to compel an authority to perform its obligations under s 14(8) at the instance of a person who needs but has not obtained permission to apply unless s 14A(6) applies.[151]

12.56 When it is considering whether to invoke s 14A(6) the court should consider carefully the manner in which it should use its powers under s 14A(9). In some cases the information which is required under the Special Guardianship Regulations 2005 will be before it in a different form, for example in adoption proceedings. In such a case the court should adopt a commonsense approach. The material can be cross-referenced and need not be duplicated in a different format. In other cases the information may not be before the court and the authority may well be required to conduct a fresh application and prepare a fresh report without preconceptions.[152] However, the court cannot define or limit the requirements of a local authority to investigate and report.[153]

Contents of the report

12.57 The importance of a detailed assessment of the child and the prospective special guardians is underlined by the words of Lord Justice Wall in *Re S (Adoption Order or Special Guardianship Order)*:[154]

> 'The carefully constructed statutory regime (notice to the local authority, leave requirements in certain cases, the role of the court and the report from the local authority even where the order is made by the court of its own motion) demonstrates the care which is required before making a special guardianship order, and that it is only appropriate if, in the particular circumstances of the particular case, it is best fitted to meet the needs of the child or children concerned.'

12.58 The information to be sought includes not only information relevant for assessing the suitability of the special guardian but also information about the natural family which may be helpful to the child and special guardian in the future.

12.59 The Schedule to the Special Guardianship Regulations 2005[155] prescribes a number of matters with which the report has to deal.

---

[151] [2006] EWCA Civ 1748, [2007] 1 FLR 564, at [103].

[152] *Re S (Adoption Order or Special Guardianship) (No 2)* [2007] EWCA Civ 54, [2007] 1 FLR 819, at [14].

[153] *Birmingham City Council v R* [2006] EWCA Civ 1748, [2007] 1 FLR 564, at [77] and *Re S (Adoption Order Or Special Guardianship) (No 2)* [2007] EWCA Civ 54, [2007] 1 FLR 819, at [17]–[18].

[154] [2007] EWCA Civ 54 , [2007] 1 FLR 819, at [47].

[155] SI 2005/1109.

The child

12.60 The matters under this part include the child's immigration status, racial origin and background and religious persuasion. Details of siblings must be given and the extent of the child's contact with his relatives and any other person the authority considers relevant must be considered. The report must describe the child's personality, development (including educational attainment) and health and educational history and address his needs. Details of any orders made under the Children Act 1989 must be given.

The child's family

12.61 The required details include basic information about the family-parents and siblings – and the health history (including any hereditary disease, disorder or disability), religious persuasion, educational and employment history and personality and interests as well as a photograph of the parents. If the identity and whereabouts of the father is not known, the report must contain the information which has been ascertained and from whom and the steps which have been taken to establish paternity.

The wishes and feelings of the child and others

12.62 This includes the wishes and feelings of the child and each parent regarding special guardianship, his religious and cultural upbringing and contact between the child, his parents, relatives and any other person the local authority considers relevant as well as the wishes and feelings of any of the child's relatives or any other person the local authority considers relevant.

The prospective special guardians

12.63 The required information includes the basic details of the prospective special guardian's nationality, immigration status (where appropriate) racial origin and cultural and linguistic background, parents and siblings, health, educational and employment history, personality and interests and details of other members of the prospective guardian's household, home and neighbourhood. Details must be given of any past or present, marriages, civil partnerships or current relationships and, where there is to be a joint application the nature of the applicants' relationship and its stability must be assessed. If there is to be a sole application by someone who is a member of a couple, the reason for this must be given.

The authority has to enquire into the prospective special guardian's previous experience of caring for children, any past assessments as a prospective adopter, foster parent or special guardian, any involvement in any previous family court proceedings, and provide a description of how he relates to children in general.

The authority must report on whether the prospective guardian is willing to follow any wishes of the child or his parents in relation to religious or cultural upbringing and the prospective special guardian's views in relation to contact between the child and his relatives and any other person the authority considers relevant.

The hopes and expectations the prospective special guardian holds for the child and his reasons for applying for and the extent of his understanding of the nature and effect of special guardianship must be ascertained.

The prospective special guardian has to nominate three personal referees and the report has to include details of the interviews carried out by the referees.

An assessment has to be carried out of the prospective special guardian's and his family's relationship with the child and his ability or suitability to bring up the child.

The local authority

12.64 The authority must report on the prospective special guardian's past involvement with the authority and, where the reporting authority is looking after the child and the prospective special guardian lives in an area of another authority,[156] details of the enquiries made of that other authority.

The authority must provide a summary of the special guardianship support services (see **12.72**) provided by the authority, the period of time for which they are to be provided or, if they are not to be provided, the reasons for this.

Medical information

12.65 A summary must be prepared by the medical professional who provided the medical information relating to the child and the prospective special guardian.

The implications of making a special guardianship order

12.66 The report must assess the implications of the making of a special guardianship order for the child, his parents, the prospective special guardian and his family and any other person the authority considers relevant.

Relative merits of a special guardianship order and other orders which may be made

12.67 The report must consider the relative merits of a special guardianship order and other orders which may be made under the Children Act 1989 or the Adoption and Children Act 2002 together with an assessment of whether the child's long-term interests would best be met by a special guardianship order.

---

[156] CA 1989, s 14A(7).

Recommendation

12.68 The report must contain a recommendation of whether or not the special guardianship order should be made and, if not, any alternative proposal in respect of the child.

Contact

12.69 The report must contain a recommendation as to what arrangements there should be for contact between the child and his relatives or any person the authority considers relevant.

12.70 Where a child is being 'looked after'[157] whether under a voluntary arrangement with those with parental authority or under a care order, the local authority has various additional duties under the Arrangements for Placement of Children by Voluntary Organisations and Others (England) Regulations 2011[158] which may apply when the authority is considering whether to approve an application for a special guardianship order or whether to place the child with the prospective adopters.[159]

12.71 Some statutory guidance to local authorities on carrying out the assessment of prospective special guardians is contained in *Friends and Family Care: Statutory Guidance for Local Authorities*.[160]

Local authority support

12.72 As well as reporting to the court, the relevant local authority will have duties after the order is made, regardless of whether the child was in care or was being looked after. It must make arrangements to provide special guardianship support services which are counselling, advice and information as well as such other services as may be prescribed,[161] including the provision of financial support.[162]

12.73 The difficulties experienced by some kinship carers have been recognised for some time. In 2001 the late Alison Richards conducted a Home Office-funded survey of 180 grandparent carers.[163] The majority of carers were aged between 55 and 65 and just under half had long-term health problems or disabilities that impaired their ability to look after the children. Approximately one-third were lone grandparents. Three-quarters said that their social life had altered significantly. They received little assistance in caring for children with

---

[157]   As defined in CA 1989, s 22(1).

[158]   SI 2011/582.

[159]   These lie outside the scope of this Handbook. They are discussed in detail in Mitchell *Adoption and Special Guardianship: A Permanency Handbook* (Jordans, 2009), ch 10.

[160]   (Department for Education, 2011).

[161]   CA 1989, s 14F(1).

[162]   Ibid, s 14F(2). And see Special Guardianship Regulations 2005 (SI 2005/1109) and *Special Guardianship Guidance* (DfES, 2005).

[163]   'Second time around – a survey of grandparents raising their grandchildren' (Family Rights Group, 2001), [2003] Fam Law 749.

special needs and seven in ten found it hard to adapt to the physical and emotional demands of young children. Several spoke of the strain which was placed on their relationship with their partners and the child's' parents.

12.74 Some of these difficulties might be expected because Richards's carers were exclusively grandparents but in a later study[164] Hunt and others found similar problems in a non-exclusive sample.

'Carers highlighted how taking on care affected them in many dimensions, including life plans and expectations, freedom to pursue outside interest/maintain peer group relationships and the loss of the expected "grandparent" relationship with the child.'

Just over one-third of the placements were problem free, just under half had some problems and one in five, 'major problems'. Half of the carers had felt like giving up at some point.

12.75 These findings were confirmed in 2011 by a study conducted by Nandy and Selwyn which used Census microdata to examine the extent and nature of kinship care in the UK.[165] One of the most notable features was the fact that older children, particularly aged between 15 and 17 were most likely to be living with kin. Most kinship carers were grandparents in their late 50s and early 60s but one in four grandparents were aged 65 or older. Over one-third reported a limiting long-term illness or disability which restricted their daily activities. Most kinship carers, whether grandparents or siblings, lived in poor and deprived conditions. About 71% of kinship children experienced multiple deprivation (two or more forms of deprivation[166]) compared with 29% of children in the general population.

Types of need

12.76 The types of needs can be analysed on a number of matrices:

- One off needs/ongoing needs.

- Needs at the outset of the placement/needs occurring later.

- Needs apparent at the outset of the placement/ unforeseen needs.

- Needs associated with the personal circumstances of the carer, the child, the parents.

---

[164] Op cit.
[165] *Spotlight on Kinship Care* (University of Bristol, 2011).
[166] Defined by *Families At Risk* (Social Exclusion Task Force, 2008) as no parent in the family working; family living in poor quality or overcrowded housing; no parent with any qualifications; mother with mental health problems; at least one parent with a longstanding limiting illness, disability or infirmity; family with low income (below 60% of median income) and a family who cannot afford a number of food and clothing items.

- Financial/non financial needs.

- Specific needs/need for general support and advice.

Research has highlighted commonly occurring problems.

Financial difficulties

12.77 An 'overwhelming' majority of Richards's respondents reported financial difficulties including paying for school uniforms and meals. Seven in ten said they had made financial sacrifices and two in five (from a sample not all of whom had been employed) had had to stop working or reduce their working hours. It was unusual for parents to contribute towards the costs of raising their children in cases where the child had moved to grandparents following a crisis such as bereavement, relationship breakdown or where there were child protection concerns. Hunt too found that finance was an issue for many carers. Only just over one-third managed without difficulty and several suffered financial strain. Support was inconsistent. Some received grants for start-up costs, extensions and special expenses as well as a regular allowance while others received very little.

Emotional difficulties

12.78 In Hunt's survey one-third of the children had abnormal scores on a standardised test 'well-being' compared with 10% of the general population. Over one-third of the children were receiving specialised help, usually from mental health services but there was evidence of unmet need in a few cases. Forty-five per cent of the carers had an abnormal or borderline score on a standardised test of wellbeing, more than twice that expected in the general population.

Respite care

12.79 In Hunt's study respite care was rarely given and practical help from the extended family was less frequent than emotional support. Although most enjoyed some support from their family 'this was typically emotional rather than practical and occasional rather than regular'.[167]

Contact

12.80 See **12.38**.

Assistance with legal services

12.81 In Richards's sample nearly all (86%) of the carers who had been involved in proceedings had been legally represented but only 54% had been

---

[167] Op cit, at p 173.

eligible for legal aid. Two-fifths of all who were involved in proceedings reported that this had caused financial hardship with many saying that they had to use all their savings. Overall, one-third of all carers – whether involved in proceedings or not – had not been able to obtain information on their legal rights and responsibilities.

In *Re L (Special Guardianship: Surname)*[168] the Court of Appeal noted that the litigation had placed grandparents who were applying for special guardianship 'under considerable stress and had taken its toll on their resilience. They are not far short of breaking point. Their financial position is such that they are not eligible for legal aid. By contrast, of course the parents are.'[169]

Assistance from social services

12.82 In the past, support by social services has been perceived to be patchy. In Richards' sample, although just under half were having or had had some contact with social services, there was a general criticism for the lack of support. Hunt's findings were more positive but not overwhelmingly so. In those cases still 'open', one-third were judged to be well supported, just under half to have some support and one-fifth, little or no support. A few carers in closed cases needed more sustained support but had mixed experiences when seeking it. Overall a quarter of carers had nothing positive to say about social services.

The effect on outcome

12.83 Special guardians are likely to need assistance at some stage during the life of the order. This is echoed by the experience of a large number of organisations. In *The Role of the State in Supporting Relatives Raising Children Who Cannot Live with Their Parents*[170] the Family Policy Alliance, formed of 14 organisations such as Barnados, the British Association for Adoption and Fostering (BAAF) and the Grandparents Association submitted that:

> 'It is crucial that the support needs of family and friends are addressed if these children [who could be placed with their extending family rather than state care] are to reach their full potential. The overwhelming evidence from the advice work of our respective organisations is that the more informal the arrangement, the less likely the family member who takes on care is to receive support. This lack of support is likely to have a detrimental effect on the child and sometimes causes the placement to break down and the children to end up in state care after all.'

Hunt considered that the research provided some grounds for thinking that better service provision might have improved outcomes. About half of the

---

[168] [2007] EWCA Civ 196, [2007] 2 FLR 50.
[169] Per Ward LJ, at [22].
[170] (2007) A response to the Green Paper Care Matters co-ordinated by the Family Rights Group.

premature terminations of placement might have been prevented and the risk might have been reduced in half of the placements which were continuing but were vulnerable.

12.84 The quality and range of the assistance required to meet the needs is important.

> 'The literature suggests that service provision needs to meet a number of cross-cutting requirements. It should, for example, be customized – tailored not only to the unique needs of kinship families in general but to the needs of the individual family in particular: kinship carers are a heterogeneous group and needs will change over time. It needs to be holistic, addressing the needs of the whole family, not just the child or the carers. The aim should be to develop 'wrap-around' services which address the whole range of need. It should be culturally attuned, recognising the specific needs of different ethnic minority groups. Finally, it should be enabling, building on the family's strengths.'[171]

Special Guardianship Support Services

12.85 The framework for the assessment and provision of adoption support services is provided by s 14F of the Children Act 1989 and the Special Guardianship Regulations 2005.[172] Guidance on the regulations is provided by *The Special Guardianship Guidance*[173] (the Guidance) which is issued under s 7 of the Local Authority Social Services Act 1970 and as Black J pointed out in *B v Lewisham London Borough Council*[174] 'whilst the document does not have the full force of statute, it should be complied with unless local circumstances indicate exceptional reasons which justify a variation'.[175] In *Munjaz v Ashworth Hospital*[176] Lord Bingham said of similar guidance:

> 'The Code does not have the binding effect which a statutory provision or statutory instrument would have. It is what it purports to be, guidance and not instruction. But ... the guidance should be given great weight. It is not instruction but it is much more than mere advice which the addressee is free to follow or not as it chooses. It is guidance which [any authority] should consider with great care and from which it should depart only if it has cogent reasons for so doing.'[177]

---

[171] Hunt 'Substitute care of children by members of their extended families and social networks: An overview' in Ebtehaj, Lindley and Richards (eds) *Kinship Matters* (Hart Publishing, 2006), at p 127.

[172] SI 2005/1109 (SGR 2005). For a detailed account of the scheme for assessing the need for and provision of support including support after a family leaves the local authority's area, see Mitchell *Adoption and Special Guardianship: A Permanency Handbook* op cit, ch 11.

[173] (DfCS, 2005).

[174] [2008] EWHC 738 (Admin).

[175] Ibid, at [20].

[176] [2005] UKHL 58, [2006] 4 All ER 736.

[177] Ibid, at [21]. See also *R v Islington LBC ex p Rixon* [1996] 32 BMLR 136, at 140.

12.86 Each local authority must 'make arrangements for the provision within their area of special guardianship support services which means a) counselling, advice and information and b) such other services as are prescribed'.[178] 'Prescribed services' consist of:

- financial support;

- services to enable children, parents, special guardians and prospective special guardians to discuss matters relating to special guardianship;

- assistance including mediation services in relation to contact;

- services relating to the therapeutic needs of the child;

- assistance to ensure the continuance of the relationship between the children, the special guardian or a prospective special guardian including training, respite care and mediation.[179]

The services can be provided either by the local authority or through other organisations of a specified nature and except as regards counselling, advice and information, can be provided by a cash payment to enable the recipient to purchase the services.[180] The Guidance provides the illustrations of giving a special guardian cash to pay a babysitter or for petrol to travel to contact. 'When cash is provided in this way it should not be means tested as it is being provided as part of a service rather than financial support.'[181]

12.87 The Guidance states that special guardianship support services should not be seen in isolation from mainstream services. 'It is vital to ensure that children and families involved in special guardianship arrangements are assisted in accessing mainstream services and are aware of their entitlement to social services benefits and tax credits as appropriate.'[182]

12.88 The key to the provision of services is a proper assessment of the needs of the special guardian, natural parents and the child. Section 14F(3)–(8) of the Act and regs 11–16 make detailed provision for:

- an assessment of a person's need for special guardianship support services as defined in s 14(1).

- a plan of the services to be provided.

---

[178] CA 1989, s 14F(1).
[179] SGR 2005, reg 3.
[180] SGR 2005, reg 4.
[181] Op cit, para 27.
[182] Op cit, para 26. See also reg 12(3) for the duty when relevant to consult health organisations and local education authorities when assessing needs.

Needs for services must be assessed at the time the s 14A report is being prepared but an assessment may also be requested before or after the report and the making of the order.

12.89 The report made to the court under s 14A(8) must include a 'summary' of any special guardianship support services provided, the period for which they are to be provided and where the authority has decided not to provide support, the reasons for this.[183]

12.90 Regularly occurring types of support include the following.[184]

Financial support

12.91 Regulation 6(1) enables financial support to be given to the special guardian or prospective special guardian:

- to facilitate arrangements for a person to become a special guardian where the local authority consider such arrangements to be beneficial to the child's welfare; or

- to support the continuation of such arrangements after an order.

However, by virtue of reg 6(2) it is payable only if the local authority considers it is necessary to ensure that the special guardian or prospective special guardian:

- can look after the child; or

- considers that the child needs special care which requires a greater expenditure of resources than would otherwise be the case because of his illness, disability, emotional or behavioural difficulties or the consequences of past abuse and neglect; or

- considers it appropriate to help meet legal expenses; or

- considers it appropriate to contribute to expenditure necessary for accommodating or maintaining the child.

It can be paid periodically if there is likely to be a recurring need or by a single payment which can, with the consent of the recipient, be paid by instalments.

12.92 Paragraph 37 of the Guidance stipulates that 'Financial issues should not be the sole reason for a special guardianship arrangement failing to survive'. However, following the principle that support should not be seen in isolation from mainstream services, regard must be had to welfare benefits

---

[183]   SGA 2005, Sch, paras 5(d) and (e).
[184]   See also Mitchell 'Supporting Special Guardianship' [2008] Fam Law 760.

available to the population at large. Paragraph 63 states that it is important that local authorities help special guardians to take advantage of all benefits and tax credits available.

> 'Financial support under [The Special Guardianship] Regulations cannot duplicate any other payment available.'

Unlike local authority foster parents, special guardians are entitled to child benefit. Like adoption allowances, special guardianship allowances are disregarded in full for income support and income-based jobseeker's allowance. It is taken into account for housing benefit and council tax benefit but only to the level of the child's personal allowance and any disabled child premium. Conversely, when a carer's means are assessed for the purpose of special guardianship financial support, welfare benefits are taken into account.[185]

12.93 Each local authority is able to decide its own scheme of payments after having regard to the Guidance. This is already an area of dispute. In *B v Lewisham London Borough Council*[186] the respondent local authority's scheme fixed the maximum allowances in the mid-range of the authorities which had agreed rates but these were very significantly below the national minimum allowance prescribed by the DfES for foster carers. Mrs Justice Black quashed the scheme on the basis that Lewisham had failed to have proper regard to para 65, which provided that 'the local authority should have regard to the amount of fostering allowance which could have been payable if the child were fostered. The local authority's core allowance plus any enhancement that would be payable in respect of the particular child, will make up the maximum payment the local authority could consider paying the family'. This was interpreted by Mrs Justice Black[187] as 'a ranging shot for the local authority's consideration of what their special guardianship provision should be or at last be held firmly in mind when fixing that provision'. In *R (L (A Child)) v Manchester City Council*[188] Mr Justice Munby had held that it was unlawful for a local authority to pay short-term kinship foster carers at a much lower rate than that paid to other foster carers.

12.94 Financial support may include an element of renumeration, but only where the decision is taken before the order is granted, the local authority considers it necessary and the recipient had been a local authority foster carer for the child and in receipt of renumeration.[189] This element can be paid for only 2 years from the making of the order unless the local authority considers it necessary having regard to the exceptional needs of the child or any other exceptional circumstances. The ability to make 'one off' payments is important. The grandmother in *B v Lewisham London Borough Council*, for example, was given £839 so that she could buy essential equipment and furniture.

---

[185] SGA 2005, reg 13(2).
[186] [2008] EWHC 738 (Admin), [2008] 2 FLR 523.
[187] Ibid, at [47].
[188] [2001] EWHC Admin 707, [2002] 1 FLR 43.
[189] SGA 2005, reg 7.

Legal costs

12.95 Given the possible difficulties in obtaining and sustaining special guardianship orders, including negotiating support services, it is obviously desirable that applicants have access to legal advice. Richards drew attention to the financial and other difficulties encountered by grandparents who were unrepresented or had to meet their own costs. If legal aid is available, it is unlikely that local authority assistance will be provided bearing in mind reg 13(2) which requires the authority to take account of any other resource available. However, where it is not available (and in Hunt's sample although 86% of carers had been involved in legal proceedings, only 54% were eligible) the authority can provide assistance under reg 6(2)(c) towards legal costs not only for obtaining a special guardianship order but also when an application is made to vary or discharge the order as well as a s 8 order. The costs of applying for a special guardianship order are not subject to financial assessment, provided the child is being looked after by the authority[190] but authorities are not expected to meet legal costs of an application for a special guardianship order when they oppose the application.[191]

Contact

12.96 The support which the authority can provide includes:

• counselling, advice and information;[192]

• assistance including mediation.[193] This could presumably include facilitating family group conferences as recommended by Hunt and supervision;

• travel costs;[194]

• legal costs in relation to a s 8 application.[195]

Respite care

12.97 In Hunt's study respite care was rarely given and practical help from the extended family was less frequent than emotional support. Respite care is part of the 'prescribed services'[196] but by virtue of reg 3(3), if it is met by the provision of accommodation, it must be by way of s 23 of the Act (accommodation for looked after children) or by a voluntary organisation. Paragraph 28 of the Guidance notes that 'this requires that appropriate safeguards are in place ... and that any foster parent providing respite care has

---

[190] SGA 2005, reg 13(4).
[191] Guidance, para 70.
[192] CA 1989, s 14F(1)(a), SGA 2005, reg 3(1)(b).
[193] SGA 2005, reg 3(1)(c).
[194] Ibid, reg 3(1)(b) or, if on a recurring basis, reg 6(2)(b); Guidance, paras 26 and 41.
[195] Ibid, reg 6(2)(c).
[196] Ibid, reg 3(1)(e)(ii).

been approved under the Fostering Services Regulations 2002'. Carers will therefore be unable to make their own arrangements if they need financial assistance to obtain the care. As one of the argued benefits of special guardianship is the autonomy of the carer,[197] this may not be attractive for special guardians.

Supervision orders and Family assistance orders

12.98 At the same time as making a special guardianship order the court may make a family assistance order for any period up to 12 months, the order being made to either Cafcass or (with its consent) a local authority (see **Chapter 13**). Alternatively in public law proceedings provided the s 31 threshold test is satisfied, a supervision order may be made under s 35 to a local authority for initially 12 months but extendable for up to 3 years.[198] A supervision order (but not a family assistance order) may direct the child to take part in certain activities or, subject to the child's consent if he has sufficient understanding to make an informed decision, to undergo a psychiatric or medical examination. The order may include a requirement that any person who has parental responsibility for the child or with whom the child lives complies with the requirement that the child takes part in the activities or is examined, subject to that person consenting.[199]

Variation and discharge

Application without leave

12.99 The court may vary or discharge a special guardianship order on an application by:

(1)   the special guardian;

(2)   any individual in whose favour a residence order is in force;

(3)   a local authority designated in a care order with respect to the child.[200]

Application with leave

12.100 The following applicants require leave:

(1)   the child himself;

(2)   any parent or guardian;

(3)   any step-parent who has acquired and not lost parental responsibility;

---

[197]   *Adoption – A New approach* (2000) Cm 5017.
[198]   CA 1989, Sch 3, para 6.
[199]   Ibid, Sch 3, para 3.
[200]   Ibid, s 14D(2).

(4)   any individual not being the child's special guardian, parent or guardian or a person in whose favour a residence order is in force who has or immediately before the making of the special guardianship order had parental responsibility for the child.[201]

No other person may apply.

Where the applicant is the child concerned, the court may grant leave only if it is satisfied that he has sufficient understanding to make the proposed application.[202] The court may not grant leave to anyone other than the child if it is satisfied that there has been a significant change in circumstances since the making of the order.[203]

12.101   The test for granting leave under s 10(9) to apply for a s 8 order (see **Chapter 15**) is not the same as for applying for leave under s 14D although the same individual factors may be relevant. In *Re G (Special Guardianship Order)*[204] the Court of Appeal stated that statutory tests expressed in much the same language should, if possible be approached in the same way. The s 14D test is very similar to the test under s 24(3) of the ACA 2002 for granting leave to apply for the revocation of a placement order namely that the court cannot grant leave 'unless it is satisfied that there has been a change in circumstances since the order was made'. The court should therefore adopt the guidance given as regards s 24(3) by the Court of Appeal in *M v Warwickshire CC*[205] namely:

> '[On] establishment of a change in circumstances, a discretion arises in which the welfare of the child and the prospect of success should both be weighed. My view is that the requisite analysis of the prospect of success will almost always include the requisite analysis of the welfare of the child ... Conversely, were there not to be any such real prospect, it is hard to conceive that it would serve the welfare of the child for the application for leave to be granted. But I hesitate to suggest that analysis of welfare will always be satisfactorily subsumed within an analysis of prospect.'[206]

It should be noted that the first stages of the two tests are different namely in the degree of change required in circumstances. It is only at the second, discretionary, stage that *M v Warwickshire CC* applies.

---

[201]   CA 1989, s 14D(3).
[202]   Ibid, s 14D(4).
[203]   Ibid, s 14D(5).
[204]   [2010] EWCA Civ 300, [2010] 2 FLR 696.
[205]   [2007] EWCA Civ 1084, [2008] 1 FLR 1093.
[206]   Ibid, per Ward LJ at [29].

Orders without an application

12.102 The court may vary or discharge a special guardianship order in any family proceedings[207] in which a question arises as to the welfare of the child if it considers that it should be varied or discharged even though no application has been made.[208]

Discharging the order

12.103 The test to be applied when a court is considering discharging a special guardianship order is the s 1 welfare test.

In *Kijowski v Poland*[209] the European Court of Human Rights held that Art 8 included a right for a parent to have measures taken with a view to his being reunited with his child, not just in care proceedings but also in private proceedings involving members of the family. However as in all Art 8 cases, this right must be balanced against considerations of the child's welfare. See **3.34**.

---

[207] As defined by s 8(3).
[208] CA1989, s 14D(2).
[209] (Application No 33829/07) [2011] 2 FLR 650.

Chapter 13

FAMILY ASSISTANCE ORDERS

INTRODUCTION

13.1 Section 16 of CA 1989 gives the court power in any family proceedings to require Cafcass to make an officer available or a local authority to make a social worker available 'to advise, assist and (where appropriate) befriend' any person named in the order. Unless a shorter period is specified, a family assistance order (FAO) lasts for a period of 12 months. There is no provision in the section for extending the order, but if the proceedings are still continuing, a further order can be made.[1]

The FAO may name any parent or guardian of the child, any person with whom the child is living or in whose favour a contact order is in force with respect to the child and the child himself. Although most orders will name the child, it is possible for the order to name, for example, just a parent. However, an FAO cannot be made unless every person named (other than the child) consents.

The FAO may direct any person named in it to take such steps as may be specified to enable the officer concerned to be kept informed of the address of any person named in the FAO and to be allowed to visit such person.

13.2 If the court makes an FAO with respect to a child and the order is to be in force at the same time as a s 8 order, the FAO may direct the officer concerned to report to the court on such matters relating to the s 8 order as the court may require (including the question whether the s 8 order ought to be varied or discharged).[2] In addition, if the court makes an FAO with respect to a child and the order is to be in force at the same time as a contact order made with respect to the child, the FAO may direct the officer concerned to give advice and assistance as regards establishing, improving and maintaining contact to such of the persons named in the order as may be specified in the order.[3]

---

[1] *Re M (Contact: Family Assistance: McKenzie Friend* [1999] 1 FLR 75 and *Re E (Family Assistance Order)* [1999] 2 FLR 512.

[2] CA 1989, s 16(6).

[3] Ibid, s 16(4A).

SHOULD THE ORDER BE MADE TO CAFCASS OR TO A LOCAL AUTHORITY?

13.3   The consent of Cafcass is not required before an order is made. In theory, the consent of the local authority is not required provided the child lives or will live in its area.[4] However, the court is unlikely to impose an order on a local authority that is reluctant to accept an order, especially if it lacks the necessary resources.[5] In most cases, therefore, an order should be made to Cafcass.

13.4   Before making an FAO, whether to Cafcass or a local authority, the court must have obtained the written or oral opinion of the appropriate officer of the service or local authority about whether it would be in the best interests of the child in question for an FAO to be made and, if so, how the FAO could operate and for what period. In addition, it must give any person whom it proposes be named in the order an opportunity to comment upon any opinion given by the appropriate officer.[6]

WHEN SHOULD A FAMILY ASSISTANCE ORDER BE MADE?

13.5   An FAO can be made only if the circumstances of the case are exceptional.[7] As always, when the legislature uses such a phrase in practice this means that the court will make an order whenever it considers an order is necessary. No further guidance is provided by the Act but non-statutory sources give some assistance.

13.6   The Law Commission report, *Family Law: Review of Child Law: Guardianship and Custody*,[8] stated that the purpose of the order is to:

> '... formalise the involvement of a welfare officer for a short period in helping the family to overcome the problems and conflicts associated with their separation or divorce ... The distinction in effect between this type of order and the conventional supervision order should be clear. The order may include requirements for the people named in it to keep in touch with the welfare officer but not the much wider range of requirements which may be included in a full supervision order.'[9]

---

4   CA 1989, s 16(7).
5   *Re C (Family Assistance Order)* [1996] 1 FLR 424. For an example of an order being imposed on a reluctant authority see *Re E (Family Assistance Order)* [1999] 2 FLR 512, discussed at **13.10**.
6   *Practice Direction: Family Assistance Orders: Consultation 3 September 2007* [2007] 2 FLR 626 (now FPR 2010, PD 12M).
7   CA 1989, s 16(3).
8   Law Com No 172 (1988).
9   Ibid, para 5.19.

The Department of Health, in its guidance on CA 1989,[10] adopted this description, adding that 'help may well be focused more on the adults than the child'.

13.7 The highest number of FAOs made in any one year has been 1,060 in 1996; 1,009 were made in 1997 and 864 in 1998.[11] The vagueness of the statutory test has contributed to the lack of a consistent approach by the courts towards making orders and the Probation Service (now Cafcass) towards their implementation. Research carried out between 1996 and 1998 found that central statistics regarding orders were unreliable.[12] Just over half (55%) of the orders in the survey were made without a recommendation from the court welfare officer but this figure varied from area to area. In one area, for example, 90% followed a recommendation while in another area the figure was only 47%. The child was named in 71%, 9% naming the child exclusively. Just over half (55%) named children together with their parents and 8% with other adults. Many court welfare officers were ambivalent about supervising orders because of the lack of funding and low priority being given to allocation of time to spend on the cases. Work with the child was carried out in only three in five (62%) of cases where the child was named.

In 2009/10 Cafcass responded to 390 Family Assistance Orders compared with over 16,000 requests for section 7 welfare reports.[13]

13.8 This background suggests that making of FAOs should be approached with care. The court needs to be satisfied that the local authority or the local Cafcass office will be able to allocate a welfare officer. The purpose of the order needs to be made clear and all the parties need to be aware of what will be required of them. Making an order which is not carried out is likely to result in the parties and the child becoming disillusioned and feeling let down.

13.9 FAOs should not be used solely to provide an escort for contact visits[14] but they can be a useful tool for securing successful contact. FAOs are usually thought about in the context of a final order but there is nothing in the Act which prevents a court making an order during the proceedings whether or not it makes any other order.[15] It might be used, for example, where contact has

---

10 *The Children Act 1989 Guidance and Regulations* Vol 1 Court Orders (HMSO, 1991), para 2.50.
11 *Making Contact Work: A Consultation Paper* Children Act Sub-Committee of the Lord Chancellor's Advisory Board on Family Law (Lord Chancellor's Department, 2001).
12 James and Sturgeon-Adams *Helping Families after Divorce: Assistance by Order?* (Policy Press, 1999) discussed in Sturgeon-Adams and James 'Assisting families – Section 16 orders under the Children Act 1989' [1999] Fam Law 471 and 'The use of family assistance orders in divorce and separation cases' *Findings* 579 (Joseph Rowntree Foundation).
13 *CAFCASS Annual Report 2009/10*. Higher figures quoted in Little 'Family Assistance Orders: Rising to the Challenge [2009] Fam Law 435 at 438 are based on the HMCS Family Management System which are often inaccurate.
14 *S v P (Contact Application: Family Assistance Order)* [1997] 2 FLR 277.
15 CA 1989, s 16(1).

broken down in circumstances which cannot easily be solved by one or two mediation appointments, to try to bring about a change.[16]

Examples

Re E (Family Assistance Order)[17]

13.10   The mother of a 2-year-old child was convicted of the manslaughter of the child's father and detained under the Mental Health Act 1993. The child went to live with her paternal aunt. A year later, the court ordered that there should be contact between mother and child every 6–8 weeks. At first, the local authority where the child lived assisted with the contact arrangements but the aunt and child then moved. Their new local authority was unwilling to help. In what he called 'a highly unusual and highly exceptional situation', Bennett J made an FAO to be supervised by the new authority, despite their objection and the resource implications, because everybody including the Official Solicitor agreed that it was overwhelmingly in the child's interests for contact to continue and if there was no FAO the likelihood was that contact would stop.

Re M (Contact: Family Assistance: McKenzie Friend)[18]

13.11   A father sought contact with his three young sons. The trial judge found that, although there was a sustained relationship between the father and the boys, direct contact would damage the children because of the effect on them of their mother's genuinely held fears. However, he made an order for indirect contact. The Court of Appeal upheld the order, but indicated that it would also make an FAO, provided the mother consented. Both the father and the mother were in need of advice and assistance. The court also applied subtle pressure to try to ensure that the mother's consent to the making of the order would be forthcoming. If she did not consent, that would be some indication that she was not prepared to put herself to the test of co-operating with indirect contact and this might justify the father in seeking a review of the contact order. On the other hand, if she did consent, an order would be made under s 91(4) preventing the father making any application without permission other than one to renew the FAO before the first FAO expired.

Re L (Contact: Transsexual Applicant)[19]

13.12   The court made an FAO when the applicant father was undergoing treatment to assist in undergoing a transition from male to female. The mother strongly resisted the father continuing contact with their daughter and it had been arranged that the family members would receive specialist therapy. Thorpe LJ said that the father's transsexuality was:

---

[16]   For an interesting discussion of this possibility, see Posner 'In praise of family assistance orders' [2000] Fam Law 435.
[17]   [1999] 2 FLR 512.
[18]   [1999] 1 FLR 75.
[19]   [1995] 2 FLR 438.

'... a huge challenge for [this] family, particularly when its emergence post-dates the breakdown of the relationship ...

... The family assistance order seems to me ... obviously required. If ever there was a family that needed assistance it is this, not just in its reaction to dramatic development but also on a practical plane ... There will be practical problems that need to be overcome in referring the individual members to [the unit], in getting that referral financed and in arranging financial support to meet the cost of attendance.'[20]

CAFCASS AND THE FAMILY ASSISTANCE ORDER

13.13 It is Cafcass policy[21] that its practitioners should consider recommending an FAO to the court where there are identified child welfare needs which are likely to be met only with assistance from Cafcass and where the adults who would be named in the order are likely to give their informed consent to it. This guidance sets out some suggested criteria to help practitioners decide if an FAO appears appropriate. 'A family assistance order should be recommended when there is an identifiable and consensually agreed task concerning the child's welfare which is too difficult for a family to undertake without specialist assistance from Cafcass or a local authority.'

13.14 When thinking through the suitability of an FAO it suggests that it may be helpful to consider the following criteria:

- Would an FAO contribute to improved safeguarding of the child/ren?

- Does the initial assessment indicate that the issues in dispute can be identified, narrowed and agreed by the parents and child (subject to age and understanding) and given a specific focus suitable for an FAO?

- Does the initial assessment identify sufficient potential for parental cooperation to make an FAO appropriate?

- In the professional judgment of the practitioner, are the parents/carers sufficiently able to differentiate their needs from those of their child so as to make an FAO a viable means of post-proceedings intervention?

- Can practical outcomes be identified which are clearly beneficial for the child/ren?

- Has the child been enabled (subject to age and understanding) to express their views about what s/he might like to happen in the family? Can the child play an active part in the FAO?

---

[20] Ibid, at 442–443.
[21] Family Assistance Order Policy (Cafcass, 2008), available at: www.cafcass.gov.uk/pdf/Family%20Assistance%20Order%20Policy.pdf.

- Are there additional resources which may support the sustainability of an FAO for this child and family? (ie support from the extended family, or the support of other agencies for the child and/or family members).

- What report, if any, might most appropriately be provided to the court at the conclusion of the order and/or during its operation?

13.15 If the practitioner believes that an FAO would safeguard and promote the welfare of a child, this should be reflected in the Analysis and Recommendation report to the court. In some cases, where the proposal for an FAO originates from the court itself, it may be necessary to request an adjournment to allow sufficient time to assess the family and to make sure there is a full and informed agreement of the adults who are to be named in the order. Though not a statutory requirement, it is good practice to ascertain the views of the affected child/children about the proposed order.

13.16 The Policy continues by pointing out that as in all Cafcass involvement it is important to involve the family in the analysis and decision-making process. However, in the case of an FAO this is particularly important, because an order can only be made with the consent of the adults who are named in the order. As part of securing the adults' informed consent to the making of an order, they should be provided with a copy of the Cafcass case plan (see **13.19**) which would be implemented if an FAO were to be made.

13.17 Similar guidance is not provided to local authorities but both they and the Cafcass officers are required by the Act to keep under consideration whether it is appropriate to refer to the court the question of whether any s 8 order should be varied or discharged.[22]

13.18 It is the policy of Cafcass[23] that in all cases, an FAO will be allocated to a Family Court Adviser who will act as case manager. The case manager may carry out some of the work under the FAO him or herself, or it may be carried out by another professional within Cafcass, such as a Cafcass Family Support Worker (FSW) or by another agency.

13.19 When providing services to a family under an FAO the following practices are expected to be followed:

- If any new concerns emerge during an FAO which gives cause to suspect that the child is at risk of harm, it must be brought to the attention of the case manager immediately. The case manager must ensure that Cafcass responds according to the Cafcass Safeguarding Framework.

---

22   CA 1989, s 16(6).
23   Family Assistance Order Policy, op cit.

- During the course of the FAO, it is good practice for the case manager or FSW periodically to review progress towards meeting the goals set out in the case plan. The goals should then be revised or added to as necessary.

- The case plan should set out the nature of the interventions to be carried out by Cafcass and other agencies, including their frequency, duration and the locations where the interventions are to take place.

13.20 Cafcass may arrange for services under the FAO to be provided by an external agency or agencies. A decision to refer a case to another agency for additional services will be taken by the case manager who may arrange a multi-agency meeting to identify how the range of services will be delivered and to clarify the role of Cafcass and other agencies in coordinating and reviewing the delivery of services. Everyone named in the FAO should be invited to the meeting.

13.21 The case manager or FSW should ensure that the child, everyone named in the FAO and other professionals involved are aware of the exact terms of the FAO, exactly what work the court wants to take place under it, and of the steps the court wants the case manager to take. The case manager or FSW should also make sure that those named in the order are clear about the circumstances which may cause the case to be referred back to the court. For example, the case manager may need to report to court on progress (or lack of progress) or seek a further order or an extension to the current order.

The conclusion of a family assistance order

13.22 As the order approaches its end date, the case manager should arrange a final review with the family to review what has been achieved and to identify what should be reported back to the court (if required by the terms of the FAO), what ongoing needs remain and how these might best be met, including through referral to another agency.[24]

PROPOSALS FOR CHANGE

13.23 The Children Act Sub-Committee of the Lord Chancellor's Advisory Board on Family Law in its working paper, *Making Contact Work: A Consultation Paper*,[25] sought views on whether the order should be abolished or amended. In its final report, *Making Contact Work*,[26] it saw FAOs 'as potentially a very useful facility if operated by CAFCASS and as part of a planned and specific programme of intervention':

> 'The scope for the use of such orders is, we think, substantial. They could, appropriately operated, provide the focus for necessary work with the family

---

[24] Ibid.
[25] (Lord Chancellor's Department, 2001), paras 3.37–3.43.
[26] (Lord Chancellor's Department, 2002), Chapter 11.

concerned by Cafcass after a contact order has been made; they could also provide a basis for intervention to implement court orders in intractable cases, as an alternative to other, more draconian, methods of enforcement.'

However, a number of changes would be required:

- FAOs should cease to be directed to local authorities;

- the time-limit of 6 (now 12) months should be reduced and be replaced by a time frame identified by the court as being required for the particular task to be undertaken; orders should not be open-ended;

- the phrase 'exceptional circumstances' has little meaning and should be dropped (this has been done);

- the ability of a person named to refuse to consent to the order should be abolished;

- Cafcass should prepare specific programmes which could be operated under an FAO, including 'educational' programmes for parents, packages of support in monitoring contract agreements, support for indirect contact and direct assistance for children (this has been done).

In its response to the report,[27] the Government accepted that FAOs had not worked as effectively as they could and agreed to review their operation. It was unlikely, however, that it would agree that all FAOs should be addressed to Cafcass.

13.24 Subsequent policy discussion on the role of family assistance orders has been limited.[28] Although it has been stressed that 'emphasis should be placed on overcoming problems through Cafcass intervention and education programmes',[29] a role which Cafcass indicated it would undertake 'as soon as courts are consistently able to reduce the number of reports ordered',[30] it is hindered by lack of resources despite the Government's belief that 'it is providing Cafcass with sufficient resources for the new service'.[31] In its report of the responses to the consultation on *Parental Separation: Children's Needs and Parents' Responsibilities: Next Steps*[32] it repeated its proposal set out in

---

[27] *Government's Response to the Report of the Children Act Sub-Committee of the Lord Chancellor's Advisory Board on Family Law, 'Making Contact Work'* (Lord Chancellor's Department, 2002).

[28] For a discussion of the history of the proposals for change, see Little 'Family assistance orders: rising to the challenge' [2009 Fam Law 435.

[29] *Family Justice: the operation of the family courts* House of Commons Constitutional Affairs Committee (2005) HC 116–1, para 111.

[30] Ibid, at para 118.

[31] The Government Response to the Constitutional Affairs Select Committee Report Cm 6507 (2005), para 26.

[32] Cm 6452 (2005), para 96.

Next Steps[33] to look more closely at whether legislation is necessary to extend the flexibility of FAOs and to make them more effective.

13.25 To a limited extent some assistance in contact cases may be available through contact activities (see Chapter 11). In other cases help can be provided by the court ordering an addendum s 7 report[34] which will often operate in practice as an informal family assistance order.

---

[33] *Parental Separation: Children's Needs and Parents' Responsibilities* Cm 6273 (2004) at para 81.
[34] See **Chapter 19**.

Chapter 14

RESTRICTIONS ON ORDERS

INTRODUCTION

14.1 The Children Act 1989 contains a number of restrictions which relate to the making of s 8 orders. The fundamental position which lies behind these restrictions is that those who have the care of a child – whether a natural person or a local authority – should be able to make everyday decisions about the child without being concerned with 'the judge over the shoulder':

> 'The person looking after the child has to be able to take decisions in the child's best interests as and when they arise. Some may have to be taken very quickly. In reality, as we pointed out in our Working Paper on Custody, it is that person who will have to put these decisions into effect and that person who has the degree of practical control over the child to be able to do so. The child may well suffer if that parent is prevented by the other's disapproval and thus has to go to court to resolve the matter, still more if the parent is inhibited by the fear that the other will disapprove or by difficulties of contacting him or of deciding whether what is proposed is or is not a major matter requiring consultation. In practice, when the parents disagree about a matter of upbringing the burden should be on the one seeking to prevent a step which the other is proposing or to impose a course of action which only the other can put into effect, to take the matter to court. Otherwise the court might be inundated with cases, disputes might escalate well beyond their true importance, and in the meantime, the children might suffer.'[1]

Most of the restrictions relate to children being 'looked after' by local authorities but others emphasise the importance of residence and contact orders by restricting the use of specific issue and prohibited steps orders. The use of wardship proceedings is also restricted, it being the intention of the legislation that it should be used to supplement s 8 orders and then only exceptionally rather than as a substitute for them.

CHILDREN BEING LOOKED AFTER BY A LOCAL AUTHORITY

14.2 The Act imposes restrictions on the courts' private law jurisdiction when children are in the care of a local authority (ie are subject to a care order)[2] or are being provided with care by a local authority under s 20. Such children are

---

1. *Review of Child Law: Guardianship and Custody* (1988) Law Com No 172, para 2.10.
2. CA 1989, s 31(11).

referred to in the Act as being 'looked after' by the local authority.[3] There are restrictions on who can apply for an order and on the type of order which can be made.

This is in keeping with the intention of the legislature that once a child has been placed in the care of a local authority, that body should be responsible for all decisions relating to his welfare:

> 'A report made to ministers by an inter-departmental working party *Review of Child Care Law* (September 1995) drew attention to some of the policy considerations. The particular strength of the courts lies in the resolution of disputes; its ability to hear all sides of the case, to decide issues of fact and law, and to make a firm decision on a particular issue at a particular time. But a court cannot have day-to-day responsibility for a child. The court cannot deliver the services which may best serve a child's needs. Unlike a local authority the court does not have close, personal and continuing knowledge of the child. The court cannot respond with immediacy and informality to practical problems and changed circumstances as they arise. Supervision by the court would encourage "drift" in decision making, a perennial problem in children cases. Nor does a court have the task of managing the financial and human resources available to a local authority for dealing with all children in need.'[4]

When a child is in care, the only orders which may be sought are residence orders (which have the effect of discharging the child from care and therefore do not offend the principle that it is for local authorities to control the care of the child) and contact orders, made under s 34 in public law proceedings instead of s 8 in private law proceedings. Two questions had to be asked: who can apply and what applications can be made?

Restrictions placed on applicants

Foster parents

14.3 No one who is or has at any time within the last 6 months been a local authority foster parent of a child may apply for leave to apply for a s 8 order with respect to the child unless:

- he has the consent of the authority;

- he is a relative of the child; or

- the child has lived with him for at least 1 year preceding the application.[5]

---

3   CA 1989, s 22(1).

4   *Re S (Minors) (Care Order: Implementation of Care Plan); Re W (Minors) (Care Order: Adequacy of Care Plan)* [2002] UKHL 10, [2002] 1 FLR 815, per Lord Nicholls of Birkenhead at [27].

5   CA 1989, s 9(3) as amended by ACA 2002, s 133(a).

'Relative' is defined as being a grandparent, brother, sister, uncle or aunt (whether of full blood or half blood or affinity) or step-parent.[6]

However, a local authority foster parent is entitled to apply without leave for a residence order or special guardianship order with respect to a child who has lived with him for at least 1 year immediately preceding the application.[7]

Applicants requiring permission to apply for a section 8 order

14.4 When an applicant requires permission to apply for a s 8 order (see Chapter 15) in respect of a child who is being looked after, two of the factors which the court has to consider under s 10(9) are the authority's plans for the child's future and the wishes and feelings of the child's parents.

Applicants who do not require permission

14.5 An applicant for a residence or contact order with respect to a child in care who otherwise would require the permission of the court to make the application may apply without leave provided he has the consent of the local authority.[8]

Applications for permission are considered in Chapter 15.

Restrictions on the applications which can be made

Residence orders

14.6 A court may not make a residence order in favour of a local authority.[9] Instead, the local authority has to apply for a care order under s 31.

The making of a residence order discharges any care order which is in force.[10] Therefore, any proceedings in respect of the application are 'specified proceedings' under s 41(6) with the effect that the rules relevant to public law applications apply.

Contact orders

14.7 A court may not make a contact order in favour of a local authority.[11]

When a child is in care, no court may make a s 8 contact order in respect of him.[12] Instead, an application for an order under s 34(2) should be made.

---

6   CA 1989, s 10(5)(l).
7   Ibid, ss 10(5A), 14A(5)(d).
8   Ibid, s 10(5)(c)(ii).
9   Ibid, s 9(2).
10   Ibid, s 91(1).
11   Ibid, s 9(2).
12   Ibid, s 9(1).

Other section 8 orders

14.8   When a child is in care, no court may make a s 8 order other than a residence order.[13] If contact is sought, an application has to be made under s 34. However, this restriction does not apply to special guardianship orders.

OTHER RESTRICTIONS

Specific issue order or prohibited steps order

14.9   No court may make a specific issue order or prohibited steps order with a view to achieving a result which could be achieved by making a residence or contact order.[14] For example, a specific issue order cannot be made declaring that a child shall spend half its time with one parent and the rest with the other. Either a joint residence order should be made or a residence order in favour of one parent and a contact order in favour of the other.

No court may make a specific issue order or prohibited steps order in any way which is denied to the High Court by s 100(2) in the exercise of its inherent jurisdiction.[15] Section 100(2) prevents the inherent jurisdiction being used to place a child in the care or under the supervision of a local authority, requiring a child to be accommodated by a local authority, making a child who is in care a ward of court or conferring on any local authority power to determine any questions which have arisen or may arise in connection with any aspect of parental responsibility for the child.

Age of the child

14.10   No court may make a s 8 order which is to have effect for a period which will end after the child has reached the age of 16 unless it is satisfied that the circumstances are exceptional.[16] If in the case of a residence order the period is extended to 18 under s 12(5). Likewise, no court may make any s 8 order other than one varying or discharging an order in respect of a child who has reached the age of 16 unless it is satisfied that the circumstances are exceptional.[17] In *Re F (Mental Health Act: Guardianship)*,[18] a 17-year-old girl suffering from mental impairment was made a ward in order to supplement the shortcomings of the mental health legislation if only for the 10 months remaining until she reached her majority.

---

13   CA 1989, s 9(1).
14   Ibid, s 9(5).
15   Ibid, s 10(5).
16   Ibid, s 9(6).
17   Ibid, s 9(7).
18   [2000] 1 FLR 192.

Chapter 15

APPLICATIONS BY NON-PARENTS

INTRODUCTION

15.1 Most applicants, other than the parents of the child, need the permission of the court before an application for a s 8 order can be made. When considering the application, the court has to consider a number of factors, including the likelihood of the application succeeding, but the hearing is not to be treated as a hearing of the substantive application nor are the interests of the child paramount. When the applicant is the child himself, the court can grant permission only if it is satisfied that he has sufficient understanding to make the proposed application.

If a special guardianship order (SGO) is in force, no one may apply for a residence order without leave.[1]

SECTION 10

15.2 Applicants for s 8 orders are divided into three groups:

- those who need no permission to apply for any s 8 order;

- those who need no permission to apply for a residence or contact order but who need permission to apply for any other order; and

- those who need permission to apply for any order.

This last group comprises two sub-groups, one of which having to meet certain requirements before they can apply for permission and the other, the child himself.

Applicants who need no permission

15.3 These are:

- any parent or guardian of the child;

---

1   CA 1989, s 10(7A).

- any person who by virtue of s 4A has parental responsibility for the child;[2]

- any person in whose favour a residence order is in force with respect to the child;[3]

- in respect of an order for the variation or discharge of an order, any person who was the applicant for that order, or in the case of a contact order, is named in that order.[4]

Applicants who need no permission to apply for a residence or contact order but need permission for other orders

15.4

The following persons are entitled to apply for a residence or contact order with respect to a child:

- any party to a marriage (whether or not subsisting) in relation to whom the child is a child of the family;[5]

- any civil partner in a civil partnership (whether or not subsisting) in relation to whom the child is a child of the family;[6]

- any person with whom the child has lived for a period of at least 3 years;[7]

- any person who:

  - in any case where a residence order is in force with respect to the child, has the consent of each of the persons in whose favour the order was made;
  - in any case where the child is in the care of a local authority, has the consent of that authority; or
  - in any other case, has the consent of each of those (if any) who have parental responsibility for the child;[8]

- (residence only) a local authority foster parent if the child has lived with him for a period of at least one year immediately preceding the application.[9]

---

[2]   A woman with parental responsibility under s 4ZA is a parent by virtue of s 43 of the Human Fertilisation and Embryology Act 2008 (see **6.21**).
[3]   Ibid, s 10(2).
[4]   Ibid, s 10(6).
[5]   CA 1989, s 10(5).
[6]   Ibid.
[7]   Ibid.
[8]   Ibid.
[9]   Ibid, s 10(5A).

15.5 However, as explained previously, when an SGO is in force no one may apply for a residence order without the leave of the court.[10]

Applicants who need permission to apply for a s 8 order

15.6 Any one not included in the above groups.[11] This includes the child himself.

Applicants who have to satisfy certain requirements

15.7 Any person who is or was at any time within the last 6 months, a local authority foster parent of a child may not apply for leave to apply for a s 8 order with respect to the child unless:

- he has the consent of the authority;

- he is a relative of the child; or

- the child has lived with him for at least 1 year preceding the application.[12]

'Relative' is defined as being a grandparent, brother, sister, uncle or aunt (whether of full blood or half blood or affinity) or step-parent.[13]

The child need not be subject to a care order – he can be in what is often called 'voluntary care' (ie being provided with accommodation under s 20).

The child

15.8 Where the person applying for leave is the child concerned, the court may grant leave only if it is satisfied that he has sufficient understanding to make the proposed application[14] (see also **4.79** and **15.60**).

The adopted child

15.9 From the date of the adoption order an adopted child is treated in law as if:

- born as the legitimate child of the adopters or adopter;[15] and

---

[10]   CA 1989, s 10(7A).
[11]   Ibid, s 10(1).
[12]   Ibid, s 9(3).
[13]   Ibid, s 105(1).
[14]   Ibid, s 10(8).
[15]   ACA 2002, s 67(1), (2).

- if adopted by a couple, or one of a couple under the Adoption and Children Act 2002 (ACA 2002), s 51(2) as the child of the relationship of the couple in question;[16] and

- as not being the child of any person other than the adopters, or as the case may be, the adopter or, if adopted by one of a couple under s 51(2), the adopter and the other one of the couple.[17]

Parental responsibility held by anyone at the time of the adoption is also extinguished.[18] However, the making of an adoption order under s 51(2) of the 2002 Act does not affect the parental responsibility of a parent who is the partner of the adopter.[19]

15.10 The child's birth parents and relatives will therefore not be treated as parents or relatives for the purpose of CA 1989, s 10 and will require the leave of the court to apply for any s 8 order.

15.11 For further discussion and the procedure to be followed when making the application, see **15.48**.

Children born as a result of artificial insemination

15.12 Applications relating to a child born as a result of artificial insemination can be very complicated and reference should be made to **Chapter 6** as to who is the child's parent. For example, in *J v C (Void Marriage: Status of Children)*[20] the applicant and a woman went through a ceremony of marriage. The applicant had lived for many years as a man but was, unknown to the woman, genetically a woman. A child was conceived as a result of the woman undergoing artificial insemination before the commencement of s 28 of the Human Fertilisation and Embryology Act 1990. Three years after the child was born, the couple separated. The applicant changed gender and obtained a gender recognition certificate showing himself to be a man. He also applied for contact. The Court of Appeal held that in order for the applicant to be the child's parent under the Family Law Reform Act 1987 which governed the situation, he had to be 'the other party' to a marriage with the mother. However, there was no marriage and he therefore required leave to make his application. Although the provisions of the 1990 Act were different, he would not have qualified as a father under that Act either. There was no marriage and at the time of the treatment he had not been a man because the grant of a gender recognition certificate was not for this purpose retrospective.[21]

---

16   ACA 2002, s 67(2).
17   Ibid, s 67(3).
18   Ibid, s 46(2).
19   Ibid, s 46(3).
20   [2006] EWCA Civ 551, [2006] 2 FLR 1098. See also *ST (Formerly J) v J (Transexual: Ancillary Relief)* [1997] 1 FLR 402.
21   Ibid, per Wall LJ at [37]; Gender Recognition Act 2004, s 9.

GRANTING PERMISSION – THE BACKGROUND

15.13 If parents who have a residence order agree to an application for a s 8 order for residence or contact being made, no leave is required.[22] It follows that whenever an application for leave is made in respect of a child who is not in the care of a local authority but whose parents are aware of the application, there is usually parental opposition to some degree. The tension then arises between making orders which may otherwise be for the benefit of the child and the opposition of the parents which in itself may be detrimental to the child's welfare.

Suppose, for example, that following the separation of a child's parents, the father dies. The child's mother subsequently restricts or denies the paternal grandmother's contact with the child. The child may in the past have had a friendly relationship with her grandmother, seeing her regularly. Her mother now has a new partner. Should leave be granted? And how much weight, if any, should the wishes of a parent carry when the welfare test is applied?

15.14 In the United States, the Supreme Court has held that state legislation which allowed an application for contact to be brought by someone who was not a parent without imposing a screening provision violated a parent's right to make decisions about her children.[23] Justice O'Connor called this right 'perhaps the oldest of the fundamental liberty issues recognised by the court'. The legislation contained no requirement that the court accord the parent's decision any presumption of validity or any weight whatsoever. It meant that a judge could disregard and overturn any decision by a fit custodial parent concerning contact based solely on the judge's determination of what was best for the child.[24]

The Law Commission's views

15.15 The requirement that non-parents seek leave before applying for a s 8 order and the factors contained in s 10 are attempts to remove this tension. One problem is that s 10 applies in a variety of situations, from close family members to comparative strangers. The Law Commission[25] recognised this and thought that its proposals (which were similar to s 10) would pose few difficulties in practice:

> 'The object of this scheme is to enable anyone with a genuine interest in a child's welfare to make applications relating to his upbringing, as at present can be done by making the child a ward of court ... The requirement of leave is intended as a filter to protect the child and his family against unwarranted interference in their

---

[22] CA 1989, s 10(4).

[23] *Troxel v Granville* 530 US 2000 decided on the facts of the example.

[24] The decision in *Troxel* is discussed and compared to the position in England by Crook in 'Grandparent visitation rights in the United States Supreme Court' [2001] CFLQ 101.

[25] *Family Law Review of Child Law: Guardianship and Custody* (1988) Law Com (No 172) at para 4.41. One of the Commissioners was Professor Brenda Hoggett, now Baroness Hale of Richmond.

comfort and security, while ensuring that the child's interests are properly respected. Leave will be a considerable hurdle to any outsider who cannot establish an obvious connection with the child and a good reason for wanting to bring the case before the court. There will hardly ever be a good reason for interfering in a parent's exercise of their responsibilities unless the child's welfare is seriously at risk from their decision to take, or more probably, not to take, a particular step, and only the people involved in taking that step for them would have the required degree of interests (the obvious example is medical treatment). On the other hand, leave will scarcely be a hurdle at all to close relatives such as grand-parents, uncles and aunts, brothers and sisters, who wish to care for or visit the child and who have no difficulty in obtaining leave in divorce proceedings at present. The new scheme will enable such issues to come before the courts whenever there is good reason to believe that the child's welfare will benefit.'

Articles 6 and 8 of the European Convention on Human Rights

15.16 The enforceability of Convention rights in domestic law inevitably raises the question of whether s 10 breaches the right to respect for family life under Art 8 and the right of access to courts under Art 6. There are no decisions either from the European Court of Human Rights or the former Commission which deal with the issue of family life and the wider family in a private as opposed to a public law context. Some general principles are, however, clear. First, family life can include ties between relatives such as siblings, grandparents and uncles and aunts.[26] Secondly, the existence of family life is a question of fact dependent upon evidence of close personal ties.[27] In *Price v United Kingdom*,[28] the Commission drew a distinction between the relationship between a child and its parents and between a child and its wider relatives:

> 'In normal circumstances the relationship between grandparents and grandchildren is different in nature and degree from the relationship between parent and child ... When a parent is denied access to a child taken into public care this would constitute in most cases an interference with the parent's rights to respect for family life as protected by Article 8(1), but this would not necessarily be the case where grandparents are concerned ... there may be interference by the local authority if it diminishes contacts by refusing to grandparents what is in all the circumstances the reasonable access necessary to preserve a normal grandparent–grandchild relationship.'

15.17   Any interference with family life has to be:

*   in accordance with the law;

*   necessary, among other things, for the protection of health and morals or for the protection of the rights and freedoms of others; and

---

[26]   *Marckx v Belgium* (1979–80) 2 EHRR 330; *Boyle v United Kingdom* (1995) 19 EHRR 179 and *L v Finland* [2000] 2 FLR 118.

[27]   *K v United Kingdom* (1986) 50 DR 199.

[28]   Price v United Kingdom (1988) 55 DR 199, E Com HR.

- proportionate to the aim sought.

15.18 There may be a clash between the wish of relatives to have contact with the child and the rights and freedoms of the parents. In *Boyle v United Kingdom*,[29] the Commission appeared to suggest that parents have a right to control access to their child which is recognised under the Convention as being lawful:

> 'Access by relatives to a child is normally at the discretion of the child's parents and, where a care order has been made in respect of the child, this control of access passes to the local authority. A restriction of access which does not deny a recoverable opportunity to maintain the relationship will not of itself show a lack of respect for family life.'

This discretion is not, however, absolute. Particular importance is attached to the best interests of the child, which, depending on their nature and seriousness, may override those of the parent. In particular, a parent is not entitled to act in a way which will harm a child's health and development.[30]

15.19 Article 6(1) affords a right of access to a court to have disputes decided,[31] but the right is not absolute and may be subject to limitations which pursue a legitimate aim, are reasonably proportionate to that aim and which do not restrict the right of access in such a way that the very essence of the right is impaired.[32] A preliminary sifting of claims by the court may therefore be compatible with Art 6(1).

15.20 Although the question has not been tested either at Strasbourg or in the English domestic courts, there appear to be strong grounds for arguing that s 10 is compatible with both Arts 6 and 8. No one is excluded from applying for leave, although applications by non-parents in relation to children in care may require the consent of the local authority which, being a public authority, has its own duties towards the applicants under both Articles. The matters to be considered by the court are relevant to the welfare of the child but not restrictive of the discretion. In contrast, where the child applies for leave, the exercise of the discretion is restricted to cases where the court considers that he has sufficient understanding to make the proposed application. However, the European Commission of Human Rights in the case of *M v United Kingdom*[33] recognised that:

> 'In the majority of the contracting states, the right of access to court is regulated in respect of minors, vexatious litigants, persons of unsound mind and persons declared bankrupt. Such regulations are not in principle contrary to Article 6 of the Convention where the aim pursued is legitimate and the means employed to achieve the aim is proportionate.'

---

29   (1994) 19 EHRR 179.
30   *L v Finland* [2000] 2 FLR 118.
31   *Golder v United Kingdom* (1979–80) 1 EHRR 524.
32   *Ashingdane v United Kingdom* (1985) 7 EHRR 528.
33   (1985) 52 DR 269.

15.21 The application of s 10 must however be proportionate in the context of the individual case.[34]

HOW OFTEN ARE SECTION 10 APPLICATIONS MADE?

15.22 The Court Service does not publish statistics relating to s 10 applications. However, in 1998 researchers[35] found that out of 345 cases studied, 6% of s 8 applications were made by grandparents and 4% by other non-parents. Eight per cent of applications for residence orders were by grandparents and 5% by other non-parents. Grandparents made 4% of contact applications and non-parents, 3%. A number of studies have shown that grandparents are probably discouraged by professionals from seeking s 8 orders and that solicitors seldom ask divorce clients about grandparent contact.[36]

TEST FOR GRANTING PERMISSION

15.23 Where a person applying for leave is not the child himself, the court when deciding whether or not to grant permission must have particular regard to:

- the nature of the proposed application;

- the applicant's connection with the child;

- any risk that the proposed application might disrupt the child's life to such an extent that he would be harmed by it; and

- where the child is being looked after (ie, subject to a care order or in voluntary care)[37] by a local authority:

  - the authority's plans for the child's future; and
  - the wishes and feelings of the child's parents.[38]

Although not part of the checklist, the court will also consider how likely it is that the substantive application would be successful.[39]

---

[34] See *Re J (Leave to Issue Applications for a Residence Order)* [2003] 1 FLR 114.

[35] Bailey-Harris and others *Monitoring Private Law Applications under the Children Act: A Research Report to the Nuffield Foundation* (University of Bristol, 1998). This is summarised in part in Pearce, Davis and Barron 'Love in a cold climate – Section 8 applications under the Children Act 1989' [1999] Fam Law 22.

[36] See, for example, Kaganas and Piper 'Grandparents and contact: "rights v welfare" revisited' (2001) 15 *International Journal of Law, Policy and the Family* 250.

[37] CA 1989, s 22(1).

[38] Ibid, s 10(9).

[39] *G v Kirklees MBC* [1993] 1 FLR 805.

GRANTING PERMISSION

15.24 The welfare checklist does not apply to application for leave to apply for s 8 orders and the child's welfare is not the paramount consideration.[40] In *Re M (Care: Contact: Grandmother's Application for Leave)*[41] the Court of Appeal had held that when considering whether to give leave the court should have regard to the likelihood of the substantive application succeeding. This is no longer the test. In *Re J (Leave to Issue Applications for a Residence Order)*,[42] Thorpe LJ said that:

> 'I am particularly anxious at the development of a practice that seems to substitute the test, "has the applicant satisfied the court that he or she has a good arguable case" for the test that Parliament applied in s 10(9). That anxiety is heightened in modern times where applicants under s 10(9) manifestly enjoy Art 6 rights to a fair trial and, in the nature of things, are also likely to enjoy Art 8 rights.
>
> Whilst the decision in *Re M (Care: Contact: Grandmother's Application for Leave)* no doubt served a valuable purpose in its day and in relation to s 34(3) applications, it is important that trial judges should recognise the greater appreciation that has developed of the value of what grandparents have to offer, particularly to children of disabled parents. Judges should be careful not to dismiss such opportunities without full inquiry. That seems to me to be the minimum essential protection of Arts 6 and 8 rights that Mrs J enjoys, given the very sad circumstances of the family.'[43]

However, this does not prohibit a 'broad assessment of the case' as opposed to a determination of the application on the 'no reasonable prospects of success' criterion.[44]

15.25 Although most applications will be heard on the basis only of the statements,[45] in some cases it may be necessary for limited oral evidence to be heard. In *Re M (Care: Contact: Grandmother's Application for Leave)*,[46] for example, a grandmother applied for contact with her four grandchildren, stating that she had seen them regularly until 4 months previously and had a close relationship with them. The children's parents, however, stated that she interfered and was not interested in seeing them. Cazelet J held that because there were two competing factual accounts of the circumstances, magistrates should have heard oral evidence so as to form a view on the disputed facts 'broadly' as to the merits of the application and as to any risk of it disrupting the children's lives to such an extent as they would be harmed by it. However,

---

40 *Re A and W (Minors) (Residence Order: Leave to Apply)* [1992] 2 FLR 154.
41 [1995] 2 FLR 86.
42 [2003] 1 FLR 114.
43 Ibid, at para 18.
44 *Re R (Adoption: Contact)* [2005] EWCA Civ 1128, [2006] 1 FLR 373, per Wall LJ at [46]. See also *Re H* [2003] EWCA Civ 369.
45 *Re A (Section 8 Order: Grandparent Contact)* [1995] 2 FLR 153, per Butler-Sloss LJ at 157.
46 [1995] 2 FLR 86.

this use predated *Re J (Leave to Issue Applications for a Residence Order)* (see **15.24**) and because the test is now less stringent, such an approach may now be less appropriate.

Nature of the proposed application

15.26   The nature of the application needs to be considered, including, if the application is for contact, whether the contact sought is direct or indirect or whether it is sought in relation to an adopted child.[47]

Applicant's connection with the child

15.27   There is no presumption that permission is likely to be granted merely because the applicant stands in a particular biological relationship to the child.[48] The psychological relation of *this* applicant to *this* child is what has to be considered:

> 'The more meaningful and important the connection is to the child, the greater is the weight to be given to this factor. Grandparents ought to have a special place in any child's affection worthy of being maintained by contact but it is easy to envisage family circumstances, very much like those before us in this case where, however loving the grandparent may be, life's wheel of misfortune has diminished the importance to the child of that blood tie and may, for example, have strengthened the claims for contact of former foster-parents who have forged close attachment to the child. The fact is that Parliament has refused to place grandparents in a special category ...'[49]

Risk that the proposed application might disrupt the child's life to such an extent that he would be harmed by it

15.28   The harm envisaged by the section means impairment to health or development[50] and a child's upset, unhappiness, confusion or anxiety needs to be sufficiently severe before it can amount to an impairment of emotional, social or behavioural impairment. In addition, it has to arise from the proposed application:

> 'The very knowledge that litigation is pending can be ... sufficiently disruptive if it involves the children in more interviews, psychiatric investigations and so forth. The stressfulness of litigation may impair the ability of those who have care of the child properly to discharge their responsibility to the child's detriment. Questions of that sort are the narrow focus of the court's attention in weighing this factor.'[51]

---

47   *Re R (Adoption: Contact)* [2005] EWCA Civ 1128, [2006] 1 FLR 373, per Wall LJ at [45].
48   *Re A (Section 8 Order: Grandparent Application)* [1995] 2 FLR 153.
49   *Re M (Care: Contact: Grandmother's Application for Leave)* [1995] 2 FLR 86, per Ward LJ at 95.
50   CA 1989, s 105(1).
51   *Re M (Care: Contact: Grandmother's Application for Leave)* [1995] 2 FLR 86, per Ward LJ at 96.

Disruption may be a crucial factor, especially if the child is in care:

> 'The child will only have come into care if life had already been so thoroughly
> disrupted that such intervention was judged to be necessary. The need then for
> stability and security is usually vital.'[52]

Where the child is looked after by a local authority

The authority's plans for the child's future[53]

15.29 These are very material, although not determinative:

> 'The court should approach the application for leave on the basis that the
> authority's plans for the child's future are designed to safeguard and promote the
> child's welfare and that any departure from those plans might well disrupt "the
> child's life to such an extent that he would be harmed by it".'[54]

The wishes and feelings of the child's parents

15.30 In *G v Kirklees Metropolitan Borough Council*,[55] an aunt was refused
permission to apply for a residence or alternatively a contact order with a child
subject to care proceedings for whom the local authority's plans were adoption.
The mother was strongly opposed to any member of her family having contact
with the child. Booth J observed that:

> 'It would only be in the most exceptional circumstances that a court would
> sanction a family placement contrary to the strongly held wishes of the mother.'

G v F (Contact and Shared Residence: Applications for Leave)[56]

15.31 The former partner of a lesbian mother was granted permission to
apply for contact and shared residence. The applicant had played a full part in
the child's life for the first 2 years of life and the contact application at least had
a 'very substantial' prospect of success.

C v Salford City Council[57]

15.32 A couple who had fostered a child of 3½ with Down's Syndrome for
2½ years and who had a very strong bond with her were given permission to
apply for a residence order against the wishes of the child's parents.

---

52 [1995] 2 FLR 86, per Ward LJ at 95.
53 See also **Chapter 13**.
54 *Re A and W (Minors) (Residence Order: Leave to Apply)* [1992] 2 FLR 154, per Balcombe LJ
    at 161.
55 [1993] 1 FLR 805.
56 [1998] 2 FLR 799.
57 [1994] 2 FLR 926. And see also *Re P (Section 91(14) Guidelines) (Residence and Religious
    Heritage)* [1999] 2 FLR 573.

Undertakings and agreements

15.33 The court has to consider the need for the application and may be influenced by the respondent's willingness to agree to or to undertake a particular course of action. In *J v C (Void Marriage: Status of Children)*[58] where children (now aged 20 and 14) were born to the respondent as a result of artificial insemination, she believing she was married to the applicant who was in fact a woman (see **15.12**), the court refused the applicant permission to apply for prohibited steps orders designed to ensure that the younger child was not told about her parentage until such time as a child expert advised it as appropriate to do so. The mother had agreed not to tell the children before taking the advice of a consultant psychiatrist. In the highly unusual circumstances of the case, Richards LJ in the Court of Appeal expressed the view that, he did not think the court could, or should, ask her to do more. The applicant had achieved all he could reasonably expect and the continued prosecution of the proceedings only served unnecessarily to prolong what had been an unduly extended court involvement.[59]

GRANDPARENTS

Background

15.34 As is apparent from the authorities already cited, a large proportion of the applications made under s 10 are made by grandparents. Over the years there has been pressure to allow grandparents to make s 8 applications without having to apply for leave[60] and in 2005 the House of Commons Constitutional Affairs Committee[61] recommended that the law should be changed. The Government responded by recognising that 'most children see their grandparents as important figures in their lives, who frequently have a stabilising influence'.[62] However, although it indicated that it would consider whether the legislation needed to be amended to make the process of applying for permission as simple as possible, no promise was made to remove the need to apply. 'The Government believes that it is usually more fruitful for parents and grandparents to work cooperatively to ensure that children have ongoing contact where that is in their best interests.'

15.35 In 2003 researchers at Cardiff University studied the role played by grandparents when parents separated.[63] They found that grandparenting seems to be characterised by asymmetry. Maternal grandparents appear to be more significant in the life of their grandchildren both before and after divorce than

---

58　　[2006] EWCA Civ551, [2006] 2 FLR 1098.

59　　Ibid, at [42].

60　　See, for example, Kaganas 'Grandparents' rights and grandparents' campaigns' [2007] CFLQ 17 and Deech 'Sisters sisters and other family matters' [2010] Fam Law 375, at 377.

61　　*Family Justice: the operation of the family courts* [2005] HC 116–1, para 64.

62　　The Government response to the Constitutional Affairs Select Committee [2005] Cm 6507, para 33.

63　　Richards 'Second time around for grandparents' [2003] Fam Law 749.

paternal grandparents and grandmothers more than grandfathers. Two norms were recognised and accepted both by grandparents and parents, the norm of obligation, expressed by 'being there' and providing a wide range of financial and non-financial support and the norm of non-interference which appeared to run very deep, namely, that grandparents should not interfere in the lives of their offspring.

15.36 The team gained the impression that grandchildren were usually more important to grandparents than vice versa and there may be a tendency for grandparents to overestimate the closeness of the relationship. However, the study was small and was not intended to be representative and the authors point out that:

'It would be wrong to conclude that grandparents are not important to their grandchildren. Some children were particularly close and strongly valued the time spent with their grandparents; they showed them care and affection and were highly appreciative of the attention their grandparents paid to them. But generally they did not talk of their grandparents in the same way they did of their parents.'

15.37 The researchers found that only a minority of parents and ex-parents in law maintained good relationships after divorce. Paternal grandparents saw less of the children than maternal grandparents. Before divorce just under three-fifths had seen them at least 13 times a year. After divorce this fell to 44%. One-third had had contact at least once a week but after divorce this fell to 14%. Despite this the researchers recommended that s 10 should remain.

'There is a very wide range of grand-parenting styles and a significant diversity in the quality of family relationships across the generations which makes it dangerous to generalise about the value of grandparents to their grandchildren ... The current legal position correctly requires grandparents to justify their claim to legal protection on the basis of the actual relationship they have had with their grandchildren rather than on the basis of their "status" as grandparents alone.'

15.38 What is clear from the research is that there are 'grave dangers' in making general statements about the roles grandparents play in the lives of their grandchildren. These differ from family to family and must not be assessed in isolation from the parent-child relationships.[64]

15.39 Kaganas comments that:

'The explanation for the higher profile of grandparents cannot lie in any compelling empirical evidence of the importance and benefits to children *in general* [emphasis added] of grandparent contact; the evidence is not really conclusive. It must therefore lie in the pervasiveness of the myths about the relationships between grandparents and grandchildren that have been fostered by

---

[64] Herring 'Grandparenthood', ch 7 in *Older People in Law and Society* (Oxford University Press, 2009), at p 236.

or at least reinforced by the campaigns of lobbying groups ... The welfare principle is being re-interpreted to designate as harmful any resistance to contact by resident mothers.'[65]

The Family Justice Review[66] considered whether the need for grandparents to apply should remain. The respondents to the Interim Report were divided. The Review concluded that although grandparents are often extremely important to children, and continue to be so if parents separate and recommended that this be emphasised in the process by which parents should seek to reach an agreement about their future care, its members continued to feel that the requirement to seek leave was not overly burdensome and should remain.

> 'As a matter of principle we agree with the many in the call for evidence who argued that just as contact is a right of the child not of the parents so also grandparents do not have a 'right' to contact. We noted in our interim report research showing that grandparents are unlikely to lose contact with a grandchild if they had meaningful contact whilst the parental relationship was still in being and if they resist taking sides after the separation. We do not believe that courts refuse leave unreasonably or that seeking leave is slow or expensive for grandparents. Rather, the requirement to seek leave prevents hopeless or vexatious applications that are not in the interests of the child.'[67]

In its *Response to the Family Justice Review*[68] the Government accepted the recommendation.

Grandparents as carers

15.40 Whereas most applications by grandparents in private law proceedings are thought to be for contact, applications for residence orders are more common in care proceedings. In 2000 a survey of grandparents as carers was carried out by the Family Rights Group.[69] The authors found that grandparent carers faced significant difficulties while at the same time experiencing emotional rewards. The overwhelming majority reported financial difficulties. Three-quarters found that their social life had altered significantly. Nearly a half were having to deal with long-term health problems and just under seven in ten found it hard to adapt to the physical and emotional demands of young children. However the grandparents emphasised the importance of providing a safe and stable home for their grandchildren within the family.

15.41 The need that grandparents have for support is discussed further in **Chapter 12**.

---

[65] 'Grandparents' rights and grandparents' campaigns' op cit, at p 40.
[66] (Ministry of Justice, 2011), Part 4.
[67] Ibid, para 4.46.
[68] (Ministry of Justice, 2011), at p 22.
[69] Richards 'Second time around for grandparents' [2003] Fam Law 749.

Grandparents and the law

15.42 'Grandparents' are not mentioned in CA 1989 but undoubtedly their relationship – biological, social or psychological – with their grandchildren can constitute family life under Art 8. In *L v Finland*[70] the European Court of Human Rights commented that:

'The Court recalls that the mutual enjoyment by parent and child, as well as by grandparent and child, of each other's company constitutes a fundamental element of family life, and domestic measures hindering such enjoyment amount to an interference with the right protected by Art 8 of the Convention (see, among others, *Johansen v Norway* (1996) 23 EHRR 33, para 52).'

However, it has been argued[71] that this relationship may not be treated as having the same weight as the relationship between the child and its parents. That may be so where the Art 8 rights of parents and grandparents conflict but domestic courts put significant weight on the perceived benefits to a child offered by grandparents.

15.43 In *Re W (A Child) (Contact Application: Procedure)*[72] Lord Justice Wilson commented that although there was no presumption:

'currently written into our jurisprudence that it is in the interests of a grandchild to have contact with a grandparent: see *Re A (Section 8 Order: Grandparent Application)*.[73] I anticipate that, when the Human Rights Act 1998 comes into force, it will be argued that a child's right to respect for his or her family life under Art 8 of the Convention requires the absence of such a presumption in the case of a grandparent to be revisited.'

15.44 However, even before the inception of the 1998 Act, the Court of Appeal had emphasised what it saw to be the general importance of the grandparental relationship but was careful to recognise that each case depended on its own facts. In *Re M (Care: Contact: Grandmother's Application for Leave)*[74] Lord Justice Ward said:

'Grandparents ought to have a special place in any child's affection worthy of being maintained by contact but it is easy to envisage family circumstances, very much like those before us in this case where, however loving the grandparent may be, life's wheel of misfortune has diminished the importance to the child of that blood tie and may, for example, have strengthened the claims for contact by former foster-parents who have forged close attachment to the child. The fact is that Parliament has refused to place grandparents in a special category or to accord them special treatment. Nevertheless, by virtue of Sch 2, para 15, contact between a child [who is in the care of a local authority] and his or her family will be assumed to be beneficial and the local authority will need to file evidence to justify

---

[70]   [2000] 2 FLR 118, at 134.
[71]   See Herring op cit, at p 252.
[72]   [2000] 1 FLR 263, at 269.
[73]   [1995] 2 FLR 153, per Butler-Sloss LJ at 157B–157C.
[74]   [1995] 2 FLR 86, per Ward LJ at 95.

why they have considered that it is not reasonably practicable or consistent with the child's welfare to promote that contact.'

15.45 After the 1998 Act was implemented, Lord Justice Thorpe in *Re J (Leave to Issue Applications for a Residence Order)*[75] commented that:

'It is important that trial judges should recognise the greater appreciation that has developed of the value of what grandparents have to offer, particularly to children of disabled parents. Judges should be careful not to dismiss such opportunities without full inquiry. That seems to me to be the minimum essential protection of Arts 6 and 8 rights that Mrs J enjoys, given the very sad circumstances of the family.'

15.46 The current position therefore is as follows:

• grandparents require leave to apply for a s 8 order unless they qualify under one of the exceptions;

• there is no presumption that leave will be granted;[76] but

• they are likely to find it easier to obtain leave than members of the wider family or non-family members.[77]

Example

Re A (A Minor) (Contact: Leave to Apply)[78]

15.47 A paternal grandmother sought leave to apply for a contact order in relation to her grandchild who was one year old. The court found that there was long-standing and serious disharmony between the grandmother and the child's parents and refused leave on the basis that the application would disrupt that child's life and harm him. Brown J dismissed the grandmother's appeal.

'The consequences are obvious and do not need a psychiatrist or a psychologist to point them out. Not even with the assistance of a skilled welfare officer could the degree of hostility in this case be overcome to provide beneficial contact for this child. The reverse is likely to be the situation, that it would be harmful contact; not that the grandmother herself would in any way set out to harm the child, any court would be confident of that without having heard her, but inevitably there would be emotional disruption to this little boy once he begins to realize that the lady who he is seeing regularly, who tells him she is his grandmother, is someone who plays no other part in his life, unlike any other grandmother, is not a visitor or welcome at his home and who is almost certainly not mentioned in conversation by these parents who have this fundamental disagreement with the grandmother. This little boy would become almost inevitably disturbed as a resulting of being made to see someone who had no other obvious connexion with his life and whom

---

75   [2003] 1 FLR 114 and see **15.24**.
76   *Re A (Section 8 Order, Grandparent Application)* [1995] 2 FLR 153.
77   Herring op cit, at 247.
78   [1995] 3 FCR 543.

he would learn fairly quickly was at odds with his parents. If there was some sound welfare reason for permitting this application to proceed, then that would be a different matter, but as the magistrate rightly took into account, this is a little boy where there are no welfare or health concerns and it would be, in his judgment and in mine, quite wrong to disturb this happy situation by the introduction of a grandmother who is sadly at odds with his parents.'

THE ADOPTED CHILD

15.48 As discussed at **15.9** an adopted child's birth parents and relatives are not be treated as parents or relatives for the purpose of CA 1989, s 10 and will require the leave of the court to apply for any s 8 order.

15.49 When a birth parent or sibling seeks permission to apply for a contact order, the adoption agency who placed the child for adoption should be given notice of the application. The adopters should not be given notice of the application but notice should only be given to the adopters if the court was satisfied that the applicant had a prima facie case for leave. The court should have as much relevant information as possible at the preliminary hearing but the application for leave should not be treated as if it were the substantive application.[79] Although Thorpe J said in *Re C (A Minor) (Adopted Child: Contact)*[80] that the Official Solicitor should also be made a party and that he, and not the court, should be responsible for notifying the adopters after the preliminary hearing if the court considered that there was a prima facie case, the Court of Appeal in *Re T (Adopted Children: Contact)*[81] expressed the view that this was not required in every case. Presumably, with the subsequent change in the Official Solicitor's responsibility, Cafcass or Cafcass Legal should be involved if necessary but not be made parties.

There is no general rule that such applications should be transferred to the High Court or that the child should be made a party.[82] It would be prudent however for the proceedings to be transferred from a family proceedings court to a county court.

15.50 Contact between adopted children and their birth parents and family is perhaps the most contentious issue in adoption. While there is general agreement that both direct and indirect contact has the potential for benefiting the child, extensive research, while generating fierce academic debate, is far from satisfying neutral commentators that as a general rule, there should be more contact than hitherto.

---

[79] *Re T (Adopted Children: Contact)* [1995] 2 FLR 792.
[80] [1993] 2 FLR 431. Approved by the Court of Appeal in *Re T (Adopted Child: Contact)*.
[81] [1995] 2 FLR 792.
[82] Ibid.

15.51 Courts have historically been reluctant to make orders for post-adoption contact, especially where adopters have not consented. In 1998 the House of Lords addressed the issue in the leading case of *Re C (A Minor) (Adoption Order: Conditions)*.[83]

> 'It seems to me essential that, in order to safeguard and promote the welfare of the child throughout his childhood, the court should retain the maximum flexibility given to it by the Act and that unnecessary fetters should not be placed upon the exercise of the discretion entrusted to it by Parliament. The cases to which I have referred illustrate circumstances in which it was clearly in the best interests of the child to allow access to a member of the child's natural family. The cases rightly stress that in normal circumstances it is desirable that there should be a complete break, but that each case has to be considered on its own particular facts. No doubt the court will not, except in the most exceptional case, impose terms or conditions as to access to members of the child's natural family to which the adopting parents do not agree. To do so would be to create a potentially frictional situation which would be hardly likely to safeguard or promote the welfare of the child. Where no agreement is forthcoming the court will, with very rare exceptions, have to choose between making an adoption order without terms or conditions as to access, or to refuse to make such an order and seek to safeguard access through some other machinery, such as wardship. To do otherwise would be merely inviting future and almost immediate litigation.'

15.52 Following the passing of the ACA 2002, the House of Lords again examined the issue of post-adoption contact in the light of changes in adoption practice approach from exclusively 'closed' adoption to some acceptance of 'open' adoptions. In *Down Lisburn Health and Social Services Trust v H*[84] Baroness Hale of Richmond commented that:

> '[Preserving] some limited contact between an adopted child and her birth family ... might serve two rather different functions. One, which can often be accomplished by life story books and occasional letters and cards, is to help the adopted child develop her sense of identity and self as she grows up. Another, which may indicate the occasional face to face meeting, is to preserve significant attachments, prevent the feelings of loss and rejection which the child who remembers her birth family may feel if she is completely cut off from her past and help her not to worry about the family she has left behind, including siblings (see Department of Health, *Adoption Now. Messages from Research*, 1999). This form of contact requires the birth parents to be able to put their own feelings of grief and anger aside so that they do not use their contact to undermine the adoptive placement. But if they can do this it can be a great help to the child in making the transition to her new 'family for life'. Hence the case for some form of post adoption contact may be strongest when the adoption itself is particularly contentious. The parents may rightly feel that they have something to offer the child even if she can no longer live with them. The problem for the court is to enable all the competing issues to be properly tried and resolved.'

---

[83]   [1988] 2 FLR 159, per Lord Ackner at 167.

[84]   [2006] UKHL 36, [2007] 1 FLR 121, at [6]–[7]. See also *Re G (Adoption: Contact)* [2002] EWCA Civ 761, [2003] 1 FLR 270, per Ward LJ at [14]. For a full discussion of adoption and contact, see Mitchell *Adoption and Special Guardianship: A Permanency Handbook* (Jordans, 2009) ch 13, paras 13.47 to 13.162.

15.53 *Down Lisburn* recognises that it may be beneficial for an adopted child to have some contact with his or her birth family but the consent or otherwise of the adopters remains a difficult and sensitive issue. 'Contact once a child becomes a member of a new family, while it may still be very desirable, is a more complex issue [than contact when a child is in care] because of the need to protect the privacy and autonomy of the new family'.[85] In *Oxfordshire CC v X*[86] for example, the Court of Appeal allowed an appeal by adoptive parents against an order that they annually supply the birth parents with a photograph of the child rather than the parents being allowed to view the photograph at social services offices. Being able to place a photograph on the internet could help the birth parents to trace the child. Furthermore, irrespective of the objective level of risk, the disturbing effect of the order on the adoptive parents and the consequent risk of emotional destabilisation of the household outweighed the value to the child of her birth parents having rather than seeing the photograph.

15.54 These difficulties influence the approach taken when a court 'considers an application by birth parents for permission to bring a contact application. Permission will not be readily granted. The court is bound to have regard to the fact that, under current jurisprudence contact orders in adoption proceedings are unusual and 'extremely unusual' when adopters do not consent.[87] Furthermore neither s 10(9) or the jurisprudence prohibit a broad assessment of the merits of a particular application. Rather, what they prohibit is the determination of the application on the 'no reasonable prospects of success' criterion.[88]

> 'So having regard to s 10(9)(a) the nature of the proposed application in this case inevitably involves, in my view, a consideration of the jurisprudence surrounding the circumstances in which such orders may or may not be made. In my view, the judge was plainly entitled in those circumstances to take into account that the court would be reluctant to make an order in the face of reasonable opposition from the prospective adopters.'[89]

15.55 Sometimes, proposed adopters and the birth parents have reached either an agreement as to future contact or a consent order is made.[90] If the adopters later want to resile from their agreement, Butler-Sloss LJ indicated in *Re T (Adoption: Contact)*[91] should inform the other party to the agreement, giving their reasons clearly. A simple explanation of their reasons in non-legal terms is all that is required and adopters should not fear that the reasons will be subjected to critical legal analysis. However, if they do not provide reasons or

---

85 Ibid, per Baroness Hale of Richmond at [33].
86 [2010] EWCA Civ 581.
87 And see also *Oxfordshire CC v X* [2010] EWCA Civ 581, per Lord Neuberger of Abbotsbury MR at [8].
88 *Re R (Adoption: Contact)* [2005] EWCA Civ 1128, [2006] 1 FLR 373, per Wall LJ at [45].
89 Ibid, per Wall LJ at [49]–[50].
90 See *Adoption and Special Guardianship* op cit, at paras 13.143–13.147.
91 *Re T (Adoption: Contact)* [1995] 2 FLR 251, per Butler-Sloss LJ at 256. See also *Re T (Adopted Children: Contact)* [1995] 2 FLR 792, per Balcombe LJ at 798.

the reasons turn out to be inadequate, wrong or unjust, the adopters should know that the other party will be able to seek leave to apply for leave to apply for a contact order.

15.56   Such a situation occurred in an identically entitled case, *Re T (Adopted Children: Contact)*.[92] A young woman was given permission to apply for a contact order in respect of her half siblings who had been adopted, the adopters having failed to provide annual reports as agreed. The Court of Appeal allowed her appeal against the dismissal of her application at the preliminary stage. The application was limited to the production of an annual report; no explanation had been given for the refusal to provide the report as agreed and there was no evidence that the proposed application might disrupt the children's life to such an extent that they might be harmed by it.

In *Re B (Adoption: Contact Order)*[93] the birth mother of an adopted child was given permission to apply for contact for herself and her younger son who remained in her care when the original care plan had provided for contact which had not taken place.

> 'It is unnecessary to express any view as to ... what will be the ultimate outcome. It is in my view simply enough to see that there is something that merits investigation. That is said on behalf of the applicant mother, but it can be said even more forcefully on behalf of Z who, after all, is a full brother who is only two years younger and who has a very strong Article 8 right to have a relationship with his brother as opposed to simply knowing of his brother's existence.'[94]

Examples
Re C (A Minor) (Adopted Child: Contact)[95]

15.57   A mother applied for leave to apply for contact to her 5-year-old son who had been removed from her care one month after he was born and whom she had last seen 4 years earlier, before his adoption. Leave was refused. A fundamental matter such as contact, albeit indirect, should not be reopened unless there was a fundamental change in circumstances of which there was none in the present case.

Re S (Contact: Application by Sibling)[96]

15.58   A 9-year-old girl, Y, applied, by her next friend and adoptive mother and supported by psychiatric evidence, for leave to apply for contact to her 7-year-old half-brother, S, who had been taken into care at the age of 1, adopted at the age of 3 and who had cystic fibrosis. Y was very distressed by her separation from S. S's adoptive mother said she did not intend to inform S

---

92   [1995] 2 FLR 792.
93   [2011] EWCA Civ 509, [2011] 2 FLR 1179.
94   Ibid, per Thorpe LJ at [9].
95   [1988] 2 FLR 159.
96   [1998] 2 FLR 897.

of his adoptive status until he was much older and vehemently opposed contact. The application was dismissed on the basis that it was S's welfare which was paramount , not Y's and that there would be a real risk of disruption to his life to the extent that he would be harmed if the application proceeded. Because S was adopted, the court had to be satisfied that the adopter's decision was sufficiently contrary to the child's best interests or sufficiently unreasonable to warrant the court overriding the adopter's discretion.

Re R (Adoption: Contact)[97]

15.59 K, aged 17, applied for leave to seek, at the hearing of the adoption application, contact with her half sister, L, aged nearly 7, in respect of whom she had been the main carer until L was taken into care at the age of 4. The Adoption Panel recommended that there should be direct contact three times a year. Post-placement K sought an increase in contact but the local authority and the proposed adopters then proposed reducing direct contact to once a year. The Court of Appeal upheld the dismissal of the application. Although post-adoption contact had become more common, the imposition of contact orders without the agreement of the adopters was extremely unusual. The prospective adopters had not resiled completely from their agreement: had they done so, leave would have been granted.

APPLICATIONS BY CHILDREN

15.60 Under s 8, the court has to be satisfied that the child has sufficient understanding to make the application. The factors to be considered by a court are discussed in **Chapter 11**. The test is the child's understanding and not his age. The judge has to do his best, on the evidence before him, to assess the understanding of the individual child in the context of the proceedings in which he seeks to participate:

> 'Where any sound judgment on these issues calls for insight and imagination which only maturity and experience can bring, both the court and the solicitor will be slow to conclude that the child's understanding is sufficient.'[98]

Although the s 10(3) and the s 1 checklists do not expressly apply, the court should consider the likelihood of the application succeeding as well as the views of the child's parents and (if he is in the care of a local authority) their views.[99] The best interests of the child are also important although not paramount.[100]

---

[97]   [2005] EWCA Civ 1128, [2006] 1 FLR 373.
[98]   *Re S (A Minor) (Independent Representation)* [1993] 2 FLR 437, per Sir Thomas Bingham MR at 444G.
[99]   *Re SC (A Minor) (Leave to Seek a Residence Order)* [1994] 1 FLR 96.
[100] *Re C (Residence: Child's Application for Leave)* [1995] 1 FLR 927.

15.61   Applications by a child should be brought in or transferred to the High Court.[101]

Examples

Re C (A Minor) (Leave to Seek Section 8 Order)[102]

15.62   C, a 15-year-old girl, applied for permission to apply for a residence order and a specific issue order against her parents. The girl was living with another family and the application concerned her wish to go on holiday to Bulgaria with the family. Johnson J said that C had been given rights by statute and the court should not seek to impede her exercise of those rights. Nevertheless, in her best interests, permission should be refused. This decision should be read in the light of the judge's view that a residence order was not necessary because C's parents were not going to force her to return home. He believed that the best way forward was by negotiation. He also took into account the relatively trivial nature of the issue she wanted the court to decide.

Re Alayn (Non-Molestation Proceedings by a Child)[103]

15.63   Parents lived together with their 12-year-old child. The child alleged that his mother was violent towards him when his father was absent and applied to the High Court of Northern Ireland for a non-molestation order and an occupation order against her. The High Court dismissed the application for an occupation order and gave the boy leave to withdraw his application for a non-molestation order on the basis that his father would apply to the family proceedings court for a residence order.

Two separate issues needed to be considered. First, the court could not, except in the most exceptional circumstances, exercise its discretion to grant leave to a child to commence proceedings without his solicitor's written assessment of the child's understanding. Secondly, in cases such as this, the court would require evidence as to whether, prior to proceedings being brought by the child active consideration had been given to whether it was more appropriate for proceedings to be begun by the other parent in a Family Proceedings Court. If the child had not agreed to discontinue the non-molestation proceedings then the court would have dismissed them on the basis that there was insufficient evidence as to his understanding and on the basis that there was inadequate information available to the court to exercise discretion as to whether to grant leave to commence proceedings.[104]

---

[101]   Practice Direction: Children Act 1989 – Applications by Children (22 February 1993) [1993] 1 FLR 668. This is not expressly referred to in the Allocation and Transfer of Proceedings Order 2008, SI 2008/2836 and Practice Direction 3 November 2008 [2009] 1 FLR 365.

[102]   [1994] 1 FLR 26.

[103]   [2009] NIFam 22, [2010] 1 FLR 1363.

[104]   See also *Re H (Residence Order: Child's Application for Leave)* [2000] 1 FLR 780 where it was said that although it was clear that the 12-year-old child had sufficient understanding, there was no argument which he could put which could not be put on behalf of his father in regard

Re SC (A Minor) (Leave to Seek a Residence Order)[105]

15.64 A 14-year-old girl who was in care was given permission to apply for an order that she live with a friend's family.

Re C (Residence: Child's Application for Leave)[106]

15.65 A 14-year-old was granted permission to apply for an order against her father that she be allowed to live with her mother.

PROCEDURE

15.66 The procedure to be followed is set out in FPR 2010. The applicant must file a written request in Form C, setting out the reasons for the application and a draft of the application. The court will either grant the application or fix a date for hearing the request, in which case it will give directions about who should be notified.

15.67 The granting of leave is a substantial judicial decision and in almost all cases should be heard in the presence of the parties.[107] A failure to follow this procedure is likely to result in the decision being overturned on appeal and the application reheard. Likewise, parents of children in care should be given notice of any application for permission.[108]

---

to an application that he live with him. See also Fortin *Children's Rights and the Developing Law* (3rd edn, Cambridge University Press, 2009), p 137 in relation to applications by children for residence orders.

[105] [1994] 1 FLR 96.
[106] [1995] 1 FLR 927.
[107] *Re W (Contact Application: Procedure)* [2000] 1 FLR 263.
[108] *Re A and W (Minors) (Residence Order: Leave to Apply)* [1992] 2 FLR 154.

Re SC (A Minor) (Leave to Seek a Residence Order) [19..]

13.54 A 14-year-old girl who was in care was given permission to apply for an order that she live with a friend's family.

Re C (A Residence: Child's Application for Leave) [19..]

13.55 A 12-year-old was granted permission to apply for an order against her father that she be allowed to live with her mother.

PROCEDURE

13.56 The procedure to be followed is set out in FPR 2010. The applicant must file a written request in form C..., setting out the reasons for the application and a draft of the application. The court will either grant the application or fix a date for hearing the request, in which case it will give directions about who should be notified.

13.57 The granting of leave is a substantial judicial decision and in almost all cases should be heard in the presence of the parties. A failure to follow this procedure is likely to result in the decision being overturned on appeal and the application refused. Likewise, parents of children in care should be given notice of any application for permission.

Chapter 16

COMMENCING PROCEEDINGS

BEFORE THE ISSUE OF PROCEEDINGS

Solicitors and their own clients

16.1 The philosophy of the CA 1989, that parents are normally the most appropriate people to make decisions about their children and that courts should only make orders if they are positively satisfied that doing so is better than making no order, means that proceedings should normally only be commenced if all other reasonable avenues have been considered and found to be inappropriate or unworkable or if this is the only way to offer the parties the opportunity of a mediated settlement.[1] To this end, the Law Society's *Family Law Protocol*[2] provides that solicitors should encourage clients to remember that in most cases they will be continuing to co-parent with the other party and it is better to acknowledge the other party's strengths as a parent rather than to condemn his or her weakness. It warns however that this approach may not be appropriate in cases involving domestic violence or dealing with a parent exhibiting an aggressive, controlling or oppositional approach to the case to the detriment of the child's welfare. They are advised at the first meeting with the client:

- to emphasise the need for parents to accept parental responsibility for their children;

- to promote the child's welfare as the paramount consideration;

- to encourage separation of addressing the children's needs from those of the parents;

- to encourage the use of mediation and other methods of dispute resolution;

- to provide information about local support/guidance services and

- to provide information about parenting apart.[3]

---

[1]   *Family Law Protocol* (The Law Society, 2010), para 5.81.
[2]   Ibid, para 5.9.13.
[3]   Ibid, para 1.5.1.

Solicitors and the other party

16.2 The tone of the initial letter to the other party is important. It should briefly address the issues and avoid protracted, clearly one-sided and unnecessary arguments or assertions. All letters should focus on the identification of issues and their resolution. Protracted, unnecessary, hostile and inflammatory exchanges and 'trial by correspondence' should be avoided. The *Family Law Protocol*[4] advises that solicitors should communicate in a non-confrontational and constructive manner designed to preserve dignity and encourage agreements. According to Resolution, an association of family lawyers:

> 'The criticisms and shortcomings of lawyers' correspondence are extensive and many of the complaints made to Resolution are received from clients who are aggrieved by the content of correspondence written either by their own lawyer, or by the lawyer acting for the other party.'[5]

The Law Society recommends that Resolution's *Guide to Good Practice on Correspondence* should be followed.

16.3 Prior to issuing proceedings, solicitors should notify the intended respondent of their intention to commence proceedings at least 7 days in advance unless there is good reason not to do so.[6] The Protocol comments that it is bad practice for respondents then to issue proceedings to pre-empt applicants issuing unless there is good reason for doing so. If respondents want to do this, their solicitors must warn them of the court's disapproval of such action, the possible cost implications and the impact of such action on the rest of the case.[7]

ALTERNATIVE DISPUTE RESOLUTION

16.4 In recent years there has been a growing recognition that court litigation should be the last and not the first recourse where adults cannot agree issues concerning children.[8] The Family Justice Review,[9] for example, stated that 'the emphasis throughout should be on enabling people to resolve their disputes safely outside court wherever possible'. It recommended that all applicants should be required to attend a mediation information and assessment meeting prior to making an application. It recognised that respondents could not be compelled to attend but they should be encouraged to do so.

---

4   *Family Law Protocol*, para 1.9.1.
5   *Guide to Good Practice on Correspondence* (2009) Resolution, available from: www.resolution. org.uk/site_content_files/files/good_practice_guide_2009_for_web_2.pdf.
6   *Family Law Protocol*, para 1.11.1.
7   Ibid, para 1.11.1.
8   For international support from the council of Europe, see Roberts 'Council of Europe mediation: 10th anniversary' [2008] Fam Law 932.
9   Final Report (Ministry of Justice, 2011), para 4.69.

16.5 To this end the Family Procedure Rules 2010 (FPR 2010)[10] state that the court's duty to further the overriding objective of enabling the court to deal with cases justly, having regard to any welfare issues involved, includes actively encouraging the parties to use an alternative dispute resolution procedure if the court considers that appropriate and helping the parties to settle the whole or part of the case.[11]

16.6 Practice Direction 3A states that:

'There is a general acknowledgement that an adversarial court process is not always best-suited to the resolution of family disputes, particularly private law disputes between parents relating to children, with such disputes often best resolved through discussion and agreement, where that can be managed safely and appropriately ... There is growing recognition of the benefits of early information and advice about mediation and of the need for those wishing to make an application to court, whether publicly-funded or otherwise, to consider alternative means of resolving their disputes, as appropriate ... Against that background, it is likely to save court time and expense if the parties take steps to resolve their dispute without pursuing court proceedings. Parties will therefore be expected to explore the scope for resolving their dispute through mediation before embarking on the court process.'

Types of ADR

16.7 Alternative Dispute Resolution (ADR) takes a number of forms. The following are the most common.

Mediation

16.8 A recognition of the benefits of ADR including mediation has lead to similar encouragement in civil cases[12] but some scepticism has been expressed about about whether mediation is always appropriate. Professor Hazel Genn. while being clear about mediation being an important supplement to courts and believing that the public and legal profession should be properly educated about the potential of mediation from the earliest possible moment and that mediation facilities should be made easily available to anyone contemplating litigation expressed three concerns in the 2008 Hamlyn Lectures.[13] First, mediation is most appropriate and successful when the process is voluntary. Secondly, ADR cannot supplant the machinery of civil justice[14] because the threat of litigation is necessary to bring people to the negotiating table and finally and most importantly, she was concerned that:

---

[10] SI 2010/2955.
[11] FPR 2010, r 1.4(2)(e) and (f).
[12] See Lord Woolf *Access to Justice: Final Report* (Lord Chancellor's Department, 1996), section 1, paras 8 and 9.
[13] *Judging Civil Justice* (Cambridge University Press, 2010) ch 3.
[14] Genn was principally but not solely writing about civil justice but her comments seem applicable to family cases, especially those involving intractable contact disputes.

'... the case for mediation has routinely been made not so much on the strength of its special benefits but by setting it up in opposition to adjudication and promoting it through anti-adjudication and anti-law discourse ... It is a cruder message that has been picked up by government and used to justify a helpfully economical policy of diverting cases way from court.'[15]

The importance of voluntary participation was underlined in *Twisting arms: court referred and court linked mediation under judicial pressure*[16], research which Professor Genn carried out for the Ministry of Justice:

'Information from [the pilots] suggest that the motivation and willingness of parties to negotiate and compromise is critical to the success of mediation. Facilitation and encouragement together with selective and appropriate pressure are likely to be more effective and possibly more efficient than blanket coercion to mediate.'[17]

16.9 Research by Trinder and Kellett into long-term outcomes of in-court conciliation in the family justice system[18] found that conciliation was an effective way of reaching agreements and restoring contact over the short-term but was often followed by further litigation and had very limited impact on making contact actually work well for children. The first significant problem was that in-court conciliation alone was not enough to provide a two-year, let alone a longer-term, solution to cases.

'What this suggests is that many parents are not able to reach workable agreements in conciliation and conciliation is often not equipping parents to be able to renegotiate agreements by themselves as circumstances change. For many parents, therefore, the high agreement rates reached in conciliation proved a false dawn.'

The second, and probably the more significant problem, concerned the outcomes for children. Even after 2 years most co-parental relationships were not improved simply by the exercise of contact. For the majority of parents co-parental relationships were competitive or non-existent, trust was low and conflict was high.

'Agreements and court orders alone are likely to increase significantly the chances of contact occurring but are far less likely to shift parental attitudes and behaviour. It is vital to recognise that the quality of co-parental relationships and the quality of contact for children is not the icing on the cake.'

They concluded that the messages from their research and that of others gave compelling reasons for focusing interventions on trying to shift parental attitudes and behaviour in conflicted cases or at the very minimum to help

---

[15]   *Judging Civil Justice* op cit, at p 80.
[16]   Genn, Fenn and others (Ministry of Justice, 2007) Research Series 1/07.
[17]   Ibid, at p v.
[18]   Trinder and Kellett *The Longer-term Outcomes of In-court Conciliation* (Ministry of Justice, 2007) Research Series 15/07, summarised in *Conciliation Report* [2008] Fam Law 81 and Trinder 'Conciliation, the Private Law Programme and children's well-being: Two steps forward, one step back?' [2008] Fam Law 338.

parents find ways to assist children with dealing with the conflict rather than doing what courts did namely to concentrate on providing a dispute resolution process addressing contact timetables – the quantity of contact – rather than understanding and addressing, the wider circumstances surrounding the dispute 'It seems that simply providing a dispute resolution process does not in itself have further interpersonal or communicative or therapeutic consequences.' A recent study[19] also found little improvement in communication or shared decision making amongst former clients of out-of-court mediation, even where a full agreement had been reached. In contrast, mediation with a clearly therapeutic orientation and emotionally-informed content could have a profound and enduring impact on relationships.

> 'This is not to suggest that courts should abandon the goal of achieving contact, or establishing a contact timetable. A timetable is critical for good contact but it is not sufficient. Rather interventions are needed where the primary goal is to address parental attitudes and the parental alliance and give children the best shot at contact that works for them, rather than for their parents or the courts.'[20]

Mediation in practice

16.10 Independent mediation is governed by four principles.

- It is a voluntary process.

- It is a confidential process.

- The mediator acts in an impartial way.

- Decision making rests with the participants to the mediation.

These principles are central to the delivery of an independent family mediation process and govern the way in which all recognised family mediators work. Mediators cannot dilute these principles which are embedded in Code/s of Practice applied by all mediation representative and regulatory bodies and in documentation provided by mediators to clients.[21]

16.11 There are a number of models of mediation. 'Co-mediation' involves two mediators. A variation is 'anchor mediation' with one main mediator, a second one being used from time to time. Some mediators will use 'shuffle mediation' with the parties starting in separate rooms with the mediator going backwards and forwards with the aim of eventually working in the same room. In 'caucusing' mediators will meet separately with each party in order to reduce

---

19   Walker et al *Picking up the Pieces: Marriage and Divorce Two Years after Information Provision* (Department for Constitutional Affairs, 2004).
20   *The Longer-term Outcomes of In-court Conciliation* op cit, pp 50–51.
21   *Practice Guidance: Independent Mediation* (Family Justice Council, 2011) [2011] Fam Law 301.

tension and defensive attitudes. In caucusing the mediator may keep each party's position secret whereas shuttle mediation usually assumes that all information will be shared.[22]

16.12   The *Family Law Protocol*[23]published by the Law Society gives advice on obtaining a mediator and lists mediation organisations who belong to the Family Mediation Council. Information can also be found from local family courts and from the Community Legal Advice Helpline.[24]

16.13   While the parties' views that their case is not suitable for mediation may be based on a misunderstanding or too pessimistic a view of mediation, it may be inappropriate in private law cases where:

* domestic abuse has occurred or is still occurring;

* the imbalance between parties is or may be such that a mediator cannot rebalance it;

* relationship counselling or marital therapy may be more appropriate prior to mediation.[25]

16.14   For the use of mediation in relocation cases, see **9.60**. For the use of mediation to resolve issues relating to shared care, see *Shared Care Disputes in Mediation*.[26]

16.15   Mediation may be desirable in a particular case but may not be effective at the particular stage the dispute has reached. In the jargon of mediators, is the time 'ripe'? Four models of 'ripeness' have been proposed.[27]

* the *hurting stalemate model* where no party can envisage a successful outcome or an end to unbearable costs;

* the *imminent mutual catastrophe model* where both parties face an undeniable disaster, for example a huge increase in costs or public funding is withdrawn;

* the *entrapment model* where parties are reluctant to withdraw because of the financial or emotional investments made in winning;

---

22   *Family Law Protocol*, ch 2; Stirum 'Mediation in high conflict or intractable cases' [2010] Fam Law 1228.

23   Family Law Protocol, ch 2.

24   CLA Direct, tel 0845 345 4345 or www.direct.gov.uk. For further discussions of mediation, see Turner 'Family mediation: The future and FMA' [2009] Fam Law 745 and 'Family mediation: The future and NFM' [2009] Fam Law 746.

25   *Family Law Protocol*, para 2.2.11. See also Parkinson 'Gateways to mediation' [2010] Fam Law 867.

26   Davies [2011] Fam Law 1385.

27   See Wilson 'Dispute 'ripeness' timing and mediation' [2005] Fam Law 162 citing Mitchell 'The right moment: notes on four models of "ripeness"' [1995] 9(2) *Paradigms* 38.

- the *enticing opportunity model* which envisages the parties being rewarded by adopting alternatives to their present course.

Wilson argues that there may be many 'ripe' moments when mediation can profitably be attempted and clients who initially reject mediation out of hand often change their minds once they have met the mediator.

16.16 The strong judicial support given to alternative methods of dispute resolution and the effectiveness of ADR in most cases can be illustrated by *Al-Khatib v Masry*[28] in which a father had removed his five children from the United Kingdom to Saudi Arabia following the collapse of his marriage. The parties attempted mediation – unfortunately though through mediators specialising in commercial litigation. Mediation failed but after further encouragement from the Court of Appeal it was reattempted with the parties eventually agreeing to a settlement of their various disputes. Thorpe LJ commented:

> '[This case] supports our conviction that there is no case, however conflicted, which is not potentially open to successful mediation, even if mediation has not been attempted or has failed during the trial process. It also demonstrates how vital it is for there to be judicial supervision of the process of mediation. It is not enough, in a difficult case such as this, for [the judge] directing mediation simply to make the order and thereafter that there will be a smooth passage to the initial meeting. The selection of the appropriate mediator in a difficult case is crucial and the availability of the supervising judge to deal with crisis is equally important.'[29]

Collaborative law

16.17 In recent years interest has been shown in using a collaborative law model to resolve disputes without recourse to litigation. Essentially parties and their lawyers sign a participation agreement by which they commit themselves to a 'transparent search for fair solutions' and which forbids them issuing or pursuing proceedings. If negotiations become stuck the parties may be referred to an external mediator or external counselling ('coaching') which aims to provide them with the emotional tools and techniques to deal with any difficulties.[30] If agreement still remains impossible the parties will need to instruct new solicitors.[31] There are many advantages in the model. The clients play a greater part in negotiations with increased satisfaction. There is a greater chance of transparency and honesty. There is greater flexibility and matters proceed at a pace which is comfortable for the parties. The requirement that the parties will have to instruct new solicitors if the process fails makes agreement more likely.[32] The extent to which this approach can be effective or appropriate for all cases remains to be seen. For example, can it be effective in cases where one unrepresented party may cause a disparity in the pressure tying the parties

---

[28] [2004] EWCA Civ 1353, [2005] 1 FLR 381.
[29] Ibid, at [17].
[30] See Pirrie 'Collaborative family law – perspectives from training' [2004] Fam Law 216.
[31] 'The main cornerstoner of the collaborative process' *Family Law Protocol*, para 2.3.3.
[32] Pirrie 'Collaborative law update' [2004] Fam Law 603.

to the process? What can prevent a party who secretly wants to obstruct contact whilst seeming to support it in principle using the process to cause delay? There will also be cases where it will be inappropriate, at least initially, for example where a risk to a party or child requires an urgent order. A small scale study by Wright[33] found that the benefit of collaborative law is that it appears to build on the strengths and overcomes the weaknesses of both mediation and the traditional negotiating model. However '… [the] process … has the potential to lead to outcomes which reflect current imbalances of power or feelings of guilt in a couple's relationship'[34] and 'it may be questioned whether clients are entirely aware of the implications for them of the system'.[35]

Family Group Conferences

16.18 A Family Group Conference (FGC) is 'a decision making meeting in which the child's wider family network makes a plan about the future arrangements for the child, which will ensure that s/he is safe and his/her well-being promoted.'[36] FGCs started in New Zealand in 1989, primarily in relation to restorative justice[37] but became recognised as a key decision-making process by which families make decisions about children and young people in need of care or protection ('child welfare FGCs') They were first introduced into this country nearly 16 years ago, since when a number of local authorities and agencies (for example, the Family Rights Group) have encouraged and facilitated their use. Although they are mainly used in public law cases, they can be valuable in private law cases where there is an involved, extended family.

16.19 The aim of FGCs is to achieve the best possible decisions and outcomes for children through a collaborative approach.

'Family group conferences promote the involvement of the wider family in the decision-making process to achieve a resolution of difficulties and permanence for their children. There are different approaches to their use, and when they are used. It is clear that they can have a beneficial effect on the decision making process, and often empower the family to develop the supports that are required. Children and young people have also said that they would like them to be used as much as possible, as they see them as promoting family and friends care, which they clearly prefer.'[38]

16.20 However, although there appears to be a high level of participation by family members, particularly mothers, and a higher attendance of fathers than at other meetings, for example child protection case conferences, and very high

---

[33] 'The evolving role of the family lawyer' [2011] CFLQ 370.

[34] Ibid, at 385.

[35] Ibid, at 392.

[36] *Using Family Group Conferences for children who are or may become subject to public law proceedings* (Family Rights Group, 2008) available for download at www.frg.org.uk.

[37] Gelsthorpe and Skinns 'Repairing harm through kith and kin' in Ebtehaj, Lindley and Richards (eds) *Kinship Matters* (Hart Publishing, 2006), at p 157.

[38] *Friends and Family Care (Kinship Care) Current Policy Framework, Issues and Options: Discussion paper* (DCSF, 2002), at paras 26 and 27.

participant satisfaction,[39] there appears to be little research, nationally or internationally which examines placements within the family made as a result of FGCs. However, what research there is seems to suggest that FGCs are effective in involving family members and are more likely to result in kinship placement than other methods of decision making.[40] They produce plans which local authorities feel able to support in over 90% of cases. They have, and children feel they have, increased contact with the wider family. However, they have been under-used for families from the black and minority ethnic communities and there is evidence that families do not always receive the support and resources needed to implement their plan.

16.21 Family Rights Group has developed a Guide on the use of FGCs in public law proceedings, which has been endorsed by Cafcass and the Family Justice Council.[41] The NSPCC[42] and Cafcass[43] have also produced fact sheets.

Parenting agreements/plans

16.22 The *Family Justice Review*[44] noted that the family justice system places too great a focus on parental rights rather than responsibilities and the terms used 'foster a sense of winning or losing'. It recommended that, instead, parents should be encouraged to develop a Parenting Agreement to set out the arrangements for the care of their children post-separation. Its aim would be to support parents to focus on the best interests of their child and make agreements on the range of issues about their care post separation, rather than just the narrow issues of contact and residence so that.

- focus remained on the details of a child's day-to-day arrangements and care rather than on status in relation to residence or contact;

- the agreement would set out in advance what the ground rules were for the child's care in certain given situations (for example how decisions about future schooling are to be approached, or the division of time between one parent's home and the other), so that both parents know the position; and

- the number of potentially disputed issues was reduced.

---

[39] Gelsthorpe op cit, at pp 165–166.
[40] Hunt *Family and Friends Carers* Scoping Paper (Department of Health, 2001) at p 77 and *Using Family Group Conferences for children who are or may become subject to public law proceedings* op cit.
[41] *Using Family Group Conferences for children who are or may become subject to public law proceedings* op cit.
[42] Family Group Conferences in child protection: NSPCC factsheet (2009) available from: www.nspcc.org.uk/inform/research.
[43] Available from: www.cafcass.gov.uk.
[44] Op cit at paras 4.49 to 4.51.

16.23 Cafcass has produced a guide on parenting plans[45] to help parents to work out the best possible arrangements for all aspects of their children's lives to try to ensure they are clear, consistent and reliable for everyone involved. It makes the point that every family and their circumstances are different and families will need to work out what suits them all best, remembering that children's needs and circumstances change so that arrangements will need to be revised from time to time.

ADR and the courts

16.24 The strong judicial support given to ADR and in particular to mediation in family cases is illustrated by *Al-Khatib v Masry*[46] in which a father had removed his five children from the United Kingdom to Saudi Arabia following the collapse of his marriage. The parties attempted mediation which failed but after further encouragement from the Court of Appeal it was reattempted with the parties eventually agreeing to a settlement. Thorpe LJ commented:

> '[This case] supports our conviction that there is no case, however conflicted, which is not potentially open to successful mediation, even if mediation has not been attempted or has failed during the trial process. It also demonstrates how vital it is for there to be judicial supervision of the process of mediation. It is not enough, in a difficult case such as this, for [the judge] directing mediation simply to make the order and thereafter that there will be a smooth passage to the initial meeting. The selection of the appropriate mediator in a difficult case is crucial and the availability of the supervising judge to deal with crisis is equally important.'

16.25 Practice Direction 3A of the Family Procedure Rules 2010 sets out a Pre-Action Protocol and the court will expect all applicants to comply with it before commencing proceedings. Before an applicant makes an application to the court for an order in relevant family proceedings, the applicant should contact a family mediator to arrange for the applicant to attend an information meeting about family mediation and other forms of alternative dispute resolution ('a Mediation Information and Assessment Meeting' (MIAM)). However an applicant is not expected to attend a MIAM where any of the circumstances set out in Annex C apply. These include situations where:

- The mediator is satisfied that mediation is not suitable because another party to the dispute is unwilling to attend a MIAM and consider mediation.[47]

- The mediator determines that the case is not suitable for a MIAM.

---

45   *Parenting Plans. Putting Your Children First* available at: www.cafcass.gov.uk.
46   [2004] EWCA Civ 1353, [2005] 1 FLR 381, at [17].
47   Absent the other party being unwilling to attend a MIAM or a decision having been taken in the past 4 months, there is no exception to attending a MIAM based on the mediator not considering the case is suitable for mediation.

- A mediator has made a determination within the previous 4 months that the case is not suitable for a MIAM or for mediation.

- Any party has, to the applicant's knowledge, made an allegation of domestic violence against another party and this has resulted in a police investigation or the issuing of civil proceedings for the protection of any party within the last 12 months.

- The parties are in agreement and there is no dispute to mediate.

- The whereabouts of the other party are unknown to the applicant.

- The prospective application is for an order in relevant family proceedings which are already in existence and are continuing.

- The prospective application is to be made without notice to the other party.

- The prospective application is urgent, meaning:

  – there is a risk to the life, liberty or physical safety of the applicant or his/her family or home; or
  – any delay caused by attending a MIAM would cause a risk of significant harm to a child, a significant risk of a miscarriage of justice, unreasonable hardship to the applicant or irretrievable problems in dealing with the dispute (such as an irretrievable loss of significant evidence).

- There is current social services involvement as a result of child protection concerns in respect of any child who would be the subject of the prospective application.

- A child would automatically be a party to the prospective application by virtue of FPR 2010, r 12.3(1). The only application to which this currently applies for the purpose of private law proceedings is an application for a special guardianship order when the child is subject to a care order.

- The applicant has contacted three mediators within 15 miles of the applicant's home and none is able to conduct a MIAM within 15 working days of the date of contact.

16.26 If the parties are willing to attend together, the MIAM may be conducted jointly, but where necessary separate meetings may be held. If the applicant and respondent(s) do not attend a joint meeting, the mediator will invite the respondent(s) to a separate meeting unless any of the circumstances set out in Annex C applies. The mediator who arranges a MIAM with one or more parties to a dispute should consider with the party concerned whether public funding may be available to meet the cost of the meeting and any subsequent mediation. Where none of the parties is eligible for, or wishes to seek, public funding, any charge made by the mediator for the MIAM will be the responsibility of the party or parties attending, in accordance with any agreement made with the mediator.

16.27 If following a MIAM the applicant makes an application to the court in respect of the dispute, the applicant should at the same time file a completed Family Mediation Information and Assessment Form (Form FM1) confirming attendance at a MIAM or giving the reasons for not attending.[48] Non-compliance with the Protocol does not prevent an application being issued but at the first hearing the court will wish to know whether mediation has been considered by the parties. In considering the conduct of any relevant family proceedings, the court will take into account any failure to comply with the Protocol[49] and may refer the parties to a meeting with a mediator before the proceedings continue further.[50] However, the court cannot compel parties to mediate.[51]

16.28 Mediation meetings (not MIAM) are privileged and anything which is said will be reported to the court only if both parties agree.

> 'It is, however, plain that parents will not succeed in composing their differences or achieving a working compromise through the good offices of a third party unless they approach the process of conciliation in an open and unreserved manner, prepared to give as well as to take and to make admissions and conciliatory gestures with a view to reaching an accord. If the parties remain in their entrenched positions no armistice will be reached in no-man's land. But it is plan that the parties will not make admissions or conciliatory gestures, or dilute their claims, or venture out of their entrenched positions unless they can be confident that their concessions and admissions cannot be used as weapons against them if conciliation fails and full-blooded litigation follows. To be effective, any attempt at conciliation must be off the record.[52]

Confidentiality does not attach to a statement clearly indicating that the maker has in the past caused or is likely in the future to cause serious harm to the well-being of a child. However, even in cases falling within this narrow exception, the judge retains a discretion whether or not to admit the evidence. He will admit it only if, in his judgment, the public interest in protecting the

---

48 For the requirements as to who could complete, sign or countersign the form, see the *Family Law Protocol*, para 9.

49 For example, when considering whether to make a costs order. For civil cases, see *Dunnett v Railtrack plc* [2002] EWCA Civ 2003; *Hurst v Leeming* [2001] EWHC 1051 (Ch); *Royal Bank of Canada Trust Corporation Ltd v Secretary of State for Defence* [2003] EWHC 1479 (Ch). However, all factors have to be considered including whether the successful party who declined mediation reasonably thought they would win and whether the unsuccessful party could show that mediation had a reasonable prospect of success: *Halsey v Milton Keynes General NHS Trust* [2004] EWCA Civ 576.

50 PD 3A, Part 4.1.

51 *Halsey v Milton Keynes General NHS Trust* [2004] EWCA Civ 576.

52 *Re D (Minors) (Conciliation: Privilege) (Disclosure of Information)* [1993] 1 FLR 932, per Sir Thomas Bingham MR at 934.

interests of the child outweighs the public interest in preserving the confidentiality of attempted conciliation.[53]

16.29 Rule 3.2 of the FPR 2010 provides that the court must consider, at every stage in proceedings, whether ADR is appropriate.[54] If it considers that it is, it may direct, on an application or of its own initiative that the proceedings or a hearing be adjourned for such specified period as it considers appropriate:

- to enable the parties to obtain information and advice about alternative dispute resolution; and

- where the parties agree, to enable alternative dispute resolution to take place.

Where the court directs an adjournment it will give directions about the timing and method by which the parties must tell the court if any of the issues in the proceedings have been resolved. If they do not comply the court will give such directions as to the management of the case as it considers appropriate.

WHAT APPLICATIONS ARE MADE?

16.30 In 2010, the High Court, county courts or family proceedings courts in England and Wales dealt with 7,430 applications by fathers and others seeking orders granting them parental responsibility. In the same year, the courts disposed of 113,010 applications for s 8 orders. Applications for residence orders accounted for 40,420 or 35.75% of all applications. 46,350 applications concerned contact (41%), 17,730, prohibited steps (15.7%) and 8,510 specific issues (7.5%).[55]

16.31 A study of three county courts[56] found that of residence and contact applications issued in 2000, 59% were for residence and 41% for contact. Of the residence applications, half were made by mothers, a third by fathers and the remainder were predominantly made by grandparents or other family members. Interestingly mothers comprised 46% of the respondents. In other words mothers were as likely to be defending residence applications as fathers but were more likely to initiate applications.[57] Of the contact cases, 86% were made by fathers, 8% by mothers and most of the remaining 6% by grandparents.

---

[53] [1993] 1 FLR 932, per Sir Thomas Bingham MR at 938.
[54] And see also FPR 2010. r 1.4(e).
[55] *Judicial Statistics* (Ministry of Justice, 2010).
[56] Smart, May, Wade, Furniss *Residence and Contact disputes in Court* vol 1 (Department for Constitutional Affairs, 2003) Research Series 6/03.
[57] For a further discussion of the research, see **10.8**.

DO THE COURTS HAVE JURISDICTION?

Section 4 orders

16.32 Exceptionally, there is no restriction on the courts' jurisdiction to grant an order for parental responsibility and all that may be required is some connection with England and Wales. In *Re S (Parental Responsibility: Jurisdiction)*,[58] the Court of Appeal held that an application under s 4 could be entertained in respect of a child born to unmarried English parents despite the fact that the child was born abroad, resided abroad, was not present and had never been present in the jurisdiction. The court did not state what connection was required and it is not clear from the report whether the parents were domiciled in England, although both resided here.

Section 8 orders

16.33 The court's jurisdiction to grant a s 8 order varies depending on whether or not there are continuing matrimonial proceedings. It is regulated by the Family Law Act 1986 and, where jurisdiction is sought to be conferred on another member state of the European Union, Council Regulation (EC) No 2201/2003 ('Brussels II bis').

Matrimonial proceedings

16.34 A court in England and Wales has jurisdiction to grant a s 8 order with respect to a child in or in connection with matrimonial proceedings within the jurisdiction if the child is a child of both parties to the matrimonial proceedings or a child of the family. Either the court must have jurisdiction to entertain the matrimonial proceedings under Brussels II bis or 'Part I' orders[59] which include s 8 orders or the condition contained in s 2A of the Family Law Act 1986 must be satisfied.[60] In short, s 2A provides that:

- proceedings for divorce or nullity must be continuing;[61] or

- proceedings for judicial separation are continuing and there are no proceedings for divorce or nullity continuing in Scotland or Northern Ireland after the grant of the decree of judicial separation; or

- the application for the order was made on or before the dismissal of the matrimonial proceedings.

---

[58]   [1998] 2 FLR 921.
[59]   Defined in Family Law Act 1986, s 1.
[60]   Family Law Act 1986, s 2(1).
[61]   They are not concluded until after the grant of decree absolute or dismissal of the petition, notwithstanding that the proceedings do not impinge on the children: *Re L (Residence, Jurisdiction)* [2006] EWHC 3374 (Fam), [2007] 1 FLR 1686.

No matrimonial proceedings

16.35 Where there are no continuing matrimonial proceedings, a court in England and Wales has the jurisdiction to grant a s 8 order if, on the date the application is made (or if no application has been made, the date when the court is considering whether to make or vary the order), the child is:

- habitually resident in England and Wales or is present in England and Wales; and

- not habitually resident in any part of the United Kingdom or a specified dependent territory.[62]

Brussels II bis

16.36 Brussels II bis is a jurisdictional code which binds all member states of the European Union except Denmark and provides a regulatory framework for the recognition and enforcement of judgments and for granting jurisdiction to try disputes about 'parental responsibility'.[63]

16.37 Recital 12 of the Regulation states that:

'The grounds of jurisdiction in matters of parental responsibility established in the present Regulation are shaped in the light of the best interests of the child, in particular on the criterion of proximity. This means that jurisdiction should lie in the first place with the Member State of the child's habitual residence, except for certain cases of a change in the child's residence or pursuant to an agreement between the holders of parental responsibility.'

Article 8(1) follows this by providing that:

'The courts of a Member State shall have jurisdiction in matters of parental responsibility over a child who is habitually resident in that Member State at the time the court is seised.'

In *Bush v Bush*[64] Lord Justice Lawrence Collins commented that:

'This must mean that acceptance of jurisdiction of a court other than that of the child's habitual residence is not lightly to be inferred, and that the paradigm case will be actual agreement by the parents at the time the matrimonial proceedings are instituted.'

For the purpose of the Regulation 'parental responsibility' consists of:

---

62 Family Law Act 1986, ss 2(2) and 3.
63 For a detailed guide, see Ranton 'Brussels II revisited' [2005] Fam Law 254 and Thomas 'Brussels II and the SFLA Guide: International aspects of family law' [2004] Fam Law 754.
64 [2008] EWCA Civ 865, [2008] 2 FLR 1437, at [53].

'... all rights and duties relating to the person and property of a child which are given by a natural or legal person by judgment, by operation of law or by agreement having legal effect. The term shall include rights of custody and rights of access.'[65]

The treaty cascades the right to exercise jurisdiction.

- The member state in which the child is habitually resident has jurisdiction.[66]

- If the child's habitual residence cannot be established, jurisdiction is given to the member state where a child is physically present.[67]

- Jurisdiction may be prorogued (extended):

  – to a court of a member state which is seised of matrimonial proceedings involving at least one party with 'parental responsibility' for the child if both parties and anyone else with 'parental responsibility' unequivocally accept that that court should have jurisdiction to deal with an issue of 'parental responsibility' and the prorogation is in the 'superior interests' of the child;[68]
  – to a court of a member state with which a child has 'substantial connections' including whether a holder of 'parental responsibility' is habitually resident in or the child is a citizen of that member state provided both parties and anyone else with 'parental responsibility' unequivocally accept that that court should have jurisdiction to deal with an issue of 'parental responsibility' and the prorogation is in the 'superior interests' of the child;[69]

- If the child lawfully moves from one member state to another, a court in the first state which has made a decision about access rights retains jurisdiction for 3 months provided the person with access rights remains habitually resident in that state and does not agree to participate in proceedings in the second state.[70]

- If the child has been unlawfully removed from one member state to another, jurisdiction remains with the first state until the child acquires habitual residence in the second state and every person or institution with rights of custody acquiesces in the removal[71] or the child acquires habitual

---

65 Brussels II bis, art 2(7)i.
66 Ibid, art 8.
67 Ibid, art 13.
68 Ibid, art 12(1).
69 Ibid, art 12(3). An agreement that a court should have jurisdiction cannot be unilaterally terminated nor may the court be deprived of jurisdiction by a decision of a court of the child's new habitual residence: *AP v TD (Relocation: Retention of Jurisdiction)* [2010] EWHC 2040 (Fam), [2011] 1 FLR 1851.
70 Brussels II bis, art 9.
71 Ibid, art 10(a).

residence in the second state, resides there for over a year and becomes settled there and every person or institution with rights of custody (within a year of knowing where the child is) fails to make a request for the child's return.[72]

- Where no court has jurisdiction by virtue of the above facts, jurisdiction is to be determined according to the domestic law of each member state.[73]

16.38 The Regulation provides four ways in which a court can exercise jurisdiction notwithstanding that the child is habitually resident elsewhere.

16.39 First, art 15 permits the court first seised of the matter to allow another more convenient country to exercise jurisdiction.

> 'By way of exception, the courts of a Member State having jurisdiction as to the substance of the matter may, if they consider that a court of another Member State, with which the child has a particular connection, would be better placed to hear the case, or a specific part thereof, and where this is in the best interests of the child: (a) stay the case or the part thereof in question and invite the parties to introduce a request before the court of that other Member State in accordance with paragraph 4; or (b) request[74] a court of another Member State to assume jurisdiction in accordance with paragraph 5.'

16.40 Secondly, art 12 provides that:

> '1 The courts of a Member State exercising jurisdiction by virtue of Article 3 on an application for divorce, legal separation or marriage annulment shall have jurisdiction in any matter relating to parental responsibility connected with that application where:
>
> (a)   at least one of the spouses has parental responsibility in relation to the child; and
> (b)   the jurisdiction of the courts has been accepted expressly or otherwise in an unequivocal manner by the spouses and by the holders of parental responsibility, at the time the court is seised, and is in the superior interests of the child.
>
> 2. The jurisdiction conferred in paragraph 1 shall cease as soon as:
>
> (a)   the judgment allowing or refusing the application for divorce, legal separation or marriage annulment has become final;
> (b)   in those cases where proceedings relating to parental responsibility are still pending on the date referred to in (a), a judgment in these proceedings has become final;
> (c)   the proceedings referred to in (a) and (b) have come to an end for another reason.

---

[72]   Brussels II bis, art 10(b).
[73]   Ibid, art 14.
[74]   See *AB v JLB (Brussels II Revised: Art 15)* [2008] EWHC 2965 (Fam), [2009] 1 FLR 517.

16.41   In *Re I (A Child) (Contact Application: Jurisdiction)*[75] Baroness Hale of Richmond said that art 12 applies even if the child is lawfully resident outside the European Union.

16.42   The meaning of 'the superior interests of the child' in art 12(1) has been the subject of debate. In *Bush v Bush*[76] Thorpe LJ considered it meant 'the best interests of the child'. In *Re I (A Child) (Contact Application: Jurisdiction)*[77] Baroness Hale of Richmond limited its meaning to the question of where the substantive issue should be litigated.

> '"[The] best interests of the child" in article 12.3, "the superior interests of the child" in article 12.1 and "the child's interest" in article 12.4 ... must mean the same thing, which is that it is in the child's interests for the case to be determined in the courts of this country rather than elsewhere. This question is quite different from the substantive question in the proceedings, which is "what outcome to these proceedings will be in the best interests of the child?" It will not depend upon a profound investigation of the child's situation and upbringing but upon the sort of considerations which come into play when deciding upon the most appropriate *forum*. The fact that the parties have submitted to the jurisdiction and are both habitually resident within it is clearly relevant though by no means the only factor.'[78]

16.43   When deciding whether to accept jurisdiction under art 12(1) the court has to consider which is the more appropriate court, the court of the child's habitual residence or the court seised with the parental divorce. Any such proportionate judgment must have regard to all the familiar considerations that dictate the determination of a *forum conveniens* issue, namely the balance of fairness including convenience.[79]

16.44   Thirdly, art 12(3) provides:

> '3. The courts of a Member State shall also have jurisdiction in relation to parental responsibility in proceedings other than those referred to in paragraph 1 where:
>
> (a)   the child has a substantial connection with that Member State, in particular by virtue of the fact that one of the holders of parental responsibility is habitually resident in that Member State or that the child is a national of that Member State; and
>
> (b)   the jurisdiction of the courts has been accepted expressly or otherwise in an unequivocal manner by all the parties to the proceedings at the time the court is seised[80] and is in the best interests of the child.'

---

[75]   [2009] UKSC 10, [2010] 1 FLR 361, at [17].
[76]   [2008] EWCA Civ 865, [2008] 2 FLR 1437, at [43].
[77]   [2009] UKSC 10, [2010] 1 FLR 361, at [36].
[78]   See also Lord Collins, ibid, at [50].
[79]   *Bush v Bush* [2008] EWCA Civ 865, [2008] 2 FLR 1437, per Thorpe LJ at [44].
[80]   For which see art 16.

16.45 There is some uncertainty about the meaning of art 12(3)(b).

- Do the words describe the time at which the parties have accepted jurisdiction? Or

- Do they describe the parties whose acceptance is required? In other words, does art 12(3)(b) mean 'the jurisdiction of the courts was accepted when the proceedings began by all those who were then parties'? Or

- Do they mean 'the jurisdiction of the courts has been accepted at any time after the proceedings have begun by all those who were parties when they began'?

In *Re I (A Child) (Contact Application: Jurisdiction)*[81] the Supreme Court considered but did not resolve the issue. Baroness Hale of Richmond noted that it might in an appropriate case have to be the subject of a referral to the European Court of Justice[82] but commented that it may not matter much in practice.

> 'Even if the words "at the time the court is seised" qualify the parties' acceptance, and refer only to the precise date when the proceedings are initiated rather than to once they have begun, the court is entitled to look at the parties' conduct after the proceedings have begun in order to decide whether they had accepted jurisdiction at the time the proceedings did begin … Whichever is the correct interpretation, the acceptance in question must be that of the parties to the proceedings at the time when the court is seised. Later parties cannot come along and upset the agreement which the original parties have made.'

Lord Collins,[83] with whom Lord Kerr agreed, expressed the view that a sensible and attractive but by no means an inevitable or a clear construction would be to treat the words 'at the time the court is seised' as qualifying the words 'by the holders of parental responsibility' in art 12(1) and the words 'all the parties to the proceedings' in art 12(3). Lord Clarke of Stone-Cum-Ebony[84] considered that the time for parties to decide in what jurisdiction to proceed was before issuing the relevant proceedings. What is clear is that the problem should be tackled at the outset rather than starting proceedings without jurisdiction in the hope that the other party will agree later or do something which could be construed as unequivocal acceptance of jurisdiction.[85]

16.46 In *C v C*[86] Hedley J held that the fundamental approach to the question of whether parties had accepted the jurisdiction should be objective: what inference should be drawn from their litigation conduct? If complete

---

81   Op cit, at [30]–[32].
82   [2009] UKSC 10, [2010] 1 FLR 361, at [30]–[32].
83   Ibid, at [62]–[63].
84   Ibid, at [89].
85   Ibid, at [90].
86   [2006] EWHC 3247 (Fam), at [17] cited in *AP v TD (Relocation: Retention of Jurisdiction)* [2010] EWHC 2040 (Fam), [2011] 1 FLR 1851, at [66].

acceptance, the court should ask whether a failure to challenge the jurisdiction vitiates what otherwise appears to be an unequivocal acceptance. In the circumstances of the instant case, absence of advice on the party's right to object did not vitiate the unequivocal acceptance otherwise established. 'The court should be looking at what the parties have actually done rather than the reasons (or lack of them) for doing it, absent, of course, fraud or misrepresentation.'[87]

16.47 Applying for a 'mirror order' (see **9.59**) does not equate with accepting the primary jurisdiction of the court.[88]

16.48 A party's acceptance of the jurisdiction cannot be unilaterally withdrawn,[89] at least once all other parties have accepted the jurisdiction.

Once jurisdiction is exercised under art 12, it displaces the jurisdiction of courts of another member state based on habitual residence.[90] However, the court with jurisdiction has a discretion to decline to exercise it. In *B v B (Brussels II Revised: Jurisdiction)*[91] Holman J declined to continue to exercise the court's jurisdiction under Art 12(3) after the child and his mother had moved to Germany and 3 months had passed despite the father currently being unable to travel to Germany to contest proceedings brought there by the mother which involved contact, the English court already having made a contact order in favour of the father. 'I cannot see that it is in the best interests of this child that this court, at a distance, should assert some continuing authority over him.'

16.49 The last way in which a court can exercise jurisdiction notwithstanding that the child is habitually resident elsewhere is provided by art 20.

> '1 In urgent cases, the provisions of this Regulation shall not prevent the courts of a Member State from taking such provisional, including protective, measures in respect of persons or assets in that State as may be available under the law of that Member State, even if, under this Regulation, the court of another Member State has jurisdiction as to the substance of the matter.
>
> 2 The measures referred to in paragraph 1 shall cease to apply when the court of the Member State having jurisdiction under this Regulation as to the substance of the matter has taken the measures it considers appropriate.'

Article 20 is mirrored by s 2(3)(b)(ii) of the Family Law Act 1986. The concept of urgency in that provision relates both to the situation of the child and to the

---

87 For an example of this process being followed, see *AP v TD (Relocation: Retention of Jurisdiction)* [2010] EWHC 2040 (Fam), [2011] 1 FLR 1851 and *Re A (Removal Outside Jurisdiction: Habitual Residence)* [2011] EWCA Civ 265.
88 *Re W (Jurisdiction: Mirror Orders)* [2011] EWCA Civ 703.
89 Ibid, at [76].
90 *Re S-R (Jurisdiction: Contact)* [2008] 2 FLR 1741.
91 [2010] EWHC 1989 (Fam), [2011] 1 FLR 54.

impossibility in practice of bringing the application concerning parental responsibility before the court with jurisdiction as to the substance.[92]

16.50 When a court is seised of the matter, parties cannot, other than under art 12(1), consent to or act in a way, for example by acknowledging the jurisdiction of the courts of another country or agreeing to the child habitually residing in the other jurisdiction, so as to confer jurisdiction on those courts.[93] Nor can the jurisdiction of the court be terminated by a court in another jurisdiction.[94]

16.51 If the child is habitually resident in England and Wales, jurisdiction is retained even though the child may be temporarily present in another country.[95] Nor is jurisdiction lost if a child, habitually resident in England and Wales is unlawfully removed to another country and the courts of that jurisdiction decline to order a summary return under the provisions of the Hague Convention on the Civil Aspects of International Child Abduction 1980.[96]

16.52 Notwithstanding the provisions of the Family Law Act 1986 and Brussels II bis it is sometimes argued that there may be a residual discretion under the inherent jurisdiction if an urgent and serious issue arose. In *Re B, RB v FB and MA (Forced Marriage: Wardship: Jurisdiction)*[97] Hogg J considered that she could exercise the wardship jurisdiction over a girl born, raised and habitually resident in Pakistan because she had British nationality and in dire circumstances required the court's protection against a threatened forced marriage.[98] In *Al Habtoor v Fotheringham*,[99] however, the Court of Appeal had rejected that argument that nationality by itself could found jurisdiction. In *B v H (Habitual Residence: Wardship)*[100] Charles J found that he had jurisdiction in wardship over a baby born and present in Bangladesh where his mother and three siblings, all of whom were habitually resident in England and Wales were being unlawfully detained.

16.53 In general an argument for a residual jurisdiction does not find favour. In *Re A (Wardship: Habitual Residence)*,[101] for example, Sir Mark Potter P declined to exercise the wardship jurisdiction over a child who had previously

---

92   *Detiček v Sgueglia* (Case C-403/09) [2010] 1 FLR 1381 European Court of Justice. See also *P v G (Family Law Act 1986: Jurisdiction)* [2010] EWHC 1311 (Fam), [2010] 2 FLR 1888.
93   See, for example, *Bush v Bush* [2008] EWCA Civ 865, [2008] 2 FLR 1437 and *JK v KC (Jurisdiction)* [2011] Fam Law 1204.
94   *AP v TD (Relocation: Retention of Jurisdiction)* [2010] EWHC 2040 (Fam), [2011] 1 FLR 1851, at [70].
95   See, for example, *P v P* [2006] EWHC 2410 (Fam), [2007] 2 FLR 439.
96   *Re H (Jurisdiction)* [2009] EWHC 2280 (Fam), [2010] 1 FLR 598.
97   [2008] EWHC 1436 (Fam), [2008] 2 FLR 1624.
98   In fact, jurisdiction was not exercised because Scottish courts became seised of the matter. See also *H v H (Jurisdiction to Grant Wardship)* [2011] EWCA Civ 796, [2012] 1 FLR 23.
99   [2001] EWCA Civ 186, [2001] 1 FLR 951.
100   [2002] 1 FLR 388.
101   [2006] EWHC 3338 (Fam), [2007] 1 FLR 1589, at [50].

been habitually resident in England and Wales but had been physically resident in Iraq where he was now habitually resident for the past 2 years. 'The jurisdiction of the court rests upon the fact-based concept of habitual residence in relation to the child who is the subject of the proceedings'. Sumner J in *Re L (Residence: Jurisdiction)*[102] stated that he would be most reluctant to contemplate, save for the most compelling reasons, that the High Court in England and Wales had jurisdiction on matters of residence over a child who was habitually resident in another jurisdiction and had only once visited England and in *H v H (Jurisdiction to Grant Wardship)*[103] the Court of Appeal held that the court did not have jurisdiction over a child who is not and has never been habitually resident or present in England and Wales.[104] This is so even where it might be thought that exercising jurisdiction would be in the best interests of the child.

Proceedings within the United Kingdom

16.54 Section 2 of the Family Law Act 1986 applies as much to possible jurisdictional clashes between courts in different parts of the United Kingdom as it does to those between courts of the United Kingdom and other countries. It and Brussels II bis are concerned with jurisdictions rather than states. However, the Act makes a number of additional provisions regulating jurisdictions within the various jurisdictions of the United Kingdom.

16.55 Although generally courts in England and Wales have jurisdiction to make Part 1 orders if the child is habitually resident in England and Wales,[105] ss 3(2) and 6(3) exclude it if, when the application is issued or, if there is no application, the court considers varying an order[106] where matrimonial proceedings are continuing in a court in Scotland or Northern Ireland in respect of the marriage of the parents of the child concerned.

16.56 A second difference is that under s 6(1) when an order made by a court in Scotland or Northern Ireland (or a variation of such an order) comes into force with respect to a child at a time when an order made by a court in England and Wales has effect with respect to him, the latter order ceases to have effect so far as it makes provision for any matter for which the same or different provision is made by (or by the variation of) the order made by the court in Scotland or Northern Ireland. Once the order has ceased to have effect so far as it makes provision for any matter, a court in England or Wales no longer has jurisdiction to vary the order so as to make provision for that matter.

---

[102]   [2006] EWHC 3374 (Fam), [2007] 1 FLR 1686, at [34].
[103]   [2011] EWCA Civ 796.
[104]   See also *Mercredi v Chaffe* [2011] EWCA Civ 272, [2011] 2 FLR 515 and *Re F (Abduction: Unborn Child)* [2006] EWHC 2199 (Fam), [2007] 1 FLR 627. *B v H (Habitual Residence: Wardship)* [2002] 1 FLR 388 might be explained on its own exceptional facts.
[105]   Family Law Act 1986, s 2(1)(b)(ii) and s 3(1).
[106]   Family Law Act 1986, s 7(c) – 'the relevant date'.

16.57 Thirdly, special provision is made for deciding habitual residence. Under s 41, where a child who has not attained the age of 16 and is habitually resident in a part of the United Kingdom becomes habitually resident outside that part of the United Kingdom because he is removed from or retained outside, or himself leaves or remains outside, the part of the United Kingdom in which he was habitually resident before his change of residence

(a) without the agreement of the person or all the persons having, under the law of that part of the United Kingdom, the right to determine where he is to reside; or

(b) in contravention of an order made by a court in any part of the United Kingdom

he is to be treated as continuing to be habitually resident in that part of the United Kingdom for the period of one year beginning with the date on which those circumstances arise. In *P v G (Family Law Act 1986: Jurisdiction)*[107] a mother (M) removed her daughter (C) from Scotland where she was habitually resident without the consent of her father (F) and commenced s 8 proceedings in England. F issued proceedings in Scotland in relation to C and the High Court in England, after making orders for the protection of C, subsequently stayed the English proceedings. Eleanor King J held s 41 was unambiguous and an argument based on concepts of *forum conveniens* had no place in its context. Although the English court had rightly exercised its powers under s 2(3)(b)(ii), this was an exceptional jurisdiction depending on the need for it being 'immediate' and 'necessary for the child's protection'. Thereafter the court cannot retain it on the basis of convenience.

16.58 There is potential for courts in two jurisdictions to disagree. In *B v B*[108] a mother (M) removed her daughter (C) from her home in Scotland in September 2000 without the consent of C's father (F) and set up home in England. She successfully applied to a county court without giving notice to F for residence and prohibited steps orders. After November 2001, ie more than one year after C's arrival in England, F applied to the High Court under the Child Abduction and Custody Act 1985 for an order returning C to Scotland. This was rejected on the basis that C was by then habitually resident in England and Wales. His application to transfer all the s 8 proceedings to Scotland was also rejected. His appeal to the Court of Appeal failed. Although the order made in the county court in 2000 was made without jurisdiction, it was not a nullity, remaining in force until discharged.[109] Before the appeal was heard F had issued divorce and custody proceedings in Scotland. After the appeal was heard M successfully persuaded the Sheriff to stay the custody proceedings because it was more convenient for the custody proceedings to continue in England. The Inner House of the Court of Session in *RAB v MIB*[110] allowed

---

[107] [2010] EWHC 1311 (Fam), [2010] 2 FLR 1888.
[108] [2004] EWCA Civ 681, [2004] 2 FLR 741.
[109] See *Hadkinson v Hadkinson* [1952] P 285.
[110] [2008] CSIH 52, [2009] 1 FLR 602.

F's appeal and doubted that the effect of s 41 was automatically to confer habitual residence after the period of one year. Inglis and Manderson[111] argue that the Inner House was correct. 'It is axiomatic that habitual residence cannot by changed by the unilateral action of a parent who shares parental responsibility with another.'

Stay

16.59 Section 5 of the Family Law Act 1986 provides that a court in England and Wales which has jurisdiction to make a Part I order may refuse an application for the order in any case where the matter in question has already been determined in proceedings outside England and Wales.

In addition, where, at any stage of the proceedings on an application made to a court in England and Wales for or for a variation of a Part I order other than proceedings governed by the Regulation, it appears to the court:

(a)   that proceedings with respect to the matters to which the application relates are continuing outside England and Wales; or

(b)   that it would be more appropriate for those matters to be determined in proceedings to be taken outside England and Wales,

the court may stay the proceedings on the application. In addition to any other power to remove the stay, the court may remove the stay if it appears to the court that there has been unreasonable delay in the taking or prosecution of the other proceedings or that those proceedings are stayed[112] or concluded.

16.60 In *M v M (Stay of Proceedings: Return of Proceedings)*,[113] for example, proceedings were stayed to allow courts in South Africa to decide where the children should live. Although they and their mother were habitually resident in England, the case was fundamentally a South African one. The family were South African citizens; their first language was Afrikaans; all the extended family lived in South Africa; the parents had always intended to return to South Africa and the mother had commenced divorce proceedings there before issuing Children Act proceedings in England.

---

[111]   'Bairns and borders: problems within the Family Law Act 1986' [2009] Fam Law 1157.
[112]   In Scotland, 'sisted'.
[113]   [2005] EWHC 1159 (Fam), [2006] 1 FLR 138.

Habitual residence

16.61 'Habitual residence' is not defined by the Family Law Act 1986, the Child Abduction and Custody Act 1985 or Brussels II bis.[114] However, there are many cases, particularly under the latter statute, in which the phrase has been analysed.[115]

Whether or not a person is habitually resident in a particular case is a question of fact to be decided by reference to all the circumstances of the case.[116]

'Habitual residence' means a person's abode in that place which he has adopted voluntarily and for a settled period of time, however limited.[117] So, a stay for a holiday is not the same as habitual residence.[118] The person must be present in the place before it can be said that he is habitually resident there. While 'habitual residence' can be lost in a day, it cannot be acquired so quickly.[119] If a person has two homes between which he divides his time, habitual residence in both places is possible.[120] The fact that a person is illegally present in a country does not prevent him being habitually resident.[121]

16.62 A child will normally have the same habitual residence as the parent who has its day-to-day care.[122] However, because a child cannot be habitually resident in a country he has never visited (see **16.53**) it follows that a child may – but does not necessarily – have the same habitual residence as his parent. A parent without parental responsibility cannot unilaterally change the child's habitual residence by unlawfully removing him to another jurisdiction.[123]

A child who divides his time under a shared residence order between two parents, each living in a different country, can be habitually resident in both countries.[124]

---

[114] *L-K v – K (No 2)* [2006] EWHC 3280 (Fam), [2007] 2 FLR 729, per Singer J at [33].

[115] For a discussion of the concept of 'habitual residence' under the 1985 Act, see Schuz 'Habitual residence of children under the Hague Child Abduction Convention – Theory and practice' [2001] CFLQ 1.

[116] *C v S (Minor: Abduction: Illegitimate Child)* [1990] 2 AC 562, [1990] 2 FLR 442.

[117] *Shah v Barnet LBC* [1983] 2 AC 309.

[118] See, for example, *Re D (Abduction: Habitual Residence)* [2005] EWHC 518 (Fam).

[119] See for example *A v P (Habitual Residence)* [2011] EWHC 1530 (Fam), [2012] 1 FLR 125. However, in *Re S (Habitual Residence)* [2009] EWCA Civ 1021, 7–8 weeks residence was found, on balance, to be enough.

[120] *Ikimi v Ikimi* [2001] 2 FLR 1288.

[121] *Mark v Mark* [2005] UKHL 42, [2005] 2 FLR 1193.

[122] *Re J (A Minor) (Abduction: Custody Rights)* [1990] 2 AC 562, [1990] 2 FLR 442.

[123] Ibid; *Re P-J (Abduction: Habitual Residence: Consent)* [2009] EWCA Civ 588 [2009] 2 FLR 1051; *SH v MM* [2011] EWHC 3314 (Fam).

[124] *M v H* [2005] EWHC 1186 (Fam). For another summary of the authorities, see *Re P-J (Abduction: Habitual Residence: Consent)* [2009] EWCA Civ 588, [2009] 2 FLR 1051, per Ward LJ at [26].

16.63 The meaning of 'habitual residence' in European jurisprudence may not be the same as in the courts of England and Wales.[125] In *Marinos v Marinos*[126] Munby J accepted that in European Jurisprudence the phrase 'habitually resident' in Brussels II bis has the meaning given to that phrase in the decisions of the European Court of Justice (ECJ) encapsulated by Dr Borrás in para [32] of his Explanatory Report on the earlier Regulation, Brussels II,[127] namely:

> '... the place where the person had established, on a fixed basis, his permanent or habitual centre of interests, with all the relevant facts being taken into account for the purpose of determining such residence'

and by the Cour de Cassation in *Moore v McLean*[128] 'the place where the party involved has fixed, with the wish to vest it with a stable character, the permanent or habitual centre of his or her interests'. Munby J added that in deciding where the habitual centre of someone's interests had been established, it was to have regard to the context. Many of the ECJ cases were cases where the issue was the entitlement of a worker to social security benefit. In those cases the claimant's place of work was obviously an important factor in ascertaining the location for that purpose of the habitual centre of his interests. In contrast, where the issue was as to the identification of the court which had jurisdiction in relation to family matters, the place where the matrimonial home is to be found, the place where the family lives, *qua* family, was equally obviously an important factor in ascertaining the location for that rather different purpose of the habitual centre of a spouse's interests.[129] Unlike the domestic approach determinative significance is not accorded to the length of time a person spends in or out of the country and a person may have only one place of habitual residence.[130]

16.64 Notwithstanding these differences, the expression 'habitually resident' must be given the same meaning and effect under the laws of all the Contracting States in which Brussels II bis has effect.[131] Therefore a different approach may be taken when domestic courts are considering domestic legislation or Brussels II bis, although in practice this may make little difference to the decision in a particular case.[132]

---

[125] *Marinos v Marinos* [2007] EWHC 2047 (Fam), [2007] 2 FLR 1018, per Munby LJ at [18].
[126] Ibid.
[127] (1998) OJ C 221/27.
[128] iv iere 14 December 2005 B No 506.
[129] See also *L-K v L-K (No 2)* [2006] EWHC 3280 (Fam), [2007] 2 FLR 729; *Munro v Munro* [2007] EWHC 3315 (Fam), [2008] 1 FLR 1613 and *Z v Z (Divorce: Jurisdiction)* [2009] EWHC 2626 (Fam); [2010] 1 FLR 694.
[130] *Marinos v Marinos* [2007] EWHC 2047 (Fam), [2007] 2 FLR 1018, at [32] and [41] and *Z v Z (Divorce: Jurisdiction)* [2009] EWHC 2626 (Fam); [2010] 1 FLR 694, per Ryder J at [40].
[131] *C v RC (Brussels II: Free-Standing Application for Parental Responsibility)* [2004] 1 FLR 317, ECJ, at [98], approved by Munby J in *Marinos v Marinos* [2007] EWHC 2047 (Fam), [2007] 2 FLR 1018, at [18].
[132] See also *Olafisoye v Olafisoye* [2010] EWHC 3539 (Fam), [2011] 2 FLR 553 and *V v V (Divorce Jurisdiction)* [2011] EWHC 1190 (Fam), [2011] 2 FLR 778.

WHICH COURT?

16.65 The allocation of proceedings between courts is governed by the Allocation and Transfer of Proceedings Order 2008[133] (ATPO 2008), supplemented by Practice Direction-Allocation and Transfer of Proceedings[134] and Practice Direction 12B of FPR 2010. The rules are designed to make sure that cases are heard at the appropriate level of judicial expertise, that all issues concerning the child are heard together and that the general principle that any delay is likely to prejudice the child is observed. The objective of the Practice Direction 'is to ensure that the criteria for the transfer of proceedings are applied in such way that proceedings are heard at the appropriate level of court, that the capacity of the magistrates' courts is properly utilised and that proceedings are only dealt with in the High Court if the relevant criteria are met'.[135] These recently introduced Rules and Practice Directions reflect previous guidance either given generally or in individual cases but are far more prescriptive than the rules they replace. Three important factors in whether they succeed in achieving one of the desired objectives namely an increase in the use of the family proceedings court (FPC) are whether the FPC will have sufficient time available, whether judicial continuity can be secured (see **16.109**) and whether the remuneration of advocates when parties are publicly funded will be sufficient to secure proper representation.

16.66 The following summary relates only to private law proceedings.

Where should proceedings start?

16.67 Subject to exceptions the following applications must be commenced in the FPC:[136]

- section 4 of CA 1989 (acquisition of parental responsibility by father);

- section 4A of CA 1989 (acquisition of parental responsibility by step-parent).

The exceptions are that the proceedings:

(a) concern a child who is the subject of proceedings which are pending in a county court or the High Court; and

(b) arise out of the same circumstances as gave rise to those proceedings in which case they may be started in the court in which those proceedings are pending;[137] or

---

[133] SI 2008/2836.
[134] 3 November 2008.
[135] PD 12B, para 1.2.
[136] ATPO 2008, art 5(2).
[137] Ibid, art 5(3).

(c)   are proceedings for parental responsibility under s 4 or 4A of the CA 1989
       which are started at the same time as proceedings in a county court or the
       High Court for an order under s 8 of the 1989 Act (residence, contact and
       other applications in relation to children) in relation to the same child in
       which case they must be started in the court in which proceedings under
       s 8 are started.[138]

16.68   Subject to art 7 (applications which may be brought in the High Court),
applications for leave brought by an applicant who is under the age of 18 under
s 10(2)(b), 11J(6) or 11O(7) of, or para 9(6) of Sch A1 to, the CA 1989 must be
brought in the county court.[139]

16.69   Other than under ATPO 2008, art 5(4) there is no rule that proceedings
must be commenced in the High Court. There is a converse rule though that
proceedings may not be commenced in the High Court unless:

- arts 5(3), 5(4) or 8 apply; or

- the proceedings are exceptionally complex; or

- the outcome of the proceedings is important to the public in general; or

- there is another substantial reason for the proceedings to be started in the
  High Court.[140]

A substantial reason for starting proceedings in the High Court will only exist
where the nature of the proceedings or the issues raised are such that they
ought to be heard in the High Court.[141]

16.70   Where adoption proceedings are pending which concern the same child,
the following proceedings must be started in the court in which the adoption
proceedings are pending:[142]

- leave to apply for a residence order under s 29(4)(b) of the Adoption and
  Children Act 2002 (ACA 2002);

- leave to apply for a special guardianship order under s 29(5)(b) of the
  ACA 2002;

- applications under s 8 of the CA 1989 where s 28(1)(a) or 29(4)(b) of
  ACA 2002 (leave obtained to make application for a residence order)
  applies;

---

[138]   ATPO 2008, art 5(4).
[139]   Ibid, art 6.
[140]   Ibid, art 7.
[141]   PD 12B, para 5.4.
[142]   ATPO 2008, art 8.

- applications under s 14A of the CA 1989 where s 28(1)(b) or 29(5)(b) of the ACA 2002 applies (leave obtained to make application for a special guardianship order).

Transferring applications between courts

16.71 Proceedings may be transferred at any stage of the proceedings, whether or not the proceedings have already been transferred.[143] The issue as to which court is the most appropriate hearing venue must be addressed by the court speedily as soon as there is sufficient information to determine whether the case meets the criteria for hearing in that court. At the First Hearing Dispute Resolution Appointment (FHDRA – see **17.26**) the case must be transferred to the FPC unless one of the exceptions specified in ATPO 2008 applies.[144] The question of transfer must then be kept under effective review at all times. It should not be assumed that proceedings will necessarily remain in the court in which they were started or to which they have been transferred. For example, proceedings that have been transferred to a county court because one or more of the criteria in art 15 applies should be transferred back to the magistrates' court if the reason for transfer falls away. Conversely, an unforeseen late complication may require a transfer from a magistrates' court to a county court.[145]

16.72 In *Re C (Children Proceedings: Powers of the Court)*[146] Wilson LJ said that orders for transfer should not be made by the court without notice to the parties. FPR 2010, r 4.3 (see **17.15**) now gives the court power to make orders of its own initiative without giving the parties prior notice but it is suggested that save in the case of emergency, the forum for the case is of such importance that parties should be given the prior opportunity of making submissions especially as, if a review of the order under FPR 2010, r 4.3(5) results in a re-transfer, the original date fixed for the trial or important hearing may have been lost.

16.73 When making any decision about the transfer of proceedings the court must have regard to the need to avoid delay in the proceedings and ATPO 2008, arts 16 and 19 do not apply if the transfer of proceedings would cause the determination of the proceedings to be delayed.[147] Therefore the listing availability of the court in which the proceedings have been started and in neighbouring FPCs and county courts must always be ascertained before deciding where proceedings should be heard. If an FPC is considering transferring proceedings to a county court or a county court is considering transferring proceedings to the High Court but that decision is finely balanced, the proceedings should not be transferred if the transfer would lead to delay. Conversely, if the High Court is considering transferring proceedings to a

---

143 ATPO 2008, art 13.
144 PD 12B, para 5.7.
145 PD, para 3.1.
146 [2008] EWCA Civ 502, [2008] 2 FLR 815.
147 ATPO 2008, art 13.

county court or a county court is considering transferring proceedings to an FPC but that decision is finely balanced, the proceedings should be transferred if retaining them would lead to delay. Transferring proceedings may mean that there will be a short delay in the proceedings being heard since the papers may need to be sent to the court to which they are being transferred. The court will determine whether the delay is significant, taking into account the circumstances of the case and with reference to the interests of the child.[148]

Transfer of proceedings from one FPC to another

16.74 An FPC (the 'transferring court') may transfer proceedings to another FPC (the 'receiving court') only if the transferring court considers that:

- the transfer will significantly accelerate the determination of the proceedings;

- it is more convenient for the parties or for the child who is the subject of the proceedings for the proceedings to be dealt with by the receiving court; or

- there is another good reason for the proceedings to be transferred.[149]

Where an FPC is considering transferring proceedings to another FPC or a county court is considering transferring proceedings to another county court, the court will take into account the following factors (which are not exhaustive) when considering whether it would be more convenient for the parties for the proceedings to be dealt with by the other court:

- the fact that a party is ill or suffers a disability which could make it inconvenient to attend at a particular court;

- the fact that the child lives in the area of the other court;

- the need to avoid delay.[150]

Transfer of proceedings from FPC to county court

16.75 An FPC may transfer the whole or any part of proceedings to a county court only if the FPC considers that:

- the transfer will significantly accelerate the determination of the proceedings;

---

148 PD 12B, paras 4.1–4.3.
149 ATPO 2008, art 14.
150 PD 12B, para 7.

- there is a real possibility of difficulty in resolving conflicts in the evidence of witnesses;

- there is a real possibility of a conflict in the evidence of two or more experts;

- there is a novel or difficult point of law;

- there are proceedings concerning the child in another jurisdiction; or

- there are international law issues;

- there is a real possibility that enforcement proceedings may be necessary and the method of enforcement or the likely penalty is beyond the powers of a magistrates' court;

- there is a real possibility that a guardian ad litem will be appointed for the child;[151]

- there is a real possibility that a party to proceedings is a person lacking capacity within the meaning of the Mental Capacity Act 2005 to conduct the proceedings;[152] or

- there is another good reason for the proceedings to be transferred.[153]

Certain proceedings (which are not of relevance to proceedings covered in the Handbook) may not be transferred.

16.76 Where an FPC is considering whether one or more of the criteria in art 15(1) (except art 15(1)(g) (guardian) and (h) (issue of capacity)) apply such that the proceedings ought to be heard in the county court, the FPC must first consider whether another FPC would have suitable experience to deal with the issues which have given rise to consideration of art 15. If so, the FPC will then consider whether the proceedings could be dealt with more quickly or within the same time if they were transferred to the other FPC rather than a county court. If so, the FPC will transfer the proceedings to the other FPC rather than a county court.[154]

16.77 An FPC may only transfer proceedings to a county court under art 15(1)(a) if it considers that the transfer will significantly accelerate the determination of the proceedings. Before considering a transfer on this ground, FPC must obtain information about the hearing dates available in other FPCs and in the relevant county court. The fact that a hearing could be arranged in a county court at an earlier date than in any appropriate FPC does not by itself

---

[151] However, the FPC now has power to make the child a party – see **4.71**.
[152] However, the FPC now has power to appoint a litigation friend – see **17.113**.
[153] ATPO 2008, art 15(1).
[154] PD 12B, para 8.1.

justify the transfer of proceedings under art 15(1)(a); the question of whether the determination of the proceedings would be significantly accelerated must be considered in the light of all the circumstances.[155]

Transfer of proceedings from county court to FPC

16.78   A county court must transfer to an FPC:

* proceedings which were transferred under art 15(1) if the county court considers that none of the criteria in the article applies;[156]

* proceedings that have previously been transferred where the county court considers that none of the criteria in art 15(1) apply.[157] 'Does not apply' should be given a liberal construction.[158] In particular, proceedings transferred to a county court by a magistrates' court for resolution of a single issue, for example, use of the inherent powers of the High Court in respect of medical testing of a child or disclosure of information by HM Revenue and Customs, should be transferred back to the magistrates' court once the issue has been resolved.[159] However, it is difficult to envisage a situation where it would be appropriate to transfer an issue to the FPC for determination;[160]

* subject to arts 5(3) and (4), 6 and 8, proceedings which were started in the county court if the county court considers that none of the criteria in art 15(1)(b) to (i) applies.[161]

16.79   Subject to arts 5(3), 6, 8 and 13 and para 4 of the PD (delay) straightforward proceedings started in a county court for:

* a s 8 order;

* a special guardianship order; or

* an order under Pt 4 of the Family Law Act 1996,

should be transferred to a magistrates' court if the county court considers that none of the criteria in art 15(1)(b) to (i) apply to those proceedings.[162]

---

155   PD 12B, para 8.2.
156   ATPO 2008, art 16(1).
157   Ibid.
158   *Re C (Children Proceedings: Powers of Transfer)* [2008] EWCA Civ 502, [2008] 2 FLR 815.
159   PD 12B, para 9.1.
160   *Re C (Children Proceedings: Powers of Transfer)* [2008] EWCA Civ 502, [2008] 2 FLR 815, per Wilson LJ at [18].
161   ATPO 2008, art 16(2).
162   PD 12B, para 9.2.

Transfer of proceedings from one county court to another

16.80 Subject to art 16 (see **16.78**), a county court may transfer proceedings to another county court (the 'receiving court') only if the transferring court considers that:

- the transfer will significantly accelerate the determination of the proceedings;

- it is more convenient for the parties or for the child who is the subject of the proceedings for the proceedings to be dealt with by the receiving court; or

- there is another good reason for the proceedings to be transferred.[163]

Transfer of proceedings from county court to High Court

16.81 Under art 18 a county court may transfer proceedings to the High Court only if the county court considers that:

- the proceedings are exceptionally complex;

- the outcome of the proceedings is important to the public in general; or

- there is another substantial reason for the proceedings to be transferred.

16.82 A court will take into account the following factors (which are not exhaustive) when considering whether the criteria in arts 7 (see **16.69**)) or 18 apply, such that the proceedings ought to be heard in the High Court:

- there is alleged to be a risk that a child concerned in the proceedings will suffer serious physical or emotional harm in the light of:

  – the death of another child in the family, a parent or any other material person; or
  – the fact that a parent or other material person may have committed a grave crime, for example, murder, manslaughter or rape, in particular where the essential factual framework is in dispute or there are issues over the causation of injuries or a material conflict of expert evidence; or

- the application concerns medical treatment for a child which involves a risk to the child's physical or emotional health which goes beyond the normal risks of routine medical treatment; or

- factors relating to adoption; or

---

[163] ATPO 2008, art 17.

- it is likely that the proceedings will set a significant new precedent or alter existing principles of common law.[164]

16.83 The following proceedings are likely to fall within the criteria for hearing in the High Court unless the nature of the issues of fact or law raised in the proceedings may make them more suitable to be dealt with in a county court:

- proceedings involving a contested issue of domicile;

- proceedings in which an application is opposed on the grounds of want of jurisdiction;

- proceedings in which there is a complex foreign element or where the court has invited submissions to be made under art 11(7) of Brussels II bis concerning jurisdiction and the recognition and enforcement of judgments in matrimonial matters and the matters of parental responsibility;

- proceedings in which there is an application to remove a child permanently or temporarily from the jurisdiction to a non-Hague Convention country;

- interlocutory applications involving (among other applications) search orders.[165]

16.84 Proceedings will not normally be suitable to be dealt with in the High Court merely because of any of the following:

- intractable problems with regard to contact;

- sexual abuse;

- injury to a child which is neither life-threatening nor permanently disabling;

- routine neglect, even if it spans many years and there is copious documentation;

- temporary or permanent removal to a Hague Convention country;

- standard human rights issues;

- uncertainty as to immigration status;

---

[164] PD 12B, para 5.1.
[165] PD 12B, para 5.2.

- the celebrity of the parties;

- the anticipated length of the hearing;

- the quantity of evidence;

- the number of experts;

- the possible availability of a speedier hearing.[166]

Transfer of proceedings from High Court

16.85 The High Court must transfer to a county court or an FPC any proceedings which were started in, or transferred to, the High Court if the High Court considers that none of the criteria in art 18 applies.

16.86 Where proceedings have been started in the High Court under art 7(c) or para 11.2(4) of the Practice Direction and the High Court considers that there is no substantial reason for them to have been started there, the High Court will transfer the proceedings to a county court or a magistrates' court and may make any orders about costs which it considers appropriate.[167]

Procedure

16.87 FPR 2010, rr 12.9–12.11 deal with the procedure to be followed when proceedings are transferred or a transfer is refused.

Which county court?

16.88 County courts with jurisdiction to hear family proceedings are divided into three classes:[168]

- *divorce county courts*, which have to transfer applications unless they are also family hearing centres;

- *family hearing centres* designated in Sch 1 to the Order;

- *care centres* designated in Sch 1 to the Order.

Courts may belong to one or more class. The Principal Registry of the Family Division is treated as if it were a divorce county court, a family hearing centre and a care centre.[169]

---

166 PD 12B, para 5.3.
167 PD 12B, para 5.4.
168 ATPO 2008, art 2.
169 Ibid, art 3.

Applications under Part I of CA 1989 (which includes applications under s 8 or for parental responsibility (but subject to any requirement to commence in an FPC – see **16.67**) or special guardianship must be commenced in a family hearing centre.

THE APPLICATION

16.89 The application is made using the appropriate Forms specified in PD 5A, Table 1. The main forms are:

- C1 (with C1A if allegations of domestic abuse are being made);

- C2: application for permission to apply for an order (see **Chapter 15**) or to be joined as a party;

- C4: application for an order for the disclosure of a child's whereabouts (see **22.15**);

- C66: application for an order under the inherent jurisdiction.[170]

16.90 Proceedings are started when a court officer issues an application at the request of the applicant. An application is issued on the date entered in the application form by the court officer.[171]

Disclosure of personal details

16.91 Unless the court directs otherwise, a party is not required to reveal:

- the party's home address or other contact details;

- the address or other contact details of any child; or

- the name of a person with whom the child is living, if that person is not the applicant.

A party who does not wish to reveal any of these particulars must give notice of those particulars to the court[172] and the particulars will not be revealed to any person unless the court directs otherwise. Where a party changes home address during the course of proceedings, that party must give notice of the change to the court.

---

[170]   For which see FPR 2010, Pt 12, ch 5.
[171]   FPR 2010, r 5.3.
[172]   Form C8.

THE PARTIES

16.92   FPR 2010, Pt12.3 sets out who the respondents to the applications must be:

- every person whom the applicant believes has parental responsibility;

- where the child is subject to a care order, every person whom the applicant believes had parental responsibility before the order was made;

- where the application is to extend, vary or discharge an existing order, the parties to the proceedings in which the order was made.

Note: the child's father is not required to be a respondent unless he has parental responsibility. Nor is the child required to be a party unless the proceedings have been specified under CA 1989, s 41(6).[173]

SERVICE

16.93   FPR 2010, Pt 6, along with PD 6A (service within the jurisdiction) and PD 6B (service out of the jurisdiction), deal with the rules relating to service. PD 6C deals with applications for the disclosure by government departments of addresses of respondents.

APPLICATIONS TO BE JOINED

Procedure

16.94   A person who wishes to be joined as a party or who wishes to cease being a party must file a request in Form C2. The court may grant the request that a person cease to be a party without a hearing but otherwise a date for hearing the request will be fixed with notice to all parties or all parties will be invited to make written representations within a specified period, after which the court may consider the request without a hearing.

Exercise of the court's discretion

16.95   Joining parties inappropriately may have implications for the trial by increasing the length of the hearing. Where any of the parties is publicly funded, it will have cost implications, both directly in relation to the party's own costs and indirectly by increasing the fee payable to counsel acting for any publicly-funded party. Effective case management is seen as the key to ensuring

---

[173] Currently none have been specified for the purpose of private law proceedings unless the child is in care, in which case see FPR 2010, r 12.27.

that wider family members are joined as parties only where this is necessary. The welfare test of s 1 does not apply to the issue of whether someone should be joined as a party.[174]

16.96 A request to be joined made by a person with parental responsibility must be granted as that person should have been made a respondent when the application was issued (see **16.92**).

16.97 An application by a father without parental responsibility to be joined should normally be allowed. However, any application should be made promptly and delay which would cause the hearing to be postponed may mean the application being refused.[175]

16.98 Where the person wishing to be joined wishes to apply for a s 8 order, the court has to consider the factors set out in s 10(9) before granting permission[176] (see **Chapter 15**).

Where the person wishing to be joined is not seeking a s 8 order, permission should not usually be granted unless he has a separate point of view which needs to be put forward. Where the proposed party's role is essentially to support another party, the appropriate way of proceeding is for him to give evidence on behalf of that party rather than being joined:[177]

> 'There were before the judge ... five parties: the father as applicant, the mother, the very proper intervention of the local authority and equally proper appointment of a guardian ad litem in a most difficult case. However, the maternal grandparents sought, and were granted, leave to intervene and appeared by counsel and solicitors throughout the 20 days of the hearing. Part of the philosophy of the Children Act 1989 is to bring before the court all parties relevant to the welfare of the children. These grandparents have offered an alternative home for their grandchildren in the event that their daughter was not considered suitable by the court to have their care, what might be called a fall-back position to keep the children within the maternal family ... The grandparents, however, unlike many cases which come before the courts, were not at odds with their daughter. Their interests are identical, and I cannot see the purpose of their being separately represented for the very lengthy hearing when they could have been called as witnesses for the mother and their offer could have been presented to the court both by the mother, and at least communicated, even if not endorsed, by the guardian ad litem. Their intervention had lengthened the proceedings and thereby increased the costs of all the parties. I should not like it to be thought that because the Children Act 1989 and the Family Proceedings Rules 1991, in particular r 4.7, provide for grandparents, among others, to be parties where appropriate, they should in fact intervene unless they have a separate point of view to put forward.'

---

[174]   *North Yorkshire County Council v G* [1993] 2 FLR 732.
[175]   *Re P (Care Proceedings: Father's Application to be Joined as Party)* [2001] 1 FLR 781.
[176]   *G v Kirklees Metropolitan Borough Council* [1993] 1 FLR 805.
[177]   See, for example, *Re M (Minors) (Sexual Abuse: Evidence)* [1993] 1 FLR 822, per Butler-Sloss LJ at 825.

16.99 Where a local authority has been directed to file a report under s 37[178] but has declined to commence care proceedings, it should not be allowed to be joined as a party to private law proceedings.[179]

The child as a party

16.100 This is discussed in **Chapter 4**.

WHICH JUDGE?

16.101 The jurisdiction of magistrates and judges to hear applications under CA 1989 is strictly controlled. In relation to judges, the control is exercised by the *Family Proceedings (Allocation to Judiciary) Directions 2009*. The following outline is not exhaustive but is confined only to those matters which are the subject of the Handbook.

Family proceedings courts

16.102 Family proceedings courts have to be composed of two or three lay justices or a district judge as chairman and one or two lay justices or, if it is not practicable for such a court to be composed, a district judge (magistrates' court) sitting alone.[180] Save in the case of a district judge (magistrates' court) sitting alone, the court should, so far as is practicable, include both a man and a woman.[181]

Lay magistrates

16.103 A lay justice must be a member of a family panel, that is, a panel of lay justices specially appointed to deal with family proceedings.[182]

District judges (magistrates' court)

16.104 For the purpose of the *Family Proceedings (Allocation to Judiciary) Directions 2009* a district judge (magistrates' court) who is nominated to sit in a FPC is treated the same as a county court district judge.[183]

---

[178] See **Chapter 20**.
[179] *F v Cambridgeshire County Council* [1995] 1 FLR 516. In *Re M (Minors) (Sexual Abuse: Evidence)* [1993] 1 FLR 822, there were consolidated s 8 and care proceedings.
[180] For the power for a single justice to exercise specific functions, see FPR 2010, r 2.6.
[181] Magistrates' Court Act 1980, s 66.
[182] Ibid. s 67(2) and Family Proceedings Court (Constitution) Rules 1991, SI 1991/1405, r 10.
[183] Magistrates' Court Act 1980, s 67 and reg 7 of the Family Proceedings (Allocation to Judiciary) Directions 2009.

High Court and county court

16.105   For circuit judges, recorders and district and deputy district judges, the key is whether or not they are authorised to hear public law or private law matters.

High Court judges and deputy High Court judges

16.106   All High Court judges of the Family Division or a deputy (s 9)[184] High Court judge (with certain exceptions) have jurisdiction to hear all Children Act applications.

Circuit judge or recorder

16.107

- A circuit judge, deputy circuit judge or recorder nominated for public law family proceedings has jurisdiction to hear all private law Children Act applications.

- A circuit judge, deputy circuit judge or recorder[185] nominated for private law family proceedings has jurisdiction to hear all private law applications unless, in the case of applications for a residence order or special guardianship order the child is subject to a care order or a placement order under the ACA 2002 or is placed for adoption.

District judge

16.108

- A district or deputy district judge of the Principal Registry or a district judge nominated for public law proceedings has jurisdiction to hear all private law Children Act applications.

- A district judge nominated for private law proceedings has jurisdiction to hear all private law applications unless, in the case of applications for a residence order or special guardianship order, the child is subject to a care order or a placement order under the ACA 2002 or is placed for adoption.

Judicial continuity

16.109   The continuity provided by the same judge hearing proceedings concerning the same child is important. Inevitably, a judge will have formed a view of the family situation and the parties will know that the judge has formed a particular view about one or both of them. Unless there are grounds

---

[184]   Of the Senior Courts Act 1981.
[185]   Including a district judge or district judge (magistrates' courts) nominated for public law proceedings.

(excluding findings and conclusions properly reached in earlier proceedings) for saying that a litigant can reasonably take the view that the judge is biased against him, those findings and conclusions, far from disqualifying him, make it more desirable that he should hear the subsequent proceedings.[186] Where there is a split hearing, for example a fact finding hearing followed by a final hearing, there must be judicial continuity. 'Split hearings are one thing; split judging is quite another.'[187]

To this end, FPR 2010, PD 12AB, para 2.2 provides that the court must consider judicial continuity at the FHDRA. See also **5.59** and **11.168**.

A litigant cannot seek a transfer because he disagrees with a view the judge has formed of him. In addition, the court will be very slow to transfer an intractable contact case to another judge.[188]

16.110 Judicial continuity may be difficult to achieve before lay magistrates.

---

[186] *Re M (Minors) (Judicial Continuity)* [1993] 1 FLR 903.
[187] *Re B (Children)* [2008] UKHL 35, [2008] 2 FLR 141, per Baroness Hale of Richmond at [61].
[188] *Re C-W (Enforcement and Committal: Contact)* [2010] EWCA Civ 1253, [2011] 1 FLR 1095, per Munby LJ at [12].

Chapter 17

DIRECTIONS APPOINTMENTS

THE FAMILY PROCEDURE RULES 2010

17.1 Proceedings under the Children Act 1989, are governed by the Family Procedure Rules 2010[1] (FPR 2010). The FPR are self-contained with one exception – costs in the High Court and county courts for which parts of the Civil Procedure Rules 1998 (CPR) apply.[2] They apply to all family proceedings and to all family courts.[3]

17.2 For the first time, family proceedings are governed by the same rules regardless of whether they are taking place in, the High Court, county court or family proceedings courts (FPC).

Practice Directions

17.3 Based on the model of the Civil Procedure Rules 1998 the FPR 2010 are extensively supplemented by Practice Directions given by the President of the Family Division.

17.4 Practice Directions provide an indication of the normal practice of the courts although, at best, they are a weak aid to the interpretation of the rules themselves. They differ from procedural rules, such as the FPR in that, in general, they provide guidance that should be followed but does not have binding effect. One exception is where a rule expressly incorporates a requirement set out in a practice direction.[4] Practice Directions are subordinate to and should yield to the procedural rules and statutory instruments where there is clear conflict between them.[5]

17.5 When the court gives directions it will take into account whether or not a party has complied with any relevant pre-action protocol.[6]

---

[1] SI 2010/2955.
[2] FPR 2010, r 2.2.
[3] FPR 2010, r 2.1. For a short overview of the FPR 2010, see Burrows 'The Family Procedure Rules 2010' [2011] Fam Law 186 and the more detailed Adam 'The Family Procedure Rules 2010: A District Judge's Perspective' [2011] Fam Law 244.
[4] For example, FPR 2010, r 5.1 provides that the forms 'referred to in a practice direction shall be used in the cases to which they apply'.
[5] *Godwin v Swindon BC* [2001] EWCA Civ 1478, [2002] 1 WLR 996, per May LJ at [11]; *R (Mount Cook Land Limited) v Westminster City Council* [2003] EWCA Civ 1346, per Auld LJ at [68]; *Re C (Legal Aid: Preparation of Bill of Costs)* [2001] 1 FLR 602, per Hale LJ at [21].
[6] FPR 2010, r 4.1(5).

The overriding objective

17.6   Like the CPR[7] and the FPAR 2005 the FPR 2010 contain an overriding objective which governs the exercise of the courts' case management powers. Its purpose, like that of the objective in other rules, is to provide 'a compass to guide courts and litigants and legal advisers as to their general course'.[8] As Lord Woolf wrote in *Access to Justice Final Report*[9]:

> 'Rules of court are not like an instruction manual for operating a piece of machinery. Ultimately their purpose is to guide the court and the litigants towards the just resolution of the case. Although the rules can offer detailed directions for the technical steps to be taken, the effectiveness of those steps depends upon the spirit in which they are carried out. That in turn depends on an understanding of the fundamental purpose of the rules and the underlying system of procedure.'

17.7   Pt1.1 defines the objective as 'enabling the court to deal with cases justly, having regard to the welfare issues involved.'

17.8   'Dealing with a case justly' includes, so far as is practicable:

- ensuring that it is dealt with expeditiously and fairly;

- dealing with the case in ways which are proportionate to the nature, importance and complexity of the issues;

- ensuring that the parties are on an equal footing;

- saving expense; and

- allotting to it an appropriate share of the court's resources, while taking into account the need to allot resources to other cases.[10]

17.9   In applying the objective, the court has to balance all the factors without giving undue weight to any of them[11].

17.10   The court must seek to give effect to the overriding objective when it exercises any power given to it by the rules or interprets any rule.[12] It controls the exercise of the court's discretion as s 1 of the Children Act 1989 controls discretion in substantive matters. However, like s 1, it does not confer any power on the court to take particular action. Those powers are contained generally in Part 4 and in the various other Parts.

---

7   CPR 1998, r 1.1.
8   Lord Woolf *Access to Justice Final Report* (1996), at p 275.
9   Ibid, at p 274.
10   FPR 2010, r 1.1(2). For a detailed discussion of the difficulties in applying these goals 'which are capable of pointing in different directions', see *Zuckerman on Civil Procedure* (2nd edn, Sweet & Maxwell, 2006), at paras 1.7–1.38.
11   *Holmes v SGB Services Plc* [2001] EWCA CIv 354, per Buxton LJ at [38].
12   FPR 2010, r 1.2.

17.11 The parties are required to help the court to further the overriding objective[13].

Court's duty to manage cases

17.12 The court must further the overriding objective by actively managing cases.[14] This includes:[15]

- encouraging the parties to co-operate with each other in the conduct of the proceedings;

- identifying at an early stage:

  - the issues; and
  - who should be a party to the proceedings;

- deciding promptly;

  - which issues need full investigation and hearing and which do not; and
  - the procedure to be followed in the case;

- deciding the order in which issues are to be resolved;

- encouraging the parties to use an alternative dispute resolution procedure if the court considers that appropriate and facilitating the use of such procedure;

- helping the parties to settle the whole or part of the case;

- fixing timetables or otherwise controlling the progress of the case;

- considering whether the likely benefits of taking a particular step justify the cost of taking it;

- dealing with as many aspects of the case as it can on the same occasion;

- dealing with the case without the parties needing to attend at court;

- making use of technology;[16] and

- giving directions to ensure that the case proceeds quickly and efficiently.

---

13 FPR 2010, r 1.3.
14 Ibid, r 1.4.
15 Ibid, r 1.4.
16 For example, by conducting case management conferences by telephone or taking evidence over a video link (r 22.3 and PD 22A, Annex 3).

THE COURT'S GENERAL CASE MANAGEMENT POWERS

17.13   Rule 4.1 gives the court general powers of management. Except where the rules provide otherwise, the court may

- extend or shorten the time for compliance with any rule, practice direction or court order (even if an application for extension is made after the time for compliance has expired);

- make such order for disclosure and inspection, including specific disclosure of documents, as it thinks fit;

- adjourn or bring forward a hearing;

- require a party or a party's legal representative to attend the court;

- hold a hearing and receive evidence by telephone or by using any other method of direct oral communication;

- direct that part of any proceedings be dealt with as separate proceedings;

- stay the whole or part of any proceedings or judgment either generally or until a specified date or event;

- consolidate proceedings;

- hear two or more applications on the same occasion;

- direct a separate hearing of any issue;

- decide the order in which issues are to be heard;

- exclude an issue from consideration;

- dismiss or give a decision on an application after a decision on a preliminary issue;

- direct any party to file and serve an estimate of costs; and

- take any other step or make any other order for the purpose of managing the case and furthering the overriding objective.

Conditions

17.14   When the court makes an order, it may:

- make it subject to conditions, including a condition to pay a sum of money into court; and

- specify the consequence of failure to comply with the order or a condition.[17]

Orders of the court's own intiative

17.15   Except where an enactment provides otherwise, the court may exercise its powers on an application or of its own initiative. Where it proposes to make an order of its own initiative it may give any person likely to be affected by the order an opportunity to make representations in which case it must specify the time by and the manner in which the representations must be made.[18] Where it proposes to hold a hearing to decide whether to make the order, it must give each party likely to be affected by the order at least 5 days' notice of the hearing.[19] However the court may make an order of its own initiative without hearing the parties or giving them an opportunity to make representations.[20] Where the court does make such an order, a party affected by the order may apply to have it set aside, varied or stayed[21] and the order must contain a statement of the right to make such an application within such period as may be specified. If the court does not specify a period, the application must be made within 7 days beginning with the date on which the order was served on the party making the application.[22]

Power to strike out applications

17.16   The court's general powers to strike out applications under FPR 2010, r 4.4 do not apply to proceedings under Parts 12–14 which involve children. However the court does have an inherent power to deal summarily with applications – see **17.46** and **20.12**.

Failure to comply with Rules, Practice Directions or Orders

17.17   Where there has been an error of procedure such as a failure to comply with a rule or practice direction the error does not invalidate any step taken in the proceedings unless the court so orders and the court may make an order to remedy the error.[23] However, where a party has failed to comply with a rule,

---

17   FPR 2010, r 4.1(4).
18   Ibid, r 4.3(2).
19   Ibid, r 4.3(3).
20   Ibid, r 4.3(4).
21   Ibid, r 4.3(5).
22   Ibid, r 4.3(6).
23   Ibid, r 4.7.

practice direction or court order, any sanction for failure to comply imposed by the rule, practice direction or court order has effect unless the party in default applies for and obtains relief from the sanction.[24] But where the sanction is the payment of costs, the party in default may only obtain relief by appealing against the order for costs.

17.18 Where a rule, practice direction or court order requires a party to do something within a specified time and specifies the consequence of failure to comply, the time for doing the act in question may not be extended by agreement between the parties.[25]

17.19 On an application for relief from any sanction imposed for a failure to comply with any rule, practice direction or court order the court will consider all the circumstances including:

(a)   the interests of the administration of justice;

(b)   whether the application for relief has been made promptly;

(c)   whether the failure to comply was intentional;

(d)   whether there is a good explanation for the failure;

(e)   the extent to which the party in default has complied with other rules, practice directions, court orders and any relevant pre-action protocol;

(f)   whether the failure to comply was caused by the party or the party's legal representative;

(g)   whether the hearing date or the likely hearing date can still be met if relief is granted;

(h)   the effect which the failure to comply had on each party; and

(i)   the effect which the granting of relief would have on each party or a child whose interest the court considers relevant.[26]

An application for relief must be supported by evidence.[27]

17.20 The list is not exhaustive. For example in civil cases, where the applicant is the defendant, the court is entitled to consider the merits of the defence.[28] Likewise in family proceedings, the court should consider whether and to what extent granting or refusing the application will affect the child's welfare.

---

[24]   FPR 2010, r 4.5.
[25]   Ibid, r 4.5(3).
[26]   Ibid, r 4.6(1).
[27]   Ibid, r 4.6(2).
[28]   *Chapple v Williams* [1999] CPLR 731.

17.21 In *Woodhouse v Consignia Plc*[29] the Court of Appeal said, in relation to the similar CPR, r 3.9:

> 'The circumstances in which a court may be asked to make a decision of this kind are infinitely varied. This is why the rule instructs the court to consider all the circumstances of the particular case, including the nine listed items. On the other hand, the rule would lose much of its praiseworthy purpose of encouraging structured decision-making if courts did not consciously go through the exercise of considering all the items on the list when determining how, on balance, it should exercise its discretion. Provided it does so, and in this way ensures that the risk of omitting any material consideration is minimised, it is most unlikely that an appeal court will interfere with its decision. If it fails to do so, an appeal court may not be able to detect that it has taken all material matters into account, and it may be obliged to exercise its discretion afresh for this reason.'

Subsequently in *Khatib v Ramco International*[30] Lloyd LJ said that there was no need for the judgment to address each factor expressly. While the judge had to make it reasonably apparent that he was aware of the rule and of the particular factors said on either side to be relevant, according to the evidence and the circumstances of the particular case, and to conduct an appropriate review and balancing exercise, it would be wrong to insist on a more fully formulated judgment as the minimum required in order to demonstrate that the judge's task under the rule had been properly discharged. However, as when applying the s 1(3) welfare checklist (see **25.62**), addressing each factor can be a useful discipline.

STEPS AFTER THE APPLICATION IS FILED

17.22 When the proceedings have been issued the court may set a date for the First Hearing Dispute Resolution Appointment (FHDRA).[31] See **17.25**.

17.23 The respondent must file and serve on the parties an answer to the application for an order in private law proceedings within 14 days, beginning with the date on which the application is served.[32]

17.24 Where a Cafcass officer has filed a risk assessment with the court (see **5.43**) (subject to safeguarding provisions), the court officer will as soon as practicable serve copies of the risk assessment on each party.[33]

---

29 [2002] EWCA Civ 275, [2002] 1 W.L.R. 2558, at [33].
30 [2011] EWCA Civ 605, at [64].
31 FPR 2010, r 12.31.
32 Ibid, r 12.32.
33 Ibid, r 12.34.

FIRST HEARING DISPUTE RESOLUTION APPOINTMENT

17.25 Provisions relating to the timing of and issues to be considered at the FHDRA are contained in PD 12B.

17.26 Parties need to prepare carefully for the first appointment, even if it is expected that the court will not be in a position to make a substantive order or even an interim one. They should focus on the issues, including the question of how crucial facts are to be proved, the legal framework and the evidence needed to support the case.[34]

The first appointment should be used imaginatively, anticipating problems and addressing them in advance.[35]

BACKGROUND

17.27 Before 2010 the first hearings of applications for s 8 orders were usually used by the court to give directions. Local procedures developed whereby Cafcass officers would attend in order to speak to the parties in order to try to limit or resolve disputes. District judges too would attempt to persuade the litigants that if an agreement could be reached without a forensic investigation and trial it could benefit the child and themselves.

17.28 Between 1996 and 1997, researchers from Bristol University studied family proceedings in four county courts in the South West of England and four other courts in other parts of the country. They found that the courts all had highly developed systems for managing cases, encompassing first appointments and review hearings. While these provided for the formal legal progress of the case, they were also occasions when often the parties could meet a Cafcass officer and which, with an input, sometimes in the form of a quite powerful intervention from the district judge, were negotiating opportunities. They also provided target dates by which it was hoped that the parties would have made substantive, as well as procedural, progress which they could report to the court, ideally as an agreed final outcome. The study[36] found that a high proportion of applications for contact or residence orders settled, a quarter (24%) after only one directions appointment and a further quarter (26%) after two. Nearly half (46%) settled within 3 months of the application being issued:

> 'We had gone looking for an old-fashioned, red in tooth and claw, welfare officer reporting and district judge adjudicating court and we could not find one.'[37]

---

34   *The Handbook of Best Practice*, ch 4.
35   Ibid.
36   As reported in Bailey-Harris and others 'Settlement culture and the use of the "no order" principle under the Children Act 1989' [1999] CFLQ 53.
37   Davis and Pearce 'A view from the trenches – practice and procedure in section 8 applications' [1999] Fam Law 457.

In comparison, FPCs offered little judicial intervention other than approving whatever orders, whether procedural or substantive, the parties asked them to make.

17.29 This use of directions hearings had obvious advantages. It enabled the parties to reach agreement rather than have one imposed by the court and there was an argument that such agreements were more likely to adhere to them.[38] Certainly, recent research which studied applications which were the subject of a welfare report found that although almost all parents, irrespective of the outcome, were dissatisfied with the court procedure, parents whose cases settled before a hearing were much more likely to be satisfied with both the process and the outcome of contact applications.[39] The possibility of mediation provided by Cafcass either at the court or by appointment later or by local mediation services, enabled parents to understand the stance of the other parent a little better and open the way not just to the current problem being resolved but to the creation of a structure for the resolution of future disagreements. Thirdly, the practice reduces the costs of disputes, whether in terms of direct legal costs, usually borne by the Legal Services Commission, or in terms of judicial time.

17.30 Following the Family Resolutions Pilot Project in 2004,[40] the Private Law Programme[41] in 2004, followed in 2010 by the Revised Private Law Programme,[42] established a national scheme designed to:

> '... assist parties to reach safe agreements where possible, to provide a forum in which to find the best way to resolve issues in each individual case and to promote outcomes that are sustainable, that are in the best interests of children and that take account of their perspectives.'[43]

This has now been replaced by Practice Direction 12B.

17.31 In 2005 a study was made on three models of in-court conciliation with varying degrees of judicial control and involvement and the role played by the Cafcass officer.[44] Whichever model was used, over half of parents reported that they were quite or very anxious. Consistent with previous research all three models had high though varying agreement rates which reflected the approach to conciliation rather than case characteristics. High judicial control had poorer

---

38 See a further article by Davis and Pearce, 'On the trail of the welfare principle' [1999] Fam Law 144.

39 Buchanan, Hunt and others *Families in Conflict* (The Policy Press, 2001).

40 For which see Maclean 'The family resolutions pilot project' [2004] Fam Law 687 and *Parental Separation: Children's Needs and Parents' Responsibilities* Cm 6273 (Department for Constitutional Affairs, 2004), at paras 68–72.

41 President's Guidance 2004, followed in 2010 by the Revised Guidance.

42 [2010] 2 FLR 717.

43 Ibid, para 1.6.

44 Trinder, Connolly and others *Making contact happen or making contact work?* (Department for Constitutional Affairs, 2006) DCA Research Series 3/06 summarised in [2006] Fam Law 416. See also Trinder 'Conciliation, the Private Law Programme and children's well-being: two steps forward, one step back?' [2008] Fam Law 338.

outcomes than the other two models. Non-resident parents were significantly more satisfied with the agreements reached than resident parents. Overall satisfaction was modest but not reaching agreements attracted even more dissatisfaction. Parents were asked which aspects in the conciliation process they would like to change. By far the most popular change was the opportunity to speak to Cafcass separately from the other parent. About a third wanted more time to be available and a third for the meeting to be held away from court. Few parents opted for changes to professional roles but resident parents were significantly more likely to want to retain or expand the role of lawyers. Outcomes 6 months later were mixed. 'In some respects the very brief intervention has had quite a marked impact' – only a fifth of agreements did not work at all; most agreements were intact or had been extended; most cases were closed with low relitigation rates; many more children were having more contact; more parents were satisfied with the quantity and quality of contact and parents and children were doing better than at baseline.

> 'What is significant … is having an agreement or the case being closed. It seems that having an agreement generates its own momentum, at least in the short term.'

By this stage, the influence of which model was used appeared to have disappeared. An important factor was the parental relationship: conciliation appeared to work best with less entrenched cases. The analysis also highlighted real and enduring problems. The relitigation rate was low, but the majority of cases required more professional input than a single conciliation session, raising concerns about the ongoing ability of parents to adapt arrangements to suit changing needs and circumstances. Parental satisfaction and parent and child well-being did improve from baseline to follow up, but overall levels remained low. Only just under three in five parents whose cases were closed were satisfied with arrangements.

17.32 The authors identified strengths in the process, namely its ability to deliver agreements and contact, but it had limited scope to make contact work, to minimise coercion and to address risk and involve children.[45]

> 'The "one size fits all" approach was ill-suited to dealing with cases raising serious risk issues and could be coercive. The rapid processing of cases and focus on settlement also meant that children were excluded from the process or risked becoming responsible for decisions.'[46]

> 'Perhaps the most pressing concern, however, is how little impact the conciliation session and the adoption of new contact arrangements had on parental relationship quality, shared decision making and contact problems. It is these issues, rather than the mere quantity of contact, that are most likely to impact on children's adjustment. The quantity of contact alone was not related to child wellbeing in this study.'[47]

45　*Making contact happen or making contact work?* op cit, at p 98.
46　Ibid, at p 100.
47　Ibid, at p 85.

'In sum, for a very brief intervention, in-court conciliation does have much to offer as a dispute-resolution process in contact cases. However, in-court conciliation is not suitable for all cases nor is it likely to be sufficient by itself in the majority of cases.'[48]

17.33 Practice Direction 12B does not prescribe how conciliation should be used at the FHDRA but the messages from the research are useful. Each party should see the Cafcass officer separately and judges should step back from the conciliation and leave it to Cafcass.

Attendance at the hearing

17.34 The parties must attend the hearing.[49]

'Consideration and discussion of all issues will not take place until the FHDRA when parties are on an equal footing and can hear what is said to and by each other.'[50]

The purpose of the hearing

17.35 At the FHDRA the court shall consider in particular:

- Whether and the extent to which the parties can safely resolve some or all of the issues with the assistance of the Cafcass Officer and any available mediator.

- Risk identification followed by active case management including risk assessment, and compliance with the Practice Direction (14 January 2009): 'Residence and Contact Orders: Domestic Violence and Harm'.

- Further dispute resolution.

- The avoidance of delay through the early identification of issues and timetabling, subject to the allocation order.

- Judicial scrutiny of the appropriateness of consent orders.

- Judicial consideration of the way to involve the child.

- Judicial continuity.[51]

---

[48] *Making contact happen or making contact work?* op cit, at p 100. Similar reservations were expressed about the Private Law Programme in 'Conciliation, The Private Law Programme and children's well-being: two steps forward, one step back?' op cit, at p 342.

[49] PD 12B, para 4.1.

[50] Ibid, para 2.2.

[51] Ibid.

Matters to be considered[52]

Safeguarding

17.36

- The court must inform the parties of the content of any screening report or other information which has been provided by Cafcass, unless it considers that to do so would create a risk of harm to a party or the child. The court may need to consider whether and how any information contained in the checks should be disclosed to the parties if Cafcass have not disclosed it.

- Is a risk assessment required and when?

- Is a fact finding hearing needed to determine allegations whose resolution is likely to affect the decision of the court?

Dispute resolution

17.37 At every FHDRA there will be a period in which the Cafcass officer, 'with the assistance of any Mediator and in collaboration with the court, will seek to conciliate and explore with the parties the resolution of all or some of the issues between them. The procedure to be followed in this connection at the hearing will be determined by local arrangements'.

- What is the result of any such meeting at court?

- What other options there are for resolution, eg may the case be suitable for further intervention by Cafcass; mediation by an external provider; collaborative law or use of a parenting plan?

- Would the parties be assisted by attendance at Parenting Information Programmes or other activities, whether by formal statutory provision under s 11 of the CA 1989 or otherwise?[53]

See **11.66**.

Consent orders

17.38 Where agreement is reached at any hearing or submitted in writing to the court, no order will be made without scrutiny by the court. Where safeguarding checks or risk assessment work remain outstanding, the making of a final order may be deferred for such work. In such circumstances the court must adjourn the case for no longer than 28 days to a fixed date. A written notification of this work is to be provided by Cafcass in accordance with the

---

52   PD 12B, para 5.1.
53   Ibid, para 5.2.

timescale specified by the court. If satisfactory information is then available, the order may be made at the adjourned hearing in the agreed terms without the need for attendance by the parties. If satisfactory information is not available, the order will not be made, and the case will be adjourned for further consideration with an opportunity for the parties to make further representations.[54]

17.39 There have been recurrent concerns that 'agreements' are imposed on parties either by their advisers or by the court, rather than representing a genuine agreement. Davis and Pearce comment that:

> 'Agreement is preferred as a matter of course, no matter that this "agreement" may be the product of highly pressurised lawyer negotiation. This pressure to settle contested applications without resort to trial finds no place in family law text books, which are geared to the study of judicially decided cases – and yet it is fundamental to parents' experience of the legal process.'[55]

17.40 Where there are serious and, from a legal point of view, relevant disputes of fact, an agreement which is not based on a finding or acceptance of fact may break down or may even be contrary to the interests of the child. Allegations of domestic violence are an obvious example of such a case. A failure to take into account a child's wishes is another. There is a danger that cases may drift in the hope that the problems will resolve themselves without a need for facts to be found and issues properly addressed.

17.41 In order to avoid these dangers, legal advisers need to be alert to the importance of ensuring that the parties genuinely agree with the course proposed, need to identify disputed issues which have to be resolved and need to remember that the 'checklist' is just as relevant at directions hearings as at a full hearing. When cases are brought back on a review, the question of whether a hearing at that stage is necessary needs to be addressed.

Reports

17.42

- Are there welfare issues or other specific considerations which should be addressed in a section 7 report by Cafcass or a s 7 or s 37 report by the local authority? See **Chapter 19**.

- Is any expert evidence required in compliance with the Experts' Practice Direction?[56] See **Chapter 18**.

---

54 PD 12B, para 5.3.
55 Davis and Pearce 'A view from the trenches – practice and procedure in section 8 applications' [1999] Fam Law 457.
56 PD 12B, para 5.4.

Wishes and feelings of the child

17.43 (See **Chapter 4**.)

• Is the child aware of the proceedings? How are the wishes and feelings of the child to be ascertained (if at all)?

• How is the child to be involved in the proceedings, if at all, and whether at or after the FHDRA?

• Who will inform the child of the outcome of the case where appropriate?

Case management

17.44

• What, if any, issues are agreed and what are the key issues to be determined? See **17.46**.

• Are there any interim orders which can usefully be made (eg indirect, supported or supervised contact) pending final hearing?

• What directions are required to ensure the application is ready for final hearing – statements, reports etc?

• List for final hearing, consider the need for judicial continuity (especially if there has been or is to be a fact finding hearing or a contested interim hearing).[57]

Transfer to FPC

17.45 See **16.78**.

Issues

17.46 The keystone of case management is the early identification and continuous reviewing of issues. Without this, disclosure, witness statements,[58] expert evidence[59] and s 7 and s 37 reports will lack focus. As FPR 2010, r 1.4(2) states: active case management includes:

• identifying at an early stage the issues;

---

57 PD 12B, para 5.6. See **16.109**.
58 See FPR 2010, r 22.1.
59 See ibid, r 25.1, PD 25A, para 4.3(c).

- deciding promptly which issues need full investigation and hearing and which do not;[60]

- deciding the order in which issues are to be resolved.

17.47 Judges are expected to be robust in identifying issues and should not assume that their views on what issues are important will be readily accepted.

17.48 For example, in *Re P (Non Disclosure of HIV Status)*[61] Bodey J decided on appeal that the issue of the mother's HIV status was not relevant to a review of a contact order made in favour of the father. There was no reason therefore why she should be compelled to disclose her status to the father.

Disclosure

17.49 FPR 2010, Pt 21 and PD 21A govern orders by the court for disclosure of documents.

In family proceedings other than proceedings for a financial remedy, where the court orders disclosure, the normal order will be for disclosure by each party setting out, in a list or questionnaire, the documents material to the proceedings, of the existence of which that party is aware and which are or have been in that party's control. This process is known as 'standard disclosure'.[62] In addition, the court – either on its own initiative or on the application of the other party – may order a party to clarify any matter which is in dispute in the proceedings or give additional information in relation to any such matter, whether or not the matter is contained in or referred to in the application or in the answer.[63]

The court may also order 'specific disclosure', which is an order that a party must disclose documents or classes of documents specified in the order, carry out a search to the extent stated in the order or disclose any documents located as a result of that search.

17.50 In the family courts disclosure has never routinely formed part of litigation involving children and an order for general disclosure will rarely, if ever, be made. Before making an order for specific disclosure, the court will need to be satisfied that it is required in relation to an issue in the case.

17.51 Some specific disclosure orders are not infrequently made, for example of a parent's medical records if the parent's mental or physical capacity to look after a child either full time or at contact is in dispute. However, where the

---

[60] For example, a mother's HIV status was not relevant to a contact dispute in *Re P (Non Disclosure of HIV Status)* [2006] 2 FLR 50 and therefore did not have to be disclosed to the father.

[61] [2006] 2 FLR 50.

[62] PD 21A, para 2.1.

[63] Ibid, para 2.3.

documents are personal records, the court will need to balance the rights of the child under Art 6 of the European Convention for the Protection of Human Rights and Fundamental Freedoms 1950 (ECHR) and the other party to have access to relevant information against the Art 8 ECHR rights of the party whose records are sought to respect for their private life.

For the withholding of documents and other evidence, see **Chapter 22**.

Documents in the possession of non-parties

17.52 Documents in the possession of non-parties, for example, social service records, require special consideration. If the non-party will not voluntarily provide a copy of the document, a witness summons requiring the document to be produced can be sought under RSC Ord 38, r 13 in the High Court or CCR Ord 20, r 12 in the county court[64] or s 97 of the Magistrates' Court Act 1980. A party who has not complied with an order for disclosure may not produce a document at a directions appointment or a hearing without the permission of the court.[65]

17.53 There are three ways in which family courts may order the production of documents which are not in the possession or control of a party.

Orders under FPR r 21.2

17.54 The High Court[66] and the county court[67] both have power to order a non-party to give disclosure. The procedure is governed by FPR 2010, r 21.2 which provides that the application for disclosure may be made without notice but must be supported by evidence.[68]

The court may grant the order only where disclosure is necessary in order to dispose fairly of the proceedings or to save costs.[69] This is different from CPR, r 31.17 which provides that the first condition is that the document is likely[70] to support the case of the applicant or adversely affect the case of one of the other parties.

17.55 The order under this rule must:

(a)   specify the documents or the classes of documents which the respondent must disclose; and

---

64   *Re A and B (Minors) (No 2)* [1995] 1 FLR 351.
65   Ibid.
66   Senior Courts Act 1981, s 34.
67   County Courts Act 1984, s 63.
68   FPR 2010, r 21.2(2).
69   Ibid, r 21.2(3).
70   Interpreted in *Three Rivers District Council v Bank of England (No 4)* [2002] EWCA Civ 1182, [2003] 1 WLR 210 as meaning 'may well'.

(b)   require the respondent, when making disclosure, to specify any of those documents:

    (i)   which are no longer in his control; or

    (ii) in respect of which he claims a right or duty to withhold inspection.[71]

The order may also:

(a)   require the respondent to indicate what has happened to any documents which are no longer in his control; and

(b)   specify the time and place for disclosure and inspection.[72]

17.56   The order must not compel a person to produce any document which that person could not be compelled to produce at the final hearing.[73]

17.57   Rather than issuing a formal order, courts may make an order merely 'requesting' the named person to provide the documents.

17.58   The person against who an order is made may apply, without notice, for an order permitting that person to withhold disclosure of a document on the ground that disclosure would damage the public interest.[74]

Witness summons

17.59   A party may apply for a witness summons under the procedure set out in FPR 2010, r 22.9 for the person in possession of the documents to attend a hearing and produce the named documents. The hearing need not be the final hearing and it may be more convenient to have the documents produced at an early directions hearing, thereby allowing them to be considered in advance of the main hearing.

Directing a party to obtain and disclose documents

17.60   Sometimes a party may not have a copy of the document, for example, minutes of a child protection conference, but is able to request a copy. The court can order the party to take such steps as are necessary to obtain and disclose the document.

17.61   In *SM v Local Authority*[75] a mother was engaged in private law proceedings in the country court and asked her local authority to produce all data it held concerning her and the children. It disclosed some but refused to

---

[71]   FPR 2010, r 21.2(4).
[72]   Ibid, r 21.2(5).
[73]   Ibid, r 21.2(6).
[74]   Ibid, r 21.3.
[75]   [2011] EWHC 3465 (Admin).

disclose information it held about her husband without his permission. He refused to grant permission. The mother issued a claim seeking access to the non-disclosed documents under ss 7 and 35 of the Data Protection Act 1998. Disclosure was refused because although the Administrative Court could have reviewed all the documents to see whether they were necessary for the family proceedings, the family court was much better placed to do so. The claim was transferred to the county court.

Requests for information

17.62   Specific provision for disclosure of information by government agencies and the police has been made by free standing practice directions.

Information from the police

17.63   The *ACPO Police/Family Disclosure Protocol: Disclosure of Information in Family Proceedings* deals with requests for disclosure of information held by the police and for compliance with such requests.[76]

It states that police information will not be disclosed unless there are important considerations of public interest to depart from the general rule of confidentiality. The protection of children is one of the areas where exceptions may be made. All parties should use the protocol proportionately having regard to what is reasonable, directly relevant and necessary when seeking disclosure from any third party.

Information supplied in pursuance of the Protocol is subject to the following implicit undertakings on the part of the parties and their legal representatives unless otherwise specifically directed by the court:

- any material disclosed will only be used for the purposes of, and preparation for, the current proceedings unless the permission of the court is obtained;

- it will only be disclosed to professionals in the proceedings (and the parties) unless the permission of the court is obtained;

- the material will otherwise be kept confidential and copying should be kept to the minimum necessary to avoid the proliferation of copies of sensitive material;

- where there is a Best Evidence or other video recorded interview (see **4.30**) one copy will normally be made available on request as soon as police investigations allow either by providing one copy to the local authority (if a party to the proceedings) or via the solicitors acting for either party in

---

[76]   (2004)   available   at: www.met.police.uk/scd/specialist_units/Police_Family_Disclosure_Protocol.pdf. See also [2006] Fam Law 895.

private law proceedings. Copies will not be provided to unrepresented parties. Copying of video evidence should be kept to a minimum and consideration should be given to the parties attending the appropriate police station or local authority premises in order to view the copy video evidence at a mutually convenient time. Where this is not possible and the evidence has to be further copied, the party(ies) will meet the police reasonable costs of copying unless alternative arrangements have been agreed between the police and the parties legal representatives for making copies;

- in relation to any Best Evidence or other interview, parties' representatives will sign and abide by the terms of the police Standard Form of Undertaking.[77] Where the party is able to say that it is or is not necessary for the purpose of the proceedings for the video to be copied or available for viewing, the party should state so;

- that the police will not transcribe or make arrangements to transcribe any video interviews or tape-recorded interviews unless this has already been done in connection with a criminal prosecution/investigation.

17.64 It is incumbent on parties to give very early consideration to what material held by the police may be relevant to the care or family proceedings. Whenever possible an early request for documents should be made to police prior to any hearing or application being made to the court. As soon as possible and not later than 10 working days before the hearing at which a request for disclosure is to be made the solicitors for any party who proposes to ask the court for a direction requiring the Chief Officer of any Police Force to disclose any information must send the Standard Request Form[78] to the nominated police disclosure officer.[79] It should set out the following information:

- the names and dates of birth of the parties including any relevant children and where possible, brief details of the circumstances of the incident(s) in respect of which the request is made;

- any relevant addresses;

- the date and place of the specific incident or incidents upon which information is sought;

- the crime reference number (if known);

- the name and 'collar' number (if known) of the officer(s) in the case(s);

- the nature and relevance of the material sought;

---

[77] Set out in Annex A of the Protocol.
[78] Annex B of the Protocol.
[79] Identified in the Schedule.

- the date of the hearing at which the formal direction is to be sought;

- a draft of the proposed direction, including the date by which the documents, records or other evidential material is likely to be directed to be disclosed;

- the likely legal (and where applicable, social work) timetable;

- whether and if so what date has been fixed by the court for any final hearing or fact finding hearing and whether the officer in the case is likely to be required at that hearing to give evidence.

17.65 The police will normally respond to the request within 5 working days in accordance with the Standard Reply Form.[80] If police are unable or unwilling to disclose the information without a court order the requesting party should make the appropriate application to the court.

17.66 At the hearing where the request is made for disclosure the court should consider:

- the necessity and relevance to the issues required to be determined by the court, of the information sought to be disclosed;

- the wording of the proposed direction for disclosure;

- the timing of any direction for disclosure with specific reference to any written representations by the police. All disclosure directions should allow sufficient time for compliance which should in normal circumstances be 14 days;

- requesting the court staff to expedite the order so that it can be served within 24 hours by the court upon the nominated police disclosure officer;

- directing the party making the request for disclosure to inform the nominated officer within 24 hours of the hearing and to serve the order within 2 days of the hearing.

Information from the Home Office and Border Agency

17.67 For the importance of obtaining accurate information about a party or child's immigration status, see *Re M and N (Parellel Family and Immigration Proceedings)*.[81] The *Practice Direction: Communicating With the Home Office in Family Proceedings*[82] provides that where an order for disclosure of information (for example regarding the immigration status of a party or child)

---

80   Annex C of the Protocol.
81   [2008] EWHC 2281 (Fam), [2008] 2 FLR 2030.
82   October 2010 [2011] 1 FLR 1442. Reissued March 2012.

is made against the Home Office in family proceedings, the court order[83] will be accompanied by the Court Service form EX660[84] which requires the details of the relevant family members and their relationship to the child including details of both mother and father if known, whether or not they are involved in the proceedings. The request or order should identify the questions it wishes to be answered by the Home Office. Parties should provide the name and contact details of someone who has agreed and is able to provide further information should it be needed, together with such information as is sufficient to enable the Home Office to understand the nature of the case, to identify whether the case involves an adoption, and to identify whether the immigration issues raised might relate to an asylum or non-asylum application. The order and EX660 should clearly state the time by which the information is required. The order should be drawn and sent the same day. Where this will not be possible the court should allow any additional time necessary for the preparation and sending of the order in order to ensure that the Home Office has 4 weeks from the time it receives the order to provide a response. Any reduction in this period may result in a request by the Home Office for further time in which to reply.

17.68 The sealed order and the completed EX660 should be sent immediately to the Home Office Liaison Officer (HOLO) of the Court Service,[85] who will then send the form and order to an appropriate officer in the Home Office.

17.69 All information provided in EX660 will be forwarded to the Home Office. Parties should ensure that any additional information, such as a case synopsis, which it wishes the Home Office to view, has the required leave of the court, set out in the order, to be disclosed to the Home Office.

17.70 The HOLO will follow up the request as required in order to ensure that the information is received by the court in time. The Home Office will send the information to the HOLO who will forward it to the parties as instructed by the court.

Information from the Office of International Family Justice

17.71 The Head of International Family Justice is a Lord Justice. His Office is able to offer informal advice to judges on issues involving courts of another jurisdiction The requests are usually made when there is a need for direct communication between judges from England and Wales and another jurisdiction including contact under the UK-Pakistan Judicial Protocol on Child Contact and Abduction[86] or where a judge needs advice and assistance relating to an international family law matter.[87]

---

83 For a draft, see the Annex to the Practice Direction.
84 Ibid.
85 See **Appendix 6**.
86 (2003). See [2003] Fam Law 919.
87 For a description of the work of the Office of International Family Justice, see [2009] Fam Law 349.

Statements

17.72 FPR 2010, r 22.1(1) states that the court may control the evidence by giving directions as to:

- the issues on which it requires evidence;

- the nature of the evidence which it requires to decide those issues; and

- the way in which the evidence is to be placed before the court.

The court may use its power under this rule to exclude evidence that would otherwise be admissible.[88]

17.73 The general rule is that any fact which needs to be proved by the evidence of witnesses is to be proved:

(a)   at the final hearing, by their oral evidence; and

(b)   at any other hearing, by their evidence in writing.

17.74 The court may give directions as to service on the other parties of any witness statement of the oral evidence on which a party intends to rely in relation to any issues of fact to be decided at the final hearing.[89] Normally, parties will be ordered to file witness statements.

17.75 The court may give directions as:

- the order in which witness statements are to be served; and

- whether or not the witness statements are to be filed.[90]

17.76 Practice Direction 22A prescribes the form of the statement and how documents should be exhibited as well as the certificate to be attached if the maker is unable to read or sign the statement. FPR 2010, Pt 17 deals with statements of truth.

Children giving evidence

17.77 The topic of children giving evidence is discussed at **4.23**. In *Re W (Children) (Family Proceedings: Oral Evidence)*[91] Baroness Hale of Richmond said that:

---

88   FPR 2010, r 22.1(2).
89   Ibid, r 22.5(1).
90   Ibid, r 22.5(2).
91   [2010] UKSC 12, [2010] 1 FLR 1485, at [31].

'The issue [of whether a child should give evidence] should be addressed at the case management conference in care proceedings or the earliest directions hearing in private law proceedings. It should not be left to the party to raise. This is not, however, an invitation to elaborate consideration of what will usually be a non-issue.'

Where there are or may be concurrent criminal proceedings, there is a need to consider the impact directions made in family proceedings may have on the criminal process. Ideally, any decision which may have a mutual effect should be taken at a joint case management hearing but, as the Law Society guide, *Related Family Criminal Proceedings*[92] notes, very few cases have been so managed through local schemes. However, even if a joint management hearing is impractical, there are real advantages to be gained from co-operation between the two jurisdictions.

17.78 The judicial role is the critical one not only in managing joint directions but in the identification of cases for which joint directions may be suitable. This must involve, as a minimum, both the existence of other proceedings being a standard question in all case management hearings and the copying across of orders between jurisdictions so that any subsequent judge is alerted to the question. The Crown Court Plea and Case Management Hearing form requires details of any concurrent family proceedings to be entered. Likewise at the FDHRA the court should be made aware of any linked proceedings.[93] It would be helpful if the alleged perpetrator's family solicitors were directed to file the contact details of those involved in the criminal proceedings using the Solicitor's Information Sheet set out in Appendix 1 to *Related Family Criminal Proceedings*.

17.79 The questions which will need to be considered include:

- Which proceedings can and should be heard first?

- Should the child be cross-examined or re-interviewed in the family proceedings before giving evidence in the criminal proceedings?

- If so, what input should the CPS have in relation to the questions to be asked? The defendant/intervenor in the family proceedings will usually be the defendant in the criminal proceedings.

- Should the child have the same witness supporter (and, if one is required, intermediary) in both proceedings?

---

[92] (Law Society, 2007), at p 47: www.judiciary.gov.uk/NR/rdonlyres/41A222FE-54B2-4EC1-A169-48C0A5FAC343/0/RelatedFamCrimPro.pdf. This has been approved by the President of the Family Division and the Family Justice Council and is a valuable guide to all aspects of linked criminal and family proceedings.
[93] Ibid, at p 49.

- What steps should be taken to ensure that any preparation does not prejudice the criminal proceedings?

- If the child is to be cross-examined or re-interviewed in the family proceedings before the criminal proceedings, should the evidence be video-recorded and should the recording or transcript be disclosed to the parties in the criminal proceedings?

In any case where a child is to give evidence the court will also have to consider:

- the use of other 'special measures' in particular live video link and screens;

- the full range of special measures in light of the child's wishes and needs;

- advance judicial approval of any questions proposed to be put to the child;

- the need for ground rules to be discussed ahead of time by the judge, lawyers (and intermediary, if applicable) about the examination;

- information about the child's communication skills, length of concentration span and level of understanding, eg from an expert or an intermediary or other communication specialist;

- the need for breaks;

- the involvement and identity of a supporter for the child;

- the timetable for children's evidence to minimise time at court and give them a fresh clear start in the morning;

- the child's dates to avoid attending court;

- the length of any ABE recording, the best time for the child and the court to view it (the best time for the child may not be when the recording is viewed by the court);

- admissions of as much of the child's evidence as possible in advance, including locations, times, and lay-outs;

- save in exceptional circumstances, agreement as to:

    - the proper form and limit of questioning;[94] and
    - the identity of the questioner.[95][96]

---

[94]   Ibid.
[95]   See **17.163**.

Assessments

17.80 In private law proceedings the court has no jurisdiction to order a residential assessment of the child with one parent against the wishes of the other parent.[97]

For assessments for the purpose of a report by an expert, see **Chapter 18**.

Directions for a final hearing

17.81 On transfer to a court of proceedings or the postponement or adjournment of any hearing or the conclusion of any hearing at which the proceedings are not finally determined, the court will set a date for the proceedings to come before the court again for the purposes of giving directions or for such other purposes as the court directs.[98]

At any hearing the court may:

- confirm a date for the final hearing or the week within which the final hearing is to begin (where a date or period for the final hearing has already been set);

- set a timetable for the final hearing unless a timetable has already been fixed, or the court considers that it would be inappropriate to do so; or

- set a date for the final hearing or a period within which the final hearing of the application is to take place.[99]

The order

17.82 The Order must set out in particular:

- the issues about which the parties are agreed;

- the issues that remain to be resolved;

- the steps that are planned to resolve the issues;

- any interim arrangements pending such resolution, including arrangements for the involvement of children;

---

[96] *Guidelines in relation to children giving evidence in family proceedings* (Family Justice Council, 2011) [2012] Fam Law 79. See also Mitchell 'Children giving evidence: the practical implications of *Re W*' [2011] Fam Law 817.

[97] *R v R (Private Law Proceedings: Residential Assessment)* [2002] 2 FLR 953.

[98] FPR 2010, r 12.13(1).

[99] Ibid, r 12.13(2).

- the timetable for such steps and, where this involves further hearings, the date of such hearings;

- a statement as to any facts relating to risk or safety; insofar as they are resolved the result will be stated and, insofar as not resolved, the steps to be taken to resolve them will be stated;

- if it be the case, the fact of the transfer of the case to the FPC with the date and purpose of the next hearing;

- if it be the case, the fact that the case cannot be transferred to the FPC and the reason for the decision;

- whether in the event of an order, by consent or otherwise, or pending such an order, the parties are to be assisted by participation in mediation, Parenting Information Programmes, or other types of parenting intervention, and to detail any contact activity directions or conditions imposed by the court.[100]

FURTHER HEARINGS

17.83   After the FADRH, further directions hearings may be necessary. It may be that orders for interim contact have been made and that subsequently it is possible to resolve any dispute without a trial. Or, if a trial is necessary, further directions may be required. If a s 7 welfare report has been ordered, it is good practice to hold a pre-trial review before the trial in order to consider the report's recommendations and give any consequential directions for the trial.

17.84   FPR 2010, r 27.3 provides that unless directed otherwise a party shall attend any directions appointments.[101]

17.85   Proceedings or any part of them shall take place in the absence of any party, including a party who is a child, if:

- the court considers it in the interests of the party, having regard to the matters to be discussed or the evidence likely to be given; and

- the party is represented by a children's guardian or solicitor.

When considering the interests of a child who is a party the court shall give the children's guardian, the solicitor for the child and, if of sufficient understanding and the court thinks it appropriate, the child, an opportunity to make representations.[102]

---

[100]   PD 12B, para 6.1.
[101]   Also, FPR 2010, r 12.14(2).
[102]   Ibid, r 27.4(1).

17.86 Where the applicant appears but one or more of the respondents do not, the court may proceed with the hearing or appointment, provided:

- it is proved to the satisfaction of the court that the respondent received reasonable notice of the date of the hearing; or

- the court is satisfied that the circumstances of the case justify proceeding with the hearing.[103]

17.87 Where one or more of the respondents appear but the applicant does not, the court may refuse the application or, if sufficient evidence has previously been received, proceed in the absence of the applicant.[104]

17.88 Where, at the time and place appointed for a hearing or directions appointment, neither the applicant nor any respondent appears, the court may refuse the application.[105]

17.89 Where a party does not attend a hearing or directions appointment and the court gives judgment or makes an order against him, the party who failed to attend may apply for the judgment or order to be set aside. An application to set aside an order must be supported by evidence.

17.90 The court may grant the application only if the applicant:

(a) acted promptly on finding out that the court had exercised its power to enter judgment or make an order against the applicant;

(b) had a good reason for not attending the hearing or directions appointment; and

(c) has a reasonable prospect of success at the hearing or directions appointment.[106]

WITHDRAWING APPLICATIONS

17.91 Applications relating to the welfare or upbringing of a child or where either of the parties is a protected party may only be withdrawn with the permission of the court.

A person seeking permission to withdraw an application must file a written request for permission setting out the reasons for the request but the request may be made orally to the court if the parties are present.

---

[103] FPR 2010, r 27.4(2) and (3).
[104] Ibid, r 27.4(4).
[105] Ibid, r 27.4(5).
[106] Ibid, r 27.5.

The court may deal with a written request without a hearing if the other parties, and any other persons directed by the court, have had an opportunity to make written representations to the court about the request.[107]

17.92 The judge may decline to grant leave to withdraw, for example if there are still issues of alleged domestic violence which require to be heard or if he considers that an order restraining the making of further applications may be needed under CA 1989, s 91(14).[108]

DISMISSAL OF APPLICATIONS WITHOUT A FULL HEARING

17.93 Courts hearing applications under the Children Act have a wide discretion to deal with cases in a way which is both in the best interests of the child and the interests of natural justice. There is no 'right' to a full hearing. In appropriate circumstances, such as an application which is doomed to failure or which seeks to revisit an earlier decision which was not appealed or was unsuccessfully appealed and where there has been no relevant change in circumstances, the court may dismiss the application without a full hearing.[109] However, if there is a demonstrably arguable issue, the judge should hear evidence and argument.[110]

PROTECTED PARTIES

17.94 A 'protected party' means a party or intended party who lacks capacity within the meaning of the Mental Capacity Act 2005 to conduct proceedings.[111]

17.95 A protected party must have a litigation friend to conduct proceedings on that party's behalf.[112]

17.96 FPR 2010, Pt 15 and PD 15A contain special provisions which apply in proceedings involving protected parties, including who can be a litigation friend and how one is appointed.

17.97 FPR 2010, Pt 16 and PD 16A contain special provisions which apply when a child is a party to the proceedings and requires a litigation friend. Such circumstances will rarely arise in private law proceedings.

---

107 FPR 2010, r 29.4.
108 *Re F (Restrictions on Applications)* [2005] EWCA Civ 499, [2005] 2 FLR 950.
109 *Cheshire County Council v M* [1993] 1 FLR 463 and *Re I and H (Contact: Right to Give Evidence)* [1998] 1 FLR 876 and *Re D (Children) (Contact: Conduct of Hearing)* [2006] All ER (D) 85 (Feb, CA).
110 *Re C (A Child) (Contact: Conduct of Hearing)* [2006] All ER (D) 214 (Jan).
111 FPR 2010, r 2.3.
112 Ibid, r 15.2.

Lack of capacity

17.98 For the purposes of the Mental Capacity Act 2005, a person lacks capacity in relation to a matter if at the material time he is unable to make a decision for himself in relation to the matter because of an impairment of, or a disturbance in the functioning of, the mind or brain. It does not matter whether the impairment or disturbance is permanent or temporary.[113]

When deciding whether someone has capacity, the court has to have regard to the following principles:

- A person must be assumed to have capacity unless it is established that he lacks capacity[114] and any question whether a person lacks capacity within the meaning of this Act must be decided on the balance of probabilities.[115]

- A person is not to be treated as unable to make a decision unless all practicable steps to help him to do so have been taken without success.

- A person is not to be treated as unable to make a decision merely because he makes an unwise decision.[116]

17.99 A person is not to be regarded as unable to understand the information relevant to a decision if he is able to understand an explanation of it given to him in a way that is appropriate to his circumstances (using simple language, visual aids or any other means).[117] The fact that a person is able to retain the information relevant to a decision for a short period only does not prevent him from being regarded as able to make the decision.[118]

17.100 A person is unable to make a decision for himself if he is unable:

- to understand the information relevant to the decision;[119]

- to retain that information;

- to use or weigh that information as part of the process of making the decision; or

---

[113] Mental Capacity Act 2005, s 2(1) and (2).
[114] Ibid, s 1(2).
[115] Ibid, s 2(4).
[116] Ibid, s 1. Subsections 1(5) and (6) do not apply because under the Adoption and Children Act 2002 there is no power for anyone to give consent on behalf of the person whose consent is required. And see s 27(1)(e) and (f) of the 2005 Act.
[117] Mental Capacity Act 2005, s 3(2).
[118] Ibid, s 3(3).
[119] Ibid, s 3(1)(a). See s 3(4).

- to communicate his decision (whether by using sign language or any other means).[120]

17.101 The information relevant to a decision includes information about the reasonably foreseeable consequences of:

- deciding one way or another; or

- failing to make the decision.[121]

17.102 A lack of capacity cannot be established merely by reference to:

- a person's age or appearance; or

- a condition of his, or an aspect of his behaviour, which might lead others to make unjustified assumptions about his capacity[122].

17.103 Tests of capacity are decision specific, that is one has to consider the question of capacity in relation to the particular transaction (its nature and complexity) in respect of which the decisions as to capacity fall to be made. 'It is not difficult to envisage claimants in personal injury actions with capacity to deal with all matters and take all "lay client" decisions related to their actions up to and including a decision whether or not to settle, but lacking capacity to decide (even with advice) how to administer a large award.'[123] Even within the types of functions where capacity has to be considered there may be different gradations of complexity. For example:

> 'In the case of ... a gift inter vivos, whether by deed or otherwise, the degree required varies with the circumstances of the transaction. Thus, at one extreme, if the subject matter and value of a gift are trivial in relation to the donor's other assets a low degree of understanding will suffice. But, at the other extreme, if its effect is to dispose of the donor's only asset of value and thus, for practical purposes, to pre-empt the devolution of his estate under his will or on his intestacy, then the degree of understanding required is as high as that required for a will, and the donor must understand the claims of all of the potential donees and the extent of the property to be disposed of.'[124]

17.104 In addition to the general principles for deciding capacity, the test set out in *Masterman-Lister v Brutton & Co* [125] still applies when a court is considering capacity to conduct proceedings:

---

[120] Mental Capacity Act 2005, s 3(1). See also *Re MB* [1997] 2 FLR 426.

[121] Ibid, s 3(4).

[122] Mental Capacity Act 2005, s 2(3).

[123] *Masterman-Lister v Brrutton and Co* [2002] EWCA Civ 1889, [2003] 3 All ER 162, per Kennedy LJ at [27].

[124] *Re Beaney (Deceased)* [1978] 1 WLR 770, per Martin Nourse QC (sitting as a deputy judge of the High Court) at 774.

[125] [2002] EWCA Civ 1889, [2003] 3 All ER 162, per Chadwick LJ at [75].

'The test to be applied ... is whether the party to legal proceedings is capable of understanding, with the assistance of such proper explanation from legal advisers and experts in other disciplines as the case may require, the issues on which his consent or decision is likely to be necessary in the course of those proceedings. If he has capacity to understand that which he needs to understand in order to pursue or defend a claim, I can see no reason why the law – whether substantive or procedural – should require the interposition of a ... litigation friend.'

17.105 The Equal Treatment Bench Book[126] comments that legal advisers may have little experience of assessing capacity and may make false assumptions on the basis of factors that do not relate to the individual's actual understanding. Even where the issue does not seem to be contentious, a judge who is responsible for case management may[127] require the assistance of an expert's report. This may be a pre-existing report or one commissioned for the purpose. It no longer needs to be by a medical practitioner but could, where appropriate, be a clinical psychologist. The judge may be assisted by seeing the person alleged to lack capacity. In case of dispute, capacity is a question of fact for the court to decide on the balance of probabilities, with a presumption of capacity. Evidence should be admitted not only from those who can express an opinion as experts but also those who know the individual. The Official Solicitor may be able to give advice where assistance is not available from another source, for example a mental health social worker allocated to the party.[128] It is important that anyone asked to provide a report is aware of the need to address capacity to conduct the litigation in question.

Litigation friend

Need for a litigation friend

17.106 A person[129] may not without the permission of the court take any step in proceedings except filing an application form or applying for the appointment of a litigation friend until the protected party has a litigation friend. If during proceedings a party lacks capacity (within the meaning of the 2005 Act) to continue to conduct proceedings, no party may take any step in proceedings without the permission of the court until the protected party has a litigation friend. Any step taken before a protected party has a litigation friend has no effect unless the court orders otherwise.[130]

---

[126] (Judicial College, 2004) ch 5.4.

[127] The Equal Treatment Bench Book states 'will' but in some cases the lack will be obvious and undisputed.

[128] See also *Assessment of Mental Capacity (EPUB version) A Practical Guide for Doctors and Lawyers* (3rd edn, British Medical Association and The Law Society, 2011). Advice on the steps local authorities should take in public law proceedings concerning parents who may lack capacity was given by the Court of Appeal in *RP v Nottinghamshire City Council and the Official Solicitor (Mental Capacity of Parent)* [2008] EWCA Civ 462, [2008] 2 FLR 1516.

[129] 'Any person' – not just a person who requires a litigation friend.

[130] FPR 2010, r 15.3.

Appointment of a litigation friend

17.107 A person with authority as a deputy[131] to conduct the proceedings in the name of a protected party or on that party's behalf is entitled to be the litigation friend of the protected party in any proceedings to which that person's authority extends.[132] Such a person must file an official copy of the order, declaration or other document which confers that person's authority to act.[133]

17.108 If there is no person with authority as a deputy to conduct the proceedings in the name of a protected party a person may act as a litigation friend if that person:

- can fairly and competently conduct proceedings on behalf of the protected party;

- has no interest adverse to that of the protected party and

- if not the Official Solicitor, undertakes to pay any costs which the protected party may be ordered to pay in relation to the proceedings, subject to any right that person may have to be repaid from the assets of the protected party.[134]

Such person, other than the Official Solicitor, must file, at the time when they first take a step in the proceedings on behalf of the protected party, a certificate of suitability stating that they satisfy the conditions specified above.[135]

17.109 The court may, of its own initiative or on an application, supported by evidence, by a person who wishes to be a litigation friend or a party to the proceedings, if:

- the person to be appointed so consents; and

- it is satisfied that the person to be appointed complies with the conditions specified,

make an order appointing:

- a person other than the Official Solicitor; or

- the Official Solicitor,

---

131 As defined by Mental Capacity Act 2005 s 16(2)(b).
132 FPR 2010, r 15.4(2).
133 Ibid, r 15.5(2).
134 Ibid, r 15.4(3) and (4).
135 Ibid, r 15.5(3).

as a litigation friend.[136]

17.110 An order appointing the Official Solicitor should be expressed as being made subject to his consent.[137]

17.111 The court may at any time direct that a party make an application for an order appointing a litigation friend.[138]

Removal of a litigation friend

17.112 The court may:

- direct that a person may not act as a litigation friend;

- terminate a litigation friend's appointment; or

- appoint a new litigation friend in substitution for an existing one.[139]

An application for such an order or direction must be supported by evidence.[140]

Litigation friends in the family proceedings court

17.113 For the first time the Rules give the FPC jurisdiction to appoint litigation friends. As a consequence there may be a number of cases where the FPC may be an appropriate forum. However, there will be cases where a transfer to the county court is appropriate under the Allocation and Transfer of Proceedings Order 2008[141] (see **16.75**). Examples are:

- where the court has to make a finding of capacity either because the party disputes an expert opinion on capacity or refuses to be assessed or the experts disagree;

- the party is a litigant in person who is likely to dispute any assessment of capacity or to attend for assessment;

- the consequence of being a protected party will complicate or prolong proceedings.[142]

---

[136] FPR 2010, r 15.6.
[137] 'Practice Note : Official Solicitor: Appointment in Family Proceedings' [2001] 2 FLR 155.
[138] Ibid.
[139] FPR 2010, r 15.7.
[140] Ibid.
[141] SI 2008/2836.
[142] Justices' Clerks Society (with the approval of the President of the Family Division) *Guidance Note to Family Proceedings Court* [2011] Fam Law 1024.

The Official Solicitor

17.114 A summary of the functions of the office of the Official Solicitor was provided in the annex to the judgment of the Court of Appeal in *RP v Nottinghamshire City Council and the Official Solicitor (Mental Capacity of Parent)*.[143] A primary duty is the representation of children who are not themselves the subject of proceedings, or adults who lack capacity to conduct proceedings, in county court or High Court proceedings in England and Wales, and also in the FPC in proceedings under the Adoption and Children Act 2002, and in proceedings in the Court of Protection, by acting as their next friend, guardian ad litem or litigation friend. He may also be asked to provide an advocate to the court or to act under a *Harbin v Masterman*[144] direction to make enquiries and to report about such matters as the court thinks fit. He has a duty to review all committals to prison for contempt of court and to take such action as is considered necessary. He generally becomes involved in litigation because he is invited to do so either by the court or by some other party to the proceedings, although he can and does initiate proceedings on behalf of a non-subject child or protected party where some responsible person or body brings the facts to his attention and it appears that the person on whose behalf he as being invited to act has a good cause of action.

> 'It is a matter for my discretion whether or not I consent to act. I cannot be compelled to act. As a matter of long-established practice, therefore, my appointment by the court and any direction given to me by the court is expressed as being subject to my consent.'[145]

17.115 The Official Solicitor is subject to severe budgetary constraints which may create difficulties in his acting as a litigation friend. Guidance on when he will accept such a role has been issued by the Official Solicitor and the President of the Family Division.[146] In all cases before accepting a case, he will need to be satisfied of the following criteria:

- satisfactory evidence or a finding by the court that the party lacks capacity to conduct the proceedings and is therefore a protected party;

- confirmation that there is security for the costs of legal representation;

- there is no other person who is suitable and willing to act as guardian ad litem/litigation friend.

Parties may need reminding of the need to provide confirmation of these matters immediately on approaching the Official Solicitor's office.

---

[143] [2008] EWCA Civ 462, [2008] 2 FLR 1516.

[144] [1896] 1 Ch 351.

[145] *RP v Nottinghamshire City Council and the Official Solicitor (Mental Capacity of Parent)* [2008] EWCA Civ 462, [2008] 2 FLR 1516, Supplement, para 11.

[146] *Guidance in Cases Involving the Official Solicitor* (2010) [2011] Fam Law 194.

17.116 In order to assist the Official Solicitor in the decisions he makes about allocating case workers, in certain cases, judges should consider whether it may be appropriate to indicate with as much particularity as possible the relative urgency of the proceedings and the likely effect upon the child (and family) of delay. The Official Solicitor will very carefully consider giving priority to such cases.[147]

17.117 The Official Solicitor aims to provide a response to any invitation within 10 working days. He will be unable to consent to act for an adult until satisfied that the party is a 'patient'. A further directions appointment after 28 days may therefore be helpful. If he accepts appointment the Official Solicitor will need time to prepare the case on behalf of the child or patient and may wish to make submissions about any substantive hearing date. The following documents should be forwarded to the Official Solicitor without delay:

- a copy of the order inviting him to act (with a note of the reasons approved by the judge if appropriate);

- the court file;

- if available, a bundle with summary, statement of issues and chronology.

It is often helpful to discuss the question of appointment with the Official Solicitor or one of his staff.[148]

17.118 The Official Solicitor will normally instruct private solicitors to act on his instructions. His standard instructions are available on his website.[149]

The role of the litigation friend

17.119 It is the duty of a litigation friend fairly and competently to conduct proceedings on behalf of a protected party. The litigation friend must have no interest in the proceedings adverse to that of the protected party and all steps and decisions the litigation friend takes in the proceedings must be taken for the benefit of the protected party.[150] There is no absolute duty for the litigation friend to employ legal representatives but where the issues in the litigation are complex and the litigation friend lacks the necessary expertise, a failure to instruct lawyers might justify his being replaced.

17.120 There is no reason in most civil litigation, personal injury or clinical negligence cases, why a lay person, including a family member, with appropriate legal advice should not be the litigation friend of the claimant. But it is of the essence of such an appointment that the litigation friend has no conflict of

---

[147] See also *Parents who lack capacity to conduct public law proceedings* (Family Justice Council) which annexes draft letters of instruction and the Official Solicitor's capacity certificate.

[148] Practice Note : Official Solicitor: Appointment in Family Proceedings op cit.

[149] Available at: www.justice.gov.uk/guidance/protecting-the-vulnerable/official-solicitor.

[150] PD 15A, para 2.1.

interest with the protected party.[151] In family cases it may be that the prospective litigation may have a conflict of interest and the court will be alert to the risk.

17.121 The appointment of a litigation friend does not mean that the protected party makes no contribution to the proceedings. A lack of capacity to conduct litigation does not necessarily indicate a lack of capacity to give evidence. In many cases litigation friends will be able to and should ascertain the views of the protected party and give appropriate weight to them depending on the extent of understanding while at the same time exercising an independent judgment.

UNREPRESENTED LITIGANTS

17.122

> 'The principle of equality of arms – one of the elements of the broader concept of a fair trial – requires that each party should be afforded a reasonable opportunity to present his or her case under conditions that do not place him or her at a substantial disadvantage vis-à-vis his or her opponent'[152]

Background

17.123 Many litigants, especially fathers, will not qualify for public funding and cannot afford to be represented. As noted by Thorpe LJ in 2005 in *Re G (Litigants in Person)*:[153]

> 'There has been a significant increase in the percentage of family cases in which one or other of the parties is unrepresented for all or part of the proceedings. There are no statistics to substantiate that assertion but it is universally recognised as the reality by all specialists in this field. The provision of legal aid in family proceedings is a shrinking rather than an expanding welfare service.'

17.124 In 2011 *Access to Justice for Litigants in Person*,[154] prepared by a working group of the Civil Justice Council, examined the position in relation to civil proceedings. It concluded that:

> 'It is a reality that those who cannot afford legal services and those for whom the state will not provide legal aid comprise the larger part of the population of England and Wales. Thus for most members of the public who become involved in legal proceedings they will have to represent themselves. The thing that keeps that reality below the surface is simply the hope or belief on the part of most people

---

[151] *RP v Nottinghamshire City Council and the Official Solicitor (Mental Capacity of Parent)* [2008] EWCA Civ 462, [2008] 2 FLR 1516, per Wall LJ at [130].

[152] *Moser v Austria* (Application No 12643/02) [2007] 1 FLR 702, ECHR, at [86]. See also Mitchell 'Representing the unrepresented litigant' [2007] Fam Law 43.

[153] [2003] EWCA Civ 1055, [2003] 2 FLR 963.

[154] (Family Justice Council, 2011). See [2012] Fam Law 95.

that they will not have a civil dispute. Every informed prediction is that, by reason of the forthcoming reductions and changes in legal aid, the number of self-represented litigants will increase, and on a considerable scale. Such litigants will be the rule rather than the exception. Where there is not an increase the reason will be that the individual was resigned to accepting that the civil justice system was not open to them even if they had a problem it could solve or it could give access to the rights they were entitled to.'[155]

The same is true for family proceedings.

17.125 The reality behind these perceptions was examined by a study of three county courts in 2004/05, commissioned by the Department for Constitutional Affairs.[156] In private law litigation involving children, a quarter of cases where both parties played an active part involved at least one litigant in person. It was difficult to ascertain from court records whether the proportion was increasing but interview evidence suggested that there had been an increase in recent years but it was too soon to say whether this was part of a trend. Litigants represented themselves for three main reasons: an inability to afford representation, a perception that lawyers were not always necessary or best placed to assist and a belief that courts were open to and supported unrepresented litigants. As might be expected many unrepresented parties experienced problems. They were more likely to make errors and the errors made were likely to be more serious. In more than half the cases the litigant in person filed at least one flawed document. They had difficulty in identifying which legally relevant issues were in dispute and sometimes struggled with the nature of the dispute itself. Cases involving them were less likely to settle but there was only modest evidence to suggest that cases took longer. The evidence of the problems faced by unrepresented litigants, their lack of active defence, their generally higher error rates and lower levels of participation prejudiced the interests of unrepresented litigants and placed extra burdens on the other party.

17.126 The study found that a significant proportion of unrepresented litigants had sought advice from solicitors, Citizen Advice Bureaux or friends but this assistance appeared to be at a fairly low level. Help was sought from the court staff but as Moorhead and Sefton comment, there is a limit to what staff who are not usually trained and may be inexperienced can or should do. In addition 'inexpert, sometimes emotional and procedurally naïve litigants pose a number of ethical and managerial problems for judges who were conscious of their role as a neutral arbiter of an adversarial process but also of the need to focus on substantive justice'.[157] Although judges were found to adopt various strategies for dealing with litigants in person they tended to interpret their duty of ensuring a fair hearing in terms of maximising the

---

[155] Ibid, ch 2, paras 14–15.
[156] Moorhead and Sefton *Litigants in person – Unrepresented litigants in first instance proceedings* (Department for Constitutional Affairs, 2005) Research Series 2/05.
[157] Ibid, at p 192.

opportunities for litigants to get help rather than ensuring that they understood the law which was applicable to their situation.

17.127   The provisions of Art 6 ECHR make it important that those who need assistance with the presentation of their case should receive it, if necessary by having someone beside them in court to prompt, take notes and quietly give advice ('a *McKenzie* friend'). In proceedings in open court, there is a presumption (which is not a right) that a party should have the assistance of a *McKenzie* friend unless the court is satisfied that the fairness and interests of justice do not require it. Although the position used to be different for proceedings in chambers,[158] there is now a presumption that litigants there should also be permitted a *McKenzie* friend:

> 'It is very important in family proceedings that litigants in person ranged up against solicitors and counsel should have the assistance that they think appropriate, particularly if it is going to contribute to their sense of confidence in the proceedings. So whilst I recognise the judge's right to exclude a particular *McKenzie* friend for good reason, it seems to me that the presumption in favour of permitting a *McKenzie* friend is a strong one.'[159]

Thorpe LJ stated in *Re M (Contact: Family Assistance: McKenzie Friend)*:[160]

> 'Provided that the *McKenzie* friend acts with restraint, he is often a useful assistance to the conduct of the litigation.'

Guidance

17.128   The FPR 2010 make no special provision for unrepresented litigants in person save to provide that parties disclose any information relating to the proceedings to a lay adviser or McKenzie Friend in order to obtain advice or assistance in relation to the proceedings.[161] Detailed guidance is however contained in *Practice Guidance: McKenzie Friends*[162] which summarises and replaces the previous guidance including that given by the President of the Family Division[163] and case law in both the civil and family jurisdictions including the decision of the Court of Appeal in *O (Children) (Hearing in Private: Assistance), Re*.[164] It applies to proceedings in both the civil and the family jurisdictions and is issued as guidance (not as a Practice Direction) to remind courts and litigants of the principles set out in the authorities.

Main points include the following.

---

[158]   See *R v Bow County Court ex parte Pelling* [1999] 2 FLR 149.
[159]   *Re H (McKenzie Friend: Pre-Trial Determination)* [2002] 1 FLR 39, per Thorpe LJ at [11]. See also *Guidance from the President's Office* [2005] Fam Law 405.
[160]   [1999] 1 FLR 75.
[161]   PD 14E, para 1.3. See also **22.54**.
[162]   [2010] 2 FLR 962.
[163]   *President's Guidance: McKenzie Friends* [2008] 2 FLR 110.
[164]   [2005] EWCA Civ 759.

The right to reasonable assistance

17.129 Litigants have the right to have reasonable assistance from a layperson, sometimes called a McKenzie Friend. Litigants assisted by a McKenzie Friend remain litigants-in- person. McKenzie Friends have no independent right to provide assistance. They have no right to act as advocates or to carry out the conduct of litigation.

What McKenzie Friends may do

17.130 McKenzie Friends may:

* provide moral support for litigants;

* take notes;

* help with case papers;

* quietly give advice on any aspect of the conduct of the case.

What McKenzie Friends may not do

17.131 McKenzie Friends may not:

* act as the litigants' agent in relation to the proceedings;

* manage litigants' cases outside court, for example by signing court documents; or

* address the court, make oral submissions or examine witnesses.

Exercising the right to reasonable assistance

17.132 While litigants ordinarily have a right to receive reasonable assistance from McKenzie Friends the court retains the power to refuse to permit such assistance. The court may do so where it is satisfied that, in that case, the interests of justice and fairness do not require the litigant to receive such assistance.

17.133 A litigant who wishes to exercise this right should inform the judge as soon as possible indicating who the McKenzie Friend will be. The proposed McKenzie Friend should produce a short curriculum vitae or other statement setting out relevant experience, confirming that he or she has no interest in the case and understands the McKenzie Friend's role and the duty of confidentiality.[165]

---

[165] *Access to Justice for Litigants in Person* op cit contains a suggested draft Notice of McKenzie Friend at Appendix 4.

17.134 If the court considers that there might be grounds for circumscribing the right to receive such assistance, or a party objects to the presence of, or assistance given by a McKenzie Friend, it is not for the litigant to justify the exercise of the right. It is for the court or the objecting party to provide sufficient reasons why the litigant should not receive such assistance.

17.135 When considering whether to circumscribe the right to assistance or refuse a McKenzie Friend permission to attend the right to a fair trial is engaged. The matter should be considered carefully. The litigant should be given a reasonable opportunity to argue the point. The proposed McKenzie Friend should not be excluded from that hearing and should normally be allowed to help the litigant.

17.136 Where proceedings are in *closed court*, eg where they relate to a child, the litigant is required to justify the McKenzie Friend's presence. The presumption in favour of permitting a McKenzie Friend to attend such hearings, and thereby enable litigants to exercise the right to assistance, is a strong one.

17.137 The court may refuse to allow a litigant to exercise the right to receive assistance at the start of a hearing. The court can also circumscribe the right during the course of a hearing. It may be refused at the start of a hearing or later circumscribed where the court forms the view that a MF may give, has given, or is giving, assistance which impedes the efficient administration of justice. However, the court should also consider whether a firm and unequivocal warning to the litigant and/or McKenzie friend might suffice in the first instance.[166]

17.138 A decision by the court not to curtail assistance from a McKenzie Friend should be regarded as final, save on the ground of subsequent misconduct by the McKenzie Friend or on the ground that the McKenzie Friend's continuing presence will impede the efficient administration of justice. In such event the court should give a short judgment setting out the reasons why it has curtailed the right to assistance. Litigants may appeal such decisions. McKenzie Friends have no standing to do so.

17.139 The following factors should not be taken to justify the court refusing to permit a litigant receiving such assistance:

- the case or application is simple or straightforward, or is, for instance, a directions or case management hearing;

- the litigant appears capable of conducting the case without assistance;

- the litigant is unrepresented through choice;

---

[166] *Access to Justice for Litigants in Person* op cit contains a suggested draft Code of Conduct for McKenzie Friends at Appendix 5.

- the other party is not represented;

- the proposed McKenzie Friend belongs to an organisation that promotes a particular cause;

- the proceedings are confidential and the court papers contain sensitive information relating to a family's affairs.

17.140 A litigant may be denied the assistance of a McKenzie Friend because its provision might undermine or has undermined the efficient administration of justice.[167] Examples of circumstances where this might arise are:

- the assistance is being provided for an improper purpose;

- the assistance is unreasonable in nature or degree;

- the McKenzie Friend is subject to a civil proceedings order or a civil restraint order;

- the McKenzie Friend is using the litigant as a puppet;

- the McKenzie Friend is directly or indirectly conducting the litigation;

- the court is not satisfied that the McKenzie Friend fully understands the duty of confidentiality.[168]

17.141 Legal representatives should ensure that documents are served on litigants in good time to enable them to seek assistance regarding their content from McKenzie Friends in advance of any hearing or advocates' meeting. See also **17.162**.

17.142 The High Court can, under its inherent jurisdiction, impose a civil restraint order on McKenzie Friends who repeatedly act in ways that undermine the efficient administration of justice.

Rights of audience and rights to conduct litigation

17.143 McKenzie Friends do not have a right of audience or a right to conduct litigation. It is a criminal offence to exercise rights of audience or to conduct litigation unless properly qualified and authorised to do so by an appropriate regulatory body or, in the case of an otherwise unqualified or

---

[167] See, for example, *Paragon Finance plc v Noueri* [2001] EWCA Civ 1402, [2001] 1 WLR 2357 and *R (Morris) v North Somerset Council* [2003] EWCA Civ 183, [2003] 2 All ER 1114.

[168] See, for example, *IIBCC v LG (By Her Litigation Friend The Official Solicitor)* [2010] EWHC 1527 (Fam), [2011] 1 FLR 463, at [150]–[152] where the court addressed the possible conflict for an elected representative between his role as a representative of a constituent and his role as a McKenzie Friend.

unauthorised individual (ie a lay individual including a McKenzie Friend), the court grants such rights on a case-by-case basis.[169]

17.144 Courts should be slow to grant any application from a litigant for a right of audience or a right to conduct litigation to any lay person, including a McKenzie Friend. This is because a person exercising such rights must ordinarily be properly trained, be under professional discipline (including an obligation to insure against liability for negligence) and be subject to an overriding duty to the court. These requirements are necessary for the protection of all parties to litigation and are essential to the proper administration of justice. Any application for a right of audience or a right to conduct litigation to be granted to any lay person should therefore be considered very carefully. The court should only be prepared to grant such rights where there is good reason to do so taking into account all the circumstances of the case, which are likely to vary greatly.[170] Such grants should not be extended to lay persons automatically or without due consideration. They should not be granted for mere convenience.

17.145 Examples of the type of special circumstances which have been held to justify the grant of a right of audience to a lay person, including a McKenzie Friend, are:

• that person is a close relative of the litigant;

• health problems preclude the litigant from addressing the court, or conducting litigation, and the litigant cannot afford to pay for a qualified legal representative;

• the litigant is relatively inarticulate and prompting by that person may unnecessarily prolong the proceedings.

17.146 It is for the litigant to persuade the court that the circumstances of the case are such that it is in the interests of justice for the court to grant a lay person a right of audience or a right to conduct litigation.

17.147 The grant of a right of audience or a right to conduct litigation to lay persons who hold themselves out as professional advocates or professional McKenzie Friends or who seek to exercise such rights on a regular basis, whether for reward or not, will however only[171] be granted in exceptional circumstances. To do otherwise would tend to subvert the will of Parliament.

17.148 If a litigant wants a lay person to be granted a right of audience, an application must be made at the start of the hearing. If a right to conduct litigation is sought such an application must be made at the earliest possible

---

[169]   Under the Legal Services Act 2007.

[170]   See, for example, *Re N (McKenzie Friend: Rights of Audience)* [2008] EWHC 2042 (Fam), [2008] 2 FLR 1899.

[171]   Highlighted in bold in the original.

time and must be made, in any event, before the lay person does anything which amounts to the conduct of litigation. It is for litigants to persuade the court, on a case-by-case basis, that the grant of such rights is justified.

17.149 Rights of audience and the right to conduct litigation are separate rights. The grant of one right to a lay person does not mean that a grant of the other right has been made. If both rights are sought their grant must be applied for individually and justified separately.

17.150 Having granted either a right of audience or a right to conduct litigation, the court has the power to remove either right.[172] The grant of such rights in one set of proceedings cannot be relied on as a precedent supporting their grant in future proceedings.

Remuneration

17.151 Litigants can enter into lawful agreements to pay fees to McKenzie Friends for the provision of reasonable assistance in court or out of court by, for instance, carrying out clerical or mechanical activities, such as photocopying documents, preparing bundles, delivering documents to opposing parties or the court, or the provision of legal advice in connection with court proceedings. Such fees cannot be lawfully recovered from the opposing party.

17.152 Fees said to be incurred by McKenzie Friends for carrying out the conduct of litigation, where the court has not granted such a right, cannot lawfully be recovered from either the litigant for whom they carry out such work or the opposing party.

17.153 Fees said to be incurred by McKenzie Friends for carrying out the conduct of litigation after the court has granted such a right are in principle recoverable from the litigant for whom the work is carried out. Such fees cannot be lawfully recovered from the opposing party.

17.154 Fees said to be incurred by McKenzie Friends for exercising a right of audience following the grant of such a right by the court are in principle recoverable from the litigant on whose behalf the right is exercised. Such fees are also recoverable, in principle, from the opposing party as a recoverable disbursement.[173]

Personal Support Unit and Citizen's Advice Bureau

17.155 Litigants should also be aware of the services provided by local Personal Support Units and Citizens' Advice Bureaux. The PSU at the Royal

---

[172] If granted for a directions hearing, it may be illogical to withdraw rights of audience at a later stage – *Re J (Residential Assessment: Rights of Audience)* [2009] EWCA Civ 1210, [2010] 1 FLR 1290, per Wall LJ at [14].

[173] CPR, rr 48.6(2) and 48(6)(3)(ii).

Courts of Justice in London can be contacted on 020 7947 7701, by e-mail at cbps@bello.co.uk or at the enquiry desk. The CAB at the Royal Courts of Justice in London can be contacted on 020 7947 6564 or at the enquiry desk.

The court and litigants in person

17.156 The difficulties faced by the court when one or both parents are unrepresented was recognised by *Access to Justice for Litigants in Person*.[174]

> 'Judges are committed to delivering fair hearings ... A challenge lies in how this translates when there is one or more self-represented litigants in a case. It involves helping one side rather than the other, and often giving more help to one side than another.'

In *Re R (Residence Order)*,[175] for example, a represented mother objected when the unrepresented father did not cross-examine her himself but the judge asked her questions before asking the father if there were other issues he wanted to raise. That ground of appeal was rejected.

> 'As more and more parties are forced to appear in person, so judges are frequently required delicately to maintain a level balance to the playing field. Give the litigant in person no help and he will complain: take too active a role and the other side complains. There is no easy way out of that dilemma. It must be left to the individual good sense of the judge to decide how and when to intervene, the circumstances varying infinitely. Here I am totally satisfied that the judge preserved his neutrality. He was helpful but not hostile. The questions were asked courteously and invariably couched in the language of leading evidence-in-chief rather than of cross-examination, wholly consistent with the non-adversarial atmosphere judges strive to achieve in family proceedings.'[176]

17.157 *Access to Justice for Litigants in Person* proposed a 'modest and sensible check-list'[177] including many things that many courts and tribunals do already, but not all and not always.[178]

- The court should ensure that hearings are arranged when required under FPR 2010, particularly early in proceedings, rather than leaving this to the parties.

- There should be encouragement for parties to engage in mediation.

- The distinction between which provisions of FPR 2010 are mandatory and which are not should be clearer.

---

[174] Op cit, at p 34.
[175] [2009] EWCA Civ 445, [2010] 1 FLR 509.
[176] Ibid, per Ward LJ at [16].
[177] Op cit, at p 37.
[178] References to FPR 2010 are substituted for those in the original to the Civil Procedure Rules, SI 1998/3132.

- There should be a starting presumption that provisions of the CPR that are mandatory should be strictly enforced.

- Guidance by a judge to parties on which specific parts of FPR 2010 are likely to be critical to a case, should be included in notices of hearings.

- Decisions should always be justified by reasons, and parties should be notified of the specific provision of FPR 2010 that has been applied in reaching significant decisions.

- Reasons should be given when parties are notified of decisions taken on applications that are determined without a hearing.

- Litigants should be given advance notice of the amount of time they are likely to be given to outline their evidence/arguments, and then allowed that amount of time to present their evidence/argument at the hearing.

- The documentation should be read by the judge prior to the hearing.

- The judge should clarify the parts of FPR 2010, or forms of evidence, that will be crucial to the case at the commencement of the hearing (reinforcing the earlier notification suggested above), and thus help make clear the scope of the hearing.[179]

17.158 It may also help if litigants in person are provided with a copy of s 1 of the Children Act 1989 in order to focus their preparation of the case.

17.159 When exercising its power to make orders, for example an order under s 91(14),[180] without an application by a party having been made, the court should ensure that litigants in person are given sufficient notice of the court's intention and, if required, an adjournment to prepare a response should be granted.[181]

Litigants in person and legal representatives

17.160 One party being unrepresented may also create difficulties for the legal representatives of the other party. It should not be forgotten that FPR 2010, r 1.3 imposes a duty on the parties to help the court further the overriding objective to deal with cases justly and to ensure, as far as is practicable that the parties are on an equal footing.

---

[179] Op cit at p 37.
[180] See **Chapter 21**.
[181] *Re G (Residence: Restrictions on Further applications)* [2008] EWCA Civ 1468, [2009] 1 FLR 894.

17.161   *Access to Justice for Litigants in Person*[182] contains a suggested draft Guidance for legal professionals appearing against a litigant in person. This includes:

> 'Where a self-represented litigant is involved in a case the court will expect the legal representatives for other parties in the case to do what they reasonably can to ensure that the self-represented litigant has a fair opportunity to prepare and put his or her case.'

17.162   It also provides a suggested draft statement of what a litigant in person is entitled to expect from the other party's legal representatives.[183] This states:

> 'If you are representing yourself in a case and there are legal professionals representing other parties in the case, then among the things you are entitled to expect from those legal professionals are:
>
> •   That they will treat you with courtesy and respect.
> •   That they will keep diligently to the timetable and the directions that the court has given in the case, but give you advance notice when the timetable cannot be met.
> •   That they will co-operate if you require additional time and it is reasonable to agree that time.
> •   That unless the court otherwise directs or allows, they will copy to you at the same time as they are provided to the court, every communication with the court in relation to the case, including written arguments.
> •   That, unless it is wholly unavoidable, they will provide you with any written arguments and documents in good time before any hearing.
> •   That before any hearing at court, they will be ready and willing to speak to you about any matter which can reasonably be answered and discussed prior to the hearing if you have any questions or wish to raise any matter.
> •   That after any hearing at court, and unless there is good reason to the contrary, they will be ready and willing to speak to you about the outcome of the hearing and any orders made by the Court.'

Litigants in person and cross-examination of children and vulnerable witnesses

17.163   In criminal trials ss 34 and 35 of the Youth Justice and Criminal Evidence Act 1999 prohibit unrepresented defendants cross-examining child (and some other) witnesses to sexual offences. In family proceedings the issue of the unrepresented alleged perpetrator is more challenging especially when he is not entitled as of right to legal aid. It may be very difficult to arrange representation.[184] In some cases it may be possible, if funds are available, for the child to be interviewed pre-trial by an independent expert.[185] This may require the child to be made a party if he or she is the subject of the

---

[182]   Op cit, at Appendix 2.
[183]   Ibid, Appendix 3.
[184]   See, for example, *H v L and R* [2006] EWHC 3099 (Fam), [2007] 2 FLR 162.
[185]   See **4.35**.

proceedings.[186] If this is not possible, the balancing of the defendant's Art 6 ECHR rights against the Art 8 ECHR rights of the witness may result in the child not being questioned, especially if young. In other cases, for example, that of a 17-year-old stepchild who may be suspected of fabrication, fairness may require that the witness is directly questioned and a way of dealing with this will have to be found.

17.164 The Family Justice Council Guidelines in relation to children giving evidence in family proceedings[187] state that:

> 'A child should never be questioned directly by a litigant in person who is an alleged perpetrator.'

17.165 If an interview away from court is not possible, it may be necessary for the judge to question the child neutrally on topics which the litigant in person appropriately wishes to explore. Pre- the 1999 Act, the Court of Appeal indicated in *R v Brown (Milton)*[188] that it might be necessary for the judge in a criminal trial to question the witness.

> 'The trial judge's duty is to ensure to the utmost of his ability that the defendant, even if unrepresented, or perhaps particularly if unrepresented, has a fair trial.'

The Lord Chief Justice referred to guidance which was given by the court in *R v De Oliveira*[189] that 'when the situation arises in which an unrepresented defendant is statutorily prohibited from cross-examining, it will generally be desirable that the trial judge should ask such questions as he sees fit, to test the accuracy and reliability and the possibility of collusion between the prosecution witnesses'. He then continued:

> 'Without either descending into the arena on behalf of the defence or, generally speaking, putting any sort of positive case on behalf of the defence, this is a difficult tight-rope for the trial judge to walk. However, he must do his best according to the circumstances of the particular case. It is also open to the judge in an appropriate case to ask a defendant whether there are matters which he wishes to have put to a witness. However, it would be for the judge to decide whether and how to put questions in relation to those matters.'

17.166 This was done in slightly different circumstances in *R v Leon Cameron*[190] where a 14-year-old complainant, giving evidence by live-link, refused to continue to be cross-examined by the defendant's counsel. The judge switched off the link, asked counsel to provide him with the material he wished to have put and indicated where he would be prepared to ask questions and where he would not, for instance on the ground that the question proposed was

---

[186] See **4.64**. See Practice Direction 16A.
[187] (2011) [2012] Fam Law 79, at para 17.
[188] [1998] 2 Cr App Rep 364.
[189] (Unreported) 15 November 1996.
[190] [2001] EWCA Crim 562.

mere comment or would unproductively inflame the witness. The Court of
Appeal saw no ground for criticising his approach.

17.167 For obvious reasons there will be a judicial reluctance in family
proceedings to walk this tightrope. In *H v L*[191] for example, Wood J said whilst
not regarding it as impossible, he felt 'a profound unease' at the thought of
conducting such an exercise in the family jurisdiction. 'If it falls to a judge to
conduct the exercise it should do so only in exceptional circumstances.'

---

[191]   [2006] EWHC 3099 (Fam), [2007] 2 FLR 162.

Chapter 18

EXPERT EVIDENCE

INTRODUCTION

18.1 Civil Evidence Act 1972, s 3 allows an expert to give his opinion on any relevant matter, notwithstanding that it is an issue which it is for the court ultimately to decide. In the past, there was resistance to the use of expert evidence in cases involving children who were not suffering from an identifiable illness but its value in difficult cases gradually came to be appreciated. *J v C*,[1] a decision of the House of Lords reported in 1970, marked the watershed. Lord Upjohn drew a distinction between a child who required treatment for a psychological condition when expert evidence would weigh heavily with the court and a normal child who was seen for the sole purpose of calling the practitioner to give 'quite general evidence' on the dangers of taking this or that course. Lord MacDermott, in contrast, noted that growing experience had shown that not all upset caused by a change of custody was transient and such a change 'will often be worthy of close and anxious attention'. That view came to prevail as judges became more aware of the problems which breaking a child's attachment to its carer could cause and expert evidence gradually became more common.

18.2 During the last 40 years, courts have concentrated not so much on the admissibility of evidence as on controlling the ways in which the evidence is obtained. More recently, with increased concern about the delay which can be caused by the instruction of experts and (to a lesser extent), the cost to the public purse, attention is being given to identifying those cases where expert evidence is needed, rather than merely helpful.

18.3 In *Re M and R (Child Abuse: Evidence)*,[2] Butler Sloss LJ described the court's approach to such evidence as follows:

> 'In cases involving children, expert medical and psychiatric evidence from paediatricians and allied disciplines is quite often indispensable to the court. As Parker LCJ said in *Director of Public Prosecutions v A and BC Chewing Gum Ltd*[3] the court needs "all the help it can get". But that dependence in no way compromises the fact that the final decision in the case is the judge's and his alone.

---

[1]   [1970] AC 668.

[2]   [1996] 2 FLR 195, at 205. The judgment contains an interesting analysis of the change in the approach of courts to the introduction of expert evidence in all cases and not just those involving children.

[3]   [1968] 1 QB 159, at 165A.

... So the passing of [the Civil Evidence Act] should not operate to force the court to, in Wigmore's words, "waste its time in listening to superfluous and cumbersome testimony" provided that the judge never loses sight of the central truths: namely that the ultimate decision is for him and that all questions of relevance and weight are for him ... The modern view is to regulate such matters by way of weight rather than admissibility.'

CONTROL OF EXPERT EVIDENCE

The need for judicial control

18.4   Over the years, a variety of rules – both statutory and judge-made – developed to govern the obtaining and admission of evidence. There are a number of reasons for this control. Instructing experts is likely to delay the final hearing. Suitably qualified and experienced experts are both in short supply and tend to have busy clinical practices, and it can be difficult to find an expert who is able to provide a report and attend the trial within a reasonable time.[4] Recently, a series of widely published cases such as *R v Clark*[5] and associated disciplinary proceedings (see **18.59** and **22.61**) have exacerbated the problem by making experts less willing to expose themselves to criticism.[6] In addition, the length of the hearing may be increased.[7]

18.5   Courts are mindful of the considerable cost of instructing an expert, usually at public expense.[8] Recent changes in legal aid will make it less easy, and in some private law cases, impossible, for an expert to be instructed.

18.6   Although courts are more aware than previously that a properly conducted investigation by an experienced child psychiatrist is unlikely to cause distress, there remains a justifiable concern that an inappropriate interview can harm the child. In *Re C (Minors) (Wardship: Medical Evidence)*,[9] a consultant paediatrician instructed in a private law case by the father quickly formed a view that the child had been physically ill-treated by his mother. In order to establish the seriousness of the finding, he closely questioned the child on seven occasions over 4 days. The Official Solicitor later described these interviews as in themselves a form of child abuse.

18.7   Courts have also identified a need to control inappropriate investigation by well-meaning but inexperienced experts. Such investigations not only carry a

---

4   See, for example, Sturge and Bhari 'Experts: maintaining the pool' [2005] Fam Law 156.
5   [2003] EWCA Civ 1020.
6   See, for example, Williams 'Bearing good witness: the reluctant expert' [2008] Fam Law 157.
7   The Children Act Advisory Committee *Annual Reports 1992/3* and *1993/94* (The Lord Chancellor's Department), *Scoping Study on Delay in Children Act Cases* (Lord Chancellor's Department, 2002), summarised in [2002] Fam Law 492. See also Chapter 2.
8   See, for example, *Re G (Minors) (Expert Witnesses)* [1994] 2 FLR 291, per Wall J at 297. See also Collier 'Experts' fees' [2007] Fam Law 460 and *Legal Aid Reform in England and Wales: The Government Response* Cm 8072 (Ministry of Justice, 2011) Appendix I.
9   [1987] 1 FLR 418.

risk to the child but can also prevent a proper investigation by others by muddying the waters. In cases of alleged sexual abuse, the notorious divergence of professional opinion on such topics as the use of anatomically correct dolls, investigative interviews and reflex and dilatation have made it necessary for courts to control the nature of the investigation, if necessary by instructing the Official Solicitor (now, by appointing a Cafcass Legal Services guardian) or actively encouraging the use of a reputable single joint expert.

18.8 Finally, there is a need to protect both the confidentiality of the proceedings and, under Art 8 of the European Convention, to protect the privacy of the parties and the child by preventing the unnecessary disclosure of information to third parties.

18.9 In *Re G (Minors) (Expert Witnesses)*,[10] one of a number of cases in which he examined the practice and usage of expert evidence in cases involving children, Wall J said:

> 'In *Re M (Minors) (Care Proceedings) (Child's Wishes)*[11] I set out my thoughts on the manner in which expert witnesses should be instructed in children's proceedings ...
>
> I also emphasised the non-adversarial nature of children's proceedings and stressed the vital importance of expert evidence in assisting the judge to reach the right solutions ...
>
> My judgments in *Re M (Minors)* and *Re MD and TD (Minors) (Time Estimates)*[12] were based on a number of assumptions. Principal amongst these were the propositions: (a) that not only is leave required before the papers in a public or private law Children Act case can be shown to an expert; but also (b) that the court has a proactive role in the grant of leave. Thus in my judgment the court in each case:
>
> (1) has the duty to analyse the evidence and decide the areas in which expert evidence is necessary; and
> (2) both the power and the duty:
>> (a) to limit expert evidence to given categories of expertise; and
>> (b) to specify the number of experts to be called.
>
> A further assumption behind both judgments was that the court should also be proactive: (a) in laying down a timetable for the filing of expert evidence; (b) in making arrangements for the dissemination of reports; and (c) in giving directions for experts to confer.'

In practice, the need to have the court's permission to disclose information or documents to an expert, or (under FPR 2010, r 12.20[13]) to have the child examined or assessed, means that in proceedings relating to children the court

---

10   [1994] 2 FLR 291.
11   [1994] 1 FLR 749.
12   [1994] 2 FLR 336.
13   SI 2010/2955.

strictly controls the number, fields of expertise and identity of the experts who may be first instructed and then called.[14]

THE CONTROLS

18.10   The instruction of expert witnesses is controlled by Part 25 of the Family Procedure Rules 2010 supplemented by Practice Direction 25A. The purpose of the Practice Direction is to:

(a)   provide the court with early information to determine whether expert evidence or assistance will help the court;

(b)   help the court and the parties to identify and narrow the issues in the case and encourage agreement where possible;

(c)   enable the court and the parties to obtain an expert opinion about a question that is not within the skill and experience of the court;

(d)   encourage the early identification of questions that need to be answered by an expert; and

(e)   encourage disclosure of full and frank information between the parties, the court and any expert instructed.[15]

18.11   The 2010 Rules make it clear that no party may call an expert or rely on an expert's report without the court's permission. Rule 12.74 goes further and provides that no party may instruct an expert for any purpose relating to proceedings without the court's permission. However r 12.75 and Practice Direction 25A, para 1.8 (see below) appear to allow a party to communicate information to a prospective expert without risking being in contempt of court to enable advice to be obtained as to whether or not the expert might be able to assist if instructed.[16]

18.12   Under the previous and, in effect, identical regime governing the instruction of experts, it was assumed in *Re J (Application for a Shadow Expert)*[17] that permission was required to instruct a 'shadow' expert, that is, someone who would not give expert evidence but to whom the evidence would be disclosed for the purpose of analysing expert evidence and to assist the instructing party's representatives to frame questions for cross-examination. Permission was refused. The legal basis for giving permission was dubious. Moreover, confidential information should not be disclosed to non-parties unless it was completely necessary and it would be wholly wrong for any opinion given by the shadow expert to be withheld from the court and the other

---

14   PD 25A, para 1.7.
15   PD 25A, para 1.3.
16   And see also ibid, para 1.8.
17   [2008] 1 FLR 1501.

parties. In addition allowing a shadow expert to formulate questions would risk imputing an unwarranted status to the questions. Whether or not the same approach would be adopted if the party seeking permission were unrepresented remains to be considered.[18]

OBTAINING PERMISSION FOR AN EXPERT

18.13 Any application for permission to instruct an expert or to use expert evidence should be raised with the court – and, where appropriate, with the other parties – as soon as possible. This will normally mean by or at the First Hearing Dispute Resolution Appointment.[19]

18.14 Before permission is obtained from the court to instruct an expert in proceedings relating to children, it will be necessary for the party seeking permission to make enquiries of the expert in order to provide the court with information to enable it to decide whether to give permission. In practice, enquiries may need to be made of more than one expert for this purpose. This will in turn require each expert to be given sufficient information about the case to decide whether or not he or she is in a position to accept instructions. Such preliminary enquiries, and the disclosure of information about the case which is a necessary part of such enquiries, will not require the court's permission and will not amount to a contempt of court.[20]

18.15 The court will need the following information:

- the category of expert evidence sought to be adduced;

- the name of the expert;

- his availability for reporting, meeting with other experts and attendance at court;

- the relevance of the expert evidence to the issues in the case;

- whether the evidence can properly be obtained by both parties jointly instructing one expert (see **18.28**);

- whether expert evidence may properly be adduced by one party only (eg the guardian);

- the fee to be charged including the hourly rate and the estimated number of hours required to read the papers, carry out any interviews and assessments and to prepare the report as well as the fee for attending court.

---

[18] 'Shadow experts' in civil proceedings has not found favour.
[19] PD 25A, para 1.11.
[20] Ibid, para 1.8.

18.16   If permission is granted it will be in relation only to the expert named or the field identified.[21] The court may limit the amount of a party's expert's fees and expenses that may be recovered from any other party.[22]

WHEN IS EXPERT EVIDENCE APPROPRIATE?

18.17   FPR 2010, r 25.1 states that expert evidence will be restricted to that which is reasonably required to resolve the proceedings.

18.18   The evidence must, first, be relevant to an issue which the court has to decide. Secondly, it must be a necessary or desirable tool to enable the judge to decide the issue. Thirdly, the expense of obtaining the evidence and the delay to the hearing which may be caused by the evidence being obtained must be proportionate to the benefit to the child of the evidence being available.

18.19   To adopt the words of Lord Upjohn in *J and Another v C and Others*,[23] 'quite general evidence' on the dangers of taking this or that course, for example, in relation to contact with a child who has no behavioural problems, is unlikely to be necessary or proportionate. On the other hand, evidence of the effect on a severely handicapped child of being moved from an established carer to someone who is inexperienced in caring for him will be both necessary and proportionate. Many cases will lie between the two extremes and no formula can be given which can provide the result in every case. Where a child is moderately disturbed, psychiatric evidence may be helpful if the judge is uncertain whether the order sought may increase that disturbance. When allegations are made of sexual abuse, the evidence of a paediatrician on the interpretation of physical signs will normally be necessary, as will psychiatric evidence on the validity of statements made by the child. Where an adult is alleged to abuse alcohol or drugs or is suffering from mental illness, the evidence of an adult psychiatrist may be useful.[24]

18.20   On the other hand, where the issue is a difficult one and lies within a recognised discipline, instructing an expert may be justified. In *Re T (Contact: Alienation: Permission to Appeal)*[25] the Court of Appeal directed the joint instruction of a child psychiatrist in a case where an 11-year-old child who had been enjoying regular staying contact with his father, expressed a very strong disinclination to see him after an incident in which the maternal uncle was alleged to have assaulted the father.

---

21   FPR 2010, r 25.4(3).
22   Ibid, r 25.4(4).
23   [1970] AC 668.
24   But not always. See *Re B (Children) (Expert Evidence)* [2005] All ER (D) 244 (March) and **17.18**. For a discussion of expert evidence relating to the relationship between a parent and child, see Tyler 'The observation of contact in expert assessments of parenting capacity: Is your client at a disadvantage?' [2011] Fam Law 719.
25   [2002] EWCA Civ 1736, [2003] 1 FLR 531, per Thorpe LJ at para [27].

'The nature of the issue is in many respects more suitable for investigation by a mental health expert than by a judge. An expert is not confined by the walls of the court. He can visit the home and talk directly to [the child] and the relevant adults in whatever circumstances he thinks fit. He has the qualifications and the experience to perceive the underlying realities to which even the adults themselves may be blind.'

18.21 However, in *Re B (children) (expert evidence)*[26] the Court of Appeal did not criticise a judge for refusing to allow the father to instruct an expert in alcoholism when he was applying for residence against the mother's admitted past alcoholism and evidence from her general practitioner showed continued stability and abstinence. 'Expert evidence had been commissioned too readily in matters such as the instant case and the judge had been right to have regard to the necessity and cost of such instruction.'

18.22 Psychometric testing does not ordinarily have a place in cases where the issue is a parent's parenting skills and cannot be used to resolve such issues unless validated by other evidence. Nor should it be used to assess credibility, which is the judge's role. If a judge is exceptionally minded to rely on the results of personality tests, he has to assess their validity, not only for the purpose of the case but also generally.[27]

18.23 An example of too many unnecessary experts being instructed is provided by *Re CB and JB (Care Proceedings: Guidelines)*.[28] A child was the subject of two shaking episodes and the only factual issue was which parent was responsible. In care proceedings, evidence was filed from 13 expert witnesses – three consultant paediatricians, a professor of paediatric radiology, a paediatric neurosurgeon, a consultant paediatric neurologist, a consultant ophthalmic surgeon, two consultant clinical psychologists, a consultant forensic psychiatrist, a consultant forensic psychologist, a chartered psychologist and a consultant child and adolescent psychiatrist. At trial, Wall J excluded the evidence of all psychologists and psychiatrists bar two:

'I was not willing to admit a blanket volume of psychiatric and psychological evidence going to propensity and psychological methodology in a case which seemed to me to turn exclusively on a simple issue of fact.'

Having heard the evidence of the two remaining psychologists, the judge found that:

'All the remaining psychiatric and psychological evidence [with the exception of a small matter] was irrelevant and leave to obtain it should not have been granted.'

---

26 [2005] All ER (D) 244 (Mar).
27 *Re S (Care: Parenting Skills: Personality Tests)* [2004] EWCA Civ 1029, [2005] 2 FLR 658. See also Westmacott 'Psychiatric and psychological reports: how well do family courts use them?' [2011] Fam Law 81.
28 [1998] 2 FLR 211.

The relevant issue

18.24   Care has to be taken to define the relevant issue with a reasonable degree of precision. Evidence of propensity or a psychiatric assessment of one of the parties is unlikely to be of any assistance in resolving a purely factual issue.[29] A general feeling that 'this is a difficult case and the court will need help' is likely to result in merely general advice, especially if the letter of instruction is equally vague.

18.25   Advice is often sought on the issue of the risk posed by a party. Advocates should remember that advice can be given on mitigating factors and warning signs:

> 'The clinician may be asked the question "Will [this person] be violent in the future?" From a scientific perspective this question is impossible to answer because it is based on an unscientific assumption about dangerousness, namely that it is a stable and consistent quality existing within the individual. The scientific translation of this question might be something like: "What are the psychological, social and biological factors bearing on [his] violent behaviour and what are the implications for future violence and the potential for change?"'[30]

18.26   Risk assessment involves asking the following questions:

- What harmful outcome is potentially present in this situation?

- What is the probability of this outcome coming about?

- What risks are probable in this situation in the short, medium and long term?

- What are the factors that could increase or decrease the risk that is probable?

- What measures are available whose deployment could mitigate the risks that are probable?[31]

18.27   As noted in *Re M (Care Disclosure to Police)*[32] increasingly, the same experts are being used in both family and criminal proceedings.

---

[29]   *Re CB and JB (Care Proceedings: Guidelines)* [1998] 2 FLR 211.

[30]   Pollock and Webster 'The clinical assessment of dangerousness' in Bluglass and Bowden (eds) *Principles and Practice of Forensic Psychiatry* (1990).

[31]   Mahendra 'Psychiatric risk assessment in family and child law' [2008] Fam Law 569. See also Mahendra 'Risk assessments: lessons from business for child protection' [2009] Fam Law 619.

[32]   [2008] 2 FLR 390, per Baron J at [14]. The judge recommended that very clear guidelines should be produced by the relevant Royal Colleges. However this does not appear to have been done. The current guidance to doctors on giving evidence is *Medical Expert Witnesses: Guidance from the Academy of Medical Royal Colleges* (2005) www.aomrc.org.uk

As a matter of practicality, this may be a necessity. But experts 'wearing two hats' have to be clear about the boundaries and limits of their role. As a counsel of perfection, it would be preferable if different professionals were used, but in the real world, that may not be possible. For example, when it is alleged that a father seeking contact drinks too much, it is unsatisfactory for an adult psychiatrist to be asked merely whether it is in the child's best interest to have contact. Relevant issues will include the likelihood of the father's attending contact in a state which would upset the child or place its safety at risk, of abusing the mother and of failing to maintain a regular pattern of contact. Relevant questions will include:

- How much control can and does the father exercise over his drinking?

- What steps can he take to increase his control?

- How strong is his motivation?

- Within what timescale can he be expected to attain such control as would make it unlikely that he would be unfit to have contact?

- What factors will tend to diminish his control or moderate his drinking?

- How can his current state be monitored both before and at the start of contact?[33]

SINGLE JOINT EXPERT

18.28 In his report *Access to Justice: Final Report to the Lord Chancellor on the Civil Justice System in England and Wales*[34] Lord Woolf stated that:

> 'The traditional English way of deciding contentious expert issues is for a judge to decide between two contrary views. This is not the best way of achieving a just result. There might be some large, complex and strongly contested cases where the full adversarial system would be the best way of producing a just result, particularly where there are several tenable schools of thought or where the boundaries of knowledge are being extended.'

However where this was not the case, as a general principle, an expert appointed jointly by the parties should be used. As a result of the 'Woolf reforms', Part 38.5 of the Civil Procedure Rules 1998 allowed the court to direct the use of single joint experts (SJEs'). By this time there was a similar trend in family cases. In *Re B (Sexual Abuse: Expert's Report)*,[35] a father in a private law matter appealed against an order, refusing to allow the joint

---

33 See also *Richmond CBC v B, W, B and CB* [2010] EWHC 2903 (Fam), [2011] 1 FLR 1345 for a discussion on the problems with hairstrand testing.

34 (Stationery Office, 1996) ch 13.

35 [2000] 1 FLR 871, per Thorpe LJ at 873.

instruction of an impartial psychiatrist but allowing evidence by a doctor previously instructed solely by the mother. The Court of Appeal allowed the appeal, holding that it was important that any instructions to a forensic expert are impartial and, wherever possible, are joint and agreed with the other side:

> 'A unilateral appeal to an expert for a partial report is something which should have disappeared from the litigation scene many years ago.'

FPR 2010, r 25.7 provides that where two or more parties wish to submit expert evidence on a particular issue, the court may direct that the evidence on that issue is to be given by an SJE. If the parties who wish to submit the evidence cannot agree who should be the SJE, the court may select the expert from a list prepared or identified by the parties or direct that the expert be selected in such other manner as the court may direct.

18.29   Where the court gives a direction for an SJE to be used, the instructions have to be contained in a jointly agreed letter unless the court directs otherwise. In default of agreement the instructions may be determined by the court on the written request of any relevant party copied to the other relevant parties. However the court can permit the parties to give separate instructions to an SJE in which case each instructing party must, when giving instructions to the expert, at the same time send a copy of the instructions to the other relevant parties.[36]

18.30   The court may give directions about the payment of the expert's fees and expenses and any inspection, examination or assessments which the expert wishes to carry out. It may, before an expert is instructed, limit the amount that can be paid by way of fees and expenses to the expert. Unless the court directs otherwise, the relevant parties are jointly and severally liable for the payment of the expert's fees and expenses.[37]

18.31   When a single joint expert has reported, one party may be dissatisfied with the report and seek permission to call additional evidence. There is no rule forbidding permission being given and the court will have to have regard to the Art 6 right to a fair trial. In the civil case of *Daniels v Walker*,[38] the Court of Appeal held that a defendant who disagreed with the opinion of a single joint expert ought to be allowed to instruct his own expert where the disagreement had serious consequences. A distinction was drawn between an expert being instructed to give advice and being allowed to give evidence. It would be for the trial judge to decide whether he should be allowed to call his expert once the results of the experts' meeting were known. Before the court gives permission for a further joint expert to be instructed it will consider whether the party should first put questions to the expert (see **18.42**).

---

[36]   FPR 2010, r 28.8(3).
[37]   Ibid, r 25.8(4)–(6).
[38]   [2000] 1 WLR 1382.

CONTROVERSIAL OR DISPUTED EXPERT EVIDENCE

18.32 In a case where there is a conflict between experts the court has to address and, where possible, resolve that conflict insofar as it is relevant to the issues before the court. Provided proper reasons are given, it is entitled to prefer the opinion of one expert against the other.[39]

18.33 Normally, the experts will apply generally accepted knowledge to the facts of a particular case, but occasionally the expert will base his opinion on a theory which is not generally accepted by his peers. One example of this was the theory of 'temporary brittle bone disease' which, expressed crudely, argued that unexplained fractures in children could be explained by the child suffering from osteogenesis imperfecta; the fact that no more fractures were suffered when the child was removed from his usual carer was explained by the fact that the condition was temporary.[40] Such evidence causes problems even in the High Court and is particularly dangerous in lower courts which might uncritically accept the evidence. It is not the function of the court to become involved in medical controversy except in rare cases where such controversy is an issue in the case.[41] In *Re AB (Child Abuse: Expert Witnesses)*,[42] Wall J noted that, while 'general acceptance' is a factor to be considered when admitting or weighing the evidence, it cannot be an absolute test. He referred to two papers in the medical literature which urged that 'only after there has been [peer group] scrutiny followed by acceptance of the validity of the expert's evidence should evidence be presented in court'. While he agreed with the broad thrust of this assertion, he entered a caveat that there are sometimes extremely rare cases where there was genuine disagreement on a scientific issue when the judge has to assess the state of knowledge.

18.34 When approaching evidence of this nature judges have to remember that it is possible that later research may undermine the accepted wisdom of the present.

> '"Never say never" is a phrase which we have heard in many contexts from expert witnesses. That does not normally provide a basis for rejecting the expert evidence, or indeed for conjuring up fanciful doubts about the possible impact of later research.'[43]

Courts should continue to deal with medical evidence on the basis of generally recognised medical opinion and the reasoning that lies behind it while giving appropriate weight to any challenge to that opinion, the reasons for the challenge and, for example, new research.[44] An interesting example of expert

---

[39] *A County Council v K, D & L* [2005] EWHC 144 (Fam), [2005] 1 FLR 851, at para [55].

[40] Another is 'parental alienation syndrome' which is discussed in **Chapter 11**. An example is *R v Cannings* [2004] EWCA Crim 1, [2004] 1 All ER 725. A useful account of the dangers is Foster *Judging Science* (MIT Press, 1999).

[41] *The Handbook of Best Practice*, ch 5, para 61.

[42] [1995] 1 FLR 181.

[43] *R v Cannings* [2004] EWCA Crim 1, [2004] 1 All ER 725 per Judge LJ at para [178].

[44] *A County Council v K, D & L* [2005] EWHC 144 (Fam), [2005] 1 FLR 851, per Charles J at

evidence being rejected in favour of generally accepted medical wisdom is provided by *Re C (Welfare of Child: Immunisation)*[45] when Sumner J rejected evidence that the triple vaccine against measles, mumps and rubella (MMR) might cause side effects. The expert's evidence was rejected because she had not complied with the duty placed on experts and her reliance on published research had been partial and misleading. In contrast, the evidence of the other experts was based on 'learning and informed research and practical experience'.

18.35 The material available to the judge in civil proceedings is likely to be more extensive than that which would be admitted in criminal proceedings but, in both jurisdictions, the tribunal of fact needs to be on its guard against 'the over-dogmatic expert ... whose reputation or amour propre is at stake or the expert who has developed a scientific prejudice'.[46]

18.36 The dangers of such evidence may be lessened if the expert complies with his duty imposed by PD 25A, para 3 (see **18.39**). In *Re AB (Child Abuse: Expert Witnesses)*,[47] for example, Wall J rejected the evidence of an expert because

'... by failing to disclose the controversial nature of his research [the doctor] lacked objectivity and omitted factors which do not support his opinion'.

Where the basis of evidence is the subject of scientific controversy, the instruction of a single joint expert is unlikely to be appropriate.[48] The Family Justice Council has provided guidelines for the instruction of overseas experts.[49]

THE ORDER

18.37 As set out in *The Handbook of Best Practice*,[50] the court has a positive duty to enquire into the information provided by the party seeking permission. It should never make a generalised order for leave to disclose the papers to an expert.

The order should deal in particular with:

---

para [57]. See also *R v Henderson* [2010] EWCA Crim 1269, [2011] 1 FLR 547, at [6]–[7]. The medical profession cannot look to the court to resolve medical controversy independent from the issues in the particular case.

45   [2003] EWHC 1376 (Fam), [2003] 2 FLR 1054, upheld on appeal [2003] EWCA Civ 1148, [2003] 2 FLR 1095.

46   *Re U (Serious Injury: Standard of Proof); Re B* [2004] EWCA Civ 567, [2004] 2 FLR 263, per Butler-Sloss P at para [23].

47   [1995] 1 FLR 181.

48   Lord Woolf MR *Access to Justice: Final Report*, ch 13.

49   Guidelines for the Instruction of Medical Experts from Overseas in Family Cases (Family Justice Council, 2011).

50   Children Act Advisory Committee (Lord Chancellor's Department, 1997).

- the party who is to be responsible for drafting the letter of instruction and providing the documents to the expert;

- the issues identified by the court and the questions about which the expert is to give an opinion;

- the timetable within which the report is to be prepared, filed and served;

- the disclosure of the report to the parties and to any other expert;

- the organisation of, preparation for and conduct of an experts' discussion (see **18.44**);

- the preparation of a statement of agreement and disagreement by the experts following an experts' discussion;

- making available to the court at an early opportunity the expert reports in electronic form;

- the attendance of the expert at court to give oral evidence (alternatively, the expert giving his or her evidence in writing or remotely by video link), whether at or for the Final Hearing or another hearing.[51]

It is also good practice for the order to specify whether the expert has permission to examine or interview the child. A copy of the order should be sent to the expert with his letter of instruction.[52]

INSTRUCTING THE EXPERT

18.38 Practice Direction 28A provides guidelines.

Within 5 working days of the hearing the instructing party has to file and serve a letter of instruction to the expert, if appropriate, agreed with the other parties, which sets out:

- the context in which the expert's opinion is sought (including any ethnic, cultural, religious or linguistic contexts);

- the specific questions which the expert is required to answer, ensuring that they:

    - are within the ambit of the expert's area of expertise;
    - do not contain unnecessary or irrelevant detail;
    - are kept to a manageable number and are clear, focused and direct; and reflect what the expert has been requested to do by the court;

---

[51] PD 28, para 4.4.
[52] PD 25, para 4.5(c).

as well as a wide range of other information including a copy of the relevant parts of the Practice direction.

The Annex to PD 25A sets out suggested questions in letters of instruction to child mental health professionals or paediatricians and adult psychiatrists and applied psychologists.

The instructing solicitor is under a duty to ensure that an expert who is to give oral evidence is kept up to date with relevant developments in the case.[53] The advocate calling an expert is under a similar duty to ensure that the expert has seen all fresh relevant material and is aware of new developments before he is called. A breach of these duties renders the solicitor or advocate liable to a wasted costs order.[54]

THE EXPERT'S DUTIES

18.39 Experts have a duty to help the court on matters within their expertise which overrides any obligation to the person from whom experts have received instructions or by whom they are paid.[55]

18.40 Their specific duties include:

- assisting the court in accordance with the overriding objective (see **17.6**);

- providing advice to the court that conforms to the best practice of the expert's profession;

- providing an opinion that is independent of the party or parties instructing the expert;

- confining their opinion to matters material to the issues between the parties and in relation only to questions that are within the expert's expertise, skill and experience;

- where a question has been put which falls outside the expert's expertise, stating this at the earliest opportunity and to volunteer an opinion as to whether another expert is required to bring expertise not possessed by those already involved or, in the rare case, as to whether a second opinion is required on a key issue and, if possible, what questions should be asked of the second expert;

- in expressing an opinion, taking into consideration all of the material facts including any relevant factors arising from ethnic, cultural, religious or linguistic contexts at the time the opinion is expressed;

53　PD 25A, para 5.7.
54　*Re G, S and M (Wasted Costs)* [2000] 1 FLR 52.
55　FPR 2010, r 25.3.

- informing those instructing the expert without delay of any change in the opinion and of the reason for the change.[56]

THE REPORT

18.41 The report must be filed in accordance with the court's timetable[57] and comply with the requirements set out in Practice Direction 25A.[58]

It must:

- give details of the expert's qualifications and experience;

- include a statement identifying the document(s) containing the material instructions and the substance of any oral instructions and, as far as necessary to explain any opinions or conclusions expressed in the report, summarising the facts and instructions which are material to the conclusions and opinions expressed;

- state who carried out any test, examination or interview which the expert has used for the report and whether or not the test, examination or interview has been carried out under the expert's supervision;

- give details of the qualifications of any person who carried out the test, examination or interview;

- in expressing an opinion to the court:

    – take into consideration all of the material facts including any relevant factors arising from ethnic, cultural, religious or linguistic contexts at the time the opinion is expressed, identifying the facts, literature and any other material including research material that the expert has relied upon in forming a opinion;

    – describe their own professional risk assessment process and process of differential diagnosis, highlighting factual assumptions, deductions from the factual assumptions, and any unusual, contradictory or inconsistent features of the case;

    – indicate whether any proposition in the report is an hypothesis (in particular a controversial hypothesis), or an opinion deduced in accordance with peer reviewed and tested technique, research and experience accepted as a consensus in the scientific community;

    – indicate whether the opinion is provisional (or qualified, as the case may be), stating the qualification and the reason for it, and identifying what further information is required to give an opinion without qualification;

---

[56] PD 25A, para 3.2.
[57] Ibid, para 3.3.
[58] FPR 2010, r 25.10.

- where there is a range of opinion on any question to be answered by the expert:

    - summarise the range of opinion;
    - identify and explain, within the range of opinions, any 'unknown cause' whether arising from the facts of the case (for example, because there is too little information to form a scientific opinion) or from limited experience or lack of research, peer review or support in the relevant field of expertise;
    - give reasons for any opinion expressed. The use of a balance sheet approach to the factors that support or undermine an opinion can be of great assistance to the court;
    - contain a summary of the expert's conclusions and opinions;

- contain a statement that the expert:

    - has no conflict of interest of any kind, other than any conflict disclosed in his or her report;
    - does not consider that any interest disclosed affects his or her suitability as an expert witness on any issue on which he or she has given evidence;
    - will advise the instructing party if, between the date of the expert's report and the final hearing, there is any change in circumstances which affects the expert's answers;
    - understands their duty to the court and has complied with that duty; and
    - is aware of the requirements of Part 25 and PD 25A;

- be verified by a statement of truth in the following form:

    'I confirm that I have made clear which facts and matters referred to in this report are within my own knowledge and which are not. Those that are within my own knowledge I confirm to be true. The opinions I have expressed represent my true and complete professional opinions on the matters to which they refer.'

QUESTIONS TO THE EXPERT

18.42 A party may put proportionate written questions to an expert only to clarify his report. They must be put not later than 10 days after receipt of the report or according to the court's timetable.[59] They must be sent to the other parties at the same time.[60] The answers, which will be treated as part of the report,[61] have to be answered according to the timetable fixed by the court.[62] If

---

[59]   FPR 2010, r 25.6.
[60]   PD 25A, para 6.1.
[61]   FPR 2010, r 25.6(3).
[62]   PD 25A, para 6.1,

the questions are not answered the court may refuse to allow the instructing party to rely on the report and/or refuse to allow the instructing party to recover the cost of instructing any other party. These two sanctions are likely to have little effect in children's cases, first because the child's interests may require the report to be admitted and also because orders for costs are rare (see **Chapter 24**). Directing the expert to answer the questions and, if necessary backing it with a penal notice is more likely to bring results.

18.43 An expert who refused at trial to comment on another expert's opinion was criticised by the Court of Appeal in *Re W (Care: Threshold Criteria)*.

> 'We find it both regrettable and surprising that JS was not prepared to assist the judge by commenting on what Miss R had observed. The basic function of an expert witness is to advise the court on matters which are within the expertise of the witness and outwith the expertise of the judge. The judge has to make findings of fact, and to draw inferences from the facts found. The task of experts is to assist judges in that process, not by telling them what the facts are or should be, but by giving them the benefit of expert opinion on questions within the area of the experts' expertise. This is, we think, elementary. JS's refusal to comment on Miss R's observations (whether they were accurate or inaccurate) has, we think two consequences. It not only put the judge in an extremely difficult position by depriving him of important expert evidence on a critical part of the case ... it also strikes us as a sufficient derogation from the basic duty owed by an expert witness to the court to cast doubt on the objectivity and soundness of JS's evidence.'[63]

DISCUSSIONS BETWEEN EXPERTS

18.44 The court may, at any stage, direct a discussion between experts for the purpose of requiring the experts to identify and discuss the expert issues in the proceedings and where possible, reach an agreed opinion on those issues. The court may specify the issues which the experts must discuss and may direct that following the discussion the experts must prepare a statement for the court setting out those issues on which they agree and disagree, with a summary of their reasons for disagreeing.[64] Practice Direction 25A, para 6.3 contains detailed guidance on the arrangement and conduct of the meetings.

18.45 In civil proceedings, experts' meetings can raise concerns that one expert, possibly less experienced or distinguished than the other, may too readily make concessions.[65] Although still a possibility this is less likely to be a significant problem in children's cases because the meeting will be chaired by the child's solicitor or guardian if there is one and because parties are less likely to be restricted in challenging their experts' concessions and are unable to settle cases without the consent of the court.

---

[63]   [2007] EWCA Civ 102, [2007] 2 FLR 98, per Wall LJ at [46].
[64]   FPR 2010, r 25.12.
[65]   See, for example, *Hubbard v Lambeth Southwark and Lewisham Health Authority* [2001] EWCA Civ 1455 and *Jones v Kaney* [2011] UKSC 13, [2011] 2 FLR 312.

THE EXPERTS AT TRIAL

18.46 Solicitors and advocates must consider the manner in which the evidence is to be given and additional information which needs to be given to the experts at an early stage and must keep this under review. Where there are two or more experts, their discussing their reports will often result in a limiting of issues and even agreement. Where there are two experts, an experts' meeting should be timetabled so that a schedule of agreed and unresolved issues can be prepared.

18.47 When the same conclusion is reached by the experts and the evidence points to only one possible result, the solicitor for the party adversely affected must draw the matter to the attention of the LSC.[66] Medical experts should not be required to give oral evidence unless their attendance is absolutely necessary. Advocates are under an ongoing duty to keep this necessity under review.[67] Where it becomes clear that an expert's report is uncontentious and that he will not be required to give oral evidence, he must be notified at the earliest opportunity. Whenever attendance is necessary, the court should always try to interpose the evidence at a given time. If possible experts should be timetabled together so that each can listen to the evidence of the other and comment on it.[68]

THE COURT AND THE EXPERT

18.48 At any stage in the proceedings an expert witness may seek directions of the court. The expert must, unless the court directs otherwise, provide a copy of the request to the instructing party at least 7 days in advance and to all other parties at least 4 days in advance.[69]

18.49 The court should not receive information 'in confidence' from experts, nor can experts receive such information from the parties. All relevant information must normally be shared with the other parties and experts must be prepared for everything they did and said to be the subject of challenge.[70]

18.50 The court will be bound by the uncontroverted evidence of an expert on a matter solely within the expert's expertise if the judge accepts the evidence as being reliable. For example, the judge cannot find that a child has not suffered a fracture in the face of uncontradicted evidence from a reliable doctor that he had. In many areas, however, the evidence will be persuasive but not binding. In such cases the court will adopt an approach similar to the one adopted to Cafcass reports. Provided the court takes into account the views of the expert, it is not bound to follow his recommendations. The judge has to have regard to

---

[66]   *Re N (Contested Care Application)* [1994] 2 FLR 992.
[67]   *Merton London Borough Council v K; Re K (Care: Representation: Public Funding)* [2005] EWHC 167 (Fam), [2005] 2 FLR 422, at [81].
[68]   *Handbook of Best Practice.*
[69]   FPR 2010, r 25.13.
[70]   *A County Council v SB, MA and AA* [2010] EWHC 2528 (Fam), [2011] 1 FLR 651.

the relevance of cach piece of evidence in relation to the other evidence and exercise an overview of the totality of the evidence.[71] For example, a judge is entitled to prefer the empirical or factual evidence before him to a prognosis derived from a psychological profile.[72] The judge should, however, indicate in his judgment or reasons, preferably expressly, the reasons for not following the recommendations. The recommendations should be carefully explored in cross-examination.[73] Where there are clear-cut recommendations and warnings of risk in reports, the judge should not depart from them without first hearing evidence from the expert.[74] This is not to say that the court should never depart from the recommendations without hearing from the expert, especially where neither party has requested his attendance.[75] However, it is not open to the judge to reject expert evidence about a parent's ability or lack of it solely on the basis of his impression of that parent in the witness box.[76]

Examples

Re B (Care: Expert Witnesses)[77]

18.51 A child of 3 months suffered serious injuries when in the care of her father. In care proceedings, the trial judge found that the father was responsible for his daughter's injuries but that, contrary to the evidence of a jointly instructed consultant paediatrician, the mother was capable of meeting her needs. The Court of Appeal upheld the decision of the trial judge. The findings were not against the weight of the evidence as a whole and the judge had given proper reasons for departing from the doctor's recommendations and those of the guardian ad litem:

'Another success of the Children Act has been the training, including and especially the training in related disciplines, which all judges receive. By their special allocation to this work they acquire a body of knowledge which, strictly speaking, cannot be substituted for the evidence received, but which can be deployed to spot any weakness in the expert evidence. The expert advises, but the judge decides. The judge decides on the evidence. If there is nothing before the court, no facts or no circumstances shown which throw doubt on the expert evidence, then, if that is all with which the court is left, the court must accept it. There is, however, no rule that a judge suspends judicial belief simply because the evidence is given by an expert.'[78]

Butler-Sloss LJ added:[79]

---

71 *Re T (Abuse: Standard of Proof)* [2004] EWCA Civ 558, [2004] 2 FLR 838, at [33].
72 *Re D (Care Order: Evidence)* [2010] EWCA Civ 1000, [2011] 1 FLR 447.
73 *Re P (Custody of Children: Split Custody Order)* [1991] 1 FLR 337. *Re M-W (Care Proceedings: Expert Evidence)* [2010] EWCA Civ 12.
74 *Re CB (Access: Attendance of Court Welfare Officer)* [1995] 1 FLR 622.
75 *Re L (Residence: Justices' Reasons)* [1995] 2 FLR 445.
76 *Re M (Residence)* [2002] 2 FLR 1059.
77 [1996] 1 FLR 667.
78 Ibid, per Ward LJ at 670.
79 Ibid, at 674.

'It is, however, necessary for a judge to give reasons for disagreeing with experts' conclusions or recommendations ... A judge cannot substitute his views for that of experts without some evidence to support what it is that he concludes.'

Re B (Non-Accidental Injury: Compelling Medical Evidence)[80]

18.52 A 10-month-old child, K, in the care of his mother and her partner, suffered a series of 94 injuries which led to his death. In subsequent care proceedings in respect of the mother's older child, expert medical evidence was given to the effect that no child subjected to injuries of the kind suffered by K could have presented as other than a child in desperate need of medical attention. The trial judge found that the injuries were caused by the mother's partner and that she had not failed to protect the child. The Court of Appeal allowed an appeal against the findings in respect of the mother:

'The expert evidence as to how seriously injured children react and present ... [cannot] simply be dismissed on the basis that it was speculation.

As Butler-Sloss said in *Re B (Split Hearings: Jurisdiction)*:[81] "The credibility or otherwise of the lay witnesses on the facts of this case, in my view, cannot stand so high as to make the evidence of the two consultant radiologists of no effect."'[82]

SANCTIONS

18.53 Although experts' overriding duty is owed to the court, following the decision of the Supreme Court in *Jones v Kaney*[83] they are no longer immune from sanctions for breaches of that and their other duties. Despite concern by Lord Hope and Baroness Hale of Richmond that abolishing the previous immunity could reduce the number of experts willing to give evidence[84] and make them vulnerable to 'harassing litigation at the instance of an aggressive client'[85] the majority of the Court agreed with Lord Phillips.

'The expert witness has this in common with the advocate. Each undertakes a duty to provide services to the client. In each case those services include a paramount duty to the court and the public, which may require the advocate or the witness to act in a way which does not advance the client's case. The advocate must disclose to the court authorities that are unfavourable to his client. The expert witness must give his evidence honestly, even if this involves concessions that are contrary to his client's interests. The expert witness has far more in common with the advocate than he does with the witness of fact ... I conclude that no justification has been

---

80   [2002] 2 FLR 599.
81   [2000] 1 FLR 334, at 339.
82   [2002] 2 FLR 599, per Thorpe LJ at 605.
83   [2011] UKSC 13, [2011] 2 FLR 312. See Cooper *'Jones v Kaney*: A curse on family court experts?' [2011] Fam Law 642.
84   [2011] UKSC 13, [2011] 2 FLR 312, at [168] and [188].
85   Ibid, at [166] and [189].

shown for continuing to hold expert witnesses immune from suit in relation to the evidence they give in court or for the views they express in anticipation of court proceedings.'[86]

18.54 There are a number of sanctions which may be used.

Wasted costs orders

18.55 Like legal representatives expert witnesses may be ordered to pay costs wasted by reason of their improper, unreasonable or negligent act or omission.[87]

Action based on breach of contract or negligence

18.56 As Lord Phillips pointed out in *Jones v Kaney*,[88] where an expert witness is retained:

'... it is likely to be, as it was in the present case, on terms that the expert will perform the functions specified in the [Procedural Rules]. The expert agrees with his client that he will perform the duties that he owes to the court. Thus there is no conflict between the duty that the expert owes to his client and the duty that he owes to the court. Furthermore, a term is implied into the contract under section 13 of the Supply of Goods and Services Act 1982, that the expert will exercise reasonable skill and care in carrying out the contractual services.'

18.57 However, in any civil litigation the court will have to be vigilant in ensuring that the expert's overriding duty to the court is safeguarded and not eroded by any perceived duty to the client. Giving an opinion without ensuring that all the documents disclosed have been read or which cannot be supported by factual evidence or any respectable body of expertise is one matter; honestly changing one's opinion for good reason is another.

18.58 In some instances an aggrieved litigant will be seeking to sue an expert whom he did not instruct. The only basis of this could be negligence and not contract and the extent of an expert's duty to someone who had not instructed him is unclear. In *X v Bedfordshire CC*[89] the House of Lords held that professionals involved in deciding whether or not to institute proceedings to protect a child from abuse did not owe him a duty of care. However, in *D v East Berkshire Community NHS Trust*[90] which was not appealed, the Court of Appeal held that doctors and social workers did owe a duty of care to the child when conducting child protection investigations. In *Jones v Kaney*[91] Baroness Hale commented that:

---

[86]   [2011] UKSC 13, [2011] 2 FLR 312, at [50], [61].
[87]   Senior Courts Act 1981, s 51(6); *Philips v Symes (No 2)* [2004] EWHC 2330 (Ch), [2005] 1 WLR 2043 and *Jones v Kaney* [2003] EWCA Civ 1151, [2004] QB 558, at [44].
[88]   [2003] EWCA Civ 1151, [2004] QB 558.
[89]   [1995] 2 AC 633.
[90]   [2003] EWCA Civ 1151, [2004] QB 558.
[91]   [2003] EWCA Civ 1151, [2004] QB 558, at 186.

'To that extent, therefore, the view taken in *X v Bedfordshire* has been superseded by later authority ... There may, therefore, be a relatively clear dividing line between conducting the examinations and investigations, on the one hand, and preparing for and giving evidence, on the other.'

Disciplinary Proceedings

18.59 Both the court or aggrieved parties may report experts to their professional bodies on the grounds of unprofessional misconduct.[92]

18.60 Without requiring the permission of the court, the party or legal adviser may communicate information relating to proceedings to the General Medical Council for the purpose of a complaint.[93]

---

[92] The then President of the Family Division reported a doctor to the General Medical Council after he had three times been criticised in court ([1991] 1 FLR 291); [1995] 1 FLR 181: he was struck off the Medical Register. See also *General Medical Council v Meadow* [2006] EWCA Civ 1390, [2007] 1 FLR 1398.

[93] FPR 2010, r 8.78(1)(b), PD 14E.

Chapter 19

SECTION 7 REPORTS AND SECTION 37 REPORTS

INTRODUCTION

19.1 In most children cases, the evidence available to the courts is partisan, no matter how candid the parent giving it tries to be. Courts need reliable, objective information about the child and the circumstances of the family. They can obtain this by requesting agencies to provide reports on the child. These are:

- welfare (otherwise known as s 7) reports;

- reports following a direction for an investigation under s 37.

Section 7 reports

19.2 Welfare reports are produced either by a Children and Family Reporter employed by the Children and Family Advisory and Support Service (Cafcass) (see **19.4**) or by a social worker employed by a local authority or such other person as the local authority considers appropriate (a 'welfare officer'). The purpose of such reports is to 'report to the court on such matters relating to the welfare of the child as are required to be dealt with'.[1]

Section 37 reports

19.3 A s 37 order is a direction to the local authority to carry out an inquiry into the child's circumstances with a report being provided only if the authority decides not to apply for a care or supervision order. In practice, however, an authority will provide a report whether or not it decides to apply. The direction is given to the local authority in whose area the child is ordinarily resident or, where the child is not ordinarily resident in any area in England and Wales, the authority within whose area any circumstances arose in consequence of which the direction for a report is given.

The court can direct such an investigation only where it appears to the court that it may be appropriate for a care or supervision order to be made in respect of the child.

---

[1] CA 1989, s 7(1).

The authority must:

• undertake an investigation into the child's circumstances;

• consider whether it should:

  _ apply for a care or supervision order;
  _ provide any services or assistance for the child and his family; or
  _ take any other action in respect of the child;

If it decides not to apply for a care or supervision order, it must consider if it would be appropriate to review the case at some later date and, if it decides to do so, must fix a date for the review. If it decides not to apply for a care or supervision order, it must inform the court of:

• its reasons for deciding not to apply;

• the services and assistance it has provided or intends to provide; and

• any other action which it has taken or proposes to take.

The information must be given to the court before the end of the period of 8 weeks, beginning with the date of the direction for the investigation or by such other time as the court may direct.

Practice Direction 12B states that at the First Hearing Dispute Resolution Appointment, the Court must consider:

• Are there welfare issues or other specific considerations which should be addressed in a report by Cafcass or the local authority?

• Is there a need for an investigation under CA 1989, s 37?[2]

CAFCASS

19.4 Family courts have used social worker services to assist them in investigating what are now called 'private law' cases since the late nineteenth century. The initial role of 'court missionary' developed to that of the family court welfare officer who was part of the Probation Service and then, in 2001, to the family court adviser. During this period, the officers have been at the forefront of implementing policies designed to shore up 'failing families'.[3] In recent years, for a variety of reasons including a desire to replace court based resolution of disputes to one of assisted 'private ordering', most applications

---

2   PD 12B, para 5.4.
3   Cretney *Family Law in the Twentieth Century* (Oxford University Press, 2003) at pp 770–773; Doughty 'From court missionaries to conflict resolution: A century of court welfare' (2008) CFLQ 131.

being issued being resolved at early hearings rather than by way of trial, an increased demand placed on its officers in public law cases where they act as guardians and a lack of resources, the emphasis in private law has changed from an evidential enquiry to provide information upon which the court can base its decision to relying on Cafcass to remove as many cases as possible from the court system.[4]

19.5 The Children and Family Advisory and Support Service (Cafcass) came into existence on 1 April 2001. Its functions include safeguarding and promoting the welfare of children, giving advice to the court, providing for the representation of children in family proceedings and providing information, advice and support to children and their families.[5] Its aims were laudable[6] but it soon ran into difficulties.[7] In 2010 the House of Commons Public Accounts Committee[8] described it, in language which many with every day experience of the service might regard as exaggerated, as being 'not fit-for-purpose'. Many areas did not provide a timely service to the courts. Nevertheless judges remained satisfied with the quality of reports to the courts,[9] but caseloads carried by family court advisers have been increasing, which brings new risks to the quality of service provided to the courts and families.

19.6 In an attempt to relieve pressure on Cafcass, in 2009 the President of the Family Division issued temporary guidance on how the service should be used[10] and renewed it in a revised form in 2010. By July 2011 a review concluded that the Guidance had achieved its temporary aim and the President and the Chief Executive decided that it did not need to be reviewed.[11]

19.7 The history of these difficulties, which may recur, means that courts need to be persuaded that a child's welfare specifically requires a s 7 report before one is ordered and that the order should identify the issue(s) upon which the report is needed. To do otherwise delays a final hearing and increases the burden placed on local Cafcass offices.

---

4   (2008) CFLQ 131, at 153.
5   Criminal Justice and Court Service Act 2000, s 12.
6   See Fricker 'The new Children and Family Advisory Service' [2000] Fam Law 102.
7   Tross 'Cafcass present and future' [2004] Fam Law 731; 'Pressure on Cafcass' [2009] Fam Law 913.
8   Sixth Report *Cafcass's Response to Increased Demand for Its Services* (3 November 2010). Summarised in 'Cafcass and the Public Accounts Committee' [2011] Fam Law 4. See also *Operation of the Family Courts* (House of Commons Justice Committee 14 July 2011), ch 6.
9   See, for example, 'Cafcass reports: delay and quality' [2011] Fam Law 784.
10   *Practice Guidance: Interim Guidance to Assist CAFCASS 30 July 2009* [2009] 2 FLR 1407.
11   *Practice Guidance: Renewed Interim Guidance to Assist CAFCASS 1 April 2010* [2010] 2 FLR 725.

WHEN SHOULD A SECTION 7 REPORT BE ORDERED?

19.8 A report can be ordered only where there is a live issue to be resolved, for example, whether a child's residence should change.[12]

Practice Direction 12B states that before a report is ordered, the court should consider alternative ways of working with the parties such as are referred to in PD 12B, para 5.2. If a report is ordered in accordance with s 7, it should be directed specifically towards and limited to those issues. General requests should be avoided and the court should state in the order the specific factual and other issues that are to be addressed in a focused report.[13]

19.9 In all cases, the provision of welfare reports is helpful and in some cases it is essential.[14] However, a lack of resources and the delay which the preparation of a report will cause mean that the court usually has to balance the need for a report against the effect which delay may cause, not just in the instant case but in other cases.

19.10 A *Best Practice Note* was issued by the Children Act Advisory Committee in 1995.[15]

• A report may only be ordered pursuant to s 7 of the Children Act 1989 ie when a court 'considering any question with respect to a child under [the] Act "requires a report" on such matters relating to the welfare of that child as are required to be dealt with in the report'. A report may not be ordered for any other purpose.

• Before a report is ordered consideration should be given to the court's powers to refer parties to mediation (with the consent of the parties). This may be to a mediation service or the court welfare officer, depending on local arrangements. It is important that this should not be confused with a welfare report and that any court welfare officer who may have been involved in any privileged mediation proceedings should not be the officer who undertakes the preparation of a welfare report.

• The ordering of a welfare officer's report is a judicial act requiring inquiry into the circumstances of the child. A report should never be ordered when there is no live issue under the Children Act before the court; for example, a report must not be ordered when no formal proceedings have yet been instituted. Furthermore, save in exceptional circumstances, a report should not be ordered in response to a written request by the parties.

---

[12] *The Children Act Advisory Committee Handbook of Best Practice in Children Act Cases* (Lord Chancellor's Department, 1997), App A VI.

[13] PD 12B, para 5.4.

[14] *Re H (Minors) (Welfare Reports)* [1990] 2 FLR 172, per Balcombe LJ at 176.

[15] See *Handbook of Best Practice* (1997) op cit.

- When a welfare report is ordered the court should explain briefly to the parties what will be involved and should emphasise the need to co-operate with the welfare officer and specifically to keep any appointments made. In particular, when the principle of contact is in dispute the parties should be told that the welfare officer will probably wish to see the applicant parent alone with the child. It should also be emphasised that the report, when received, is a confidential document and must not be shown to anyone who is not a named party to the application.

- The order should specify the date by which the report should be filed and, if possible, indicate the date of the substantive hearing. The solicitors for the applicant should be handed a pro forma in a prescribed form and asked to complete details such as name, address and telephone number on the front of the form. The court should complete the rear of the pro forma which sets out the reasons for the report and the concern of the court; this should set out succinctly the issues on which the officer is being asked to report. This part of the form should specify any documents which are to be sent to the welfare officer. This form must be fully completed and attached to the court file before the court disposes of the case.

- An addendum report may be ordered e g for the purpose of testing an agreement between the parties or where there has been a substantial change in circumstances. However, an addendum report should not be ordered merely because of a delay or adjournment in the listing of the substantive hearing.

- The court will not order both a welfare report and s 37 report.

- It should be noted that court welfare officers do not normally travel outside the UK;[16] International Social Services are available to meet this need.[17]

- A court welfare officer will not attend a hearing unless specifically directed to do so by the court). When such a direction is given the court should ensure that the officer gives evidence as soon as possible after the case has opened (and in any event on the first day) and is released after that evidence has been completed.'

19.11 In deciding whether a report should be ordered, the following questions need to be considered:

- What are the issues which require a report and how important are they? If the parents agree that there should be contact, is the issue whether there

---

[16] See *Enquiries Abroad/Overseas Travel Policy* (Cafcass, 2006).
[17] See ibid, Appendix 1.

should be staying contact, the length or frequency of contact or the arrangements for the non-resident parent to meet the child at the start of contact?

- Are these issues likely to be resolved by mediation? If so, the court should consider whether a decision on ordering a report can be postponed until mediation has taken place.[18]

- Is the report likely to produce factual information which the court needs to resolve the issues? In disputed residence cases, cases where the resident parent objects to contact or cases where there are issues relating to violence, the answer may be 'yes'. In other cases, for example a dispute as to whether contact should last for 3 or 4 hours, the answer is likely to be 'probably not'.

- Does the court need professional advice? The answer to this will depend not only on the nature of the issues but also on the experience of the judge.

- What delay will the preparation of the report cause? How detrimental will this be?

- Is it appropriate to delay a decision on whether to order a report? For example, when a non-resident father seeks contact, including staying contact, with a young child where there is no pattern of regular contact, the court may take the view that visiting contact should first be established and the decision on whether a report on the issue of staying contact is needed be delayed to see whether a pattern of contact can be established. If it is, the parents may then agree how staying contact is to progress without the need for a report.

19.12 In March 2005 The President of the Family Division and the Chief Executive of Cafcass issued a memorandum to emphasise some key issues of the *Private Law Programme*.

'We should like to see ... more focussed reports from CAFCASS which get to the heart of the issues facing a particular child, and not text which duplicates information or assessments available to the court and parties in other ways. The CAFCASS practitioners' contribution is unique and we would wish to see an emphasis in reports on the key issues at stake, with professional analysis and judgment designed to assist the court reach the best decision. Judges should, where appropriate direct focussed reports, and should be clear about the precise points of information, analysis and judgment they are looking for. The need to produce long reports should be rare, and reserved for the most complex of situations. In particular, in private law cases where a s 7 report is directed, a report should generally be short and limited to the issue(s) identified in the court direction, unless unusually other more serious issues arise in the course of investigating the

---

18   *Handbook of Best Practice*, op cit.

family. In some cases where there is a return to court before the same judge, an oral report or very short email should often be sufficient.'

19.13 When more cases are resolved at an early stage, then fewer cases will need reports. It is reasonable to suppose that those cases which do not settle will be more complex and intractable requiring reports at least as detailed as those currently provided. While there have long been complaints of the delay in producing reports, there is no evidence that courts are receiving more information than they require. One study of families who had been the subject of s 7 reports, *Families in Conflict*[19] found that three-quarters of parents felt that the reporters should have more time to prepare the report and two-thirds did not believe that the amount of time available allowed the investigation to be thorough enough. More people, for example teachers and other family members, should be interviewed. Half the parents would have liked the reporters to have spent more time talking with the children. The House of Commons Constitutional Affairs Committee in 2005 received evidence which suggested that there are risks that if report writing were reduced there would be an impact on the ability of the court to obtain detailed evidence about the child's 'perspective in the dispute'.[20] Some way has to be found to ensure that the child's voice is heard effectively, especially when cases have to proceed to trial. At present the s 7 report is the only way this can be achieved in the majority of cases, a lack of resources not permitting guardians to be appointed in private law matters in other than exceptional cases.

When should a section 7 report be provided by Cafcass?

19.14 Practice Direction 12B states that when determining whether a request for a report should be directed to the relevant local authority or to Cafcass, the court should consider such information as Cafcass has provided about the extent and nature of the local authority's current or recent involvement with the subject of the application and the parties, and any relevant protocol between Cafcass and the Association of Directors of Children's Services.[21]

Reports can be expedited, but this will prejudice other cases and expedition should be ordered rarely and only after discussion between the judge and the Children and Family Reporter or local Cafcass manager.

19.15 Cafcass's *Safeguarding Framework*[22] states that there should be a priority allocation system for private law work following the First Hearing. The local service manager should keep all cases which are either unallocated or allocated to a duty worker, under regular review. Cases should receive particular priority for allocation based on current vulnerability. Where the

---

[19]   Hunt, Bretherton and Bream (2001) Nuffield Foundation (and see also *Families in Conflict* [2001] Fam Law 900).

[20]   *Family Justice: the operation of the family courts* (2005) HC 116–1, para 121.

[21]   PD 12B, para 5.4.

[22]   Working Together Update (2010), p 69.

issues are not sufficiently clear to enable this prioritisation to be undertaken, then clarification from the court should be sought.

High priority should be given in cases of:

- risk factors identified in the work to First Hearing, along with the need for more detailed assessment;

- child displaying disturbed behaviour;

- substantial contact suddenly stopped;

- recent change of residence – refusing to return child after contact;

- application to remove child from jurisdiction;

- one or both parents below the age of 18;

- parents living in the same household.

Medium priority should be given in cases of:

- allegations of unfit parenting (drugs/alcohol/mental health) but no current safeguarding concerns;

- extended family member application for residence;

- domestic violence allegations from the past but no current safeguarding concerns;

- child split between carers;

- application to remove child to another area.

Low priority should be given in cases of:

- extended family applications for contact;

- applications for parental responsibility;

- applications for variation in contact where there is ongoing contact;

- order for further work (e g addendum report) where the previous Cafcass report has identified no constructive role for Cafcass at this stage.

A s 7 report should not be ordered if a s 37 report is ordered.[23]

---

23   *Best Practice Note.*

When should a section 7 report by a local authority be ordered?

19.16   When deciding which type of s 7 report to order, courts should bear in mind that Children and Family Reporters are accustomed to the court process. Social workers may have more limited experience and frequently their role will be confined to fact-finding reports which do not involve making recommendations.[24]

19.17   If a Cafcass report can be ordered, there is often no point in ordering a report from a local authority unless it is currently investigating or assisting the family because there may be no social worker allocated to the family. If, however, the local authority is carrying out a child protection investigation under s 47 of CA 1989, a s 7 report is appropriate and should be ordered before a Cafcass report.[25] If the child is subject to a child protection plan, there should be a named key social worker responsible for coordinating the plan.

19.18   If the child is or has been the subject of a child protection investigation, a report on the investigation will be produced for the child protection conference and parents are entitled to receive a copy of the report and of the minutes of child protection conferences.[26] The parents can therefore be ordered to serve and file copies and these are likely to be available sooner than any s 7 report. If there is such an investigation, the court should ensure that the agencies who are involved, including the police, are told of the court's involvement and of any concern the court may have about the timetable of the investigation.

WHEN SHOULD A SECTION 37 INVESTIGATION BE ORDERED?

19.19   The court cannot direct a s 37 investigation unless it appears that a care or supervision order may be appropriate. A sense of proportion needs to be preserved and the criteria for making a care or supervision order must be borne in mind.[27] There is no point in ordering a s 37 report if it will not result in a local authority taking action.[28]

In private law proceedings, a direction should not be given as a device for enabling the court to appoint a litigation friend for the child.[29]

---

[24]   *Re W (Welfare Reports)* [1995] 2 FLR 142.

[25]   *Re A and B (Minors) (No 2)* [1995] 1 FLR 351.

[26]   *Working Together to Safeguard Children* (Department for Children, Schools and Families, 2010), para 5.112. See also *R v Cornwall County Council ex parte LH* [2000] 1 FLR 236.

[27]   *Re CE (Section 37 Direction)* [1995] 1 FLR 26; *Re L (Section 37 Direction)* [1999] 1 FLR 984. See also *Re F (Family Proceedings: Section 37 Investigations)* [2005] EWHC 2935 (Fam), [2006] 1 FLR 1122, per Sumner J at [137].

[28]   *Re R (Residence)* [2009] EWCA Civ 358, [2009] 2 FLR 819, per Wall J at [76]–[81].

[29]   'Best Practice Guidance on s 37(1) Directions', *Handbook of Best Practice in Children Act Cases*, Appendix A.

The purpose of a direction is to cause the local authority to consider whether a care or supervision order is appropriate. It is not to provide a general welfare report. If such a report is needed, a s 7 report should be ordered.[30]

If a s 37 direction is given, the court should not seek to fetter the local authority in the way it carries out its investigation, eg by asking the Official Solicitor or a guardian ad litem to monitor the investigation.[31]

Examples

Re H (A Minor) (Section 37 Direction)[32]

19.20 A lesbian couple applied for a residence order in respect of a baby who was not their own and there were concerns about their future ability to look after the baby. The court held that a s 37 investigation was appropriate.

Re L (Section 37 Direction)[33]

19.21 This was a contact dispute between a father and the grandmother and an allegation was made that the child was behaving in a disturbed way. The Court of Appeal held that a s 37 investigation should not have been directed. Thorpe LJ said:

'A sense of proportion needs to be preserved in all private law proceedings. Here there was very little in dispute save as to quantum and detail of contact ... This is not the sort of case which was anywhere near the threshold.'

Re F (Family Proceedings: Section 37 Investigation)[34]

19.22 A mother's contact with her two children aged 9 and 7 ceased because of their expressed hostility to her. The judge found that the father's attitude towards her, his refusal to allow the children to be seen and his complete subjugation to their views were all likely to cause them significant harm. A s 37 report was justified unless he agreed to allow a child psychiatrist to see the children.

---

[30] 'Best Practice Guidance on s 37(1) Directions', *Handbook of Best Practice in Children Act Cases*, Appendix A.

[31] *Re M (Official Solicitor's Role)* [1998] 2 FLR 815.

[32] [1993] 2 FLR 541.

[33] [1999] 1 FLR 984.

[34] [2005] EWHC 2935 (Fam).

PROCEDURE

Section 37 directions

19.23 The order must contain the date by which the report must be filed. This must be 8 weeks, unless the court directs otherwise. The date for the next hearing must be fixed.

If the court is considering making or has made an interim care order under s 41, the court has to appoint a guardian ad litem unless satisfied that it is not necessary to do so in order to safeguard the child's interests.[35]

The court should consider which parts of the documentary evidence should be served on the local authority.

It is important that the authority should be told about the order as quickly as possible. An immediate phone call should be confirmed in writing. A copy of the order must be served as soon as is practicable.

The reporter will not attend the hearing unless ordered to do so. The court will therefore consider whether to give such a direction after the report is filed.[36]

Making the order does not make the local authority a party to the proceedings. The reporter will not therefore be legally represented.

Practice Direction 12B states that:

> 'A copy of the Order requesting the report and any relevant court documents are to be sent to Cafcass or, in the case of the Local Authority, to the Legal Adviser to the Director of the Local Authority Children's Services and, where known, to the allocated social worker by the court forthwith.'[37]

PREPARING THE SECTION 7 OR 37 REPORT

19.24 It is the duty of the officer preparing the report to comply with any request for a report under this rule and to provide the court with such other assistance as it may require. The court officer will notify the officer of a direction given at a hearing at which the officer was not present but the welfare report was considered.[38]

Under Practice Direction 16A the officer must make such investigations as may be necessary to perform the officer's powers and duties and must, in particular:

---

[35] CA 1989, s 41(1).
[36] *Re CE (Section 37 Direction)* [1995] 1 FLR 26.
[37] PD 12B, para 5.4.
[38] Family Procedure Rules 2010 (SI 2010/2955), r 16.33.

- contact or seek to interview such persons as appear appropriate or as the court directs; and

- obtain such professional assistance as is available which the children and family reporter thinks appropriate or which the court directs be obtained;

- notify the child of such contents of the report (if any) as the officer considers appropriate to the age and understanding of the child, including any reference to the child's own views on the application and the recommendation; and

- if the child is notified of any contents of the report, explain them to the child in a manner appropriate to the child's age and understanding;

- attend hearings as directed by the court;

- advise the court of the child's wishes and feelings;

- advise the court if the officer considers that the joining of a person as a party to the proceedings would be likely to safeguard the interests of the child;

- consider whether it is in the best interests of the child for the child to be made a party to the proceedings, and if so, notify the court of that opinion together with the reasons for that opinion; and

- where the court has directed that a written report be made he must file the report, serve a copy on the other parties and on any children's guardian in accordance with the timetable set by the court.[39]

19.25 CAFCASS's *Safeguarding Framework*[40] provides useful guidance on matters which should be considered when preparing a report.

In addition, guidance on child protection is provided by *Working Together to Safeguard Children*[41] and on assessing the needs of children in *Framework for the Assessment of Children in Need and their Families*.[42] Although the latter guide is concerned with assessing children in need (and of course, most children who are the subjects of s 7 Cafcass reports are not 'children in need') it contains a valuable discussion on the assessment process which is applicable to all reports:

'The approach must be child centred. This means that the child is kept in focus throughout the assessment and that account is always taken of the child's perspective. In complex situations where much is happening, attention can be

---

[39] PD 16A, para 9.
[40] Op cit.
[41] (Department for Education, 2010).
[42] (Department of Health, 1999).

diverted from the child to other issues which the family may be facing, such as a high level of conflict between adult family members or depression being experienced by the mother or acute housing problems ... This can result in the child becoming lost during assessment and the impact of the family and environmental circumstances on the child not being clearly identified and understood.'[43]

19.26 It is important that the assessment is based on a full understanding of what is happening to the child in the context of the family and the wider community. Positive as well as negative influences must be identified:

'Nothing can be assumed: the facts must be sought, the meaning attached to them explored and weighed up with the family. Sometimes assessments have been largely in terms of ... difficulties. What is working well or what may be acting as positive factors for the child and family may be overlooked. For example, a single mother, in crisis over health, financial and housing problems may still be managing to get her child up in time in the mornings, washed, dressed, breakfasted and off to school each day. An older child living in a family periodically disrupted by domestic violence, may be provided with welcome respite care on a regular basis by a grandmother living locally. Working with a child or family's strengths may be an important part of a plan to resolve difficulties.'[44]

If a Children and Family Reporter has previously been involved in mediation with the parents, a different reporter should provide the report in order to preserve any confidences.

19.27 The Reporter needs to consider whether to see the parties together. Doing so can promote parental responsibility and can assist them to reach agreements but they should be informed in writing in plain terms that they are free to choose whether to attend a joint meeting or be seen separately and that their choice will not be to the detriment of their case. They should be advised to take legal advice if they are unsure of their position. The Reporter must exercise particular care in cases in which violence has been alleged and a joint interview should not be arranged if it can be reasonably be foreseen that the safety or well-being of either party must be jeopardised.

19.28 A Children and Family Reporter will usually see the child and the non-resident parent together as well as the child separately. If a child is not seen, the reasons for this should be reported to the court. The Reporter should make it clear to children that their views will be reported to the court and that their parents will be made aware of them. However, children should never be forced to express a view, nor should they be made to feel that they are taking responsibility for decisions about them which will properly belong with adults.

19.29 Difficult issues arise when a Children and Family Reporter discovers information during the course of enquiries which indicates that a child may

---

[43] Ibid, para 1.31.
[44] *Framework for the Assessment of Children and their Families* (Department of Health, 1999), at para. 1.44.

have been abused or is at risk of being abused. The *Safeguarding Framework* states that the Reporter should report her concern to social services in accordance with local child protection procedures. The court should also be informed and the Reporter should suspend the enquiries pending further directions from the court.[45]

19.30 The Reporter should keep the parties informed of his thinking so that the final report does not come as a surprise.

Cafcass will normally send a copy of the report directly to the parties' legal advisers (or the parties if they are representing themselves). Local authorities will send reports to the court, which will forward copies to the parties.

Child protection

19.31 Sometimes the Reporter finds evidence that the child may have suffered abuse and this gives rise to sensitive issues relating to the boundaries between a court's control of proceedings and the responsibility of child care professionals to report concerns to the relevant social services department. Cafcass' *Safeguarding Framework*[46] states that its practitioners should make referrals to:

- Children's Services if a child appears to be suffering or likely to suffer significant harm (type A);

- Children's Services if a child appears to be in need (ie whose health and development will be significantly impaired without the provision of services (type B);

- any other agency in order to promote the welfare of a child, usually through use of the Common Assessment Framework (type C).

It provides detailed guidance on the process to be followed.

19.32 In *Re M (A Child) (Children and Family Reporter: Disclosure)*,[47] Thorpe LJ expressed the view that this was well written but that the final phrase went too far. The decision to suspend the enquiry must be a decision of the judge and not the Children and Family Reporter. He went on to give guidance on whether Children and Family Reporters needed the permission of the court before disclosing information to social services or the police.

19.33 The relationship between the Children and Family Reporter and the judge is collaborative. Each has distinct functions and responsibilities in the discharge of which they can act independently. Where, in the course of

---

45 *Safeguarding Framework*, para 4.3; *Re M (A Child) (Children and Family Reporter: Disclosure)* [2002] 4 All ER 401.
46 Op cit, Section B, para 4.2.
47 [2002] EWCA Civ 1199, [2002] 2 FLR 893.

preparing a report in private law proceedings, a Children and Family Reporter becomes aware that a child may have been abused, the following matters should be considered:

- Is this:

  - a discovery or direct report; or
  - is the Children and Family Reporter listening to an account of someone's discovery or a second-hand report?

- If the latter:

  - has the information been relayed to social services or the police already?
  - is there a history or pattern of past complaints?
  - how plausible is the report?
  - is the informant a party to the proceedings? If he is, has he put the statement in evidence?

- Would the abuse if established amount to significant harm or the risk of significant harm within the meaning of s 31?

- Is there a need for urgent action? What are the risks of delay?

The Children and Family Reporter should always be alert to the dangers of becoming enmeshed in the strategy of the manipulative litigant. Maintaining the independence and impartiality of the Children and Family Reporter is crucial. It will seldom be necessary for the Children and Family Reporter to relay second-hand reports to social services. Furthermore, such reports are unlikely to be urgent and there will ordinarily be no obstacle to the Children and Family Reporter consulting the judge before taking any action. Where the information is received first hand, an immediate report to social services or the police may be indicated and in such a situation the Children and Family Reporter must exercise an unfettered independent discretion. However, he must inform the judge of the steps he has taken at the earliest opportunity so that the judge can consider the impact of the development and the need for consequential directions.

Withholding the report from the parties

19.34 Exceptionally, the court may withhold copies from the parties but before doing so it must apply the threefold test set out by the House of Lords in *Re D (Adoption Reports: Confidentiality)*.[48] The court should first consider whether the disclosure of the whole or part of the report will involve a real possibility of significant harm to the child. If it would, the court next has to consider whether the overall interests of the child will benefit from

---

[48] [1995] 2 FLR 687.

non-disclosure, weighing the interests of the child in having the material properly tested against the magnitude of the risk that harm will occur and the gravity of the risk. If the court is satisfied that the interests of the child point towards non-disclosure, the final step is to weigh that consideration against the interests of the adult parties in having an opportunity to see and respond to the material, taking into account the importance of the material to the issues in the case:

> 'Non-disclosure should be the exception and not the rule. The court should be rigorous in its examination of the risk and gravity of the feared harm to the child and should order non-disclosure only when the case for doing so is compelling.'[49]

Judges speaking to the reporter privately

19.35   Although there may be circumstances when it may be appropriate for the judge to have a private conversation with the reporter, these circumstances must be exceptional. If such a conversation took place absent such circumstances, this will constitute 'a grave irregularity' which will result in a rehearing being ordered.[50]

THE REPORTER AND THE HEARING

19.36   A report to the court is confidential (see **Chapter 22**).[51]

A party may question the officer about oral or written advice tendered by that officer to the court.[52]

19.37   The Reporter will not attend the hearing unless ordered to do so. Any request for the Reporter to attend will be examined carefully and will not be granted as a matter of course. The *Memorandum from the President of the Family Division and the Chief Executive of CAFCASS*[53] states that:

> 'We hope to achieve a position where CAFCASS practitioners, who are busy people, only attend court when they clearly need to be there. Some judges allow them to leave … when the practitioner has given evidence … We should like to remind judges, court managers and administrators of the pressure on CAFCASS practitioners and the need to minimise their unnecessary attendance at court, particularly time waiting if this can be avoided.'

Where there are clear-cut recommendations and warnings of risk in reports, the judge should not depart from them without first hearing evidence from the

---

49   [1995] 2 FLR 687, per Lord Mustill at 701.
50   *Re B (A Minor) (Irregularity of Practice)* [1990] 1 FLR 300, per Glidewell LJ at 303. See too, *Re W (Cross-Examination)* [2010] EWCA Civ 1449, [2011] 1 FLR 1979 (guardian).
51   Family Procedure Rules 2010, r 16.33.
52   Ibid.
53   *Memorandum from the President of the Family Division and the Chief Executive of CAFCASS*, 9 March 2005.

Reporter.[54] Apart from this, it is a matter for the judge whether or not he adjourns a hearing to allow the Reporter to be present. Before such a direction is made, enquiry should be made to ensure that the Reporter will be available.[55]

19.38 Although the *Handbook of Best Practice* states that the court should allow the Reporter to give evidence first and then be released, there are cases where it is preferable for the Reporter to hear the evidence of the parties before giving evidence. Unfortunately, limited resources often mean that the stage at which the evidence is given is governed solely by the availability of the Reporter.

19.39 Provided the judge takes into account the views of the Reporter, he is not bound to follow his or her recommendations. The judge should, however, indicate in his judgment, preferably expressly, his reasons for not following the recommendations.[56] The recommendations should be carefully explored in cross-examination.[57]

---

[54] *Re CB (Access: Attendance of Court Welfare Officer)* [1995] 1 FLR 622.

[55] *Handbook of Best Practice*, para 4.53.

[56] See, for example, *Re M (Residence)* [2004] EWCA Civ 1574, [2005] 1 FLR 656; *Re R (Residence Order)* [2009] EWCA Civ 445; [2010] 1 FLR 509. See also **25.60**.

[57] *Re P (Custody of Children: Split Custody Order)* [1991] 1 FLR 337.

Chapter 20

TRIAL

TRIAL BUNDLE

20.1 A detailed Practice Direction[1] deals with the preparation of a trial bundle for all hearings which are not listed for one hour or less or any urgent applications if and to the extent that it is impossible to comply with it. It applies to all family courts with the exception of the family proceedings court (FPC).

A bundle should be prepared by the applicant, containing all documents relevant to the hearing in chronological order, paginated, indexed and divided into separate sections as follows:

(a)   applications and orders;

(b)   statements and affidavits;

(c)   experts' reports and other reports;

(d)   other documents divided into further sections as necessary.

At the front of the bundle there should be:

(a)   a summary of the background to the hearing limited, if practicable, to one A4 page;

(b)   a statement of the issue or issues to be decided;

(c)   a summary of the order or directions sought by each party;

(d)   a chronology if there is a final hearing or if the summary is insufficient – although the practice directions does not require it, if possible the chronology should be cross-referenced to the bundle;

(e)   skeleton arguments may be appropriate together with copies of all authorities relied on.

---

[1]   Practice Direction 27A: Family Proceedings Court Bundles, President's Direction, 27 July 2006 [2006] 2 FLR 199.

If possible, the bundle should be agreed. An index should be provided to all parties. It should be lodged with the court 2 clear days before the hearing unless an order for earlier lodgment is made.

The party preparing it should ensure that there is a copy at court for use by the witnesses.

20.2 A paginated bundle for the use of the court at the hearing shall be provided by the party in the position of applicant at the hearing (or, if there are cross-applications, by the party whose application was first in time) or, if that person is a litigant in person, by the first listed respondent who is not a litigant in person.[2]

20.3 The bundle must contain copies of all documents relevant to the hearing, in chronological order from the front of the bundle, paginated and indexed, and divided into separate sections (each section being separately paginated) as follows:

- preliminary documents and any other case management documents required by any other practice direction. These include:

    - an up to date summary of the background to the hearing confined to those matters which are relevant to the hearing and the management of the case and limited, if practicable, to one A4 page;
    - a statement of the issue or issues to be determined (1) at that hearing and (2) at the final hearing;
    - a position statement by each party including a summary of the order or directions sought by that party (1) at that hearing and (2) at the final hearing;
    - an up-to-date chronology, if it is a final hearing or if the summary is insufficient;
    - skeleton arguments, if appropriate, with copies of all authorities relied on; and
    - a list of essential reading for that hearing.

- applications and orders;

- statements and affidavits (which must be dated in the top right corner of the front page);

- experts' reports and other reports (including those of a guardian, children's guardian or litigation friend); and

- other documents, divided into further sections as may be appropriate.

---

2   FPR 2010, PD 27A, para 3.

- Copies of notes of contact visits should normally not be included in the bundle unless directed by a judge.[3]

The summary of the background, statement of issues, chronology, position statement and any skeleton arguments must be cross-referenced to the relevant pages of the bundle.[4]

20.4 The summary of the background, statement of issues, chronology and reading list must in the case of a final hearing and so far as practicable in the case of any other hearing, each consist of an agreed single document. Where the parties disagree as to the content the fact of their disagreement and their differing contentions shall be set out at the appropriate places in the document.[5]

20.5 Where the nature of the hearing is such that a complete bundle of all documents is unnecessary, the bundle (which need not be repaginated) may comprise only those documents necessary for the hearing, but the summary must commence with a statement that the bundle is limited or incomplete and the bundle shall if reasonably practicable be in a form agreed by all parties.[6]

20.6 Provision is made for updating the bundle[7] and its format.[8]

20.7 The party preparing the bundle must, provide a paginated index to all other parties not less than 4 working days before the hearing. With the exception of the preliminary documents if they are not then available, it must be lodged with the court not less than 2 working days before the hearing, or at such other time as may be specified by the judge.[9]

20.8 Provision is made for how the bundle is to be lodged, both generally and also at the Royal Courts of Justice and the Principal Registry at First Avenue House.[10]

20.9 A failure to comply with any part of the practice direction may result in the judge removing the case from the list or putting the case further back in the list and may also result in a 'wasted costs' order against the lawyer responsible in accordance with CPR, r 48.7 or some other adverse costs order.[11]

> 'There is [also] the risk that those who default may find their cases put to the end of the list – and I should like to emphasise that the plea "but the case will only take 30 minutes, including reading time" will not necessarily save defaulters from

---

3   PD 27A, paras 4.1 and 4.2.
4   Ibid, para 4.4.
5   Ibid, para 4.5.
6   Ibid, para 4.6.
7   Ibid, para 4.7.
8   Ibid, para 5.1.
9   Ibid, para 7.
10 Ibid, para 8.
11 See **24.25**.

this salutary fate. Why, after all, should others in a busy list who have complied with the Practice Direction be held up? Sometimes ... there will be no option but to take the case out of the list altogether – to adjourn to a date which may or may not be in the near future. In particularly egregious cases, defaulters may find themselves publicly identified in judgments delivered in open court. It would not, in my judgment, be fair or just to expose a practitioner to this last sanction without fair public warning having been given that the sanction is available and that it may be applied in appropriate cases. I have therefore not identified anyone involved in either of the cases to which I have referred. But the professions have now been warned. Next time a defaulter may not be so lucky.'[12]

TIME ESTIMATES

20.10 In every case a time estimate (which shall be inserted at the front of the bundle) must be prepared which shall so far as practicable be agreed by all parties. It must:

- specify separately:

  - the time estimated to be required for judicial pre-reading;
  - the time required for hearing all evidence and submissions; and
  - the time estimated to be required for preparing and delivering judgment; and

- be prepared on the basis that before they give evidence all witnesses will have read all relevant filed statements and reports.[13]

Once a case has been listed, any change in time estimates must be notified immediately by telephone (and then immediately confirmed in writing) in the case of hearings in the Royal Courts of Justice, to the Clerk of the Rules and in the case of hearings elsewhere, to the relevant listing officer.[14]

TAKING CASES OUT OF THE LIST

20.11 As soon as it becomes known that a hearing will no longer be effective, whether as a result of the parties reaching agreement or for any other reason, the parties and their representatives must immediately notify the court by telephone and by letter. The letter, which shall wherever possible be a joint letter sent on behalf of all parties with their signatures applied or appended, must include:

---

[12] *Re X and Y (Bundles)* [2008] EWHC 2058 (Fam), [2008] 2 FLR 2053. Other judicial complaints have been made about bundles, most memorably by Sir Stephen Sedley who drafted 12 laws of documents which include the Third Law: 'No two copies of any bundle shall have the same pagination' and the Seventh Law: 'As many photocopies as practicable shall be blurred, truncated or cropped'. See Sedley 'The Laws of Documents in Ashes and Sparks' (Cambridge University Press, 2011) at pp 228–230.

[13] PD 27A, para 10.1.

[14] Ibid, para 10.2.

- a short background summary of the case;

- the written consent of each party who consents and, where a party does not consent, details of the steps which have been taken to obtain that party's consent and, where known, an explanation of why that consent has not been given;

- a draft of the order being sought; and

- enough information to enable the court to decide whether to take the case out of the list and whether to make the proposed order.[15]

THE MODE OF TRIAL

20.12 The court has a broad discretion to conduct the case as is most appropriate for the issues involved and the evidence available. There is a spectrum of procedure from the ex parte application on minimal evidence to full and detailed investigations on oral evidence. Considerations in deciding whether to hold a full hearing include:

- whether there is sufficient evidence on which to make the relevant decision;

- whether the proposed evidence (which should be available at least in outline) which the applicant wishes to adduce is likely to affect the outcome of the proceedings;

- whether the opportunity to cross-examine the witnesses for the other party, in particular expert witnesses, is likely to affect the outcome of the proceedings;

- the welfare of the child and the effect of further litigation – whether the delay caused by holding a full hearing will be so detrimental to the child's well-being that exceptionally there should not be a full hearing;

- the prospects of success of the application on a full trial;

- whether the justice of the case requires a full investigation with oral evidence.[16]

---

[15] PD 27A, para 11.
[16] See also *Re N; Av G and N* [2009] EWHC 1807 (Fam), [2010] 1 FLR 272; *W v Ealing LBC* [1993] 2 FLR 788; *S v S* [2008] EWHC 2288 (Fam), [2009] 1 FLR 241; *Re B (Minors) (Contact)* [1994] 2 FLR 1.

Dismissal of an application without permitting an applicant to give oral evidence is, however, an exceptional course for a court to take.[17] If the court hears from a witness or Children and Family Reporter, a party should be allowed to ask questions.[18]

20.13 The judge should not have a private discussion with counsel,[19] the guardian (if any)[20] or, save in very exceptional circumstances, the Children and Family Reporter.[21]

HEARINGS IN PUBLIC OR IN PRIVATE

Background to the rule

20.14 Historically, wardship hearings involving the welfare of children were always held in private. The classic justification for this was set out by Lord Haldane LC in 1913.

> 'The Court is really sitting primarily to guard the interests of the ward ... Its jurisdiction is in this respect parental and administrative and the disposal of controverted questions is an incident only in the jurisdiction. It may often be necessary, in order to achieve its primary object, that the Court should exclude the public.'[22]

In recent years, however, there has been increasing pressure for hearings to be held in public. In 2005, for example, the House of Commons Constitutional Affairs Committee in its report, *Family Justice: the Operation of the Family Courts*[23] said:

> 'A greater degree of transparency is required in the family courts. An obvious move would be to allow the press and public into the family courts under appropriate reporting restrictions, and subject to the judge's discretion to exclude the public. Anonymised judgments should normally be delivered in public unless the judge in question specifically chooses to make an order to the contrary. This would make it possible for the public to have a more informed picture of what happens in the family courts and would give the courts the "open justice" which characterises our judicial system while protecting the parties.'

---

[17] *Re M (Contact)* [1995] 1 FLR 1029, *Re C (A Child) (Contact: Conduct of Hearing)* [2006] EWCA Civ 144, [2006] 2 FLR 289.

[18] *Re I and H (Contact: Right to Give Evidence)* [1998] 1 FLR 876.

[19] *Re Z (Unsupervised Contact: Allegations of Domestic Violence)* [2009] EWCA Civ 430, [2009] 2 FLR 877.

[20] *Re W (Cross-Examination)* [2010] EWCA Civ 1449, [2011] 1 FLR 1979.

[21] See **19.35**.

[22] *Scott v Scott* [1913] AC 417 at 437.

[23] [2005] HC116–1, at para 144.

20.15 In its Response to the Report[24] the Government recognised that there was a growing consensus that family courts lacked transparency and that this lay the system open to unfounded accusations of bias and injustice. 'There is a clear need to ensure that these accusations can readily be rebutted through greater openness.' However, the interests of the children involved were paramount and no steps would be taken to increase transparency unless it could be certain that children were protected. For a further discussion of transparency, see **22.62**.

Article 6(1)

20.16 Article 6(1) of the European Convention for the Protection of Human Rights (ECHR) provides for the public hearing and the public pronouncement of judgment of cases but with the proviso that the press and public may be excluded 'in the interest of morals, public order or national security in a democratic society, where the interest of juveniles or the protection of the private life of the parties so requires'.

20.17 The European Court of Human Rights examined the implications of Art 6 for England and Wales in *B v United Kingdom; P v United Kingdom*,[25] cases brought by fathers who had been refused permission to have their applications for residence orders held in open court. The Court found that there had been no violation of the applicants' rights to a fair trial.

The Court observed that the public character of judicial proceedings protected litigants against the administration of justice in secret with no public scrutiny and was one of the means whereby confidence in the court could be maintained. It contributed to the achievement of the aim of Art 6(1), namely a fair hearing which was one of the foundations of a democratic society. However, the requirement to hold a hearing in public was subject to certain exceptions. It might on occasion be necessary to limit the open and public nature of the proceedings, for example, to protect the safety or privacy of witnesses or to promote the free exchange of information and opinion in the pursuit of justice.

'The proceedings which the present applicants wished to take place in public concerned the residence of each man's son following the parents' divorce or separation. The court considers that such proceedings are prime examples of cases where the exclusion of the press and public may be justified to protect the privacy of the child and parties and to avoid prejudicing the interests of justice. To enable the deciding judge to gain as full and accurate picture as possible of the advantages and disadvantages of the various residence and contact options open

---

24 *The Government Response to the Constitutional Affairs Select Committee Report: Family Justice: the Operation of the Family Courts* (2005) Cm 6507, at paras 45–47.
25 (Applications 36337/97 and 35974/97) [2001] 2 FLR 261.

to the child, it is essential that the parents and other witnesses feel able to express themselves candidly on highly personal issues without fear of public curiosity or comment.'[26]

The English procedural law relating to hearings in private could therefore be seen as a specific reflection of the general exceptions provided for by Art 6(1).

20.18   The form of publicity given to a judgment had to be assessed in the special light of the proceedings in question and by reference to the object and purpose of Art 6(1). The Court noted that anyone who could establish an interest could consult or obtain a copy of the full text of the orders or judgments at first instance and that judgments of the Court of Appeal and of first instance courts in cases of special interest were routinely published.

'Having regard to the nature of the proceedings and the form of publicity applied by national law, the Court considers that a literal interpretation of the terms of Art 6(1) ... would not only be unnecessary for the purposes of public scrutiny but might even frustrate the primary aim of Art 6(1) which is to secure a fair hearing.'[27]

The past practice of English courts

20.19   In *Re PB (Hearings in Open Court)*[28] (which gave rise to *B v United Kingdom; P v United Kingdom*) the Court of Appeal had held that in the absence of unusual circumstances, the normal practice of conducting first instance hearings in private would continue. 'The exercise of discretion [to allow the hearing to be conducted in public] remains in the hands of the trial judge and it is a matter for the judge in each case to exercise that discretion if called upon to do so.'[29] Following *B v United Kingdom; P v United Kingdom*, one of the applicants returned to the Court of Appeal to argue that r 4.16(7) of the Family Proceedings Rules was incompatible with Arts 6 and 8.[30] Not surprisingly the Court rejected his appeal on the grounds that his arguments had already been rejected in his earlier appeal and by the European Court of Human Rights. However, while it remained justifiable to hold hearings in private, greater justification was required for refusing to pronounce judgment in public given the almost universal practice of anonymising public judgments in Children Act cases.

'It is not so evident that either the inherent or the statutory jurisdiction justifies the imposition of an automatic restriction without the exercise of a specific discretion in the individual case.'

---

[26]   [2001] 2 FLR 261, at para 38.
[27]   Ibid, at para 48.
[28]   [1996] 2 FLR 765.
[29]   Per Butler-Sloss LJ at 769.
[30]   *Pelling v Bruce-Williams (Secretary of State for Constitutional Affairs Intervening)* [2004] EWCA Civ 845, [2004] 2 FLR 823.

So rarely are applications made that the exercise of the discretion might be prejudiced by the tradition of privacy or an unconscious preference for the atmosphere created in chambers. 'Judges need to be aware of this and be prepared to consider another course where appropriate.'

20.20 Following *Pelling v Bruce-Williams*, the House of Lords in *Re S (Identification: Restrictions on Publication)*[31] held, in a case concerning restricting the identity of a child in a criminal trial, that the coming into force of the Human Rights Act 1998 made it unnecessary to consider the preceding case law about the existence and scope of the High Court's inherent jurisdiction to restrain publicity. The foundation of the jurisdiction now derived from rights under the Convention. The importance of the freedom of both the national and local press and the Art 10 right to freedom of expression needs to be addressed.

20.21 There were no reported cases of applications under the Children Act being held in public at first instance. However, there were a number of cases where judgment had been given in public because of their public rather than legal importance. Most common were decisions about the future medical care of children, for example, *Re L (A Child) (Medical Treatment: Benefit)*.[32] Usually the decisions were anonymised but this was not always the case. The child was named in *Portsmouth NHS Trust v Wyatt, Southampton NHS Trust Intervening*[33] because the matter had already received widespread publicity. Munby J gave his judgment in *Re D (Intractable Contact Dispute: Publicity)*[34] in public as a contribution to the debate about the role of courts in contact and residence disputes.[35] *Blunkett v Quinn*[36] was a rare example of a judgment in a non-medical treatment case being given in an unanonymised form.[37] Ryder J justified this 'having regard to the quantity of material that is in the public domain, some of it even in the most responsible commentaries wholly inaccurate'.

20.22 After much debate,[38] and consultations by the Department for Constitutional Affairs which included seeking the views of children,[39] the Family Proceedings Rules 1991 and the Family Proceedings (Children

---

[31] [2004] UKHL 47, [2005] 1 FLR 591.

[32] [2004] EWHC 2713 (Fam), [2005] 1 FLR 491.

[33] [2004] EWHC 2247 (Fam), [2005] 1 FLR 21.

[34] [2004] EWHC 727 (Fam), [2004] 1 FLR 1226.

[35] It certainly received attention. *The Sun*, for example, gave it the headline: 'Judge: law fails love split dads'.

[36] [2004] EWHC 2816 (Fam), [2005] 1 FLR 648.

[37] Compare, for example, *Re Z (A Minor) (Freedom of Publication)* [1996] 1 FLR 191. This may however be the start of a change in approach. See, for example, *In the Matter of the Children of Mr O'Connell, Mr Whelan and Mr Watson* [2005] EWCA Civ 615, [2005] 2 FLR 967.

[38] See, for example, Wall 'Opening up the family courts: a personal view' [2006] Fam Law 747, Macdonald 'Openness – refocusing the debate' [2006] Fam Law 855.

[39] *Confidence and Confidentiality: Improving Transparency and Privacy in Family Courts*, Cm 6886 (2006) [2006] Fam Law 620 and 826; *Confidence and Confidentiality: Openness in family courts – a new approach*, Cm 7036 (2007); *Family Justice in View*, Cm 7502 (2008). See also *Family Justice: the operation of the family courts*, (House of Commons Constitutional Affairs

Act 1989) Rules 1991 were changed[40] as from the 27 April 2009 to permit representatives of the media to attend hearings subject to the discretion of the court to exclude them. The rule change as supplemented by two practice directions[41] and Guidance from the President of the Family Division.[42] After the expected initial flurry of interest[43] which gave the opportunity to the higher courts to consider some of the issues involved, there was little change to the factual norm that family proceedings are held only in the presence of parties, their representatives and witnesses.

The Rule

20.23   The earlier rule changes and guidance are now contained in FPR 2010, r 27.11, PD 27B[44] and PD 27C.[45]

20.24   Private law proceedings to which these rules apply will be held in private and the general public have no right to be present unless the rules or any other enactment provide otherwise; or the court directs otherwise.[46] Where they are held in private, no one shall be present other than:

- an officer of the court;

- a party to the proceedings;

- a litigation friend for any party, or legal representative instructed to act on that party's behalf;

- an officer of Cafcass or Welsh family proceedings officer;

- a witness;

Committee, Fourth Report of Session 2004–05) HC 116-1, at paras 132–144. For a description of the debate, see Munby 'Lost opportunities: law reform and transparency in the family courts' [2010] CFLQ 273, at pp 282–284.

40   By r 10.28 and r 16A respectively.

41   *Practice Direction: Attendance of Media Representatives at Hearings in Family Proceedings* 20 April 2009 [2009] 2 FLR 157 and *Practice Direction: Attendance of Media Representatives at Hearings in Family Proceedings* (20 April 2009) [2009] 2 FLR 162.

42   *President's Guidance in Relation to Applications Consequent upon the Attendance of the Media in Family Proceedings* [2009] 2 FLR 167.

43   'One could hardly move in the Royal Courts of Justice on 27 April 2009 without seeing some representative of the media, yet the fact is that the media, with the exception of only a few cases, have been conspicuously absent from family courts ever since.' *Spencer v Spencer* [2009] EWHC 1529 (Fam), [2009] 2 FLR 1416, per Munby J at [64].

44   High Court and county court.

45   The family proceedings court.

46   FPR 2010, r 27.11.

- duly accredited[47] representatives of news gathering and reporting organisations; and

- any other person whom the court permits to be present.[48]

20.25 At any stage of the proceedings the court may direct that persons permitted to be present as set out above shall not attend the proceedings or any part of them if it is satisfied that:

(a) this is necessary:

    (i) in the interests of any child concerned in, or connected with, the proceedings;

    (ii) for the safety or protection of a party, a witness in the proceedings, or a person connected with such a party or witness; or

    (iii) for the orderly conduct of the proceeding;s or

(b) justice will otherwise be impeded or prejudiced.[49]

20.26 The court may exercise the power to exclude duly accredited representatives of its own initiative or pursuant to representations made by:

- a party to the proceedings;

- any witness in the proceedings;

- where appointed, any children's guardian;

- where appointed, an officer of Cafcass or Welsh family proceedings officer, on behalf of the child the subject of the proceedings;

- the child, if of sufficient age and understanding.

Before doing so the court must give duly accredited representatives who are present an opportunity to make representations.[50]

20.27 This rule does not affect any power of the court to direct that witnesses shall be excluded until they are called for examination.[51]

---

[47] Ie accredited in accordance with any administrative scheme for the time being approved for the purposes of the rule by the Lord Chancellor: FPR 2010, r 27.11(7). See also PD 27B and PD 27C, para 4.
[48] FPR 2010, r 27.11(2).
[49] Ibid, r 27.11(3).
[50] Ibid, r 27.11(4)–(5).
[51] Ibid, r 27.11(6).

20.28 The Practice Directions deal with:

- identification of media representatives as 'accredited';

- the exercise of the discretion to exclude media representatives from all or part of the proceedings; and

- applications to exclude media representatives.

20.29 Both state that:

> 'While the guidance does not aim to cover all possible eventualities, it should be complied with so far as consistent in all the circumstances with the just determination of the proceedings.'[52]

The courts' approach to the Rule

20.30 In *Re X (A Child) (Residence and Contact: Rights of Media Attendance)*[53] Sir Mark Potter P held that the media should be excluded from a hearing in private law proceedings involving residence and contact disputes where the child's father was a celebrity subject to a high level of media attention and both the Cafcass officer and a consultant child and adolescent psychiatrist who aws going to give expert evidence expressed concern about the effect on the child's welfare if the media were present. In addition the expert raised a concern that the child had given him information in confidence on the understanding that it would be shared only with the court and the parents.

20.31 In summary his lordship held:

- the rules for excluding the press (in FPR 2010, r 27.11)[54] (see **20.25**) are in broad terms and comply with Art 6 ECHR. Ground (a)(i) is within the legitimate aim of protecting the interests of juveniles and Grounds (a)(ii), (iii) and (b) are legitimised under the heading of 'special circumstances where publicity would prejudice the interests of justice'.

- Nothing in the rule provides for exclusion of the press where the Art 8 interests of the parties (as opposed to those of the child) so require.

> 'However, one can envisage a situation where a ground for exclusion, at least for part of the proceedings, might be required to protect the Article 8 interests of the parties which could properly justify exclusion of the media under ground (b) to prevent the press from hearing and/or reporting allegations of an outrageous or intimate nature before the Court's decision as to whether or not they were established. This might well constitute a

---

52   PD 27B, para 3.2.
53   [2009] EWHC 1728 (Fam), [2009] 2 FLR 1467.
54   The President referred to FPR 1991, r 10.28(4).

serious and irredeemable invasion of the privacy and/or family life of an adult party if the press were not excluded.'[55]

- When deciding whether to exclude the press in the welfare or privacy interests of a party or third party the court has to balance the parties' Art 8 rights against the Art 10 right of freedom of expression which includes the freedom to receive and impart information and ideas without interference by public authorities. Under the principles enunciated in *Campbell*:[56]

  'First, neither Article has as such precedence over the other. Secondly, where the values under the two articles are in conflict, an intense focus on the comparative importance of the specific rights being claimed in the individual case is necessary. Thirdly, the justifications for interfering with or restricting each right must be taken into account. Finally, the proportionality test must be applied to each. For convenience I will call this the ultimate balancing test.'

- Whilst the principle of open justice is important in proceedings concerning children, the need for their protection from publicity in the course of proceedings which concern them, recognised at common law in *Scott v Scott*,[57] is provided for in the statutory provisions as to identification (see **22.30**).[58]

- It is important to remember that the purpose of the application is not to limit the media's reporting rights, but to exclude the media from their exercising presumptive rights under the Rule to be present for the purpose of exercising a watchdog role, albeit with limited reporting rights under the terms of the Administration of Justice Act [1960].[59]

- Private law family cases concerning the children of celebrities are no different in principle from those involving the children of anyone else.[60]

- When considering whether or not to exclude the press under Ground (a)(i), the focus is upon the interests of the child and not the parents. 'It is almost axiomatic that the press interest in and surrounding the case will be more intense in the case of children of celebrities; and the need for protection of the child from intrusion or publicity, and the danger of leakage of information to the public will similarly be the more intense.'[61]

---

[55]   [2009] EWHC 1728 (Fam), [2009] 2 FLR 1467, at [45].

[56]   *Campbell v MGN Ltd* [2004] UKHL 22, [2004] 2 AC 457 as paraphrased by Lord Steyn in *Re S (Identification: Restrictions on Publication)* [2004] UKHL 47, [2005] 1 FLR 591, at [17].

[57]   [1913] AC 417.

[58]   [2009] EWHC 1728 (Fam), [2009] 2 FLR 1467, at [48].

[59]   Ibid, at [49].

[60]   Ibid, at [51] and see *C v Crown Prosecution Service* [2008] EWHC 854 (Admin), per Thomas LJ at [34]–[35].

[61]   [2009] EWHC 1728 (Fam), [2009] 2 FLR 1467, at [52].

- In order to exclude the press on any of the grounds the court must be satisfied that it is necessary to do so.[62]

  '"Necessary" has been strongly interpreted; it is not synonymous with "indispensable", neither has it the flexibility of such expressions as "admissible", "ordinary", "useful", "reasonable" or "desirable": *Handyside v United Kingdom*[63]. One must consider whether the interference complained of corresponds to a pressing social need, whether it is proportionate to the legitimate aim pursued and whether the reasons given by the national authority to justify it are relevant and sufficient under Article 10(2): *The Sunday Times v United Kingdom*[64]'[65]

- The question of necessity must be approached on the basis set out by Lord Bingham in *Shayler*,[66] in the context of the particular facts of the case, and with an eye to the question whether any information received in confidence is involved and therefore at risk by reason of press attendance.[67]

- When applying the test of necessity, the court carries out the balancing exercise by making a value judgment as to the conflicts which arise rather than regarding the matter simply as an exercise of discretion as between two equally legitimate courses.[68]

- The burden of satisfying the court of the exclusion grounds is on the party who seeks exclusion (or the court itself where it takes steps of its own motion, to exclude the press). 'This will be an easier burden to satisfy in the case of temporary exclusion in the course of the proceedings, in order to meet concerns arising from the evidence of the particular witness or witnesses.'[69]

- 'In deciding whether or not the grounds advanced for exclusion are sufficient to override the presumptive right of the press to be present and in particular whether or not an order for total exclusion is proportionate, it will be relevant to have regard to the nature and sensitivities of the evidence and the degree to which the watchdog function of the media may be engaged, or whether its apparent interests lie in observing, and reporting on matters relating to the child which may well be the object of interest, in the sense of curiosity, on the part of the public but which are confidential and private and do not themselves involve matters of public interest properly so called. However, while this may be a relevant

---

62 [2009] EWHC 1728 (Fam), [2009] 2 FLR 1467, at [53].
63 [1976] 1 EHRR 737, 754, at [48].
64 (1979) 2 EHRR 245, 277–278, at [62].
65 *R v Shayler* [2003] 1 AC 247, 268, per Lord Bingham of Cornhill at [23].
66 Ibid.
67 [2009] EWHC 1728 (Fam), [2009] 2 FLR 1467, at [55].
68 Ibid, at [56] and see *Interbrew SA v Financial Times* [2002] EWCA Civ 274, [2002] 2 Lloyd's Rep 229, per Sedley LJ at [58].
69 [2009] EWHC 1728 (Fam), [2009] 2 FLR 1467, at [57].

consideration, it in no sense creates or places any burden of proof or justification upon the media. The burden lies upon the applicant to demonstrate that the matter cannot be appropriately dealt with by allowing the press to attend, subject as they are to the statutory safeguards in respect of identity and under the provisions of s.12 of the 1960 Act.'[70]

20.32 In *Spencer v Spencer*[71] Munby J refused to exclude the media from a hearing of an application for financial relief following a divorce. He considered exclusion on what is now Ground (b) namely that if the media were not excluded, 'justice will otherwise be impeded or prejudiced' and guidance given in what is now PD 27B, at para 5.4:

'Examples of circumstances where the impact on justice of continued attendance might be sufficient to necessitate exclusion may include –

...

(b)   any hearing at which a witness (other than a party) states for credible reasons that he or she will not give evidence in front of media representatives, or where there appears to the court to be a significant risk that a witness will not give full or frank evidence in the presence of media representatives.'

He said that that was unlikely in the general run of cases. The ground focuses upon the case of a specific witness who, there is credible reason to believe, will either not give evidence at all, or not give full or frank evidence, if the media are present. In such a case it would be a proper basis for excluding the media from that particular part of the proceedings where the condition is satisfied in relation to a particular witness. But 'I have some difficulty in seeing how it could ever realistically be a reason for excluding the media from the hearing as a whole.'[72]

In *Re X (A Child) (Residence and Contact: Rights of Media Attendance)*[73] the President said that he agreed in general with the proposition but would not accept its universal application.

Disclosure of documents to members of the media at the hearing

20.33 Unless media representatives are allowed access to documents such as expert reports and, with more advocacy taking place by way of written material such as skeleton arguments and position statements, their ability to understand what is taking place will be compromised and this would defeat the purpose of their being present.[74] In civil proceedings, where hearings take place in open court, there is what may be described as a presumption in favour of providing

---

[70]   Ibid at [58].
[71]   [2009] EWHC 1529 (Fam), [2009] 2 FLR 1416.
[72]   Ibid, at [60].
[73]   Ibid, at [65].
[74]   *Norfolk County Council v Webster* [2006] EWHC 2898 (Fam), [2007] 2 FLR 415, at [34].

to third parties documents which were relied upon by the court in reaching its decision,[75] though not the entire court file.[76]

20.34   No such provision has been made in FPR 2010. The President of the Family Division, Sir Nicholas Wall, said he would like to see a practice develop, in which expert reports would be routinely disclosed, and the media able to comment both on the report and on the use to which they were put in the proceedings.[77] In *Norfolk County Council v Webster*[78] Munby J permitted a media representative to have a copy of the position statements.

20.35   No guidance has yet been given on how a request for documents should be approached. The view of the parties should be sought. The court should have regard to the purpose of granting the request namely to assist the representative's right to be present and to understand the proceedings. Therefore the need for disclosure of the particular document will have to be considered. The right to be present does not yet include the right to have access to all the papers in the trial bundle whether referred to or not. The court will also have to decide whether the representative should be allowed to take a copy away from the court. Preferably such matters should be considered in advance of the dealing with the representative present. There may be little time on the day an expert witness gives evidence to consider these novel issues.

Reporting the proceedings

20.36   The restrictions on the reporting of proceedings held in private is discussed at **22.22**. Reference should also be made to *The Family Courts: Media Access & Reporting*.[79]

Proposals for further reform

20.37   Part II of the Children, Schools and Families Act 2010 which is not yet in force makes proposals for:

- amending the restriction on publication of information relating to family proceedings;[80]

- authorising publication of court orders and judgments by an acredited news publication[81] provided certain conditions[82] are met;[83]

---

75   *Dain AO v Davis Frankel and Mead* [2004] EWHC 2662 (Comm), [2005] 1 WLR 2951; *Cleveland Bridge UK Ltd v Multiplex Constructions (UK) Limited* [2005] EWHC 2101 (TCC).

76   See Wolanski and Wilson 'The Family Courts: Media Access & Reporting' (2011), a paper commissioned and endorsed by the President of the Family Division and the Executive Director of the Society of Editors, at [35].

77   *X (Children) (Expert Witness), Re* [2011] EWHC 1157 (Fam), at [97].

78   [2006] EWHC 2898 (Fam), [2007] 2 FLR 415.

79   Op cit.

80   Children, Schools and Families Act 2010, s 11.

81   Ibid, s 13.

82   Ibid, ss 14–16.

- providing a defence to a contempt of court by reason of breach of s 11 if the person proves that at the time of the publication the person did not know and had no reason to suspect that the information published was information relating to the proceedings.[84]

20.38 Lord Justice Munby, writing extra-judicially has expressed doubt about these proposed changes. They are far from comprehensive and represent a lost opportunity which, if anything, is likely to reduce rather than increase the amount of information about children and other family proceedings which finds its way into the public domain.[85]

WITNESSES

Witness summons

20.39 The court's power to compel a witness to attend court to give evidence or produce documents by use of a witness summons is set out in FPR 2010, rr 24.2–24.6 and PD 24, paras 1–3.

Order of witnesses

20.40 The court may give directions as to the order of speeches and evidence at a hearing or directions appointment. Subject to this, the parties will conventionally adduce their evidence in the following order:

(1) the applicant;

(2) any party with parental responsibility for the child;

(3) other respondents;

(4) the guardian ad litem (if any).

However, it may be more appropriate for witnesses to be heard in a different order, for example lay witnesses including parents giving evidence as to what happened to a child before he was taken to hospital suffering from injuries before expert evidence as to whether the factual evidence is consistent with the injuries.[86] Where objection is taken to this, the matter will need to be resolved by reference both to Art 6 ECHR as well as to the overriding objective (see **17.6**).

---

83 Children, Schools and Families Act 2010, s 12.
84 Ibid, s 17.
85 *Lost opportunities: law reform and transparency in the family courts* op cit, at p 289.
86 See *Lancashire CC v R* [2008] EWHC 2959 (Fam), [2010] 1 FLR 387, per Munby J at [70]. Munby J used the phrase 'severely compromised'.

Evidence by video-link

20.41 FPR 2010, r 1.4 includes in the concept of 'active case management' 'making the use of technology'. Taking evidence over a video–link[87] is one such use. It may be a convenient way of dealing with any part of proceedings and can make considerable savings in time and cost. Its use for the taking of evidence from overseas witnesses will, in particular, be likely to achieve a material saving of costs, and such savings may also be achieved by its use for taking domestic evidence. However, as PD 22A points out, it is, inevitably not as ideal as having the witness physically present in court. Its convenience should not therefore be allowed to dictate its use. A judgment must be made in every case in which its use is being considered not only as to whether it will achieve an overall cost saving but as to whether its use will be likely to be beneficial to the efficient, fair and economic disposal of the litigation. In particular, it needs to be recognised that the degree of control a court can exercise over a witness at the remote site is or may be more limited than it can exercise over a witness physically before it.[88]

20.42 When used for the taking of evidence, the objective should be to make the VCF session as close as possible to the usual practice in court where evidence is taken in open court. To gain the maximum benefit, several differences have to be taken into account. Some matters, which are taken for granted when evidence is taken in the conventional way, take on a different dimension when it is taken by VCF – for example, the administration of the oath, ensuring that the witness understands who is at the local site and what their various roles are, the raising of any objections to the evidence and the use of documents.

20.43 Consideration will need to be given in advance to the documents to which the witness is likely to be referred. The parties should endeavour to agree on this. It will usually be most convenient for a bundle of the copy documents to be prepared in advance, which the VCF arranging party should then send to the remote site. Additional documents may sometimes need to be introduced during the course of a witness's evidence. To cater for this, the VCF arranging party should ensure that equipment is available to enable documents to be transmitted between sites during the course of the VCF transmission.[89]

20.44 The parties, their advisers and the court need to be aware that, even with the most advanced systems, there are the briefest of delays between the receipt of the picture and that of the accompanying sound. If due allowance is not made for this, there will be a tendency to 'speak over' the witness, whose voice will continue to be heard for a millisecond or so after he or she appears on the screen to have finished speaking. With current technology, picture

---

[87] Referred to in FPR 2010 and PD 22A as 'video-conferencing' or 'VCF'.
[88] PD 21A, Annex 3, para 3.
[89] Ibid, paras 18 and 19.

quality is good, but not as good as a television picture. The quality of the picture is enhanced if those appearing on VCF monitors keep their movements to a minimum.[90]

20.45 Annex 3 to PD 22A gives detailed guidance on its use both for taking evidence from witnesses within the jurisdiction and those elsewhere (where the implications of different time zones[91] and local rules about permitting the taking of evidence by courts in other jurisdictions[92] need to be considered). A list of the sites which are available for video conferencing can be found on Her Majesty's Court Service's website.[93]

Concurrent witness evidence

20.46 Concurrent evidence, otherwise known as 'hot-tubbing' is a procedure which enables expert witnesses to give evidence at the same time with far more testimonial attitude than would normally be permitted. Originating in Australia,[94] its form was described by Ryder J in *A Local Authority v A (No 2)*.[95] Out of the experts' reports and discussions the court and the parties drafted an agenda of topics which were relevant to the key issues. The witnesses were sworn together and the court asked each witness the same questions under each topic, taking a topic at a time. The experts were encouraged to add or explain their own or another's evidence so that a healthy discussion ensued, chaired by the court. Each advocate is permitted to examine or cross examine and where appropriate re-examine each witness after the court has elicited evidence on a topic.

> 'The resulting coherence of evidence and attention to the key issues rather than adversarial point scoring is marked. The evidence of experts who might have been expected to fill 2 days of court time was completed within 4 hours.'

HEARSAY EVIDENCE

20.47 By virtue of the Children (Admissibility of Hearsay Evidence) Order 1993[96] in civil proceedings before the High Court, county court and in the FPC, evidence given in connection with the upbringing, maintenance or welfare of a child is admissible notwithstanding any rule of law relating to hearsay.

20.48 The weight to be given to hearsay evidence must be assessed with care and the rules of natural justice and the right to a fair trial under Art 6 ECHR

---

90   PD 21A, Annex 3, paras 7 and 8.
91   Ibid, para 6.
92   Ibid, para 5.
93   www.hm-courts-service.gov.uk.
94   See Edmond 'Secrets of the "hot tub": expert witnesses, concurrent evidence and judge-led law reform in Australia' [2008] CFLQ 51.
95   [2011] EWHC 590 Fam, [2011] 2 FLR 162, at [22] and [23].
96   SI 1993/621.

observed.[97] As a matter of practice, it is prudent for courts to have regard to the matters set out in s 4 of the Civil Evidence Act 1995. Regard should be had to any circumstances from which any inference can reasonably be drawn as to the reliability or otherwise of the evidence. Regard may be had in particular to the following:

- whether it would have been reasonable and practicable for the party by whom the evidence was adduced to have produced the maker of the original statement as a witness;

- whether the original statement was made contemporaneously with the occurrence or existence of the matters alleged;

- whether the evidence involves multiple hearsay;

- whether any person involved had any motive to conceal or misrepresent matters;

- whether the original statement was an edited account or was made in collaboration with another or for a particular person;

- whether the circumstances in which the evidence is adduced as hearsay are such as to suggest an attempt to prevent a proper evaluation of its weight.[98]

STANDARD OF PROOF

20.49 The standard of proof in Children Act proceedings is the same as in other civil proceedings, namely the balance of probability:

'The balance of probability standard means that the court is satisfied an event occurred if the court considers that, on the evidence, the occurrence of the event was more likely than not. When assessing the probabilities the court will have in mind as a factor, to whatever extent is appropriate in the particular case, that the more serious the allegation the less likely it is that the event occurred and, hence, the stronger should be the evidence before the court concludes that the allegation is established on the balance of probability. Fraud is less usually likely than negligence. Deliberate physical injury is usually less likely than accidental physical injury. A stepfather is usually less likely to have repeatedly raped and had non-consensual oral sex with his under-age stepdaughter than on some occasion to have lost his temper and slapped her. Built into the preponderance of probability standard is a serious degree of flexibility in respect of the seriousness of the allegation.

---

[97]   See *R v B County Council ex parte P* [1991] 1 FLR 470.
[98]   Although FCC rr 23.2 to 23.5 contain rules about hearsay, it does not apply to evidence where the Children (Admissibility of Hearsay Evidence) Order 1993 (SI 1993/ 621) applies – see FPR 2010, r 23.1.

Although the result is much the same, this does not mean that where a serious allegation is in issue the standard of proof required is higher.'[99]

20.50 In *Re B (Children) (Sexual Abuse: Standard of Proof)*[100] Baroness Hale of Richmond criticised Lord Nicholls for continuing and saying 'This approach also provides a means by which the balance of probability standard can accommodate one's instinctive feeling that even in civil proceedings a court should be more sure before finding serious allegations proved than when deciding less serious or trivial matters.'[101] Her Ladyship said:

> 'Lord Nicholls' nuanced explanation left room for the nostrum, "the more serious the allegation, the more cogent the evidence needed to prove it", to take hold and be repeated time and time again in fact-finding hearings in care proceedings (see, for example, the argument of counsel for the local authority in *Re U (A Child) (Department for Education and Skills intervening)*[102]. It is time for us to loosen its grip and give it its quietus.'

She continued:

> 'I would go further and announce loud and clear that the standard of proof in finding the facts necessary to establish the threshold under section 31(2) or the welfare considerations in section 1 of the 1989 Act is the simple balance of probabilities, neither more nor less. Neither the seriousness of the allegation nor the seriousness of the consequences should make any difference to the standard of proof to be applied in determining the facts. The inherent probabilities are simply something to be taken into account, where relevant, in deciding where the truth lies.'[103]

20.51 As to the seriousness of the consequences, they are serious either way. A child may find her relationship with her family seriously disrupted; or she may find herself still at risk of suffering serious harm. A parent may find his relationship with his child seriously disrupted; or he may find himself still at liberty to maltreat this or other children in the future.

20.52 There is no logical or necessary connection between seriousness and probability.

> 'Some seriously harmful behaviour, such as murder, is sufficiently rare to be inherently improbable in most circumstances. Even then there are circumstances, such as a body with its throat cut and no weapon to hand, where it is not at all improbable. Other seriously harmful behaviour, such as alcohol or drug abuse, is regrettably all too common and not at all improbable. Nor are serious allegations

---

[99] *Re H (Minors) (Sexual Abuse: Standard of Proof)* [1996] 1 FLR 80, per Lord Nicholls of Birkenhead at 96. See also, *A Local Authority v S, W and T (By His Guardian)* [2004] EWHC 1270 (Fam), [2004] 2 FLR 129; *Re T (Abuse: Standard of Proof)* [2004] EWCA Civ 558, [2004] 2 FLR 838 and *A v A* [2010] EWHC 1282 (Fam), [2010] 2 FLR 1173.
[100] [2008] UKHL 35, [2008] 2 FLR 141, at [64].
[101] Ibid.
[102] [2004] EWCA Civ 567, [2005] Fam 134, at 137.
[103] [2008] UKHL 35, [2008] 2 FLR 141, at [70]–[71].

made in a vacuum. Consider the famous example of the animal seen in Regent's Park. If it is seen outside the zoo on a stretch of greensward regularly used for walking dogs, then of course it is more likely to be a dog than a lion. If it is seen in the zoo next to the lions' enclosure when the door is open, then it may well be more likely to be a lion than a dog.'[104]

JUDGMENT

20.53 After the final hearing, the court has to deliver its judgment as soon as is practicable.[105] If judgment is reserved, judges are required to deliver judgment no later than one month after the hearing, unless the circuit presider gives permission for a later delivery.

Reasons

20.54 The extent to which reasons for decisions are required is discussed at **25.57**.

Draft judgments

20.55 Sometimes a judge will send the parties a draft judgment before it is handed down. Its purpose is to enable the parties to spot typographical, spelling and minor factual errors which have escaped the judge's eye. It is also to give the parties the opportunity to save costs by attempting to reach agreement on costs and to consider whether they wish to appeal.

Judgments do not take effect until formally handed down and parties may not reveal the content of draft judgments, including the decision reached to anyone until then. In civil proceedings, CPR, PD40E states that:

> 'A copy of the draft judgment may be supplied, in confidence, to the parties provided that –
>
> (a) neither the draft judgment nor its substance is disclosed to any other person or used in the public domain; and
> (b) no action is taken (other than internally) in response to the draft judgment, before the judgment is handed down.'[106]

No similar rule exists in family proceedings but reserved judgments will be handed down on the same basis.

20.56 Circulation of the draft is not intended to provide counsel with an opportunity to re-argue the issues in the case. Only in the most exceptional circumstances is it appropriate to ask the judge to reconsider a point of

---

104 [2008] UKHL 35, [2008] 2 FLR 141, at [72].

105 Family Proceedings Rules 1991, r 4.21(3); Family Proceedings Court (Children Act 1989) Rules 1991, r 21(4).

106 CPR, PD 40E, para 2.4.

substance. Those circumstances might be, for example, where counsel feels that the judge had not given adequate reasons for some aspect of his/her decision. Then it may be appropriate to send a note to the judge asking him/her to explain the reasons more fully. Another example is if the judge has decided the case on a point which was not properly argued or has relied on an authority which was not considered. Then the appropriate course will be to ask him/her either to reconvene for further argument or to receive written submissions from both sides. Letters which seek to reopen the argument on a wide variety of points, should not be sent and such a practice is deprecated.[107]

Should the judgment be given in public?

20.57 Judgments in private law proceedings are normally given in private. Following *Re PB (Hearings in Open Court)*[108] in 1996 Butler Sloss LJ said that where issues of public interest arise it would seem 'entirely appropriate' to give judgment in open court providing, where desirable in the interests of the child, appropriate directions are given to avoid identification. Butler-Sloss LJ issued a memorandum of administrative directions:[109]

'Where applications for the variation, discharge or revocation of final orders are made, Judges should consider issuing in public at the conclusion of the case suitably anonymised judgments ... It is also worth giving consideration to increasing the frequency with which anonymised Family Court judgments in general are made public. According to current convention, judgments are usually made public where they involve some important principle of law which in the opinion of the judge makes the case of interest to law reporters. In view of the current climate and increasing complaints of 'secrecy' in the Family Justice system, a broader approach to making judgments public may be desirable.'

20.58 In *Clayton v Clayton)*[110] Wall LJ said given judgments publicly assisted open justice by:

• enabling informed and proper public scrutiny of the administration of family justice;

• facilitating informed public knowledge, understanding and discussion of the important social, medical and ethical issues which are litigated in the family justice system;

• facilitating the dissemination of information useful to other professions and organisations in the multi-disciplinary working of family law.[111]

---

[107] *Egan v Motor Services (Bath)* [2007] EWCA Civ 1002, [2008] 1 FLR 1294, per Smith LJ at [49]–[51].
[108] [1996] 2 FLR 765, at 769.
[109] 28 January 2004.
[110] [2006] EWCA Civ 878, [2007] 1 FLR 11, at [85].
[111] See also *Re H (Freeing Order: Publicity)* [2005] EWCA Civ 1325, [2006] 1 FLR 815, per Wall LJ at [31]–[33] and *Medway Council v G* [2008] EWHC 1681 (Fam), [2008] 2 FLR 1687.

The Family Courts Information Pilot which published 165 anonymised judgments and written reasons in public proceedings in five family courts on the internet between November 2009 and December 2010 found no evidence of any press interest. Only 10 members of the public replied to an online survey on the site.[112]

Varying judgments

20.59 Courts had before the introduction of the CPR, and continue to have, an inherent power in exceptional circumstances to reconsider and alter a judgment or order before the order is drawn.[113] In *Compagnie Noga D'Importation et D'Exportation SA v Abacha*[114] Rix LJ said that:

> '[The] reference to exceptional circumstances is not a statutory definition and the ultimate interests involved, whether before or after the introduction of the CPR, are the interests of justice. On the one hand the court is concerned with finality, and the very proper consideration that too wide a discretion would open the floodgates to attempts to ask the court to reconsider its decision in a large number and variety of cases, rather than to take the course of appealing to a higher court. On the other hand, there is a proper concern that courts should not be held by their own decisions in a straitjacket pending the formality of the drawing up of ... Provided that the formula of "exceptional circumstances" is not turned into a straitjacket of its own, and the interests of justice and its constituents as laid down in the overriding principle are held closely to mind, I do not think that the proper balance will be lost. Clearly, it cannot be in every case that a litigant should be entitled to ask the judge to think again. Therefore, on one ground or another, the case must raise considerations, in the interests of justice, which are out of the ordinary, extraordinary, or exceptional. An exceptional case does not have to be uniquely special. "Strong reasons" is perhaps an acceptable alternative to "exceptional circumstances". It will necessarily be in an exceptional case that strong reasons are shown for reconsideration.'[115]

In *K v K (Abduction) (No 2)*[116] Sumner J, who relied on the decision of the Court of Appeal in *Paulin v Paulin*[117] which discussed *Re Barrell*, similarly held that an application to reconsider or reverse a judgment before the order is drawn must satisfy a test of strong reasons or exceptional circumstances.

Judgments in the family proceedings court

20.60 After a hearing in the FPC, the court will make its decision as soon as is practicable.[118] It must give written reasons for its decision.[119]

---

112   (Ministry of Justice, 2011).
113   *Re Barrell Enterprises* [1973] 1 WLR 19, CA. See also *Zuckerman on Civil Procedure: Principles of Practice* (2nd edn, Sweet & Maxwell, 2006), at paras 22.32–22.39.
114   [2001] 3 All ER 513.
115   Ibid at [42]–[43]. See also *Robinson v Bird* [2003] EWCA Civ 1820.
116   [2009] EWHC 3378 (Fam), [2010] 1 FLR 1310.
117   [2009] EWCA Civ 221, [2009] 2 FLR 354 and in particular, the judgment of Wilson LJ at [30].
118   FPR 2010, r 27.2(2).
119   Ibid, r 27.2(3).

Where the court comprises of lay magistrates the justices' clerk must, before the court makes an order or refuses an application or request, make notes of:

- the names of the justice or justices constituting the court by which the decision is made; and

- in consultation with the justice or justices, the reasons for the court's decision.[120]

20.61 The Best Practice Guidance of July 1997[121] contains guidance from Mr Justice Cazalet on the preparation of justices' written reasons including on how to set out reasons and findings of fact.

20.62 The clerk must make a written record of the reasons for the court's decision.[122]

20.63 When making an order or refusing an application, the court, or one of the justices constituting the court by which the decision is made, will announce its decision and:

- the reasons for that decision; or

- a short explanation of that decision.[123]

20.64 Subject to any other rule or practice direction, the court officer will, by close of business on the day when the court announces its decision or where that time is not practicable and the proceedings are on notice, no later than 72 hours from the time when the court announced its decision, supply a copy of the order and the reasons for the court's decision to:

- the parties (unless the court directs otherwise);

- any person who has actual care of a child who is the subject of proceedings, or who had such care immediately prior to the making of the order;

- in the case of an emergency protection order and a recovery order, the local authority in whose area the child lives or is found;

- any other person who has requested a copy if the court is satisfied that it is required in connection with an appeal or possible appeal.[124]

---

[120] FPR 2010, r 27.2(4)–(5).
[121] *Children Act Advisory Committee Handbook of Best Practice in Children Act Cases.*
[122] FPR, r 27.2(6).
[123] Ibid, r 27.2(7).
[124] Ibid, r 27.2 (8) and (9).

Publication of judgments

20.65 Judgments in private law proceedings cannot be published, save to persons and for the purpose identified in PD 12G, para 2.1 without the court's permission (see **22.22**). When the court grants permission a rubric will be attached stating:

> 'This judgment was handed down in private but the judge hereby gives leave for it to be reported in the form in which it here appears. The judgment is being distributed on the strict understanding that in any report no person other than the advocates (and other persons identified by name in the judgment itself) may be identified by name or location and that in particular the anonymity of the children and the adult members of their family must be strictly preserved.'

20.66 This does not prevent a party identifying themselves in public as people involved in the proceedings or, subject to compliance with s 12 of the Administration of Justice Act 1960 discussing in public the nature of the dispute in the proceedings. Nor is there anything to prevent them making whatever use they wish of the judgment in the anonymous form in which leave was given for it to be reported. However they cannot link themselves with the judgment to say that, for example, the Mrs B referred to in my judgment is in fact Mrs Brown and that the child, J, is in fact James.[125]

20.67 For examples of applications to remove anonymity, see *Z County Council v TS, DS, ES and A*[126] and *Medway Council v G*.[127]

MATTERS TO BE CONSIDERED POST-JUDGMENT

20.68 The matters which may need to be considered following the judgment include:

- Should the judge be asked to amplify any reason? See **25.57**.

- Who should explain the decision to the child?[128] The child's guardian (if there is one) or the Cafcass officer who provided any s 7 report may be the appropriate person.

- In addition to the above, should the judge write to the child to explain the decision? Considerations may include the age and wishes of the child and whether the judge has met the child (for which see **4.48**).

- Who should communicate the decision to any expert evidence? If a transcript of the judgment is to be prepared, should a copy be sent to the

---

[125] *Re B; X Council v B (No 2)* [2008] EWHC 270 (Fam), [2008] 1 FLR 1460, per Munby J at [13].
[126] [2008] EWHC 1773 (Fam), [2008] 2 FLR 1800.
[127] [2008] EWHC 1681 (Fam), [2008] 2 FLR 1687.
[128] PD 12B, para 5.5(d).

expert together with a copy of the order explaining the purpose of disclosing the judgment and limiting any further publication?[129]

- Should any future applications be reserved to the judge who heard the proceedings?[130]

- Is permission to appeal sought? See **25.22**.

ORDERS

20.69   A judgment or order takes effect from the day when it is given or made, or such later date as the court may specify.[131]

The court may at any time correct an accidental slip or omission in a judgment or order and a party may apply for a correction without notice.[132] Orders, whether made by consent or otherwise can be corrected under this rule only if it does not express the court's intended meaning at the time it was made.[133]

---

[129]   For example, 'only for his information and no other purpose'.
[130]   If this is done, the order should recite an obligation on anyone issuing such an application to draw the attention of the court staff to the reservation.
[131]   FPR 2010, r 29.15.
[132]   Ibid, r 29.16.
[133]   See, for example. *Re N, A v G and N* [2009] EWHC 1807 (Fam), [2010] 1 FLR 272, at [179] and *A v Ward (No 2)* [2010] EWHC 538 (Fam), [2010] 2 FLR 159, at [11].

Chapter 21

RESTRAINING FURTHER APPLICATIONS

INTRODUCTION

21.1 Section 91(14) of CA 1989 enables courts to control any further applications in respect of the child by imposing a restraining order:

> 'On disposing of any application for an order under this Act, the court may, (whether or not it makes any other order in response to the application) order that no application for an order under this Act of any specified kind may be made in respect of the child concerned by any person named in the order without leave of the court.'

Any such order therefore has:

- to be made at the time an application under CA 1989 is disposed of;

- to specify the kind of order which cannot be made without leave;

- to name the person who cannot make the order without leave.

21.2 Such orders are exceptional and it is important that guidance given by the Court of Appeal (see **21.4**) is followed. The Law Reports contain many examples of such orders being overturned on appeal because they are not justified or were improperly made.[1]

REASON FOR THE POWER

21.3 The purpose of s 91(14) is to protect the other parties and the child from unnecessary involvement in the proposed proceedings and unwarranted investigations into the circumstances of the child:[2]

> 'Those of us who frequently determine applications for orders to change a child's residence can forget the weight of the emotional assault upon the resident parent which they engender ... Apart from the unlawful abduction of a child ... nothing can raise the temperature of a family dispute more than an ill-considered, unfounded application for a residence order.'[3]

---

[1] *Re A (Contact: Section 91(14))* [2009] EWCA Civ 1548, [2010] 2 FLR 151, per Wilson LJ at [71].

[2] *Re P (Section 91(14) Guidelines) (Residence and Religious Heritage)* [1999] 2 FLR 573.

[3] *Re R (Residence: Contact: Restricting Applications)* [1998] 1 FLR 749, per Wilson J at 759.

There will often be a background of failed applications but this is not a pre-requisite for an order. In some cases, a limited restriction may be justified to provide a breathing space for the child and the carers. In some cases it may be justified in order to ensure future compliance with court procedure.[4]

PRINCIPLES TO BE APPLIED

21.4 The test when a court is considering exercising its powers is the welfare test. In *Re P (Section 91(14) Guidelines) (Residence and Religious Heritage)*,[5] the Court of Appeal summarised existing authority in a set of guidelines while stressing that these were only guidelines intended to assist and not replace the wording of the section:

(1) Section 91(14) should be read in conjunction with s 1(1) which makes the welfare of the child the paramount consideration.

(2) The power to restrict applications to the court is discretionary and in the exercise of its discretion the court must weigh in the balance all the relevant circumstances.

(3) An important consideration is that to impose a restriction is a statutory intrusion into the right of a party to bring proceedings before the court and to be heard in matters affecting his/her own child.

(4) The power has therefore to be used with great care and sparingly – the exception and not the rule.

(5) It is generally to be seen as a useful weapon of last resort in cases of repeated and unreasonable applications.[6]

(6) In suitable circumstances (and on clear evidence), a court may impose the leave restriction in cases where the welfare of the child requires it, although there is no past history of making unreasonable applications.[7]

(7) In cases under para (6) above, the court will need to be satisfied first that the facts go beyond the commonly encountered need for a time to settle a regime ordered by the court and the all too common situation where there is animosity between the adults in dispute or between the local authority and the family and secondly that there is a serious risk that, without the imposition of the restriction, the child or the primary carers will be subject to unacceptable strain.

---

4   *C v W (Contact: Leave to Apply)* [1999] 1 FLR 916.
5   [1999] 2 FLR 573.
6   See also *Re A (Contact: Section 91(14))* [2009] EWCA Civ 1548, [2010] 2 FLR 151.
7   For example, *Re F (Children) (Restriction on Applications)* [2005] EWCA Civ 499, *Re M (A Child) (Restriction on Applications)* [2005] All ER (D) 84 (Dec, CA).

(8) A court may impose the restriction on making applications in the absence of a request from any of the parties, subject, of course, to the rules of natural justice such as an opportunity for the parties to be heard on the point.

(9) A restriction may be imposed with or without limitation of time.

(10) The degree of restriction should be proportionate to the harm it is intended to avoid. Therefore, the court imposing the restriction should carefully consider the extent of the restriction to be imposed and specify, where appropriate, the type of application to be restrained and the duration of the order.

The court cannot impose a condition that any application for leave must be accompanied by psychiatric or other medical evidence because to do so will fetter in advance the discretion of the judge hearing any application for permission.[8]

21.5 However, a court may, when making a s 91(14) order identify an issue and suggest to the party affected that unless he can show that the particular issue has been addressed, any application for permission to apply to the court was unlikely to be successful.[9]

21.6 Orders are a last resort.

'There is a view among some family lawyers that the requirement of leave to make an application is a reasonable feature of many branches of the law and may be particularly valuable in family proceedings and that it casts no undue hardship upon a parent (or other person) to be required to show to the court an arguable case in support of a proposed application under the Act before being permitted to make it. Indeed I myself might, in other circumstances, have had some sympathy for that view. But that view is, as all we family lawyers know, emphatically not the view taken in our jurisprudence about the circumstances in which it is appropriate to make an order under s.91(14) of the Act. Ever since the enunciation by Butler-Sloss LJ of 11 guidelines in *Re P (Section 91(14) Guidleines) (Residence and Religious Heritage)* we have known that the power to make such an order is, pursuant to her fourth guideline, to be used with great care and sparingly and is, pursuant to her fifth guideline, generally to be seen as a weapon of last resort in cases of repeated and unreasonable applications.'[10]

An immediate, perhaps instinctive reaction to the case might be that it is preferable for the child if, for a time, future litigation should be controlled by the court but this is not a legitimate foundation for making the order.[11]

---

8 *Stringer v Stringer Ltd* [2006] EWCA Civ 1617, [2007] 1 FLR 1532. See also *Re S (Contact: Prohibition of Applications)* [1994] 2 FLR 1057.
9 *Stringer v Stringer Ltd* [2006] EWCA Civ 1617, [2007] 1 FLR 1532, at [10].
10 *Re A (Contact: Section 91(14))* [2009] EWCA Civ 1548, [2010] 2 FLR 151, per Wilson LJ at [16].
11 Ibid, at [17].

21.7   Although orders made be made to last indefinitely or until the child reaches the age of 16 or even 18, this should be the exception rather than the rule.[12] For an example of where such an order was upheld in relation to a 14-year-old child, see *Re J (A Child) (Restriction on Applications)*.[13]

PROCEDURE

21.8   It is undesirable in other than the most exceptional cases for the order to be made without notice to all parties.[14] However, there will be cases in which the question of a s 91(14) order arises either during or at the end of a hearing, on the application of one of the parties, or on the court's own initiative. In addition one or more of the parties before the court may be unrepresented.

21.9   In *Re C (Litigant in Person: Section 91(14) Order)*[15] Wall LJ gave guidance on the procedure which should be followed in these circumstances.

- The court may make an order under s 91(14);

- It is of the utmost importance that the party or parties or other persons affected by the order, particularly if they are in person:

  - understand that such an application is being made, or that consideration is being given to making a s 91(14) order;
  - understand the meaning and effect of such an order. This will involve the court telling the parties in ordinary language what a s 91(14) order is;
  - have a proper opportunity to make submissions to the court in answer to the application or to the suggestion that a s 91(14) order be made. This may mean adjourning the application for it to be made in writing and on notice;
  - If there is a substantive objection on which a litigant wishes to seek legal advice the court should either normally not make an order; alternatively it can make an order and give the recipient permission to apply to set it aside within a specified time.

- Where the parties (and in particular the person affected by the s 91(14) order) are unrepresented, it may be possible for the court to deal with the matter in argument without a formal application, although if the representative for the party affected seeks a short adjournment to take instructions, such an application should normally be granted. If there is a

---

12   *Re S (Permission to Seek Relief)* [2006] EWCA Civ 1190, [2007] 1 FLR 482.

13   [2007] EWCA Civ 906, [2008] 1 FLR 369.

14   *Re P (Section 91(14) Guidelines) (Residence and Religious Heritage)* [1999] 2 FLR 573 at 593. See also *Re C-J (Section 91(14) Order)* [2006] EWHC 1491 (Fam), [2006] 2 FLR 1213 and *Re C (Litigant in Person: Section 91(14) Order)* [2009] EWCA Civ 674, [2009] 2 FLR 1461.

15   Ibid, at [13]. The form and sequence of the guidance has been amended slightly.

substantive objection to the s 91(14) order, then the court should require the application to be made formally on notice in the normal way.

His Lordship added that none of this guidance was designed to address the merits of s 91(14) orders, which are exceptional.

HUMAN RIGHTS CONSIDERATIONS

21.10 Article 6(1) of the European Convention for the Protection of Human Rights and Fundamental Freedoms 1950 impliedly contains a right of access to courts,[16] but this right is not absolute. States may regulate the right so long as they do so in pursuit of a legitimate aim and the restrictions are proportionate to that aim.[17] Any restrictions must not impair the essence of the right to access.[18] The European Commission on Human Rights has held that restrictions requiring vexatious litigants to obtain permission before commencing proceedings are, in principle, legitimate.[19]

21.11 In *Re P (Section 91(14) Guidelines) (Residence and Religious Heritage)*,[20] the President held that s 91(14) does not offend Art 6(1):

'The applicant is not denied access to the court. It is a partial restriction in that it does not allow him the right to an immediate inter partes hearing. It thereby protects the other parties and the child from being drawn into the proposed proceedings unless or until a court has ruled that the application should be allowed to proceed. On an application for leave, the applicant must persuade the judge that he has an arguable case with some chance of success. That is not a formidable hurdle to surmount. If the application is hopeless and refused the other parties and the child will have been protected from unnecessary involvement in the proposed proceedings and unwarranted investigations into the present circumstances of the child.'

Examples

Re T (A Minor) (Parental Responsibility: Contact)[21]

21.12 A father's application for parental responsibility and contact was dismissed in circumstances where the father had treated the mother with violence, displayed hostility towards her and had failed to return the child after contact. A s 91(14) order was made restraining any applications for s 8 orders without permission for a period of 3 years.

---

[16] *Golder v United Kingdom* (1979–80) 1 EHRR 524.
[17] *Lithgow v United Kingdom* (1986) 8 EHRR 329.
[18] *Stubbings v UK* (1997) 23 EHRR 213, [1997] 1 FLR 105.
[19] *M v United Kingdom* (1985) 52 DR 269.
[20] [1999] 2 FLR 573, at 593.
[21] [1993] 2 FLR 450.

Re R (Residence: Contact: Restricting Applications)[22]

21.13   A father was prevented from making any application for contact or residence without permission for an unlimited time against a background of a turbulent and violent marriage and three failed applications for residence orders, at least one of which was expressed in intemperate terms.

C v W (Contact: Leave to Apply)[23]

21.14   An order was made in relation to any s 8 application for an unlimited period. The father had removed the 3-year-old child from the mother on three occasions. He had failed to co-operate with the court welfare officer's arrangements for supervised contact, had failed to file a statement as directed and failed to attend the final hearing.

Re P (Section 91(14) Guidelines) (Residence and Religious Heritage)[24]

21.15   A s 91(14) order was made without restriction of time to prevent Jewish parents re-applying for a residence order in respect of their daughter who had Down's Syndrome and who was living with Roman Catholic foster parents in circumstances where a further application would submit the foster parents to 'corrosive' tension.

Re B (Section 91(14) Order: Duration)[25]

21.16   A father had not seen his 9-year-old daughter for 6 years. Because of certain difficulties only indirect contact was ordered although the medium- to long-term objective remained the establishment of direct contact. The Court of Appeal allowed an appeal against an indefinite s 91(14) order in relation to any contact application made on the ground that applications were likely to damage the emotional development and well-being of the child and her mother. Such an order was incompatible with the primary objective of restoring the child's relationship with her father. The order would be restricted to applications for direct contact within a 2-year period.

Re F (children) (restrictions on applications)[26]

21.17   Against a background of domestic violence in 2003 and 2004 the Cafcass officer recommended that there should be only indirect contact because direct contact would alarm and unsettle the children. The father's appeal against a s 91(14) order restraining him from making any s 8 application

---

22   [1998] 1 FLR 749.
23   [1999] 1 FLR 916.
24   [1999] 2 FLR 573.
25   [2003] EWCA Civ 1966, [2004] 1 FLR 871.
26   [2005] EWCA Civ 499.

for a period of two-and-a-half years was dismissed although the period was 'perhaps towards the top end of the appropriate bracket'.

Applying for leave

21.18 On an application for leave, the applicant must persuade the judge that he has an arguable case with some chance of success. In *Re P (Section 91(14) Guidelines) (Residence and Religious Heritage)*,[27] the President said that is not a formidable hurdle to surmount.

The simplest of tests should be applied. Does the application show that there is a need for renewed judicial application? The criteria imposed by s 10(9) and elaborated in cases concerned with that sub-section do not govern the application for leave under s 91(14).[28]

The granting of permission does not mean that the client is automatically entitled to a full hearing. In some cases, the application may be able to be decided at a directions hearing if any additional information shows that it should go no further.[29]

The appropriate procedure for applying for leave is to issue the application on Form C2 for a direction in the proceedings in which the s 91(14) order was made.[30] The application should normally be heard on notice[31] but it can be heard without notice to all or some of the other parties in order to protect the other parties from the very upset that the order was made to avoid.[32]

Examples

Re F (Contact: Restraint Order)[33]

21.19 Leave was granted to a father to apply for contact given where the s 91(14) order had been made in order to allow the children to be assessed by a child psychiatrist and the mother had failed to co-operate with the assessment. The original purpose of the order had failed.

Re A (Application for Leave)[34]

21.20 A s 91(14) order had been made against the mother of three children who lived with their father. Eighteen months later, she applied for permission to apply for contact with three of the children, the third having left her father's home and joined her mother. The Court of Appeal held that the mother should

---

27 [1999] 2 FLR 573, at 593.
28 *Re A (Application for Leave)* [1998] 1 FLR 1.
29 Ibid, at 4.
30 Ibid, at 3.
31 Ibid.
32 *Re G and M (Child Orders: Restricting Applications)* [1995] 2 FLR 416.
33 [1995] 1 FLR 956.
34 [1998] 1 FLR 1.

have been granted permission. Too much emphasis had been laid on past history and too little on developments since the order.

EXPIRY OF ORDER

21.21   Even after expiry of the s 91(14) order by efluxion of time the court will still be able to exercise its other powers[35] and in particular, the power of summary dismissal of an application which is unmeritorious or the pursuit of which is not in the child's best interests.[36]

GREPE V LOAM RESTRICTIONS

21.22   Courts were able to restrain parties from issuing proceedings or applications within proceedings without first obtaining permission[37] and before the introduction of the Family Procedure Rules 2010 there appeared to be no reason why such a power could not be exercised in the family jurisdiction in the High Court. Although there are few reported cases in which the power has been exercised, undoubtedly it was used in practice. Because it is an inherent jurisdiction, there was some doubt whether county courts, being created by statute, possess the power. However, in *Ebert v Venvil*,[38] Lord Woolf MR appeared to assume that the county court had such a power, both the county court and the High Court being part of the same civil justice system. There can be no doubt however that family proceedings courts cannot make *Grepe v Loam* orders. The extent to which such restrictions have survived the power to make civil restraint orders (see **21.25**) is uncertain. It is likely it no longer exists, or, if it does, should not be exercised.

Example

Re K (Replacement of Guardian ad Litem)[39]

21.23   Both parents were restricted from making any further applications in wardship proceedings in order to afford the child a period of stability.

21.24   In addition, if the Court of Appeal refuses an application for permission to appeal and considers that the application is totally without merit, its order must so record.[40] At the same time it must consider whether it is appropriate to make a limited, extended or general civil restraint order[41] under

---

35   Analysed in *Re N, A v G and N* [2009] EWHC 1807 (Fam), [2010] 1 FLR 454, at [219]–[234].
36   *Re N (Section 91(14))* [2009] EWHC 3055 (Fam), [2010] 1 FLR 1110.
37   *Grepe v Loam* (1887) 37 Ch D 168. See also *Bhamjee v Forsdick (No 2)* [2003] EWCA Civ 1113, *The Times*, 31 July. In civil proceedings the matter is now governed by the Civil Procedure Rules 1998, r 3.11 (civil restraint orders).
38   [2000] Ch 484, at 498.
39   [2001] 1 FLR 663.
40   CPR, r 52.10(5).
41   As defined by CPR PD 3C and in the conditions required by CPR Part 3.

CPR 2.3.1.[42] Such a power is also available to the court when dismissing an appeal if it considers it is totally without merit, although it would be unusual for such a finding to be made if the appeal had been brought with leave.

Civil restraint orders

21.25 The High Court and county court have power to make civil restraint orders against a party who has made applications which are 'totally without merit'.[43] The orders prevent applications being made without prior permission of a named judge. The powers of the court to make civil restraint orders are separate from and do not replace the powers given to the court by CA 1989, s 91(14).[44]

The procedure and effect of the orders are governed by Practice Direction 4B.

There are three types of orders which can be made.

Limited civil restraint orders

21.26 A limited civil restraint order may be made by a judge of the High Court or a county court where a party has made two or more applications which are totally without merit.[45]

Where the court makes a limited civil restraint order, the party against whom the order is made:

(a) is restrained from making any further applications in the proceedings in which the order is made without first obtaining the permission of a judge identified in the order;

(b) may apply for amendment or discharge of the order, but only with the permission of a judge identified in the order; and

(c) may apply for permission to appeal the order and if permission is granted, may appeal the order.[46]

Extended civil restraint order

21.27 An extended civil restraint order may be made by a judge of the High Court but not a district judge where a party has persistently made applications which are totally without merit.[47]

---

[42] See *Re A (A Child)* [2009] EWCA Civ 1249 and *Re N (Section 91(14))* [2009] EWHC 3055 (Fam), [2010] 1 FLR 1110, at [39].
[43] FPR 2010, r 4.8.
[44] PD 4B, para 1.1.
[45] Ibid, para 2.1.
[46] Ibid, para 2.2.
[47] Ibid, para 3.1.

Unless the court orders otherwise, where the court makes an extended civil restraint order, the party against whom the order is made:

(a)   is restrained from making applications in any court concerning any matter involving or relating to or touching upon or leading to the proceedings in which the order is made without first obtaining the permission of a judge identified in the order;

(b)   may apply for amendment or discharge of the order, but only with the permission of a judge identified in the order; and

(c)   may apply for permission to appeal the order and if permission is granted, may appeal the order.[48]

General civil restraint order

21.28   A general civil restraint order may be made by a judge of the High Court but not a district judge where, the party against whom the order is made persists in making applications which are totally without merit, in circumstances where an extended civil restraint order would not be sufficient or appropriate.[49]

Unless the court otherwise orders, where the court makes a general civil restraint order, the party against whom the order is made:

(a)   is restrained from making any application in any court without first obtaining the permission of a judge identified in the order;

(b)   may apply for amendment or discharge of the order, but only with the permission of a judge identified in the order; and

(c)   may apply for permission to appeal the order and if permission is granted, may appeal the order.[50]

---

[48]   PD 4B, para 3.2.
[49]   Ibid, para 4.1.
[50]   Ibid, para 4.2.

Chapter 22

DUTY TO DISCLOSE AND NOT TO DISCLOSE

INTRODUCTION

22.1 It is clearly in the interest of children that courts have access to all information which may be relevant to their welfare. But there is a tension between this and a litigant's right to be able to consult frankly with his or her lawyer without what is said becoming known to the court and the other parties. Likewise, until recently there had long been a belief that litigation about intimate family matters should be conducted in private. A tension arises, however, when information which becomes known in these proceedings may be relevant for other purposes, for example, for the prosecution of alleged child abuse. The importance of the public understanding the workings of the family justice system has prompted a debate about the reporting of proceedings which would otherwise be closed to the public. Some of the issues have been resolved by statute. Other issues, although the subject of judicial pronouncement, remain unresolved.[1]

DUTIES TO DISCLOSE

Parties

22.2 In all cases where the welfare of a child is the court's paramount consideration, there is a duty on all parties to make a full and frank disclosure of all matters material to the welfare of the child and the issues before the court, whether or not the matters are favourable or adverse to their case.[2] This includes frankness not just in written and oral evidence but also in conversations with family and court reporters and in disclosing material documents.

22.3 When reports have been obtained with the permission of the court, they too must be disclosed, whether or not the report is favourable and whether or not the party obtaining the report wishes to use it in evidence.[3] The House of

---

1   For further discussion of all aspects of disclosure, see Brasse 'The duty of disclosure in children cases' [1996] Fam Law 358.
2   *Oxfordshire County Council v P* [1995] 1 FLR 552, per Ward J at 557A.
3   *Re L (Police Investigation: Privilege)* [1996] 1 FLR 731, per Lord Jauncey of Tullichettle at 741.

Lords, in the leading case of *Re L (Police Investigation: Privilege)*,[4] left open the question of whether or not a report had to be disclosed if it had been obtained in circumstances where permission was not required, that is where the child was not interviewed and documents confidential to the proceedings were not seen by the person preparing the report.

22.4 A party in private law proceedings has greater protection from self-incrimination than one in public law proceedings. He is able to refuse to answer any question put to him in the course of giving evidence on the ground that doing so might incriminate himself or his spouse. This common law protection[5] is denied a witness in public law proceedings by s 98, although some limited degree of protection is afforded by the proviso that a statement or admission made in the proceedings shall not be admissible in evidence against the person making it in proceedings for an offence other than perjury.[6]

Legal representatives

22.5 The position of lawyers who have material information which their clients have not disclosed is unclear. Certainly they are under a duty not to mislead the court.[7] If they know, as opposed to suspect, that their client has lied when giving oral evidence or in a statement or has failed to make proper disclosure of documents, they, like legal representatives in all cases, are under a duty to cease acting for the client unless matters are put right.

22.6 The uncertainty arises over the issue of whether they are under a positive duty to make full disclosure of matters within their knowledge if their client refuses to allow them to do so. In *Essex County Council v R*,[8] Thorpe J (as he then was) seemed to accept that there was no such duty although he thought there should be:

> 'For my part, I would wish to see case-law go yet further and to make it plain that the legal representatives in possession of such material relevant to determination but contrary to the interests of their client, not only are unable to resist disclosure by reliance on legal professional privilege, but have a positive duty to disclose to the other parties and to the court.'

In addition, he held that legal professional privilege cannot be used as a defence to resist disclosure.

22.7 In *Re DH (A Minor) (Child Abuse)*,[9] Wall J went further than Thorpe J, holding, obiter, that a duty to disclose already existed:

---

4   *Re L (Police Investigation: Privilege)* [1996] 1 FLR 731, per Lord Jauncey of Tullichettle at 741.
5   *Blunt v Park Lane Hotels* [1942] 2 KB 253.
6   CA 1989, s 98(2).
7   *The Guide to the Professional Conduct of Solicitors* (8th edn, The Law Society), Principle 21.01.
8   [1993] 2 FLR 826, at 828.
9   [1994] 1 FLR 679, at 704.

'... the client needs to be told authoritatively at an early stage in the relationship that whilst the advocate has a duty to present the client's case to the best of his or her ability, the advocate has a higher duty to the court and to the child whose interests are paramount to disclose relevant material to the court even if that disclosure is not in the interests of the client.'

22.8 In *Vernon v Bosley (No 2)*,[10] Thorpe LJ agreed there was such a duty in all cases:

'If counsel's duty goes no further than requiring his withdrawal from the case there seems to me to be a remaining risk of injustice.'

22.9 The issue was considered by the House of Lords in *Re L (Police Investigation: Privilege)*.[11] Lord Jauncey of Tullichettle, in the leading speech, which was supported by Lord Lloyd of Berwick and Lord Steyn, expressly left the matter open for future consideration. Lord Nicholls of Birkenhead, supported by Lord Mustill, however, rejected the argument that the duty existed:

'I do not believe that the Children Act 1989 was intended to abrogate legal professional privilege in family proceedings, or that it has done so. Legal professional privilege is deeply embedded in English law. This was confirmed recently by your Lordship's House in *R v Derby Magistrates' Court ex parte B*.[12] The privilege against non-disclosure prevails even where the privileged material might assist the defence of a person charged with murder.

Clear words, therefore, or a compelling context are needed before Parliament can be taken to have intended that the privilege should be ousted in favour of another interest. The Children Act contains neither.'[13]

'Indeed, it must be doubtful whether a parent who is denied the opportunity to obtain legal advice in confidence is accorded the fair hearing to which he is entitled under Art 6(1) read in conjunction with Art 8 of the European Convention for the Protection of Human Rights and Fundamental Freedoms.

... The paramountcy principle must not be permitted to become a loose cannon, destroying all else around it.'[14]

This uncertainty leaves the lawyer in a very difficult position, at risk of alienating the client, an action for breach of confidence and, in theory at least, of disciplinary action from his or her professional body.

As the Court of Appeal pointed out in *Re D (A Child)*[15] counsel and solicitors need to be familiar with 'the full ramifications' of the law relating to waiver of

---

10 [1998] 1 FLR 304, at 346.
11 [1996] 1 FLR 731.
12 [1996] 1 FLR 513.
13 [1996] 1 FLR 731, at 742.
14 [1996] 1 FLR 731, at 744.
15 [2011] EWCA Civ 684, per Ward LJ at [24].

professional privilege and should be on guard to protect their client from revealing, either in written evidence or when giving oral evidence, advice which has prompted to prompt the change of heart or change of attitude. Judges must also be astute to anticipate an unintentional observation which results in privilege being waived and must be ready to warn a witness of any such danger.

22.10   The *Solicitors Code of Conduct*[16] provides some assistance for solicitors. There is a 'fundamental'[17] duty of confidence to the client:

> 'You and your firm must keep the affairs of clients and former clients confidential except where disclosure is required or permitted by law or by your client (or former client).'[18]

22.11   The *Code of Conduct for the Bar*[19] similarly states:

> 'Whether or not the relation of counsel and client continues a barrister must preserve the confidentiality of the lay client's affairs and must not without the prior consent of the lay client or as permitted by law lend or reveal the contents of the papers in any instructions to or communicate to any third person (other than another barrister, a pupil ... or any other person who needs to know it for the performance of their duties) information which has been entrusted to him in confidence or use such information to the lay client's detriment or to his own or another client's advantage.'

22.12   Guidance to the *Solicitors' Code of Conduct* adds the following:

> 'In proceedings under the Children Act 1989 you are under a duty to reveal experts' reports commissioned for the purpose of proceedings, as these reports are not privileged. The position in relation to voluntary disclosure of other documents or solicitor/client communications is uncertain. ... An advocate is under a duty not to mislead the court ... Therefore, if you are an advocate and have certain knowledge which you realise is adverse to the client's case you may be extremely limited in what you state in the client's favour. In this situation, you should seek the client's agreement for full voluntary disclosure for three reasons:
>
> (i)   the matters the client wants to hide will probably emerge anyway;
> (ii)   you will be able to do a better job for the client if all the relevant information is presented to the court;
> (iii) if the information is not voluntarily disclosed you may be severely criticised by the court.
>
> If the client refuses to give you authority to disclose the relevant information you are entitled to refuse to continue to act for the client if to do so will place you in breach of your obligations to the court.'[20]

---

[16]   (Solicitors Regulation Authority, 2007).
[17]   Ibid, Guidance to Rule 4 Note 3.
[18]   Ibid, Rule 4.01.
[19]   Bar Standards Board (8th edn, 2004) Section 1 Pt VII Rule 702. See also Langdale and Miller 'Professional ethics: counsel acting in family proceedings' [2010] Fam Law 718.
[20]   Ibid, note 14.

If the advocate is in any doubt about what course should be taken, he or she should discuss the matter with a partner or senior member of chambers. If doubts remain, advice should be sought from his or her professional body.

22.13 Legal advisers may in exceptional circumstances consider revealing confidential information to relevant authorities such as social services:

'There may be exceptional circumstances involving children where a solicitor should consider revealing confidential information to an appropriate authority. This may be where the child is a client and the child reveals information which indicates continuing sexual or other physical abuse but refuses to allow disclosure of such information. Similarly there may be situations where an adult discloses abuse either by himself or herself or by another adult against a child but refuses to allow any disclosure. The solicitor must consider whether the threat to the child's life or health, both mental and physical is sufficiently serious to justify a breach of the duty of confidentiality.'[21]

22.14 The Law Society's *Family Law Protocol*[22] states that in 'appropriate circumstances' solicitors must make their clients aware of this principle and in cases concerning allegations of domestic abuse and child abuse, should wherever possible encourage clients to confirm the appropriate authority:[23]

'However, solicitors should always bear in mind that they owe a duty of confidentiality to their clients and may have to justify any breach of that duty to their professional body. It is always advisable to seek advice from the Law Society's Professional Ethics section (tel 0870 606 2555)[24] and ... other members of the profession, partners in the firm and professional insurers.'[25]

Unless the court directs otherwise, a party is not required to reveal

- their home address or other contact details;

- the address or other contact details of any child;

- the name of a person with whom the child is living, if that person is not the applicant; or

- in relation to an application for permission to change a child's surname under s 28(2) of the Adoption and Children Act 2002, the proposed new surname of the child.[26]

Where a party does not wish to reveal any of these particulars, that party must give notice of those particulars to the court and the particulars will not be

---

[21] Ibid, note 13.
[22] (The Law Society, 3rd edn, 2010), para 3.3.6.
[23] Ibid, para 5.3.1.
[24] The telephone number of the Ethical Enquiries line of the Bar Council is 020 7611 1307.
[25] *Family Law Protocol*, para 5.3.6.
[26] FPR 2010, r 29.1.

revealed to any person unless the court directs otherwise.[27] However, where a party changes home address during the course of proceedings, that party must give notice of the change to the court.[28]

Missing children

22.15   The court has powers under Family Law Act 1986, s 33 to order any person to disclose information concerning the whereabouts of a child. Before the order is made, there must be proceedings to which Part 1 of the Family Law Act 1986 applies (ie proceedings for s 8 orders, care orders, freeing orders, orders for the delivery of a child or made under the Child Abduction and Custody Act 1985,[29] but seemingly not parental responsibility orders). Adequate information as to where the child is must not be otherwise available to the court. In addition, the court must have reason to believe that the person against whom the order is sought may have relevant information. As under CA 1989, s 98, a person cannot be excused from complying with the order on the ground that doing so might incriminate himself or his spouse but the same limited protection in relation to evidence being admissible in criminal proceedings is available.[30] It should be noted that these protections apply only to spouses and do not extend to information likely to incriminate the other parent or the parent's cohabitee if they and the person giving evidence or complying with the order are not married to each other.

22.16   Orders under s 33 can be made against legal advisers.[31]

22.17   The *Family Law Protocol* advises that if a client discloses to a solicitor any threat to abduct a child, the solicitor should discuss the issue with the Law Society's Professional Ethics department.[32]

A DUTY NOT TO DISCLOSE

Disclosure forbidden by statute and the Family Proceedure Rules

22.18   The principle that there should be 'open justice' is well established in common law and is now buttressed by Arts 6 and 10 of the European Convention on Human Rights and Fundamental Freedoms 1950 (ECHR).

> 'The principle of open justice represents an element of democratic accountability, and the vigorous manifestation of the principle of freedom of expression. Ultimately it supports the rule of law itself ... [It] encompasses the entitlement of the media to impart and the public to receive information in accordance with article 10 of the European Convention of Human Rights. Each element of the

---

27   FPR 2010, r 29.2.
28   Ibid, r 29.3.
29   Family Law Act 1986, s 1(1).
30   CA 1989, s 33(2).
31   *Re H (Abduction: Whereabouts Order to Solicitors)* [2000] 1 FLR 766.
32   *Family Law Protocol*, para 7.2.3.

media must be free to decide for itself what to report ... It is, of course, elementary that the courts do not function in order to provide the media with copy, or to provide ammunition for the media, or for that matter private individuals, to berate the government or the opposition of the day, or for that matter to berate or laud anyone else. They function to enable justice to be done between parties. However where litigation has taken place and judgment given, any disapplication of the principle of open justice must be rigidly contained, and even within the small number of permissible exceptions, it should be rare indeed for the court to order that any part of the reasoning in the judgment which has led it to its conclusion should be redacted. As a matter of principle it is an order to be made only in extreme circumstances.'[33]

22.19 Proceedings relating to the welfare of children are, however, held in private and hitherto the legislature and the courts have been anxious to protect the privacy and confidentiality of what the House of Lords in *Scott v Scott*[34] called 'truly domestic affairs' and the judicial process concerned with exercising a paternalistic, parental, quasi-domestic and essentially administrative jurisdiction. To allow the proceedings to be reported, whether formally through the media or informally by parties disseminating information, would be to risk children suffering emotional harm from publicity,[35] to deter both lay and professional witnesses from giving evidence thereby prejudicing the judicial process and encouraging witnesses to be less than frank. The importance of telling 'the truth, the whole truth and nothing but the truth' in cases involving children is illustrated by s 98 of the Act which provides that in care proceedings no one shall be excused from giving evidence or answering any questions put to him in the course of giving evidence on the ground that to do so might incriminate him or his spouse or civil partner of an offence.

22.20 In recent years there has been a perception, strengthened by the debate about contact between children and their non-resident fathers, that the public want family proceedings to be more open. How far this perception is based on fact rather than an assertion by journalists, is unclear.[36] The result according to Sir Nicholas Wall P and Bob Satchwell, the Executive Director of the Society of Editors, is that:

> 'There is no more difficult issue in family justice than the reporting of cases. There is a tension between concerns about "secret justice" and legitimate expectations of privacy and confidentiality for the family. Both standpoints are valid and the question is whether they are irreconcilable.'[37]

---

[33] *R (Binyam Mohamed) v Secretary of State for Foreign and Commonwealth Affairs* [2010] EWCA Civ 65, [2011] QB 218 per Lord Judge CJ at [39]–[42]. See also Wolanski and Wilson *The Family Courts: Media Access & Reporting* (Judicial Office, 2011), paras 3–6.

[34] [1913] AC 417, per Lord Shaw at 482 and Viscount Haldane at 437.

[35] See, for example, *Re Z (A Minor) (Freedom of Publication)* [1996] 1 FLR 191 noted at **22.48**.

[36] The Family Courts Information Pilot which published 165 anonymised judgments and written reasons in public proceedings in five family courts on the internet between November 2009 and December 2010 found no evidence of any press interest. Only 10 members of the public replied to an online survey on the site (Ministry of Justice, 2011).

[37] Preface to *The Family Courts: Media Access & Reporting*, op cit.

The complexities of the debate have been deepened by the difficulties in controlling publication by means of the internet.[38]

22.21 The question of what information about private law children proceedings can be made public has to be examined in a number of ways: the default position established by legislation; when courts can increase protection and when it can decrease it. Whatever approach is used, there is no overall rule: revealing the identity of the child involved has to be distinguished from other information, for example, the evidence or the identity of adult witnesses. The issue of what can be disclosed is a complex one, governed not by a single Code but by various statutes. The position is usefully summarised by Wolanski and Wilson in *The Family Courts: Media Access and Reporting* which was jointly commissioned by the President of the Family Division and the Society of Editors.

Disclosure forbidden by statute and the Family Proceedure Rules 2010

Information

22.22 The keystone of protection is provided by s 12(1) of the Administration of Justice Act 1960 (AJA 1960) which states that the publication of information relating to proceedings before any court sitting in private[39] shall not of itself be contempt of court except where the proceedings:[40]

- relate to the exercise of the inherent jurisdiction of the High Court with respect to minors;

- are brought under the Children Act 1989; or

- otherwise relate wholly or mainly to the maintenance or upbringing of a minor;

- where the court (having power to do so) expressly prohibits the publication of all information relating to the proceedings or of information of the description which is published.

22.23 'Publication' is not confined to information communicated through the media but includes private communication to individuals. It can be oral or written. Save where an individual communicates information to a professional, each acting to protect children, there is publication whenever the law of defamation would treat it as being publication.[41]

---

[38]   Op cit.
[39]   Including a court sitting in camera or in chambers (s 12(3)).
[40]   There are other exceptions not related to cases involving children.
[41]   *Re B (A Child) (Disclosure)* [2004] EWHC 411 (Fam), [2004] 2 FLR 142, per Munby J at [68], [72].

22.24 The section is not confined to wardship proceedings and its protection extends to the Children Act 1989.[42]

22.25 The scope of s 12(1) was extensively reviewed by Munby J (now Munby LJ) in *Re B (A Child) (Disclosure)*.[43]

The information which is protected relates only to information concerning the proceedings. Events in the lives of the children in the present case which are already in the public domain or which do not relate to the proceedings can be the subject of publication.[44]

22.26 Section 12(1) does not of itself prohibit the publication of:

- the fact, if it be the case, that a child is a ward of court and is the subject of wardship proceedings or that a child is the subject of residence or other proceedings under the Children Act 1989 or of proceedings relating wholly or mainly to his maintenance or upbringing;

- the name, address or photograph of such a child;

- the name, address or photograph of the parties (or, if the child is a party, the other parties) to such proceedings;

- the date, time or place of a past or future hearing of such proceedings;

- the nature of the dispute in such proceedings;

- anything which has been seen or heard by a person conducting himself lawfully in the public corridor or other public precincts outside the court in which the hearing in private is taking place;

- the name, address or photograph of the witnesses who have given evidence in such proceedings;

- the party on whose behalf such a witness has given evidence; and

- the text or summary of the whole or part of any order made in such proceedings.

It does however prohibit publication of:

- accounts of what has gone on in front of the judge sitting in private;

- documents such as affidavits, witness statements, reports, position statements, skeleton arguments or other documents filed in the

---

[42]   *Her Majesty's Attorney General v Pelling* [2005] EWHC 414 (Admin), [2006] 1 FLR 93.
[43]   Ibid, at [82].
[44]   *X v Dempster* [1999] 1 FLR 894.

proceedings, transcripts or notes of the evidence or submissions, and transcripts or notes of the judgment (this list is not necessarily exhaustive);

- extracts or quotations from such documents;

- summaries of such documents.

These prohibitions apply whether or not the information or the document being published has been anonymised.

22.27   Section 12 of the AJA 1960 prohibits disclosure by anyone and not just the parties. In *A v Payne and Williams; A v G and N*,[45] for example, a guardian was held in contempt for sending reports to the staff at a centre which the parents had been ordered to attend for therapy and parenting classes, without first obtaining the court's permission. No penalty was imposed but the centre was ordered to return the reports.

22.28   As most cases involving children will be heard in private at first instance, s 12(1) of the AJA 1960 will inhibit what of the proceedings can be reported even though the media may be allowed access to the courtroom (for which see **20.24**). There are additional prohibitions in the Family Proceedings Court. Section 71 of the Magistrates' Courts Act 1980 prohibits the printing or publishing, or a person causing or procuring to be printed or published, in a newspaper or periodical or in a programme included in a programme service (within the meaning of the Broadcasting Act 1990) for reception in Great Britain:

- the names, addresses and occupations of the parties and witnesses;

- the grounds of the application, and a concise statement of the charges, defences and counter-charges in support of which evidence has been given;

- submissions on any point of law arising in the course of the proceedings and the decision of the court on the submissions;

- the decision of the court, and any observations made by the court in giving it.

However, nothing in this section prohibits the printing or publishing of any matter in a newspaper or periodical of a technical character bona fide intended for circulation among members of the legal or medical professions.[46]

---

[45]   [2009] EWHC 736 (Fam), [2009] 2 FLR 463.
[46]   Magistrates Courts Act 1980, s 71(5).

22.29 The Court of Appeal will usually sit in public when the statutory prohibitions imposed by AJA 1960, s 12(1) does not apply.

The identity of the child

22.30 Section 97(2) of the Children Act 1989 makes it an offence for anyone to publish to the public at large or any section of the public any material which is intended, or likely, to identify:

- any child as being involved in any proceedings before the High Court, a county court or a magistrates' court but not the Court of Appeal,[47] in which any power under the Act or the Adoption and Children Act 2002 may be exercised by the court with respect to that or any other child; or

- an address or school as being that of a child involved in any such proceedings.

It is a defence for the accused to prove that he did not know, and had no reason to suspect, that the published material was intended, or likely, to identify the child.

The court or, if the Lord Chief Justice agrees, the Lord Chancellor, may, if satisfied that the welfare of the child requires it, dispense with the requirements of s 97(2) to such extent as may be specified in the order.[48]

For the purposes of the section 'publish' includes inclusion in a programme service (within the meaning of the Broadcasting Act 1990) and 'causing to be published' and "material' includes any picture or representation.[49] It does not cover a child and family reporter reporting suspicion of child abuse to social services or the police.[50]

22.31 Importantly, and unlike s 12(1) the prohibition lasts only for the duration of the proceedings.[51]

Orders

22.32 Section 12(1) of AJA 1960 does not prevent the publication of the text or a summary of the whole or part of an order made by a court sitting in private. Publication will not of itself be contempt of court except where the court (having power to do so) expressly prohibits the publication.[52]

---

[47] *Pelling v Bruce Williams* [2004] EWCA Civ 845, [2004] 2 FLR 823, at [53].

[48] CA 1989, s 97(4).

[49] Ibid, s 97(5).

[50] *Re M (Disclosure: Children and Family Reporter)* [2002] 2 FLR 893. See also **19.31**.

[51] *Clayton v Clayton* [2006] EWCA Civ 878, [2007] 1 FLR 11, per Sir Mark Potter P at [52].

[52] AJA 1960, s 12(3).

Access to information held by the court

22.33   The public (including the media) are not entitled to peruse the court file.[53]

The court's power to prevent the disclosure of further information

22.34   The High Court (which includes the Court of Appeal) has a discretionary power to prevent disclosure of information which could otherwise be disclosed.

22.35   In addition, s 39 of the Children and Young Persons Act 1933 gives any court the power to prohibit publication of certain matter in newspapers regardless of the nature of the proceedings or whether the court was sitting in public or private. The prescribed matters are:

- the name, address or school, or include any particulars calculated to lead to the identification, of any child or young person concerned in the proceedings, either as being the person or against or in respect of whom the proceedings are taken, or as being a witness;

- any picture which is or includes a picture of any child or young person so concerned in the proceedings.

22.36   These powers are not, unlike s 92(4) of the Children Act 1989 restricted to preventing publication only for so long as the proceedings continue.

Disclosure forbidden by court order

22.37   When considering whether to grant such an order, the court has to bear in mind the right of freedom of expression granted by Art 10 of the ECHR. Not only must the restriction be necessary, it must be proportionate to the perceived harm and must be no wider than is necessary. When an order against everyone is sought, the order should be granted only if the proposed publication is directly about a child whose care and upbringing are being supervised by the court and is such as might threaten the effective working of the court's jurisdiction or the ability of the child's carers to look after him:

> 'No child, simply by being a child, is entitled to a right of privacy or confidentiality.[54] That is as true of a ward of court (or child in respect of whom the inherent jurisdiction is otherwise invoked) as of any other child. Any element of confidentiality concerning a child in respect of whom the court's jurisdiction is invoked belongs not to the child but to the court. It is imposed to protect the

---

[53]   Wolanski and Wilson *The Family Courts: Media Access and Reporting* op cit, para 31.
[54]   Since the implementation of the Human Rights Act 1998, a child and its parents have a right to privacy under Art 8 and cases may arise where this might give rise to injunctions irrespective of any need to assisting the functioning of the court's jurisdiction.

proper functioning of the court's own jurisdiction, and will not be imposed to any further extent than is necessary to afford that protection ...'[55]

Given the existence of the statutory provisions and the impact of Art 10, there may be fewer cases than previously where it will be seen to be legitimate to invoke this jurisdiction especially against everyone.[56] In appropriate cases, orders can be made to prevent solicitation of information from the child, his carers and witnesses or potential witnesses and to protect them against abuse or even criticism arising from their actions in the litigation.

22.38 Guidance on applying for reporting restrictions is contained in a Practice Direction issued by the President of the Family Division,[57] supplemented by advice from the Official Solicitor.[58] Orders can be made only in the High Court and if the need for an order arises in proceedings in the county court, judges should either transfer the application to the High Court or consult their Family Division Liaison Judge. Legal advisers to the media are used to participating in hearings at very short notice and making without notice orders will be exceptional. An order will always give persons affected permission to apply to vary it on short notice. The Practice Note of the Official Solicitor contains a useful draft order. Service of the order on the national media can now be effected by means of the Press Association's Copy Direct Service and this should be the norm.

The Court of Appeal

22.39 By 1998 the Court of Appeal had established a standard practice of requiring the anonymising of any report of appeals in Children Act proceedings if, as is usually the case, the appeal was held in public. In *Re R (Minor) (Court of Appeal: Order against Identification)*[59] Lord Woolf, then Master of the Rolls, said that the reason was that:

'... it is appreciated that in the court below the hearing is in chambers (in normal circumstances the public will have no access to those proceedings unless they make special arrangements to hear them; in children proceedings the public do not normally have access; the matter is subject to the Family Proceedings Rules 1991, r 4.16(7)), while in this court the proceedings are in public. It is considered highly desirable that appellate proceedings wherever possible should be in open court, and the judgment which is given should be available to the public and the profession through the normal court reporting procedures. In the great majority of cases, this could have adverse consequences so far as children are concerned. In a case where a child's parents are in dispute as to how the child should be brought

---

55 *R v Central Independent Television plc* [1994] 2 FLR 151, per Waite LJ at 165.

56 *Harris v Harris; Attorney-General v Harris* [2001] 2 FLR 895, per Munby J. The judgment contains an exhaustive review of the authorities. The leading authority of the Court of Appeal is *Re Z (A Minor) (Freedom of Publication)* [1996] 1 FLR 191.

57 *President's Practice Direction (Applications for Reporting Restriction Orders)* [2005] 2 FLR 120.

58 *Practice Note (Official Solicitor: Deputy Director of Legal Services: CAFCASS: Application for Reporting Restriction Orders)* [2005] 2 FLR 111.

59 [1999] 2 FLR 145.

up or cared for, to identify the child might subject that child to stress and anxiety. It is important that the child, who cannot be said to be other than entirely innocent, should not be damaged by the fact that his or her parents are not in a position to agree amicably as to the future care for that child, or because there are some other disputes as to the child's upbringing. It is therefore accepted by this court that in general the identity of the child should be protected.'

22.40 In 2004 in *Pelling v Bruce-Williams* the Court of Appeal expressed the view that it appeared desirable for the Master of the Rolls and the President to review this automatic practice to reflect developments since the decision pronounced in *Re R (Minor) (Court of Appeal: Order Against Identification)*. Whether or not such a review has happened, the practice remains as before.

Preventing disclosure of evidence, reports and documents to a party

22.41 An entitlement to a fair trial under Art 6 of the ECHR does not confer an unqualified right to see all the evidence. The court can, if the situation demands it, limit the disclosure of parts of the evidence to a party. Exceptionally, the court can withhold part of the evidence from a party, but before doing so it must apply the threefold test set out by the House of Lords in *Re D (Adoption Reports: Confidentiality)*:[60]

'The court should first consider whether the disclosure of the [whole or part of the evidence] would involve a real possibility of significant harm to the child.

If it would, the court should next consider whether the overall interests of the child would benefit from non-disclosure, weighing on the one hand the interest of the child in having the material properly tested, the magnitude of the risk that harm will occur and the gravity of the harm if it does occur. If the court is satisfied that the interests of the child point towards non-disclosure, the final step is for the court to weigh that consideration ... against the interest of the parent or other party in having an opportunity to see and respond to the material. In the latter regard the court should take into account the importance of the material to the issues in the case.

Non-disclosure should be the exception and not the rule. The court should be rigorous in its examination of the risk and gravity of the feared harm to the child, and should order non-disclosure only when the case for doing so is compelling. [Non-disclosure must be limited to what the situation imperatively demands. The court has to be rigorous in its examination of the feared harm and any difficulty caused to the party counterbalanced by other features which may ensure a fair trial.]'[61]

22.42 In *Re M (Disclosure)*[62] Lord Justice Thorpe identified the following principles.

---

[60] [1995] 2 FLR 687, per Lord Mustill at 700.
[61] *Re B (Disclosure to Other Parties)* [2001] 2 FLR 1017.
[62] [1998] 2 FLR 1028.

- '• It is a fundamental principle of fairness that a party is entitled to the disclosure of all materials which may be taken into account by the court when reaching a decision adverse to that party ...
- • ... the court should first consider whether disclosure of the material would involve a real possibility of significant harm to the child.
- • If it would, the court should next consider whether the overall interests of the child would benefit from non-disclosure, weighing on the one hand the interest of the child in having the material properly tested, and on the other both the magnitude of the risk that harm will occur and the gravity of the harm if it does occur.
- • If the court is satisfied that the interests of the child point towards non-disclosure, the next and final step is for the court to weigh that consideration, and its strength in the circumstances of the case, against the interest of the parent or other party in having an opportunity to see and respond to the material. In the latter regard the court should take into account the importance of the material to the issues in the case.
- • Non-disclosure should be the exception not the rule. The court should be rigorous in its examination of the risk and gravity of the feared harm to the child, and should order non-disclosure only when the case for doing so is compelling.'

22.43 These principles remain applicable after the coming into force of the Human Rights Act 1998. In addition the Art 8 rights of adults may justify non-disclosure where the risk is of harm to them rather than the child.

22.44 In *A v A Local Authority*[63] Hedley J refused to withhold information on the sexual behaviour of a mother, her aunt and sister from a Muslim Asian father in care proceedings despite assertions that their safety and lives would be in danger. The information was relevant to her capacity to parent the child and in the context of the case non-disclosure would be justified only if there were or on further investigation there might reasonably be expected to be a real risk of death or at least bodily harm. However disclosure was postponed for 2 weeks to consider how the order should be implemented and any consequences of disclosure handled.

22.45 When the court considers whether to withhold information, it has to bear in mind what Sedley LJ in a different context, referred to as the 'sobering experience' of practitioners and judges that the court cannot be sure of anything, including the relevance of information, until all the evidence has been heard. Any non-disclosure therefore needs to be kept under review throughout the case.

---

[63] [2009] EWHC 1574 (Fam).

Examples

Re C (A Minor) (No 2) (Wardship: Publication of Information)[64]

22.46 Newspapers were prohibited from publishing the name of a terminally ill child, that of her parents, the local authority and the area health authority concerned and the hospital where she was being treated.

Re M and N (Wards) (Publication of Information)[65]

22.47 Newspapers were forbidden to publish the identity of children, their foster parents and school, the children having been moved from foster parents by a local authority in whose care they were.

Re Z (A Minor) (Freedom of Publication)[66]

22.48 A mother was forbidden to take part in making a film about her handicapped daughter in circumstances where the court considered that the child's identity should not, for other reasons connected with her welfare, be made known.

Re Roddy (A Child) (Identification: Restriction on Publication)[67]

22.49 Care proceedings were instituted in relation to a 12-year-old child who had become pregnant. Following press reports that the Roman Catholic church had paid her not to have an abortion, an order was made protecting the identity both of the mother and the putative father, a boy of the same age. The baby was later adopted, the court dispensing with the consent of the mother. When she was 17 she approached a newspaper, indicating that she was willing to be named in an article and for her photograph to be published. The court held that the matter raised important issues of public interest. A proper balance between the competing Art 8 rights would be struck by preserving the anonymity of the child and the father and preventing solicitation of information about them but allowing the mother to be identified and permitting her story and the father's story to be published.

PERMITTED DISCLOSURE

22.50 Parties are free under FPR 2010 to disclose information in circumstances which would otherwise be prohibited by reason of the restrictions discussed above without requiring the court's permission. In

---

64   [1990] 1 FLR 263.
65   [1990] 1 FLR 149.
66   [1996] 1 FLR 191.
67   [2003] EWHC 2927 (Fam), [2004] 2 FLR 949.

addition, as the statutory restrictions all allow the court to give directions to the contrary, the court may in an individual case permit disclosure which would otherwise be prohibited.

22.51 There are a variety of circumstances where a party may wish to disclose information or where the disclosure would be in the public interest or in the interests of the child concerned. In care proceedings, for example, the local authority might seek permission to disclose information about child abuse to the police or the Crown Prosecution Service. In private law cases, one party might wish to use the CAFCASS report for the purpose of civil proceedings.[68] Contact proceedings may reveal issues of child protection that should be referred to social services.[69] A parent may wish to bring proceedings or make a claim under the Criminal Injuries Compensation Scheme on behalf of the child and to use information arising from the Children Act proceedings. A party may wish to use material for the purpose of his or her defence in criminal proceedings.[70] It may be suggested that information should be disclosed to the employer or professional body of a party or witness if it related to the person's fitness to do his work.

General permission to disclose

22.52 Rule 12.73 of the FPR 2010 permits the communication of information relating to proceedings held in private (whether or not contained in a document filed with the court) to be communicated to certain people connected with the proceedings or to other defined persons for specified purposes. However nothing in r 12.73 permits the communication to the public at large, or any section of the public, of any information relating to the proceedings nor does it allow the disclosure of an unapproved draft judgment handed down by any court.[71]

22.53 The persons connected to the proceedings to whom disclosure is permitted for any purpose are:

- a party;

- the legal representative of a party;

- a professional legal adviser;

- an officer of the service or a Welsh family proceedings officer;

- the welfare officer;

---

68   *B v M (Disclosure of Welfare Report)* [1990] 2 FLR 46.
69   For example, *Re D and M (Disclosure: Private Law)* [2002] EWHC 2820 (Fam), [2003] 1 FLR 647.
70   *Re Z (Children) (Disclosure: Criminal Proceedings)* [2003] EWHC 61 (Fam), [2003] 1 FLR 1194.
71   FPR 2010, r 12.73(2) and (3).

- the Legal Services Commission;

- an expert whose instruction by a party has been authorised by the court for the purposes of the proceedings;

- a professional acting in furtherance of the protection of children;

- an independent reviewing officer[72] appointed in respect of a child who is, or has been, subject to proceedings to which this rule applies.[73]

In *Re M (Children and Family Reporter: Disclosure)*[74] the Court of Appeal gave guidance on how Cafcass should deal with concerns about a child's welfare which arise during an investigation. See also **19.32**.

22.54 The persons who may disclose information for a specific purpose, the person to whom disclosure may be made and the specified purposes are defined by FPR 2010, r 12.73 and Practice Direction 12G. They include:

- A party to a lay adviser, a McKenzie Friend[75] or a person arranging pro bono legal services for the purpose of enabling the party to obtain advice or assistance in relation to the proceedings.

- A party to a health care professional[76] or a children or family counsellor for the purpose of enabling the party or any child of the party to obtain health care or counselling. It is important to note that the disclosure is for the purpose of the child or the party by whom the disclosure is made to receive therapy. Disclosure, for example, by a guardian to enable a parent to receive therapy is not covered and express permission is required.[77]

- A party to the European Court of Human Rights for the purpose of making an application to the Court or to a Minister of the Crown with responsibility for a government department engaged or potentially engaged in such an application for the purpose of providing the department with relevant or potentially relevant information.

- A legal representative or professional legal adviser to a person or body responsible for investigating or determining complaints relating to legal representatives or professional legal advisers for the purpose of such an investigation.

---

[72] An Independent Reviewing Officer is appointed by a local authority to perform various supervisory functions in relation to a child in their care. See the Arrangements for Placement of Children by Voluntary Organisations and Others (England) Regulations 2011, SI 2011/582.

[73] FPR 2010, r 12.73(1)(a).

[74] [2002] EWCA Civ 1199, [2002] 2 FLR 893.

[75] See **17.127**.

[76] Defined as a registered medical practitioner, a registered nurse or midwife, a clinical psychologist or a child psychotherapist: PD 12G para 6.1.

[77] *A v Payne and Williams; A v G and N* [2009] EWHC 736 (Fam), [2009] 2 FLR 463.

- A party may disclose the text or summary of the whole or part of the judgment to a police officer for the purpose of a criminal investigation and a party or person lawfully in receipt of information may disclose the text or summary of the whole or part of the judgment to the Crown Prosecution Service to enable it to discharge its statutory functions. So, for example, a police officer to whom the judgment has been disclosed may pass it on to the CPS. Prior to the enactment of the Family Proceedings Rules 1991, r 11.5–11.8 in 2009 this was a common ground for seeking specific permission to disclose. Such applications are no longer necessary unless information other than the judgment, for example, witness statements, are required. The new rule should assist the police in deciding whether or not to seek specific disclosure. However, parties wishing to use the judgment for the purpose of defending themselves in criminal proceedings and being able to show it to their legal representatives in those proceedings will still need specific permission to do so.

22.55 It should be noted that PD 12G is more restrictive than PD 14F, which covers disclosure in adoption proceedings and its predecessor, Family Procedure Rules 1991, r 11. For example is does not permit:

- disclosure to the General Medical Council for the purpose of making a complaint;[78]

- disclosure to a mediator;

- disclosure to an elected representative (which would include a Minister of the Crown). In *Re B (A Child) (Disclosure)*[79] Mr Justice Munby held that under AJA 1960, s 12(1) it is not lawful to give information to a Law Officer or the Minister of State for children without the permission of the court.

22.56 The omission of elected representatives and Ministers from the list may cause difficulties. In *Re C (Children Disclosure)*[80] Lord Justice Thorpe fully understood that a party might want to discuss what may be his predicament with his local member councillor or his Member of Parliament. 'That is, I believe, commonplace not only in public law proceedings but also in private law proceedings.' However what must be questioned was the wisdom of a pre-arranged interview between the Member of Parliament and the children involved with the plain express purpose of ascertaining their wishes and feelings.

'It seems to me that whatever responsibility a Member of Parliament may feel in relation to the constituent, great care should be taken before acceding to a request that the children be brought to a constituency surgery to enable the Member to

---

[78] Compare the position under FPR 1991 r 11, *Re N (Family Proceedings: Disclosure)* [2009] EWHC 1663 (Fam), [2009] 2 FLR 1152.
[79] [2004] EWHC 411 (Fam), [2004] 2 FLR 142.
[80] [2010] EWCA Civ 239, [2010] 2 FLR 22.

ascertain their wishes and feelings. What is the purpose of that? What will the Member of Parliament do with the information? Before acceding to such a request, any Member of Parliament would be wise to seek clear information as to the nature of the proceedings within the family justice system, the stage that they have reached and what other steps have been or will be taken in order to ascertain the wishes and feelings of the children ... [It] does seem to me that any Member of Parliament has to ask himself the question: why am I being asked to do this? Am I being manipulated by my constituent or may I be in danger of manipulation, am I invading territory that has been rightly assigned by Parliament to other professionals?'[81]

No reference was made in the judgment to the legality of the disclosure on information to the MP.

Specific permission to disclose

22.57 Parties can seek permission to disclose specific information to specified persons.

22.58 The factors to be considered are set out in the judgment of Balcombe LJ in *Re Manda (Wardship: Disclosure of Evidence)*:[82]

'(1) The interests of the particular child concerned will always be the most important factor, since it is to protect those interests that the court imposes the curtain of privacy.

(2) When the child is still a minor, the court will have to decide where his interests lie, although the older the child, the more relevant are his own views and wishes.

(3) Where the child concerned has attained majority, he or she alone (unless mentally incompetent) is entitled to decide what are his or her interests. This is the inevitable consequence under our law of the attainment of adult status.

(4) If, as is usually the case, the material is to be disclosed for use in other proceedings, the public interest in the administration of justice requires that all relevant information should be available for use in those proceedings.

(5) If it be the case that, in particular proceedings relating to children, information has been obtained on an express assurance of confidentiality, that must also be a very relevant factor. It would, however, be most undesirable for such an express assurance to be given unless the information could not otherwise be obtained.

(6) Where no such express assurance has been given, persons who give evidence in child proceedings, may normally assume that their evidence will remain confidential. They are not entitled, however, to assume that it will remain confidential in all circumstances ...'

---

[81] See also *R v P, Nottingham City Council and the Official Solicitor (Mental Capacity of Parent)* [2008] EWCA Civ 462, [2008] 2 FLR 1516.

[82] [1993] 1 FLR 205, at 215.

In *Re L (Police Investigation: Privilege)*,[83] Sir Thomas Bingham MR added:

'I doubt whether the discretion to order or refuse disclosure is properly described as unfettered, since every judicial discretion must be exercised judicially. The authorities show that many factors are potentially relevant ... Where material has come into existence in the course of proceedings to determine ... how the welfare of the child will be best served, it is plain that consideration of the welfare of the child will be a major factor in the exercise of the discretion: if disclosure will promote the welfare of the child it will readily be ordered; if disclosure will not affect the welfare of the child, other considerations are likely to carry the day one way or the other, if disclosure will prejudice the welfare of the child, disclosure may nevertheless be ordered if there are potent arguments for disclosure, but the court will be more reluctant to make the order. It is plain that the public interest in the fair administration of justice and the right of a criminal defendant to defend himself are accepted as potent reasons for disclosure. If, on the other hand, it could be shown that disclosure would for some reason be unfair or oppressive to a party ... that would weigh against disclosure.'

The application for permission must be made to the court seised of the Children Act proceedings.[84]

The following are examples of situations where permission is commonly sought.

Criminal investigations and proceedings

22.59 Courts have tended to favour disclosure of information for the purpose of criminal investigations and prosecution while noting the tension between the public interest in the prosecution of offences and avoiding miscarriages of justice and the interest in child proceedings in encouraging candour by use of confidentiality which, however, cannot be guaranteed.[85] In *Re Z (Children) (Disclosure: Criminal Proceedings)*[86] Mr Justice Munby (as he was) observed:

'To refuse disclosure might deny [the defendant] a fair trial, exposing him to the possibility of a wrongful conviction and thereby producing a miscarriage of justice. But there is another and equally important aspect of the interests of justice which is here in play: the interest of the Crown in ensuring that there is not the miscarriage of justice which would be brought about were the [defendant] able to secure a wrongful acquittal by suggesting to the jury, disclosure not having been ordered, that if only his counsel had been able to cross-examine [a prosecution witness] on the contents of a document – the family court statement – which is

---

83 [1995] 1 FLR 999, at 1019, approved by the House of Lords in *Re L (Police Investigation: Privilege)* [1996] 1 FLR 731, at 741.
84 *B v M (Disclosure of Welfare Reports)* [1990] 2 FLR 46.
85 See *Re Manda (Wardship: Disclosure of Evidence)* [1993] 1 FLR 205. In care proceedings but not private law proceedings, s 98 of the CA 1989 both removes the ability of witnesses to refuse to answer questions on the ground that doing so might incriminate them while also limiting the way in which their answers can be used against them. See also Edwards 'Disclosure: Sacrificing the Privilege of Self-Incrimination For the Greater Good of Child Protection?' [2007] Fam Law 510.
86 [2003] EWHC 61 (Fam), [2003] 1 FLR 1194, at [13].

known to exist, but whose contents are unknown because the family court has refused to sanction their disclosure, he might be able to discredit the [witness's] evidence, but where the circumstances are in truth such that were the jury in fact able to hear that cross-examination they would nonetheless convict. A wrongful acquittal is as much a miscarriage of justice as a wrongful conviction. Accordingly, as it seems to me, the Crown also has an interest in the family court statement being disclosed ...'

These considerations also have to be balanced against the interests of the child involved.[87] In striking a balance, the interests of the child are not paramount.[88] In *Re P (Care Proceedings: Disclosure)*,[89] permission to disclose a transcript of care proceedings and the agreed Schedule of Findings to the police to reopen a criminal investigation of the two highly vulnerable parents was refused although an expert report on the father's level of functioning was disclosed. The focus of the proceedings had been on whether the child should return home. Reopening the criminal investigation could have a catastrophic impact on the parents' ability to care for the child.

22.60 The reasons for disclosure for the purposes of criminal proceedings are varied. In *Re X (Disclosure for the Purpose of Criminal Proceedings)*,[90] for example, permission for the disclosure of information relating to care proceedings was given to the police and the Crown Prosecution Service for the purposes of the trial, to the child victim's mother to enable her to write her victim impact statement and in order to claim criminal injury compensation and to adult social services who were supporting the child victim who was aged 16 and autistic. In *Re Z (Children) (Disclosure: Criminal Proceedings)*[91] the father was given permission to use a statement made by the mother in care proceedings for the purpose of his defence in criminal proceedings. In *Northumberland CC v Z*,[92] an adoption case which involved child trafficking, permission was given to disclose documents to government departments and Interpol to minimise the risk of further abduction, to assist communication between Kenya and other countries concerning child abduction and to assist the investigation and pursuit of criminal proceedings. Disclosure to the police of DNA results taken in care proceedings was permitted, subject to safeguards, in *Lewisham London Borough Council v D (Local Authority Disclosure of DNA Samples to Police)*.[93] Although the disclosure interfered with the children's Art 8 rights, disclosure was proportionate and necessary in order to assist police to investigate allegations of child traffficking.

---

87   See also *Re X (Disclosure of Information)* [2001] 2 FLR 440.
88   *Re X Children* [2007] EWHC 1719 (Fam), at [24].
89   [2008] EWHC Fam 2197, [2009] 2 FLR 1039.
90   [2008] EWHC 242 (Fam), [2008] 2 FLR 944.
91   [2003] EWHC 61 (Fam), [2003] 1 FLR 1194.
92   [2009] EWHC 498 (Fam), [2009] 2 FLR 696.
93   [2010] EWHC 1238 (Fam), [2011] 1 FLR 895.

Disciplinary proceedings and employment issues

22.61 Courts will give permission to a party to disclose information to the professional body of a witness, or even a party, if there is cause for considering that there are grounds for believing that the documents should be disclosed in order to allow the body to carry out its duties, subject to also considering the welfare of the child.[94] In *Re A (Disclosure of Medical Records to the GMC)*[95] permission was given to the General Medical Council to obtain the transcript of a judgment which criticised an expert witness together with a copy of the expert's report. Cazalet J commented that it is always open to any judge as a person acting in a public capacity to send a letter of complaint and information to a disciplinary body if the judge is of the view that the conduct of an expert giving evidence before him appears to merit it. In *Re R (Disclosure)*[96] the court disclosed psychiatric reports on a father who was employed as a court welfare officer to his employer. Notwithstanding that the welfare of the children might be compromised by adverse publicity and the father losing his job, the balance of public interest fell heavily in favour of disclosure with safeguards, for example, not publishing the names and identity of the children.

Disclosure in order to assist publicity

22.62 There have been a number of cases in recent years where restraints against publicity have been listed either in order to allow publicity not to a limited number of people (for the GMC) but to the public at large or to avoid accusations of 'secret justice'. In *Re O (Children) (Hearing in Private: Assistance)*,[97] the Court of Appeal allowed the names of the father appellants to be published, presumably at their request, although to do so might have resulted in the children being identified. In *Re Webster: Norfolk County Council v Webster*[98] the court allowed the media to be present at and to report the trial in care proceedings. The background was unusual[99] and Munby J considered that four factors in particular were significant when considering whether reporting restrictions constituted a disproportionate interference with the rights of the media and the parents: the parents alleged that the case and the previous proceedings involving their other children amounted to a miscarriage of justice; the parents' own wish for publicity; the extensive publicity which had already occurred and the need for the full facts to emerge in a way which would command public confidence in the family justice system.[100] In *Doncaster MBC v Haigh*[101] the President allowed a judgment in care proceedings to be

---

94 Ibid. See also *Re B (Child Abuse: Expert Witnesses)* [1995] 1 FLR 181.
95 [1998] 1 FLR 433.
96 [1998] 1 FLR 433.
97 [2005] EWCA Civ 759, [2005] 2 FLR 967.
98 [2006] EWHC 2733 (Fam), [2007] 1 FLR 1146.
99 For the background, and the outcome, see [2006] EWHC 549 (Fam), [2007] EWHC 1566 (Fam) and [2009] EWCA Civ 59.
100 For which, see for example, *Re H (Freeing Orders: Publicity)* [2005] EWCA Civ 1325, [2006] 1 FLR 815, per Wall LJ at [31] and [33]. See also *Re B, C and D (By the Children's Guardian)* [2010] EWHC 262 (Fam), [2010] 1 FLR 1708.
101 [2011] EWHC 2412 (Fam).

published because although the trial judge had found that the child, X, had not been sexually abused by her father as her mother had alleged, the mother had subsequently put into the public domain the false allegations that she had not had justice and that X, contrary to two judges' findings, has been sexually abused by her father.

> 'There is, sadly, a tendency for those who wish to criticise the family justice system to publish the leaked version put forward by one side and to ignore any corrected version, notably the judgment given by the judge: – see, for example, the recent case of *Re L (A Child: Media Reporting)*[102] in which a journalist published one side's version and ignored what the judge said about it. I called attention to the dangers of this course a long time ago: – see my reported decision of *Re H (Freeing Orders: Publicity)*[103] ... Ms. Watson,[104] [who supported the mother] ... has publicised a tendentious version, which two judges, on investigation, have found to be untrue. In so doing, moreover, she has breached the court's order. It follows, in my judgment, that the record must be put straight. How is this to be achieved? It is, I think, trite law that I have the power to release information into the public domain. Judges regularly do so, for example, when an abducted child needs to be traced. My personal experience of this has been entirely positive. I have found the media helpful and cooperative, and, with their assistance, the child has usually been found. Here, of course, the situation is different. There is, however, a need to put material into the public domain. It is important for the world to know that two judges have found that Mr. Tune is not a paedophile and that it is in the interests of his daughter to live with him. It is also important for me, having examined the record, having read all the papers in the case, to state that I have reached the same conclusion. Since there is already much information about X in the public domain, including the names of her parents, why am I forbidding future publication of her name? The answer is not, I think, far to seek, and I have already touched upon it. Above all, I adhere strongly to the principle that children should not be named in Children Act proceedings. Children are nearly always the victims of their parents' misbehaviour. In this case the mother happens to be the abusive parent, but the principle is firm; the child should be protected as much as possible.'

Permission was given to the local authority to publish the judgment of the trial judge but with X's name redacted.

22.63 Local authorities, judges, guardians or social workers cannot claim immunity of protection from their names being mentioned in legitimate media reporting and can be named.[105] In *Ward (A Child) Re*[106] Munby LJ held that any assumption or expectation of anonymity on the part of expert witnesses is not justified in principle or in practice. Whatever may be the situation in relation to other witnesses or other professional witnesses, there are, as already observed, powerful arguments, founded in the public interest, for denying

---

102 [2011] EWHC 1285 (Fam).

103 [2005] EWCA Civ 1325, [2006] 1 FLR 815.

104 Mrs Watson was committed to prison for 9 months for breaching an order restricting the reporting of specified information about X – *Doncaster MBC v Watson* [2011] EWHC 2376 (Fam).

105 *Re B, C and D (By the Children's Guardian)* [2010] EWHC 262 (Fam), [2010] 1 FLR 1708.

106 [2010] EWHC 16 (Fam, [2010] 1 FLR 1497, at [150].

expert witnesses anonymity: see *BBC v Cafcass Legal*.[107] There might be cases
where the evidence established fears of targeting, harassment and vilification
which would justify a different conclusion, though those would probably be
cases where the risk is peculiar to a particular individual rather than generic to
a whole class of expert witnesses. The same applies to social workers.[108] The
child's carers are however in a different position if only because publicity might
affect their ability to care for the child.[109]

---

[107] [2007] EWHC 616 (Fam), [2007] 2 FLR 765.

[108] *Ward (A Child) Re* [2010] EWHC 16 (Fam, [2010] 1 FLR 1497, at [160]–[171], *Re W (Care Proceedings: Witness Anonymity)* [2002] EWCA Civ 1626, [2003] 1 FLR 329, at [13], *BBC v Rochdale MBC* [2005] EWHC 2862 (Fam), [2007] 1 FLR 101.

[109] See, for example, *Re Webster: Norfolk County Council v Webster* [2006] EWHC 2733 (Fam), [2007] 1 FLR 1146, at [125], para 8 of the order made. See also *Re X, Y and Z (Expert Witnesses)* [2011] EWHC 1157 (Fam).

Chapter 23
ENFORCEMENT

INTRODUCTION

23.1 Although courts are occasionally required to enforce s 8 orders other than those for contact, it is the question of how to enforce contact orders which causes most problems and concern. The question should however be rephrased: How can effective contact best be established and maintained? For, as Wall LJ commented in a paper in 2004:

> 'The message is that, if in the forensic process, we get to enforcement we have failed. The order we have made is not working. The first proposition, therefore is that we should try never to get to the stage of enforcement.'[1]

Even when imprisonment is used as a matter of last resort, it may not ensure compliance.[2]

The problem of making effective contact orders is extensively discussed in **Chapter 11** but the issue of how courts should react when a carer refuses to comply with an order made after proper consideration, and often after extensive investigation, cannot be avoided.

Cases brought under the European Convention for the Protection of Human Rights and Fundamental Freedoms 1950 (ECHR) make it clear that courts have a duty under Arts 6 and 8 to assist litigants to enforce orders within a reasonable time. However, a study in 2002 by the Children Act Sub-Committee of the Lord Chancellor's Advisory Board on Family Law, *Making Contact Work*, concluded that the current system was 'seriously deficient' in the means available to enforce orders. Although courts are more willing than previously to impose the sanction of imprisonment, this is a sanction of 'last resort'. The object of any enforcement exercise is to enforce the breached order in the sense of getting it working, or putting something more workable in its place.[3]

---

[1] Wall 'Enforcement of Contact Orders' [2005] Fam Law 26, at p 30.

[2] See, for example, *Re D (Intractable Contact Dispute: Publicity)* [2004] EWHC 727 (Fam), [2004] 1 FLR 1226. Mother continued to breach orders despite a suspended order of 7 days' imprisonment and then an immediate term of 14 days.

[3] *Thomason v Thomason* [1985] FLR 214.

BACKGROUND

23.2 It is unknown for certain how many of the 40,000 or so contact orders made each year are successful in the sense of regular contact taking place. Many orders, no doubt made by consent, as an adjunct to residence orders and without the matter having to be resolved by a formal judicial investigation, are successful. A study of fathers in 1997[4] found that seven out of ten non-resident fathers reported having contact with their children and almost half reported seeing them every week. Lone mothers, however, reported lower levels of contact between non-resident fathers and children. In other cases, contact will drop away for a variety of reasons: the residential parent or the non-resident parent moves away and distance becomes a factor, the non-resident parent forms a new relationship and transfers his paternal feelings to children with whom he lives. Children grow older and transfer their alliances to their peer group. The non-resident parent may find the weekly separation too painful or may decide that, in an atmosphere of continuing tension, it is fairer on the other parent or the children to discontinue contact or just lose interest. The resident parent may be unco-operative and may be influenced by a relationship with a new partner. The lack of co-operation may not be deliberate but rather a reflection of a reaction to the separation or a desire to end a continuing painful relationship with the other parent. For example, a study of Contact Centres carried out in 2000[5] found that the use of Centres seemed to make little difference to the parents. Communication between them did not increase and parents moved, if at all, from high conflict to wanting nothing to do with each other. Only a small number could talk to the other parent about the child. And yet, a significant proportion of non-resident parents do have continuing contact.

23.3 Following a call for more information by the Children Act Sub-Committee of the Lord Chancellor's Advisory Board on Family Law,[6] the Government commissioned a report to examine the outcomes of applications to court for contact orders. *Outcomes of applications to court for contact orders after parental separation or divorce*[7] was based on a sample of 300 court files covering cases heard at all three levels of court. It found that 10% of applications made by non-resident parents were brought, in part at least, to give effect to orders or agreements made in earlier proceedings. Moreover 6% of concluded cases in the sample returned to court in the survey period because of non-compliance, the researchers considering this figure probably being an underestimate. Practitioners who were interviewed generally expressed the view

---

4   Burgess and others *Fathers and Fatherhood in Britain* (Family Policy Studies Centre) summarised in 'Fathers and fatherhood in Britain', *Findings* 120 (Joseph Rowntree Foundation).

5   Furniss 'The process of referral to a Family Contact Centre: policy and practice' [2000] CFLQ 255.

6   *Making Contact Work: A Report to the Lord Chancellor's* Department (2002) summarised in [2002] Fam Law 164.

7   Hunt and Macleod *Outcomes of applications to Court for Contact Orders after Parental Separation or Divorce* (Ministry of Justice, 2008).

that 'something' needed to be done but recognised that the courts' enforcement powers were of limited utility being impracticable, counter-productive or likely to have an adverse effect on the child.

> 'Many resident parents express a degree of hostility to contact at the outset of proceedings ... but persistent hostility was generally seen by interviewees as quite unusual ... Where possible courts seek to overcome a resident parent's objections through encouragement and persuasion but when these efforts are ineffective sterner methods come into play. However it is unusual for sanctions to be actually employed and judicial interviews revealed a general reluctance to go down this road. Hence at the end of the day there are some cases in which the court may eventually and very reluctantly have to admit defeat[8] ... Children who steadfastly resist contact present the court with an even more difficult challenge. It is quite common for children to be said to be opposed to contact at the outset of proceedings ... When resistance is not seen to be well founded the courts adopt a range of strategies to try to address the problem but there are again some cases where they have to call a halt to proceedings.'[9]

23.4 New statutory enforcement powers were introduced in the Children Act 1989 by the Children and Adoption Act 2006 but a small scale study by the University of Cardiff in 2008[10] found that many professionals questioned doubted the extent to which they would resolve problems. Their responses indicated a number of recurring themes:

- delay in handling cases;

- resident parents manipulating the views of children;

- the family justice system, despite being viewed as less adversarial than other jurisdictions, remains an arena for point scoring;

- parents disregarding the authority of the court.[11]

23.5 Speaking extra-judicially in 2010, Mr Justice Coleridge said although less complex children cases now move through the system with greater fluency and take up less court time, there had been almost no improvement in the dispatch of the complex and time consuming cases, either private or public.

> 'The cause is at least in part, if not in large part of our own making. In short the population do not generally take our decisions seriously enough and do not obey the orders promptly and fully. And it is this attitude which leads to ever more hearings and ever more interventions by guardians, social workers, Cafcass officers

---

8   See, for example, *Re S (Contact: Promoting Contact with Absent Parent)* [2004] EWCA Civ 18, [2004] 1 FLR 1279 and **11.139**.

9   *Outcomes of applications to Court for Contact Orders after Parental Separation or Divorce*, op cit, p 223.

10 Dyer, McCrum, Thomas, Ward and Wookey 'Making contact work: is the Children and Adoption Act 2006 enough for resident parents and children?' [2008] Fam Law 1237.

11 For another survey of professionals, see also *Outcomes of applications to Court for Contact Orders after Parental Separation or Divorce*, op cit, p 225.

and child experts of all descriptions ... In short we are demonstrating insufficient authority in our handling of cases and our orders are regarded as helpful advice rather than binding edicts to be obeyed ... Once a decision and order is made, the consequences of breach must be spelled out with perlucid clarity and then, where breach occurs, the order must be swiftly and rigorously enforced.'[12]

ENFORCEMENT REFORM

Making contact work

23.6 In 2001, the Children Act Sub-Committee of the Lord Chancellor's Advisory Board on Family Law invited responses to a Consultation Paper on the facilitation of arrangements for contact between children and their non-residential parents and the enforcement of court orders for contact. The Sub-Committee reported in February 2002.[13]

The Sub-Committee agreed with the majority of the respondents to the Consultation Paper that the court needs to retain its powers to compel obedience to contact orders and that fines and imprisonment are part of that process, albeit that imprisonment should be a matter of last resort. However, it concluded that:

'Fines and committals are not only very crude methods of enforcement: they are wholly inadequate as a means of addressing the problem of contact orders ... The result is that the current system is seriously deficient in the means available to enforce its orders.'[14]

23.7 The Sub-Committee recommended that courts needed to be given much wider powers designed to meet the circumstances of the individual case. The following powers were essential:

- the power to refer a defaulting parent to a variety of resources including information meetings, meetings with a counsellor, parenting programmes/ classes designed to deal with contact disputes;

- the power to refer to a psychiatrist or psychologist (publicly funded in the first instance);

- the power to refer a non-resident parent who is violent or in breach of an order to an education programme or perpetrator programme;

- the power to place on probation with a condition of treatment or attendance at a given class or programme;

---

[12] 'The authority of the Family Court' [2011] Fam Law 96.
[13] *Making Contact Work: A Report to the Lord Chancellor* (Lord Chancellor's Department, 2002).
[14] Ibid, at paras 14.47–14.48.

- the power to impose a community service order, with programmes specifically designed to address the default in question;

- the power to award financial compensation from one parent to another (for example, where the cost of a holiday has been lost).[15]

There should be two stages to the enforcement proceedings. The first would be essentially non-punitive. The resident parent could, for example, be directed to attend an information meeting or parenting programme designed to address intractable contact disputes or required to seek psychiatric advice. If that did not work and the contact remained unabated, the court could impose an order with a penal sanction such as community service or regular attendance at a parenting class. Any question of fines or imprisonment would then genuinely be an issue of last resort.[16]

Response by the Government

23.8 The Lord Chancellor's Department responded in August 2002.[17] A review of research on contact was being undertaken and the Office of National Statistics had been asked to conduct a survey to investigate how contact was agreed, whether parents were happy with the arrangements and what barriers there were to effective contact. It supported measures such as the development of contact centres and the use of mediation. It was giving further consideration to the proposals concerning enforcement. However, it was concerned that:

'... a more prescriptive approach in all cases, such as non-punitive and then punitive steps may be too rigid. We need to allow for diversity in family circumstances'.

Parental Separation: Children's Needs and Parents' Responsibilities: Next Steps[18]

23.9 Following further consultation, Next Steps announced proposals in the Children (Contact) and Adoption Bill which would prepare the way for effective contact by empowering courts to refer parents to parenting programmes, classes or information sessions before a contact order was made or by way of conditions attached to orders (see **Chapter 11**). Where an order was breached, new sanctions would be introduced to impose community-based orders for unpaid work or curfew (this latter proposal was soon dropped after

---

[15] *Making Contact Work: A Report to the Lord Chancellor* (Lord Chancellor's Department, 2002), para 14.55.

[16] Ibid, para 14.53.

[17] *Government's Response to the Report of the Children Act Sub-Committee of the Lord Chancellor's Advisory Board on Family Law: 'Making Contact Work'* (Lord Chancellor's Department, 2002).

[18] Department of Constitutional Affairs [2005] Fam Law 96.

the draft Bill was published) and awarding financial compensation. 'As a last resort courts will have the power to fine or commit a parent to prison where a contact order has been breached.'[19]

The new powers were introduced in to the Children Act 1989 as ss 11A–11P by the Children and Adoption Act 2006.[20] It is to be noted that they do not include the power to refer a defaulting parent to a psychiatrist or psychologist nor to place him or her on probation as recommended by the Children Act sub-committee (see **23.7**). They are markedly different from those contained in *Making Contact Work* which included referrals to parenting classes in its package of sanctions and the change may indicate that lessons had been learnt from the Australian experience. In 2000 a framework had been introduced in Australia whereby the party in breach of a contact order or, if necessary, both parties were directed to attend a post-separation parenting programme. Earlier pilot projects had found that often it was the non-resident rather than the resident parent who needed to attend a parenting class and that a large number of cases were complicated by a range of relationship issues which suggested there was a greater need for counselling rather than education. A study of the revised system[21] argued that few of those involved – parents, practitioners, service providers or judges – were satisfied with the scheme. Behind disputes lay diverse factors.

> 'Clearly the solution to all these issues cannot be found in the one remedy. Yet, while it appears to have embraced an approach that recognises the limits of penalties and the importance of supporting parents after their relationship breaks down, the new scheme remains essentially a sentencing code for dealing with breaches of court orders. Its staged measures framework ... means that the kind of response a parent receives depends on the chronology of their litigation rather than the nature of the problem.'

Rhoades also pointed to the difficulties caused by a failure to select appropriate programmes for individuals. Amendments were proposed to the scheme but 'agencies have made it clear that the services that are most needed are those with significant resource implications'.

In addition, the proposals in *Making Contact Work* had met with some criticism in the UK. For example, Professor Fortin found in them 'a rather chilly authoritarianism, perhaps reflecting a greater concern to prevent judicial orders being scoffed at than to fulfil children's interests'.[22]

---

19   Ibid, at para 100.
20   See Mahmood 'The enforcement of contact orders: the never ending story' [2010] Fam Law 727.
21   Rhoades 'Contact enforcement and parenting programmes – policy aims in confusion?' [2004] CFLQ 1. See also Rhoades 'Revising Australia's parenting laws: a plea for a rational approach to children's best interests' [2010] CFLQ 172.
22   Fortin *Children's Rights and the Developing Law* (2nd edn, 2003), p 406. This comment does not appear in the 3rd edition (2009).

In 2005 the House of Commons Constitutional Affairs Committee[23] had recognised that enforcing orders has always been fraught with difficulties. 'There are obvious practical problems with fining or imprisoning recalcitrant parents – especially those who live with the children in the case – since the main impact of doing so will be to injure the children's interests.' Nevertheless:

'It is pointless for the courts to make orders if those orders are not then enforced. There is a legitimate public interest in ensuring that where an order is made by the court it is subsequently obeyed. Failure to enforce contact orders is the basis of some of the claims that the system is "biased against fathers." Furthermore, a failure of the State to enforce orders in this sphere has been held by the European Court of Human Rights to amount to a breach of the State's positive obligations under the European Convention on Human Rights.'[24]

Recognising that forcing parents to do things they might not consider to be in their child's best interests was problematical, the Committee recommended that emphasis should be placed on overcoming problems through Cafcass intervention and education programmes rather than the traditional method of a system of sanctions.

ARTICLES 6 AND 8

23.10 Enforcement of s 8 orders engages both Arts 6 and 8 of the ECHR.[25]

Article 6

23.11 Article 6 is engaged because the determination of civil rights and obligations includes the enforcement of judgments.[26] The courts, as public authorities, are therefore under an obligation to provide judicial opportunities to enforce orders within a reasonable time. The reasonableness of the length of the proceedings has to be considered in the light of the complexity of the case, the conduct of the applicant and the relevant authorities including the court and welfare services. The importance of what is at stake for the applicant also has to be taken into account. It is essential that contact and residence cases are dealt with speedily.[27] The European Court of Human Rights has found that there is no fundamental defect in the structure in UK courts for enforcing orders relating to contact and residence.[28]

---

[23] *Family Justice: The Operation of the Family Courts*, HC 116–1, March 2005.
[24] Ibid, at paras 104–105.
[25] *Hokkanen v Finland* (1994) 19 EHRR 139, [1996] 1 FLR 289.
[26] *Hornsby v Greece* (1997) 24 EHRR 250.
[27] *Hokkanen v Finland* [1996] 1 FLR 289, at 308 and *Glasner v United Kingdom* [2001] 1 FLR 153, at 175.
[28] *Glasner v United Kingdom* [2001] 1 FLR 153, at 169.

Article 8

23.12 Article 8 is engaged because a denial of contact can be an interference with the right to family life. It includes the right of a parent to have measures taken with a view to being reunited with the child and there is an obligation on national authorities to take action. Both contact and residence rights are protected. However, the obligation of the authorities to take measures is not absolute. For example, reunion of a parent with a child who has lived for some time with other people may not be able to take place immediately and may require preparation. The nature and extent of such preparation will depend on the circumstances of each case, but the understanding and concern of all concerned will always be an important ingredient. While national authorities must do their utmost to facilitate such co-operation, any obligation to apply coercion must be limited because the rights and freedoms of all concerned must be taken into account, especially the best interests of the child and its rights under the Article. Where contact with a parent appears to threaten or interfere with those rights, the national authority has to strike a fair balance between them. Coercive measures may, in themselves, present a risk of damage to the child. What is decisive is whether the national authorities have taken all necessary steps to facilitate reunion as can reasonably be demanded in the special circumstances of each case.[29] Applicants cannot leave it to the national authorities to take action. They bear a substantial responsibility and their active participation can hardly be dispensed with in normal cases. They have to make normal and proper use of the remedies available.[30]

Glasner v United Kingdom[31]

23.13 The European Court of Human Rights found no violation of a father's Art 6 and Art 8 rights in relation to enforcing contact orders against a mother who moved from England to a secret address in Scotland. The case presented considerable complexity. The history of the family showed that the children's welfare required that further undue stress be avoided and work had to be done to rebuild their trust and confidence in the father. The Court held that the father could have pursued the committal of the children's mother for failing to comply with a contact order but had failed to do so. On the other hand, in the circumstances of the case, the courts would have been irresponsible if they imposed stringent coercive measures on the mother without proper and careful investigation of the children's circumstances.

Hokkanen v Finland[32]

23.14 The European Court of Human Rights found that the Finnish courts had breached a father's Art 8 rights in failing to take effective steps to enforce a

---

[29]   *Hokkanen v Finland* [1996] 1 FLR 289, at 305; *Glasner v United Kingdom* [2001] 1 FLR 153, at 169; *Kaleta v Poland* (Application No 11375/02) [2009] 1 FLR 927.

[30]   *Glasner v United Kingdom* [2001] 1 FLR 153, at 169.

[31]   Ibid. See also *Kosmopolou v Greece* (Application No 60457/00) [2004] 1 FLR 800.

[32]   (1994) 19 EHRR 139, [1996] 1 FLR 289.

contact order made in respect of a 10-year-old girl who had lived with her maternal grandparents since she was 18 months old. They had placed a burden on the father of having to have constant recourse to a succession of time-consuming and ultimately ineffectual remedies to enforce his rights against grandparents who had consistently refused to comply with the decisions of the courts.

Nuutinen v Finland[33]

23.15 The European Court of Human Rights found, in another very difficult contact case, that there had been no breach of the father's Art 8 rights. The national authorities had taken all necessary steps as could reasonably be demanded. However, the overall time the proceedings took – the child was nearly 2 when a contact order was made and nearly 7 by the time the order was revoked because of the mother's fear of the father – breached his Art 6 rights. In all, there had been four hearings (taking 11 months) before the father's paternity was decided and interim contact was ordered, two hearings (taking 6 months) before a final contact order was made and seven enforcement hearings (including appeals) taking 3 years. The court criticised delays in producing welfare reports of 9 and 8 months.

Hansen v Turkey[34]

23.16 The father failed to return his two children, aged 9 and 8, to their mother after a holiday. After court proceedings, which lasted 6 years, she was granted contact but efforts to see them on more than three occasions before they were 18 were unsuccessful. The European Court of Human Rights held that her Art 8 rights had been breached. Even in difficult circumstances the authorities had failed to enable the mother to have contact during the protracted proceedings. In particular they had failed to take the advice of social services, psychologists or child psychiatrists in order to facilitate a reunion and to create a more co-operative atmosphere between the parents. Although there were occasions when the children had refused to see their mother, they were never given a real opportunity to develop a relationship with her in a calm environment where they could freely express their feelings for her without outside pressure.

METHODS OF ENFORCEMENT

23.17 Most of the reported cases are concerned with contact orders and the remedies will be discussed in relation to contact. Save for enforcement orders under s 115 of the Act, they are, however, equally applicable in residence cases or those involving specific issues or prohibited steps orders.

---

[33]   (2002) 34 EHRR 15.
[34]   (Application No 36141/97) [2004] 1 FLR 142.

Practice Direction: Applications in Magistrates' Courts to Enforce Contact Orders[35] provides guidance for how such applications are to be heard.

Warning notices

23.18 Where the court makes (or varies) a contact order, it is to attach to the contact order (or the order varying the contact order) a notice warning of the consequences of failing to comply with the contact order.[36]

The warning placed on orders by HM Courts and Tribunal Service reads:

> **'[Name]: Take note:** If you do not comply with this contact order –
>
> a)   you may be held in contempt of court and be committed to prison or fined and/or
>
> b)   the Court may make an order requiring you to undertake unpaid work ("an enforcement order") and/or an order that you pay financial compensation.'

23.19 In addition, whatever the possible method of enforcement, it is important that the order states precisely what it is that the resident parent is required to do.[37] An order that 'there be contact between F [the father] and C [the child] every Saturday' is insufficient. It does not direct the resident parent to do anything nor does it state a time for the compliance. Nor will an order that the resident parent (RP) 'shall allow F to have contact with C and make him available every Saturday from 12 noon to 6pm' suffice as the basis for an enforcement or committal order based on the resident parent taking the child to contact but not encouraging or ensuring that C goes with F.

> 'The [resident parent] father's obligations under [an order in this form] is to "allow" contact and "make [C] available" for contact. To "allow" is to concede or to permit; to "make available" is to put at one's disposal or within one's reach. That was the father's obligation; no more and no less. But that is not how [the judge] treated the orders. Running through all his judgments is the assumption ... that the father's obligation was to "make sure" or "ensure" that [C] went and that contact took place. The father's obligation, according to [the judge] was to "make sure that he did all that was necessary so that that child would go" and to take "whatever other steps within the exercise of his parental responsibility were necessary to make sure that he went". The father may have been under a parental or moral obligation to do these things, but on the wording of these orders he was not, in my judgment, under any legal obligation such as to render him in breach of the orders for failing to do them, let alone for failing to achieve – to "ensure" – that contact actually took place.'[38]

---

35   6 November 2008 [2009] 1 FLR 371.

36   Children Act 1989, s 11I.

37   *Re S-C (Contempt)* [2010] EWCA Civ 21, [2010] 1 FLR 1478 per Wall LJ at [17] and *Re L-W (Enforcement and Committal: Contact); CPL v CH-W* [2010] EWCA Civ 1253, [2011] 1 FLR 1095, per Munby LJ at [34].

38   *Re L-W (Enforcement and Committal: Contact); CPL v CH-W* [2010] EWCA Civ 1253, [2011] 1 FLR 1095, per Munby LJ at [76].

23.20 The order needs to be drafted for the specific circumstances of each case. A sample order might read:

> '[Name] shall ensure that [name of child] has contact with [name of non resident parent] every Saturday from [time] until [time], the first contact to take place on [date]. [Name] shall deliver [name of child] to [name of non resident parent] at [place] promptly at the start of contact and shall collect [him] from the same place at the end of contact.

Enforcement by the Tipstaff or police

23.21 When a person is required by an order specified in Part I of the Family Law Act 1986 (which includes s 8 orders) or an order for the enforcement of a Part I order, the court (which includes not just the High Court and county courts but also magistrates' courts) may make an order authorising an officer of the court or a police officer to 'take charge of the child and deliver him to the person concerned'. Similar additional powers exist in the High Court, where the 'officer of the court' will also include the Tipstaff. Unless there is an imminent threat of danger, the police should not be asked to act.[39] It is 'highly questionable' that, given the very specialist skills and experience of the Tipstaff, using him to move a child from one home to another is in breach of the child's ECHR, Art 5 rights (right to liberty and security). It is 'strongly arguable', that in any event it would be covered by the Art 5(2) exception (the lawful detention for non-compliance with a court order or in order to fulfil any obligation prescribed by law).[40]

Although this section can in theory be used to enforce a contact order, it should not be used for this purpose.[41]

Compensation for financial loss

The order

23.22 If the court is satisfied that:

- an individual has failed to comply with the contact order; and

- a person falling within s 110(6)[42] has suffered financial loss by reason of the breach; and

---

[39]   *R v Chief Constable of Cheshire ex parte K* [1990] 1 FLR 70.
[40]   *Re S (a Child) (Transfer of Residence: Judge's Discretion)* [2010] EWCA Civ 325, per Thorpe LJ at [17].
[41]   *A v N (Committal: Refusal of Contact)* [1997] 1 FLR 533 and *Making Contact Work* (Lord Chancellor's Department, 2002), para 14.30.
[42]   See **23.24**.

- before the failure occurred the individual had been given (in accordance with rules of court) a copy of, or otherwise informed of the terms of the contact order backed by a warning notice and of the most recent of any order varying the contact order.[43]

it may, make an order requiring the individual in breach to pay the person compensation in respect of his financial loss.[44] However the court may not make such an order if it is satisfied that the individual in breach had a reasonable excuse for failing to comply with the contact order.[45] For a discussion of 'reasonable excuse' see **23.32**.The burden of proof as to 'reasonable loss' lies on the individual claiming to have had a reasonable excuse.[46]

23.23   The court may not make an order:

- if it is satisfied that the individual in breach had a reasonable excuse for failing to comply with the contact order;[47]

- in respect of a failure to comply with a contact order where the failure occurred before the individual attained the age of 18;[48]

- if the contact order is an excepted order.[49]

An 'excepted order' is a contact order with respect to a child which:

- it is made in proceedings that include proceedings on an application for a relevant adoption order[50] in respect of the child; or

- it makes provision as regards contact between the child and a person who would be a parent or relative of the child but for the child's adoption by an order falling within subs (5).[51]

---

43   Children Act 1989, s 11P(1).
44   Ibid, s 11O(2).
45   Ibid, s 11O(3).
46   Ibid, s 11O(4).
47   Ibid, s 11O(3).
48   Ibid, s 11P(2).
49   Ibid, s 11P(3).
50   Ie an adoption order within the meaning of s 46(1) of the Adoption and Children Act 2002 other than an order made on an application under s 50 by a couple one of whom is the mother or the father of the person to be adopted or on an application under s 51 (adoption by one person) – CA 1989, s 11B(6).
51   Ie a relevant adoption order, an adoption order, within the meaning of s 72(1) of the Adoption Act 1976, other than an order made by virtue of s 14 of that Act on the application of a married couple one of whom is the mother or the father of the child; a Scottish adoption order, within the meaning of the Adoption and Children Act 2002, other than an order made by virtue of s 14 of the Adoption (Scotland) Act 1978 on the application of a married couple one of whom is the mother or the father of the child or by virtue of s 15(1)(aa) of that Act or a Northern Irish adoption order, within the meaning of the Adoption and Children Act 2002,

Application

23.24 The order may be made only on an application by a person claiming to have suffered financial loss.[52] A person falls within the meaning of this phrase if he is:

- the person who is, for the purposes of the contact order, the person with whom the child concerned lives or is to live;

- the person whose contact with the child concerned is provided for in the contact order;

- an individual subject to a condition under s 11(7)(b)[53] or a contact activity condition imposed by the contact order;[54] or

- the child concerned, in which case the child must obtain the leave of the court before making the application.[55] The court may grant leave only if it is satisfied that the child has sufficient understanding to make the proposed application.[56]

Making the order

23.25 The amount of compensation is to be determined by the court, but may not exceed the amount of the applicant's financial loss.[57]

In determining the amount of compensation payable, the court must take into account:

- the individual's financial circumstances;[58]

- the welfare of the child concerned.[59]

Enforcing the order

23.26 An amount ordered to be paid as compensation may be recovered by the applicant as a civil debt due to him.[60] Enforcement is under CPR, r 70.5

---

other than an order made by virtue of art 14 of the Adoption (Northern Ireland) Order 1987 on the application of a married couple one of whom is the mother or the father of the child: CA 1989, s 11B(5)(b).

[52] Ibid, s 11O(5).
[53] Ie Contact conditions which may be imposed on any person in whose favour the order is made; who is a parent of the child ,who is not a parent of his but who has parental responsibility for him or with whom the child is living.
[54] Ibid, s 11O(6).
[55] Ibid, s 11O(6), (7).
[56] Ibid, s 11O(8).
[57] Ibid, s 11O(9).
[58] Ibid, s 11O(10).
[59] Ibid, s 11O(14).
[60] Ibid, s 11O(11).

and PD 70. The application may be made without notice and must be made to the court for the district where the person against whom the order is sought, resides or carries on business, unless the court otherwise orders. The application notice must be in the form and contain the information required by PD 70. A copy of the decision or compromise must be filed with the application notice.

Enforcement orders

23.27   The provisions relating to the making and enforcing of an enforcement order are complicated and are set out below. As the order is penal in nature, it is important that there is strict compliance with the procedures.

The order

23.28   An enforcement order is an order imposing on a person an unpaid work requirement[61] for not more than 200 hours[62] to be performed during a period of 12 months.[63]

23.29   The court may not make an enforcement order:

* if the person in respect of any failure to comply is alleged had not attained the age of 18 before the failure occurred;

* if the person is not habitually resident in England and Wales;

* if the contact order is an excepted order (see **23.23**).[64]

23.30   The court may suspend an enforcement order for such period as it thinks fit.[65] An enforcement order ceases to have effected if the person named ceases to be habitually resident in England and Wales.[66]

Nothing in s 11J prevents the court making more than one enforcement order in relation to the same person on the same occasion.[67]

Application

23.31   The court may make an enforcement order in relation to the contact order only on the application of:

---

[61]   Children Act 1989, s 11J(2).
[62]   Ibid, Sch A1, para 3(3).
[63]   Ibid, Sch A1, para 3(4).
[64]   Ibid, s 11K(2)–(4).
[65]   Ibid, s 11J(9).
[66]   Ibid, s 11K(4).
[67]   Ibid, s 11J(10).

- the person who is, for the purposes of the contact order, the person with whom the child concerned lives or is to live;

- the person whose contact with the child concerned is provided for in the contact order;

- any individual subject to a condition under s 11(7)(b) or a contact activity condition imposed by the contact order; or

- the child concerned who must obtain the leave of the court before making such an application. The court may grant leave only if it is satisfied that he has sufficient understanding to make the proposed application.[68]

Making the order

23.32 The court may make an enforcement order only if:

- it is satisfied that before the failure occurred the person had been given (in accordance with rules of court) a copy of, or otherwise informed of the terms of the contact order backed by a warning notice (see **23.18**) and of the most recent of any order varying the contact order;[69] and

- it is satisfied beyond reasonable doubt (ie to the criminal standard) that a person has failed to comply with the contact order;[70] and

- it is not satisfied that the person had a reasonable excuse for failing to comply with the contact order. The burden of proof as to 'reasonable excuse' lies on the person claiming to have had such an excuse, and the standard of proof is the balance of probabilities (ie the civil standard);[71] and

- it is satisfied that making the enforcement order proposed is necessary to secure the person's compliance with the contact order or any contact order that has effect in its place;[72] and

- it is satisfied that the likely effect on the person of the enforcement order proposed to be made is proportionate to the seriousness of the breach of the contact order;[73] and

---

[68] Children Act 1989, s 11J(5)–(7).
[69] Ibid, s 11K(1).
[70] Ibid, s 11J(2).
[71] Ibid, s 11J(2)–(4).
[72] Ibid, s 11L(1).
[73] Ibid, s 11L(1).

- it is satisfied that that provision for the person to work under an unpaid work requirement imposed by an enforcement order can be made in the local justice area in which the person in breach resides or will reside.[74]

The phrase 'a reasonable excuse' was discussed by the Court of Appeal in *Re L-W (Enforcement and Committal: Contact*.[75] It is to be distinguished from force majeure, events beyond the person's control, which mean that there is no breach at all.

> 'For example, if a parent taking a child for contact is prevented from going on or is delayed by unforeseen and insuperable transport or weather problems – one thinks of the sudden and unexpected grounding of the nation's airlines by volcanic ash – then there will be no breach. Reasonable excuse, in contrast, arises where, although it was within the power of the defendant to comply, he has some good reason, specifically, a "reasonable excuse", for not doing so. A typical case might be where a child suddenly falls ill and the defendant, reasonably in the circumstances, takes the child to the doctor rather than going to contact.'[76]

23.33 When making the order, the court must take account of the welfare of the child[77] but his welfare is not paramount.

23.34 Before making an enforcement order as regards a person in breach of a contact order, the court must obtain and consider information about the person and the likely effect of the enforcement order on him. Information about the likely effect of the enforcement order may, in particular, include information as to:

- any conflict with the person's religious beliefs;

- any interference with the times (if any) at which he normally works or attends an educational establishment.[78]

A court that proposes to make an enforcement order may ask an officer of Cafcass or a Welsh family proceedings officer to provide the court with information as to the matters set out in s 11L(2) (availability of provision) and s 11L(3) (information about the person) and Cafcass or the officer must comply with the request.[79]

23.35 When the court makes an enforcement order a notice warning of the consequences of failing to comply with the order must be attached to the order.[80]

---

[74] Children Act 1989, s 11L(2).
[75] *Re L-W (Enforcement and Committal: Contact); CPL v CH-W* [2010] EWCA Civ 1253, [2011] 1 FLR 1095.
[76] Ibid, per Munby LJ at [40].
[77] Children Act 1989, s 11L(2).
[78] Ibid, s 11L(2) and (3).
[79] Ibid, s 11L(5) and (6).
[80] Ibid, s 11N.

Operation of the order

23.36 On making an enforcement order the court has to ask an officer of Cafcass or a Welsh family proceedings officer:

- to monitor, or arrange for the monitoring of, the person's compliance with the unpaid work requirement imposed by the order;

- to report to the court if a report following a breach of the order (see **23.42**) is made in relation to the person;

- to report to the court on such other matters relating to the person's compliance as may be specified in the request;

- to report to the court if the person is, or becomes, unsuitable to perform work under the requirement.[81]

It is the duty of the Cafcass or Welsh family proceedings officer to comply with any request under this section.[82]

Varying the order

23.37 On an application by the person subject to the enforcement order, or of its own motion,[83] if the court is satisfied that the person has changed, or proposes to change, his residence from the local justice area specified in the order to another local justice area, the court may amend the order by substituting the other area for the area specified.[84]

23.38 On an application by the person subject to the enforcement order or of its own motion[85] if it appears to the court that, having regard to circumstances that have arisen since the enforcement order was made, it would be appropriate to do so, the court may reduce the number of hours specified in the order (but not below a minimum of 40 hours).[86] In amending the order the court must be satisfied that the effect on the person of the enforcement order as proposed to be amended is no more than is required to secure his compliance with the contact order or any contact order that has effect in its place.[87]

23.39 On an application by the person subject to the enforcement order, or of its own motion,[88] if it appears to the court that, having regard to circumstances

---

[81] Children Act 1989, s 11M(1).
[82] Ibid, s 11M(2).
[83] Ibid, Sch A1, para 5(3).
[84] Ibid, Sch A1, para 5(2).
[85] Ibid, Sch A1, para 6(4).
[86] Ibid, Sch A1, para 6(2); Criminal Justice Act 2003, s 199(2)(a).
[87] Ibid, Sch A1, para 6(3).
[88] Ibid, Sch A1, para 7(3).

that have arisen since the enforcement order was made, it would be appropriate to do so, the court may extend the period of 12 months.[89]

23.40 The order may also be extended or varied following a breach (see **23.43**).

Revoking the order

23.41 On an application by the person subject to the enforcement order, or of its own motion,[90] the court may revoke the enforcement order if it appears to the court that:

- in all the circumstances no enforcement order should have been made;

- having regard to circumstances which have arisen since the enforcement order was made, it would be appropriate for the enforcement order to be revoked; or

- having regard to the person's satisfactory compliance with the contact order or any contact order that has effect in its place, it would be appropriate for the enforcement order to be revoked.[91]

In deciding whether to revoke the enforcement order on the ground that having regard to circumstances which have arisen since the enforcement order was made, it would be appropriate for the enforcement order to be revoked, the court has to take into account:

- the extent to which the person subject to the enforcement order has complied with it; and

- the likelihood that the person will comply with the contact order or any contact order that has effect in its place in the absence of an enforcement order.[92]

In deciding whether to revoke the enforcement order on the ground of satisfactory compliance the court has to take into account the likelihood that the person will comply with the contact order or any contact order that has effect in its place in the absence of an enforcement order.[93]

Enforcing the order

23.42 Paragraphs 8 and 9 of Sch A1 to the Act contain detailed provisions relating to breach. If the person responsible for ensuring compliance ('the

---

[89]   Children Act 1989, Sch A1, para 7(2).
[90]   Ibid, Sch A1, para 4(3).
[91]   Ibid, Sch A1, para 4(2).
[92]   Ibid, Sch A1, para 4(4).
[93]   Ibid, Sch A1, para 4(5).

responsible officer') is of the opinion that the order has been breached he must give the person a specified warning unless a warning has already been given in the previous 12 months or he reports that matter to the monitoring Cafcass officer.

23.43 If the court is satisfied:

- beyond reasonable doubt that the person has failed to comply with the unpaid work requirement imposed by the first order;[94] and

- before the failure occurred the person had been given (in accordance with rules of court) a copy of, or otherwise informed of the terms of, a notice under s 11N relating to the first order (see **23.35**)[95]

it may:

- amend the first order so as to make the requirement more onerous by increasing the hours up to the maximum or extending the period of the order beyond 12 months;[96] or

- make an enforcement order ('the second order') in relation to the person and (if the first order is still in force) provide for the second order to have effect either in addition to or in substitution for the first order.[97]

However, the court may not exercise these powers if it is satisfied that the person had a reasonable excuse for failing to comply with the unpaid work requirement imposed by the first order. The burden of proof lies on the person claiming to have had a reasonable excuse, and the standard of proof is the balance of probabilities.[98]

23.44 The court may exercise its powers in relation to the first order only:

- on the application of a person who would be able to apply for an enforcement order (see **23.34**)[99] and, if that person is the child, with the leave of the court;[100] and

- if the application is made while the first order is in force.[101]

---

[94] Children Act 1989, Sch A1, para 9(2).
[95] Ibid, Sch A1, para 9(8).
[96] Ibid, Sch A1, para 9(2) and (9).
[97] Ibid, Sch A1, para 9(2).
[98] Ibid, Sch A1, para 9(3) and (4).
[99] Ibid, Sch A1, para 9(5).
[100] Ibid, Sch A1, para 9(6).
[101] Ibid, Sch A1, para 9(7).

23.45 In exercising its powers the court must be satisfied that, taking into account the extent to which the person has complied with the unpaid work requirement imposed by the first order, the effect on the person of the proposed exercise of those powers:

• is no more than is required to secure his compliance with the contact order or any contact order that has effect in its place; and

• is no more than is proportionate to the seriousness of his failures to comply with the contact order and the first order.

Discussion

23.46 Although enforcement orders are a useful alternative to committal, the need to obtain detailed information, the possibility that suitable work will not be available, the fact that the person subject to the order has 12 months in which to carry out the requirement and the limited sanctions available for non-compliance mean that the order does not offer what the then Mr Justice Munby said in *Re D (Intractable Contact Dispute: Publicity)*[102] was required namely 'swift, efficient enforcement of existing court orders'. There is as yet no reported guidance from the Family Division or the Court of Appeal on the use of enforcement orders.[103] However, given the draconian nature of committal it is important that before a court makes a committal order it considers making an enforcement order and, if it does not make it, gives cogent reasons why the order is not appropriate and why committal is both necessary and proportionate.

Committals and fines

23.47 NB Both the High Court and the county court have power to commit anyone who fails to comply with an order to do an act within a stated time or failing to obey an order to refrain from doing an act.

23.48 The High Court can grant injunctions in support of s 8 orders and the injunctions, if breached, can be enforced by committal. However, county courts have no inherent power to grant injunctions[104] and family proceedings courts have no power at all. However, prohibited steps orders are in the nature of injunctions and may be enforced in the county court as if they were. In some cases, it may be appropriate for a court to grant a non-molestation order under Part IV of the Family Law Act 1996, with or without a power of arrest being added and this can be done in proceedings under the CA 1989 without an application having to be made under the 1996 Act.[105] This was done, for

---

[102] [2004] EWHC 727 (Fam), [2004] 1 FLR 1226. See **11.172**.
[103] They were briefly discussed in *Re L-W (Enforcement and Committal: Contact): CPL v CH-W* [2010] EWCA Civ 1253, [2011] 1 FLR 1095, per Munby LJ at [35]–[40].
[104] *Devon County Council v B* [1997] 1 FLR 591.
[105] Family Law Act 1996, s 42(2).

example, in *G v C (Residence Order: Committal)*,[106] when a judge granted a father a contact order but ordered him not to harass, threaten or pester the mother, not to have contact with her save in emergency through a third party and not to use violence towards her.

In order for injunctions and prohibited steps orders to be enforceable, it is necessary for them to be drafted in such a way as to order a named person to carry out or refrain from carrying out a specific act. A requirement to carry out a specific act must state the time within which the act is to be carried out. The importance of careful drafting is discussed at **23.18**.

23.49 Courts view committal orders in cases under the Children Act as matters of last resort (see below) and courts should not exercise their discretion to direct that a penal notice is added to an order unless it is justified[107] and unless the court thinks that committal may be appropriate in the particular case.

23.50 In addition there are a number of important preconditions before the order can be enforced:

• the order must be served personally;

• if the order requires an act to be performed, it must be served before expiry of the time;

• the order must contain a warning ('the penal notice') that disobeying the order will be a contempt of court punishable by imprisonment.[108]

23.51 The High Court and the county courts may dispense with the requirement that the order be served if it thinks it just to do so.[109] For example, the person to whom the order is addressed may be present in court when it is made and the order and the power of committal are made clear. However, good practice requires the service of the order in most cases. Then, there can be no doubt that the person served knew what was to be done, and the penalties for non-compliance, and he would have a copy of the order to remind him. However, on an application for committal, the court may enforce an order requiring a person to abstain from doing an act if the judge is satisfied that the person to whom the order is directed had notice, either because he was present when it was made or was notified of its terms whether by phone or otherwise.[110] There appears to be no reason why 'texting' should not be used in an appropriate case.

---

[106] [1998] 1 FLR 43.
[107] See, for example, *Re N (A Minor) (Access: Penal Notice)* [1992] 1 FLR 134.
[108] For the enforcement of undertakings see FPR 2010, PD 33A.
[109] RSC Ord 45, r 7(7), CCR Ord 29, r 1(7) and the Civil Procedure Rules Practice Direction on Committal, applied to family proceedings by FPR 2010, r 33.1(2).
[110] RSC Ord 45, r 7(6), CCR Ord 29, r 1(6), *Lewis v Lewis* [1991] 2 FLR 43.

Procedure

23.52   The procedure to be followed is set out in Family Procedure Rules 2010, Pt 33, RSC Ord 52, r 4(1) (High Court), CCR Ord 29, r 1 (County Court) and the Practice Direction on Committals (both courts). The summons or application must identify the provisions of the injunction which are alleged to have been breached and detail the alleged breaches. It must be supported by an affidavit and be served personally at least 2 clear days before the hearing. The Civil Procedure Rules Practice Direction on committal which requires full compliance with the ECHR must be observed. For the purposes of Art 6, the proceedings are criminal proceedings. Alleged breaches must be proved on the criminal standard of proof, ie beyond all reasonable doubt. Hearsay evidence will probably be inadmissible or, if strictly admissible, given little or no weight.[111] A respondent is not obliged to give evidence.[112]

23.53   In all applications for committal – in civil as well as family cases – it is important that a respondent has the opportunity of being represented and, if necessary, the proceedings should be adjourned for representation to be obtained. Committal proceedings are criminal in nature and Art 6 of the ECHR guarantees the following minimum rights:

(a)   to be informed promptly in a language he understands and in detail the nature and cause of what is being alleged;

(b)   to have adequate time and facilities for the preparation of his defence;

(c)   to defend himself in person or through legal assistance of his own choosing or, if he has not sufficient means to pay for legal assistance, to be given it free when the interests of justice so require;

(d)   to examine or have examined witnesses against him and to obtain the attendance and examination of witnesses on his behalf under the same conditions as witnesses against him;

(e)   to have the free assistance of an interpreter if he cannot understand or speak the language used in court.

If the respondent wants legal representation, the court itself cannot grant it but should consider inviting a solicitor to represent him by providing 'Help at Court'.[113] If an interpreter is needed, the court must provide one.[114]

---

[111]   *C v C (Contempt: Evidence)* [1993] 1 FLR 220.
[112]   *Hammerton v Hammerton* [2007] EWCA Civ 248, [2007] 2 FLR 1133.
[113]   See Administration of Justice Act 1999, Pt 1.
[114]   See *Guidance: Arranging interpreters for people with a hearing impairment and for foreign languages* (Court Service, September 2003).

23.54 As in all cases involving committal, it is important not to allow 'speed to degenerate into haste'.[115] Even where great pains have been taken to ensure representation, the Court of Appeal may still find that extra steps should be taken. In *Re K (Contact: Committal Order)*[116] a mother consistently refused to allow contact. At a hearing when she was represented by counsel instructed by the Bar Pro Bono Unit, but not with a solicitor, a suspended committal order was made on terms that she complied with the contact order. When the father applied for the suspension to be lifted because she had not complied, she was still unrepresented and the hearing was adjourned for a week for her to consult the Royal Courts of Justice Advice Bureau. After a further breach, she was again unrepresented. The Bar Pro Unit had expressed doubts about whether it was right to take the case without papers and without a solicitor being instructed. The judge lifted the suspension and issued a warrant for the mother's arrest and granting residence to the father. The Court of Appeal allowed the mother's appeal. While Art 6 does not entitle someone to indefinite offers of legal assistance if they behave so unreasonably as to make it impossible for the funders to provide it, in the instant case the question of legal aid had not been specifically addressed. The Legal Services Commission should have expedited an application for emergency public funding to be represented by solicitor and counsel. The Court also made the point that representation was desirable for reasons in addition to the Art 6 requirements. Psychiatric advice on the mother might have been helpful to try to resolve the situation and a fuller investigation of whether it was appropriate for residence to be granted to the father could have been carried out. The court may conclude that had the respondent been offered the opportunity of representation, she would have refused it.[117]

A committal application should not be heard at the same time as an application for contact. The evidential structure for the former is more formal and regulated than that normally applicable in private law proceedings which are quasi-inquisitorial and the court's objective is not primarily to grant relief to one party or the other, but to reach a solution which is in the best interests of the child or children involved, whose welfare is the court's paramount concern. As a result, the evidential rules in such proceedings are more relaxed. Hearsay is admissible, and facts have to be established on the balance of probabilities, not beyond reasonable doubt. Judges must pause for thought, if they are asked to hear both at the same time.

> 'I do not say that a judge can never take that course. There may well be cases in which the factual matrix for the committal proceedings is so inter-twined with that giving rise to the Part II proceedings, that there is no sensible alternative but to hear them together. However, if a judge does take that course, he or she must be astute to differentiate between the two sets of proceedings when it comes to findings of fact and disposal. contact.'[118]

---

[115] *Newman v Modern Bookbinders Ltd* [2000] 2 All ER 814, per Sedley LJ at [25].
[116] [2002] EWCA Civ 1559, [2003] 1 FLR 277.
[117] *G v G* [2007] EWCA Civ 680, [2007] 2 FLR 1127.
[118] *Hammerton v Hammerton* [2007] EWCA Civ 248, [2007] 2 FLR 1133, per Ward LJ at [31].

In addition, to be able to defend himself against the allegations, it is important that the respondent should be given the opportunity specifically to address the court on the question of sentence.[119]

23.55 In an appropriate case the court can deal with a committal application in the absence of the respondent. The decision to do so has to be viewed within the factual context of the case as a whole. Thus the Court of Appeal in one case held where the mother had failed to attend the last five hearings and had informed her solicitors on the morning of the committal hearing that she would not attend court because she had no one to look after her child, the judge had been entitled to conclude that her excuse for not attending lacked substance and was entitled to proceed in her absence.[120]

23.56 The Children Act 1989, s 14 gives the court the power to enforce a residence order as if it was an order for the production of a child and contact orders too can be enforced under s 63.[121]

23.57 The same requirement about when, where and by whom specified acts must be done applies to orders sought to be enforced under s 63 as applies to orders in the High Court and county court. So too does the advice that committals should be a matter of last resort.[122] Any failure to comply with the order must be deliberate.[123]

Should an order be made?

23.58 Committal is only appropriate where there is a continuing course of deliberate refusal to comply with the order and all other efforts to resolve the situation have been unsuccessful.[124] The impact of the order on the child should also be considered,[125] although the child's welfare is not the paramount consideration.[126] Courts have repeatedly stated that committal of a parent for non-compliance with a contact order is a matter of last resort, but in recent years the emphasis has shifted from a position that it should never be used to one that it may be justified. The two positions can be illustrated from two dicta of the Court of Appeal, 13 years apart. In *Churchard v Churchard*,[127] Ormrod LJ said:

> 'There is no doubt and it should be clearly understood ... that an application for committal for breach of orders relating to access ... are inevitably futile and

---

[119] *G v G* [2007] EWCA Civ 680, [2007] 2 FLR 1127.

[120] *Re P (Committal for Breach of Contact Order: Reasons)* [2006] EWCA Civ 1792, [2007] 1 FLR 1820.

[121] *Re K (A Minor) (Access: Breach)* [1977] 2 All ER 737.

[122] *Re H (Contact: Enforcement)* [1996] 1 FLR 614.

[123] *Patterson v Walcott* [1984] FLR 408.

[124] *Re M (Minors) (Access: Contempt: Committal)* [1991] 1 FLR 355 and *Re M (Contact Order)* [2005] EWCA Civ 615, [2005] 2 FLR 1006.

[125] *Re M (Contact Order: Committal)* [1999] 1 FLR 810.

[126] *A v N (Committal: Refusal of Contact)* [1997] 1 FLR 533.

[127] [1984] FLR 635, at 638.

should not be made. The damage they cause is appalling ... To apply for a legalistic but futile remedy, because it is the only thing left to do is ... the last hope of the destitute.'

In 1997, Ward LJ disagreed in *A v N (Committal: Refusal of Contact)*:[128]

'... it is perhaps appropriate that the message goes out in loud and clear terms that there does come a limit to the tolerance of the court to see its orders flouted by mothers even if they have to care for their young children. If she goes to prison it is her own fault ... [The judge] did not commit this young mother to preserve his own dignity ... He was essentially concerned to do what he thought best for the child in the long term which is to give her the chance to know her father.'

23.59 Immediate orders are expected to be rare. Every opportunity is usually given for the defaulting parent to comply. As in *Re K (Contact: Committal Order)*[129] warning is given with a return to court, preferably the following week, to monitor compliance, then a suspended sentence before finally an immediate order is made.

Sentence

23.60 The maximum sentence for breaches of injunctions or a failure to comply with orders backed by a penal notice in the High Court or county court is 2 years' imprisonment or, in family proceedings courts, 1 month or a fine (in the case of family proceedings courts, not exceeding £2,500) or both,[130] The sentence of imprisonment can be suspended, for example, on terms that the contemnor obeys the order. However, on an application to purge contempt, a suspended order cannot be substituted for an order of immediate imprisonment.[131]

23.61 Applicants for committal are discouraged from participating in the sentence exercise which is a matter for the court.[132] The applicant may appeal a refusal to make a committal order but requires leave to do so.[133]

23.62 In *Re D (Intractable Contact Dispute: Publicity)*[134] Munby J said that although committal is the remedy of last resort, a case strategy may properly involve imprisonment.

'There is no reason why in a case of serious recalcitrance or defiance where it is possible to establish a breach of the order the court should not, there and then, make an immediate suspended committal order so that the mother can be told in very plain terms that if she again prevents contact taking place the following

---

[128] [1997] 1 FLR 533, at 541.
[129] [2002] EWCA Civ 1559, [2003] 1 FLR 277.
[130] Contempt of Court Act 1981, s 14.
[131] *Harris v Harris* [2002] 1 FLR 248.
[132] *M v M (Breaches of Orders: Committal)* [2005] EWCA Civ 1722, [2006] 1 FLR 1154.
[133] Ibid.
[134] [2004] EWHC 727 (Fam), [2004] 1 FLR 1226.

Saturday she is likely to find herself in prison the following week ... A willingness to impose very short sentences – 1, 2 or 3 days – may suffice to achieve the necessary deterrent or coercive effect without significantly impairing a mother's ability to look after her children.'[135]

It should be noted though that sentences of less than a week are likely to result in the contemnor's immediate release. Remission is available, the day the sentence is imposed is counted towards the term and civil prisoners due for release at a weekend are released on the previous Friday. For this reason judges are advised on courses run by the Judicial Studies Board that no committal order in proceedings under Part IV of the Family Law Act 1996 should be made for a term of less than 8 days.[136]

23.63 In *Hale v Tanner*[137] Hale LJ gave important guidance on how the sentencing exercise should be carried out.

- 'I would not wish to suggest that there should be any general principle that the statutory provisions relating to sentencing in ordinary criminal cases should be applied to sentencing for contempt. The circumstances surrounding contempt cases are much more various and the objectives underlying the court's actions are also much more various.'

- 'Family cases, it has long been recognised, raise different considerations from those elsewhere in the civil law. The two most obvious are the heightened emotional tensions that arise between family members and often the need for those family members to continue to be in contact with one another because they have children together or the like. Those two factors make the task of the court, in dealing with these issues, quite different from the task when dealing with commercial disputes or other types of case in which sometimes, in fact rarely, sanctions have to be imposed for contempt of court.'

- Committal is the only procedure which is available. [Note This is no longer the case as an enforcement order can now be made.] The court has to direct its mind to whether or not committal to prison is the appropriate order but it does not follow from that that imprisonment is to be regarded as the automatic consequence of the breach of an order. There is, however, no principle that imprisonment is not to be imposed at the first occasion.[138] Nevertheless, it is a common practice, and usually appropriate in view of the sensitivity of the circumstances of these cases, to take some other course on the first occasion.

---

[135] [2004] EWHC 727 (Fam), [2004] 1 FLR 1226, at [56]–[57].
[136] See Platt 'Sentencing for contempt' [2009] Fam Law 519 which contains a table showing the effect of sentences of varying length.
[137] [2000] 2 FLR 879, at 883–885.
[138] See *Thorpe v Thorpe* [1998] 2 FLR 127, CA.

- Alternatives are limited. The full range of sentencing options is not available for contempt of court. Nevertheless, there is a range of things that the court can consider. It may do nothing, make no order. It may adjourn, and in a case where the alleged contemnor has not attended court, that may be an appropriate course to take, although I would not say so in every case. It depends on the reasons that may be thought to lie behind the non-attendance. There is a power to fine. There is a power of requisition of assets and there are mental health orders. All of those may, in an appropriate case, need consideration, particularly in a case where the court has not found any actual violence proved.

- If imprisonment is appropriate, the length of the committal should be decided without reference to whether or not it is to be suspended. A longer period of committal is not justified because its sting is removed by virtue of its suspension.

- The length of the committal has to depend upon the court's objectives. 'There are two objectives always in contempt of court proceedings. One is to mark the court's disapproval of the disobedience to its order. The other is to secure compliance with that order in the future. Thus, the seriousness of what has taken place is to be viewed in that light as well as for its own intrinsic gravity.'

- The length of the committal has to bear some reasonable relationship to the maximum of 2 years.

- Suspension is possible in a much wider range of circumstances than it is in criminal cases. It does not have to be the exceptional case. Indeed, it is usually the first way of attempting to secure compliance with the court's order.

- The length of the suspension requires separate consideration, although it is often appropriate for it to be linked to continued compliance with the order underlying the committal.

- The court has to bear in mind the context which may be an aggravating or mitigating factor. The context is often the break-up of an intimate relationship in which emotions run high and people behave in silly ways. The context of having children together, if that be the case, cannot be ignored. Sometimes that means that there is an aggravation of what has taken place, because of the greater fear that is engendered from the circumstances. Sometimes it may be mitigating, because there is reason to suppose that once the immediate emotions have calmed down, the molestation and threats will not continue.

- In many cases, the court will have to bear in mind that there are concurrent proceedings in another court based on either the same facts or some of the same facts which are before the court on the contempt proceedings. The court cannot ignore those parallel proceedings. It may have to take into account their outcome in considering what the practical effect is upon the contempt proceedings. They do have different purposes and often the overlap is not exact, but nevertheless the court will not want, in effect, the contemnor to suffer punishment twice for the same events.

• It will usually be desirable for the court to explain very briefly why it has made the choices that it has made in the particular case before it. It would be appropriate in most cases for the contemnor to know why he or she was being sentenced to a period of imprisonment; why it was the length that it was; if it was suspended, why the suspension was as it was, but only very briefly.

• An important part of the exercise is that the contemnor should understand the importance of keeping court orders, of not breaking them and the likely consequences if they are so broken.

23.64 When the contemnor has already been punished by a criminal court for offences arising from the same incident, the civil court must be careful to reflect the prior sentence in its own sentence.

'However effectively the proceedings are managed, a perpetrator may face sentence for the same act which amounts to both a breach of an injunction made in family proceedings and also a crime under the Protection from Harassment Act 1997. Of course the sentencing courts do not share the same objective and operate in different ranges. The judge in family proceedings has to fit a custodial sentence within a range of 0–24 months. An important objective for him is to uphold the authority of the court by demonstrating that its orders cannot be flouted with impunity. Nevertheless there will be a shared deterrent objective in the punishment of domestic violence by imprisonment. Clearly, therefore, the first court to sentence must not anticipate or allow for a likely future sentence. It is for the second court to sentence to reflect *the prior sentence* [italics added] in its judgment in order to ensure that the defendant is not twice punished for the same act. It is essential that the second court should be fully informed of the factors and circumstances reflected in the first sentence.'[139]

'No doubt the seriousness or otherwise of the breach of the obligation to the civil court, whether undertaken or imposed by injunction, will in part be informed by what one might call its *context*, namely (for example) by whether it was the first breach or the last in a series of breaches, by the existence or otherwise of warnings of the consequences of a breach or further breaches and by the propinquity in time between the creation of the obligation and the breach. But how much further can the judge go into the circumstances or *content* of the breach without sentencing for the conduct for which sentence has already been passed? In the most general terms the judge must surely be entitled to assess the conduct's gravity: for the graver the conduct, the more serious the contempt of the civil court. But, so it seems to me, any more profound assessment risks trespass upon the area for which sentence has already been passed. And, even when the breach is

---

[139] *Lomas v Parle* [2003] EWCA Civ 1804, [2004] 1 FLR 812, per Thorpe LJ at [46]–[47].

serious, the civil court must rigorously remind itself that, however problematical, its function is to sentence only for the fact of a serious contempt and not for the content of the serious contempt.'[140]

See also *Hale v Tanner* (above).

Examples

23.65

- *C v C (Access Order: Enforcement)*[141] committal for 7 days upheld on appeal;

- *A v N (Committal: Refusal of Contact)*[142] suspended sentence of 6 weeks activated, upheld by the Court of Appeal;

- *F v F (Contact: Committal)*[143] committal order of 7 days suspended for 6 months, upheld by the Court of Appeal.

- *S (Contact Dispute: Committal)*[144] application for committal adjourned for 6 weeks when the mother agreed to allow contact. When she again refused, a committal order for 7 days was made, suspended on condition that she allow contact on the following Saturday and thereafter. She failed to comply and the order was activated with the child living with the father under an interim residence order. The mother's appeal was dismissed. The judge had no alternative and would have been failing in her duty had she not upheld the authority of the court.

- *Re M (Contact Order)*[145] conditions imposed on a contact order requiring the child's father to collect the child from school and return her to her mother at 4 pm. In committal proceedings brought by the mother the judge found that the father had returned her at 4.10 pm and sentenced him to a term of 7 days suspended for 6 months. The Court of Appeal allowed his appeal. A custodial sentence should be imposed only where justified. It was contrary to principle to impose such a sentence merely because the contemnor lacked the means to pay a fine.

- *B v S (Contempt: Imprisonment of Mother)*[146] A mother persisted in failing to comply with a contact order ('a particularly serious history of a refusal') and, in addition to the three alleged breaches, also failed to comply with the order after the judge had adjourned the committal

---

[140] *Slade v Slade* [2009] EWCA Civ 748, [2010] 1 FLR 160, per Wilson LJ at [23].
[141] [1990] 1 FLR 462.
[142] [1997] 1 FLR 533.
[143] [1998] 2 FLR 237.
[144] [2004] EWCA Civ 1790, [2005] 1 FLR 812.
[145] [2005] EWCA Civ 615, [2005] 2 FLR 1006.
[146] [2009] EWCA Civ 548, [2009] 2 FLR 1005

proceedings in order to give her another opportunity to comply. She was sentenced to three concurrent terms of 28 days each. The Court of Appeal remitted the matter to the trial judge for resentencing because the mother was still breast feeding a 3-month-old baby who had not been allowed to join her in prison. The Court directed that the prison governor should be asked to authorise the admission of the baby and Wilson LJ warned that 'The days are long gone when mothers can assume that their role of carers of children protects them from being sentenced to immediate terms of imprisonment for clear, repeated and deliberate breaches of contact orders.'

- *Re X (A Child by His Litigation Friend)*[147] A mother was ordered to return her child, a ward, from Nigeria. Under a consent order she authorised the child's aunt with whom he was staying and the child's school to return his passport and take him to the airport. However, by a second letter she countermanded the instructions. Despite an adjournment of the committal proceedings she failed to sign further letters to facilitate his return. The Court of Appeal dismissed her appeal against a sentence of 8 months. The committal proceedings were not an enquiry as to whether the child would have been returned had it not been for his mother's actions but rather into the seriousness of her beach of the order. This was an active breach of an order rather than a mere failure to comply with it and her actions had been intended totally to frustrate the order.

- *Re C (Children)*[148] Mother breached two injunctions restraining her from going to her children's foster home and damaging the foster carer's property. Committal orders totaling 4 months reduced on appeal to 3 months because of her emotional state at the time of the breach.

Purging contempt

23.66 The court may, on the application of any person committed to prison for any contempt of court, discharge him.[149]

23.67 In *CJ v Flintshire Borough Council*[150] the Court of Appeal gave guidance on how a court should approach the matter. Lord Justice Atkins said that the court has to consider two broad issues.

- Despite the fact that the contemnor has not served the term originally imposed, has the contemnor demonstrated that he has now received sufficient punishment for his breach of the court's injunction? In this regard, the court will examine among possible other matters, at the least, whether the contemnor now not only accepts that he has been guilty of his contempt, but also that 'he is genuinely sorry for his misdeeds and repents

---

147 [2011] EWCA Civ 555, [2011] 2 FLR 793.
148 [2011] EWCA Civ 1230.
149 RSC, Ord 52, r 8(1).
150 [2010] EWCA Civ 393, [2010] 2 FLR 1224.

them'. If the answer to the question is 'no, the contemnor has not so demonstrated that he has received sufficient punishment for the breach', it is difficult to see how a court can consider an early release unless there are other, extenuating circumstances which require that the court consider the exercise of its power to grant an early release.

- If the answer to that first question is 'yes', the court must ask whether the interests of justice be best served in permitting his early discharge? The matters that the court will consider will depend on the type of case in hand.[151]

In addition:

'it seems to me that when a court is considering whether to commit for contempt in the first place and also when a court is asked to make an order for early release, it must consider the extent to which an order imprisoning a person for contempt is necessary and is proportionate in the interests of the prevention of disorder or crime and to uphold the rule of law and the lawful orders of the court.'[152]

23.68 However, Lord Justice Sedley pointed out that there are no unfettered discretions.

- A judge cannot let a contemnor out because he feels sorry for him or because he would not himself have imposed so long a sentence. There has to be a reason for discharge known to the law

- It is for the contemnor to advance such a reason for discharge, not for the court to find a reason for refusing it.

- Purging is not a matter of practice or parlance but a matter of substantive justice. This is why the vocabulary of judgment is more relevant than the vocabulary of discretion.

- It is at the point of sentence that necessity and proportionality govern judgment. When a judge comes to consider discharge from a sentence which has already been found both necessary and proportionate, he or she is looking at new factors, if there are any, albeit these may modify what is now necessary and what is now proportionate.[153]

23.69 Lord Justice Wilson pointed out that:

'Although a person committed to prison for breach of a mandatory order to do an act (such as to hand over a child[154]) may reasonably be said to purge his contempt if he thereupon does the act or causes it to be done, the notion is less easily applied

---

[151] Ibid, at [28]–[29].
[152] Ibid, at [30].
[153] Ibid, at [37].
[154] For example as in *Corcoran v Corcoran* [1950] 1 All ER 495.

to an act which amounts to the breach of a prohibitory order and which, once done, cannot be undone. In such cases the court could ask

- Can it conclude, in all the circumstances as they now are, that the contemnor has suffered punishment proportionate to his contempt?
- Would the interest of the state in upholding the rule of law be significantly prejudiced by early discharge?
- How genuine is the contemnor's expression of contrition?
- Has he done all that he reasonably can to demonstrate a resolve and an ability not to commit a further breach if discharged early?
- In particular has he done all that he reasonably can (bearing in mind the difficulties of his so doing while in prison) in order to construct for himself proposed living and other practical arrangements in the event of early discharge in such a way as to minimise the risk of his committing a further breach?
- Does he make any specific proposal to augment the protection against any further breach of those whom the order which he breached was designed to protect?
- What is the length of time which he has served in prison, including its relation to (a) the full term imposed upon him and (b) the term which he will otherwise be required to serve prior to release pursuant to s 258(2) of the Criminal Justice Act 2003?
- Are there any special factors which impinge upon the exercise of the discretion in one way or the other?

The success of an application for an order for early discharge does not depend on favourable answers to all the questions. Nevertheless the first is a general question which ... probably needs an affirmative answer before early discharge should be ordered. The second will surely require a negative answer. An affirmative answer to the third will usually although not always[155] ... Subject to [this], answers to the questions go into the melting pot; and out of it, once they have melted together, comes the conclusion.'[156]

23.70 When contempt is purged, the court cannot partially suspended part of the sentence, for example, the unserved part of the sentence originally imposed.[157]

SEQUESTRATION OF ASSETS

23.71 Where a person has been committed for failing to comply with a judgment or order requiring him to deliver any thing to some other person or to deposit it in court or elsewhere, the High Court may issue a writ of sequestration to enforce that judgment or order.[158] An application for permission to issue a writ of sequestration must be made in accordance with

---

[155] For example, *Enfield LBC v Mahoney* [1983] 1 WLR 749.

[156] *CJ v Flintshire Borough Council* [2010] EWCA Civ 393, [2010] 2 FLR 1224, at [21]–[22].

[157] *Harris v Harris* [2001] EWCA Civ 1645, [2002] 1 FLR 248, *Doncaster MBC v Watson* [2011] EWHC 2498 (Fam) (for which see also [2011] EWHC B15 (Fam) and [2011] EWHC 2376 (Fam)).

[158] RSC, Ord 52, r 8(2); Ord 46, r 5.

CPR, Part 23. Tthe application notice, stating the grounds of the application and accompanied by a copy of the witness statement or affidavit in support of the application, must be served personally on the person against whose property it is sought to issue the writ. The court may dispense with service of the application notice under this rule if it thinks it just to do so. The judge hearing an application for permission to issue a writ of sequestration may sit in private in any case in which, if the application were for an order of committal, he would be entitled to do so by virtue of RSC, Ord 52, r 6 but, except in such a case, the application shall be heard in public.[159]

23.72 In *H v N*[160] a mother, in breach of an order that her child should not be removed from the jurisdiction, failed to return the child to his father at the end of contact and abducted him to India. The mother was found, in her absence, to be guilty of contempt of court and the judge granted the father leave to issue a writ of sequestration, which he did later the same day. An order was then made directing the sequestrators to pay the father £25,000 from the sequestrated assets, to be used to help recover the child from India, and for the payment of his solicitors' costs.

Magistrates' Courts Act 1980, s 63

23.73 Committal for breaches of orders of magistrates' courts are possible under Magistrates' Courts Act 1980, s 63. Section 63(1) provides that, where a court has power to require the doing of anything other than the payment of money or to prohibit the doing of anything, that power may contain such provisions for the manner in which anything is to be done, for the time within which anything is to be done or during which anything is not to be done and generally for giving effect to the order as the court thinks fit. Section 63(3) states that, where anybody disobeys the order, the court may order him to pay a sum not exceeding £50 for every day he is in breach, to a limit of £5,000 or commit him to prison until he has remedied his default or for a period not exceeding 2 months.

23.74 In *Thomason v Thomason*[161] Bush J warned that the use of s 63 to enforce access orders should be approached with the greatest of caution, both by the lawyers acting for the parties and also by the magistrates. Questions of punishment for past behaviour or concepts of the damage to the dignity of the court if an order were disobeyed should not enter into consideration in a domestic jurisdiction of this kind. The object of the exercise is to enforce the breached order for access in the sense of getting it working, or putting something more workable in its place.

---

[159] RSC, Ord 46, r 5.
[160] [2009] EWHC 640 (Fam), [2009] 2 FLR 211.
[161] [1985] FLR 214 at 216. See *also Re H (Contact: Enforcement)* [1996] 1 FLR 614 and *I v D (Access Order: Enforcement)* [1988] 2 FLR 286.

'This is rarely achieved by sending a parent to prison or by fining them. Indeed, the odds are that such an approach will only serve to aggravate the hostility that already may exist between the parties.'

Changing the child's residence

23.75 Although in some cases a persistent refusal by a parent to co-operate with contact may justify changing a child's residence if overall that is in the child's best interests, such an order should not be made merely to enforce a contact order. The Lord Chancellor's Sub-Committee disapproved of the use or threat of a residence application as a means of achieving contact:

'It is a legitimate complaint by women's groups that abused women are sometimes induced to agree to unsuitable and unsafe contact with violent fathers by their belief in unfounded threats that their children will either be transferred to the father or taken into care. At the same time there will be cases in which a refusal of contact will be sufficiently damaging to the child as to outweigh the trauma caused by removing the child from the care of the residential parent. [Cases may include a mother who has placed herself in a socially isolated position with the child and is thoroughly over-protective of him], where children are being brought up in the false belief that they have been sexually abused by the absent parent or where children of mixed race are being brought up in the belief that the race to which the absent parent belongs consists of people who are dangerous and/or bad.'[162]

In *Re M (A Child: Residence Order)*,[163] the Court of Appeal dismissed a mother's appeal against a transfer of residence of a 5-year-old girl to her father after she had confirmed that she had no intention of complying with a contact order. The judge had conducted a full hearing and given full and clear facts. Even leaving aside the issue of contact, the father had the strongest case to provide primary care to the child.

23.76 Changing residence if a prolonged resistance to contact by the resident parent has damaged the parent/child relationship is obviously very difficult.[164] In extreme cases, as illustrated by *Re M (Intractable Contact, Interim Care Order)*[165] a child can be placed in the interim care of a local authority as a prelude to being moved to the other parent. Whatever method is used, success is not guaranteed.[166]

23.77 This topic is discussed more fully at **11.176**.

---

[162] *Making Contact Work*, ibid, para 14.27.
[163] [2002] All ER (D) 226 (May).
[164] See, for example, *Re K (Contact: Committal Order)* [2002] EWCA Civ 1558, [2003] 1 FLR 277, per Hale J at [28].
[165] [2003] EWHC 1024 (Fam), [2003] 2 FLR 636.
[166] See, for example, *Re S (Transfer of Residence)* [2011] 1 FLR 1789 and [2010] EWHC192 (Fam), [2010] 1 FLR 1785 and [2010] EWCA Civ 219 (sub nom *Re S (A Child)*).

Chapter 24

COSTS

COSTS IN THE FAMILY PROCEEDINGS COURT

24.1 In family proceedings the court may at any time make such order as to costs as it thinks just.[1] However, it is not usual for a costs order to be made in children's cases.[2] The approach to the exercise of the discretion is discussed below at **24.4**.

24.2 There are three possible courses that the court can take to quantify the costs, none of them being wholly satisfactory because justices are inexperienced in assessing large amounts of costs:

- It can assess the amount payable there; and then

- It can adjourn until a bill has been prepared or, in the case of a LSC-funded receiving party, an assessment of the LSC costs has taken place; or

- In the case of a LSC-funded receiving party, it can order the paying party to pay a proportion of the assessed LSC costs.[3] This later course has the disadvantage that the paying party has no opportunity of making representations as to the amount and should be the least preferred option. However, this difficulty can be overcome to some extent by the court imposing a maximum amount payable.

COSTS IN THE COUNTY COURT AND THE HIGH COURT

24.3 Both the award of costs and their assessment are covered by Parts 43, 44 (except rr 44.3(2) and (3), 44.9 to 44.12C, 44.13(1A) and 44.18 to 44.20), r 45.6, Parts 47 and 48 of CPR 1998 and the accompanying Practice Directions.[4]

The orders which a court can make include an order that a party pay:

- a proportion of another party's costs;

---

[1]   Family Procedure Rules 2010, SI 2010/2955, r 28.1.
[2]   *Gojkovic v Gojkovic (No 2)* [1991] 2 FLR 233.
[3]   *Sutton BC v Davis (Costs) (No 2)* [1994] 2 FLR 569.
[4]   FPR 2010, r 28.2.

- a stated amount in respect of another party's costs;

- costs from or until a certain date;

- costs incurred before proceedings have begun;

- costs relating to particular steps taken in the proceedings;

- costs relating only to a distinct part of the proceedings; and

- interest on costs from or until a certain date including a date before judgment (CPR 1998, r 44.3(6)).

One of the aims of the CPR 1998 is to simplify the regime for the assessment of costs and so, when a court is considering making a costs order relating to a distinct part of the proceedings, it must instead, if practicable, order that the party pay a proportion of the overall costs or a stated amount.[5]

In family proceedings, the need to avoid the expense, delay and aggravation involved in protracted assessment proceedings, especially in complex cases, may make it desirable for courts to continue the practice set out in the pre-CPR 1998 cases of *Leary v Leary*[6] and *Newton v Newton*[7] and order a fixed sum to be paid rather than a sum ascertained by summary or detailed assessment.[8]

DISCRETION

24.4 The court has a discretion to order costs. The 'general' rule applicable in civil proceedings, that the unsuccessful party will be ordered to pay the costs of the successful party but it may make a different order,[9] does not apply to family proceedings.[10] However, the rest of CPR 1998, r 44.3 applies and so the court must have regard to all the circumstances, including:

- the conduct of all the parties which includes:

  - conduct before as well as during the proceedings and in particular the extent to which the parties followed any particular protocol;
  - whether it was reasonable for a party to raise, pursue or contest a particular allegation or issue;
  - the manner in which a party has pursued or defended his case or a particular allegation or issue; and

---

5   CPR 1998, r 44.3(7).
6   [1987] 1 FLR 384.
7   [1990] 1 FLR 33.
8   *Q v Q (Costs: Summary Assessment)* [2002] 2 FLR 668.
9   CPR 1998, r 44.3(2).
10   Family Proceedings Rules 1991, r 10.27(1).

  – whether a party who has succeeded in his case, in whole or in part, exaggerated his case;

• whether a party has succeeded on part of his case even if he has not been wholly successful;

• any admissible offer to settle made by a party which is drawn to the court's attention (CPR 1998, r 44.3(4) and (5)).

24.5 At the present time, there is no Pre-action Protocol relating to children cases, but the court might take into account the extent to which the parties have attempted to negotiate with all cards on the table before commencing proceedings and the extent to which the *Family Law Protocol* issued by The Law Society has been followed.

24.6 Notwithstanding the need to take into account these factors, the award of costs remains discretionary. In family proceedings the starting-point is that costs follow the event but this may be displaced much more easily than, and in circumstances which would not apply, in other Divisions of the High Court. In children's cases it is variously been described as unusual,[11] 'exceptional'[12] and 'wholly exceptional'[13] to order costs. The reasons why this practice has developed perhaps fall into four categories. The first is general to all family proceedings. Orders for costs between the parties will diminish the funds available to meet the needs of the family.[14] The second is that proceedings relating to children are more inquisitorial. The court's concern is to discover what will be best for the child. People who have a reasonable case to put forward as to what will be in the best interests of the child should not be deterred from doing so by the threat of a costs order against them if they are unsuccessful.[15] 'That is indeed the major reason in children cases why the court is reluctant to add to the existing deterrents which all litigants face in coming to court.'[16] The third reason is that the parties are likely to have to co-operate in the future and courts are anxious to avoid anything which may impede this. There is a possibility that in effect a costs order will add insult to the injury of having lost in the debate as to what is to happen to the child in the future; it is likely therefore to exacerbate rather than to calm down the existing tensions; and this will not be in the best interests of the child.[17] Nevertheless, the court has a broad discretion under FPR 2010, r 28.1 to make such order as it thinks 'just'.[18]

---

[11] *Gojkovic v Gojkovic (No 2)* [1991] 2 FLR 233.
[12] *Re T (Order for Costs)* [2005] EWCA Civ 311, [2005] 2 FLR 681, per Wall LJ at [36] and [46].
[13] *Re B (Indemnity Costs)* [2007] EWCA Civ 921, [2008] 1 FLR 205, per Wall LJ at [12].
[14] *Gojkovic v Gojkovic (No 2)* [1991] 2 FLR 233, at 237.
[15] *R v R (Costs: Child Case)* [1997] 2 FLR 95, at 97.
[16] Ibid, per Hale J.
[17] *London Borough of Sutton (Costs) (No 2)* [1994] 2 FLR 569; *Re M (Local Authority's Costs)* [1995] 1 FLR 533, *Re T (Order for Costs)* [2005] EWCA Civ 311, [2005] 2 FLR 681.
[18] *R v A (Costs in Children Proceedings)* [2011] EWHC 1158 (Fam), [2011] 2 FLR 672, per Sir Nicholas Wall P at [17].

24.7 Notwithstanding these important differences between cases under the Children Act 1989 and civil litigation, it is recognised that it may be appropriate to order one party to pay the whole or part of the costs of the other. The main reason for a costs orders being made is when one party has engaged in 'litigation misconduct'.

> 'It is, of course, right in principle that in Children Act proceedings orders for costs against a parent are exceptionally rare, but that is as against a parent acting responsibly and it seems to me that Circuit Judges should have recourse to [order costs] in cases in which they conclude that a parent has acted irresponsibly both in relation to [the other parent] and in relation to the child and in relation to public funds.'[19]

24.8 Litigation misconduct is not to be confused with unreasonableness in relation to the substantive issues. The court should ask whether there was conduct in relation to the litigation which went way beyond the usual sort of attitude which concerned parents show in relation to the future of their child.

> 'Of course, the parties should not be deterred, by the prospect of having to pay costs, from putting before the court that which they think to be in the best interests of the child, but there have to be limits. Children should not be put through the strain of being subject to claims which have little real prospect of success ...'[20]

24.9 At the same time, when considering litigation misconduct, the court has to remember the strain which family proceedings often causes.

> 'We recognise that irrational behaviour is commonplace in complex contact disputes, and that such behaviour may well be exacerbated by the personality of the individual parent. There is, however, in our judgment, a limit to which allowance can be made for a parent who deliberately and unreasonably obstructs contact by the other parent in circumstances where, on any objective analysis, contact is in the interests of the child and should take place. Of course there is a whole range of cases in which opposition to contact is reasonable.'[21]

24.10 Examples of such litigation misconduct may include the following.

- **Reprehensible conduct** — In *Re A (Family Proceedings: Expert Witnesses)*,[22] a father who made unwarranted personal attacks on the integrity of a family centre was ordered to pay its costs of intervening. See also *R v A (Costs in Children Proceedings)*[23] where costs in a dispute about habitual residence were awarded against a party who had made 'highly unpleasant and irrelevant' allegations.

---

[19] *Khatun v Fayez* 2 March 1998, unreported, CA, per Thorpe LJ.
[20] *R v R (Costs: Child Case)* [1997] 2 FLR 95, per Hale J at 98.
[21] *Re T (Order for Costs)* [2005] EWCA Civ 311, [2005] 2 FLR 681, per Wall LJ at [50].
[22] [2001] 1 FLR 723.
[23] [2011] EWHC 1158 (Fam), [2011] 2 FLR 672.

- **Commencing or continuing the proceedings when it was no longer reasonable to do so** — In *Re B (Costs)*,[24] a father who persisted with an application for a residence order on the grounds that the mother posed a risk to the children after two psychiatrists advised to the contrary, was ordered to pay 80% of the mother's costs from the date when the psychiatrists filed their joint accord.

- **Failing to comply with contact orders made after a full investigation**

  'Where a judge, as here, carefully investigates the disputed areas of fact which have given rise to a parent's objections to contact, and where the judge, as here, has found in terms that the child enjoys a good relationship with the non-resident parent; that there is no reason for the resident parent to have any concerns; and that there is no reason why contact should not take place, a reasonable parent, even if still anxious, has no proper grounds for failing to implement the order. If, in these circumstances, the resident parent unreasonably fails to implement the order or an agreement as to contact, and if the matter has to return to court, it will be open to the court to find that that parent is acting unreasonably.'[25]

- **Issuing appropriate proceedings** — 'Wholly inappropriate' attempts to use family proceedings for collateral and impermissible purposes (for example, issuing wardship proceedings to obstruct the proper use of immigration powers) or for purposes which are otherwise an abuse of process) may result in a costs order.[26]

- **Unreasonable litigation conduct** — See *Re S (Leave to Remove: Costs)*.[27]

24.11 In most cases, the proper consideration of all the factors will lead to there being no order for costs. Where, however, an order is made, it ought to be made clear in the judgment or, preferably, on the face of the order itself, why the order was made.[28]

24.12 There are other reasons where it may be appropriate to make a costs order. One reason may be when there is a marked disparity in the respective wealth of the parties such that the costs of one would bear harshly on his or her economy but could be discharged by the other without a similar impact.[29]

---

[24] [1999] 2 FLR 221.

[25] *Re T (Order for Costs)* [2005] EWCA Civ 311, [2005] 2 FLR 681, per Wall LJ at [51].

[26] *S v S* [2008] EWHC 2288 (Fam), [2009] 1 FLR 241, per Munby J at [37].

[27] [2010] 1 FLR 834. Costs awarded against a father who had made attempts to denigrate the mother as a person and a mother which had added to the preparation and hearing time and the expense of the litigation. See also *Kent CC v A Mother* [2011] EWHC 1267 (Fam) and *Re R (Costs: Contact Enforcement)* [2011] EWHC 2777 (Fam).

[28] *Re G (Costs: Child Case)* [1999] 2 FLR 250.

[29] *Kv K (Legal Aid: Costs)* [1995] 1 FLR 259, at 265.

24.13 It may also be appropriate to make a costs order in relation to fact finding hearings where serious and relevant allegations of misconduct (for example, domestic violence) are found proved.[30]

24.14 This general rule relating to costs in children's proceedings does not apply to appeals where the judge hearing the appeal has a broad judicial discretion over costs.[31] At first instance, nobody knows what the judge is going to find. For example, it may be reasonable for a parent to advance a view to the judge at first instance which, even if was rejected, was one which was genuinely held. It was only when that party's litigation conduct became unreasonable, when, for example, refusing to accept findings made by the judge, that the litigation conduct could be said to have become unreasonable and thus vulnerable to a costs order. A further difference is that a party who faces an appeal has the opportunity to take stock, and to make offers to compromise it. This is not to say that an order for costs will inevitably be made. 'Clearly, there will be circumstances in which the judge will refuse to make an order for costs: there will equally be circumstances in which the judge will make such an order.'[32]

24.15 Clear principles for rehearings are more difficult to state. Some rehearings will be much closer to an original hearing, for example, because new evidence or further reports are introduced which require the case to be reassessed or where the judgment at first instance was so flawed that justice could only be served by a rehearing with a fresh assessment of the witnesses. It is likely that in such instances the principles on costs are more likely to follow those applicable at the original hearing. Other cases will lack that element of a complete rehearing and the judge or court on appeal may have expressed some views on the outcome but nevertheless permitted a rehearing. There the principles applicable on the rehearing will more naturally follow those applicable to an appeal.[33]

24.16 In most cases, the proper consideration of all the factors will lead to there being no order for costs. Where, however, an order is made, it ought to be made clear in the judgment or, preferably, on the face of the order itself why the order was made.[34]

Examples

M v H (Costs: Residence Proceedings)[35]

24.17 A father seeking orders for a shared residence and defined contact orders who had unreasonably rejected a proposal to resolve the matter by

---

[30] *Re J (Costs)* [2009] EWCA Civ 1350, [2010] 1 FLR 1893.

[31] *EM v SW* [2009] EWCA Civ 311; *Re S (Leave to Remove: Costs)* [2010] 1 FLR 834.

[32] *EM v SW* [2009] EWCA Civ 311, per Wall LJ at [22].

[33] *Re S (Leave to Remove: Costs)* [2010] 1 FLR 834 per Sir Christopher Sumner, at [73]–[74].

[34] *Re G (Costs: Child Case)* [1999] 2 FLR 250.

[35] [2000] 1 FLR 394.

mediation unless the mother agreed to a shared residence order, who 'took every possible basis for criticising the mother and blowing it into an issue of her parental fitness', who continued with his application for a shared residence order despite the recommendations of the Children and Family Reporter until 4 days before the start of a hearing listed for 3 days and who had taken advantage of his financial superiority over the mother, was ordered to pay 75% of her costs.

Q v Q (Costs: Summary Assessment)[36]

24.18 A father who should never have applied for a residence order and who had failed to undergo medical tests designed to establish whether he was abusing alcohol and drugs and who had failed to attend interviews with a clinical psychologist who had been instructed to interview both parents and the child was ordered to pay 'a significant' part of the mother's costs.

T v T (A Child: Costs Order)[37]

24.19 The mother's opposition to the father taking their son abroad on holiday related only to an issue of whether it was a prelude to three possible future visits. When this was made clear at the hearing, the father offered an undertaking which the mother accepted. Sumner J held that the mother's failure to clarify matters earlier was unreasonable and irresponsible and ordered her to pay half of his costs.

Re T (Order for Costs)[38]

24.20 An intractable contact dispute in which there were three hearings when the judge found that the mother's concerns were unfounded, rejected later allegations of sexual abuse and finally made a residence order in favour of the father. The Court of Appeal dismissed the mother's appeal against an order that she pay the father's costs of all three hearings on the grounds that she had behaved unreasonably both in regard to the welfare of the child and to the conduct of the litigation. The trial judge had been justified in feeling that despite aspects of the mother's personality which allowed suspicions to take hold, 'it would be an affront to justice to expect the father to pay the costs of defending himself against these most serious allegations'. Wall LJ added:[39]

> 'We do not think that the orders for costs which we have upheld are either likely to
> or should deter a resident parent from advancing a reasonable opposition to
> contact which is genuinely based on a proper perception of the child's interests.
> But those who unreasonably frustrate contact need to be aware that the court has

[36] [2002] 2 FLR 668.
[37] [2004] EWHC 1067 (Fam), Sumner J, unreported.
[38] [2005] EWCA Civ 1029, [2005] 2 FLR 681.
[39] Ibid, at [56].

power to make cost orders in appropriate cases and that the consequences of such unreasonable behaviour may well be an order for costs against the resident parent who has behaved unreasonably.'

Re F (Family Proceedings: Costs)[40]

24.21 In proceedings brought by a father for a residence order his allegations that the mother's partner had sexually abused the child were dismissed as were M's allegations that F had abused the child. Findings were made that the partner had inappropriately spanked the child. The trial judge found that F had behaved vindictively and in a harassing manner throughout the proceedings and ordered him to pay M's costs. On appeal the Court of Appeal reduced the order to one that F pay half of the costs because he had acted properly in instituting the proceedings.

Re J (Costs of Fact-Finding Hearing)[41]

24.22 A fact-finding hearing in contact proceedings was devoted exclusively to consideration of serious and relevant allegations against the father. Over two-thirds of the mother's allegations were true. Less than one-third of them were not established yet were not found to be untrue. Of the true allegations, nine had been falsely denied by F; and all but one of the remainder had been admitted by him only in part. The Court of Appeal held that the case was one in which a proper exercise of discretion on the part of the trial judge called for an order for costs to be made against F. In the light of the allegations which M failed to establish, and of the limited admissions made by F prior to the hearing, he was ordered to pay two-thirds of M's costs of and incidental to the fact-finding hearing.

STANDARD OR INDEMNITY BASIS?

24.23 Where the court is to assess the amount of costs (whether by summary or detailed assessment) it will assess the costs on either the standard or the indemnity basis. In both cases, costs will not be allowed which have been unreasonably incurred or are unreasonable in amount. However, where the amount of costs is to be assessed on the standard basis, the court will only allow costs which are proportionate to the matters in issue and will resolve any doubt which it may have as to whether costs were reasonably incurred or reasonable and proportionate in amount in favour of the paying party. Where the amount of costs is to be assessed on the indemnity basis, there is no requirement of proportionality and any doubt as to whether costs were reasonably incurred or were reasonable is resolved in favour of the receiving party.[42]

---

40   [2008] EWCA Civ 938, [2008] 2 FLR 1662.
41   [2009] EWCA Civ 1350, [2010] 1 FLR 1893.
42   Civil Procedure Rules 1998, r 44.4.

24.24 An indemnity costs order carries some stigma. It is of its nature penal rather than exhortatory. Such an order for costs is only justified where the paying party has been guilty of conduct which is unreasonable to a high degree. This does not mean merely wrong or misguided in hindsight.[43] An order for indemnity costs is a wholly exceptional order to make in family proceedings and needs to be very carefully thought through and justified.[44]

WASTED COSTS ORDERS

24.25 The court may disallow costs (eg on a solicitor/client assessment or public funded costs assessment) or order the legal or other representative to pay them.[45] Where costs are incurred by a party as a result of:

- any improper, unreasonable or negligent act or omission on the part of a legal or other representative; or

- which, in the light of any such act or omission after they have been incurred, the court considers it unreasonable to expect that party to pay.

'Improper' covers, but is not restricted to, conduct which might lead to a serious professional penalty or offends professional consensus as to what is professional conduct. 'Unreasonable' includes conduct which is vexatious or harasses other parties, designed to harass the other side rather than advance the resolution of the case. It does not include an approach which merely leads to an unsuccessful result or which a more cautious representative might not have adopted. The acid test is whether the conduct permits of a reasonable explanation. 'Negligent' should be approached in a non-technical way. It may include failing to act with the competence reasonably to be expected of a member of the legal profession.[46] It is not limited to the representative's conduct when exercising a right of audience. Negligence in advising or in drafting documents is also included.[47]

24.26 Lawyers should not however be penalised merely for pursuing a hopeless case:

> 'Parents [in care proceedings] are at risk of losing their children; no decision could be more important … and all parents at such risk are entitled to proper representation and to have their cases put.'[48]

---

[43] *Kiam v MGM* [2002] EWCA Civ 66, [2002] 1 WLR 2810, per Sedley LJ at [12].
[44] *Re B (Indemnity Costs)* [2007] EWCA Civ 921, [2008] 1 FLR 205, per Wall LJ at [12]; *Re F (Family Proceedings: Costs)* [2008] EWCA Civ 938, [2008] 2 FLR 1662.
[45] Supreme Court Act 1981, s 51(6).
[46] *Ridehalgh v Horsefield* [1994] 2 FLR 194.
[47] *Medcalf v Mardell* [2002] 3 All ER 721.
[48] *Re G, S and M (Wasted Costs)* [2000] 1 FLR 52, per Wall J at 60.

The procedure is governed by CPR 1998, r 48.7. In *Ridehalgh v Horsefield*,[49] the Court of Appeal gave guidance on how the issue should be approached:

- Has the legal representative acted improperly, unreasonably or negligently?

- If so, did the conduct cause the party to incur unnecessary costs?

- If so, is it in all the circumstances just to order the legal representative to compensate the party for the whole or any part of the costs?

- The representative should be given the opportunity of making representations either at the time or on a subsequent occasion in which case the notice of the hearing should state the reasons why the court is considering making the order;

- The order should state:

  – the reasons why it is made; and
  – the amount to be paid or disallowed.

24.27 The issue of client confidentiality may give rise to difficulties in the representative defending himself and, save in the clearest case, the application should be decided at a separate hearing.[50] Often, the circumstances of the litigation may make it necessary to reserve the issue until after the conclusion of the case but this may not be necessary, for example, when the client has ceased to instruct the representative, or the case does not involve issues of client confidentiality or the matter is simple and straightforward:[51]

'When a wasted costs order is sought against a practitioner precluded by legal professional privilege from giving his full answer to the application, the court should not make a wasted costs order unless, proceeding with extreme care, it is satisfied (a) that there is nothing the practitioner could say, if unconstrained, to resist the order and (b) that it is in all the circumstances fair to make the order.'[52]

Examples

Re G, S and M (Wasted Costs)[53]

24.28 An order was made against counsel because of its failure to ensure that expert witnesses had seen all the relevant information before giving oral evidence.

---

[49]   [1994] 2 FLR 194.
[50]   *Medcalf v Mardell* [2002] 3 All ER 721.
[51]   See, for example, *B v B (Wasted Costs: Abuse of Process)* [2001] 1 FLR 843.
[52]   *Medcalf v Mardell* [2002] 3 All ER 721, per Lord Bingham of Cornhill at 734.
[53]   [2000] 1 FLR 52.

B v B (Wasted Costs: Abuse of Process)[54]

24.29 An order was made against counsel (75%) and solicitor (25%) because they were pursuing a hopeless appeal in a publicly funded case without reporting to the Legal Services Commission.

COSTS AGAINST NON-PARTIES

24.30 In principle a costs order can be made against someone who is not a party to the proceedings. In *Phillips v Symes*[55] Peter Smith J held that costs could be ordered against an expert witness who by his evidence caused significant expense to be incurred in flagrant disregard of his duties to the court. Orders against expert witnesses have rarely, if ever, been made.

ASSESSMENT OF COSTS

24.31 When the court orders a party to pay costs, it may either assess costs summarily or make an order for detailed assessment.[56] However, the court cannot summarily assess costs to be paid to (as opposed to by) an LSC-funded litigant.[57] A summary assessment of costs to be paid by an LSC-funded party is not by itself a determination of that person's liability to pay (for which see CPR 1998, r 44.17 and Costs PD Sections 21–23).

The general rule is that there should be summary assessment at the conclusion of any hearing which has lasted for no more than 1 day unless there is good reason not to do so (eg where the paying party shows substantial grounds for disputing the amount claimed that cannot be dealt with summarily or there is insufficient time to carry out a summary assessment). There is a move towards summary assessment, even for the costs of longer hearings. Summary assessment is appropriate in family proceedings because it avoids delay and expense.[58] However, summary assessment is not appropriate where the length and complexity of the hearing requires a detailed assessment of a fully drawn bill of costs.[59]

If that hearing disposes of the case, the court may deal with the costs of the whole of the case. Otherwise, it will deal with only the costs of the particular

---

[54] [2001] 1 FLR 843.
[55] [2004] EWHC 2330 (Ch), [2005] 4 All ER 519. Experts no longer enjoy immunity in respect of their participation in a trial: *Jones v Kaney* [2011] UKSC 13, [2011] 2 FLR 312.
[56] CPR 1998, r 44.7.
[57] CPR PD 44, para 13.9.
[58] *Q v Q (Costs: Summary Assessment)* [2002] 2 FLR 668. Strictly speaking, this is not a case where costs were assessed summarily but one where the paying party was ordered to pay a stated amount towards the receiving party's costs (estimated at £336,000).
[59] *Re F (Family Proceedings: Costs)* [2008] EWCA Civ 938, [2008] 2 FLR 1662.

hearing.[60] When the court has ordered a party to pay costs, but does not proceed to assess them immediately, it can order the paying party to pay an amount on account.[61]

Summary assessment

Procedure

24.32 The procedure for assessing costs summarily is set out in PD 44 at Section 13.

A written statement of costs should be filed and served no less than 24 hours before the hearing. A failure to serve the statement does not prevent the court dealing summarily with the assessment.[62] The court can:

- deal with the assessment without a statement;

- adjourn for a few minutes to enable a statement to be prepared;

- adjourn the summary assessment to a short appointment. If it does this, it must be before the same judge[63] and the failure to serve the statement will be taken into account in deciding what order to make about the costs of the application and the further hearing;[64]

- order a detailed assessment.

Basis for assessment

24.33 The following points need to be borne in mind.

- Costs must be reasonably incurred, reasonable in amount and (if awarded on the standard basis) proportionate to the matters in issue bearing in mind the importance of the case, the complexity of the issues and the financial position of each party.[65]

- The court also has to have regard to:

  - the conduct of all parties before as well as during the proceedings;
  - the efforts made if any, before and during the proceedings in order to try to resolve the dispute;
  - the importance of the matter to all parties;

60　CPR PD Costs, Section 13.
61　CPR 1998, r 44.3.
62　*Macdonald v Taree Holdings Ltd* (2000) *The Times*, 28 December.
63　CPR PD Costs, Section 13.
64　CPR PD Costs, para 13.6.
65　CPR 1998, rr 44.4 and 44.5, PD Costs, Section 11.

– the particular complexity of the matter or the difficulty or novelty of the questions raised;

– the skill, effort, specialised knowledge and responsibility involved;

– the time spent on the case;

– the place where and the circumstances in which the work or any part of it was done.[66]

- Care must be taken not to be affected by hindsight, especially where investigations are concerned otherwise there will be tendency to pay by result.[67]

- If the costs claimed as a whole do not appear to be disproportionate, all that is normally required is that each item should have been reasonably incurred and reasonable in amount. If, however, the costs appear to be disproportionate the court will need to be satisfied that the work in relation to each item was both necessary and was reasonable in amount.[68]

- Guidelines of hourly rates for solicitors in different parts of the country are regularly published by the Supreme Court Costs Office but these are broad approximations only. The cost schedule provided by the paying party may give further guidance if both solicitors are based in the same area.[69] When a party has used a solicitor who is not local to the court or who charges higher rates:

  'The focus is primarily upon the reasonable interests of the [party] so that, in relation to broad categories of costs ... one looks to see whether, having regard to the extent and importance of the litigation to the reasonably minded [litigant] a reasonable choice or decision has been made.'[70]

- If the cost of using a solicitor advocate is more than the cost of instructing counsel, the higher cost is unlikely to be recoverable.[71] Bear in mind that a solicitor advocate would charge at an hourly rate for preparing for the hearing, travelling to and from court and waiting, in addition to the hearing. On the other hand, if counsel is used, the instructing solicitor will have to spend time preparing the brief and counsel may be attended at the hearing by a fee earner.

- A receiving party who is a litigant in person may be entitled to compensation for the time reasonably spent in preparing and conducting

---

[66] CPR 1998, r 44.5.

[67] *Francis v Francis and Dickerson* [1955] 3 All ER 836.

[68] *Lownds v Home Office* [2002] EWCA Civ 365, [2002] 4 All ER 775.

[69] *Guide to the Summary Assessment of Costs* (SCCO).

[70] *Truscott v Truscott; Wraith v Sheffield Forgemasters Ltd* [1998] 1 All ER 82.

[71] *Guide to the Summary Assessment of Costs.*

the case, either at no more than two-thirds of the hourly rate which a solicitor would charge if he can show actual financial loss or at the prescribed rate of £9.25 an hour.[72]

- Routine letters out and telephone calls will in general be allowed on a unit basis of 6 minutes each (ie charged at one tenth of the hourly rate). Emails and letters received will not normally be allowed.[73]

- The cost of postage, couriers and outgoing phone calls are not allowed as disbursements except in unusual circumstances or where the cost is unusually heavy.[74]

- The cost of making copies of documents is not allowed except in exceptional circumstances or where the documents copied are exceptionally numerous.[75]

- Local (generally within 10 miles of the court) travelling expenses will not be allowed.[76]

Payment of costs

24.34   Unless the court orders otherwise, the costs must be paid within 14 days of the assessment.[77]

---

[72]   CPR 1998, r 48.6.
[73]   CPR PD 43, paras 4.6 and 4.16.
[74]   CPR PD 43, para 4.16.
[75]   Ibid.
[76]   Ibid.
[77]   CPR 1998, r 44.8.

Chapter 25

APPEALS

FORUM AND PROCEDURE

The principles of the appeal system

25.1 In 1997 the *Report to the Lord Chancellor by the Review of the Court of Appeal (Civil Division)*[1] – 'the Bowman Report' – recommended that civil appeals should be dealt with in ways which reflect the principles which Lord Woolf recommended the civil justice system should meet.

- An appeal should not be seen as an automatic further stage in a case.

- An individual who has grounds for dissatisfaction with the outcome of his or her case should always be able to have the case looked at by a higher court so that it can consider whether there appears to have been an injustice and, if so, allow an appeal to proceed.

- An appeal process should ensure that, so far as is practical, uncertainty and delay are reduced to a minimum.

- There is a private and a public purpose of appeals in civil cases. The private purpose is to correct an error, unfairness or wrong exercise of discretion which has led to an unjust result. The public purpose is to ensure public confidence in the administration of justice and, in appropriate cases, to:

  - clarify and develop the law, practice and procedure; and
  - help maintain the standards of first instance courts and tribunals.

- Appeals should be dealt with in ways that are proportionate to the grounds of complaint and the subject matter of the dispute.

- More than one level of appeal cannot normally be justified except in restricted circumstances where there is an important point of principle or practice or one which for some other special reason should be considered by the CA.

These principles have informed the rules governing appeals in children cases.

---

[1]   Lord Chancellor's Department; www.dca.gov.uk/civil/bowman/bowfr.htm.

Rules

25.2   Appeals under the Children Act 1989 are covered by two sets of rules. Part 30 of the Family Procedure Rules 2010 (FPR 2010) apply to appeals from the family proceedings court (FPC) to the county court and from a district judge to a circuit judge (in the county court) or a High Court judge (in the High Court).[2] The Civil Procedure Rules (CPR) 1998, Part 52 applies to appeals from a circuit judge or a High Court judge to the Court of Appeal. Although the procedure and the powers of the appellate court are similar, there is an important difference. Permission to appeal is not required for appeals from the FPC under FPR 2010, Pt 8 but is required for all other appeals including those under CPR, Pt 52 other than where the appeal is against a committal order or a secure accommodation order or a refusal to grant habeas corpus.[3]

Family proceedings court

25.3   Since 2009 an appeal from the FPC lies to the county court against the making of any order or a refusal to make any order under the Children Act 1989.[4] However, where the court has power to decline jurisdiction because it considers that the case can more conveniently be dealt with by another court, no appeal lies.[5] For appeals relating to the transfer or refusal to transfer proceedings, see FPR 2010, r 12.10.

25.4   Permission to appeal is required.

Appeals from district judges in the county court or High Court

25.5   Permission to appeal is required unless the appeal is against a committal order or a secure accommodation order.[6]

25.6   Appeals from district judges in the county court lie to a circuit judge and from a district judge in the High Court or the Principal Registry of the Family Division to a judge of the High Court.[7] They are governed by FPR 2010, Pt 30 and Practice Direction 30A.

25.7   Appeals to the High Court must be filed in the Principal Registry of the Family Division or the district registry nearest to the court from which the appeal lies.[8]

---

[2]   FPR 2010, r 30.1.

[3]   FPR 2010, r 30.3; CPR, r 52.3(1).

[4]   Children Act 1989, s 94(1); Access to Justice Act 1999 (Destination of Appeals) (Family Proceedings) Order 2009 (SI 2009/871).

[5]   CA 1989, s 94(2).

[6]   FPR 2010, r 30.3.

[7]   Access to Justice Act 1999 (Destination of Appeals) (Family Proceedings) Order 2009, arts 2 and 3.

[8]   PD 30A, para 8.1.

25.8 The Designated Circuit Judge for the area in consultation with the relevant Family Liaison Judge has responsibility for allocating appeals to a circuit judge.[9]

Appeals from a circuit judge or High Court judge

25.9 Appeals from a circuit judge or judge of the High Court are to the Court of Appeal and are governed by CPR Pt 52 and CPR PD 52.

25.10 Permission to appeal is required unless the appeal is against a committal order or a secure accommodation order or a refusal to grant habeas corpus.[10]

PROCEDURE

Appellant's notice

25.11 Within 21 days of the decision being appealed or such other time as the court may direct the appellant must file with the court and serve as soon as practicable, and in any event no later than 7 days after filing, on:

- each respondent to the proceedings in the court below; and

- where the appeal is not to the Court of Appeal, any children's guardian;

- where applicable any local authority which had prepared a special guardianship report (see **12.54**); and

- if the appeal is from the FPC, the court officer,

a notice of appeal setting out the grounds of appeal including, if permission is required, a request for permission and an appeal bundle which includes the documents specified in the relevant Practice Directions.[11] These are:

- a sealed or stamped copy of the appellant's notice;

- a sealed or stamped copy of the order being appealed, or a copy of the notice of the making of an order;

- a copy of any order giving or refusing permission to appeal, together with a copy of the court's reasons for allowing or refusing permission to appeal;

---

9   PD 30A, para 9.1.
10 CPR, r 52.3(1).
11 FPR 2010, r 30.4 and CPR, r 52.4; FPR 2010, PD 30A, paras 5.8 and 5.9 and CPR PD 52, paras 5.6 and 5.6A.

- any affidavit or witness statement filed in support of any application included in the appellant's notice;

- where the appeal is against a consent order, a statement setting out the change in circumstances since the order was agreed or other circumstances justifying a review or re-hearing;

- a copy of the appellant's skeleton argument;

- a transcript or note of judgment or, in a magistrates' court, written reasons for the court's decision (see **12.54**), and in cases where permission to appeal was given by the lower court or is not required those parts of any transcript of evidence which are directly relevant to any question at issue on the appeal;

- the application form;

- any application notice (or case management documentation) relevant to the subject of the appeal;

- any other documents which the appellant reasonably considers necessary to enable the appeal court to reach its decision on the hearing of the application or appeal;

- such other documents as the court may direct.

All documents extraneous to the appeal must be excluded.[12] The trial bundle must also contain a certificate from the appellant's legal representative (if any) that PD 30A, para 5.10/PD 52, para 5.6A(2) has been read and complied with.[13] Where it is not possible to file all the required documents an explanation must be given and the documents must be filed as soon as reasonably practicable.[14]

Respondent's notice

25.12 A respondent who seeks permission to appeal or who wishes to ask the appellate court to uphold the decision of the lower court for reasons different from or additional to those given by the lower court must file a respondent's notice within:

- such period as directed by the lower court; or

- where there is no such direction, 14 days after the date when:

---

[12] FPR 2010, PD 30A, paras 5.9 and 5.10; CPR PD 52, para 5.6A(2).
[13] FPR 2010, PD 30A, para 5.11; CPR PD 52, para 5.6A(3).
[14] FPR 2010, PD 30A, para 5.12; CPR PD 52, para 5.7.

- she is served with the appellant's notice (if he did not require permission to appeal or the lower court gave permission); or
- the date when she was notified the Court of Appeal had given permission.

It must be served as soon as is practicable and in any event no later than 7 days after it is filed.[15]

GROUNDS OF APPEAL

25.13 The grounds of appeal should:

- set out clearly the reasons why it is said the decision of the lower court was wrong or unjust because of a serious procedural or other irregularity in the proceedings in the lower court;[16] and

- specify in respect of each ground, whether the ground raises an appeal on a point of law or is an appeal against a finding of fact.[17]

25.14 At the hearing of the appeal a party may not rely on a matter not contained in that party's appeal notice unless the appeal court gives permission.[18]

SKELETON ARGUMENTS

25.15 The Practice Directions[19] require that the appellant's argument must be accompanied by a skeleton argument (which does not form part of the notice) unless the appellant is not represented (although he is encouraged to be so since it will be helpful to the court).[20]. Where it is impracticable for the appellant's skeleton argument to accompany the appellant's notice it must be filed and served on all respondents within 14 days of filing the notice.

25.16 A skeleton argument must contain a concise numbered list of the points both defining and confining the areas of controversy. Each point should be stated as concisely as the nature of the case allows. It must state, in respect of each authority cited the proposition of law that the authority demonstrates; and the identified parts of the authority that support the proposition. If more than one authority is cited in support of a given proposition, the reason for this must be stated briefly, showing the relevance of the authority to the argument; and that the citation is necessary. The appellant should consider what other

---

15 FPR 2010, r 30.5; CPR, r 52.5.
16 FPR 2010, r 30.12(3); CPR, r 52.11(3)
17 FPR 2010, PD 30A, para 3.2; CPR PD 52, para 3.2.
18 FPR 2010, r 30.12(5); CPR, r 52.11(5).
19 FPR 2010, PD 30A, para 5.13; CPR PD 52, para 5.9–5.11.
20 FPR 2010, PD 30A, para 5.13; CPR PD 52, paras 5.9–5.10.

information the appeal court will need. This may include a list of persons who feature in the case or glossaries of technical terms. A chronology of relevant events will be necessary in most appeals.

25.17 The cost of preparing a skeleton argument which does not comply with the Practice Direction or was not filed within the time limits will not be allowed on assessment of costs except to the extent that the court otherwise directs.

RECORD OF THE PROCEEDINGS BELOW

25.18 Where the judgment to be appealed has been officially recorded by the court, an approved transcript of that record should accompany the appellant's notice. However, where there is no officially recorded judgment, the following documents are acceptable:

• written judgments endorsed with the judge's signature;

• written reasons from the FPC;

• note of judgment when judgment was not officially recorded or made in writing a note of the judgment (agreed between the appellant's and respondent's advocates) should be submitted for approval to the judge whose decision is being appealed. If the parties cannot agree on a single note of the judgment, both versions should be provided to that judge with an explanatory letter. For the purpose of an application for permission to appeal the note need not be approved by the respondent or the lower court judge;

• advocates' notes of judgments where the appellant is unrepresented. When the appellant was unrepresented in the lower court it is the duty of any advocate for the respondent to make the advocate's note of judgment promptly available, free of charge to the appellant where there is no officially recorded judgment or if the court so directs. Where the appellant was represented in the lower court it is the duty of the appellant's own former advocate to make that advocate's note available in these circumstances. The appellant should submit the note of judgment to the appeal court.[21]

25.19 An advocates' brief (or, where appropriate, refresher) fee includes:

• remuneration for taking a note of the judgment of the court;

• having the note transcribed accurately;

• attempting to agree the note with the other side if represented;

---

[21] FPR 2010, PD 30A, paras 5.23–5.24; PD 52, paras 5.12–5.15.

- submitting the note to the judge for approval where appropriate;

- revising it if so requested by the judge,

- providing any copies required for the appeal court, instructing solicitors and lay client; and

- providing a copy of the note to an unrepresented appellant.[22]

25.20 When the evidence is relevant to the appeal an official transcript of the relevant evidence must be obtained. Transcripts or notes of evidence are generally not needed for the purpose of determining an application for permission to appeal. If this evidence was not officially recorded, a typed version of the judge's (including a district judge (magistrates' courts) or justices' clerk's notes of evidence must be obtained.[23]

25.21 Where the lower court or the appeal court is satisfied that an unrepresented appellant; or an appellant whose legal representation is provided free of charge to the appellant and not funded by the Community Legal Service, is in such poor financial circumstances that the cost of a transcript would be an excessive burden the court may certify that the cost of obtaining one official transcript should be borne at public expense. In the case of a request for an official transcript of evidence or proceedings to be paid for at public expense, the court must also be satisfied that there are reasonable grounds for appeal. Whenever possible a request for a transcript at public expense should be made to the lower court when asking for permission to appeal.[24]

PERMISSION TO APPEAL

Requesting permission to appeal

25.22 When permission to appeal is required an application for permission to appeal may be made to the lower court at the hearing at which the decision to be appealed was made; to or the appeal court in an appeal notice.

25.23 Where the lower court refuses an application for permission to appeal, a further application for permission to appeal may be made to the appeal court. Where the appeal court, without a hearing, refuses permission to appeal, within 7 days beginning with the date on which the notice that permission has been refused was served the person seeking permission may request the decision to be reconsidered at a hearing.[25] Where the appellant is in receipt of services funded by the Legal Services Commission (or legally aided) and permission to

---

[22] FPR 2010 PD 30A, para 5.25; CPR PD 52, para 5.14.
[23] FPR 2010 PD 30A, paras 5.31–5.32; CPR PD 52, paras 5.15–5.16.
[24] FPR 2010 PD 30A, paras 5.33–5.34; CPR PD 52, paras 5.17–5.18.
[25] FPR 2010, r 30.3; CPR, r 52.3.

appeal has been refused by the appeal court without a hearing, the appellant must send a copy of the reasons the appeal court gave for refusing permission to the relevant office of the Legal Services Commission as soon as it has been received from the court. The court will require confirmation that this has been done if a hearing is requested to re-consider the question of permission.[26]

25.24   Where an appellant, who is represented, makes a request for a decision to be reconsidered at an oral hearing, the appellant's advocate must, at least 4 days before the hearing, in a brief written statement:

- inform the court and the respondent of the points which the appellant proposes to raise at the hearing;

- set out the reasons why permission should be granted notwithstanding the reasons given for the refusal of permission; and

- confirm, where applicable, that the Legal Services Commission has been informed.

The respondent will be given notice of a permission hearing, but is not required to attend unless requested by the court to do so. If the court requests the respondent's attendance at the permission hearing, the appellant must supply the respondent with a copy of the appeal bundle within 7 days of being notified of the request, or such other period as the court may direct. The costs of providing that bundle shall be borne by the appellant initially, but will form part of the costs of the permission application.[27]

Granting permission to appeal

25.25   Permission to appeal may be given only where:

- the court considers that the appeal would have a real prospect of success; or

- there is some other compelling reason why the appeal should be heard.[28]

25.26   The test applied to the condition of 'a real prospect of success' is the same as that set for obtaining summary judgment in civil proceedings[29] as explained by the leading case of *Swain v Hillman*.[30]

---

[26]   FPR 2010 PD 30A, para 4.17; CPR PD 52, para 4.17.
[27]   Ibid.
[28]   Ibid.
[29]   Under CPR Pt 24. For the application of the *Swain v Hillman* exposition to appeals, see *Tanfern Ltd v Cameron-Macdonald* [2000] 2 All ER 801, per Booke LJ at para 21.
[30]   [2001] All ER 91.

'The word "real" distinguishes fanciful prospects of success or, as Mr Bidder QC submits, they direct the court to the need to see whether there is a "realistic" as opposed to a "fanciful" prospect of success.'[31]

'This is simple language, not susceptible to much elaboration, even forensically. If there is a real prospect of success, the discretion to give summary judgment does not arise merely because the court concludes that success is improbable. If that were the court's conclusion, then it is provided with a different discretion, which is that the case should proceed but subject to appropriate conditions imposed by the court.'[32]

25.27 The condition of 'some other compelling reason' enables the Court of Appeal or the Supreme Court to provide an authoritative ruling on a matter of public importance even though an appeal in the instant case would not otherwise justify an appeal.[33]

25.28 An order giving permission may:

- limit the issues to be heard; and

- be made subject to conditions.[34]

25.29 Practice Direction 52, para 4.4 contains special provisions for appeals to the Court of Appeal from case management decisons. There are no similar provisions in Practice Direction 30A.

25.30 Case management decisions include decisions about:

- disclosure;

- filing of witness statements or expert's reports;

- directions about the timetable of the claim;

- adding a party to a claim; and

- security for costs.

Where the application is for permission to appeal from a case management decision, the court dealing with the application may take into account whether:

- the issue is of sufficient significance to justify the costs of an appeal;

- the procedural consequences of an appeal (e g loss of trial date) outweigh the significance of the case management decision;

---

[31] Ibid, per Lord Woolf MR at 92.
[32] Ibid, per Judge LJ at 96.
[33] *Zuckerman on Civil Procedure* (Sweet & Maxwell, 2nd edn, 2007), at para 23-110.
[34] FPR 2010 r 30.3; CPR r 52.3

- it would be more convenient to determine the issue at or after trial.

SECOND APPEALS

25.31 Permission is required from the Court of Appeal for any appeal (including an appeal against committal) to that court from a decision of a county court or the High Court which was itself made on appeal.[35] The Court of Appeal will not give permission unless it considers that:

- the appeal would raise an important point of principle or practice; or

- there is some other compelling reason for the Court of Appeal to hear it.[36]

25.32 The Court of Appeal in its civil jurisdiction has emphasised that Parliament has made it clear that it is only in an exceptional case that a second appeal may be sanctioned.

'This reform introduces a major change to our appeal procedures. It will no longer be possible to pursue a second appeal to the Court of Appeal merely because the appeal is "properly arguable" or "because it has a real prospect of success". The new statutory provision is even tougher—the relevant point of principle or practice must be an important one—and it has effect even if the would-be appellant won in the lower court before losing in the appeal court. The decision of the first appeal court is now to be given primacy unless the Court of Appeal itself considers that the appeal would raise an important point of principle or practice, or that there is some other compelling reason for it to hear this second appeal.'[37]

25.33 In *Re B (Residence: Second Appeal)*[38] the Court of Appeal made it equally clear that the same approach applied to appeals in family cases.

'Where either arguability or even a strong prospect of success to constitute a compelling reason for a second appeal, there would be no difference between first and second appeals, and the statute would be deprived of its meaning and effect. In our judgment, that must equally be so in family appeals. The strength of the case does not, of itself, provide a compelling reason to hear an appeal.'

However the Rule might not be limited to clarifying important questions of principle.

'It may also be the case – we did not hear argument on the point and have reached no concluded view – that the effect of a decision relating to the welfare or future upbringing of a child may itself constitute a compelling reason for hearing a second appeal. The importance of such decisions for the children and adults

---

[35] Access to Justice Act 1999, s 55; CPR, r 52.13.
[36] Ibid.
[37] *Tanfern Ltd v Cameron-MacDonald* [2000] 2 All ER 801, per Brooke LJ at [41]–[42].
[38] [2009] EWCA Civ 545, [2009] 2 FLR 632, per Wall LJ at [12]–[14].

concerned cannot be over-emphasised. Moreover, the fact that two courts have reached different conclusions *may* (a word we emphasise) reinforce the justification for hearing the appeal.'[39]

STAYS

25.34 Issuing a notice of appeal does not operate to stay the order which is being appealed.[40] However, all appellate courts – and the court below if asked during the time for appealing – has power to grant a stay.

THE POWERS OF THE APPELLATE COURT

25.35 The appellate court has all the powers of the court below. In addition it may:

- affirm, set aside or vary any order or judgment made or given by the lower court;

- refer any application or issue for determination by the lower court;

- order a new trial or hearing;

- make a costs order.[41]

25.36 The appellate courts are very reluctant to order a rehearing in children's cases.

> 'The desirability of putting an end to litigation is particularly strong because the longer the legal proceedings last, the more are the children, whose welfare is at stake, likely to be disturbed by the uncertainty.'[42]

25.37 In managing the appeal, where there is a compelling reason for doing so, the appeal court can

- strike out the whole or part of an appeal notice;

- set aside permission to appeal in whole or in part;

- impose or vary conditions upon which an appeal may be brought.[43]

---

[39] Ibid.

[40] FPR 2010, r 8.1(6); CPR, r 52.7.

[41] FPR 2010, r 30.11; CPR, r 52.10(2).

[42] *G v G (Minors: Custody Appeal)* [1985] FLR 894, per Lord Fraser of Tullybelton at 898.

[43] FPR 2010, r 30.10; CPR, r 52.9. See, for example, *Re M (Placement Order)* [2010] EWCA Civ 1257, [2011] Fam Law 129 where an appeal brought by a litigant in person was struck out for failing to comply with directions.

It will make considerable allowance for the difficulties faced by unrepresented appellants. However, 'rules require compliance'[44] – because otherwise, the appeal cannot be fairly heard – and although further time for compliance may be given, any urgency of achieving finality may be 'a potent consideration'.[45]

Directions

25.38   In addition it has the power to give directions whether to supplement or vary the general directions contained in the Rules. Such directions are given for a purpose and must be obeyed.[46] A failure to do so may result in an order for costs or wasted costs.

Extension of time

25.39   The court has power to extend or shorten the time for compliance with any rule, practice direction or court order (even if an application for extension is made after the time for compliance has expired) and this includes time for appealing.[47] However, an application to vary the time limit for filing an appeal notice must be made to the appeal court and time cannot be extended merely by the parties agreeing.[48] The Bowman Committee[49] recommended that the same time limits should be imposed on litigants in person in so far as possible in the same way as for represented appellants.

The importance of speed

25.40   Regardless of the time limits for appealing, it is important that appeals involving children should be pursued with expedition. It may take some 21 days between the lower court refusing a stay and the matter reaching the Court of Appeal with a further delay before a judge can consider the papers especially in the vacation. All this leaves creates uncertainty about the child's future. In *Re P (Residence: Appeals)*[50] the trial judge enabled an appeal relating to the transfer of residence to be heard within 15 days by staying the order but reducing the time for appealing to 3 days thereby making it necessary for the appellant to seek urgent directions from the Court of Appeal

25.41   Emergency facilities in the Court of Appeal are always available to deal with urgent child cases and can be accessed by telephone where necessary. The trial judge should immediately be asked for permission to appeal and to stay the order pending appeal or at least for such period as would allow the appellant to seek directions from the Court of Appeal.[51] If this is refused the

---

44   Ibid, at [18] per Wilson LJ.
45   Ibid.
46   *Re M-W (Care Proceedings)* [2010] EWCA Civ 46, [2010] 2 FLR 46, per Wall LJ at [6].
47   FPR 2010, r 30.7; CPR, r 52.6.
48   FPR 2010, r 30.8; CPR, rr 52.6–52.7.
49   Op cit, ch 9.
50   [2007] EWCA Civ 1053, [2008] 1 FLR 198.
51   Ibid.

appellant should contact the Court of Appeal (in cases out of hours by contacting the duty officer through the security offices of the Royal Courts of Justice (0207 947 6260). If there was a particular reason for expedition, or if an advocate wished to engage the Court of Appeal as a matter of urgency, he or she should either speak to a Deputy Master on the telephone, or ask to be put through to a Lord Justice with family experience. In cases of lesser urgency, but which still required expedition, the advocate should invite the office to place the papers before such a Lord Justice as a matter of urgency. If the Court is satisfied either that permission to appeal should be granted or that an application for permission should be listed at short notice, it will give such a direction.[52]

25.42 Similar local arrangements will be in place for appeals from a family proceedings court and with a county court or the High Court.

Striking out appeals

25.43 The appellate court has jurisdiction to strike out an appeal for non-compliance with the rules or for failure to comply with an order for directions.[53] Notice should be taken of the particular difficulties faced by a litigant in person and some leeway may be allowed which would not be given to a represented party.

25.44 If the appeal court:

- refuses an application for permission to appeal;

- strikes out an appellant's notice; or

- dismisses an appeal,

and it considers that the application, the appellant's notice or the appeal is totally without merit, then:

- the court's order must record the fact that it considers the application, the appellant's notice or the appeal to be totally without merit; and

- the court must at the same time consider whether it is appropriate to make a civil restraint order (see **21.25**).[54]

---

[52] *Re S (Child Proceedings: Urgent Appeals)* [2007] EWCA Civ 958, [2007] 2 FLR 1044; *Re P and P (Care Proceedings: Appointment of Experts)* [2009] EWCA Civ 610, [2009] 2 FLR 1370.
[53] *MH v Lancashire CC* [2010] EWCA Civ 1257, at [15].
[54] FPR 2010, r 30.11(4) and (5); CPR, r 52.10(5) and (6).

FRESH EVIDENCE

25.45 Unless it orders otherwise, the appeal court will not receive oral evidence or evidence which was not before the lower court. It may draw any inference of fact which it considers justified on the evidence.[55]

25.46 However, an appeal court in proceedings concerning the welfare of children is not strictly bound by the rule in *Ladd v Marshall*,[56] namely that evidence not placed before the trial judge ('fresh evidence') will not be admitted unless:

• it is shown that the evidence could not have been obtained with reasonable diligence for use at the trial;

• the evidence is such that, if given, it would probably have an important influence on the result of the case although need not be decisive; and

• the evidence must be such as is presumably to be believed or, in other words, it must be apparently credible although it need not be incontrovertible.

25.47 The court has the discretion to admit oral or further evidence as it considers relevant and on such terms as it considers appropriate.[57] It is not strictly bound by the rules in *Ladd v Marshall*:[58]

'If the discretion is at all times the judge's discretion the parties are entitled to have the judge's decision on these matters if they choose to appeal. Consequently they must be in a position to introduce before him [subject to rules about the filing of evidence] any evidence which is admissible and relevant. It may be that the circumstances have changed in some way since the hearing ... so that the evidence requires bringing up to date. It may be that in the course of hearing before [the court below] some problem arose or there was some doubt about some particular point. Clearly, therefore, either party should be able to clear up these matters when the matter comes before the judge and put before him their cases in full as they wish and without any restriction.'[59]

However, because the appellate judge has a discretion as to how the appeal will be heard, additional evidence will not ordinarily be admitted unless there is good reason to do so.[60] Because the court has to have regard to considerations of justice, it may be necessary to admit fresh evidence even though the *Ladd v*

---

55   FPR 2010, r 30.12; CPR, r 52.11.
56   [1954] 1 WLR 1489, per Lord Denning LJ at 1491.
57   FPR 2010, r 30.12(2); CPR 1998, r 52.11(2).
58   *Marsh v Marsh* [1993] 1 FLR 467.
59   *G (formerly P) v P (Ancillary Relief: Appeal)* [1977] 1 WLR 1376, per Ormrod LJ at 1382.
60   *Marsh v Marsh* [1993] 1 FLR 467, applying *Walters v Walters* [1992] 2 FLR 337.

Marshall test is not met.[61] Appeals should not present an opportunity to seek to call new experts in the hope that they might do better than those whose evidence was rejected at trial.[62]

25.48 Where there is fresh evidence which justifies a revision to the facts found by the court below but this does not result in the appeal being allowed, a summary of those facts should be appended to the order or the judgment dismissing the appeal so that they are not forgotten.[63] The court will be vigilant to see that the material is genuinely fresh and not a further manifestation of what was before the judge. There is a real difference between a child reacting adversely and dramatically to an order, for example refusing hysterically to go on contact, and one merely repeating what was said earlier to the Children and Family Reporter. The same applies to other evidence. Does it constitute something new or is it another example of material before the trial judge?[64]

Any attempt to adduce evidence from the child by way of a witness statement will be seriously deprecated.[65]

REOPENING APPEALS

25.49 Every appeal will be limited to a review of the decision of the lower court unless:

- an enactment or practice direction makes different provision for a particular category of appeal; or

- the court considers that in the circumstances of an individual appeal it would be in the interests of justice to hold a re-hearing.

The appeal court will allow an appeal where the decision of the lower court was:

- wrong; or

- unjust because of a serious procedural or other irregularity in the proceedings in the lower court.

25.50 Few cases involving the welfare of children are decided on points of law. Sometimes appeals allege errors in procedure but the majority are concerned

---

61   *Couwenbergh v Valkova* [2004] EWCA Civ 676, at [68].
62   *R v Henderson* [2010] EWCA Crim 1269, [2011] 1 FLR 547, at [3].
63   *Re I (Care Proceedings: Fresh Evidence)* [2010] EWCA Civ 319, [2010] 2 FLR 1462.
64   See, for example, *Re P (Custody of Children) (Split Custody Order)* [1991] 1 FLR 337.
65   *Re M (Family Proceedings: Affidavits)* [1995] 2 FLR 100.

with whether the trial judge's exercise of a wide discretion was wrong. In such appeals the test propounded by the House of Lords in *G v G (Minors: Custody Appeal)*[66] is still applicable:

'The reason for the limited role of the Court of Appeal in custody cases is not that appeals in such cases are subject to any special rules, but that there are often two or more possible decisions, any one of which might reasonably be thought to be the best, and any one of which therefore a judge may make without being held to be wrong.

'In cases dealing with the custody of children, the desirability of putting an end to litigation, which applies to all classes of case, is particularly strong because the longer legal proceedings last, the more are children, whose welfare is at stake, likely to be disturbed by the uncertainty.

'Nevertheless there will be some cases in which the Court of Appeal decides that the judge at first instance has come to a wrong conclusion. In such cases it is the duty of the Court of Appeal to substitute its own decision for that of the judge ... the appellate court should only interfere if they consider that the judge of first instance has not merely preferred an imperfect solution which the Court of Appeal might or would have adopted but has exceeded the generous ambit within which a reasonable disagreement is possible.'[67][68]

25.51 The discretion applies equally to findings of fact and of credibility, the evaluation of factors and apportioning weight to those factors. In *Re J (Child Returned Abroad: Convention Rights)*[69] Baroness Hale emphasised in the House of Lords:

'If there is indeed a discretion in which various factors are relevant, the valuation and balancing of those factors is also a matter for the trial judge. Only if his decision is so plainly wrong that he must have given far too much weight to a particular factor is the appellate court entitled to interfere: see *G v G* [reference given]. Too ready an interference by the appellate court, particularly if it always seems to be in the direction of one result rather than the other, risks robbing the trial judge of the discretion entrusted to him by the law. In short, if trial judges are led to believe that, even if they direct themselves impeccably on the law, make findings of fact which are open to them on the evidence, and are careful, as this judge undoubtedly was, in the evaluation and weighing of the relevant factors, their decisions are liable to be overturned unless they reach a particular conclusion, they will come to believe that they do not in fact have any choice or discretion in the matter.'[70]

25.52 Until recently, courts adopted the approach that, where an appeal lay from a district judge to a circuit judge, the circuit judge had to exercise his own

---

[66] [1985] FLR 894.
[67] 'The [judge's] "zone of reasonableness" – the area within which he has discretion to decide a case either way without disgracing himself.' Posner *How Judges Think* (Harvard University Press, 2008), at p 86.
[68] [1985] FLR 894, per Lord Fraser of Tullybelton at 898–899.
[69] [2005] UKHL 40, [2005] 2 FLR 802.
[70] Ibid, at para 12.

discretion, giving such weight to the factors found by the district judge as he thought fit – the '*Marsh v Marsh*' approach. In 1998, however, the Family Appeals Review Group, chaired by Thorpe LJ recommended that appeals under s 94 should be decided by applying *G v G* principles. In 1999, the President held in *Re W, Re A, Re B (Change of Name)*[71] that *G v G* principles should govern all Children Act appeals where all levels of judiciary (including magistrates) have the same jurisdiction and no fresh evidence is adduced:

'The trial judge sees and hears the oral evidence and has the inestimable feel of the case, denied as much to the circuit judge on appeal as to the Court of Appeal.'

This approach has now been adopted for all family appeals.[72]

APPEALS FROM CASE MANAGEMENT DECISIONS

25.53 Both civil[73] and family appellate courts will be slow to overturn case management decision, believing that the judge in the court below is likely to have a better understanding of the issues and the practicality of the alternatives. The court will be particularly reluctant to allow an appeal where this will mean the loss of the trial date. However, crucial decisions which could have a serious impact on the outcome of the trial, for example, the instruction of an expert witness, will need to be settled before the trial. It is important therefore that any appeal against a case management decision is brought and pursued expeditiously.

'Case management decisions by the High Court and the circuit bench are not to be challenged on a whim, or because one party simply happens to disagree with them. They are discretionary decisions in which the allocated judge enjoys a very wide discretion to deal with the case within the confines of the overriding objective and taking into account the best interests of the child. There must be a point of substance which requires an urgent challenge and speedy resolution. In the overwhelming majority of cases, no such point will arise. Where it does, however, speed is of the essence. Delay, as the 1989 Act makes clear, is usually contrary to the interests of children, as well as being the enemy of justice in most child cases.'[74]

25.54 In 2010 the President gave guidance on appeals from case management decisions.[75] In it he said:

'As a general proposition, and as a matter of policy, appellate courts recognise that decisions at first instance are often taken quickly and under pressure both of time and other work. It follows that the instinct of the appellate court is to support the

---

71 [1999] 2 FLR 930.
72 *Cordle v Cordle* [2002] 1 FLR 207.
73 See *Zuckerman on Civil Procedure* op cit, at paras 23-132–23-133.
74 *Re P and P (Care Proceedings: Appointment of Experts)* 2009] EWCA Civ 610, [2009] 2 FLR 1370, per Wall LJ at [17].
75 *President's Guidance (Case Management Decisions and Appeals Therefrom)* [2010] Lexis Citation 59; [2011] Fam Law 189.

decision made below, unless that decision is – as both Asquith LJ and Lord Fraser emphasise "plainly wrong" – see below. Judicial decisions under the Act are mostly discretionary. A judicial discretion must, of course, be exercised judicially. That said, the discretion is, usually, a wide one, particularly in relation to case management decisions. It is worth remembering always what Atkin LJ said in *Bellenden (formerly Sattersthwaite) v Sattersthwaite*[76] namely:

> "It is, of course, not enough ... to establish that this court might, or would, have made a different order. We are here concerned with a judicial discretion, and it is of the essence of such a discretion that on the same evidence two minds may reach different conclusions in relation to the same subject matter without either being wrong: or, to put it another way, an appellate court cannot reverse a court of first instance unless the decision at first instance is plainly wrong."

When exercising a first instance discretion, it is essential for the tribunal to take all relevant matters into account and to exclude all irrelevant matters. The pros and cons should then be weighed and a decision reached. The decision itself must be reasoned and clearly articulated. Provided it follows these rules, the decision should be fireproof.'

APPEALS FROM INTERIM ORDERS

25.55 The appellate courts are reluctant to hear appeals on interim matters. If there has been a change in circumstances, the proper course is to apply for further directions to the court below. However, it will hear appeals in respect of issues determined as a preliminary part of the case without waiting for the second part of a split trial.[77] A similar reluctance applies to appeals from case management decisions (see **25.53**).

GROUNDS OF APPEAL[78]

25.56 It is notoriously difficult to prophesy which appeals will engage the Court of Appeal to such an extent that the appellate judges will interfere with the discretion of the trial judge. Some issues occur regularly.

Failure of the trial judge to give sufficient reasons

25.57 Courts must give proper reasons for their decisions and a failure to do so will vitiate the decision.[79] This was so before the advent of the Human Rights Act 1998 and now, a failure to give reasons will breach the Art 6 right to a fair trial.

---

[76] [1948] 1 All ER 343, at 345 (cited by Lord Fraser in *G v G* [1985] 1 WLR 647, at 651–652, [1985] FLR 894, at 898).

[77] *Re B (Split Hearings: Jurisdiction)* [2000] 1 FLR 334.

[78] See also *English v Emery Reimbold and Strick Ltd* [2002] EWCA Civ 605, [2002] 1 WLR 2409.

[79] *W v Hertfordshire CC* [1993] 1 FLR 118; *T v W (Contact: Reasons for Refusing Leave)* [1996] 2 FLR 473, an appeal from a family proceedings court.

The reasons should include:

- a statement of the issues;

- the court's findings of fact on those issues;

- its reasons for preferring the evidence of a witness on those issues to that of another witness, for disagreeing with the recommendation of a Children and Family Reporter, guardian ad litem or expert witness and its reasons for reaching its decision.

The appellate court (and the parties) must be able to be satisfied that the trial court took into account all the relevant matters and did not take into account irrelevant ones. Justices' reasons should not be approached in the same way as a judgment but the appellate court might be less ready to assume that magistrates had taken relevant factors into account if they had not referred to them than it might in the case of an experienced judge.[80] Justices cannot supplement their original reasons later.[81] There is a distinction between a court giving no reasons or inadequate reasons and one which fails expressly to mention everything. If the judgment as a whole explains the reasons for the decision, the precise format and phraseology are a matter for the judge.[82]

The more experienced the judge the more likely it is that he will display 'the virtue of brevity'.[83]

When a judgment is given, an advocate ought immediately as a matter of courtesy to draw the judge's attention to any material omission which he believes exists. It is open for the judge then to amend his judgment at any time prior to the order being drawn up.[84] If an application for permission to appeal on the ground of lack of reasons is made to the trial judge, the judge should consider adjourning in order to remedy any defect by the provision of additional reasons before refusing permission to appeal.

25.58 This is procedure not always understood by advocates.

'It is high time that the Family Bar woke up to *English v Emery Reimbold & Strick Ltd* ... I wish to make it as clear as possible that after a judge has given

---

[80] *Re M (Section 94 Appeals)* [1995] 1 FLR 546.
[81] *Hillingdon LBC v H* [1992] 2 FLR 372.
[82] *Re V (Residence: Review)* [1995] 2 FLR 1010; *English v Emery Reimbold & Strick Ltd; DJ and Withers (Farms) Ltd v Ambic Equipment Ltd; Verrechia (trading as Freightmaster Commercials) v Commissioner of Police for the Metropolis* [2002] EWCA Civ 605, [2002] 1 WLR 2409; *Re F (Shared Residence Order)* [2009] EWCA Civ 313, [2010] 1 FLR 354.
[83] *Re B (Appeal: Lack of Reasons)* [2003] EWCA Civ 881, [2003] 2 FLR 1035, per Thorpe LJ at para [11].
[84] *Re T (Contact: Alienation: Permission to Appeal)* [2002] EWCA Civ 1736, [2003] 1 FLR 531, per Arden LJ at para [41]. Approved in *Re B (Appeal: Lack of Reasons)* [2003] EWCA Civ 881, [2003] 2 FLR 1035. See also *Re A and C (Appeal: Fact-Finding)* [2011] EWCA Civ 1205, [2012] 1 FLR 134.

judgment, counsel have a positive duty to raise with the judge not just any alleged deficiency in the judge's reasoning process but any genuine query or ambiguity which arises on the judgment. Judges should welcome this process[85].'[86]

25.59 To assist, Practice Direction 30A contains specific advice.[87] Where a party's advocate considers that there is a material omission from a judgment of the lower court or, in a magistrates' court, the written reasons for the decision of the lower court (including inadequate reasons for the lower court's decision), the advocate should before the drawing of the order give the lower court which made the decision the opportunity of considering whether there is an omission and should not immediately use the omission as grounds for an application to appeal. Where the application for permission to appeal is made to the lower court, (but not where the lower court is an FPC) the court which made the decision must consider whether there is a material omission (adjourning for that purpose if necessary) and where the conclusion is that there has been such an omission, provide additions to the judgment.

Where the application for permission to appeal is made to the appeal court, the appeal court must consider whether there is a material omission; and where the conclusion is that there has been such an omission, may adjourn the application and remit the case to the lower court with an invitation to provide additions to the judgment.

Children and Family Reporter

25.60 Provided the judge takes into account the views of the Children and Family Reporter, he is not bound to follow his/her recommendations. The judge should, however, indicate in his judgment or reasons, preferably expressly, the reasons for not following the recommendations. The recommendations should be carefully explored in cross-examination.[88] It has been said that even the most experienced judge is not entitled to overrule 'the measured and careful assessments of the attitude of a party merely by observing their conduct during the course of the hearing', but this may depend on the relative opportunities to observe the parties. Where there are clear-cut recommendations and warnings of risk in reports, the judge should not depart from them without first hearing evidence from the Children and Family Reporter.[89] This is not to say that the court should never depart from the recommendations without hearing from the

---

85   Judges are less likely to welcome attempts to ask them to reconsider their conclusions save in the most exceptional circumstances – a growing practice in some courts which has been deprecated: *Egan v Motor Services (Bath) Ltd* [2007] EWCA Civ 1002, [2008] 1 FLR 1346, per Smith LJ at [49]–[51] and *Re N (Payments For Benefit Of Child)* [2009] EWHC 11 (Fam), [2009] 1 FLR 1442, per Munby J at [106].

86   *Re M (Fact-Finding Hearing: Burden of Proof)* [2008] EWCA Civ 1261, [2009] 1 FLR 1177, per Wall LJ at [36], [38].

87   At paras 4.6–4.9.

88   *Re P (Custody of Children: Split Custody Order)* [1991] 1 FLR 337. See also *Re M (Residence)* [2004] EWCA Civ 1574, [2005] 1 FLR 656.

89   *Re CB (Access: Attendance of Court Welfare Officer)* [1995] 1 FLR 622; *Re R (Residence Order)* [2009] EWCA Civ 445, [2010] 1 FLR 509.

Children and Family Reporter especially where neither party has requested the Children and Family Reporter's attendance.[90]

Experts

25.61 Similar considerations apply to recommendations from expert witnesses.

Failing to apply the welfare checklist or art 8

25.62 A version of an allegation that the trial judge failed to give sufficient reasons for his decision and that he misapplied the welfare checklist is the allegation that he failed to have regard to all the factors set out in the checklist or failed to mention Art 8 of the European Convention for the Protection of Human Rights and Fundamental Freedoms. Guidance from the Court of Appeal on whether the judge needs to deal specifically with each item may appear to be inconsistent. In *EH v LB Greenwich AA and A (Children)*,[91] for example, Baron J said that:

> 'The judge was making a very Draconian order[92]. As such, he was required to balance each factor within the welfare checklist in order to justify his conclusions and determine whether the final outcome was appropriate. Accordingly, because this analysis is entirely absent, his failure to mention the provisions of the Children Act 1989 and deal with each part of s 1(3) undermines his conclusions and his orders.'

Her Ladyship also criticised the judge for failing to mention Art 8. Two and a half months later in *D MCG v Neath Talbot County Borough Council*[93] Wilson LJ, sitting in a differently constituted court, commented:

> 'It goes without saying that, in making placement orders, a judge must not infringe rights under Art 8 and that in some cases the safest means of avoiding infringement may be for him expressly to consider the rights and the circumstances in which interference with them is permissible. We are also extremely conscious of the desirability that this court should speak with one voice, even beyond the realms in which the doctrine of binding precedent so dictates. That said, it is, of course, unusual for a judge to be required to include any particular set of words in his judgment. The more usual approach is to assume, unless he has demonstrated to the contrary, that the judge knew how to perform his functions and what matters to take into account: *Piglowska v Piglowski*.'[94]

---

[90] *Re L (Residence: Justices' Reasons)* [1995] 2 FLR 445.
[91] [2010] EWCA Civ 344, [2010] 2 FLR 661, at [60].
[92] An order allowing a local authority to place a child for adoption.
[93] [2010] EWCA Civ 821, [2010] 2 FLR 1827, at [22].
[94] [1999] 1 WLR 1360, [1999] 2 FLR 763, at 1372G and 784 respectively, per Lord Hoffmann.

25.63   A commonly accepted approach appears to be as follows.

- The trial judge has to reach a decision having regard to all the circumstances of the case including those set out in the checklist.

- As a general rule, the trial judge does not need to recite a mantra referring to all the circumstances in the checklist.

- The more experienced the judge the more likely it is that an appellate court will accept that he had regard to all the circumstances.

- Where a particular circumstance is relevant in an individual case the parties and the appellate court must be able see how the judge approached the matter and understand how it influenced the decision.

- The more difficult the decision, the more useful it may be for the trial judge to consider each item separately.

The same approach applies to Art 8.

'Misapplication' of the welfare test and the checklist

25.64   There are no presumptions when the s 1 checklist is applied. Every case must be decided on its own facts:

> 'The only direction that can be given to the trial judge is to apply the welfare principle and the welfare checklist ... to the facts of the specific case.'[95]

Therefore, an appeal which relies, for example, on the assertion that a judge was 'wrong' to grant a father a residence order in relation to an infant or to separate siblings contrary to some perceived principle or norm is unlikely to succeed.

The more difficult the decision and finely balanced the conclusion, the less prospect there is of the decision being successfully appealed:

> 'If, as I suspect, [this hopeless appeal] has been brought on public funds, then it is another of the all-too-frequent examples of public money being spent to no good effect and, indeed, in an adverse way, because it continues to raise the temperature, to exacerbate the unhappy feelings between the parents and to have an adverse effect upon the children who are the subject of the proceedings ... these are appeals brought in, perhaps, the height of emotion and understandable upset by a parent, where it requires a particular degree of detachment and common sense from the legal advisers not to be carried away by the enthusiasm, frustration and hurt of their lay clients.'[96]

---

[95]   *S v M (Access Order)* [1997] 1 FLR 980, per Thorpe LJ at 370.
[96]   *Re N (Residence: Hopeless Appeals)* [1995] 2 FLR 230, per Butler-Sloss LJ at 231.

Legal advisers who bring hopeless appeals are vulnerable to a wasted costs order.[97]

Findings of fact

25.65 Although it is possible to appeal against a finding of fact, it is notoriously difficult to succeed in so doing. Where findings of fact are made based on the demeanour of a witness, the appeal court will seldom interfere because the trial judge has the special advantage over the appellate judge.[98] An appellate court is severely handicapped in judging the credibility of oral evidence, even though transcripts are provided, because it has not heard and seen the witnesses giving evidence nor observed their demeanour.[99] Although it may be easier for an appellate court to interfere with an inference drawn from primary facts,[100] the appellate court has to remember that specific findings of fact are inherently an incomplete statement of the impression made on the trial judge by the primary evidence and that such findings are always surrounded by a penumbra of imprecision as to emphasis, relative weight, minor qualification and nuance.[101] It is therefore necessary for the appellate court to treat the judge's findings with 'appropriate respect'. 'It must be very slow indeed to interfere with any such findings. That, however, does not mean that an appeal on fact can never succeed. If this court is convinced that the judge was plainly wrong, then it is its duty to interfere.'[102]

MEDIATION

25.66 Attempting to resolve disputes by mediation is just appropriate in appeals as for cases at first instance and the Court of Appeal has its own Alternative Dispute Resolution scheme operated by the Centre of Effective Dispute Resolution (CEDR). In *Al-Khatib v Masry*[103] Thorpe LJ said:

> '[This case] supports our conviction that there is no case, however conflicted, which is not potentially open to successful mediation, even if mediation has not been attempted or has failed during the trial process. It also demonstrates how vital it is for there to be judicial supervision of the process of mediation. It is not enough, in a difficult family case such as this, for the supervising Lord Justice or the Lord Justice directing mediation simply to make the order and thereafter

---

97 *B v B (Wasted Costs: Abuse of Process)* [2001] 1 FLR 843. See Chapter 23.

98 *Re S (Abduction: Custody Rights)* [2002] EWCA Civ 908, [2002] 2 FLR 815, per Ward LJ at [25].

99 *Sherrington v Sherrington* [2005] EWCA Civ 326, [2005] 3 FCR 538, per Peter Gibson at [33].

100 *Benmax v Austin Motor Co Ltd* [1955] AC 370.

101 *Biogen Inc v Medeva plc* [1997] 38 BMLR 149.

102 *Sherrington v Sherrington* [2005] EWCA Civ 326, [2005] 3 FCR 538, per Peter Gibson at [33]. See also *AA v NN* [2010] EWHC 1282 (Fam), [2010] 2 FLR 1173.

103 [2004] EWCA Civ 1353, [2005] 1 FLR 381.

assume that there will be a smooth passage to an initial meeting. The selection of the appropriate mediator is crucial and the availability of the supervising judge to deal with crisis is equally important.'[104]

25.67 The scheme has a relatively low take up from family appeals but an encouragingly high success rate.[105]

25.68 If the parties arrive at a compromise of the appeal, the court will uphold and enforce the compromise, absent some vitiating element.[106]

REOPENING APPEALS

25.69 The High Court and the Court of Appeal but not the county court have a residual jurisdiction to hear second appeals if:

- it is necessary to do so in order to avoid real injustice;

- the circumstances are exceptional and make it appropriate to reopen the appeal; and

- there is no alternative effective remedy.[107]

Permission is required from the Court of Appeal – applied for in writing – whether or not the original appeal required permission[108] and the prospective appellant needs to show that a significant injustice has probably occurred and there is no alternative effective remedy. The effect of reopening the appeal on others and the extent to which the effective appellant is the author of his own misfortune will also be important considerations. Where the alternative remedy is an appeal to the House of Lords, the Court of Appeal will only give permission to reopen the appeal if it is satisfied that the House of Lords would not give leave to appeal.[109] The jurisdiction can only be properly revoked where it is shown that the integrity of the earlier litigation process has been critically undermined.[110]

In *Re U (Re-Opening of Appeal)*,[111] for example, permission to reopen an appeal on the ground that there was fresh medical evidence relating to a child's injuries was refused. If the discovery of fresh evidence is to justify the reopening of an appeal, not only must the *Ladd v Marshall* test be satisfied, there must also be shown a 'powerful probability' that an error has resulted and

---

[104] [2004] EWCA Civ 1353, [2005] 1 FLR 381, at [17].
[105] *Rothwell v Rothwell* [2008] EWCA Civ 1600, [2009] 2 FLR 96, per Thorpe LJ at [8].
[106] Ibid.
[107] FPR 2010, r 30.14(1); CPR, r 52.17(1).
[108] FPR 2010, r 30.14(4); PD 30A, para 18; PD 52, para 25;CPR, 52.17(4).
[109] *Taylor v Lawrence* [2002] EWCA Civ 90, [2003] QB 528.
[110] *Re U (Re-opening of Appeal)* [2005] EWCA Civ 52, [2005] 2 FLR 444.
[111] Ibid.

the injustice was so grave as to 'overbear the pressing claims of finality in litigation'.[112] That was not the case in the instant appeal.

---

[112] Per Butler-Sloss P at paras [21]–[22].

Appendix 1

STATUTORY MATERIAL

CHILDREN ACT 1989

PART I
INTRODUCTORY

1 Welfare of the child

(1)   When a court determines any question with respect to –

  (a)   the upbringing of a child; or

  (b)   the administration of a child's property or the application of any income arising from it,

the child's welfare shall be the court's paramount consideration.

(2)   In any proceedings in which any question with respect to the upbringing of a child arises, the court shall have regard to the general principle that any delay in determining the question is likely to prejudice the welfare of the child.

(3)   In the circumstances mentioned in subsection (4), a court shall have regard in particular to –

  (a)   the ascertainable wishes and feelings of the child concerned (considered in the light of his age and understanding);

  (b)   his physical, emotional and educational needs;

  (c)   the likely effect on him of any change in his circumstances;

  (d)   his age, sex, background and any characteristics of his which the court considers relevant;

  (e)   any harm which he has suffered or is at risk of suffering;

  (f)   how capable each of his parents, and any other person in relation to whom the court considers the question to be relevant, is of meeting his needs;

  (g)   the range of powers available to the court under this Act in the proceedings in question.

(4)   The circumstances are that –

  (a)   the court is considering whether to make, vary or discharge a special guardianship order or a section 8 order, and the making, variation or discharge of the order is opposed by any party to the proceedings; or

  (b)   the court is considering whether to make, vary or discharge an order under Part IV.

(5)   Where a court is considering whether or not to make one or more orders under this Act with respect to a child, it shall not make the order or any of the orders unless it considers that doing so would be better for the child than making no order at all.

Amendments—Adoption and Children Act 2002, s 115(2), (3).

2 Parental responsibility for children

(1)   Where a child's father and mother were married to each other at the time of his birth, they shall each have parental responsibility for the child.

(1A) Where a child –

- (a)   has a parent by virtue of section 42 of the Human Fertilisation and Embryology Act 2008; or
- (b)   has a parent by virtue of section 43 of that Act and is a person to whom section 1(3) of the Family Law Reform Act 1987 applies,

the child's mother and the other parent shall each have parental responsibility for the child.

(2)   Where a child's father and mother were not married to each other at the time of his birth –

- (a)   the mother shall have parental responsibility for the child;
- (b)   the father shall have parental responsibility for the child if he has acquired it (and has not ceased to have it) in accordance with the provisions of this Act.

(2A) Where a child has a parent by virtue of section 43 of the Human Fertilisation and Embryology Act 2008 and is not a person to whom section 1(3) of the Family Law Reform Act 1987 applies –

- (a)   the mother shall have parental responsibility for the child;
- (b)   the other parent shall have parental responsibility for the child if she has acquired it (and has not ceased to have it) in accordance with the provisions of this Act.

(3)   References in this Act to a child whose father and mother were, or (as the case may be) were not, married to each other at the time of his birth must be read with section 1 of the Family Law Reform Act 1987 (which extends their meaning).

(4)   The rule of law that a father is the natural guardian of his legitimate child is abolished.

(5)   More than one person may have parental responsibility for the same child at the same time.

(6)   A person who has parental responsibility for a child at any time shall not cease to have that responsibility solely because some other person subsequently acquires parental responsibility for the child.

(7)   Where more than one person has parental responsibility for a child, each of them may act alone and without the other (or others) in meeting that responsibility; but nothing in this Part shall be taken to affect the operation of any enactment which requires the consent of more than one person in a matter affecting the child.

(8)   The fact that a person has parental responsibility for a child shall not entitle him to act in any way which would be incompatible with any order made with respect to the child under this Act.

(9)   A person who has parental responsibility for a child may not surrender or transfer any part of that responsibility to another but may arrange for some or all of it to be met by one or more persons acting on his behalf.

(10)   The person with whom any such arrangement is made may himself be a person who already has parental responsibility for the child concerned.

(11)   The making of any such arrangement shall not affect any liability of the person making it which may arise from any failure to meet any part of his parental responsibility for the child concerned.

Amendments—Adoption and Children Act 2002, s 111(5); Human Fertilisation and Embryology Act 2008, s 56, Sch 6, Pt 1, para 26.

3 Meaning of 'parental responsibility'

(1)   In this Act 'parental responsibility' means all the rights, duties, powers, responsibilities and authority which by law a parent of a child has in relation to the child and his property.

(2)   It also includes the rights, powers and duties which a guardian of the child's estate (appointed, before the commencement of section 5, to act generally) would have had in relation to the child and his property.

(3)   The rights referred to in subsection (2) include, in particular, the right of the guardian to receive or recover in his own name, for the benefit of the child, property of whatever description and wherever situated which the child is entitled to receive or recover.

(4)   The fact that a person has, or does not have, parental responsibility for a child shall not affect –

    (a)   any obligation which he may have in relation to the child (such as a statutory duty to maintain the child); or

    (b)   any rights which, in the event of the child's death, he (or any other person) may have in relation to the child's property.

(5)   A person who –

    (a)   does not have parental responsibility for a particular child; but

    (b)   has care of the child,

may (subject to the provisions of this Act) do what is reasonable in all the circumstances of the case for the purpose of safeguarding or promoting the child's welfare.

4 Acquisition of parental responsibility by father

(1)   Where a child's father and mother were not married to each other at the time of his birth the father shall acquire parental responsibility for the child if –

    (a)   he becomes registered as the child's father under any of the enactments specified in subsection (1A);

    (b)   he and the child's mother make an agreement (a 'parental responsibility agreement') providing for him to have parental responsibility for the child; or

    (c)   the court, on his application, orders that he shall have parental responsibility for the child.

(1A)   The enactments referred to in subsection (1)(a) are –

    (a)   paragraphs (a), (b) and (c) of section 10(1) and of section 10A(1) of the Births and Deaths Registration Act 1953;

    (b)   paragraphs (a), (b)(i) and (c) of section 18(1), and sections 18(2)(b) and 20(1)(a) of the Registration of Births, Deaths and Marriages (Scotland) Act 1965; and

    (c)   sub-paragraphs (a), (b) and (c) of Article 14(3) of the Births and Deaths Registration (Northern Ireland) Order 1976.

(1B)   The Secretary of State may by order amend subsection (1A) so as to add further enactments to the list in that subsection.

(2)   No parental responsibility agreement shall have effect for the purposes of this Act unless –

    (a)   it is made in the form prescribed by regulations made by the Lord Chancellor; and

    (b)   where regulations are made by the Lord Chancellor prescribing the manner in which such agreements must be recorded, it is recorded in the prescribed manner.

(2A)   A person who has acquired parental responsibility under subsection (1) shall cease to have that responsibility only if the court so orders.

(3)   The court may make an order under subsection (2A) on the application –

    (a)   of any person who has parental responsibility for the child; or

    (b)   with the leave of the court, of the child himself,

subject, in the case of parental responsibility acquired under subsection (1)(c), to section 12(4).

(4)   The court may only grant leave under subsection (3)(b) if it is satisfied that the child has sufficient understanding to make the proposed application.

Amendments—Adoption and Children Act 2002, s 111(1), (2), (3), (4), (7), SI 2003/3191.

4ZA Acquisition of parental responsibility by second female parent

(1)   Where a child has a parent by virtue of section 43 of the Human Fertilisation and Embryology Act 2008 and is not a person to whom section 1(3) of the Family Law Reform Act 1987 applies, that parent shall acquire parental responsibility for the child if –

    (a)   she becomes registered as a parent of the child under any of the enactments specified in subsection (2);

    (b)   she and the child's mother make an agreement providing for her to have parental responsibility for the child; or

    (c)   the court, on her application, orders that she shall have parental responsibility for the child.

(2)   The enactments referred to in subsection (1)(a) are –

    (a)   paragraphs (a), (b) and (c) of section 10(1B) and of section 10A(1B) of the Births and Deaths Registration Act 1953;

    (b)   paragraphs (a), (b) and (d) of section 18B(1) and sections 18B(3)(a) and 20(1)(a) of the Registration of Births, Deaths and Marriages (Scotland) Act 1965; and

    (c)   sub-paragraphs (a), (b) and (c) of Article 14ZA(3) of the Births and Deaths Registration (Northern Ireland) Order 1976.

(3) The Secretary of State may by order amend subsection (2) so as to add further enactments to the list in that subsection.

(4) An agreement under subsection (1)(b) is also a 'parental responsibility agreement', and section 4(2) applies in relation to such an agreement as it applies in relation to parental responsibility agreements under section 4.

(5) A person who has acquired parental responsibility under subsection (1) shall cease to have that responsibility only if the court so orders.

(6) The court may make an order under subsection (5) on the application –

(a)   of any person who has parental responsibility for the child; or
(b)   with the leave of the court, of the child himself,

subject, in the case of parental responsibility acquired under subsection (1)(c), to section 12(4).

(7) The court may only grant leave under subsection (6)(b) if it is satisfied that the child has sufficient understanding to make the proposed application.

Amendments—Inserted by Human Fertilisation and Embryology Act 2008, s 56, Sch 6, Pt 1, para 27.

4A   Acquisition of parental responsibility by step-parent

(1)   Where a child's parent ('parent A') who has parental responsibility for the child is married to, or a civil partner of, a person who is not the child's parent ('the step-parent') –

(a)   parent A or, if the other parent of the child also has parental responsibility for the child, both parents may by agreement with the step-parent provide for the step-parent to have parental responsibility for the child; or
(b)   the court may, on the application of the step-parent, order that the step-parent shall have parental responsibility for the child.

(2)   An agreement under subsection (1)(a) is also a 'parental responsibility agreement', and section 4(2) applies in relation to such agreements as it applies in relation to parental responsibility agreements under section 4.

(3)   A parental responsibility agreement under subsection (1)(a), or an order under subsection (1)(b), may only be brought to an end by an order of the court made on the application –

(a)   of any person who has parental responsibility for the child; or
(b)   with the leave of the court, of the child himself.

(4)   The court may only grant leave under subsection (3)(b) if it is satisfied that the child has sufficient understanding to make the proposed application.

Amendments—Adoption and Children Act 2002, s 112(7); Civil Partnership Act 2004, s 75(1), (2).

5   Appointment of guardians

(1)   Where an application with respect to a child is made to the court by any individual, the court may by order appoint that individual to be the child's guardian if –

(a)   the child has no parent with parental responsibility for him; or
(b)   a residence order has been made with respect to the child in favour of a parent, guardian or special guardian of his who has died while the order was in force; or

(c)　　paragraph (b) does not apply, and the child's only or last surviving special guardian dies.

(2)　The power conferred by subsection (1) may also be exercised in any family proceedings if the court considers that the order should be made even though no application has been made for it.

(3)　A parent who has parental responsibility for his child may appoint another individual to be the child's guardian in the event of his death.

(4)　A guardian of a child may appoint another individual to take his place as the child's guardian in the event of his death;and a special guardian of a child may appoint another individual to be the child's guardian in the event of his death.

(5)　An appointment under subsection (3) or (4) shall not have effect unless it is made in writing, is dated and is signed by the person making the appointment or –

(a)　　in the case of an appointment made by a will which is not signed by the testator, is signed at the direction of the testator in accordance with the requirements of section 9 of the Wills Act 1837; or

(b)　　in any other case, is signed at the direction of the person making the appointment, in his presence and in the presence of two witnesses who each attest the signature.

(6)　A person appointed as a child's guardian under this section shall have parental responsibility for the child concerned.

(7)　Where –

(a)　　on the death of any person making an appointment under subsection (3) or (4), the child concerned has no parent with parental responsibility for him; or

(b)　　immediately before the death of any person making such an appointment, a residence order in his favour was in force with respect to the child, or he was the child's only (or last surviving) special guardian

the appointment shall take effect on the death of that person.

(8)　Where, on the death of any person making an appointment under subsection (3) or (4) –

(a)　　the child concerned has a parent with parental responsibility for him; and

(b)　　subsection (7)(b) does not apply,

the appointment shall take effect when the child no longer has a parent who has parental responsibility for him.

(9)　Subsections (1) and (7) do not apply if the residence order referred to in paragraph (b) of those subsections was also made in favour of a surviving parent of the child.

(10)　Nothing in this section shall be taken to prevent an appointment under subsection (3) or (4) being made by two or more persons acting jointly.

(11)　Subject to any provision made by rules of court, no court shall exercise the High Court's inherent jurisdiction to appoint a guardian of the estate of any child.

(12)　Where the rules of court are made under subsection (11) they may prescribe the circumstances in which, and conditions subject to which, an appointment of such a guardian may be made.

(13)   A guardian of a child may only be appointed in accordance with the provisions of this section.

Amendments—Adoption and Children Act 2002, s 115(2), (4)(a), (b), (c).

6 Guardians: revocation and disclaimer

(1)   An appointment under section 5(3) or (4) revokes an earlier such appointment (including one made in an unrevoked will or codicil) made by the same person in respect of the same child, unless it is clear (whether as the result of an express provision in the later appointment or by any necessary implication) that the purpose of the later appointment is to appoint an additional guardian.

(2)   An appointment under section 5(3) or (4) (including one made in an unrevoked will or codicil) is revoked if the person who made the appointment revokes it by a written and dated instrument which is signed–

(a)   by him; or
(b)   at his direction, in his presence and in the presence of two witnesses who each attest the signature.

(3)   An appointment under section 5(3) or (4) (other than one made in a will or codicil) is revoked if, with the intention of revoking the appointment, the person who made it –

(a)   destroys the instrument by which it was made; or
(b)   has some other person destroy that instrument in his presence.

(3A)   An appointment under section 5(3) or (4) (including one made in an unrevoked will or codicil) is revoked if the person appointed is the spouse of the person who made the appointment and either–

(a)   a decree of a court of civil jurisdiction in England and Wales dissolves or annuls the marriage, or.
(b)   the marriage is dissolved or annulled and the divorce or annulment is entitled to recognition in England and Wales by virtue of Part II of the Family Law Act 1986,

unless a contrary intention appears by the appointment.

(3B)   An appointment under section 5(3) or (4) (including one made in an unrevoked will or codicil) is revoked if the person appointed is the civil partner of the person who made the appointment and either –

(a)   an order of a court of civil jurisdiction in England and Wales dissolves or annuls the civil partnership, or
(b)   the civil partnership is dissolved or annulled and the dissolution or annulment is entitled to recognition in England and Wales by virtue of Chapter 3 of Part 5 of the Civil Partnership Act 2004,

unless a contrary intention appears by the appointment.

(4)   For the avoidance of doubt, an appointment under section 5(3) or (4) made in a will or codicil is revoked if the will or codicil is revoked.

(5)   A person who is appointed as a guardian under section 5(3) or (4) may disclaim his appointment by an instrument in writing signed by him and made within a reasonable time of his first knowing that the appointment has taken effect.

(6)   Where regulations are made by the Lord Chancellor prescribing the manner in which such disclaimers must be recorded, no such disclaimer shall have effect unless it is recorded in the prescribed manner.

(7)   Any appointment of a guardian under section 5 may be brought to an end at any time by order of the court–

(a)   on the application of any person who has parental responsibility for the child;
(b)   on the application of the child concerned, with leave of the court; or
(c)   in any family proceedings, if the court considers that it should be brought to an end even though no application has been made.

Amendments—Law Reform (Succession) Act 1995, s 4(1); Civil Partnership Act 2004, s 76.

Prospective amendments—Family Law Act 1996, s 66(1), Sch 8, para 41 (2).

7 Welfare reports

(1)   A court considering any question with respect to a child under this Act may –

(a)   ask an officer of the Serviceor a Welsh family proceedings officer; or
(b)   ask a local authority to arrange for –
(i)   an officer of the authority; or
(ii)   such other person (other than an officer of the Service or a Welsh family proceedings officer) as the authority considers appropriate,

to report to the court on such matters relating to the welfare of that child as are required to be dealt with in the report.

(2)   The Lord Chancellor may, after consulting the Lord Chief Justice, make regulations specifying matters which, unless the court orders otherwise, must be dealt with in any report under this section.

(3)   The report may be made in writing, or orally, as the court requires.

(4)   Regardless of any enactment or rule of law which would otherwise prevent it from doing so, the court may take account of –

(a)   any statement contained in the report; and
(b)   any evidence given in respect of the matters referred to in the report,

in so far as the statement or evidence is, in the opinion of the court, relevant to the question which it is considering.

(5)   It shall be the duty of the authority or officer of the Service or a Welsh family proceedings officer to comply with any request for a report under this section.

(6)   The Lord Chief Justice may nominate a judicial office holder (as defined in section 109(4) of the Constitutional Reform Act 2005) to exercise his functions under subsection (2).

Amendments—Criminal Justice and Court Services Act 2000, s 74, Sch 7, paras 87, 88; Children Act 2004, s 40, Sch 3, paras 5, 6; Constitutional Reform Act 2005, s 15(1), Sch 4, Pt 1, paras 203, 204(1), (2), (3).

PART II
ORDERS WITH RESPECT TO CHILDREN IN FAMILY PROCEEDINGS

General

8 Residence, contact and other orders with respect to children

(1) In this Act –

'a contact order' means an order requiring the person with whom a child lives, or is to live, to allow the child to visit or stay with the person named in the order, or for that person and the child otherwise to have contact with each other;

'a prohibited steps order' means an order that no step which could be taken by a parent in meeting his parental responsibility for a child, and which is of a kind specified in the order, shall be taken by any person without the consent of the court;

'a residence order' means an order settling the arrangements to be made as to the person with whom a child is to live; and

'a specific issue order' means an order giving directions for the purpose of determining a specific question which has arisen, or which may arise, in connection with any aspect of parental responsibility for a child.

(2) In this Act 'a section 8 order' means any of the orders mentioned in subsection (1) and any order varying or discharging such an order.

(3) For the purposes of this Act 'family proceedings' means any proceedings–

(a) under the inherent jurisdiction of the High Court in relation to children; and

(b) under the enactments mentioned in subsection (4),

but does not include proceedings on an application for leave under section 100(3).

(4) The enactments are –

(a) Parts I, II and IV of this Act;

(b) the Matrimonial Causes Act 1973;

(ba) Schedule 5 to the Civil Partnership Act 2004;

(c) …

(d) the Adoption and Children Act 2002;

(e) the Domestic Proceedings and Magistrates' Courts Act 1978;

(ea) Schedule 6 to the Civil Partnership Act 2004;

(f) …

(g) Part III of the Matrimonial and Family Proceedings Act 1984;

(h) the Family Law Act 1996;

(i) sections 11 and 12 of the Crime and Disorder Act 1998.

Amendments—Family Law Act 1996, s 66(1), Sch 8, Pt III, para 60; Crime and Disorder Act 1998, s 119, Sch 8, para 68; Adoption and Children Act 2002, s 139(1), Sch 3, paras 54, 55; Civil Partnership Act 2004, s 261(1), Sch 27, para 129(1), (2), (3). Prospectively amended by Family Law Act 1996, s 66(1), Sch 8, para 41(3).

9 Restrictions on making section 8 orders

(1) No court shall make any section 8 order, other than a residence order, with respect to a child who is in the care of a local authority.

(2) No application may be made by a local authority for a residence order or contact order and no court shall make such an order in favour of a local authority.

(3)   A person who is, or was at any time within the last six months, a local authority foster parent of a child may not apply for leave to apply for a section 8 order with respect to the child unless –

   (a)   he has the consent of the authority;
   (b)   he is relative of the child; or
   (c)   the child has lived with him for at least one year preceding the application.

(4)   (*repealed*)

(5)   No court shall exercise its powers to make a specific issue order or prohibited steps order–

   (a)   with a view to achieving a result which could be achieved by making a residence or contact order; or
   (b)   in any way which is denied to the High Court (by section 100(2)) in the exercise of its inherent jurisdiction with respect to children.

(6)   No court shall make a specific issue order, contact order or prohibited steps order is to have effect for a period which will end after the child has reached the age of sixteen unless it is satisfied that the circumstances of the case are exceptional.

(7)   No court shall make any section 8 order, other than one varying or discharging such an order, with respect to a child who has reached the age of sixteen unless it is satisfied that the circumstances of the case are exceptional.

Amendments—Adoption and Children Act 2002, ss 113(a), (b), 114(2), 139(3), Sch 5; Children and Young Persons Act 2008, s 37(1).

10 Power of court to make section 8 orders

(1)   In any family proceedings in which a question arises with respect to the welfare of any child, the court may make a section 8 order with respect to the child if –

   (a)   an application for the order has been made by a person who –
      (i)   is entitled to apply for a section 8 order with respect to the child; or
      (ii)   has obtained the leave of the court to make the application; or
   (b)   the court considers that the order should be made even though no such application has been made.

(2)   The court may also make a section 8 order with respect to any child on the application of a person who–

   (a)   is entitled to apply for a section 8 order with respect to the child; or
   (b)   has obtained the leave of the court to make the application.

(3)   This section is subject to the restrictions imposed by section 9.

(4)   The following persons are entitled to apply to the court for any section 8 order with respect to a child –

   (a)   any parent, guardian or special guardian of the child;
   (aa)   any person who by virtue of section 4A has parental responsibility for the child;
   (b)   any person in whose favour a residence order is in force with respect to the child.

(5)   The following persons are entitled to apply for a residence or contact order with respect to a child –

(a) any party to a marriage (whether or not subsisting) in relation to whom the child is a child of the family;

(aa) any civil partner in a civil partnership (whether or not subsisting) in relation to whom the child is a child of the family;

(b) any person with whom the child has lived for a period of at least three years;

(c) any person who–

    (i) in any case where a residence order is in force with respect to the child, has the consent of each of the persons in whose favour the order was made;

    (ii) in any case where the child is in the care of a local authority, has the consent of that authority; or

    (iii) in any other case, has the consent of each of those (if any) who have parental responsibility for the child.

(5A) A local authority foster parent is entitled to apply for a residence order with respect to a child if the child has lived with him for a period of at least one year immediately preceding the application.

(5B) A relative of a child is entitled to apply for a residence order with respect to the child if the child has lived with the relative for a period of at least one year immediately preceding the application.

(6) A person who would not otherwise be entitled (under the previous provisions of this section) to apply for the variation or discharge of a section 8 order shall be entitled to do so if–

(a) the order was made on his application; or

(b) in the case of a contact order, he is named in the order.

(7) Any person who falls within a category of person prescribed by rules of court is entitled to apply for any such section 8 order as may be prescribed in relation to that category of person.

(7A) If a special guardianship order is in force with respect to a child, an application for a residence order may only be made with respect to him, if apart from this subsection the leave of the court is not required, with such leave.

(8) Where the person applying for leave to make an application for a section 8 order is the child concerned, the court may only grant leave if it is satisfied that he has sufficient understanding to make the proposed application for the section 8 order.

(9) Where the person applying for leave to make an application for a section 8 order is not the child concerned, the court shall, in deciding whether or not to grant leave, have particular regard to–

(a) the nature of the proposed application for the section 8 order;

(b) the applicant's connection with the child;

(c) any risk there might be of that proposed application disrupting the child's life to such an extent that he would be harmed by it; and

(d) where the child is being looked after by a local authority–

    (i) the authority's plans for the child's future; and

    (ii) the wishes and feelings of the child's parents.

(10) The period of three years mentioned in subsection (5)(b) need not be continuous but must not have begun more than five years before, or ended more than three months before, the making of the application.

Amendments—Adoption and Children Act 2002, s 139(1), Sch 3, paras 54, 56; Civil Partnership Act 2004, s 77; Children and Young Persons Act 2008, s 36.

11 General principles and supplementary provisions

(1) In proceedings in which any question of making a section 8 order, or any other question with respect to such an order, arises, the court shall (in the light of any rules made by virtue of subsection (2)) –

    (a)   draw up a timetable with a view to determining the question without delay; and

    (b)   give such directions as it considers appropriate for the purpose of ensuring, so far as is reasonably practicable, that that timetable is adhered to.

(2) Rules of court may –

    (a)   specify periods within which specified steps must be taken in relation to proceedings in which such questions arise; and

    (b)   make other provision with respect to such proceedings for the purpose of ensuring, so far as is reasonably practicable, that such questions are determined without delay.

(3) Where a court has power to make a section 8 order, it may do so at any time during the course of the proceedings in question even though it is not in a position to dispose finally of those proceedings.

(4) Where a residence order is made in favour of two or more persons who do not themselves all live together, the order may specify the periods during which the child is to live in the different households concerned.

(5) Where –

    (a)   a residence order has been made with respect to a child; and

    (b)   as a result of the order the child lives, or is to live, with one of two parents who each have parental responsibility for him,

the residence order shall cease to have effect if the parents live together for a continuous period of more than six months.

(6) A contact order which requires the parent with whom a child lives to allow the child to visit, or otherwise have contact with, his other parent shall cease to have effect if the parents live together for a continuous period of more than six months.

(7) A section 8 order may –

    (a)   contain directions about how it is to be carried into effect;

    (b)   impose conditions which must be complied with by any person –

        (i)   in whose favour the order is made;

        (ii)   who is a parent of the child concerned;

        (iii)   who is not a parent of his but who has parental responsibility for him; or

        (iv)   with whom the child is living,

        and to whom the conditions are expressed to apply;

    (c)   be made to have effect for a specified period, or contain provisions which are to have effect for a specified period;

    (d)   make such incidental, supplemental or consequential provision as the court thinks fit.

11A Contact activity directions

(1) This section applies in proceedings in which the court is considering whether to make provision about contact with a child by making –

   (a)   a contact order with respect to the child, or

   (b)   an order varying or discharging a contact order with respect to the child.

(2) The court may make a contact activity direction in connection with that provision about contact.

(3) A contact activity direction is a direction requiring an individual who is a party to the proceedings to take part in an activity that promotes contact with the child concerned.

(4) The direction is to specify the activity and the person providing the activity.

(5) The activities that may be so required include, in particular –

   (a)   programmes, classes and counselling or guidance sessions of a kind that –
      (i)   may assist a person as regards establishing, maintaining or improving contact with a child;
      (ii)   may, by addressing a person's violent behaviour, enable or facilitate contact with a child;

   (b)   sessions in which information or advice is given as regards making or operating arrangements for contact with a child, including making arrangements by means of mediation.

(6) No individual may be required by a contact activity direction –

   (a)   to undergo medical or psychiatric examination, assessment or treatment;

   (b)   to take part in mediation.

(7) A court may not on the same occasion –

   (a)   make a contact activity direction, and

   (b)   dispose finally of the proceedings as they relate to contact with the child concerned.

(8) Subsection (2) has effect subject to the restrictions in sections 11B and 11E.

(9) In considering whether to make a contact activity direction, the welfare of the child concerned is to be the court's paramount consideration.

Amendments—Inserted by Children and Adoption Act 2006, s 1.

11B Contact activity directions: further provision

(1) A court may not make a contact activity direction in any proceedings unless there is a dispute as regards the provision about contact that the court is considering whether to make in the proceedings.

(2) A court may not make a contact activity direction requiring an individual who is a child to take part in an activity unless the individual is a parent of the child in relation to whom the court is considering provision about contact.

(3) A court may not make a contact activity direction in connection with the making, variation or discharge of a contact order, if the contact order is, or would if made be, an excepted order.

(4) A contact order with respect to a child is an excepted order if –

(a)   it is made in proceedings that include proceedings on an application for a relevant adoption order in respect of the child; or

(b)   it makes provision as regards contact between the child and a person who would be a parent or relative of the child but for the child's adoption by an order falling within subsection (5).

(5) An order falls within this subsection if it is –

(a)   a relevant adoption order;

(b)   an adoption order, within the meaning of section 72(1) of the Adoption Act 1976, other than an order made by virtue of section 14 of that Act on the application of a married couple one of whom is the mother or the father of the child;

(c)   a Scottish adoption order, within the meaning of the Adoption and Children Act 2002, other than an order made –

(i)   by virtue of section 14 of the Adoption (Scotland) Act 1978 on the application of a married couple one of whom is the mother or the father of the child, or

(ii)   by virtue of section 15(1)(aa) of that Act; or

(iii)   by virtue of an application under section 30 of the Adoption and Children (Scotland) Act 2007 where subsection (3) of that section applies; or

(d)   a Northern Irish adoption order, within the meaning of the Adoption and Children Act 2002, other than an order made by virtue of Article 14 of the Adoption (Northern Ireland) Order 1987 on the application of a married couple one of whom is the mother or the father of the child.

(6) A relevant adoption order is an adoption order, within the meaning of section 46(1) of the Adoption and Children Act 2002, other than an order made –

(a)   on an application under section 50 of that Act by a couple (within the meaning of that Act) one of whom is the mother or the father of the person to be adopted, or

(b)   on an application under section 51(2) of that Act.

(7) A court may not make a contact activity direction in relation to an individual unless the individual is habitually resident in England and Wales; and a direction ceases to have effect if the individual subject to the direction ceases to be habitually resident in England and Wales.

Amendments—Children and Adoption Act 2006, s 1; SI 2011/1740.

11C Contact activity conditions

(1) This section applies if in any family proceedings the court makes –

(a)   a contact order with respect to a child, or

(b)   an order varying a contact order with respect to a child.

(2) The contact order may impose, or the contact order may be varied so as to impose, a condition (a 'contact activity condition') requiring an individual falling within subsection (3) to take part in an activity that promotes contact with the child concerned.

(3) An individual falls within this subsection if he is –

(a)   for the purposes of the contact order so made or varied, the person with whom the child concerned lives or is to live;

(b)   the person whose contact with the child concerned is provided for in that order; or

(c)   a person upon whom that order imposes a condition under section 11(7)(b).

(4) The condition is to specify the activity and the person providing the activity.

(5) Subsections (5) and (6) of section 11A have effect as regards the activities that may be required by a contact activity condition as they have effect as regards the activities that may be required by a contact activity direction.

(6) Subsection (2) has effect subject to the restrictions in sections 11D and 11E.

Amendment—Inserted by Children and Adoption Act 2006, s 1.

11D Contact activity conditions: further provision

(1) A contact order may not impose a contact activity condition on an individual who is a child unless the individual is a parent of the child concerned.

(2) If a contact order is an excepted order (within the meaning given by section 11B(4)), it may not impose (and it may not be varied so as to impose) a contact activity condition.

(3) A contact order may not impose a contact activity condition on an individual unless the individual is habitually resident in England and Wales; and a condition ceases to have effect if the individual subject to the condition ceases to be habitually resident in England and Wales.

Amendment—Inserted by Children and Adoption Act 2006, s 1.

11E Contact activity directions and conditions: making

(1) Before making a contact activity direction (or imposing a contact activity condition by means of a contact order), the court must satisfy itself as to the matters falling within subsections (2) to (4).

(2) The first matter is that the activity proposed to be specified is appropriate in the circumstances of the case.

(3) The second matter is that the person proposed to be specified as the provider of the activity is suitable to provide the activity.

(4) The third matter is that the activity proposed to be specified is provided in a place to which the individual who would be subject to the direction (or the condition) can reasonably be expected to travel.

(5) Before making such a direction (or such an order), the court must obtain and consider information about the individual who would be subject to the direction (or the condition) and the likely effect of the direction (or the condition) on him.

(6) Information about the likely effect of the direction (or the condition) may, in particular, include information as to –

(a)   any conflict with the individual's religious beliefs;

(b)   any interference with the times (if any) at which he normally works or attends an educational establishment.

(7) The court may ask an officer of the Service or a Welsh family proceedings officer to provide the court with information as to the matters in subsections (2) to (5); and it shall be the duty of the officer of the Service or Welsh family proceedings officer to comply with any such request.

(8) In this section 'specified' means specified in a contact activity direction (or in a contact activity condition).

Amendment—Inserted by Children and Adoption Act 2006, s 1.

11F Contact activity directions and conditions: financial assistance

(1) The Secretary of State may by regulations make provision authorising him to make payments to assist individuals falling within subsection (2) in paying relevant charges or fees.

(2) An individual falls within this subsection if he is required by a contact activity direction or condition to take part in an activity that promotes contact with a child, not being a child ordinarily resident in Wales.

(3) The National Assembly for Wales may by regulations make provision authorising it to make payments to assist individuals falling within subsection (4) in paying relevant charges or fees.

(4) An individual falls within this subsection if he is required by a contact activity direction or condition to take part in an activity that promotes contact with a child who is ordinarily resident in Wales.

(5) A relevant charge or fee, in relation to an activity required by a contact activity direction or condition, is a charge or fee in respect of the activity payable to the person providing the activity.

(6) Regulations under this section may provide that no assistance is available to an individual unless –

    (a)   the individual satisfies such conditions as regards his financial resources as may be set out in the regulations;

    (b)   the activity in which the individual is required by a contact activity direction or condition to take part is provided to him in England or Wales;

    (c)   where the activity in which the individual is required to take part is provided to him in England, it is provided by a person who is for the time being approved by the Secretary of State as a provider of activities required by a contact activity direction or condition;

    (d)   where the activity in which the individual is required to take part is provided to him in Wales, it is provided by a person who is for the time being approved by the National Assembly for Wales as a provider of activities required by a contact activity direction or condition.

(7) Regulations under this section may make provision –

    (a)   as to the maximum amount of assistance that may be paid to or in respect of an individual as regards an activity in which he is required by a contact activity direction or condition to take part;

    (b)   where the amount may vary according to an individual's financial resources, as to the method by which the amount is to be determined;

    (c)   authorising payments by way of assistance to be made directly to persons providing activities required by a contact activity direction or condition.

Amendment—Inserted by Children and Adoption Act 2006, s 1.

11G Contact activity directions and conditions: monitoring

(1) This section applies if in any family proceedings the court –

(a) makes a contact activity direction in relation to an individual, or

(b) makes a contact order that imposes, or varies a contact order so as to impose, a contact activity condition on an individual.

(2) The court may on making the direction (or imposing the condition by means of a contact order) ask an officer of the Service or a Welsh family proceedings officer –

(a) to monitor, or arrange for the monitoring of, the individual's compliance with the direction (or the condition);

(b) to report to the court on any failure by the individual to comply with the direction (or the condition).

(3) It shall be the duty of the officer of the Service or Welsh family proceedings officer to comply with any request under subsection (2).

Amendment—Inserted by Children and Adoption Act 2006, s 1.

11H Monitoring contact

(1) This section applies if in any family proceedings the court makes –

(a) a contact order with respect to a child in favour of a person, or

(b) an order varying such a contact order.

(2) The court may ask an officer of the Service or a Welsh family proceedings officer –

(a) to monitor whether an individual falling within subsection (3) complies with the contact order (or the contact order as varied);

(b) to report to the court on such matters relating to the individual's compliance as the court may specify in the request.

(3) An individual falls within this subsection if the contact order so made (or the contact order as so varied) –

(a) requires the individual to allow contact with the child concerned;

(b) names the individual as having contact with the child concerned; or

(c) imposes a condition under section 11(7)(b) on the individual.

(4) If the contact order (or the contact order as varied) includes a contact activity condition, a request under subsection (2) is to be treated as relating to the provisions of the order other than the contact activity condition.

(5) The court may make a request under subsection (2) –

(a) on making the contact order (or the order varying the contact order), or

(b) at any time during the subsequent course of the proceedings as they relate to contact with the child concerned.

(6) In making a request under subsection (2), the court is to specify the period for which the officer of the Service or Welsh family proceedings officer is to monitor compliance with the order; and the period specified may not exceed twelve months.

(7) It shall be the duty of the officer of the Service or Welsh family proceedings officer to comply with any request under subsection (2).

(8) The court may order any individual falling within subsection (3) to take such steps as may be specified in the order with a view to enabling the officer of the Service or Welsh family proceedings officer to comply with the court's request under subsection (2).

(9) But the court may not make an order under subsection (8) with respect to an individual who is a child unless he is a parent of the child with respect to whom the order falling within subsection (1) was made.

(10) A court may not make a request under subsection (2) in relation to a contact order that is an excepted order (within the meaning given by section 11B(4)).

Amendment—Inserted by Children and Adoption Act 2006, s 2.

11I Contact orders: warning notices

Where the court makes (or varies) a contact order, it is to attach to the contact order (or the order varying the contact order) a notice warning of the consequences of failing to comply with the contact order.

Amendment—Inserted by Children and Adoption Act 2006, s 3.

11J Enforcement orders

(1) This section applies if a contact order with respect to a child has been made.

(2) If the court is satisfied beyond reasonable doubt that a person has failed to comply with the contact order, it may make an order (an 'enforcement order') imposing on the person an unpaid work requirement.

(3) But the court may not make an enforcement order if it is satisfied that the person had a reasonable excuse for failing to comply with the contact order.

(4) The burden of proof as to the matter mentioned in subsection (3) lies on the person claiming to have had a reasonable excuse, and the standard of proof is the balance of probabilities.

(5) The court may make an enforcement order in relation to the contact order only on the application of –

    (a)   the person who is, for the purposes of the contact order, the person with whom the child concerned lives or is to live;

    (b)   the person whose contact with the child concerned is provided for in the contact order;

    (c)   any individual subject to a condition under section 11(7)(b) or a contact activity condition imposed by the contact order; or

    (d)   the child concerned.

(6) Where the person proposing to apply for an enforcement order in relation to a contact order is the child concerned, the child must obtain the leave of the court before making such an application.

(7) The court may grant leave to the child concerned only if it is satisfied that he has sufficient understanding to make the proposed application.

(8) Subsection (2) has effect subject to the restrictions in sections 11K and 11L.

(9) The court may suspend an enforcement order for such period as it thinks fit.

(10) Nothing in this section prevents a court from making more than one enforcement order in relation to the same person on the same occasion.

(11) Proceedings in which any question of making an enforcement order, or any other question with respect to such an order, arises are to be regarded for the purposes of section 11(1) and (2) as proceedings in which a question arises with respect to a section 8 order.

(12) In Schedule A1 –

    (a)   Part 1 makes provision as regards an unpaid work requirement;

    (b)   Part 2 makes provision in relation to the revocation and amendment of enforcement orders and failure to comply with such orders.

(13) This section is without prejudice to section 63(3) of the Magistrates' Courts Act 1980 as it applies in relation to contact orders.

Amendment—Inserted by Children and Adoption Act 2006, s 4(1).

11K Enforcement orders: further provision

(1) A court may not make an enforcement order against a person in respect of a failure to comply with a contact order unless it is satisfied that before the failure occurred the person had been given (in accordance with rules of court) a copy of, or otherwise informed of the terms of –

    (a)   in the case of a failure to comply with a contact order that was varied before the failure occurred, a notice under section 11I relating to the order varying the contact order or, where more than one such order has been made, the last order preceding the failure in question;

    (b)   in any other case, a notice under section 11I relating to the contact order.

(2) A court may not make an enforcement order against a person in respect of any failure to comply with a contact order occurring before the person attained the age of 18.

(3) A court may not make an enforcement order against a person in respect of a failure to comply with a contact order that is an excepted order (within the meaning given by section 11B(4)).

(4) A court may not make an enforcement order against a person unless the person is habitually resident in England and Wales; and an enforcement order ceases to have effect if the person subject to the order ceases to be habitually resident in England and Wales.

Amendment—Inserted by Children and Adoption Act 2006, s 4(1).

11L Enforcement orders: making

(1) Before making an enforcement order as regards a person in breach of a contact order, the court must be satisfied that –

    (a)   making the enforcement order proposed is necessary to secure the person's compliance with the contact order or any contact order that has effect in its place;

    (b)   the likely effect on the person of the enforcement order proposed to be made is proportionate to the seriousness of the breach of the contact order.

(2) Before making an enforcement order, the court must satisfy itself that provision for the person to work under an unpaid work requirement imposed by an enforcement order can be made in the local justice area in which the person in breach resides or will reside.

(3) Before making an enforcement order as regards a person in breach of a contact order, the court must obtain and consider information about the person and the likely effect of the enforcement order on him.

(4) Information about the likely effect of the enforcement order may, in particular, include information as to –

(a)   any conflict with the person's religious beliefs;

(b)   any interference with the times (if any) at which he normally works or attends an educational establishment.

(5) A court that proposes to make an enforcement order may ask an officer of the Service or a Welsh family proceedings officer to provide the court with information as to the matters in subsections (2) and (3).

(6) It shall be the duty of the officer of the Service or Welsh family proceedings officer to comply with any request under this section.

(7) In making an enforcement order in relation to a contact order, a court must take into account the welfare of the child who is the subject of the contact order.

Amendment—Inserted by Children and Adoption Act 2006, s 4(1).

11M Enforcement orders: monitoring

(1) On making an enforcement order in relation to a person, the court is to ask an officer of the Service or a Welsh family proceedings officer –

(a)   to monitor, or arrange for the monitoring of, the person's compliance with the unpaid work requirement imposed by the order;

(b)   to report to the court if a report under paragraph 8 of Schedule A1 is made in relation to the person;

(c)   to report to the court on such other matters relating to the person's compliance as may be specified in the request;

(d)   to report to the court if the person is, or becomes, unsuitable to perform work under the requirement.

(2) It shall be the duty of the officer of the Service or Welsh family proceedings officer to comply with any request under this section.

Amendment—Inserted by Children and Adoption Act 2006, s 4(1).

11N Enforcement orders: warning notices

Where the court makes an enforcement order, it is to attach to the order a notice warning of the consequences of failing to comply with the order.

Amendment—Inserted by Children and Adoption Act 2006, s 4(1).

11O Compensation for financial loss

(1) This section applies if a contact order with respect to a child has been made.

(2) If the court is satisfied that –

(a)   an individual has failed to comply with the contact order, and

(b)   a person falling within subsection (6) has suffered financial loss by reason of the breach,

it may make an order requiring the individual in breach to pay the person compensation in respect of his financial loss.

(3) But the court may not make an order under subsection (2) if it is satisfied that the individual in breach had a reasonable excuse for failing to comply with the contact order.

(4) The burden of proof as to the matter mentioned in subsection (3) lies on the individual claiming to have had a reasonable excuse.

(5) An order under subsection (2) may be made only on an application by the person who claims to have suffered financial loss.

(6) A person falls within this subsection if he is –

(a)   the person who is, for the purposes of the contact order, the person with whom the child concerned lives or is to live;

(b)   the person whose contact with the child concerned is provided for in the contact order;

(c)   an individual subject to a condition under section 11(7)(b) or a contact activity condition imposed by the contact order; or

(d)   the child concerned.

(7) Where the person proposing to apply for an order under subsection (2) is the child concerned, the child must obtain the leave of the court before making such an application.

(8) The court may grant leave to the child concerned only if it is satisfied that he has sufficient understanding to make the proposed application.

(9) The amount of compensation is to be determined by the court, but may not exceed the amount of the applicant's financial loss.

(10) In determining the amount of compensation payable by the individual in breach, the court must take into account the individual's financial circumstances.

(11) An amount ordered to be paid as compensation may be recovered by the applicant as a civil debt due to him.

(12) Subsection (2) has effect subject to the restrictions in section 11P.

(13) Proceedings in which any question of making an order under subsection (2) arises are to be regarded for the purposes of section 11(1) and (2) as proceedings in which a question arises with respect to a section 8 order.

(14) In exercising its powers under this section, a court is to take into account the welfare of the child concerned.

Amendment—Inserted by Children and Adoption Act 2006, s 5.

11P Orders under section 11O(2): further provision

(1) A court may not make an order under section 11O(2) requiring an individual to pay compensation in respect of a failure by him to comply with a contact order unless it is satisfied that before the failure occurred the individual had been given (in accordance with rules of court) a copy of, or otherwise informed of the terms of –

(a) in the case of a failure to comply with a contact order that was varied before the failure occurred, a notice under section 11I relating to the order varying the contact order or, where more than one such order has been made, the last order preceding the failure in question;

(b) in any other case, a notice under section 11I relating to the contact order.

(2) A court may not make an order under section 11O(2) requiring an individual to pay compensation in respect of a failure by him to comply with a contact order where the failure occurred before the individual attained the age of 18.

(3) A court may not make an order under section 11O(2) requiring an individual to pay compensation in respect of a failure by him to comply with a contact order that is an excepted order (within the meaning given by section 11B(4)).

Amendment—Inserted by Children and Adoption Act 2006, s 5.

12 Residence orders and parental responsibility

(1) Where the court makes a residence order in favour of the father of a child it shall, if the father would not otherwise have parental responsibility for the child, also make an order under section 4 giving him that responsibility.

(1A) Where the court makes a residence order in favour of a woman who is a parent of a child by virtue of section 43 of the Human Fertilisation and Embryology Act 2008 it shall, if that woman would not otherwise have parental responsibility for the child, also make an order under section 4ZA giving her that responsibility.

(2) Where the court makes a residence order in favour of any person who is not the parent or guardian of the child concerned that person shall have parental responsibility for the child while the residence order remains in force.

(3) Where a person has parental responsibility for a child as a result of subsection (2), he shall not have the right –

(a) ...

(b) to agree, or refuse to agree, to the making of an adoption order, or an order under section 84 of the Adoption and Children Act 2002, with respect to the child; or

(c) to appoint a guardian for the child.

(4) Where subsection (1) or (1A) requires the court to make an order under section 4 or 4ZA in respect of the parent of a child, the court shall not bring that order to an end at any time while the residence order concerned remains in force.

(5), (6) (*repealed*)

Amendments—Adoption and Children Act 2002, ss 114(1), 139(1), (3), Sch 3, paras 54, 57(a), (b), Sch 5; Human Fertilisation and Embryology Act 2008, s 56, Sch 6, Pt 1, para 28, Children and Young Persons Act 2008, ss 37(2), 42, Sch 4.

13 Change of child's name or removal from jurisdiction

(1) Where a residence order is in force with respect to a child, no person may –

(a) cause the child to be known by a new surname; or

(b) remove him from the United Kingdom;

without either the written consent of every person who has parental responsibility for the child or the leave of the court.

(2) Subsection (1)(b) does not prevent the removal of a child, for a period of less than one month, by the person in whose favour the residence order is made.

(3) In making a residence order with respect to a child the court may grant the leave required by subsection (1)(b), either generally or for specified purposes.

14 Enforcement of residence orders

(1) Where–

    (a)   a residence order is in force with respect to a child in favour of any person; and

    (b)   any other person (including one in whose favour the order is also in force) is in breach of the arrangements settled by that order,

the person mentioned in paragraph (a) may, as soon as the requirement in subsection (2) is complied with, enforce the order under section 63(3) of the Magistrates' Courts Act 1980 as if it were an order requiring the other person to produce the child to him.

(2) The requirement is that a copy of the residence order has been served on the other person.

(3) Subsection (1) is without prejudice to any other remedy open to the person in whose favour the residence order is in force.

Special guardianship

14A Special guardianship orders

(1) A 'special guardianship order' is an order appointing one or more individuals to be a child's 'special guardian' (or special guardians).

(2) A special guardian –

    (a)   must be aged eighteen or over; and

    (b)   must not be a parent of the child in question,

and subsections (3) to (6) are to be read in that light.

(3) The court may make a special guardianship order with respect to any child on the application of an individual who –

    (a)   is entitled to make such an application with respect to the child; or

    (b)   has obtained the leave of the court to make the application,

or on the joint application of more than one such individual.

(4) Section 9(3) applies in relation to an application for leave to apply for a special guardianship order as it applies in relation to an application for leave to apply for a section 8 order.

(5) The individuals who are entitled to apply for a special guardianship order with respect to a child are –

    (a)   any guardian of the child;

    (b)   any individual in whose favour a residence order is in force with respect to the child;

    (c)   any individual listed in subsection (5)(b) or (c) of section 10 (as read with subsection (10) of that section);

    (d)   a local authority foster parent with whom the child has lived for a period of at least one year immediately preceding the application;

(e)　　a relative with whom the child has lived for a period of at least one year immediately preceding the application.

(6)　The court may also make a special guardianship order with respect to a child in any family proceedings in which a question arises with respect to the welfare of the child if –

(a)　　an application for the order has been made by an individual who falls within subsection (3)(a) or (b) (or more than one such individual jointly); or

(b)　　the court considers that a special guardianship order should be made even though no such application has been made.

(7)　No individual may make an application under subsection (3) or (6)(a) unless, before the beginning of the period of three months ending with the date of the application, he has given written notice of his intention to make the application –

(a)　　if the child in question is being looked after by a local authority, to that local authority, or

(b)　　otherwise, to the local authority in whose area the individual is ordinarily resident.

(8)　On receipt of such a notice, the local authority must investigate the matter and prepare a report for the court dealing with –

(a)　　the suitability of the applicant to be a special guardian;

(b)　　such matters (if any) as may be prescribed by the Secretary of State; and

(c)　　any other matter which the local authority consider to be relevant.

(9)　The court may itself ask a local authority to conduct such an investigation and prepare such a report, and the local authority must do so.

(10)　The local authority may make such arrangements as they see fit for any person to act on their behalf in connection with conducting an investigation or preparing a report referred to in subsection (8) or (9).

(11)　The court may not make a special guardianship order unless it has received a report dealing with the matters referred to in subsection (8).

(12)　Subsections (8) and (9) of section 10 apply in relation to special guardianship orders as they apply in relation to section 8 orders.

(13)　This section is subject to section 29(5) and (6) of the Adoption and Children Act 2002.

Amendments—Adoption and Children Act 2002, s 115(1); Children and Young Persons Act 2008, s 38.

14B Special guardianship orders: making

(1)　Before making a special guardianship order, the court must consider whether, if the order were made –

(a)　　a contact order should also be made with respect to the child,

(b)　　any section 8 order in force with respect to the child should be varied or discharged.

(c)　　where a contact order made with respect to the child is not discharged, any enforcement order relating to that contact order should be revoked, and

(d)　　where a contact activity direction has been made as regards contact with the child and is in force, that contact activity direction should be discharged.

(2)   On making a special guardianship order, the court may also –

(a)   give leave for the child to be known by a new surname;

(b)   grant the leave required by section 14C(3)(b), either generally or for specified purposes.

Amendments—Adoption and Children Act 2002, s 115(1); Children and Adoption Act 2006, s 15, Sch 2, paras 7, 8(a), Sch 3.

14C Special guardianship orders: effect

(1)   The effect of a special guardianship order is that while the order remains in force –

(a)   a special guardian appointed by the order has parental responsibility for the child in respect of whom it is made; and

(b)   subject to any other order in force with respect to the child under this Act, a special guardian is entitled to exercise parental responsibility to the exclusion of any other person with parental responsibility for the child (apart from another special guardian).

(2)   Subsection (1) does not affect –

(a)   the operation of any enactment or rule of law which requires the consent of more than one person with parental responsibility in a matter affecting the child; or

(b)   any rights which a parent of the child has in relation to the child's adoption or placement for adoption.

(3)   While a special guardianship order is in force with respect to a child, no person may –

(a)   cause the child to be known by a new surname; or

(b)   remove him from the United Kingdom,

without either the written consent of every person who has parental responsibility for the child or the leave of the court.

(4)   Subsection (3)(b) does not prevent the removal of a child, for a period of less than three months, by a special guardian of his.

(5)   If the child with respect to whom a special guardianship order is in force dies, his special guardian must take reasonable steps to give notice of that fact to –

(a)   each parent of the child with parental responsibility; and

(b)   each guardian of the child,

but if the child has more than one special guardian, and one of them has taken such steps in relation to a particular parent or guardian, any other special guardian need not do so as respects that parent or guardian.

(6)   This section is subject to section 29(7) of the Adoption and Children Act 2002.

Amendments—Inserted by Adoption and Children Act 2002, s 115(1).

14D Special guardianship orders: variation and discharge

(1)   The court may vary or discharge a special guardianship order on the application of –

(a)   the special guardian (or any of them, if there are more than one);

(b)   any parent or guardian of the child concerned;

(c)   any individual in whose favour a residence order is in force with respect to the child;

(d)   any individual not falling within any of paragraphs (a) to (c) who has, or immediately before the making of the special guardianship order had, parental responsibility for the child;

(e)   the child himself; or

(f)   a local authority designated in a care order with respect to the child.

(2)   In any family proceedings in which a question arises with respect to the welfare of a child with respect to whom a special guardianship order is in force, the court may also vary or discharge the special guardianship order if it considers that the order should be varied or discharged, even though no application has been made under subsection (1).

(3)   The following must obtain the leave of the court before making an application under subsection (1) –

(a)   the child;

(b)   any parent or guardian of his;

(c)   any step-parent of his who has acquired, and has not lost, parental responsibility for him by virtue of section 4A;

(d)   any individual falling within subsection (1)(d) who immediately before the making of the special guardianship order had, but no longer has, parental responsibility for him.

(4)   Where the person applying for leave to make an application under subsection (1) is the child, the court may only grant leave if it is satisfied that he has sufficient understanding to make the proposed application under subsection (1).

(5)   The court may not grant leave to a person falling within subsection (3)(b)(c) or (d) unless it is satisfied that there has been a significant change in circumstances since the making of the special guardianship order.

Amendments—Inserted by Adoption and Children Act 2002, s 115(1).

14E Special guardianship orders: supplementary

(1)   In proceedings in which any question of making, varying or discharging a special guardianship order arises, the court shall (in the light of any rules made by virtue of subsection (3)) –

(a)   draw up a timetable with a view to determining the question without delay; and

(b)   give such directions as it considers appropriate for the purpose of ensuring, so far as is reasonably practicable, that the timetable is adhered to.

(2)   Subsection (1) applies also in relation to proceedings in which any other question with respect to a special guardianship order arises.

(3)   The power to make rules in subsection (2) of section 11 applies for the purposes of this section as it applies for the purposes of that.

(4)   A special guardianship order, or an order varying one, may contain provisions which are to have effect for a specified period.

(5)   Section 11(7) (apart from paragraph (c)) applies in relation to special guardianship orders and orders varying them as it applies in relation to section 8 orders.

Amendments—Inserted by Adoption and Children Act 2002, s 115(1).

14F Special guardianship support services

(1)   Each local authority must make arrangements for the provision within their area of special guardianship support services, which means –

(a)   counselling, advice and information; and
(b)   such other services as are prescribed,

in relation to special guardianship.

(2)   The power to make regulations under subsection (1)(b) is to be exercised so as to secure that local authorities provide financial support.

(3)   At the request of any of the following persons –

(a)   a child with respect to whom a special guardianship order is in force;
(b)   a special guardian;
(c)   a parent;
(d)   any other person who falls within a prescribed description,

a local authority may carry out an assessment of that person's needs for special guardianship support services (but, if the Secretary of State so provides in regulations, they must do so if he is a person of a prescribed description, or if his case falls within a prescribed description, or if both he and his case fall within prescribed descriptions).

(4)   A local authority may, at the request of any other person, carry out an assessment of that person's needs for special guardianship support services.

(5)   Where, as a result of an assessment, a local authority decide that a person has needs for special guardianship support services, they must then decide whether to provide any such services to that person.

(6)   If –

(a)   a local authority decide to provide any special guardianship support services to a person, and
(b)   the circumstances fall within a prescribed description,

the local authority must prepare a plan in accordance with which special guardianship support services are to be provided to him, and keep the plan under review.

(7)   The Secretary of State may by regulations make provision about assessments, preparing and reviewing plans, the provision of special guardianship support services in accordance with plans and reviewing the provision of special guardianship support services.

(8)   The regulations may in particular make provision –

(a)   about the type of assessment which is to be carried out, or the way in which an assessment is to be carried out;
(b)   about the way in which a plan is to be prepared;
(c)   about the way in which, and the time at which, a plan or the provision of special guardianship support services is to be reviewed;
(d)   about the considerations to which a local authority are to have regard in carrying out an assessment or review or preparing a plan;

(e)   as to the circumstances in which a local authority may provide special guardianship support services subject to conditions (including conditions as to payment for the support or the repayment of financial support);

(f)   as to the consequences of conditions imposed by virtue of paragraph (e) not being met (including the recovery of any financial support provided);

(g)   as to the circumstances in which this section may apply to a local authority in respect of persons who are outside that local authority's area;

(h)   as to the circumstances in which a local authority may recover from another local authority the expenses of providing special guardianship support services to any person.

(9)   A local authority may provide special guardianship support services (or any part of them) by securing their provision by –

(a)   another local authority; or

(b)   a person within a description prescribed in regulations of persons who may provide special guardianship support services,

and may also arrange with any such authority or person for that other authority or that person to carry out the local authority's functions in relation to assessments under this section.

(10)   A local authority may carry out an assessment of the needs of any person for the purposes of this section at the same time as an assessment of his needs is made under any other provision of this Act or under any other enactment.

(11)   Section 27 (co-operation between authorities) applies in relation to the exercise of functions of a local authority under this section as it applies in relation to the exercise of functions of a local authority under Part 3.

Amendments—Inserted by Adoption and Children Act 2002, s 115(1).

****

Family assistance orders

16 Family assistance orders

(1)   Where, in any family proceedings, the court has power to make an order under this Part with respect to any child, it may (whether or not it makes such an order) make an order requiring –

(a)   an officer of the Service or a Welsh family proceedings officer to be made available; or

(b)   a local authority to make an officer of the authority available,

to advise, assist and (where appropriate) befriend any person named in the order.

(2)   The persons who may be named in an order under this section ('a family assistance order') are –

(a)   any parent, guardian or special guardian of the child;

(b)   any person with whom the child is living or in whose favour a contact order is in force with respect to the child;

(c)   the child himself.

(3)   No court may make a family assistance order unless –

(a)   ....

(b)   it has obtained the consent of every person to be named in the order other than the child.

(4)   A family assistance order may direct –

(a)   the person named in the order; or

(b)   such of the persons named in the order as may be specified in the order,

to take such steps as may be so specified with a view to enabling the officer concerned to be kept informed of the address of any person named in the order and to be allowed to visit any such person.

(4A)   If the court makes a family assistance order with respect to a child and the order is to be in force at the same time as a contact order made with respect to the child, the family assistance order may direct the officer concerned to give advice and assistance as regards establishing, improving and maintaining contact to such of the persons named in the order as may be specified in the order.

(5)   Unless it specifies a shorter period, a family assistance order shall have effect for a period of twelve months beginning with the day on which it is made.

(6)   If the court makes a family assistance order with respect to a child and the order is to be in force at the same time as a section 8 order made with respect to the child, the family assistance order may direct the officer concerned to report to the court on such matters relating to the section 8 order as the court may require (including the question whether the section 8 order ought to be varied or discharged).

(7)   A family assistance order shall not be made so as to require a local authority to make an officer of theirs available unless –

(a)   the authority agree; or

(b)   the child concerned lives or will live within their area.

(8), (9)   *(repealed)*

Amendments—Criminal Justice and Court Services Act 2000, s 74, Sch 7, paras 87, 89, Sch 8; Adoption and Children Act 2002, s 139(1), Sch 3, paras 54, 58; Children Act 2004, s 40, Sch 3, paras 5, 7; Children and Adoption Act 2006, ss 6, 15(2), Sch 3.

****

PART IV
CARE AND SUPERVISION

General

31 Care and supervision orders

(1)   On the application of any local authority or authorised person, the court may make an order –

(a)   placing the child with respect to whom the application is made in the care of a designated local authority; or

(b)   putting him under the supervision of a designated local authority

(2)   A court may only make a care order or supervision order if it is satisfied –

(a)   that the child concerned is suffering, or is likely to suffer, significant harm; and

(b)   that the harm, or likelihood of harm, is attributable to –

> (i)   the care given to the child, or likely to be given to him if the order were not made, not being what it would be reasonable to expect a parent to give to him; or
> (ii)   the child's being beyond parental control.

(3)   No care order or supervision order may be made with respect to a child who has reached the age of seventeen (or sixteen, in the case of a child who is married).

(3A)   No care order may be made with respect to a child until the court has considered a section 31A plan.

(4)   An application under this section may be made on its own or in any other family proceedings.

(5)   The court may –

> (a)   on an application for a care order, make a supervision order;
> (b)   on an application for a supervision order, make a care order.

(6)   Where an authorised person proposes to make an application under this section he shall–

> (a)   if it is reasonably practicable to do so; and
> (b)   before making the application,

consult the local authority appearing to him to be the authority in whose area the child concerned is ordinarily resident.

(7)   An application made by an authorised person shall not be entertained by the court if, at the time when it is made, the child concerned is –

> (a)   the subject of an earlier application for a care order, or supervision order, which has not been disposed of; or
> (b)   subject to –
>> (i)   a care order or supervision order;
>> (ii)   a youth rehabilitation order within the meaning of Part 1 of the Criminal Justice and Immigration Act 2008; or
>> (iii) (*applies to Scotland only*)

(8)   The local authority designated in a care order must be –

> (a)   the authority within whose area the child is ordinarily resident; or
> (b)   where the child does not reside in the area of a local authority, the authority within whose area any circumstances arose in consequence of which the order is being made.

(9)   In this section–

'authorised person' means –

> (a)   the National Society for the Prevention of Cruelty to Children and any of its officers; and
> (b)   any person authorised by order of the Secretary of State to bring proceedings under this section and any officer of a body which is so authorised;

'harm' means ill-treatment or the impairment of health or development including, for example, impairment suffered from seeing or hearing the ill-treatment of another ;

'development' means physical, intellectual, emotional, social or behavioural development;

'health' means physical or mental health; and

'ill-treatment' includes sexual abuse and forms of ill-treatment which are not physical.

(10)   Where the question of whether harm suffered by a child is significant turns on the child's health or development, his health or development shall be compared with that which could reasonably be expected of a similar child.

(11)   In this Act–

'a care order' means (subject to section 105(1)) an order under subsection (1)(a) and (except where express provision to the contrary is made) includes an interim care order made under section 38; and

'a supervision order' means an order under subsection (1)(b) and (except where express provision to the contrary is made) includes an interim supervision order made under section 38.

Amendments—Criminal Justice and Court Services Act 2000, ss 74, 75, Sch 7, paras 87, 90, Sch 8; Powers of Criminal Courts (Sentencing) Act 2000, s 165, Sch 9, para 127; Adoption and Children Act 2002, ss 120, 121(1); Criminal Justice and Immigration Act 2008, ss 6(2), Sch 4, Pt 1, paras 33, 35.

****

Effect and duration of orders etc

91 Effect and duration of orders etc

(1)   The making of a residence order with respect to a child who is the subject of a care order discharges the care order.

(2)   The making of a care order with respect to a child who is the subject of any section 8 order discharges that order.

(2A)   Where a contact activity direction has been made as regards contact with a child, the making of a care order with respect to the child discharges the direction.

(3)   The making of a care order with respect to a child who is the subject of a supervision order discharges that other order.

(4)   The making of a care order with respect to a child who is a ward of court brings that wardship to an end.

(5)   The making of a care order with respect to a child who is the subject of a school attendance order made under section 437 of the Education Act 1996 discharges the school attendance order.

(5A)   The making of a special guardianship order with respect to a child who is the subject of –

(a)   a care order; or

(b)   an order under section 34,discharges that order.

(6)   Where an emergency protection order is made with respect to a child who is in care, the care order shall have effect subject to the emergency protection order.

(7)   Any order made under section 4(1), 4ZA(1), 4A(1) or 5(1) shall continue in force until the child reaches the age of eighteen, unless it is brought to an end earlier.

(8)   Any–

    (a)   agreement under section 4, 4ZA or 4A; or

    (b)   appointment under section 5(3) or (4),

shall continue in force until the child reaches the age of eighteen, unless it is brought to an end earlier.

(9)   An order under Schedule 1 has effect as specified in that Schedule.

(10)   A section 8 order other than a residence order shall, if it would otherwise still be in force, cease to have effect when the child reaches the age of sixteen, unless it is to have effect beyond that age by virtue of section 9(6)

(11)   Where a section 8 order has effect with respect to a child who has reached the age of sixteen, it shall, if it would otherwise still be in force, cease to have effect when he reaches the age of eighteen.

(12)   Any care order, other than an interim care order, shall continue in force until the child reaches the age of eighteen, unless it is brought to an end earlier.

(13)   Any order made under any other provision of this Act in relation to a child shall, if it would otherwise still be in force, cease to have effect when he reaches the age of eighteen.

(14)   On disposing of any application for an order under this Act, the court may (whether or not it makes any other order in response to the application) order that no application for an order under this Act of any specified kind may be made with respect to the child concerned by any person named in the order without leave of the court.

(15)   Where an application ('the previous application') has been made for –

    (a)   the discharge of a care order;

    (b)   the discharge of a supervision order;

    (c)   the discharge of an education supervision order;

    (d)   the substitution of a supervision order for a care order; or

    (e)   a child assessment order,

no further application of a kind mentioned in paragraphs (a) to (e) may be made with respect to the child concerned, without leave of the court, unless the period between the disposal of the previous application and the making of the further application exceeds six months.

(16)   Subsection (15) does not apply to applications made in relation to interim orders.

(17)   Where –

    (a)   a person has made an application for an order under section 34;

    (b)   the application has been refused; and

    (c)   a period of less than six months has elapsed since the refusal,

that person may not make a further application for such an order with respect to the same child, unless he has obtained the leave of the court.

Amendments—Education Act 1996, s 582(1), Sch 37, Pt I, para 90; Adoption and Children Act 2002, ss 114(3), 139(1), Sch 3, paras 54, 68; Children and Adoption Act 2006, s 15(1), Sch 2, paras 7, 9; Human Fertilisation and Embryology Act 2008, s 56, Sch 6, Pt 1, para 29; Children and Young Persons Act 2008, ss 37(3), 42, Sch 4.

****

94 Appeals

(1)   Subject to any express provision to the contrary made by or under this Act, an appeal shall lie to a county court against–

(a)   the making by a magistrates' court of any order under this Act or the Adoption and Children Act 2002; or

(b)   any refusal by a magistrates' court to make such an order.

(2)   Where a magistrates' court has power, in relation to any proceedings under this Act or the Adoption and Children Act 2002, to decline jurisdiction because it considers that the case can more conveniently be dealt with by another court, no appeal shall lie against any exercise by that magistrates' court of that power.

(3)   ...

(4)   On an appeal under this section, a county court may make such orders as may be necessary to give effect to its determination of the appeal.

(5)   Where an order is made under subsection (4) a county court may also make such incidental or consequential orders as appear to it to be just.

(6)   ...

(7)   ...

(8)   ...

(9)   Any order of a county court made on an appeal under this section (other than one directing that an application be re-heard by a magistrates' court) shall, for the purposes –

(a)   of the enforcement of the order; and

(b)   of any power to vary, revive or discharge orders,

be treated as if it were an order of the magistrates' court from which the appeal was brought and not an order of a county court.

(10)   The Lord Chancellor, after consulting the Lord Chief Justice, may by order make provision as to the circumstances in which appeals may be made against decisions taken by courts on questions arising in connection with the transfer, or proposed transfer, of proceedings by virtue of any order under paragraph 2 of Schedule 11.

(11)   Except to the extent provided for in any order made under subsection (10), no appeal may be made against any decision of a kind mentioned in that subsection.

(12)   ...

Amendments—Courts and Legal Services Act 1990, s 116, Sch 16, para 23; Adoption and Children Act 2002, s 100; Constitutional Reform Act 2005, s 15(1), Sch 4, Pt 1, paras 203, 206(1)–(3); SI 2009/871.

****

96   Evidence given by, or with respect to, children

(1)   Subsection (2) applies where a child who is called as a witness in any civil proceedings does not, in the opinion of the court, understand the nature of an oath.

(2)   The child's evidence may be heard by the court if, in its opinion—

(a) he understands that it is his duty to speak the truth; and

(b) he has sufficient understanding to justify his evidence being heard.

(3)   The Lord Chancellor may, with the concurrence of the Lord Chief Justice, by order make provision for the admissibility of evidence which would otherwise be inadmissible under any rule of law relating to hearsay.

(4)–(7)   ...

97   Privacy for children involved in certain proceedings

(1)   Family Procedure Rules may make provision for a magistrates' court to sit in private in proceedings in which any powers under this Act or the Adoption and Children Act 2002 may be exercised by the court with respect to any child.

(2)   No person shall publish to the public at large or any section of the public any material which is intended, or likely, to identify –

(a)   any child as being involved in any proceedings before the High Court, a county court or a magistrates' court in which any power under this Act or the Adoption and Children Act 2002 may be exercised by the court with respect to that or any other child; or

(b)   an address or school as being that of a child involved in any such proceedings.

(3)   In any proceedings for an offence under this section it shall be a defence for the accused to prove that he did not know, and had no reason to suspect, that the published material was intended, or likely, to identify the child.

(4)   The court or the Lord Chancellor may, if satisfied that the welfare of the child requires it and, in the case of the Lord Chancellor, if the Lord Chief Justice agrees, by order dispense with the requirements of subsection (2) to such extent as may be specified in the order.

(5)   For the purposes of this section –

'publish' includes –
(a)   include in a programme service (within the meaning of the Broadcasting Act 1990); or
(b)   cause to be published; and

'material' includes any picture or representation.

(6)   Any person who contravenes this section shall be guilty of an offence and liable, on summary conviction, to a fine not exceeding level 4 on the standard scale.

(7)   Subsection (1) is without prejudice to –

(a)   ...
(b)   any other power of a magistrates' court to sit in private.

(8)   Sections 69 (sittings of magistrates' courts for family proceedings) and 71 (newspaper reports of certain proceedings) of the Act of 1980 shall apply in relation to any proceedings (before a magistrates' court) to which this section applies subject to the provisions of this section.

(9)   The Lord Chief Justice may nominate a judicial office holder (as defined in section 109(4) of the Constitutional Reform Act 2005) to exercise his functions under subsection (4).

Amendments—Broadcasting Act 1990, s 203(1), Sch 20, para 53; Courts and Legal Services Act 1990, s 116, Sch 16, para 24; SI 1992/709; Access to Justice Act 1999, s 72; Adoption and Children Act 2002, s 101(3); Courts Act 2003, s 109(1), Sch 8, para 337(1), (2); Children Act 2004, s 62(1); Constitutional Reform Act 2005, s 15(1), Sch 4, Pt 1, paras 203, 208(1)–(3).

****

105 Interpretation

(1) In this Act –

...

'care order' has the meaning given by section 31(11) and also includes any order which by or under any enactment has the effect of, or is deemed to be, a care order for the purposes of this Act; and any reference to a child who is in the care of an authority is a reference to a child who is in their care by virtue of a care order;

'child' means, subject to paragraph 16 of Schedule 1, a person under the age of eighteen;

...

'child of the family', in relation to parties to a marriage, or to two people who are civil partners of each other, means –
  (a)   a child of both of them, and
  (b)   any other child, other than a child placed with them as foster parents by a local authority or voluntary organisation, who has been treated by both of them as a child of their family;

...

'family proceedings' has the meaning given by section 8(3);

...

'harm' has the same meaning as in section 31(9) and the question of whether harm is significant shall be determined in accordance with section 31(10);

...

'ill-treatment' has the same meaning as in section 31(9);

...

'relative', in relation to a child, means a grandparent, brother, sister, uncle or aunt (whether of the full blood or half blood or by marriage or civil partnership) or step-parent;

(2) References in this Act to a child whose father and mother were, or (as the case may be) were not, married to each other at the time of his birth must be read with section 1 of the Family Law Reform Act 1987 (which extends the meaning of such references).

(3) References in this Act to –

  (a)   a person with whom a child lives, or is to live, as the result of a residence order; or
  (b)   a person in whose favour a residence order is in force,

shall be construed as references to the person named in the order as the person with whom the child is to live.

(4) References in this Act to a child who is looked after by a local authority have the same meaning as they have (by virtue of section 22) in Part III.

...

(6)   In determining the 'ordinary residence' of a child for any purpose of this Act, there shall be disregarded any period in which he lives in any place –

(a)   which is a school or other institution;

(b)   in accordance with the requirements of a supervision order under this Act

(ba)   in accordance with the requirements of a youth rehabilitation order under Part 1 of the Criminal Justice and Immigration Act 2008; or

(c)   while he is being provided with accommodation by or on behalf of a local authority.

...

Amendments—Local Government (Wales) Act 1994, Sch 10, para 13, Sch 18; Health Authorities Act 1995, ss 2(1), 5(1), Sch 1, Pt III, para 118(1), (10), Sch 3; Jobseekers Act 1995, s 41(4), Sch 2, para 19; Education Act 1996, s 582(1), Sch 37, Pt I, para 91; Family Law Act 1996, s 52, Sch 6, para 5; Care Standards Act 2000, ss 116, 117(2), Sch 4, para 14(1), (23)(a), Sch 6; Criminal Justice and Court Services Act 2000, s 74, Sch 7, paras 87, 95; Local Government Act 2000, s 107, Sch 5, para 22; Powers of Criminal Courts (Sentencing) Act 2000, s 165, Sch 9, para 129; SI 2000/90; Adoption and Children Act 2002, ss 139(1), Sch 3, paras 54, 70(a); SI 2002/2469; Children Act 2004, s 40, Sch 3, paras 5, 11; Civil Partnership Act 2004, s 75(1), (3); Childcare Act 2006, s 103, Sch 2, para 17, Sch 3, Pt 2; National Health Service (Consequential Provisions) Act 2006, s 2, Sch 1, paras 124, 125; SI 2007/961; Welfare Reform Act 2007, s 28(1), Sch 3, para 6(1), (5); Children and Adoption Act 2006, s 15(1), Sch 2, paras 7, 11; Human Fertilisation and Embryology Act 2008, s 56, Sch 6, Pt 1, para 31; Criminal Justice and Immigration Act 2008, ss 6(2), 149, Sch 4, Pt 1, paras 33, 36, Sch 28, Pt 1; Children and Young Persons Act 2008, s 8(2), Sch 1, para 3; SI 2010/1158; SI 2010/813.

FAMILY LAW REFORM ACT 1969

****

PART III
PROVISIONS FOR USE OF SCIENTIFIC TESTS IN DETERMINING PARENTAGE

Amendments—Family Law Reform Act 1987, s 33(1), Sch 2, paras 21–24.

20 Power of court to require use of scientific tests

(1) In any civil proceedings in which the parentage of any person falls to be determined, the court may, either of its own motion or on an application by any party to the proceedings, give a direction –

(a)   for the use of scientific tests to ascertain whether such tests show that a party to the proceedings is or is not the father or mother of that person; and

(b)   for the taking, within a period specified in the direction, of bodily samples from all or any of the following, namely, that person, any party who is alleged to be the father or mother of that person and any other party to the proceedings;

and the court may at any time revoke or vary a direction previously given by it under this subsection.

(1A)   Tests required by a direction under this section may only be carried out by a body which has been accredited for the purposes of this section by –

(a)   the Lord Chancellor, or

(b)   a body appointed by him for the purpose.

(2)   The individual carrying out scientific tests in pursuance of a direction under subsection (1) above shall make to the court a report in which he shall state –

(a)   the results of the tests;

(b)   whether any party to whom the report relates is or is not excluded by the results from being the father or mother of the person whose parentage is to be determined; and

(c)   in relation to any party who is not so excluded, the value, if any, of the results in determining whether that party is the father or mother of that person;

and the report shall be received by the court as evidence in the proceedings of the matters stated in it.

(2A)   Where the proceedings in which the parentage of any person falls to be determined are proceedings on an application under 55A or 56 of the Family Law Act 1986, any reference in subsection (1) or (2) of this section to any party to the proceedings shall include a reference to any person named in the application.

(3)   A report under subsection (2) of this section shall be in the form prescribed by regulations made under section 22 of this Act.

(4)   Where a report has been made to a court under subsection (2) of this section, any party may, with the leave of the court, or shall, if the court so directs, obtain from the tester a written statement explaining or amplifying any statement made in the report, and that statement shall be deemed for the purposes of this section (except subsection (3) thereof) to form part of the report made to the court.

(5)   Where a direction is given under this section in any proceedings, a party to the proceedings, unless the court otherwise directs, shall not be entitled to call as a witness the tester, or any other person by whom any thing necessary for the purpose of enabling those tests to be carried out was done, unless within fourteen days after receiving a copy of the report he serves notice on the other parties to the proceedings, or on such of them as the court may direct, of his intention to call the tester or that other person; and where the tester or any such person is called as a witness the party who called him shall be entitled to cross-examine him.

(6)   Where a direction is given under this section the party on whose application the direction is given shall pay the cost of taking and testing bodily samples for the purpose of giving effect to the direction (including any expenses reasonably incurred by any person in taking any steps required of him for the purpose), and of making a report to the court under this section, but the amount paid shall be treated as costs incurred by him in the proceedings.

Amendments—Family Law Reform Act 1987, ss 23(1), 33(1), Sch 2, paras 21–24; Child Support, Pensions and Social Security Act 2000, ss 82(1), (2), 83(5), Sch 8, para 9.

21 Consents, etc, required for taking of bodily samples

(1)   Subject to the provisions of subsections (3) and (4) of this section, a bodily sample which is required to be taken from any person for the purpose of giving effect to a direction under section 20 of this Act shall not be taken from that person except with his consent.

(2)   The consent of a minor who has attained the age of sixteen years to the taking from himself of a bodily sample shall be as effective as it would be if he were of full age; and where a minor has by virtue of this subsection given an effective consent to the taking of a bodily sample it shall not be necessary to obtain any consent for it from any other person.

(3)   A bodily sample may be taken from a person under the age of sixteen years, not being such a person as is referred to in subsection (4) of this section,

   (a)   if the person who has the care and control of him consents; or
   (b)   where that person does not consent, if the court considers that it would be in his best interests for the sample to be taken.

(4)   A bodily sample may be taken from a person who lacks capacity (within the meaning of the Mental Capacity Act 2005) to give his consent, if consent is given by the court giving the direction under section 20 or by –

   (a)   a donee of an enduring power of attorney or lasting power of attorney (within the meaning of that Act), or
   (b)   a deputy appointed, or any other person authorised, by the Court of Protection,

with power in that respect.

(5)   The foregoing provisions of this section are without prejudice to the provisions of section 23 of this Act.

Amendments—Mental Health Act 1983, s 148, Sch 4, para 25; Family Law Reform Act 1987, s 33(1), Sch 2, para 22; Child Support, Pensions and Social Security Act 2000, s 82(1), (3); Mental Capacity Act 2005, s 67(1), Sch 6, para 15.

22 Power to provide for manner of giving effect to direction of use of scientific tests

(1)   The Lord Chancellor may by regulation make provision as to the manner of giving effect to directions under section 20 of this Act and, in particular, any such regulations may –

(a)   provide that bodily samples shall not be taken except by registered medical practitioners or members of such professional bodies as may be prescribed by the regulations;

(aa)   prescribe the bodily samples to be taken;

(b)   regulate the taking, identification and transport of bodily samples;

(c)   require the production at the time when a bodily sample is to be taken of such evidence of the identity of the person from whom it is to be taken as may be prescribed by the regulations;

(d)   require any person from whom a bodily sample is to be taken, or, in such cases as may be prescribed by the regulations, such other person as may be so prescribed, to state in writing whether he or the person from whom the sample is to be taken, as the case may be, has during such period as may be specified in the regulations suffered from any such illness or condition or undergone any such treatment as may be so specified or received a transfusion of blood;

(e)   prescribe conditions which a body must meet in order to be eligible for accreditation for the purposes of section 20 of this Act;

(f)   prescribe the scientific tests to be carried out and the manner in which they are to be carried out;

(g)   regulate the charges that may be made for the taking and testing of bodily samples and for the making of a report to a court under section 20 of this Act;

(h)   make provision for securing that so far as practicable the bodily samples to be tested for the purpose of giving effect to a direction under section 20 of this Act are tested by the same person;

(i)   prescribe the form of the report to be made to a court under section 20 of this Act.

(j)   make different provision for different cases or for different descriptions of case.

(2)   The power to make regulations under this section shall be exercisable by statutory instrument which shall be subject to annulment in pursuance of a resolution of either House of Parliament.

Amendments—Family Law Reform Act 1987, s 33(1), Sch 2, para 23; SI 1992/709; Child Support, Pensions and Social Security Act 2000, s 82(1), (4).

23 Failure to comply with direction for takingscientific tests

(1)   Where a court gives a direction under section 20 of this Act and any person fails to take any step required of him for the purpose of giving effect to the direction, the court may draw such inferences, if any, from that fact as appear proper in the circumstances.

(2)   Where in any proceedings in which the parentage of any person falls to be determined by the court hearing the proceedings there is a presumption of law that that person is legitimate, then if –

(a)   a direction is given under section 20 of this Act in those proceedings, and

(b)   any party who is claiming any relief in the proceedings and who for the purpose of obtaining that relief is entitled to rely on the presumption fails to take any step required of him for the purpose of giving effect to the direction, the court may adjourn the hearing for such period as it thinks fit to enable that party to take that step, and if at the end of that period he has failed without reasonable cause to take it the court may, without prejudice to subsection (1) of this section, dismiss his claim for relief notwithstanding the absence of evidence to rebut the presumption.

(3)   Where any person named in a direction under section 20 of this Act fails to consent to the taking of a bodily sample from himself or from any person named in the direction of whom he has the care and control, he shall be deemed for the purposes of this section to have failed to take a step required of him for the purpose of giving effect to the direction.

Amendments—Family Law Reform Act 1987, s 33(1), Sch 2, para 24.

24 Penalty for personating another, etc, for purpose of providing bodily sample

If for the purpose of providing a bodily sample for a test required to give effect to a direction under section 20 of this Act any person personates another, or proffers a child knowing that it is not the child named in the direction, he shall be liable –

(a)   on conviction on indictment, to imprisonment for a term not exceeding two years, or

(b)   on summary conviction, to a fine not exceeding the prescribed sum.

Amendments—Magistrates' Courts Act 1980, s 32(2); Family Law Reform Act 1987, s 33(1), Sch 2, para 25.

25   Interpretation of Part III

In this Part of this Act the following expressions have the meanings hereby respectively assigned to them, that is to say –

'bodily sample' means a sample of bodily fluid or bodily tissue taken for the purpose of scientific tests;

'excluded' means excluded subject to the occurrence of mutation to section 27 of the Family Law Reform Act 1987, to sections 27 to 29 of the Human Fertilisation and Embryology Act 1990 and to sections 33 to 47 of the Human Fertilisation and Embryology Act 2008.

'scientific tests' means scientific tests carried out under this Part of this Act and made with the object of ascertaining the inheritable characteristics of bodily fluids or bodily tissue.

Amendments—Family Law Reform Act 1987, s 23; Human Fertilisation and Embryology Act 1990, s 49(5), Sch 4, para 1; Human Fertilisation and Embryology Act 2008, s 56, Sch 6, Pt 1, para 13.

PART IV
MISCELLANEOUS AND GENERAL

26   Rebuttal of presumption as to legitimacy and illegitimacy

Any presumption of law as to the legitimacy or illegitimacy of any person may in any civil proceedings be rebutted by evidence which shows that it is more probable than not that that person is illegitimate or legitimate, as the case may be, and it shall not be necessary to prove that fact beyond reasonable doubt in order to rebut the presumption.

****

FAMILY LAW ACT 1986

****

Chapter II
Jurisdiction of Courts in England and Wales

2 Jurisdiction: general

(1)   A court in England and Wales shall not make a section 1(1)(a) order with respect to a child unless

   (a)   it has jurisdiction under the Council Regulation, or

   (b)   the Council Regulation does not apply but

       (i)   the question of making the order arises in or in connection with matrimonial proceedings or civil partnership proceedings and the condition in section 2A of this Act is satisfied, or

       (ii)   the condition in section 3 of this Act is satisfied.

(2A)   A court in England and Wales shall not have jurisdiction to make a special guardianship order under the Children Act 1989 unless the condition in section 3 of this Act is satisfied.

(2B)   A court in England and Wales shall not have jurisdiction to make an order under section 26 of the Adoption and Children Act 2002 unless the condition in section 3 of this Act is satisfied.

(3)   A court in England and Wales shall not make a section 1(1)(d) order unless

   (a)   it has jurisdiction under the Council Regulation, or

   (b)   the Council Regulation does not apply but

       (i)   the condition in section 3 of this Act is satisfied, or

       (ii)   the child concerned is present in England and Wales on the relevant date and the court considers that the immediate exercise of its powers is necessary for his protection.

Amendments—Children Act 1989, s 108, Sch 13, para 64; Adoption and Children Act 2002, s 139(1), Sch 3, paras 46, 48; SI 2005/265; SI 2005/3336.

2A Jurisdiction in or in connection with matrimonial proceedings or civil partnership proceedings

(1)   The condition referred to in section 2(1) of this Act is that the proceedings are proceedings in respect of the marriage or civil partnership of the parents of the child concerned and–

   (a)   the proceedings –

       (i)   are proceedings for divorce or nullity of marriage, or dissolution or annulment of a civil partnership, and

       (ii)   are continuing;

   (b)   the proceedings –

       (i)   are proceedings for judicial separation or legal separation of civil partners,

       (ii)   are continuing,

and the jurisdiction of the court is not excluded by subsection (2) below; or

   (c)   the proceedings have been dismissed after the beginning of the trial but –

(i)   the section 1(1)(a) order is being made forthwith, or

(ii)   the application for the order was made on or before the dismissal.

(2)   For the purposes of subsection (1)(b) above, the jurisdiction of the court is excluded if –

(a)   after the grant of a decree of judicial separation, on the relevant date, proceedings for divorce or nullity in respect of the marriage, or

(b)   after the making of a separation order, on the relevant date, proceedings for dissolution or annulment in respect of the civil partnership,

are continuing in Scotland or Northern Ireland.

(3)   Subsection (2) above shall not apply if the court in which the other proceedings there referred to are continuing has made –

(a)   an order under section 13(6) or 19A(4) of this Act (not being an order made by virtue of section 13(6)(a)(i)), or a corresponding dependent territory order, or

(b)   an order under section 14(2) or 22(2) of this Act, or a corresponding dependent territory order, which is recorded as being made for the purpose of enabling Part I proceedings to be taken in England and Wales with respect to the child concerned.

(4)   Where a court –

(a)   has jurisdiction to make a section 1(1)(a) order by virtue of section 2(1)(b)(i) of this Act, but

(b)   considers that it would be more appropriate for Part I matters relating to the child to be determined outside England and Wales,

the court may by order direct that, while the order under this subsection is in force, no section 1(1)(a) order shall be made by any court by virtue of section 2(1)(b)(i) of this Act.

Amendments—Children Act 1989, s 108, Sch 13, para 64; SI 1991/1723; SI 1995/756; SI 2005/265; SI 2005/3336.

Prospective amendments—Family Law Act 1996, s 66(1), Sch 8, para 37(3), (5).

3   Habitual residence or presence of child

(1)   The condition referred to in section 2(1)(b)(ii) of this Act is that on the relevant date the child concerned –

(a)   is habitually resident in England and Wales, or

(b)   is present in England and Wales and is not habitually resident in any part of the United Kingdom or a specified dependent territory,

and, in either case, the jurisdiction of the court is not excluded by subsection (2) below.

(2)   For the purposes of subsection (1) above, the jurisdiction of the court is excluded if, on the relevant date, matrimonial proceedings or civil partnership proceedings are continuing in a court in Scotland, Northern Ireland or a specified dependent territory in respect of the marriage or civil partnership of the parents of the child concerned.

(3)   Subsection (2) above shall not apply if the court in which the other proceedings there referred to are continuing has made –

(a)   an order under section 13(6) or 19A(4) of this Act (not being an order made by virtue of section 13(6)(a)(i)), or a corresponding dependent territory order, or

(b)   an order under section 14(2) or 22(2) of this Act, or a corresponding
       dependent territory order, which is recorded as made for the purpose of
       enabling Part I proceedings with respect to the child concerned to be taken in
       England and Wales,

and that order is in force.

(4)–(6)   *(repealed)*

Amendments—Children Act 1989, s 108, Sch 13, para 65, Sch 15; SI 1991/1723; SI 1995/756; SI 2005/265;
SI 2005/3336.

****

41   Habitual residence after removal without consent, etc

(1)   Where a child who –

(a)   has not attained the age of sixteen, and
(b)   is habitually resident in a part of the United Kingdom or in a specified
       dependent territory,

becomes habitually resident outside that part of the United Kingdom or that territory in
consequence of circumstances of the kind specified in subsection (2) below, he shall be
treated for the purposes of this Part as continuing to be habitually resident in that part
of the United Kingdom or that territory for the period of one year beginning with the
date on which those circumstances arise.

(2)   The circumstances referred to in subsection (1) above exist where the child is
removed from or retained outside, or himself leaves or remains outside, the part of the
United Kingdom or the territory in which he was habitually resident before his change
of residence –

(a)   without the agreement of the person or all the persons having, under the law of
       that part of the United Kingdom or that territory, the right to determine
       where he is to reside, or
(b)   in contravention of an order made by a court in any part of the United
       Kingdom or in a specified dependent territory.

(3)   A child shall cease to be treated by virtue of subsection (1) above as habitually
resident in a part of the United Kingdom or a specified dependent territory if, during
the period there mentioned –

(a)   he attains the age of sixteen, or
(b)   he becomes habitually resident outside that part of the United Kingdom or
       that territory with the agreement of the person or persons mentioned in
       subsection (2)(a) above and not in contravention of an order made by a court
       in any part of the United Kingdom or in any specified dependent territory.

****

Amendments—SI 1991/1723.

55A   Declarations of parentage

(1)   Subject to the following provisions of this section, any person may apply to the
High Court, a county court or a magistrates' court for a declaration as to whether or not
a person named in the application is or was the parent of another person so named.

(2)   A court shall have jurisdiction to entertain an application under subsection (1) above if, and only if, either of the persons named in it for the purposes of that subsection –

(a)   is domiciled in England and Wales on the date of the application, or

(b)   has been habitually resident in England and Wales throughout the period of one year ending with that date, or

(c)   died before that date and either –

(i)   was at death domiciled in England and Wales, or

(ii)   had been habitually resident in England and Wales throughout the period of one year ending with the date of death.

(3)   Except in a case falling within subsection (4) below, the court shall refuse to hear an application under subsection (1) above unless it considers that the applicant has a sufficient personal interest in the determination of the application (but this is subject to section 27 of the Child Support Act 1991).

(4)   The excepted cases are where the declaration sought is as to whether or not –

(a)   the applicant is the parent of a named person;

(b)   a named person is the parent of the applicant; or

(c)   a named person is the other parent of a named child of the applicant.

(5)   Where an application under subsection (1) above is made and one of the persons named in it for the purposes of that subsection is a child, the court may refuse to hear the application if it considers that the determination of the application would not be in the best interests of the child.

(6)   Where a court refuses to hear an application under subsection (1) above it may order that the applicant may not apply again for the same declaration without leave of the court.

(7)   Where a declaration is made by a court on an application under subsection (1) above, the prescribed officer of the court shall notify the Registrar General, in such a manner and within such period as may be prescribed, of the making of that declaration.

Amendments—Child Support, Pensions and Social Security Act 2000, s 83(1), (2).

****

HUMAN RIGHTS ACT 1998

Schedule 1
The Articles

****

PART I
THE CONVENTION — RIGHTS AND FREEDOMS

Article 2
Right to life

1

Everyone's right to life shall be protected by law. No one shall be deprived of his life intentionally save in the execution of a sentence of a court following his conviction of a crime for which this penalty is provided by law.

2

Deprivation of life shall not be regarded as inflicted in contravention of this Article when it results from the use of force which is no more than absolutely necessary –

(a) in defence of any person from unlawful violence;
(b) in order to effect a lawful arrest or to prevent the escape of a person lawfully detained;
(c) in action lawfully taken for the purpose of quelling a riot or insurrection.

Article 3
Prohibition of torture

No one shall be subjected to torture or to inhuman or degrading treatment or punishment.

****

Article 5
Right to liberty and security

1

Everyone has the right to liberty and security of person. No one shall be deprived of his liberty save in the following cases and in accordance with a procedure prescribed by law –

(a) the lawful detention of a person after conviction by a competent court;
(b) the lawful arrest or detention of a person for non-compliance with the lawful order of a court or in order to secure the fulfilment of any obligation prescribed by law;
(c) the lawful arrest or detention of a person effected for the purpose of bringing him before the competent legal authority on reasonable suspicion of having committed an offence or when it is reasonably considered necessary to prevent his committing an offence or fleeing after having done so;

(d) the detention of a minor by lawful order for the purpose of educational supervision or his lawful detention for the purpose of bringing him before the competent legal authority;

(e) the lawful detention of persons for the prevention of the spreading of infectious diseases, of persons of unsound mind, alcoholics or drug addicts or vagrants;

(f) the lawful arrest or detention of a person to prevent his effecting an unauthorised entry into the country or of a person against whom action is being taken with a view to deportation or extradition.

2

Everyone who is arrested shall be informed promptly, in a language which he understands, of the reasons for his arrest and of any charge against him.

3

Everyone arrested or detained in accordance with the provisions of paragraph 1(c) of this Article shall be brought promptly before a judge or other officer authorised by law to exercise judicial power and shall be entitled to trial within a reasonable time or to release pending trial. Release may be conditioned by guarantees to appear for trial.

4

Everyone who is deprived of his liberty by arrest or detention shall be entitled to take proceedings by which the lawfulness of his detention shall be decided speedily by a court and his release ordered if the detention is not lawful.

5

Everyone who has been the victim of arrest or detention in contravention of the provisions of this Article shall have an enforceable right to compensation.

Article 6
Right to a fair trial

1

In the determination of his civil rights and obligations or of any criminal charge against him, everyone is entitled to a fair and public hearing within a reasonable time by an independent and impartial tribunal established by law. Judgment shall be pronounced publicly but the press and public may be excluded from all or part of the trial in the interest of morals, public order or national security in a democratic society, where the interests of juveniles or the protection of the private life of the parties so require, or to the extent strictly necessary in the opinion of the court in special circumstances where publicity would prejudice the interests of justice.

2

Everyone charged with a criminal offence shall be presumed innocent until proved guilty according to law.

3

Everyone charged with a criminal offence has the following minimum rights –

(a)   to be informed promptly, in a language which he understands and in detail, of the nature and cause of the accusation against him;

(b)   to have adequate time and facilities for the preparation of his defence;

(c)   to defend himself in person or through legal assistance of his own choosing or, if he has not sufficient means to pay for legal assistance, to be given it free when the interests of justice so require;

(d)   to examine or have examined witnesses against him and to obtain the attendance and examination of witnesses on his behalf under the same conditions as witnesses against him;

(e)   to have the free assistance of an interpreter if he cannot understand or speak the language used in court.

****

Article 8
Right to respect for private and family life

1

Everyone has the right to respect for his private and family life, his home and his correspondence.

2

There shall be no interference by a public authority with the exercise of this right except such as is in accordance with the law and is necessary in a democratic society in the interests of national security, public safety or the economic well-being of the country, for the prevention of disorder or crime, for the protection of health or morals, or for the protection of the rights and freedoms of others.

Article 9
Freedom of thought, conscience and religion

1

Everyone has the right to freedom of thought, conscience and religion; this right includes freedom to change his religion or belief and freedom, either alone or in community with others and in public or private, to manifest his religion or belief, in worship, teaching, practice and observance.

2

Freedom to manifest one's religion or beliefs shall be subject only to such limitations as are prescribed by law and are necessary in a democratic society in the interests of public safety, for the protection of public order, health or morals, or for the protection of the rights and freedoms of others.

Article 10
Freedom of expression

1

Everyone has the right to freedom of expression. This right shall include freedom to hold opinions and to receive and impart information and ideas without interference by public authority and regardless of frontiers. This Article shall not prevent States from requiring the licensing of broadcasting, television or cinema enterprises.

2

The exercise of these freedoms, since it carries with it duties and responsibilities, may be subject to such formalities, conditions, restrictions or penalties as are prescribed by law and are necessary in a democratic society, in the interests of national security, territorial integrity or public safety, for the prevention of disorder or crime, for the protection of health or morals, for the protection of the reputation or rights of others, for preventing the disclosure of information received in confidence, or for maintaining the authority and impartiality of the judiciary.

****

Article 12
Right to marry

Men and women of marriageable age have the right to marry and to found a family, according to the national laws governing the exercise of this right.

****

Article 14
Prohibition of discrimination

The enjoyment of the rights and freedoms set forth in this Convention shall be secured without discrimination on any ground such as sex, race, colour, language, religion, political or other opinion, national or social origin, association with a national minority, property, birth or other status.

****

Article 17
Prohibition of abuse of rights

Nothing in this Convention may be interpreted as implying for any State, group or person any right to engage in any activity or perform any act aimed at the destruction of any of the rights and freedoms set forth herein or at their limitation to a greater extent than is provided for in the Convention.

Article 18
Limitation on use of restrictions on rights

The restrictions permitted under this Convention to the said rights and freedoms shall not be applied for any purpose other than those for which they have been prescribed.

****

UN CONVENTION ON THE RIGHTS OF THE CHILD 1989

Adopted and opened for signature, ratification and accession by General Assembly resolution 44/25 of 20 November 1989

Entry into force 2 September 1990, in accordance with article 49

Preamble

The States Parties to the present Convention,

Considering that, in accordance with the principles proclaimed in the Charter of the United Nations, recognition of the inherent dignity and of the equal and inalienable rights of all members of the human family is the foundation of freedom, justice and peace in the world,

Bearing in mind that the peoples of the United Nations have, in the Charter, reaffirmed their faith in fundamental human rights and in the dignity and worth of the human person, and have determined to promote social progress and better standards of life in larger freedom,

Recognizing that the United Nations has, in the Universal Declaration of Human Rights and in the International Covenants on Human Rights, proclaimed and agreed that everyone is entitled to all the rights and freedoms set forth therein, without distinction of any kind, such as race, colour, sex, language, religion, political or other opinion, national or social origin, property, birth or other status,

Recalling that, in the Universal Declaration of Human Rights, the United Nations has proclaimed that childhood is entitled to special care and assistance,

Convinced that the family, as the fundamental group of society and the natural environment for the growth and well-being of all its members and particularly children, should be afforded the necessary protection and assistance so that it can fully assume its responsibilities within the community,

Recognizing that the child, for the full and harmonious development of his or her personality, should grow up in a family environment, in an atmosphere of happiness, love and understanding,

Considering that the child should be fully prepared to live an individual life in society, and brought up in the spirit of the ideals proclaimed in the Charter of the United Nations, and in particular in the spirit of peace, dignity, tolerance, freedom, equality and solidarity,

Bearing in mind that the need to extend particular care to the child has been stated in the Geneva Declaration of the Rights of the Child of 1924 and in the Declaration of the Rights of the Child adopted by the General Assembly on 20 November 1959 and recognized in the Universal Declaration of Human Rights, in the International Covenant on Civil and Political Rights (in particular in articles 23 and 24), in the International Covenant on Economic, Social and Cultural Rights (in particular in article 10) and in the statutes and relevant instruments of specialized agencies and international organizations concerned with the welfare of children,

Bearing in mind that, as indicated in the Declaration of the Rights of the Child, 'the child, by reason of his physical and mental immaturity, needs special safeguards and care, including appropriate legal protection, before as well as after birth',

Recalling the provisions of the Declaration on Social and Legal Principles relating to the Protection and Welfare of Children, with Special Reference to Foster Placement and Adoption Nationally and Internationally; the United Nations Standard Minimum Rules for the Administration of Juvenile Justice (The Beijing Rules); and the Declaration on the Protection of Women and Children in Emergency and Armed Conflict, Recognizing that, in all countries in the world, there are children living in exceptionally difficult conditions, and that such children need special consideration,

Taking due account of the importance of the traditions and cultural values of each people for the protection and harmonious development of the child, Recognizing the importance of international co-operation for improving the living conditions of children in every country, in particular in the developing countries,

Have agreed as follows:

****

Article 2

1. States Parties shall respect and ensure the rights set forth in the present Convention to each child within their jurisdiction without discrimination of any kind, irrespective of the child's or his or her parent's or legal guardian's race, colour, sex, language, religion, political or other opinion, national, ethnic or social origin, property, disability, birth or other status.

2. States Parties shall take all appropriate measures to ensure that the child is protected against all forms of discrimination or punishment on the basis of the status, activities, expressed opinions, or beliefs of the child's parents, legal guardians, or family members.

Article 3

1. In all actions concerning children, whether undertaken by public or private social welfare institutions, courts of law, administrative authorities or legislative bodies, the best interests of the child shall be a primary consideration.

2. States Parties undertake to ensure the child such protection and care as is necessary for his or her well-being, taking into account the rights and duties of his or her parents, legal guardians, or other individuals legally responsible for him or her, and, to this end, shall take all appropriate legislative and administrative measures.

3. States Parties shall ensure that the institutions, services and facilities responsible for the care or protection of children shall conform with the standards established by competent authorities, particularly in the areas of safety, health, in the number and suitability of their staff, as well as competent supervision.

****

Article 5

States Parties shall respect the responsibilities, rights and duties of parents or, where applicable, the members of the extended family or community as provided for by local custom, legal guardians or other persons legally responsible for the child, to provide, in a manner consistent with the evolving capacities of the child, appropriate direction and guidance in the exercise by the child of the rights recognized in the present Convention.

Article 6

1. States Parties recognize that every child has the inherent right to life.

2. States Parties shall ensure to the maximum extent possible the survival and development of the child.

Article 7

1. The child shall be registered immediately after birth and shall have the right from birth to a name, the right to acquire a nationality and. as far as possible, the right to know and be cared for by his or her parents.

2. States Parties shall ensure the implementation of these rights in accordance with their national law and their obligations under the relevant international instruments in this field, in particular where the child would otherwise be stateless.

Article 8

1. States Parties undertake to respect the right of the child to preserve his or her identity, including nationality, name and family relations as recognized by law without unlawful interference.

2. Where a child is illegally deprived of some or all of the elements of his or her identity, States Parties shall provide appropriate assistance and protection, with a view to re-establishing speedily his or her identity.

Article 9

1. States Parties shall ensure that a child shall not be separated from his or her parents against their will, except when competent authorities subject to judicial review determine, in accordance with applicable law and procedures, that such separation is necessary for the best interests of the child. Such determination may be necessary in a particular case such as one involving abuse or neglect of the child by the parents, or one where the parents are living separately and a decision must be made as to the child's place of residence.

2. In any proceedings pursuant to paragraph 1 of the present article, all interested parties shall be given an opportunity to participate in the proceedings and make their views known.

3. States Parties shall respect the right of the child who is separated from one or both parents to maintain personal relations and direct contact with both parents on a regular basis, except if it is contrary to the child's best interests.

4. Where such separation results from any action initiated by a State Party, such as the detention, imprisonment, exile, deportation or death (including death arising from any cause while the person is in the custody of the State) of one or both parents or of the child, that State Party shall, upon request, provide the parents, the child or, if appropriate, another member of the family with the essential information concerning the whereabouts of the absent member(s) of the family unless the provision of the information would be detrimental to the well-being of the child. States Parties shall further ensure that the submission of such a request shall of itself entail no adverse consequences for the person(s) concerned.

Article 10

1. In accordance with the obligation of States Parties under article 9, paragraph 1, applications by a child or his or her parents to enter or leave a State Party for the purpose of family reunification shall be dealt with by States Parties in a positive,

humane and expeditious manner. States Parties shall further ensure that the submission of such a request shall entail no adverse consequences for the applicants and for the members of their family.

2. A child whose parents reside in different States shall have the right to maintain on a regular basis, save in exceptional circumstances personal relations and direct contacts with both parents. Towards that end and in accordance with the obligation of States Parties under article 9, paragraph 1, States Parties shall respect the right of the child and his or her parents to leave any country, including their own, and to enter their own country. The right to leave any country shall be subject only to such restrictions as are prescribed by law and which are necessary to protect the national security, public order (ordre public), public health or morals or the rights and freedoms of others and are consistent with the other rights recognized in the present Convention.

Article 11

1. States Parties shall take measures to combat the illicit transfer and non-return of children abroad.

2. To this end, States Parties shall promote the conclusion of bilateral or multilateral agreements or accession to existing agreements.

Article 12

1. States Parties shall assure to the child who is capable of forming his or her own views the right to express those views freely in all matters affecting the child, the views of the child being given due weight in accordance with the age and maturity of the child.

2. For this purpose, the child shall in particular be provided the opportunity to be heard in any judicial and administrative proceedings affecting the child, either directly, or through a representative or an appropriate body, in a manner consistent with the procedural rules of national law.

Article 13

1. The child shall have the right to freedom of expression; this right shall include freedom to seek, receive and impart information and ideas of all kinds, regardless of frontiers, either orally, in writing or in print, in the form of art, or through any other media of the child's choice.

2. The exercise of this right may be subject to certain restrictions, but these shall only be such as are provided by law and are necessary:

(a)   For respect of the rights or reputations of others; or
(b)   For the protection of national security or of public order (ordre public), or of public health or morals.

Article 14

1. States Parties shall respect the right of the child to freedom of thought, conscience and religion.

2. States Parties shall respect the rights and duties of the parents and, when applicable, legal guardians, to provide direction to the child in the exercise of his or her right in a manner consistent with the evolving capacities of the child.

3. Freedom to manifest one's religion or beliefs may be subject only to such limitations as are prescribed by law and are necessary to protect public safety, order, health or morals, or the fundamental rights and freedoms of others.

Article 15

1. States Parties recognize the rights of the child to freedom of association and to freedom of peaceful assembly.

2. No restrictions may be placed on the exercise of these rights other than those imposed in conformity with the law and which are necessary in a democratic society in the interests of national security or public safety, public order (ordre public), the protection of public health or morals or the protection of the rights and freedoms of others.

Article 16

1. No child shall be subjected to arbitrary or unlawful interference with his or her privacy, family, or correspondence, nor to unlawful attacks on his or her honour and reputation.

2. The child has the right to the protection of the law against such interference or attacks.

****

COUNCIL REGULATION (EC) NO 2201/2003

of 27 November 2003

concerning jurisdiction and the recognition and enforcement of judgments in matrimonial matters and the matters of parental responsibility, repealing Regulation (EC) No 1347/2000

THE COUNCIL OF THE EUROPEAN UNION,

Having regard to the Treaty establishing the European Community, and in particular Article 61(*c*) and Article 67(1) thereof,

Having regard to the proposal from the Commission,

Having regard to the opinion of the European Parliament,

Having regard to the opinion of the European Economic and Social Committee,

Whereas:

(1) The European Community has set the objective of creating an area of freedom, security and justice, in which the free movement of persons is ensured. To this end, the Community is to adopt, among others, measures in the field of judicial cooperation in civil matters that are necessary for the proper functioning of the internal market.

(2) The Tampere European Council endorsed the principle of mutual recognition of judicial decisions as the cornerstone for the creation of a genuine judicial area, and identified visiting rights as a priority.

(3) Council Regulation (EC) No 1347/2000 sets out rules on jurisdiction, recognition and enforcement of judgments in matrimonial matters and matters of parental responsibility for the children of both spouses rendered on the occasion of the matrimonial proceedings. The content of this Regulation was substantially taken over from the Convention of 28 May 1998 on the same subject matter.

(4) On 3 July 2000 France presented an initiative for a Council Regulation on the mutual enforcement of judgments on rights of access to children.

(5) In order to ensure equality for all children, this Regulation covers all decisions on parental responsibility, including measures for the protection of the child, independently of any link with a matrimonial proceeding.

(6) Since the application of the rules on parental responsibility often arises in the context of matrimonial proceedings, it is more appropriate to have a single instrument for matters of divorce and parental responsibility.

(7) The scope of this Regulation covers civil matters, whatever the nature of the court or tribunal.

(8) As regards judgments on divorce, legal separation or marriage annulment, this Regulation should apply only to the dissolution of matrimonial ties and should not deal with issues such as the grounds for divorce, property consequences of the marriage or any other ancillary measures.

(9) As regards the property of the child, this Regulation should apply only to measures for the protection of the child, i.e. (i) the designation and functions of a person or body having charge of the child's property, representing or assisting the child, and (ii) the administration, conservation or disposal of the child's property. In this context, this Regulation should, for instance, apply in cases where the parents are in dispute as

regards the administration of the child's property. Measures relating to the child's property which do not concern the protection of the child should continue to be governed by Council Regulation (EC) No 44/2001 of 22 December 2000 on jurisdiction and the recognition and enforcement of judgments in civil and commercial matters.

(10) This Regulation is not intended to apply to matters relating to social security, public measures of a general nature in matters of education or health or to decisions on the right of asylum and on immigration. In addition it does not apply to the establishment of parenthood, since this is a different matter from the attribution of parental responsibility, nor to other questions linked to the status of persons. Moreover, it does not apply to measures taken as a result of criminal offences committed by children.

(11) Maintenance obligations are excluded from the scope of this Regulation as these are already covered by Council Regulation No 44/2001. The courts having jurisdiction under this Regulation will generally have jurisdiction to rule on maintenance obligations by application of Article 5(2) of Council Regulation No 44/2001.

(12) The grounds of jurisdiction in matters of parental responsibility established in the present Regulation are shaped in the light of the best interests of the child, in particular on the criterion of proximity. This means that jurisdiction should lie in the first place with the Member State of the child's habitual residence, except for certain cases of a change in the child's residence or pursuant to an agreement between the holders of parental responsibility.

(13) In the interest of the child, this Regulation allows, by way of exception and under certain conditions, that the court having jurisdiction may transfer a case to a court of another Member State if this court is better placed to hear the case. However, in this case the second court should not be allowed to transfer the case to a third court.

(14) This Regulation should have effect without prejudice to the application of public international law concerning diplomatic immunities. Where jurisdiction under this Regulation cannot be exercised by reason of the existence of diplomatic immunity in accordance with international law, jurisdiction should be exercised in accordance with national law in a Member State in which the person concerned does not enjoy such immunity.

(15) Council Regulation (EC) No 1348/2000 of 29 May 2000 on the service in the Member States of judicial and extrajudicial documents in civil or commercial matters should apply to the service of documents in proceedings instituted pursuant to this Regulation.

(16) This Regulation should not prevent the courts of a Member State from taking provisional, including protective measures, in urgent cases, with regard to persons or property situated in that State.

(17) In cases of wrongful removal or retention of a child, the return of the child should be obtained without delay, and to this end the Hague Convention of 25 October 1980 would continue to apply as complemented by the provisions of this Regulation, in particular Article 11. The courts of the Member State to or in which the child has been wrongfully removed or retained should be able to oppose his or her return in specific, duly justified cases. However, such a decision could be replaced by a subsequent decision by the court of the Member State of habitual residence of the child prior to the wrongful removal or retention. Should that judgment entail the return of the child, the

return should take place without any special procedure being required for recognition and enforcement of that judgment in the Member State to or in which the child has been removed or retained.

(18) Where a court has decided not to return a child on the basis of Article 13 of the 1980 Hague Convention, it should inform the court having jurisdiction or central authority in the Member State where the child was habitually resident prior to the wrongful removal or retention. Unless the court in the latter Member State has been seised, this court or the central authority should notify the parties. This obligation should not prevent the central authority from also notifying the relevant public authorities in accordance with national law.

(19) The hearing of the child plays an important role in the application of this Regulation, although this instrument is not intended to modify national procedures applicable.

(20) The hearing of a child in another Member State may take place under the arrangements laid down in Council Regulation (EC) No 1206/2001 of 28 May 2001 on cooperation between the courts of the Member States in the taking of evidence in civil or commercial matters.

(21) The recognition and enforcement of judgments given in a Member State should be based on the principle of mutual trust and the grounds for non-recognition should be kept to the minimum required.

(22) Authentic instruments and agreements between parties that are enforceable in one Member State should be treated as equivalent to "judgments" for the purpose of the application of the rules on recognition and enforcement.

(23) The Tampere European Council considered in its conclusions (point 34) that judgments in the field of family litigation should be "automatically recognised throughout the Union without any intermediate proceedings or grounds for refusal of enforcement". This is why judgments on rights of access and judgments on return that have been certified in the Member State of origin in accordance with the provisions of this Regulation should be recognised and enforceable in all other Member States without any further procedure being required. Arrangements for the enforcement of such judgments continue to be governed by national law.

(24) The certificate issued to facilitate enforcement of the judgment should not be subject to appeal. It should be rectified only where there is a material error, i.e. where it does not correctly reflect the judgment.

(25) Central authorities should cooperate both in general matter and in specific cases, including for purposes of promoting the amicable resolution of family disputes, in matters of parental responsibility. To this end central authorities shall participate in the European Judicial Network in civil and commercial matters created by Council Decision 2001/470/EC of 28 May 2001 establishing a European Judicial Network in civil and commercial matters.

(26) The Commission should make publicly available and update the lists of courts and redress procedures communicated by the Member States.

(27) The measures necessary for the implementation of this Regulation should be adopted in accordance with Council Decision 1999/468/EC of 28 June 1999 laying down the procedures for the exercise of implementing powers conferred on the Commission.

(28) This Regulation replaces Regulation (EC) No 1347/2000 which is consequently repealed.

(29) For the proper functioning of this Regulation, the Commission should review its application and propose such amendments as may appear necessary.

(30) The United Kingdom and Ireland, in accordance with Article 3 of the Protocol on the position of the United Kingdom and Ireland annexed to the Treaty on European Union and the Treaty establishing the European Community, have given notice of their wish to take part in the adoption and application of this Regulation.

(31) Denmark, in accordance with Articles 1 and 2 of the Protocol on the position of Denmark annexed to the Treaty on European Union and the Treaty establishing the European Community, is not participating in the adoption of this Regulation and is therefore not bound by it nor subject to its application.

(32) Since the objectives of this Regulation cannot be sufficiently achieved by the Member States and can therefore be better achieved at Community level, the Community may adopt measures, in accordance with the principle of subsidiarity as set out in Article 5 of the Treaty. In accordance with the principle of proportionality, as set out in that Article, this Regulation does not go beyond what is necessary in order to achieve those objectives.

(33) This Regulation recognises the fundamental rights and observes the principles of the Charter of Fundamental Rights of the European Union. In particular, it seeks to ensure respect for the fundamental rights of the child as set out in Article 24 of the Charter of Fundamental Rights of the European Union,

HAS ADOPTED THE PRESENT REGULATION:

Chapter I
Scope and Definitions

Article 1
Scope

1 This Regulation shall apply, whatever the nature of the court or tribunal, in civil matters relating to:

    (a)   divorce, legal separation or marriage annulment;
    (b)   the attribution, exercise, delegation, restriction or termination of parental responsibility.

2 The matters referred to in paragraph 1(b) may, in particular, deal with:

    (a)   rights of custody and rights of access;
    (b)   guardianship, curatorship and similar institutions;
    (c)   the designation and functions of any person or body having charge of the child's person or property, representing or assisting the child;
    (d)   the placement of the child in a foster family or in institutional care;
    (e)   measures for the protection of the child relating to the administration, conservation or disposal of the child's property.

3 This Regulation shall not apply to:

    (a)   the establishment or contesting of a parent-child relationship;
    (b)   decisions on adoption, measures preparatory to adoption, or the annulment or revocation of adoption;
    (c)   the name and forenames of the child;
    (d)   emancipation;
    (e)   maintenance obligations;

(*f*)   trusts or succession;

(*g*)   measures taken as a result of criminal offences committed by children.

Article 2
Definitions

For the purposes of this Regulation:

1 the term "court" shall cover all the authorities in the Member States with jurisdiction in the matters falling within the scope of this Regulation pursuant to Article 1;

2 the term "judge" shall mean the judge or an official having powers equivalent to those of a judge in the matters falling within the scope of the Regulation;

3 the term "Member State" shall mean all Member States with the exception of Denmark;

4 the term "judgment" shall mean a divorce, legal separation or marriage annulment, as well as a judgment relating to parental responsibility, pronounced by a court of a Member State, whatever the judgment may be called, including a decree, order or decision;

5 the term "Member State of origin" shall mean the Member State where the judgment to be enforced was issued;

6 the term "Member State of enforcement" shall mean the Member State where enforcement of the judgment is sought;

7 the term "parental responsibility" shall mean all rights and duties relating to the person or the property of a child which are given to a natural or legal person by judgment, by operation of law or by an agreement having legal effect. The term shall include rights of custody and rights of access;

8 the term "holder of parental responsibility" shall mean any person having parental responsibility over a child;

9 the term "rights of custody" shall include rights and duties relating to the care of the person of a child, and in particular the right to determine the child's place of residence;

10 the term "rights of access" shall include in particular the right to take a child to a place other than his or her habitual residence for a limited period of time;

11 the term "wrongful removal or retention" shall mean a child's removal or retention where:

(*a*)   it is in breach of rights of custody acquired by judgment or by operation of law or by an agreement having legal effect under the law of the Member State where the child was habitually resident immediately before the removal or retention; and

(*b*)   provided that, at the time of removal or retention, the rights of custody were actually exercised, either jointly or alone, or would have been so exercised but for the removal or retention. Custody shall be considered to be exercised jointly when, pursuant to a judgment or by operation of law, one holder of parental responsibility cannot decide on the child's place of residence without the consent of another holder of parental responsibility.

****

Section 2
Parental responsibility

Article 8
General jurisdiction

1 The courts of a Member State shall have jurisdiction in matters of parental responsibility over a child who is habitually resident in that Member State at the time the court is seised.

2 Paragraph 1 shall be subject to the provisions of Articles 9, 10 and 12.

Article 9
Continuing jurisdiction of the child's former habitual residence

1 Where a child moves lawfully from one Member State to another and acquires a new habitual residence there, the courts of the Member State of the child's former habitual residence shall, by way of exception to Article 8, retain jurisdiction during a three-month period following the move for the purpose of modifying a judgment on access rights issued in that Member State before the child moved, where the holder of access rights pursuant to the judgment on access rights continues to have his or her habitual residence in the Member State of the child's former habitual residence.

2 Paragraph 1 shall not apply if the holder of access rights referred to in paragraph 1 has accepted the jurisdiction of the courts of the Member State of the child's new habitual residence by participating in proceedings before those courts without contesting their jurisdiction.

****

Article 12
Prorogation of jurisdiction

1 The courts of a Member State exercising jurisdiction by virtue of Article 3 on an application for divorce, legal separation or marriage annulment shall have jurisdiction in any matter relating to parental responsibility connected with that application where:

(a)   at least one of the spouses has parental responsibility in relation to the child; and

(b)   the jurisdiction of the courts has been accepted expressly or otherwise in an unequivocal manner by the spouses and by the holders of parental responsibility, at the time the court is seised, and is in the superior interests of the child.

2 The jurisdiction conferred in paragraph 1 shall cease as soon as:

(a)   the judgment allowing or refusing the application for divorce, legal separation or marriage annulment has become final;

(b)   in those cases where proceedings in relation to parental responsibility are still pending on the date referred to in (a), a judgment in these proceedings has become final;

(c)   the proceedings referred to in (a) and (b) have come to an end for another reason.

3 The courts of a Member State shall also have jurisdiction in relation to parental responsibility in proceedings other than those referred to in paragraph 1 where:

(*a*)   the child has a substantial connection with that Member State, in particular by virtue of the fact that one of the holders of parental responsibility is habitually resident in that Member State or that the child is a national of that Member State; and

(*b*)   the jurisdiction of the courts has been accepted expressly or otherwise in an unequivocal manner by all the parties to the proceedings at the time the court is seised and is in the best interests of the child.

4 Where the child has his or her habitual residence in the territory of a third State which is not a contracting party to the Hague Convention of 19 October 1996 on jurisdiction, applicable law, recognition, enforcement and cooperation in respect of parental responsibility and measures for the protection of children, jurisdiction under this Article shall be deemed to be in the child's interest, in particular if it is found impossible to hold proceedings in the third State in question.

Article 13
Jurisdiction based on the child's presence

1 Where a child's habitual residence cannot be established and jurisdiction cannot be determined on the basis of Article 12, the courts of the Member State where the child is present shall have jurisdiction.

2 Paragraph 1 shall also apply to refugee children or children internationally displaced because of disturbances occurring in their country.

Article 14
Residual jurisdiction

Where no court of a Member State has jurisdiction pursuant to Articles 8 to 13, jurisdiction shall be determined, in each Member State, by the laws of that State.

****

Appendix 2

PROCEDURAL RULES

FAMILY PROCEDURE RULES 2010

SI 2010/2955

PART 1
OVERRIDING OBJECTIVE

CONTENTS OF THIS PART

1.1 The overriding objective

(1) These rules are a new procedural code with the overriding objective of enabling the court to deal with cases justly, having regard to any welfare issues involved.

(2) Dealing with a case justly includes, so far as is practicable –

    (a) ensuring that it is dealt with expeditiously and fairly;

    (b) dealing with the case in ways which are proportionate to the nature, importance and complexity of the issues;

    (c) ensuring that the parties are on an equal footing;

    (d) saving expense; and

    (e) allotting to it an appropriate share of the court's resources, while taking into account the need to allot resources to other cases.

1.2 Application by the court of the overriding objective

The court must seek to give effect to the overriding objective when it –

    (a) exercises any power given to it by these rules; or

    (b) interprets any rule.

1.3 Duty of the parties

The parties are required to help the court to further the overriding objective.

1.4 Court's duty to manage cases

(1) The court must further the overriding objective by actively managing cases.

(2) Active case management includes –

(*a*)   encouraging the parties to co-operate with each other in the conduct of the proceedings;

(*b*)   identifying at an early stage –
    (i)   the issues; and
    (ii)   who should be a party to the proceedings;

(*c*)   deciding promptly –
    (i)   which issues need full investigation and hearing and which do not; and
    (ii)   the procedure to be followed in the case;

(*d*)   deciding the order in which issues are to be resolved;

(*e*)   encouraging the parties to use an alternative dispute resolution procedure if the court considers that appropriate and facilitating the use of such procedure;

(*f*)   helping the parties to settle the whole or part of the case;

(*g*)   fixing timetables or otherwise controlling the progress of the case;

(*h*)   considering whether the likely benefits of taking a particular step justify the cost of taking it;

(*i*)   dealing with as many aspects of the case as it can on the same occasion;

(*j*)   dealing with the case without the parties needing to attend at court;

(*k*)   making use of technology; and

(*l*)   giving directions to ensure that the case proceeds quickly and efficiently.

****

PART 3
ALTERNATIVE DISPUTE RESOLUTION: THE COURT'S POWERS

CONTENTS OF THIS PART

3.1 Scope of this Part

(1) This Part contains the court's powers to encourage the parties to use alternative dispute resolution and to facilitate its use.

(2) The powers in this Part are subject to any powers given to the court by any other rule or practice direction or by any other enactment or any powers it may otherwise have.

3.2 Court's duty to consider alternative dispute resolution

The court must consider, at every stage in proceedings, whether alternative dispute resolution is appropriate.

3.3 When the court will adjourn proceedings or a hearing in proceedings

(1) If the court considers that alternative dispute resolution is appropriate, the court may direct that the proceedings, or a hearing in the proceedings, be adjourned for such specified period as it considers appropriate –

(*a*)   to enable the parties to obtain information and advice about alternative dispute resolution; and

(*b*)   where the parties agree, to enable alternative dispute resolution to take place.

(2) The court may give directions under this rule on an application or of its own initiative.

(3) Where the court directs an adjournment under this rule, it will give directions about the timing and method by which the parties must tell the court if any of the issues in the proceedings have been resolved.

(4) If the parties do not tell the court if any of the issues have been resolved as directed under paragraph (3), the court will give such directions as to the management of the case as it considers appropriate.

(5) The court or court officer will –

    (*a*)   record the making of an order under this rule; and

    (*b*)   arrange for a copy of the order to be served as soon as practicable on the parties.

(6) Where the court proposes to exercise its powers of its own initiative the procedure set out in rule 4.3(2) to (6) applies.

    (By rule 4.1(7), any direction given under this rule may be varied or revoked.)

****

PART 4
GENERAL CASE MANAGEMENT POWERS

CONTENTS OF THIS PART

4.1 The court's general powers of management

(1) In this Part, "statement of case" means the whole or part of, an application form or answer.

(2) The list of powers in this rule is in addition to any powers given to the court by any other rule or practice direction or by any other enactment or any powers it may otherwise have.

(3) Except where these rules provide otherwise, the court may –

    (*a*)   extend or shorten the time for compliance with any rule, practice direction or court order (even if an application for extension is made after the time for compliance has expired);

    (*b*)   make such order for disclosure and inspection, including specific disclosure of documents, as it thinks fit;

    (*c*)   adjourn or bring forward a hearing;

    (*d*)   require a party or a party's legal representative to attend the court;

    (*e*)   hold a hearing and receive evidence by telephone or by using any other method of direct oral communication;

(*f*)   direct that part of any proceedings be dealt with as separate proceedings;

(*g*)   stay the whole or part of any proceedings or judgment either generally or until a specified date or event;

(*h*)   consolidate proceedings;

(*i*)   hear two or more applications on the same occasion;

(*j*)   direct a separate hearing of any issue;

(*k*)   decide the order in which issues are to be heard;

(*l*)   exclude an issue from consideration;

(*m*)   dismiss or give a decision on an application after a decision on a preliminary issue;

(*n*)   direct any party to file and serve an estimate of costs; and

(*o*)   take any other step or make any other order for the purpose of managing the case and furthering the overriding objective.

(Rule 21.1 explains what is meant by disclosure and inspection.)

(4) When the court makes an order, it may –

(*a*)   make it subject to conditions, including a condition to pay a sum of money into court; and

(*b*)   specify the consequence of failure to comply with the order or a condition.

(5) Where the court gives directions it will take into account whether or not a party has complied with any relevant pre-action protocol(GL).

(6) A power of the court under these rules to make an order includes a power to vary or revoke the order.

(7) Any provision in these rules –

(*a*)   requiring or permitting directions to be given by the court is to be taken as including provision for such directions to be varied or revoked; and

(*b*)   requiring or permitting a date to be set is to be taken as including provision for that date to be changed or cancelled.

(8) The court may not extend the period within which an application for a section 89 order must be made.

Amendments-SI 2012/0000.

4.2 Court officer's power to refer to the court

Where a step is to be taken by a court officer –

(*a*)   the court officer may consult the court before taking that step;

(*b*)   the step may be taken by the court instead of the court officer.

4.3 Court's power to make order of its own initiative

(1) Except where an enactment provides otherwise, the court may exercise its powers on an application or of its own initiative.

(Part 18 sets out the procedure for making an application.)

(2) Where the court proposes to make an order of its own initiative –

(*a*)   it may give any person likely to be affected by the order an opportunity to make representations; and (*b*) where it does so it must specify the time by and the manner in which the representations must be made.

(3) Where the court proposes –

(*a*) to make an order of its own initiative; and
(*b*) to hold a hearing to decide whether to make the order,

it must give each party likely to be affected by the order at least 5 days' notice of the hearing.

(4) The court may make an order of its own initiative without hearing the parties or giving them an opportunity to make representations.

(5) Where the court has made an order under paragraph (4) –

(*a*) a party affected by the order may apply to have it set aside, varied or stayed; and
(*b*) the order must contain a statement of the right to make such an application.

(6) An application under paragraph (5)(*a*) must be made –

(*a*) within such period as may be specified by the court; or
(*b*) if the court does not specify a period, within 7 days beginning with the date on which the order was served on the party making the application.

(7) If the High Court or a county court of its own initiative strikes out a statement of case or dismisses an application (including an application for permission to appeal) and it considers that the application is totally without merit –

(*a*) the court's order must record that fact; and
(*b*) the court must at the same time consider whether it is appropriate to make a civil restraint order.

4.4 Power to strike out a statement of case

(1) Except in proceedings to which Parts 12 to 14 apply, the court may strike out^(GL) a statement of case if it appears to the court –

(*a*) that the statement of case discloses no reasonable grounds for bringing or defending the application;
(*b*) that the statement of case is an abuse of the court's process or is otherwise likely to obstruct the just disposal of the proceedings;
(*c*) that there has been a failure to comply with a rule, practice direction or court order; or
(*d*) in relation to applications for matrimonial and civil partnership orders and answers to such applications, that the parties to the proceedings consent.

(2) When the court strikes out a statement of case it may make any consequential order it considers appropriate.

(3) Where –

(*a*) the court has struck out an applicant's statement of case;
(*b*) the applicant has been ordered to pay costs to the respondent; and
(*c*) before paying those costs, the applicant starts another application against the same respondent, arising out of facts which are the same or substantially the same as those relating to the application in which the statement of case was struck out,

the court may, on the application of the respondent, stay that other application until the costs of the first application have been paid.

(4) Paragraph (1) does not limit any other power of the court to strike out a statement of case.

(5) If the High Court or a county court strikes out an applicant's statement of case and it considers that the application is totally without merit –

(*a*)   the court's order must record that fact; and
(*b*)   the court must at the same time consider whether it is appropriate to make a civil restraint order.

4.5 Sanctions have effect unless defaulting party obtains relief

(1) Where a party has failed to comply with a rule, practice direction or court order, any sanction for failure to comply imposed by the rule, practice direction or court order has effect unless the party in default applies for and obtains relief from the sanction.

> (Rule 4.6 sets out the circumstances which the court may consider on an application to grant relief from a sanction.)

(2) Where the sanction is the payment of costs, the party in default may only obtain relief by appealing against the order for costs.

(3) Where a rule, practice direction or court order –

(*a*)   requires a party to do something within a specified time; and
(*b*)   specifies the consequence of failure to comply,

the time for doing the act in question may not be extended by agreement between the parties.

4.6 Relief from sanctions

(1) On an application for relief from any sanction imposed for a failure to comply with any rule, practice direction or court order the court will consider all the circumstances including –

(*a*)   the interests of the administration of justice;
(*b*)   whether the application for relief has been made promptly;
(*c*)   whether the failure to comply was intentional;
(*d*)   whether there is a good explanation for the failure;
(*e*)   the extent to which the party in default has complied with other rules, practice directions, court orders and any relevant pre –action protocol(GL);
(*f*)   whether the failure to comply was caused by the party or the party's legal representative;
(*g*)   whether the hearing date or the likely hearing date can still be met if relief is granted;
(*h*)   the effect which the failure to comply had on each party; and
(*i*)   the effect which the granting of relief would have on each party or a child whose interest the court considers relevant.

(2) An application for relief must be supported by evidence.

4.7 General power of the court to rectify matters where there has been an error of procedure

Where there has been an error of procedure such as a failure to comply with a rule or practice direction –

(*a*)   the error does not invalidate any step taken in the proceedings unless the court so orders; and

(*b*)   the court may make an order to remedy the error.

4.8 Power of the court to make civil restraint orders

Practice Direction 4B sets out –

(*a*)   the circumstances in which the High Court or a county court has the power to make a civil restraint order against a party to proceedings;

(*b*)   the procedure where a party applies for a civil restraint order against another party; and

(*c*)   the consequences of the court making a civil restraint order.

****

PART 12
PROCEEDINGS RELATING TO CHILDREN EXCEPT PARENTAL ORDER PROCEEDINGS AND PROCEEDINGS FOR APPLICATIONS IN ADOPTION, PLACEMENT AND RELATED PROCEEDINGS

CONTENTS OF THIS PART

Chapter 1
Interpretation and Application of this Part

12.1 Application of this Part

(1) The rules in this Part apply to –

    (*a*)   emergency proceedings;

    (*b*)   private law proceedings;

    (*c*)   public law proceedings;

    (*d*)   proceedings relating to the exercise of the court's inherent jurisdiction (other than applications for the court's permission to start such proceedings);

    (*e*)   proceedings relating to child abduction and the recognition and enforcement of decisions relating to custody under the European Convention;

    (*f*)   proceedings relating to the Council Regulation or the 1996 Hague Convention in respect of children; and

    (*g*)   any other proceedings which may be referred to in a practice direction.

    (Part 18 sets out the procedure for making an application for permission to bring proceedings.)

    (Part 31 sets out the procedure for making applications for recognition and enforcement of judgments under the Council Regulation or the 1996 Hague Convention.)

(2) The rules in Chapter 7 of this Part also apply to family proceedings which are not within paragraph (1) but which otherwise relate wholly or mainly to the maintenance or upbringing of a minor.

12.2 Interpretation

In this Part –

    "the 2006 Act" means the Childcare Act 2006;

    "advocate" means a person exercising a right of audience as a representative of, or on behalf of, a party;

    "care proceedings" means proceedings for a care order under section 31(1)(*a*) of the 1989 Act;

"Case Management Order" means an order in the form referred to in Practice Direction 12A which may contain such of the provisions listed in that practice direction as may be appropriate to the proceedings;

"child assessment order" has the meaning assigned to it by section 43(2) of the 1989 Act;

"contact activity condition" has the meaning assigned to it by section 11C(2) of the 1989 Act;

"contact activity direction" has the meaning assigned to it by section 11A(3) of the 1989 Act;

"contribution order" has the meaning assigned to it by paragraph 23(2) of Schedule 2 to the 1989 Act;

"education supervision order" has the meaning assigned to it by section 36(2) of the 1989 Act;

"emergency proceedings" means proceedings for –

(a)   the disclosure of information as to the whereabouts of a child under section 33 of the 1986 Act;

(b)   an order authorising the taking charge of and delivery of a child under section 34 of the 1986 Act;

(c)   an emergency protection order;

(d)   an order under section 44(9)(b) of the 1989 Act varying a direction in an emergency protection order given under section 44(6) of that Act;

(e)   an order under section 45(5) of the 1989 Act extending the period during which an emergency protection order is to have effect;

(f)   an order under section 45(8) of the 1989 Act discharging an emergency protection order;

(g)   an order under section 45(8A) of the 1989 Act varying or discharging an emergency protection order in so far as it imposes an exclusion requirement on a person who is not entitled to apply for the order to be discharged;

(h)   an order under section 45(8B) of the 1989 Act varying or discharging an emergency protection order in so far as it confers a power of arrest attached to an exclusion requirement;

(i)   warrants under sections 48(9) and 102(1) of the 1989 Act and under section 79 of the 2006 Act; or

(j)   a recovery order under section 50 of the 1989 Act;

"emergency protection order" means an order under section 44 of the 1989 Act;

"enforcement order" has the meaning assigned to it by section 11J(2) of the 1989 Act;

"financial compensation order" means an order made under section 11O(2) of the 1989 Act;

"interim order" means an interim care order or an interim supervision order referred to in section 38(1) of the 1989 Act;

"private law proceedings" means proceedings for –

(a)   a section 8 order except a residence order under section 8 of the 1989 Act relating to a child who is the subject of a care order;

(b)   a parental responsibility order under sections 4(1)(c), 4ZA(1)(c) or 4A(1)(b) of the 1989 Act or an order terminating parental responsibility under sections 4(2A), 4ZA(5) or 4A(3) of that Act;

(c)   an order appointing a child's guardian under section 5(1) of the 1989 Act or an order terminating the appointment under section 6(7) of that Act;

(*d*)   an order giving permission to change a child's surname or remove a child from the United Kingdom under sections 13(1) or 14C(3) of the 1989 Act;

(*e*)   a special guardianship order except where that order relates to a child who is subject of a care order;

(*f*)   an order varying or discharging such an order under section 14D of the 1989 Act;

(*g*)   an enforcement order;

(*h*)   a financial compensation order;

(*i*)   an order under paragraph 9 of Schedule A1 to the 1989 Act following a breach of an enforcement order;

(*j*)   an order under Part 2 of Schedule A1 to the 1989 Act revoking or amending an enforcement order; or

(*k*)   an order that a warning notice be attached to a contact order;

"public law proceedings" means proceedings for –

(*a*)   a residence order under section 8 of the 1989 Act relating to a child who is the subject of a care order;

(*b*)   a special guardianship order relating to a child who is the subject of a care order;

(*c*)   a secure accommodation order under section 25 of the 1989 Act;

(*d*)   a care order, or the discharge of such an order under section 39(1) of the 1989 Act;

(*e*)   an order giving permission to change a child's surname or remove a child from the United Kingdom under section 33(7) of the 1989 Act;

(*f*)   a supervision order under section 31(1)(*b*) of the 1989 Act, the discharge or variation of such an order under section 39(2) of that Act, or the extension or further extension of such an order under paragraph 6(3) of Schedule 3 to that Act;

(*g*)   an order making provision regarding contact under section 34(2) to (4) of the 1989 Act or an order varying or discharging such an order under section 34(9) of that Act;

(*h*)   an education supervision order, the extension of an education supervision order under paragraph 15(2) of Schedule 3 to the 1989 Act, or the discharge of such an order under paragraph 17(1) of Schedule 3 to that Act;

(*i*)   an order varying directions made with an interim care order or interim supervision order under section 38(8)(*b*) of the 1989 Act;

(*j*)   an order under section 39(3) of the 1989 Act varying a supervision order in so far as it affects a person with whom the child is living but who is not entitled to apply for the order to be discharged;

(*k*)   an order under section 39(3A) of the 1989 Act varying or discharging an interim care order in so far as it imposes an exclusion requirement on a person who is not entitled to apply for the order to be discharged;

(*l*)   an order under section 39(3B) of the 1989 Actvarying or discharging an interim care order in so far as it confers a power of arrest attached to an exclusion requirement;

(*m*)   the substitution of a supervision order for a care order under section 39(4) of the 1989 Act;

(*n*)   a child assessment order, or the variation or discharge of such an order under section 43(12) of the 1989 Act;

(*o*)   an order permitting the local authority to arrange for any child in its care to live outside England and Wales under paragraph 19(1) of Schedule 2 to the 1989 Act;

(*p*)   a contribution order, or revocation of such an order under paragraph 23(8) of Schedule 2 to the 1989 Act;

(*q*)   an appeal under paragraph 8(1) of Schedule 8 to the 1989 Act;

"special guardianship order" has the meaning assigned to it by section 14A(1) of the 1989 Act;

"supervision order" has the meaning assigned to it by section 31(11) of the 1989 Act;

"supervision proceedings" means proceedings for a supervision order under section 31(1)(*b*) of the 1989 Act;

"warning notice" means a notice attached to an order pursuant to section 8(2) of the Children and Adoption Act 2006.

(The 1980 Hague Convention, the 1996 Hague Convention, the Council Regulation, and the European Convention are defined in rule 2.3.)

Chapter 2
General Rules

12.3 Who the parties are

(1) In relation to the proceedings set out in column 1 of the following table, column 2 sets out who may make the application and column 3 sets out who the respondents to those proceedings will be.

Proceedings for	*Applicants*	*Respondents*
A parental responsibility order (section 4(1)(*c*), 4ZA(1)(*c*), or section 4A(1)(*b*) of the 1989 Act).	The child's father; the step parent; or the child's parent (being a woman who is a parent by virtue of section 43 of the Human Fertilisation and Embryology Act 2008 and who is not a person to whom section 1(3) of the Family Law Reform Act 1987 applies) (sections 4(1)(*c*), 4ZA(1)(*c*) and 4A(1)(*b*) of the 1989 Act).	Every person whom the applicant believes to have parental responsibility for the child; where the child is the subject of a care order, every person whom the applicant believes to have had parental responsibility immediately prior to the making of the care order; in the case of an application to extend, vary or discharge an order, the parties to the proceedings leading to the order which it is sought to have extended, varied or discharged; in the case of specified proceedings, the child.

Proceedings for	Applicants	Respondents
An order terminating a parental responsibility order or agreement (section 4(2A), 4ZA(5) or section 4A(3) of the 1989 Act).	Any person who has parental responsibility for the child; or with the court's permission, the child (section 4(3), 4ZA(6) and section 4A(3) of the 1989 Act).	As above.
An order appointing a guardian (section 5(1) of the 1989 Act).	An individual who wishes to be appointed as guardian (section 5(1) of the 1989 Act).	As above.
An order terminating the appointment of a guardian (section 6(7) of the 1989 Act).	Any person who has parental responsibility for the child; or with the court's permission, the child (section 6(7) of the 1989 Act).	As above.
A section 8 order.	Any person who is entitled to apply for a section 8 order with respect to the child (section 10(4) to (7) of the 1989 Act); or with the court's permission, any person (section 10(2)(*b*) of the 1989 Act).	As above.
An enforcement order (section 11J of the 1989 Act).	A person who is, for the purposes of the contact order, a person with whom the child concerned lives or is to live; any person whose contact with the child concerned is provided for in the contact order; any individual subject to a condition under section 11(7)(*b*) of the 1989 Act or a contact activity condition imposed by a contact order; or	The person the applicant alleges has failed to comply with the contact order.

Proceedings for	Applicants	Respondents
	with the court's permission, the child (section 11J(5) of the 1989 Act).	
A financial compensation order (section 11O of the 1989 Act).	Any person who is, for the purposes of the contact order, a person with whom the child concerned lives or is to live; any person whose contact with the child concerned is provided for in the contact order; any individual subject to a condition under section 11(7)(*b*) of the 1989 Act or a contact activity condition imposed by a contact order; or with the court's permission, the child (section 11O(6) of the 1989 Act).	The person the applicant alleges has failed to comply with the contact order.
An order permitting the child's name to be changed or the removal of the child from the United Kingdom (section 13(1), 14C(3) or 33(7) of the 1989 Act).	Any person (section 13(1), 14C(3), 33(7) of the 1989 Act).	As for a parental responsibility order.
A special guardianship order (section 14A of the 1989 Act).	Any guardian of the child; any individual in whose favour a residence order is in force with respect to the child; any individual listed in subsection (5)(*b*) or (*c*) of section 10 (as read with subsection (10) of that section) of the 1989 Act;	As above, and if a care order is in force with respect to the child, the child.

Proceedings for	Applicants	Respondents
	a local authority foster parent with whom the child has lived for a period of at least one year immediately preceding the application; or any person with the court's permission (section 14A(3) of the 1989 Act) (more than one such individual can apply jointly (section 14A(3) and (5) of that Act)).	
Variation or discharge of a special guardianship order (section 14D of the 1989 Act).	The special guardian (or any of them, if there is more than one); any individual in whose favour a residence order is in force with respect to the child; the local authority designated in a care order with respect to the child; any individual within section 14D(1)(d) of the 1989 Act who has parental responsibility for the child; the child, any parent or guardian of the child and any step-parent of the child who has acquired, and has not lost, parental responsibility by virtue of section 4A of that Act with the court's permission; or	As above.

Proceedings for	Applicants	Respondents
	any individual within section 14D(1)(*d*) of that Act who immediately before the making of the special guardianship order had, but no longer has, parental responsibility for the child with the court's permission.	
A secure accommodation order (section 25 of the 1989 Act).	The local authority which is looking after the child; or the Health Authority, Primary Care Trust, National Health Service Trust established under section 25 of the National Health Service Act 2006 or section 18(1) of the National Health Service (Wales) Act 2006, National Health Service Foundation Trust or any local authority providing accommodation for the child (unless the child is looked after by a local authority).	As above.
A care or supervision order (section 31 of the 1989 Act).	Any local authority; the National Society for the Prevention of Cruelty to Children and any of its officers (section 31(1) of the 1989 Act); or any authorised person.	As above.
An order varying directions made with an interim care or interim supervision order (section 38(8)(*b*) of the 1989 Act).	The parties to proceedings in which directions are given under section 38(6) of the 1989 Act; or any person named in such a direction.	As above.

Proceedings for	Applicants	Respondents
An order discharging a care order (section 39(1) of the 1989 Act).	Any person who has parental responsibility for the child; the child; or the local authority designated by the order (section 39(1) of the 1989 Act).	As above.
An order varying or discharging an interim care order in so far as it imposes an exclusion requirement (section 39(3A) of the 1989 Act).	A person to whom the exclusion requirement in the interim care order applies who is not entitled to apply for the order to be discharged (section 39(3A) of the 1989 Act).	As above.
An order varying or discharging an interim care order in so far as it confers a power of arrest attached to an exclusion requirement (section 39(3B) of the 1989 Act).	Any person entitled to apply for the discharge of the interim care order in so far as it imposes the exclusion requirement (section 39(3B) of the 1989 Act).	As above.
An order substituting a supervision order for a care order (section 39(4) of the 1989 Act).	Any person entitled to apply for a care order to be discharged under section 39(1) (section 39(4) of the 1989 Act).	As above.
A child assessment order (section 43(1) of the 1989 Act).	Any local authority; the National Society for the Prevention of Cruelty to Children and any of its officers; or any person authorised by order of the Secretary of State to bring the proceedings and any officer of a body who is so authorised (section 43(1) and (13) of the 1989 Act).	As above.

Proceedings for	Applicants	Respondents
An order varying or discharging a child assessment order (section 43(12) of the 1989 Act).	The applicant for an order that has been made under section 43(1) of the 1989 Act; or the persons referred to in section 43(11) of the 1989 Act (section 43(12) of that Act).	As above.
An emergency protection order (section 44(1) of the 1989 Act).	Any person (section 44(1) of the 1989 Act).	As for a parental responsibility order.
An order extending the period during which an emergency protection order is to have effect (section 45(4) of the 1989 Act).	Any person who – has parental responsibility for a child as the result of an emergency protection order; and is entitled to apply for a care order with respect to the child (section 45(4) of the 1989 Act).	As above.
An order discharging an emergency protection order (section 45(8) of the 1989 Act).	The child; a parent of the child; any person who is not a parent of the child but who has parental responsibility for the child; or any person with whom the child was living before the making of the emergency protection order (section 45(8) of the 1989 Act).	As above.
An order varying or discharging an emergency protection order in so far as it imposes the exclusion requirement (section 45(8A) of the 1989 Act).	A person to whom the exclusion requirement in the emergency protection order applies who is not entitled to apply for the emergency protection order to be discharged (section 45(8A) of the 1989 Act).	As above.

Proceedings for	Applicants	Respondents
An order varying or discharging an emergency protection order in so far as it confers a power of arrest attached to an exclusion requirement (section 45(8B) of the 1989 Act).	Any person entitled to apply for the discharge of the emergency protection order in so far as it imposes the exclusion requirement (section 45(8B) of the 1989 Act).	As above.
An emergency protection order by the police (section 46(7) of the 1989 Act).	The officer designated officer for the purposes of section 46(3)(*e*) of the 1989 Act (section 46(7) of the 1989 Act).	As above.
A warrant authorising a constable to assist in exercise of certain powers to search for children and inspect premises (section 48 of the 1989 Act).	Any person attempting to exercise powers under an emergency protection order who has been or is likely to be prevented from doing so by being refused entry to the premises concerned or refused access to the child concerned (section 48(9) of the 1989 Act).	As above.
A warrant authorising a constable to assist in exercise of certain powers to search for children and inspect premises (section 102 of the 1989 Act).	Any person attempting to exercise powers under the enactments mentioned in section 102(6) of the 1989 Act who has been or is likely to be prevented from doing so by being refused entry to the premises concerned or refused access to the child concerned (section 102(1) of that Act).	As above.
An order revoking an enforcement order (paragraph 4 of Schedule A1 to the 1989 Act).	The person subject to the enforcement order.	The person who was the applicant for the enforcement order; and where the child was a party to the proceedings in which the enforcement order was made, the child.

Proceedings for	Applicants	Respondents
An order amending an enforcement order (paragraphs 5 to 7 of Schedule A1 to the 1989 Act).	The person subject to the enforcement order.	The person who was the applicant for the enforcement order. (Rule 12.33 makes provision about applications under paragraph 5 of Schedule A1 to the 1989 Act.)
An order following breach of an enforcement order (paragraph 9 of Schedule A1 to the 1989 Act).	Any person who is, for the purposes of the contact order, the person with whom the child lives or is to live; any person whose contact with the child concerned is provided for in the contact order; any individual subject to a condition under section 11(7)(*b*) of the 1989 Act or a contact activity condition imposed by a contact order; or with the court's permission, the child (paragraph 9 of Schedule A1 to the 1989 Act).	The person the applicant alleges has failed to comply with the unpaid work requirement imposed by an enforcement order; and where the child was a party to the proceedings in which the enforcement order was made, the child.
An order permitting the local authority to arrange for any child in its care to live outside England and Wales (Schedule 2, paragraph 19(1), to the 1989 Act).	The local authority (Schedule 2, paragraph 19(1), to the 1989 Act).	As for a parental responsibility order.
A contribution order (Schedule 2, paragraph 23(1), to the 1989 Act).	The local authority (Schedule 2, paragraph 23(1), to the 1989 Act).	As above and the contributor.
An order revoking a contribution order (Schedule 2, paragraph 23(8), to the 1989 Act).	The contributor; or the local authority.	As above.

Proceedings for	Applicants	Respondents
An order relating to contact with the child in care and any named person (section 34(2) of the 1989 Act) or permitting the local authority to refuse contact (section 34(4) of that Act).	The local authority; or the child (section 34(2) or 34(4) of the 1989 Act).	As above; and the person whose contact with the child is the subject of the application.
An order relating to contact with the child in care (section 34(3) of the 1989 Act).	The child's parents; any guardian or special guardian of the child; any person who by virtue of section 4A of the 1989 Act has parental responsibility for the child; a person in whose favour there was a residence order in force with respect to the child immediately before the care order was made; a person who by virtue of an order made in the exercise of the High Court's inherent jurisdiction with respect to children had care of the child immediately before the care order was made (section 34(3)(*a*) of the 1989 Act); or with the court's permission, any person (section 34(3)(*b*) of that Act).	As above; and the person whose contact with the child is the subject of the application.
An order varying or discharging an order for contact with a child in care under section 34 (section 34((9) of the 1989 Act).	The local authority; the child; or any person named in the order (section 34(9) of the 1989 Act).	As above; and the person whose contact with the child is the subject of the application.
An education supervision order (section 36 of the 1989 Act).	Any local authority (section 36(1) of the 1989 Act).	As above; and the child.

Proceedings for	Applicants	Respondents
An order varying or discharging a supervision order (section 39(2) of the 1989 Act).	Any person who has parental responsibility for the child; the child; or the supervisor (section 39(2) of the 1989 Act).	As above; and the supervisor.
An order varying a supervision order in so far as it affects the person with whom the child is living (section 39(3) of the 1989 Act).	The person with whom the child is living who is not entitled to apply for the order to be discharged (section 39(3) of the 1989 Act).	As above; and the supervisor.
An order varying a direction under section 44(6) of the 1989 Act in an emergency protection order (section 44(9)(*b*) of that Act).	The parties to the application for the emergency protection order in respect of which it is sought to vary the directions; the children's guardian; the local authority in whose area the child is ordinarily resident; or any person who is named in the directions.	As above, and the parties to the application for the order in respect of which it is sought to vary the directions; any person who was caring for the child prior to the making of the order; and any person whose contact with the child is affected by the direction which it is sought to have varied.
A recovery order (section 50 of the 1989 Act).	Any person who has parental responsibility for the child by virtue of a care order or an emergency protection order; or where the child is in police protection the officer designated for the purposes of section 46(3)(*e*) of the 1989 Act (section 50(4) of the 1989 Act).	As above; and the person whom the applicant alleges to have effected or to have been or to be responsible for the taking or keeping of the child.
An order discharging an education supervision order (Schedule 3, paragraph 17(1), to the 1989 Act).	The child concerned; a parent of the child; or the local authority concerned (Schedule 3, paragraph 17(1), to the 1989 Act).	As above; and the local authority concerned; and the child.

Proceedings for	Applicants	Respondents
An order extending an education supervision order (Schedule 3, paragraph 15(2), to the 1989 Act).	The local authority in whose favour the education supervision order was made (Schedule 3, paragraph 15(2), to the 1989 Act).	As above; and the child.
An appeal under paragraph (8) of Schedule 8 to the 1989 Act.	A person aggrieved by the matters listed in paragraph 8(1) of Schedule 8 to the 1989 Act.	The appropriate local authority.
An order for the disclosure of information as to the whereabouts of a child under section 33 of the 1986 Act.	Any person with a legitimate interest in proceedings for an order under Part 1 of the 1986 Act; or a person who has registered an order made elsewhere in the United Kingdom or a specified dependent territory.	Any person alleged to have information as to the whereabouts of the child.
An order authorising the taking charge of and delivery of a child under section 34 of the 1986 Act.	The person to whom the child is to be given up under section 34(1) of the 1986 Act.	As above; and the person who is required to give up the child in accordance with section 34(1) of the 1986 Act.
An order relating to the exercise of the court's inherent jurisdiction (including wardship proceedings).	A local authority (with the court's permission); any person with a genuine interest in or relation to the child; or the child (wardship proceedings only).	The parent or guardian of the child; any other person who has an interest in or relationship to the child; and the child (wardship proceedings only and with the court's permission as described at rule 12.37).

Proceedings for	Applicants	Respondents
A warrant under section 79 of the 2006 Act authorising any constable to assist Her Majesty's Chief Inspector for Education, Children's Services and Skills in the exercise of powers conferred on him by section 77 of the 2006 Act.	Her Majesty's Chief Inspector for Education, Children's Services and Skills.	Any person preventing or likely to prevent Her Majesty's Chief Inspector for Education, Children's Services and Skills from exercising powers conferred on him by section 77 of the 2006 Act.
An order in respect of a child under the 1980 Hague Convention.	Any person, institution or body who claims that a child has been removed or retained in breach of rights of custody or claims that there has been a breach of rights of access in relation to the child.	The person alleged to have brought the child into the United Kingdom; the person with whom the child is alleged to be; any parent or guardian of the child who is within the United Kingdom and is not otherwise a party; any person in whose favour a decision relating to custody has been made if that person is not otherwise a party; and any other person who appears to the court to have sufficient interest in the welfare of the child.
An order concerning the recognition and enforcement of decisions relating to custody under the European Convention.	Any person who has a court order giving that person rights of custody in relation to the child.	As above.
An application for the High Court to request transfer of jurisdiction under Article 15 of the Council Regulation or Article 9 of the 1996 Hague Convention (rule 12.65).	Any person with sufficient interest in the welfare of the child and who would be entitled to make a proposed application in relation to that child, or who intends to seek the permission of the court to make such application if the transfer is agreed.	As directed by the court in accordance with rule 12.65.

Proceedings for	Applicants	Respondents
An application under rule 12.71 for a declaration as to the existence, or extent, of parental responsibility under Article 16 of the 1996 Convention.	Any interested person including a person who holds, or claims to hold, parental responsibility for the child under the law of another State which subsists in accordance with Article 16 of the 1996 Hague Convention following the child becoming habitually resident in a territorial unit of the United Kingdom	Every person whom the applicant believes to have parental responsibility for the child; any person whom the applicant believes to hold parental responsibility for the child under the law of another State which subsists in accordance with Article 16 of the 1996 Hague Convention following the child becoming habitually resident in a territorial unit of the United Kingdom; and where the child is the subject of a care order, every person whom the applicant believes to have had parental responsibility immediately prior to the making of the care order
A warning notice.	The person who is, for the purposes of the contact order, the person with whom the child concerned lives or is to live; the person whose contact with the child concerned is provided for in the contact order; any individual subject to a condition under section 11(7)(*b*) of the 1989 Act or a contact activity condition imposed by the contact order; or with the court's permission, the child.	Any person who was a party to the proceedings in which the contact order was made. (Rule 12.33 makes provision about applications for warning notices).

(2) The court will direct that a person with parental responsibility be made a party to proceedings where that person requests to be one.

(3) Subject to rule 16.2, the court may at any time direct that –

    (*a*)   any person or body be made a party to proceedings; or (*b*)   a party be removed.

(4) If the court makes a direction for the addition or removal of a party under this rule, it may give consequential directions about –

(*a*)   the service of a copy of the application form or other relevant documents on the new party;

(*b*)   the management of the proceedings.

(5) In this rule –

"a local authority foster parent" has the meaning assigned to it by section 23(3) of the 1989 Act; and

"care home", "independent hospital", "local authority" and "Primary Care Trust" have the meanings assigned to them by section 105 of the 1989 Act.

(Part 16 contains the rules relating to the representation of children.)

12.4 Notice of proceedings to person with foreign parental responsibility

(1) This rule applies where a child is subject to proceedings to which this Part applies and –

(*a*)   a person holds or is believed to hold parental responsibility for the child under the law of another State which subsists in accordance with Article 16 of the 1996 Hague Convention following the child becoming habitually resident in a territorial unit of the United Kingdom; and

(*b*)   that person is not otherwise required to be joined as a respondent under rule 12.3.

(2) The applicant shall give notice of the proceedings to any person to whom the applicant believes paragraph (1) applies in any case in which a person whom the applicant believed to have parental responsibility under the 1989 Act would be a respondent to those proceedings in accordance with rule 12.3.

(3) The applicant and every respondent to the proceedings shall provide such details as they possess as to the identity and whereabouts of any person they believe to hold parental responsibility for the child in accordance with paragraph (1) to the court officer, upon making, or responding to the application as appropriate.

(4) Where the existence of a person who is believed to have parental responsibility for the child in accordance with paragraph (1) only becomes apparent to a party at a later date during the proceedings, that party must notify the court officer of those details at the earliest opportunity.

(5) Where a person to whom paragraph (1) applies receives notice of proceedings, that person may apply to the court to be joined as a party using the Part 18 procedure.

12.5 What the court will do when the application has been issued

When the proceedings have been issued the court will consider –

(*a*)   setting a date for –

(i)   a directions appointment;

(ii)   in private law proceedings, a First Hearing Dispute Resolution Appointment;

(iii)   in care and supervision proceedings and in so far as practicable other public law proceedings, the First Appointment; or

      (iv)   the hearing of the application or an application for an interim order, and if the court sets a date it will do so in accordance with rule 12.13 and Practice Directions 12A and 12B;

(b)   giving any of the directions listed in rule 12.12 or, where Chapter 6, section 1 applies, rule 12.48; and

(c)   doing anything else which is set out in Practice Directions 12A or 12B or any other practice direction.

(Practice Directions 12A and 12B supplementing this Part set out details relating to the First Hearing Dispute Resolution Appointment and the First Appointment.)

12.6 Children's guardian, solicitor and reports under section 7 of the 1989 Act

As soon as practicable after the issue of proceedings or the transfer of the proceedings to the court, the court will –

(a)   in specified proceedings, appoint a children's guardian under rule 16.3(1) unless –

      (i)   such an appointment has already been made by the court which made the transfer and is subsisting; or

      (ii)   the court considers that such an appointment is not necessary to safeguard the interests of the child;

(b)   where section 41(3) of the 1989 Act applies, consider whether a solicitor should be appointed to represent the child, and if so, appoint a solicitor accordingly;

(c)   consider whether to ask an officer of the service or a Welsh family proceedings officer for advice relating to the welfare of the child;

(d)   consider whether a report relating to the welfare of the child is required, and if so, request such a report in accordance with section 7 of the 1989 Act.

(Part 16 sets out the rules relating to representation of children.)

12.7 What a court officer will do

(1) As soon as practicable after the issue of proceedings the court officer will return to the applicant the copies of the application together with the forms referred to in Practice Direction 5A.

(2) As soon as practicable after the issue of proceedings or the transfer of proceedings to the court or at any other stage in the proceedings the court officer will –

(a)   give notice of any hearing set by the court to the applicant; and

(b)   do anything else set out in Practice Directions 12A or 12B or any other practice direction.

12.8 Service of the application

The applicant will serve –

(a)   the application together with the documents referred to in Practice Direction 12C on the persons referred to and within the time specified in that Practice Direction; and

(b)   notice of any hearing set by the court on the persons referred to in Practice Direction 12C at the same time as serving the application.

12.9 Request for transfer from magistrates' court to county court or to another magistrates' court

(1) In accordance with the Allocation Order, a magistrates' court may order proceedings before the court (or any part of them) to be transferred to another magistrates' court or to a county court.

(2) Where any request to transfer proceedings to another magistrates' court or to a county court is refused, the court officer will send a copy of the written record of the reasons for refusing the transfer to the parties.

12.10 Procedure following refusal of magistrates' court to order transfer

(1) Where a request under rule 12.9 to transfer proceedings to a county court in accordance with the provisions of the Allocation Order is refused, a party to the proceedings may apply to a county court for an order transferring proceedings from the magistrates' court.

(2) Such an application must be made in accordance with Part 18 and the Allocation Order.

12.11 Transfer of proceedings from one court to another court

Where proceedings are transferred from one court to another court in accordance with the provisions of the Allocation Order, the court officer from the transferring court will notify the parties of any order transferring the proceedings.

12.12 Directions

(1) This rule does not apply to proceedings under Chapter 6 of this Part.

(2) At any stage in the proceedings, the court may give directions about the conduct of the proceedings including –

  (a)   the management of the case;
  (b)   the timetable for steps to be taken between the giving of directions and the final hearing;
  (c)   the joining of a child or other person as a party to the proceedings in accordance with rules 12.3(2) and (3);
  (d)   the attendance of the child;
  (e)   the appointment of a children's guardian or of a solicitor under section 41(3) of the 1989 Act;
  (f)   the appointment of a litigation friend;
  (g)   the service of documents;
  (h)   the filing of evidence including experts' reports; and
  (i)   the exercise by an officer of the Service, Welsh family proceedings officer or local authority officer of any duty referred to in rule 16.38(1).

(3) Paragraph (4) applies where –

  (a)   an officer of the Service or a Welsh family proceedings officer has filed a report or a risk assessment as a result of exercising a duty referred to in rule 16.38(1)(a); or
  (b)   a local authority officer has filed a report as a result of exercising a duty referred to in rule 16.38(1)(b).

(4) The court may –

(a) give directions setting a date for a hearing at which that report or risk assessment will be considered; and

(b) direct that the officer who prepared the report or risk assessment attend any such hearing.

(5) The court may exercise the powers in paragraphs (2) and (4) on an application or of its own initiative.

(6) Where the court proposes to exercise its powers of its own initiative the procedure set out in rule 4.3(2) to (6) applies.

(7) Directions of a court which are still in force immediately prior to the transfer of proceedings to another court will continue to apply following the transfer subject to –

(a) any changes of terminology which are required to apply those directions to the court to which the proceedings are transferred; and

(b) any variation or revocation of the direction.

(8) The court or court officer will –

(a) take a note of the giving, variation or revocation of a direction under this rule; and

(b) as soon as practicable serve a copy of the note on every party.

(Rule 12.48 provides for directions in proceedings under the 1980 Hague Convention and the European Convention.)

12.13 Setting dates for hearings and setting or confirming the timetable and date for the final hearing

(1) At the –

(a) transfer to a court of proceedings;

(b) postponement or adjournment of any hearing; or

(c) conclusion of any hearing at which the proceedings are not finally determined,

the court will set a date for the proceedings to come before the court again for the purposes of giving directions or for such other purposes as the court directs.

(2) At any hearing the court may –

(a) confirm a date for the final hearing or the week within which the final hearing is to begin (where a date or period for the final hearing has already been set);

(b) set a timetable for the final hearing unless a timetable has already been fixed, or the court considers that it would be inappropriate to do so; or

(c) set a date for the final hearing or a period within which the final hearing of the application is to take place.

(3) The court officer will notify the parties of –

(a) the date of a hearing fixed in accordance with paragraph (1);

(b) the timetable for the final hearing; and

(c) the date of the final hearing or the period in which it will take place.

(4) Where the date referred to in paragraph (1) is set at the transfer of proceedings, the date will be as soon as possible after the transfer.

(5) The requirement in paragraph (1) to set a date for the proceedings to come before the court again is satisfied by the court setting or confirming a date for the final hearing.

12.14 Attendance at hearings

(1) This rule does not apply to proceedings under Chapter 6 of this Part except for proceedings for a declaration under rule 12.71.

(2) Unless the court directs otherwise and subject to paragraph (3), the persons who must attend a hearing are –

    (*a*)   any party to the proceedings;

    (*b*)   any litigation friend for any party or legal representative instructed to act on that party's behalf; and

    (*c*)   any other person directed by the court or required by Practice Directions 12A or 12B or any other practice direction to attend.

(3) Proceedings or any part of them will take place in the absence of a child who is a party to the proceedings if –

    (*a*)   the court considers it in the interests of the child, having regard to the matters to be discussed or the evidence likely to be given; and

    (*b*)   the child is represented by a children's guardian or solicitor.

(4) When considering the interests of the child under paragraph (3) the court will give –

    (*a*)   the children's guardian;

    (*b*)   the solicitor for the child; and

    (*c*)   the child, if of sufficient understanding,

an opportunity to make representations.

(5) Subject to paragraph (6), where at the time and place appointed for a hearing, the applicant appears but one or more of the respondents do not, the court may proceed with the hearing.

(6) The court will not begin to hear an application in the absence of a respondent unless the court is satisfied that –

    (*a*)   the respondent received reasonable notice of the date of the hearing; or

    (*b*)   the circumstances of the case justify proceeding with the hearing.

(7) Where, at the time and place appointed for a hearing one or more of the respondents appear but the applicant does not, the court may –

    (*a*)   refuse the application; or

    (*b*)   if sufficient evidence has previously been received, proceed in the absence of the applicant.

(8) Where at the time and place appointed for a hearing neither the applicant nor any respondent appears, the court may refuse the application.

(9) Paragraphs (5) to (8) do not apply to a hearing where the court –

    (*a*)   is considering –

        (i)   whether to make a contact activity direction or to attach a contact activity condition to a contact order; or

        (ii)   an application for a financial compensation order, an enforcement order or an order under paragraph 9 of Schedule A1 to the 1989 Act following a breach of an enforcement order; and

    (*b*)   has yet to obtain sufficient evidence from, or in relation to, the person who may be the subject of the direction, condition or order to enable it to determine the matter.

(10) Nothing in this rule affects the provisions of Article 18 of the Council Regulation in cases to which that provision applies.

> (The Council Regulation makes provision in Article 18 for the court to stay proceedings where the respondent is habitually resident in another Member State of the European Union and has not been adequately served with the proceedings as required by that provision.)

12.15 Steps taken by the parties

If –

    (a)   the parties or any children's guardian agree proposals for the management of the proceedings (including a proposed date for the final hearing or a period within which the final hearing is to take place); and

    (b)   the court considers that the proposals are suitable,

it may approve them without a hearing and give directions in the terms proposed.

12.16 Applications without notice

(1) This rule applies to –

    (a)   proceedings for a section 8 order;

    (b)   emergency proceedings; and

    (c)   proceedings relating to the exercise of the court's inherent jurisdiction (other than an application for the court's permission to start such proceedings and proceedings for collection, location and passport orders where Chapter 6 applies).

(2) An application in proceedings referred to in paragraph (1) may, in the High Court or a county court, be made without notice in which case the applicant must file the application –

    (a)   where the application is made by telephone, the next business day after the making of the application; or

    (b)   in any other case, at the time when the application is made.

(3) An application in proceedings referred to in paragraph (1)(a) or (b) may, in a magistrates' court, be made with the permission of the court, without notice, in which case the applicant must file the application at the time when the application is made or as directed by the court.

(4) Where –

    (a)   a section 8 order;

    (b)   an emergency protection order;

    (c)   an order for the disclosure of information as to the whereabouts of a child under section 33 of the 1986 Act; or

    (d)   an order authorising the taking charge of and delivery of a child under section 34 of the 1986 Act,

is made without notice, the applicant must serve a copy of the application on each respondent within 48 hours after the order is made.

(5) Within 48 hours after the making of an order without notice, the applicant must serve a copy of the order on –

    (a)   the parties, unless the court directs otherwise;

    (*b*)   any person who has actual care of the child or who had such care immediately prior to the making of the order; and

    (*c*)   in the case of an emergency protection order and a recovery order, the local authority in whose area the child lives or is found.

(6) Where the court refuses to make an order on an application without notice it may direct that the application is made on notice in which case the application will proceed in accordance with rules 12.3 to 12.15.

(7) Where the hearing takes place outside the hours during which the court office is normally open, the court or court officer will take a note of the proceedings.

> (Practice Direction 12E (Urgent Business) provides further details of the procedure for out of hours applications. See also Practice Direction 12D (Inherent Jurisdiction (including Wardship Proceedings).)

> (Rule 12.47 provides for without-notice applications in proceedings under Chapter 6, section 1 of this Part, (proceedings under the 1980 Hague Convention and the European Convention).)

12.17 Investigation under section 37 of the 1989 Act

(1) This rule applies where a direction is given to an appropriate authority by the court under section 37(1) of the 1989 Act.

(2) On giving the direction the court may adjourn the proceedings.

(3) As soon as practicable after the direction is given the court will record the direction.

(4) As soon as practicable after the direction is given the court officer will –

    (*a*)   serve the direction on –
        (i)   the parties to the proceedings in which the direction is given; and
        (ii)   the appropriate authority where it is not a party;
    (*b*)   serve any documentary evidence directed by the court on the appropriate authority.

(5) Where a local authority informs the court of any of the matters set out in section 37(3)(*a*) to (*c*) of the 1989 Act it will do so in writing.

(6) Unless the court directs otherwise, the court officer will serve a copy of any report to the court under section 37 of the 1989 Act on the parties.

> (Section 37 of the 1989 Act refers to the appropriate authority and section 37(5) of that Act sets out which authority should be named in a particular case.)

12.18 Disclosure of a report under section 14A(8) or (9) of the 1989 Act

(1) In proceedings for a special guardianship order, the local authority must file the report under section 14A(8) or (9) of the 1989 Act within the timetable fixed by the court.

(2) The court will consider whether to give a direction that the report under section 14A(8) or (9) of the 1989 Act be disclosed to each party to the proceedings.

(3) Before giving a direction for the report to be disclosed, the court must consider whether any information should be deleted from the report.

(4) The court may direct that the report must not be disclosed to a party.

(5) The court officer must serve a copy of the report in accordance with any direction under paragraph (2).

(6) In paragraph (3), information includes information which a party has declined to reveal under rule 29.1(1).

12.19 Additional evidence

(1) This rule applies to proceedings for a section 8 order or a special guardianship order.

(2) Unless the court directs otherwise, a party must not –

    (*a*)   file or serve any document other than in accordance with these rules or any practice direction;

    (*b*)   in completing a form prescribed by these rules or any practice direction, give information or make a statement which is not required or authorised by that form; or

    (*c*)   file or serve at a hearing –

        (i)   any witness statement of the substance of the oral evidence which the party intends to adduce; or

        (ii)   any copy of any document (including any experts' report) which the party intends to rely on.

(3) Where a party fails to comply with the requirements of this rule in relation to any witness statement or other document, the party cannot seek to rely on that statement or other document unless the court directs otherwise.

12.20 Expert evidence – examination of child

(1) No person may cause the child to be medically or psychiatrically examined, or otherwise assessed, for the purpose of preparation of expert evidence for use in the proceedings without the court's permission.

(2) Where the court's permission has not been given under paragraph (1), no evidence arising out of an examination or assessment referred to in that paragraph may be adduced without the court's permission.

12.21 Hearings

(1) The court may give directions about the order of speeches and the evidence at a hearing.

(2) Subject to any directions given under paragraph (1), the parties and the children's guardian must adduce their evidence at a hearing in the following order –

    (*a*)   the applicant;

    (*b*)   any party with parental responsibility for the child;

    (*c*)   other respondents;

    (*d*)   the children's guardian;

    (*e*)   the child, if the child is a party to proceedings and there is no children's guardian.

****

Chapter 4
Special Provisions about Private Law Proceedings

12.31 The First Hearing Dispute Resolution Appointment

(1) The court may set a date for the First Hearing Dispute Resolution Appointment after the proceedings have been issued.

(2) The court officer will give notice of any of the dates so fixed to the parties.

> (Provisions relating to the timing of and issues to be considered at the First Hearing Dispute Resolution Appointment are contained in Practice Direction 12B.)

12.32 Answer

A respondent must file and serve on the parties an answer to the application for an order in private law proceedings within 14 days beginning with the date on which the application is served.

12.33 Applications for warning notices or applications to amend enforcement orders by reason of change of residence

(1) This rule applies in relation to an application to the High Court or a county court for –

    (a)   a warning notice to be attached to a contact order; or

    (b)   an order under paragraph 5 of Schedule A1 to the 1989 Act to amend an enforcement order by reason of change of residence.

(2) The application must be made without notice.

(3) The court may deal with the application without a hearing.

(4) If the court decides to deal with the application at a hearing, rules 12.5, 12.7 and 12.8 will apply.

12.34 Service of a risk assessment

(1) Where an officer of the Service or a Welsh family proceedings officer has filed a risk assessment with the court, subject to paragraph (2), the court officer will as soon as practicable serve copies of the risk assessment on each party.

(2) Before serving the risk assessment, the court must consider whether, in order to prevent a risk of harm to the child, it is necessary for –

    (a)   information to be deleted from a copy of the risk assessment before that copy is served on a party; or

    (b)   service of a copy of the risk assessment (whether with information deleted from it or not) on a party to be delayed for a specified period,

and may make directions accordingly.

12.35 Service of enforcement orders or orders amending or revoking enforcement orders

(1) Paragraphs (2) and (3) apply where the High Court or a county court makes –

    (a)   an enforcement order; or

    (b)   an order under paragraph 9(2) of Schedule A1 to the 1989 Act (enforcement order made following a breach of an enforcement order).

(2) As soon as practicable after an order has been made, a copy of it must be served by the court officer on –

(a)   the parties, except the person against whom the order is made;

(b)   the officer of the Service or the Welsh family proceedings officer who is to comply with a request under section 11M of the 1989 Act to monitor compliance with the order; and

(c)   the responsible officer.

(3) Unless the court directs otherwise, the applicant must serve a copy of the order personally on the person against whom the order is made.

(4) The court officer must send a copy of an order made under paragraph 4, 5, 6 or 7 of Schedule A1 to the 1989 Act (revocation or amendment of an enforcement order) to –

(a)   the parties;

(b)   the officer of the Service or the Welsh family proceedings officer who is to comply with a request under section 11M of the 1989 Act to monitor compliance with the order;

(c)   the responsible officer; and

(d)   in the case of an order under paragraph 5 of Schedule A1 to the 1989 Act (amendment of enforcement order by reason of change of residence), the responsible officer in the former local justice area.

(5) In this rule, "responsible officer" has the meaning given in paragraph 8(8) of Schedule A1 to the 1989 Act.

Chapter 5
Special Provisions about Inherent Jurisdiction Proceedings

12.36 Where to start proceedings

(1) An application for proceedings under the Inherent Jurisdiction of the court must be started in the High Court.

(2) Wardship proceedings, except applications for an order that a child be made or cease to be a ward of court, may be transferred to the county court unless the issues of fact or law make them more suitable for hearing in the High Court.

> (The question of suitability for hearing in the High Court is explained in Practice Direction 12D (Inherent Jurisdiction (including Wardship Proceedings)).)

12.37 Child as respondent to wardship proceedings

(1) A child who is the subject of wardship proceedings must not be made a respondent to those proceedings unless the court gives permission following an application under paragraph (2).

2) Where nobody other than the child would be a suitable respondent to wardship proceedings, the applicant may apply without notice for permission to make the wardship application –

(a)   without notice; or

(b)   with the child as the respondent.

12.38 Registration requirements

The court officer will send a copy of every application for a child to be made a ward of court to the principal registry for recording in the register of wards.

12.39 Notice of child's whereabouts

(1) Every respondent, other than a child, must file with the acknowledgment of service a notice stating –

    (*a*)   the respondent's address; and

    (*b*)   either –

        (i)   the whereabouts of the child; or

        (ii)   that the respondent is unaware of the child's whereabouts if that is the case.

(2) Unless the court directs otherwise, the respondent must serve a copy of that notice on the applicant.

(3) Every respondent other than a child must immediately notify the court in writing of –

    (*a*)   any subsequent changes of address; or

    (*b*)   any change in the child's whereabouts,

and, unless the court directs otherwise, serve a copy of that notice on the applicant.

(4) In this rule a reference to the whereabouts of a child is a reference to –

    (*a*)   the address at which the child is living;

    (*b*)   the person with whom the child is living; and

    (*c*)   any other information relevant to where the child may be found.

12.40 Enforcement of orders in wardship proceedings

The High Court may secure compliance with any direction relating to a ward of court by an order addressed to the tipstaff.

> (The role of the tipstaff is explained in Practice Direction 12D (Inherent Jurisdiction (including Wardship Proceedings)).)

12.41 Child ceasing to be ward of court

(1) A child who, by virtue of section 41(2) of the Senior Courts Act 1981, automatically becomes a ward of court on the making of a wardship application will cease to be a ward on the determination of the application unless the court orders that the child be made a ward of court.

(2) Nothing in paragraph (1) affects the power of the court under section 41(3) of the Senior Courts Act 1981 to order that any child cease to be a ward of court.

12.42 Adoption of a child who is a ward of court

An application for permission –

    (*a*)   to start proceedings to adopt a child who is a ward of court;

    (*b*)   to place such a child for adoption with parental consent; or

    (*c*)   to start proceedings for a placement order in relation to such a child,

may be made without notice in accordance with Part 18.

****

PART 15
REPRESENTATION OF PROTECTED PARTIES

CONTENTS OF THIS PART

15.1 Application of this Part

This Part contains special provisions which apply in proceedings involving protected parties.

15.2 Requirement for litigation friend in proceedings

A protected party must have a litigation friend to conduct proceedings on that party's behalf.

15.3 Stage of proceedings at which a litigation friend becomes necessary

(1) A person may not without the permission of the court take any step in proceedings except –

    (*a*)   filing an application form; or
    (*b*)   applying for the appointment of a litigation friend under rule 15.6,

until the protected party has a litigation friend.

(2) If during proceedings a party lacks capacity (within the meaning of the 2005 Act) to continue to conduct proceedings, no party may take any step in proceedings without the permission of the court until the protected party has a litigation friend.

(3) Any step taken before a protected party has a litigation friend has no effect unless the court orders otherwise.

15.4 Who may be a litigation friend for a protected party without a court order

(1) This rule does not apply if the court has appointed a person to be a litigation friend.

(2) A person with authority as a deputy to conduct the proceedings in the name of a protected party or on that party's behalf is entitled to be the litigation friend of the protected party in any proceedings to which that person's authority extends.

(3) If there is no person with authority as a deputy to conduct the proceedings in the name of a protected party or on that party's behalf, a person may act as a litigation friend if that person –

(*a*)   can fairly and competently conduct proceedings on behalf of the protected party;

(*b*)   has no interest adverse to that of the protected party; and

(*c*)   subject to paragraph (4), undertakes to pay any costs which the protected party may be ordered to pay in relation to the proceedings, subject to any right that person may have to be repaid from the assets of the protected party.

(4) Paragraph (3)(*c*) does not apply to the Official Solicitor.

("deputy" is defined in rule 2.3.)

15.5 How a person becomes a litigation friend without a court order

(1) If the court has not appointed a litigation friend, a person who wishes to act as a litigation friend must follow the procedure set out in this rule.

(2) A person with authority as a deputy to conduct the proceedings in the name of a protected party or on that party's behalf must file an official copy[(GL)] of the order, declaration or other document which confers that person's authority to act.

(3) Any other person must file a certificate of suitability stating that that person satisfies the conditions specified in rule 15.4(3).

(4) A person who is to act as a litigation friend must file –

(*a*)   the document conferring that person's authority to act; or

(*b*)   the certificate of suitability,

at the time when that person first takes a step in the proceedings on behalf of the protected party.

(5) A court officer will send the certificate of suitability to every person on whom, in accordance with rule 6.28, the application form should be served.

(6) This rule does not apply to the Official Solicitor.

15.6 How a person becomes a litigation friend by court order

(1) The court may, if the person to be appointed so consents, make an order appointing –

(*a*)   a person other than the Official Solicitor; or

(*b*)   the Official Solicitor,

as a litigation friend.

(2) An order appointing a litigation friend may be made by the court of its own initiative or on the application of –

(*a*)   a person who wishes to be a litigation friend; or

(*b*)   a party to the proceedings.

(3) The court may at any time direct that a party make an application for an order under paragraph (2).

(4) An application for an order appointing a litigation friend must be supported by evidence.

(5) Unless the court directs otherwise, a person appointed under this rule to be a litigation friend for a protected party will be treated as a party for the purpose of any provision in these Rules requiring a document to be served on, or sent to, or notice to be given to, a party to the proceedings.

(6) Subject to rule 15.4(4), the court may not appoint a litigation friend under this rule unless it is satisfied that the person to be appointed complies with the conditions specified in rule 15.4(3).

15.7 Court's power to change litigation friend and to prevent person acting as litigation friend

(1) The court may –

  (*a*)   direct that a person may not act as a litigation friend;
  (*b*)   terminate a litigation friend's appointment; or
  (*c*)   appoint a new litigation friend in substitution for an existing one.

(2) An application for an order or direction under paragraph (1) must be supported by evidence.

(3) Subject to rule 15.4(4), the court may not appoint a litigation friend under this rule unless it is satisfied that the person to be appointed complies with the conditions specified in rule 15.4(3).

15.8 Appointment of litigation friend by court order – supplementary

(1) A copy of the application for an order under rule 15.6 or 15.7 must be sent by a court officer to –

  (*a*)   every person on whom, in accordance with rule 6.28, the application form should be served; and
  (*b*)   unless the court directs otherwise, the protected party.

(2) A copy of an application for an order under rule 15.7 must also be sent to –

  (*a*)   the person who is the litigation friend, or who is purporting to act as the litigation friend, when the application is made; and
  (*b*)   the person, if not the applicant, who it is proposed should be the litigation friend.

15.9 Procedure where appointment of litigation friend comes to an end

(1) When a party ceases to be a protected party, the litigation friend's appointment continues until it is brought to an end by a court order.

(2) An application for an order under paragraph (1) may be made by –

  (*a*)   the former protected party;
  (*b*)   the litigation friend; or
  (*c*)   a party.

(3) On the making of an order under paragraph (1), the court officer will send a notice to the other parties stating that the appointment of the protected party's litigation friend to act has ended.

PART 16
REPRESENTATION OF CHILDREN AND REPORTS IN PROCEEDINGS INVOLVING CHILDREN

CONTENTS OF THIS PART

Chapter 1
Application of this Part

Chapter 8
Duties of Solicitor Acting for the Child

Chapter 10
Children and Family Reporter and Welfare Officer

Chapter 1
Application of this Part

16.1 Application of this Part

This Part –

    (a)   sets out when the court will make a child a party in family proceedings; and

    (b)   contains special provisions which apply in proceedings involving children.

****

Chapter 8
Duties of Solicitor Acting for the Child

16.29 Solicitor for child

(1) Subject to paragraphs (2) and (4), a solicitor appointed –

    (a)   under section 41(3) of the 1989 Act; or

    (b)   by the children's guardian in accordance with the Practice Direction 16A,

must represent the child in accordance with instructions received from the children's guardian.

(2) If a solicitor appointed as mentioned in paragraph (1) considers, having taken into account the matters referred to in paragraph (3), that the child –

    (a)   wishes to give instructions which conflict with those of the children's guardian; and

    (b)   is able, having regard to the child's understanding, to give such instructions on the child's own behalf,

the solicitor must conduct the proceedings in accordance with instructions received from the child.

(3) The matters the solicitor must take into account for the purposes of paragraph (2) are –

    (a)   the views of the children's guardian; and

(*b*)   any direction given by the court to the children's guardian concerning the part to be taken by the children's guardian in the proceedings.

(4) Where –

(*a*)   no children's guardian has been appointed; and
(*b*)   the condition in section 41(4)(*b*) of the 1989 Act is satisfied,

a solicitor appointed under section 41(3) of the 1989 Act must represent the child in accordance with instructions received from the child.

(5) Where a solicitor appointed as mentioned in paragraph (1) receives no instructions under paragraphs (1), (2) or (4), the solicitor must represent the child in furtherance of the best interests of the child.

(6) A solicitor appointed under section 41(3) of the 1989 Act or by the children's guardian in accordance with Practice Direction 16A must serve documents, and accept service of documents, on behalf of the child in accordance with rule 6.31 and, where the child has not been served separately and has sufficient understanding, advise the child of the contents of any document so served.

(7) Where the child wishes an appointment of a solicitor –

(*a*)   under section 41(3) of the 1989 Act; or
(*b*)   by the children's guardian in accordance with the Practice Direction 16A,

to be terminated –

(i)   the child may apply to the court for an order terminating the appointment; and
(ii)   the solicitor and the children's guardian will be given an opportunity to make representations.

(8) Where the children's guardian wishes an appointment of a solicitor under section 41(3) of the 1989 Act to be terminated –

(*a*)   the children's guardian may apply to the court for an order terminating the appointment; and
(*b*)   the solicitor and, if of sufficient understanding, the child, will be given an opportunity to make representations.

(9) When terminating an appointment in accordance with paragraph (7) or (8), the court will give its reasons for so doing, a note of which will be taken by the court or a court officer.

(10) The court or a court officer will record the appointment under section 41(3) of the 1989 Act or the refusal to make the appointment.

****

Chapter 10
Children and Family Reporter and Welfare Officer

16.33 Request by court for a welfare report in respect of the child

(1) Where the court is considering an application for an order in proceedings, the court may ask –

(*a*)   in proceedings to which Parts 12 and 14 apply, a children and family reporter; or
(*b*)   in proceedings to which Part 12 applies, a welfare officer,

to prepare a report on matters relating to the welfare of the child, and, in this rule, the person preparing the report is called "the officer".

(2) It is the duty of the officer to –

    (*a*)   comply with any request for a report under this rule; and

    (*b*)   provide the court with such other assistance as it may require.

(3) A report to the court under this rule is confidential.

(4) The officer, when carrying out duties in relation to proceedings under the 1989 Act, must have regard to the principle set out in section 1(2) and the matters set out in section 1(3)(*a*) to (*f*) of that Act as if for the word "court" in that section there were substituted the words "children and family reporter" or "welfare officer" as the case may be.

(5) A party may question the officer about oral or written advice tendered by that officer to the court.

(6) The court officer will notify the officer of a direction given at a hearing at which –

    (*a*)   the officer is not present; and

    (*b*)   the welfare report is considered.

(7) The officer's duties must be exercised in accordance with Practice Direction 16A

    ("children and family reporter" and "welfare officer" are defined in rule 2.3)

****

PART 17
STATEMENTS OF TRUTH

CONTENTS OF THIS PART

17.1 Interpretation

In this Part "statement of case" has the meaning given to it in Part 4 except that a statement of case does not include –

    (*a*)   an application for a matrimonial or a civil partnership order or an answer to such an application;

    (*b*)   an application under Article 56 of the Maintenance Regulation made on the form in Annex VI or VII to that Regulation.

    (Rule 4.1 defines "statement of case" for the purposes of Part 4.)

Amendment—Substituted by SI 2011/1328.

17.2 Documents to be verified by a statement of truth

(1) Subject to paragraph (9), the following documents must be verified by a statement of truth –

(*a*)   a statement of case;

(*b*)   a witness statement;

(*c*)   an acknowledgement of service in a claim begun by the Part 19 procedure;

(*d*)   a certificate of service;

(*e*)   a statement of arrangements for children;

(*f*)   a statement of information filed under rule 9.26(1)(*b*); and

(*g*)   any other document where a rule or practice direction requires it.

(2) Where a statement of case is amended, the amendments must be verified by a statement of truth unless the court orders otherwise.

(3) If an applicant wishes to rely on matters set out in the application form or application notice as evidence, the application form or notice must be verified by a statement of truth.

(4) Subject to paragraph (5), a statement of truth is a statement that –

(*a*)   the party putting forward the document;

(*b*)   in the case of a witness statement, the maker of the witness statement; or

(*c*)   in the case of a certificate of service, the person who signs the certificate,

believes the facts stated in the document are true.

(5) If a party is conducting proceedings with a litigation friend, the statement of truth in –

(*a*)   a statement of case; or

(*b*)   an application notice,

is a statement that the litigation friend believes the facts stated in the document being verified are true.

(6) The statement of truth must be signed by –

(*a*)   in the case of a statement of case –

    (i)   the party or litigation friend; or

    (ii)   the legal representative on behalf of the party or litigation friend; and

(*b*)   in the case of a witness statement or statement of arrangements for children, the maker of the statement.

(7) A statement of truth, which is not contained in the document which it verifies, must clearly identify that document.

(8) A statement of truth in a statement of case may be made by –

(*a*)   a person who is not a party; or

(*b*)   by two parties jointly,

where this is permitted by a practice direction.

(9) An application that does not contain a statement of facts need not be verified by a statement of truth.

(Practice Direction 17A sets out the form of statement of truth.)

17.3 Failure to verify a statement of case

(1) If a party fails to verify that party's statement of case by a statement of truth –

(*a*)   the statement of case shall remain effective unless struck out; but (*b*)   the party may not rely on the statement of case as evidence of any of the matters set out in it.

(2) The court may strike out$^{(GL)}$ a statement of case which is not verified by a statement of truth.

(3) Any party may apply for an order under paragraph (2).

17.4 Failure to verify a witness statement

If the maker of a witness statement fails to verify the witness statement by a statement of truth, the court may direct that it shall not be admissible as evidence.

17.5 Power of the court to require a document to be verified

(1) The court may order a person who has failed to verify a document in accordance with rule 17.2 to verify the document.

(2) Any party may apply for an order under paragraph (1).

17.6 False statements

(1) Proceedings for contempt of court may be brought against a person who makes, or causes to be made, a false statement in a document verified by a statement of truth without an honest belief in its truth.

(2) Proceedings under this rule may be brought only –

(*a*)   by the Attorney General, or
(*b*)   with the permission of the court.

(3) This rule does not apply to proceedings in a magistrates' court.

****

PART 25
EXPERTS AND ASSESSORS

CONTENTS OF THIS PART

25.1 Duty to restrict expert evidence

Expert evidence will be restricted to that which is reasonably required to resolve the proceedings.

25.2 Interpretation

(1) A reference to an "expert" in this Part –

    (*a*)   is a reference to a person who has been instructed to give or prepare expert evidence for the purpose of family proceedings; and

    (*b*)   does not include –

        (i)   a person who is within a prescribed description for the purposes of section 94(1) of the 2002 Act (persons who may prepare a report for any person about the suitability of a child for adoption or of a person to adopt a child or about the adoption, or placement for adoption, of a child); or

        (ii)   an officer of the Service or a Welsh family proceedings officer when acting in that capacity.

    (Regulation 3 of the Restriction on the Preparation of Adoption Reports Regulations 2005 (S.I. 2005/1711) sets out which persons are within a prescribed description for the purposes of section 94(1) of the 2002 Act.)

(2) "Single joint expert" means an expert instructed to prepare a report for the court on behalf of two or more of the parties (including the applicant) to the proceedings.

25.3 Experts – overriding duty to the court

(1) It is the duty of experts to help the court on matters within their expertise.

(2) This duty overrides any obligation to the person from whom experts have received instructions or by whom they are paid.

25.4 Court's power to restrict expert evidence

(1) No party may call an expert or put in evidence an expert's report without the court's permission.

(2) When parties apply for permission they must identify –

    (*a*)   the field in which the expert evidence is required; and

    (*b*)   where practicable, the name of the proposed expert.

(3) If permission is granted it will be in relation only to the expert named or the field identified under paragraph (2).

(4) The court may limit the amount of a party's expert's fees and expenses that may be recovered from any other party.

25.5 General requirement for expert evidence to be given in a written report

(1) Expert evidence is to be given in a written report unless the court directs otherwise.

(2) The court will not direct an expert to attend a hearing unless it is necessary to do so in the interests of justice.

25.6 Written questions to experts

(1) A party may put written questions about an expert's report (which must be proportionate) to –

    (*a*)   an expert instructed by another party; or

    (*b*)   a single joint expert appointed under rule 25.7.

(2) Written questions under paragraph (1) –

    (*a*)   may be put once only;

    (*b*)   must be put within 10 days beginning with the date on which the expert's report was served; and

    (*c*)   must be for the purpose only of clarification of the report,

unless in any case –

    (i)   the court directs otherwise; or

    (ii)   a practice direction provides otherwise.

(3) An expert's answers to questions put in accordance with paragraph (1) are treated as part of the expert's report.

(4) Where –

    (*a*)   a party has put a written question to an expert instructed by another party; and

    (*b*)   the expert does not answer that question,

the court may make use of one or both of the following orders in relation to the party who instructed the expert –

    (i)   that the party may not rely on the evidence of that expert; or

    (ii)   that the party may not recover the fees and expenses of that expert from any other party.

25.7 Court's power to direct that evidence is to be given by a single joint expert

(1) Where two or more parties wish to submit expert evidence on a particular issue, the court may direct that the evidence on that issue is to be given by a single joint expert.

(2) Where the parties who wish to submit the evidence ("the relevant parties") cannot agree who should be the single joint expert, the court may –

    (*a*)   select the expert from a list prepared or identified by the instructing parties; or

    (*b*)   direct that the expert be selected in such other manner as the court may direct.

25.8 Instructions to a single joint expert

(1) Where the court gives a direction under rule 25.7(1) for a single joint expert to be used, the instructions are to be contained in a jointly agreed letter unless the court directs otherwise.

(2) Where the instructions are to be contained in a jointly agreed letter, in default of agreement the instructions may be determined by the court on the written request of any relevant party copied to the other relevant parties.

(3) Where the court permits the relevant parties to give separate instructions to a single joint expert, each instructing party must, when giving instructions to the expert, at the same time send a copy of the instructions to the other relevant parties.

(4) The court may give directions about –

> (*a*)   the payment of the expert's fees and expenses; and
> (*b*)   any inspection, examination or assessments which the expert wishes to carry out.

(5) The court may, before an expert is instructed, limit the amount that can be paid by way of fees and expenses to the expert.

(6) Unless the court directs otherwise, the relevant parties are jointly and severally liable for the payment of the expert's fees and expenses.

25.9 Power of court to direct a party to provide information

(1) Subject to paragraph (2), where a party has access to information which is not reasonably available to another party, the court may direct the party who has access to the information to prepare, file and serve a document recording the information.

(2) In proceedings under Part 14 (procedure for applications in adoption, placement and related proceedings), –

> (*a*)   the court may direct the party with access to the information to prepare and file a document recording the information; and
> (*b*)   a court officer will send a copy of that document to the other party.

25.10 Contents of report

(1) An expert's report must comply with the requirements set out in Practice Direction 25A.

(2) At the end of an expert's report there must be a statement that the expert understands and has complied with their duty to the court.

(3) The instructions to the expert are not privileged against disclosure.

> (Rule 21.1 explains what is meant by disclosure.)

25.11 Use by one party of expert's report disclosed by another

Where a party has disclosed an expert's report, any party may use that expert's report as evidence at any relevant hearing.

25.12 Discussions between experts

(1) The court may, at any stage, direct a discussion between experts for the purpose of requiring the experts to –

> (*a*)   identify and discuss the expert issues in the proceedings; and
> (*b*)   where possible, reach an agreed opinion on those issues.

(2) The court may specify the issues which the experts must discuss.

(3) The court may direct that following a discussion between the experts they must prepare a statement for the court setting out those issues on which –

> (*a*)   they agree; and
> (*b*)   they disagree,

with a summary of their reasons for disagreeing.

25.13 Expert's right to ask court for directions

(1) Experts may file written requests for directions for the purpose of assisting them in carrying out their functions.

(2) Experts must, unless the court directs otherwise, provide copies of the proposed request for directions under paragraph (1) –

(*a*)   to the party instructing them, at least 7 days before they file the requests; and
(*b*)   to all other parties, at least 4 days before they file them.

(3) The court, when it gives directions, may also direct that a party be served with a copy of the directions.

25.14 Assessors

(1) This rule applies where the court appoints one or more persons under section 70 of the Senior Courts Act 1981 or section 63 of the County Courts Act 1984 as an assessor

(2) An assessor will assist the court in dealing with a matter in which the assessor has skill and experience.

(3) The assessor will take such part in the proceedings as the court may direct and in particular the court may direct an assessor to –

(*a*)   prepare a report for the court on any matter at issue in the proceedings; and
(*b*)   attend the whole or any part of the hearing to advise the court on any such matter.

(4) If the assessor prepares a report for the court before the hearing has begun –

(*a*)   the court will send a copy to each of the parties; and
(*b*)   the parties may use it at the hearing.

(5) Unless the court directs otherwise, an assessor will be paid at the daily rate payable for the time being to a fee-paid deputy district judge of the principal registry and an assessor's fees will form part of the costs of the proceedings.

(6) The court may order any party to deposit in the court office a specified sum in respect of an assessor's fees and, where it does so, the assessor will not be asked to act until the sum has been deposited.

(7) Paragraphs (5) and (6) do not apply where the remuneration of the assessor is to be paid out of money provided by Parliament.

****

PART 30
APPEALS

CONTENTS OF THIS PART

30.1 Scope and interpretation

(1) The rules in this Part apply to appeals to –

(*a*)   the High Court; and
(*b*)   a county court.

(2) This Part does not apply to an appeal in detailed assessment proceedings against a decision of an authorised court officer.

> (Rules 47.20 to 47.23 of the CPR deal with appeals against a decision of an authorised court officer in detailed assessment proceedings.)

(3) In this Part –

"appeal court" means the court to which an appeal is made;
"appeal notice" means an appellant's or respondent's notice;
"appellant" means a person who brings or seeks to bring an appeal;
"lower court" means the court from which, or the person from whom, the appeal lies; and
"respondent" means –

(*a*)   a person other than the appellant who was a party to the proceedings in the lower court and who is affected by the appeal; and
(*b*)   a person who is permitted by the appeal court to be a party to the appeal.

(4) This Part is subject to any rule, enactment or practice direction which sets out special provisions with regard to any particular category of appeal.

30.2 Parties to comply with the practice direction

All parties to an appeal must comply with Practice Direction 30A.

30.3 Permission

(1) An appellant or respondent requires permission to appeal –

(*a*)   against a decision in proceedings where the decision appealed against was made by a district judge or a costs judge, unless paragraph (2) applies; or
(*b*)   as provided by Practice Direction 30A.

(2) Permission to appeal is not required where the appeal is against –

(*a*)   a committal order; or
(*b*)   a secure accommodation order under section 25 of the 1989 Act.

(3) An application for permission to appeal may be made –

(*a*)   to the lower court at the hearing at which the decision to be appealed was made; or
(*b*)   to the appeal court in an appeal notice.

(Rule 30.4 sets out the time limits for filing an appellant's notice at the appeal court. Rule 30.5 sets out the time limits for filing a respondent's notice at the appeal court. Any application for permission to appeal to the appeal court must be made in the appeal notice (see rules 30.4(1) and 30.5(3)).)

(4) Where the lower court refuses an application for permission to appeal, a further application for permission to appeal may be made to the appeal court.

(5) Where the appeal court, without a hearing, refuses permission to appeal, the person seeking permission may request the decision to be reconsidered at a hearing.

(6) A request under paragraph (5) must be filed within 7 days beginning with the date on which the notice that permission has been refused was served.

(7) Permission to appeal may be given only where –

(a)   the court considers that the appeal would have a real prospect of success; or
(b)   there is some other compelling reason why the appeal should be heard.

(8) An order giving permission may –

(a)   limit the issues to be heard; and
(b)   be made subject to conditions.

(9) In this rule "costs judge" means a taxing master of the Senior Courts.

30.4 Appellant's notice

(1) Where the appellant seeks permission from the appeal court it must be requested in the appellant's notice.

(2) Subject to paragraph (3), the appellant must file the appellant's notice at the appeal court within –

(a)   such period as may be directed by the lower court (which may be longer or shorter than the period referred to in sub-paragraph (b)); or
(b)   where the court makes no such direction, 21 days after the date of the decision of the lower court against which the appellant wishes to appeal.

(3) Where the appeal is against an order under section 38(1) of the 1989 Act, the appellant must file the appellant's notice within 7 days beginning with the date of the decision of the lower court.

(4) Unless the appeal court orders otherwise, an appellant's notice must be served on each respondent and the persons referred to in paragraph (5) –

(a)   as soon as practicable; and
(b)   in any event not later than 7 days,

after it is filed.

(5) The persons referred to in paragraph (4) are –

(a)   any children's guardian, welfare officer, or children and family reporter;
(b)   a local authority who has prepared a report under section 14A(8) or (9) of the 1989 Act;
(c)   an adoption agency or local authority which has prepared a report on the suitability of the applicant to adopt a child;
(d)   a local authority which has prepared a report on the placement of the child for adoption; and
(e)   where the appeal is from a magistrates' court, the court officer.

30.5 Respondent's notice

(1) A respondent may file and serve a respondent's notice.

(2) A respondent who –

(*a*) is seeking permission to appeal from the appeal court; or
(*b*) wishes to ask the appeal court to uphold the order of the lower court for reasons different from or additional to those given by the lower court,

must file a respondent's notice.

(3) Where the respondent seeks permission from the appeal court it must be requested in the respondent's notice.

(4) A respondent's notice must be filed within –

(*a*) such period as may be directed by the lower court; or
(*b*) where the court makes no such direction, 14 days beginning with the date referred to in paragraph (5).

(5) The date referred to in paragraph (4) is –

(*a*) the date on which the respondent is served with the appellant's notice where –
permission to appeal was given by the lower court; or
permission to appeal is not required;
(*b*) the date on which the respondent is served with notification that the appeal court has given the appellant permission to appeal; or
(*c*) the date on which the respondent is served with notification that the application for permission to appeal and the appeal itself are to be heard together.

(6) Unless the appeal court orders otherwise, a respondent's notice must be served on the appellant, any other respondent and the persons referred to in rule 30.4(5) –

(*a*) as soon as practicable; and
(*b*) in any event not later than 7 days,

after it is filed.

(7) Where there is an appeal against an order under section 38(1) of the 1989 Act –

(*a*) a respondent may not, in that appeal, bring an appeal from the order or ask the appeal court to uphold the order of the lower court for reasons different from or additional to those given by the lower court; and
(*b*) paragraphs (2) and (3) do not apply.

30.6 Grounds of appeal

The appeal notice must state the grounds of appeal.

30.7 Variation of time

(1) An application to vary the time limit for filing an appeal notice must be made to the appeal court.

(2) The parties may not agree to extend any date or time limit set by –

(*a*) these rules;
(*b*) Practice Direction 30A; or
(*c*) an order of the appeal court or the lower court.

(Rule 4.1(3)(*a*) provides that the court may extend or shorten the time for compliance with a rule, practice direction or court order (even if an application for extension is made after the time for compliance has expired).)

(Rule 4.1(3)(*c*) provides that the court may adjourn or bring forward a hearing.)

30.8 Stay

Unless the appeal court or the lower court orders otherwise, an appeal does not operate as a stay(GL) of any order or decision of the lower court.

30.9 Amendment of appeal notice

An appeal notice may not be amended without the permission of the appeal court.

30.10 Striking out appeal notices and setting aside or imposing conditions on permission to appeal

(1) The appeal court may –

    (*a*)   strike out(GL) the whole or part of an appeal notice;

    (*b*)   set aside(GL) permission to appeal in whole or in part;

    (*c*)   impose or vary conditions upon which an appeal may be brought.

(2) The court will only exercise its powers under paragraph (1) where there is a compelling reason for doing so.

(3) Where a party was present at the hearing at which permission was given that party may not subsequently apply for an order that the court exercise its powers under paragraphs (1)(*b*) or (1)(*c*).

30.11 Appeal court's powers

(1) In relation to an appeal the appeal court has all the powers of the lower court.

(Rule 30.1(4) provides that this Part is subject to any enactment that sets out special provisions with regard to any particular category of appeal.)

(2) The appeal court has power to –

    (*a*)   affirm, set aside(GL) or vary any order or judgment made or given by the lower court;

    (*b*)   refer any application or issue for determination by the lower court;

    (*c*)   order a new hearing;

    (*d*)   make orders for the payment of interest;

    (*e*)   make a costs order.

(3) The appeal court may exercise its powers in relation to the whole or part of an order of the lower court.

(Rule 4.1 contains general rules about the court's case management powers.)

(4) If the appeal court –

    (*a*)   refuses an application for permission to appeal;

    (*b*)   strikes out an appellant's notice; or

    (*c*)   dismisses an appeal,

and it considers that the application, the appellant's notice or the appeal is totally without merit, the provisions of paragraph (5) must be complied with.

(5) Where paragraph (4) applies –

(*a*)   the court's order must record the fact that it considers the application, the appellant's notice or the appeal to be totally without merit; and

(*b*)   the court must at the same time consider whether it is appropriate to make a civil restraint order.

30.12 Hearing of appeals

(1) Every appeal will be limited to a review of the decision of the lower court unless –

(*a*)   an enactment or practice direction makes different provision for a particular category of appeal; or

(*b*)   the court considers that in the circumstances of an individual appeal it would be in the interests of justice to hold a re-hearing.

(2) Unless it orders otherwise, the appeal court will not receive –

(*a*)   oral evidence; or

(*b*)   evidence which was not before the lower court.

(3) The appeal court will allow an appeal where the decision of the lower court was –

(*a*)   wrong; or

(*b*)   unjust because of a serious procedural or other irregularity in the proceedings in the lower court.

(4) The appeal court may draw any inference of fact which it considers justified on the evidence.

(5) At the hearing of the appeal a party may not rely on a matter not contained in that party's appeal notice unless the appeal court gives permission.

30.13 Assignment of appeals to the Court of Appeal

(1) Where the court from or to which an appeal is made or from which permission to appeal is sought ("the relevant court") considers that –

(*a*)   an appeal which is to be heard by a county court or the High Court would raise an important point of principle or practice; or

(*b*)   there is some other compelling reason for the Court of Appeal to hear it,

the relevant court may order the appeal to be transferred to the Court of Appeal.

(2) This rule does not apply to proceedings in a magistrates' court.

30.14 Reopening of final appeals

(1) The High Court will not reopen a final determination of any appeal unless –

(*a*)   it is necessary to do so in order to avoid real injustice;

(*b*)   the circumstances are exceptional and make it appropriate to reopen the appeal; and

(*c*)   there is no alternative effective remedy.

(2) In paragraphs (1), (3), (4) and (6), "appeal" includes an application for permission to appeal.

(3) This rule does not apply to appeals to a county court.

(4) Permission is needed to make an application under this rule to reopen a final determination of an appeal.

(5) There is no right to an oral hearing of an application for permission unless, exceptionally, the judge so directs.

(6) The judge will not grant permission without directing the application to be served on the other party to the original appeal and giving that party an opportunity to make representations.

(7) There is no right of appeal or review from the decision of the judge on the application for permission, which is final.

(8) The procedure for making an application for permission is set out in Practice Direction 30A.

****

FAMILY PROCEDURE RULES: SUPPLEMENTARY PRACTICE DIRECTIONS

PRACTICE DIRECTION 3A –
PRE-APPLICATION PROTOCOL FOR MEDIATION INFORMATION AND ASSESSMENT

This Practice Direction supplements FPR Part 3 (Pre-Application Protocol for Mediation Information and Assessment)

Introduction

1.1 This Practice Direction applies where a person is considering applying for an order in family proceedings of a type specified in Annex B (referred to in this Direction as "relevant family proceedings").

1.2 Terms used in this Practice Direction and the accompanying Pre-action Protocol have the same meaning as in the FPR.

1.3 This Practice Direction is supplemented by the following Annexes:

(i) Annex A: The Pre-application Protocol ("the Protocol"), which sets out steps which the court will normally expect an applicant to follow before an application is made to the court in relevant family proceedings;

(ii) Annex B: Proceedings which are "relevant family proceedings" for the purposes of this Practice Direction; and

(iii) Annex C: Circumstances in which attendance at a Mediation Information and Assessment Meeting is not expected.

Aims

2.1 The purpose of this Practice Direction and the accompanying Protocol is to:

(a) supplement the court's powers in Part 3 of the FPR to encourage and facilitate the use of alternative dispute resolution;

(b) set out good practice to be followed by any person who is considering making an application to court for an order in relevant family proceedings; and

(c) ensure, as far as possible, that all parties have considered mediation as an alternative means of resolving their disputes.

Rationale

3.1 There is a general acknowledgement that an adversarial court process is not always best suited to the resolution of family disputes, particularly private law disputes between parents relating to children, with such disputes often best resolved through discussion and agreement, where that can be managed safely and appropriately.

3.2 Litigants who seek public funding for certain types of family proceedings are (subject to some exceptions) already required to attend a meeting with a mediator as a pre-condition of receiving public funding.

3.3 There is growing recognition of the benefits of early information and advice about mediation and of the need for those wishing to make an application to court, whether publicly funded or otherwise, to consider alternative means of resolving their disputes, as appropriate.

3.4 In private law proceedings relating to children, the court is actively involved in helping parties to explore ways of resolving their dispute. The Private Law Programme, set out in Practice Direction 12B, provides for a first hearing dispute resolution appointment ('FHDRA'), at which the judge, legal advisor or magistrates, accompanied by an officer from Cafcass (the Children and Family Court Advisory and Support Service), will discuss with parties both the nature of their dispute and whether it could be resolved by mediation or other alternative means and can give the parties information about services which may be available to assist them. The court should also have information obtained through safeguarding checks carried out by Cafcass, to ensure that any agreement between the parties, or any dispute resolution process selected, is in the interests of the child and safe for all concerned.

3.5 Against that background, it is likely to save court time and expense if the parties take steps to resolve their dispute without pursuing court proceedings. Parties will therefore be expected to explore the scope for resolving their dispute through mediation before embarking on the court process.

The Pre-application Protocol

4.1 To encourage this approach, all potential applicants for a court order in relevant family proceedings will be expected, before making their application, to have followed the steps set out in the Protocol. This requires a potential applicant except in certain specified circumstances, to consider with a mediator whether the dispute may be capable of being resolved through mediation. The court will expect all applicants to have complied with the Protocol before commencing proceedings and (except where any of the circumstances In Annex C applies) will expect any respondent to have attended a Mediation Information and Assessment Meeting, if invited to do so. If court proceedings are taken, the court will wish to know at the first hearing whether mediation has been considered by the parties. In considering the conduct of any relevant family proceedings, the court will take into account any failure to comply with the Protocol and may refer the parties to a meeting with a mediator before the proceedings continue further.

4.2 Nothing in the Protocol is to be read as affecting the operation of the Private Law Programme, set out in Practice Direction 12B, or the role of the court at the first hearing in any relevant family proceedings.

ANNEX A – THE PRE-APPLICATION PROTOCOL

1 This Protocol applies where a person ("the applicant") is considering making an application to the court for an order in relevant family proceedings.

2 Before an applicant makes an application to the court for an order in relevant family proceedings, the applicant (or the applicant's legal representative) should contact a family mediator to arrange for the applicant to attend an information meeting about family mediation and other forms of alternative dispute resolution (referred to in this Protocol as "a Mediation Information and Assessment Meeting").

3 An applicant is not expected to attend a Mediation Information and Assessment Meeting where any of the circumstances set out in Annex C applies.

4 Information on how to find a family mediator may be obtained from local family courts, from the Community Legal Advice Helpline – CLA Direct (0845 345 4345) or at www.direct.gov.uk.

5 The applicant (or the applicant's legal representative) should provide the mediator with contact details for the other party or parties to the dispute ("the respondent(s)"), so that the mediator can contact the respondent(s) to discuss that party's willingness and availability to attend a Mediation Information and Assessment Meeting.

6 The applicant should then attend a Mediation Information and Assessment Meeting arranged by the mediator. If the parties are willing to attend together, the meeting may be conducted jointly, but where necessary separate meetings may be held. If the applicant and respondent(s) do not attend a joint meeting, the mediator will invite the respondent(s) to a separate meeting unless any of the circumstances set out in Annex C applies.

7 A mediator who arranges a Mediation Information and Assessment Meeting with one or more parties to a dispute should consider with the party or parties concerned whether public funding may be available to meet the cost of the meeting and any subsequent mediation. Where none of the parties is eligible for, or wishes to seek, public funding, any charge made by the mediator for the Mediation Information and Assessment Meeting will be the responsibility of the party or parties attending, in accordance with any agreement made with the mediator.

8 If the applicant then makes an application to the court in respect of the dispute, the applicant should at the same time file a completed Family Mediation Information and Assessment Form (Form FM1) confirming attendance at a Mediation Information and Assessment Meeting or giving the reasons for not attending.

9 The Form FM1, must be completed and signed by the mediator, and countersigned by the applicant or the applicant's legal representative, where either:

- (*a*)   the applicant has attended a Mediation Information and Assessment Meeting; or
- (*b*)   the applicant has not attended a Mediation Information and Assessment Meeting and
  - (i)   the mediator is satisfied that mediation is not suitable because another party to the dispute is unwilling to attend a Mediation Information and Assessment Meeting and consider mediation;
  - (ii)   the mediator determines that the case is not suitable for a Mediation Information and Assessment Meeting; or
  - (iii)   a mediator has made a determination within the previous four months that the case is not suitable for a Mediation Information and Assessment Meeting or for mediation.

10 In all other circumstances, the Form FM1 must be completed and signed by the applicant or the applicant's legal representative.

11 The form may be obtained from magistrates' courts, county courts or the High Court or from www.direct.gov.uk.

ANNEX B – PROCEEDINGS WHICH ARE "RELEVANT FAMILY PROCEEDINGS" FOR THE PURPOSES OF THIS PRACTICE DIRECTION

1 Private law proceedings relating to children, except:

- proceedings for an enforcement order, a financial compensation order or an order under paragraph 9 or Part 2 of Schedule Al to the Children Act 1989;
- any other proceedings for enforcement of an order made in private law proceedings; or
- where emergency proceedings have been brought in respect of the same child(ren) and have not been determined.

("Private law proceedings" and "emergency proceedings" are defined in Rule 12.2)

2 Proceedings for a financial remedy, except:

- Proceedings for an avoidance of disposition order or an order preventing a disposition;
- Proceedings for enforcement of any order made in financial remedy proceedings.

("Financial remedy" is defined in Rule 2.3(1) and "avoidance of disposition order" and "order preventing a disposition" are defined in Rule 9.3(1))

ANNEX C – A PERSON CONSIDERING MAKING AN APPLICATION TO THE COURT IN RELEVANT FAMILY PROCEEDINGS IS NOT EXPECTED TO ATTEND A MEDIATION INFORMATION AND ASSESSMENT MEETING BEFORE DOING SO IF ANY OF THE FOLLOWING CIRCUMSTANCES APPLIES:

1 The mediator is satisfied that mediation is not suitable because another party to the dispute is unwilling to attend a Mediation Information and Assessment Meeting and consider mediation.

2 The mediator determines that the case is not suitable for a Mediation Information and Assessment Meeting.

3 A mediator has made a determination within the previous four months that the case is not suitable for a Mediation Information and Assessment Meeting or for mediation.

4 *Domestic abuse*

Any party has, to the applicant's knowledge, made an allegation of domestic violence against another party and this has resulted in a police investigation or the issuing of civil proceedings for the protection of any party within the last 12 months.

5 *Bankruptcy*

The dispute concerns financial issues and the applicant or another party is bankrupt.

6 The parties are in agreement and there is no dispute to mediate.

7 The whereabouts of the other party are unknown to the applicant.

8 The prospective application is for an order in relevant family proceedings which are already in existence and are continuing.

9 The prospective application is to be made without notice to the other party.

10 *Urgency*

The prospective application is urgent, meaning:

    (*a*)   there is a risk to the life, liberty or physical safety of the applicant or his or her family or his or her home; or

    (*b*)   any delay caused by attending a Mediation Information and Assessment Meeting would cause a risk of significant harm to a child, a significant risk of a miscarriage of justice, unreasonable hardship to the applicant or irretrievable problems in dealing with the dispute (such as an Irretrievable loss of significant evidence).

11 There is current social services involvement as a result of child protection concerns in respect of any child who would be the subject of the prospective application.

12 A child would be a party to the prospective application by virtue of Rule 12.3(1).

13 The applicant (or the applicant's legal representative) contacts three mediators within 15 miles of the applicant's home and none is able to conduct a Mediation Information and Assessment Meeting within 15 working days of the date of contact.

****

PRACTICE DIRECTION 6C – DISCLOSURE OF ADDRESSES BY GOVERNMENT DEPARTMENTS (AMENDING PD OF 13 FEBRUARY 1989 [AS AMENDED BY PRACTICE DIRECTION 20 JULY 1995])

This Practice Direction supplements FPR Part 6

The arrangements set out in the Registrar's Direction of 26 April 1988 whereby the court may request the disclosure of addresses by government departments have been further extended. These arrangements will now cover:

(a)   tracing the address of a person in proceedings against whom another person is seeking to obtain or enforce an order for financial provision either for himself or herself or for the children of the former marriage; and,

(b)   tracing the whereabouts of a child, or the person with whom the child is said to be, in proceedings under the Child Abduction and Custody Act 1985 or in which a [Part I order] is being sought or enforced.

Requests for such information will be made officially by the [district judge]. The request, in addition to giving the information mentioned below, should certify:

1 *In financial provision applications either*

(a)   that a financial provision order is in existence, but cannot be enforced because the person against whom the order has been made cannot be traced; or

(b)   that the applicant has filed or issued a notice, petition or originating summons containing an application for financial provision which cannot be served because the respondent cannot be traced.

[A "financial provision order" means any of the orders mentioned in s 21 of the Matrimonial Causes Act 1973, except an order under s 27(6) of that Act].

2 *In wardship proceedings* that the child is the subject of wardship proceedings and cannot be traced, and is believed to be with the person whose address is sought.

3 (*deleted*)

The following notes set out the information required by those departments which are likely to be of the greatest assistance to an applicant.

(1) Department of Social Security

The department most likely to be able to assist is the Department of Social Security, whose records are the most comprehensive and complete. The possibility of identifying one person amongst so many will depend on the particulars given. An address will not be supplied by the department unless it is satisfied from the particulars given that the record of the person has been reliably identified.

The applicant or his solicitor should therefore be asked to supply as much as possible of the following information about the person sought:

(i)   National Insurance number;

(ii)   surname;

(iii)   forenames in full;

(iv)   date of birth (or, if not known, approximate age);

(v)   last known address, with date when living there;

(vi)   any other known address(es) with dates;

(vii)   if the person sought is a war pensioner, his war pension and service particulars (if known);

and in applications for financial provision:

(viii) the exact date of the marriage and the wife's forenames.

Enquiries should be sent by the [district judge] to:

Contribution Agency
Special Section A, Room 101B
Longbenton
Newcastle upon Tyne
NE98 1YX

The department will be prepared to search if given full particulars of the person's name and date of birth, but the chances of accurate identification are increased by the provision of more identifying information.

Second requests for records to be searched, provided that a reasonable interval has elapsed, will be met by the Department of Social Security.

Income Support [/Supplementary Benefit]

Where, in the case of applications for financial provision, the wife is or has been in receipt of [income support/supplementary benefit], it would be advisable in the first instance to make enquiries of the manager of the local Social Security office for the area in which she resides in order to avoid possible duplication of enquiries.

(2) [Office for National Statistics]

National Health Service Central Register

[The Office for National Statistics] administers the National Health Service Central Register for the Department of Health. The records held in the Central Register include individuals' names, with dates of birth and National Health Service number, against a record of the Family Practitioner Committee area where the patient is currently registered with a National Health Service doctor. The Central Register does not hold individual patients' addresses, but can advise courts of the last Family Practitioner Committee area registration. Courts can then apply for information about addresses to the appropriate Family Practitioner Committee for independent action.

When application is made for the disclosure of Family Practitioner Committee area registrations from these records the applicant or his solicitor should supply as much as possible of the following information about the person sought:

(i) National Health Service number;
(ii) surname;
(iii) forenames in full;
(iv) date of birth (or, if not known, approximate age);
(v) last known address;
(vi) mother's maiden name.

Enquiries should be sent by the [district judge] to:

[The Office for National Statistics]
National Health Service Central Register
Smedley Hydro, Trafalgar Road
Southport
Merseyside PR8 2HH

(3) Passport Office

If all reasonable enquiries, including the aforesaid methods, have failed to reveal an address, or if there are strong grounds for believing that the person sought may have made a recent application for a passport, enquiries may be made to the Passport Office. The applicant or his solicitor should provide as much of the following information about the person as possible:

(i) surname;
(ii) forenames in full;
(iii) date of birth (or, if not known, approximate age);
(iv) place of birth;
(v) occupation;
(vi) whether known to have travelled abroad, and, if so, the destination and dates;
(vii) last known address, with date living there;
(viii) any other known address(es), with dates.

The applicant or his solicitor must also undertake in writing that information given in response to the enquiry will be used solely for the purpose for which it was requested, ie to assist in tracing the husband in connection with the making or enforcement of a financial provision order or in tracing a child in connection with a [Part 1 order] or wardship proceedings, as the case may be.

Enquiries should be sent to:

The Chief Passport Officer
[UK Passport Agency]
Home Office
Clive House, Petty France
London SW1H 9HD

(4) Ministry of Defence

In cases where the person sought is known to be serving or to have recently served in any branch of HM Forces, the solicitor representing the applicant may obtain the address for service of financial provision or [Part I] and wardship proceedings direct from the appropriate service department. In the case of army servicemen, the solicitor can obtain a list of regiments and of the various manning and record offices from the Officer in Charge, Central Manning Support Office, Higher Barracks, Exeter EC4 4ND.

The solicitor's request should be accompanied by a written undertaking that the address will be used for the purpose of service of process in those proceedings and that so far as is possible the solicitor will disclose the address only to the court and not to the applicant or any other person, except in the normal course of the proceedings.

Alternatively, if the solicitor wishes to serve process on the person's commanding officer under the provisions contained in s 101 of the Naval Act 1957, s 153 of the Army Act 1955 and s 153 of the Air Force Act 1955 (all of which as amended by s 62 of the Armed Forces Act 1971) he may obtain that officer's address in the same way.

Where the applicant is acting in person the appropriate service department is prepared to disclose the address of the person sought, or that of his commanding officer, to a [district judge] on receipt of an assurance that the applicant has given an undertaking that the information will be used solely for the purpose of serving process in the proceedings.

In all cases, the request should include details of the person's full name, service number, rank or rating, and his ship, arm or trade, corps, regiment or unit or as much of this information as is available. The request should also include details of his date of birth, or, if not known, his age, his date of entry into the service and, if no longer serving, the date of discharge, and any other information, such as his last known address. Failure to quote the service number and the rank or rating may result in failure to identify the serviceman or at least in considerable delay.

Enquiries should be addressed as follows:

[(a)	Officers of Royal Navy and Women's Royal Naval Service	The Naval Secretary Room 161 Victory Building HM Naval Base Portsmouth Hants PO1 3LS
	Ratings in the Royal Navy WRNS Ratings QARNNS Ratings	Captain Naval Drafting Centurion Building Grange Road Gosport Hants PO13 9XA
	RN Medical and Dental Officers	The Medical Director General (Naval) Room 114 Victory Building HM Naval Base Portsmouth Hants PO1 3LS
	Naval Chaplains	Director General Naval Chaplaincy Service Room 201 Victory Building HM Naval Base Portsmouth Hants PO1 3LS

(*b*)	Royal Marine Officers	The Naval Secretary
		Room 161
		Victory Building
		HM Naval Base
		Portsmouth
		Hants PO1 3LS
	Royal Marine Ranks	HQRM (DRORM)
		West Battery
		Whale Island
		Portsmouth
		Hants PO2 8DX
(*c*)	Army Officers (including WRAC and QARANC)	Army Officer Documentation Office
		Index Department
		Room F7
		Government Buildings
		Stanmore
		Middlesex
	Other Ranks, Army	The Manning and Record Office which is appropriate to the Regiment or Corps
(*d*)	Royal Air Force Officers and Other Ranks Women's Royal Air Force Officers and Other Ranks (including PMRA FNS)	Ministry of Defence
		RAF Personnel Management
		2b1(a) (RAF)
		Building 248
		RAF Innsworth
		Gloucester
		GL3 1EZ]

General notes

Records held by other departments are less likely to be of use, either because of their limited scope or because individual records cannot readily be identified. If, however, the circumstances suggest that the address may be known to another department, application may be made to it by the [district judge], all relevant particulars available being given.

When the department is able to supply the address of the person sought to the [district judge], it will be passed on by him to the applicant's solicitor (or, in proper cases, direct to the applicant if acting in person) on an understanding to use it only for the purpose of the proceedings.

Nothing in this practice direction affects the service in matrimonial causes of petitions which do not contain any application for financial provision, etc. The existing arrangements whereby the Department of Social Security will at the request of the solicitor forward a letter by ordinary post to a party's last known address remain in force in such cases.

The Registrar's Direction of 26 April 1988 is hereby revoked.

Issued [in its original form] with the concurrence of the Lord Chancellor.

****

PRACTICE DIRECTION 12B –
THE REVISED PRIVATE LAW PROGRAMME

This Practice Direction supplements FPR Part 12

1 Introduction

1.1 The Private Law Programme has achieved marked success in enabling the resolution of the majority of cases by consent at the First Hearing Dispute Resolution Appointment ("FHDRA"). It has been revised to build on the successes of the initial programme and to take account of recent developments in the law and practice associated with private family law.

1.2 In particular, there have been several legislative changes affecting private family law. The Allocation and Transfer of Proceedings Order 2008 (the "Allocation Order"), requires the transfer of cases from the County Court to the Family Proceedings Court (FPC). Sections 1 to 5 and Schedule 1 of the Children and Adoption Act 2006 which came into force on 8th December 2008, amends the Children Act 1989 by introducing Contact Activity Directions, Contact Activity Conditions, Contact Monitoring Requirements, Financial Compensation Orders and Enforcement Orders.

1.3 There has been growing recognition of the impact of domestic violence and abuse, drug and alcohol misuse and mental illness, on the proper consideration of the issues in private family law; this includes the acceptance that Court orders, even those made by consent, must be scrutinised to ensure that they are safe and take account of any risk factors. Coupled with this is the need to take account of the duty on Cafcass, pursuant to s 16A Children Act 1989, to undertake risk assessments where an officer of the Service ("Cafcass Officer") suspects that a child is at risk of harm (References to Cafcass include CAFCASS CYMRU and references to the Cafcass Officer include the Welsh family proceedings officer in Wales).

1.4 There is awareness of the importance of involving children where appropriate in the decision making process.

1.5 The Revised Programme incorporates these developments. It also retains the essential feature of the FHDRA as the forum for the parties to be helped to reach agreement as to, and understanding of, the issues that divide them. It recognises that having reached agreement parties may need assistance in putting it into effect in a co-operative way.

1.6 The Revised Programme is designed to provide a framework for the consistent national approach to the resolution of the issues in private family law whilst enabling local practices and initiatives to be operated in addition and within the framework.

1.7 The Revised Programme is designed to assist parties to reach safe agreements where possible, to provide a forum in which to find the best way to resolve issues in each individual case and to promote outcomes that are sustainable, that are in the best interests of children and that take account of their perspectives.

2 Principles

2.1 Where an application is made to a court under Part II of the Children Act 1989, the child's welfare is the court's paramount concern. The court will apply the principle of the "Overriding Objective" to enable it to deal with a case justly, having regard to the welfare principles involved. So far as practicable the Court will –

(a)   Deal expeditiously and fairly with every case;
(b)   Deal with a case in ways which are proportionate to the nature, importance and complexity of the issues;
(c)   Ensure that the parties are on an equal footing;
(d)   Save unnecessary expense;
(e)   Allot to each case an appropriate share of the court's resources, while taking account of the need to allot resources to other cases.

2.2 The court will give effect to the overriding objective when applying this programme and when exercising its powers to manage cases.

The parties are required to help the court further the overriding objective and promote the welfare of the child by the application of the welfare principle, pursuant to s 1(1) of the Children Act 1989.

This Programme provides that consideration and discussion of all issues will not take place until the FHDRA when parties are on an equal footing and can hear what is said to and by each other. This excludes the safety checks and enquiries carried out by Cafcass before the first hearing that are required for that hearing and deal only with safety issues.

At the **FHDRA** the Court shall consider in particular –

(a)   Whether and the extent to which the parties can safely resolve some or all of the issues with the assistance of the Cafcass Officer and any available mediator.
(b)   Risk identification followed by active case management including risk assessment, and compliance with the Practice Direction 14th January 2009: "Residence and Contact Orders: Domestic Violence and Harm".
(c)   Further dispute resolution.
(d)   The avoidance of delay through the early identification of issues and timetabling, subject to the Allocation Order.
(e)   Judicial scrutiny of the appropriateness of consent orders.
(f)   Judicial consideration of the way to involve the child.
(g)   Judicial continuity.

3 Practical arrangements before the FHDRA

3.1 Applications shall be issued on the day of receipt in accordance with the appropriate Rules of Procedure. It is important that the form C100 is fully completed, especially on pages 1, 2, 3, and 5 otherwise delay may be caused by requests for information.

3.2 If possible at the time of issue, and in any event by no later than 24 hours after issue, or in courts where applications are first considered on paper, by no later than 48 hours after issue, the court shall

(i)   send or hand to the Applicant
(ii)   send to Cafcass

the following:

(a)   a copy of the Application Form C100, (together with Supplemental Information Form C1A) (if provided) (references to form C1A are to be read as form C100A following the introduction of this replacement form),
(b)   the Notice of Hearing,
(c)   the Acknowledgment Form C7,

(*d*)   a blank Form C1A,
(*e*)   the Certificate of Service Form C9,
(*f*)   information leaflets for the parties.

3.3 Save in urgent cases that require an earlier listing, the fully effective operation of this Practice Direction requires the FHDRA to take place within **4** weeks of the application. Where practicable, the first hearing must be listed to be heard in this period and in any event no later than within **6** weeks of the application. Where, at the time of introduction of this Programme, the Designated Family Judge/Justices' Clerk determines that it is not practicable to list the first hearing within 4 weeks, they should, in consultation with HMCS and Cafcass, formulate a timetable for revisiting the position and managing to list the FHDRA within 4 weeks.

3.4 Copies of each Application Form C100 and Notice of Hearing shall be sent by the court to Cafcass in accordance with 3.2 above.

3.5 The Respondent shall have at least 14 days notice of the hearing where practicable, but the court may abridge this time.

3.6 The Respondent should file a response on the Forms C7/C1A no later than 14 days before the hearing.

3.7 A copy of Forms C7/C1A shall be sent by the court to Cafcass on the day of receipt.

3.8 **NOTE:** This provision relates to cases that are placed in the FHDRA list for hearing other than by direct application in accordance with the procedure referred to in paragraph 3.1. Such listing may follow an application under the Family Law Act 1996, or a direction by the Court in other proceedings. In all such cases, or where the Court adjourns proceedings to a 'dispute resolution hearing' (sometimes called 'conciliation'), this will be treated as an adjournment to a FHDRA, and the documents referred to in para 3.2 must be filed and copied to parties and Cafcass for safety checks and enquiries, in the same way.

3.9 Before the FHDRA Cafcass shall identify any safety issues by the steps outlined below. Such steps shall be confined to matters of safety. Neither Cafcass nor a Cafcass Officer shall discuss with either party before the FHDRA any matter other than relates to safety. The Parties will not be invited to talk about other issues, for example relating to the substance of applications or replies or about issues concerning matters of welfare or the prospects of resolution. If such issues are raised by either party they will be advised that such matters will be deferred to the FHDRA when there is equality between the parties and full discussion can take place which will also be a time when any safety issues that have been identified also can be taken into account.

(*a*)   In order to inform the court of possible risks of harm to the child in accordance with its safeguarding framework Cafcass will carry out safeguarding enquiries, including checks of local authorities and police, and telephone risk identification interviews with parties.
(*b*)   If risks of harm are identified, Cafcass may invite parties to meet separately with the Cafcass Officer before the FHDRA to clarify any safety issue.
(*c*)   Cafcass shall record and outline any safety issues for the court.
(*d*)   The Cafcass Officer will not initiate contact with the child prior to the FHDRA. If contacted by a child, discussions relating to the issues in the case will be postponed to the day of the hearing or after when the Cafcass officer will have more knowledge of the issues.

(*e*)   At least 3 days before the hearing the Cafcass Officer shall report the outcome of risk identification work to the court by completing the Form at Schedule 2.

4 The First Hearing Dispute Resolution Appointment.

4.1 The parties and Cafcass Officer shall attend this hearing. A mediator may attend where available.

4.2 At the hearing, which is not privileged, the court should have the following documents:

(*a*)   C100 application, and C1A if any
(*b*)   Notice of Hearing
(*c*)   C7 response and C1A if any
(*d*)   Schedule 2 safeguarding information

4.3 The detailed arrangements for the participation of mediators will be arranged locally. These will include:

(*a*)   Arrangements for the mediator to ask the parties in a particular case to consent to the mediator seeing the papers in the case where it seems appropriate to do so.
(*b*)   Arrangements for the mediator to ask the parties to waive privilege for the purpose of the first hearing where it seems to the mediator appropriate to do so in order to assist the work of the mediator and the outcome of the first hearing.
(*c*)   In all cases it is important that such arrangements are put in place in a way that avoids any pressure being brought to bear in this connection on the parties that is inconsistent with general good mediation practice.

4.4 At the FHDRA the Court, in collaboration with the Cafcass Officer, and with the assistance of any mediator present, will seek to assist the parties in conciliation and in resolution of all or any of the issues between them. Any remaining issues will be identified, the Cafcass Officer will advise the court of any recommended means of resolving such issues and directions will be given for the future resolution of such issues. At all times the decisions of the Court and the work of the Cafcass Officer will take account of any risk or safeguarding issues that have been identified.

4.5 The Cafcass Officer shall, where practicable, speak separately to each party at court and before the hearing.

4.6 In the County Court, the Court shall have available a telephone contact to the Family Proceedings Court listing manager, diary dates for the appropriate Family Proceedings Court, or other means by which the County Court, at the time of the hearing, will be able to list subsequent hearings in the Family Proceedings Court.

5 Conduct of the Hearing. The following matters shall be considered

5.1 **Safeguarding:**

(*a*)   The court shall inform the parties of the content of any screening report or other information which has been provided by Cafcass, unless it considers that to do so would create a risk of harm to a party or the child. The court may need to consider whether and how any information contained in the checks should be disclosed to the parties if Cafcass have not disclosed it.
(*b*)   Whether a risk assessment is required and when.

(c) Whether a fact finding hearing is needed to determine allegations whose resolution is likely to affect the decision of the court.

5.2 Dispute Resolution:

(a) There will be at every FHDRA a period in which the Cafcass Officer, with the assistance of any Mediator and in collaboration with the Court, will seek to conciliate and explore with the parties the resolution of all or some of the issues between them. The procedure to be followed in this connection at the hearing will be determined by local arrangements between the Cafcass manager, or equivalent in Wales, and the Designated Family Judge or the Justices' Clerk where appropriate.

(b) What is the result of any such meeting at Court?

(c) What other options there are for resolution e.g. may the case be suitable for further intervention by Cafcass; mediation by an external provider; collaborative law or use of a parenting plan?

(d) Would the parties be assisted by attendance at Parenting Information Programmes or other activities, whether by formal statutory provision under section 11 Children Act 1989 as amended by Children and Adoption Act 2006 or otherwise?

5.3 Consent Orders:

Where agreement is reached at any hearing or submitted in writing to the court, no order will be made without scrutiny by the court. Where safeguarding checks or risk assessment work remain outstanding, the making of a final order may be deferred for such work. In such circumstances the court shall adjourn the case for no longer than 28 days to a fixed date. A written notification of this work is to be provided by Cafcass in accordance with the timescale specified by the court. If satisfactory information is then available, the order may be made at the adjourned hearing in the agreed terms without the need for attendance by the parties. If satisfactory information is not available, the order will not be made, and the case will be adjourned for further consideration with an opportunity for the parties to make further representations.

5.4 Reports:

(a) Are there welfare issues or other specific considerations which should be addressed in a report by Cafcass or the Local Authority? Before a report is ordered, the court should consider alternative ways of working with the parties such as are referred to in paragraph 5.2 above. If a report is ordered in accordance with Section 7 of the Children Act 1989, it should be directed specifically towards and limited to those issues. General requests should be avoided and the Court should state in the Order the specific factual and other issues that are to be addressed in a focused report. In determining whether a request for a report should be directed to the relevant local authority or to Cafcass, the court should consider such information as Cafcass has provided about the extent and nature of the local authority's current or recent involvement with the subject of the application and the parties, and any relevant protocol between Cafcass and the Association of Directors of Children's Services.

(b) Is there a need for an investigation under S 37 Children Act 1989?

(c) A copy of the Order requesting the report and any relevant court documents are to be sent to Cafcass or, in the case of the Local Authority, to the Legal Adviser to the Director of the Local Authority Children's Services and, where known, to the allocated social worker by the court forthwith.

(*d*)　Is any expert evidence required in compliance with the Experts' Practice Direction?

5.5 Wishes and feelings of the child:

(*a*)　Is the child aware of the proceedings?
How are the wishes and feelings of the child to be ascertained (if at all)?
(*b*)　How is the child to be involved in the proceedings, if at all, and whether at or after the FHDRA?
(*c*)　If consideration is given to the joining of the child as a party to the application, the court should consider the current Guidance from the President of the Family Division. Where the court is considering the appointment of a guardian ad litem, it should first seek to ensure that the appropriate Cafcass manager has been spoken to so as to consider any advice in connection with the prospective appointment and the timescale involved. In considering whether to make such an appointment the Court shall take account of the demands on the resources of Cafcass that such appointment would make.
(*d*)　Who will inform the child of the outcome of the case where appropriate?

5.6 Case Management:

(*a*)　What, if any, issues are agreed and what are the key issues to be determined?
(*b*)　Are there any interim orders which can usefully be made (e.g. indirect, supported or supervised contact) pending final hearing?
(*c*)　What directions are required to ensure the application is ready for final hearing – statements, reports etc?
(*d*)　List for final hearing, consider the need for judicial continuity (especially if there has been or is to be a fact finding hearing or a contested interim hearing).

5.7 Transfer to FPC:

The case should be transferred to the FPC, pursuant to the Allocation and Transfer of Proceedings Order 2008 unless one of the specified exceptions applies. The date should be fixed at court and entered on the order.

6 The Order

6.1 The Order shall set out in particular:

(*a*)　The issues about which the parties are agreed
(*b*)　The issues that remain to be resolved
(*c*)　The steps that are planned to resolve the issues
(*d*)　Any interim arrangements pending such resolution, including arrangements for the involvement of children.
(*e*)　The timetable for such steps and, where this involves further hearings, the date of such hearings.
(*f*)　A statement as to any facts relating to risk or safety; in so far as they are resolved the result will be stated and, in so far as not resolved, the steps to be taken to resolve them will be stated.
(*g*)　If it be the case, the fact of the transfer of the case to the Family Proceedings Court with the date and purpose of the next hearing
(*h*)　If it be the case, the fact that the case cannot be transferred to the Family Proceedings Court and the reason for the decision.
(*i*)　Whether in the event of an order, by consent or otherwise, or pending such an order, the parties are to be assisted by participation in mediation, Parenting

Information Programmes, or other types of parenting intervention, and to detail any contact activity directions or conditions imposed by the court.

6.2 A suggested template order is available as set out in Schedule 1 below.

7 Commencement and Implementation

7.1 This Practice Direction will come into effect on April 1st 2010. So that procedural changes can be made by all agencies, the requirement for full implementation of the provisions is postponed, but in any event it should be effected by no later than October 4th 2010.

SCHEDULE 1

The suggested form of Order which courts may wish to use is PLP10 which is available from Her Majesty's Court Service.

SCHEDULE 2

Report Form on outcome of safeguarding enquiries. See version for Cafcass in England and for CAFCASS CYMRU in Wales.

****

PRACTICE DIRECTION 12G – COMMUNICATION OF INFORMATION

This Practice Direction supplements FPR Part 12, Chapter 7

1.1 Chapter 7 deals with the communication of information (whether or not contained in a document filed with the court) relating to proceedings which relate to children.

1.2 Subject to any direction of the court, information may be communicated for the purposes of the law relating to contempt in accordance with paragraphs 2.1, 3.1 or 4.1.

Communication of information by a party etc. for other purposes

2.1 A person specified in the first column of the following table may communicate to a person listed in the second column such information as is specified in the third column for the purpose or purposes specified in the fourth column –

| A party | A lay adviser, a McKenzie Friend, or a person arranging or providing pro bono legal services | Any information relating to the proceedings | To enable the party to obtain advice or assistance in relation to the proceedings |

A party	A health care professional or a person or body providing counselling services for children or families	To enable the party or any child of the party to obtain health care or counselling
A party	The Child Maintenance and Enforcement Commission, a McKenzie Friend, a lay adviser or the First-tier Tribunal dealing with an appeal made under section 20 of the Child Support Act 1991	For the purposes of making or responding to an appeal under section 20 of the Child Support Act 1991 or the determination of such an appeal
A party	An adoption panel	To enable the adoption panel to discharge its functions as appropriate
A party	The European Court of Human Rights	For the purpose of making an application to the European Court of Human Rights
A party or any person lawfully in receipt of information	The Children's Commissioner or the Children's Commissioner for Wales	To refer an issue affecting the interests of children to the Children's Commissioner or the Children's Commissioner for Wales
A party, any person lawfully in receipt of information or a proper officer	A person or body conducting an approved research project	For the purpose of an approved research project

A legal representative or a professional legal adviser	A person or body responsible for investigating or determining complaints in relation to legal representatives or professional legal advisers	For the purposes of the investigation or determination of a complaint in relation to a legal representative or a professional legal adviser	
A legal representative or a professional legal adviser	A person or body assessing quality assurance systems	To enable the legal representative or professional legal adviser to obtain a quality assurance assessment	
A legal representative or a professional legal adviser	An accreditation body	Any information relating to the proceedings providing that it does not, or is not likely to, identify any person involved in the proceedings	To enable the legal representative or professional legal adviser to obtain accreditation
A party	A police officer	The text or summary of the whole or part of a judgment given in the proceedings	For the purpose of a criminal investigation
A party or any person lawfully in receipt of information	A member of the Crown Prosecution Service	To enable the Crown Prosecution Service to discharge its functions under any enactment	

Communication for the effective functioning of Cafcass and CAFCASS CYMRU

3.1 An officer of the Service or a Welsh family proceedings officer, as appropriate, may communicate to a person listed in the second column such information as is specified in the third column for the purpose or purposes specified in the fourth column –

A Welsh family proceedings officer	A person or body exercising statutory functions relating to inspection of CAFCASS CYMRU	Any information relating to the proceedings which is required by the person or body responsible for the inspection	For the purpose of an inspection of CAFCASS CYMRU by a body or person appointed by the Welsh Ministers

An officer of the Service or a Welsh family proceedings officer	The General Social Care Council or the Care Council for Wales	Any information relating to the proceedings providing that it does not, or is not likely to, identify any person involved in the proceedings	For the purpose of initial and continuing accreditation as a social worker of a person providing services to Cafcass or CAFCASS CYMRU in accordance with section 13(2) of the Criminal Justice and Courts Services Act 2000 or section 36 of the Children Act 2004 as the case may be
An officer of the Service or a Welsh family proceedings officer	A person or body providing services relating to professional development or training to Cafcass or CAFCASS CYMRU	Any information relating to the proceedings providing that it does not, or is not likely to, identify any person involved in the proceedings without that person's consent	To enable the person or body to provide the services, where the services cannot be effectively provided without such disclosure
An officer of the Service or a Welsh family proceedings officer	A person employed by or contracted to Cafcass or CAFCASS CYMRU for the purposes of carrying out the functions referred to in column 4 of this row	Any information relating to the proceedings	Engagement in processes internal to Cafcass or CAFCASS CYMRU which relate to the maintenance of necessary records concerning the proceedings, or to ensuring that Cafcass or CAFCASS CYMRU functions are carried out to a satisfactory standard

Communication to and by Ministers of the Crown and Welsh Ministers

4.1 A person specified in the first column of the following table may communicate to a person listed in the second column such information as is specified in the third column for the purpose or purposes specified in the fourth column –

A party or any person lawfully in receipt of information relating to the proceedings	A Minister of the Crown with responsibility for a government department engaged, or potentially engaged, in an application before the European Court of Human Rights relating to the proceedings	Any information relating to the proceedings of which he or she is in lawful possession	To provide the department with information relevant, or potentially relevant, to the proceedings before the European Court of Human Rights
A Minister of the Crown	The European Court of Human Rights	For the purpose of engagement in an application before the European Court of Human Rights relating to the proceedings	
A Minister of the Crown	Lawyers advising or representing the United Kingdom in an application before the European Court of Human Rights relating to the proceedings	For the purpose of receiving advice or for effective representation in relation to the application before the European Court of Human Rights.	
A Minister of the crown or a Welsh Minister	Another Minister, or Ministers, of the Crown or a Welsh Minister	For the purpose of notification, discussion and the giving or receiving of advice regarding issues raised by the information in which the relevant departments have, or may have, an interest	

5.1 This paragraph applies to communications made in accordance with paragraphs 2.1, 3.1 and 4.1 and the reference in this paragraph to "the table" means the table in the relevant paragraph.

5.2 A person in the second column of the table may only communicate information relating to the proceedings received from a person in the first column for the purpose or purposes –

(a)   for which he or she received that information; or

(b)   of professional development or training, providing that any communication does not, or is not likely to, identify any person involved in the proceedings without that person's consent.

6.1 In this Practice Direction –

"accreditation body" means –
- (a)   The Law Society,
- (b)   Resolution, or
- (c)   The Legal Services Commission;

"adoption panel" means a panel established in accordance with regulation 3 of the Adoption Agencies Regulations 2005 or regulation 3 of the Adoption Agencies (Wales) Regulations 2005;

"approved research project" means a project of research –
- (a)   approved in writing by a Secretary of State after consultation with the President of the Family Division,
- (b)   approved in writing by the President of the Family Division, or
- (c)   conducted under section 83 of the Act of 1989 or section 13 of the Criminal Justice and Court Services Act 2000;

"body assessing quality assurance systems" includes –
- (a)   The Law Society,
- (b)   The Legal Services Commission, or
- (c)   The General Council of the Bar;

"body or person responsible for investigating or determining complaints in relation to legal representatives or professional legal advisers" means –
- (a)   The Law Society,
- (b)   The General Council of the Bar,
- (c)   The Institute of Legal Executives,
- (d)   The Legal Services Ombudsman; or
- (e)   The Office of Legal Complaints.

"Cafcass" has the meaning assigned to it by section 11 of the Criminal Justice and Courts Services Act 2000;

"CAFCASS CYMRU" means the part of the Welsh Assembly Government exercising the functions of Welsh Ministers under Part 4 of the Children Act 2004;

"criminal investigation" means an investigation conducted by police officers with a view to it being ascertained –
- (a)   whether a person should be charged with an offence, or
- (b)   whether a person charged with an offence is guilty of it;

"health care professional" means –
- (a)   a registered medical practitioner,
- (b)   a registered nurse or midwife,
- (c)   a clinical psychologist, or
- (d)   a child psychotherapist;

"lay adviser" means a non-professional person who gives lay advice on behalf of an organisation in the lay advice sector;

"McKenzie Friend" means any person permitted by the court to sit beside an unrepresented litigant in court to assist that litigant by prompting, taking notes and giving him advice; and "social worker" has the meaning assigned to it by section 55 of the Care Standards Act 2000.

****

PRACTICE DIRECTION 12I –
APPLICATIONS FOR REPORTING RESTRICTION ORDERS

This Practice Direction supplements FPR Part 12

1 This direction applies to any application in the Family Division founded on Convention rights for an order restricting publication of information about children or incapacitated adults.

2 Applications to be heard in the High Court

Orders can only be made in the High Court and are normally dealt with by a Judge of the Family Division. If the need for an order arises in existing proceedings in the county court, judges should either transfer the application to the High Court or consult their Family Division Liaison Judge. Where the matter is urgent, it can be heard by the Urgent Applications Judge of the Family Division (out of hours contact number 020 7947 6000).

3 Service of application on the national news media

Section 12(2) of the Human Rights Act 1998 means that an injunction restricting the exercise of the right to freedom of expression must not be granted where the person against whom the application is made is neither present nor represented unless the court is satisfied (*a*) that the applicant has taken all practicable steps to notify the respondent, or (*b*) that there are compelling reasons why the respondent should not be notified.

Service of applications for reporting restriction orders on the national media can now be effected via the Press Association's CopyDirect service, to which national newspapers and broadcasters subscribe as a means of receiving notice of such applications.

The court will bear in mind that legal advisers to the media (i) are used to participating in hearings at very short notice where necessary; and (ii) are able to differentiate between information provided for legal purposes and information for editorial use. Service of applications via the CopyDirect service should henceforth be the norm.

The court retains the power to make without notice orders, but such cases will be exceptional, and an order will always give persons affected liberty to apply to vary or discharge it at short notice.

4 Further guidance

The *Practice Note Applications for Reporting Restriction Orders* dated 18 March 2005 and issued jointly by the Official Solicitor and the Deputy Director of Legal Services, provides valuable guidance and should be followed.

5 Issued with the concurrence and approval of the Lord Chancellor.

PRACTICE DIRECTION 12J –
RESIDENCE AND CONTACT ORDERS: DOMESTIC VIOLENCE AND HARM

This Practice Direction supplements FPR Part 12

1 This Practice Direction applies to any family proceedings in the High Court, a county court or a magistrates' court in which an application is made for a residence order or a contact order in respect of a child under the Children Act 1989 ("the 1989 Act") or the Adoption and Children Act 2002 ("the 2002 Act") or in which any question arises about residence or about contact between a child and a parent or other family member.

2 The practice set out in this Direction is to be followed in any case in which it is alleged, or there is otherwise reason to suppose, that the subject child or a party has experienced domestic violence perpetrated by another party or that there is a risk of such violence. For the purpose of this Direction, the term 'domestic violence' includes physical violence, threatening or intimidating behaviour and any other form of abuse which, directly or indirectly, may have caused harm to the other party or to the child or which may give rise to the risk of harm.

> ('Harm' in relation to a child means ill-treatment or the impairment of health or development, including, for example, impairment suffered from seeing or hearing the ill-treatment of another: Children Act 1989, ss 31(9), 105(1))

General principles

3 The court must, at all stages of the proceedings, consider whether domestic violence is raised as an issue, either by the parties or otherwise, and if so must:

- identify at the earliest opportunity the factual and welfare issues involved;
- consider the nature of any allegation or admission of domestic violence and the extent to which any domestic violence which is admitted, or which may be proved, would be relevant in deciding whether to make an order about residence or contact and, if so, in what terms;
- give directions to enable the relevant factual and welfare issues to be determined expeditiously and fairly.

4 In all cases it is for the court to decide whether an order for residence or contact accords with Section 1(1) of the 1989 Act or section 1(2) of the 2002 Act, as appropriate; any proposed residence or contact order, whether to be made by agreement between the parties or otherwise must be scrutinised by the court accordingly. The court shall not make a consent order for residence or contact or give permission for an application for a residence or contact order to be withdrawn, unless the parties are present in court, except where it is satisfied that there is no risk of harm to the child in so doing.

5 In considering, on an application for a consent order for residence or contact, whether there is any risk of harm to the child, the court shall consider all the evidence and information available. The court may direct a report under Section 7 of the 1989 Act either orally or in writing before it makes its determination; in such a case, the court may ask for information about any advice given by the officer preparing the report to the parties and whether they or the child have been referred to any other agency, including local authority children's services. If the report is not in writing, the court shall make a note of its substance on the court file.

Issue

6 Immediately on receipt of an application for a residence order or a contact order, or of the acknowledgement of the application, the court shall send a copy of it, together with any accompanying documents, to Cafcass or Cafcass Cymru, as appropriate, to enable Cafcass or Cafcass Cymru to undertake initial screening in accordance with their safeguarding policies.

Liaison

7 The Designated Family Judge, or in the magistrates' court the Justices' Clerk, shall take steps to ensure that arrangements are in place for:

- the prompt delivery of documents to Cafcass or Cafcass Cymru in accordance with paragraph 6
- any information obtained by Cafcass or Cafcass Cymru as a result of initial screening or otherwise and any risk assessments prepared by Cafcass or Cafcass Cymru under section 16A of the 1989 Act to be placed before the appropriate court for consideration and directions
- a copy of any record of admissions or findings of fact made pursuant to paragraphs 12 & 21 below to be made available as soon as possible to any Officer of Cafcass or Welsh family proceedings officer or local authority officer preparing a report under section 7 of the 1989 Act.

Response of the court on receipt of information

8 Where any information provided to the court before the first hearing, whether as a result of initial screening by Cafcass or Cafcass Cymru or otherwise, indicates that there are issues of domestic violence which may be relevant to the court's determination, the court may give directions about the conduct of the hearing and for written evidence to be filed by the parties before the hearing.

9 If at any stage the court is advised by Cafcass or Cafcass Cymru or otherwise that there is a need for special arrangements to secure the safety of any party or child attending any hearing, the court shall ensure that appropriate arrangements are made for the hearing and for all subsequent hearings in the case, unless it considers that those are no longer necessary.

First hearing

10 At the first hearing, the court shall inform the parties of the content of any screening report or other information which has been provided by Cafcass or Cafcass Cymru, unless it considers that to do so would create a risk of harm to a party or the child.

(Specific provision about service of a risk assessment under section 16A of the 1989 Act is made by rule 12.34 of the Family Procedure Rules 2010.)

11 The court must ascertain at the earliest opportunity whether domestic violence is raised as an issue and must consider the likely impact of that issue on the conduct and outcome of the proceedings. In particular, the court should consider whether the nature and effect of the domestic violence alleged is such that, if proved, the decision of the court is likely to be affected.

Admissions

12 Where at any hearing an admission of domestic violence to another person or the child is made by a party, the admission should be recorded in writing and retained on the court file.

Directions for a fact-finding hearing

13 The court should determine as soon as possible whether it is necessary to conduct a fact-finding hearing in relation to any disputed allegation of domestic violence before it

can proceed to consider any final order(s) for residence or contact. Where the court determines that a finding of fact hearing is not necessary, the order shall record the reasons for that decision.

14 Where the court considers that a fact-finding hearing is necessary, it must give directions to ensure that the matters in issue are determined expeditiously and fairly and in particular it should consider:

- directing the parties to file written statements giving particulars of the allegations made and of any response in such a way as to identify clearly the issues for determination;
- whether material is required from third parties such as the police or health services and may give directions accordingly;
- whether any other evidence is required to enable the court to make findings of fact in relation to the allegations and may give directions accordingly.

15 Where the court fixes a fact-finding hearing, it must at the same time fix a further hearing for determination of the application. The hearings should be arranged in such a way that they are conducted by the same judge or, in the magistrates' court, by at least the same chairperson of the justices.

Reports under Section 7

16 In any case where domestic violence is raised as an issue, the court should consider directing that a report on the question of contact, or any other matters relating to the welfare of the child, be prepared under section 7 of the 1989 Act by an Officer of Cafcass or a Welsh family proceedings officer (or local authority officer if appropriate), unless the court is satisfied that it is not necessary to do so in order to safeguard the child's interests. If the court so directs, it should consider the extent of any enquiries which can properly be made at this stage and whether it is appropriate to seek information on the wishes and feelings of the child before findings of fact have been made.

Representation of the child

17 Subject to the seriousness of the allegations made and the difficulty of the case, the court shall consider whether it is appropriate for the child who is the subject of the application to be made a party to the proceedings and be separately represented. If the case is proceeding in the magistrates' court and the court considers that it may be appropriate for the child to be made a party to the proceedings, it may transfer the case to the relevant county court for determination of that issue and following such transfer the county court shall give such directions for the further conduct of the case as it considers appropriate.

Interim orders before determination of relevant facts

18 Where the court gives directions for a fact-finding hearing, the court should consider whether an interim order for residence or contact is in the interests of the child; and in particular whether the safety of the child and the residential parent can be secured before, during and after any contact.

19 In deciding any question of interim residence or contact pending a full hearing the court should: –

(*a*) take into account the matters set out in section 1(3) of the 1989 Act or section 1(4) of the 2002 Act ('the welfare check-list'), as appropriate;

(*b*)   give particular consideration to the likely effect on the child of any contact and any risk of harm, whether physical, emotional or psychological, which the child is likely to suffer as a consequence of making or declining to make an order;

20 Where the court is considering whether to make an order for interim contact, it should in addition consider

(*a*)   the arrangements required to ensure, as far as possible, that any risk of harm to the child is minimised and that the safety of the child and the parties is secured; and in particular:

(i)   whether the contact should be supervised or supported, and if so, where and by whom; and

(ii)   the availability of appropriate facilities for that purpose

(*b*)   if direct contact is not appropriate, whether it is in the best interests of the child to make an order for indirect contact.

The fact-finding hearing

21 At the fact-finding hearing, the court should, wherever practicable, make findings of fact as to the nature and degree of any domestic violence which is established and its effect on the child, the child's parents and any other relevant person. The court shall record its findings in writing, and shall serve a copy on the parties. A copy of any record of findings of fact or of admissions must be sent to any officer preparing a report under Section 7 of the 1989 Act.

22 At the conclusion of any fact-finding hearing, the court shall consider, notwithstanding any earlier direction for a section 7 report, whether it is in the best interests of the child for the court to give further directions about the preparation or scope of any report under section 7; where necessary, it may adjourn the proceedings for a brief period to enable the officer to make representations about the preparation or scope of any further enquiries. The court should also consider whether it would be assisted by any social work, psychiatric, psychological or other assessment of any party or the child and if so (subject to any necessary consent) make directions for such assessment to be undertaken and for the filing of any consequent report.

23 Where the court has made findings of fact on disputed allegations, any subsequent hearing in the proceedings should be conducted by the same judge or, in the magistrates' court, by at least the same chairperson of the justices. Exceptions may be made only where observing this requirement would result in delay to the planned timetable and the judge or chairperson is satisfied, for reasons recorded in writing, that the detriment to the welfare of the child would outweigh the detriment to the fair trial of the proceedings.

In all cases where domestic violence has occurred

24 The court should take steps to obtain (or direct the parties or an Officer of Cafcass or a Welsh family proceedings officer to obtain) information about the facilities available locally to assist any party or the child in cases where domestic violence has occurred.

25 Following any determination of the nature and extent of domestic violence, whether or not following a fact-finding hearing, the court should consider whether any party should seek advice or treatment as a precondition to an order for residence or contact being made or as a means of assisting the court in ascertaining the likely risk of harm to the child from that person, and may (with the consent of that party) give directions for such attendance and the filing of any consequent report.

Factors to be taken into account when determining whether to make residence or contact orders in all cases where domestic violence has occurred

26 When deciding the issue of residence or contact the court should, in the light of any findings of fact, apply the individual matters in the welfare checklist with reference to those findings; in particular, where relevant findings of domestic violence have been made, the court should in every case consider any harm which the child has suffered as a consequence of that violence and any harm which the child is at risk of suffering if an order for residence or contact is made and should only make an order for contact if it can be satisfied that the physical and emotional safety of the child and the parent with whom the child is living can, as far as possible, be secured before during and after contact.

27 In every case where a finding of domestic violence is made, the court should consider the conduct of both parents towards each other and towards the child; in particular, the court should consider;

(a)   the effect of the domestic violence which has been established on the child and on the parent with whom the child is living;

(b)   the extent to which the parent seeking residence or contact is motivated by a desire to promote the best interests of the child or may be doing so as a means of continuing a process of violence, intimidation or harassment against the other parent;

(c)   the likely behaviour during contact of the parent seeking contact and its effect on the child;

(d)   the capacity of the parent seeking residence or contact to appreciate the effect of past violence and the potential for future violence on the other parent and the child;

(e)   the attitude of the parent seeking residence or contact to past violent conduct by that parent; and in particular whether that parent has the capacity to change and to behave appropriately.

Directions as to how contact is to proceed

28 Where the court has made findings of domestic violence but, having applied the welfare checklist, nonetheless considers that direct contact is in the best interests of the child, the court should consider what if any directions or conditions are required to enable the order to be carried into effect and in particular should consider:

(a)   whether or not contact should be supervised, and if so, where and by whom;

(b)   whether to impose any conditions to be complied with by the party in whose favour the order for contact has been made and if so, the nature of those conditions, for example by way of seeking advice or treatment (subject to any necessary consent);

(c)   whether such contact should be for a specified period or should contain provisions which are to have effect for a specified period;

(d)   whether or not the operation of the order needs to be reviewed; if so the court should set a date for the review and give directions to ensure that at the review the court has full information about the operation of the order.

29 Where the court does not consider direct contact to be appropriate, it shall consider whether it is in the best interests of the child to make an order for indirect contact.

The reasons of the court

30 In its judgment or reasons the court should always make clear how its findings on the issue of domestic violence have influenced its decision on the issue of residence or contact. In particular, where the court has found domestic violence proved but nonetheless makes an order, the court should always explain, whether by way of reference to the welfare check-list or otherwise, why it takes the view that the order which it has made is in the best interests of the child.

31 This Practice Direction is issued by the President of the Family Division, as the nominee of the Lord Chief Justice, with the agreement of the Lord Chancellor.

****

PRACTICE DIRECTION 12L –
CHILDREN ACT 1989: RISK ASSESSMENTS UNDER SECTION 16A

This Practice Direction supplements FPR Part 12

1 This Practice Direction applies to any family proceedings in the High Court, a county court or a magistrates' court in which a risk assessment is made under section 16A of the Children Act 1989 ("the 1989 Act"). It has effect from 1st October 2007.

2 Section 16A(2) of the 1989 Act provides that, if in carrying out any function to which the section applies (as set out in section 16A(1)), an officer of the Service or a Welsh family proceedings officer is given cause to suspect that the child concerned is at risk of harm, the officer must make a risk assessment in relation to the child and provide the risk assessment to the court.

3 The duty to provide the risk assessment to the court arises irrespective of the outcome of the assessment. Where an officer is given cause to suspect that the child concerned is at risk of harm and makes a risk assessment in accordance with section 16A(2), the officer must provide the assessment to the court, even if he or she reaches the conclusion that there is no risk of harm to the child.

4 The fact that a risk assessment has been carried out is a material fact that should be placed before the court, whatever the outcome of the assessment. In reporting the outcome to the court, the officer should make clear the factor or factors that triggered the decision to carry out the assessment.

5 Issued by the President of the Family Division, as the nominee of the Lord Chief Justice, with the agreement of the Lord Chancellor.

PRACTICE DIRECTION 12M –
FAMILY ASSISTANCE ORDERS: CONSULTATION

This Practice Direction supplements FPR Part 12

1 This Practice Direction applies to any family proceedings in the High Court, a county court or a magistrates' court in which the court is considering whether to make a family assistance order under section 16 of the Children Act 1989, as amended ("the 1989 Act"). It has effect from 1st October 2007.

2 Before making a family assistance order the court must have obtained the opinion of the appropriate officer about whether it would be in the best interests of the child in question for a family assistance order to be made and, if so, how the family assistance order could operate and for what period.

3 The appropriate officer will be an officer of the Service, a Welsh family proceedings officer or an officer of a local authority, depending on the category of officer the court proposes to require to be made available under the family assistance order.

4 The opinion of the appropriate officer may be given orally or in writing (for example, it may form part of a report under section 7 of the 1989 Act).

5 Before making a family assistance order the court must give any person whom it proposes be named in the order an opportunity to comment upon any opinion given by the appropriate officer.

6 Issued by the President of the Family Division, as the nominee of the Lord Chief Justice, with the agreement of the Lord Chancellor

****

PRACTICE DIRECTION 27A –
FAMILY PROCEEDINGS: COURT BUNDLES (UNIVERSAL PRACTICE TO BE APPLIED IN ALL COURTS OTHER THAN THE FAMILY PROCEEDINGS COURT)

This Practice Direction supplements FPR Part 27

1.1 The President of the Family Division has issued this practice direction to achieve consistency across the country in all family courts (other than the Family Proceedings Court) in the preparation of court bundles and in respect of other related matters.

Application of the practice direction

2.1 Except as specified in para 2.4, and subject to specific directions given in any particular case, the following practice applies to:

   (a)   all hearings of whatever nature (including but not limited to hearings in family proceedings, Civil Procedure Rules 1998 Part 7 and Part 8 claims and appeals) before a judge of the Family Division of the High Court wherever the court may be sitting;
   (b)   all hearings in family proceedings in the Royal Courts of Justice (RCJ);
   (c)   all hearings in the Principal Registry of the Family Division (PRFD) at First Avenue House; and
   (d)   all hearings in family proceedings in all other courts except for Family Proceedings Courts.

2.2 'Hearings' includes all appearances before a judge or district judge, whether with or without notice to other parties and whether for directions or for substantive relief.

2.3 This practice direction applies whether a bundle is being lodged for the first time or is being re-lodged for a further hearing (see para 9.2).

2.4 This practice direction does not apply to:

   (a)   cases listed for one hour or less at a court referred to in para 2.1(c) or 2.1(d); or
   (b)   the hearing of any urgent application if and to the extent that it is impossible to comply with it.

2.5 The designated family judge responsible for any court referred to in para 2.1(c) or 2.1(d) may, after such consultation as is appropriate (but in the case of hearings in the

PRFD at First Avenue House only with the agreement of the Senior District Judge), direct that in that court this practice direction shall apply to all family proceedings irrespective of the length of hearing.

Responsibility for the preparation of the bundle

3.1 A bundle for the use of the court at the hearing shall be provided by the party in the position of applicant at the hearing (or, if there are cross-applications, by the party whose application was first in time) or, if that person is a litigant in person, by the first listed respondent who is not a litigant in person.

3.2 The party preparing the bundle shall paginate it. If possible the contents of the bundle shall be agreed by all parties.

Contents of the bundle

4.1 The bundle shall contain copies of all documents relevant to the hearing, in chronological order from the front of the bundle, paginated and indexed, and divided into separate sections (each section being separately paginated) as follows:

- (*a*) preliminary documents (see para 4.2) and any other case management documents required by any other practice direction;
- (*b*) applications and orders;
- (*c*) statements and affidavits (which must be dated in the top right corner of the front page);
- (*d*) care plans (where appropriate);
- (*e*) experts' reports and other reports (including those of a guardian, children's guardian or litigation friend); and
- (*f*) other documents, divided into further sections as may be appropriate.

Copies of notes of contact visits should normally not be included in the bundle unless directed by a judge.

4.2 At the commencement of the bundle there shall be inserted the following documents (the preliminary documents):

- (i) an up to date summary of the background to the hearing confined to those matters which are relevant to the hearing and the management of the case and limited, if practicable, to one A4 page;
- (ii) a statement of the issue or issues to be determined (1) at that hearing and (2) at the final hearing;
- (iii) a position statement by each party including a summary of the order or directions sought by that party (1) at that hearing and (2) at the final hearing;
- (iv) an up to date chronology, if it is a final hearing or if the summary under (i) is insufficient;
- (v) skeleton arguments, if appropriate, with copies of all authorities relied on; and
- (vi) a list of essential reading for that hearing.

4.3 Each of the preliminary documents shall state on the front page immediately below the heading the date when it was prepared and the date of the hearing for which it was prepared.

4.4 The summary of the background, statement of issues, chronology, position statement and any skeleton arguments shall be cross-referenced to the relevant pages of the bundle.

4.5 The summary of the background, statement of issues, chronology and reading list shall in the case of a final hearing, and shall so far as practicable in the case of any other hearing, each consist of a single document in a form agreed by all parties. Where the parties disagree as to the content the fact of their disagreement and their differing contentions shall be set out at the appropriate places in the document.

4.6 Where the nature of the hearing is such that a complete bundle of all documents is unnecessary, the bundle (which need not be repaginated) may comprise only those documents necessary for the hearing, but

(i)   the summary (para 4.2(i)) must commence with a statement that the bundle is limited or incomplete; and

(ii)   the bundle shall if reasonably practicable be in a form agreed by all parties.

4.7 Where the bundle is re-lodged in accordance with para 9.2, before it is re-lodged:

(*a*)   the bundle shall be updated as appropriate; and

(*b*)   all superseded documents (and in particular all outdated summaries, statements of issues, chronologies, skeleton arguments and similar documents) shall be removed from the bundle.

Format of the bundle

5.1 The bundle shall be contained in one or more A4 size ring binders or lever arch files (each lever arch file being limited to 350 pages).

5.2 All ring binders and lever arch files shall have clearly marked on the front and the spine:

(*a*)   the title and number of the case;

(*b*)   the court where the case has been listed;

(*c*)   the hearing date and time;

(*d*)   if known, the name of the judge hearing the case; and

(*e*)   where there is more than one ring binder or lever arch file, a distinguishing letter (A, B, C etc).

Timetable for preparing and lodging the bundle

6.1 The party preparing the bundle shall, whether or not the bundle has been agreed, provide a paginated index to all other parties not less than 4 working days before the hearing (in relation to a case management conference to which the provisions of the *Protocol for Judicial Case Management in Public Law Children Act Cases* [2003] 2 FLR 719 apply, not less than 5 working days before the case management conference).

6.2 Where counsel is to be instructed at any hearing, a paginated bundle shall (if not already in counsel's possession) be delivered to counsel by the person instructing that counsel not less than 3 working days before the hearing.

6.3 The bundle (with the exception of the preliminary documents if and insofar as they are not then available) shall be lodged with the court not less than 2 working days before the hearing, or at such other time as may be specified by the judge.

6.4 The preliminary documents shall be lodged with the court no later than 11 am on the day before the hearing and, where the hearing is before a judge of the High Court and the name of the judge is known, shall at the same time be sent by email to the judge's clerk.

Lodging the bundle

7.1 The bundle shall be lodged at the appropriate office. If the bundle is lodged in the wrong place the judge may:

(a) treat the bundle as having not been lodged; and

(b) take the steps referred to in para 12.

7.2 Unless the judge has given some other direction as to where the bundle in any particular case is to be lodged (for example a direction that the bundle is to be lodged with the judge's clerk) the bundle shall be lodged:

(a) for hearings in the RCJ, in the office of the Clerk of the Rules, 1st Mezzanine (Rm 1M), Queen's Building, Royal Courts of Justice, Strand, London WC2A 2LL (DX 44450 Strand);

(b) for hearings in the PRFD at First Avenue House, at the List Office counter, 3rd floor, First Avenue House, 42/49 High Holborn, London, WC1V 6NP (DX 396 Chancery Lane); and

(c) for hearings at any other court, at such place as may be designated by the designated family judge or other judge at that court and in default of any such designation at the court office of the court where the hearing is to take place.

7.3 Any bundle sent to the court by post, DX or courier shall be clearly addressed to the appropriate office and shall show the date and place of the hearing on the outside of any packaging as well as on the bundle itself.

Lodging the bundle – additional requirements for cases being heard at First Avenue House or at the RCJ

8.1 In the case of hearings at the RCJ or First Avenue House, parties shall:

(a) if the bundle or preliminary documents are delivered personally, ensure that they obtain a receipt from the clerk accepting it or them; and

(b) if the bundle or preliminary documents are sent by post or DX, ensure that they obtain proof of posting or despatch.

The receipt (or proof of posting or despatch, as the case may be) shall be brought to court on the day of the hearing and must be produced to the court if requested. If the receipt (or proof of posting or despatch) cannot be produced to the court the judge may: (i) treat the bundle as having not been lodged; and (ii) take the steps referred to in para 12.

8.2 For hearings at the RCJ:

(a) bundles or preliminary documents delivered after 11 am on the day before the hearing will not be accepted by the Clerk of the Rules and shall be delivered:

(i) in a case where the hearing is before a judge of the High Court, directly to the clerk of the judge hearing the case;

(ii) in a case where the hearing is before a Circuit Judge, Deputy High Court Judge or Recorder, directly to the messenger at the Judge's entrance to the Queen's Building (with telephone notification to the personal assistant to the Designated Family Judge, 020 7947 7155, that this has been done).

(b) upon learning before which judge a hearing is to take place, the clerk to counsel, or other advocate, representing the party in the position of applicant shall no later than 3 pm the day before the hearing:

     (i)   in a case where the hearing is before a judge of the High Court, telephone the clerk of the judge hearing the case;

     (ii)   in a case where the hearing is before a circuit judge, deputy high court judge or recorder, telephone the personal assistant to the designated family judge;

to ascertain whether the judge has received the bundle (including the preliminary documents) and, if not, shall organise prompt delivery by the applicant's solicitor.

Removing and re-lodging the bundle

9.1 Following completion of the hearing the party responsible for the bundle shall retrieve it from the court immediately or, if that is not practicable, shall collect it from the court within 5 working days. Bundles which are not collected in due time may be destroyed.

9.2 The bundle shall be re-lodged for the next and any further hearings in accordance with the provisions of this practice direction and in a form which complies with para 4.7.

Time estimates

10.1 In every case a time estimate (which shall be inserted at the front of the bundle) shall be prepared which shall so far as practicable be agreed by all parties and shall:

    (*a*)   specify separately: (i) the time estimated to be required for judicial pre-reading; and (ii) the time required for hearing all evidence and submissions; and (iii) the time estimated to be required for preparing and delivering judgment; and

    (*b*)   be prepared on the basis that before they give evidence all witnesses will have read all relevant filed statements and reports.

10.2 Once a case has been listed, any change in time estimates shall be notified immediately by telephone (and then immediately confirmed in writing):

    (*a*)   in the case of hearings in the RCJ, to the Clerk of the Rules;

    (*b*)   in the case of hearings in the PRFD at First Avenue House, to the List Officer at First Avenue House; and

    (*c*)   in the case of hearings elsewhere, to the relevant listing officer.

Taking cases out of the list

11.1 As soon as it becomes known that a hearing will no longer be effective, whether as a result of the parties reaching agreement or for any other reason, the parties and their representatives shall immediately notify the court by telephone and by letter. The letter, which shall wherever possible be a joint letter sent on behalf of all parties with their signatures applied or appended, shall include:

    (*a*)   a short background summary of the case;

    (*b*)   the written consent of each party who consents and, where a party does not consent, details of the steps which have been taken to obtain that party's consent and, where known, an explanation of why that consent has not been given;

    (*c*)   a draft of the order being sought; and

    (*d*)   enough information to enable the court to decide (i) whether to take the case out of the list and (ii) whether to make the proposed order.

Penalties for failure to comply with the practice direction

12.1 Failure to comply with any part of this practice direction may result in the judge removing the case from the list or putting the case further back in the list and may also result in a "wasted costs" order in accordance with CPR, Part 48.7 or some other adverse costs order.

Commencement of the practice direction and application of other practice directions

13.1 This practice direction replaces *Practice Direction (Family Proceedings: Court Bundles) (10 March 2000)* [2000] 1 WLR 737, [2000] 1 FLR 536 and shall have effect from 2 October 2006.

14.1 Any reference in any other practice direction to *Practice Direction (Family Proceedings: Court Bundles) (10 March 2000)* shall be read as if substituted by a reference to this practice direction.

15.1 This practice direction should where appropriate be read in conjunction with *Practice Direction (Family Proceedings: Human Rights)* [2000] 1 WLR 1782, [2000] 2 FLR 429 and with *Practice Direction (Care Cases: Judicial Continuity and Judicial Case Management)* appended to the *Protocol for Judicial Case Management in Public Law Children Act Cases*. In particular, nothing in this practice direction is to be read as removing or altering any obligation to comply with the requirements of the *Public Law Protocol*.

This Practice Direction is issued:

(i)   in relation to family proceedings, by the President of the Family Division, as the nominee of the Lord Chief Justice, with the agreement of the Lord Chancellor; and

(ii)   to the extent that it applies to proceedings to which s 5 of the Civil Procedure Act 1997 applies, by the Master of the Rolls as the nominee of the Lord Chief Justice, with the agreement of the Lord Chancellor.

PRACTICE DIRECTION 27B –
ATTENDANCE OF MEDIA REPRESENTATIVES AT HEARINGS IN FAMILY PROCEEDINGS (HIGH COURT AND COUNTY COURTS)

This Practice Direction supplements FPR Part 27

1 Introduction

1.1 This Practice Direction supplements rule 27.11 of the Family Procedure Rules 2010 ("FPR 2010") and deals with the right of representatives of news gathering and reporting organisations ("media representatives") to attend at hearings of family proceedings which take place in private subject to the discretion of the court to exclude such representatives from the whole or part of any hearing on specified grounds[1] It takes effect on 27 April 2009.

---

1   It does not, accordingly, apply where hearings are held in open court where the general public including media representatives may attend as of right, such as committal hearings or the hearing of matrimonial or civil partnership causes.

2 Matters unchanged by the rule

2.1 Rule 27.11(1) contains an express exception in respect of hearings which are conducted for the purpose of judicially assisted conciliation or negotiation and media representatives do not have a right to attend these hearings. Financial Dispute Resolution hearings will come within this exception. First Hearing Dispute Resolution appointments in private law Children Act cases will also come within this exception to the extent that the judge plays an active part in the conciliation process. Where the judge plays no part in the conciliation process or where the conciliation element of a hearing is complete and the judge is adjudicating upon the issues between the parties, media representatives should be permitted to attend, subject to the discretion of the court to exclude them on the specified grounds. Conciliation meetings or negotiation conducted between the parties with the assistance of an officer of the service or a Welsh Family Proceedings officer, and without the presence of the judge, are not "hearings" within the meaning of this rule and media representatives have no right to attend such appointments.

The exception in rule 27.11(1) does not operate to exclude media representatives from:

- Hearings to consider applications brought under Parts IV and V of the Children Act 1989, including Case Management Conferences and Issues Resolution Hearings
- Hearings relating to findings of fact
- Interim hearings
- Final hearings.

The rights of media representatives to attend such hearings are limited only by the powers of the court to exclude such attendance on the limited grounds and subject to the procedures set out in paragraphs (3)–(5) of rule 27.11.

2.2 During any hearing, courts should consider whether the exception in rule 27.11(1) becomes applicable so that media representatives should be directed to withdraw.

2.3 The provisions of the rules permitting the attendance of media representatives and the disclosure to third parties of information relating to the proceedings do not entitle a media representative to receive or peruse court documents referred to in the course of evidence, submissions or judgment without the permission of the court or otherwise in accordance with Part 12, Chapter 7 of the Family Procedure Rules 2010 and Practice Direction 12G (rules relating to disclosure to third parties). (This is in contrast to the position in civil proceedings, where the court sits in public and where members of the public are entitled to seek copies of certain documents[1]).

1   See *GIO Services Ltd v Liverpool and London Ltd* [1999] 1 WLR 984.

2.4 The question of attendance of media representatives at hearings in family proceedings to which rule 27.11 and this guidance apply must be distinguished from statutory restrictions on publication and disclosure of information relating to proceedings, which continue to apply and are unaffected by the rule and this guidance.

2.5 The prohibition in section 97(2) of the Children Act 1989, on publishing material intended to or likely to identify a child as being involved in proceedings or the address or school of any such child, is limited to the duration of the proceedings[1]. However, the limitations imposed by section 12 of the Administration of Justice Act 1960 on publication of information relating to certain proceedings in private[2] apply during and after the proceedings. In addition, in proceedings to which s 97(2) of the Children Act 1989 applies the court should continue to consider at the conclusion of the proceedings whether there are any outstanding welfare issues which require a continuation of the protection afforded during the course of the proceedings by that provision.

1   See *Clayton v Clayton* [2006] EWCA Civ 878.

2   In particular proceedings which

    (*a*)   relate to the exercise of the inherent jurisdiction of the High Court with respect to minors;

    (*b*)   are brought under the Children Act 1989; or

    (*c*)   otherwise relate wholly or mainly to the maintenance or upbringing of a minor.

3 Aims of the guidance

3.1 This Practice Direction is intended to provide guidance regarding:

- the handling of applications to exclude media representatives from the whole or part of a hearing; and
- the exercise of the court's discretion to exclude media representatives whether upon the court's own motion or any such application.

3.2 While the guidance does not aim to cover all possible eventualities, it should be complied with so far as consistent in all the circumstances with the just determination of the proceedings.

4 Identification of media representatives as "accredited"

4.1 Media representatives will be expected to carry with them identification sufficient to enable court staff, or if necessary the court itself, to verify that they are "accredited" representatives of news gathering or reporting organisations within the meaning of the rule.

4.2 By virtue of paragraph (7) of the rule, it is for the Lord Chancellor to approve a scheme which will provide for accreditation. The Lord Chancellor has decided that the scheme operated by the UK Press Card Authority provides sufficient accreditation; a card issued under that scheme will be the expected form of identification, and production of the Card will be both necessary and sufficient to demonstrate accreditation.

4.3 A media representative unable to demonstrate accreditation in accordance with the UK Press Card Authority scheme, so as to be able to attend by virtue of paragraph (2)(*f*) of the rule, may nevertheless be permitted to attend at the court's discretion under paragraph (2)(*g*).

5 Exercise of the discretion to exclude media representatives from all or part of the proceedings

5.1 The rule anticipates and should be applied on the basis that media representatives have a right to attend family proceedings throughout save and to the extent that the court exercises its discretion to exclude them from the whole or part of any proceedings on one or more of the grounds set out in paragraph (3) of the rule.

5.2 When considering the question of exclusion on any of the grounds set out in paragraph (3) of the rule the court should –

- specifically identify whether the risk to which such ground is directed arises from the mere fact of media presence at the particular hearing or hearings the subject of the application or whether the risk identified can be adequately addressed by exclusion of media representatives from a part only of such hearing or hearings;
- consider whether the reporting or disclosure restrictions which apply by operation of law, or which the court otherwise has power to order will provide

sufficient protection to the party on whose behalf the application is made or any of the persons referred to in paragraph (3)(*a*) of the rule;

- consider the safety of the parties in cases in which the court considers there are particular physical or health risks against which reporting restrictions may be inadequate to afford protection;

- in the case of any vulnerable adult or child who is unrepresented before the court, consider the extent to which the court should of its own motion take steps to protect the welfare of that adult or child.

5.3 Paragraph (3)(*a*)(iii) of the rule permits exclusion where necessary "for the orderly conduct of proceedings". This enables the court to address practical problems presented by media attendance. In particular, it may be difficult or even impossible physically to accommodate all (or indeed any) media representatives who wish to attend a particular hearing on the grounds of the restricted size or layout of the court room in which it is being heard. Court staff will use their best efforts to identify more suitable accommodation in advance of any hearing which appears likely to attract particular media attention, and to move hearings to larger court rooms where possible. However, the court should not be required to adjourn a hearing in order for larger accommodation to be sought where this will involve significant disruption or delay in the proceedings.

5.4 Paragraph (3)(*b*) of the rule permits exclusion where, unless the media are excluded, justice will be impeded or prejudiced for some reason other than those set out in sub-paragraph (*a*). Reasons of administrative inconvenience are not sufficient. Examples of circumstances where the impact on justice of continued attendance might be sufficient to necessitate exclusion may include:

- a hearing relating to the parties' finances where the information being considered includes price sensitive information (such as confidential information which could affect the share price of a publicly quoted company); or

- any hearing at which a witness (other than a party) states for credible reasons that he or she will not give evidence in front of media representatives, or where there appears to the court to be a significant risk that a witness will not give full or frank evidence in the presence of media representatives.

5.5 In the event of a decision to exclude media representatives, the court should state brief reasons for the decision.

6 Applications to exclude media representatives from all or part of proceedings

6.1 The court may exclude media representatives on the permitted grounds of its own motion or after hearing representations from the interested persons listed at paragraph (5) of the rule. Where exclusion is proposed, any media representatives who are present are entitled to make representations about that proposal. There is, however, no requirement to adjourn proceedings to enable media representatives who are not present to attend in order to make such representations, and in such a case the court should not adjourn unless satisfied of the necessity to do so having regard to the additional cost and delay which would thereby be caused.

6.2 Applications to exclude media representatives should normally be dealt with as they arise and by way of oral representations, unless the court directs otherwise.

6.3 When media representatives are expected to attend a particular hearing (for example, where a party is encouraging media interest and attendance) and a party intends to apply to the court for the exclusion of the media, that party should, if practicable, give advance notice to the court, to the other parties and (where appointed) any children's guardian, officer of the service or Welsh Family Proceedings officer, NYAS or other representative of the child of any intention to seek the exclusion of media representatives from all or part of the proceedings. Equally, legal representatives and parties should ensure that witnesses are aware of the right of media representatives to attend and should notify the court at an early stage of the intention of any witness to request the exclusion of media representatives

6.4 Prior notification by the court of a pending application for exclusion will not be given to media interests unless the court so directs. However, where such an application has been made, the applicant must where possible, notify the relevant media organisations [and should do so by means of the Press Association CopyDirect service, following the procedure set out in the Official Solicitor/CAFCASS *Practice Note* dated 18 March 2005][1].

1 The additional words in square brackets were added by the President in *Re Child X (Residence and Contact: Rights of Media Attendance – FPR r 10.28(4))* [2009] 2 FLR 1467, para [87].

****

PRACTICE DIRECTION 30A –
APPEALS

This Practice Direction supplements FPR Part 30

1.1 This practice direction applies to all appeals to which Part 30 applies.

Routes of appeal

2.1 The following table sets out to which court or judge an appeal is to be made (subject to obtaining any necessary permission) –

Decision of:	Appeal made to:
Magistrates' Court	Circuit judge
District judge of a county court	Circuit judge
District judge of the High Court	High Court judge
District judge of the principal registry of the Family Division	High Court judge
Costs judge	High Court Judge
Circuit judge or recorder	Court of Appeal
High Court judge	Court of Appeal

(Provisions setting out routes of appeal include section 16(1) of the Senior Courts Act 1981 (as amended); section 77(1) of the County Courts Act 1984 (as amended) and the Access to Justice Act 1999 (Destination of Appeals) (Family Proceedings) Order 2009 (see paragraphs 9.1 to 9.12 below. The Family Proceedings (Allocation to Judiciary) (Appeals) Directions 2009 provide for an appeal from a magistrates' court to be heard by a Circuit judge.

The routes of appeal from an order or decision relating to contempt of court of a magistrates' court under section 63(3) of the Magistrates' Courts Act 1980 and of a county court and the High Court are set out in section 13(2) of the Administration of Justice Act 1960. Appeals under section 8(1) of the Gender Recognition Act 2004 lie to the High Court (see section 8 of the 2004 Act). The procedure for appeals to the Court of Appeal is governed by the Civil Procedure Rules 1998, in particular CPR Part 52.).

2.2 Where the decision to be appealed is a decision in a Part 19 (Alternative Procedure For Applications) application on a point of law in a case which did not involve any substantial dispute of fact, the court to which the appeal lies, where that court is the High Court or a county court and unless the appeal would lie to the Court of Appeal in any event, must consider whether to order the appeal to be transferred to the Court of Appeal under rule 30.13 (Assignment of Appeals to the Court of Appeal).

Grounds for appeal

3.1 Rule 30.12 (hearing of appeals) sets out the circumstances in which the appeal court will allow an appeal.

3.2 The grounds of appeal should –

(a)　set out clearly the reasons why rule 30.12 (3)(a) or (b) is said to apply; and

(b)　specify in respect of each ground, whether the ground raises an appeal on a point of law or is an appeal against a finding of fact.

Permission to appeal

4.1 Rule 30.3 (Permission) sets out the circumstances when permission to appeal is required. At present permission to appeal is required where the decision appealed against was made by a district judge or a costs judge. However, no permission is required where rule 30.3(2) (appeals against a committal order or a secure accommodation order under section 25 of the Children Act 1989) applies.

(The requirement of permission to appeal may be imposed by a practice direction – see rule 30.3(1)(b) (Permission).).

Court to which permission to appeal application should be made

4.2 An application for permission should be made orally at the hearing at which the decision to be appealed against is made.

4.3 Where –

(a)　no application for permission to appeal is made at the hearing; or

(b)　the lower court refuses permission to appeal,

an application for permission to appeal may be made to the appeal court in accordance with rules 30.3(3) and (4) (Permission).

(Rule 30.1(3) defines 'lower court'.)

4.4 Where no application for permission to appeal has been made in accordance with rule 30.3(3)(a) (Permission) but a party requests further time to make such an application the court may adjourn the hearing to give that party an opportunity to do so.

4.5 There is no appeal from a decision of the appeal court to allow or refuse permission to appeal to that court (although where the appeal court, without a hearing, refuses permission to appeal, the person seeking permission may request that decision to be reconsidered at a hearing- see section 54(4) of the Access to Justice Act 1999 and rule 30.3(5) (Permission)).

Material omission from a judgment of the lower court

4.6 Where a party's advocate considers that there is a material omission from a judgment of the lower court or, in a magistrates' court, the written reasons for the decision of the lower court (including inadequate reasons for the lower court's decision), the advocate should before the drawing of the order give the lower court which made the decision the opportunity of considering whether there is an omission and should not immediately use the omission as grounds for an application to appeal.

4.7 Paragraph 4.8 below applies where there is an application to the lower court for permission to appeal on the grounds of a material omission from a judgment of the lower court. Paragraph 4.9 below applies where there is an application for permission to appeal to the appeal court on the grounds of a material omission from a judgment of the lower court. Paragraphs 4.8 and 4.9 do not apply where the lower court is a magistrates' court.

4.8 Where the application for permission to appeal is made to the lower court, the court which made the decision must –

(a) consider whether there is a material omission and adjourn for that purpose if necessary; and

(b) where the conclusion is that there has been such an omission, provide additions to the judgment.

4.9 Where the application for permission to appeal is made to the appeal court, the appeal court –

(a) must consider whether there is a material omission; and

(b) where the conclusion is that there has been such an omission, may adjourn the application and remit the case to the lower court with an invitation to provide additions to the judgment.

Consideration of Permission without a hearing

4.10 An application for permission to appeal may be considered by the appeal court without a hearing.

4.11 If permission is granted without a hearing the parties will be notified of that decision and the procedure in paragraphs 6.1 to 6.8 will then apply.

4.12 If permission is refused without a hearing the parties will be notified of that decision with the reasons for it. The decision is subject to the appellant's right to have it reconsidered at an oral hearing. This may be before the same judge.

4.13 A request for the decision to be reconsidered at an oral hearing must be filed at the appeal court within 7 days after service of the notice that permission has been refused. A copy of the request must be served by the appellant on the respondent at the same time.

Permission hearing

4.14 Where an appellant, who is represented, makes a request for a decision to be reconsidered at an oral hearing, the appellant's advocate must, at least 4 days before the hearing, in a brief written statement –

(a)   inform the court and the respondent of the points which the appellant proposes to raise at the hearing;

(b)   set out the reasons why permission should be granted notwithstanding the reasons given for the refusal of permission; and

(c)   confirm, where applicable, that the requirements of paragraph 4.17 have been complied with (appellant in receipt of services funded by the Legal Services Commission).

4.15 The respondent will be given notice of a permission hearing, but is not required to attend unless requested by the court to do so.

4.16 If the court requests the respondent's attendance at the permission hearing, the appellant must supply the respondent with a copy of the appeal bundle (see paragraph 5.9) within 7 days of being notified of the request, or such other period as the court may direct. The costs of providing that bundle shall be borne by the appellant initially, but will form part of the costs of the permission application.

Appellants in receipt of services funded by the Legal Services Commission applying for permission to appeal

4.17 Where the appellant is in receipt of services funded by the Legal Services Commission (or legally aided) and permission to appeal has been refused by the appeal court without a hearing, the appellant must send a copy of the reasons the appeal court gave for refusing permission to the relevant office of the Legal Services Commission as soon as it has been received from the court. The court will require confirmation that this has been done if a hearing is requested to re-consider the question of permission.

Limited permission

4.18 Where a court under rule 30.3 (Permission) gives permission to appeal on some issues only, it will –

(a)   refuse permission on any remaining issues; or

(b)   reserve the question of permission to appeal on any remaining issues to the court hearing the appeal.

4.19 If the court reserves the question of permission under paragraph 4.18(b), the appellant must, within 14 days after service of the court's order, inform the appeal court and the respondent in writing whether the appellant intends to pursue the reserved issues. If the appellant does intend to pursue the reserved issues, the parties must include in any time estimate for the appeal hearing, their time estimate for the reserved issues.

4.20 If the appeal court refuses permission to appeal on the remaining issues without a hearing and the applicant wishes to have that decision reconsidered at an oral hearing, the time limit in rule 30.3(6) (Permission) shall apply. Any application for an extension of this time limit should be made promptly. The court hearing the appeal on the issues for which permission has been granted will not normally grant, at the appeal hearing, an application to extend the time limit in rule 30.3(6) for the remaining issues.

4.21 If the appeal court refuses permission to appeal on remaining issues at or after an oral hearing, the application for permission to appeal on those issues cannot be renewed at the appeal hearing (see section 54(4) of the Access to Justice Act 1999).

Respondents' costs of permission applications

4.22 In most cases, applications for permission to appeal will be determined without the court requesting –

(*a*)   submissions from; or
(*b*)   if there is an oral hearing, attendance by,

the respondent.

4.23 Where the court does not request submissions from or attendance by the respondent, costs will not normally be allowed to a respondent who volunteers submissions or attendance.

4.24 Where the court does request –

(*u*)   submissions from; or
(*b*)   attendance by the respondent,

the court will normally allow the costs of the respondent if permission is refused.

Appellant's notice

5.1 An appellant's notice must be filed and served in all cases. Where an application for permission to appeal is made to the appeal court it must be applied for in the appellant's notice.

Human Rights

5.2 Where the appellant seeks –

(a)   to rely on any issue under the Human Rights Act 1998; or
(b)   a remedy available under that Act,

for the first time in an appeal the appellant must include in the appeal notice the information required by rule 29.5(2).

5.3 Practice Direction 29A (Human Rights, Joining the Crown) will apply as if references to the directions hearing were to the application for permission to appeal.

Extension of time for filing appellant's notice

5.4. If an extension of time is required for filing the appellant's notice the application must be made in that notice. The notice should state the reason for the delay and the steps taken prior to the application being made.

5.5 Where the appellant's notice includes an application for an extension of time and permission to appeal has been given or is not required the respondent has the right to be heard on that application and must be served with a copy of the appeal bundle (see paragraph 5.9). However, a respondent who unreasonably opposes an extension of time runs the risk of being ordered to pay the appellant's costs of that application.

5.6 If an extension of time is given following such an application the procedure at paragraphs 6.1 to 6.8 applies.

Applications

5.7 Notice of an application to be made to the appeal court for a remedy incidental to the appeal (e.g. an interim injunction under rule 20.2 (Orders for interim remedies)) may be included in the appeal notice or in a Part 18 (Procedure For Other Applications in Proceedings) application notice.

(Paragraph 13 of this practice direction contains other provisions relating to applications.).

Documents

5.8 The appellant must file the following documents together with an appeal bundle (see paragraph 5.9) with his or her appellant's notice –

(*a*)   two additional copies of the appellant's notice for the appeal court;

(*b*)   one copy of the appellant's notice for each of the respondents;

(*c*)   one copy of the appellant's skeleton argument for each copy of the appellant's notice that is filed;

(*d*)   a sealed or stamped copy of the order being appealed or a copy of the notice of the making of an order;

(*e*)   a copy of any order giving or refusing permission to appeal, together with a copy of the court's reasons for allowing or refusing permission to appeal;

(*f*)   any witness statements or affidavits in support of any application included in the appellant's notice.

5.9 An appellant must include the following documents in his or her appeal bundle –

(*a*)   a sealed or stamped copy of the appellant's notice;

(*b*)   a sealed or stamped copy of the order being appealed, or a copy of the notice of the making of an order;

(*c*)   a copy of any order giving or refusing permission to appeal, together with a copy of the court's reasons for allowing or refusing permission to appeal;

(*d*)   any affidavit or witness statement filed in support of any application included in the appellant's notice;

(*e*)   where the appeal is against a consent order, a statement setting out the change in circumstances since the order was agreed or other circumstances justifying a review or re-hearing;

(*f*)   a copy of the appellant's skeleton argument;

(*g*)   a transcript or note of judgment or, in a magistrates' court, written reasons for the court's decision (see paragraph 5.23), and in cases where permission to appeal was given by the lower court or is not required those parts of any transcript of evidence which are directly relevant to any question at issue on the appeal;

(*h*)   the application form;

(*i*)   any application notice (or case management documentation) relevant to the subject of the appeal;

(*j*)   any other documents which the appellant reasonably considers necessary to enable the appeal court to reach its decision on the hearing of the application or appeal; and

(*k*)   such other documents as the court may direct.

5.10 All documents that are extraneous to the issues to be considered on the application or the appeal must be excluded. The appeal bundle may include affidavits, witness statements, summaries, experts' reports and exhibits but only where these are directly relevant to the subject matter of the appeal.

5.11 Where the appellant is represented, the appeal bundle must contain a certificate signed by the appellant's solicitor, counsel or other representative to the effect that the appellant has read and understood paragraph 5.10 and that the composition of the appeal bundle complies with it.

5.12 Where it is not possible to file all the above documents, the appellant must indicate which documents have not yet been filed and the reasons why they are not currently available. The appellant must then provide a reasonable estimate of when the missing document or documents can be filed and file them as soon as reasonably practicable.

Skeleton arguments

5.13 The appellant's notice must, subject to paragraphs 5.14 and 5.15, be accompanied by a skeleton argument. Alternatively the skeleton argument may be included in the appellant's notice. Where the skeleton argument is so included it will not form part of the notice for the purposes of rule 30.9 (Amendment of appeal notice).

5.14 Where it is impracticable for the appellant's skeleton argument to accompany the appellant's notice it must be filed and served on all respondents within 14 days of filing the notice.

5.15 An appellant who is not represented need not file a skeleton argument but is encouraged to do so since this will be helpful to the court.

5.16 A skeleton argument must contain a numbered list of the points which the party wishes to make. These should both define and confine the areas of controversy. Each point should be stated as concisely as the nature of the case allows.

5.17 A numbered point must be followed by a reference to any document on which the party wishes to rely.

5.18 A skeleton argument must state, in respect of each authority cited –

   (*a*)   the proposition of law that the authority demonstrates; and
   (*b*)   the parts of the authority (identified by page or paragraph references) that support the proposition.

5.19 If more than one authority is cited in support of a given proposition, the skeleton argument must briefly state the reason for taking that course.

5.20 The statement referred to in paragraph 5.19 should not materially add to the length of the skeleton argument but should be sufficient to demonstrate, in the context of the argument –

   (a)   the relevance of the authority or authorities to that argument; and
   (b)   that the citation is necessary for a proper presentation of that argument.

5.21 The cost of preparing a skeleton argument which –

   (a)   does not comply with the requirements set out in this paragraph; or
   (b)   was not filed within the time limits provided by this Practice Direction (or any further time granted by the court),

will not be allowed on assessment except to the extent that the court otherwise directs.

5.22 The appellant should consider what other information the appeal court will need. This may include a list of persons who feature in the case or glossaries of technical terms. A chronology of relevant events will be necessary in most appeals.

Suitable record of the judgment

5.23 Where the judgment to be appealed has been officially recorded by the court, an approved transcript of that record should accompany the appellant's notice. Photocopies will not be accepted for this purpose. However, where there is no officially recorded judgment, the following documents will be acceptable –

Written judgments – Where the judgment was made in writing a copy of that judgment endorsed with the judge's signature.

Written reasons – in a magistrates' court, a copy of the written reasons for the court's decision.

Note of judgment – When judgment was not officially recorded or made in writing a note of the judgment (agreed between the appellant's and respondent's advocates) should be submitted for approval to the judge whose decision is being appealed. If the parties cannot agree on a single note of the judgment, both versions should be provided to that judge with an explanatory letter. For the purpose of an application for permission to appeal the note need not be approved by the respondent or the lower court judge.

Advocates' notes of judgments where the appellant is unrepresented – When the appellant was unrepresented in the lower court it is the duty of any advocate for the respondent to make the advocate's note of judgment promptly available, free of charge to the appellant where there is no officially recorded judgment or if the court so directs. Where the appellant was represented in the lower court it is the duty of the appellant's own former advocate to make that advocate's note available in these circumstances. The appellant should submit the note of judgment to the appeal court.

5.24 An appellant may not be able to obtain an official transcript or other suitable record of the lower court's decision within the time within which the appellant's notice must be filed. In such cases the appellant's notice must still be completed to the best of the appellant's ability on the basis of the documentation available. However it may be amended subsequently with the permission of the appeal court in accordance with rule 30.9 (Amendment of appeal notice).

Advocates' notes of judgments

5.25 Advocates' brief (or, where appropriate, refresher) fee includes –

(a) remuneration for taking a note of the judgment of the court;
(b) having the note transcribed accurately;
(c) attempting to agree the note with the other side if represented;
(d) submitting the note to the judge for approval where appropriate;
(e) revising it if so requested by the judge,
(f) providing any copies required for the appeal court, instructing solicitors and lay client; and
(g) providing a copy of the note to an unrepresented appellant.

Appeals from decision made by a family proceedings court under Parts 4 and 4A of the Family Law Act 1996

5.26 Where the appeal is brought against the making of a hospital order or a guardianship order under the Mental Health Act 1983, the court officer for the court from which the appeal is brought must send a copy of any written evidence considered by the magistrates under section 37(1)(a) of that Act to the appeal court.

Appeals under section 8(1) of the Gender Recognition Act 2004

5.27 Paragraph 5.28 to 5.30 apply where the appeal is brought under section 8(1) of the Gender Recognition Act 2004 to the High Court on a point of law against a decision by the Gender Recognition Panel to reject the application under sections 1(1), 5(2), 5(A)(2) or 6(1) of the 2004 Act.

5.28 The appeal notice must be –

(a)   filed in the principal registry of the Family Division; and
(b)   served on the Secretary of State and the President of the Gender Recognition Panels.

5.29 The Secretary of State may appear and be heard in the proceedings on the appeal.

5.30 Where the High Court issues a gender recognition certificate under section 8(3)(*a*) of the Gender Recognition Act 2004, the court officer must send a copy of that certificate to the Secretary of State.

Transcripts or Notes of Evidence

5.31 When the evidence is relevant to the appeal an official transcript of the relevant evidence must be obtained. Transcripts or notes of evidence are generally not needed for the purpose of determining an application for permission to appeal.

Notes of evidence

5.32 If evidence relevant to the appeal was not officially recorded, a typed version of the judge's (including a district judge (magistrates' courts) or justices' clerk's /assistant clerk's notes of evidence must be obtained.

Transcripts at public expense

5.33 Where the lower court or the appeal court is satisfied that –

(a)   an unrepresented appellant; or
(b)   an appellant whose legal representation is provided free of charge to the appellant and not funded by the Community Legal Service,

is in such poor financial circumstances that the cost of a transcript would be an excessive burden the court may certify that the cost of obtaining one official transcript should be borne at public expense.

5.34 In the case of a request for an official transcript of evidence or proceedings to be paid for at public expense, the court must also be satisfied that there are reasonable grounds for appeal. Whenever possible a request for a transcript at public expense should be made to the lower court when asking for permission to appeal.

Filing and service of appellant's notice

5.35 Rule 30.4 (Appellant's notice) sets out the procedure and time limits for filing and serving an appellant's notice. Subject to paragraph 5.36, the appellant must file the appellant's notice at the appeal court within such period as may be directed by the lower court, which should not normally exceed 14 days or, where the lower court directs no such period within 21 days of the date of the decision that the appellant wishes to appeal.

5.36 Rule 30.4(3) (Appellant's notice) provides that unless the appeal court orders otherwise, where the appeal is against an order under section 38(1) of the 1989 Act, the appellant must file the appellant's notice within 7 days beginning with the date of the decision of the lower court.

5.37 Where the lower court announces its decision and reserves the reasons for its judgment or order until a later date, it should, in the exercise of powers under rule 30.4(2)(*a*))(Appellant's notice), fix a period for filing the appellant's notice at the appeal court that takes this into account.

5.38 Except where the appeal court orders otherwise a sealed or stamped copy of the appellant's notice, including any skeleton arguments must be served on all respondents and other persons referred to in rule 30.4(5) (Appellant's notice) in accordance with the timetable prescribed by rule 30.4(4)) (Appellant's notice) except where this requirement is modified by paragraph 5.14 in which case the skeleton argument should be served as soon as it is filed.

5.39 Where the appellant's notice is to be served on a child, then rule 6.33 (supplementary provision relating to service on children) applies and unless the appeal court orders otherwise a sealed or stamped copy of the appellant's notice, including any skeleton arguments must be served on the persons or bodies mentioned in rule 6.33(2). For example, the appeal notice must be served on any children's guardian, welfare officer or children and family reporter who is appointed in the proceedings.

5.40 Unless the court otherwise directs, a respondent need not take any action when served with an appellant's notice until such time as notification is given to the respondent that permission to appeal has been given.

5.41 The court may dispense with the requirement for service of the notice on a respondent.

5.42 Unless the appeal court directs otherwise, the appellant must serve on the respondent the appellant's notice and skeleton argument (but not the appeal bundle),where the appellant is applying for permission to appeal in the appellant's notice.

5.43 Where permission to appeal –

    (*a*)   has been given by the lower court; or
    (*b*)   is not required,

the appellant must serve the appeal bundle on the respondent and the persons mentioned in paragraph 5.39 with the appellant's notice.

Amendment of Appeal Notice

5.44 An appeal notice may be amended with permission. Such an application to amend and any application in opposition will normally be dealt with at the hearing unless that course would cause unnecessary expense or delay in which case a request should be made for the application to amend to be heard in advance.

Procedure after permission is obtained

6.1 This paragraph sets out the procedure where –

    (*a*)   permission to appeal is given by the appeal court; or
    (*b*)   the appellant's notice is filed in the appeal court and –
        (i)   permission was given by the lower court; or

(ii)   permission is not required.

6.2 If the appeal court gives permission to appeal, the appeal bundle must be served on each of the respondents within 7 days of receiving the order giving permission to appeal.

6.3 The appeal court will send the parties –

(*a*)   notification of the date of the hearing or the period of time (the 'listing window') during which the appeal is likely to be heard;

(*b*)   where permission is granted by the appeal court a copy of the order giving permission to appeal; and

(*c*)   any other directions given by the court.

6.4 Where the appeal court grants permission to appeal, the appellant must add the following documents to the appeal bundle –

(*a*)   the respondent's notice and skeleton argument (if any);

(*b*)   those parts of the transcripts of evidence which are directly relevant to any question at issue on the appeal;

(*c*)   the order granting permission to appeal and, where permission to appeal was granted at an oral hearing, the transcript (or note) of any judgment which was given; and

(*d*)   any document which the appellant and respondent have agreed to add to the appeal bundle in accordance with paragraph 7.16.

6.5 Where permission to appeal has been refused on a particular issue, the appellant must remove from the appeal bundle all documents that are relevant only to that issue.

Time estimates

6.6 If the appellant is legally represented, the appeal court must be notified, in writing, of the advocate's time estimate for the hearing of the appeal.

6.7 The time estimate must be that of the advocate who will argue the appeal. It should exclude the time required by the court to give judgment.

6.8 A court officer will notify the respondent of the appellant's time estimate and if the respondent disagrees with the time estimate the respondent must inform the court within 7 days of the notification. In the absence of such notification the respondent will be deemed to have accepted the estimate proposed on behalf of the appellant.

Respondent

7.1 A respondent who wishes to ask the appeal court to vary the order of the lower court in any way must appeal and permission will be required on the same basis as for an appellant.

(Paragraph 3.2 applies to grounds of appeal by a respondent.).

7.2 A respondent who wishes to appeal or who wishes to ask the appeal court to uphold the order of the lower court for reasons different from or additional to those given by the lower court must file a respondent's notice.

7.3 A respondent who does not file a respondent's notice will not be entitled, except with the permission of the court, to rely on any reason not relied on in the lower court. This paragraph and paragraph 7.2 do not apply where the appeal is against an order under section 38(1) of the 1989 Act (see rule 30.5(7) (Respondent's notice)).

7.4 Paragraphs 5.3 (Human Rights and extension for time for filing appellant's notice) and 5.4 to 5.6 (extension of time for filing appellant's notice) of this practice direction also apply to a respondent and a respondent's notice.

Time limits

7.5 The time limits for filing a respondent's notice are set out in rule 30.5(4) and (5) (Respondent's notice).

7.6 Where an extension of time is required the extension must be requested in the respondent's notice and the reasons why the respondent failed to act within the specified time must be included.

7.7 Except where paragraphs 7.8 and 7.10 apply, the respondent must file a skeleton argument for the court in all cases where the respondent proposes to address arguments to the court. The respondent's skeleton argument may be included within a respondent's notice. Where a skeleton argument is included within a respondent's notice it will not form part of the notice for the purposes of rule 30.9 (Amendment of appeal notice).

7.8 A respondent who –

(a)   files a respondent's notice; but
(b)   does not include a skeleton argument with that notice,

must file the skeleton argument within 14 days of filing the notice.

7.9 A respondent who does not file a respondent's notice but who files a skeleton argument must file that skeleton argument at least 7 days before the appeal hearing.

(Rule 30.5(4) (Respondent's notice) sets out the period for filing a respondent's notice.).

7.10 A respondent who is not represented need not file a skeleton argument but is encouraged to do so in order to assist the court.

7.11 The respondent must serve the skeleton argument on –

(a)   the appellant; and
(b)   any other respondent;

at the same time as the skeleton argument is filed at court. Where a child is an appellant or respondent the skeleton argument must also be served on the persons listed in rule 6.33(2) unless the court directs otherwise.

7.12 A respondent's skeleton argument must conform to the directions at paragraphs 5.16 to 5.22 with any necessary modifications. It should, where appropriate, answer the arguments set out in the appellant's skeleton argument.

Applications within respondent's notices

7.13 A respondent may include an application within a respondent's notice in accordance with paragraph 5.7.

Filing respondent's notices and skeleton arguments

7.14 The respondent must file the following documents with the respondent's notice in every case –

(a)   two additional copies of the respondent's notice for the appeal court; and
(b)   one copy each for the appellant, any other respondents and any persons referred to in paragraph 5.39.

7.15 The respondent may file a skeleton argument with the respondent's notice and –

(a)   where doing so must file two copies; and
(b)   where not doing so must comply with paragraph 7.8.

7.16 If the respondent considers documents in addition to those filed by the appellant to be necessary to enable the appeal court to reach its decision on the appeal and wishes to rely on those documents, any amendments to the appeal bundle should be agreed with the appellant if possible.

7.17 If the representatives for the parties are unable to reach agreement, the respondent may prepare a supplemental bundle.

7.18 The respondent must file any supplemental bundle so prepared, together with the requisite number of copies for the appeal court, at the appeal court—

(a)   with the respondent's notice; or
(b)   if a respondent's notice is not filed, within 21 days after the respondent is served with the appeal bundle.

7.19 The respondent must serve –

(a)   the respondent's notice;
(b)   the skeleton argument (if any); and
(c)   the supplemental bundle (if any),

on—

(i)   the appellant; and
(ii)   any other respondent;

at the same time as those documents are filed at the court. Where a child is an appellant or respondent the documents referred to in paragraphs (a) to (c) above must also be served on the persons listed in rule 6.33(2) unless the court directs otherwise.

Appeals to the High Court

Application

8.1 The appellant's notice must be filed in –

(a)   the principal registry of the Family Division; or
(b)   the district registry which is nearest to the court from which the appeal lies.

8.2 A respondent's notice must be filed at the court where the appellant's notice was filed.

8.3 In the case of appeals from district judges of the High Court, applications for permission and any other applications in the appeal, appeals may be heard and directions in the appeal may be given by a High Court Judge or by any person authorised under section 9 of the Senior Courts Act 1981 to act as a judge of the High Court.

Appeals to a county court

Appeals to a judge of a county court from a district judge

9.1 The Designated Family Judge in consultation with the Family Division Liaison Judges has responsibility for the allocation of appeals from decisions of district judges to circuit judges.

Appeals to a county court from a magistrates' court

Appeals under section 111A of the Magistrates' Courts Act 1980 ("the 1980 Act") from a magistrates' court to a county court on the ground that the decision is wrong in law or in excess of jurisdiction

9.2 As a result of an amendment to section 111 of the 1980 Act by the Access to Justice Act 1999 (Destination of Appeals) (Family Proceedings) Order 2009 ("the Destination Order") an application to have a case stated for the opinion of the High Court under section 111 of that Act may not be made in relation to family proceedings. Family proceedings for those purposes are defined as –

(a)   proceedings which, by virtue of section 65 of the 1980 Act, are or may be treated as family proceedings for the purposes of that Act; and
(b)   proceedings under the Child Support Act 1991.

9.3 Section 111A of the 1980 Act, which is inserted by article 4(3) of the Destination Order, provides that in family proceedings as defined in paragraph 9.2 above a person may appeal to a county court on the ground that a decision is wrong in law or is in excess of jurisdiction; this appeal to a county court replaces the procedure for making an application to have a case stated. Section 111A(3)(*a*) provides that no appeal may be brought under section 111A if there is a right of appeal to a county court against the decision otherwise than under that section.

9.4 Subject to section 111A of the 1980 Act and any other enactment, the following rules in Part 30 apply to appeals under section 111A of the 1980 Act –

(*a*)   30.1 (scope and interpretation);
(*b*)   30.2 (parties to comply with the practice direction);
(*c*)   30.4 (appellant's notice);
(*d*)   30.6 (grounds of appeal);
(*e*)   30.8 (stay); and
(*f*)   30.9 (amendment of appeal notice).

9.5 Section 111A(4) of the 1980 Act provides that the notice of appeal must be filed within 21 days after the day on which the decision of the magistrates' court was given. The notice of appeal should also be served within this period of time. The time period for filing the appellant's notice in rule 30.4(2) does not apply. There can be no extension of this 21 day time limit under rule 4.1(3)(*a*).

Other statutory rights of appeal from a magistrates' court and the court at which the appellant's notice is to be filed-provisions applying to those appeals and appeals under section 111A of the 1980 Act

9.6 The effect of the Destination Order is that appeals against decisions of magistrates' courts in family proceedings shall lie to a county court instead of to the High Court. In addition to replacing appeals by way of case stated by amending the 1980 Act as outlined above, the Destination Order amends the statutory provisions listed in paragraph 9.7 below to provide for the appeals under those provisions to lie to a county court instead of to the High Court Paragraph 9.7 also refers to the amendment to the 1980 Act for completeness.

9.7 Paragraph 9.8 and 9.9 below apply to appeals under –

(*a*)   section 4(7) of the Maintenance Orders Act 1958;
(*b*)   section 29 of the Domestic Proceedings and Magistrates' Courts Act 1978;
(*c*)   section 60(5) of the Family Law 1986;
(*d*)   section 94(1) to (9) of the Children Act 1989;

(*e*)　　section 61 of the Family Law Act 1996;

(*f*)　　sections 10(1)(*a*) to (3) and 13 (1) and (2) of the Crime and Disorder Act 1998; or

(*g*)　　section 111A of the 1980 Act.

9.8 Subject to any enactment or to any directions made by the President of the Family Division in exercise of the powers conferred on him under section 9 of the Courts and Legal Services Act 1990, a district judge may –

(*a*)　　dismiss an appeal;

　　(i)　　for want of prosecution; or

　　(ii)　　with the consent of the parties; or

(*b*)　　give leave for the appeal to be withdrawn,

and may deal with any question of costs arising out of the dismissal or withdrawal. Unless the court directs otherwise, any interlocutory application in an appeal under the statutory provisions listed in paragraph 9.7 may be made to a district judge.

9.9 Subject to paragraph 9.10 below, the appellant's notice and other documents required to be filed by rule 30.4 and this practice direction shall where the appeal is against the making by a magistrates' court of any order or any refusal by a magistrates' court to make such an order –

(*a*)　　in proceedings listed in Schedule 1 to this Practice Direction, be filed in a care centre within the meaning of article 2(*b*) of the Allocation and Transfer of Proceedings Order 2008;

(*b*)　　in proceedings under the Adoption and Children Act 2002, be filed in an adoption centre or an intercountry adoption centre within the meaning of article 2(*c*) and (*d*) of the Allocation and Transfer of Proceedings Order 2008; and

(*c*)　　in any other case, be filed in a family hearing centre within the meaning of article 2(*a*) of that Order.

9.10 Where the appeal is an appeal from a decision of a magistrates' court under section 94 of the 1989 Act or section 61 of the Family Law Act 1996, the documents required to be filed by rule 30.4 and this practice direction may be filed in the principal registry of the Family Division of the High Court.

9.11 Article 11 of the Destination Order amends article 3 of the Allocation and Transfer of Proceedings Order 2008 to provide that the principal registry of the Family Division of the High Court is treated as a county court for the purposes of appeals from decisions of a magistrates' court under section 94 of the Children Act 1989 and section 61 of the Family Law Act 1996.

9.12 This practice direction applies to appeals under the statutory provisions listed in paragraph 9.7 with the following modifications and any other necessary modifications –

(*a*)　　after paragraph 5.6 insert –

"5.6A Paragraphs 5.4 to 5.6 do not apply to an appeal to a county court under section 111A of the Magistrates' Courts Act 1980."

(*b*)　　in paragraph 5.35, insert "and 5.36A" after " subject to paragraph 5.36";

(*c*)　　after paragraph 5.36 insert –

"5.36A Where the appeal is to a judge of a county court under section 111A of the Magistrates' Courts Act 1980, the appellant's notice must be filed and served within 21 days after the day on which the decision of the lower court was given.".

Appeals to a county court from the Child Maintenance and Enforcement Commission ("the Commission"): Deduction order appeals

9.13 A "deduction order appeal" is an appeal under regulation 25AB(1)(*a*) to (*d*) of the Child Support (Collection and Enforcement) Regulations 1992 (S.I. 1992/1989)("the Collection and Enforcement Regulations").A deduction order appeal is an appeal against –

(*a*)   the making of a regular deduction order under section 32A of the Child Support Act 1991 ("the 1991 Act");

(*b*)   a decision on an application to review a regular deduction order;

(*c*)   a decision to withhold consent to the disapplication of sections 32G(1) and 32H(2)(*b*) of the 1991 Act which has the effect of unfreezing funds in the liable person's account; or

(*d*)   the making of a final lump sum deduction order under section 32F of the 1991 Act.

A deduction order appeal lies to a county court from the Commission as a result of regulation 25AB(1) of the Collection and Enforcement Regulations.

9.14 The rules in Part 30 apply to deduction order appeals with the amendments set out in paragraphs 9.15 to 9.27 and 9.29 and 9.30 below. The rules in Part 30 also apply to appeals against the decision of a district judge in proceedings relating to a deduction order appeal with the amendments set out in paragraph 9.28 below.

9.15 "The respondent" means –

(*a*)   the Commission and any person other than the appellant who was served with an order under section 32A(1), 32E(1) or 32F(1) of the 1991 Act; and

(*b*)   a person who is permitted by the appeal court to be a party to the appeal.

9.16 The appellant will serve the appellant's notice on the Commission and any other respondent.

9.17 The appellant shall file and serve the appellant's notice, within 21 days of –

(*a*)   where the appellant is a deposit-taker, service of the order;

(*b*)   where the appellant is a liable person, receipt of the order; or

(*c*)   where the appellant is either a deposit-taker or a liable person, the date of receipt of notification of the decision.

9.18 For the purposes of paragraph 9.17 –

(*a*)   references to "liable person" and "deposit-taker" are to be interpreted in accordance with section 32E of the 1991 Act and regulation 25A(2) of the Collection and Enforcement Regulations and section 54 of the 1991 Act, respectively; and

(*b*)   the liable person is to be treated as having received the order or notification of the decision 2 days after it was posted by the Commission.

9.19 Rule 4.1(3)(*a*) (court's power to extend or shorten the time for compliance with a rule, practice direction or court order) does not apply to an appeal against the making of a lump sum deduction order under section 32F of the 1991 Act in so far as that rule gives the court power to extend the time set out in paragraph 9.17 for filing and serving an appellant's notice after the time for filing and serving the that notice set out in paragraph 9.17 has expired.

9.20 The Commission shall provide to the court and serve on all other parties to the appeal any information and evidence relevant to the making of the decision or order being appealed, within 14 days of receipt of the appellant's notice.

9.21 Subject to paragraph 9.23, a respondent who wishes to ask the appeal court to uphold the order or decision of the Commission for reasons different from or in additional to those given by the Commission must file a respondent's notice.

9.22 A respondent's notice must be filed within 14 days of receipt of the appellant's notice.

9.23 Where the Commission as a respondent, wishes to contend that its order or decision should be –

(a)   varied, either in any event or in the event of the appeal being allowed in whole or in part; or

(b)   affirmed on different grounds from those on which it relied when making the order or decision,

it shall, within 14 days of receipt of the appellant's notice, file and serve on all other parties to the appeal a respondent's notice.

9.24 In so far as rule 30.7 (Variation of time) may permit any application for variation of the time limit for filing an appellant's notice after the time for filing the appellant's notice has expired, that rule shall not apply to an appeal made against an order under section 32F(1) of the Act of 1991.

9.25 Rule 30.8 (stay) shall not apply to an appeal made against an order under section 32F(1) of the Act of 1991.

9.26 A district judge may hear a deduction order appeal.

9.27 Rule 30.11 (appeal court's powers) does not apply to deduction order appeals.

9.28 Rule 30.11(2)(d) (making orders for payment of interest) does not apply in the case of an appeal against a decision of a district judge in proceedings relating to a deduction order appeal.

9.29 In the case of a deduction order appeal –

(a)   the appeal court has power to –
   (i)   affirm or set aside the order or decision;
   (ii)   remit the matter to the Commission for the order or decision to be reconsidered, with appropriate directions;
   (iii) refer any application or issue for determination by the Commission;
   (iv)   make a costs order; and

(b)   the appeal court may exercise its powers in relation to the whole or part of an order or decision of the Commission.

9.30 In rule 30.12 (Hearing of appeals) –

(a)   at the beginning of paragraph (1), for "Every" substitute "Subject to paragraph (2A), every";

(b)   at the beginning of paragraph (2), for "Unless" substitute "Subject to paragraph (2A), unless";

(c)   after paragraph (2), insert –
"(2A) In the case of a deduction order appeal, the appeal will be a re-hearing, unless the appeal court orders otherwise.";

(d) in paragraph (3), after "lower court" insert "or, in a deduction order appeal, the order or decision of the Commission"; and

(e) for sub-paragraph (b) of paragraph (3), substitute –

"(b) unjust because of a serious procedural or other irregularity in –

(i) the proceedings in the lower court; or

(ii) the making of an order or decision by the Commission."

Information about the Commission's decision

9.31 In relation to the deduction order appeals listed in column 1 of the table in Schedule 2 to this Practice Direction-

(a) the documents to be filed and served by the appellant include the documents set out in Column 3; and

(b) the relevant information to be provided by the Commission in accordance with paragraph 9.20 above includes the information set out in Column 4.

The court at which the appeal notice is to be filed

9.32 In relation to a deduction order appeal, the appellant's notice and other documents required to be filed with that notice shall be filed in a county court (the Collection and Enforcement Regulations 25AB(1)).

The Commission's address for service

9.33 For the purposes of a deduction order appeal the Commission's address for service is –

Commission Legal Adviser
Deduction Order Team
Legal Enforcement (Civil)
Antonine House
Callendar Road
Falkirk
FK1 1XT

All notices or other documents for CMEC relating to a deduction order appeal should be sent to the above address.

9.34 This practice direction applies to deduction order appeals and appeals against the decision of a district judge in proceedings relating to a deduction order appeal with the following modifications and any other necessary modifications-

(a) in paragraph 5.35, insert "and 5.36B" after " subject to paragraph 5.36A";

(b) after paragraph 5.36A insert –

"5.36A Where the appeal is a deduction order appeal, the appellant's notice must be filed and served within 21 days of –

(a) where the appellant is a deposit-taker, service of the order;

(b) where the appellant is a liable person, receipt of the order; or

(c) where the appellant is either a deposit-taker or a liable person, the date of receipt of notification of the decision the lower court was given.".

Appeal against the court's decision under rules 31.10, 31.11 or 31.14

10.1 The rules in Part 30 apply to appeals against the court's decision under rules 31.10, 31.11 or 31.14 with the amendments set out in paragraphs 10.2 to 10.5 below.

Rules 31.15 and 31.16 apply to these appeals. These modifications do not apply to appeals against the decision made on appeal under rule 31.15.

10.2 Rule 30.3 (permission to appeal) does not apply.

10.3 The time for filing an appellant's notice at the appeal court in rule 30.4(2) does not apply. Rule 31.15 sets out the time within which an appeal against the court's decision under rules 31.10, 31.11 or 31.14 must be made to a judge of the High Court.

10.4 Rule 4.1(3)(*a*) (court's power to extend or shorten the time for compliance with a rule, practice direction or court order) does not apply to an appeal against the court's decision under rules 31.10, 31.11 or 31.14 in so far as that rule gives the court power to extend the time set out in rules 31.15 for filing an appellant's notice.

10.5 Rules 30.7 (variation), 30.8 (stay of proceedings), 30.10 (striking out appeal notices, setting aside or imposing conditions on permission to appeal) and 30.12 (hearing of appeals) do not apply.

Appeals against pension orders and pension compensation sharing orders

11.1 Paragraph 11.2 below applies to appeals against –

(*a*) a pension sharing order under section 24B of the Matrimonial Causes Act 1973 or the variation of such an order under section 31 of that Act;

(*b*) a pension sharing order under Part 4 of Schedule 5 to the Civil Partnership Act 2004 or the variation of such an order under Part 11 of Schedule 5 to that Act;

(*c*) a pension compensation sharing order under section 24E of the Matrimonial Causes Act 1973 or a variation of such an order under section 31 of that Act; and

(*d*) a pension compensation sharing order under Part 4 of Schedule 5 to the Civil Partnership Act 2004 or a variation of such an order under Part 11 of Schedule 5 to that Act.

11.2 Rule 4.1(3)(*a*) (court's power to extend or shorten the time for compliance with a rule, practice direction or court order) does not apply to an appeal against the making of the orders referred to in paragraph 11.1 above in so far as that rule gives the court power to extend the time set out in rule 30.4 for filing and serving an appellant's notice after the time for filing and serving that notice has expired .

11.3 In so far as rule 30.7 (Variation of time) may permit any application for variation of the time limit for filing an appellant's notice after the time for filing the appellant's notice has expired, that rule shall not apply to an appeal made against the orders referred to in paragraph 11.1 above.

Appeals to a court under section 20 of the 1991 Act (appeals in respect of parentage determinations)

12.1 The rules in Chapters 1 and 5 of Part 8 will apply as appropriate to an appeal under section 20(1) of the 1991 Act where that appeal must be made to a court in accordance with the Child Support Appeals (Jurisdiction of Courts) Order 2002.

12.2 The respondent to such an appeal will be the Child Maintenance and Enforcement Commission.

12.3 Where the justices' clerk or the court is considering whether or not to transfer appeal proceedings under section 20(1) of the 1991 Act, rules 12.9 to 12.11 will apply as appropriate.

Applications

13.1 Where a party to an appeal makes an application whether in an appeal notice or by Part 18 (Procedure For Other Applications in Proceedings) application notice, the provisions of Part 18 will apply.

13.2 The applicant must file the following documents with the notice –

(*a*)　　one additional copy of the application notice for the appeal court, one copy for each of the respondents and the persons referred to in paragraph 5.39;

(*b*)　　where applicable a sealed or stamped copy of the order which is the subject of the main appeal or a copy of the notice of the making of an order;

(*c*)　　a bundle of documents in support which should include –

(i)　　the Part 18 application notice; and

(ii)　　any witness statements and affidavits filed in support of the application notice.

Appeals against consent orders

14.1 The rules in Part 30 and the provisions of this Practice Direction apply to appeals relating to orders made by consent in addition to orders which are not made by consent. An appeal is the only way in which a consent order can be challenged.

Disposing of applications or appeals by consent

15.1 An appellant who does not wish to pursue an application or an appeal may request the appeal court for an order that the application or appeal be dismissed. Such a request must state whether the appellant is a child, or a protected person.

15.2 The request must be accompanied by a consent signed by the other parties stating whether the respondent is a child, or a protected person and consents to the dismissal of the application or appeal.

Allowing unopposed appeals or applications on paper

16.1 The appeal court will not normally make an order allowing an appeal unless satisfied that the decision of the lower court was wrong, but the appeal court may set aside or vary the order of the lower court with consent and without determining the merits of the appeal, if it is satisfied that there are good and sufficient reasons for doing so. Where the appeal court is requested by all parties to allow an application or an appeal the court may consider the request on the papers. The request should state whether any of the parties is a child, or protected person and set out the relevant history of the proceedings and the matters relied on as justifying the proposed order and be accompanied by a copy of the proposed order.

Summary assessment of costs

17.1 Costs are likely to be assessed by way of summary assessment at the following hearings –

(*a*)　　contested directions hearings;

(*b*)　　applications for permission to appeal at which the respondent is present;

(c) appeals from case management decisions or decisions made at directions hearings; and

(d) appeals listed for one day or less.

(Provision for summary assessment of costs is made by section 13 of the Practice Direction supplementing CPR Part 44)

17.2 Parties attending any of the hearings referred to in paragraph 17.1 should be prepared to deal with the summary assessment.

Reopening of final appeals

18.1 This paragraph applies to applications under rule 30.14 (Reopening of final appeals) for permission to reopen a final determination of an appeal.

18.2 In this paragraph, "appeal" includes an application for permission to appeal.

18.3 Permission must be sought from the court whose decision the applicant wishes to reopen.

18.4 The application for permission must be made by application notice and supported by written evidence, verified by a statement of truth.

18.5 A copy of the application for permission must not be served on any other party to the original appeal unless the court so directs.

18.6 Where the court directs that the application for permission is to be served on another party, that party may within 14 days of the service on him or her of the copy of the application file a written statement either supporting or opposing the application.

18.7 The application for permission, and any written statements supporting or opposing it, will be considered on paper by a single judge, and will be allowed to proceed only if the judge so directs.

SCHEDULE 1

Description of proceedings

(1) Proceedings under section 25 of the Children Act 1989;

(2) Proceedings under Parts IV and V of the Children Act 1989;

(3) Proceedings under Schedules 2 and 3 to the Children Act 1989;

(4) Applications for leave under section 91(14),(15) or (17) of the Children Act 1989;

(5) Proceedings under section 102 of the Children Act 1989 or section 79 of the Childcare Act 2006;

(6) Proceedings for a residence order under section 8 of the Children Act 1989 or for a special guardianship order under section 14A of the Children Act 1989 with respect to a child who is the subject of a care order.

(7) Proceedings for a residence order under section 8 of the Children Act 1989 where either section 28(1) (child placed for adoption) or 29(4) (placement order in force) of the Adoption and Children Act 2002 applies;

(8) Proceedings for a special guardianship order under section 14A of the Children Act 1989 where either section 28(1)(child placed for adoption) or section 29(5) (placement order in force) of the Adoption and Children Act 2002 applies.

SCHEDULE 2

Appeal	Relevant legisation	Appellant information	Commission information
Appeal against the making of a regular deduction order (under section 32A of the 1991 Act)	Section 32C(4)(*a*) of the 1991 Act The Collection and Enforcement Regula-tions 25AB(1)(*a*) (appeals)	A copy of the order; A covering letter explaining that the order has been made and the reasons for the order namely that there are arrears of child maintenance and/or no other arrangements have been made for the payment of child maintenance, including arrears	The amount of the current maintenance calculation, the period of debt and the total amount of arrears (including account breakdown if appropriate) and the reasons for the Commission's decision, details of all previous attempts to negotiate payment i.e. phone calls and letters to the non resident parent, details of any previous enforcement action taken
Appeal against a decision on an application for a review of a regular deduction order	Sections 32C(4)(*b*) 32C(2)(*k*) of the 1991 Act The Collection and Enforcement Regulations 25G (review of a regular deduction order) and 25AB(1)(*b*) (appeals)	A decision notification setting out whether or not the review has been agreed by the Commission and the resulting action to be taken if agreed; with an enclosure setting out the specific reasons for the Commission's decision	The reasons for the Commission's decision in respect of the application for review and any evidence supporting that decision

Appeal against the withholding of consent to the disapplication of sections 32G(1) and 32H(2)(*b*) of the 1991 Act	Section 32I(4) of the 1991 Act The Collection and Enforcement Regulations 25N (disapplication of sections 32G(1) and 32H(2)(*b*) of the 1991 Act) and 25AB(1)(*c*) (appeals)	A decision notification setting out that either: *a*) consent has been refused; or *b*) consent has been given in relation to part of the application i.e. that only some of the funds which were requested to be released have been agreed to be released (the right of appeal will lie in respect of the part of the application which has been refused). There will be an enclosure with the notification setting out the reasons for the decision on the application.	The reasons for the Commission's decision in respect of the application for consent and any evidence supporting that decision
Appeal against the making of a final lump sum deduction order (under section 32F of the 1991 Act)	Section 32J(5) of the 1991 Act Collection and Enforcement Regula-tions 25AB(1)(*d*) (appeals)	A copy of the order; A covering letter explaining that the order has been made and the reasons for the order namely that there are arrears of child maintenance and/or no other arrangements have been made for the payment of child maintenance, including arrears	The amount of the current maintenance calculation (if applicable), the period of debt and the total amount of arrears (including account breakdown if appropriate) and the reasons for the Commission's decision, details of all previous attempts to negotiate payment i.e. phone calls and letters to the non resident parent, details of any previous enforcement action taken.

****

Appendix 3

PRINCIPLES OF CONTACT

RE O (CONTACT: IMPOSITION OF CONDITIONS)

Court of Appeal

Sir Thomas Bingham MR, Simon Brown and Swinton Thomas LJJ

14 March 1995

SIR THOMAS BINGHAM MR:

...

It may perhaps be worth stating in a reasonably compendious way some very familiar but none the less fundamental principles. First of all, and overriding all else as provided in s 1(1) of the 1989 Act, the welfare of the child is the paramount consideration of any court concerned to make an order relating to the upbringing of a child. It cannot be emphasised too strongly that the court is concerned with the interests of the mother and the father only insofar as they bear on the welfare of the child.

Secondly, where parents of a child are separated and the child is in the day-to-day care of one of them, it is almost always in the interests of the child that he or she should have contact with the other parent. The reason for this scarcely needs spelling out. It is, of course, that the separation of parents involves a loss to the child, and it is desirable that that loss should so far as possible be made good by contact with the non-custodial parent, that is the parent in whose day-to-day care the child is not. This has been said on a very great number of occasions and I cite only two of them. In *Re H (Minors) (Access)* [1992] 1 FLR 148 at p 151A, Balcombe LJ quoted, endorsing as fully as he could, an earlier passage in a judgment of Latey J in which that judge had said:

> '... where the parents have separated and one has the care of the child, access by the other often results in some upset in the child. Those upsets are usually minor and superficial. They are heavily outweighed by the long-term advantages to the child of keeping in touch with the parent concerned so that they do not become strangers, so that the child later in life does not resent the deprivation and turn against the parent who the child thinks, rightly or wrongly, has deprived him, and so that the deprived parent loses interest in the child and therefore does not make the material and emotional contribution to the child's development which that parent by its companionship and otherwise would make.'

My second citation is from *Re J (A Minor) (Contact)* [1994] 1 FLR 729 at p 736B–C, where Balcombe LJ said:

> 'But before concluding this judgment I would like to make three general points. The first is that judges should be very reluctant to allow the implacable hostility of one parent (usually

the parent who has a residence order in his or her favour), to deter them from making a contact order where they believe the child's welfare requires it. The danger of allowing the implacable hostility of the residential parent (usually the mother) to frustrate the court's decision is too obvious to require repetition on my part.'

Thirdly, the court has power to enforce orders for contact, which it should not hesitate to exercise where it judges that it will overall promote the welfare of the child to do so. I refer in this context to the judgment of the President of the Family Division in *Re W (A Minor) (Contact)* [1994] 2 FLR 441 at p 447H, where the President said:

'However, I am quite clear that a court cannot allow a mother, in such circumstances, simply to defy the order of the court which was, and is, in force, that is to say that there should be reasonable contact with the father. That was indeed made by consent as I have already observed. Some constructive step must be taken to permit and encourage the boy to resume contact with his father.'

At p 449A the President added:

'I wish to make it very clear to the mother that this is an order of the court. The court cannot be put in a position where it is told, "I shall not obey an order of the court".'

Fourthly, cases do, unhappily and infrequently but occasionally, arise in which a court is compelled to conclude that in existing circumstances an order for immediate direct contact should not be ordered, because so to order would injure the welfare of the child. In *Re D (A Minor) (Contact: Mother's Hostility)* [1993] 2 FLR 1 at p 7G, Waite LG said:

'It is now well settled that the implacable hostility of a mother towards access or contact is a factor which is capable, according to the circumstances of each particular case, of supplying a cogent reason for departing from the general principle that a child should grow up in the knowledge of both his parents. I see no reason to think that the judge fell into any error of principle in deciding, as he clearly did on the plain interpretation of his judgment, that the mother's present attitude towards contact puts D at serious risk of major emotional harm if she were to be compelled to accept a degree of contact to the natural father against her will.'

I simply draw attention to the judge's reference to a serious risk of major emotional harm. The courts should not at all readily accept that the child's welfare will be injured by direct contact. Judging that question the court should take a medium-term and long-term view of the child's development and not accord excessive weight to what appear likely to be short-term or transient problems. Neither parent should be encouraged or permitted to think that the more intransigent, the more unreasonable, the more obdurate and the more unco-operative they are, the more likely they are to get their own way. Courts should remember that in these cases they are dealing with parents who are adults, who must be treated as rational adults, who must be assumed to have the welfare of the child at heart, and who have once been close enough to each other to have produced the child. It would be as well if parents also were to bear these points in mind.

Fifthly, in cases in which, for whatever reason, direct contact cannot for the time being be ordered, it is ordinarily highly desirable that there should be indirect contact so that the child grows up knowing of the love and interest of the absent parent with whom, in due course, direct contact should be established. This calls for a measure of restraint, common sense and unselfishness on the part of both parents. If the absent parent deluges the child with presents or writes long and obsessive screeds to the child, or if he or she uses his or her right to correspond to criticise or insult the other parent, then inevitably those rights will be curtailed. The object of indirect contact is to build up a relationship between the absent parent and the child, not to enable the absent parent to pursue a feud with the caring parent in a manner not conducive to the welfare of the child.

The caring parent also has reciprocal obligations. If the caring parent puts difficulties in the way of indirect contact by withholding presents or letters or failing to read letters to a child who cannot read, then such parent must understand that the court can compel compliance with its orders; it has sanctions available and no residence order is to be regarded as irrevocable. It is entirely reasonable that the parent with the care of the child should be obliged to report on the progress of the child to the absent parent, for the obvious reason that an absent parent cannot correspond in a meaningful way if unaware of the child's concerns, or of where the child goes to school, or what it does when it gets there, or what games it plays, and so on. Of course judges must not impose duties which parents cannot realistically be expected to perform, and it would accordingly be absurd to expect, in a case where this was the case, a semi-literate parent to write monthly reports. But some means of communication, directly or indirectly, is essential if indirect contact is to be meaningful, and if the welfare of the child is not to suffer.

...

Appendix 4

DOMESTIC VIOLENCE AND CONTACT

RE L (CONTACT: DOMESTIC VIOLENCE); RE V (CONTACT: DOMESTIC VIOLENCE); RE M (CONTACT: DOMESTIC VIOLENCE); RE H (CONTACT: DOMESTIC VIOLENCE)[1]

Court of Appeal

Dame Elizabeth Butler-Sloss P, Thorpe and Waller LJJ

19 June 2000

DAME ELIZABETH BUTLER-SLOSS P:

...

There are however a number of general comments I wish to make on the advice given to us [by Drs Sturge and Glaser]. The family judges and magistrates need to have a heightened awareness of the existence of and consequences (some long term), on children of exposure to domestic violence between their parents or other partners. There has, perhaps, been a tendency in the past for courts not to tackle allegations of violence and to leave them in the background on the premise that they were matters affecting the adults and not relevant to issues regarding the children. The general principle that contact with the non-resident parent is in the interests of the child may sometimes have discouraged sufficient attention being paid to the adverse effects on children living in the household where violence has occurred. It may not necessarily be widely appreciated that violence to a partner involves a significant failure in parenting – failure to protect the child's carer and failure to protect the child emotionally.

In a contact or other s 8 application, where allegations of domestic violence are made which might have an effect on the outcome, those allegations must be adjudicated upon and found proved or not proved. It will be necessary to scrutinise such allegations which may not always be true or may be grossly exaggerated. If however there is a firm basis for finding that violence has occurred, the psychiatric advice becomes very important. There is not, however, nor should there be, any presumption that, on proof of domestic violence, the offending parent has to surmount a prima facie barrier of no contact. As a matter of principle, domestic violence of itself cannot constitute a bar to contact. It is one factor in the difficult and delicate balancing exercise of discretion. The court deals with the facts of a specific case in which the degree of violence and the seriousness of the impact on the child and on the resident parent have to be taken into account. In cases of proved domestic violence, as in cases of other proved harm or risk of harm to the child, the court has the task of weighing in the balance the seriousness of the

[1]   [2000] 2 FLR 334.

domestic violence, the risks involved and the impact on the child against the positive factors (if any), of contact between the parent found to have been violent and the child. In this context, the ability of the offending parent to recognise his past conduct, be aware of the need to change and make genuine efforts to do so, will be likely to be an important consideration. Wall J in *Re M (Contact: Violent Parent)* [1999] 2 FLR 321 suggested at 333 that often in cases where domestic violence had been found, too little weight had been given to the need for the father to change. He suggested that the father should demonstrate that he was a fit person to exercise contact and should show a track record of proper behaviour. Assertions, without evidence to back it up, may well not be sufficient.

In expressing these views I recognise the danger of the pendulum swinging too far against contact where domestic violence has been proved. It is trite but true to say that no two child cases are exactly the same. The court always has the duty to apply s 1 of the Children Act 1989 that the welfare of the child is paramount and, in considering that welfare, to take into account all the relevant circumstances, including the advice of the medical experts as far as it is relevant and proportionate to the decision in that case. It will also be relevant in due course to take into account the impact of Art 8 of the European Convention for the Protection of Human Rights and Fundamental Freedoms 1950 on a decision to refuse direct contact.

The propositions set out above are not, in my view, in any way inconsistent with earlier decisions on contact. The fostering of a relationship between the child and the non-resident parent has always been and remains of great importance. It has equally been intended to be for the benefit of the child rather than of the parent. Over the last 40 years there has been a movement away from rights towards responsibilities of the parents and best interests of the child. In *Re M (Contact: Welfare Test)* [1995] 1 FLR 274, Wilson J, referring to the general principles on contact laid down in *Re H (Minors) (Access)* [1992] 1 FLR 148 (and which were endorsed in *Re O (Contact: Imposition of Conditions)* [1995] 2 FLR 124) said at 278–279:

> 'I personally find it helpful to cast the principles into the framework of the checklist of considerations set out in s 1(3) of the Children Act 1989 and to ask whether the fundamental emotional need of every child to have an enduring relationship with both his parents (s 1(3)(b)) is outweighed by the depth of harm which, in the light, inter alia, of his wishes and feelings (s 1(3)(a)), this child would be at risk of suffering (s 1(3)(e)) by virtue of a contact order.'

I find that a helpful summary of the proper approach to a contact application where domestic violence is a factor.

In the decision in *Re O (Contact: Imposition of Conditions)* [1995] 2 FLR 124, Sir Thomas Bingham MR reviewed the leading authorities on contact and restated the main principles with which I respectfully agree. In that case an intransigent mother refused the father contact to his child aged 2. Although there was a non-molestation order breached by the father who received a short suspended sentence for contempt, it was not a case of domestic violence. Sir Thomas Bingham said at 128:

> 'First of all, and overriding all else as provided in s 1(1) of the 1989 Act, the welfare of the child is the paramount consideration of any court concerned to make an order relating to the upbringing of a child. It cannot be emphasised too strongly that the court is concerned with the interests of the mother and the father only insofar as they bear on the welfare of the child.

Secondly, where parents of a child are separated and the child is in the day-to-day care of one of them, it is almost always in the interests of the child that he or she should have contact with the other parent. The reason for this scarcely needs spelling out. It is, of course, that the separation of parents involves a loss to the child, and it is desirable that that loss should so far as possible be made good by contact with the non-custodial parent, that is the parent in whose day-to-day care the child is not.'

He said at 129:

'... cases do, unhappily and infrequently but occasionally, arise in which a court is compelled to conclude that in existing circumstances an order for immediate direct contact should not be ordered, because so to order would injure the welfare of the child.'

This passage was followed by a quotation from Waite LJ in *Re D (A Minor) (Contact: Mother's Hostility)* [1993] 2 FLR 1. The Master of the Rolls then said at 129–130:

'The courts should not at all readily accept that the child's welfare will be injured by direct contact. Judging that question the court should take a medium-term and long-term view of the child's development and not accord excessive weight to what appear likely to be short-term or transient problems. Neither parent should be encouraged or permitted to think that the more intransigent, the more unreasonable, the more obdurate and the more unco-operative they are, the more likely they are to get their own way.'

With all those observations I respectfully agree, but it is clear that the Master of the Rolls was considering the risk of emotional harm to the child from the implacable hostility of the mother to contact and not to the entirely different circumstances of domestic violence proved against the parent seeking contact. The issues with which we are concerned in these appeals relate to violence or threats of violence that have been proved, where the fears of the resident parent are reasonable and where serious issues arise as to the risks of emotional harm to the children, a far cry from the unreasonable implacable hostility cases (see also *Re D (Contact: Reasons for Refusal)* [1997] 2 FLR 48).

In conclusion, on the general issues, a court hearing a contact application in which allegations of domestic violence are raised should consider the conduct of both parties towards each other and towards the children, the effect on the children and on the residential parent and the motivation of the parent seeking contact. Is it a desire to promote the best interests of the child or a means to continue violence and/or intimidation or harassment of the other parent? In cases of serious domestic violence, the ability of the offending parent to recognise his or her past conduct, to be aware of the need for change and to make genuine efforts to do so, will be likely to be an important consideration.

On an application for interim contact, when the allegations of domestic violence have not yet been adjudicated upon, the court should give particular consideration to the likely risk of harm to the child, whether physical or emotional, if contact is granted or refused. The court should ensure, as far as it can, that any risk of harm to the child is minimised and that the safety of the child and the residential parent is secured before, during and after any such contact.

...

THORPE LJ:

... Domestic violence is one of a catalogue of factors that may operate to offset the assumption for contact but it has not been separately categorised in either statute or case-law nor, in my opinion, should it be. However it is worth noting that the last of the four general principles underlying Parts II and III of the Family Law Act 1996 (yet to come into force and only of application to the families on the verge of divorce or judicial separation) is:

> '(d) that any risk to one of the parties to a marriage, and to any children, of violence from the other party should, so far as reasonably practicable, be removed or diminished.'

The reported cases on the topic are sparse: *Re A (Contact: Domestic Violence)* [1998] 2 FLR 171, *Re P (Contact: Discretion)* [1998] 2 FLR 696, *Re H (Contact: Domestic Violence)* [1998] 2 FLR 42 and *Re M (Contact: Violent Parent)* [1999] 2 FLR 321. This constellation of cases may suggest an emerging modern problem, although certainly not one created by any shift in the pattern of human behaviour.

In giving the leading judgment in the case of *Re H (Contact: Domestic Violence)* [1998] 2 FLR 42 in this court Wall J said (at 56):

> 'The point that has troubled me most on this aspect of the case is the question of domestic violence. Can it be said, as a matter of principle, that it is in the interests of children to impose an order for contact on a mother who is caring for them well in favour of a father who has treated her with such violence as to give her good and valid reasons to oppose contact?
>
> Having asked the question, however, the answer must be that, as a matter of principle, domestic violence of itself cannot constitute a bar to contact. Each case must inevitably be decided on its facts. Domestic violence can only be one factor in a very complex equation. There will be contact cases in which it is decisive against contact. There will be others in which it will be peripheral. For example, *Re D*, to which I have already referred, demonstrates that domestic violence may both provide a powerful basis for a mother's objection to contact and demonstrate in a given case the father's unfitness to exercise contact.
>
> The matter is therefore not one of principle, but of discretion, and there thus remains the question whether or not, on the facts of this case, the recorder erred in what is conventionally called the balancing exercise.'

I am in complete agreement with that analysis. Wall J went on to emphasise the obligation on the father first to acknowledge and then to address his maltreatment of the mother. Wall J was in my view absolutely right to introduce this vital consideration, although its introduction only reveals the limitations on the court's powers to direct and supervise the delivery of, as well as the father's engagement in, available therapeutic services.

Wall J returned to that theme when deciding an appeal from the family proceedings court in *Re M (Contact: Violent Parent)* [1999] 2 FLR 321. In that case he said towards the conclusion of his judgment (at 333):

> 'Often in these cases where domestic violence has been found, too little weight in my judgment is given to the need for the father to change. It is often said that, not withstanding the violence, the mother must none the less bring up the children with full knowledge and a positive image of their natural father and arrange for the children to be available for contact. Too often it seems to me the courts neglect the other side of that equation, which is that a

father, like this father, must demonstrate that he is a fit person to exercise contact; that he is not going to destabilise the family, that he is not going to upset the children and harm them emotionally.'

Apart from Wall J's contribution in these judgments he has done most valuable work as Chairman of the Children Act Sub-Committee of the Lord Chancellor's Advisory Board on Family Law culminating in his recently published report to the Lord Chancellor. The report is obviously of great value not least because it digests a wide range of responses to a well publicised consultation.

The extent to which judges throughout the jurisdiction have been elevating a presumption in favour of a contact order too high or trivialising a history of domestic violence must remain uncertain. Certainly applications and appeals to the Court of Appeal over the course of the past 5 years do not suggest that contact orders have been made when plainly they should have been refused. Nor have other professions brought their concerns to the President's interdisciplinary family law committee, save in one instance. However I have been impressed by the research of Professor Bailey-Harris and others into the presumption of contact in practice: reported at (1999) *International Journal of Law, Policy and the Family* 111 and I must acknowledge the help that I have drawn from this article. That research demonstrates that:

- Solicitors and district judges in their daily work in the field of contact concentrate on future arrangements and discourage the ventilation of past history. They consistently set the presumption in favour of contact high.

- Research evidence, particularly the reports of Hester and Radford in 1995 and 1996, demonstrated that children are seriously harmed by witnessing family violence and that violent fathers use the opportunity of contact to continue abuse.

- The research was recognised by court welfare officers but remained unknown to the legal professions. The court welfare officers sensed a need to educate the judges.

- Nevertheless during the period of investigation, January 1996 to May 1997, there was little evidence of any shift of approach and therefore outcome.

This research demonstrates to me the value of the work that Wall J has done in drawing attention to the need to re-evaluate domestic violence in its impact on continuing relationships within the family after separation.

... the factors that may offset the assumption in favour of contact are probably too legion to be either listed or categorised. Abuse must form the largest compartment: as well as physical abuse of the other parent and/or a child there is equally sexual and emotional abuse within the family. Then there is the self abuse of either drugs or alcohol and the failure to maintain sexual boundaries appropriate to the development of the child. Additionally mental illness or personality disorder may be a dominant factor as may be malign motives prompting the applicant to pursue a seemingly justifiable application for the covert purpose of threatening or dominating the primary carer. This uncomprehensive catalogue only demonstrates that the factor of domestic violence must be kept in proportion and must not be elevated either to reduce the focus on other factors that may counter the assumption in favour of contact or otherwise distort the paramount judicial task. My primary conclusion is that listing of the present appeals and the great assistance given by the Official Solicitor, by Mr Posnansky QC and by the Sturge/Glaser report does not call for any adjustment of the approach adopted by Wall J in the passages that I have cited from his judgments in *Re H (Contact: Domestic Violence)* [1998] 2 FLR 42 and in *Re M (Contact: Violent Parent)* [1999] 2 FLR 321. The danger of elevating any one factor in what will always be an extremely complex evaluation is to move the pendulum too far and thus to create an excessive concentration on past history and an over-reflection of physical abuse within the determination of individual cases. I would not adopt the suggestion in the Sturge/Glaser report ([2000] Fam Law 615, 623):

> 'From all that is written above, it will be clear that we consider that there should be no automatic assumption that contact to a previously or currently violent parent is in the child's interests; if anything the assumption should be in the opposite direction and the case of the non-residential parent one of proving why he can offer something of such benefit not only to the child but to the child's situation ... that contact should be considered.'

As the quotation itself suggests there is a spectrum within the broad categorisation of domestic violence from the slap that may have been provoked to premeditated murder. There is the equally obvious distinction between past abuse which has been acknowledged and addressed and a continuing risk of future violence if any opportunity is created. In my opinion the only direction that can be given to the trial judge is to apply the welfare principle and the welfare checklist, s 1(1) and (3) of the Children Act 1989, to the facts of the particular case. It follows that I am doubtful as to whether specific guidelines are now required but my preference would be for brevity and simplicity always bearing in mind the risk of creating satellite litigation as to how the guidelines should be construed and applied.

WALLER LJ:

... Without being exhaustive the key points which it may be helpful for me to emphasise appear to be the following:

(1)   the effect of children being exposed to domestic violence of one parent as against the other *may* up until now have been underestimated by judges, and advisers alike;

(2)   it follows that alleged domestic violence is a matter that ought to be investigated, and on which findings of fact should be made because if it is established, its effect on children exposed to it, and the risk to the residential carer are highly relevant factors in considering orders for contact and their form;

(3)   in assessing the relevance of past domestic violence, it is likely to be highly material whether the perpetrator has shown an ability to recognise the wrong he (or less commonly she) has done, and the steps taken to correct the deficiency in the perpetrator's character;

(4)   there should however be no presumption against contact simply because domestic violence is alleged or proved; domestic violence is not to be elevated to some special category; it is one highly material factor amongst many which may offset the assumption in favour of contact when the difficult balancing exercise is carried out by the judge applying the welfare principle and the welfare checklist, s 1(1) and (3) of the Children Act 1989.

Appendix 5

RESEARCH INTO CONTACT

RESEARCH

Blackwell and Dawe 'Non-Resident Parental Contact' (Office of National Statistics, 2002)

Based on the National Statistics Omnibus Survey of a representative sample of adults aged 16 or over, living in private households in Great Britain. There were 935 adults who were non-resident or parents with care.

Summarised in [2004] Fam Law 480.

www.statistics.gov.uk

Wikeley, Barnett and others 'National Survey of Child Support Agency Clients' (Research Report No 152, Department of Work and Pensions, 2001)

Based on a survey drawn from a 5% scan of all cases on the Agency's data base in 1999. The response rate was 38% – 38% of non-resident parents and 59% of parents with care. Interviews were conducted with 1017 non-resident parents and 1392 parents with care.

Summarised in [2002] Fam Law 522.

www.dwp.gov.uk

Smart, May, Wade and Furniss 'Residence and Contact Disputes in Court' (Department for Constitutional Affairs)

Volume 1 (2003) DCA Research Series No 6103

Summarised in [2004] Fam Law 36.

Volume 2 (2005) DCA Research Series 4105

Based on 430 cases derived from a random sample of court files concerning s 8 cases which commenced in three county courts in 2000.

www.dca.gov.uk

Trinder, Beek and Connolly 'Making Contact: How Parents and Children Negotiate and Experience Contact after Divorce' (Joseph Rowntree Foundation, 2002)

Based on interviews with 61 families recruited from a variety of resources.

Summarised in *Findings 092*.

www.jrf.org.uk

Trinder, Connolly and others 'A Profile of Applicants and Respondents in Contact Cases in Essex' (Research series 1/05, Department of Constitutional Affairs, 2005)

Summarised in [2004] Fam Law 877.

Based on 59 contact cases in one county in 2003.

Trinder, Connolly and others 'Making Contact Happen or Making Contact Work?' (Research Series, Department for Constitutional Affairs, 2006)

The process and outcome of in-court conciliation.

Trinder and Kellett 'The Longer-Term Outcomes of In-Court Conciliation' (Ministry of Justice Research Series 15/07 2007)

A two year follow up of the families studied in 'Making Contact Happen or Making Contact Work'.

Hunt and Macleod 'Outcomes of Applications to Court for Contact Orders after Parental Separation or Divorce' (Oxford Centre for Family Law and Policy, 2008)

Based on a sample of 300 files covering cases heard in the Family Proceedings Court, county court and High Court.

NOTE

Surveys invariably show a divergence between reports on the frequency and quality of contact reported by non-resident parents from that reported by parents with care.

LITERATURE REVIEW

Douglas and others 'Research on Divorce, Separation and Family Change: Messages for Practitioners' (Joseph Rowntree Foundation, 2004)

Summarises key messages and themes from 12 research projects about the effects of divorce and separation.

www.jrf.org.uk

Hunt and Roberts 'Child Contact with Non-Resident Parents' (Family Policy Briefing 3, University of Oxford Department of Social Policy and Social Work, 2004)

Hunt and Roberts 'Intervening in Litigated Contact: Ideas from other Jurisdictions' (Family Policy Briefing 4, University of Oxford Department of Social Policy and Social Work, 2005)

Summarised in [2005] Fam Law 1000.

www.apsoc.ox.ac.uk/Publications_PublishedPapers.html

Appendix 6

USEFUL ADDRESSES

Royal Courts of Justice
Strand, London WC2A 2CC
Tel: 020 7947 6000 (This is also the out-of-hours emergency number.)

Family Justice Council
WG32A, E201 East Block, Royal Courts of Justice, Strand, London WC2A 2GL
Tel: 020 7947 7333
Fax: 020 7947 7875
www.judiciary.gov.uk/about-the-judiciary/advisory-bodies/fjc

The Ministry of Justice
102 Petty France, London SW1H 9AJ
Tel: 020 3334 3555
www.justice.gov.uk

Children and Family Court Advisory and Support Services (Cafcass)
6th Floor, Sanctuary Buildings, Great Smith Street, London SW1P 3BT
Tel: 0844 353 3350
Fax: 0844 353 3351
www.cafcass.gov.uk

Cafcass Legal Services
Details as above.

European Court of Human Rights Database (Hudoc)
www.echr.coe.int/Hudoc.htm

Family Rights Group
The Print House, 18 Ashwin Street, London E8 3DL
Tel: 0208 7923 2628
Fax: 020 7923 2683
email: office@frg.org.uk
www.frg.org.uk

Home Office Liaison Officer
Her Majesty's Courts and Tribunals Service
Arnhem House, PO Box 6987, Leicester LE1 6ZX
Email: homeofficeliaison@hmcts.gsi.gov.uk
Telephone: 0116 249 4309
Fax: 0116 249 4400

The National Association of Child Contact Centres
1 Heritage Mews, High Pavement, Nottingham NG1 1HN
Tel: 0845 4500 280
Fax: 0845 4500 420
www.nacc.org.uk

The National Youth Advocacy Service (NYAS)
Everton House, Tower Road, Birkenhead, Wirral, Merseyside, CH41 1FN
Tel: 0151 649 8700
www.nyas.net

Joseph Rowntree Foundation
The Homestead, 40 Water End, York, North Yorkshire YO30 6WP
Tel: 01904 629241
Fax: 01904 620072
www.jrf.org.uk
The website provides access to Findings, the summary of research commissioned by the JRF.

INDEX

References are to paragraph numbers.